MSU LIBRARIES
3 2109 00094 4943
WITHDRAWN
D1307144

Historical Sets, Collected Editions, and Monuments of MUSIC

Historical Sets, Collected Editions, and Monuments of MUSIC

A Guide to Their Contents

Compiled by ANNA HARRIET HEYER

Consultant on Music Library Materials
Texas Christian University
Fort Worth, Texas
Formerly
Music Librarian and
Assistant Professor of Library Service
North Texas State University
Denton, Texas

Second Edition

AMERICAN LIBRARY ASSOCIATION

Chicago, 1969

Standard Book Number 8389–0037–2 (1969)

Library of Congress Catalog Card Number 68–21021

Manufactured in the United States of America

Copy 4

REFERENCE
ML
113
H52
1969
cop. 4

Dedicated to
the memory of my parents
HARRIET G. and ARTHUR W. HEYER

RC 9-28770

Preface

Aim. The first compilation of HISTORICAL SETS, COLLECTED EDITIONS, AND MONUMENTS OF MUSIC appeared in 1957. The aim of the work was to present a list of those publications, with complete bibliographical information about each, and to list the contents of each. This second, revised edition continues the aim of the original work and supersedes the former edition. Much of the material in the first edition has been retained and, when necessary, revised to correct errors, to complete entry or contents listings, and to note volumes published or announced since the first edition. Many new entries have been added to fill some gaps in the first edition and to include recently published works.

Scope. The general policy of the first edition has been followed in the present work. It thus includes the complete editions of the music of individual composers and major collections of music that have been published or are in the process of publication. For purposes of this compilation, major collections of music are collections, anthologies, or monumental sets of music considered by the author to have historical value, musical worth, reliable editing, or significance to music research. More detailed contents than are found in the first edition are given in this edition for some titles, such as Delsarte's *Archives du chant* and the collected works of Palestrina. Also included are detailed contents for (1) the collected works of Berlioz and Monteverdi, which were analyzed by the Music Library Association in the first two numbers of the M.L.A. Index Series, and (2) the complete works of Bach, Beethoven, Brahms, and Mozart, which appeared in reprint form as the first four numbers of the Edwards Brothers music reprints, Series A, *Complete works and monumenta.* For collections whose contents are not presented in detail in this compilation, further work of this kind remains for such projects as the M.L.A. Index Series.

Folk music has been excluded (except for a few comprehensive sets or general collections and collections which include other material in addition to folk music) since good lists of folk-song material are otherwise available. Collections of songs are outside the scope of this work, also, except for monumental works and such comprehensive sets as Richard Strauss's *Lieder.* Reproductions of original editions are included if they are facsimile editions, but microfilm copies of books and music have been omitted.

Although the basic purpose of this work is to list publications of music, when a publication contains volumes both of music and of literature, all volumes of the entry are included. For example, volumes of literature are found in the supplements to the reprint edition of *Denkmäler deutscher Tonkunst* [1.Folge] and in the publications of the Institute of Mediaeval Music.

Entries. The form of entry of the new edition is the same as that of the old and follows, in the main, the form of the Library of Congress card. Each entry contains, when known, the composer or compiler of the collection, the title (a title entry instead of compiler for some distinctive titles), the place of publication, the publisher, the date of publication, the paging or number of volumes, and a brief description of illustrative material. After any special notes, a listing of the contents is given. For works in more than one volume, each volume is itemized with its contents. For single-volume works containing a few selections, specific titles of the compositions are given. For miscellaneous collections, either the composers included are listed after the words "Contains compositions by," or the contents are omitted entirely. Contents are intentionally omitted for collections containing many miscellaneous examples of music, such as Schering's *Geschichte der Musik in Beispielen* and Riemann's *Musikgeschichte in Beispielen,* because of the extensiveness of these collections and the short length of many of the examples.

Usually, the language used in the entry came from the publication itself. However, when a copy of the publication was not available for examination or for verification, the entry is in the language of the descriptive notice or announcement released by the music publisher or dealer or in the language of the source from which it was taken. The music in the publication, rather than the language in which it was published, was the determining factor in the decision to include the compilation. More than ten languages are represented in this edition, with the Roman alphabet used throughout. Russian entries are either translated or transliterated.

To describe pagination for sets in the process of publication, when the total number of volumes planned for the set was known, the collation appears as: 5v. (In progress), the number of volumes depending upon the particular set. When the total number of volumes was unknown, the collation appears as: v.1– . If an approximate total number of volumes has been announced, a note is made stating this, "Proposed set about 10v." If the set has been announced, but no volumes have been published, the collation appears as: v.1– , and a note "To be published" is made. With a set consisting of numbers instead of volumes, the term "nos." is used instead of "v." When the paging of a one-volume work is unknown, the collation appears as: p.1– , or as 1v.

Generally, the form used in the entries for names and for dates of birth and death are established by information from Library of Congress cards. When Library of Congress information was not used, the principal sources for determining names and dates were: *Grove's Dictionary of music and musicians* (5th ed.; St. Martin's Press, Inc.; Macmillan and Co., Ltd., 1954; Suppl. 1961); *Baker's Biographical dictionary of musicians* (5th ed.; G. Schirmer, 1958); *Moser's Musik Lexikon* (4th ed.; Musikverlag Hans Sikorski, 1955); *Riemann Musik Lexikon* (12th ed.; B. Schott's Söhne, 1959–61); and *Die Musik in Geschichte und Gegenwart* (Bärenreiter-Verlag, 1949–). Other music reference tools were used as needed.

Variations of a name in different volumes of a set, or in different sets, are retained in contents listings as they appear in each volume. Thus, forms of a name are not always uniform in these listings, such as the initials for Biber in volumes of *Denkmäler der Tonkunst in Österreich,* and "Campion" in the *Euterpe* entry but "Campian" in the Fellowes collections. It is in the Index entries that these variations are brought together under one established form of the name.

Cross references appear for titles of works that are entered under composer or compiler and for alternate spellings of names. Works entered under title generally have cross references for the editor. With the exception of cross references to the complete works of a composer when such a compilation is a part of a larger collection, cross references are made only to names and titles that appear in the main entry itself.

Abbreviations used in the text are explained in the *List of Abbreviations* on page xiii.

Index. Following the main body of the book is an index to the contents of the collections, listed (1) by composers, (2) by titles for title entries, and (3) by form or medium. Under each composer's name is a listing of his works, each entry followed by the name and volume number of the collection in which the work is found. Whole works appear first, followed by individual listings from collections. Miscellaneous selections precede the alphabetical listing of specific types or titles of music. Individual listings are arranged by key word rather than by the first word of the entry, as: concertos, masses, motets, sonatas, symphonies. Keyboard music for two hands, except organ, is grouped together under the word "Keyboard." Organ music is listed under "Keyboard music—Organ." The language used in listing a title in the Index is the same as the one used for that title in the main body of the book. If the identity of a composer for an entry is uncertain, the source of the entry is preceded by a question mark.

Cross references are made in the Index from most alternate spellings of a name, as they appear in the main body of the book, to the one selected as the entry in the Index. These alternate forms or spellings are also listed with the Index entry, preceded by "var. sp." (variant spelling). Both "see" and "see also" references are used, the "see" referring to the entry under which the material has been listed and the "see also" referring to other subject entries dealing with a similar subject.

The Index also brings together those works or volumes which emphasize a musical form or medium, as Dances, Lute Music, Madrigals, Violin, but it does not attempt to analyze the collections by listing all the types and forms of music contained in them. Collections emphasizing special countries are brought together in the Index under the name of the country, as England—Music, France—Music, Germany—Music.

Alphabetizing. In both the main body of the book and the Index, the names are alphabetized on a letter-by-letter basis. Thus, Lanner comes before La Rue. Words with an umlaut are alphabetized as spelled, the umlaut being ignored, so that Halle comes before Händel. Where words or names are better known written with the "e" rather than with the umlaut, as "ae", "oe", these are spelled with the "e" and alphabetized as spelled. Mc is alphabetized as Mac.

Title entries are alphabetized on a word-by-word basis, thus *Alte salzburger Meister der kirchenlichen Tonkunst* comes before *Altenglische Violenmusik zu drei Stimmen.* Titles under a name entry are generally arranged in alphabetical order, except that complete editions precede partial collections, with earliest works usually listed first.

Coverage. The second, revised edition attempts to be as complete as possible for publications of the nineteenth and twentieth centuries, with emphasis on current publications. Works published before the nineteenth century were included as information could be found about them. No attempt has been made to list very early works, although Berg's *Patrocinium musices* is entered as an example of this period. Where a reprint has been made of an early work, as Petrucci's *Harmonice musices Odhecaton A,* this is listed instead of the original work, since it would be more available.

A limiting date has been placed on this edition, as was done with the first edition. Spring, 1966, was selected as the latest date for an overall coverage of new publications, although some new titles coming within the scope of this work, and new volumes of sets in the process of publication appearing after this date, have been added. Also, some recent death dates have been included with name entries. Proposed volumes which were not published by Spring, 1966, but which were announced, are included.

The following statistics will serve to compare the first compilation of HISTORICAL SETS, COLLECTED EDITIONS, AND MONUMENTS OF MUSIC with the new one. In the first edition, there were more than 550 entries. In the new edition, nearly 100 of these carry additional or changed information. This information either fills in gaps, adds contents not listed before, or adds volumes published after the first edition was compiled. In addition, more than 350 new entries have been added. Of these, more than 190 were published after June, 1956, the limiting date of the first edition. A total of more than 900 entries are listed in the new edition.

Although the new edition fills many of the gaps in the first edition and adds many new titles, some entries still are incomplete, and some titles which would come within the scope of this work have undoubtedly been omitted. Since it was not possible to complete all gaps or to make a more exhaustive survey of the field without much additional searching and delay, the second edition has been completed for publication with the realization that these gaps and omissions occur.

Due to the increased interest in the publication of collected editions of music, new compilations are appearing frequently. It is, therefore, impossible to complete a work of this kind and have it currently up to date. The author, anticipating that supplements to the second, revised edition will be needed from time to time to add material not included in the present edition, requests that she be advised of information pertaining to gaps, omissions, or corrections in the present list.

Acknowledgments. Acknowledgments are due many individuals, music publishers, and dealers for their valuable help in making the present compilation possible:

To Miss Marion Dittman, Managing Editor, Publishing Department, American Library Association, for her valuable assistance in editing the manuscript. Recognition is due her for the many hours she spent checking details of form and accuracy. The author is greatly indebted to her for the benefit of her counsel and advice.

To Mrs. Harriet Nicewonger of the Music Library, University of California at Berkeley, for making available the resources of the California Library and for her helpful suggestions concerning titles in the list. To Fred Blum of the Music Division, Library of Congress, for his generous contribution of material and for reading the manuscript. To the editorial staff of the Publishing Department of the American Library Association—Mrs. Pauline J. Love, Director; Miss Pauline Cianciolo, Assistant to the Director; and Miss Marion Dittman, Managing Editor—for their assistance concerning detail and for their editorial advice. To H. Baron of London, England, for the *Euterpe* and *Sammlung russischer Romanzen* entries and for the work of checking publications in the British Museum. To Dan Fog of Copenhagen, Denmark, for the list of the *Samfundet til Udgivelse af dansk Musik.* To Åke Lellky, Librarian, Kungliga Musikaliska Akademiens Bibliotek, Stockholm, Sweden, for the *Musikaliska konstföreningen* list. To Kenneth Mummery of Bournemouth, England, for assistance on the *Istituzioni e monumenti dell' arte musicale italiana, Monumenta musicae sacrae,* and *Monumenta musicae svecicae* sets and the collected works of Vivaldi. To the late Henry Cowell and to Calvert Bean, Jr., Director of Publications of Theodore Presser Co., for their help with the *New music* entry. To John Bice, Agnes M. Fleming, and Gustav Reese of Carl Fischer, Inc., for their assistance with the Societas Universalis Sanctae Ceciliae publications. To Luther A. Dittmer, of the Institute of Mediaeval Music, for the list of the publications of this organization. To Edward N. Waters and Carroll Wade of the Music Division, Library of Congress; Brooks Shepard, Jr., of the Music Library, Yale University; and Miss Sirvart Poladian and the late Mrs. Catharine Keyes Miller, of the New York Public Library, for their help in supplying information that was requested. To the Music Library Association for use of material in the M.L.A. Index Series.

To the following music publishers and dealers for their invaluable assistance: American Institute of Musicology; A.-R. Editions, Inc.; Associated Music Publishers, Inc.; Boosey & Hawkes, Inc.; Broude Brothers, granting permission to quote from their catalogs listing collected editions; Alexander Broude; Franco Colombo, Inc.; Concordia Publishing House; H. W. Gray Co.; Leeds Music Corp.; McGinnis & Marx; New Valley Music Press; C. F. Peters Corp.; G. Schirmer, Inc., granting permission to use the list of the Wa-Wan Press publications of American music—all of these publishers of the United

States; Athenaeum Cremonense of Cremona, Italy; Bärenreiter-Antiquariat of Kassel, Germany, granting permission to use the *Gesamtausgabe* listings in *Die Musik in Geschichte und Gegenwart;* Breitkopf & Härtel of Wiesbaden, Germany; Creyghton of Bilthoven, Holland; Editions de l'Oiseau-Lyre of Les Remparts, Monaco; Heugel & Cie. of Paris, France; C. F. Kahnt of Leipzig, Germany; F. Kistner & C. F. W. Siegel of Lippstadt, Germany; Librairie Encyclopédique of Brussels, Belgium; Macmillan and Co., Ltd., granting permission to quote listings of contents found in the 1916 and 5th editions of *Grove's Dictionary of music and musicians;* Hermann Moeck Verlag of Celle, Germany; Möseler Verlag of Wolfbüttel, Germany; Munksgaard of Copenhagen, Denmark; Martinus Nijhoff of The Hague, Netherlands; Schott & Co., Ltd., of London, England; Stainer & Bell, Ltd., of London, England; and Ugrino Verlag of Hamburg, Germany. And to the many other individuals, publishers, and dealers, too numerous to mention, who contributed to the compilation.

To the following for their help with language problems in the manuscript: Dr. Jacob Hieble of the Department of Foreign Languages, North Texas State University, Denton; Dr. Harry Poppers and Dr. Bita May Hall of the Department of Foreign Languages, Texas Christian University, Fort Worth; and Dr. Michael Winesanker, Head of the Department of Music, Texas Christian University, Fort Worth.

Finally, to Mrs. Edna Mae Sandborn, Assistant Music Librarian, Music Library, North Texas State University, Denton, for her assistance in checking material in that library; and to Dr. David A. Webb, Librarian of North Texas State University, Denton, and Dr. Paul Parham, Librarian of Texas Christian University, Fort Worth, for their help and cooperation with the problems involved in assembling the manuscript. All of this support and assistance is gratefully acknowledged.

Anna Harriet Heyer
Texas Christian University
Fort Worth, Texas

List of Abbreviations

The abbreviations listed here include those for which some explanation or translation seemed needed. Abbreviations which appear in a single work or in only a few titles are explained in the entry in which they are used. Abbreviations found on title pages or in listings within sets which are not explained in the set are not always identified in this compilation. Shortened forms of names and abbreviations that appear self-explanatory, as Co., Inc., Ltd., Soc., have not been included here.

A.: *alto*
a 4, a 5, etc.: *for 4, for 5* [*voices*]
Abt. (Ger.) Abteilung: *part, section, division*
acc., accomp.: *accompaniment*
a.d. (Ger.) an der: *on the*
ad lib. (Lat.) ad libitum: *freely*
aflg. (Dutch) aflevering: *part*
Aflg. (Ger.) Auflage: *edition*
Anh. (Ger.) Anhang: *appendix*
arr., arrang.: *arranged, arranger*
Ausg. (Ger.) Ausgabe: *printing, edition*
ausgew. (Ger.) ausgewählte: *selected*

B.: *bass*
b.: *born*
B. & H. (Ger.) : *Breitkopf & Härtel*
B.C. (It.) basso continuo: *continuous bass*
Bd. (Ger.) Band: *volume*
bearb. (Ger.) bearbeitet: *revised*
bzw. (Ger.) beziehungsweise: *respectively; or else*

c., ca.: *circa*
c' Blockflöte (Ger.) : *tenor recorder*
cf. (Lat.) confer: *see, compare*
col.: *colored*
coll.: *collection*
cop.: *copyright*
cuad. (Sp.) cuaderno: *quire (of sheets)*

d.: *died*
diagr.: *diagram*

ed.: *edited, edition, editor*

F.: *Antonio Fanna listing of Vivaldi's works*
f' Blockflöte (Ger.) : *treble recorder*
facsim.: *facsimile*
fasc. (Lat.) fasciculus: *fascicle, fascicule*
fl.: *flourished*
front.: *frontispiece*

geistl. (Ger.) geistlich: *sacred*
gem. (Ger.) gemischt: *mixed*
G.m.b.H. (Ger.) Gesellschaft mit beschränkter Haftung: *corporation with limited liability*
Greg.: *Gregorian*

h. (Ger.) hoch: *high* [*voice*]
H.G. (Ger.) Händelgesellschaft: *Breitkopf & Härtel (1858–1894, 1902) edition of Händel's works*
Hoboken (Ger.) Hoboken Verzeichnis: *Hoboken catalog for Haydn's works*
hrsg. (Ger.) herausgegeben: *published, edited*

illus.: *illustrated, illustrations*
incl.: *including*

Jahrg. (Ger.) Jahrgang: *annual volume*
Jahrh. (Ger.) Jahrhundert: *century*
Jg. (Ger.) Jahrgang: *annual volume*

K., K.V. (Ger.) Köchel Verzeichnis: *Köchel catalog for Mozart's works*

L.: *leaf, leaves*
Lfng. (Ger.) Lieferung: *part, section, number*
Lief. (Ger.) Lieferung: *part, section, number*
livr. (Fr.) livraison: *part, issue*
loc.cit. (Lat.) loco citato: *in the place cited*

ms., mss.: *manuscript, manuscripts*
mz.: *mezzo*

n.d.: *no date*
Neuaus., Neuausg. (Ger.) Neuausgabe: *new edition*
No., nos.: *number, numbers*
n.p.: *no place mentioned*
Nr. (Ger.) Nummer: *number*
numb.: *numbered*

obl. (It.) obbligato: *obbligato*
od. (Ger.) oder: *or*
oeuv. (Fr.) oeuvre: *work*
op.: *opus*
op.cit. (Lat.) opere citato: *in the work cited*

p.: *page*
Part. (Ger.) Partitur: *score*
passim (Lat.) : *scattered throughout*
pfte: (It.) pianoforte: *piano*
pl.: *plate, plates*
p.L.: *preliminary leaves*
port., ports.: *portrait, portraits*
posth.: *posthumous*
prakt. (Ger.) praktisch: *practical*
pref.: *preface*
ps.: *psalm*
pt., pts.: *part, parts*
pub.: *published, publisher*

quad. (It.) quadèrno: *quire (of sheets)*
q.v. (Lat.) quod vide: *which see*

Resp. (Lat.) Responsoria: *Responses*
rev.: *revised*

s. (Ger.) siehe: *see*
S.A.T.B.: *soprano, alto, tenor, bass*
ser.: *series*
sér. (Fr.) série: *series*
Sgst. (Ger.) Singstimme: *singing voice*
Singst. (Ger.) Singstimme: *singing voice*
St. (Ger.) Stimme: *voice, part*
stg., stgn. (4stg., 4stgn.; 5stg., 5stgn.; etc.) (Ger.) -stimmig, -stimmigen: [*4*]*-voiced,* [*5*]*-voiced*
Streichor. (Ger.) Streichorchester: *string orchestra*
supp., suppl.: *supplement*

T. (Ger.) Teil: *part*
t. (Ger.) tief: *low* [*voice*]
T.: *tenor*
tom. (Lat.) tomus: *volume*

u.A. (Ger.) und Andere: *and others*
unacc.: *unaccompanied*
usw. (Ger.) und so weiter: *and so forth*

v.: *voice*
v. (4v., 5v., etc.) : *volume*
var. sp.: *variant spelling*
vergl. (Ger.) vergleiche: *see, compare*
Verz. (Ger.) Verzeichnis: *list, catalog*
vgl. (Ger.) vergleiche: *see, compare*
voc. (It.) voce: *voice, voices*
vol.: *volume*

weltl. (Ger.) weltlich: *secular*
w.w.: *woodwind*

z.T. (Ger.) zum Teil: *partly*

* indicates *unpublished volumes*

Historical Sets, Collected Editions, and Monuments of MUSIC

ABEL, KARL FRIEDRICH, 1723–1787.
Kompositionen, Gesammelt, neueingerichtet und hrsg. von Walter Knape. Cuxhaven, [Ger.], W. Knape, [195?–].
v.1 – .
"Revisionsbericht" in pocket or bound in each volume.
Contents:
Ser.A: Sinfonien.
I. Sechs Sinfonien, Op.1. 1962.
II. Sechs Sinfonien, Op.4. 1962.
III. Sechs Sinfonien, Op.7. 1963.
IV. Sechs Sinfonien, Op.10. 1962.
Ser.B: Konzerte.
I. Flötenkonzerte Nr.1–6. Violoncello-Konzert (Nr.7). 1963.
Ser.C: Streichquartette.
Ser.D: Streichtrios.
Ser.E: Sonaten.

Achtzig Choralvorspiele deutscher Meister des 17. und 18. Jahrhunderts, *see* Keller, Hermann. Achtzig Choralvorspiele deutscher Meister des 17. und 18. Jahrhunderts.

ADAM DE LA HALLE, ca.1235–ca.1288.
Oeuvres complètes du trouvère Adam de la Halle (poésies et musique). Publiées sous les auspices de la Société des Sciences, des Lettres, et des Arts de Lille, par C. E. H. de Coussemaker. Paris, Durand & Pédone-Lauriel, 1872.
lxxxiv p., 1L., 440p. 1 plate.

Additional settings of certain of the canticles at mattins and evensong, *see* Plainsong and Mediaeval Music Society. Additional settings of certain of the canticles at mattins and evensong.

Adler, Guido, 1855–1941, ed. Musikalische Werke der Kaiser Ferdinand III, Leopold I, und Joseph I, *see* Musikalische Werke der Kaiser Ferdinand III, Leopold I, und Joseph I.

AGRICOLA, ALEXANDER, 1446–1506.
Opera omnia. Ed. by Edward R. Lerner. Rome, American Institute of Musicology, 1961– .
5v. (in progress). (Corpus mensurabilis musicae. No.22).
Contents:
Vol.1. Missa La serviteur, Missa Malheur me bat, Missa Je ne demande, Missa In myne zyn. 1961.
Vol.2. Missa Paschalis, Missa primi toni, Missa secundi toni, Missa sine nomine, Credo Je ne vis Oncques I, Credo Je ne vis Oncques II, Credo Vilayge, Credo Sanctus sine nomine.
Vol.3. Lamentationes, hymni, magnificat. 1966.
Vol.4. Motetta, contrafacta. 1966.

AICH, ARNT VON, d.1530.
Das Liederbuch des Arnt von Aich (Köln um 1510). Erste Partitur-Ausgabe der 75 vierstimmigen Tonsätze, von Eduard Bernoulli und Hans Joachim Moser . . . Kassel, Bärenreiter-Verlag, 1930.
xvi, 133p. facsims. (Bärenreiter-Ausgabe. [Nr.] 386).
German words; music for 4 voices.
Twelve of the songs are identified as being by: Adam von Fulda, Jörg Brack, Wolfgang Grefinger, Paul Hofhaimer, Heinrich Isaac, Erasmus Lapicida, Mattheus Pipelare, and Adam Reiner.

Akademie der Wissenschaften. Musikalische Denkmäler, *see* Musikalische Denkmäler.

ALAIN, JEHAN, 1911–1940.
L'oeuvre d'orgue, de Jehan Alain. Paris, Alphonse Leduc, [cop.1936–52].
3v.

ALBERT, PRINCE CONSORT OF QUEEN VICTORIA, 1819–1861.
The collected compositions of His Royal Highness, the Prince Consort, ed. by W. G. Cusins. London, Metzler & Co., [1882?].
221p.
Contains 30 songs and a vocal trio, with German words; Invocazione all'armonia, with Italian words, for chorus and solo; for chorus, with English words; Te Deum, Jubilata, Sanctus, Responses, Anthem (Out of the deep), Christmas hymn and a Choral, all with piano or organ acc.; also Melody for the violin.

ALBERT, HEINRICH, 1870–1950. ed.
Die Gitarre in der Haus- und Kammermusik vor 100 Jahren (1780–1820). Neuausg. von Meisterwerken der klassischen Gitarrezeit. Leipzig, Zimmermann, 1921.
14 nos.
Contents:
No.1. Diabelli, A. Op.68. Sonatine A dur für Gitarre und Hammerklavier.
No.2. Carulli, Ferd. Op.21, Nr.1. Sonate A dur für Gitarre und Hammerklavier.
No.3. Carulli, Ferd. Op.21, Nr.2. Sonate D dur für Gitarre und Hammerklavier.
No.4. Gragnani, Filippo. Op.8, Nr.1. Sonate D dur für Violine und Gitarre.
No.5, 6. Gragnani, Filippo. Op.8, Nr.2 und 3. Zweite und dritte Sonate C dur und A moll für Violine und Gitarre.
No.7. Giuliani, Mauro. Op.25. Sonate für Violine und Gitarre.

No.8. Molino, Francesco. Op.45. Trio D dur für Flöte, Viola und Gitarre.
No.9. Kreutzer, Jean. Trio A dur für Flöte, Klarinette und Gitarre.
No.10. Call, Leonhard von. Op.134. Trio C dur für Violine oder Flöte, Viola und Gitarre.
No.11. Matijegka, W. Op.26. Serenade für Flöte, Viola und Gitarre.
No.12. Call, Leonhard von. Op.26. Leichtes Trio für 3 Gitarren.
No.13. Gragnani, Filippo. Op.12. Trio für 3 Gitarren.
No.14. Giuliani, Mauro. Op.71. Trio für 3 Gitarren.

Album nordischer Komponisten für Orgel, *see* Gerhardt, Paul. Album nordischer Komponisten für Orgel.

Äldre svensk musik, *see* Svenska Samfundet för Musikforskning. Äldre svensk musik.

ALFIERI, PIETRO, 1801–1863. ed.
Raccolta di musica sacra in cui contengonsi i capi lavori de' più celebri compositori italiani, consistente in messe, sequenze, offertori, mottetti, salmi, inni, responsori . . . Roma, P. Pittarelli e Comp., 1841–46.
7v.
Contents (from *Grove's Dictionary of music and musicians,* 1916, Vol.1, p.66):
Vol.1.
Messe scelte di G. P. da Palestrina.
Messa di Papa Marcello.
Messa per I Defonti, a 5 voci.
Messa. Canonica, a 4.
Messa. O regem coeli, a 4.
Messa. Aeterna Christi munera, a 4.
Messa. Dies sanctificatus, a 4.
Messa. De feria, a 4.
Messa. Breve, a 4.
Messa. Ego enim accepti, a 8.

Vol.2.
Motetti a 5 voci di G. P. da Palestrina.
Adjuro vos.
Ave Trinitatis sacrarium.
Beatus Laurentius.
Canite tuba in Sion.
Caput ejus.
Caro mea.
Coenantibus illis.
Crucem sanctam subiit.
Derelinquat impius.
Descendit in hortum meum.
Dilectus meus descendit.
Dilectus meus mihi.
Domine secundum actum meum.
Duo ubera tua.
Ecce tu pulcher es.
Exi cito in plateas.
Exultate Deo adjutori nostro.
Fasciculus myrrhae.
Guttur tuum.
Introduxit me Rex.
Lapidabant Stephanum.
Leva ejus.
Manus tuae Domine.
Nigra sum, sed formosa.
O admirabile commercium.
O beata, et benedicta, et gloriosa Trinitas.
O sacrum convivium.
O vera summa sempiterna Trinitas.
Osculetur me osculo.
Parce mihi Domine.
Pater noster.
Paucitas dierum meorum.
Peccantem me quotidie.
Peccavi quid faciam tibi.
Peccavimus cum patribus nostris.
Pulcra es amica mea.
Pulcrae sunt genuae tuae.
Quae est ista quae progreditur.
Quam pulcra es.
Quam pulcri sunt gressus tui.
Rorate coeli.
Salve regina.
Si ignoras te.
Sicut lilium inter spinas.
Surgam, et circuibo civitatem.
Surge amica mea.
Surge propera.
Tota pulcra es.
Trahe me post te.
Tribulationes civitatum.
Veni veni dilecte mi.
Vineam meam.
Vox dilecti mei.
Vulnerasti cor meum.

Vol.3.
(Palestrina).
Hymni totius anni Romae. 1589.

Vol.4.
Lamentazioni di G. P. da Palestrina. Liber tre.

Vol.5.
Offertorii a 5 voci di G. P. da Palestrina. (Offertoria totius anni . . . quinque vocibus concinenda . . . Romae, 1593).

Vol.6.
Motet a 6. Jerusalem cito veniet. 2da pars. Ego enim.
Motet a 6. Veni Domine. 2da pars. Excita Domine.
Motet a 6. O magnum mysterium. 2da pars. Quem vidistis pastores?
Antiphona a 6. Cum ortus fuerit sol.
Antiphona a 6. Responsum accepit Simeon.
Antiphona a 6. Cum inducerent.
Motet a 6. Sancta et immaculata. 2da pars. Benedicta tu.
Motet a 6. Haec dies.
Motet a 6. Viri Galilaei. 2da pars. Ascendit Deus.
Motet a 6. Dum complerentur.
Motet a 6. Tu es Petrus. 2da pars. Quodcumque ligaveris.
Motet a 6. Solve jubente Deo. 2da pars. Quodcumque ligaveris.
Motet a 6. Deus qui Ecclesiam tuam.
Motet a 6. Vidi turbam magnam. 2da pars. Et omnes angeli.

Motet a 6. Columna es immobilis.
Motet a 6. Cantabo Domino. 2da pars. Deficiant peccatores.
Antiphona a 6. Regina mater misericordiae.
Motet a 7. Tu es Petrus.
Motet. Virgo prudentissima. (Motet. 2da pars). Maria Virgo.
Motet a 8. Surge illuminare. 2da pars. Et ambulabunt.
Motet. Caro mea vere est cibus. 2da pars. Hic est panis.
Motet. Laudate Dominum.
Motet a 4. 2 Choirs. Alma redemptoris mater.
Antiphona a 8. Ave regina coelorum.
Psalmi a 8. Jubilate Deo. Laudate pueri. 2da pars. Quis sicut Dominus.
Sequentiae a 8. Victimae paschali.
Sequentiae a 8. Veni spiritus.
Sequentiae a 8. Stabat mater.

Vol.7.
Hymnus a 12. O gloriosa virginum.
Sequentia a 12. Stabat mater.
Absolutio in messa defunct. a 4. Libera me, Kyrie, etc.
Motet in messa defunct. a 4. Ne recorderis. Domine secundum actum meum.
Motet a 4. Innocentes pro Christo.
Motet a 4. Valde honorandus.
Motet a 4. Deus qui animae famuli Gregorii.
Motet a 4. Ascendens Christus.
Motet a 4. Princeps gloriosissime Michael.
Hymnus a 4. Gaude Barbara.
Psalmus a 5. Venite.
Motet a 5. Cantantibus organis Caecilia. 2da pars. Biduanis.
Motet a 6. Assumpta est Maria. 2da pars. Quae est ista.
Motet a 6. Cum autem esset Stephanus. 2da pars. Positis autem.
Motet a 6. Hic est beatissimus Evangelista. 2da pars. Hic est discipulus.
Motet a 8. Fratres ego enim.
Motet a 8. Jesus junxit se. 2da pars. Et increpavit eos.
Motet. Spiritus sanctus.
Magnificat a 8. Imi toni.
Magnificat. Imi toni a 5 and 6.
Magnificat. 2di toni a 5 and 6.
Magnificat. 3ti toni a 6.
Magnificat. 8vi toni a 6.
Magnificat octo tonorum a 4. Pars 1: 1, 2, 3, 4, 5, 6, 7, 8. Altera pars: 1, 2, 3, 4, 5, 6, 7, 8.
Catalogo di tutte le opere del Palestrina.
Elziarii Genet. Lamentatio a 4.
Claudii Goudimel. Motet a 4.
Const. Festa. Te Deum a 4.
Christ. Morales. Motet a 5.

Alphenaar, Gerard. Organ masters of the Baroque period, *see* Organ masters of the Baroque period.

Alt-italienische Versetten, *see* Kastner, Macário Santiago. Alt-italienische Versetten.

Alte Hausmusik für Klavier (1550–1780), *see* Rehberg, Willy. Alte Hausmusik für Klavier (1550–1780).

Alte Klavier-Musik, *see* Pauer, Ernst. Alte Klavier-Musik.

Alte Klavier-Musik, *see* Roitzsch, Ferd. August. Alte Klavier-Musik.

Alte Lautenkunst aus drei Jahrhundertern, *see* Bruger, Hans Dagobert. Alte Lautenkunst aus drei Jahrhundertern.

Alte Meister, *see* Pauer, Ernst. Alte Meister.

Alte Meister, *see* Straube, Karl. Alte Meister.

Alte Meister aus der Frühzeit des Orgelspiels, *see* Schering, Arnold. Alte Meister aus der Frühzeit des Orgelspiels.

Alte Meister des Bel Canto, *see* Landshoff, Ludwig. Alte Meister des Bel Canto.

Alte Meister des deutschen Liedes, *see* Moser, Hans Joachim. Alte Meister des deutschen Liedes.

Alte Meister des Orgelspiels, *see* Straube, Karl. Alte Meister des Orgelspiels.

Alte Meister des Violinspiels für den praktischen Gebrauch zum ersten Mal, *see* Schering, Arnold. Alte Meister des Violinspiels für den praktischen Gebrauch zum ersten Mal.

ALTE MUSIK. (REIHE "LEUCKARTIANA"). Klassische Bläsermusik. München, Leipzig, F. E. C. Leuckart, 19?– .
v.1 – .
Contents:
Danzi, Franz. Bläserquintett B-Dur, Op.56, Nr.1. (Weigelt).
—— Bläserquintett G-moll, Op.56, Nr.2. (Weigelt).
Mozart, W. A. Adagio B-Dur, K.V.411. Für Flöte, Oboe, Klarinette, Horn und Fagott. (Weigelt).
—— Divertimento Nr.8, F-Dur, K.V.213. Für Flöte, Oboe, Klarinette, Horn und Fagott. (Weigelt).
—— Divertimento Nr.9, B-Dur, K.V.240. Für Flöte, Oboe, Klarinette, Horn und Fagott. (Weigelt).
—— Divertimento Nr.13, F-Dur, K.V.253. Für Flöte, Oboe, Klarinette, Horn und Fagott. (Weigelt).
—— Divertimento Nr.14, B-Dur, K.V.270. Für Flöte, Oboe, Klarinette, Horn und Fagott. (Weigelt).
Onslow, George. Bläserquintett F-Dur, Op.81, Nr.3. (Redel).
Reicha, Anton. Bläserquintett Es-Dur, Op.88, Nr.2. (Weigelt).
—— Bläserquintett B-Dur, Op.88, Nr.5. (Seydel).
Stamitz, Karl. Bläserquintett Es-Dur, Op.8, Nr.2. (Weigelt).
Telemann, G.P. Ouvertüren-Suite. Für 2 Oboen, 2 Hörner und Fagott (Original) oder Flöte, Oboe, Klarinette, Horn und Fagott. (Hinnenthal).

Alte salzburger Meister der kirchlichen Tonkunst, *see* Messner, Joseph. Alte salzburger Meister der kirchlichen Tonkunst.

Altenglische Violenmusik zu drei Stimmen, *see* Giesbert, Franz Julius. Altenglische Violenmusik zu drei Stimmen.

Die ältesten musikalischen Denkmäler, *see* Zagiba, František. Die ältesten musikalischen Denkmäler.

Altniederländische Meister für Orgel oder Harmonium, *see* Peeters, Flor. Altniederländische Meister für Orgel oder Harmonium.

AMBROS, AUGUST WILHELM, 1816–1876.
Auserwählte Tonwerke der berühmtesten Meister des 15. und 16. Jahrhunderts. Eine Beispielsammlung zu dem dritten Bande der Musikgeschichte von A. W. Ambros nach dessen unvollendet hinterlassenem Notenmaterial mit zahlreichen Vermehrungen, hrsg. von Otto Kade. Dritte unveränderte Auflage. Leipzig, F. E. C. Leuckart, 1911.
lxviii, 605p. (Geschichte der Musik von August Wilhelm Ambros. Fünfter Band. Beispielsammlung zum dritten Bande. Ausgestattet von Otto Kade. Dritte unveränderte Auflage).
2d edition, 1889.
Contains compositions by Alexander Agricola, Florentinus Alexander, Francesco d'Ana, Bartholomeus de Florentia, Arnoldus de Bruck, Antonius Brumel, Loyset Compère, Benedict Ducis, Bartolomeo Escobedo, Antonius Fevin, Heinrich Finck, Jacobus Gallus, Gaspar, Eleazar Genet genannt Carpentras, Johannes Ghiselin, Nicolaus Gombert, Matthes Greiter, Hans Leo von Hassler, Jacob Hobrecht, Paulus Hoffheimer, Josquin de Près, Henricus Isaac, David Köler, Franciscus de Layolle, Matthaeus le Maistre, Rogier Michael, Cristophero Morales, Joannes Okeghem, Marbriano de Orto, Pierre de la Rue, Antonius Scandellus, Leonhart Schröter, Paulus Scotus, Ludwig Senfl, Thomas Stoltzer, Thomas Walliser, Johann Walter, Adrian Willaert, and Johann Baptist Zesso.

Ameln, Konrad, 1899– , ed. Das Locheimer Liederbuch, *see* Das Locheimer Liederbuch.

AMERICAN MUSICOLOGICAL SOCIETY. Studies and documents.
No.1 – .
Contents:
No.1, *see* Ockeghem, Jean de. Collected works. Vol.2.
No.2, *see* Musica Britannica. Vol.8. Dunstable, John. Complete works.
No.3, *see* Ockeghem, Jean de. Collected works. Vol.1.

Les anciens maîtres espagnols. Pièces pour orgue, *see* Piedelievre, Paule. Les anciens maîtres espagnols. Pièces pour orgue.

Ancient Scotish melodies, from a manuscript of the reign of King James VI, *see* Dauney, William. Ancient Scotish melodies, from a manuscript of the reign of King James VI.

Anglo-French sequelae. Hughes, Anselm, *Father, see* Plainsong and Mediaeval Music Society. Hughes, Anselm, *Father.* Anglo-French sequelae.

ANNIBALE PADOVANO, 1527–1575.
. . . Ricercari; publiés par N. Pierront et J. P. Hennebaine d'après l'unique exemplaire du Çollège Royal de Musique à Londres. Paris, Éditions de l'Oiseau Lyre, L. B. M. Dyer, 1934.
104p. illus. (facsims.).
For organ.
With facsimiles of original dedication and title page of tenor part: . . . Il primo libro de ricercari a quattro ucci . . . In Venetia appresso di Antonio Gardano, 1556.
First published in parts: Cantus, Altus, Tenor, Bassus.
350 copies printed.

Annunzio, Gabriele d', 1864–1938, ed. I classici della musica italiana, *see* I classici della musica italiana.

The anthems of the Blessed Virgin Mary according to the season, *see* Plainsong and Mediaeval Music Society. The anthems of the Blessed Virgin Mary according to the season.

ANTHOLOGIA ANTIQUA. Classic works for the organ . . . New York, J. Fischer & Bro., [1935–52].
8v.
Contents:
Vol.1. XVII Century masters. Transcribed by Joseph W. Clokey. (Compositions by Arcangelo Corelli, L. N. Clérambault, J. S. Bach).
Vol.2. XVII and XVIII Century masters. Transcribed by Garth Edmundson. (Compositions by J. François d'Andrieu, J. C. F. Bach, G. F. Handel, Jean Baptiste de Lully, G. Sammartini, G. Tartini).
Vol.3. Handel. Suite from Water music. Transcribed by Carl McKinley.
Vol.4. French clavecin composers. Transcribed by Joseph W. Clokey. (Compositions by Fr. Couperin, J. Philip Rameau).
Vol.5. Buxtehude, Dietrich. Six chorale preludes for organ. Edited, collected, and arranged by Seth Bingham.
Vol.6. Telemann, G. Suite baroque. Arranged for organ by Ludwig Altman.
Vol.7. Couperin, François. Suite for organ from Solemn mass for parish use. Edited, collected, and arranged by Seth Bingham.
Vol.8. Buxtehude, Dietrich. Magnificat–shorter version; Chaconne in E minor; Passacaglia. Wie schön leuchtet der Morgenstern; Canzonetta in G major. Edited, collected, and annotated by Seth Bingham.

Anthologia polyphonica auctorum saeculi XVI paribus vocibus, *see* Casimiri, Raffaele Casimiro.

Anthologia polyphonica auctorum saeculi XVI paribus vocibus.

Anthologia pro organo, *see* Peeters, Flor. Anthologia pro organo.

Anthologie de cent chansons de trouvères et de troubadours des XIIe et XIIIe siècles, *see* Beck, Jean Baptiste. Anthologie de cent chansons de trouvères et de troubadours des XIIe et XIIIe siècles.

Anthologie de l'orgue, *see* Froidebise, Pierre. Anthologie de l'orgue.

Anthologie de la chanson parisienne au XVIe siècle, *see* Lesure, François. Anthologie de la chanson parisienne au XVIe siècle.

Anthologie de maîtres religieux anciens pour chant ou orgue. Sér.1, *see* Anthologie des maîtres religieux primitifs des XVe, XVIe et XVIIe siècles.

Anthologie de musique sacrée des maîtres anciens, *see* Expert, Henry. Anthologie de musique sacrée des maîtres anciens.

Anthologie des maîtres français du clavecin des XVIIe et XVIIIe siècles, *see* Brunold, Paul. Anthologie des maîtres français du clavecin des XVIIe et XVIIIe siècles.

ANTHOLOGIE DES MAÎTRES RELIGIEUX PRIMITIFS DES XVe, XVIe ET XVIIe SIÈCLES. Édition populaire à l'usage des maîtrises et des amateurs, en notation moderne avec clefs usuelles, nuances et indications d'exécution et réduction des voix au clavier, par Charles Bordes . . . Année 1–3. Paris, Bureau d'Édition Schola Cantorum, Soc. de Musique Religieuse, [etc., etc.], 1893–[98].
3 année. (Anthologie de maîtres religieux anciens pour chant ou orgue. Sér.1).
Quarterly.
At head of title: Répertoire des Chanteurs de Saint-Gervais.
Année 1 (1893) in two volumes, "Masses" and "Motets," with imprint: Paris, Assoc. des Chanteurs de Saint-Gervais, [etc., etc.]. Année 1 comprises a reissue of material which appeared in Vol.1 of the original quarterly).
Ceased publication with Année 3.
Contents:
No.3. Palestrina, G. P. da. Messe. Ascendo ad Patrem. a 5 voix.
No.7. Palestrina, G. P. da. Messe. O Regem coeli. a 4 voix.
No.8. Palestrina, G. P. da. Messe. Papae Marcelli. a 6 voix.
No.19. Palestrina, G. P. da. Messe. Sine nomine. a 4 voix.

An anthology of early French organ music, *see* Bonnet, Joseph. An anthology of early French organ music.

Anthology of early keyboard music, *see* Schott's anthology of early keyboard music.

ANTHOLOGY OF MUSIC. A collection of complete musical examples illustrating the history of music, ed. by K. G. Fellerer. Köln, Arno Volk Verlag, [c195?–].
v.1– .
Also published in German under the title: Das Musikwerk.
To be completed in about 32v.
Contents:
Vol.1. Georgii, Walter, ed. Four hundred years of European keyboard music. 1959.
Vol.2. Gennrich, Friedrich, ed. Troubadours, trouvères, minnesang and meistergesang. 1960.
Vol.3. Engel, Hans, ed. The sixteenth-century part song in Italy, France, England and Spain. 1961.
Vol.4. Wiora, Walter, ed. European folksongs.
Vol.5. Abert, Anna Amalie, ed. Opera from its beginnings to the beginning of the nineteenth century. 1962.
Vol.6. Stephenson, Kurt, ed. The classics. 1962.
Vol.7. Schenk, Erich, ed. The Italian trio sonata. 1955.
Vol.8. Kahl, Willi, ed. The character piece. 1961.
Vol.9. Husmann, Heinrich, ed. Medieval polyphony. 1962.
Vol.10. Osthoff, Helmuth, ed. The German part song. 1955.
Vol.11. Fischer, Karl von, ed. The variation. 1962.
Vol.12. Ferand, Ernst Thomas, ed. Improvisation. 1961.
Vol.13. Wellesz, Egon, ed. The music of the Byzantine church. 1959.
Vol.14. Moser, Hans Joachim, ed. The German solo song and the ballad. 1958.
Vol.15. Giegling, Franz, ed. The solo sonata. 1960.
Vol.16. Noske, Frits, ed. The solo song outside German-speaking countries. 1958.
Vol.17. Valentin, Erich, ed. The toccata. 1958.
Vol.18. Tack, Franz, ed. Gregorian chant. 1960.
Vol.19. Adrio, Adam, ed. The fugue. Vol.1. 1961.
Vol.20. Werner, Eric, ed. Hebrew music. 1961.
Vol.21. Stephenson, Kurt, ed. Romanticism in music. 1961.
Vol.22. Lenaerts, René, ed. Music of the Netherlands. 1964.
Vol.23. Engel, Hans, ed. The concerto grosso. 1964.
Vol.24. Becker, Heinz, ed. History of instrumentation. 1964.
Vol.25. Engel, Hans, ed. The solo concerto. 1964.
Vol.26. Beck, Hermann, ed. The suite. 1966.
Vol.27. Reichert, Ernst, ed. The dance.
Vol.28. Fellerer, Karl Gustav, ed. Pre-classical polyphony. 1965.

ANTICA MUSICA STRUMENTALE ITALIANA. Italian instrumental music of the 17th and 18th century. Roma, I Virtuosi di Roma (Collegium Musicum Italicum).
v.1– .
Ser.I.
Vol.1. Albinoni, Tomaso. Concerto in C, Op.9, No.9 (2 oboes, strings, cembalo).

Vol.2. Albinoni, Tomaso. Concerto in F, Op.9, No.10 (violin solo, strings, cembalo).
Vol.3. Albinoni, Tomaso. Sinfonia No.5 in D (strings).
Vol.4. Albinoni, Tomaso. Sonata in A, Op.2, No.3 (strings, cembalo).
Vol.5. Bellini, Vincenzo. Concerto in E flat (oboe solo, strings).
Vol.6. Bonporti, Francesco. Concerto in B flat, Op.11, No.3 (violin solo, strings, cembalo).
Vol.7. Bonporti, Francesco. Concerto in B flat, Op.11, No.4 (violin solo, strings, cembalo).
Vol.8. Cambini, Giovanni. Concerto in G, Op.15, No.3 (piano solo, strings).
Vol.9. Cirri, Giovanni Battista. Concerto in A, Op.14, No.1 (violoncello solo, strings).
Vol.10. Viotti, Giovanni. Concerto in G minor (piano solo, orchestra).
Ser.II.
Vol.11. Albinoni, Tomaso. Sinfonia No.3 in G (strings).
Vol.12. Clementi, Muzio. Symphony in B flat, Op.44 (formerly Op.18).
Vol.13. Galuppi, Baldassare. Concerto No.6 in C minor (strings).
Vol.14. Giordani, Tommaso. Concerto No.3 in C (cembalo solo, strings).
Vol.15. Giordani, Tommaso. Concerto No.5 in D (cembalo solo, strings).
Vol.16. Pergolesi, Giovanni. Concertino in E flat (strings).
Vol.17. Pergolesi, Giovanni. Concertino No.1 in G (strings).
Vol.18. Puccini, Domenico V. M. Concerto in B flat (piano, orchestra).
Vol.19. Scarlatti, Alessandro. Concerto No.6 in E (2 violin soli, strings, cembalo).
Vol.20. Valentini, Giuseppe. Concerto No.3 in C (oboe, violin soli, strings, cembalo).
Ser.III.
Vol.21. Clementi, Muzio. Symphony in D, Op.44 (formerly Op.18).
Vol.22. Marcello, Benedetto. Concerto No.5 in F, Op.1, No.4 (strings, cembalo).
Vol.23. Salieri, Antonio. Symphony in D (Veneziana).
Vol.24. Salieri, Antonio. Symphony in D (Patron Saints' Day).
Vol.25. Locatelli, Antonio. Concerto grosso in G minor, Op.1, No.2 (strings).
In preparation:
Abaco, Evaristo Felice dall'. Sonata, Op.3, No.3, for organ, strings.
Albinoni, Tomaso. Concerto in G for 7 strings, basso continuo.
—— Sonata in G minor, Op.6, No.2, for strings, cembalo.
Clementi, Muzio. Concerto in C.
Galuppi, Baldassare. L'ero cincese for oboes, horns, strings.
Legrenzi, Giovanni. 3 sonatas from the opera La cetra, for strings, basso continuo.
Leo, Leonardo. Concerto for cello and strings.
Locatelli, Antonio. Il pianto di Arianna, for strings.
Marcello. Benedetto. Concerto, Op.1, No.3.
Paisiello, Giovanni. Concerto in F for 2 horns, strings, cembalo.
Reali. La follia.
Scarlatti, Alessandro. Concerto in F.
Tartini, Giuseppe. Concerto.
Viotti, Giovanni. Concerto No.19 in G minor for violin, orchestra.

Antichi maestri italiani, *see* Boghen, Felice. Antichi maestri italiani.

Antiphonae Beatae Mariae Virginis, *see* Plainsong and Mediaeval Music Society. Antiphonae Beatae Mariae Virginis.

Antiphonale Sarisburiense. Catholic Church, Roman. Liturgy and ritual. Antiphonary. Salisbury, *see* Plainsong and Mediaeval Music Society. Catholic Church, Roman. Liturgy and ritual. Antiphonary. Salisbury. Antiphonale Sarisburiense.

Antiphons for the Psalms, *see* Plainsong and Mediaeval Music Society. Antiphons for the Psalms.

The antiphons upon the Magnificat and Nunc dimittis, *see* Plainsong and Mediaeval Music Society. The antiphons upon the Magnificat and Nunc dimittis.

ANTIQUA CHORBUCH. Hrsg. von Helmut Mönkemeyer. Mainz, B. Schott's Söhne, [cop. 1951–52].
2v. (Edition Schott 4251–4260).
German words.
Contents:
Vol.1. Heft 1–5. Geistliche Chorwerke. Deutscher Meister.
Vol.2. Heft 1–5. Weltliche Chorwerke. Deutscher Meister.
Vol.1.
Heft 1 contains compositions by Martin Agricola, Sixt Dietrich, Benedict Ducis, Heinrich Finck, Lupus Hellingk, Heinrich Isaac, Johann Kugelmann, Stephan Mahu, Leonhard Paminger, Balthasar Resinarius, Ludwig Senfl, Thomas Stoltzer, and Martin Wolff, and the Glogauer Liederbuch.
Heft 2 contains compositions by Jobst vom Brant, Arnold von Bruck, Georg Forster, Christian Hollander, Balduin Hoyoul, Jacobus de Kerle, Mattheus le Maistre, Antonius Scandellus, Leonhard Schröter, and Johann Walther.
Heft 3 contains compositions by Joachim von Burck, Sethus Calvisius, Andreas Crappius, Gallus Dressler, Johann Eccard, Gotthard Erythräus, Cornelius Freundt, Jacobus Gallus, Bartholomäus Gesius, Orlando di Lasso, Leonhard Lechner, Lucas Osiander, Ivo de Vento, and Melchior Vulpius.
Heft 4 contains compositions by Gregor Aichinger, Johann Christenius, Joachim Decker, Johann Christoph Demantius, Adam Gumpelzhaimer, Otto Siegfried Harnisch, Hans Leo Hassler, Rudolf di Lasso,Hieronymus Praetorius, Michael Praetorius, Andreas

Raselius, Andreas Rauch, Melchior Schaerer, and Nicolaus Zangius.
Heft 5 contains compositions by Johann Rudolf Ahle, Johann Sebastian Bach, Dietrich Buxtehude, Johann Crüger, Johann Georg Ebeling, Philipp Heinrich Erlebach, Melchior Franck, Andreas Hammerschmidt, Stephan Otto, Johann Hermann Schein, Heinrich Schütz, Johann Staden, and Johann Stobäus.
Vol.2.
Heft 1 contains compositions by Jobst vom Brant, Benedict Ducis, Heinrich Eitelwein, Heinrich Finck, Georg Forster, Wolfgang Grefinger, Matthias Greiter, Wolff Heintz, Paul Hofhaimer, Heinrich Isaac, Johann Leonhard von Langenau, Erasmus Lapicida, Lorenz Lemlin, Stephan Mahu, Oswald Reytter, Georg Schönfelder, Thomas Stoltzer, and Johann Walther, and the Lochamer Liederbuch, Schedelsches Liederbuch, and Glogauer Liederbuch.
Heft 2 contains compositions by Arnold von Bruck, Anton Gosswin, Mattheus le Maistre, Caspar Othmayr, Clemens non Papa, Wolfgang Schmeitzel, Ludwig Senfl, and Alexander Utendal.
Heft 3 contains compositions by Johann Christoph Demantius, Conrad Hagius, Otto Siegfried Harnisch, Gregor Lange, Orlando di Lasso, Leonhard Lechner, Jacob Regnart, Melchior Schaerer, and Ivo de Vento.
Heft 4 contains compositions by Henning Dedekind, Johann Eccard, Adam Gumpelzhaimer, Hanns Christoph Haiden, Hans Leo Hassler, Valentin Haussmann, Michael Praetorius, Andreas Rauch, Nicolaus Rosthius, Paul Sartorius, Melchior Vulpius, and Erasmus Widmann.
Heft 5 contains compositions by Johann Rudolf Ahle, Heinrich Albert, Johann Sebastian Bach, Melchior Franck, Daniel Friderici, Georg Friedrich Händel, Michael Jacobi, Paul Peuerl, Johann Hermann Schein, Johannes Schultz, Heinrich Schütz, and Johann Staden.

ANTIQUA EDITION. Eine Sammlung alter Musik.
Mainz, B. Schott, 1933– .
No.1– .
Contents (incomplete):
Von zwei Instrumenten an.
Abel, K. F. Sonate E-moll für Viola da Gamba, Cembalo (Klavier) und Bass-Instrument ad lib.
—— Ausgabe für Violoncello und Klavier.
Bach, J. Chr. Sonate Es-dur für Violine und Cembalo (Klavier).
Hammer, F. X. Sonate D-dur (Nr.5) für Viola da Gamba, Cembalo (Klavier) und Bass-Instrument ad lib.
—— Ausgabe für Violoncello und Klavier.
Kühnel, A. Drei Sonaten (Nr.7–9) für Viola da Gamba, Cembalo (Klavier) und Bass-Instrument ad lib.
—— Nr.7, G-dur; Nr.8, A-dur; Nr.9, D-dur.
—— Ausgabe für Violoncello und Klavier.
Leclair, J. M. Sonate G-dur für Flöte (Violine), Cembalo (Klavier) und Bass-Instrument ad lib.
Marais, M. Suite D-moll für Viola da Gamba, Cembalo (Klavier) und Bass-Instrument ad lib.
—— Ausgabe für Violoncello und Klavier.
Ortiz, D. Recercada (Ricercare).
Pisendel, J. G. Sonate für Violine und Cembalo (Klavier).
Platti, G. Drei Sonaten für Flöte oder Violine, Klavier und Bass-Instrument ad lib.
—— Ausgabe für Flöte: Nr.1, E-moll; Nr.2, G-dur; Nr.3, A-dur.
—— Ausgabe für Violine: Nr.1, E-moll; Nr.2, G-dur; Nr.3, A-dur.
Richter, Fr. X. Sonate in G für Flöte (Violine) und Cembalo (Klavier). Violoncello ad lib.
Rolla, A. Drei Duos für Violine und Violoncello.
—— Nr.1, B-dur; Nr.2, C-dur; Nr.3, A-dur.
Simpson, Chr. Variationen über zwei Bassthemen für Viola da Gamba und Cembalo (Klavier).
—— Ausgabe für Violoncello und Klavier.
Stamitz, K. Sonate D-dur für Viola d'Amore und Cembalo (Klavier). Bass-Instrument ad lib.
Telemann, G. Ph. Sonata in G für Flöte (Violine) und Cembalo (oder Klavier). Bass-Instrument ad lib.
Vivaldi, A. Sonate C-moll für Oboe (Flöte oder Violine) und Basso Continuo (Cembalo, Violoncello oder Fagott).
—— Zwei Sonaten für Violine und Klavier (Cembalo), Violoncello (Gambe) ad lib.

Von drei Instrumenten an.
Bach, J. S. Trio-Sonate C-dur für 2 Violinen, Tasten-Instrument und Bass-Instrument ad lib.
Beethoven, L. v. 6 Gesellschafts-Menuette für 2 Violinen und Bass (Violoncello). Klavier ad lib.
Boccherini, L. Sechs Trios für zwei Violinen und Violoncello, Op.35.
Buxtehude, D. Sonate A-moll, Op.1, Nr.3.
—— für Violine, Viola da Gamba, Cembalo (Klavier) und Bass-Instrument ad lib.
—— für Violine (Flöte), Violoncello, Cembalo (Klavier) und Bass-Instrument ad lib.
Camerloher, P. v. Vier Sonaten für 2 Violinen und Klavier, Bass-Instrument ad lib.
Corelli, A. Zwei Kirchensonaten (C, D) für zwei Violinen, Tasten-Instrument und Bass-Instrument ad lib.
Frescobaldi, G. Fünf Canzonen für zwei beliebige hohe Instrumente (Streicher, Bläser oder gemischt), Tasten-Instrument und Bass-Instrument ad lib.
Fux, J. Sonata a tre für 3 Violinen.
Händel, G. F. Trio-Sonate F-dur, Op.5 VI, für zwei Violinen, Tasten-Instrument und Bass-Instrument ad lib.
Haydn, J. Weiner Hofball-Menuette für 2 Violinen und Bass (Violoncello). Klavier ad lib.
—— 2 Divertimenti a tre für Baryton (Viola da Gamba oder Violine), Viola und Violoncello: Nr.109, C-dur; Nr.113, D-dur.
Haydn, J. M. Divertimento C-dur für Violine, Violoncello (Viola) und Violone (Kontrabass oder Violoncello II).
Holzbauer, J. Sinfonia a tre für 2 Violinen und Bass.

Leclair, J. M. Sonate VIII D-dur aus Op.2:
—— für Violine (Flöte), Viola da Gamba, Cembalo (Klavier) und Bass-Instrument ad lib.
—— für Violine (Flöte), Violoncello, Cembalo (Klavier) und Bass-Instrument ad lib.
—— für Violine (Flöte), Viola, Cembalo (Klavier) und Bass-Instrument ad lib.
Purcell, H. Zwei Trio-Sonaten (Gm, B) für zwei Violinen, Cembalo (Klavier) und Bass-Instrument ad lib.
Scheidt, S. 15 Symphonien für 2 Violinen (oder andere Melodie-Instrumente), Violoncello, Bass ad lib., Klavier (Orgel).
Stamitz, J. Orchester-Trios für 2 Violinen und Violoncello (einfach oder chorisch besetzt) mit Kontrabass, Viola und Cembalo (oder Klavier) ad lib. Op.1: Nr.1 in C-dur; Nr.5 in B-dur.
Vivaldi, A. Zwei Sonaten, Op.2, für Violine, Cembalo (Klavier) und Bass-Instrument.
Willaert, A. Neuen Ricercari für drei beliebige Instrumente (Violine, Viola, Violoncello, Blockflöten oder andere Bläser; Streicher und Bläser gemischt).

Von vier Instrumenten an.
Bach, J. Chr. Quartett für Violine, Viola, Violoncello und Klavier (Cembalo).
Boccherini, L. Fünf Leichte Tänzweisen für zwei Violinen, Viola, Violoncello I und Violoncello II ad lib.
Gabrieli, G. Canzoni per sonar, für vier beliebige Instrumente (Violine I/II, Viola, Bass, Blockflöten oder andere Bläser; Streicher und Bläser gemischt) und Tasten-Instrument ad lib.
Händel, G. F. Concerto I a 4, D-moll, für Flöte (Violine), Violine, Violoncello, Tasten-Instrument und Bass-Instrument ad lib.
—— Concerto II a 4, D-dur, für zwei Violinen, Violoncello, Tasten-Instrument und Bass-Instrument ad lib.
Locke, Matthew. Consort zu 4 Stimmen (6 Suiten) für Violen- und Blockflötenchor oder Streichquartett.
Mozart, W. A. Die Mailänder Quartette für zwei Violinen, Viola und Violoncello.
—— Nr.1, A-dur; Nr.2, B-dur; Nr.3, C-dur; Nr.4, Es-dur.
—— 6 Quartetti capricciosi (Leichte Streichquartette) für zwei Violinen, Viola und Violoncello (K.V., Anh.291a).
Paganini, N. Quartetto für Violine, Viola, Violoncello und Gitarre (oder Cembalo).
Palestrina, G. P. da. Ricercare für vier beliebige Instrumente (Violine I/II, Viola, Violoncello, Blockflöten oder andere Bläser; Streicher und Bläser gemischt) oder für ein Tasten-Instrument.
Purcell, H. Pavane und Chaconne für drei hohe Instrumente (Streicher; Blockflöten oder andere Bläser; Streicher und Bläser gemischt) und ein Bass-Instrument.
Telemann, G. Ph. Sonata a 4 per Flauto traverso due Viole di Gamba e Cembalo.
—— für Flöte, zwei Gamben, Cembalo (Klavier) und Bass-Instrument ad lib.
—— für Flöte (Violine), Viola, Gambe, Cembalo (Klavier) und Bass-Instrument ad lib.
—— für Flöte (Violine), zwei Violoncelli, Cembalo (Klavier) und Bass-Instrument ad lib.
—— für Flöte (Violine), Viola, Violoncello, Cembalo (Klavier) und Bass-Instrument ad lib.
—— Sonata a 4, C-dur, für 4 Violinen.
—— Concerto a 4 für 4 Violinen.

Von fünf Instrumenten an.
Stoltzer, Th. Fantasien für fünf beliebige Instrumente (Violine I/II, Viola I/II, Violoncello; Blockflöten oder andere Bläser; Streicher und Bläser gemischt).

Solo-Instrument mit Begleitung.
Bach, J. Chr. Concerto II, A-dur, für Cembalo (Klavier) und Streichorchester.
—— Konzert G-dur für Klavier und Streichorchester.
Bach, W. Fr. Concerto C-moll für Cembalo (Klavier) und Streichorchester.
Mozart, W. A. Drei Konzerte für Cembalo (Klavier) mit Streichorchester.
—— Nr.1, D-dur; Nr.2, G-dur; Nr.3, Es-dur.
Vivaldi, A. 6 Konzerte für Flauto traverso, Streichorchester und Cembalo, Op.10.
—— Konzert in D-dur für Violoncello, Streichorchester und Cembalo.
Vogler, G. J. Variationen und Capriccio über "Malbrough s'en va-t-en guerre" für Klavier (Cembalo) und kleines Kammerorchester.

Instrumente mit Singstimmen.
Gibbons, O. Londoner Strassenrufe für fünf Instrumente (Streicher; Blockflöten oder andere Bläser; Streicher und Bläser gemischt) mit Chor (ad lib.).
Benedicamus Domino. Drei dreistimmige Organa aus der Zeit um 1200 für Singstimmen oder hohe Instrumente (Streicher; Blockflöten oder andere Bläser; Streicher und Bläser gemischt).

Ein Tasten-Instrument allein. (Cembalo bzw. Klavier oder Orgel).
Händel, G. F. Pieces for harpsichord. 76 Stücke für Clavicembalo oder Klavier.
Palestrina, G. P. da. Ricercari für vier beliebige Instrumente oder ein Tasten-Instrument.

ANTIQUITATES MUSICAE IN POLONIA. Redaktion: Prof. Dr. Hieronim Feicht. Warschau, Polnischer Wissenschaftlicher Verlag, 196? – .
v.1– .
To be published.
Contents (proposed):
Ser.I.
Bd.1: Pelpliner Tabulatur. Thematischer Katalog.
Bd.2–7: Pelpliner Tabulatur. Faksimile.
Bd.8–10: Pelpliner Tabulatur. Transkriptionen.
Bd.11: Missale plenarium. Faksimile.
Bd.12: Monumenta Poloniae neumatica. Faksimile.
Bd.13: Mittelalterliche polyphonie. Faksimile.
Bd.14: Mittelalterliche polyphonie. Transkriptionen.

ANTOLOGIA DE COMPOSITORES ARGENTINOS.
Obras para piano y para canto con acompañamiento de piano. (A. Williams). Buenos Aires, 1941.
p.1– .
Contains compositions by J. B. Alberdi, A. Alcorta, and J. P. Esnaola.

Antología de organistas clásicos españoles (siglos XVI, XVII e XVIII), *see* Pedrell, Felipe. Antología de organistas clásicos españoles (siglos XVI, XVII y XVIII).

Antologia di musica antica e moderna per pianoforte, *see* Tagliapietra, Gino. Antologia di musica antica e moderna per pianoforte.

Antología musical; Siglo de oro de la música litúrgica de España, *see* Elúsitiza, Juan B. de. Antología musical; Siglo de oro de la música litúrgica de España.

Antologia polifonica sacra, *see* Rubio, Samuel. Antologia polifonica sacra.

Apel, Willi, 1893– , ed. Corpus of early keyboard music, *see* Corpus of early keyboard music.

APEL, WILLI, 1893– . ed.
French secular music of the late fourteenth century. Edition of the literary texts by Robert W. Linker and Urban T. Holmes, Jr.; with foreword by Paul Hindemith. Cambridge, Mass., Mediaeval Academy of America, 1950.
xii, 39, 133p. 8 plates. (facsims., part col.) (The Mediaeval Academy of America. Publication No.55).
"81 compositions . . . [including] the complete output of the five most prolific composers . . . Matheus de Perusio . . . Anthonellus de Caserta . . . Solage, Trebor and Senleches."

Apel, Willi, 1893– , ed. Historical anthology of music, *see* Davison, Archibald Thompson. Historical anthology of music.

APEL, WILLI, 1893– . ed.
Musik aus früher Zeit für Klavier. Musique du moyen âge pour piano. Music of early times for piano (1350–1650). Hrsg. von Willi Apel . . . Mainz and Leipzig, B. Schott's Söhne; London, Schott & Co., Ltd., [cop. 1934].
2v. (Edition Schott. No.2341–2342).
English edition by American Music Press, 194?– .
Compositions for lute, organ, harpsichord, and other keyboard instruments.
Annotations in German, French, and English.
Contents:
Bd.1. Germany and Italy. (Germany: Conrad Paumann, Paumgartner [a.d. Buxheimer Orgelbuch um 1450], Hans Judenkünig, Hans Kotter, Leonhard Kleber, Hans Neusiedler, Elias Nic. Ammerbach, Augustus Nörmiger, Samuel Scheidt, Erasmus Kindermann; Italy: Joanambrosio Dalza, Franciscus Bossinensis, Girolamo Cavazzoni, Francesco Bendusi, Giov. Gabrieli, Girolamo Diruta, Gio. Maria Trabaci, Adriano Banchieri, Girolamo Frescobaldi).
Bd.2. England, Spain, France. (England: Hugh Aston, John Bull, William Byrd; Spain: Don Luis Milán, Luis de Narvaéz, Enriquez de Valderrábano, Miguel de Fuenllana, Antonio de Cabezón; France: Joh. Bapt. Besardus, Jacques Champion de Chambonnières, Denis Gaultier, Louis Couperin).

Apparatus musico-organisticus, *see* Muffat, Georg. Apparatus musico-organisticus.

Arbeitsgemeinschaft für rheinische Musikgeschichte, *see* Denkmäler rheinischer Musik.

ARCADELT, JACOB, ca.1514–ca.1575.
Opera omnia. Ed. by Albert Seay. Rome, American Institute of Musicology, 19?– .
v.1– . (Corpus mensurabilis musicae. No.31).
Proposed set about 12v.
Contents:
Vol.1. Missa Noe noe, Missa Ave Regina caelorum, Missa de Beata Virgine.

Archives des maîtres de l'orgue des XVIe et XVIIe et XVIIIe siècles, *see* Guilmant, Alexandre. Archives des maîtres de l'orgue des XVIe et XVIIe et XVIIIe siècles.

Archives du chant, *see* Delsarte, François. Archives du chant.

ARCHIVIUM MUSICES METROPOLITANUM MEDIOLANENSE. [Milano], Veneranda Fabbrica del Duomo di Milano, 1958 .
v.1– .
Contents:
Vol.1. Gaffurio, Franchino. Messe.
Vol.2. Gaffurio, Franchino. Messe.
Vol.3. Gaffurio, Franchino. Messe.
Vol.4. Gaffurio, Franchino. Magnificat.
Vol.5. Gaffurio, Franchino. Motetti.
Vol.6, 7, 8. Anonymous composers. Messe, Magnificat, and motetti.
Vol.9. Anonymous composers. Motetti.
Vol.10. Isaac, Heinrich. Messe.
Vol.11. Weerbecke, Gaspar van. Messe e motetti.
Vol.12. Martini, Johannes. Magnificat e messe.

. . . ARCHIVO DE MÚSICA COLONIAL VENEZOLANA. Cuaderno No.1–12. Montevideo, 1942–43.
12 nos.
Issued by the Dirección de Cultura of the Ministerio de Educación Nacional in Caracas, in collaboration with the Instituto Interamericano de Musicología at Montevideo.
Contents:
No.1. Landaeta, J. J. Pésame a la Vírgen. 1942.
No.2. Lamas, J. A. Tres lecciones para el oficio de difuntos. 1942.
No.3. Carreño, Cayetano. Tristis est. 1942.
No.4. Olivares, J. M. Salve. 1943.
No.5. Lamas, J. A. Salve Regina. 1942.

No.6. Carreño, Cayetano. In Monte Oliveti. 1943.
No.7. Lamas, J. A. Populе meus. 1943.
No.8. Caro de Boesi, J. A. Christus factus est. 1943.
No.9. Nolasco Colón, Pedro. Llorad mortales. Partitura para voces y orquesta. 1943.
No.10. Velásquez, José Francisco. Niño mío. Partitura para voces y orquesta. 1943.
No.11. Landaeta, Juan José. Salve Regina. Partitura para voces y orquesta. 1943.
No.12. Velásquez, José Francisco. Tercera lección de difuntos. Partitura para voces y orquesta. 1943.

Archivo de música religiosa, *see* Lange, Francisco Curt. Archivo de música religiosa.

Arie antiche, *see* Parisotti, Alessandro. Arie antiche.

ARION. Ed. by Sir C. Hubert H. Parry, Messrs. Lionel S. Benson and W. Barclay Squire. Laudy and Co., [1899].
3v.
Collection of madrigals and part-songs.
Contents (Vol.1, 3 from *Grove's Dictionary of music and musicians,* 1916, Vol.1, p.105):
Vol.1.
Anon. Amor che deggio far. Filles de Lyon.
Bertani, L. Ch'ami la vita mia.
Sweelinck, J. P. Tu es tout seul.
Franck, Melchior. Whoso doth love must suffer.
Friederici, Daniel. As Cupid once.
Lichfild, Henry. All yee that sleepe in pleasure.
Gibbons, Orlando. Trust not too much.
Weelkes, Th. Lady your eie.
Quintiani, L. At sound of his sweet voice.
Palestrina, G. Mori quasi il mio core.
Lasso, O. di. O let me look on Thee.
—— I know a young maiden.
Tessier, Charles. Au joli bois.
Wilbye, J. Love me not for comely grace.

Vol.2.
Rendall, E. D. Ballet madrigal, S.S.A.T.B.
Dvořák, A. A Slavonic cradle song. S.A.T.B.
Korsakoff, R. Peaceful and still. S.A.T.B.
Rendall, E. D. Dame music. S.A.T.B.
—— Spring the sweet spring. S.A.T.B.
Selimer, J. The broken vow. Trio. S.S.A.
—— The herdsman's call. Trio. S.S.A.
—— Swedish folk-song. Trio. S.S.A.
—— Rosamond. Trio. S.S.A.
—— The fraticide. Trio. S.S.A.
—— Norwegian folk-song. Trio. S.S.A.
Blumenthal, J. White-heart cherries. (Das Herzlein). Soprano solo and chorus.
Henschel, G. To music. S.S.A.T.B.
Gray, A. The midhour of night. S.A.T.B.
Grieg, E. The bearhunter. S.A.T.B.
Benson, L. S. Long time ago. S.A.T.B.

Vol.3.
Josquin des Près. Petite camusette.
Clemens non Papa. La, la, Maistre Pierre.
Vecchi, Orazio. O bella, O bianca.
Calvisius, Sethus. Joseph, lieber Joseph mein.
Weelkes, Th. Loe countrie sports.
Wilbye, J. Adew, sweet Amarillis.
—— When shall my wretched life.
Lefevre, Jacques. Aime-moi bergère.
Vecchi, Orazio. Leggiadretto Clorino.
Albert, Heinrich. Hasten hither.
Anon. Cuckow.
Wizlav, Prince. Mancher Thor.
Spervogel. Tritt ein reines Weib.
Anon. Das Waldvöglein.
Verdelot, Philippe. I vostr'-acuti dardi.
Goudimel, Claude. Psalm CV.
Wilbye, J. Sweet love.
Stabile, Annibale. Io non sò.
Bateson, Th. Phillis, farewell.

ARKWRIGHT, GODFREY EDWARD PELLEW, 1864–1944. ed.
The Old English edition; ed. by G. E. P. Arkwright. No.1–25. London, J. Williams, 1889–1902.
25v.
Contents:
Vol.1. Campion, T. Masque in honour of the marriage of Lord Hayes. 1889.
Vol.2. Arne, T. A. 6 Songs. 1890.
Vol.3–5. Kirbye, G. Madrigals to 4, 5, and 6 voices. 1891–92.
Vol.6. 14 Songs to 3 voices. 1892.
Vol.7–9. Byrd, W. Songs of sundry natures. 1892–93.
Vol.10. Tye, C. Mass to 6 voices. "Euge bone." 1893.
Vol.11–12. Ferrabosco, A. Madrigals from Musica transalpina, 1588. 1894.
Vol.13–15. Weelkes, T. Ballets and madrigals. 1895.
Vol.16–17. Weelkes, T. Airs or fantastic spirits. 1895–96.
Vol.18–20. Pilkington, F. The first book of songs or airs of 4 parts. 1897–98.
Vol.21. Anthems and motets by Robert White, George Kirbye, John Wilbye, and William Daman. 1898.
Vol.22. Milton, John. 6 Anthems. 1900.
Vol.23. Blow, John. 6 Songs, selected from the Amphion anglicus, 1700. 1900.
Vol.24. Purcell, H. 6 Songs, selected from the Orpheus britannicus. 1901.
Vol.25. Blow, J. Venus and Adonis. 1902.

ARNOLD, SAMUEL, 1740–1802. ed.
Cathedral music, being a collection in score of the most valuable and useful compositions for the service by the several English masters of the last 200 years . . . Selected and revised. London, D'Almaine & Co., 1790.
4v.
A reprint was issued by Edward Francis Rimbault in 1843.
Contents (Vol.1, 3–4 from *Grove's Dictionary of music and musicians,* 1916, Vol.1, p.110):
(Abbreviations: M. and E., Morning and Evening; F.A., Full Anthem; V.A., Verse Anthem; S.A., Solo Anthem; Serv., Service).
Vol.1.
Patrick. M. and E. Serv. G minor.

Child. M. and E. Serv. E minor.
—— F.A. If the Lord.
—— F.A. O pray.
Clark. Sanctus.
Kent. F.A. Hearken unto.
Croft. V.A. I will give.
King. F.A. Hear, O Lord.
—— F.A. Rejoice in the Lord.
—— M. and E. Serv. B flat.
Croft. M. Serv. B minor.
Aldrich. M. and E. Serv. in A.
—— 2 chants.
Purcell. V.A. Blessed are they.
Tallis. F.A. All people.
Goldwin. M. and E. Serv. in F.
Weldon. Solo A. O God, Thou hast.
Aldrich. F.A. We have heard.
Goldwin. F.A. Behold my servant.
Aldrich. F.A. Not unto us.
—— F.A. O praise.

Vol.2.
Greene. M. and E. Serv. in C.
—— Solo A. Praise the Lord.
—— V.A. Like as the hart.
Croft. V.A. Be merciful.
King. M. and E. Serv. in F.
—— F.A. O pray.
Greene. V.A. O Lord, I will.
—— V.A. I will magnify.
King. M. and E. Serv. in A.
Tudway. V.A. Thou, O Lord.
Weldon. F.A. Who can tell.
Greene. V.A. O praise.
Bryan. M. and E. Serv. in G.
Travers. M. Serv. in F.

Vol.3.
Boyce. M. Serv. in A.
—— Solo A. Lord, what is.
—— F.A. Save me, O God.
Chants by Savage, Travers, Nares, Kent.
Boyce. Solo A. Lord, teach us.
Tallis. F.A. Hear the voice.
Aldrich. V.A. I am well pleased.
Travers. S.A. Ponder my words.
Nares. M. and E. Serv. in F.
—— F.A. Blessed is he.
—— F.A. O Lord, grant.
—— F.A. Try me.
—— Chant.
Travers. Te Deum in D.
King. M. and E. Serv. in C.
—— V.A. Wherewithal.
Greene. V.A. Hear my prayer.
Boyce. S.A. Turn Thee
—— F.A. Blessing and glory.
King. M. Serv. in A.
Hall and Hine. Te Deum and Jubilate.
Greene. V.A. O God, Thou hast.
Ayrton. Chant.
Travers. V.A. Ascribe.
Aldrich. E. Serv. in F.
Dupuis. Chant.
Boyce. S.A. Ponder my words.
Greene. S.A. O Lord God.

Vol.4.
The organ part to the foregoing.

Arnt von Aich, *see* Aich, Arnt von.

Arras, Chansonnier d', *see* Chansonnier d'Arras.

Arsenal, Le chansonnier de l', *see* Paris. Bibliothèque de l'Arsenal. Mss. (No.5198). Le chansonnier de l'Arsenal.

L'art harmonique aux XIIe et XIIIe siècles, *see* Coussemaker, Edmond de. L'art harmonique aux XIIe et XIIIe siècles.

The art of the suite, *see* Pessl, Yella. The art of the suite.

L'arte musicale in Italia, *see* Torchi, Luigi. L'arte musicale in Italia.

ASENJO Y BARBIERI, FRANCISCO, 1823–1894. ed.
Cancionero musical de los siglos XV y XVI, transcrito y comentado por Francisco Asenjo y Barbieri, individuo de número de la Real Academia de Bellas Artes de San Fernando. Publícalo la Misma Academia. Madrid, Tip. de los Huérfanos, [1890].
636, [2] p.
The original of the Cancionero forms Ms. 2–I–5 of the Royal Library (Real Biblioteca), Madrid.
"Notas biográficas de los autores contenidos en el códice": p.18–49.
Reprint: Buenos Aires, Editorial Schapire, 1945.
See another edition by Querol Gavaldá under Monumentos de la música española, Vol.8–9.
Contents:
Preliminaries; Cancionero (Poesias); Partituras; Apéndices.

ASOCIACIÓN PATRIÓTICA ESPAÑOLA.
Clásicos españoles de la música, publicados por la Asociación Patriótica Española. Dirección de Ernesto Mario Barreda. Buenos Aires, 1938.
1 v.
Contents:
Vol.1. Narváez, Luis de. Tema y variaciones sobre un aire popular. 1938.

Association Internationale des Bibliothèques Musicales. 2. Reihe: Handschriften-Faksimiles, *see* Documenta musicologica. 2. Reihe: Handschriften-Faksimiles.

Atkins, Ivor Algernon, 1869–1953, ed. The great advent antiphons, *see* Plainsong and Mediaeval Music Society. Atkins, Ivor Algernon. The great advent antiphons.

ATTAINGNANT, PIERRE, fl.1528–1549. ed.
Chansons und Tänze; Pariser Tabulaturdrucke für Tasteninstrumente aus dem Jahre 1530, von Pierre Attaingnant, nach dem einzigen bekannten Exemplar in der K. Hof.- und

Staatsbibliothek zu München, hrsg. von Eduard Bernoulli . . . München, C. Kuhn, 1914.
5v. (Added title page: Seltenheiten aus Süddeutschen Bibliotheken in getreuen Nachbildungen, hrsg. unter Leitung von Ernst Freys, Otto Glauning, Erich Petzet. Bd.3).
Vol.I–IV, photographie facsimiles.

ATTAINGNANT, PIERRE, fl.1528–1549. ed.
Transcriptions of chansons for keyboard. Ed. by Dr. Albert Seay. Rome, American Institute of Musicology, 1961.
3v. in 1. (204p.) (Corpus mensurabilis musicae. No.20).
70 pieces.

ATTAINGNANT, PIERRE, fl.1528–1549. ed.
Treize livres de motets parus chez Pierre Attaingnant en 1534 et 1535; réédités par A. Smijers . . . [Paris, Éditions de l'Oiseau Lyre, cop.1934–36; Monaco, Éditions de l'Oiseau Lyre, 1960–].
v.1– .
The later volumes were edited by A. Tillman Merritt.
Contents:
Livre 1 contains 4-part motets by Bouteillier, Claudin, Couillart, Gascongne, Gombert, Lhéritier, Lupus, Mouton, Richafort, Sermisy, Verdelot, Vermont Primus, and Willaert. 1934.
Livre 2 contains compositions by Bouteillier, Claudin, Consilium, Du Lot, Gascongne, Gombert, Lhéritier, Mathias, Mouton, Richafort, Verdelot, and Willaert. 1936.
Livre 3 contains compositions by Claudin, De Ferrare, De la Fage, De Silva, Hesdin, Heurteur, Mouton, Penet, Piéton, Verdelot, and Vermont Primus. 1936.
Livre 4 contains compositions by Consilium, Courtoys, De la Fage, De Silva, Gombert, Hesdin, Heurteur, Josquin des Près, Mathias, Richafort, Verdelot, Vermont Primus, and Willaert. 1960.
Livre 5 contains compositions by Barra, Claudin, Cybot, Du Lot, Fevin, Hesdin, Heurteur, Jacotin, Le Brun, Manchicourt, Mornable, and Penet. 1960.
Livre 6 contains compositions by Claudin, De Billon, Divitis, Du Hamel, Gascongne, Heurteur, Jacotin, Lhéritier, Mouton, and Richafort. 1960.
Livre 7 contains compositions by Certon, Claudin, Consilium, Gombert, Gosse, Hesdin, Heurteur, Hotinet [Barra], Le Roy, Manchicourt, Mornable, Mouton, Rousée, Vermont Primus, and Willaert. 1962.
Livre 8 contains compositions by Consilium, De Ferrare, Gombert, Hesdin, Lasson, Le Brun, Lhéritier, Lupus, Mouton, Richafort, Rousée, and Willaert. 1962.
Livre 9 contains compositions by Briant, Claudin, Gascongne, Gosse, Guyon, Heurteur, Jacotin, Lhéritier, Lupus, Mouton, and Vermont Primus. 1962.
Livre 10 contains compositions by Claudin, Divitis, Fevin, Jacquet, Lenfant, Louvet, Moulu, and Verdelot. 1962.
Livre 11 contains compositions by Claudin, Consilium, De la Fage, Fevin, Gascongne, Lasson, Longueval, Mouton, Passereau, Verdelot, Vermont Primus, and Willaert. 1962.
Livre 12 contains compositions by Barra, Bourguignon, Claudin, Consilium, De Silva, Georget, Gombert, Josquin [des Près], Lhéritier, Moulu, Richafort, Rousée, Sohier, Vermond Primus, and Willaert. 1963.
Livre 13 contains compositions by Cadéac, Claudin, Gombert, Jacquet, Jarsins, Jodon, Joris, Lasson, Lhéritier, Lupi, Manchicourt, Margot, Roger, and Villain. 1963.
Livre 14. Manchicourt, Pierre de. 19 "Musices cantiones." (Published by Attaingnant and entitled by him "Liber decimus quartus"). 1964.

ATTAINGNANT, PIERRE, fl.1528–1549. ed.
Zwei- und dreistimmige Solostücke für die Laute. Hrsg. von Hans Dagobert Bruger. Wolfenbüttel, Gg. Kallmeyer, 1927.
35p. (Beiheft 2 zur "Schule des Lautenspiels").

AUBRY, PIERRE, 1874–1910. ed.
. . . Cent motets du XIIIe siècle publiés d'après le Manuscrit Ed.IV. 6 de Bamberg, par Pierre Aubry . . . Paris, A. Rouart, Lerolle & Co., [1908].
3v. plates, facsims. (Publications de la Société Internationale de Musique. Section de Paris).
Title within ornamental border.
Contents: I. Réproduction phototypique du manuscrit original; II. Transcription en notation moderne et mise en partition; III. Études et commentaires.

Aubry, Pierre, 1874–1910, ed. Le chansonnier de l'Arsenal, *see* Paris. Bibliothèque de l'Arsenal. Mss. (No.5198). Le chansonnier de l'Arsenal.

Aubry, Pierre, 1874–1910, ed. Mélanges de musicologie critique, *see* Mélanges de musicologie critique.

AULER, WOLFGANG, 1904– . ed.
Spielbuch für Kleinorgel, oder andere Tasteninstrumente (Orgel, Cembalo Klavier), Werke alter Meister, mit Registervorschlägen für Positiv und Cembalo, hrsg. von Wolfgang Auler . . . New York, London [etc.], C. F. Peters Corp., cop.1942, 1951.
2v. (On cover: Edition Peters. No.4527 a–b).
Contents:
Vol.1. 16./17. Jahrhundert. Contains compositions by Antonio de Cabezón, Girolamo Frescobaldi, Johann Jakob Froberger, Johann Kaspar Kerll, Florentio Maschera, Johann Pachelbel, Samuel Scheidt, Adam Steigleder, Jan Pieters Sweelinck, Matthias Weckmann.
Vol.2. 17./18. Jahrhundert. Contains compositions by Johann Philipp Krieger, Johann Krieger, Franz Xaver Murschhauser, Johann Pachelbel, Wilhelm Hieronymus Pachelbel, Georg Andreas Sorge, Johann Gottfried Walther.

Aus Natur und Geisteswelt . . . Bd.439, *see* Einstein, Alfred. Beispielsammlung zur älteren Musikgeschichte.

Aus Richard Buchmayers historischen Klavierkonzerten, *see* Buchmayer, Richard. Aus Richard Buchmayers historischen Klavierkonzerten.

Auserwählte Tonwerke der berühmtesten Meister des 15. und 16. Jahrhunderts, *see* Ambros, August Wilhelm. Auserwählte Tonwerke der berühmtesten Meister des 15. und 16. Jahrhunderts.

Ausgewählte Madrigale und mehrstimmige Gesänge, *see* Squire, William Barclay. Ausgewählte Madrigale und mehrstimmige Gesänge.

Ausgewählte Stücke aus dem Fitzwilliam virginal book, *see* The Fitzwilliam virginal book. Ausgewählte Stücke aus dem Fitzwilliam virginal book.

Auswahl vorzüglicher Musik-Werke, *see* Königliche Akademie der Künste. Berlin. Musicalische Section. Auswahl vorzüglicher Musik-Werke.

BACH, CARL PHILIPP EMANUEL, 1714–1788.
. . . Die sechs Sammlungen von Sonaten, freien Fantasien und Rondos für Kenner und Liebhaber. Urtextausgabe herausgegeben von Carl Krebs. Nach dem Erstdruck neu durchgesehen von Lothar Hoffmann-Erbrecht . . . Leipzig, Breitkopf & Härtel, [1953].
6v.
Contents:
Vol.1. Sechs Clavier-Sonaten.
Vol.2. Clavier-Sonaten nebst einigen Rondos fürs Forte-Piano.
Vol.3. Clavier-Sonaten nebst einigen Rondos fürs Forte-Piano.
Vol.4. Clavier-Sonaten und freie Fantasien nebst einigen Rondos fürs Forte-Piano.
Vol.5. Clavier-Sonaten und freie Fantasien nebst einigen Rondos fürs Forte-Piano.
Vol.6. Clavier-Sonaten und freie Fantasien nebst einigen Rondos fürs Forte-Piano.

BACH, JOHANN SEBASTIAN, 1685–1750.
Johann Sebastian Bachs Werke. Hrsg. von der Bach-Gesellschaft. Leipzig, Breitkopf & Härtel, 1851–1926.
61v. in 47. illus.
Issued in 47 Jahrgängen (61 Lieferungen). Each Lieferung has special title page and separate paging.
Editors: Jahrg.1–2, 8, Moritz Hauptmann; Jahrg.3, C. F. Becker; Jahrg.4, 6, Julius Rietz; Jahrg.5, 7, 9–13, 15–23, 25, 28, Wilhelm Rust; Jahrg.$_1$14, Franz Kroll; Jahrg.24, 26–27, 31^{1-2}, 35, 37, 41, 45^2, Alfred Dörffel; Jahrg.29–30, 31^3, 34, 43, Paul Waldersee; Jahrg. 32, 36, 38, 40, 42, 45^1, Ernst Naumann; Jahrg.33, 39, Franz Wüllner; Jahrg.44, 46, Hermann Kretzschmar; Jahrg.47, Wolfgang Graeser.
Pages 155–306 of the first issue of Jahrg.6 have been replaced by the corrected version.
An extensive account of this work may be found in Grove's *Dictionary of music and musicians* under "Bach Gesellschaft."
Contents:
Vol.1. Kirchencantaten. Erster Band. No.1–10.
1. Wie schön leuchtet der Morgenstern.
2. Ach Gott, vom Himmel sieh darein.
3. Ach Gott, wie manches Herzeleid.
4. Christ lag in Todesbanden.
5. Wo soll ich fliehen hin.
6. Bleib' bei uns, denn es will Abend werden.
7. Christ unser Herr zum Jordan kam.
8. Liebster Gott, wann werd' ich sterben?
9. Es ist das Heil uns kommen her.
10. Meine Seel' erhebt den Herren.
Vol.2. Kirchencantaten. Zweiter Band. No.11–20.
11. Lobet Gott in seinen Reichen.
12. Weinen, Klagen, Sorgen, Zagen.
13. Meine Seufzer, meine Thränen.
14. Wär' Gott nicht mit uns diese Zeit.
15. Denn du wirst meine Seele nicht in der Hölle lassen.
16. Herr Gott dich loben wir.
17. Wer Dank opfert, der preiset mich.
18. Gleich wie der Regen und Schnee vom Himmel fällt.
19. Es erhub sich ein Streit.
20. O Ewigkeit, du Donnerwort.
Vol.3. Clavierwerke. Erster Band.
Funfzehn Inventionen und funfzehn Symphonien.
Clavierübung.
Erster Theil. Sechs Partiten.
Zweiter Theil. Ein Concert und eine Partita.
Dritter Theil. Choralvorspiele und Duetten.
Vierter Theil. Aria mit 30 Veränderungen.
Toccata. (Fis moll).
Toccata. (C moll).
Fuga. (A moll).
Vol.4. Passionsmusik nach dem Evangelisten Matthäus.
Vol.5. Part 1. Kirchencantaten. Dritter Band. No.21–30.
21. Ich hatte viel Bekümmerniss.
22. Jesus nahm zu sich die Zwölfe.
23. Du wahrer Gott und Davids Sohn.
24. Ein ungefärbt Gemüthe.
25. Es ist nichts Gesundes an meinem Leibe.
26. Ach wie flüchtig, ach wie nichtig.
27. Wer weiss, wie nahe mir mein Ende.
28. Gottlob! nun geht das Jahr zu Ende.
29. Wir danken dir Gott, wir danken dir.
30. Freue dich, erlöste Schaar.
Vol.5. Part 2. Weihnachts-Oratorium nach dem Evangelisten. Lucas, Cap.2, v.1–21; und Matthäus, Cap.2, v.1–12.
Vol.6. Messe. (H moll).
Vol.7. Kirchencantaten. Vierter Band. No.31–40.
31. Der Himmel lacht, die Erde jubiliret.
32. Liebster Jesu, mein Verlangen.
33. Allein zu dir, Herr Jesu Christ.
34. O ewiges Feuer, o Ursprung der Liebe.
35. Geist und Seele wird verwirret.
36. Schwingt freudig euch empor.

37. Wer da glaubet und getauft wird.
38. Aus tiefer Noth schrei ich zu dir.
39. Brich dem Hungrigen dein Brod.
40. Dazu ist erschienen der Sohn Gottes.

Vol.8. Messen. (F dur, A dur, G moll, G dur).

Vol.9. Kammermusik. Erster Band.
Drei Sonaten für Clavier und Flöte.
Suite für Clavier und Violine.
Sechs Sonaten für Clavier und Violine.
Drei Sonaten für Clavier und Viola da Gamba.
Sonate für Flöte, Violine und bezifferten Bass.
Sonate für zwei Violinen und bezifferten Bass.
Anhang.

Vol.10. Kirchencantaten. Fünfter Band. No.41–50.
41. Jesu, nun sei gepreiset.
42. Am Abend aber desselbigen Sabbaths.
43. Gott fähret auf mit Jauchzen.
44. Sie werden euch in den Bann thun.
45. Es ist dir gesagt, Mensch was gut ist.
46. Schauet doch und sehet, ob irgend ein Schmerz sei.
47. Wer sich selbst erhöhet, der soll erniedriget werden.
48. Ich elender Mensch, wer wird mich erlösen.
49. Ich geh' und suche mit Verlangen.
50. Nun ist das Heil und die Kraft.

Vol.11. Part 1. Magnificat, D dur, und vier Sanctus, C dur, D dur, D moll, G dur.
Anhang.

Vol.11. Part 2. Kammermusik für Gesang. Erster Band.
Der Streit zwischen Phoebus und Pan.
"Weichet nur, betrübte Schatten."
"Amore traditore."
Von der Vergnügsamkeit.
Der zufriedengestellte Aeolus.

Vol.12. Part 1. Passionsmusik nach dem Evangelisten Johannes.

Vol.12. Part 2. Kirchencantaten. Sechster Band. No.51–60.
51. Jauchzet Gott in allen Landen.
52. Falsche Welt, dir trau ich nicht.
53. Schlage doch, gewünschte Stunde.
54. Widerstehe doch der Sünde.
55. Ich armer Mensch, ich Sündenknecht.
56. Ich will den Kreuzstab gerne tragen.
57. Selig ist der Mann.
58. Ach Gott, wie manches Herzeleid. Zweite Composition.
59. Wer mich liebet, der wird mein Wort halten. Erste Composition.
60. O Ewigkeit, du Donnerwort. Zweite Composition.

Vol.13. Part 1. Trauungs-Cantaten.
Dem Gerechten muss das Licht.
Der Herr denket an uns.
Gott ist uns're Zuversicht.
Drei Choräle:
"Was Gott thut, das ist wohlgethan."
"Sei Lob und Ehr' dem höchsten Gut."
"Nun danket alle Gott."

Vol.13. Part 2. Clavierwerke. Zweiter Band.
Sechs grosse Suiten, genannt Englische Suiten.
Sechs kleine Suiten, genannt Französische Suiten.

Vol.13. Part 3. Trauer-Ode, auf das Ableben der Gemahlin August des Starken "Christiane Eberhardine." Königen von Polen und Churfürstin zu Sachsen.

Vol.14. Clavierwerke. Dritter Band.
Das Wohltemperirte Clavier.
Erster Theil. 1722.
Zweiter Theil. 1744.
Anhang. Varianten und Erläuterungen.

Vol.15. Orgelwerke. Erster Band.
Sechs Sonaten für zwei Clavier und Pedal.
Sechs Praeludien und Fugen. Erste Folge.
Sechs Praeludien und Fugen. Zweite Folge.
Sechs Praeludium und Fugen. Dritte Folge.
Drei Toccaten.
Passacaglia.

Vol.16. Kirchencantaten. Siebenter Band. No.61–70.
61. Nun komm, der Heiden Heiland. Erste Composition (1714).
62. Nun komm, der Heiden Heiland. Zweite Composition.
63. Christen, ätzet diesen Tag.
64. Sehet, welch' eine Liebe hat une der Vater erzeiget.
65. Sie werden aus Saba Alle kommen.
66. Erfreut euch, ihr Herzen.
67. Halt' im Gedächtniss Jesum Christ.
68. Also hat Gott die Welt geliebt.
69. Lobe den Herrn, meine Seele.
70. Wachet, betet, seid bereit allezeit.

Vol.17. Kammermusik. Zweiter Band.
Sieben Concerte für Clavier mit Orchesterbegleitung. Nr.1, D moll. Nr.2, E dur. Nr.3, D dur. Nr.4, A dur. Nr.5, F moll. Nr.6, F dur. Nr.7, G moll.
Tripel-Concert für Clavier, Flöte und Violine mit Orchesterbegleitung. A moll.
Anhang.

Vol.18. Kirchencantaten. Achter Band. No.71–80.
71. Gott ist mein König. Componirt 1708.
72. Alles nur nach Gottes Willen.
73. Herr, wie du willt, so schick's mit mir.
74. Wer mich liebet, der wird mein Wort halten. Zweite, grössere Bearbeitung.
75. Die Elenden sollen essen.
76. Die Himmel erzählen die Ehre Gottes. Componirt 1723.
77. Du sollst Gott, deinen Herren, lieben.
78. Jesu, der du meine Seele.
79. Gott, der Herr, ist Sonn' und Schild.
80. Ein' feste Burg ist unser Gott.

Vol.19. Kammermusik. Dritter Band.
Concert in F dur für zwei Hörner, drei Oboen, Fagott, concertirende Quart-Geige, zwei Violinen, Viola, Violoncell und Continuo.
Concert in F dur für concertirende Trompete, Flöte, Oboe und Violine mit Begleitung von zwei Violinen, Viola und Continuo.
Concert in G dur für drei Violinen, drei Violen, drei Violoncelle und Continuo.
Concert in G dur für concertirende Violine mit Begleitung von zwei Flöten (Flûtes à bec), zwei Violinen, Viola, Violoncell und Continuo.
Concert in D dur für Clavier, Flöte und Violine mit Begleitung von Violine, Viola, Violoncell und Continuo.

Concert in B dur für zwei Violen, zwei Gamben, Violoncell und Continuo.
Vol.20. Part 1. Kirchencantaten. Neunter Band. No.81–90.
81. Jesus schläft, was soll ich hoffen?
82. Ich habe genug.
83. Erfreute Zeit im neuen Bunde.
84. Ich bin vergnügt mit meinem Glücke.
85. Ich bin ein guter Hirt.
86. Wahrlich, ich sage euch.
87. Bisher habt ihr nichts gebeten in meinem Namen.
88. Siehe, ich will viel Fischer aussenden, spricht der Herr.
89. Was soll ich aus dir machen, Ephraim?
90. Es reifet euch ein schrecklich Ende.
Vol.20. Part 2. Kammermusik für Gesang. Zweiter Band.
Drama aus das Geburts-Fest August III. Königs von Polen, Churfürsten von Sachsen, etc. "Schleicht, spielende Wellen".
Drama zu einer Universitätsfeier, als Dr. Gottlieb Kortte die Professor erhielt. "Vereinigte Zwietracht der wechselnden Saiden."
Anhang. Drama zum Namenstage des Königs Augustus. "Auf, schmetternde Töne der muntern Trompeten."
Vol.21. Part 1. Kammermusik. Vierter Band.
Concerte für Violine mit Orchesterbegleitung.
No.1 in A moll für eine Violine.
No.2 in E dur für eine Violine.
No.3 in D moll für zwei Violinen.
No.4 in D dur. Sinfoniesatz für concertirende Violine.
Vol.21. Part 2. Kammermusik. Fünfter Band.
Drei Concerte für zwei Claviere mit Orchesterbegleitung.
No.1 in C moll. No.2 in C dur. No.3 in C moll.
Vol.21. Part 3. Oster-Oratorium. "Kommt, eilet und laufet."
Vol.22. Kirchencantaten. Zehnter Band. No.91–100.
91. Gelobet seist du, Jesu Christ.
92. Ich hab' in Gottes Herz und Sinn.
93. Wer nur den lieben Gott lässt walten.
94. Was frag' ich nach der Welt.
95. Christus, der ist mein Leben.
96. Herr Christ, der ein'ge Gottessohn.
97. In allen meinen Thaten.
98. Was Gott thut, das ist wohlgethan. Erste Composition. B dur.
99. Was Gott thut, das ist wohlgethan. Zweite Composition. G dur.
100. Was Gott thut, das ist wohlgethan. Dritte Composition. G dur.
Anhang.
Vol.23. Kirchencantaten. Elfter Band. No.101–110.
101. Nimm von uns, Herr, du treuer Gott.
102. Herr, deine Augen sehen nach dem Glauben.
103. Ihr werdet weinen und heulen.
104. Du Hirte Israël, höre.
105. Herr, gehe nicht in's Gericht.
106. Gottes Zeit ist die allerbeste Zeit.
107. Was willst du dich betrüben.
108. Es ist euch gut, dass ich hingehe.
109. Ich glaube, lieber Herr.
110. Unser Mund sei voll Lachens.
Vol.24. Kirchencantaten. Zwölfter Band. No.111–120.
111. Was mein Gott will, das g'scheh' allzeit.
112. Der Herr ist mein getreuer Hirt.
113. Herr Jesu Christ, du höchstes Gut.
114. Ach, lieben Christen, seid getrost.
115. Mache dich, mein Geist, bereit.
116. Du Friedefürst, Herr Jesu Christ.
117. Sei Lob und Ehr' dem höchsten Gut.
118. O Jesu Christ, mein's Lebens Licht.
119. Preise, Jerusalem, den Herrn.
120. Gott, man lobet dich in der Stille.
Vol.25. Part 1. Die Kunst der Fuge. 1749–1750.
Anhang. Das Berliner Autograph in Anordnung und Lesarten.
Vol.25. Part 2. Orgelwerke. Zweiter Band.
I. Orgelbüchlein. Cöthen 1717–1723.
II. Sechs Choräle, die sogenannten Schübler-schen. 1747–1749.
III. Achtzehn Choräle, die sogenannten grossen mit dem Schwanenliede "Vor deinen Thron tret' ich."
Anhang.
a. Zwei ältere Lesarten zu Sammlung I.
b. Fünfzehn ältere Lesarten zu Sammlung III.
Alphabetisches Inhaltsverzeichniss.
Vol.26. Kirchencantaten. Dreizehnter Band. No.121–130.
121. Christum wir sollen loben schon.
122. Das neugebor'ne Kindelein.
123. Liebster Immanuel, Herzog der Frommen.
124. Meinen Jesum lass' ich nicht.
125. Mit Fried' und Freud' ich fahr' dahin.
126. Erhalt' uns, Herr, bei deinem Wort.
127. Herr Jesu Christ, wahr'r Mensch und Gott.
128. Auf Christi Himmelfahrt allein.
129. Gelobet sei der Herr, mein Gott.
130. Herr Gott, dich loben alle wir.
Vol.27. Part 1. Kammermusik. Sechster Band.
Solowerke für Violine.
Solowerke für Violoncello.
Vol.27. Part 2. Thematisches Verzeichniss der Kirchencantaten. No.1–120.
Enthalten in den Jahrgängen 1, 2, 5 (erste Lieferung), 7, 10, 12 (zweite Lieferung), 16, 18, 20 (erste Lieferung), 22, 23 und 24 der Ausgabe der Bach-Gesellschaft.
Vol.28. Kirchencantaten. Vierzehnter Band. No.131–140.
131. Aus der Tiefe rufe ich, Herr, zu dir.
132. Bereitet die Wege, bereitet die Bahn.
133. Ich freue mich in dir.
134. Ein Herz, das seinen Jesum lebend weiss.
135. Ach Herr, mich armen Sünder.
136. Erforsche mich, Gott, und erfahre mein Herz.
137. Lobe den Herren, den mächtigen König der Ehren.
138. Warum betrübst du dich, mein Herz.
139. Wohl dem, der sich auf seinen Gott.
140. Wachet auf, ruft uns die Stimme.
Anhang.

Zwei ältere Bearbeitungen der Cantate No.134.
a. Mit Gnaden bekröne der Himmel die Zeiten.
b. Ein Herz, das seinen Jesum lebend weiss.
Vol.29. Kammermusik für Gesang. Dritter Band.
Cantate. Was mir behagt, ist nur die muntre Jagd.
Cantate. Non sa che sia dolore.
Hochzeits-Cantate. O holder Tag, erwünschte Zeit.
Cantate. Höchsterwünschtes Freudenfest.
Cantate. Schweigt stille, plaudert nicht.
Cantate. Mir habn en neue Oberkeet.
Anhang.
I. Gratulations-Cantate. Mit Gnaden bekröne der Himmel die Zeiten.
II. Cantate. O, angenehme Melodei.
III. Instrumentalsatz für Violine, Hoboe und Continuo.
Vol.30. Kirchencantaten. Fünfzehnter Band.
No.141–150.
141. Das ist je gewisslich wahr.
142. Uns ist ein Kind geboren.
143. Lobe den Herrn, meine Seele.
144. Nimm, was dein ist, und gehe hin.
145. So du mit deinem Munde bekennest Jesum.
146. Wir müssen durch viel Trübsal in das Reich Gottes eingehen.
147. Herz und Mund und That und Leben.
148. Bringet dem Herrn Ehre seines Namens.
149. Man singet mit Freuden vom Sieg.
150. Nach dir, Herr, verlanget mich.
Vol.31. Part 1. Orchesterwerke.
Ouverturen in C dur, H moll, D dur, D dur.
Sinfonia in F dur.
Vol.31. Part 2. Musikalisches Opfer. 1747.
Anhang.
Auflösungen der Canons.
Auflösung der canonischen Fuge in der Quinte.
Das sechstimmige Ricercare nach dem Autograph Bach's.
Cembalostimme zu dem Trio.
Vol.31. Part 3. Kammermusik. Siebenter Band.
Zwei Concerte für drei Claviere mit Orchesterbegleitung.
No.1 in D moll. No.2 in C dur.
Vol.32. Kirchencantaten. Sechzehnter Band.
No.151–160.
151. Süsser Trost, mein Jesus kommt.
152. Tritt auf die Glaubensbahn.
153. Schau', lieber Gott, wie meine Feind .
154. Mein liebster Jesus ist verloren.
155. Mein Gott, wie lang', ach lange.
156. Ich steh' mit einem Fuss im Grabe.
157. Ich lasse dich nicht, du segnest mich denn.
158. Der Friede sei mit dir.
159. Sehet, wir geh'n hinauf gen Jerusalem.
160. Ich weiss, das mein Erlöser lebt.
Vol.33. Kirchencantaten. Siebzehnter Band.
No.161–170.
161. Komm, du süsse Todesstunde.
162. Ach, ich sehe, jetzt da ich zur Hochzeit gehe.
163. Nur Jedem das Seine.
164. Ihr, die ihr euch von Christo nennet.
165. O heil'ges Geist- und Wasserbad.
166. Wo gehest du hin.
167. Ihr Menschen, rühmet Gottes Liebe.
168. Thue Rechnung! Donnerwort.
169. Gott soll allein mein Herze haben.
170. Vergnügte Ruh', beliebte Seelenlust.
Vol.34. Kammermusik für Gesang. Vierter Band.
Serenata. Durchlaucht'ster Leopold.
Cantata. Schwingt freudig euch empor.
Cantata. Die Freude reget sich.
Dramma per musica. Lasst uns sorgen, lasst uns wachen.
Dramma per musica. Tönet, ihr Pauken! Erschallet, Trompeten!
Cantata gratulatoria in adventum regis. Preise dein Glücke, gesegnetes Sachsen.
Anhang.
I. Dramma per musica. Angenehmes Wiederau.
II. Dramma per musica. Auf, schmetternde Töne der muntern Trompeten.
Vol.35. Kirchencantaten. Achtzehnter Band.
No.171–180.
171. Gott, wie dein Name, so ist auch dein Ruhm.
172. Erschallet, ihr Lieder.
173. Erhöhtes Fleisch und Blut.
174. Ich liebe den Höchsten von ganzem Gemüthe.
175. Er rufet seinen Schafen mit Namen.
176. Es ist ein trotzig und verzagt Ding.
177. Ich ruf' zu dir, Herr Jesu Christ.
178. Wo Gott der Herr nicht bei uns hält.
179. Siehe zu, dass deine Gottesfurcht nicht Heuchelei sei.
180. Schmücke dich, o liebe Seele.
Vol.36. Clavierwerke. Vierter Band.
Suiten, Toccaten, Präludien, Fugen, Fantasieen und andere Stücke.
Anhang I. Varianten zu den vorstehenden Claviercompositionen, sowie zu einigen Stücken des dritten Bandes derselben.
Anhang II. Suiten-Fragmente, verschiedene einzelne Sätze und unvollendete Stücke.
Vol.37. Kirchencantaten. Neunzehnter Band.
No.181–190.
181. Leichtgesinnte Flattergeister.
182. Himmelskönig, sei willkommen.
183. Sie werden euch in den Bann thun. (Zweite Composition).
184. Erwünschtes Freudenlicht.
185. Barmherziges Herze der ewigen Liebe.
186. Ärg're dich, o Seele, nicht.
187. Es wartet Alles auf dich.
188. Ich habe meine Zuversicht.
189. Meine Seele rühmt und preist.
190. Singet dem Herrn ein neues Lied. (Lobe, Zion, deinen Gott.
Vol.38. Orgelwerke. Dritter Band.
Erste Abtheilung.
Praeludien, Fugen, Fantasieen und andere Stücke.
Zweite Abtheilung.
Concerte nach Antonio Vivaldi.
Anhang I. Variante zu Nr.XIV und unvollendete Stücke.

Anhang II. Compositionen, deren Aechtheit nicht völlig verbürgt ist.
Anhang III. Erster Satz des zweiten Concertes in Vivaldi's Original.
Vol.39. Motetten, Choräle und Lieder.
Erste Abtheilung. Die Motetten.
No.1. Singet dem Herrn ein neues Lied, für acht Singstimme.
No.2. Der Geist hilft unsrer Schwachheit auf, für acht Singstimme.
No.3. Jesu, meine Freude.
No.4. Fürchte dich nicht, ich bin bei dir, für acht Singstimme.
No.5. Komm, Jesu, komm, für acht Singstimme.
No.6. Lobet den Herrn, alle Heiden, für vier Singstimme und Continuo.
Anhang zur ersten Abtheilung.
I. Instrumentalbegleitung und bezifferte Orgelstimme zu der Motette "Der Geist hilft unsrer Schwachheit auf."
II. Motette. "Ich lasse dich nicht, du segnest mich denn." Für acht Singstimmen.
III. Motette. "Sei Lob und Preis mit Ehren." Für vier Singstimmen.
Zweite Abtheilung. Choräle und Lieder.
Choräle für vier Singstimmen aus der Sammlung von Carl Philipp Emanuel Bach.
Lieder und Arien aus Schemelli's Gesangbuch und aus dem "Notenbuch" der Anna Magdalena Bach.
Vol.40. Orgelwerke. Vierter Band.
Erste Abtheilung. Choralvorspiele in Kirnberger's Sammlung.
Zweite Abtheilung. Übrige Choralvorspiele.
Dritte Abtheilung. Choralvariationen.
Anhang I. Varianten und Bruchstücke.
Anhang II. Compositionen, welche mangelhaft überliefert oder als ächt nicht sicher verbürgt sind.
Vol.41. Kirchenmusikwerke.
Ergänzungsband.
Kirchencantate Nr.191. Gloria in excelsis Deo.
Drei unvollständige Kirchencantaten.
1. Nun danket alle Gott.
2. Ihr Pforten zu Zion.
3. Ehre sei Gott in der Höhe.
Zwei unvollständige Trauungscantaten.
1. O ewiges Feuer, o Ursprung der Liebe.
2. Herr Gott, Beherrscher aller Dinge.
Einzelne Sätze.
Anhang I. Vier Kirchencantaten, deren Ächtheit als Sebastian Bach'sche Compositionen nicht sicher verbürgt ist.
1. Gedenke, Herr, wie es uns gehet.
2. Gott der Hoffnung erfülle euch.
3. Siehe, es hat überwunden der Löwe.
4. Lobt ihn mit Herz und Munde.
Anhang II. Verzeichniss von Kirchencompositionen des Johann Ludwig Bach in Meiningen.
Nachträge und Bemerkungen.
Vol.42. Clavierwerke. Fünfter Band.
Umarbeitungen eigener und fremder Compositionen.
Verschiedene Präludien, Fugen und andere Stücke, deren Ächtheit wahrscheinlich ist.
Anhang I. Compositionen, deren Ächtheit nicht sicher verbürgt ist, und einige Varianten.
Anhang II. Concert Nr.2 von Vivaldi und Fuge von Erselius in der Originalgestalt.
Vol.43. Part 1. Kammermusik. Achter Band.
Drei Sonaten für Flöte und bezifferten Bass. C dur, E moll, E dur.
Sonate (E moll) und Fuge für Violine und bezifferten Bass.
Sonate für zwei Claviere. F dur.
Concert für vier Claviere nach Antonio Vivaldi.
Anhang. Concert für vier Violinen von Antonio Vivaldi in der Originalgestalt.
Vol.43. Part 2. Musikstücke in den Notenbüchern der Anna Magdalena Bach.
Vol.44. Handschrift in zeitlich geordneten Nachbildungen.
Vol.45. Part 1. Clavierwerke. Zweiter Band.
Neue berichtigte Ausgabe.
Sechs grosse Suiten, genannt Englische Suiten. A dur, A moll, G moll, F dur, E moll, D moll.
Sechs kleine Suiten, genannt Französische Suiten. D moll, C moll, H moll, Es dur, G dur, E dur.
Vol.45. Part 2. Instrumentalwerke. Ergänzungsband.
Canons.
Verschiedene Instrumentalcompositionen.
Clavier-Büchlein für Wilhelm Friedemann Bach.
Angefangen in Cöthen den 22 Januar 1720.
Anhang.
I. Zu dem Violinconcert in A moll.
II. Zu der Cantate No.188, "Ich habe meine zuversicht."
III. Zu dem Wohltemperirten Clavier, Theil I, Theil II.
Vol.45. Part 3. Passionsmusik nach dem Evangelisten Lucas.
Vol.46. Schlussband.
Bericht und Verzeichnisse.
Die Gesangeswerke Bach's.
Thematisches Verzeichniss.
Kirchencantaten.
Oratorien.
Passionsmusiken.
Messen und Mess-Sätze.
Magnificat.
Trauer-Ode.
Trauungs-Cantaten.
Motetten.
Choräle und Lieder.
Kammermusik.
Die Instrumentalwerke Bach's.
Thematisches Verzeichniss.
Namen- und Sachregister.
Vol.47. Die Kunst der Fuge, 1750; in ihre ursprünglichen Form wiederhergestellt und von neuem Hrsg.

BACH, JOHANN SEBASTIAN, 1685–1750.
Werke. Leipzig, Bach-Gesellschaft, [1851–99. Ann Arbor, Michigan, J. W. Edwards, 1947].
60v. in 46 (bound in 47). illus. (Edwards music reprints. Ser.A. Complete works and monumenta, No.1).
"Photolithographischer Neudruck."
Jahrgang 47 not reproduced in this issue.

BACH, JOHANN SEBASTIAN, 1685–1750.
Veröffentlichungen der neuen Bachgesellschaft. Jahrg.1– . Leipzig, Breitkopf & Härtel, 1901– .
v.1– .
Contents:
Jahrg.1.
Bach, J. S. 83 Geistliche Lieder und Arien aus Schemellis Gesangbuch und dem Notenbuch der Anna Magdalena Bach. Für eine Singstimme mit Klavier, Orgel oder Harmonium. Bearb. von Ernst Naumann.
Bach, J. S. 75 Geistliche Lieder und Arien aus Schemellis Gesangbuch und dem Notenbuch der Anna Magdalena Bach. Für gemischten Chor. Bearb. von Franz Wüllner.
Jahrg.2.
Bach, J. S. Orgelbüchlein. 46 kürzere Choralbearbeitungen, für Klavier zu vier Händen. Eingerichtet von B. Fr. Richter.
Bach, J. S. Kirchenkantaten. Heft 1. Klavierauszug. Eingerichtet von Gustav Schreck und Ernst Naumann.
Jahrg.3.
Bach, J. S. Kirchenkantaten. Heft 2. Klavierauszug. Eingerichtet von Gustav Schreck und Ernst Naumann.
Bach, J. S. Drei Sonaten (Nr.1–3). Für Klavier und Violine. Eingerichtet von Ernst Naumann.
Jahrg.4.
Bach, J. S. Drei Sonaten (Nr.4–6). Für Klavier und Violine. Eingerichtet von Ernst Naumann.
Bach, J. S. Bildnis in Heliogravüre. (Nach dem von Fritz Volbach aufgefundenen Ölbild).
Jahrg.5.
Fest-Gottesdienst zum Zweiten Deutschen Bachfest in der Thomaskirche zu Leipzig.
Bach, J. S. Ausgewählte Arien. Mit einem obligaten Instrument und Klavier- oder Orgelbegleitung. 1. Abt.: Arien für Sopran. Bearb. von Eusebius Mandyczewski.
Bach-Jahrbuch 1904.
Jahrg.6.
Bach, J. S. Ausgewählte Arien. Mit einem obligaten Instrument und Klavier- oder Orgelbegleitung. 2. Abt.: Arien für Alt. Bearb. von Eusebius Mandyczewski.
Bach, J. S. Ausgewählte Duette. Mit einem obligaten Instrument und Klavier- oder Orgelbegleitung. 3. Abt.: Duette, Bearb. von Eusebius Mandyczewski.
Bach-Jahrbuch 1905.
Jahrg.7.
Bach, J. S. Kantate Nr.88. "Siehe, ich will viel Fischer aussenden." Partitur zum praktischen Gebrauch. Bearb. von Max Seiffert.
Bach, J. S. Kantate Nr.88. Klavierauszug. Bearb. von Otto Taubmann.
Bach-Jahrbuch 1906.
Jahrg.8.
Bach, J. S. Violinkonzert Nr.2 in E dur. Partitur zum praktischen Gebrauch. Bearb. von Max Seiffert.
Bach, J. S. Violinkonzert Nr.2 in E dur. Klavierauszug. Bearb. von A. Saran.
Bach-Jahrbuch 1907.
Jahrg.9.
Bach, J. S. Kantate Nr.85. "Ich bin guter Hirt." Partitur zum praktischen Gebrauch. Bearb. von Max Seiffert.
Bach, J. S. Kantate Nr.85. "Ich bin guter Hirt." Klavierauszug mit Text. Bearb. von Max Schneider.
Bach, J. S. Brandenburgisches Konzert Nr.3. Partitur zum praktischen Gebrauch. Bearb. von Max Seiffert.
Bach, J. S. Brandenburgisches Konzert Nr.3. Bearbeitung für Klavier zu vier Händen von Max Schneider.
Bach-Jahrbuch 1908.
Jahrg.10.
Bach, J. S. Ausgewählte Arien. Mit einem obligaten Instrument und Klavier- oder Orgelbegleitung. 4. Abt.: Arien für Tenor. Bearb. von Eusebius Mandyczewski.
Bach, J. S. Brandenburgischen Konzert Nr.1. Partitur zum praktischen Gebrauch. Bearb. von Max Seiffert.
Bach, J. S. Brandenburgisches Konzert Nr.1. Bearbeitung für Klavier zu vier Händen von Max Schneider.
Bach-Jahrbuch 1909.
Jahrg.11.
Bach, J. S. Ausgewählte Arien. Mit einem obligaten Instrument und Klavier- oder Orgelbegleitung. 5. Abt.: Arien für Bass. Bearb. von Eusebius Mandyczewski.
Bach-Jahrbuch 1910.
Jahrg.12.
Bach, J. S. Ausgewählte Arien. Mit einem obligaten Instrument und Klavier- oder Orgelbegleitung. 6. Abt.: Arien für Sopran, Heft 2. Bearb. von Eusebius Mandyczewski.
Bach-Jahrbuch 1911.
Jahrg.13.
Bach, J. S. Ausgewählte Arien. Mit obligaten Instrumenten und Klavierbegleitung. 7. Abt.: Arien für Sopran. Heft 3. Weltliche Arien. Bearb. von Eusebius Mandyczewski.
Bach, J. S. Solokantate für Sopran. "Mein Herze schwimmt im Blut." Partitur, hrsg. von C. A. Martienssen.
Bach, J. S. Solokantate für Sopran. "Mein Herze schwimmt im Blut." Klavierauszug mit Text. Bearb. von Max Schneider.
Bach-Jahrbuch 1912.
Jahrg.14.
Bach, J. S. Kantatentexte. Hrsg. und mit Anmerkungen versehen von Rudolf Wustmann.
Bach-Jahrbuch 1913.
Jahrg.15.
Bach, J. S. Ausgewählte Arien. Mit einem obligaten Instrument und Klavier- oder Orgelbegleitung. 8. Abt.: Arien für Alt. Heft 2. Bearb. von Eusebius Mandyczewski.

Bach-Jahrbuch 1914.
Jahrg.16.
Das Bachbildnis der Thomasschule zu Leipzig. Nach seiner Wiederherstellung im Jahre 1913. Gemalt von E. G. Haussmann. 1746.
Bach-Jahrbuch 1915.
Jahrg.17.
Bach, J. S. Motette "O Jesu Christ, mein's Lebens Licht." Partitur. Nach Bachs Handschrift hrsg. von Max Schneider.
Bach, J. S. Motette "O Jesu Christ, mein's Lebens Licht." Klavierauszug mit Text. Bearb. von Max Schneider.
Bach-Urkunden. Ursprung der musikalisch-Bachischen Familie. Nachrichten über Joh. Seb. Bach von Carl Phil. Em. Bach. Hrsg. von Max Schneider.
Bach-Jahrbuch 1916.
Jahrg.18.
Bach, J. S. Konzert in D moll. Partitur nach der ursprünglichen Fassung für Violine, wiederhergestellt von Robert Reitz.
Bach, J. S. Konzert in D moll. Für Violine und Klavier.
Bach-Jahrbuch 1917.
Jahrg.19.
Bach-Jahrbuch 1918.
Verzeichnis der Sammlung alter Musikinstrumente in Bachhause zu Eisenach.
Jahrg.20.
Bach, J. S. Kantate Nr.71. "Gott ist mein König." Klavierauszug mit Text. Bearb. von Otto Schröder.
Bach-Jahrbuch 1919.
Jahrg.21.
Bach, J. S. Ausgewählte Arien. Mit einem obligaten Instrument und Klavier- oder Orgelbegleitung. 9. Abt.: Arien für Tenor. Heft 2. Bearb. von Eusebius Mandyczewski.
Bach-Jahrbuch 1920.
Jahrg.22.
Bach, J. S. Bachs Choralspiel. 22 Orgelchoräle Joh. Seb. Bachs aus Lüneburger bis Weimarer Zeit. Hrsg. von Hans Luedtke.
Bach-Jahrbuch 1921.
Jahrg.23.
Bach, J. S. Kantate Nr.160. "Ich weiss, dass mein Erlöser lebt." Klavierauszug mit Text. Bearb. von Otto Schröder.
Bach-Jahrbuch 1922.
Jahrg.24.
Bach, J. S. Ausgewählte Arien. Mit einem obligaten Instrument und Klavier- oder Orgelbegleitung. 10. Abt.: Arien für Tenor. Heft 3. Bearb. von Eusebius Mandyczewski.
Bach-Jahrbuch 1923.
Jahrg.25.
Bach, J. S. Kantate Nr.142. "Uns ist ein Kind geboren." Klavierauszug mit Text. Bearb. von Otto Schröder.
Bach, J. S. Ausgewählte Arien. Mit einem obligaten Instrument und Klavier- oder Orgelbegleitung. 11. Abt.: Arien für Alt. Heft 3. Bearb. von Eusebius Mandyczewski.
Bach-Jahrbuch 1924.
Jahrg.26.
Bach, J. S. Ausgewählte vierstimmige Chöre zu gottesdienstl. Gebrauch. Bearb. von Julius Röntgen und Otto Schröder.
Bach, J. S. Ausgewählte Duette. Mit obligaten Instrumenten und Klavier- oder Orgelbegleitung. Abt. 12. Heft 2. Bearb. von Eusebius Mandyczewski.
Bach-Jahrbuch 1925.
Jahrg.27.
Bach, J. S. Kantate Nr.106. "Gottes Zeit ist die allerbeste Zeit." (Actus tragicus). Klavierauszug mit Text. Bearb. von Otto Schröder.
Bach-Jahrbuch 1926.
Jahrg.28.
Bach, J. S. Die Kunst der Fuge, 1750. In der Neuordnung von Wolfgang Graeser.
Bach, J. S. Ausgewählte Duette. Mit einem obligaten Instrument und Klavier- oder Orgelbegleitung. Abt. 13. Heft 3. Bearb. von Eusebius Mandyczewski.
Bach-Jahrbuch 1927.
Jahrg.29.
Schütz, Heinrich. Musikalische Exequien. Deutsche Totenmesse. Bearb. von Georg Schumann. Partitur.
Bach, J. S. Trio aus dem Musikalischen Opfer. Bearb. von Max Seiffert.
Bach-Jahrbuch 1928.
Jahrg.30.
Bach, J. S. Sonate G dur für Violine und beziffertem Bass.
Bachs Choralvorspiel, 2. Teil. Leipziger Orgelchoräle. Hrsg. von Hans Luedtke.
Bach-Jahrbuch 1929.
Jahrg.31.
Bach, J. S. Trio für 2 Violinen, Violoncell und Cembalo. Bearb. von Max Seiffert.
Bach, J. S. Kantate Nr.18. "Gleich wie der Regen und Schnee." Klavierauszug mit Text. Bearb. von Otto Schröder.
Bach-Jahrbuch 1930.
Jahrg.32.
Bach-Jahrbuch 1931.
Bach, J. S. Quodlibet. Ein Fragment für 4 Singstimmen mit Generalbass. Erstmals veröffentlicht von Max Schneider.
Ein Bachscher Familientag. Ein fröhliches Spiel um Bachs Hochzeits–Quodlibet und weitl. Kantaten von Hans Joachim Moser.
Jahrg.33.
Bach-Jahrbuch 1932.
Eisenacher Dokumente um Sebastian Bach. Hrsg. von Conrad Freyse.
Jahrg.34.
Weber, Bernhard Christian. Das Wohltemperierte Klavier. 24 Präludien und Fugen durch alle Tonarten für die Orgel. Hrsg. von Max Seiffert.
Bach, J. S. Vom Himmel hoch da komm ich her, per Canones für die Orgel mit 2 Klavieren und Pedal.
Bach-Jahrbuch 1933.
Jahrg.35.
Altnikol, Johann Christoph. Motette für 4 Singstimmen. Befiehlt du deine Wege.
Bach-Jahrbuch 1934.
Matthäus-Passion. Klavierauszug.
Jahrg.36.
Heft 2. Schering, Arnold. Johann Sebastian

Bachs Leipziger Kirchenmusik. 1936.
Jahrg.37.
Heft 2. Bach, J. S. Die Kunst der Fuge, für Klavier zu 4 Händen. Bearb. von Bruno G. Seidhofer.
Jahrg.38.
Heft 2. Verzeichnis der Sammlung alter Musikinstrumente im Bachhause zu Eisenach. 3. ed. [pref. 1939].
Jahrg.39.
Heft 2. Bach, Johann Christoph. Aria Eberliniana. 1940.
Jahrg.41–46. Heft 1. Neumann, Werner. Handbook of Joh. Seb. Bach's cantatas. 1947.
Jahrg.48–50. Heft 1–2. Bach, J. S. Kantate Nr.152. 1950.

BACH, JOHANN SEBASTIAN, 1685–1750.
Die neue Bach-Ausgabe. Hrsg. von Johann-Sebastian-Bach-Institut, Göttingen, und vom Bach-Archiv, Leipzig. Kassel und Basel, Bärenreiter Verlag, 1954– .
8 series. (86v. or 87v. proposed).
To be completed over a period of approximately 15 years.
A "Kritische Bericht" is planned with most of the volumes; also pocket scores, piano scores, and parts for individual works.
Contents (proposed):
Ser.I: Cantatas. (41v. proposed) (Asterisk indicates unpublished volumes).
Vol.1. Advent cantatas.
Vol.2. Cantatas for the first day of Christmas.
*Vol.3. Cantatas for the second and third day of Christmas and the Sunday after Christmas.
*Vol.4. Cantatas for New Year and the Sunday after New Year.
*Vol.5. Cantatas from Epiphany to the 2nd Sunday after Epiphany.
*Vol.6. Cantatas for the 3rd and 4th Sunday after Epiphany.
Vol.7. Cantatas for Septuagesima and Sexagesima.
*Vol.8. Cantatas for Estomihi until Palm Sunday.
*Vol.9. Cantatas for the 1st day of Easter.
Vol.10. Cantatas for the 2nd and 3rd day of Easter.
*Vol.11. Cantatas for Quasimodogeniti until Jubilate.
Vol.12. Cantatas for Cantate until Exaudi.
Vol.13. Cantatas for the 1st day of Whitsun.
Vol.14. Cantatas for the 2nd and 3rd day of Whitsun.
*Vol.15. Cantatas for Trinity and the 1st Sunday after Trinity.
*Vol.16. Cantatas for the 2nd and 3rd Sunday after Trinity.
*Vol.17. Cantatas for the 4th to 6th Sunday after Trinity.
Vol.18. Cantatas for the 7th and 8th Sunday after Trinity. 1966.
*Vol.19. Cantatas for the 9th and 10th Sunday after Trinity.
*Vol.20. Cantatas for the 11th and 12th Sunday after Trinity.
Vol.21. Cantatas for the 13th and 14th Sunday after Trinity.
*Vol.22. Cantatas for the 15th Sunday after Trinity.
*Vol.23. Cantatas for the 16th and 17th Sunday after Trinity.
*Vol.24. Cantatas for the 18th and 19th Sunday after Trinity.
*Vol.25. Cantatas for the 20th and 21st Sunday after Trinity.
*Vol.26. Cantatas for the 22nd and 23rd Sunday after Trinity.
*Vol.27. Cantatas for the 24th until 27th Sunday after Trinity.
*Vol.28. Cantatas for Lady Day.
*Vol.29. Cantatas for St. John's Day.
*Vol.30. Cantatas for Michaelmas.
*Vol.31. Cantatas for Reformation Festival and Dedication of an organ.
*Vol.32. Cantatas for Council election.
Vol.33. Wedding cantatas.
*Vol.34. Cantatas for funerals and various occasions.
Vol.35. Homage cantatas for Weimar, Weissenfels and Cöthen.
Vol.36. Homage cantatas in honour of the Electoral House of Saxony I.
Vol.37. Homage cantatas in honour of the Electoral House of Saxony II.
Vol.38. Festival cantatas for Leipzig University ceremonies.
*Vol.39. Festival cantatas for Leipzig Council and School ceremonies. Homage cantatas for nobles and burghers.
*Vol.40. Wedding cantatas and various works.
*Vol.41. Cantatas of doubtful authenticity.
*Volume of libretti (works of which the music is missing).
Ser.II: Masses, passions, and oratorical works. (9v. proposed).
Vol.1. Missa, Symbolum Nicenum, Sanctus, Osanna, Benedictus, Agnus Dei et Dona nobis pacem, later called Mass in B minor.
*Vol.2. Masses and separate Mass movements.
Vol.3. Magnificat.
*Vol.4. St. John Passion.
*Vol.5. St. Matthew and St. Mark Passion.
Vol.6. Christmas oratorio.
*Vol.7. Easter and Ascension oratorio.
*Vol.8. Arrangements of other composers' works.
*Vol.9. Works of doubtful authenticity.
*Volume of libretti (works of which the music is missing).
Ser.III: Motets, chorales, songs. (3v. proposed).
*Vol.1. Motets.
*Vol.2. Chorales and songs.
*Vol.3. Works of doubtful authenticity.
Ser.IV: Organ works. (9v. proposed).
*Vol.1. Chorale arrangements I. (Little organ book and chorale variations).
Vol.2. Chorale arrangements II. (Schübler chorales and 18 chorales).
Vol.3. Chorale arrangements III.
*Vol.4. Clavierübung. Part III.
*Vol.5/6. Preludes (toccatas, fantasias) and fugues I, II. (Vol.6 published 1964).

*Vol.7. Organ trios and various works.
*Vol.8. Arrangements of other composers' works.
*Vol.9. Works of doubtful authenticity.
Ser.V: Keyboard and lute works. (12v. proposed).
*Vol.1. Clavierübung. Part I.
*Vol.2. Clavierübung. Parts II and IV.
Vol.3. [v.4?] Notebooks for Anna Magdalena Bach, Inventions and sinfonias.
Vol.4. [v.5?] Clavierbüchlein for Wilhelm Friedemann Bach.
*Vol.5. The well-tempered clavier. Part I.
*Vol.6. The well-tempered clavier. Part II.
*Vol.7. English suites, French suites.
*Vol.8. Preludes and fugues, fantasias, toccatas, etc.
*Vol.9. Single suites and suite movements, Capricci, Aria variata, Sonatas; Lute works.
*Vol.10. Arrangements of other composers' works.
*Vol.11. Works of doubtful authenticity.
*Vol.12.
Ser.VI: Chamber music works. (4v. proposed).
Vol.1. Works for violin (Sonatas and Partitas for violin solo, Sonatas for violin and b.c., 6 Sonatas for violin and harpsichord obbligato).
Vol.2. [v.3?]. Works for flute, violoncello, gamba and mixed ensemble (Sonata for flute solo, Sonatas for flute and b.c., Sonatas for flute and obbligato harpsichord, 6 Suites for violoncello solo, 3 Sonatas for viola da gamba and obbligato harpsichord. Trio in G major, instrumental movement in F major).
*Vol.3. Works of doubtful authenticity.
*Vol.4.
Ser.VII: Orchestral works. (6v. proposed).
Vol.1. Orchestral suites. Overtures BWV 1066, 1067, 1068, 1096. 1967.
Vol.2. Brandenburg concertos.
*Vol.3. Concertos for violin, Triple concerto in A minor, Sinfonia in F major.
*Vol.4. Concertos for clavier and orchestra.
*Vol.5. Concertos for 2 claviers and orchestra.
*Vol.6. Arrangements of works of other composers, or presumably other composers.
Ser.VIII: Canons, Musical offering, Art of fugue. (2v. proposed).
*Vol.1. Canons, Musical offering.
*Vol.2. Art of fugue.
For all series together: Catalogue of the water marks appearing in the original manuscripts.

BACH, JOHANN SEBASTIAN, 1685–1750.
Johann Sebastian Bach's Compositionen für die Orgel. Kritisch-korrecte Ausgabe Friedrich Conrad Griepenkerl und Ferdinand Roitzsch. Leipzig, C. F. Peters, n.d.
9v. (Edition Peters. No.240–247, 2067).
Contents (capital letter indicates major key; small letter indicates minor key):
Vol.1. Passacaglia (c); Pastorale (F); 6 Trio sonatas.
Vol.2. Fantasy and fugue (g [Great]); 9 Preludes and fugues (C [Weimar], G [Great], A, f, c [Great], C [Leipzig], a [Great], e [Wedge or scissors], b [Great]).
Vol.3. Fantasy and fugue (c); 6 Preludes and fugues (E♭ [St. Anne's or Trinity]), d [Violin fugue] (g, C, a, e [Cathedral, Little or Night-watchman]); 3 Toccatas and fugues (F, d [Dorian], C).
Vol.4. Canzone (d); 2 Fantasies (G, c); 4 Fugues (c [Legrenzi or Double fugue], g [Little or Folksong], b [on a theme by Corelli], c); Praeludium (a); 4 Preludes and fugues (C [Trumpet], G, D, C [Arnstadt]); Toccata and fugue (d); Trio (d).
Vol.5. 5 Canons on "Vom Himmel hoch"; 7 Chorale preludes; Chorale variations on "Christ, der Du bist der helle Tag" (7 Partitas), "O Gott, du frommer Gott" (9 Partitas), "Sei gegrusset Jesu guetig" (11 Variations); 56 Short chorale preludes.
Vol.6. Chorale preludes (Chorales A to J), incl. Schuebler chorales, No.5; 18 Great chorales, No.3, 5, 12, 13–16; Clavieruebung III, No.7–11, 16–21.
Vol.7. 29 Chorale preludes (Chorales K–Z), incl. No.60; Wir glauben all an einem Gott [The great fugue or The credo; Schuebler chorales, No.1–4, 6; 18 Great chorales, No.1, 2, 4, 6–11, 17, 18; Clavieruebung III, No.1–6, 12–15.
Vol.8. Allabreve (D); 4 Concerti (G, a [Vivaldi], C [Vivaldi], c); Fantasy (C); 2 Fugues (C [Hexachord], g); 3 Preludes (C, C, G); 8 Short preludes and fugues (C, d, e, F, G, g, a, B♭).
Vol.9. Aria (F); 14 Chorale preludes; Partita (Chorale variations on "Ach, was soll ich Suender machen"); Fantasia (G [Concerto]); Fantasia con imitazione (b); Fantasy and fugue (a); 2 Fugues (G [Fugue a la Gigue], G); A short harmonical labyrinthus (c); Pedalexercitium; 3 Trios (G, G [Telemann], c).

BACH, JOHANN SEBASTIAN, 1685–1750.
. . . Complete organ works. W. T. Best edition. Newly revised by Dr. A. Eaglefield Hull . . . London, Augener, Ltd., [cop.1914].
10v. (Augener's Edition. No.9971–9980).
Contents:
Vol.1. The great preludes and fugues.
Vol.2. Preludes, fugues, fantasia and toccatas.
Vol.3. Toccatas, fugues, passacaglia, fantasias.
Vol.4.
Vol.5. Early works and the four concertos.
Vol.6.
Vol.7. The great choral-preludes.
Vol.8. Short choral-preludes.
Vol.9. Choral-preludes, preludes and fugues, and partitas.
Vol.10. Fugues, chorales, variations, etc.

BACH, JOHANN SEBASTIAN, 1685–1750.
. . . Complete organ works. A critico-practical edition in eight volumes. Provided with a Preface containing general observations on the manner of performing the preludes and

fugues and suggestions for the interpretation of the compositions contained in each volume by Charles Marie Widor . . . and Dr. Albert Schweitzer . . . New York, G. Schirmer, Inc., cop.1940– .
8v.
Editor of v.6–8: Eduard Nies-Berger.
Vol.1. Preludes and fugues of the youthful period.
Vol.2. Preludes and fugues of the first master-period.
Vol.3–4. Preludes and fugues of the mature master-period.
Vol.5. Organ concertos and organ sonatas.
Vol.6. Miscellaneous compositions on the chorale.
Vol.7. Catechism hymns; The Orgelbüchlein from Clavierübung, Part III.
Vol.8. To be published.

BACH, JOHANN SEBASTIAN, 1685–1750.
Oeuvres complètes pour orgue, doigtées, annotées par Marcel Dupré. Paris, S. Bornemann, 19?– .
12v.

BACH, JOHANN SEBASTIAN, 1685–1750.
. . . Klavierübung . . . Nach dem erstdruck revidiert und hrsg. von Kurt Soldan. Fingersatz von C. A. Martienssen. New York, London, C. F. Peters, cop.1937.
4v. in 5. (Edition Peters. No.4463a/b–4465, 4462).
Contents:
Vol.1. Pt.1. Partiten. Nr.1–3.
Vol.1. Pt.2. Partiten. Nr.4–6.
Vol.2. Italienisches Konzert. Französisches Ouverture.
Vol.3. Vier Duette.
Vol.4. Aria mit verschiedenen Veränderungen. (Goldberg-Variationen).

BACH, JOHANN SEBASTIAN, 1685–1750.
Klavierwerke von Joh. Seb. Bach. Hrsg. von Czerny, Griepenkerl, und Roitzsch. London, New York [etc.], C. F. Peters, n.d.
23v. (Edition Peters. No.1a–b, 200–219, 1959).
Contents:
Vol.1–2. Wohltemperirtes Klavier.
Vol.3. Kleine Präludien und Fughetten.
Vol.4. Zwei- und dreistimmige Inventionen.
Vol.5. Französische Suiten.
Vol.6–7. Englische Suiten.
Vol.8–9. Partiten.
Vol.10. Italienische Konzert, Chromatische Phantasie usw.
Vol.11. Ouverture, Phantasie, Capriccio usw.
Vol.12. Goldberg-Variationen.
Vol.13. Vier Toccaten und Fugen.
Vol.14. Toccata, Präludium, Phantasie.
Vol.15. Phantasien, Fugen, Suite F moll usw.
Vol.16. Sonaten A moll, C dur, D moll.
Vol.17. Präludien, Fugen, Suiten.
Vol.18. Phantasien, Aria, Toccata.
Vol.19. Capriccio, Sonate, Fugen.
Vol.20. 16 Konzerte nach Vivaldi usw. für Klavier.
Vol.21. Die Kunst der Fuge. Klavier-Ausgabe.
Vol.22. Das Musikalische Opfer.
Vol.23. Klaviermusik. Supplement. (Seiffert).

BACH, WILHELM FRIEDEMANN, 1710–1784.
Ausgewählte Instrumentalwerke. Hrsg. von der Abteilung für Musik der Preussischen Akademie der Künste. Leipzig, Breitkopf & Härtel, 1934.
1 v.
Contents:
Vol.1 contains 4 Trios. (12 parts in 1 v.).

BACH, WILHELM FRIEDEMANN, 1710–1784.
. . . Complete works for organ. Three fugues and seven choral preludes. Ed. by E. Power Biggs. New York, Music Press, Inc., [cop.1947].
32p.

BACH FAMILY.
Die Kunst des Bachsen Geschlechts, hrsg. von A. Fareanu. Leipzig, Breitkopf & Härtel, 1920– .
4v.
Contents (v.1–3 between 1920–23; v.4 between 1924–28):
No.1. Bach, Johann Bernhard. Erste Ouvertüre für Sologeige und Streichorchester, hrsg. von Alexander Fareanu.
No.2. Bach, Nicolaus. Messe (Em) für gemischtem Chor mit Streichorchester und Pianoforte (Cembalo). Ausgabe für den praktischen Gebrauch von Victor Junk.
No.3. Bach, Johann Nicolaus. Der jenaische Wein- und Bierrufer. Komisches Singspiel. Für die Aufführung bearb. von Fritz Stein.
No.4. Bach, Johann Christoph. Motetten. No.1. Fürchte dich nicht! (5 stimmig). No.2. Lieber Herre Gott, wecke uns auf! (8 stimmig für Doppelchor). No.3. Herr, nun lässest du deinen Diener. (8 Stimmig für Doppelchor). Partitur.

BAL Y GAY, JESÚS. arr.
Romances y villancicos españoles del signo XVI. Dispuestos en edición moderna para canto y piano por Jesús Bal y Gay. Ser.1– . México, La Casa de España, 1939– .
v.1– .
Transcribed for 1 voice and piano from lute tablature. Spanish words. "Las fuentes utilizadas para esta edición." Ser.1, p.7.
Contents:
Ser.1. Triste estaba; Sospirastes. Valdovinos; Durandarte, por Luis Milán. De Antequera sale el moro, por Cristóbal de Morales. Mira Nero de Tarpeya, por Juan Bermudo. De dóndevents, amore? por Enríquez de Valderrábano. Falai, miñ' amor, por Luis Milán. Con qué la lavaré? De los á lamos vengo; En la fuente del rosel. Como queréis, madre? Vos me matastes; Quiero dormir, y no puedo, por Juan Vásquez. Ardé, corazón, ardé, por Luis de Narváez. Si la noche hace escura, por Diego Pisador.

BALAKIREV, MILIĬ ALEKSEEVICH, 1836–1910.
Complete piano works. Moscow, State Music Publishers, 1952– .
v.1– .
Contents:

Vol.2. 3 Scherzi; 7 Mazurkas; 3 Nocturnes; 7 Waltzes. 1952.
Vol.3. Pt.1. The desert (Romance). Transcribed for piano; 4 Compositions on folk themes and themes by other composers; 8 transcriptions and arrangements of works by Russian composers; 4 Arrangements of works by western composers; Original compositions for piano (four hands); 5 Sacred works; 7 old Russian epics (Bilini); 10 Wedding songs; 3 Round songs; 5 Slow songs; Suite for piano (four hands); On the Volga (four hands). 1954.
Vol.3. Pt.2. (Two pianos). Concerto in E flat major; Concerto in F sharp minor; Grand fantasy on Russian folk songs; Quartet in F minor (Beethoven, Op.95, transcribed). 1954.

The ballad literature and popular music of the olden time, *see* Chappell, William. The ballad literature and popular music of the olden time; Old English popular music.

Balli antichi veneziani per cembalo, *see* Jeppesen, Knud. Balli antichi veneziani per cembalo.

BANNISTER, HENRY MARRIOTT, 1854–1919.
Monumenti Vaticani di paleografia musicale latina, raccolti ed. illustrati da Enrico Marriott Bannister . . . Editi a cura della Biblioteca Vaticana. Lipsia, O. Harrassowitz, 1913.
lxi, 280, 4p. [addenda] and portfolio of 2p.L., v, 130 (i.e., 132) pl. (facsims.). (Added title page: Codices e Vaticanis selecti phototypice expressi iussu Pii p.x consilio et opera Curator um Bybliothecae Vaticanae. [Series maior]. Vol.XII).
"Principali opere citate nelle mote e siglo relative": p.[xv].
Contents:
Vol.1. Text.
Vol.2. Plates.

Barbieri, Francisco Asenjo y, *see* Asenjo y Barbieri, Francisco.

BARBIREAU, JACQUES, ca.1420–1491.
Opera omnia, ed. by Bernhard Meier. Rome, American Institute of Musicology in Rome, 1954–57.
2v. (Corpus mensurabilis musicae. No.7).
Contents:
Vol.1. All the masses: Missa Virgo parens Christi, Missa faulx perverse, Kyrie paschale, Missa terribilment. 1954.
Vol.2. Motet, chansons. 1957.

BARCELONA. BIBLIOTECA CENTRAL. SECCIÓN DE MÚSICA.
Publicaciones. No.1–15. Barcelona, Institut d'Estudis Catalans, 1921–51.
15v. plates, ports.
Vol.1– , issued by the section and library under an earlier name: Biblioteca de Catalunya. Departámento de Música (varies slightly).
Contents:
Vol.1. Pedrell, Felipe and Higinii Anglès. Els madrigals i la missa de difunts d'en Brudieu. Transcriptión y notas históricas y críticas por Felipe Pedrell e Higinii Anglès. 1921.
Vol.2. Pedrell, Felipe. Catàleg dels manuscrits musicals de la collecció Pedrell, por Higinii Anglès. 1921.
Vol.3, 7. Pujol, Johannis. Opera omnia. Transcripción y revisión crítica por Higinii Anglès. v.1–2. 1926, 1932.
Vol.4, 8, 13. Cabanilles, Johannis. Musici organici. Opera omnia. Transcripción y revisión crítica por Hyginii Anglès. v.1–3. 1927, 1933, 1936.
Vol.5. Rojo, Casiano and Germán Prado. El canto Mozárabe. Estudio histórico-crítico de su antigüedad y estado actual. 1929.
Vol.6. Las Huelgas de Burgos, Spain. (Cisterican Nunnery). El còdex musical de Las Huelgas (Música a veus dels segles XIII–XIV). Introducció, facsímil y transcripció per Higini Anglès. Tres tomos. 1931.
Vol.7. *See* Vol.3.
Vol.8. *See* Vol.4.
Vol.9. Soler, Antoni. Sis quintets per a instruments d'arc i orgue o clave obligat. Transcripció i revisió per Robert Gerhard. Introducció i estudi d'Higini Anglès. 1933.
Vol.10. Anglès, Higini. La música a Catalunya fins al segle XIII, por Higini Anglès. 1935.
Vol.11. Hidalgo, Juan. Celos aun del aire matan. Ópera del siglo XVII. Texto de calderón y música de Juan Hidalgo. Transcripción y estudio por José Subirá. 1933.
Vol.12. Ripollés Pérez, Vicente. El villancico i la cantata del segle XVIII a València. Transcripción y notas históricas por Vicente Ripollés, Canónigo de la Seo de Valencia. 1935.
Vol.13. *See* Vol.4.
Vol.14. Terradelles, Domingo. La merope. Ópera en tres actos de Domingo Terradelles (siglo XVIII). Transcripción y revisión por Roberto Gerhard. 1951.
Vol.15. Anglès, Higini. Las cantigas de Santa María del Rey D. Alfonso el Sabio (1252–1284). Reproducción del Codice princeps J.B.2 de El Escorial y transcripción crítica de todas las melodiás existentes, por Higini Anglès. Vol.1, Facsímil. Vol.II, Transcripción musical. 1943. Vol.III, Estudios.

Barfark, V. *see* Greff, Valentin.

Barreda, Ernesto Mario, 1883– , ed., *see* Asociación Patriótica Española. Clásicos españoles de la música.

BASILICA. MESSEN UND MOTETTEN ALTKLASSISCHER VOKALPOLYPHONIE. Hrsg. von Prof. Dr. H. Lemacher und Prof. Dr. K. G. Fellerer. Düsseldorf, Schwann, 1952–
No.1– .
Contents (arranged by date):
Monte, Philippus de. Missa sine nomine. S.S.A.T.B.B. 1952.
Palestrina, G. P. da. Missa brevis. S.A.T.B. 1952.
Antonelli, Abondio. Missa brevis. S.A.T.B. 1953.

Cifra, Antonio. Missa s'allor che più sperai. S.A.T.B. 1953.
Cannicciari, Pompeo. Missa cum organo. S.A.T.B. and organ. 1954.
Lasso, Orlando di. Missa super passio sparsio. S.A.T.B. 1954.
Palestrina, G. P. da. Missa iste confessor. S.A.T.B. 1958.

BASSES DANSES.
. . . Le manuscrit dit Des basses danses de la Bibliothèque de Bourgogne; introduction et transcription par Ernest Closson. [Bruxelles, 1912].
2p.L., 77, [17] p. facsim.: [46] p. facsim., col. coat of arms. (Société des Bibliophiles et Iconophiles de Belgique. Publication No.4).
"Ce volume a été tiré à 250 exemplaires numérotés à la presse et signés . . ."

BÄUMKER, WILHELM, 1842–1905. ed.
Das katholische deutsche Kirchenlied in seinen Singweisen von den frühesten Zeiten . . . Auf grund handschriftlicher und gedruckter Quellen bearb. von Wilhelm Bäumker. Freiburg im Breisgau, St. Louis, Mo. [etc.], Herder, 1883–1911.
4v.
Vol.1 published 1886; v.2, 1883. Imprint varies.
Vols.1–2: Von den frühesten Zeiten bis gegen Ende des siebzehnten Jahrhunderts. Vol.2 ("Begonnen von Karl Severin Meister") was written originally as a continuation of a work of same title by Meister, of which the first and only volume was published in 1862.
Vol.3, which deals with the 18th century, has title: Das katholische deutsche Kirchenlied in seinen Singweisen. Dritte (schluss-) band. Mit Nachträgen zu den zwei ersten Bänden . . .
In Vol.4, which covers the 19th century, title reads: . . . Vierter und letzter Band. Mit Nachträgen zu den drei ersten Bänden. Auf grund handschriftlicher und gedruckter Quellen bearb. von Wilhelm Bäumker . . . Nach dem Tode des Verfassers hrsg. von Joseph Gotzen.
"Literatur" and "Bibliographie": v.1, p.40–124; v.2, p.20–43; v.3, p.19–118; v.4, p.16–287.

BAUSTEINE FÜR MUSIKERZIEHUNG UND MUSIKPFLEGE. Mainz, Verlag Junge Musik (Schott), 1951– .
v.1– .
Werkreihe.
Contents:
B 101. Jöde, Fritz. Der Singkreisel. Kanons für alle Gelegenheiten des Lebens.
B 102. Zipp, Friedrich. Kein schöner Land. Kleinste Volksliedkantaten in einfacher Besetzung mit Blockflöten, Geigen und Triangel.
B 103. Bialas, Günter. Die alte Weise im neuen Satz, für gemischten Chor zu drei Stimmen.
B 104. Bresgen, Cesar. Die Bettlerhochzeit. Eine kleine Kantate zum Singen, Spielen und Tanzen für Kinderchor, Schulflöten und Schlagzeug.
B 105. Werdin, Eberhard. Kommt, ihr G'spielen. Volkslieder zum Singen und Spielen mit allerlei Instrumenten (Blockflöte, Geige, Schlaginstrumente).
B 106. Maasz, Gerhard. Klingende Jahreszeiten. Kleine Liedvariationen für Gesang, Schulflöte und Geige.
B 107. Hindemith, Paul. Wer sich die Musik erkiest. Bewährte Sing- und Spielmusik für die Jugend/Zusammengestellt von Fritz Jöde.
B 108. Twittenhoff-Kaestner. Das erste Spiel auf der Schulflöte. Spielanweisung für die Sopranflöte C dur (deutsche oder barocke Griffweise).
B 109. Jöde, Fritz. Die Musikantenfibel. (Neuausgabe). Mit vielen vierfarbigen Illustrationen von Heiner Rothfuchs.
B 110. Reusch, Fritz. Elementares Musikschaffen. Band I. "Wir finden Melodien und Begleitformen."
B 111. Bräutigam, Helmut. Tänzerische Spielmusik, für 2 Flöten (auch Sopran- und Altblockflöte), 2 Violinen und Cello (Bass).
B 112. Klein, Richard Rudolf. Das Bauernjahr. Zwölf Bauernregeln zum Singen und Spielen mit 1 bis 2 Singstimmen und 1 bis 2 Geigen.
B 113. Reusch, Fritz. Das Christkindelspiel. Ein Weichnachtsspiel für Kinder zum Singen und Spielen mit 2 und 3 Melodie-Instrumenten.
B 114. Kukuck, Felicitas. Komm, wir wollen tanzen. Neue Jugendtänze für ein und mehr Instrumente. Tanzanweisungen von Karl Lorenz und Thilde Lorenz-Ringlage.
B 115. Bresgen, Cesar. Sonne, Sonne, scheine. Lieder zum Singen und Spielen für Kinder- oder Jugendchor und beliebige Instrumente.
B 116. Reusch, Fritz. Elementares Musikschaffen. Band II.
B 117. Metzler, Friedrich. Die güldene Sonne. Drei kleine Liedkantaten zum Tagesbeginn für Singstimmen und Instrumente.
B 118. Singt dem Kindelein. Kleine Weihnachtsmusiken mit Stimmen und Instrumenten von Cesar Bresgen, Gerhard Maasz, Ilse Sachs und Wilhelm Twittenhoff.
B 119. Bresgen, Cesar. Das Riesenspiel. Eine kleine szenische Kantate für Kinderchor, Schulflöten und Schlagzeug.
B 120. Nitsche, Paul. Die Pflege der Kinderstimme II.
B 121. Höckner, Hilmar. Violin-Übung am Volkslied. Ein methodischer Lehrgang für den elementaren Violin-Unterricht.
B 122. Zanoskar, Hubert. Das Spiel auf der Altfidel. Ein methodischer Lehrgang für die Altfidel in Quart-Terz-Stimmung.
B 123. Jöde, Fritz. Egon Kraus. Der Fünfton. Pentatonische Weisen zum Singen und Spielen.
B 124. Keller, Wilhelm. Quibus, quabus. Neue Weisen für Kinder und Eltern zum Singen und Spielen.
B 125. Rohwer, Jens. Einfache Singsätze, zum Zusammenbauen aus selbständigen Stimmen für gleiche oder gemischte Stimmen.
B 126. Werdin, Eberhard. Die Heinzelmännchen. Ein musikalisches Stegreifspiel zum Singen

und Spielen mit Melodie-Instrumenten und kleinem Schlagwerk.
B 127. Bresgen, Cesar. Uns ist kommen ein liebe Zeit. Kantate nach den Tanzweisen des Neidhardt von Reuenthal zum Singen, Spielen und Tanzen.
B 128. Träder, Willi. Über Jahr und Tag. Liedsätze zum Singen und Spielen.
B 129. Zipp, Friedrich. Heiteres Tierliederspiel, mit verbindenden Reimen von Margareta Fries.
B 130. Bresgen, Cesar. Das Schlaraffenland. Kleine szenische Kantate für 1–3 stimmigen Jugendchor und Instrumente.
B 131. Thiel, Jörn. Ene mene Tintenfass. Szenisches Schulspiel für Kinder zum Singen, Spielen und Tanzen.
B 132. Schroeder, Hermann. Die Weihnachtsgeschichte, für Vorsänger, zweistimmigen Kinderchor und 2 Instrumente (Altflöte, Violine).
B 133. Zipp. Friedrich. Fest und Feier. Kleine Liedkantaten und Instrumentalstücke in einfacher Besetzung.
B 134. Biebl, Franz. Was wir gerne tun. Kinderspiel für 1 und 2 Singstimmen, Sopranflöte (auch andere Melodie-Instrumente) und kleines Schlagwerk (Handtrommel, Triangel usw.).
B 135. Hirtenweihnacht. Fröhliche Hirtenlieder aus Bayern und Österreich zum Singen und Spielen mit Blockflöte, Gitarre und Orff-Instrumenten. Herausgegeben von Sigrid Abel-Struth, Sätze von Günter Bialas.
B 136. Rohwer, Jens. Drei hübsche Mädchen. 15 Liedsätze mit Vorspann-Kanons zum Singen und Spielen-Tenor ad lib.
B 137. Werdin, Eberhard. Verzierte Volksliedsätze, für drei gemischte Stimmen mit Instrumenten.
B 138. Bresgen, Cesar. Das improvisierte Chorlied. 20 europäische Volksliedbeispiele und eine Einführung in die mehrstimmige vokale Improvisation.
B 139. Der Tanzmusikant. Volkstänze für drei beliebige Melodie-Instrumente oder Klavier/Akkordeon, Gitarre ad lib. Herausgegeben von Herbert Oetke.
B 140. Träder, Willi. Singt im Chor. Leichte Volksliedsätze für gemischten Chor.
B 141. Zipp, Friedrich. Fröhlicher Jahrmarkt. Kantate für ein- und zweistimmigen Kinderchor und Instrumente. Text von Hanna Schachenmeier.
B 142. Fegers, Karl. Sechs kleine Weisen, nach Texten von Ringelnatz für hohe Singstimme (Chor), zwei Sopranflöten und Schlagwerk.
B 143. Indo-Amerikanische Tänze, für Sopran- und Altflöte, Gitarre (Laute), Kontrabass und Schlagwerk. Herausgegeben von Guillermo Graetzer.
B 144. Bresgen, Cesar. Morgenmusik, für Blockflötenchor und kleines Schlagzeug.
B 145. Schroeder, Hermann. Uns kommt ein Schiff gefahren. 20 Weihnachtslieder zum Singen und Spielen mit Blockflöte C dur oder F moll oder Violine und Klavier oder Blockflöte, Violine und Violoncello.

BECK, JEAN BAPTISTE, 1881–1943. ed.
Anthologie de cent chansons de trouvères et de troubadours des XIIe et XIIIe siècles . . . [Philadelphia, University of Pennsylvania Press, 1939?].
1p.L., 102p.
Reprinted from Le chansonnier Cangé, t.2.

BECK, JEAN BAPTISTE, 1881–1943. ed.
. . . Les chansonniers des troubadours et des trouvères, publiés en facsimilé et transcrits en notation moderne par Jean Beck . . . No.1–2. Philadelphia, (Penn.), The University of Pennsylvania Press; Paris, H. Champion, 1927–38.
2v. in 4 parts. (Corpus cantilenarum medii aevi. 1.Sér.).
Subtitle varies slightly.
Imprint varies: No.2, Philadelphia, (Penna.), The University of Pennsylvania Press; London, Oxford University Press, H. Milford.
"Revue bibliographique des travaux sur la musique des troubadours et des trouvères: [No.1], t.1, p.vii–xii.
Contents:
No.1, t.1–2. Le chansonnier Cangé, manuscrit français No.846 de la Bibliothèque Nationale de Paris. 1927; No.2, t.1–2. Le manuscrit du roi, fonds français No.844 de la Bibliothèque Nationale, reproduction phototypique. 1938.

Beck, Sydney, ed. Early symphonies and concertos, *see* Early symphonies and concertos.

Beck, Sydney, ed. English instrumental music of the 16th and 17th centuries from manuscripts in the New York Public Library, *see* English instrumental music of the 16th and 17th centuries from manuscripts in the New York Public Library.

Bedbrook, G. S., ed. Early Italian keyboard music, *see* Early Italian keyboard music.

BEDELL, ROBERT LEECH. ed.
. . . The French organist. (L'organiste français). Album of masterpieces of the French and Belgian repertoire. Ed. and compiled by Robert Leech Bedell. New York, Edward B. Marks Music Co., [cop.1944].
2v.
Contents:
Vol.1 contains compositions by Leon Boellmann, Edouard Commette, Theodore Dubois, Eugène Gigout, Joseph Jongen, Henri Libert, Clément Loret, Gabriel Pierné, Charles Quef, J. Guy Ropartz, Charles Tournemire, Louis Vierne, and Charles Marie Widor.
Vol.2 contains compositions by Leon Boellmann, Charles Chaix, Gaston Dethier, Daniel Fleuret, Eugène Gigout, Joseph Jongen, Paul de Maleingreau, Henri Mulet, J, Guy Ropartz, Charles Tournemire, Louis Vierne, and Charles Marie Widor.

BEETHOVEN, LUDWIG VAN, 1770–1827.
Ludwig van Beethovens Werke. Vollständige kritisch durchgesehene überall berechtigte Ausgabe. Mit Genehmigung aller Originalverleger. Ser.1–25. Leipzig, Breitkopf & Härtel, [1864–90].
25 series.
Issued in 25 series, numb.1–311 (No.104, 199–202 assigned but not used; No.17a, 36a, 70a, 111a, 207a–207d added). Most numbers have special title pages and separate paging.
Editors: Guido Adler (Ser.25, No.310–311), Selmar Bagge, Ferdinand David, Franz Espagne, Eusebius Mandyczewski (Ser.25, No.264–309), Gustav Nottebohm, Carl Reinicke, E. F. Richter, and Julius Reitz.
cf. Verzeichnis des Musikalien-Verlages von Breitkopf & Härtel (1892), v.2, p.187.
An account of this work appears in Schweizerisches Jahrbuch für Musikwissenschaft, v.5, p.164–66.
Ser.25, No.311, erroneously assigned to Beethoven, is the 1st movement of a piano concerto in D major by Johann Josef Rösler. cf. Neues Beethoven-Jahrbuch, v.2, p.167–82.
Principally scores. Where required, parts were issued.
Contents:
Ser.1. Symphonien für grosses Orchester.
No.1. C dur, Op.21.
No.2. D dur, Op.36.
No.3. Es dur, Op.55.
No.4. B dur, Op.60.
No.5. C moll, Op.67.
No.6. F dur, Op.68.
No.7. A dur, Op.92.
No.8. F dur, Op.93.
No.9. D moll, Op.125.
Ser.2. Orchester-Werke.
No.10. Wellington's Sieg oder die Schlacht bei Vittoria. Op.91.
No.11. Die Geschöpfe des Prometheus. Ballet. Op.43.
No.12. Musik zu Goethe's Trauerspiel Egmont. Op.84.
No.13. Allegretto in Es.
No.14. Marsch aus Tarpeja in C.
No.15. Militär-Marsch.
No.16. 12 Menuetten.
No.17. 12 deutsche Tänze.
No.17a. 12 Contretänze.
Ser.3. Ouverturen für Orchester.
No.18. Ouverture zu Coriolan. Op.62 in C moll.
No.19. Ouverture zu Leonore. (Fidelio). No.1. Op.138 in C.
No.20. Ouverture zu Leonore. (Fidelio). No.2. Op.72 in C.
No.21. Ouverture zu Leonore. (Fidelio). No.3. Op.72 in C.
No.22. Ouverture. Op.115 (Namensfeier) in C.
No.23. Ouverture zu König Stephan. Op.117 in Es.
No.24. Ouverture. Op.124 (Weihe des Hauses) in C.
No.25. Ouverture zu Prometheus. Op.43 in C.
No.26. Ouverture zu Fidelio. Op.72 in E.
No.27. Ouverture zu Egmont. Op.84 in F moll.
No.28. Ouverture zu Ruinen von Athen. Op.113 in B.
Ser.4. Für Violine und Orchester.
No.29. Concert. Op.61 in D.
No.30. Romanze. Op.40 in G.
No.31. Romanze. Op.50 in F.
Ser.5. Kammermusik für fünf und mehrere Instrumente.
No.32. Septett für Violine, Bratsche, Horn, Clarinette, Fagott, Violoncell und Contrabass. Op.20 in Es.
No.33. Sextett für 2 Violinen, Bratsche, Violoncell und 2 obligate Hörner. Op.81b in Es.
No.34. Quintett für 2 Violinen, 2 Bratschen und Violoncell. Op.29 in C.
No.35. Fuge für 2 Violinen, 2 Bratschen und Violoncell. Op.137 in D.
No.36. Quintett für 2 Violinen, 2 Bratschen und Violoncell. Op.4 in Es. Nach dem Octett. Op.103.
No.36a. Quintett für 2 Violinen, 2 Bratschen und Violoncell. Op.104 in C moll. Nach dem Trio. Op.1, No.3.
Ser.6. Quartett für 2 Violinen, Bratsche und Violoncell.
Erster Band.
No.37. No.1. Op.18, No.1, in F.
No.38. No.2. Op.18, No.2, in G.
No.39. No.3. Op.18, No.3, in D.
No.40. No.4. Op.18, No.4, in Cm.
No.41. No.5. Op.18, No.5, in A.
No.42. No.6. Op.18, No.6, in B.
No.43. No.7. Op.59, No.1, in F.
No.44. No.8. Op.59, No.2, in Em.
No.45. No.9. Op.59, No.3, in C.
Zweiter Band.
No.46. No.10. Op.74 in Es.
No.47. No.11. Op.95 in Fm.
No.48. No.12. Op.127 in Es.
No.49. No.13. Op.130 in B.
No.50. No.14. Op.131 in Cism.
No.51. No.15. Op.132 in Am.
No.52. No.16. Op.135 in F.
No.53. Grosse Fuge. Op.133 in B.
Ser.7. Trios für Violine, Bratsche und Violoncell.
No.54. No.1. Op.3 in Es.
No.55. No.2. Op.9, No.1, in G.
No.56. No.3. Op.9, No.2, in D.
No.57. No.4. Op.9, No.3, in Cm.
No.58. Serenade. Op.8 in D.
Ser.8. Für Blasinstrumente.
No.59. Octett für 2 Oboen, 2 Clarinetten, 2 Hörner und 2 Fagotte. Op.103 in Es.
No.60. Rondino für 2 Oboen, 2 Clarinetten, 2 Hörner und 2 Fagotte. Op.103 in Es.
No.61. Sextett für 2 Clarinetten, 2 Hörner und 2 Fagotte. Op.71 in Es.
No.62. Serenade für Flöte, Violine und Bratsche. Op.25 in D.
No.63. Trio für 2 Oboen und englisches Horn. Op.87 in C.
No.64. 3 Duos für Clarinette und Fagott in C, F, B.

Ser.9. Für Pianoforte und Orchester.
No.65. Erstes Concert. Op.15 in C.
No.66. Zweites Concert. Op.19 in B.
No.67. Drittes Concert. Op.37 in Cm.
No.68. Viertes Concert. Op.58 in G.
No.69. Fünftes Concert. Op.73 in Es.
No.70. Concert für Pianoforte, Violine und Violoncell. Op.56 in C.
No.71. Phantasie mit Chor. Op.80 in Cm.
No.72. Rondo in B.
No.73. Pianofortestimme zu dem Violin-Concert. Op.61 in D.
Ser.10. Pianoforte-Quintett und Quartette.
No.74. Quintett für Pianoforte, Oboe, Clarinette, Horn und Fagott. Op.16 in Es.
No.75. Quartett für Pianoforte, Violine, Bratsche und Violoncell. No.1 in Es.
No.76. Quartett für Pianoforte, Violine, Bratsche und Violoncell. No.2 in D.
No.77. Quartett für Pianoforte, Violine, Bratsche und Violoncell. No.3 in C.
No.78. Quartett für Pianoforte, Violine, Bratsche und Violoncell, nach dem Quintett, Op.16.
Ser.11. Trios für Pianoforte, Violine und Violoncell.
No.79. No.1. Trio. Op.1, No.1, in Es.
No.80. No.2. Trio. Op.1, No.2, in G.
No.81. No.3. Trio. Op.1, No.3, in Cm.
No.82. No.4. Trio. Op.70, No.1, in D.
No.83. No.5. Trio. Op.70, No.2, in Es.
No.84. No.6. Trio. Op.97 in B.
No.85. No.7. Trio in B, in 1 Satze.
No.86. No.8. Trio in Es.
No.87. Adagio, Rondo und Variationen. Op.121a in G.
No.88. 14 Variationen. Op.44 in Es.
No.89. Trio für Pianoforte, Clarinette oder Violine und Violoncell. Op.11 in B.
No.90. Trio für Pianoforte, Violine und Violoncell nach der Symphonie No.2 in D.
No.91. Trio für Pianoforte, Clarinette oder Violine und Violoncell. Op.38 in Es, nach dem Septett, Op.20.
Ser.12. Für Pianoforte und Violine.
No.92. No.1. Sonate. Op.12, No.1, in D.
No.93. No.2. Sonate. Op.12, No.2, in A.
No.94. No.3. Sonate. Op.12, No.3, in Es.
No.95. No.4. Sonate. Op.23 in Am.
No.96. No.5. Sonate. Op.24 in F.
No.97. No.6. Sonate. Op.30, No.1, in A.
No.98. No.7. Sonate. Op.30, No.2, in Cm.
No.99. No.8. Sonate. Op.30, No.3, in G.
No.100. No.9. Sonate. Op.47 in A.
No.101. No.10. Sonate. Op.96 in G.
No.102. Rondo in G.
No.103. Variationen (Se vuol ballare) in F.
Ser.13. Für Pianoforte und Violoncell.
No.105. No.1. Sonate. Op.5, No.1, in F.
No.106. No.2. Sonate. Op.5, No.2, in Gm.
No.107. No.3. Sonate. Op.69 in A.
No.108. No.4. Sonate. Op.102, No.1, in C.
No.109. No.5. Sonate. Op.102, No.2, in D.
No.110. 12 Variationen über ein Thema aus Händel's Judas Maccabäus, in G.
No.111. 12 Variationen über ein Thema aus Mozart's Zauberflöte "Ein Mädchen oder Weibchen." Op.66 in F.
No.111a. 7 Variationen über ein Thema aus Mozart's Zauberflöte "Bei Männern welche Liebe fühlen," in Es.
Ser.14. Für Pianoforte und Blasinstrumente.
No.112. Sonate für Pianoforte und Horn. Op.17 in F.
No.113. 6 Themen für Pianoforte und Flöte oder Violine (ad lib.). Op.105. Heft 1.
No.114. 6 Themen für pianoforte und Flöte oder Violine (ad lib.). Op.105. Heft 2.
No.115. 10 Themen für Pianoforte und Flöte oder Violine (ad lib.). Op.107. Heft 1.
No.116. 10 Themen für Pianoforte und Flöte oder Violine (ad lib.). Op.107. Heft 2.
No.117. 10 Themen für Pianoforte und Flöte oder Violine (ad lib.). Op.107. Heft 3.
No.118. 10 Themen für Pianoforte und Flöte oder Violine (ad lib.). Op.107. Heft 4.
No.119. 10 Themen für Pianoforte und Flöte oder Violine (ad lib.). Op.107. Heft 5.
Ser.15. Für Pianoforte zu 4 Händen.
No.120. Sonate. Op.6 in D.
No.121. 3 Märsche. Op.45 in C, Es, D.
No.122. Variationen (über ein Thema vom Grafen Waldstein) in C.
No.123. 6 Variationen (Lied mit Veränderungen) in D.
Ser.16. Sonaten für das Pianoforte.
Erster Band.
No.124. No.1. Sonate. Op.2, No.1, in Fm.
No.125. No.2. Sonate. Op.2, No.2, in A.
No.126. No.3. Sonate. Op.2, No.3, in C.
No.127. No.4. Sonate. Op.7 in Es.
No.128. No.5. Sonate. Op.10, No.1, in Cm.
No.129. No.6. Sonate. Op.10, No.2, in F.
No.130. No.7. Sonate. Op.10, No.3, in D.
No.131. No.8. Sonate. Op.13 in Cm. (Pathétique).
No.132. No.9. Sonate. Op.14, No.1, in E.
No.133. No.10. Sonate. Op.14, No.2, in G.
No.134. No.11. Sonate. Op.22 in B.
No.135. No.12. Sonate. Op.26 in As.
Zweiter Band.
No.136. No.13. Sonate. Op.27, No.1, in Es (quasi fantasia).
No.137. No.14. Sonate. Op.27, No.2, in Cism (quasi fantasia).
No.138. No.15. Sonate. Op.28 in D.
No.139. No.16. Sonate. Op.31, No.1, in G.
No.140. No.17. Sonate. Op.31, No.2, in Dm.
No.141. No.18. Sonate. Op.31, No.3, in Es.
No.142. No.19. Sonate. Op.49, No.1, in Gm.
No.143. No.20. Sonate. Op.49, No.2, in G.

No.144. No.21. Sonate. Op.53 in C.
No.145. No.22. Sonate. Op.54 in F.
No.146. No.23. Sonate. Op.57 in Fm.
No.147. No.24. Sonate. Op.78 in Fis.
Dritter Band.
No.148. No.25. Sonate. Op.79 in G.
No.149. No.26. Sonate. Op.81a in Es.
No.150. No.27. Sonate. Op.90 in Em.
No.151. No.28. Sonate. Op.101 in A.
No.152. No.29. Sonate. Op.106 in B. (Hammerklavier).
No.153. No.30. Sonate. Op.109 in E.
No.154. No.31. Sonate. Op.110 in As.
No.155. No.32. Sonate. Op.111 in Cm.
No.156. No.33. Sonate in Es.
No.157. No.34. Sonate in Fm.
No.158. No.35. Sonate in D.
No.159. No.36. Sonate in C (leicht).
No.160. No.37. Sonate. No.1 in G (leicht).
No.161. No.38. Sonate. No.2 in F (leicht).
Ser.17. Variationen für das Pianoforte.
No.162. 6 Variationen. Op.34 in F.
No.163. 15 Variationen (mit Fuge). Op.35 in Es.
No.164. 6 Variationen. Op.76 in D.
No.165. 33 Veränderungen über einen Walzer von A. Diabelli. Op.121 in C.
No.166. 9 Variationen über einen Marsch von Dressler in Cm.
No.167. 9 Variationen über das Thema "Quanto è bello l'amor contadino" von Paisiello in A.
No.168. 6 Variationen über das Duett "Nel cor più non mi sento" von Paisiello in G.
No.169. 12 Variationen über das Menuett à la Vigano von Haibl in C.
No.170. 12 Variationen über den russischen Tanz aus dem Ballet: Das Waldmädchen in A.
No.171. 8 Variationen über das Thema "Une fièvre brûlante" von Grétry in C.
No.172. 10 Variationen über das Thema "La stessa, la stessissima" von Salieri in B.
No.173. 7 Variationen über das Quartett "Kind willst du ruhig schlafen" von Winter in F.
No.174. 8 Variationen über das Trio "Tändeln und Scherzen" von Süssmayr in F.
No.175. 13 Variationen über das Thema "Es war einmal ein alter Mann" von Dittersdorf in A.
No.176. 6 Leichte Variationen in G.
No.177. 6 Leichte Variationen über ein Schweizerlied in F.
No.178. 24 Variationen über die Ariette "Vieni amore" von V. Righini in D.
No.179. 7 Variationen über das Volkslied "God save the King" in C.
No.180. 5 Variationen über das Volkslied "Rule Britannia" in D.
No.181. 32 Variationen in Cm.
No.182. 8 Variationen über das Lied "Ich hab' ein kleines Hüttchen nur" in B.
Ser.18. Kleinere Stücke für das Pianoforte.
No.183. 7 Bagatellen. Op.33.
No.184. 2 Praeludien. Op.39.
No.185. Rondo. Op.51, No.1, in C.
No.186. Rondo. Op.51, No.2, in G.
No.187. Phantasie. Op.77 in Gm.
No.188. Polonaise. Op.89 in C.
No.189. 12 Neue Bagatellen. Op.119.
No.190. 6 Bagatellen. Op.126.
No.191. Rondo a capriccio. Op.129.
No.192. Andante favori in F.
No.193. Menuett in Es.
No.194. 6 Menuetten.
No.195. Praeludium in Fm.
No.196. Rondo in A.
No.197. 6 Ländrische Tänze.
No.198. 7 Ländrische Tänze.
Ser.19. Kirchenmusik.
No.203. Missa solennis. Op.123 in D.
No.204. Missa. Op.86 in C.
No.205. Christus am Oelberge. Oratorium. Op.85.
Ser.20. Dramatische Werke.
No.206. Fidelio (Leonore). Oper von Sonnleithner und Treitschke. Op.72.
No.207. Die Ruinen von Athen. Fest- und Nachspiel von A. von Kotzebue. Op.113.
No.207a. Marsch und Chor aus den Ruinen von Athen etc. Op.114.
No.207b. König Stephan. Vorspiel von A. von Kotzebue.
No.207c. Schlussgesang: "Es ist vollbracht" aus dem patriotischen Singspiel: Die Ehrenpforten.
No.207d. Schlussgesang: "Germania, wie stehst du jetzt" aus dem Singspiel: Die gute Nachricht.
Ser.21. Cantaten.
No.208. Der glorreiche Augenblick. Op.136.
No.209. Meeresstille und glückliche Fahrt. Op.112.
Ser.22. Gesänge mit Orchester.
No.210. Scene und Arie: Ah! perfido, für Sopran mit Begleitung des Orchesters. Op.65.
No.211. Terzett: Tremate, empj, tremate, für Sopran, Tenor und Bass mit Begleitung des Orchesters. Op.116.
No.212. Opferlied für eine Singstimme mit Chor und Orchesterbegleitung. Op.121b.
No.213. Bundeslied für 2 Solo- und 3 Chorstimmen mit Begleitung von 2 Clarinetten, 2 Fagotten und 2 Hörnern. Op.122.
No.214. Elegischer Gesang für 4 Singstimmen mit Begleitung von 2 Violinen, Bratsche und Violoncell. Op.118.
Ser.23. Lieder und Gesänge mit Begleitung des Pianoforte.
No.215. An die Hoffnung. Op.32.
No.216. Adelaide. Op.46.
No.217. 6 Lieder von Gellert. Op.48.
No.218. 8 Gesänge und Lieder. Op.52.
No.219. 6 Gesänge. Op.75.
No.220. 4 Arietten und 1 Duett. Op.82.
No.221. 3 Gesänge von Goethe. Op.83.
No.222. Das Glück der Freundschaft (Lebensglück). Op.88.
No.223. An die Hoffnung. Op.94.
No.224. An die ferne Geliebte (Liederkreis). Op.98.

No.225. Der Mann von Wort. Op.99.
No.226. Merkenstein. Op.100.
No.227. Der Kuss. Op.128.
No.228. Schilderung eines Mädchens.
No.229. An einen Säugling.
No.230. Abschiedsgesang an Wien's Bürger.
No.231. Kriegslied der Oestreicher.
No.232. Der freie Mann.
No.233. Opferlied.
No.234. Der Wachtelschlag.
No.235. Als die Geliebte sich trennen wollte. (Empfindungen bei Lydien's Untreue).
No.236. Lied aus der Ferne.
No.237. Der Jüngling in der Fremde.
No.238. Der Liebende.
No.239. Sehnsucht: Die stille Nacht.
No.240. Des Kriegers Abschied.
No.241. Der Bardengeist.
No.242. Ruf vom Berge.
No.243. An die Geliebte.
No.243a. Dasselbe. (Frühere Bearbeitung).
No.244. So oder so.
No.245. Das Geheimniss.
No.246. Resignation.
No.247. Abendlied unterm gestirnten Himmel.
No.248. Andenken.
No.249. Ich liebe dich.
No.250. Sehnsucht von Goethe. (4mal componirt).
No.251. La partenza. (Der Abschied).
No.252. In questa tomba oscura.
No.253. Seufzer eines Ungeliebten.
No.254. Die laute Klage.
No.255. Gesang der Mönche: Rasch tritt der Tod etc., für 3 Männerstimmen (ohne Begleitung).
No.256. Canons.

Ser.24. Lieder mit Pianoforte, Violine und Violoncell.
No.257. 25 Schottische Lieder. Op.108.
No.258. Irische Lieder.
No.259. Englische, Schottische, Irische und Italienische Lieder.
No.260. 12 Schottische Lieder.
No.261. 25 Irische Lieder.
No.262. 20 Irische Lieder.
No.263. 26 Wallisische Lieder.

Ser.25. Supplement.
Gesang-Musik.
No.264. Cantate auf den Tod Kaiser Joseph des Zweiten. Für Solo, Chor und Orchester.
No.265. Cantate auf die Erhebung Leopold des Zweiten zur Kaiserwürde. Für Solo, Chor und Orchester.
No.266. Chor zum Festspiel: Die Weihe des Hauses. Für Solo, Chor und Orchester.
No.267. Chor auf die verbündeten Fürsten. Für vier Singstimmen und Orchester.
No.268. Opferlied. Für drei Solostimmen, Chor und kleines Orchester.
No.269. Zwei Arien für eine Bassstimme mit Orchesterbegleitung.
No.270. Zwei Arien zu Ignaz Umlauf's Singspiel "Die schöne Schusterin."
No.271. Arie "Primo amore piacer del ciel" für Sopran mit Orchesterbegleitung.
No.272. Musik zu Friedrich Duncker's Drama: Leonore Prohaska. No.1. Krieger-Chor. No.2. Romanze. No.3. Melodram. No.4. Trauermarsch.
No.273. Abschiedsgesang. Für drei Männerstimmen.
No.274. Lobkowitz-Cantate für drei Singstimmen mit Clavierbegleitung.
No.275. Ich, der mit flatterndem Sinn. Lied für eine Singstimme mit Clavierbegleitung.
No.276. Merkenstein. Für eine Singstimme mit Clavierbegleitung.
No.277. Der Gesang der Nachtigall. Für eine Singstimme mit Clavierbegleitung.
No.278. Lied (für Frau von Weissenthurn). Für eine Singstimme mit Clavierbegleitung.
No.279. Lied aus Metastasio's "Olimpiade." Für eine Singstimme mit Clavierbegleitung.
No.280. An Minna. Lied für eine Singstimme mit Clavierbegleitung.
No.281. Gedenke mein! Lied für eine Singstimme mit Clavierbegleitung.
No.282. Trinklied (beim Abschied zu singen). Für eine Singstimme mit Clavierbegleitung.
No.283. Klage. Für eine Singstimme mit Clavierbegleitung.
No.284. Elegie auf den Tod eines Pudels. Für eine Singstimme mit Clavierbegleitung.
No.285. Fünf Canons. No.1. Te solo adoro. No.2. Freundschaft. No.3. Glaube und hoffe! No.4. Gedenket heute an Baden! No.5. Freu' dich des Lebens!

Instrumental-Musik.
No.286. Musik zu einem Ritterballet.
No.1. Marsch.
No.2. Deutscher Gesang.
No.3. Jagdlied.
No.4. Romanze.
No.5. Kriegslied.
No.6. Trinklied.
No.7. Deutscher Tanz.
No.8. Coda.
No.287. Zwei Märsche für Militärmusik. Verfasst zum Carroussel an dem glorreichen Namensfeste Ihrer k. k. Majestät Maria Ludovika in dem k. k. Schlossgarten zu Laxenburg.
No.288. Marsch (Zapfenstreich) für Militärmusik.
No.289. Polonaise für Militärmusik.
No.290. Ecossaise für Militärmusik.
No.291. Sechs ländlerische Tänze für zwei Violinen und Bass.
No.292. Marsch für zwei Clarinetten, zwei Hörner und zwei Fagotte.
No.293. Drei Equale für vier Posaunen.
No.294. Trio für Clavier, Flöte und Fagott.
No.295. Sonatine für die Mandoline.

No.296. Adagio für die Mandoline.
No.297. Zwei Bagatellen für Clavier.
No.298. Clavierstück in A moll.
No.299. Allegretto in C moll für Clavier.
No.300. Lustig. Traurig. Zwei kleine Clavierstücke.
No.301. Clavierstücke in B dur.
No.302. Sechs Ecossaisen für Clavier.
No.303. Walzer in Es dur für Clavier.
No.304. Walzer in D dur für Clavier.
No.305. Ecossaise in Es dur für Clavier.
No.306. Ecossaise in G dur für Clavier.
No.307. Allemande in A dur für Clavier.
No.308. Sechs Deutsche für Clavier und Violine.
No.309. Zweistimmige Fuge für Orgel. Revisionsbericht zum Supplement-Bande.
No.310. Konzert in Es dur für das Pianoforte.
No.311. Konzert in D dur, erster Satz, für das Pianoforte.

BEETHOVEN, LUDWIG VAN, 1770–1827.
Ludwig van Beethovens Werke. Another issue. Ann Arbor, Mich., J. W. Edwards, 1949.
25 series in 24v. (Edwards music reprints. Ser.A. Complete works and monumenta, No.2).
"Photolithographischer Neudruck."
Ser.25, No.310–311, not reproduced in this issue. Parts for Ser.10–14, 24 reproduced.
"Inhalt der Serien": v.24, p.[ix]–xv.
"Systematisches Verzeichnis": v.24, p.[xi]–xv.
"Verzeichnis nach Opus Nummern": v.24, p.[xvii]–xviii.

BEETHOVEN, LUDWIG VAN, 1770–1827.
Veröffentlichungen der Beethovenhauses Bonn. Im Auftrage des Vorstandes hrsg. von Ludwig Schiedermair. Bonn, Beethovenhaus; Leipzig, Quelle & Meyer, 1920–33.
9v.
Contents:
Vol.1. Unger, Max. Beethoven über ein Gesamtausgabe seiner Werke . . . 1920.
Vol.2. Beethoven, Ludwig van. Beethovens Streichquartett, Op.18, No.1, und seine erste Fassung. 1922.
Vol.3. Schmitz, Arnold. Beethoven, unbekannte Skizzen und Entwürfe. 1924.
Vol.4. Unger, Max. Beethovens Handschrift. 1926.
Vol.5. Schmidt, Josef. Unbekannte Manuskripte zu Beethovens Weltlicher und Geistlicher Gesangsmusik. 1928.
Vol.6. Schiedermair, Ludwig. Beethoven: Beiträge zum Leben und Schaffen . . . 1930.
Vol.7–8. Haas, Wilhelm. Systematische Ordnung Beethovenscher Melodien. 1932.
Vol.9. Heer, Joseph. Der Graf von Waldstein und sein Verhältnis zu Beethoven. 1933.

BEETHOVEN, LUDWIG VAN, 1770–1827.
Veröffentlichungen des Beethovenhauses in Bonn. Neue Folge. Im Auftrage des Vorstandes hrsg. von Prof. Dr. Joseph Schmidt-Görg. Bonn, Beethovenhaus.
v.1– .
Contents:
1. Reihe. Beethoven. Skizzen und Entwürfe. Erste kritische Gesamtausgabe.
   1. Bd. Drei Skizzenbücher zur Missa Solemnis.
      1. Ein Skizzenbuch aus den Jahren 1819/20.
   2. Bd. Ein Skizzenbuch zur Chorfantasie Op. 80 und zu anderen Werken.
2. Reihe. Beethoven-Jahrbuch.
3. Reihe. Beethoven. Ausgewählte Handschriften in Faksimile-Ausgabe.
   1. Bd. Entwurf einer Denkschrift an das Appellationsgericht in Wien vom 18. Februar 1820.
   2. Bd. Klaviersonate in C-dur, Op.53. (Waldsteinsonate).
   3. Bd. Dreizehn unbekannte Briefe an Josephine Gräfin Deym, geb. v. Brunsvik.
4. Reihe. Schriften zur Beethovenforschung.
   1. Bd. Beethoven. Die Geschichte seiner Familie von Joseph Schmidt-Görg.
   2. Bd. Textkritische Untersuchungen bei Beethoven von Paul Mies.
   3. Bd. Die Faktoren der Einheit in der Mehrsätzigkeit der Werke Beethovens von Ludwig Misch.

Sonderveröffentlichung.
Festschrift. Joseph Schmidt-Görg zum 60. Geburtstag.

BEETHOVEN, LUDWIG VAN, 1770–1827.
[Unvollendete Gesamtausgabe erschienen in:] Wien, Haslinger, 1828– .
Ser.1– .
Contents:
Ser.I: Sonaten für das Pianoforte.
Nr.1. 1. Werk. No.1. [Ohne Umschlag, aber mit dem Widmungsblatt und der Beglaubigung, die mit Beethovens Unterschrift in Facsimile abschliesst; vergleiche Abbildung bei E. Bücken; Ludwig van Beethoven, Potsdam, 1934]. Es- dur. Nottebohm.
Nr.2. 1. Werk. No.2. . . . F moll. Nottebohm.
Nr.3. 1. Werk. No.3. . . . D dur. Nottebohm.
Nr.4. 10. Werk. No.1. . . . C moll. Op.10. Nr.1.
Nr.5. 10. Werk. No.2. . . . F dur. Op.10. Nr.2.
Nr.20. 29. Werk. No.2. . . . D moll. Op.31. Nr.2. [Mit abweichendem Titel: "Section I" und Nouvelle Edition exacte. S. 2 unten a.d. Platte: "Beethoven, I. No.20. Verlag von Josef Czerny in Wien. Mit dessen Einwilligung in diese Gesamtausgabe aufgenommen. Wien, bei Tobias Haslinger"].
Nr.22. 57. Werk. . . . F moll. Op.57.
Nr.23. 78. Werk. . . . Fis dur. Op.78.
Nr.25. 81. Werk. . . . Es dur. Op.81a.
Nr.26. 90. Werk. . . . E moll. Op.90.
Nr.27. 101. Werk. . . . A dur. Op.101.
Nr.28. 109. Werk. . . . E dur. Op.109.
Nr.29. 110. Werk. . . . As dur. Op.110.
Nr.30. 111. Werk. . . . C moll. Op.111.

Ser.II: Kleinere Kompositionen für das Pianoforte allein.

Nr.2. [Teil 2]. Prélude. No.29 . . . Präludium F moll. Nottebohm.

Ser.V: Duetten für Pianoforte und Violine.
Nr.1. 17. Werk. . . . Sonate für Pianoforte und Horn, F dur. Op.17, arrangiert für Pianoforte und Violine [s. Anmerkung].
Nr.2. 23. Werk. . . . A moll. Sonate. Op.23.
Nr.3. 24. Werk. . . . F dur. Sonate. Op.24.
Nr.4. 30. Werk. No.1. . . . A dur. Sonate. Op.30. Nr.1.
Nr.5. 30. Werk. No.2. . . . G dur. Sonate. Op.30. Nr.3.
Nr.6. 30. Werk. No.3. . . . C moll. Sonate. Op.30. Nr.2.
Nr.7. 47. Werk. . . . A dur. Sonate. Op.47.
Nr.8. 96. Werk. . . . G dur. Sonate. Op.96.

Ser.VI: Duetten für Pianoforte und Violoncello.
Nr.1. Sonate. 17. Werk (in F dur) für Pianoforte und Violoncell (Flöte oder Horn oder Violine oder Viola) [spätere Abzug mit der Verlags-Bezeichnung. Wien, Carl Haslinger Qm. Tobias . . .].

Ser.VII: Trios für Pianoforte, Violine und Violoncell.
Nr.1. 1. Werk. No.1. Es dur.
Nr.2. 1. Werk. No.2. G dur.
Nr.3. 1. Werk. No.3. C moll.
Nr.5. 97. Werk. B dur.

Ser.IX: Sämmtliche Concerte in Partitur.
Nr.(1). Werk. Concert für das Pianoforte, mit Beleitung des Orchesters [s. Anmerkung].

Ser.XI: Quartetten für zwei Violinen, Viola und Violoncello.
[Stimmen].
Nr.4. 18. Werk. No.4. C moll.
Nr.9. 59. Werk. No.3. C dur.
Nr.11. 95. Werk. F moll.

BEETHOVEN, LUDWIG VAN, 1770–1827.
Ludwig van Beethovens Werke. Neue kritisch durchgesehene Gesamtausgabe für Unterricht und praktischen Gebrauch. (Orchester für Klavier übertragen) . . . Leipzig, Breitkopf & Härtel, [1888–92].
20v.
Contents:
Gesangwerke.
Bd.1. 132 Volkslieder.
Bd.2. 107 Lieder und Gesänge.
Bd.3. Kirchenmusik.
Bd.4. Dramatische Werke.
Bd.5. Kantaten und Gesange.

Klavierwerke.
Bd.6. Gesammelte Werke für Klavier.
Bd.7. Sonaten. Abt.1–2.
Bd.8. Variationen.
Bd.9. Koncerte. Abt.1–2.

Orchesterwerke. (für Klavier übertragen).
Bd.10. Gesammelte Orchesterwerke.
Bd.11. Symphonien.
Bd.12. Ouverturen.

Kammermusik.
Bd.13. Septett, Sextett, Quintette für Streichinstrumente. 10 parts in 1 v.
Bd.14. Streichquartette. Abt.1–4.
Bd.15. Streichtrios. 3 parts in 1 v.
Bd.16. Kammermusik für Blas Instrumente. 16 parts in 1 v.
Bd.17. Klavier-Quintett und -Quartette. 8 parts in 1 v.
Bd.18. Klavier-Trios. Abt.1–3.
Bd.19. Werke für Klavier und Violoncell. [Abt. 1–2].
Bd.20. Werke für Klavier und Violine. Abt.1–2.

BEETHOVEN, LUDWIG VAN, 1770–1827.
Sämtliche Werke. Ed. by Schmidt-Görg. Munich, G. Henle Verlag, 1960– .
14 series.
Proposed set will consist of about 40v.
Contents:
Abt.I. Symphonien.
Abt.II. Andere Orchesterwerke.
Abt.III. Werke für ein und mehrere Soloinstrumente mit Orchester.
Abt.IV. Kammermusik mit Klavier.
Abt.V. Duos mit Klavier.
Abt.VI. Kammermusik ohne Klavier.
Bd.3. Streichquartette I, Op.18, Nr.1–6. 1962.
Abt.VII. Werke für Klavier.
Bd.5. Variationen für Klavier. 1960.
Abt.VIII. Geistliche Chorwerke.
Abt.IX. Dramatische Werke.
Abt.X. Kantaten und Gesänge mit Orchester.
Abt.XI. Mehrstimmige Gesänge ohne Begleitung.
Abt.XII. Lieder und Gesänge mit Trio-Begleitung.
Abt.XIII. Lieder mit Klavier.
Abt.XIV. Nachtrag.

BEETHOVEN, LUDWIG VAN, 1770–1827.
Sämtliche Werke. Supplemente zur Gesamtausgabe. Hrsg. von Willy Hess. Wiesbaden, Breitkopf & Härtel, [cop.1959–].
v.1– .
Contents:
Bd.1. Mehrstimmige Italienische Gesänge ohne Begleitung. 1959.
Bd.2. Gesänge mit Orchester. 1960.
Bd.3. Werke für Soloinstrumente und Orchester. Band I. 1960.
Bd.4. Werke für Orchester. 1961.
Bd.5. Lieder und Gesänge mit Klavierbegleitung, Kanons und Musikalische Scherze. 1962.
Bd.6. Duette, Trios, Quartette, Quintette für Streichinstrumente.
Bd.7. Kammermusik für Blasinstrumente, Kammermusik für Bläser und Streicher, Werke für ein mechanisches Laufwerk.
Bd.8. Original-Klavierauszüge zweihändig und vierhändig.

BEETHOVEN, LUDWIG VAN, 1770–1827.
. . . Klavierstücke. Hrsg. und mit Fingersatz versehen von Louis Köhler und Adolf Ruthardt. Frankfurt, New York [etc.], Peters Edition, n.d.
7v. (Edition Peters. No.296a/b, 1231, 297, 298a/b, 144).

Contents:
Vol.1–2. Sonaten.
Vol.3. Sechs Sonatinen.
Vol.4. Stücke, Rondos, Bagatellen.
Vol.5–6. Variationen.
Vol.7. Konzerte und Phantasie. Op.80.

BÈGUE, NICOLAS ANTOINE LE, ca.1630–1702.
Oeuvres de clavecin. Oeuvres complètes. (Premier et deuxième livres). Ed. Norbert Dufourcq. Monaco, Éditions de l'Oiseau-Lyre, 19?– .
89p.

Beispielsammlung zur älteren Musikgeschichte, *see* Einstein, Alfred. Beispielsammlung zur älteren Musikgeschichte.

Belgische Vereniging voor Muziekwetenschap, *see* Société Belge de Musicologie.

Benedicamus Domino, *see* Schmidt-Garre, Helmut. Benedicamus Domino.

Benedictines of Solesmes. Paléographie musicale, *see* Paléographie musicale.

BENEVENUTI, GIACOMO, 1885– . ed.
Cembalisti italiani del settecento. Diciotto sonate. Mailand, G. Ricordi, 1926.
147p.
Includes 18 sonatas from the Hoffner collection.
Preface notes are in Italian, French, and English.
Contains compositions by Ferdinando Bertoni, Baldassare Galuppi, (il Buranello), Vincenzo Manfredini, Giovanni Antonio Paganelli, Giuseppe Paladini, Pietro Domenico Paradies (known mostly as Domenico), Padre Fulgenzio Peroti, Giovanni Battista Pescetti, Giovanni Maria Rutini (he also used the names of Giovanni Marco and Giovanni Placido), Pietro Pompeo Sales, Giovanni Battista Sammartini, and Giovanni Battista Serini.

BENEVOLI, ORAZIO, 1605–1672.
Opera omnia. [Rome], Societas Universalis Sanctae Ceciliae, 1966– .
13v. (Monumenta liturgiae polychoralis sanctae ecclesiae romanae).
Editor: v.1– , Laurentius Feininger.
Contents (in progress). (Asterisk indicates unpublished volumes):
Vol.1. Missarum XVI vocum. Tomus I.
No.1. Missa sine nomine XVI vocum. 1966.
No.2. Missa Victoria XVI vocum. 1966.
No.3. Missa Benevola XVI vocum. 1966.
Vol.2. Missarum XVI vocum. Tomus II.
No.1. Missa Tiracorda XVI vocum. 1967.
*No.2. Si Deus pro nobis.
*No.3. In diluvium.
Vol.3. Missarum XVI vocum. Tomus III.
*No.1. In angustia pestilentiae.
*No.2. Tu es Petrus.
*No.3. Cum complerentur.
Vol.4. Missae XII vocum.
*No.1. Angelus Domini.
*No.2. Ecce sacerdos magnus.
*No.3. Onde tolse amore.
*Vol.5. Missae X vocum.
*Vol.6. Missae IX, VIII et V vocum.
*Vol.7. Missa Salisburgensis, in facsimile.
*Vol.8. Psalmi XXIV et XVI vocum.
*Vol.9. Psalmi XIV et XII vocum.
*Vol.10. Psalmi X et IX vocum.
*Vol.11. Psalmi VIII vocum.
*Vol.12. Antiphonae, motecta et varia.
*Vol.13. Catalogus thematicus et bibliographicus, cum adnotationibus criticis and opera omnia ac singula.

BERG, ADAM, d.1610. music printer.
Patrocinium musices. Munich, 1573–98.
12v.
Contents (from *Grove's Dictionary of music and musicians.* 5th ed. New York, St. Martin's Press, Inc.; London, Macmillan and Co., Ltd., 1954 [reprint 1966]. Vol.1, p.635):
Vol.1. Lassus. 12 Cantiones. (4v.). 1573.
Vol.2. Lassus. 5 Masses. 1574.
Vol.3. Lassus. Officia. 1574.
Vol.4. Lassus. Passio. (5v.). etc. 1575.
Vol.5. Lassus. 10 Settings of Magnificat. (4 to 8v.). 1576.
Vol.6. Ludwig Daser. Passion. (4v.). 1578.
Vol.7. Lassus. 13 Settings of Magnificat. (4 to 6v.). 1587.
Vol.8. Lassus. 6 Masses. 1589.
Vol.9. Francesco di Sale. Officie. (5 and 6v.). 1589.
Vol.10. Blasius Amon. Masses. (4v.). 1591.
Vol.11. Caesar de Zacchariis. Intonationes. 1594.
Vol.12. Francesco di Sale. Mass. (5v.). 1598.

BERLIN. INSTITUT FÜR MUSIKFORSCHUNG.
Veröffentlichungen. Berlin, Verlag Merseburger, cop.1955– .
v.1– .
Contents:
Reihe 1: Heft 1–37: Buxtehude, Dietrich. Kantaten.

BERLIOZ, HECTOR, 1803–1869.
Hector Berlioz Werke. Hrsg. von Charles Malherbe und Felix Weingartner. Band I–XX in 18v. Leipzig, Breitkopf & Härtel, 1900–1907.
20v.
Contents:
Vol.1.
Symphonie fantastique. Op.14.
Symphonie funèbre et triomphale. Op.15.
Vol.2.
Harold en Italie. Op.16.
Vol.3.
Roméo et Juliette (Symphonie dramatique). Op.17.
Vol.4.
Les francs Juges. Overture. Op.3.
Rob-Roy. Overture.
Roi Lear. Overture. Op.4.
Waverley. Overture. Op.1 bis.
Vol.5.
Beatrice et Benedict. Op.27. Overture.
Benvenuto Cellini. Op.23. Overture.
Le carnaval romain. Overture. Op.9.

Le corsaire. Overture. Op.21.
L'enfance du Christ. Op.25. Overture to Part II (La fuite en Egypte).
Les Troyens à Carthage. Op.29b. Overture.
Vol.6.
Fugue à deux choeurs et deux contre-sujets.
Fugue à trois sujets.
Hamlet. Marche funèbre. Op.18. No.3.
Hymne pour l'élévation.
Marche funèbre pour la dernière scène d'Hamlet. Op.18. No.3.
Marche troyenne (from La prise de Troie) (arr. for concert use).
Les Troyens à Carthage. Prélude.
Rêverie et caprice (Romance). Op.8 (violin & orchestra) & (violin & piano).
Sérénade agreste à la Madone.
Toccata.
Vol.7.
Coro dei Maggi.
Requiem (Grande Messe des morts, Op.5).
Resurrexit.
Tantum ergo.
Veni Creator.
Vol.8.
Te Deum. Op.22.
Vol.9.
L'enfance du Christ. Op.25.
Vol.10.
Faust. Huit scènes. Op.1.
Vol.11–12.
La damnation de Faust. Op.24.
Vol.13.
Le cinq mai (Chant sur la mort de l'Empereur Napoleon). Op.6.
Lelio, ou le retour à la vie. Op.14b (Monodrame lyrique).
Vol.14.
Chant des chemins de fer. Op.19. No.3.
Chant sacré. Op.2. No.6 (chorus & orchestra).
Hélène (Ballade). Op.2. No.2 (chorus & orchestra.
Hymne à la France. Op.20. No.2.
Méditation religieuse. Op.18, No.1.
La menace des francs (Marche et choeur). Op.20. No.1 (voices & orchestra).
La mort d'Ophélie. Op.18. No.2 (chorus & orchestra).
Sara la baigneuse (chorus & orchestra).
Vol.15.
Absence. Op.7. No.4 (voice & orchestra).
Au cimetière (Clair de lune). Op.7. No.5 (voice & orchestra).
La belle voyageuse. Op.2. No.4 (voice & orchestra).
La captive (Rêverie). Op.12 (voice & orchestra).
Le chasseur danois. Op.19. No.6 (voice & orchestra).
Cléopâtre (Scène lyrique).
Herminie (Scène lyrique).
L'île inconnue. Op.7. No.6 (voice & orchestra).
Le jeune pâtre breton. Op.13. No.4 (voice & orchestra).
Les nuits d'été. Op.7 (voice & orchestra).
Le spectre de la rose. Op.7. No.2 (voice & orchestra).
Sur les lagunes. Op.7. No.3 (voice & orchestra).
Villanelle. Op.7. No.1 (voice & orchestra).
Zaïde (Boléro). Op.19. No.1 (voice & orchestra).
Vol.16.
Amitié, reprends ton empire.
L'apothéose (Chant héroïque).
Le ballet des ombres (Ronde nocturne). Op.2.
Canon libre à la quinte à deux voix.
Chanson à boire. Op.2. No.5.
Le chant des bretons. Op.13. No.5 (chorus).
Chant guerrier. Op.2. No.3.
Chant sacré. Op.2. No.6 (chorus & piano).
Hélène (Ballade). Op.2. No.2 (2 voices & piano).
Hymne pour la consécration du nouveau tabernacle.
La menace des francs (Marche et choeur). Op.20. No.1 (voices & piano).
Le montagnard exilé (Chant élégiaque).
La mort d'Ophélie. Op.18. No.2 (chorus & piano).
Pleure, pauvre Colette (Romance).
Prière du matin (Choeur d'enfants). Op.19. No.4.
Sara la baigneuse (2 voices & piano).
Le temple universel. Op.28.
Le trébuchet (Scherzo). Op.13. No.3.
Vol.17.
Absence. Op.7. No.4 (voice & piano).
Adieu, Bessy. Op.2. No.8.
Au cimetière (Clair de lune). Op.7. No.5 (voice & piano).
La belle Isabeau (Conte pendant l'orage). Op.19. No.5.
La belle voyageuse. Op.2. No.4 (voice & piano).
La captive (Rêverie). Op.12 (voice & piano).
Les champs (Aubade). Op.19. No.2.
Chant de bonheur.
Le chant des bretons. Op.13. No.5 (solo).
Le chasseur danois. Op.19. No.6 (voice & piano).
Le coucher du soleil (Rêverie). Op.2. No.1.
Le dépit de la bergère (Romance).
Elégie. Op.2. No.9.
L'île inconnue. Op.7. No.6 (voice & piano).
L'impériale (Cantate à deux choeurs). Op.26.
Je crois en vous.
Le jeune pâtre breton. Op.13. No.4 (voice & piano).
Le matin. Op.13. No.1.
Le maure jaloux (Romance).
La mort d'Ophélie. Op.18. No.2 (solo voice & piano).
Les nuits d'été. Op.7 (voice & piano).
L'origine de la harpe (Ballade). Op.2. No.7.
Page d'album.
Le pêcheur.
Petit oiseau (Chanson de paysan). Op.13. No.2.
Premiers transports.
Le spectre de la rose. Op.7. No.2 (voice & piano).
Sur les lagunes. Op.7. No.3 (voice & piano).
Toi qui l'aimas, verse des pleurs (Romance).
Villanelle. Op.7. No.1 (voice & piano).
Zaïde (Boléro). Op.19. No.1 (voice & piano).
Vol.18.
Les francs Juges. Overture. Op.3. Arr. for piano, four hands, by Berlioz.
Arrangements of:
Bortniansky, Adoremus.
Bortniansky. Pater Noster.
Couperin. Invitation à louer Dieu.
La Marseillaise.
Martini. Plaisir d'amour.
Schubert. Der Erlkönig.

Weber. Aufforderung zum Tanz (Invitation to the dance).
Vol.18. Act.2.
Traité d'instrumentation. Op.10 (musical examples only).
Vol.19–20.
Beatrice et Benedict. Op.27.

Besseler, Heinrich, 1900– , ed. Capella, *see* Capella.

Biblioteca de Catalunya, Barcelona. Departáment de Música, *see* Barcelona. Biblioteca Central. Sección de Música.

Biblioteca di rarità musicali, *see* Chilesotti, Oscar. Biblioteca di rarità musicali.

Bibliotheca Apostica Vaticana. Codices e Vaticanis selecti phototypice expressi, v.XII, *see* Bannister, Henry Marriott. Monumenti Vaticani di paleografia musicale latina.

Bibliotheca musico-liturgica, *see* Plainsong and Mediaeval Music Society. Bibliotheca musico-liturgica.

Bibliothèque musicologique. IV, *see* Pierre de Corbiel. Office de Pierre de Corbeil.

BIGGS, EDWARD POWER, 1906– . ed.
Treasury of early organ music, ed. by E. Power Biggs. Organ music of the 15th to 18th centuries from England, Italy, Germany and France by Dunstable, Tallis, Redford, Bull, Walond, Gabrieli (Andrea), Frescobaldi, Marcello, Sweelinck, Froberger, Buxtehude, Pachelbel, Homilius, Couperin, Raison, Clerambault, Daquin. New York, Music Press, Inc., [cop.1947].
75p.

BIGGS, EDWARD POWER, 1906– . ed.
A treasury of shorter organ classics. Ed. by E. Power Biggs. New York, Mercury Music Corp., [cop.1955].
32p.
Contains compositions by Claude Louis Balbastre, Andre Campra, Johan Ernst Eberlin, Ludwig Krebs, Richard Coeur de Lion, Benedetto Marcello, Wolfgang Amadeus Mozart, Henry Purcell, William Selby, and Antonio Soler.

BILLINGS, WILLIAM, 1746–1800.
The continental harmony. Ed. by Hans Nathan. Cambridge, Mass., Belknap Press of Harvard University Press, 1961.
xix p., facsim.: score (201p.). (The John Harvard Library).
Reproduction of the corrected issue of the original edition, with title page reading: The continental harmony, containing a number of anthems, fuges, and chorusses in several parts, never before published. Boston, I. Thomas and E. T. Andrews, 1794.

Bliss, Arthur, 1891– , ed. Alte Klavier-Musik. New edition, *see* Pauer, Ernst. Alte Klavier-Musik. New edition.

BLOW, JOHN, 1649–1708.
Complete organ works. Revised and edited, with introduction and textual notes by Watkins Shaw. London, Schott & Co., Inc.; New York, Associated Music Publishers, Inc. [etc., etc., cop.1958].
5p.L., 66p.

Blume, Friedrich, 1893– , ed. Das Chorwerk, *see* Das Chorwerk [various individual volumes].

Boepple, Paul, ed. Dessoff choir series, *see* Dessoff choir series.

BOGHEN, FELICE, 1875– . ed.
Antichi maestri italiani. Partite per clavicembalo o pianoforte, riunite, rivedute ed illustrate. Milano, New York, Ricordi, [19?–].
31p.
Contains 5 Partitas by B. Pasquini and 1 Partita by D. Zipoli.

BÖHM, GEORG, 1661–1733.
... Sämtliche Werke. Klavier- und Orgelwerke ... Auf Grund der Ausgabe von Johannes Wolgast neu hrsg. von Gesa Wolgast. Wiesbaden, Breitkopf & Härtel, [1952–].
v.1– .
Contents:
Vol.1. Freie Kompositionen und Klavier-Suiten.
Vol.2. Choralarbeiten und Anhang.
[Vol.3]. Vokalwerke. Band 1. 1963.
[Vol.4]. Vokalwerke. Band 2. 1963.

BOLETÍN LATINO-AMERICANO DE MÚSICA.
año 1– . abril 1935– . Montevideo, [etc.], 1935– .
v.1– .
No issues for 1939–1940.
At head of title, 1935–1938: Instituto de estudios superiores. Montevideo. Sección de investigaciones musicales; 1941– . Instituto interamericano de musicologia, Montevideo.
Editor: 1935– . F. C. Lange.
Vol.2 published in Lima; v.4 in Bogatá.
"Suplemento musical" issued with v.1, 3– .
Contents of "Suplemento musical":
Vol.1 contains compositions for piano by Juan José Castro, Luis Gianneo, Cárlos Isamitt, Juan Cárlos Paz; *Canciones escolares* by P. Humberto Allende, Heitor Villa-Lobos; *Canto y piano* by J. T. Wilkes, F. Eduardo Fabini, M. Camargo Guarnieri, O. Lorenzo Fernandez, Francisco Mignone; *Canto coral* by Enrique M. Casella.
Vol.2. No "Suplemento musical" was issued with vol.2.
Vol.3 contains compositions by V. Ascone (Montevideo), R. Carpio Valdés (Lima), L. Cluzeau Mortet (Montevideo), F. Gerdes (Lima), R. Gnattali (Rio de Janeiro), and anonymous composers.
Vol.4 contains *Obras para piano*: José María Castro (Buenos Aires), Domingo Santa Cruz (Santiago de Chile), Carlos Isamitt (Santiago de Chile), Alfonso Leng (Santiago de Chile), Cárlos Sánchez Malaga (Lima), Roberto García

Morillo (Buenos Aires), Samuel Negret (Santiago de Chile), Juan Cárlos Paz (Buenos Aires), Julio Percevel (Buenos Aires), Honorio Siccardi (Buenos Aires), Cárlos Suffern (Buenos Aires), Fructuoso Vianna (S. Paulo), and Heitor Villa-Lobos (Rio de Janeiro); *Obras para canto*: Carlos Posada Amador (Medellín), Guillermo Uribe Holguín (Bogatá), Alejandro Inzaurraga (Buenos Aires), Abraham Jurafsky (Buenos Aires), and Andrés Sas (Lima); *Obras corales*: Estanislao Mejia (México).

Vol.5 contains *Obras para piano*: Paul Bowles, Harold Brown, Norman Cazden, Elliott Carter, Aaron Copland, Henry Cowell, David Diamond, Alvin Etler, A. Lehman Engel, Otto Luening, George Perle, and Earl Robinson; *Obras para canto*: Ross Lee Finney, Frederick Jacobi, and Wallingford Riegger; *Música de cámara*: Marion Bauer, Henry Brant, Ruth Crawford, Paul Creston, Robert Delaney, Vivian Fine, Edward Burlinghame Hill, Mary Howe, Charles E. Ives, Cárlos Isamitt, Harrison Kerr, Gerschefski, Burril Phillips, Walter Piston, Quincy Porter, William Schuman, Charles Seeger, Gerald Strang, David Van Vactor, and Adolph Weiss.

Vol.6 contains *Obras instrumentales (Música de cámara)*: Francisco Braga, Dinorá de Carvalho, Luiz Cosme, Oscar Lorenzo Fernandez, M. Camargo Guarnieri, Radamés Gnattali, Brasílio Itibere, Francisco Curt Lange, Ibere Lemos, Francisco Mignone, Jayme Ovalle, César Guerra Peixe, Arthur Pereira, Claudio Santoro, Paulo Silva, José Síqueira, Fructuoso Vianna, José Vieira Brandão, and Heitor Villa-Lobos.

Bonaccorsi, Alfredo, 1887– , ed. Classici italiani della musica, *see* Classici italiani della musica.

BONNET, JOSEPH, 1884–1944. ed.
An anthology of early French organ music. From the XIIth to the XVIIIth century. Collected, annotated, and transcribed by Joseph Bonnet. New York, H. W. Gray Co., Inc., cop.1942.
vi, 58p.
Contains compositions by Nicolas le Bègue, Eustache du Caurroy, Jacques Champion de Chambonnières, François Couperin, Louis Couperin, Nicolas de Grigny, Pérotin le Grand, and Jean Titelouze.

BONNET, JOSEPH, 1884–1944. ed.
. . . Historical organ-recitals, in six volumes . . . Collected, edited, and annotated by Joseph Bonnet . . . New York, G. Schirmer, Inc., [cop.1917–40].
6v.
Contents:
Vol.1. Forerunners of Bach: Hofhaimer to Du Mage.
Contains compositions by Paulus Hofhaimer, Antonio de Cabezon, Andrea Gabrieli, Giovanni Pierluigi da Palestrina, Jan Pieter Sweelinck, John Bull, Jean Titelouze, Girolamo Frescobaldi, Samuel Scheidt, Peter Cornet, Nicolas le Bègue, François Couperin, Johann Jacob Froberger, Diderik Buxtehude, Georg Muffat, Johann Pachelbel, Henry Purcell, Johann Kuhnau, Louis Marchand, André Raison, Nicolas de Grigny, Louis Nicolas Clérambault, and Du Mage.
Vol.2. Johann Sebastian Bach.
Vol.3. Masters of the 18th and early 19th centuries. Handel, Mozart, etc.
Contains compositions by George Frederick Handel, Louis Claude d'Aquin, Padre Giambattista Martini, Johann Ludwig Krebs, Wolfgang Amadeus Mozart, Samuel Wesley, and Alexandre Pierre François Boëly.
Vol.4. Three composers of the Romantic period: Schumann, Mendelssohn, and Liszt.
Vol.5. Modern composers: Franck to Reger.
Contains compositions by César Auguste Franck, Jacques Nicolas Lemmens, Johannes Brahms, Camille Saint-Saëns, Alexandre Guilmant, Eugène Gigout, Charles Marie Widor, Harry Rowe Shelley, Basil Harwood, Marco Enrico Bossi, J. Guy Ropartz, Louis Vierne, Charles Tournemire, and Max Reger.
Vol.6. Old Spanish masters: Cabezón to Cabanilles.
Contains compositions by Antonio de Cabezón, Fray Tomás de Santa María, Sebastián Aguilera de Heredia, Francisco Correa de Araujo, and Juan Bautista José Cabanilles.

Bordes, Charles, 1863–1909, ed. Anthologie des maîtres religieux primitifs des XVe, XVIe et XVIIe siècles, *see* Anthologie des maîtres religieux primitifs des XVe, XVIe et XVIIe siècles.

BORDES, CHARLES, 1863–1909. ed.
. . . Chansonnier du XVe siècle. Édition populaire à l'usage des sociétés chorales et des amateurs en notation moderne, avec clefs usuelles, nuances, & indications d'exécution, par Charles Bordes . . . Préface de M. André Hallays. Édition avec réduction des voix . . . Paris, Bureau d'Édition de la Schola Cantorum, [1905].
25 nos. in 1 v.
French words with music for 4 voices.
At head of title: Répertoire des Chanteurs de Saint-Gervais et de la Schola Cantorum.
Contains songs by Pierre Certon, Claude le Jeune, Guillaume Costeley, Gascongne, Clément Jannequin, Roland de Lassus, and Claudin de Sermisy.

Borren, Charles van den, 1874– , ed. Missa Tornacensis, *see* Catholic Church, Roman. Liturgy and ritual. Missal. Missa Tornacensis.

Borren, Charles van den, 1874– , ed. Polyphonia sacra. *see* Plainsong and Mediaeval Music Society. Borren, Charles van den. Polyphonia sacra.

Borren, Charles van den, 1874– , ed. The Tournai Mass. *see* Catholic Church, Roman. Liturgy and ritual. Missal. Missa Tornacensis.

BOSSI, MARCO ENRICO, 1861–1925.
Ausgewählte Kompositionen für die Orgel, von M. Enrico Bossi . . . Leipzig, New York, [etc.], C. F. Peters, n.d.
2v. (Edition Peters. No.3590a–b).

BOSSI, MARCO ENRICO, 1861–1925. ed.
Sammlung von Stücken alter italienischer Meister für die moderne Orgel. Bearb. und hrsg. von M. Enrico Bossi . . . Leipzig, New York, [etc.], C. F. Peters, [cop.1936].
59p. (Edition Peters. No.3592).
Contains compositions by G. B. Bassani, G. Frescobaldi, G. B. Martini, Palafuti, G. B. Pescetti, C. F. Pollaroli, and D. Zipoli.

The Bottegari lutebook, *see* The Wellesley edition. No.8.

BOYCE, WILLIAM, 1710–1779. ed.
Cathedral music, being a collection in score of the most valuable and useful compositions for that service by the several English masters of the last two hundred years. The whole selected and carefully revised by Dr. William Boyce . . . London, 1760–73.
3v.
2d ed. London, J. Ashley, 1788. 3v.
Later editions: 1844; London, R. Cocks & Co., 1849. 3v.; London, J. A. Novello, [1894]. 5v.
For 1–8 voices, with figured bass.
Contents (from *Grove's Dictionary of music and musicians*, 1916, Vol.1, p.380):
(Abbreviations: M. and E., Morning and Evening; F.A., Full Anthem; V.A., Verse Anthem; Serv., Service).
Vol.1.
Tallis. Preces. M. and E. Serv.
Morley. Burial Serv. G minor.
Farrant. M. and E. Serv. G minor.
Bevin. M. and E. Serv. D minor.
Gibbons. M. and E. Serv. F.
Child. M. and E. Serv. E minor.
Rogers. M. and E. Serv. D.
Blow. M. and E. Serv. A.
Aldrich. M. and E. Serv. G.
Blow. M. and E. Serv. G.
—— Kyrie and Creed (triple measure). G.
14 Chants.

Vol.2.
Henry VIII. F.A. O Lord the Maker. 4 voices.
Tallis. F.A. I call and cry. 5v.
Tye. F.A. I will exalt Thee. 4v.
—— (2d part). Sing unto the Lord. 4v.
Farrant. F.A. Call to remembrance. 4v.
—— F.A. Hide not Thou. 4v.
Byrd. F.A. O Lord, turn. 5v.
—— F.A. (2d part). Bow Thine ear, O Lord. 5v.
—— F.A. Sing joyfully. 6v.
Gibbons. F.A. Hosanna. 6v.
—— F.A. Lift up your heads. 6v.
—— F.A. Almighty and everlasting. 4v.
—— F.A. O clap your hands. 8v.
—— (2d part). God is gone up. 8v.
Batten. F.A. Hear my prayer. 5v.
—— F.A. O praise the Lord. 4v.
—— F.A. Deliver us, O Lord. 4v.
Child. F.A. Praise the Lord. 4v.
—— F.A. O Lord, grant the King. 4v.
—— F.A. Sing we merrily. 7v.
Rogers. F.A. Behold now. 4v.
—— F.A. Teach me, O Lord. 4v.
Blow. V.A. God is our hope. 8v.
—— V.A. O God, wherefore art Thou absent. 5v.
—— V.A. Save me, O God. 4v.
—— F.A. The Lord hear Thee. 4v.
—— F.A. My God, my God. 4v.
Aldrich. V.A. Out of the deep. 4v.
—— F.A. O give thanks. 6v.
Creyghton. F.A. I will arise. 4v.
Purcell. V.A. O God, Thou art. 4v.
—— V.A. O God, Thou hast. 6v.
—— V.A. O Lord God of Hosts. 8v.
Goldwin. V.A. I have set God. 4v.
Clarke. F.A. Praise the Lord, O Jerusalem. 4v.
Croft. V.A. God is gone up. 4v.
—— V.A. Put me not to rebuke. 4v.
Weldon. V.A. In Thee, O Lord. 4v.
—— V.A. Hear my crying. 6v.
Lawes (Wm.). V.A. The Lord is my light. 4v.
Lock. V.A. Lord, let me know mine end. 5v.
Humphrey. V.A. Have mercy upon me. 3v.
—— V.A. O Lord my God. 3v.
Blow. V.A. I was in the spirit. 4v.
Wise. V.A. Prepare ye the way of the Lord. 4v.
—— V.A. Awake, put on thy strength. 3v.
Purcell. V.A. Thy way, O God. 4v.
—— V.A. Be merciful. 3v.
Clarke. V.A. How long wilt Thou. 1 v.
Croft. V.A. O praise the Lord. 3v.
—— V.A. Give the King. 5v.
5 Chants.

Vol.3.
Byrd. M. and E. Serv. D min.
Child. M. and E. Serv. D.
Blow. M. and E. Serv. E min.
Purcell. M. and E. Serv. (double), B flat.
Bull. V.A. O Lord my God. 5v.
Humphrey. V.A. Thou art my King. 4v.
—— V.A. Like as the hart. 4v.
—— V.A. Hear, O Heavens. 3v.
—— V.A. Rejoice in the Lord. 4v.
—— V.A. Haste Thee, O God. 4v.
Wise. V.A. The ways of Zion. 2v.
—— V.A. Thy beauty, O Israel. 4v.
—— V.A. Awake up, my glory. 3v.
—— V.A. Blessed is he. 3v.
Blow. V.A. O Lord, I have sinned. 4v.
—— V.A. O sing unto God. 3v.
—— V.A. O Lord Thou hast searched me out. 2v.
—— V.A. I beheld and lo! 4v.
Turner. V.A. Lord, Thou hast been our refuge. 3v.
Purcell. V.A. Behold, I bring you. 3v.
—— V.A. They that go down. 2v.
—— V.A. Thy word is a lantern. 3v.

—— V.A. O give thanks. 4v.
Clarke. V.A. I will love Thee. 2v.
Gibbons. Sanctus. 4v. in F.
Child. Sanctus. 4v. in E minor.
Rogers. Sanctus. 4v. in D.
Creyghton. Sanctus. 4v. in E flat.

BOYCE, WILLIAM, 1710–1779. ed.
Cathedral music. London, R. Cocks & Co., 1849. 3v.
Contents:
Vol.1.
Tallis, Thomas. Preces. M. and E. Serv.
Farrant, Richard. M. and E. Serv.
Byrd, William. M. and E. Serv.
Bevin, Elway. M. and E. Serv.
Morley, Thomas. Burial Serv.
Gibbons, Orlando. M. and E. Serv.
Child, William. M. and E. Serv.
—— M. and E. Serv.
Rogers, Benjamin. M. and E. Serv.
Aldrich, Henry. M. and E. Serv.
Appendix:
Tomkins, Thomas. M. and E. Serv.
Parsons, John. Burial Serv.

Vol.2.
Blow, John. M. and E. Serv.
—— M. and E. Serv.
—— Kyrie Eleeson. Nicene Creed.
—— M. and E. Serv.
Purcell, Henry. M. and E. Serv.
—— Benedicite, Jubilate, Cantate Domino. Deus misereatur.
Full Anthems:
Mundy, William. O Lord, the Maker of all.
Tye, Christopher. I will exalt Thee. (1st part).
—— Sing unto the Lord. (2d part).
Farrant, Richard. Call to remembrance.
—— Hide not Thou Thy face.
Gibbons, Orlando. Almighty and everlasting God.
Batten, Adrian. O praise the Lord, all ye heathen.
—— Deliver us, O Lord.
Child, William. Praise the Lord, O my soul.
—— O Lord, grant the King.
Rogers, Benjamin. Behold, now praise the Lord.
—— Teach me, O Lord.
Blow, John. The Lord, hear Thee.
—— My God, my God.
Creyghton, Robert. I will arise.
Clark, Jeremiah. Praise the Lord, O Jerusalem.
Tallis, Thomas. I call and cry.
Byrd, William. O Lord, turn Thy wrath. (1st part).
—— Bow Thine ear, O Lord. (2d part).
—— Sing joyfully unto God.
Gibbons, Orlando. Hosanna to the Son of David.
—— Lift up your heads.
Aldrich, Henry. O give thanks.
Appendix:
Creyghton, Robert. M. and E. Serv.
Full Anthems:
Tallis, Thomas. O Lord, give Thy Holy Spirit.
Tomkins, Thomas. Almighty and everlasting God.
—— O pray for the peace of Jerusalem.
Gibbons, Orlando. Why art Thou so full of heaviness.
—— O Lord, increase my faith.
Byrd, William. Save me, O God.

Vol.3.
Full Anthems:
Child, William. Sing we merrily.
Gibbons, Orlando. O clap your hands. (1st part).
—— God is gone up. (2d part).
Full Anthems with Verses:
Aldrich, Henry. Out of the deep have I called.
Blow, John. Save me, O God.
Purcell, Henry. O God, Thou art my God.
Goldwin, John. I have set God alway before me.
Weldon, John. In Thee, O Lord.
Croft, William. God is gone up.
—— Put me not to rebuke.
Bull, John. O Lord, my God.
Batten, Adrian. Hear my prayer, O God.
Blow, John. O God, wherefore art Thou.
Purcell, Henry. O God, Thou hast cast us out.
Weldon, John. Hear my crying, O God.
Blow, John. God is our hope.
Purcell, Henry. O Lord God of Hosts.
Verse Anthems:
Clark, Jeremiah. How long wilt Thou forget me.
Blow, John. O Lord, Thou hast searched me out.
Purcell, Henry. They that go down to the sea in ships.
—— Thy way, O God, is holy.
Wise, Michael. The ways of Zion do mourn.
Clark, Jeremiah. I will love Thee, O Lord.
Humphrey, Pelham. Have mercy upon me, O God.
—— O Lord, my God.
—— Hear, O heavens.
Blow, John. O sing unto God.
Purcell, Henry. Be merciful unto me, O God.
—— Behold! I bring you glad tidings.
—— Thy Word is a lantern.
Turner, William. Lord, Thou hast been our refuge.
Wise, Michael. Blessed is he that considereth the poor.
—— Awake up, my glory.
—— Awake, put on thy strength.
—— Thy beauty, O Israel.
Croft, William. O praise the Lord, all ye heathen.
Lawes, William. The Lord is my light.
Humphrey, Pelham. Like as the hart.
—— Thou art my King, O God.
—— Rejoice in the Lord.
—— Haste Thee, O God.
Blow, John. O Lord, I have sinned.
—— I beheld, and lo, a great multitude.
—— I was in the spirit.
Purcell, Henry. O give thanks unto the Lord.
Wise, Michael. Prepare ye the way of the Lord.

Locke, Matthew. Lord, let me know mine end.
Croft, William. Give the King thy judgments, O God.
Chants:
Single (18).
Double (6).
Appendix:
Blow, John. V.A. Lord, how are they increased that trouble me.

BRAHMS, JOHANNES, 1833–1897.
Johannes Brahms Sämtliche Werke. Ausgabe der Gesellschaft der Musikfreunde in Wien. [Hrsg. von H. Gál und E. Mandyczewski]. Leipzig, Breitkopf & Härtel, [1926–27].
26v. ports., facsims.
Vols.1–10 ed. by H. Gál; v.11–26, by E. Mandyczewski.
Contents:
Bd.1. Symphonien für Orchester I.
Symphonie Nr.1, C moll, Op.68.
Symphonie Nr.2, D dur, Op.73.
Bd.2. Symphonien für Orchester II.
Symphonie Nr.3, F dur, Op.90.
Symphonie Nr.4, E moll, Op.98.
Bd.3. Ouvertüren und Variationen für Orchester.
Akademische Festouvertüre, C moll, Op.80.
Tragische Ouvertüre, D moll, Op.81.
Variationen über ein Thema von Haydn, B dur, Op.56a.
Bd.4. Serenaden und Tänze für Orchester.
Serenade für grosses Orchester, D dur, Op.11.
Serenade für kleines Orchester, A dur, Op.16.
Ungarische Tänze, für Orchester gesetzt.
Nr.1, G moll.
Nr.2, F dur.
Nr.3, F dur.
Bd.5. Konzerte für Streichinstrumente und Orchester.
Konzert für Violine, Op.77.
Konzert für Violine und Violoncell, Op.102.
Bd.6. Konzerte für Klavier und Orchester.
Konzert Nr.1, D moll, Op.15.
Konzert Nr.2, B dur, Op.83.
Bd.7. Kammermusik für Streichinstrumente.
Sextett Nr.1 für zwei Violinen, zwei Bratschen und zwei Violoncelle, B dur, Op.18.
Sextett Nr.2 für zwei Violinen, zwei Bratschen und zwei Violoncelle, G dur, Op.36.
Quintett Nr.1 für zwei Violinen, zwei Bratschen und Violoncell, F dur, Op.88.
Quintett Nr.2 für zwei Violinen, zwei Bratschen und Violoncell, G dur, Op.111.
Quintett für Klarinette (oder Bratsche), zwei Violinen, Bratsche und Violoncell, Op.115.
Quartett Nr.1 für zwei Violinen, Bratsche und Violoncell, C moll, Op.51, Nr.1.
Quartett Nr.2 für zwei Violinen, Bratsche und Violoncell, A moll, Op.51, Nr.2.
Quartett Nr.3 für zwei Violinen, Bratsche und Violoncell, B dur, Op.67.
Bd.8. Klavier-Quintett und -Quartette.
Quintett für Klavier, 2 Violinen, Bratsche und Violoncell, F moll, Op.34.
Quartett Nr.1 für Klavier, Violine, Bratsche und Violoncell, G moll, Op.25.
Quartett Nr.2 für Klavier, Violine, Bratsche und Violoncell, A dur, Op.26.
Quartett Nr.3 für Klavier, Violine, Bratsche und Violoncell, C moll, Op.60.
Bd.9. Klavier-Trios.
Trio Nr.1 für Pianoforte, Violine und Violoncell, H dur, Op.8. Erste Fassung.
Trio Nr.1, H dur, Op.8. Spätere Fassung.
Trio Nr.2 für Pianoforte, Violine und Violoncell, C dur, Op.87.
Trio Nr.3 für Pianoforte, Violine und Violoncell, C moll, Op.101.
Trio für Pianoforte, Violine und Waldhorn (oder Violoncell oder Bratsche), Es dur, Op.40.
Trio für Pianoforte, Klarinette (oder Bratsche) und Violoncell, A moll, Op.114.
Bd.10. Klavier-Duos.
Sonate Nr.1 für Pianoforte und Violine, G dur, Op.78.
Sonate Nr.2 für Pianoforte und Violine, A dur, Op.100.
Sonate Nr.3 für Pianoforte und Violine, D moll, Op.108.
Sonatensatz (Scherzo) für Pianoforte und Violine.
Sonate Nr.1 für Pianoforte und Violoncell, E moll, Op.38.
Sonate Nr.2 für Pianoforte und Violoncell, F dur, Op.99.
Sonate Nr.1 für Pianoforte und Klarinette (oder Bratsche), F moll, Op.120, Nr.1.
Sonate Nr.2 für Pianoforte und Klarinette (oder Bratsche), Es dur, Op.120, Nr.2.
Bd.11. Werke für zwei Klaviere zu vier Händen.
Sonate nach dem Quintett, Op.34, F moll, Op.34b.
Variationen über ein Thema von Joseph Haydn, B dur, Op.56b.
Bd.12. Werke für Klavier zu vier Händen.
Variationen über ein Thema von Robert Schumann. Op.23.
Walzer, Op.39.
Liebeslieder. Walzer. Op.52a.
Neue Liebeslieder. Walzer. Op.65a.
Ungarische Tänze.
Nr.1, G moll.
Nr.2, D moll.
Nr.3, F dur.
Nr.4, F moll.
Nr.5, Fis moll.
Nr.6, Des dur.
Nr.7, A dur.
Nr.8, A moll.
Nr.9, E moll.
Nr.10, E dur.
Nr.11, D moll.
Nr.12, D moll.
Nr.13, D dur.
Nr.14, D moll.
Nr.15, B dur.
Nr.16, F moll.
Nr.17, Fis moll.
Nr.18, D dur.
Nr.19, H moll.
Nr.20, E moll.
Nr.21, E moll.

Bd.13. Sonaten und Variationen für Klavier zu zwei Händen.
Op.1. Sonate, Nr.1, C dur.
Op.2. Sonate, Nr.2, Fis moll.
Op.5. Sonate, Nr.3, F moll.
Op.9, Variationen über ein Thema von Robert Schumann, Fis moll.
Op.21. Nr.1. Variationen über ein eigenes Thema, D dur.
Op.21. Nr.2. Variationen über ein ungarisches Lied, D dur.
Op.24. Variationen und Fuge über ein Thema von Händel, B dur.
Op.35. Variationen über ein Thema von Paganini, A moll. Heft I, II.
Bd.14. Kleinere Klavierwerke.
Op.4. Scherzo, Es moll.
Op.10. Balladen.
1. "Edward," D moll.
2. Andante, D dur.
3. Intermezzo. Allegro, H moll.
4. Andante, H dur.
Op.39. Walzer.
Op.39. Walzer. Erleichterte Ausgabe.
Op.76. Acht Klavierstücke.
1. Capriccio, Fis moll.
2. Capriccio, H moll.
3. Intermezzo, As dur.
4. Intermezzo, B dur.
5. Capriccio, Cis moll.
6. Intermezzo, A dur.
7. Intermezzo, A moll.
8. Capriccio, C dur.
Op.79. Zwei Rhapsodien.
1. Agitato, H moll.
2. Molto passionato, G moll.
Op.116. Fantasien.
1. Capriccio, D moll.
2. Intermezzo, A moll.
3. Capriccio, G moll.
4. Intermezzo, E dur.
5. Intermezzo, E moll.
6. Intermezzo, E dur.
7. Capriccio, D moll.
Op.117. Drei Intermezzi.
1. Andante moderato, Es dur.
2. Andante non troppo, B moll.
3. Andante con moto, Cis moll.
Op.118. Sechs Klavierstücke.
1. Intermezzo, A moll.
2. Intermezzo, A dur.
3. Ballade, G moll.
4. Intermezzo, F moll.
5. Romanze, F dur.
6. Intermezzo, Es moll.
Op.119. Vier Klavierstücke.
1. Intermezzo, H moll.
2. Intermezzo, E moll.
3. Intermezzo, C dur.
4. Rhapsodie, Es dur.
Bd.15. Studien und Bearbeitungen für Klavier.
Etüde nach Friedrich Chopin. (Studien Nr.1).
Rondo nach C. M. von Weber. (Studien Nr.2).
Presto nach J. S. Bach. Erste Bearbeitung. Zweite Bearbeitung. (Studien Nr.3–4).
Chaconne von J. S. Bach. Für die linke Hand allein. (Studien Nr.5).
Gavotte von Christ. W. Gluck.
Impromptu von Franz Schubert. Op.90, Nr.2. Studie für die linke Hand.
Zwei Giguen. Nr.1–2.
Zwei Sarabanden. Nr.1–2.
Thema mit Variationen.
Ungarische Tänze.
Nr.1, G moll.
Nr.2, D moll.
Nr.3, F dur.
Nr.4, Fis moll.
Nr.5, Fis moll.
Nr.6, Des dur.
Nr.7, F dur.
Nr.8, A moll.
Nr.9, E moll.
Nr.10, E dur.
Kadenz zu J. S. Bachs Klavierkonzert in D moll.
Zwei Kadenzen zu W. A. Mozarts Klavierkonzert in G dur. Nr.1–2. Köchel-Verz. 453.
Kadenz zu W. A. Mozarts Klavierkonzert in D moll. Köchel-Verz. 466.
Kadenz zu W. A. Mozarts Klavierkonzert in C moll. Köchel-Verz. 491.
Zwei Kadenzen zu L. van Beethovens Klavierkonzert in G dur, Op.58.
Kadenz zu L. van Beethovens Klavierkonzert in C moll, Op.37.
51 Übungen für Pianoforte.
Bd.16. Orgelwerke.
Zwei Präludien und Fugen. 1, A moll. 2, G moll.
Fuge in As moll.
Choralvorspiel und Fuge über "O Traurigkeit, o Herzeleid."
Elf Choralvorspiele, Op.122.
1. Mein Jesu, der du mich.
2. Herzliebster Jesu.
3. O Welt, ich muss dich lassen.
4. Herzlich tut mich erfreuen.
5. Schmücke dich, o liebe Seele.
6. O wie selig seid ihr doch, ihr Frommen.
7. O Gott, du frommer Gott.
8. Es ist ein Ros' entsprungen.
9. Herzlich tut mich verlangen.
10. Herzlich tut mich verlangen.
11. O Welt, ich muss dich lassen.
Bd.17. Chorwerke mit Orchester. I.
Ein deutsches Requiem. Nach Worten der Heiligen Schrift, für Soli, Chor und Orchester. (Orgel ad lib.). Op.45.
Bd.18. Chorwerke mit Orchester. II.
Triumphlied für Achtstimmigen Chor, Bariton-Solo und Orchester. (Orgel ad lib.). Op.55.
Rinaldo von Goethe, Kantate für Tenor-Solo, Männerchor und Orchester. Op.50.
Bd.19. Chorwerke mit Orchester. III.
Rhapsodie für eine Altstimme, Männerchor und Orchester. Op.53.
Schicksalslied von Fr. Hölderlin für Chor und Orchester. Op.54.
Nänie von Fr. Schiller für Chor und Orchester. (Harfe ad lib.). Op.82.
Gesang der Parzen für Sechsstimmigen Chor und Orchester. Op.89.
Ave Maria für Frauenchor mit Orchester oder Orgel. Op.12.

Begräbnisgesang für Chor und Blasinstrumente. Op.13.
Gesänge für Frauenchor mit zwei Hörnern und Harfe. Op.17.
1. Es tont ein voller Harfenklang.
2. Lied von Shakespeare: Komm Herbei, Tod.
3. Der Gartner: Wohin ich geh und schaue.
4. Gesang aus Fingal: Wein' an den Felsen der Brausenden Winde.
Ellens zweiter Gesang aus W. Scotts "Fräulein vom See" von Franz Schubert, für Sopran, dreistimmigen Frauenchor, vier Hörner, zwei Fagotte.
Bd.20. Mehrstimmige Gesänge mit Klavier oder Orgel.
Der 13. Psalm, Op.27.
Geistliches Lied, Op.30.
Drei Quartette für 4 Solostimmen, Op.31.
Drei Quartette für 4 Solostimmen, Op.64.
Liebeslieder, Op.52.
Neue Liebeslieder, Op.65.
Quartette für Sopran, Alt, Tenor und Bass, Op.92.
Zigeunerlieder, Op.103.
Sechs Quartette für Sopran, Alt, Tenor und Bass, Op.112.
Tafellied, Op.93b.
Kleine Hochzeitskantate.
Bd.21. Mehrstimmige Gesänge ohne Begleitung.
Marienlieder. Op.22.
Zwei Motetten. Op.29.
Zwei Motetten. Op.74.
Drei Motetten. Op.110.
Fest- und Gedenksprüche. Op.109.
Drei Gesänge. Op.42.
Sieben Lieder. Op.62.
Lieder und Romanzen. Op.93a.
Fünf Gesänge. Op.104.
Deutsche Volkslieder.
Dem dunkeln Schoss der heil' gen Erde.
Töne, lindernder Klang! Kanon.
Zu Rauch. Kanon.
Drei geistliche Chöre. Op.37.
Zwölf Lieder und Romanzen. Op.44.
Dreizehn Kanons. Op.113.
Mir lächelt kein Frühling. Kanon.
Grausam erweiset sich Amor. Kanon.
O wie Sanft! Kanon.
Wann? Wann hört der Himmel auf zu strafen. Kanon.
Spruch. In dieser Welt des Trugs und Scheins. Kanon.
Fünf Lieder. Op.41.
Bd.22. Duette mit Klavierbegleitung.
Drei Duette für Sopran und Alt mit Begleitung des Pianoforte. Op.20.
1. Weg der Liebe. (1. Teil).
2. Weg der Liebe. (2. Teil).
3. Die Meere.
Vier Duette für Alt und Bariton mit Begleitung des Pianoforte. Op.28.
1. Die Nonne und die Ritter.
2. Vor der Tür.
3. Es rauschet das Wasser.
4. Der Jäger und sein Liebchen.
Vier Duette für Sopran und Alt mit Begleitung des Pianoforte. Op.61.
1. Die Schwestern.
2. Klosterfräulein.
3. Phänomen.
4. Die Boten der Liebe.
Fünf Duette für Sopran und Alt mit Begleitung des Pianoforte. Op.66.
1. Klänge. (Nr.1). Aus der Erde quellen Blumen.
2. Klänge. (Nr.2). Wenn ein müder Leib begraben.
3. Am Strande. Es sprechen und blicken die Wellen.
4. Jägerlied. Jäger, was jagst du die Häselein?
5. Hüt du dich! Ich weiss ein Mädlein hübsch und fein.
Balladen und Romanzen für zwei Singstimmen mit Pianoforte. Op.75.
1. Edward. Für Alt und Tenor.
2. Guter Rat. Für Sopran und Alt.
3. So lass uns wandern! Für Sopran und Tenor.
4. Walpurgisnacht. Für 2 Soprane.
Bd.23. Lieder und Gesänge. Für eine Singstimme mit Klavierbegleitung. I.
Sechs Gesänge für eine Tenor- oder Sopranstimme. Op.3.
Sechs Gesänge für eine Sopran- oder Tenorstimme. Op.6.
Sechs Gesänge. Op.7.
Lieder und Romanzen. Op.14.
Fünf Gedichte. Op.19.
Lieder und Gesänge. Op.32.
Romanzen aus Tiecks "Magelone." Op.33
Bd.24. Lieder und Gesänge. Für eine Singstimme mit Klavierbegleitung. II.
Vier Gesänge. Op.43.
Vier Gesänge. Op.46.
Fünf Lieder. Op.47.
Sieben Lieder. Op.48.
Fünf Lieder. Op.49.
Acht Lieder und Gesänge. Op.57.
Acht Lieder und Gesänge. Op.58.
Acht Lieder und Gesänge. Op.59.
Neun Lieder und Gesänge. Op.63.
Bd.25. Lieder und Gesänge. Für eine Singstimme mit Klavierbegleitung. III.
Neun Gesänge. Op.69.
Vier Gesänge. Op.70.
Fünf Gesänge. Op.71.
Fünf Gesänge. Op.72.
Romanzen und Lieder für eine oder zwei Stimmen. Op.84.
Sechs Lieder. Op.85.
Sechs Lieder für eine tiefere Stimme. Op.86.
Zwei Gesänge für eine Altstimme mit Bratsche. Op.91.
Fünf Lieder für eine tiefe Stimmen. Op.94.
Sieben Lieder. Op.95.
Vier Lieder. Op.96.
Sechs Lieder. Op.97.
Bd.26. Lieder und Gesänge. Für eine Singstimme mit Klavierbegleitung. IV.
Fünf Lieder für eine tiefere Stimme. Op.105.
Fünf Lieder. Op.106.
Fünf Lieder. Op.107.
Vier Ernste Gesänge für eine Bass-Stimme. Op.121.

Mondnacht.
Regenlied.
Acht Zigeunerlieder. Op.103.
Deutsche Volkslieder.
Vierzehn Volks-Konderlieder.
Achtungzwanzig Volkslieder.

BRAHMS, JOHANNES, 1833–1897.
Johannes Brahms Sämtliche Werke. Another issue. Ann Arbor, Mich., J. W. Edwards, 1949.
26v. ports., facsims. (Edwards music reprints. Ser.A. Complete works and monumenta, No.3).
"Photolithographischer Neudruck."
"In dieser Ausgabe sind eine Anzahl Fehler berichtigt, wofür wir Herrn Dr. Hans Gál, einem der Herausgeber der Original-Ausgabe, zu Danke verpflichtet sind." – v.26, p.[ii].

BRAHMS, JOHANNES, 1833–1897.
Johannes Brahms Sämtliche Werke Neuauflage. Wiesbaden, Breitkopf & Härtel, 19? .
Proposed publication date 1966.

BRAHMS, JOHANNES, 1833–1897.
Complete organ works. New edition by W. Buszin and P. Bunjes. New York, C. F. Peters, 19?– .
2v.
Contents:
Vol.1. 4 Early compositions.
Vol.2. Op.122. 11 Chorale preludes.

BRAHMS, JOHANNES, 1833–1897.
The organ works of Johannes Brahms. Revised by Gerard Alphenaar. English translation by Harold Heiberg. New York, Edward B. Marks Music Corp., cop.1948.
2v. (Marks organ library. No.82–83).
Contents:
Vol.1. 11 Chorale preludes. Op.122.
Vol.2. Miscellaneous compositions.

BRAHMS, JOHANNES, 1833–1897.
. . . Klavierwerke. Hrsg. von Emil von Sauer. Leipzig, C. F. Peters, [c19?–].
2v. (Edition Peters. No.3300a–b).
Contents:
Vol.1. Op.1, 2, 4, 5, 9, 10 (No.1–4), 21 (No.1–2), 24.
Vol.2. Op.76 (No.1–8), 79 (No.1–2), 116 (No.1–7), 117 (No.1–3), 118 (No.1–6), 119 (No.1–4), Studien No.1–5.

BRAHMS, JOHANNES, 1833–1897.
. . . Piano works. Complete in three volumes. (Authentic edition). New York, International Music Co., [1948].
3v.
Contents:
Vol.1. Op.1, 2, 5, 9, 21 (No.1–2), 24, 35.
Vol.2. Op.4, 10 (No.1–4), 39, 76 (No.1–8), 79 (No.1–2), 116 (No.1–7), 117 (No.1–3), 118 (No.1–6), 119 (No.1–4).
Vol.3. Study after Chopin; Rondo; Presto after Bach (2 versions); Chaconne after Bach; Gavotte in A major by Gluck; Impromptu by Franz Schubert; Gigue No.1–2; Sarabande No.1–2; Theme and Variations; 10 Hungarian Dances.

BRASSART, JOHANNES, 15th century.
Opera omnia. Ed. by Keith Mixter. Rome, American Institute of Musicology, 19?– .
2v. (proposed). (Corpus mensurabilis musicae. No.35).
Contents:
Vol.1. Mass sections.

Bravi, Eugenio, ed. I classici musicali italiani, *see* I classici musicali italiani.

A brief compendium of early organ music, *see* Schweiger, Hertha. A brief compendium of early organ music.

Briggs, H. B. Recent research in plainsong, *see* Plainsong and Mediaeval Music Society. Briggs, H. B. Recent research in plainsong.

BROWN, HOWARD MAYER. ed.
Theatrical chansons of the 15th and early 16th centuries. Cambridge, Mass., Harvard University Press, 1963.
188p.
Contains compositions by Noël Bauldewyn, Benedictus, Bouteiller, Jacques Buus, Doyset Compère, Antoine de Févin, Mathieu Gascongne, Godard, Gosse, Guyard, Guillaume le Heurteur, Jacotin, Clément Janequin, Johannes Japart, Lupi, Pierre de Manchicourt, Pierre Moulu, Jean Mouton, Jean Richafort, Claudin de Sermisy, Johannes Stokhem, Vaqueras (Compère?), Vuildre, and Adrian Willaert.

BRUCKNER, ANTON, 1824–1896.
Anton Bruckners Sämtliche Werke. Kritische Gesamtausgabe im Auftrage der Generaldirektion der Nationalbibliothek und der Internationalen Bruckner-Gesellschaft hrsg. von Robert Haas und Alfred Orel. Wien, Musikwissenschaftlicher Verlag (15: Augsburg-Wien, Dr. Benno Filser Verlag), 1930– .
v.1– . facsims.
Each volume has also special title page. Vols.7, 14 have imprint: Leipzig, Bruckner-Verlag; Vol.8, 13: Leipzig, Musikwissenschaftlicher Verlag; Vol.15: Augsburg, B. Filser.
Vol.1– , ed. by Robert Haas; Vol.9, by Alfred Orel.
Contents:
1. Bd. I. Symphonie, C-moll (Wiener und Linzer Fassung). Aufführungsbemerkungen von Max Reger.
2. Bd. II. Symphonie, C-moll (Originalfassung). 1938.
3. Bd. III. Symphonie D-moll (3. Fassung von 1889).
4. Bd. I.T. IV. Symphonie Es-dur (2. Fassung von 1878 mit dem Finale der 3. Fassung von 1880). Finale der 2. Fassung von 1878. 1936.
5. Bd. V. Symphonie, B-dur (Originalfassung).
6. Bd. VI. Symphonie, A-dur (Originalfassung).

7. Bd. VII. Symphonie, E-dur (Originalfassung).
8. Bd. VIII. Symphonie, C-moll (Originalfassung). 1935. (Neuauflage: Fassung von 1890).
9. Bd. IX. Symphonie, D-moll (Originalfassung). 1934.
12. Bd. Streichquartett, C-moll.
13. Bd. Messe in E-moll (Fassung 1882). 1939.
14. Bd. Messe in F-moll (Originalfassung).
15. Bd. Requiem, D-moll. Missa solemnis, B moll. 1935.
16. Bd. Messe, D-moll.
17. Bd. Messe, E-moll.
18. Bd. Messe, F-moll.
19. Bd. Te Deum.

BRUCKNER, ANTON, 1824–1896.
Anton Bruckners Sämtliche Werke. Entwürfe und Skizzen zur IX Symphonie, vorgelegt und erläutert von Alfred Orel. Sonderdruck aus 9. Band. Wien, Musikwissenschaftlicher Verlag der Internationalen Bruckner-Gesellschaft, [cop.1934].
144p.

BRUCKNER, ANTON, 1824–1896.
Anton Bruckners Sämtliche Werke. Another issue. Sämtliche Werke . . . Studienpartitur. Wiesbaden, Bruckner-Verlag, 1934– . (Neuauflage 1949–).
Miniature score (v.1–).

BRUCKNER, ANTON, 1824–1896.
Sämtliche Werke. [2. revidierte Ausgabe]. Kritische Gesamtausgabe, hrsg. von der Generaldirektion der Oesterreichischen Nationalbibliothek und der Internationalen Bruckner-Gesellschaft. unter Leitung von Leopold Nowak [und Robert Haas]. Wien, Leipzig, Musikwissenschaftlicher Verlag, 1951– .
Miniature score (v.1–).
Contents:
1. Bd. I.T. I. Symphonie, C-moll, Linzer Fassung. 2. revidierte Ausg. 1953.
2. Bd. II. Symphonie, C-moll, Fassung von 1889. 2. revidierte Ausg.
3. Bd. III.T. III. Symphonie, D-moll, Fassung von 1889. 1959.
4. Bd. II.T. IV. Symphonie, Es-dur, Fassung von 1878/80. 2. revidierte Ausg. 1953.
5. Bd. V. Symphonie, B-dur, Originalfassung. 2. revidierte Ausg. 1951.
6. Bd. VI. Symphonie, A-dur, Originalfassung. 2. revidierte Ausg. 1952.
7. Bd. VII. Symphonie, E-dur. 2. revidierte Ausg. 1954.
8. Bd. II.T. VIII. Symphonie, C-moll, Fassung von 1890. 2. revidierte Ausg. 1955.
9. Bd. IX. Symphonie, D-moll, Originalfassung. 2. revidierte Ausg. 1951.
10. Bd. Streichquartett, C-moll. 1955.
13. Bd. II.T. Streichquintett, F-dur; Intermezzo, D-moll. 1963.
14. Bd. Messe, F-moll, Originalfassung.
15. Bd. Requiem, D-moll; Missa solemnis, B-moll.
16. Bd. Messe, D-moll. 1957.
17. Bd. II.T. Messe, E-moll, Fassung von 1882. 1959.
18. Bd. Messe, F-moll. 2. revidierte Ausg. 1960.
19. Bd. Te deum, Fassung von 1884. 1962.

BRUGER, HANS DAGOBERT, 1894–1932. ed.
Alte Lautenkunst aus drei Jahrhundertern . . . Eine Sammlung der schönsten Lautenlieder und Solostücke aus den Blütezeiten aller Länder, ausgewählt und für die heutige Laute bearb. von Dr. Hans Dagobert Bruger. Berlin, N. Simrock, G.m.b.H., [cop.1923].
2v. in 1.
The songs have German, French, Italian, Spanish, or English words with acc. of lute, or lute and other instruments.
Title page illustrated.
Contents:
Heft 1. Das XVI Jahrhundert.
Heft 2. XVII und XVIII Jahrhundert.

BRUHNS, NIKOLAUS, ca. 1665–1697.
Complete organ works. Ed. by Stein. New York, C. F. Peters, 19?– .
p.1– .

Bruhns, Nikolaus, ca. 1665–1697, Gesammelte Werke, *see* Das Erbe deutscher Musik. Zweite Reihe. Landschaftsdenkmale. Schleswig-Holstein und Hansestädte. Vol.1, 2.

BRUMEL, ANTOINE, ca. 1480–ca. 1520.
Opera omnia. Edidit Armen Carapetyan. Rome, American Institute of Musicology in Rome, 1951– .
8v. (in progress). (Corpus mensurabilis musicae. No.5).
Contents:
Vol.1. Fasc.1. Missa l'Homme armé. 1951.
Vol.1. Fasc.2. Missa Je ney dueul. 1956.
Contents (proposed):
Vol.1. Fasc.3–5.
Missa Bergerette savoyenne.
Missa Ut re mi fa.
Missa Victime paschali.

BRUNOLD, PAUL, 1875– . ed.
Anthologie des maîtres français du clavecin des XVIIe et XVIIIe siècles. Ed. by H. Expert.
p.1– .

Brunswick, Germany (State). Herzog-August-Bibliothek, Wolfenbüttel. Mss. (Cod. Helmst. 628), *see* Wolfenbüttel. Herzog-August-Bibliothek. Mss. (677 [Helmst. 628]).

BUCHMAYER, RICHARD, 1856–1934. ed.
. . . Aus Richard Buchmayers historischen Klavierkonzerten. Zum Konzertgebrauch und für den Unterricht bearbeitete Klavier- und Orgelwerke des 17. Jahrhunderts . . . Leipzig, Breitkopf & Härtel, [1927].
5v. (Edition Breitkopf. Nr.5341–45).
Contents:
Vol.1. Matthias Weckmann: Tokkata E moll; Kanzone C moll; Suite H moll; Variationen über "Die lieblichen Blicke"; Orgeltokkata D moll.
Vol.2. Matthias Weckmann: Tokkata A moll; Kanzone C dur; Kanzone D moll; Suite

C moll; Fantasia D moll (Orgel); Choralbearbeitung zu "Komm, heiliger Geist, Herre Gott."
Franz Tunder: Praeludium und Fuge G moll (Orgel).
Vol.3. Matthias Weckmann: Suite A moll.
Joh. Adam Reinken: Tokkata G dur; Fuge G moll.
Franz Tunder: Praeludium und Fuge G moll (Orgel).
Vol.4. Joh. Adam Reinken: Variationen über ein "Ballett" E moll.
Georg Böhm. Praeludium, Fuge, Postludium G moll; Französische Suite D dur.
Vol.5. Christian Ritter: Suite Fis moll; Sonatina D moll (Orgel); Georg Böhm: Suite Es dur; C moll; A moll.

BUCHNER, HANS (von CONSTANZ), 1483–1538.
Fundamentbuch von Hans von Constanz; ein Beitrag zur Geschichte des Orgelspiels im 16. Jahrhundert, von Carl Paesler. In: Vierteljahrschrift für Musikwissenschaft. Vol.5. 1889.
p.1–192.
Title page of Fundamentbuch: Abschrifft M. Hansen von Constantz, des wyt beriempten Organisten fundament buch einen kinden verlossen. Bonifacii Amerbachii, Basiliensis, M.D.L1.
Contents:
1. Puer natus est nobis. Vierstimmig.
2.a. Quae est ista, quae ascendit. Vierstimmig.
b. Et universae. Dreistimmig.
3.a. Judea et Hierusalem. Vierstimmig.
b. Cras egrediemini. Vierstimmig.
4.a. Sanctus. Vierstimmig.
b. Sanctus Dominus Deus (Sabaoth). Dreistimmig.
c. Osanna in excelsis. Dreistimmig.
d. Osanna, secundum. Vierstimmig.
5.a. Sanctus, idem per semibreves. Dreistimmig.
b. Sanctus Dominus Deus (Sabaoth). Dreistimmig.
c. Osanna in excelsis, primum. Dreistimmig.
d. Osanna in excelsis, secundum. Dreistimmig.
6. Agnus Dei, qui (tollis peccata mundi). Dreistimmig.
7.a. Kyrie eleyson. Vierstimmig.
b. Kyrie, tertium. Dreistimmig.
c. Christe (eleyson). Dreistimmig.
d. Kyrie, penultimum. Fünfstimmig.
e. Kyrie, aliud penultimum. Dreistimmig.
f. Kyrie, ultimum. Vierstimmig.
8.a. Et in terra pax (hominibus bonae voluntatis). Dreistimmig.
b. Domine Deus Rex coelestis. Vierstimmig.
c. Domine Deus agnus Dei. Dreistimmig.
d. Qui sedes ad (dextram Patris, miserere nobis). Dreistimmig.
e. Tu solus Dominus. Dreistimmig.
f. Cum sancto spiritu (In gloria Dei Patris). Dreistimmig.
9.a. Sanctus, penthecostale et in summis festis. Vierstimmig.
b. Sanctus Dominus Deus Sabaoth. Dreistimmig.
c. Osanna in excelsis, primum. Vierstimmig.
d. Osanna, secundum. Dreistimmig.
10.a. Agnus Dei, primum. Zweistimmig.
b. Agnus Dei, ultimum. Dreistimmig.
11.a. Sanctus, festive in die resurrectionis. Dreistimmig.
b. Sanctus Dominus Deus (Sabaoth). Vierstimmig.
c. Osanna in excelsis, primum. Dreistimmig.
d. Osanna in excelsis, secundum. Dreistimmig.
12.a. Agnus Dei, in resurrectione Domini. Vierstimmig.
b. Agnus, ultimum. Vierstimmig.
13.a. Agnus Dei, primum, ad festum trium Regum. Vierstimmig.
b. Agnus, secundum. Vierstimmig.
14.a. Agnus Dei, ad trium Regum festum. Dreistimmig.
b. Agnus Dei, ultimum. Dreistimmig.
15.a. Sanctus, ad trium Regum (festum), tempore perfecto. Vierstimmig.
b. Sanctus Dominus (Deus Sabaoth). Dreistimmig.
c. Osanna in excelsis, primum. Vierstimmig.
d. Osanna in excelsis, secundum. Dreistimmig.
16.a. Kyrie eleyson festivum, primum. Dreistimmig.
b. Kyrie (eleyson), secundum. Dreistimmig.
c. Christe eleyson. Dreistimmig.
d. Kyrie, penultimum. Vierstimmig.
e. Kyrie, ultimum. Dreistimmig.
17.a. Et in terra pax, festivum. Dreistimmig.
b. Domine Deus Rex coelestis. Dreistimmig.
c. Domine Deus agnus Dei. Dreistimmig.
d. Qui sedes (ad dextram Dei Patris). Dreistimmig.
e. Cum sancto spiritu. Dreistimmig.
18.a. Kyrie eleyson. Angelicum sollemne, primum. Vierstimmig.
b. Kyrie eleyson, secundum. Vierstimmig.
c. Christe eleyson. Choralis in discantu. Dreistimmig.
d. Kyrie, penultimum. Fünfstimmig.
e. Kyrie, ultimum. Vierstimmig.
19.a. Et in terra pax, hominibus (bonae voluntatis), Angelicum. Vierstimmig.
b. Domine Deus Rex coelestis. Dreistimmig.
c. Domine Deus agnus Dei. Fünfstimmig.
d. Qui sedes ad dextram Dei Patris. Dreistimmig.
e. Tu solus Dominus. Vierstimmig.
f. Cum sancto spiritu. Vierstimmig.
20. Gaudeamus omnes. Vierstimmig.
21. Gaudeamus (omnes), aliud. Dreistimmig.
22.a. Congaudent angelorum. Vierstimmig.
b. Filium qui suo. Dreistimmig.
c. In terris cui quondam. Vierstimmig.
d. Qui filii. Vierstimmig.
e. Quam splendida quae omnium. Vierstimmig.
f. Te cantus melodia super. Vierstimmig.
g. Te plebis sexus. Sechsstimmig.
h. Tibi suam manifestat. Vierstimmig.
i. Ut sibi auxilio. Vierstimmig.
23. Spiritus Domini (replevit orbem terrarum). Vierstimmig.

24.a. Sancti Spiritus assit nobis gratia. Vierstimmig.
b. Expulsis inde cunctis. Fünfstimmig.
c. Infunde unctionem tuam. Vierstimmig.
d. Purifica nostri. Vierstimmig.
e. Mundi cordis. Vierstimmig.
f. Apostolos tu confortasti. Dreistimmig.
g. Tu super aquas. Vierstimmig.
h. Tu aspirando. Dreistimmig.
i. Idolatras ad cultam. Dreistimmig.
k. Sine quo preces. Dreistimmig.
l. Ipse hodie Apostolos Christi. Dreistimmig.
m. Sancti Spiritus assit nobis gratia. Vierstimmig.
25. Puer natus est nobis. Vierstimmig.
26. Gloria Patri (et Filio et Spiritui Sancto). Vierstimmig.
27.a. Notus ante secula. Vierstimmig.
b. Per quem dies et horae. Vierstimmig.
c. Hic corpus assumpserat. Vierstimmig.
d. Nec nox vacat. Dreistimmig.
e. Gaude Dei genitrix. Vierstimmig.
f. Et quorum. Dreistimmig.
g. Ut ipsos. Vierstimmig.
28. Resurrexi et adhuc tecum sum. Dreistimmig.
29. Gloria Patri, quarti toni in 1a. Fünfstimmig.
30.a. Kyrie eleyson, paschale, primum. Vierstimmig.
b. Kyrie, tertium. Dreistimmig.
c. Christe eleyson. Dreistimmig.
d. Kyrie, penultimum. Dreistimmig.
e. Kyrie, ultimum. Dreistimmig.
31.a. Et in terra (pax), paschale. Dreistimmig.
b. Domine Deus Rex coelestis. Dreistimmig.
c. Domine Deus agnus Dei. Dreistimmig.
d. Qui sedes ad dextram (Dei) Patris. Dreistimmig.
e. Tu solus Dominus. Dreistimmig.
f. Cum sancto spiritu. Dreistimmig.
32.a. Victimae paschali laudes (immolent Christiani). Dreistimmig.
b. Mors et vita duello (conflixere mirando). Vierstimmig.
c. Angelicos testes, sudarium et vestes. Vierstimmig.
d. Scimus Christum surrexisse (a mortuis vere). Dreistimmig.
33. Christ ist erstanden. Dreistimmig.
34. Quem terra, pontus. Hymnus in assumptione Beatae Mariae Virginis. Vierstimmig.
35. Veni Creator Spiritus. Hymnus de sancto spiritu. Dreistimmig.

Bull, John, 1562–1628. Virginal book, *see* Tisdall, William. Complete keyboard works.

Burgess, Francis, ed. Liturgical choir books, *see* Liturgical choir books.

BUSZIN, WALTER EDWIN, 1899– . ed.
. . . Organ series. St. Louis, Mo., Concordia Publishing House, cop.1948– cop.1950.
3v.
Contents:
Vol.1. Chorale preludes by masters of the XVII and XVIII centuries (contains compositions by Johann Friedrich Alberti, Andreas Armsdorf, Johann Christoph Bach, Johann Michael Bach, Georg Boehm, Dietrich Buxtehude, Johann Friedrich Doles, Johann Ludwig Krebs, Johann Pachelbel, Heinrich Scheidemann, Samuel Scheidt, Andreas Nicolaus Vetter, Tobias Volckmar, Johann Gottfried Walther, Matthias Weckmann, and Friedrich Wilhelm Zachow).
Vol.2. Memorial collection of organ preludes and variations by Johann Gottfried Walther.
Vol.3. Johann Sebastian Bach. Memorial collection.

BUTCHER, VERNON. ed.
English organ music of the eighteenth century, ed. by Vernon Butcher . . . London, Hinrichsen Edition; New York, Peters Edition, [cop.1951].
2v. (Hinrichsen. No.180, 293).
Vol.1 contains compositions by William Boyce, T. S. Dupuis, G. F. Handel, and John Stanley.
Vol.2 contains compositions by T. A. Arne, John Keeble, and William Walond.

BUXHEIMER ORGELBUCH.
Das Buxheimer Orgelbuch, im besitze der Kgl. Hof- und Staatsbibliothek in München, Mss. Mus. 3725. [Leipzig, Breitkopf & Härtel, 1887–88].
111, [1]p. incl. 2 facsim. (music). (Monatschefte für Musikgeschichte, 19.–20. Jahrg. Beilagen).
Caption title.
Fifty selections, including several by Conrad Paumann from the "Buxheimer Orgelbuch," a 15th-century Codex containing 258 or more organ pieces assigned to the period 1450–1460 (cf.p.4).
Ed. by Robert Eitner.
In modern notation.
"Anhang: 17 Praeludien und 1 Fantasie [aus dem Kleber'schen Orgelbuche von c.1520]": p.96–111.

BUXHEIMER ORGELBUCH.
Das Buxheimer Orgelbuch. Facsimile edition published as Reihe II (Handschriften-Faksimiles), No.1, of Documenta musicologica. Hrsg. von Bertha Antonia Wallner. Kassel und Basel, Bärenreiter-Verlag, 1955.
[2]p., facsim. (v, 167L.), vii p.

BUXHEIMER ORGELBUCH, transcribed from the 15th century MS. by Alan Booth with foreword by Anthony Lewis. [New York, London, Edition Peters, Hinrichsen Edition, 1959–60].
2v. (Hinrichsen. No.585 a–b).

An index to *Das Buxheimer Orgelbuch,* by Eileen Southern, appeared in M.L.A. *Notes,* 19, No.1: 47–50 (Dec.1961).

BUXTEHUDE, DIETRICH, 1637–1707.
Dietrich Buxtehudes Werke. [Hrsg. von der Oberleitung der Glaubensgemeinde Ugrino]. Klecken, Ugrino, Abteilung Verlag, 1925–37, 1958– .
v.1– .

Vol.4.– , pub. in Hamburg.
Vols.1–2 ed. by Willibald Gurlitt; v.3–4 by Gottlieb Harms; v.5–7 by Hilmar Trede; v.8 by Dietrich Kilian.
Critical notes for v.1–4 appear in v.4; for v.5–8 in the respective volumes.
"Errata-Verzeichnis" to Bd.4–5; leaf inserted in v.5.
Contents:
Bd.1. Nr.1–17. Solokantaten für Sopran mit Instrumenten. 1925.
Bd.2. Solokantaten für Alt, Tenor oder Bass mit Instrumenten. 1926.
Nr.18–20. Drei Kirchenkantaten für eine Altstimme.
Nr.21–24. Vier Kirchenkantaten für eine Tenorstimme.
Nr.25–27. Drei Kirchenkantaten für eine Bassstimme.
Nr.28. Trauermusik auf den Tod des Johannes Buxtehude.
Bd.3. Solokantaten für 2 Singstimmen mit Instrumenten. 1930.
Nr.29–41. Dreizehn Kirchenkantaten für zwei Singstimme.
Bd.4. Grosse Vokalwerke. 1931.
Nr.42. Missa brevis.
Nr.43. Motette Benedicam Dominum.
Nachweise zu Band I und II.
Nachweise zu Band III.
Nachweise zu Band IV.
Bd.5. 12 Kantaten und Arien für 2 Soprane und Bass mit Continuo und Instrumenten. 1933.
Nr.44. Afferte Domino gloriam, honorem.
Nr.45. Bedenke Mensch das Ende.
Nr.46. Canite Jesu nostro.
Nr.47. Cantate Domino.
Nr.48. Du Frieden Fürst Herr Jesu Christ.
Nr.49. Gott fähret aus mit Jauchzen.
Nr.50. Ich habe Lust abzuscheiden.
Nr.51. Ich habe Lust abzuscheiden. 2. Fassung.
Nr.52. In dulci jubilo.
Nr.53. Je höher du bist.
Nr.54. Jesu, meine Freude.
Nr.55. Aria sopra le nozze di Sua Maesta il Re di Svecia. (Klinget für Freuden).
Bd.6. 9 Kantaten und Arien für 2 Soprane und Bass mit Continuo und Instrumenten. 1935.
Nr.56. Kommst du, Licht der Heiden.
Nr.57. Lauda Sion Salvatorem.
Nr.58. Meine Seele, willtu Ruhn.
Nr.59. O Jesu mi dulcissime. (Fragment).
Nr.60. Salve, desiderium.
Nr.61. Surrexit Christus hodie.
Nr.62. Wachet auf, ruft uns die Stimme.
Nr.63. Welt, packe dich.
Nr.64. Wie soll ich dich empfangen.
Nachweise.
Bd.7. 11 Kirchenkantaten und eine Aria für e Singstimmen und Instrumente. 1937.
Nr.65. In Te, Domine, speravi.
Nr.66. Mein Gemüt erfreuet sich.
Nr.67. Nichts soll uns scheiden von der Liebe Gottes.
Nr.68. Was frag' ich nach der Welt.
Nr.69. Wie schmeckt es so lieblich und wohl.
No.70. An Filius non est Dei.
No.71. Aperite mihi portas justitiae.
No.72. Jesu dulcis memoria.
No.73. Jesu komm, mein Trost und Lachen.
No.74. Jesulein, du Tausendschön.
No.75. Wachet auf, ruft uns die Stimme.
No.76. Auf! Stimmet die Saiten.
Nachweise.
Bd.8. 9 Kantaten für vier Singstimmen und Instrumente. 1958.
No.77. Nun lasst uns Gott, dem Herren, Dank sagen.
Nr.78. Wär Gott nicht mit uns diese Zeit.
No.79. Walts Gott, mein Werk ich lasse.
No.80. Erhalt uns, Herr, bei deinem Wort.
No.81. Herren vår Gud.
No.82. Befiehl dem Engel, dass er komm.
No.83. Der Herr ist mit mir.
No.84. Ecce nunc benedicite Domino.
No.85. Das neugeborne Kindelein.
Kritischer Bericht.
In preparation:
Bd.9. Zehn Kantaten für vier Singstimmen und Instrumente.
Bd.10. Neun Kantaten für fünf Singstimmen und Instrumente.
Bd.11. Sieben Kantaten für fünf Singstimmen und Instrumente und zwei Kantaten für sechs Singstimmen und Instrumente.
Bd.12. Rhythmica oratio.
Bd.13. Das Jüngste Gericht.
Bd.14. Klavierwerke.
Bd.15. Orgelwerke. 1. Teil: Choralbearbeitungen.
Bd.16. Orgelwerke. 2. Teil: Freie Orgelkompositionen.
Bd.17. Instrumentalwerke. Kammermusik.
Bd.18. Ergänzungsband. Kompositionen, deren Echtheit nicht verbürgt ist.

BUXTEHUDE, DIETRICH, 1637–1707.
Dietrich Buxtehude's Orgelcompositionen, hrsg. von Philipp Spitta . . . Leipzig, Breitkopf & Härtel, 1876–78.
2v.
Another edition, 2v. in 1, 1876–1888 (v.1, 1888).
Max Seiffert made a new edition in 1903–1904 and a revised edition in 1940.
Contents:
Bd.1. Passacaglia, Ciaconen, Praeludien und Fugen, Fugen, Toccaten und Canzonetten.
Bd.2. Choralbearbeitungen.

BUXTEHUDE, DIETRICH, 1637–1707.
. . . Ausgewählte Orgelwerke; Praeludien und Fugen, Toccata, Passacaglia, Ciacona, Canzonetta. Hrsg. von Herman Keller. Frankfurt, New York, London, C. F. Peters, [cop.1938–39].
2v. (Edition Peters. No.4449, 4457).
Contents:
Vol.1. Praeludien und Fugen.
Vol.2. Choralbearbeitungen.

BUXTEHUDE, DIETRICH, 1637–1707.
. . . Orgelwerke . . . Hrsg. von Philipp Spitta, neue Ausgabe von Max Seiffert, mit einer

Einleitung von Walter Kraft. Wiesbaden, Breitkopf & Härtel, n.d.
4v.
Contents:
Vol.1–2. Freie Kompositionen.
Vol.3–4. Choralbearbeitungen.

BUXTEHUDE, DIETRICH, 1637–1707.
Sämtliche Orgelwerke. Hrsg. von Josef Hedar. København, Wilhelm Hansen Musik-Forlag; London, J. & W. Chester, Ltd., [1952].
4v.
Contents:
Vol.1. Passacaglia, Ciaconen, und Canzonen.
Vol.2. Präludien und Fugen.
Vol.3. Orgelchoräle.
Vol.4. Orgelchoräle.

BYRD, WILLIAM, 1542 (or 3)–1623.
The collected vocal works of William Byrd. Edited by Edmund H. Fellowes. London, Stainer & Bell, 1937– .
v.1– . facsims.
To be complete in about 22 v.
Vols.18–20 were published under title: The collected works of William Byrd.
Vols.12, 13, 14 are identical with vols.14, 15, 16 of the Editor's "The English madrigal school."
Contents:
Vol.1. Masses, Cantiones sacrae (1575). 1937.
Vol.2. Cantiones sacrae (1589). 1937.
Vol.3. Cantiones sacrae (1591). 1937.
Vol.4. Gradualia (1605, Part 1). 1938.
Vol.5. Gradualia (1605, Parts 2 and 3). 1938.
Vol.6–7. Gradualia (1607, Parts 1 and 2). 1938.
Vol.8. Motets for 3, 4 and 5 voices. 1939.
Vol.9. Motets for 6, 8 and 9 voices. 1939.
Vol.10. English liturgical music. 1948.
Vol.11. English anthems. 1948.
Vol.12. Psalmes, sonnets, and songs (1588). 1948.
Vol.13. Songs of sundry natures (1589). 1949.
Vol.14. Psalmes, songs and sonnets (1611). 1949.
Vol.15. Madrigals recovered from manuscript, and secular songs for solo voice. 1948.
Vol.16. Rounds and canons; and sacred songs for solo voice. 1948.
Vol.17. String fantasies, etc. 1948.
Vol.18–20. Keyboard works. 1950.
Vol.21–22. Songs for voice and instruments. (In preparation).

BYRD, WILLIAM, 1542 (or 3)–1623.
The collected vocal works of William Byrd. New edition. Ed. by Thurston Dart.
v.1– .

BYRD, WILLIAM, 1542 (or 3)–1623.
. . . Forty-five pieces for keyboard instruments. Ed. with introduction and notes by Stephen Davidson Tuttle. Paris, Éditions de l'Oiseau-Lyre, Louise B.-M. Dyer, [cop.1939].
xxix [1] 142p. incl. facsims. (music).
Most of the pieces here first published.

BYRD, WILLIAM, 1542 (or 3)–1623.
My Ladye Nevells booke [by] William Byrd; ed., with an introduction and notes, by Hilda Andrews . . . with a preface by Sir Richard Terry. London, J. Curwen & Sons, Ltd.; Philadelphia, Curwen, Inc., 1926.
xliv, 245p. front., facsims. (music).
"This manuscript, My Ladye Nevells booke, is still preserved at Eridge Castle in Sussex, the seat of the Marquess of Abergavenny."– Historical note.
"Modern editions of virginal music by Byrd": p.xxxvii.
"Ms. sources consulted": p.xxxvii.
Bibliography: p.xxxviii.

BYRD, WILLIAM, 1542 (or 3)–1623.
My Ladye Nevells booke. Reprint. New York, Broude Brothers, 1955.

Cabanilles, Juan, 1644–1712. Opera omnia, *see* Barcelona. Biblioteca Central. Sección de Música. Publicaciones. Vol.4, 8, 13.

CABANILLES, JUAN, 1644–1712.
. . . Opera selecta pro organo, nunc primum in lucem scripta, cura et studio. Hygini Anglis, . . . Prima editio practica, revista et adnotata per Charles Tournemire et Flor Peeters. Bruxelles, Paris, Schott Freres, [cop.1948].
3v. (Edition Peters. No.6011, 6012, 6013).
Contents:
Vol.1. Pasacalles. (1. modus); Tiento I. (2. modus); Tiento II. (4. modus); Tiento III. Ave maris stella. (1. modus).
Vol.2. Toccata (6. modus); Tiento. (1. modus); Pasacalles. (3. modus); Battala. (Imperial. 5. modus).
Vol.3. Tiento. (6. modus); Tiento. (1. modus); Tiento. (Pangue lingua, 5. modus).

Cabezón, Antonio de. Collected works, *see* Institute of Mediaeval Music. Collected works. (Gesamtausgaben). Vol.4.

CAECILIA; Sammlung von Choralvorspielen aus alter und neuer Zeit für Orgel oder Harmonium. Zum Gottesdienstlichen Gebrauche. Hrsg. von August Reinhard. Op.54. Leipzig, Breitkopf & Härtel, n.d.
143, [1] p. (On cover: Edition Breitkopf. Nr.5887).
Contains compositions by J. G. Albrechtsberger, J. Ch. Bach, J. S. Bach, L. H. Bodenschatz, M. G. Fischer, L. E. Gebhardi, J. W. Hässler, A. Hesse, C. Karow, A. Kehrer, J. C. Kittel, V. Klauss, J. H. Knecht, F. Kühmstedt, A. Reinhard, J. E. Rembt, J. C. H. Rinck, J. G. Vierling, and K. H. Zöllner.

CAECILIA; eine Sammlung von Tonstücken verschiedensten Charakters für die Orgel. Aus den Werken älterer und neuerer Komponisten. Bearb. und hrsg. von C. Schweich. Leipzig, Breitkopf & Härtel, n.d
123 [1] p. (Edition Breitkopf. Nr.1368).
Score for organ.
100 Orgelstücke.

California. University. Publications of music. Vol.5, *see* Jacopo da Bologna. The music of Jacopo da Bologna.

O cancioneiro musical e poetico da Biblioteca Públia Hortênsia, *see* Joaquim, Manuel. O cancioneiro musical e poetico da Biblioteca Públia Hortênsia.

Cancionero de Upsala, *see* Villancicos de diuersos autores. Cancionero de Upsala.

Cancionero musical de los siglos XV e XVI, *see* Asenjo y Barbieri, Francisco. Cancionero musical de los siglos XV y XVI.

Cancionero musical y poético del siglo XVII, *see* La Sablonara, Claudio de. Cancionero musical y poético del siglo XVII.

CANTANTIBUS ORGANIS. Sammlung von Orgelstücken alter Meister. Hrsg. von Eberhard Kraus. Kassel, Bärenreiter, 1958– .
v.1– .
Contents:
Vol.1. Die Orgel im Kirchenjahr; Advent/Weihnachten. Werke von D'Aquin, Le Bègue, Erbach, Fasolo, Grigny, Königsperger, Lasso, Muffat, Palestrina, Redford, Tallis, Titelouze. 1958.
Vol.2. Orgelmusik an Europäischen Kathedralen. Werke von Erbach, A. Gabrieli, G. Gabrieli, Guammi, Hassler, Kerll, Lasso, Merulo, Murschhauser, Paix. 1959.
Vol.3. Orgelmusik im Baierischen Raum. Werke von Anonym, Eberlin, Ett, Grätz, Hugl, Kolb, G. Muffat, Murschhauser, Vogler. 1959.
Vol.4. Die Orgel in Choralamt. IX. Messe – cum jubilo. Werke von Binchois, Buxheimer Orgelbuch, Cavassoni, Despres, Erbach, Fasolo, Mudarra, Palero. 1960.
Vol.5. Orgelmusik in Benediktinerklöstern: Kremsmünster, Prüfening, Rott am Inn. Werke von Königsperger, Metsch, Pasterwitz. 1959.
Vol.6. Orgelmusik an Europäischen Kathedralen II: St. Peter in Rom. Werke von Arcadelt, Bakfarc (Greffus), Despres, Dufay, Ferrabosco, Frescobaldi, Giovanelli, Lasso, Marenzio, Morales, De Orto, Paix, Palero, Palestrina, D. Scarlatti, B. Schmid d. A., B. Schmid d. J., Sicher, Victoria. 1961.
Vol.7. Orgelmusik in Benediktinerklöstern II: Augsburg, Garsten, St. Lambrecht, Mariazell. Werke von Aichinger, Ertel, Schmid, Woltz. 1962.
Vol.8. Ostern. Werke von Apel, Asola, Buxheimer Orgelbuch, Daca, Dandrieu, Desprez, Erbach, Fasolo, Finck, Glogauer Liederbuch, Lasso, Muffat, Nerescheimer Orgelbuch, Preston, Schmid, Sicher, Titelouze, Vasurto. 1962.
Vol.9. Orgelmusik in Benediktinerklöstern III. 1962.
Vol.10. Still unpublished.
Vol.11. Orgelmusik an Europäischen Kathedralen III: Bergamo, Passau. Werke von Ammerbach, Bassani, Brignoli, Cavaccio, Hofhaimer, Hugl, Mayr, Ponzio, Scandello, Vinco, Ziani. Hrsg. von Eberhard Kraus. 1963.

Cantaten des 17. und 18. Jahrhunderts, *see* Eitner, Robert, ed. Cantaten des 17. und 18. Jahrhunderts.

Cantica sacra, *see* Commer, Franz. Cantica sacra.

Cantica selecta musices sacrae in Polonia, *see* Gieburowski, Waclaw. Cantica selecta musices sacrae in Polonia.

CANTIO SACRA. Hrsg. von Rudolf Ewerhart. Köln, Edmund Bieler, cop.1955– .
No.1– .
Contents:
No.1. Gratiani, Bonifatio. Gaudia, Pastores, Optate. Sopran (Tenor) und Basso Continuo.
No.2. Bassani, Giovanni Battista. Nascere, Nascere, Dive Puellule. Alt und B.C.
No.3. Couperin, François. Leçons de ténèbres. Première leçon Sopran (Tenor) und B.C.
No.4. Couperin, François. Leçons de ténèbres. Seconde leçon. Sopran (Tenor) und B.C.
No.5. Viadana, Lodovico da. Drei geistliche Konzerte. Bass und B.C.
No.6. Campra, André. Quam dulce est. Inhaerere Tibi. Alt und B.C.
No.7. Monteverdi, Claudio. Salve, O Regina. Tenor (Sopran) und B.C.
No.8. Carissimi, Giacomo. Domine, Deus meus. Sopran (Tenor) und B.C.
No.9. Campra, André. Exaltabo Te. Deus meus, Rex. Bass und B.C.
No.10. Foggia, Antonio. O quam fulgido splendore. Sopran (Tenor) und B.C.
No.11. Brevi, Giovanni Battista. Catenae terrenae. Bass und B.C.
No.12. Milans, Tomas. Drei Motetten. Sopran (Tenor) und B.C., Bass und B.C.
No.13. Brossard, Sébastien de. Quemadmodum desiderat cervus. Tenor (Sopran) und B.C.
No.14. Anerio, Giovanni Francesco. Drei geistliche Konzerte. Bass und B.C.
No.15. Leo, Leonardo. Praebe, Virgo, Benignas aures. Motette a canto solo con organo obligato.
No.16. Carissimi, Giacomo. O vulnera doloris. Bass und B.C.
No.17. Campra, André. O dulcis amor. Sopran (Tenor) und B.C.
No.18. Grandi, Alessandro. Drei geistliche Konzerte. Sopran (Tenor) und B.C.
No.19. Cazzati, Mauritio. In Calvaria rupe. Bass und B.C.
No.20. Porpora, Nicolo. Vigilate, oculi mei. Sopran (Tenor) und B.C.
No.21. Spanische Meister des 18. Jahrhunderts. Drei Motetten. Alt und B.C., Tenor (Sopran) und B.C., Bass und B.C.
No.22. Benevoli, Oratio. Ego autem pro Te, Domine. Sopran (Tenor) und B.C.
No.23. Monteverdi, Claudio; Bernardi, Steffano; Grandi, Alessandro. Drei Hoheliedmotetten. Sopran (Tenor) und B.C.

No.24. Brossard, Sébastien de. O plenus irarum dies. Bass und B.C.
No.25. Brevi, Giovanni Battista. Deliciae terrenae. Sopran (Tenor) und B.C.
No.26. Charpentier, Marc-Antoine. Vier Elevations. Sopran (Tenor) und B.C., Tenor (Sopran) und B.C., Alt und B.C.
No.27. Caldara, Antonio. Veni, dilecte, veni. Sopran (Tenor) und B.C.
No.28. Foggia, Francesco. De valle lacrimarum. Sopran (Tenor) und B.C.
No.29. Brossard, Sébastien de. Sonitus armorum. Alt und B.C.
No.30. Charpentier, Marc-Antoine. Sieben Motetten. Sopran (Tenor) und B.C., Tenor (Sopran) und B.C.
No.31. Rosetti, Giovanni Antonio. Ad festa, fideles. Bass und B.C.
No.32. Campra, André. Jubilate Deo. Sopran (Tenor) und B.C.
No.33. Fiocco, Joseph Hector. Lamentatio tertia. Sopran (Tenor) und B.C.
No.34. Brevi, Giovanni Battista. O spiritus angelici. Alt und B.C.
No.35. Unbekannter spanischer Meister. Intonuit de coelo. Sopran (Tenor) und B.C.
No.36. Majo, Gian Francesco de. Sicut cerva, quae per valles. Sopran und Konzertierende Orgel.
No.37. Carissimi, Giacomo. Lucifer. Bass und B.C.
No.38. Foggia, Francesco. Cessate, deh, cessate. Sopran (Tenor) und B.C.
No.39. Gratiani, Bonifatio. Salve, Regina. Sopran (Tenor) und B.C.
No.40. Viadana, Lodovico da. Drei geistliche Konzerte. Alt und B.C.
No.41. Gratiani, Bonifatio. Pastores, dum custodistis. Sopran (Tenor) und B.C.
No.42. Piazza, Gaetano. Tonat coelum cum furore. Sopran und Konzertierende Orgel.
No.43. Giansetti, Giovanni Battista. Blandire puero. Sopran und B.C.
No.44. Bernabei, Ercole. Heu me miseram et infelicem. Sopran (Tenor) und B.C.
No.45. Morin, Jean Baptiste. Ad mensam coelitus paratam. Sopran (Tenor) und B.C.
No.46. Caprioli, Giovanni Paolo. Drei geistliche Konzerte. Sopran (Tenor) und B.C.
No.47. Terziani, Pietro. Salve, Regina. Sopran und Konzertierende Orgel.
No.48. Carissimi, Giacomo. Salve, salve, puellule. Sopran (Tenor) und B.C.
No.49. Monferrato, Natale. Alma redemptoris mater. Sopran (Tenor) und B.C.
No.50. Morin, Jean Baptiste. Venite, exsultemus Domino. Sopran (Tenor) und B.C.
No.51. Viadana, Lodovico da. Drei geistliche Konzerte. Sopran und B.C.
No.52. Bernabei, Ercole. In hymnis et canticis. Sopran (Tenor) und B.C.
No.53. Casola, Francesco. Quam candidus es. Sopran (Tenor) und B.C.
No.54. Pellegrini, Domenico. Dicite, mortales. Sopran (Tenor) und B.C.
No.55. Cazzati, Mauritio. Dulcis amor. Bass und B.C.
No.56. Campra, André. Quemadmodum desiderat cervus. Sopran (Tenor) und B.C.
No.57. Carissimi, Giacomo. O quam pulchra es. Sopran (Tenor) und B.C.

Capalavori della polifonia italiani (Sec.XVI), *see* Pistone, Pier Giovanni. Capalavori della polifonia italiana (sec.XVI).

CAPELLA. Meisterwerke mittelalterlicher Musik. Hrsg. von Heinrich Besseler. Kassel, Bärenreiter Verlag, 1950– .
v.1– .
Contents:
Vol.1. Drei- und vierstimmige Singstücke des 15. Jahrhundert von Dunstable, Dufay, Touront, Obrecht, Finck, and Josquin. 1950. 2. Auflage. 1959.
Vol.2. Dufay, Guillaume. Vierstimmige Messe "Se la face ay pale." 1951.

Capirola, Vincenzo, b.1474. Compositione. Lutebook (circa 1517), *see* La Société de Musique d'Autrefois. Publications. Textes musicaux. Tome 1.

Capolavori polifonici del secolo XVI, *see* Somma, Bonaventura. Capolavori polifonici del secolo XVI.

Caracas. Dirección de Cultura of the Ministerio de Educación Nacional, *see* Archivo de música colonial venezolana.

Carissimi, Giacomo, ca.1604–1674. Werke, *see* Istituto Italiano per la Storia della Musica. 1. Monumenti III.

Carpio, Lope Félix de Vega, *see* Vega Carpio, Lope Félix de, 1562–1635.

Carse, Adam von Ahn, 1878– , ed. Old English dance tunes, 17th century, *see* Playford, John. Old English dance tunes, 17th century.

CARVER, ROBERT, b. ca.1491.
Collected works. Ed. by Denis Stevens. [n.p.] American Institute of Musicology, 1959– .
v.1– . (Corpus mensurabilis musicae. No.16).
Proposed set: 3–5v.
Contents:
Vol.1. The two extant motets: O bone Jesu and Gaude flore Virginali. 1959.

CASIMIRI, RAFFAELE CASIMIRO, 1880–1943. ed.
Anthologia polyphonica auctorum saeculi XVI paribus vocibus. Cura et studio Raph. Casimiri . . . v.1–2. Roma, Edizioni "Psalterium," [1932?].
2v.
For 3 to 8 voices unaccompanied. Latin words.
Vol.1, 3d. ed.; v.2, cop.1932.

Casimiri, Raffaele Casimiro, 1880–1943, ed. Societas Polyphonica Romanae. Repertorium, *see* Societas Polyphonica Romanae. Repertorium.

Castrillo Hernández, Gonzalo, ed. Antología musical; Siglo de oro de la música litúrgica de España, *see* Elúsitiza, Juan B. de. Antología musical; Siglo de oro de la música litúrgica de España.

Cathedral music, *see* Arnold, Samuel. Cathedral music; Boyce, William. Cathedral music; Dupuis, Thomas Sanders. Cathedral music in score; Page, John. Harmonia sacra.

Catholic Church, Roman. Liturgy and ritual. Antiphonary. Salisbury. Antiphonale Sarisburiense, *see* Plainsong and Mediaeval Music Society. Catholic Church, Roman. Liturgy and ritual. Antiphonary. Salisbury. Antiphonale Sarisburiense.

Catholic Church, Roman. Liturgy and ritual. Graduals. Salisbury. Graduale Sarisburiense, *see* Plainsong and Mediaeval Music Society. Catholic Church, Roman. Liturgy and ritual. Graduals. Salisbury. Graduale Sarisburiense.

Catholic Church, Roman. Liturgy and ritual. Graduals. Salisbury. The plainchant of the ordinary of the Mass, *see* Plainsong and Mediaeval Music Society. Catholic Church, Roman. Liturgy and ritual. Graduals. Salisbury. The plainchant of the ordinary of the Mass.

CATHOLIC CHURCH, ROMAN. LITURGY AND RITUAL. MISSAL.
Missa Tornacensis, edidit Charles van den Borren. [Rome], American Institute of Musicology, 1957.
3p.L., xi p., 1L. (Corpus mensurabilis musicae. No.13).

CATHOLIC CHURCH, ROMAN. LITURGY AND RITUAL. TROPER.
The Winchester troper, from mss. of the Xth and XIth centuries, with other documents illustrating the history of tropes in England and France. Ed. by Walter Howard Frere . . . London, [Harrison and Sons, Printers], 1894.
xlvii, 248p. 6 pl.(music). 27 facsim. (music). (Added title page: Henry Bradshaw Society. . . [Publications] Vol.VIII).
Some of the facsimiles are accompanied by "elucidatory plates printed in music type."
"List of mss. and printed authorities": p.xlii–xliv.
Contents: The Winchester troper; The Canterbury troper; Worcester greater tropes; St. Alban's greater tropes; Dublin greater tropes; English troper in Pamelius' Liturgicon; Trope of Benedicamus. Appendix: St. Magioire troper. St. Martial troper. Extraits from the Novalaise troper.

CAUCHIE, MAURICE, 1882– . comp.
Quinze chansons françaises du XVIe siècle à quatre et cinq voix, pour soli ou choeur mixtes, mises en partition. Paris, Rouart, Lerolle & Cie., 1926.
57p. (Les concerts de la Renaissance).
Contains vocal and instrumental music of the 16th century.
Contains compositions by Jacques Arcadelt, De Bussy, Pierre Certon, Guillaume Costeley, Godard, Claude Goudimel, Nicolas Millot, Le Moyne, Passereau ou Janequin, Pierre de la Rue, P. Sandrin, Claude de Sermisy, and Guillaume du Tertre.

Cembalisti italiani del settecento, *see* Benevenuti, Giacomo. Cembalisti italiani del settecento.

Cent motets du XIIIe siècle, *see* Aubry, Pierre. Cent motets du XIIIe siècle.

Cent versets de Magnificat des XVIème, XVIIème et XVIIIème siècles pour orgue, *see* Pierront, Noëlie. Cent versets de Magnificat des XVIème, XVIIème et XVIIIème siècles pour orgue.

Cesti, Marc Antonio, 1623–1669. Cantata, *see* The Wellesley edition. No.5.

Chaĭkovskiĭ, Petr Il'ich, *see* Tchaikovskiĭ, Peter Ilich.

CHAMBONNIÈRES, JACQUES CHAMPION DE, ca.1602–ca.1672.
. . . Oeuvres complètes de Chambonnières. Publiées par Paul Brunold et André Tessier. Paris, Éditions M. Senart, 1925.
xxiii, 132p. facsims. (Les maîtres français du clavecin).

CHAMBONNIÈRES, JACQUES CHAMPION DE, ca.1602–ca.1672.
. . . Oeuvres complètes de Chambonnières. Reprint. English translation and new preface by Denise Restout. New York, Broude Brothers, [cop. 1967].
xxxv, 139p. facsims.

Le chansonnier Cangé, *see* Beck, Jean Baptiste. Anthologie de cent chansons de trouvères et de troubadours des XIIe et XIIe siècles; Beck, Jean Baptiste. Les chansonniers des troubadours et des trouvères. No.1, t.1–2.

CHANSONNIER D'ARRAS.
La chansonnier d'Arras, reproduction en phototypie; introduction par Alfred Jeanroy . . . Paris, [1925].
19p., facsim. (lxiv numb. leaves, vignettes, initials).
"Volume offert aux membres de la Société des anciens textes [français] pour le cinquantenaire, tiré à 1,000 exemplaires, dont 200 mis dans le commerce chez E. Champion, Paris . . ."
The manuscript volume which includes the Chansonnier is in the Bibliothèque Municipale, Arras, where it bears the number 139 (formerly 657). The Chansonnier (32p., numbered 129 to 160) has lost several leaves, and the remaining ones are not bound in order. It is assigned to the late 13th or early 14th century and shows a close relationship to Vatican ms. Reg. 1490. Besides the songs (with music), it includes a section of 32 *jeux partis.* cf. Introd.
Leaves of facsimile printed on one side only; arranged in proper sequence and renumbered (as in collation) by the editor.

Le chansonnier de l'Arsenal, *see* Paris. Bibliothèque de l'Arsenal. Mss. (No.5198). Le chansonnier de l'Arsenal.

Chansonnier du XVe siècle, *see* Bordes, Charles. Chansonnier du XVe siècle.

Les chansonniers des troubadours et des trouvères, *see* Beck, Jean Baptiste. Les chansonniers des troubadours et des trouvères.

Chansons und Tänze, *see* Attaingnant, Pierre. Chansons und Tänze.

Chants d'église à plusieurs voix des anciens compositeurs polonais, *see* Cichocki, Jos. Chants d'église à plusieurs voix des anciens compositeurs polonais.

Chants de France et d'Italie, *see* Expert, Henry. Chants de France et d'Italie.

Chants de la Sainte-Chapelle tirés de manuscrits du XIIIe siècle, *see* Clément, Félix. Chants de la Sainte-Chapelle tirés de manuscrits du XIIIe siècle.

CHAPPELL, WILLIAM, 1809–1888.
The ballad literature and popular music of the olden time; a history of the ancient songs, ballads and of the dance tunes of England, with numerous anecdotes and entire ballads. Also a short account of the minstrels. The whole of the airs harmonized by C. A. Macfarren. London, Chappell, [1855–59].
2v. front., facsims.
Contains music.

CHAPPELL, WILLIAM, 1809–1888.
Old English popular music, by William Chappell, F.S.A. A new ed. with a preface and notes, and the earlier examples entirely revised by H. Ellis Wooldridge . . . London, Chappell & Co., [etc.]; New York, Novello, Ewer & Co., 1893.
2v. front. (facsim.).
First published 1838–40 as "A collection of national English airs" which was afterward expanded into his "Popular music of the olden time" (1859, 2 v.). Part of the latter edition was published under title "The ballad literature and popular music of the olden time."

CHAPPELL, WILLIAM, 1809–1888.
Old English popular music. A new ed. with a preface and notes, and the earlier examples entirely revised by H. Ellis Wooldridge. New York, J. Brussel, [cop.1961].
2v. in 1.

CHARPENTIER, MARC ANTOINE, 1634–1704.
[Oeuvres, réalisées par Guy Lambert]. Paris, 1948– .
v.1– .
Ed. musicologique réalisée par subscription internationale et publ. par Guy Lambert sous l'égide du Comité Marc-Antoine Charpentier.
The edition does not have numbered volumes.
Contents (as listed in *Die Musik in Geschichte und Gegenwart*, Bd.4, *Gesamtausgaben.* 1955):
Concert pour quatrê parties de violes. 1948.
"Regina coeli" pour voce sola con flauti from Vol.8 of the "Meslanges." 1948.
"Salve Regina des Jésuites" pour taille et continuo from Vol.4 of the "Meslanges." 1949.
3. Répons: "Amicus meus" pour haute-contre et continuo from Vol.4 of the "Meslanges." 1949.
Médée, 3. Akt., 3. Scene. "Quel prix de mon amour." 1950.
Médée, 4. Akt., 9. Scene. "Noires divinitez." 1950.
"Pie Jesus" pour deux dessus et orgue from the "Messe des morts" in Vol.24 of the "Meslanges." 1951.
Antienne à la Vierge "Regina coeli" a deux dessus et orgue from Vol.23 of the "Meslanges." 1951.
Médée. 3. Akt., 3. Scene. "Que me peut demander la gloire." 1951.
Antiphona "Sub tuum praesidium" from Vol.28 of the "Meslanges." Motet pour la Vierge "Alma Dei" from Vol.21 of the "Meslanges." 1952.
Leçon de Ténèbres. 7. Répons "Seniores populi" pour haute-contre et continuo from Vol.4 of the "Meslanges." 1952.
Médée. 5. Akt., 6. Scene. "Appelez vous douceur." 1952.
Deux antiennes "Regina coeli" and "Assumpta est" pour contralto, symphonie et continuo from Vol.8 and 28 of the "Meslanges." 1953.
Prose: "Languentibus in purgatorio" pour 2 dessus et basse avec symphonie de 3 flutes, clavecin et viole from the "Supplications pour les défunts" in Vol.18 of the "Meslanges." 1953.
Leçon de Ténèbres. 1. Leçon du mercredy saint: "Plorens ploravit" pour haute-contre et continuo from Vol.4 of the "Meslanges." 1953.

LES CHEFS d'OEUVRES CLASSIQUES DE l'OPÉRA FRANÇAIS. Leipzig, Breitkopf & Härtel, cop.1880.
40v.
Contents:
Beaujoyeux. Le ballet-comique de la reine. [188?].
Cambert, R. Les peines & les plaisirs de l'amour. [188?].
—— Pomone. [188?].
Campra, A. L'Europe galante. [188?].
—— Les fêtes vénitiennes. [188?].
—— Tancrède. [188?].
Catel, C. S. Les bayadères. [188?].
Colasse, P. and J. B. Lully. Les saisons. [188?].
—— Thétis et Pélée. [188?].
Destouches, A. C. and M. R. de Lalande. Les éléments. [188?].
—— Issé. [188?].
—— Omphale. [188?].
Grétry, A. E. M. La caravane du Caire. [188?].
—— Céphale & Procris. [188?].
Le Sueur, J. F. Ossian ou les bardes. [188?].
Lully, J. B. de. Alceste. [188?].
—— Armide. [1878].

—— Atys. [188?].
—— Bellérophon. [188?].
—— Cadmus et Hermione. [188?].
—— Isis. [188?].
—— Persée. [188?].
—— Phaéton. [188?].
—— Proserpine. [188?].
—— Psyché. [1878].
—— Thésée. [1877].
Philidor, F. A. D. Ernélinde. [188?].
Piccinni, N. Didon. [188?].
—— Roland. [188?].
Rameau, J. P. Castor et Pollux. [188?].
—— Dardanus. [188?].
—— Les fêtes d'Hébé. [188?].
—— Hippolyte et Aricie. [188?].
—— Les Indes galantes. [188?].
—— Platée. [1884].
—— Zoroastre. [188?].
Sacchini, A. M. G. Chimène ou le Cid. [188?].
—— Renaud. [188?].
Saliéri, A. Les Danaïdes. [188?].
—— Tarare. [188?].

CHILESOTTI, OSCAR, 1848–1916. ed.
Biblioteca di rarità musicali. Milan, G. Ricordi, [1884–1915].
9v.
Contents:
Vol.1. Caroso, F. . . . Nobilità di dame . . . [1884?].
Vol.2. Picchi, G. Balli d'arpicordo. [1884?].
Vol.3. Stefani, G. Affetti amorosi. [1885].
Vol.4. Marcello, B. Arianna. [1885?].
Vol.5. Vecchi, O. Arie, canzonette e balli. [1892].
Vol.6. Frescobaldi, G. Partite sopra La romanesca, La monicha, Ruggiero e La follia. [1908].
Vol.7. Besard, J. B. Airs de court (secolo XVI) dal Thesaurus harmonicus.
Vol.8. Chilesotti, O., ed. Musica del passato. 1895.
Vol.9. Besard, J. B. Madrigali, villanelle ed arie di danza del cinquecento. 1915.

CHILESOTTI, OSCAR, 1848–1916. ed.
. . . Da un codice Lauten-Buch del cinquecento, trascrizioni in notazione moderna, di Oscar Chilesotti. Lipsia, Breitkopf & Härtel, [pref. 1890].
ix, 101p. facsim. (music).
Transcribed into modern notation on one staff.
Preface in Italian and German.
Title page illustrated.

CHILESOTTI, OSCAR, 1848–1916. ed.
Lautenspieler des XVI. Jahrhunderts. (Liutisti del cinquecento). Ein Beitrag zur Kenntnis des Ursprungs der modernen Tonkunst, von Oscar Chilesotti. Leipzig, Breitkopf & Härtel, [pref. 1891].
xv, 248p. facsim.
Reprinted by the publishers in 1926.
Transcribed into modern notation on one staff.
Preface in Italian and German.
Title page illustrated.
Contains compositions by William Ballet, J. C. Barbetta, Bernardo Gianoncelli detto il Barnardello, G. B. Besardo, Fabritio Caroso, Gabriel Fallamero, Francesco da Milano, Vincentio Galilei, Simon Gintzler, Gio. Battista dalla Gostena, Jacomo Gorzanis, Mersenne Marin, Joanne Matelart, Simone Molinaro, Cesare Negri, Hans Newsidler, and G. A. Terzi.

Choir responses, *see* Plainsong and Mediaeval Music Society. Choir responses.

CHOMIŃSKI, JÓZEF MICHAL, 1906– . ed.
Music of the Polish Renaissance; a selection of works from the XVIth and the beginning of the XVIIth century. Ed. by Józef M. Chomiński and Zofia Lissa. [Translation from the Polish: Claire Grece Dabrowska; English translation of the Polish songs: Przemyslaw Mroczkowski. Kraków],Polskie Wydawnictwo Muzyczne, 1955.
Score (370p.). facsims.
Partial contents: Music of the Polish Renaissance; Instrumental music; Vocal music; Translations of the Polish songs.

CHOPIN, FRYDERYK FRANCISZEK, 1810–1849.
Werke. Hrsg. von W. Bargiel, J. Brahms, A. Franchomme, F. Liszt, C. Reinecke, E. Rudorff. (Erste kritisch durchgesehene Gesamtausgabe). Leipzig, Breitkopf & Härtel, 1878–80.
14v.
Revisionsbericht in 3 pts. and Suppl. in 3 pts. Leipzig, Breitkopf & Härtel, 1878–1902.
Contents:
Vol.1. Balladen.
Vol.2. Etüden.
Vol.3. Mazurkas.
Vol.4. Notturnes.
Vol.5. Polonaisen.
Vol.6. Präludien.
Vol.7. Rondos und Scherzos.
Vol.8. Sonaten.
Vol.9. Walzer.
Vol.10. Verschiedene Werke.
Vol.11. Trio und Duos.
Vol.12. Orchesterwerke (Op.2, 11, 13, 14, 21, 22).
Vol.13. Nachlass. 35 Pianofortewerke.
Vol.14. Lieder und Gesänge.
Supplement: 3 unveröffentlichte Klavierstücke nach den im Besitz der Familie Joseph Elsner befindlichten Original-Handschriften.

CHOPIN, FRYDERYK FRANCISZEK, 1810–1849.
. . . Complete works, according to the autographs and original editions with a critical commentary. Editor, Ignacy J. Paderewski, assisted by Ludwik Bronarski and Jósef Turczyński. With reproductions of portraits and manuscripts. Warsaw, The Fryderyk Chopin Institute; Cracow Polish Music Publications, 1949– .
v.1– .
Contents:
Vol.1. Preludes for piano.
Vol.2. Studies for piano.
Vol.3. Ballades for piano.
Vol.4. Impromptus for piano.
Vol.5. Scherzos for piano.

Vol.6. Sonatas for piano.
Vol.7. Nocturnes for piano.
Vol.8. Polonaises for piano.
Vol.9. Walzes for piano.
Vol.10. Mazurkas for piano.
Vol.11. Fantasia, Berceuse, Barcarolle for piano.
Vol.12. Rondos for piano and for 2 pianos.
Vol.13. Concert allegro. Variations. For piano.
Vol.14. Concertos. Piano arrangement. Op.11, 21.
Vol.15. Works for piano and orchestra. Op.2, 13, 14.
Vol.16. Chamber music. Op.3, 8, 65. Grand duo concertant, Variations for flute.
Vol.17. Songs for solo voice with piano accompaniment. Op.74, No.1–17, Czary, and Dumka.
Vol.18. Minor works for piano. Op.19, 43, 72, No.1–5, and other pieces.
Vol.19. Concerto in E minor for piano and orchestra. Op.11. Score.
Vol.20. Concerto in F minor for piano and orchestra. Op.21. Score.
Vol.21–26. Orchestra parts.

CHOPIN, FRYDERYK FRANCISZEK, 1810–1849.
Oeuvres complètes, d'après des autographes et les premières éditions avec commentaires critiques, rédigées par Ignacy J. Paderewski en collaboration avec Ludwik Bronarski et Józef Turczyński. Varsovie, Institut Fryderyk Chopin, éditeur; exécution et dépôt central: Édition polonaise de Musique, Cracovie, 1949– .
v.1– .
Contents: v.2. Études.

CHOPIN, FRYDERYK FRANCISZEK, 1810–1849.
. . . Complete works for the piano. Ed. and fingered, and provided with an introductory note by Carl Mikuli. Historical and analytical comments by James Huneker . . . New York, G. Schirmer, Inc., cop.1934.
15v. (Schirmer's Library of musical classics. Vol.29, 35, 1546–1558).
Contents:
Vol.1. Waltzes.
Vol.2. Mazurkas.
Vol.3. Polonaises.
Vol.4. Nocturnes.
Vol.5. Ballades.
Vol.6. Impromptus.
Vol.7. Scherzi and fantasy.
Vol.8. Etudes.
Vol.9. Preludes.
Vol.10. Rondos.
Vol.11. Sonatas.
Vol.12. Various compositions.
Vol.13. Four concert pieces.
Vol.14. Concerto in E minor.
Vol.15. Concerto in F minor.

CHOPIN, FRYDERYK FRANCISZEK, 1810–1849.
Sämtliche Werke. Leipzig, C. F. Peters, 19? – .
3v. (Edition Peters. No.1900 a-c).
Contents:
Vol.1. Walzer, Mazurkas, Polonaisen, Nocturnes.
Vol.2. Balladen, Impromptus, Scherzi, Phantasie, Etüden, Präludien, Rondos.
Vol.3. Sonaten, Stücke, Konzerte.

CHOPIN, FRYDERYK FRANCISZEK, 1810–1849.
Sämtliche Werke. Neue Ausgabe von Bronislaw von Pozniak. Leipzig, C. F. Peters, 19? – .
12v. (Edition Peters. No.1901, 1804, 1902–1912).
Contents:
Vol.1. Walzer, Volksausgabe. Walzer, Prachtausgabe.
Vol.2–3. Mazurkas. Polonaisen.
Vol.4–5. Nocturnes. Balladen/Impromptus.
Vol.6–7. Scherzi/Phantasie in F. Etüden.
Vol.8–9. Präludien/Rondos. Sonaten.
Vol.10. Stücke. (Berceuse. Barcarolle usw.)
Vol.11–12. Konzerte. Konzertstücke.

CHOR-ARCHIV. Kassel, Basel [etc.], Bärenreiter, 19? – .
No.1– .
Contents:
Altniederländische Motetten von Ockeghem, Compère und Josquin des Prez für drei bis sechs gemischte Stimmen. (Besseler).
Anonymus (um 1450). In Gottes Namen fahren wir. Für achtstimmigen gemischten Chor. (Gutmann).
Crüger, Johann. Neun geistliche Lieder für vierstimmigen gemischten Chor mit zwei Melodie-Instrumenten und Generalbass (nicht ausgesetzt). (Mahrenholz).
Dufay, Guillaume. Se la face ay pale. Messe für vierstimmigen gemischten Chor. (Besseler).
Ebeling, Johann Georg. Zwölf geistliche Lieder Paul Gerhardts für vierstimmigen gemischten Chor, zwei Violinen und Generalbass (nicht ausgesetzt). (Ameln).
Franck, Melchior. Dank sagen wir alle Gott. Weihnachtsmusik zu 7 Stimmen für 2 Chöre a cappella. (Peters-Marquardt).
Gabrieli, Andrea. Quem vidistis pastores? Wen denn sahet ihr Hirten? Weihnachtsmotette für achtstimmigen Doppelchor. (Grusnick).
Hassler, Hans Leo. Angelus ad pastores ait. Der Engel sprach zu den Hirten. Weihnachtsmotette für achtstimmigen Doppelchor. (Grusnick).
—— Missa octo vocum. (Grusnick).
—— Psalmen und Christliche Gesäng Fugweiss für vierstimmigen gemischten Chor. (Saalfeld).
Kugelmann, Paul. Sieben teutsche Liedlein aus Kugelmanns Sammlung 1558 für vier bis sechs gemischte Stimmen. (Engel).
Lasso, Orlando di. Come la Notte. Madrigal für fünfstimmigen gemischten Chor. (Boetticher).
—— Drei Chansons für vierstimmigen gemischten Chor. (Boetticher).
—— Landsknechtsständchen für vierstimmigen gemischten Chor. (Grischkat).
—— Lauda Sion. Motette für sechsstimmigen gemischten Chor.
—— Missa super "Credidi propter" für fünfstimmigen gemischten Chor. (Hermelink).

—— Missa super "Frère Thibault" für vierstimmigen gemischten Chor. (Hermelink).
—— Missa super "Ite rime dolenti" für fünfstimmigen gemischten Chor. (Hermelink).
—— Missa super "Scarco di doglia" für fünfstimmigen gemischten Chor. (Hermelink).
—— Vier Motetten für gemischten Chor. (Cum rides mihi, 5st.; Data est de lachrimis, 5st.; Da pacem, Domine, 5st.; Gloria Patri, 6st). (Boetticher).
Lechner, Leonhard. Italienische Madrigale 1579 und 1585 für fünfstimmigen gemischten Chor. (Ameln).
—— Lustige teutsche Lieder für vierstimmigen gemischten Chor. (Schmid).
—— Neue deutsche weltliche Lieder 1577 für vierstimmigen gemischten Chor. (Martin). Heft 1–2.
—— Magnificat primi toni für vier gemischte Stimmen. (Lipphardt).
Michael, Rogier. Die geburt unsers Herren Jesu Christi nach den Evangelisten Lukas und Matthäus, Anno 1602. Für Evangelisten und fünf- bis sechsstimmigen gemischten Chor a cappella. (Osthoff).
Monteverdi, Claudio. Canzonetten für drei gleiche Stimmen. (Trede).
Musica Reservata. I. Vier- bis sechsstimmige Motetten von Senfl, Lasso, Stobäus. (Müller-Blattau).
Musica Reservata. II. Vier- bis sechsstimmige Motetten von Josquin, Senfl und Orlando di Lasso. (Müller-Blattau).
Othmayr, Kaspar. Geistliche Lieder zu vier Stimmen. 1546. (Ameln).
Päminger, Leonhard. Weihnachtsmotette. Exijt edictum a Caesare Augusto . . . für fünfstimmigen Chor a cappella. (Zimbauer).
Praetorius, Michael. Ein Kindelein so Löbelich. Choralmotette für achtstimmigen Doppelchor. (Grusnick).
—— Nun Lob, mein Seel, den Herren. Choralmotette für achtstimmigen Doppelchor. (Brodde).
Purcell, Henry. Evening Service. (Geistliche Abendmusik) für vier Solostimmen (oder kleinen Chor) und vierstimmigen Chor. (Just).
—— Singt, o singt dem Herrn. Anthem für Sopran, Alt, Tenor, Bass, vierstimmigen gemischten Chor und Streichorchester (2 Violinen, Viola, Violoncello). (Just).
Regnart, Jacob. Einsmals in einem Tiefen Tal. Liedmotette für fünfstimmigen Chor aus den "Newen kurtzweiligen teutschen Liedern" vom Jahre 1580. (Osthoff).
Scheidt, Samuel. Christe, der Du bist Tag und Licht. Motette für zwei vierstimmige Chöre. (Mahrenholz).
—— Duo seraphim clamabant für achtstimmigen Doppelchor. (Mahrenholz).
—— Ein Feste Burg. Motette für zwei vierstimmige Chor. (Mahrenholz).
—— Ich hebe meine Augen auf. Der 121. Psalm für achtstimmigen Doppelchor. (Mahrenholz).
—— In dulci jubilo. Motette für zwei vierstimmige Chor und zwei Trompeten ad lib. (Mahrenholz).
—— Nun komm, der Heiden Heiland für achtstimmigen Doppelchor. (Mahrenholz).
—— Zion spricht: Der Herr hat mich verlassen. Motette für zwei vierstimmige Chöre. (Mahrenholz).
Schröter, Leonhart. Wo der Herr nicht das Haus bauet. Der 127. Psalm, zu acht Stimmen für zwei Chöre. (Hofmann).
Schütz, Heinrich. Ich weiss, dass mein Erlöser lebet. Sechsstimmige Motette. (Moser).
—— Der 100. Psalm "Jauchzet dem Herrn alle Welt" für zwei vierstimmige Chöre. (Huber).
—— Singet dem Herrn ein neues Lied. Der 98. Psalm für achtstimmigen Doppelchor aus den "Psalmen Davids, 1619." (Thate).
Telemann, Georg Philipp. Der 117. Psalm. "Auf, lobet den Herrn, alle Heiden" für vierstimmigen gemischten Chor, zwei Violinen und Generalbass. (Valentin).
Zelter, Carl Friedrich. Die Gunst des Augenblicks. Kantate nach Worten von Schiller für Sopran, Alt, Tenor, Bass, vierstimmigen gemischten Chor, 2 Trompeten, 2 Hörner, Pauken, Streichorchester und Klavier. (Müller-Blattau).
—— Johanna Sebus. Nach dem Gedicht von Goethe für Sopran, Bariton, Bass, vierstimmigen gemischten Chor und Klavier oder Querflöte, Streichorchester, Klavier. (Müller-Blattau).

Chor- und Hausmusik aus älter Zeit, *see* Wolf, Johannes. Chor- und Hausmusik aus älter Zeit.

Choralis Constantinus. Book III, *see* Isaac, Heinrich. Choralis Constantinus. Book III.

Choralvorspiele alter Meister, *see* Straube, Karl. Choralvorspiele alter Meister.

CHORBUCH FÜR DIE KIRCHENCHÖRE SACHSENS, hrsg. vom Kirchenchor-Verband der Evangelisch-Lutherischen Landeskirche Sachsens. Heft D.71 ein-, zwei-, und dreistimmige Chöre mit und ohne Begleitung (insbesondere auch für Kinder- und Frauenchor verwendbar). Leipzig, Breitkopf & Härtel, 1931.
1 v.
Contains compositions by Arnoldus de Bruck, S. Calvisius, K. C. Dedekind, Adam Gumpelzhaimer, A. Hammerschmidt, J. E. Kindermann, Vincent Lübeck, Georg Neumark, Michael Prätorius, Balthasar Resinarius, J. H. Schein, Heinrich Schütz, Johann Staden, and Franz Tunder.

DAS CHORWERK. Heft 1– . Wolfenbüttel, Berlin, G. Kallmeyer, 1929– .
No.1– .
Contents:
Jahrg.1.
No.1. Deprès, Josquin. Missa "Pange lingua" zu 4 Stimmen. Hrsg. von Friedrich Blume. 1929. 4. Auflage. 1951.
No.2. Vaet, Jacobus. Sechs Motetten, zu 4–6 Stimmen. Hrsg. von Ernst Hermann Meyer. Unveränderte Neuauflage. 1929.
No.3. Deprès, Josquin. Weltliche Lieder zu 3–5 Stimmen [von Josquin des Près und

andere Meister]. Hrsg. von Friedrich Blume. Unveränderte Neuauflage. 1930.
No.4. Ockeghem, Jean de. Missa. Mi–Mi. Hrsg. von Heinrich Besseler. 1930. 2. Auflage. 1950.
No.5. Willaert, Adriano. Italienische Madrigale zu 4–5 Stimmen [von Adrian Willaert und andere Meister]. Hrsg. von Walter Wiora. Unveränderte Neuauflage. 1930.
Jahrg.2.
No.6. Stoltzer, Thomas. Der 37. Psalm, Erzürne dich nicht, zu 6 Stimmen (1526). Hrsg. von Otto Gombosi. 2. Auflage. 1953.
No.7. Isaac, Heinrich. Missa carminum. Hrsg. von Reinhold Heyden. 2. Auflage. 1950.
No.8. Willaert, Adriano. Volkstümliche Italienische Lieder, zu 3–4 Stimmen [von Adrian Willaert und andere Meister]. Hrsg. von Erich Hertzmann. Unveränderte Neuauflage. 1930.
No.9. Finck, Heinrich. Acht Hymnen, zu 4 Stimmen. Hrsg. von Rudolf Gerber. 2. Auflage. 1930.
No.10. Gabrieli, Giovanni. Drei Motetten, für 8-Stimmigen Doppelchor. Hrsg. von Heinrich Besseler. Unveränderte Neuauflage. 1931.
No.11. La Rue, Pierre de. Requiem und eine Motetten, zu 4–6 Stimmen. Hrsg. von Friedrich Blume. 2. unveränderte Auflage. 1931.
Jahrg.3.
No.12. Schein, Johann Hermann. Sechs deutsche Motetten, zu 5 Stimmen. Hrsg. von Adam Adrio. 2. unveränderte Auflage. 1931.
No.13. Lasso, Orlando di. Madrigale und Chansons, zu 4–5 Stimmen. Hrsg. von Heinrich Besseler. 2. unveränderte Auflage. 1931.
No.14. Sieben chromatische Motetten des Barock, zu 4–6 Stimmen, von Lasso, Hieron. Praetorius, Sweelinck, Hassler, und Schein. Hrsg. von Friedrich Blume. 2. unveränderte Auflage. 1931.
No.15. Lupi, Johannes. Zehn weltliche Lieder, zu 4 Stimmen. Hrsg. von Hans Albrecht. 2. unveränderte Auflage. 1931.
No.16. Theile, Johann. Zwei Kurzmessen, zu 5 Stimmen [von] Johann Theile und Christoph Bernhard. Hrsg. von Rudolf Gerber. 2. unveränderte Auflage. 1932.
No.17. Purcell, Henry. Fünf geistliche Chöre, zu 4–6 Stimmen. Hrsg. von Friedrich Blume. 2. unveränderte Auflage. 1932.
Jahrg.4.
No.18. Deprès, Josquin. Vier Motetten, zu 4 und 6 Stimmen, für Singstimmen und Instrumente. Hrsg. von Friedrich Blume. 2. Auflage. 1950.
No.19. Dufay, Guillaume. Zwölf geistliche und weltliche Werke, zu 3 Stimmen, für Singstimmen und Instrumente. Hrsg. von Heinrich Besseler. 2. Auflage. 1951.
No.20. Deprès, Josquin. Missa da pacem, zu 4 Stimmen. Hrsg. von Friedrich Blume. 2. Auflage. 1950.
No.21. Finck, Heinrich. Missa in summis, zu 6–7 Stimmen für Singstimmen und Instrumente. Hrsg. von Musik-Institut der Universität Tübingen unter Leitung von Karl Hasse. 2. unveränderte Auflage. 1932.
No.22. Binchois, Egidius. Sechzehn weltliche Lieder, zu 3 Stimmen für eine Singstimme mit Instrumenten. Hrsg. von Willibald Gurlitt. 2. unveränderte Auflage. 1933.
No.23. Deprès, Josquin. Drei Evangelien-Motetten, zu 4, 6 und 8 Stimmen. Hrsg. von Friedrich Blume. 2. Auflage. 1950.
Jahrg.5.
No.24. Franck, Melchior. Fünf Hohelied-Motetten, zu 5–6 Stimmen. Hrsg. von Anna Amalie Abert. 2. unveränderte Auflage. 1933.
No.25. Caldara, Antonio. Ein Madrigal und achtzehn Kanons, zu 3–6 Stimmen. Hrsg. von Karl Geiringer. 2. unveränderte Auflage. 1933.
No.26. Selle, Thomas. Passion nach dem Evangelisten Johannes, mit Intermedien für Solostimmen, Chor und Instrumente. Hrsg. von Rudolf Gerber. 2. unveränderte Auflage. 1933.
No.27. Demantius, Christoph. Passion nach dem Evangelisten Johannes und Weissagung des Leidens und Sterbens Jesu Christi aus dem 53. Kapitel des Propheten Elajae, zu 6 Stimmen. Hrsg. von Friedrich Blume. 2. unveränderte Auflage. 1934.
No.28. Dressler, Gallus. Fünf Motetten, zu 4–5 Stimmen. Hrsg. von Manfred Ruëtz. 2. unveränderte Auflage. 1934.
Jahrg.6.
No.29. Fünfzehn deutsche Lieder für Singstimmen und Instrumente oder für gemischten Chor. Aus Peter Schöffers Liederbuch (1513). Hrsg. von Musik-Institut der Universität Tübingen unter Leitung von Karl Hasse. 2. unveränderte Auflage. n.d.
No.30. Acht Lied- und Choralmotetten zu 4, 5 und 7 Stimmen. (Josquin des Près, Matthaeus le Maistre, Christian Hollander, Alexander Utendal, Ivo de Vento, Jacob Regnart). Hrsg. von Helmuth Osthoff. 2. unveränderte Auflage. n.d.
No.31. Aulen. Missa zu 3 Stimmen. Hrsg. von Herbert Birtner. 2. unveränderte Auflage. n.d.
No.32. Zwölf Hymnen zu 3–5 Stimmen für Singstimmen und Instrumente. (Adam von Fulda, Heinrich Finck, V. Florigal, Balthasar Hartzer, Urbanus Kingsperger). Hrsg. von Rudolf Gerber. 2. unveränderte Auflage. n.d.
No.33. Deprès, Josquin. Drei Psalmen, zu 4 Stimmen, für gemischten Chor, Frauenchor und Männerchor. Hrsg. von Friedrich Blume. 2. Auflage. 1951.
No.34. Lasso, Orlando di. Busstränen des Heiligen Petrus. Zu 7 Stimmen. Erste Folge (Nr.1–7). Hrsg. von Hans Joachim Therstappen. 2. unveränderte Auflage. n.d.

Jahrg.7.
- No.35. Neun Madrigale zu 5 Stimmen. Nordische Schüler Giovanni Gabrielis (Johann Grabbe, Mogens Pederson, Hans Nielsen). Hrsg. von Rudolf Gerber. 2. unveränderte Auflage. n.d.
- No.36. Schein, Johann Hermann. Der 116. Psalm. In Kompositionen zu 5 Stimmen von Johann Hermann Schein [und] Christoph Demantius. Hrsg. von Adam Adrio. 2. unveränderte Auflage. 1935.
- No.37. Lasso, Orlando di. Busstränen des Heiligen Petrus, zu 7 Stimmen. Zweite Folge (Nr.8–14). Hrsg. von Hans Joachim Therstappen. 2. unveränderte Auflage. 1935.

Folge II.
- No.38. Franck, Melchior. Musikalische Bergreihen zu 4 Stimmen. Hrsg. von Bruno Grusnick. 2. unveränderte Auflage. 1936.
- No.39. Demantius, Christoph. Vier deutsche Motetten, zu 6 Stimmen. Hrsg. von Anna Amalie Abert. 2. unveränderte Auflage. 1936.
- No.40. Grandi, Alessandro. Drei konzertierende Motetten, zu 5 Stimmen mit Generalbass. 2. unveränderte Auflage. 1936.

Jahrg.8.
- No.41. Lasso, Orlando di. Busstränen des Heiligen Petrus, zu 7 Stimmen. Dritte Folge (Nr.15–21; Schluss). Hrsg. von Hans Joachim Therstappen. 2. unveränderte Auflage. 1936.

Folge III.
- No.42. Deprès, Josquin. Missa de Beata Virgine, zu 4 und 5 Stimmen. Hrsg. von Friedrich Blume. 2. Auflage. 1951.
- No.43. Karnevalslieder der Renaissance, zu 3–4 Stimmen. (Heinrich Isaac, Michele Pesenti, Loyset Compère, Joh. Bapt. Zesso, P. Scotus, Jac. Fo . . . , Joan Domenico del Giovane da Nola, Giovane da Nola). Hrsg. von Kurt Westphal. 2. unveränderte Auflage. 1936.
- No.44. Galliculus, Johannes. Ostermesse, über das Lied "Christ ist erstanden," zu 4 Stimmen. Hrsg. von Friedrich Blume und Willi Schulze. 2. unveränderte Auflage. 1936.
- No.45. Deutsche Lieder des 15. Jahrhunderts aus fremden Quellen, zu 3 und 4 Stimmen. Hrsg. von Heinz Funck. 2. unveränderte Auflage. 1937.
- No.46. Martini, Johannes. Drei geistliche Gesänge, zu 4 Stimmen. Hrsg. von Rudolf Gerber. 2. unveränderte Auflage. 1937.

Jahrg.9.
- No.47. Resinarius, Balthasar. Summa passions secundum Johannem, zu 4 Stimmen. Hrsg. von Friedrich Blume und Willi Schulze. 2. unveränderte Auflage. 1937.
- No.48. Lasso, Orlando di. Prophetiae Sibyllarum, zu 4 Stimmen. Hrsg. von Joachim Therstappen. 2. unveränderte Auflage. 1937.
- No.49. Dufay, Guillaume. Sämtliche Hymnen, zu 3 und 4 Stimmen. Hrsg. von Rudolf Gerber. 2. unveränderte Auflage. 1937.
- No.50. Kühnhausen, Johannes Georg. Passion nach dem Evangelisten Matthäus, für Solostimmen, Chor und Generalbass. Hrsg. von Adam Adrio. 2. unveränderte Auflage. 1937.
- No.51. Sayve, Lambert de und Michael Praetorius. Teutsche Liedlein, zu 4 Stimmen. Hrsg. von Friedrich Blume. 2. unveränderte Auflage. 1938.
- No.52. Pfleger, Augustin. Passionsmusik über die Sieben Worte Jesu Christi am Kreuz (um 1670), für Solostimmen, Chor und Instrumente. Hrsg. von Fritz Stein. 2. unveränderte Auflage. 1938.

Neue Folge.
- No.53. Franck, Melchior. Drei Quodlibets zu 4 Stimmen. Hrsg. von Kurt Gudewill. 1955.
- No.54. Fünf Vergil-Motetten zu 4–7 Stimmen von Josquin Desprez, Adrian Willaert, Jakob Arcadelt, Cipriano de Rore. Hrsg. von Helmuth Osthoff. 1955.
- No.55. Compère, Loyset. Missa "Alles regrets" zu 4 Stimmen. Hrsg. von Lutz Finscher. 1956.
- No.56. Missa anonyma II aus dem Codex Breslau. Mf. 2016 zu 4 Stimmen. Hrsg. von Fritz Feldmann. 1955.
- No.57. Deprès, Josquin. Drei Motetten zu 4–6 Stimmen. Hrsg. von Helmuth Osthoff. 1956.
- No.58. Sechs italienische Madrigale zu 4–5 Stimmen. (Jakob Arcadelt, Constanzo Festa, Alfonso della Viola, Giovan Nasco, and Domenico Maria Ferrabosco). Hrsg. von Bernhard Meier. 1956.
- No.59. Willaert, Adrian. Drei Motetten zu fünf Stimmen. Hrsg. von Walter Gerstenberg. 1956.
- No.60. Spanisches Hymnar um 1500 zu vier Stimmen. Hrsg. von Rudolf Gerber. 1957.
- No.61. Zwölf französische Lieder aus Jacques Moderne: Le parangon des chansons (1538) zu vier Stimmen. Hrsg. von Hans Albrecht. 1956.
- No.62. Senfl, Ludwig. Zwei Marien-Motetten zu fünf Stimmen. Hrsg. von Walter Gerstenberg. 1957.
- No.63. Zehn weltliche Lieder aus Georg Forster: Frische teutsche Liedlein (Teil III bis V) zu 4, 5 und 8 Stimmen. Hrsg. von Kurt Gudewill. 1956.
- No.64. Deprès, Josquin. Zwei Psalmen zu vier und fünf Stimmen. Hrsg. von Helmuth Osthoff. 1957.
- No.65. Scandello, Antonio. Missa super Eptiaphium Mauritii zu 6 Stimmen. Hrsg. von Lothar Hoffmann-Erbrecht. 1957.
- No.66. Beber, Ambrosius. Markus-Passion, ein- bis fünfstimmig. Hrsg. von Simone Wallon. 1958.
- No.67. Gabrieli, Giovanni. Drei Motetten II zu 7–8 Stimmen zum Teil mit Generalbass. Hrsg. von Christiane Engelbrecht. 1957.
- No.68. Brumel, Antoine. Missa pro defunctis zu 4 Stimmen. Hrsg. von Albert Seay. 1958.

No.69. Drei Motetten zu 5–6 Stimmen. (Georg Hemmerley, Thomas Bachofen, Johannes Keutzenhoff). Hrsg. von Wilfried Brennecke. 1958.
No.70. Mouton, Jean. Missa "Alleluya" zu 4 Stimmen. Hrsg. von Paul Kast. 1957.
No.71. Köler, David. Drei deutsche Psalmen zu 4 und 6 Stimmen. Hrsg. von Lothar Hoffmann-Erbrecht. 1959.
No.72. Clément, Jacques. Drei Motetten zu 3–5 Stimmen. Hrsg. von Bernhard Meier. 1958.
No.73. Jannequin, Clément. Zehn Chansons zu 4 Stimmen. Hrsg. von Albert Seay. 1959.
No.74. Stoltzer, Thomas. Ostermesse zu 4 Stimmen. Hrsg. von Lothar Hoffmann-Erbrecht. 1958.
No.75. Gosswin, Anton. Newe teutsche Lieder mit dreyen Stimmen (1581). Hrsg. von Karl Gustav Fellerer. 1959.
No.76. Mouton, Jean. Fünf Motetten zu 4 und 6 Stimmen. Hrsg. von Paul Kast. 1959.

Neue Folge III.
No.77. Zarlino, Gioseffo. Drei Motetten und ein geistliches Madrigal zu 4–6 Stimmen. Hrsg. von Roman Flury. 1959.
No.78/79. Funcke, Friedrich. Matthäus-passion für Solostimmen, vierstimmigen Chor und Instrumente. Hrsg. von Joachim Birke. 1960.
No.80. Vier Madrigale von Mantuaner Komponisten zu 5 und 8 Stimmen. (Giaches de Wert, Benedetto Pallavicino, Alessandro Striggio). Hrsg. von Denis Arnold. 1960.
No.81. Isaac, Heinrich. Introiten I zu 6 Stimmen. Hrsg. von Martin Just. 1960.
No.82. Certon, Pierre. Zehn Chansons zu 4 Stimmen. Hrsg. von Albert Seay. 1961.
No.83. Divitis, Antonius. Missa "Quem dicunt homines" zu 4 Stimmen. Hrsg. von Lewis Lockwood. 1960.
No.84. Shepherd, John. Sechs Responsorien zu 4 und 6 Stimmen. Hrsg. von Frank Ll. Harrison. 1960.
No.85. Drei Weihnachtsmagnificat zu 4 Stimmen. (Johannes Galliculus and anonymous composers). Hrsg. von Winfried Kirsch. 1961.
No.86. Sayve, Lambert de. Vier Motetten zu 5–9 Stimmen. Hrsg. von Georg Rebscher. 1960.
No.87. Greiter, Matthias. Sämtliche weltliche Lieder zu 4 und 5 Stimmen. Hrsg. von Hans-Christian Müller. 1962.
No.88. Fünf Madrigale auf Texte von Francesco Petrarca zu 4–6 Stimmen. (Giovan Nasco, Stephano Rossetti, Pietro Taglia). Hrsg. von Bernhard Meier. 1961.

Neue Folge IV.
No.89. Vier Motetten der Bachschule (J. L. Krebs, J. Ph. Kirnberger, G. A. Homilius) für 4–5 Stimmen zum Teil mit Generalbass. Hrsg. von Georg Feder. 1963.
No.90. Selle, Thomas. Zwei Kurzmessen zu 8 und 5 Stimmen mit Generalbass. Hrsg. von Joachim Birke. 1962.
No.91. La Rue, Pierre de. Vier Motetten zu 4 Stimmen. Hrsg. von Nigel Davison. 1962.
No.92. Fünfzehn flämische Lieder der Renaissance zu 2 bis 5 Stimmen. Hrsg. von René Bernard Lenaerts. 1962.
No.93. Porta, Costanzo. Missa "La sol fa re mi" für 6 Stimmen. Hrsg. von Oscar Mischiati.
No.94. Drei Motetten über den Text "Quem dicunt homines" (J. Richafort, J. Pionnier, N. Gombert) zu 4 und 6 Stimmen. Hrsg. von Lewis Lockwood. 1963.
No.95. Mazzocchi, Domenico. Acht Madrigalen, für 5 Stimmen. Hrsg. von Raymond Meylan.
No.96. Gabrieli, Andrea. Drei Motetten, für 8 Stimmen. Hrsg. von Denis M. Arnold.
No.97. Fayrfax, Robert. Missa "Tecum principium" für 5 Stimmen. Hrsg. von Denis Stevens.
No.98. Hartmann, Heinrich. Motetten. Hrsg. von Adam Adrio.
No.99. Bach, Johann Ludwig. Zwei Motetten zu 6 und 8 Stimmen. Hrsg. von Karl Geiringer. 1963.
No.100. Isaac, Heinrich. Vier "Marienmotetten." Hrsg. von Martin Just. 1964.
No.101. Rener, Adam. Missa Carminum zu 4 Stimmen. Hrsg. von Jürgen Kindermann. 1966.
No.103. Goudimel, Claude. Vier Festmotetten zu 4 und 6 Stimmen. Hrsg. von Rudolf Häusler. 1966.

CHRISTOPHORUS-CHORWERK, hrsg. von Fritz Schieri. Freiburg im Breisgau, Christophorus-Verlag Herder, [cop.1954–].
v.1– .
Contents:
Heft 1. Josquin des Prez. Sequenz "Ave Maria" für vier Stimmen. Bearbeitung und deutscher Text von Walther Lipphardt. cop.1954.
Heft 2. Marx, Karl. Deutsches Proprium vom Fest Mariä Himmelfahrt, für gemischten Chor (Orgel ad lib.). cop.1954.
Heft 3. Roeseling, Kaspar. Missa in honorem sanctorum trium regum, für vier gemischte Stimmen. cop.1954.
Heft 4. Schieri, Fritz. Zwei Pfingstchöre: "Heiliger Geist!" Sequenz "Veni, Sancte Spiritus/Komm, O Geist der Heiligkeit," für Chor in verschiedener Besetzung (Orgel oder andere Instrumente ad lib.). cop.1954.
Heft 5. Fröhliche Chorlieder aus dem 16. und 17. Jahrhundert (Knöfel, Widmann, Reiner, Scandello), für vier bis sechs Stimmen. Hrsg. von Hans Kulla. cop.1954.
Heft 6. Ivo de Vento. Weltliche Chorlieder für vier Stimmen. Hrsg. von Hans Kulla. cop.1954.
Heft 7. Lechner, Leonhard. Ein Musikus wollt' fröhlich sein. Deutsche Chorlieder für vier und fünf Stimmen. Hrsg. von Walther Lipphardt. cop.1955.
Heft 8. Isaac, Heinrich. Proprium missae vom Feste Christi Himmelfahrt (Introitus, Alleluja, Sequenz, Communio), für vier Stimmen. Hrsg. von Walter Lipphardt. cop.1955.

Heft 9. Nucius, Johannes. Zwei Hohelied-Motetten für fünf- und achtstimmigen Chor. Hrsg. von Josef Güldenmeister. cop. 1955.
Heft 10. Doppelbauer, Josef Friedrich. Fünf kleine Motetten (1954), für vierstimmigen gemischten Chor. cop.1955.
Heft 11. Trinklieder alter Meister (Scandello, Widmann, Meiland) zu fünf und sechs Stimmen. Hrsg. von Hans Kulla. cop.1955.
Heft 12. Nucius, Johannes. Mariä Verkündigung 3 Motetten für vier- und fünfstimmigen Chor. Hrsg. von Josef Güldenmeister. cop.1955.
Heft 13. Roeseling, Kaspar. Kleine Anzeigen der Stadtzeitung für vierstimmigen gemischten Chor. cop.1956.
Heft 14. Humpert, Hans. Psalm 60 und 121, für gemischten Chor (vier- und sechsstimmig). cop.1956.
Heft 15. Bialas, Günter. Veni Creator Spiritus. Hymnus für fünfstimmigen gemischten Chor. cop.1956.
Heft 16. Woll, Erna. Messe in Em, für drei gleiche (oder gemischte) Stimmen. cop. 1956.
Heft 17. Humpert, Hans. Psalm 67 und 24, für gemischten Chor (vier- und fünfstimmig). cop.1956.
Heft 18. Humpert, Hans. Psalm 90, für fünfstimmigen gemischten Chor. cop.1956.
Heft 19. Nucius, Johannes. Drei Psalmen (112, 123 und 8) für sechstimmigen Chor. Hrsg. von Josef Güldenmeister. cop. 1956.
Heft 20. Clausing, Franz. Introitus, Sequenz und Psalm für vierstimmigen gemischten Chor. cop.1956.
Heft 21. Klein, Richard Rudolf. Lobe den Herren, Geistliche Kantate für gemischten Chor und kleines Orchester (2 Oboen, Streichquartette, ad lib., Cembalo oder Orgel, 2 Trompetten, Schlagzeug), auch mit Gemeindegesang. cop.1956.
Heft 22. Woll, Erna. Und alles preist dich, Gott, den Herrn. Kantate für Chor (gleiche oder gemischte Stimmen, auch einstimmig) und Instrumente (Quer- oder Blockflöte ad lib. und Streicher). cop.1956.
Heft 23. Denhoff, Joachim. Missa brevis, für vierstimmigen gemischten Chor. cop. 1957.
Heft 24. Schubert, Heino. Missa für dreistimmigen gemischten Chor und obligate Orgel. cop.1957.
Heft 25. Schieri, Fritz. Proprium in Festo Corporis Christi (Fronleichnamsproprium) für Chor. cop. 1958.
Heft 26. Motzer, Franz. Proprium vom 4. Fastensonntag. (Laetare), für vierstimmigen gemischten Chor. cop. 1958.
Heft 27. Padrós, Jaime. Katalanische und kastellanische Volkslieder, sieben Sätze für gemischten Chor. cop.1959.
Heft 28. Stingl, Anton. O Herr, mein Gott, wie bist du gross! Kantate für Kinderchor und Instrumente (Blockflöten, Stabspiele, Schlagwerk, Gitarre oder Klavier). cop. 1959.
Heft 29. Klein, Richard Rudolf. Sieben geistliche Chorlieder nach altdeutschen Texten, für vier gemischte Stimmen. cop. 1958.
Heft 30. Wilhelm, Grete. Besinnliches Singen. Neun kleine Chorstücke für Frauen- (Kinder-) Stimmen, teilweise auch für gemischten Chor oder abwechselnd zwischen Frauen- und Männerstimmen zu singen. cop. 1959.
Heft 31. Woll, Erna. Herz-Mariä-Kantate, für Chor, Gemeinde und Instrumente. cop. 1959.
Heft 32. Schieri, Fritz. Die Eigengesänge des Christkönigsfestes, für gemischten Chor. cop. 1958.
Heft 33. Quack, Erhard. Die Geburt des Herrn (Das Weihnachtsevangelium) für Vorsänger, Kinderchor und ein Tasteninstrument. cop. 1958.
Heft 34. Schubert, Heino. Ich bin das Brot des Lebens. 3 Motetten für Chor und Orgel (oder Instrumente). cop. 1960.
Heft 35. Nucius, Johannes. Salve Regina, für gemischten Chor. Hrsg. von Josef Güldenmeister. cop. 1959.
Heft 36. Denhoff, Joachim. Du bist min. Chorlieder nach Versen des Minnesangs, für gleiche oder gemischte Stimmen. cop. 1959.
Heft 37. Kulla, Hans. Lateinisches Proprium vom Ostermontag. Für dreistimmigen gemischte Chor. cop. 1960.
Heft 38. Motzer, Franz. Lateinisches Proprium von Allerheiligen. Für vierstimmigen gemischten Chor. cop. 1960.
Heft 39.
Heft 40. Roeseling, Kaspar. Psalmen und Gesänge zum Advent. Für gemischten Chor, Volk (ad lib.) und Orgel. cop. 1961.
Heft 41. Roeseling, Kaspar. Psalmen und Gesänge zur Fastenzeit. Für gemischten Chor, Volk (ad lib.) und Orgel. cop. 1961.
Heft 42. Woll, Erna. Lass den Stern mich finden. Fünf kleine Motetten für gleiche Stimmen. cop. 1960.
Heft 43. Schubert, Heino. Drei Motetten zum Feste Christi Himmelfahrt. cop. 1960.
Heft 44. Wilhelm, Grete. Sechs Chöre nach Texten von Hermann Hesse. Für 2 Frauen- und 1 Männerstimme. cop. 1960.
Heft 45. Schieri, Franz. Deutsche Ordinariumsmesse. cop. 1962.

Chrysander, Friedrich, 1826–1901, ed. Denkmäler der Tonkunst, *see* Denkmäler der Tonkunst.

Church music, Collection of ancient, *see* Motett Society. [Collection of ancient church music].

Church of England. Liturgy and ritual. Evening canticles, *see* Plainsong and Mediaeval Music Society. Church of England. Liturgy and ritual. Evening canticles.

Church of England. Liturgy and ritual. Mass for the dead, *see* Plainsong and Mediaeval Music Society. Church of England. Liturgy and ritual. Mass for the dead.

Church of England. Liturgy and ritual. The musick of the Mass for the dead, *see* Plainsong and Mediaeval Music Society. Church of England. Liturgy and ritual. The musick of the Mass for the dead.

Church of England. Liturgy and ritual. An order for compline, *see* Plainsong and Mediaeval Music Society. Church of England. Liturgy and ritual. An order for compline.

Church of England. Liturgy and ritual. Services in Holy Week, *see* Plainsong and Mediaeval Music Society. Church of England. Liturgy and ritual. Services in Holy Week.

Chybiński, Adolf, 1880– , ed. Denkmäler altpolnischer Musik. *see* Denkmäler altpolnischer Musik.

CICHOCKI, JOS. ed.
Chants d'église à plusieurs voix des anciens compositeurs polonais. Warsaw, 1838–39.
2v.
Contents:
Vol.1. Gomólka, N. Psalmen. (1539–1609). New ed. by J. W. Reiss. 1923.
Vol.2. Gorczyski, Greg. Messen. (1660–1734).

Clásicos españoles de la música, *see* Asociación Patriótica Española. Clásicos españoles de la música.

I classici del Bel Canto, *see* Landshoff, Ludwig, ed. I classici del Bel Canto.

I CLASSICI DELI A MUSICA ITALIANA. Raccolta nazionale delle musiche italiane, diretta da Gabriele d'Annunzio e dai maestri, G. F. Malipiero, Carlo Perinello, Ildebrando Pizzetti, F. Balilla Pratella. Milano, Istituto Editoriale Italiano, 1918–20.
36v.
This publication originally came out in single pamphlets. Later all works of one composer were combined in one volume (*see* entry following).
Contents:
Quad.1–3. Banchieri, A. Musiche corali. 1919. 3v.
Quad.4–8. Bassani, G. B. Cantate a una voce. 1919. 5v.
Quad.9–12. Caccini, G. Le nuove musiche. 1919. 4v.
Quad.13–18. Carissimi, G. Oratorii. 1918–19. 3v.
Quad.23–27. Cavazzoni, G. Dal I e II libro di intavolature per organo. 1919. 4v.
Quad.28–34. Corelli, A. Sonate. Op.V per violino. 1919. 7v.
Quad.35–36. Cavaliere, E. del. Dalla rappresentazione di anima et di corpo.
Quad.40–42, 303. Durante, F. Sonate, toccate e divertimenti per pianoforte. 1919.
Quad.43–47. Frescobaldi, G. Composizione per organo e cembalo. 1919. 4v.
Quad.54–58. Galuppi, B. Da "Il filosofo di campagna." 1919. 5v.
Quad.59–62. Gesualdo, C. Madrigali a 5 voci. 1919. 4v.
Quad.63–66. Jommelli, N. De la passione di Gesù Cristo. 1919. 4v.
Quad.67–69. Marcello, B. Cantate a una voce. 1919. 3v.
Quad.70–71. Marcello, B. Composizioni per cembalo od organo. 1920. 2v.
Quad.72–75. Martini, G. B. Sonate per pianoforte. 1919.
Quad.79. Monteverdi, C. Composizioni varie: Lamento d'Arianna. 1919.
Quad.80–81. Paisiello, G. Dalla "Nina". 1919. 2v.
Quad.82–84. Palestrina, G. B. P. da. Madrigali a 4 e 5 voci. 1919. 3v.
Quad.85, 88, 304–305. Paradisi, P. D. Sonate per pianoforte. 1919.
Quad.89–90. Pergolesi, G. B. La serva padrona. 1920.
Quad.91–92. Pergolesi, G. B. Livietta e tracollo. 1920.
Quad.93, 94, 306–307. Pergolesi, G. B. Stabat mater.
Quad.95–96. Peri, J. Da l'Euridice. 1919. 2v.
Quad.104–107. Porpora, N. A. Sonate per violine e pianoforte. 1919.
Quad.110–113. Rossi, M. A. Composizioni per organo e cembalo. 1920. 4v.
Quad.114–119. Sammartini, G. B. Sonate notturne. Op.VII. 1919–20. 6v.
Quad.120–125. Scarlatti, A. Cantate ad una voce. 1920. 6v.
Quad.126–130. Scarlatti, D. Sonate per pianoforte. 1919. 5v.
Quad.131–136. Tartini, G. Sonate per violino. 1919. 3v.
Quad.139–144. Veracini, F. M. Sonate per violino. 1919. 6v.
Quad.145–150. Zipoli, D. Composizioni per organo e cembalo. 1919. 6v.
Quad.155–156. Bertoni, F. G. Quartetto No.3, riduzione per pianoforte a 4 mani. 1920.
Quad.164–165. Boccherini, L. Sonate per violoncello e piano, B flat major, C major. 1919. 2v.
Quad.172–173. Cherubini, L. Arie per canto e pianoforte. 1919. 2v.
Quad.176–181. Clementi, M. Sonate per pianoforte. 1919.
Quad.205. Locatelli, P. and F. G. Bertoni. Composizioni per pianoforte a quattro mani. 1919.
Quad.224–225. Monteverdi, C. Il combattimento di Tancredi e Clorinda per canto e pianoforte. 1919.
Quad.266–267. Sandoni, P. G. Sonate per cembalo trascritte per pianoforte e cura di F. Balilla Pratella. [1921?].
Quad.276–281. Rutini, G. Sonate per pianoforte. 1919.
Quad.284. Serini, G. Sonate per cembalo. 1921.
Quad.286–288. Turrini, F. Sonate trascritte per pianoforte. 1919.
Quad.289. Corelli, A. Concerto grosso. Nr.7. Op.6. (Reduction per pianoforte a quattro mani).
Quad.290. Corelli, A. Concerto grosso. Nr.3. Op.6. (Reduction per pianoforte a quattro mani).
Quad.294–297. Vivaldi, A. Concerti delle stagioni. Op.VIII. 1920.
Quad.303. *See* Quad. 40.
Quad.304–305. *See* Quad.85.
Quad.306–307. *See* Quad.93.

I CLASSICI DELLA MUSICA ITALIANA. Raccolta nazionale diretta da Gabriele d'Annunzio. Milano, Società Anonima Notari La Santa, 1919–21.
36v.
Contents:
Bd.1. A. Banchieri: Musiche corali.
Bd.2. G. B. Bassani: Canzoni.
Bd.3. L. Boccherini: Sonate.
Bd.4. G. Caccini: Arie.
Bd.5. G. Carissimi: Oratorii.
Bd.6. G. Cavazzoni: Composizioni.
Bd.7. L. Cherubini: Le duo giornate.
Bd.8. M. Clementi: Sonate.
Bd.9. A. Corelli: Sonate.
Bd.10. E. del Cavaliere: Rappresentazione di anima e di corpo.
Bd.11. F. Durante: Sonate, toccate e divertimenti.
Bd.12. G. Frescobaldi: Sonate.
Bd.13. B. Galuppi: Il filosofo di campagna.
Bd.14. Gesualdo da Venosa: Madrigali.
Bd.15. N. Jommelli: La Passione di Gesù Cristo.
Bd.16. P. Locatelli e F. G. Bertoni: Composizioni.
Bd.17. B. Marcello: Cantate.
Bd.18. G. B. Martini: Sonate.
Bd.19. C. Monteverdi: Il combattimento di Tancredi e Clorinda.
Bd.20. G. Paisiello: La pazza per amore.
Bd.21. G. B. P. da Palestrina: Canzonette e madrigali.
Bd.22. P. D. Paradisi: Sonate.
Bd.23. G. B. Pergolesi: Opere.
Bd.24. J. Peri: L'Euridice.
Bd.25. N. A. Porpora: Sonate.
Bd.26. M. Rossi: Composizioni.
Bd.27. G. Rutini: Sonate.
Bd.28. G. B. Sammartini: Sonate.
Bd.29. P. G. Sandoni e Serini: Sonate.
Bd.30. A. Scarlatti: Cantate.
Bd.31. D. Scarlatti: Composizioni.
Bd.32. G. Tartini: Sonate per violino.
Bd.33. F. Turrini: Sonate.
Bd.34. F. M. Veracini: Sonate.
Bd.35. A. Vivaldi: Le stagioni.
Bd.36. D. Zipoli: Composizioni.

Classici italiani dell'organo, *see* Fuser, Ireneo. Classici italiani dell'organo.

CLASSICI ITALIANI DELLA MUSICA. Raccolta di inediti diretta da Alfredo Bonaccorsi sotto gli auspici del Conseil International de la Musique (UNESCO). Roma, Del Turco Editore, [1956–].
v.1– .
Contents:
Vol.1. Boccherini, Luigi. Vier quintettini, Op.30; Sechs quartettini, Op.33, piccola. [pref.1956].
Vol.2. Vivaldi, Antonio. Concerto in Do maggiore; Concerto in Fa maggiore, dai Concerti di Dresda. [1960?].
Vol.3. Brunetti, Gaetano. Il maniático. Sinfonia, No.33; Sinfonia in Sol minore, No.22. [1960?].
Vol.4. Boccherini, Luigi. Sinfonia a più istrumenti obbligati, Op.37, grande; Sinfonia a grande orchestra, Op.21/3. [1960?].

I CLASSICI MUSICALI ITALIANI. Fondazione Eugenio Bravi. Milano, I Classici Musicali Italiani. 1941–43, 1956.
15v.
Vol.14 was not published with the original set. It appeared in 1956.
Contents:
Vol.1. Cavazzoni, M. A., Fogliano, J., Segni, J., ed Anonimi. Composizioni per organo. Ricercari e Ricercate. 1941.
Vol.2. Marcello, B. Cantate per contralto e per soprano. 1941.
Vol.3. Giardini, F. Sonate per cembalo con violino o flauto traverso. Op.3. 1941.
Vol.4. Boccherini, L. Sonate Op.5 per cembalo con violino obbligato. 1941.
Vol.5. Gabrieli, A. Musiche di chiesa. 1941.
Vol.6. Giardini, F. Quartetti Op.23, Nr.3 e 4. 1941.
Vol.7. Piccinni, N. La buona figliola. 1941.
Vol.8. Marcello, B. Gioàz. 1942.
Vol.9. Monteverdi, C. L'Orfeo. 1942.
Vol.10. Sigismondo d'India. Madrigali a 5 voci. 1942.
Vol.11. Martini, G. B. Concerti per cembalo e orchestra. 1943.
Vol.12. Grazioli, G. B. Dodici sonate per cembalo. 1943.
Vol.13. Scarlatti, A. Primo e secondo libro di toccate. 1943.
Vol.14. Locatelli, P. A. Sei sonate da camera per violino e basso. Op.6. 1956.
Vol.15. Graziani, C. Sei sonate per violoncello e basso continuo. Op.3. 1943.

Claude le Jeune, *see* Le Jeune, Claude.

CLAVECINISTES FLAMANDS. Collection d'oeuvres composées par d'anciens et de célèbres clavecinistes flamands. Retrouvées et publiées par le Chevalier van Elewyck. Bruxelles, Schott Frères, 1877.
2v.
Vol.1. Gheyn, Mathias van den. Op.3. Six suites pour le clavecin; Divertimenti de Londres; Deux préludes pour orgue; Deux préludes pour carillon.
Vol.2. Extracts from works by various composers (17 composers in all).

Clemens non Papa, *see* Clément, Jacques.

CLÉMENT, FÉLIX, 1833–1885. ed.
Chants de la Sainte-Chapelle tirés de manuscrits du XIIIe siècle, traduits et mis en parties avec accompagnement d'orgue par Félix Clément . . . Avec une introduction par Didron ainé . . . Paris, V. Didron, [1849].
15p., 19L. incl. front., facsims., illus., pl.
Music for 1 to 4 voices with organ acc., Latin words, 18L. at end.
Contents: Regnantem sempiterna. Haec est clara dies. Orientis paribus. Concordi laetitia. Ecce panis. Qui regis sceptra. Salve Virgo. Domine salvam. Patrem parit. Versets et répons.

CLÉMENT, JACQUES, 16th century.
Opera omnia, edidit K. Ph. Bernet Kempers. Rome,

American Institute of Musicology, 1951– .
v.1– . (Corpus mensurabilis musicae. No.4).
Proposed set about 21v.
Contents:
Vol.1. Fasc.1. Missa Miseracorde. 1951.
Vol.1. Fasc.2. Missa Virtute magna. 1954.
Vol.1. Fasc.3. Missa En espoir. 1954.
Vol.1. Fasc.4. Missa Ecce quam bonum. 1954.
Vol.2. Souterliedekens. (Psalmi Neerlandici). 1953.
Vol.3. Motetta. 1957.
Vol.4. Magnificat. 1958.
Vol.5. Missa Spes salutis. Missa Gaude lux donatiane. Missa Languir my fault. 1958.
Vol.5. Suppl. Motet. Spes salutis (model for mass by same name in Vol.5).
Vol.6. Missa Pastores quidnam vidistis. Missa Caro mea. Missa Jay veu le cerf. 1959.
Vol.7. Missa A la fontaine du prez. Missa Quam pulchra es. Missa Panis quam ego dabo. Missa Or combien est. 1959.
Vol.8. Missa defunctorum. Kyrie paschale. Credo a 8. 1959.
Vol.9. Cantiones sacrae. 1960.
Vol.10. Chansons. 1962.
Vol.11. Chansons. 1964.
Vol.12. Cantiones ecclesiasticae, lib.1–4, 1553, 4 vocum. 1965.
Vol.13. Cantiones ecclesiasticae, lib.5–8, 5 vocum, 1553, and Psalmi selecti 5 et 6 vocum. 1553/54. 1966.
Vol.14. Cantiones sacrae 5 et 6 vocum ex typographia Phalesii, 1554. 1966.
Vol.15. Moteta ex officina Latii & Waelrandi & "del Laberinto" excusa MDLN. 1966.

CLEMENTI, MUZIO, 1752–1832. ed.
Clementi's Selection of practical harmony, for the organ or pianoforte; containing voluntaries, fugues, canons and other ingenious pieces. By the most eminent composers. To which is prefixed an epitome of counterpoint by the editor. London, Printed by Clementi, Banger, Hyde, Collard & David, No.26 Cheapside, 1811–15.
4v.
Contents (from *Grove's Dictionary of music and musicians*, 1916, Vol.3, p.804):
Vol.1.
Treatise on harmony and counterpoint by Clementi.
Kirnberger. Two voluntaries in F. Four fugues, in C sharp minor, A minor, B flat, and D minor. Gavotte in D minor. Fugue in D. Prelude and fugue in G. Fugue and polonaise in E flat. Fugue and polonaise in F minor and major. Prelude and fugue in C.
A set of canons by C. P. E. Bach, Fasch, Turini, Padre Martini, and A. da Vallerano.
Caresano. Double fugue in C.
Perti, Antonio. Fugue in D.
Bach, C. P. E. Canon in G.
Haydn, Joseph. Minuet and trio in E minor.
Bach, C. P. E. Two minuets.
Handel. Fugue in B minor.
Porpora. Six fugues, in A, G, D, B flat, G minor, and C.
Albrechtsberger. Nine fugues, in B minor, E, A minor, F, C, E flat, C, A minor, and A.
Telemann. Fughetta in D.
Eberlin, J. E. Five voluntaries and fugues in D minor, A minor, E minor, C, and F.
Umstatt. Voluntary and fugue in G minor.
Marpurg. Prelude and fugue in G.
Mozart. Fugue in D minor from the Requiem, arranged by Clementi.
Bach, C. P. E. Two voluntaries and fugues in A and D minor. Fantasia and fugue in G minor. Voluntary and fugue in F minor.
Bach, Ernest. Fantasia and fugue in F.
Bach, J. S. Organ fantasia in G, arranged. Suite (5th French) in G.

Vol.2.
Albrechtsberger. Six fugues in G, B minor, G, G minor, D, and D minor.
Eberlin. Four voluntaries and fugues in G minor, D, G, and E minor.
Mozart. Fantasia in F minor, arranged.
Bach, C. P. E. Fantasia and fugue in C minor. Fantasia in C. Voluntary and fugue in C minor. Organ sonata in B flat.
Bach, J. S. Toccata and fugue in D minor.
Handel. Eleven fugues in G minor, C minor, B flat, A minor, G, B minor, G minor, F sharp minor, D minor, F, and F minor.
Padre Martini. Four sonatas in F minor, G minor, A, and E minor.
Scarlatti, A. Fugue in F minor.
Scarlatti, D. Two fugues in D minor and G minor (the "Cat's fugue").
Frescobaldi. Two canzone in G minor and G. Three fugues in D minor, G minor, and E minor. Canzone in F. Corrente in F minor. Toccata in F.

Vol.3.
Bach, W. F. Fugue and capriccio in D minor. Two polonaises in F. Fugue in D. Adagio in B minor. Vivace in D. Polonaise in D. Fugue and polonaise in C. Two fugues in C minor and B flat. Two polonaises in B flat and G minor. Fugue and polonaise in E flat. Fugue and polonaise in E minor. Polonaise in E. Fugue and polonaise in F minor. Fugue and polonaise in C minor.
Bach, C. P. E. Fantasia in C minor. Fugue in C minor for organ [by J. S. Bach, wrongly attributed to C. P. E. Bach]. Rondo in C minor. Fantasia in C. Fugue in C minor on the name "Bach." Allegro in C. Andantino in C minor. Presto in C minor. Allegro in C. Sonate in F, and Sinfonia in F.
Bach, J. C. F. Fugue in C minor. Rondo in C. Minuet in C. Polonaise in G. Sonata in C. Two sonatas in E and C minor.
Bach, J. S. Two fugues in A minor and C.

Vol.4.
Padre Martini. Nine sonatas in E minor, B minor, D, D minor, B flat, G, C minor, C, and F.
Albrechtsberger. Twenty-one fugues in F, F minor, G, G minor, A, and A minor; (these preceded by "Cadenzas or preludes") in D, A, E, E minor,

G, B flat, and C; (these with preludes) in D minor, E minor, G, A minor, B minor; (the rest without preludes) in D minor; "Christus resurrexit" in C; "Alleluja" in C; "Alleluja"; "Ita missa est."

CLEMENTI, MUZIO, 1752–1832.
Works for pianoforte, ed. by Frank Dawes. London [etc.], Schott, 1958– .
v.1– .
Contents:
Vol.1. Sonata in F minor, Op.14, No.3. 1958.
Vol.2. Sonata in G minor, Op.34, No.2. 1958.
Vol.3. Capriccio (in forma di sonata) in C, Op.47, No.2. 1958.
Vol.4. Sonata in E flat, Op.9, No.3. 1958.

CODAX, MARTIN, 14th century.
. . . Las siete canciones de amor; Poema musical del siglo XII, publícase en facsímil, ahora por primera vez, con algunas notas recopiladas, por Pedro Vindel . . . Madrid, [Imprenta de la Sucesora de M. Minuesa de los Ríos, 1915].
14p., 10L. facsims.

CODEX ESCORIAL. CHANSONNIER. Biblioteca del Monasterio. El Escorial/Signatur. Ms.V.III.24. Hrsg. und mit einem Nachwort versehen von Wolfgang Rehm. Kassel, New York [etc.], Bärenreiter, 1958.
1p.L., 62 numb. leaves, [5]p. (Internationale Gesellschaft für Musikwissenschaft. Association Internationale des Bibliothèques Musicales. Documenta musicologica. Zweite Reihe: Handschriften-Faksimiles. 2).

Codices e Vaticanis selecti phototypice expressi iussu Pii p.x consilio et opera Curator um Bybliothecae Vaticanae. [Series maior]. Vol.XII, *see* Bannister, Henry Marriott. Monumenti Vaticani di paleografia musicale latina.

Colección de vihuelistas españoles del siglo XVI, *see* Martínez Torner, Eduardo. Colección de vihuelistas españoles del siglo XVI.

Collectio operum musicorum batavorum saeculi XVI, *see* Commer, Franz. Collectio operum musicorum batavorum saeculi XVI.

Collection d'ordre lyrique Expert-Pillard, *see* Expert, Henry. Collection d'ordre lyrique Expert-Pillard.

Collection de l'Institut Français d'Athènes. Série musicale, *see* Institut Français d'Athènes. Collection. Série musicale.

Collection espagnole, *see* Guenther, Felix. Collection espagnole.

Collection of ancient church music, *see* Motett Society. [Collection of ancient church music].

A collection of songs and madrigals by English composers of the close of the 15th century, *see* Plainsong and Mediaeval Music Society. A collection of songs and madrigals by English composers of the close of the 15th century.

COLLEGIUM MUSICAE NOVAE. Wiesbaden, Breitkopf & Härtel, 1954– .
No.1– .
Contents:
No.1. Bräutigam, Helmut. Fröhliche Musik für Flöte, Oboe und 3 Violinen. [1954].
No.2. David, Johann Nepomuk. Deutsche Tänze. Variationen über ein eigenes Thema für Streichorchester. [1954].
No.3. Fiebig, Kurt. Concertino für Violine und Streichorchester. [1954].
No.4. Knapp, Arno. Concertino für Klavier und Streichorchester. [1954].
No.5. Koerppen, Alfred. Concerto in D für Streichorchester. [1954].
No.6. Raphael, Günter. Die vier Jahreszeiten. Vier Variations. Reihen für Streichorchester. Op.77, Teil I. [1954].
No.7. Rohwer, Jens. Heptameron, eine vierstimmige Suite. [1954].
No.8. Seeboth, Max. Andreana. Suite für vier Streicher. [1954].
No.9. Strohbach, Siegfried. Festliche Ouvertüre für drei Geigen und Violoncello. [1954].
No.10. Thomas, Kurt. Erste Spielmusik, Op.18a. Suite für Schülerorchester.
No.11. Wolpert, Franz Alfons. Banchetto musicale Nr.1 für Streichorchester, Op.25. [1954].
No.12. Zender, Hans. Fünf leichte Stücke für Streichorchester, Op.7a. [1954].
No.13. Atterberg, Kurt. Suite pastorale in Modo antico, Op.34. [1955].
No.14. Bräutigam, Helmut. Kleine Musik für Streicher. [1955].
No.15. Bräutigam, Helmut. Musik für Flöte und Streichorchester, Op.55b. [1955].
No.16. Raphael, Günter. Die vier Jahreszeiten. Vier Variations. Reihen für Streichorchester, Op.77, Teil II. [1955].
No.17. Thomas, Kurt. Zweite Spielmusik, Op.22. Deutsche Tanz-Suite für Jugendorchester.
No.18. Zbinden, Julien François. Suite française für Streichorchester, Op.23. [1955].
No.19. Zender, Hans. Divertimento für Flöte, Violine, Violoncello und Streicher, Op.7b. [1955].
No.20. Benker, Heinz. Der Wächter auf dem Turme sass. Volkslieder. Rondo für Streicher und Klavier. [1955].
No.21. Erdmann, Dietrich. Serenade für Streichorchester und Bläser. [1955].
No.22. Rasch, Kurt. Moritat vom verlassenen Mariechen. [1956].
No.23. Rohwer, Jens. Wach auf, wach auf, 's ist höchste Zeit. [1956].
No.24. Fussan, Werner. Suite für Streicher. [1956].
No.25. Schibler, Armin. Kleine konzertante Suite für Streichorchester. [1956].
No.26. Benker, Heinz. Triplum humanum für Streicher und Triangel ad lib. [1956].
No.27. Gerhard, Fritz Christian. Concertino für Streichorchester. [1956].
No.28. Eder, Helmut. Musica semplice für Flöte, Cembalo und Streicher, Op.23, Nr.1. [1957].

No.29. Benker, Heinz. Praeludium pastorale für Streichorchester. [1957].
No.30. Gebhard, Hans. Konzert für Klavier, Streichorchester und Schlagzeug, Op.62.
No.31. Trapp, Klaus. Kleine Streichersinfonie. [1957].
No.32. Benker, Heinz. Colloquium musicale für zwei Solo-Violinen, Klavier und Streicher.
No.33. Gál, Hans. Musik für Streichorchester, Op.73.
No.34. David, Thomas Christian. Serenade für Streichorchester, Op.10. [1958].
No.35. Rosenstengel, Albrecht. Concertino für Schlagwerk-Solo und kleines Orchester. [1958].
No.36. Warner, Theodor. Vier Capricen für drei Bläser und Streichorchester. [1958].
No.37. Schibler, Armin. Elegische Musik für Flöte, Violoncello und Streichorchester, Op.52. [1958].
No.38. Fussan, Werner. Kleine Suite für Streichorchester und Bläser (ad lib.). [1959].
No.39. Schollum, Robert. Konturen. Fünf Stücke für Streichorchester, Op.59b. [1959].
No.40. Benker, Heinz. Rondo scherzando für Flöte und Streicher. [1959].
No.41. Hohlfeld, Christoph. Kleines Konzert für Violine und Orchester im klassischen Stil.
No.42. Gerhard, Fritz Christian. Rhapsodisches Konzert für Klavier und Streichorchester.
No.43. Finkbeiner, Reinhold. Sinfonia piccola für Streichorchester. [1961].
No.44. Baur, Jürg. Concertino für Flöte, Oboe, Klarinette, Streichorchester und Pauken. [1960].
No.45. Müller, Sigfrid Walther. Weihnachtsmusik. Kleines Konzert G-dur, Op.38b. [1959].
No.46. Eder, Helmut. Musik für zwei Trompeten und Streichorchester, Op.23, Nr.2. [1960].
No.47. Bräutigam, Helmut. Festliche Musik für Bläser und Streicher. [1960].
No.48. Koerppen, Alfred. Zwei Sätze über den Choral "Wir glauben all' an einen Gott." [1960].
No.49. Benker, Heinz. Concerto colorito für Orchester. [1961].
No.50.
No.51. Rosenstengel, Albrecht. Kleine Musik für Glockenspiel (Vibraphon) und Streicher. [1961].
No.52. Rohwer, Jens. Kammerkonzert für 2 Querflöten und Streichorchester. [1961].
No.53. Bertram, Hans Georg. Tanzende Intervalle. Suite für Kammerorchester. [1961].
No.54. Degen, Helnut. Kleine symphonische Musik für kleines Orchester. [1962].
No.55. Limmert, Erich. Russische Miniaturen nach alten ostslawischen Volksmelodien für Streichorchester. [1962].
No.56. Stadlmair, Hans. Introduktion und Fuge für Streicher. [1962].
No.57. Limmert, Erich. Suite concertante für vier Holzbläser und Streichorchester. [1963].
No.58. Ziems, H. Kammerkonzert. (Klarinette, Streicher). [1964].
No.59. Schibler, A. Festlicher Introitus. (2 Flöte, 2 Klarinette, Klavier/Cembalo, Streicher). [1964].
No.60. Rietz, J. Concertino. (Oboe, Viola, Streicher).

Collegium musicum, *see* Riemann, Hugo. Collegium musicum.

COLLEGIUM MUSICUM. [New Haven], Yale University, 1955– .
v.1– .
Contents:
Vol.1. Scarlatti, A. Passio Domini nostri Jesu Christi secundum Joannem. 1955.
Vol.2. Seay, Albert, ed. Thirty chansons for three and four voices, from Attaingnant's collections. 1960.
Vol.3. Haydn, Michael. Te Deum in C (1770). Ed. by Reinhart G. Pauly. 1961.
Vol.4. Stephens, Daphne E. R., ed. The Wickhambrook lute manuscript. 1963.
Vol.5. Planchart, Alejandro, ed. Three Caput masses. 1964.
In preparation:
[Vol.6]. Sammartini, G. B. Four symphonies. Ed. by Newell Jenkins.
[Vol.7]. Knapp, Janet, ed. An anthology of polyphonic conductus.

Collezione di trattati e musiche antiche edite in fac-simile, *see* Fantini, Girolamo. Modo per imparare a sonare di tromba; [Petrucci, Ottaviano dei]. Harmonice musices Odhecaton A.

Collins, Henry Bird, 1870–1941, ed. Missa "O quam suavis" for five voices, *see* Plainsong and Mediaeval Music Society. Missa "O quam suavis" for five voices.

Collins, Henry Bird, 1870–1941, ed. Old Hall manuscript, *see* Plainsong and Mediaeval Music Society. Old Hall manuscript.

COMES, JUAN BAUTISTA, 1568–1643.
Danzas del Santísimo Corpus Christi. Transcripción realizada por Vicente García Julbe. Biografía de Comes, Notas históricas y estudios críticos de los textos literario y musical por Manuel Palau. [Valencia], Instituto Valenciano de Musicología, Institución Alfonso el Magnánimo, Diputación Provincial de Valencia, 1952.
144p.
For chorus and harp, the latter as an unfigured bass.

Commemoration folio, *see* The Liturgical Music Press, Inc. Commemoration folio.

COMMER, FRANZ, 1813–1887. ed.
Cantica sacra. Sammlung geistlicher Gesänge aus dem 16. und 17. Jahrhundert. Berlin, Trautwein.
2v.
Contents:
Vol.1.
1. Händel. Aus einer Kantate: Ach Herr, mir armen Sünder.
2. Hasse. Miserere: Tibi soli peccavi.
3. Hasse. Miserere: Quoniam si voluisses.

4.a. Lotti. Psalm 50: Aspergas me.
b. Lotti. Psalm 50: Libera me de sanguinibus.
5. J. Haydn. Stabat Mater: Quis non posset.
6. Leo. Psalm 110: Tecum principum.
7. Durante. Lamentations Jeremiae: Pupili facti sumus.
8. Durante. Lamentations Jeremiae: Mulieres in Sion.
9. Astorga. Stabat Mater: Sancta Mater istud agas.
10. Graun. Te Deum laudamus: Te ad liberandum.
11. Graun. Te Deum laudamus: Dignare Domine die.
12. Händel. Oratorium Joseph: Du nanntest den armen Fremdling.
13. J. S. Bach. Messe: Qui tollis peccata.
14. Händel. Psalm 27: Es est der Herr, der.
15. Jomelli. Motette: Deo Patri sit gloria.
16. Händel. Psalm 95: Erhebet hoch den Herrn.
17. C. Ph. E. Bach. Oratorium, Die Israeliten in der Wüste: Warum verliessen wir.
18. Händel. Psalm 51: Rein mach' das Herz mir.
19. C. Ph. E. Bach. Oratorium, Die Israeliten in der Wüste: Wie nah' war uns der Tod.
20. Händel. Psalm 89: Wohl, ach wohl, o Herr.
21. Leo. Ave Maris Stella: Virgo singularis.
22. C. Ph. E. Bach. Oratorium, Die Israeliten in der Wüste: Beneidenswert, die ihren Sohn.
23. Hasse. Te Deum: Judex crederis esse.
24. Händel. Aus einem Psalm: Gott deine Gnade.
25. Jomelli. Offertorium: Discerne causam meam.

Vol.2.
1. Händel. Aus einem Psalm: O preist den Herrn.
2. Astorga. Aus dem Stabat Mater: Fac me plagis vulnerari.
3. Händel. Aus einem Psalm: Jehovah gedenket unser.
4. J. Haydn. Aus dem Stabat Mater: Pro peccatis suae gentis.
5. Händel. Aus einem Psalm: Du Gott bist gross.
6. J. Haydn. Aus dem Stabat Mater: Flammis orcine.
7. Händel. Arie aus dem Oratorium Debora: Gefahren verachtend.
8. Graun. Aus dem Te Deum laudamus: Salvum fac populum.
9. Händel. Aus dem Oratorium Joseph: Heilig sei dieser Tag dem Land.
10. Rolle. Aus dem Oratorium Lazarus: Wo bin ich, Wo bin ich?
11. Händel. Aus dem Oratorium Belsazar: Ihr Brüder freuet euch.
12. Rolle. Aus dem Oratorium Lazarus: O Tag des Jubels!
13. Händel. Aus dem Oratorium, Das Alexanderfest: Denn Rache, denn Rache.
14. J. S. Bach. Aus einer Messe: Domine, Deus.
15. Händel. Aus dem Oratorium Samson: Bedauernswertes Los.
16. Leonardo Leo. Aus einer Messe: Quoniam tu solus Sanctus.
17. Händel. Aus dem Oratorium Josua: Erstürmt ist endlich.
18. Rosenmüller. Aus Psalmus VI: Domine ne in furore.
19. Händel. Aus dem Oratorium Josua: Mein Mass ist voll.
20. Rosenmüller. Aus Psalmus VI: Laboravi.
21. Händel. Aus dem Oratorium, Der Messiah: Denn siehe Nacht bedecket.
22. Graun. Aus einer Passionsmusik: Nun darf ich mich nicht.
23. Händel. Aus dem Oratorium, Der Messiah: Warum toben die Heiden.
24. J. S. Bach. Aus der Kantate: Du Hirte Israel.
25. J. S. Bach. Aus der Kantate: Herr, deine Augen.

COMMER, FRANZ, 1813–1887. ed.
Collectio operum musicorum batavorum saeculi XVI, edidit Franciscus Commer. Sumptibus Societatis Batavae ad Musicam Promovendam. Berolin, Apud T. Trautwein (J. Guttentag). (V–VII: Maguntiae, Antverpiae et Bruxellarum ex Taberna Musices B. Schott Filiorum; IX–XI: Berolini apud M. Bahn; Amstelodami apud Eck, et Lefebure [Roothaan]; XII: Berlin, M. Bahn Verlag [Früher T. Trautwein]). [1844–58].
12v.
Contents:
Bd.1.
Clemens non Papa:
Vox clamantis in deserto.
Angelus Domini.
Deus in adiutorium.
Ego flos campi.
Pater peccavi in coelum.
Hollander, Christ.:
Si ignoras te o pulchra.
Hollander, Seb.:
Dum transisset Sabatum Maria.
Waelrant, Hub.:
Domine exaudi orationem.
Verba mea auribus percipe.
Willaert, Ad.:
Deus meus ad te.
Bd.2.
Clemens non Papa:
Pastores quidnam vidisti.
Ierusalem surge.
Super ripam Iordanis.
Vaet, Jac.:
Transeunte Domino clamabat.
Te Deum laudamus.
Willaert, Ad.:
Magnificat anima mea.
Cum invocarem examdivit.
In te Domine speravi.
Bd.3.
Clemens non Papa:
Ierusalem cito veniet.
Tu es Petrus.
Venit vox de coelo.
Mane nobiscum Domine.
Levavi oculos meos.
Ave martyr gloriosa.
Clemens et benigna.
Iubilate Deo.
Virgo prudentissima.
Bd.4.
Cleve, Joan. de:
Domine Iesu Christe.

Dixit ergo Iesus.
Regina coeli laetare.
Erravi sicut ovis.
Hollander, Christ.:
Saulus cum iter faceret.
Austria virtutis.
Nobile virtutum.
Vaet, Jac.:
Currite foelices.
Egressus Iesus.
Bd.5.
Hollander, Christ.:
Inter natos.
Pater peccavi.
Junior fui.
Sic Deus dilexi.
Laudate Dominum.
Deus adiutor.
O crux benedicta.
Clemens non Papa:
Tristitia obsedit.
Erravi sicut ovis.
Venit ergo Rex.
Nunc dimittis.
Vaet, Jac.:
Si qua fides.
Jam pridem.
Gratus in austriacam.
Romulidum invicti.
Miserere mei Deus.
Bd.6.
Hollander, Christ.:
Qui moritur Christo.
Repleti sunt omnes.
Agnosce Domine.
Postquam consumati.
Tres veniunt reges.
Vitam quae faciunt.
Christus resurgens.
Vos mea magnanimi.
Josquin du Pres:
Domine ne in furore.
Coeli enarrant.
Deus in nomine.
Benedicite omnia.
Monte, Philip de:
Domine Deus meus.
Bd.7.
Lassus, Orl. de:
Audi benigne.
Domine quando veneris.
In Monte Oliveti.
O quam suavis.
O mors quam amara.
Estote ergo misericordes.
In convertendo Dominus.
Josquin du Pres:
Domine Dominus noster.
Beati quorum remissae.
Miserere mei Deus.
Cantate Domino.
Rore, Cyprian de:
In convertendo Dominus.
Bd.8.
Josquin du Pres:
Ave Christe.
Sic Deus dilexit.
Christus mortuus.
Bassiron, Phil.:
Agnus Dei.
Mouton, Joan.:
Confitemini Domino.
Arcadelt, Jac.:
Pater Noster.
Canis, Corn.:
Dixit insipiens.
Gombert, Nic.:
Deus ultionum.
Peverage, And.:
O Virgo generosa.
Phinot, Dominicus:
Lamentationes Jeremiae.
Sancta Trinitas.
Jam non dicam.
Meister, Matth. le:
Estote prudentes.
Lattre, Petit Jan de:
O bone Jesu.
Buus, Jac.:
Qui inventi mulierem.
Lassus, Orl. de:
Jam lucis orto sidere.
Confitebor tibi.
Te decet hymnus.
Dixit Joseph.
Timor et tremor.
Clemens non Papa:
Qui consolabatur.
Bd.9.
Hollander, Christ.:
Valde honorandus est.
Christe salus hominum.
Educ me o Domine.
Da pacem Domine.
Auxilium meum a Domino.
Nolite mirari quia veniet.
Casta novenarum iacet.
Vaet, Jac.:
Salve Regina.
Dum complerentur dies.
Discubuit Jesus.
Euge serve bone et fidelis.
Videns Dominus flentes sorores Lazari.
Filiae Jerusalem venite.
Fortitudo et laus mea.
Heu mihi Domine.
Quoties diem illum considero.
Beata es et venerabilis Virgo.
Reges terrae congregati sunt.
Pascha nostrum immolatus est Christus.
In tenebris nostrae.
Phinot, Dominicus:
Tanto tempore vobiscum sunt.
Bd.10.
Clemens non Papa:
Nobilis illa . . . musica.
Obsecro Domine.
Domine Deus exercituum.
Domine clamavi ad te.
Adesto dolori meo.
Ego me diligentes.

Concussum est mare.
Misit me vivens.
Quam moesta dies.
O Maria vernans rosa.
In te Domine speravi.
Servus tuus ego sum.
O bone Jesu.
In honore beatissimae Annae.
Ascendit Deus.
Crecquillon, Thomas:
Cum deambularet.
Verbum caro factum.
Lassus, Orl. de:
Cognoscimus Domine.
Fili quid facisti.
Tibi laus tibi gloria.
Confisus Domino.
Peccavi quid faciam.
Bd.11.
Clemens non Papa:
Souter Liedekens: Psalm 1–150. Teil I–IV.
Bd.12.
Jannequin, Clem.:
Voulez ouyr.
Claudin:
Il me suffit de tous mes maulx.
Richafort:
De mon triste deplaisir.
Claudin:
Languir me faîs.
Dont vient cela belle.
Lupi, Joan:
Reviens vers moy.
De Roucourt:
O coeur ingrat.
Crecquillon, Thomas:
Ung gay bergier.
Le Cocq, Jean:
Les me fault il tant de mal.
Nostre vicaire ung jour.
Crecquillon, Thomas:
Du cueur le don.
Barbe, Ant.:
Ung capitaine de pillars.
Gombert, Nic.:
Le bergier et la bergiere.
Le Cocq, Jean:
Sy des haulx cieulx.
Josquin du Pres:
Douleur me bat.
Petite Camusette.
Basies moy.
Manchicourt, Peter de:
Sortes mes pleurs.
Castileti, Joan (alias Guyot):
Joyeusement sans nulz faulx.
Baston, Josquin:
C'est à grant tort.
Clemens non Papa:
Entre vous filles de XV ans.
La la la Maistre Pierre.
La belle Margaritte.
Languir me fais.
Certon:
Je ne fus jamais si ayse.
Arcadelt, Jac.:
J'ay mis mon cueur.
Gombert, Nic.:
Chant des oiseaux.
Jannequin, Clem.:
La bataille.
La chasse de lièvre.
Rore, Cyprianus de:
Calami sonum ferentes.
Lassus, Orl. de:
Si je suis brun.
Matona mia cara.

COMMER, FRANZ, 1813–1887. ed.
Compositionen für Orgel aus dem 16., 17., und 18. Jahrhundert zum Gebrauch beim Gottesdienst gesammelt: [Mit Vorbemerkungen in deutscher und französischer. Sprache]. Leipzig, Leuckart, 18? – .
6 Hefte.
Contents:
Heft 1. Praeambulen und Versetten aus dem Anhange der als zweiten Theil des "Wegweiser die Orgel recht zu schlagen" 1602 zu Augsburg erschienenen deutschen Uebersetzung der "Ars cantandi," von G. Carissimi.
Heft 2. Compositionen, von G. Frescobaldi.
Heft 3. Compositionen aus "Wegweiser die Orgel recht zu schlagen" uns aus "Manuductio ad Organum." Augsburg, 1748; Praeludium, von A. Caldara.
Heft 4. Compositionen, von F. X. A. Murschhauser.
Heft 5. Compositionen, von Joh. Speth aus "Ars magna consoni et dissoni . . ."
Heft 6. Compositionen, von Joh. Speth.

COMMER, FRANZ, 1813–1887. ed.
Geistliche und weltliche Lieder aus dem XVI.–XVII. Jahrhundert für 3, 4, 5 und 6 Stimmen Part. Berlin, Bahn, 1870.
1 v.
Contains 14 sacred songs by Chr. Hollander, A. Scandellus; 22 secular songs by A. Utendal, I. de Vento; 5 songs in the appendix by W. Briegel, Nic. Zang.

Commer, Franz, 1813–1887. ed. Musica sacra, *see* Musica sacra, hrsg. F. Commer.

COMPÈRE, LOYSET, d.1518.
Opera omnia. Edidit Ludwig Finscher. [Rome], American Institute of Musicology, 1958– .
v.1– . (Corpus mensurabilis musicae. No.15).
To be completed in about 6v.
Contents:
Vol.1. Missa l'homme armé. Missa alles regrets. [Missa brevis sine nomine]. Credo [sine nomine]. Credo Mon Père. Mon Père m'a donné mari. 1958.
Vol.2. [Missa] Galeazescha [de Beata Virgine]. [Missa de D.N.J.C.]. [Missa in nativitate D.N.J.C.]. 1959.
Vol.3. Gaude prole regia– Sancta Catherina. Quis numerare queat– Da pacem. Solo caret monstris– Fera pessima. Virgo coelesti. Magnificat 1i, 6i, 7: toni, Esurientes 4i, 8i toni. 1959.

Vol.4. Ad honorem tuum, Christe. Asperges me, Domine. Ave Maria. Crux triumphans. Officium de cruce (In nomine Jesu). O admirabile commercium. O bone Jesu. O genitrix gloriosa. Omnium bonorum plena. Paranymphus. Profitentes unitatem. Propter gravamen. Sile fragor. 1961.

Composições polifónicas, *see* Lobo, Duarte. Composições polifónicas.

Compositionen für Orgel aus dem 16., 17., und 18. Jahrhundert, *see* Commer, Franz. Compositionen für Orgel aus dem 16., 17., und 18. Jahrhundert.

Concert historique d'orgue, *see* Guilmant, Alexandre. Concert historique d'orgue.

CONCERTINO. Werke für Schul- und Laienorchester. Mainz, B. Schott's Söhne, [1958–].
v.1– .
This is an unnumbered series.
Contents (incomplete):
Albinoni, Tomaso. Sinfonia a 4 für Streichorchester. Hrsg. von Walter Kolneder. Edition Schott 4957.
—— Sinfonia G-dur für Streichorchester und Bläser ad lib. Hrsg. von Walter Kolneder. Edition Schott 4962 [cop.1959].
Bach, Johann Sebastian. Sinfonia D-dur aus der Kantate Nr.42 "Am Abend aber desselbigen Sabbats" für zwei Oboen, Fagott, Streichorchester und Basso continuo (Cembalo, Orgel). Hrsg. von Walter Kolneder. Edition Schott 4961.
Bartók, Béla. Vier kleine Tanzstücke und Sechs ungarische Volkslieder für Streichorchester. Hrsg. von Darvar. Edition Schott 4971.
—— Zehn leichte Stücke für Streichorchester. Hrsg. von Rudolf Maros. Edition Schott 4970 [cop.1961].
Beethoven, Ludwig van. Zwölf Contretänze für Orchester. Hrsg. von Walter Kolneder. Edition Schott 4964.
—— Sechs ländlerische Tänze für zwei Violinen und Bass. Hrsg. von Walter Kolneder. Edition Schott 4963.
Boismortier, Joseph Bodin de. Sonate, E-moll, für drei Melodie-Instrumente (Flöten, Violinen, Oboen) oder Streichorchester und Basso continuo, Cembalo (Pianoforte), Violoncello (Viola da gamba, Fagotto) ad lib. Op.34/3. Hrsg. von Hugo Ruf. Edition Schott 4975 [cop.1963].
—— Sonate, A-moll, für drei Melodie-Instrumente (Flöten, Violinen, Oboen) oder Streichorchester und Basso continuo, Cembalo (Pianoforte), Violoncello (Viola da gamba, Fagotto) ad lib. Op.34/6. Hrsg. von Hugo Ruf. Edition Schott 4969 [cop.1963].
Charpentier, Marc Antoine. Suite für Streichorchester. Hrsg. von Walter Kolneder. Edition Schott 4951 [cop.1958].
Corelli, Arcangelo. Concertino für 2 B-Trompeten und Streicher. Nach der Sonata da camera für 2 Violinen und Basso continuo. Hrsg. von Eberhard Werdin. Edition Schott 4954 [cop. 1958].
Ditters von Dittersdorf, Karl. Konzert in C-dur für zwei Violinen und Streichorchester. Erstmals hrsg. von Walter Lebermann. Dirigier-Klavierauszug von Helmut May. Edition Schott 5310 [1964].
Fussan, Werner. Concertino für Flöte und Streichorchester (1957). Edition Schott 4955 [cop. 1958].
Genzmer, Harald. Divertimento giocoso, für zwei Holzbläzer und Streichorchester. 1960. Edition Schott 4966 [1961].
Giornovichi, Giovanni Mane. Konzert Nr.1 in A-dur, für Violine und Orchester (1773). Hrsg. von Walter Lebermann. Dirigier-Klavierauszug von Bernhard Weigart. Edition Schott 4973 [cop.1962].
Gottron, Adam. Musik am Mainzer Hof: für Streicher und Basso continuo, Cembalo (Pianoforte), Violoncello (Viola da gamba) ad lib. Edition Schott 5306 [cop.1964].
Haydn, Joseph. Konzert F-dur, für Klavier oder Cembalo und Streicher, 2 Hörner ad lib., Hoboken XVIII:3. Hrsg. von Ewald Lassen. Kadenzen von Heinz Schröter. Edition Schott 4958 [cop.1958].
—— Klavierauszug von Wilhelm Lutz. Edition Schott 4959 [cop.1958].
Mohler, Philipp. Shakespeare-Suite; Tanzsätze von Zeitgenossen William Shakespeares für Streicher, Holzbläser und Cembalo (Laute ad lib.). Edition Schott 5309 [1964].
Mozart, Leopold. Divertimento I für zwei Violinen und Violoncello. Hrsg. von Walter Kolneder. Edition Schott 4956.
Mozart, Wolfgang Amadeus. Konzert-Rondo A-dur K.V.386, für Klavier und Orchester. Hrsg. von Badura-Skoda/Macherras. Edition Schott 4968.
—— Klavierauszug. Edition Schott 4969.
Pez, Johann Christoph. Ouvertüren-Suite, A-moll, für Streichorchester, Bläser ad lib., und Basso continuo. Cembalo (Pianoforte), Violoncello (Viola da gamba) ad lib. Hrsg. von Felix Schroeder. Edition Schott 5301 [cop.1963].
Schröter, Johann Samuel. Konzert, C-dur, für Klavier und Streichorchester, Op.3, Nr.3. Hrsg. von Karlheinz Schultz-Hauser. Edition Schott 4974 [1964].
Schubert, Franz Peter. Fünf Deutsche mit Coda und sieben Trios für Streicher (solistisch oder chorisch). Hrsg. von Walter Kolneder. Edition Schott 4965.
Stamitz, Johann Wenzel Anton. Konzert für Violine in G-dur, mit Streichorchester und 2 Hörnern ad lib. Erstmals hrsg. von Walter Lebermann. Dirigier-Klavierauszug (H. May). Edition Schott 5305 [1964].
Stamitz, Karl. Orchester-Quartett C-dur für zwei Violinen, Viola und Violoncello. Hrsg. von Mönkemeyer. Edition Schott 4960.
—— Quartetto concertante G-dur für Streicher (solistisch oder chorisch). Edition Schott 4967.
Telemann, Georg Philipp. Concerto A-moll, für zwei Altblockflöten (Querflöten), zwei Oboen (Violinen, Tenorblockflöten), zwei Violinen und Basso continuo, Cembalo (Pianoforte),

Violoncello (Viola da Gamba) ad lib. Hrsg. von Ilse Hechler. Edition Schott 4968 [1963].
Torelli, Giuseppe. Konzert für Streichorchester, Op.VI, Nr.1. Hrsg. von Walter Kolneder. Edition Schott 4661 [cop.1958].
Werdin, Eberhard. Festliche Musik für zwei Instrumentalchöre. Edition Schott 4952 [cop.1958].
Zipp, Friedrich. Musik für Orchester (1955). Edition Schott 4953 [cop.1958].

Les concerts de la Renaissance, *see* Cauchie, Maurice. Quinze chansons françaises du XVIe siècle.

CONCERTS SPIRITUELS OU RECUEIL DE MOTETS, à une, à deux, à trois, et à un plus grand numbre de voix, sur la musique de Gluck, Piccini, Sacchini, Mozart, Rossini, Beethoven, Weber & autres maîtres célèbres; pour les offices et les saluts des fêtes solennelles et pour servir à l'exercice du chant dans les étab ;sements religieux et les maisons d'éducation chrétienne. Avec accompagnement de piano (ou d'orgue) A.M.D.G. Livre I-IV. Avignon, Seguin Aîné, [cop.1840].
4v.

Conseil International de la Musique (UNESCO). Classici italiani della musica, *see* Classici italiani della musica.

Consejo Superior de Investigaciones Científicas, Instituto Español de Musicología, *see* Monumentos de la música española; Música hispana.

Consort lessons, *see* Morley, Thomas. The first book of consort lessons.

Constanz, Hans von, *see* Buchner, Hans (von Constanz).

The contemporaries of Purcell, *see* Fuller-Maitland, John Alexander. The contemporaries of Purcell.

Contemporaries of Purcell, *see* Herrmann, Kurt. Contemporaries of Purcell.

CONTEMPORARY BRITISH PIANO MUSIC. London, Schott and Co., Ltd., cop.1956.
28p.
Contains compositions by Don Banks, P. Racini Fricker, Iain Hamilton, and Humphrey Searle.

CONTEMPORARY JAPANESE MUSIC SERIES. Tokyo, Ongaku-no-Tomo-Sha, 196? – .
No.1– .
This series of separate music publications appears as a supplement to "The ongaku geijutsu" (Tokyo).
The series title appears in English only.
Contents:
No.9. Mamiya, Michio. Three movements for wind quintet. Quartet for shakuhachi, sangen, and two kotos. cop.1963.
No.10. Hayama, Mitsuaki. Piano sonata. cop. 1963.
No.11. Matsushita, Shin-ichi. Canzona da sonate. No.1 [for piano and percussion]. cop.1962.
No.12. Akutagawa, Yasushi. Music for strings. No.1. cop.1963.
No.13. Miyoshi, Akira. En blanc; four poems by Chika Sagawa. cop.1963.
No.14. Okumura, Hajime. Fourth sonatina for piano. cop.1963.

No.21. Toyama, Yuzo. Sonata for violin and piano. cop.1964.
No.22. Matsushita, Shin-ichi. Music for soprano and chamber ensemble. cop.1964.
No.23. Ishiketa, Mareo. Sonata II for violoncello and piano. cop.1964.
No.24. Mamiya, Michio. Composition for male chorus. cop.1964.
No.25. Tanaka, Toshimitsu. Adagio and Allegro for piano quartet. cop.1964.
No.26. Okumura, Hajime. Third sonatina for piano. cop.1964.
No.27. Koyama, Kiyoshige. Ainu no Uta; for string orchestra. cop.1964.
No.28. Nodah, Téryuki. Trio for violin, violoncello and piano. cop.1964.
No.29. Hachimura, Yoshio. Improvisation for piano. cop.1964.
No.30. Maruta, Shozo. Divertissement for brass quintet. cop.1965.

No.32. Miyake, Haruna. Quartet for clarinet, violin, violoncello and piano. cop.1965.

CONTEMPORARY ORGAN SERIES. General editor, William Strickland. New York, H. W. Gray Co., Inc., 1941– .
No.1– .
Contents:
No.1. Sowerby, Leo. Toccata. 1941.
No.2. Sessions, Roger. Chorale. (No.1). 1941.
No.3. Piston, Walter. Chromatic study on the name of Bach. 1941.
No.4. Moore, Douglas. Dirge. (Passacaglia).
No.5. Wagenaar, Bernard. Eclogue. 1941.
No.6. Jacobi, Frederick. Prelude. 1941.
No.7. Copland, Aaron. Episode. 1941.
No.8. James, Philip. Pantomime. 1941.
No.9. Milhaud, Darius. Pastorale. 1942.
No.10. Křenek, Ernst. Sonata. Op.92. 1942.
No.11. Bingham, Seth. Pastorale. (Op.16).
No.12. Porter, Quincy. Canon and fugue. 1944.
No.13. Schönberg, Arnold. Variations on a recitative. 1947.
No.14. Thomson, Virgil. Pastorale on a Christmas plainsong. 1942.
No.15. Beach, Mrs. H. H. A. Prelude on an old folk tune.
No.16. Cowell, Henry Dixon. Processional. 1944.
No.17. Effinger, C. Prelude and fugue.
No.18. Donovan, R. Paignion.
No.19. Kubik, G. Quiet piece.
No.20. Arnell, Richard Anthony Sayer. Baroque prelude and fantasia. 1948.
No.21. Howe, M. Elegy.
No.22. Keller, H. Fantasy and fugue.
No.23. Milhaud, Darius. Sonata. 1950.
No.24. Jacobi, F. Three quiet preludes.
No.25. Sowerby, Leo. Whimsical variations.

No.26. Kohs, E. Passacaglia. (Organ and piano duet).
No.27. Kay, U. Two meditations.
No.28. Castelnuovo-Tedesco. Fanfare.
No.29. Becker, J. J. Fantasia tragica.

The continental harmony, *see* Billings, William. The continental harmony.

Cook, Edgar Thomas, 1880–1953. The use of plainsong, *see* Plainsong and Mediaeval Music Society. Cook, Edgar Thomas. The use of plainsong.

Cooper, Gerald M., ed. The Tudor edition of old music, *see* The Tudor edition of old music.

COPENHAGEN KONGELIGE BIBLIOTEK. Mss. (Thottske Samling 291[8]).
Der kopenhagener Chansonnier; das Manuskript Thott 291[8] der Königlichen Bibliothek, Kopenhagen. Eingeleitet und hrsg. von Dr. Knud Jeppesen . . . Die Gedichte philologisch revidiert und mit einem Glossar versehen von Dr. Viggo Brøndal . . . Kopenhagen, Levin & Munksgaard; Leipzig, Breitkopf & Härtel, 1927.
cix p., 1L., 63p. incl. facsims.
"Das interessanteste und wertvollste mittelalterliche Musikmanuskript der Königlichen Bibliothek."
French words; music for 3 voices transcribed into modern notation.
33 chansons. "4 Kompositionen von Busnois, 3 von Convert, 2 von Okeghem, 2 von Morton, und je eine Komposition von Hayne (v. Ghizeghem), Baziron, Molinet, Prioris, Michelet und Magister Symon."
Facsims. printed on both sides.
Bibliographical footnotes.
"Verzeichnis der Quellen": p.[lxxi]–lxxiv.

COPENHAGEN KONGELIGE BIBLIOTEK. Mss. (Thottske Samling 291[8]).
Der kopenhagener Chansonnier. Reprint. New York, Broude Brothers, [cop.1965].

Corbeil, Pierre de, *see* Pierre de Corbeil.

CORELLI, ARCANGELO, 1653–1713.
Les oeuvres de Arcangelo Corelli. Revues par J. Joachim and F. Chrysander. London, Augener & Co., 1888–91. (Augener's Edition. No.4936A–E).
5v.
See an earlier edition under Denkmäler der Tonkunst, ed. by Fr. Chrysander, v.3, 1869.
Contents:
Vol.1. Sonate da chiesa a tre. Op.1; Sonate da camera a tre. Op.2.
Vol.2. Sonate da chiesa a tre. Op.3; Sonate da camera a tre. Op.4.
Vol.3. 6 Sonate a violino solo e violine o cimbalo. Op.5, I; Preludii, Allemande, Correnti, Gighe, Sarabande, Gavotte e Follia a violino solo e violine o cimbalo. Op.5, II.
Vol.4/5. Concerti grossi, 2 livres. Op.6.

CORNELIUS, PETER, 1824–1874.
Peter Cornelius Musikalisches Werke. Erste Gesamtausgabe im Auftrage seinen Familie hrsg. von Max Hasse und Waldemar von Baussnern. Leipzig, Breitkopf & Härtel, 1905–6.
5v.
Contents:
Bd.1. Einstimmige Lieder und Gesänge mit Pianofortebegleitung.
Bd.2. Mehrstimmige Lieder und Gesänge, Duette, Männerchöre, Gemischte Chöre.
Bd.3. Der Barbier von Bagdad. Partitur.
Bd.4. Der Cid. Partitur.
Bd.5. Gunlöd. Partitur.

CORONA. Werkereihe für Schul- und Kammerorchester. Hrsg. von Adolf Hoffmann. Wolfenbüttel, Möseler Verlag, 19? – .
v.1– .
Also published under title *Deutsche Instrumentalmusik. Werke für Kammerorchester.*
Contents:
Vol.1. Händel, G. F. Festmusik (B-dur). (Ouvertüre und Tänze) aus der Oper "Alcina" (1775) für 4stg. Streichorchester und Generalbass (Klavier).
Vol.2. Pezel, J. Feierliche Musik (E-moll) aus der "Musica Vespertina," Leipzig (1669) für 2 Violinen, 2 Violen (1 Viola, 3 Violine), Violoncello und Generalbass (Klavier).
Vol.3. Telemann, G. Ph. Lustige Suite (C-dur) für 4stg. Streichorchester und Generalbass (Klavier). Erstdruck.
Vol.4. 15 Aufzugsmusiken alter Meister für 4- bis 6stg. Streichorchester. zum Teil mit Generalbass (Klavier).
Vol.5. Gluck, Chr. W. Ballettmusik, 12 Tänze für 4stg. Streichorchester (Klavier nach Belieben).
Vol.6. Gluck, Chr. W. Sinfonie (G-dur) für 4stg. Streichorchester (Klavier nach Belieben). Erstdruck.
Vol.7. Haydn, J. Zwölf deutsche Tänze, 12 Menuette für 2 Violinen und Violoncello. Erstdruck.
Vol.8. Mozart, W. A. Zwölf deutsche Tänze, 7 Salzburger Menuette, 6 ländlerische Tänze für 2 Violinen und Violoncello.
Vol.9. Beethoven, L. v. Zwölf deutsche Tänze, 12 Menuette, 6 ländlerische Tänze für 2 Violinen und Violoncello.
Vol.10. Händel, G. F. Suite mit dem Marsch für 2 Violinen, Violoncello (Kontrabass) und Klavier.
Vol.11. 16 Märsche von Fux, Telemann, Graupner, Bach, Händel, Gluck, Mozart, Beethoven und unbekannten Meistern für 4stg. Streichorchester und zum Teil Generalbass (Klavier).
Vol.12. Telemann, G. Ph. Festliche Suite (A-dur) für 2 Violinen, Violoncello und Generalbass (Klavier). Erstdruck.
Vol.13. Praetorius, M. Sechs Tanzfolgen für 2 Violinen, Viola (für C-Tenor-Blockflöte im Viol.-Schlüssel) und Violoncello oder Blockflötenquartett (Folge 1 bis 3).

Vol.14. Praetorius, M. Sechs Tanzfolgen für 2 Violinen (Folge 5 und 6 für 3 Violinen), Viola (für Cm Tenor-Blockflöte im Viol.-Schüssel) und Violoncello oder Blockflötenquartett bzw.-quintett (Folge 4 bis 6).

Vol.15. Haydn, J. Sechs Weinzirler Trios für 2 Violinen und Violoncello, oder Violine (Flöte usw.) und Klavier. Erstdruck.

Vol.16. Niedersächsische Dorftänze für 2 Violinen, Violoncello, Klavier nach Belieben. Aus dem Tourenbuch eines Dorfmusikanten.

Vol.17. Lanner, J. Wiener Ländler und Walzer für 3 Violinen, Violoncello, Klavier nach Belieben.

Vol.18. Fux, J. J. Nürnberger Partita (1701) für Flöte, Oboe (2 F-Alt-Blockflöten oder Violinen) und Klavier (Violoncello oder Gambe nach Belieben).

Vol.19. Pamer, M. Zwölf Walzer für 2 Violinen und Violoncello, Klavier nach Belieben.

Vol.20. Haydn, J. Sechs leichte Wiener Trios für 2 Violinen und Violoncello oder Violine (Flöte usw.) und Klavier. Erstdruck.

Vol.21. Telemann, G. Ph. Konzert für 2 F-Alt-Blockflöten, 4stg. Streichorchester und Generalbass. (Klavier).

Vol.22. Mozart, W. A. Fünf Wiener Serenaden für 2 Violinen und Violoncello oder Violine (Flöte usw.) und Klavier. Gesamtausgabe.

Vol.23. Schubert, F. Deutsche Tanze, Ländler, Walzer, Menuette, Ecossaisen für 2 Violinen und Violoncello.

Vol.24. Bach, J. S. Largo aus dem Doppelkonzert für Violinen in D-moll, Sinfonien, Fugen, Kanons, Choräle, Menuette und andere Tänze, meist für 4stg. Streichorchester und Generalbass (Klavier).

Vol.25. Mozart, W. A. Drei salzburger Sinfonien ohne Bläser. (KV.136, 137, 138) für 4stg. Streichorchester und Generalbass (Klavier).

Vol.26. Händel, G. F. Rinaldo. Suite für 4stg. Streichorchester und Generalbass (Klavier), Ouvertüre, Sinfonien und Tänze aus Händels Oper "Rinaldo." (1711).

Vol.27. Graupner, Chr. Konzert für Flöte, 4stg. Streichorchester und Generalbass (Klavier).

Vol.28. Ländgraf Ludwig V. Hessen (1718). Leichte Suite für 4stg. Streichorchester und Generalbass (Klavier).

Vol.29. Händel, G. F. Zwölf Feiermusiken für 4stg. Streichorchester und Generalbass (Klavier).

Vol.30. Feiermusik von Tunder, Rosenmüller, J. C. F. Fischer, Händel, Bach, Haydn, Mozart, Beethoven, Schubert, für Violine 1 (Blockflöte 1, 2), Violine 2, 3, 4, Viola 1, 2, Violoncello (Kontrabass) und zum Teil Generalbass (Klavier).

Vol.31. Händel, G. F. Konzert für Flöte und 4stg. Streichorchester und Generalbass (Klavier). Erstdruck.

Vol.32. Bach, J. S. Konzert für Klavier (Cembalo), 2 Altblockflöten und 4stg. Streichorchester.

Vol.33. Mozart, W. A. Zwei Fugen und eine Fantaste. (KV. Nr.401, 546, 608) für 4stg. Streichorchester.

Vol.34. Telemann, G. Ph. Konzertsuite für Violoncello oder Viola da Gamba (Bratsche) 4stg. Streichorchester und Generalbass (Cembalo oder Klavier).

Vol.35. Händel, G. F. Xerxes. Ouvertüre, Sinfonie, Arien und Tänze aus der gleichnamigen Oper für 4stg. Streichorchester und Generalbass (Klavier).

Vol.36. Camerloher, Pl. v. Drei Freisinger Sinfonien für 4stg. Streichorchester. Erstdruck.

Vol.37. Telemann, G. Ph. Konzert für 2 Violinen, Streichorchester und Generalbass (Klavier). Erstdruck.

Vol.38. Stamitz, J. Drei Mannheimer Sinfonien für 4stg. Streichorchester. Erstdruck.

Vol.39. Quantz, J. J. Konzert (D-dur) für Flöte und Streichorchester (Generalbass). Bearb. von H. D. Sonntag. Erstdruck.

Vol.40. Camerloher, Pl. v. Orchesterquartett F-dur. Erstdruck.

Vol.41. Richter, F. X. Drei Sinfonien für 4stg. Streichorchester. Erstdruck.

Vol.42. Telemann, G. Ph. Ouvertüre in G-dur für 4stg. Streichorchester. Erstdruck.

Vol.43. Fasch, J. F. Sinfonie in G-dur für 4stg. Streichorchester und Generalbass (Klavier). Erstdruck.

Vol.44. Kanzonen für 4 Instrumente (Blockflöten- , Fidel- , Gamben- , Streichquartett, Lauten, zum Teil Bleckblasinstrumente) in einfacher, chorischer oder gemischter Besetzung. (Fugenbuch Teil I).

Vol.45. Ricercare (Fugenbuch Teil 2. Besetzung wie 44).

Vol.46. Fugen I, Nord- und süddeutsche Meister (Fugenbuch Teil 3. Besetzung wie 44).

Vol.47. Fugen II, Mitteldeutsche Meister (Fugenbuch Teil 4. Besetzung wie 44).

Vol.48. Choralbearbeitungen alter Meister. (Fugenbuch Teil 5. Besetzung wie 44).

Vol.49. Hassler, H. L. Kirchengesange, Psalmen und geistliche Lieder fugweis komponiert und simpliciter gesetzt. (Fugenbuch Teil 6. Besetzung wie 44).

Vol.50. Weihnachtsmusik alter Meister. (Fugenbuch Teil 7. Besetzung wie 44).

Vol.51. Haydn, J. Cassation für 5stg. Streichorchester.

Vol.52. Bach, J. S. Menuette aus einer Serenate für Flöte, 5stg. Streichorchester und Generalbass. (Klavier).

Vol.53. Mozart, W. A. Pantalon und Colombine. Musik zu einer Pantomime. Für 4stg. Streichorchester. (Violine 1. K. V. 446 nach Mozarts Autograph). Zum Teil Erstdruck.

Vol.54. Dittersdorf, K. D. v. Konzert in E-moll für Flöte, 4stg. Streichorchester und Generalbass (Klavier). Bearb. von H. D. Sonntag. Erstdruck.

Vol.55. Händel, G. F. Drei Ouvertüren. (Alexander, Berenice, Theodora) für 4stg. Streichorchester und Generalbass (Klavier).

Vol.56. Quantz, J. J. Konzert in C-dur für Flöte und 4stg. Streichorchester und Generalbass (Klavier). Bearb. von H. D. Sonntag. Erstdruck.

Vol.57. Bach, J. S. Sinfonia in C-dur, Ouvertüre

in A-moll, Sinfonia in H-moll für 4stg. Streichorchester und Generalbass (Klavier). Bearb. von A. Lunow.
Vol.58. Heinichen, J. D. Konzert in G-dur für Violine und 4stg. Streichorchester und Generalbass (Klavier). Erstdruck.
Vol.59. Fasch, J. F. Sinfonie in G-dur für 4stg. Streichorchester und Generalbass (Klavier). Erstdruck.
Vol.60. Graun, C. H. Konzert C-moll für Cembalo und 4stg. Streichorchester. Erstdruck.
Vol.61. Haydn, J. Opernsinfonie, Die wahre Beständigkeit "La vera costanza" für 4stg. Streichorchester.
Vol.62. Haydn, J. 1. Divertimento in B-dur (Op. 1, Nr.1) für 2 Violinen, Viola, Violoncello in mehrfacher oder solistischer Besetzung.
Vol.63. Haydn, J. 11. Divertimento in D-dur (Op.2, Nr.5. Besetzung wie Corona 62).
Vol.64. Haydn, J. 17. Divertimento in F-dur (Op.3, Nr.5. Besetzung wie Corona 62).
Vol.65. Fasch, J. F. Konzert in D-dur für Violine, 4stg. Streichorchester und Generalbass (Klavier).
Vol.66. Händel, G. F. Konzert, B-dur. 1961.
Vol.67. Stamitz, K. Orchesterquartett A-dur. (Hoffmann). 1961.
Vol.68. Stamitz, K. Orchesterquartett G-dur. (Hoffmann). 1961.
Vol.69. Bach, J. C. Drei Sinfonietten. 1961.
Vol.70–71. Telemann, G. P. Klingende Geographie; Ouvertürensuite. (2v.). 1961.
Vol.72. Händel, G. F. Concerto grosso B-dur. 1962.
Vol.73. Bach, J. Chr. Konzert A-dur für Cembalo. 1962.
Vol.74. Händel, G. F. Konzert, B-dur. 1962.
Vol.75. Händel, G. F. Konzert G-moll für Oboe. 1962.
Vol.76. Marcello, A. Konzert D-moll für Oboe. 1962.
Vol.77. Fasch, J. F. Konzert D-moll für Oboe oder Sopranblockflöte. 1963.
Vol.78. Telemann, G. Ph. Konzertsuite A-dur für Violine. 1963.
Vol.79. Telemann, G. Ph. Konzert G-dur für Violine. 1963.
Vol.80. Mendelssohn-Bartholdy, F. Schweizer Sinfonie C-moll. 1963.

Corpus cantilenarum medii aevi. 1. Sér., *see* Beck, Jean Baptiste. Les chansonniers des troubadours et des trouvères.

Corpus de musique marocaine, *see* Morocco. Service des Arts Indigènes. Corpus de musique marocaine.

CORPUS MENSURABILIS MUSICAE. Rome, American Institute of Musicology in Rome, 1948– .
No.1– .
Contents:
No.1, *see* Dufay, Guillaume. Opera omnia.
No.2, *see* Guillaume de Machaut. Opera.
No.3, *see* Willaert, Adrian. Opera omnia.
No.4, *see* Clément, Jacques. Opera omnia.
No.5, *see* Brumel, Antoine. Opera omnia.
No.6, *see* Gombert, Nicolas. Opera omnia.
No.7, *see* Barbireau, Jacques. Opera omnia.
No.8, *see* Pirrotta, Nino, ed. The music of fourteenth-century Italy.
No.9, *see* Regis, Johannes. Opera omnia.
No.10, *see* Gaffurio, Franchino. Collected musical works.
No.11, *see* Reaney, Gilbert, ed. Early fifteenth-century music.
No.12, *see* Gabrieli, Giovanni. Opera omnia.
No.13, *see* Catholic Church, Roman. Liturgy and ritual. Missal. Missa Tornacensis.
No.14, *see* Rore, Cipriano de. Opera omnia.
No.15, *see* Compère, Loyset. Opera omnia.
No.16, *see* Carver, Robert. Collected works.
No.17, *see* Fayrfax, Robert. Collected works.
No.18, *see* Tinctoris, Johannes. Opera omnia.
No.19, *see* Frye, Walter. Opera omnia.
No.20, *see* Attaingnant, Pierre. Transcriptions of chansons for keyboard.
No.21, *see* Turin. Biblioteca Nazionale. Mss. (J.II.9). The Cypriot-French repertory.
No.22, *see* Agricola, Alexander. Opera omnia.
No.23, *see* Ghiselin-Verbonnet, Johannes. Opera omnia.
No.24, *see* Wert, Giaches de. Opera omnia.
No.25, *see* Festa, Costanzo. Opera omnia.
No.26, *see* Vicentino, Nicola. Collected works.
No.27, *see* Ludford, Nicholas. Collected works.
No.28, *see* Verdelot, Philippe. Opera omnia.
No.29, *see* Stäblein-Harder, Hanna, ed. Fourteenth-century mass music in France.
No.30, *see* Escurel, Jehannot de l'. Collected works.
No.31, *see* Arcadelt, Jacob. Opera omnia.
No.32, *see* Pisano, Bernardo. Opera omnia.
No.33, *see* Hothby, John. The musical works.
No.34, *see* Pipelare, Matthaeus. Opera omnia.
No.35, *see* Brassart, Johannes. Opera omnia.

CORPUS MUSICAE POPULARIS HUNGARICAE. Budapest, Akadémiai Kiadó, 1953– .
v.1– . (A Magyar Népzene Tára. A Magyar Tudományos Akadémia Megbizásából, Szerkesztette Béla Bartók és Zoltán Kodály).
Contents (in progress):
Vol.1. Kerényi, György, ed. Gyermekjátékok. II. Kiadás. 1957.
Vol.2. Kerényi, György, ed. Jeles napok. 1953.
Vol.3. Kiss, Lajos, ed. Lakodalom. 2v. 1955–1956.
Vol.4. Kerényi, György, ed. Párosítók. 1959.
Vol.5. Kiss, Lajos és Rajeczky, Benjamin, ed. Siratók. 1966.
*Vol.6. Popular customs.

CORPUS OF EARLY KEYBOARD MUSIC. Willi Apel, General editor. [Rome], American Institute of Musicology, 1963– .
v.1– .
Contents:
Vol.1. Keyboard music of the fourteenth and fifteenth centuries. Ed. by Willi Apel. 1963.
Vol.2. Facoli, Marco. Collected works. Ed. by Willi Apel. 1963.
Vol.3. Salvatore, Giovanni. Collected keyboard works. Ed. by Barton Hudson. 1964.

Vol.4. Praetorius, Hieronymus. Organ magnificats. On the eight tones. Ed. by Clare G. Rayner. 1963.
Vol.5, pt.1– . Pasquini, Bernardo. Collected works for keyboard. Ed. by Maurice Brooks Haynes. Pt.1–2, 1964; pt.3, 1967.
Vol.6, pt.1– . Johannes of Lublin. Tablature of keyboard music. Vol.1– . Ed. by John Reeves White. Pt.1, 1964; pt.2–3, 1966.
Vol.7. Storace, Bernardo. Selva di varie compositioni d'intavolatura per cimbalo ed organo. Ed. by Barton Hudson. 1965.
Vol.8. Keyboard dances from the earlier sixteenth century. Ed. by Daniel Heartz. 1965.
Vol.9. Antegnati, Costanzo. L'antegnata intavolatura de ricercari d'organo. 1608. Ed. by Willi Apel. 1965.
Vol.10, pt.1– . Keyboard music from Polish manuscripts. Ed. by Jerzy Gołos and Adam Sutkowski. Pt.1. Organ chorales by Nicolaus Hasse and Ewaldt. 1965; pt.2. Organ chorales by Heinrich Scheidemann and Franz Tunder. 1967; pt.3. Fantasias from Ms. 300 R. Vv, 123, Archiwum Wojewódzkie, Gdánsk. 1967; pt.4. Organ music by D. Cato, J. Podbielski, M. Wartecki, P. Zelechowski and anonymous composers. 1967.
Vol.11. Strozzi, Gregorio. Capricci da sonare cembali et organi. Ed. by Barton Hudson. 1967.
Vol.12. Pasquini, Ercole. Collected keyboard works. Ed. by W. Richard Shindle. 1966.

Vol.15. Rossi, Michelangelo. Works for keyboard. Ed. by John R. White. 1966.

Vol.24. Neapolitan keyboard composers, circa 1600. (Ippolito, Scipione Stella, Rinaldo, Fabrizio Fillimarino, Gian Domenico Montella, Ascanio Mayone, Francesco Lambardo, and Don Carlo Gesualdo). Ed. by Roland Jackson. 1967.

Vol.27. Mareschal, Samuel. Selected works. Ed. by Jean-Marc Bonhote. 1967.

Cosyn, Benjamin, 17th century. Virginal book, *see* Fuller-Maitland, John Alexander. Twenty-five pieces for keyed instruments from Benjamin Cosyn's Virginal book; Gibbons, Orlando. Ten pieces arranged for modern organ from the Virginal book of Benjamin Cosyn.

COUPERIN, FRANÇOIS, 1668–1733.
Oeuvres complètes de François Couperin. Publiées par un Groupe de Musicologues sous la direction de Maurice Cauchie . . . Paris, Éditions de l'Oiseau Lyre, 1932–33.
12v.
Contents:
Vol.1. Oeuvres didactiques.
Vol.2–5. Musique de clavecin I–IV.
Vol.6. Musique d'orgue.
Vol.7–10. Musique de chambre I–IV.
Vol.11–12. Musique vocale I–II.

COUPERIN, FRANÇOIS, 1668–1733.
. . . Pièces de clavecin composées par François Couperin. Revues par J. Brahms & F. Chrysander . . . London, Augener, Ltd., [pref.1888].
4v. (Augener's edition. No.8100).
Contents:
Book 1. Paris, 1713.
Book 2. Paris, 1716–1717.
Book 3. Paris, 1722.
Book 4. Paris, 1730.

COUPERIN, LOUIS, ca.1626–1661.
Oeuvres complètes de Louis Couperin. Publiées par Paul Brunold. Paris, Éditions de l'Oiseau Lyre, chez Louise B. M. Dyer, [cop.1936].
2p.L., 151p.
Scores.
". . . trois cents exemplaires sur papier 'Oiseau Lyre' . . ."
Contains 138 compositions, in most part for harpsichord, with a few organ pieces and works for viols.

COUPERIN, LOUIS, ca.1626–1661.
Pièces de clavecin. Publiées par Paul Brunold et revues d'après le Manuscrit Bauyn par Thurston Dart. Monaco, Éditions de l'Oiseau-Lyre, [1959].
4p.L., 135p., 1L.

COUSSEMAKER, EDMOND DE, 1805–1876. ed.
L'art harmonique aux XIIe et XIIIe siècles, par E. de Coussemaker . . . Paris, Durand, [etc.], 1865.
xii, 292p., 2L., cv p., 1L., 123, [14]p., 1L. front. (facsim. in colors).
"Tiré à trois cents exemplaires."
Contents:
Préface. Prolégomènes: I. Description du manuscrit de Montpellier. II. Des plus anciennes compositions harmoniques. III. Des plus anciennes documents sur la musique harmonique; 1.ptie. Musique harmonique; 2.ptie. Musiciens harmonistes; 3.ptie. Monuments: I. Compositions en notation originals. II. Traductions en notation moderne.

COUSSEMAKER, EDMOND DE, 1805–1876. ed.
Messe du XIIIe siècle, traduite en notation moderne et précédée d'une introduction par E. de Coussemaker. Tournai, Impr. de Malo et Levasseur, 1861.
8, 33p. facsim.
Appeared in: Bulletin de la Société Historique de Tournai, v.8; Bulletin de la Société Antiq. de Normandie, v.3.

Crappius, Andreas, ca.1542–1623. Works, *see* Das Erbe deutscher Musik. Zweite Reihe. Landschaftsdenkmale. Niedersachsen. Vol.2.

CREMA, JOAN MARIA DA.
. . . Intavolatura di liuto. Libro primo di recercari, canzon francese, motetti, madrigali, pass' e mezzi, saltarelli, trascritto in notazione

moderna da Giuseppe Gullino. Riveduto, corretto e interpretato da Reginald Smith Brindle. Con presentazione di Federico Ghisi. Firenzi, Edizioni Musicali ditta R. Maurri, 1955.
5p.L., 64p. illus.
La presente edizione consta di 300 esemplari numerati.

Cremona, Biblioteca Governativa e Civica di, *see* Instituta et monumenta.

CROTCH, WILLIAM, 1775–1847. ed.
Specimens of various styles of music referred to in a course of lectures read at Oxford and London and adapted to keyed instruments by William Crotch. London, Robt. Birchall for the author, 18? – .
3v.
The first volume of this music was issued by subscription shortly before 1807. The second is dated, in the preface, 1808, and the third came out a little later.
Contents (from *Grove's Dictionary of music and musicians,* 1916, Vol.4, p.630–31):
Vol.1.
Handel. Symphony to Sommi Dei.
—— Symphony to jealousy.
Gluck. Part of overture to Ifigénie.
Handel. Moses and the children of Israel.
—— How excellent (opening).
—— Who is like unto Thee.
—— He rebuked, and He led them.
—— Menuet in Berenice.
Scarlatti, D. Sonata for harpsichord. (D).
Gibbons, O. Sanctus.
Haydn. Allegretto, F. (Symphony).
Jewish music. 5 examples.
Irish music. 60 examples.
Scotch music. 76 examples.
Welsh music. 42 examples.
Old English music. 37 examples.
French national music. 20 examples.
Italian national music. 1 example.
Swiss national music. 2 examples.
German national music. 8 examples.
Spanish national music. 15 examples.
Polish national music. 4 examples.
Scandinavian national music. 5 examples.
Norwegian national music. 21 examples.
Danish national music. 1 example.
Russian music. 16 examples.
Turkish music. 10 examples.
Chinese music. 5 examples.
East Indian tunes. 32 examples.
Music of North America. 6 examples.

Vol.2.
Various styles.
Ambrosian chant, AD.384.
Guido. Plain chant. (1022).
—— Other harmonies.
Franco. Harmony.
Josquin des Prés. Chant.
Martin Luther. 1st Psalm O.V.
38th Psalm O.V.
81st Psalm O.V.
French Tune. 111th Psalm O.V.
Tye. I will exalt Thee.
Farrant. Lord, for Thy tender mercies' sake.
—— Gloria Patri.
Palestrina. Deposuit potentes.
—— We have heard with our ears.
Tallis. Gloria Patri.
Marenzio. "Dissi a l'amata mia."
Byrd, William. Bow thine ear.
—— Non nobis Domine.
Morley. Double chant.
Peri. Symphony, 3 flutes.
Cavalieri, E. del. Fate festa al signore.
Gibbons, O. Hosanna.
—— Almighty and everlasting.
—— God is gone up.
—— Gloria Patri.
—— The silver swan.
Dowland. Awake, sweet love.
Carissimi. S'in ch' havro spirto.
—— Movement from Amante che dite.
—— Hodie Simon Petrus.
—— Et ululantes; Jephtha.
—— Abiit ergo in montes.
—— Plorate filiae Israel.
—— Deum de Deo.
Scarlatti, A. Part of a cantata. Fortunati miei martire.
—— Aria. Perche geme O tortorella.
—— Aria. Voglio amar.
—— Aria. Non da piu peni O cara.
—— Aria. Che piu brami.
—— Aria. Il seno de mia vita.
—— Cantata. Son ferito.
—— Aria. Strada penare.
—— Aria. Il destin.
—— Aria. Illustre il sangue mio.
—— Aria. Con l'arte del mio cor.
—— Aria. Miei fidi a vendetta.
—— Aria. L'innocente diffendete.
—— Duet. Non son piu.
—— Arie. Due bellissime pupille.
—— Arie. Il mio figlio.
—— Part of Cantata. Che mesta horti sospiro.
Rossi, L. Motet. Domine quinque talenta.
Rogers. Anthem. Teach me, O Lord.
Purcell, T. Single chant.
Anon. Aria. Opri il fato.
—— Aria. No non amero.
—— Aria. Due vaghe pupille.
—— Aria. Del tuo cor tempri.
—— Aria. Se tu credi.
—— Tanto basti per far.
—— Aria. Bella bocca de cinabro.
—— Aria. Foglio lieve.
—— Aria. Tu fuggisti, O caro.
—— Aria. Crine vezzose.
—— Aria. Dolce amor mi dice spera.
—— Aria. Lusingami speranze.
—— Aria. Begl' occhi perdonatemi.
—— Aria. Col freddo suo velen.
—— Aria. Se il mio labbro.
—— Aria. Gia che amor.
—— Aria. Se versasti da tuoi lumi.
—— Aria. Fantasmi orribili.
—— Cantata. Taci O cruda.
—— Aria. Begl' occhi d'amore.
—— Aria. Migravit Juda.
Child. Aria. Gloria Patri.
Cesti. Aria. Dormi dormi ben mio.

Stradella. Part of cantata. Dite a lei.
—— Cantata. Se gelose, sei Tu.
—— Canzonet. Chi dira.
Rosa, Salv. Aria. Vado ben spesso.
Blow. Gloria Patri.
Creyghton. Anthem. I will arise.
Durante. Duet. Dormino l'aure estive.
Corelli, A. 7th Concerto.
—— Part of 2nd Sonata, Op.1.
—— Fugue from the 4th Sonata, Op.3.
—— Part of the 7th solo.
—— Part of the 11th solo.
Aldrich. Anthem. Out of the deep.
Purcell, H. Anthem. O God, Thou hast cast us out.
Gloria Patri (4 settings).
Purcell, H. Part of 1st Sonata. 1st set.
—— From 6th Sonata. 1st set.
—— From 9th Sonata. 2nd set.
—— In guilty night.
—— Overture to King Arthur.
—— Chaconne, before the play.
—— Brave souls to be renowned.
Croft. Gloria Patri.
Steffani. Qui diligit Mariam.
Leo. Dixit Dominus.
Pergolesi. Part of a mass.
—— Euridice, dove sei (Orfeo).
—— Gloria in excelsis.
Marcello. 4th Psalm.
—— 7th Psalm.
Graun. From Der Tod Jesu.
—— Te gloriosus (Te Deum).
Hasse. Overture to I. Pellegrini.
—— Le porte noi diserra. Pellegrini.
—— Pellegrini è l'uomo. Pellegrini.
Handel. Overture to Pastor fido.
—— Aria. Son confusa (Poro).
—— He is my God (Israel in Egypt).
—— Chorus. The listening crowd.
—— Chorus. May no rash intruder.
—— Double chorus. He gave them hailstones.

Vol.3.
Bach. Fugue (in E).
Tartini. No.2 of the 12 solos for the violin.
Vinci. Air. Pupillette vezzosette, from Ormisda.
—— Air. Infelice abbandonata.
Geminiani. Concerto 6, Op.3.
Ricciotti. Concerto 2.
Paradies. Part of Sonata 10.
Jommelli. Requiem.
—— Chorus. Santa speme (Passione).
Crispi. Sonata 3.
—— Part of Sonata 4.
Bach, C. P. E. Fantasia.
Bach, J. S. Concerto for a full band.
Gluck. Overture to Iphigénie en Aulide.
Chorus. Que d'attraits.
Grétry. Overture. Pierre le Grand.
Champigny. Overture. Don Quichotte.
Vogel. Overture. Toison d'or.
Vanhall. Part of Sonata 2.
Schobert. Part of Sonata 2, Op.9.
—— Minuet and trio, Sonata 1, Op.5.
Boccherini. Part of Quintet 3, Op.12.
Kozeluch. Sonata 3, Op.23.
Pleyel. Part of Quartet 1, 8th set.
—— Part of Quartet 6, Op.8.
Krumpholtz. Part of Sonata 1, Op.12.
Hullmandel. Part of Sonata 2, Op.11.
Clementi. Part of Sonata 2, Op.4.
—— Adagio from Op.11.
—— Part of Sonata 4, Op.12.
Mozart. Recordare from Requiem.
—— Benedictus from Requiem.
—— Overture. Le nozze di Figaro.
Haydn. Part of Quartet 3, Op.76.
—— Sinfonia, in E flat.

Cuyler, Louise Elvira, 1908– , ed. Choralis Constantinus. Book III, *see* Isaac, Heinrich. Choralis Constantinus. Book III.

CVETKO, DRAGOTIN. ed.
Skladatelji Gallus, Plautzius [in] Dolar, in njihovo delo. Les compositeurs Gallus, Plautzius [et] Dolar, et leur oeuvre. Ljubljana, Slovanska Matica, 1963.
p.1– .

The Cypriot-French repertory, *see* Turin. Biblioteca Nazionale. Mss. (J.II.9). The Cypriot-French repertory.

Da un codice Lauten-Buch del cinquecento, *see* Chilesotti, Oscar. Da un codice Lauten-Buch del cinquecento.

The dancing master, *see* Playford, John. The English dancing master.

Dania sonans, *see* Samfundet til Udgivelse af dansk Musik. Ser.IV. Dania sonans.

Danish Society for the Publication of Danish Music, *see* Samfundet til Udgivelse af dansk Musik.

Danzas del Santísimo Corpus Christi, *see* Comes, Juan Bautista. Danzas del Santísimo Corpus Christi.

DARGOMIZHSKY, ALEXANDER, 1813–1869.
Complete piano works. Moscow State Music Publishers, 1959– .
v.1– .
Title page in Russian.
Vol.1. 1959.

DARGOMIZHSKY, ALEXANDER, 1813–1869.
Complete romances and songs. Moscow, State Music Publishers, 1947.
2v.
Title page in Russian.

DARGOMIZHSKY, ALEXANDER, 1813–1869.
Complete vocal ensembles and choruses. Moscow, State Music Publishers, 1950.
1p.L., 288, [2]p. front. (port.).
Title page in Russian.

DAUNEY, WILLIAM, 1800–1843. ed.
Ancient Scottish melodies, from a manuscript of the reign of King James VI. With an

introductory enquiry illustrative of the history of the music of Scotland. By William Dauney . . . Edinburgh, Edinburgh Printing and Publishing Company, 1838.

3p.L., [v]-x, 390p. illus. (music). facsims. (music).

The manuscript in question is known as the Skene manuscript.

Music: p.217–51, 342–52.

Contents:

The list of contents of the manuscript, with those of Dauney, is taken from *Grove's Dictionary of music and musicians,* 1916, Vol.4, p.480.

The first row of figures shows the order in which they appear in the original; the second is that of Mr. Dauney's volume. The asterisks point out the duplicates, and the figures after the names show their place in the manuscript. The omitted tunes are marked by daggers. The double dagger in the first line of figures between 29 and 30 shows the place of a tune omitted in Mr. Dauney's list (*Grove's, loc. cit.*).

Part I. (24 leaves).
1. 38. Male. Simme.
2. 40. Doun in yon banke.
3. 76. O sillie soule alace.
4. 10. Long ere onie old man.
5. 63. The Spanishe ladie.
6. 8. My dearest sueate is fardest fra me.
7. 41. I long for your verginitie. *48.
8. † Hutcheson's Galziard.
9. 59. Pitt in an inche and mair of it.
10. † A French volt.
11. 69. Lady Elizabeth's maske.
12. 47. Kette Bairdie.
13. 85. Trumpeters currand. *50.
14. 60. Joy to the persone.
15. 68. Comedians maske.
16. 42. Aderneis lilt.
17. 78. Sommersetts maske.
18. 36. John Devesonnes pint of wine.
19. † Horreis Galziard. *45.
20. 64. Froggis Galziard.
21. 22. I cannot liue and want thee.
22. 20. I mett her in the medowe.
23. 9. Prettie well begunn man.
24. 67. Prince Henreis maske. Finis quod Skine.

Part II. (8 leaves).
25. † Lady wilt thou love me. (Fragment).
26. 37. The lass o Glasgowe.
27. 25. Shoe looks as shoe wold lett me.
28. 1. Alace yat I came owr the moor and left my love behind me. *42.
29. 34. Bone Jeane makis meikill of me.
‡ 27. Let never crueltie dishonour bewtie.
30. 17. My love she winns not her away.
31. 18. Jennet drinks no water.

Part III. (12 leaves).
32. 84. A Frenche.
33. * Scerdustis. 66.
34. * My Ladie Rothemayes lilt. 96.
35. 21. Blue breiks.
36. † Aberdeins currand.
37. * Scullione. 83.
38. 15. My Ladie Laudians lilt. *84.
39. 35. Lesleis lilt.
40. 29. The Keiking glasse.
41. 3. To dance about the Bailzeis dubb.
42. * I left my love behind me. 28.
43. 12. Alace this night yat we suld sinder.
44. 58. Pitt on your shirt (mail) on Monday. *65.
45. † Horreis Galziard. *19. (both omitted).
46. 23. I dowe not qunne (when) cold.
47. 33. My mistress blush is bonie.
48. * I long for her verginitie. 7.
49. † A saraband.
50. * Trumpeters currant (anonymous). 13.

Part IV. (12 leaves).
51. 70. What if a day.
52. 77. Floodis of tears.
53. 66. Nightingale.
54. 74. The willow trie.
55. 55. Marie me marie me quoth the bonie lass.
56. † My Lord Haye's currand.
57. † Jeane is best of onie.
58. 72. What high offences hes my fair love taken.
59. † Alman Nicholas.
60. 54. Currand Royal (Sir John Hopes currand).
61. 46. Hunter's carrier.
62. 6. Blue ribbenn at the bound rod.
63. 49. I serue a worthie ladie.

Part V. (22 leaves).
64. 80. Canaries.
65. * Pitt on your shirt (mail) on Monday. 44.
66. 71. Scerdustis. *33.
67. 50. She mowpit it coming owr the lie.
68. 24. Adew Dundie.
69. 31. Thrie sheips skinns.
70. 65. Chrichtons gud nicht.
71. 28. Alace I lie my alon I am lik to die awid.
72. * I love for love again. 98.
73. 73. Sincopas (Cinque-pace).
74. 56. Almane Delorne.
75. 51. Who learned you to dance and a towdle?
76. 19. Remember me at evenings.
77. † Love is a labour in vaine.
78. 26. I dare not vowe I love thee..
79. † My Lord Dingwalls currand.
80. 83. Brangill of Poictu.
81. 53. Pantalone.
82. 57. Ane Almane Moreiss.
83. 81. Scullione. *37.
84. * My Ladie Laudians lilt. 38.
85. † Queins currand.

Part VI. (10 leaves).
86. 61. Then wilt thou goe and leave me her.
87. 48. I will not goe to my bed till I suld die.
88. 13. The flowres of the forest.
89. 82. The fourth measur of the buffins.
90. 39. Shackle of hay.
91. 62. Com love lett us walk into the springe.
92. 45. Sa merrie as we have bein.
93. 11. Kilt thy coat Magge, cilt thy coat ti.
94. 75. Shipeherd saw thou not.
95. 2. Peggie is ouer ye sie wi ye souldier.
96. 4. Ladye Rothemayes lilt. *34.
97. 52. Omnia vincit amor.
98. 5. O love my love for love again. *72.
99. 14. Ostend.

100. † Sir John Moresons currant.
101. † Preludium.

Part VII. (14 leaves).
102. † Exercises.
103. 44. Gilcreichs lilt.
104. 43. Blew cappe.
105. 30. Lady Cassilis lilt.
106. * Blew breiks. 35.
107. 32. Post Ballangowne.
108. 7. John Andersonne my Jo.
109. 16. Good night and God be with you.
110. † A sarabande.
111. † Lik as the dum Solsequium.
112. † Come sueat love lett sorrow cease.
113. 79. Veze setta.
114. † A sarabande.

David, Hans Theodore, 1902– , ed. Music of the Moravians in America, *see* Music of the Moravians in America.

DAVID, JOHANN NEPOMUK, 1895– .
... Choralwerk. Choralvorspiele, Partiten, Toccaten, Fantasien, Passacaglien ... Für Orgel ... Leipzig, Breitkopf & Härtel, [cop. 1932–1953–].
v.1– .
Contents:
Vol.1. No.1–6.
Vol.2. No.7–15.
Vol.3. No.16–21.
Vol.4. No.22–27.
Vol.5. No.28–32.
Vol.6. No.33. Christus, der ist mein Leben. Ein Lehrstück für Orgel.
Vol.7. No.34–36. Für Orgel-Positiv.
Vol.8. No.37. Es sungen drei Engel ein süssen Gesang. Geistliches Konzert für Orgel.
Vol.9. No.38. Unüberwindlich starker Held, Sankt Michael. Partita.
Vol.10. No.39. Es ist ein Schnitter, heisst der Tod (Dies irae). Partita.
Vol.11. Da Jesus an dem Kreuze stund. 1952.
Vol.12. Lobt Gott, ihr frommen Christen. 1953.
Vol.13. (In preparation).

DAVISON, ARCHIBALD THOMPSON, 1883– . ed.
Historical anthology of music, by Archibald T. Davison and Willi Apel. Cambridge, Mass., Harvard University Press, 1946–50.
2v.
Contents:
Vol.1. Oriental, Medieval, and Renaissance music.
Vol.2. Baroque, Rococo, and Pre-classical music.

Dawes, Frank, ed. Schott's Anthology of early keyboard music, *see* Schott's anthology of early keyboard music.

DEHN, SIEGFRIED WILHELM, 1799–1858. ed.
Sammlung älterer Musik aus dem XVI. und XVII. Jahrhundert. Hrsg. von S. W. Dehn. Berlin, Crantz, [1837–40].
12 nos. in 1 v.
For 2 to 10 unaccompanied mixed voices in open score. German or Latin words.
Issued in parts. Each part has special title page.
Contains compositions by Ferrabosco, Florius, Gosswinus, Grillo, Guami, De las Infantus, Ingegnerius, O. de Lassus, F. de Lassus, Lechner, Meloni, De Monte, Morari, Palestrina, Porta, Praetorius, De Rore, and De Wert.

De la Halle, Adam, *see* Adam de la Halle.

De la Rue, Pierre, *see* La Rue, Pierre de.

De la Sablonara, Claudio, *see* La Sablonara, Claudio de.

DELIUS, FREDERICK, 1862–1934.
Complete works. Rev. and ed. by Sir Thomas Beecham. Issued in conjunction with the Delius Trust. London, New York, Hawkes & Son, sole selling agents: Boosey & Hawkes, [1951–].
v.1– .
Contents:
Vol.1. Appalachia.
Vol.2. Piano concerto.
Vol.3. Sea drift.

DELSARTE, FRANÇOIS, 1811–1871. ed.
Archives du chant. Paris, F. Delsarte, 1860–70.
25 Livraisons.
Contents:
Livraison I.
1. St. Ambroise. Hymne du IVme siècle.
2. Guedron. Musique de cour XVIme siècle.
3. Lully. Atys.
4. Lully. Phaéton.
5. Lully. Trio de la chambre du roi.
6. Chanson à danser XVIme siècle. Aime-moi bergère.
7. Chanson à danser. C'est l'amour même.
8. Rameau. Achante et Céphise.
9. Rameau. Castor et Pollux.
10. Rameau. Dardanus.
11. Destouche. Isse.
12. Gluck. Cythère Assiegée.
13. Gluck. Telemaco.

Livraison II.
1. St. Grégoire le Grand. Hymne du VIme siècle.
2. Jacques Mauduit. Chansonnette.
3. Chanson à danser XVme siècle. Margoton va à Piau.
4. Chanson à danser XVIIe siècle. Le bergère Nanette.
5. Chanson à danser XVIe siècle. Le beau laboureur.
6. Lully. Amadis.
7. Lully. Thésée.
8. Colasse. Les saisons ballet.
9. Rameau. Hypolite et Aricie.
10. Rameau. Dardanus.
11. Grétry. L'amant jaloux.
12. Gluck. Écho et Narcisse.

Livraison III.
1. Innocent III. Hymne du XIIme siècle.
2. Lully. Acis et Galatée.
3. Lully. Amadis.

4. Lully. Phaéton.
5. Même scène.
6. Rameau. Hyppolite et Aricie.
7. Rameau. Platée.
8. Musette XVIIme siècle. Languirai-je toujours.
9. Chanson à danser. On a le coeur sensible.
10. Destouches. Omphale.
11. J. B. Stuck. Florentin. N'attendez jamais le jour.
12. Gluck. L'arbre enchanté.
13. Gretry. Le tableau parlant.

Livraison IV.
1. St. Thomas d'Aquin. Hymne du XIIIème siècle.
2. Théodore de Beze. Chant calviniste du XVIme siècle.
3. Lully. Amadis. Scène.
4. Lully. Amadis. Même scène.
5. Lully. Phaéton.
6. Lambert. Chanson avec choeur.
7. Chanson à danser XVIIe siècle. Branle.
8. Chanson à danser. Liron lirette.
9. Chanson à danser XVIe siècle. J'ai le coeur tant rejoui.
10. Rameau. Les Indes galantes.
11. Rameau. Hyppolite et Aricie.
12. Grétry. Le rival confident.

Livraison V.
1. St. Thomas d'Aquin. Hymne du XIIIme siècle.
2. Lully. Atis.
3. Lully. Fragment de ballet.
4. Lully. Cariselli. Trio des pantalons. Tiré des Intermèdes de Molière.
5. Rameau. Hyppolite et Aricie.
6. Musette. Vous qui donnez de l'amour.
7. Chanson à danser. On est lié.
8. Gluck. Telemaco.
9. Mozart. Nozze di Figaro.
10. Grétry. Anacréon.
10 bis. De basse. Le même pour voix.

Livraison VI.
1. St. Ambroise. Hymne du IVme siècle.
2. Lully. Phaéton.
3. Lully. Cadmus.
4. Lully. Amadis.
5. Rameau. Les fêtes de Polimnie.
6. Gluck. Paride e Elena.
7. Grétry. Les deux avares.
8. Chanson à danser. Jeannette.
9. Chanson à danser. Climène.
10. Monsigny. Le roi et le fermier.

Livraison VII.
1. Antienne. Ave verum.
2. Lully. Alceste.
3. Lully. La fête de Versailles.
4. Lully. Proserpine.
5. Lully. Phaéton.
6. Carles Tessier. 1597. Chanson.
7. Le même à quatre voix.
8. Chanson bretonne. Ma mie.
9. Rameau. Dardanus.
10. Orlando de Lasso. XVIme siècle.
11. Durante. Vers–1740.
12. Gluck. Alceste. 1776.
13. Noël. XVme siècle.

Livraison VIII.
1. Stabat Mater. XIIIme siècle.
2. Lully. Armide.
3. Lully. Amadis.
4. Lully. Même air.
5. Lully. Roland.
6. Galuppi. Scène et air.
7. Brunette. J'ai perdu ma liberté.
8. Rameau. Dardanus.
9. Duny. La fée Urgèle.

Livraison IX.
1. Du Carême. Kyrie.
2. Lully. Amadis.
3. Le même pour voix de contralto.
4. Lully. Atys.
5. Rameau. Hyppolite et Aricie.
6. Le même pour voix de basse.
7. Chanson à danser. Amour tu n'entends pas.
8. Chanson à danser. Toure loure.
9. Le même pour voix de soprano.
10. Gluck. Iphigénie en Aulide.
11. Phylidor. Le sorcier.
12. Phylidor. Sancho Panca.

Livraison X.
1. St. Ambroise. Hymne du IVe siècle.
2. Lully. Thesée.
3. Lully. Acis et Galatée.
4. Rameau. Les Indes galantes.
5. Rebel et Francoeur. Ballet de la paix.
6. Passerat. La premier de Mai.
7. Chanson à danser. Le mot pour rire.
8. Duny. La fée Urgèle.
9. Gluck. Spermnestre.
10. Grétry. Anacréon.
11. Mozart. Nozze di Figaro.

Livraison XI.
1. St. Bernard. Antienne à la Ste. Vierge.
2. Lully. Amadis.
3. Lully. Persée.
4. Rameau. Les fêtes d'Hébée.
5. Rameau. Dardanus.
6. Royer. Zaïde.
7. Chanson spirituelle XVIme siècle.
8. Chant béarnais. Mon doux ami.
9. Chanson bretonne. Je vous aime tant.
10. Monsigny. On ne s'avise jamais de tout.
11. Philidor. Tom Jone.
12. Grétry. Éliska.

Livraison XII.
1. Regina coeli. XIe siècle.
2. Lully. Isis.
3. Rameau. Castor et Pollux.
4. Rameau. Hippolite et Aricie.
5. Jomelli. Scène et air.
6. Chanson à danser.
7. Monsigny. On ne s'avise jamais de tout.
8. Gluck. Iphigénie en Aulide.
9. Philidor. Le sorcier.
10. Duny. La fée Urgèle.

Livraison XIII.
1. Charlemagne. Veni Creator.
2. Lully. Roland.
3. Rameau. Castor et Pollux.
4. Chanson bretonne. Rossignolet.
5. Gluck. Armide.
6. Grétry. Zémire et Azor.
7. Pergolèse. La serva padrona.
8. Handel. Les fêtes d'Alexandre.

Livraison XIV.
1. David. In exitu.
2. Martin Luther. Choral.
3. Pergolèse. Fragments du Stabat; Quis est homo; Vidit suum; Quando corpus.
4. Mozart. Don Giovanni.
5. Mozart. Il flauto magico.

Livraison XV.
1. Beethoven. Gloria Patri.
2. Nanini. Stabat.
3. Lully. Armide.
4. Handel. Te Deum.
5. Rameau. Les Indes galantes.
6. Rameau. Castor et Pollux.
7. Gluck. Alceste.
8. Mozart. Il flauto magico.
9. Mozart. Il flauto magico.
10. Haydn. Orfeo e Euridici.
11. Duny. La clochette.

Livraison XVI.
1. Orlando de Lasso. XVIme siècle.
2. Chanson d'Orlando de Lasso. Fuyons tous d'amour le jeu.
3. Lully. Le triomphe de l'amour.
4. Lully. La naissance de Venus. Fragment de ballet.
5. Al. Scarlatti. Canzonetta.
6. Rameau. Dardanus.
7. Gluck. Telemaco.
8. Haydn. La création du monde.
9. Haydn. La création du monde.
10. Mozart. Il flauto magico.
11. Chanson à danser. Margoton allant au moulin.
12. Grétry. Zémire et Azor.

Livraison XVII.
1. D'Astorga. Stabat Mater.
2. Stradella. Aria di chiesa.
3. Lully. Armide.
4. Lully. Persée.
5. Gluck. Alceste.
6. Gluck. Armide.
7. Grétry. Anacréon.

Livraison XVIII.
1. Orlando de Lasso.
2. Mystères de N.S.J.C.
3. Les IV fins de l'homme.
4. Dieu admirable. Dans ses ouvrages.
5. Brunette.
6. Destouches. Omphale.
7. Gluck. Aria.
8. Pergolèse. Sicilienne.
9. Grétry. Anacréon.
10. Grétry. La suite du Comte d'Albert.
11. Dalayrac. Léon.
12. Paesiello. Proserpine.

Livraison XIX.
1. Josepho Octavio Pitoni. Missa pro defunctis.
2. Sophie. XVIIIme siècle.
3. Duny. Les moissonneurs.
4. Monsigny. Le roi et le fermier.
5. Sacchini. Renaud.
6. Grétry. La fausse magie.
7. Grétry. Richard Coeur de Lion.
8. Gluck. Iphigénie en Tauride.
9. Gluck. Iphigénie en Aulide.

Livraison XX.
1. Marcello. Fragment du psaume. Confitebor tibi Domine.
2. Chanson de Clément Marot. L'hermite.
3. Lully. Amadis.
4. Philidor. Le maréchal ferrant.
5. Grétry. Le huron.
6. Gluck. Iphigénie en Tauride.
7. Le même pour basse.
8. Gluck. Iphigénie en Tauride.

Livraison XXI.
1. Marcello. Parte di canto Greco. Fragment du Psaume 18.
2. Lully. Le triumphe de l'amour.
3. Rameau. Hippolite et Aricie.
4. Chanson à danser. Dans notre village.
5. Monsigny. Rose et Colas.
6. Monsigny. Rose et Colas.
7. Monsigny. Le déserteur.
8. Gluck. Écho et Narcisse.
9. Sacchini. Oedipe à Colone.

Livraison XXII.
1. Couperin. Explication du Salve Regina.
2. Lully. Phaéton.
3. Handel. La resurrezione.
4. Handel. La resurrezione.
5. Handel. Rinaldo.
6. Gluck. Iphigénie en Aulide.
7. Gluck. Armide.

Livraison XXIII.
1. Couperin. Cantique sur l'Ave maris stella.
2. Cantique XVIme siècle.
3. Chanson spirituelle du XVIme siècle. Coeur à vendre.
4. Chanson spirituelle du XVIme siècle.
5. Chanson à danser. Petit bossu.
6. Dalayrac. Nina.
7. Gluck. Orphée.

Livraison XXIV.
1. Rameau. Castor et Pollux.
2. Mozart. Nozze di Figaro.
3. Gluck. Alceste.
4. Gluck. Alceste.
5. Gluck. Écho et Narcisse.
6. Gluck. Iphigénie en Tauride.
7. Monsigny. Le déserteur.
8. Grétry. Richard Coeur de Lion.

Livraison XXV.
1. Grétry. La rosière de Salenci.
2. Gluck. Iphigénie en Aulide.
3. Gluck. Iphigénie en Tauride.
4. Gluck. Armide.
5. Gluck. Armide.
6. Gluck. Écho et Narcisse.
7. Dalayrac. Léon.

Supplement.
1. La mort s'avance. Cantique.
2. Clément Marot. Chanson.
3. Lully. Amadis.
4. Lully. Le carnaval. Ballet.
5. Handel. Rinaldo.
6. Gluck. Telemaco.
7. Grétry. Lucile.
8. Monsigny. Le cadi dupé.
9. Monsigny. On ne s'avise jamais de tout.
10. Mozart. L'enlèvement du Sérail.
11. Mozart. Le sorcier.
12. Mozart. Nozze di Figaro.
13. Mozart. Il flauto magico.

DENKMÄLER ALTPOLNISCHER MUSIK. Leitung: Dr. Adolf Chybiński. Warsaw, Polskie Wydawnictwo Muzyczne, 193? – . v.1– .

Also known under title, *Wydawnictwo Dawnej Muzyki Polskiej.*

A collection of sacred and secular instrumental and choral music by Polish composers of the 17th and 18th centuries, published by the Society for the Publication of Polish Music, under the editorship of Adolf Chybiński.

Contents:

Vol.1. Szarzyński, S. S. Sonata for 2 violins and organ. 2. ed. [cop.1958].
Vol.2. Mielczewski, M. Deus in nomine tuo, concerto for bass, 2 violins, bassoon (cello) and organ. 2. ed. [cop.1961].
Vol.3. Rózycki, J. Hymni ecclesiastici for 4-part mixed chorus.
Vol.4. Pekiel, B. Audite mortales, cantata for 2 sopranos, 2 altos, tenor, bass, 2 gambas (violas or cellos), violin (cello or bass) and organ. [1928].
Vol.5. Szarzyński, S. S. Pariendo non gravaris, concerto for tenor (or soprano), 2 violins, cello and organ. 2. ed. [cop.1960].
Vol.6. Mielczewski, M. Canzone for 2 violins, bassoon, cello and organ. 1930. [193?].
Vol.7. Gorczyski, G. G. Missa paschalis for mixed chorus. 2. ed. [1964].
Vol.8. Anonymous (unknown Polish composer, 16th century). Duma for string quartet. [193?].
Vol.9. Wachaw z Szamotul (Szamotulski). In Te Domine speravi, motet for mixed chorus.
Vol.10. Szarzyński, S. S. Jesu spes mea, concerto for soprano, 2 violins, cello and organ. [193?]. 2. ed. [cop.1959].
Vol.11. Jarzebski, A. Tamburitta for violin, viola, cello and harpsichord. [1932?]. 2. ed. [cop.1960].
Vol.12. Zieleński, M. Vox in Rama, communion for mixed chorus with or without organ. 2. ed. [1964].
Vol.13. Damian, P. S. P. Veni Consolator, concerto for soprano, "clarino" (trumpet, oboe, clarinet, viol) and organ. [193?].
Vol.14. Gorczyski, G. G. Illuxit sol, concerto for 2 sopranos, alto, tenor, bass (solo and choir), string orchestra and organ. 2. ed. [1962].
Vol.15. Jarzebski, A. Nova casa, concerto for 3 viols (cello) and harpsichord. [cop.1936].
Vol.16. Rózycki, J. H. Magnificamus in cantico, concerto for 2 sopranos, bass and organ. [1937].
Vol.17. Pekiel, B. Missa pulcherrima for S.A.T.B. a cappella. 2. ed. [cop.1961].
Vol.18. Podbielski, J. Praeludium for organ or harpsichord. [cop.1957].
Vol.19. Pekiel, B. 2 Latin carols for S.A.T.B. a cappella. 2. ed. [1964].
Vol.20. Chybiński, A. E. 36 Dances from the Tablature by Jan de Lublin.
Vol.21. Jarzebski, A. Chromatica, concerto a 3 (2 violins, cello and bass). [cop.1950].
Vol.22. Polak, J. Preludes, fantasies and dances for lute.
Vol.23. Dlugoraj, W. Fantasies and villanellas for lute.
Vol.24. Cato, Diomedes. Preludes, fantasies, dances and madrigals for lute.
Vol.25. Szarzyński, S. S. Ave Regina, antiphon for solo voice, 2 violins, viola di basso and continuo. [1953].
Vol.26. Szarzyński, S. S. Ad hymnos ad cantus, motets for A.T.B. 2 violins, viola alta, viola tenore, viola bassa and organ.
Vol.27. Jarzebski, A. Bentrovala, concerto for 2 violins, cello and continuo. 2. ed. [1964].
Vol.28. Wachaw of Szamotuly. Pieśni, for S.A.T.B. a cappella. [1956].
Vol.29. Mielczewski, M. Canzona a 2 for 2 violins, cello and harpsichord. 2. ed. [cop. 1962].
Vol.30. Pekiel, B. 40 Pieces for the lute.
Vol.31. Zieleński, M. Domus mea, communio for S.A.T.B. with organ. 2. ed. [cop.1958].
Vol.32. Jarzebski, A. Sentinella, concerto for 3 violins and harpsichord. [1956].
Vol.33. Szadek, T. Dies est laetitiae, Mass for T.T.B.B. a cappella.
Vol.34. Bazylik, C. Pieśni, for S.A.T.B. a cappella. [cop.1958].
Vol.35. Leopolita, M. Missa paschalis, for S.A.T.B. a cappella. [cop.1957].
Vol.36. Zienleński, M. Exiit sermo inter fratres and Si consurrexistis cum Christo, communiones for baritone and organ. [cop.1957].
Vol.37. Gorczyski, G. G. Laetatus sum. Concerto a 9 (soprano, alto, bass, 2 violins, 2 trumpets and basso continuo). [cop.1958].
Vol.38. Mielczewski, Marcin. Veni Domine. Concerto a 3 (2 sopranos and bass with basso continuo). [cop.1958].
Vol.39. Jarzebski, Adam. Canzoni for 4 instruments and basso continuo. [cop.1958].
Vol.40. Lilius, Franciszek. Jubilate Deo omnis terra. Motet a II (2 sopranos, alto, tenor, bass, 2 violins, viola, 2 trombones, bassoon, and basso continuo).

Vol.41. Zieleński, Mikolay. Justus ut palma florebit. Offertorium for 2 voices and organ.
Vol.42. Mielczewski, Marcin. Vesperae Dominicales. Soloists, chorus, instruments and continuo. [cop.1962].
Vol.43. Rohaczewski, A. Canzon a 4. Organ (or 4 string or wind instruments) and continuo. [cop.1960].
Vol.44. Rózycki, J. Exsultemus omnes. S.S.B. soli and continuo. [cop.1960].
Vol.45. Zieleński, M. Communiones. Soprano and organ. [cop.1961].
Vol.46. Rohaczewski, A. Crucifixus surrexit. Mixed chorus. [cop.1961].
Vol.47, 48, 49. Gomólka, Mikolaj. Melodies for Polish psalter. Mixed chorus. Book I, II, III. [cop.1963].
Vol.50. Szarzyński, S. S. Veni Sancte Spiritus. Soprano, 2 violins and continuo. [1963].
Vol.51. Jarzebski, A. Concerti a 2, No.1–4. 2 instruments and continuo. [1964].
Vol.52. Pekiel, B. 2 Patrem. Male or mixed chorus a cappella.

Denkmäler der japanischen Tonkunst, *see* Die geschichtlichen Denkmäler der japanischen Tonkunst.

DENKMÄLER DER MUSIK IN POMMERN: "Pommersche Meister des 16. bis 18. Jahrhunderts." [Hrsg. von H. Engel]. Kassel, Bärenreiter-Verlag, 1930–36.
5v.
Pub. by the Musikwissenschaftliches Seminar der Universität Greifswald.
Contents:
Heft 1. Vierdanck, J. Spielmusik für zwei und drei Violinen oder andere Melodieinstrumente. 1930.
Heft 2. Luetkeman, P. Fantasien über Kirchenmelodien der pommerschen Reformationzeit (1597); für fünf Melodieinstrumente. 1931.
Heft 3. Vierdanck, J. [Geistliche Concerte. Theil 1, Nr.21] . . . Weihnachtskonzert "Ich verkündige euch grosse Freude" aus "Erster Theil geistlicher Concerten" 1641; für zwei Singstimmen, zwei Melodieinstrumente und Generalbass. (Instrumental- und Vokalchor dazu ad lib.). 1932.
Heft 4. Vierdanck, J. [Geistliche Concerte. Theil 1, Nr.17] . . . Siehe, Wie fein und lieblich, aus "Erster Theil geistlicher Concerten" 1641; für zwei Singstimmen, zwei Melodieinstrumente und Generalbass. 1933.
Heft 5. Fromm, A. [Actus musicus de Divite et Lazaro. Full score]. . . . Vom reichen Manne und Lazaro. 1936.

DENKMÄLER DER TONKUNST; hrsg. von Fr. Chrysander. Bergedorf bei Hamburg, Expedition der Denkmäler, 1869–71.
6v.
Vol.1. Palestrina. Motecta festorum. (ed. Bellermann). 1869.
Vol.2. Carissimi. Werke. Abt.1: Oratorien. Jephte, Judicium Salomonis, Jonas, Baltazar. 1869.
Vol.3. Corelli. Werke. Theil 1: Sonaten für 2 Violinen, Violoncello, und Bass. (ed. Joachim). 1869.
Vol.4. Couperin. Pièces de Clavecin. (Also in: Augener's Reprint). (ed. Brahms). 1869.
Vol.5. Urio, F. A. Te Deum. (Also in: Suppl. to Händel's Werke. vol.2). 1871.
Vol.6. Steffani. Kammerduette.

DENKMÄLER DER TONKUNST IN ÖSTERREICH. Bd.[1]– . Wien, Österreichischer Bundesverlag, 1894–19– .
v.1– .
Vol. numbers irregular; Bd.[1–34/35], 1894–1910, issued without continuous vol. numbering: Bd.[1–13], 1894–99, called Bd.1–6; Bd.[14/15–34/35], 1900–1910, called Jahrg. 7–17; Bd.36–83, 1911–38, called also Jahrg. 18–45.
Vol.44a, 1914, pub. as the first no. of a projected Ser.2.
Vol.14–15, 34–35, 42–44, 51–52 are combined issues.
Added title page: Publikationen der Gesellschaft zur Herausgabe der Denkmäler der Tonkunst in Österreich.
"Herausgegeben mit Unterstützung der K. K. Ministeriums für Kultus und Unterreicht," 1894–1918; "mit Unterstützung des Deutschösterreichischen Staatsamtes für Inneres und Unterreicht." 1919.
Editors: 1894–1938, Guido Adler; 19? – , Erich Schenk.
Pub. by Artaria, 1894–1919; by Universal Edition, 1920– , vol.84– .
Contents:
Vol.1. (Jg.I/1). J. J. Fux. Masses, ed. J. E. Habert and G. A. Glossner. 1894.
Vol.2. (Jg.I/2). Georg Muffat. Florilegium primum for strings, ed. H. Rietsch. 1894.
Vol.3. (Jg.II/1). J. J. Fux. Motets, Part i, ed. J. E. Habert. 1895.
Vol.4. (Jg.II/2). Georg Muffat. Florilegium secundum, ed. H. Rietsch. 1895.
Vol.5. (Jg.III/1). Joh. Stadlmayr. Hymns, ed. J. E. Habert. 1896.
Vol.6. (Jg.III/2). Marcantonio Cesti. Pomo d'oro, Part i (Prolog and Act 1), ed. Guido Adler. 1896.
Vol.7. (Jg.III/3). Gottlieb Muffat. Componimenti musicali, ed. Guido Adler. 1896.
Vol.8. (Jg.IV/1). J. J. Froberger. Organ and clavier works, Part i, ed. Guido Adler. 1897.
Vol.9. (Jg.IV/2). Marcantonio Cesti. Pomo d'oro, Part ii (Act 2–5), ed. Guido Adler. 1897.
Vol.10. (Jg.V/1). Heinrich Isaac. Choralis Constantinus, Book i, ed. E. Bezecny and W. Rabl. 1898.
Vol.11. (Jg.V/2). Heinrich Biber. Violin sonatas, ed. Guido Adler. 1898.
Vol.12. (Jg.VI/1). Jacob Handl (Gallus). Opus musicum, motets, Part i, ed. E. Bezecny and J. Mantuani. 1899.
Vol.13. (Jg.VI/2). J. J. Froberger. Organ and

clavier works, Part ii, ed. Guido Adler. 1899.
Vol.14–15. (Jg.VII). 6 Trent codices. Mss. of vocal works of the 15th century, ed. Guido Adler and O. Koller. 1900.
Vol.16. (Jg.VIII/1). And. Hammerschmidt. Dialogi, Part i, ed. A. W. Schmidt. 1901.
Vol.17. (Jg.VIII/2). Joh. Pachelbel. 94 Compositions for organ, ed. H. Botstiber and M. Seiffert. 1901.
Vol.18. (Jg.IX/1). O. von Wolkenstein. Lieder, ed. J. Schatz and O. Koller. 1902.
Vol.19. (Jg.IX/2). J. J. Fux. Church sonatas and overtures (instrumental music, Part i), ed. Guido Adler. 1902.
Vol.20. (Jg.X/1). Orazio Benevoli. Festmesse and Hymnus, ed. Guido Adler. 1903.
Vol.21. (Jg.X/2). J. J. Froberger. Organ and clavier works, Part iii, ed. Guido Adler. 1903.
Vol.22. (Jg.XI/1). 6 Trent codices, 15th century compositions. II, ed. Guido Adler and O. Koller. 1904.
Vol.23. (Jg.XI/2). Georg Muffat. Auserlesene, etc. Instrumental music (1701), ed. Dr. Erwin Luntz. 1904.
Vol.24. (Jg.XII/1). Jacob Handl (Gallus). Opus musicum, Part ii, ed. E. Bezecny and J. Mantuani. 1905.
Vol.25. (Jg.XII/2). H. F. Biber. 16 Violin sonatas, ed. E. Luntz. 1905.
Vol.26. (Jg.XIII/1). Antonio Caldara. Church compositions, ed. E. Mandyczewski. 1906.
Vol.27. (Jg.XIII/2). Viennese clavier and organ compositions (2d half of 17th century), ed. H. Botstiber. (Alessandro Poglietti, Ferdinand Tobias Richter, Georg Reutter). 1906.
Vol.28. (Jg.XIV/1). Heinrich Isaac. Secular compositions, ed. J. Wolf. 1907.
Vol.29. (Jg.XIV/2). Michael Haydn. Instrumental works, ed. L. H. Perger. 1907.
Vol.30. (Jg.XV/1). Jacob Handl (Gallus). Opus musicum, Part iii, ed. E. Bezecny and J. Mantuani. 1908.
Vol.31. (Jg.XV/2).. Viennese instrumental music, about 1750, ed. K. Horwitz and K. Riedel. (Johann Adam Georg Reutter, Georg Christoph Wagenseil, Georg Matthias Monn, Matthaeus Schlöger, Josef Starzer). 1908.
Vol.32. (Jg.XVI/1). Heinrich Isaac. Choralis Constantinus, Book ii, ed. J. Wolf. 1909.
Vol.33. (Jg.XVI/2). J. G. Albrechtsberger. Instrumental works, ed. O. Kapp. 1909.
Vol.34–35. (Jg.XVII). J. J. Fux. Constanza e fortezza, ed. E. Wellesz. 1910.
Vol.36. (Jg.XVIII/1). Ignaz Umlauf. Die Bergknappen, ed. R. Haas. 1911.
Vol.37. (Jg.XVIII/2). Austrian lute music of the 16th century, ed. Adolf Koczirz. (Hans Judenkünig, Hans Newsidler, Simon Gintzler, Valentin Greff Bakfark). 1911.
Vol.38. (Jg.XIX/1). 6 Trent codices, 15th century compositions. III, ed. Guido Adler and others. 1912.
Vol.39. (Jg.XIX/2). Viennese instrumental music before 1750. (*see also* v.31 [Jg.XV/2]). (Matthias Georg Monn, Johann Christoph Mann). 1912.
Vol.40. (Jg.XX/1). Jacob Handl (Gallus). Opus musicum, Part iv, ed. E. Bezecny and J. Mantuani. 1913.
Vol.41. (Jg.XX/2). Minnesinger manuscripts, ed. H. Rietsch. 1913.
Vol.42–44. (Jg.XXI/1). F. L. Gassmann. "La contessina," ed. R. Haas. 1914.
Vol.44a. (Jg.XXI/2). C. W. Gluck. Orfeo e Euridice, ed. H. Abert. 1914.
Vol.45. (Jg.XXII). Michael Haydn. Masses, ed. A. M. Klafsky. 1915.
Vol.46. (Jg.XXIII/1). Antonio Draghi. Church music (masses; sequences; hymns). 1916.
Vol.47. (Jg.XXIII/2). J. J. Fux. Concentus musico-instrumentalis, ed. H. Rietsch. 1916.
Vol.48. (Jg.XXIV). Jacob Handl (Gallus). Opus musicum, Part v, ed. E. Bezecny and J. Mantuani. 1917.
Vol.49. (Jg.XXV/1). F. H. Biber. Missa Sti Henrici; Heinrich Schmelzer. Missa nuptialis; J. C. Kerll. Missa cujus tone, Missa a 3 cori. 1918.
Vol.50. (Jg.XXV/2). Austrian lute music between 1650 and 1720, ed. A. Koczirz. (J. G. Peyer, F. I. Hinterleithner, J. G. Weichenberger, Graf Logi, Wenzel Ludwig, Freiherr von Radolt, J. T. Herold, Jacques de Saint Luc, H. J. F. Biber, Georg Muffat, Graf Tallard, Rochus Berhandizki). (*see also* v.37 [Jg.XVIII/2]). 1918.
Vol.51–52. (Jg.XXVI). Jacob Handl (Gallus). Opus musicum, Part vi, ed. E. Bezecny and J. Mantuani. 1919.
Vol.53. (Jg.XXVII/1). 6 Trent codices, 15th century compositions. IV, ed. R. Ficker and A. Orel. 1920.
Vol.54. (Jg.XXVII/2). Viennese song from 1778 to 1791, ed. M. Ansion and I. Schlaffenberg. (J. A. Steffan, Carl Friberth, Leopold Hofmann, Johann Holzer, Wilhelm Pohl, Martin Ruprecht, Leopold Kozeluch, J. J. Grünwald, M. T. Paradis, J. C. Hackel, F. A. Hoffmeister). 1920.
Vol.55. (Jg.XXVIII/1). J. E. Eberlin. Der blutschwitzende Jesus, ed. R. Haas. 1921.
Vol.56. (Jg.XXVIII/2). Viennese dance music of the second half of the 17th century, ed. P. Nettl. (J. H. Schmelzer, J. J. Hoffer, Alexander Poglietti). 1921.
Vol.57. (Jg.XXIX/1). Claudio Monteverdi. I. Ritorno d'Ulisse in patria, ed. R. Haas. 1922.
Vol.58. (Jg.XXIX/2). Gottlieb Muffat. Works for organ and piano. 1922.
Vol.59. (Jg.XXX/1). Requiem of Christopher Straus, Franz Heinrich Biber, and Johann Caspar Kerll. 1923.
Vol.60. (Jg.XXX/2). C. W. Gluck. Don Juan (pantomime ballet), ed. R. Haas. 1923.
Vol.61. (Jg.XXXI). 7 Trent codices, 15th century compositions. V, ed. R. Ficher. 1924.
Vol.62. (Jg.XXXII/1). Michael Haydn. Church compositions, ed. A. M. Klafsky. 1925.
Vol.63. (Jg.XXXII/2). Johann Strauss, Jr. 3 Valses, ed. H. Gál. 1926.
Vol.64. (Jg.XXXIII/1). German arias from

comedies (1754–58), ed. R. Haas. 1926.
Vol.65. (Jg.XXXIII/2). Joseph Lanner. Ländler und Valses, ed. A. Orel. 1926.
Vol.66. (Jg.XXXIV). Johann Schenk. Der Dorfbarbier, ed. R. Haas. 1927.
Vol.67. (Jg.XXXV/1). E. A. Förster. Chamber music, ed. K. Weigl. 1928.
Vol.68. (Jg.XXXV/2). Johann Strauss, Sr. Valses, ed. H. Gál. 1928.
Vol.69. (Jg.XXXVI/1). Steffano Bernardi. Church music, ed. K. A. Rosenthal. 1929.
Vol.70. (Jg.XXXVI/2). Paul Peuerl and Isaac Posch. Instrumental and vocal compositions, ed. K. Geiringer. 1929.
Vol.71. (Jg.XXXVII/1). Neidhart von Reuenthal. Lieder, ed. W. Schmieder and E. Wiessner. 1930.
Vol.72. (Jg.XXXVII/2). The German Gesellschaftslief in Austria, 1480–1550, ed. L. Nowak, A. Koczirz, A. Pfalz. (Arnold von Bruck, Heinrich Finck, Wolfgang Grefinger, Paul Hofhaymer, Erasmus Lapicida, Stephan Mahu, Gregor Peschin, Johann Sies, Thomas Stoltzer). 1930.
Vol.73. (Jg.XXXVIII/1). Blasius Amon. Church music, ed. P. C . Huigens. 1931.
Vol.74. (Jg.XXXVIII/2). Josef Strauss. 3 Valses, ed. H. Botstiber. 1931.
Vol.75. (Jg.XXXIX). Antonio Caldara. Chamber music, ed. E. Mandyczewski. 1932.
Vol.76. (Jg.XL). 7 Trent codices. Mss. of vocal works of the 14th and 15th centuries. VI, ed. R. Ficker. 1933.
Vol.77. (Jg.XLI). Italian musicians, 1567–1625. Works dedicated to and written for the Imperial court, ed. A. Einstein. (Filippo di Monte, Francesco Portinaro, Andrea Gabrieli, Annibale Padovano, Matteo Flecha, Carlo Luyton, Lamberto de Sayve, Giacomo Regnart, Francesco Rovigo, Alessandro Orologio, Camillo Zanotti, Giovanni Priuli). 1934.
Vol.78. (Jg.XLII/1). Jacob Handl (Gallus). 6 Masses, ed. P. A. Pisk. 1935.
Vol.79. (Jg.XLII/2). The Wiener Lied 1792–1815, ed. H. Maschek, H. Kraus. (Anton Teyber, Anton Eberl, Emilian Gottfried von Jacquin, Moriz von Dietrichstein, Johann Fuss, Sigmund Neukomm, Niklas von Krufft, Conradin Kreutzer). 1935.
Vol.80. (Jg.XLIII/1). Salzburgian church composers, C. Biber, M. S. Biechteler, J. E. Eberlin, A. C. Adlgasser; ed. K. A. Rosenthal, C. Schneider. 1936.
Vol.81. (Jg.XLIII/2). Carl Ditters von Dittersdorf. Instrumental works, ed. V. Luithlen. 1936.
Vol.82. (Jg.XLIV). C. W. Gluck. L'innocenza giustificata. Festa teatrale 1755, ed. A. Einstein. 1937.
Vol.83. (Jg.XLV). F. L. Gassmann. Church music, ed. F. Kosch. 1938.
Vol.84. Viennese lute music in the 18th century. 1942.
Vol.85. J. J. Fux. Works for keyboard instruments, ed. E. Schenk. 1947.
Vol.86. Tiroler instrumental music in the 18th century, ed. Walter Senn. (Georg Paul Falk, Johann Elias de Sylva, Franz Sebastian Haindl, Nonnosus Madlseder, Stefan Paluselli). 1949.
Vol.87. Nicolaus Zangius. Sacred and secular songs, ed. H. Sachs. 1951.
Vol.88. Georg Reutter. Church compositions, ed. P. N. Hofer. 1952.
Vol.89. Georg Muffat. Armonico tributo 1682. Exquisitioris harmoniae instrumentalis gravi-jucundae selectus primus 1701, ed. E. Schenk. 1953.
Vol.90. Netherland and Italian musicians of the Graz court orchestra of Karl II, 1564–1590, ed. H. Federhofer. (Johannes de Cleve, Lambert de Sayve, Jacob von Brouck, Annibale Padovano, Simone Gatto, Francesco Rovigo, Giovanni Battista Galeno, Pietro Antonio Bianco, Matthia Ferrabosco). 1954.
Vol.91. Antonio Caldara. Dafne, ed. C. Schneider. 1955.
Vol.92. H. I. F. Biber. Harmonia artificiosa-ariosa, ed. P. Nettl and F. Reidinger. 1956.
Vol.93. J. H. Schmelzer. Violin sonatas, ed. E. Schenk. 1958.
Vol.94/95. Jacob Handl (Gallus). 5 Masses in 7 and 8 parts, ed. P. A. Pisk. 1959.
Vol.96. H. I. F. Biber. Mensa sonora. Seu musica instrumentalis. Sonatis aliquot liberius sonantibus ad mensam (1680), ed. E. Schenk. 1960.
Vol.97. H. I. F. Biber. Fidicinium sacro-profanum. Tam choro, quam foro fluribus fidibus concinnatum et concini aptum (1683), ed. E. Schenk. 1960.
Vol.98. Jacobus Vaet. Complete works. I. Motets. Vol.1, ed. M. Steinhardt. 1961.
Vol.99. Arnold von Bruck. Complete collection of Latin motets and other unedited works, ed. O. Wessely. 1961.
Vol.100. Jacobus Vaet. Complete works. II. Motets. Vol.2, ed. M. Steinhardt. 1962.
Vol.101/102. Sacred solo motets of the 18th century, ed. Camillo Schoenbaum (Marc' Antonio Ziani, Antonio Caldara, Francesco Conti, J. J. Fux). 1962.
Vol.103/104. Jacobus Vaet. Complete works. III. Motets. Vol.3, ed. M. Steinhardt. 1963.
Vol.105. J. H. Schmelzer. Duodena selectarum sonatarum (1659), ed. E. Schenk. 1963.
Vol.106/107. H. I. F. Biber. Sonatae tam aris quam aulis servientes. 1963.
Vol.108/109. Jacobus Vaet. Complete works. IV. Masses. Vol.1, ed. M. Steinhardt. 1964.
Vol.110. Tiburtio Massaino (ca.1550–ca.1609). Liber primus cantionum ecclesiasticarium (1592); Drei instrumentalcanzonen (1608), ed. Raffaello Monterosso. 1964.
Vol.111/112. J. H. Schmelzer (ca.1620–1680). Sacro-profanus concentus musices fidium aliorumque instrumentorum (1662), ed. Erich Schenk. 1965.
Vol.113/114. Jacobus Vaet. Complete works. V. Masses. Vol.2, ed. Milton Steinhardt. 1965.
Vol.115. Franz Mathias Techelmann (ca.1649–1714). Suiten für Tasteninstrumente von und um Franz Mathias Techelmann. ed. Herwig Knaus. 1966.

DENKMÄLER DER TONKUNST IN ÖSTERREICH. Reprint. Unter Leitung von Guido Adler. Graz, Akademische Druck- und Verlagsanstalt, 1959– .
v.1– .
Reprint edition of earlier volumes. In progress.

DENKMÄLER DER TONKUNST IN WÜRTTEMBERG, hrsg. vom Musik-Institut der Universität Tübingen unter Leitung von Prof. Dr. Karl Hasse.
2v.
Heft 1, 2 publ. as Chorwerk, Heft 21, 29 respectively, 1933–34.
Contents:
Heft 1. Finck, Heinrich. Missa in summis.
Heft 2. Schöffer, Peter. Fünfzehn deutsche Lieder.

DENKMÄLER DEUTSCHER TONKUNST. [1. Folge]. Hrsg. von der Musikgeschichtlichen Kommission . . . Bd.1–65. Leipzig, Breitkopf & Härtel, 1892–1931.
65v.
Called Erste Folge from Bd.4, 1900.
1894–1900, hrsg. von eine von der Königlich Preussischen Regierung Berufenen Commission; 1901–1931, hrsg. von der Musikgeschichtlichen Kommission.
Editors: 1900–1911, Freiherr von Liliencron; 1912–18, Hermann Kretzschmar; 1927, Hermann Abert; 1928–31, Arnold Schering.
Superseded by Das Erbe deutscher Musik.
Contents:
Vol.1. Samuel Scheidt. Tabulatura nova for organ, etc., ed. M. Seiffert. 1892.
Vol.2. H. L. Hassler. Cantiones sacrae, ed. H. Gehrmann. 1894.
Vol.3. Franz Tunder. Solo cantatas and choral works, ed. M. Seiffert. 1900.
Vol.4. Johann Kuhnau. Clavier works, ed. K. Päsler. 1901.
Vol.5. J. R. Ahle. Selected vocal works, ed. J. Wolf. 1901.
Vol.6. Solo cantatas and choral works with instrumental accompaniment, ed. M. Seiffert. (Matthias Weckmann, Christoph Bernhard). 1901.
Vol.7. H. L. Hassler. Masses, ed. J. Auer. 1902.
Vol.8. Ignaz Holzbauer. Günther von Schwarzburg, opera in 3 acts, Part i, ed. J. H. Kretzschmar. 1902.
Vol.9. Ignaz Holzbauer. Günther von Schwarzburg, opera in 3 acts, Part ii, ed. J. H. Kretzschmar. 1902.
Vol.10. J. C. F. Fischer. Journal des printemps, and J. A. Schmierer. Zodiacus, ed. F. von Werra. 1902.
Vol.11. Dietrich Buxtehude. Sonatas for violin, violoncello, and harpsichord, ed. C. Stiehl. 1903.
Vol.12. Heinrich Albert. Arien, Part i, ed. E. Bernoulli. 1903.
Vol.13. Heinrich Albert. Arien, Part ii, ed. E. Bernoulli. 1904.
Vol.14. Dietrich Buxtehude. Abendmusiken and church cantatas, ed. M. Seiffert. 1903.
Vol.15. C. H. Graun. Montezuma, ed. A. Mayer-Reinach. 1904.
Vol.16. Selected instrumental compositions of Melchoir Franck and Valentin Haussmann, ed. F. Bölsche. 1904.
Vol.17. Passion-settings by Johann Sebastiani and Johann Theile, ed. Friedrich Zelle. 1904.
Vol.18. Johann Rosenmüller. Sonate da camera, ed. Karl Nef. 1904.
Vol.19. Adam Krieger. Arien, ed. A. Heuss. 1905.
Vol.20. J. A. Hasse. Conversione di Sant' Agostino, ed. Arnold Schering. 1905.
Vol.21–22. F. W. Zachau. Selected compositions, ed. M. Seiffert. 1905.
Vol.23. Hieronymus Praetorius. Selected compositions, ed. H. Leichtentritt. 1905.
Vol.24–25. H. L. Hassler. Sacri concentus, ed. J. Auer. 1906.
Vol.26–27. J. G. Walther. Complete organ works, ed. H. Leichtentritt. 1906.
Vol.28. G. P. Telemann. Tag des Gerichte, and Ino (K. W. Ramler), ed. M. Schneider. 1907.
Vol.29–30. Instrumental concertos by various German masters, ed. A. Schering. (J. G. Pisendel, J. A. Hasse, C. P. E. Bach, G. P. Telemann, Chr. Graupner, G. H. Stölzel, K. F. Hurlebusch). 1905.
Vol.31. Philippus Dulichius. Centuriae (1607), ed. R. Schwartz. 1907.
Vol.32–33. Nicolo Jommelli. Fetonte, ed. H. Abert. 1907.
Vol.34. New German sacred songs (1544), ed. J. Wolf. 1908.
Vol.35–36. Sperontes. Singende Muse an der Pleisse, ed. E. Buhle. 1909.
Vol.37–38. Reinhard Keiser. Krösus and selection from L'inganno felice, ed. M. Schneider. 1912.
Vol.39. Johann Schobert. Selected works, ed. H. Riemann. 1909.
Vol.40. Andreas Hammerschmidt. Selected works, ed. H. Leichtentritt. 1910.
Vol.41. Philippus Dulichius. Centuriae (*see* v.31), ed. R. Schwartz. 1907.
Vol.42. Songs of Ernst Bach and Valentin Herbing, ed. H. Kretzschmar. 1910.
Vol.43–44. Ballets of Florian Deller and J. J. Rudolph, ed. H. Abert. 1913.
Vol.45. Heinrich Elmenhorst. Geistliche Lieder, composed by J. W. Franck, Georg Böhm, and P. L. Wockenfuss, ed. J. Kromolicki and W. Krabbe. 1911.
Vol.46–47. P. H. Erlebach. Harmonische Freude, ed. O. Kinkeldey. 1914.
Vol.48. J. E. Bach. Passion oratorio, ed. J. Kromolicki. 1914.
Vol.49–50. Thuringian motets of the first half of the 18th century, from Ms.13661 of the Königsberger Universitätsbibliothek, ed. M. Seiffert. 1915.
Vol.51–52. Christoph Graupner. Selected cantatas, ed. F. Noack. 1926.
Vol.53–54. J. P. Krieger. Selected church compositions, ed. M. Seiffert. 1916.
Vol.55. Carlo Pallavicino. La Gerusalemme liberata, ed. H. Abert. 1916.
Vol.56. J. C. F. Bach. Die kindheit Jesu and

Die auferweckung Lazarus, ed. G. Schünemann. 1917.
Vol.57. Odes and songs of G. P. Telemann and J. V. Görner, ed. W. Krabbe. 1917.
Vol.58–59. Selected church cantatas, ed. A. Schering. (Sebastian Knüpfer, Johann Schelle, Johann Kuhnau). 1918.
Vol.60. Antonio Lotti. Masses, ed. H. Müller. 1930.
Vol.61–62. G. P. Telemann. Tafelmusik, ed. M. Seiffert. 1927.
Vol.63. Johann Pezel. Turnmusiken, ed. A. Schering. 1928.
Vol.64. Georg Benda. Der Jahrmarkt, ed. T. W. Werner. 1930.
Vol.65. Thomas Stoltzer. Complete collection of Latin hymns and psalms, ed. H. Albrecht and O. Gombosi. 1931.

DENKMÄLER DEUTSCHER TONKUNST.
[1. Folge]. Reprint. Hrsg. von der Musikgeschichtlichen Kommission unter Leitung von Prof. Dr. Arnold Schering. In Neuauflage hrsg. und kritisch revidiert von Hans Joachim Moser. Wiesbaden, Breitkopf & Härtel; Graz, Akademische Druck- und Verlagsanstalt, 1957–61.
65v. and 2 supp.
Supplement, vol.51/52: Noack, Friedrich. Christoph Graupner als Kirchenkomponist. 1960.
Supplement, vol.61/62: Seiffert, Max. Georg Philipp Telemann (1681–1767). Musique de table. 1960.

DENKMÄLER DEUTSCHER TONKUNST.
[2. Folge]. Denkmäler der Tonkunst in Bayern. Jahrg.1–38. Braunschweig, H. Litolff's Verlag, [etc., etc.], 1900–1938.
38v. illus., plates, ports., facsims.
Vols.37–38, 1936–38, issued as Das Erbe deutscher Musik. 2. Reihe. Landschaftsdenkmäler: Bayern, Bd.1–2.
Several volumes are issued in combined form.
"Veröffentlicht von der Gesellschaft zur herausgabe von Denkmälern der Tonkunst in Bayern."
Title varies: v.1–36, 1900–1931, Denkmäler deutscher Tonkunst. 2. Folge: Denkmäler der Tonkunst in Bayern; v.37–38, 1936–38, Denkmäler der Tonkunst in Bayern.
Editor: 1900– . Adolf Sandberger.
Imprint varies: v.1–31, Leipzig, Breitkopf & Härtel, 1900–1920; v.32–36, Augsburg, Dr. Benno Filser Verlag G.m.b.H. [etc.], 1924–31.
Contents:
Vol.1. E. F. Dall'Abaco. Selected works, Part i, ed. A. Sandberger. 1900.
Vol.2. (i). Joh. and W. H. Pachelbel. Clavier works, ed. M. Seiffert. 1901.
Vol.2. (ii). J. K. Kerll. Selected works, Part i, ed. A. Sandberger.
Vol.3. (i). Symphonies of the Mannheim School. (J. W. A. Stamitz, F. X. Richter, Anton Filtz). ed. H. Riemann. 1902.
Vol.3. (ii). Ludwig Senfl. Works, Vol.1, ed. T. Kroyer. 1903.
Vol.4. (i). Organ works of Johann Pachelbel, with some by W. H. Pachelbel, ed. M. Seiffert. 1903.
Vol.4. (ii). Selected works of Christian Erbach (i) and compositions of H. L. Hassler (i), ed. von Werra. 1903.
Vol.5. 2v. Works of H. L. Hassler (ii) and annotations, etc., by A. Sandberger. 1904.
Vol.6. (i). Geistliche Konzert and church cantatas by Nuremberg masters of the 17th century, ed. M. Seiffert. 1905.
Vol.6. (ii). Agostino Steffani. Selected compositions, ed. A. Einstein and A. Sandberger.
Vol.7. (i). Johann Staden. Selected works, ed. E. Schmitz. 1906.
Vol.7. (ii). Symphonies of the Mannheim School (i), ed. H. Riemann.
Vol.8. (i). Johann Staden. Selected works, ed. E. Schmitz.
Vol.8. (ii). Symphonies of the Mannheim School (ii), ed. H. Riemann. 1907.
Vol.9. (i). E. F. Dall'Abaco. Selected works, Part ii, ed. A. Sandberger. 1908.
Vol.9. (ii). Leopold Mozart. Selected works, ed. M. Seiffert.
Vol.10. (i). Gregor Aichinger. Selected works, ed. T. Kroyer.
Vol.10. (ii). Adam Gumpeltzhaimer. Selected works, ed. Mayer.
Vol.11. (i). H. L. Hassler. Works, Part iii, ed. Schwartz.
Vol.11. (ii). Agostino Steffani. Alarico, and bibliography of operas, ed. H. Riemann.
Vol.12. (i). Agostino Steffani. Selected operas, ed. H. Riemann.
Vol.12. (ii). F. A. Rössler (Rosetti). Symphonies, ed. Kaul.
Vol.13. J. E. Kindermann. Selected works, ed. Schneider.
Vol.14. (i). Tommaso Traetta. Selected works, ed. Goldschmidt. 1916.
Vol.14. (ii). C. W. Gluck. Nozze d'Ercole e d'Ebe, ed. Abert. 1914.
Vol.15–16. Chamber music of Mannheim, 18th century, ed. H. Riemann.
Vol.17. Tommaso Traetta. Selected works, Part ii, ed. Goldschmidt. 1916.
Vol.18. Selected works of Johann Krieger, F. X. A. Murschhauser, J. P. Krieger, ed. M. Seiffert. 1917.
Vol.19–20. Pietro Torri. Selected works, ed. Junker. 1920.
Vol.21–24. J. E. Kindermann. Selected works, Part ii, ed. F. Schreiber. 1924.
Vol.25. F. A. Rössler (Rosetti). Selected works, Part ii. Orchestra and chamber music, ed. O. Kaul.
Vol.26. Jacobus de Kerle. Selected works, Part i. Special pieces for the Council of Trent, ed. O. Ursprung. 1926.
Vol.27–28. J. C. Pez. Selected works, ed. B. A. Wallner. 1928.
Vol.29–30. Andreas Raselius. Sacred songs, ed. L. Roselius. 1931.
Vol.31–36. Das Erbe deutscher Musik.
Vol.37–38. Das Erbe deutscher Musik. 2. Reihe. Bayern. v.1–2. 1936, 1938.

DENKMÄLER DEUTSCHER TONKUNST.
[2. Folge]. Reprint edition planned.

DENKMÄLER RHEINISCHER MUSIK. Hrsg. von der Arbeitsgemeinschaft für rheinische Musikgeschichte. Düsseldorf, Musikverlag L. Schwann, 1951– .
v.1– .
Imprint of Vol.2: Köln und Krefeld, Staufen-Verlag, 1951.
Contents:
Vol.1. Sinfonien um Beethoven: Ferdinand Graf von Waldstein. Sinfonie in D; Neefe, Christian Gottlob. Partita in Es. Hrsg. von Ludwig Schiedermair. 1951.
Vol.2. Mies, Paul. Das kölnische Volks- und Karnevalslied; ein Beitrag zur Kulturgeschichte der Stadt Köln von 1823 bis 1923 im Lichte des Humors. 1951.
Vol.3. Rinteleus, Cunradus Hagius. Die Psalmen Davids nach Kaspar Ulenberg. (Köln, 1582). Hrsg. von Johannes Overath. [cop.1955].
Vol.4. Liederbuch der Anna von Köln (um 1500). Eingeleitet und hrsg. von Walter Salmen und Johannes Koepp. 1954.
Vol.5. Leibl, Carl. Festkantate zur Feier der Grundsteinlegung für den Fortbau der Kölner Doms 1842. Hrsg. von Paul Mies. 1955.
Vol.6. Burch, Cornelius. Geistliche Konzerte zu vier Stimmen, 1630. Hrsg. von Karlheinz Höfer. 1957.
Vol.7. Rosier, Carl. Ausgewählte Instrumentalwerke. Hrsg. von Ursel Niemöller. 1957.
Vol.8. Steffani, Agostino. Tassilone. Hrsg. von Gerhard Croll. 1958.
Vol.9. Burch, Cornelius. Geistliche Konzerte zu vier Stimmen, 1630. Zweite Folge. 1961.
Vol.10. Neefe, Christian Gottlob. Zwölf Klavier-Sonaten. (Nr.I–VI). Mit Nachwort und kritischem Bericht. Hrsg. von Walter Thoene. 1961.

DENKMÄLER THURINGISCHER MUSIK. Kassel, Bärenreiter-Verlag, 1934–36.
2v.
Contents:
Heft 1. Vulpius. Passions-Music. 1613. 1934.
Heft 2. Stölzel, G. H. Enharmonische Sonate. Für Pianoforte, hrsg. von E. W. Böhme. 1936.

DEPRÈS, JOSQUIN, d.1521.
Werken. Uitgegeven door A. Smijers. Amsterdam, G. Alsbach; Leipzig, F. Kistner and C. F. W. Siegel, 1925– .
v.1– . port., facsims.
Issued in parts.
At head of title: Vereeniging voor Nederlandsche Muziekgeschiedenis.
Editor of later volumes: Dr. Myroslaw Antonowycz.
Contents (in progress):
Vol.1. Klaagliederen op den dood van Josquin. Vinders, H. O mors benedictus. Musae Jovis. Gombert, H. Musae Jovis.
Vol.2. Motetten. Bundel I.
1. Ave Maria . . . Virgo serena. 4 voc.
1a. Ave Maria . . . Virgo serena. 6 voc.
2. Ave Maria . . . Benedicta Tu. 4 voc.
3. Mittit ad Virginem. 4 voc.
4. Christum ducem. 4 voc.
5. O admirabile commercium. 4 voc.
6. Quando natus es. 4 voc.
7. Rubum quem viderat Moyses. 4 voc.
8. Germinavit radix Jesse. 4 voc.
9. Ecce Maria genuit. 4 voc.
Vol.3. Wereldlijke werken. I.
1. Cueur langoreulx. A 5.
2. Vous ne l'aurez pas. A 6.
3. Parfons regretz. A 5.
4. Plaine de dueil. A 5.
5. Regrets sans fin. A 6.
6. Incessament. A 5.
7. Plusieurs regrets. A 5.
8. N'esse pas ung grant desplaisir. A 5.
8a. Responce: Si vous n'avez aultre desir. A 6. (Not by Deprès; by Jo. le Brung).
9. En non saichant. A 5.
10. Pour souhaitter. A 6.
11. Je me complains. A 5.
12. Se congié prens. A 6.
Vol.4. Motetten. Bundel II.
10. O Domine Jesu Christie. 4 voc.
11. Qui velatus facie fuisti. 4 vox.
12. Ave verum Corpus. 2 et 3 voc.
13. Domine, non secundum peccata. 2 et 4 voc.
14. Tu solis, qui facis mirabilia. 4 voc.
Vol.5. Wereldlijke werken. II.
13. Tenez moy en voz bras. A 6.
14. Allégez moy. A 6.
15. Faulte d'argent. A 5.
16. Vous l'arez, s'il vous plaist. A 6.
17. Petite camusette. A 6.
18. Douleur me bat. A 5.
19. Ma bouche rit. A 6.
20. Basies moy. A 6.
20a. Basiez moy. A 4.
21. Nimphes, nappés. A 6.
22. La déploration de Johan Okeghem. A 5.
23. Du mien amant. A 5.
Vol.6. Motetten. Bundel III.
15. Liber generationis Jesu Christi. 4 voc.
16. Factum est autem. 4 voc.
17. Missus est Gabriel angelus. 4 voc.
18. O bone et dulcis Domine Jesu. 4 voc.
19. Magnus es Tu, Domine. 4 voc.
20. Planxit autem David. 4 voc.
Vol.7. Motetten. Bundel IV.
21. Alma redemptoris Mater. 4 voc. Ave Regina coelorum. 4 voc.
22. Ut Phoebi radiis. 4 voc.
23. Gaude, Virgo, Mater Christi. 4 voc.
24. Valtum Tuum deprecabuntur. 4 voc.
Vol.8. Wereldlijke Werken. III.
24. Mille regretz. A 4.
24a. Tylman Susato. Les miens aussi brief. A 4.
25. L'amye a tous. A 5.
26. Cent mille regretz. A 5.
27. Incessament mon povre cueur lamente. A 5.
28. Cueurs desolez par toute nation. A 5.
29. Plus nulz regrets. A 4.
30. Plus n'estes ma maistresse. A 4.

31. Je ne me puis tenir d'aimer. A 5.
32. Cueurs desolez par toutes nations. A 4.
33. J'ay bien cause de lamenter. A 6.
34. Mi larés vous tousjours languir. A 5.

Vol.9. Motetten. Bundel V.
25. Virgo prudentissima. 4 voc.
26. Victimae Paschali laudes. 4 voc.
27. Illibata Dei Virgo nutrix. 5 voc.
28. Homo quidam fecit coenam magnam. 5 voc.
29. Requiem. 5 voc.

Aahangsel.
1. Ludovicus Senfl. Ave Maria . . . Virgo serena. 6 voc.
2. Mittit ad Virginem. Gregoriaansch.
3. O admirabile commercium. Gregoriaansch.
4. Quando natus es. Gregoriaansch.
5. Rubum quem viderat Moyses. Gregoriaansch.
6. Germinavit radix Jesse. Gregoriaansch.
7. Ecce Maria genuit. Gregoriaansch.
8. Ave verum Corpus. Gregoriaansch.
9. Domine, non secundum peccata. Gregoriaansch.
10. Liber generationis Jesu Christi. Gregoriaansch.
11. Factum est autem. Gregoriaansch.
12. Alma redemptoris Mater. Gregoriaansch.
13. Ave Regina coelorum. Gregoriaansch.
14. Virgo prudentissima. Gregoriaansch.
15. Victimae Paschali laudes. Gregoriaansch.
16. Homo quidam fecit coenam magnam. Gregoriaansch.

Vol.10. Missen I. Missa L'homme armé, super voces musicales.
Vol.11. Missen II. Missa La sol fa re mi.
Vol.12. Missen III. Missa Gaudeamus.
Vol.13. Missen IV. Missa Fortuna desperata.
Vol.14. Missen V. Missa L'homme armé, sexti toni.
Vol.15. Missen VI. Missa Ave maris stella.
Vol.16. Motetten. Bundel VI.
30. Ecce, tu pulchra es, amica mea.
31. Memor esto verbi tui.
32. Huc me sydereo descendere jussit olympo.

Vol.17. Missen VII. Missa Hercules dux Ferrariae.
Vol.18. Motetten. Bundel VII.
33. Praeter rerum seriem.
34. Ave mobilissima Creatura.
35. Virgo salutiferi.

Vol.19. Missen VIII. Missa Malheur me bat.
Vol.20. Missen IX. Missa L'ami baudichon.
Vol.21. Motetten. Bundel VIII.
36. Stabat Mater dolorosa.
37. Miserere mei, Deus.
38. Alma redemptoris Mater.
39. Domine, ne in furore tuo arguas me.

Vol.22. Missen X. Missa Una musque de Buscaya. 1948.
Vol.23. Missen XI. Missa D'ung aultere amer. 1950.
Vol.24. Motetten. Bundel IX. 1950.
40. Missus est Gabriel angelus.
41. Lectio actuum apostolorum.

Vol.25. Motetten. Bundel X. 1950.
42. Inviolata, integra et casta es, Maria.
43. Misericordias Domini in aeternum cantabo.
44. Deus, in nomine tuo salvum me fac.

Vol.26. Missen XII. Missa Mater patris. 1950.
Vol.27. Missen XIII. Missa Faisant regretz. 1951.
Vol.28. Missen XIV. Missa Ad fugam. 1951.
Vol.29. Missen XV. Missa di dadi. 1951.
Vol.30. Missen XVI. Missa de Beata Virgina (Kyrie, Gloria, Credo). 1952.
Vol.31. Missen XVI. Missa de Beata Virgina (Sanctus, Benedictus, Agnus Dei). 1952.
Vol.32. Missen XVII. Missa sine nomine. 1952.
Vol.33. Missen XVIII. Missa Pange lingua. 1952.
Vol.34. Missen XIX. Missa Da pacem. 1953.
Vol.35. Motetten. Bundel XI. 1954.
45. O Virgo prudentissima.
46. Benedicta es, caelorum Regina.
47. De profundis clamavi.
48. Salve Regina.

Vol.36. Motetten. Bundel XII. 1954.
49. Veni, Sancte Spiritus.
50. Pater noster, qui es in caelis.
51. In exitu Israël de Egypte.

Vol.37. Motetten. Bundel XIII. 1954.
52. Qui habitat in adjutorio altissimi.
53. Benedicite omnia opera Domini Domino.
54. Tribulatio et angustia invenerunt me.

Vol.38. Motetten. Bundel XIV. 1954.
55. In illo tempore stetit Jesus in medio discipulorum auorum.
56. In principio erat Verbum.
57. Deus pacis reduxit a mortuis.

Vol.39. Motetten. Bundel XV. 1955.
58. Stetit autem Salomon.
59. Domine, ne in furore tuo arguas me.
60. Usquequo, Domine, oblivisceris me.
61. Caeli enarrant gloriam Dei.

Vol.40. Motetten. Bundel XVI. 1955.
62. Beati quorum remissae sunt iniquitates.
63. Qui regis Israel, intende.
64. Domine, ne projicias me.

Vol.41. Motetten. Bundel XVII. 1955.
65. Dominus regnavit, decorem indutus est.
66. Jubilate Deo omnis terra.
67. Paratum cor meum, Deus.

Vol.42. Motetten. Bundel XVIII. 1956.
68. Laudate, pueri, Dominum.
69. Mirabilia testimonia tua, Domine.
70. Levari oculos meos in montes.

Vol.43. Missen XX. Missa Allez regretz. 1956.
Vol.44. Fragmenta missarum. 1956.
1. Gloria de beata Virgine.
2. Credo super De tous biens.
3. Credo Vilayge.

Vol.45. Motetten. Bundel XIX. 1957.
71. Nesciens Mater Virgo virum.
72. Cantate Domino canticum novum.
73. In Domino confido.

Vol.46. Motetten. Bundel XX. 1957.
74. Sancti Dei omnes.
75. Responde mihi.
76. Ave Christe.

Vol.47. Motetten. Bundel XXI. 1958.
77. Magnificat tertii toni.
78. Magnificat quarti toni.

Vol.48. Motetten. Bundel XXII. 1959.
79. In illo tempore assumpsit Jesus duodecim discipulos suos.

80. Ave verum.
81. Victimae Paschali laudes.
Vol.49. Motetten. Bundel XXIII. 1961.
82. Absolve, quaesumus, Domine.
83. O Virgo virginum.
84. Inter natos mulierum.
85. Responsum acceperat Simeon.
Vol.50. Fragmenta missarum. Bundel II. 1963.
4. Credo.
5. Credo.
6. Credo.
7. Sanctus de passione.
Vol.51. Motetten. Bundel XXIV. 1963.
86. Dic Deus dilexit mundum.
87. Christus mortuus est.
88. Verbum caro factum est.
89. Domine, Dominus noster.
90. De profundis clamavi.
Vol.52. Motetten. Bundel XXV. 1964.
91. De profundis clamavi.
92. Domine, exaudi orationem meam.
93. Nunc dimittis servum tuum, Domine.
94. Ave maris stella.
95. Salve Regina.
96. O bone et dulcissime Jesu.
Vol.53. Wereldlijke Werken. IV. 1965.
35. Adieu mes amours.
36. Bergerette savoyenne.
37. Una musque de Buscgaya.
38. Je sey bien dire.
39. Recondans de my segnora.
40. Vive le roy.
41. A l'eure que ie vous p.x.
42. La bernardina.
43. Ile fantazies de Joskin.
44. Cela sans plus.
45. La plus des plus.
46. Fortyne destrange plummaige. Pauper sum ego.
47. Que vous madame. In pace in idipsum.
48a. Fortuna desperata. (Busnoys).
48b. Fortuna desperata.
49a. De tous biens playne. (Hayne).
49b. De tous biens playne.

DEPRÈS, JOSQUIN, d. 1521.
Opera omnia. Editio altera quam edendam curavit Vereniging voor Nederlandse Muziekgeschiedenis. Amsterdam, G. Alsbach, 1957– .
v.1– .
Editor: v.1, A. Smijers.
Contents:
Vol.1. Fasc. 1. Missa L'homme armé, 1957.
Vol.1. Fasc. 2. Missa La sol fa re mi. 1957.

DESSOFF CHOIR SERIES, ed. by Paul Boepple . . . No.1–48. New York, Music Press, Inc., cop. 1941–48.
48 nos.
Scores: 1–6 solo voices and/or chorus, string and wind instruments, harpsichord, or organ.
Numbering evidently continued by Music Press, Inc. [Choral series] (q.v.).
Contents:
No.1. Palestrina, G. P. da. Assumpta est Maria.
No.2. Hassler, H. L. Ad Dominum cum tribularer.
No.3. Sweelinck, J. Psalm 90.
No.4. Sweelinck, J. Psalm 96.
No.5. Sweelinck, J. Psalm 102.
No.6. Schütz, H. 4 Psalms, 20, 84, 97, 121.
No.7. Schein, H. Christmas chorale.
No.8. Lasso, O. di. La terre les eaux va beuvant.
No.9. Lasso, O. di. Ores que je suis dispos.
No.10. Haydn, F. J. The holy ten commandments.
No.11. Lasso, O. di. Cantiones duarum vocum. Magnum opus I–XX.
No.12. Palestrina, G. P. da. Magnificat in the fourth mode.
No.13. Schütz, H. Sacred concert. Give ear, oh Lord.
No.14. Couperin, F. Troisième leçon de ténèbres.
No.15. Schubert, F. P. Serenade (Ständchen, Op.135).
No.16. Lasso, O. di. Cantiones sine textu. Magnum opus XIII–XXIV.
No.17. Schütz, H. Sacred concert. (First book, No.5). Great is our Lord.
No.18. Schütz, H. Sacred concert. (First book, No.6). O mighty Lord, our God.
No.19. Schein, H. Who with grieving soweth.
No.20. Schütz, H. Symphonia sacra (II:13). Why afflict thyself, oh my spirit.
No.21. Lasso, O. di. 3 Psalms, 25, 5, and 43.
No.22. Lasso, O. di. Lamentations of the prophet Jeremiah.
No.23. Buxtehude, D. Missa brevis. Kyrie-Gloria.
No.24. Monteverdi, C. Sacrae cantiunculae, Nos.12 and 16.
No.25. Desprès, J. Pange lingua. Pleni sunt coeli. De Beata Virgine. Agnus Dei.
No.26. Bach, J. S. Schwingt freudig euch empor. Non komm, der heiden Heiland.
No.27. Bach, J. S. Herr Jesu Christ, du höchstes Gut. Ach Herr, mein Gott, vergieb mir's doch.
No.28. Brasart, Johannes. O flos flagrans.
No.29. Dufay, G. Magnificat in the eighth mode.
No.30. Händel, G. F. Duet XVII: Beato in ver chi puo.
No.31. Handl, J. Repleti sunt.
No.32. Handl, J. Trahe me post te.
No.33. Handl, J. Regnum mundi.
No.34. Purcell, H. In the midst of life.
No.35. Purcell, H. Lord, how long wilt Thou be angry.
No.36. La Rue, Pierre de. Sicut cervus.
No.37. La Rue, Pierre de. Pourquoy non.
No.38. Binchois, A. Solus ortus cardine.
No.39. Desprès, J. Cueurs desolez.
No.40. Mouton, J. Ave Maria.
No.41. Brumel, A. Sicut lilium.
No.42. Compère, L. Le renvoy.
No.43. Desprès, J. De profundis.
No.44. Desprès, J. Ave Maria.
No.45. Desprès, J. Tu solus qui facis mirabilia.
No.46. Desprès, J. Bergerotti sayoysienne.
No.47. Desprès, J. Parfons regretz.
No.48. Desprès, J. Plus nulz regretz.

Deutsch, Otto Erich, 1883– , ed. Musikalische Seltenheiten, *see* Musikalische Seltenheiten.

Das deutsche geistliche Lied, *see* Reimann, Heinrich. Das deutsche geistliche Lied.

Deutsche Hausmusik aus vier Jahrhunderten, *see* Leichtentritt, Hugo. Deutsche Hausmusik aus vier Jahrhunderten.

Deutsche Instrumentalmusik. Werke für Kammerorchester, *see* Corona.

Deutsche Klaviermusik des 17. und 18. Jahrhunderts, *see* Oberdörffer, Fritz. Deutsche Klaviermusik des 17. und 18. Jahrhunderts.

Das deutsche Lied, *see* Reimann, Heinrich. Das deutsche Lied.

DICKINSON, CLARENCE, 1873– . ed.
Historical recital series for organ, ed. and arr. by Clarence Dickinson. New York, H. W. Gray Co., Inc., [cop.1917–cop.1920].
2v. and 8 nos.
Each number is also published separately.
Contents:
Vol.1.
No.1. Stamitz, K. Andante.
No.2. Stravinsky, I. Rondo des princesses (From "The fire bird").
No.3. Quantz, J. J. Arioso (Sonata 333).
No.4. Quantz, J. J. Presto (Sonata 333).
No.5. Rousseau, J. J. Minuet (From Le devin du village).
No.6. Bull, J. The king's hunt.
No.7. Couperin, F. Lament.
No.8. Bach, J. H. Chorale prelude. Have mercy, O Lord God.
No.9. Bach, J. C. Prelude and fugue.
No.10. Bach, J. M. Chorale prelude. When my last hour.
No.11. Bach, J. B. Variations on the chorale, Thou Prince of Peace.
No.12. Bach, J. S. Capriccio. On the departure of his beloved brother.
No.13. Bach, W. F. Chorale prelude. We thank Thee, Lord.
No.14. Bach, C. P. E. Fantasie and fugue.
No.15. Beethoven, L. Adagio sostenuto (Moonlight sonata).
No.16. Marpurg, F. W. Preludio e capriccio.
No.17. Palestrina, G. P. da. Prayer.
No.18. Froberger, J. J. Fantasie.
No.19. Tchaikowsky, P. I. Valse (From Symphony V).
No.20. Aubert, J. Forlane (La reine des peris).
Vol.2.
No.21. Dowland, J. Lachrymae paran.
No.22. Nichelmann, C. Suite.
No.23. Rameau, J. P. Minuet and gigue.
No.24. Fasch, K. F. C. Concert fugue.
No.25. Farnaby, G. Giles Farnaby's dreame.
No.26. Smetana, B. Tabor ("My country"). Arr. Urban.
No.27. Smetana, B. Blanik ("My country"). Arr. Urban.
No.28. Novák, V. In the church (From "Slovak suite"). Arr. Urban.
No.29. Fibich, Z. Paradise. Arr. Urban.
No.30. Bach, J. S. Chorale prelude. In dulci jubilo.
No.31. Clerambault, L. N. Prelude in D minor. Arr. Guilmant.
No.32. Couperin, F. Soeur Monique. Arr. Guilmant.
No.33. Krebs, J. L. Trio.
No.34. Pachelbel, J. Christmas pastorale. From heaven high.
No.35. Liszt, F. Ora pro nobis.
No.36. Gheyn, M. van den. Carillon et fugue.
No.37. Arcadelt, J. Ave Maria. Arr. Liszt.
No.38. Rinck, J. C. H. Rondo (From Concerto for flute stop).
No.39. Purcell, H. Trumpet voluntary.
No.40. Bach, J. S. Anna Magdalena's March.
Additional numbers, not included in above volumes.
No.41. Buxtehude, D. Prelude and fugue in F.
No.42. Buxtehude, D. Chorale prelude. Praise God, Ye Christians.
No.43. Traditional. Two ancient melodies.
No.44. Bach, J. S. Badinage.
No.45. Cosyn, B. The Goldfinch.
No.46. Nowakowski, D. Prayer (Ancient Hebrew melody).
No.47. Balbastre, C. Prelude on two French noels.
No.48. Couperin, F. Qui tollis peccata mundi.

DIETRICH, FRITZ. ed.
Elf Orgelchörale des siebzehnten Jahrhunderts, hrsg. von Fritz Dietrich. Notenbeilage zur "Geschichte des deutschen Orgelchorals im siebzehnten Jahrhundert" von Fritz Dietrich. Kassel, Bärenreiter-Verlag, 1932.
31p.
Contains compositions by J. F. Alberti, Andreas Armsdorf, J. M. Bach, J. H. Buttstedt, Dietrich Buxtehude, Daniel Erich, Heinrich Scheidemann, Samuel Scheidt, A. N. Vetter, and Matthias Weckmann.

DIETRICH, SIXTUS, ca.1490–1548.
Hymnen; Wittenberg, 1545. Ed. by Hermann Zenck, with an introduction by Wilibald Gurlitt. St. Louis, Concordia Pub. House, 1960.
xxii p., score (178p.). ports., facsims.
Principally for discantus, altus, tenor, and bassus.
Latin words.
Introduction and preface in German and English.

DIEUPART, CHARLES, ca.1670–1740.
Collection, publiée par Paul Brunold. Paris, Éditions de l'Oiseau Lyre, cop.1934.
2v.
Contents:
Vol.1. 6 Suites pour clavecin.
Vol.2. Airs et chansons.

DILETTO MUSICALE. Doblingers Reihe alter Musik. Wien-München, Verlag Doblinger, 19? – .
No.1– .
Contents (Hoboken: a numbering system for Haydn's works):

No.1. Haydn, J. Divertimento a tre: Trio in Es-dur für Horn, Violine und Violoncello. Hoboken IV:5.
No.2. Förster, E. A. Op.2/1. Streichquartett in C-dur.
No.3. Haydn, M. Konzert in B-dur für Violine, Streichorchester und Cembalo.
No.4. Haydn, J. Klaviertrio in F-dur. Hoboken XV:40. Viersätzige Ausgabe.
No.5. Haydn, J. Op.1/1. Streichquartett in B-dur. Hoboken III:1.
No.6. Haydn, J. Op.1/2. Streichquartett in Es-dur. Hoboken III:2.
No.7. Haydn, J. Op.3/5. Streichquartett in F-dur. Serenaden-Quartett. Hoboken III:17.
No.8. Haydn, J. Op.17/5. Streichquartett in G-dur. Hoboken III:29.
No.9. Mozart, W. A. Streichquartett in G-dur. K.V.80.
No.10. Haydn, J. Sonate in F-dur für Violine und Viola. Hoboken VI:1.
No.11. Haydn, J. Sonate in A-dur für Violine und Viola. Hoboken VI:2.
No.12. Haydn, J. Sonate in B-dur für Violine und Viola. Hoboken VI:3.
No.13. Fontana, G. B. Sechs Sonaten für Violine und Klavier. Heft 1: Sonaten Nr.1, 2.
No.14. Fontana, G. B. Heft 2: Sonaten Nr.3, 4.
No.15. Fontana, G. B. Heft 3: Sonaten Nr.5, 6.
No.16. Lully, J. B. Ballettsuite "Le triomphe de l'amour" für Streichorchester.
No.17. Haydn, J. Cantata "Miseri noi, misera patria" für Sopran und Orchester.
No.18. Haydn, J. Ouvertüre. Lo speziale. Hoboken Ia:10.
No.19. Haydn, J. Son pietosa, son bonina. Arie der Lindora in Climarosas "La Circe" für Sopran und Orchester.
No.20. Haydn, M. Sinfonia in D-dur.
No.21. Haydn, J. Concertino in C-dur für Cembalo (Klavier), 2 Violinen und Violoncello (Bass). Hoboken XIV:11.
No.22. Haydn, J. Divertimento in E-dur für Violine, Violoncello und Cembalo (Klavier). Hoboken XV:34.
No.23. Haydn, J. Divertimento (Cassatio) in C-dur, für 2 Klarinetten, 2 Hörner, 2 Violinen, 2 Violen, Violoncello (Bass). Hoboken II:17.
No.24. Haydn, M. Divertimento in B-dur für Oboe, Fagott, Violine, Viola, Contrabass. Perger-Kat. 92.
No.25. Haydn, M. Divertimento in G-dur für Flöte, Horn, Violine, Viola, Violoncello, Fagott. Perger-Kat. 94.
No.26. Haydn, M. Notturno in F-dur für 2 Hörner, 2 Violinen, Viola, Bass. Perger-Kat. 106.
No.27. Mozart, W. A. Sechs deutsche Tänze für Klavier. K.V.509.
No.28. Gassmann, F. Sinfonia (Ouvertüre) "Issipile."
No.29. Haydn, J. Divertimento Nr.1 in F-dur für 2 Oboen, 2 Fagotten, 2 Hörner. Hoboken II:15.
No.30. Haydn, J. Divertimento Nr.2 in F-dur für 2 Oboen, 2 Fagotten, 2 Hörner. Hoboken II:23.
No.31. Haydn, J. Divertimento Nr.3 in C-dur für 2 Oboen, 2 Fagotten, 2 Hörner. Hoboken II:7.
No.32. Haydn, J. Divertimento Nr.4 in C-dur für 2 Klarinetten, 2 Hörner. Hoboken II:14.
No.33. Haydn, J. Divertimento Nr.5 in D-dur für 2 Oboen, 2 Fagotten, 2 Hörner. Hoboken II:D18.
No.34. Haydn, J. Märsche für Blasinstrumente.
No.35. Haydn, J. Zwei italienische Duette für Sopran, Tenor und Klavier.
No.36. Pesenti, M. Tänze für Violine und Klavier bzw. Violine, Violoncello und Klavier.
No.37. Castello, D. Zwei Sonaten für Violine und Klavier.
No.38. Wanhal, J. B. Sinfonia in G-moll.
No.39. Haydn, J. Ouvertüre. Acide e Galatea. Hoboken Ia:5.
No.40. Anonym (18.Jh.): Drei Sinfonien für Altblockflöte und Cembalo (Klavier), mit Viola da Gamba (Violoncello) ad lib.
No.41–45. Haydn, J. Lirenkonzerte. Hoboken VIIh:1–5.
No.41. Concerto Nr.1 in C-dur.
No.42. Concerto Nr.2 in G-dur.
No.43. Concerto Nr.3 in G-dur.
No.44. Concerto Nr.4 in F-dur.
No.45. Concerto Nr.5 in F-dur.
No.46. Frescobaldi, G. Toccata per spinettina e violino.
No.47. Haydn, J. Cassatio (Divertimento) in G-dur für 2 Oboen, 2 Hörner, 2 Violinen, 2 Violen, Violoncello, Bass. Hoboken II:G1.
No.48. Haydn, J. Notturno Nr.1 in C-dur.
No.49. Frescobaldi, G. Toccata e Canzone für Cembalo und Bass.
No.50. Haydn, J. Sinfonia (Parthia) in B-dur. Hoboken I:108.
No.51. Haydn, J. Ouvertüre in D-dur. Hoboken Ia:4.
No.52. Haydn, J. Six Allemandes. Sechs deutsche Tänze für Orchester. Hoboken IX:9.
No.53. Mozart, W. A. Andante der Urfassung der 1. Pariser Symphonie. K.V.297.
No.54. Salieri, A. Concerto in C-dur für Flöte, Oboe und Orchester.
No.55. Haydn, J. Ouvertüre. Orlando Paladino. Hoboken Ia:16.
No.56. Haydn, J. Cassatio (Divertimento) a nove istromenti in F-dur. Hoboken II:20.
No.57. Haydn, J. Divertimento a sei "Dei Gebrutstag." Hoboken II:11.
No.58. Haydn, J. Ouvertüre. La fedeltà premiata. Hoboken XXVIII:1.
No.59. Haydn, J. Ouvertüre. La vera costanza. Hoboken Ia:15.
No.60. Haydn, J. Ouvertüre. L'incontro improviso. Hoboken Ia:6.
No.61. Wagenseil, G. C. Concerto in A-dur für Violoncello, Streichorchester und Cembalo.
No.62. Flackton, W. Sonata in C-dur für Viola und Klavier.
No.63. Flackton, W. Sonata in D-dur für Viola und Klavier.
No.64. Flackton, W. Sonata in G-dur für Viola und Klavier.

No.65. Hummel, J. N. Op.5/3. Sonate in Es-dur für Viola und Klavier.
No.66. Haydn, J. Cassatio in D-dur, "Hornsignal," für 4 Hörner, Violine, Viola, Violoncello (Basso). Hoboken deest.
No.67. Salieri, A. Scherzi istrumentali a quattro di stile fugato (Streichquartett).
No.68. Flackton, W. Sonata in C-dur für Violoncello und Klavier.
No.69. Flackton, W. Sonata in B-dur für Violoncello und Klavier.
No.70. Flackton, W. Sonata in F-dur für Violoncello und Klavier.
No.71–76. Haydn, J. Sechs Scherzandi. Hoboken II:33–38.
No.71. Scherzando Nr.1 in F-dur.
No.72. Scherzando Nr.2 in C-dur.
No.73. Scherzando Nr.3 in D-dur.
No.74. Scherzando Nr.4 in G-dur.
No.75. Scherzando Nr.5 in E-dur.
No.76. Scherzando Nr.6 in A-dur.
No.77. Haydn, J. Sinfonia (Overture) in D-dur. Hoboken Ia:7.
No.78. Haydn, J. Concerto in D-dur für Cembalo und Streichorchester. Hoboken XVIII:2.
No.79. Haydn, J. Concerto in G-dur für Violine und Streichorchester. Hoboken VIIIa:4.
No.80. Haydn, J. Concerto Nr.2 in C-dur für Orgel und Orchester. Hoboken XVIII:8.
No.81. Werner, G. J. Wienerischer Tandelmarkt.
No.82. Starzer, J. Konzert in F-dur für Violine und Streichorchester.
No.83. Mozart, L. Sinfonia burlesca.
No.84. Haydn, J. Divertimento Nr.6 in G-dur für 2 Oboen, 2 Fagotten, 2 Hörner. Hoboken II:3.
No.85. Haydn, J. Divertimento Nr.7 in G-dur für 2 Oboen, 2 Fagotten, 2 Hörner. Hoboken deest.
No.86. Haydn, J. Divertimento Nr.8 in D-dur für 2 Oboen, 2 Fagotten, 2 Hörner. Hoboken deest.
No.87. Frescobaldi, G. Canzonen für eine Oberstimme und Generalbass.
No.88. Frescobaldi, G. Canzonen für eine Bassstimme und Generalbass. Heft 1.
No.89. Frescobaldi, G. Canzonen für eine Bassstimme und Generalbass. Heft 2.
No.90. Haydn, J. Oratorien-Fragment. Mare clausum.
No.91. Haydn, J. Divertimento in C-dur für Cembalo (Klavier). 2 Violinen, Violoncello. Hoboken XIV:8.
No.92. Haydn, J. Divertimento in F-dur für Cembalo (Klavier). 2 Violinen, Violoncello. Hoboken XIV:9.
No.93. Haydn, J. Capriccio in A-dur für Cembalo (Klavier). Violine, Bass. Hoboken XV:35.
No.94. Galuppi, B. Concerto a quattro. Nr.1 in G-moll.
No.95. Galuppi, B. Concerto a quattro. Nr.2 in G-dur.
No.96. Bach, J. C. Overture. La clemenza di Scipione.
No.97. Reichardt, J. F. Sinfonia in G-dur.
No.98. Haydn, J. March für The Royal Society of Musicians. Hoboken VIII:3 bis.
No.99. Boccherini, L. Op.60/1. Quintetto in C-dur.
No.100. Hummel, J. N. Op.5/1. Sonate in B-dur für Violine und Klavier.
No.101. Boccherini, L. Op.60/2. Quintetto in B-dur.
No.102. Boccherini, L. Op.60/3. Quintetto in A-dur.
No.103. Boccherini, L. Op.60/5. Quintetto in G-dur.
No.104. Boccherini, L. Op.60/6. Quintetto in F-dur.
No.105. Beethoven, L. v. Streichquartett in F-dur nach der Klaviersonate in E-dur, Op. 14/1.
No.106. Fux, J. J. Capriccio und Fuge für Cembalo. K.V.404.
No.107.
No.108. Stamitz, K. Op.10/1. Duo für Violine und Viola.
No.109. Hoffmeister, F. A. Quintett in Es-dur für Horn und Streichquartett.
No.110. Fux, J. J. Ouvertüre in C.
No.111. Weber, C. M. v. Op.26. Concertino für Klarinette und Klavier in Es-dur.
No.112. Süssmayer, F. X. Quintett in D-dur für Flöte, Oboe, Violine, Viola, Violoncello.
No.113. Schenk, J. Konzert in Es-dur für Harfe und Orchester.
No.114. Boccherini, L. Op.62/1. Quintetto in C-dur.
No.115. Boccherini, L. Op.62/2. Quintetto in Es-dur.
No.116. Boccherini, L. Op.62/3. Quintetto in F-dur.
No.117. Dittersdorf, C. D. v. Sinfonia. Die vier Weltalter.
No.118. Dragonetti, D. Solo in D-dur für Kontrabass und Klavier.
No.119. Stamitz, K. Op.10/2. Duo für Violine und Viola.
No.120. Dragonetti, D. Solo in D-moll für Kontrabass und Klavier.
No.121. Wagenseil, G. C. Concerto in G-dur für Violoncello und Orchester.
No.122. Haydn, J. Streichquintett in G-dur. Hoboken II:2.
No.123. Haydn, J. Streichquintett in A-dur. Hoboken IIA1.
No.124. Haydn, J. Sonate in D-dur für Violine und Viola. Hoboken VI:4.
No.125. Haydn, J. Sonate in Es-dur für Violine und Viola. Hoboken VI:5.
No.126. Haydn, J. Sonate in C-dur für Violine und Viola. Hoboken VI:6.
No.127. Toeschi, G. Sonata für Viola d'amore und Cembalo.
No.128. Tänze aus dem 17. und 18. Jahrhundert für zwei Instrumente.
No.129. Haydn, J. Scena di Berenice für Sopran und Orchester.
No.130. Gassmann, F. Partita für 2 Klarinetten, 2 Hörner, Fagott.
No.131. Hoffmeister, F. A. Quartett für Klarinette, Violine, Viola, Violoncello.
No.132. Salieri, A. Zwei Bläserserenaden.
No.133. Avison, C. Op.3/1. Concerto grosso.

No.134. Czermák, A. G. Streichquartett. Die drohende Gefahr oder Die Vaterlandsliebe.
No.135. Salieri, A. Concerto in D-dur für Violine, Oboe, Violoncello und Orchester.
No.136. Devienne, F. Duo concertant Nr.1 für 2 Klarinetten.
No.137–140. Pleyel, I. Zwölf Duette für 2 Flöten.
No.137. Heft 1: Duette Nr.1–3.
No.138. Heft 2: Duette Nr.4–6.
No.139. Heft 3: Duette Nr.7–9.
No.140. Heft 4: Duette Nr.10–12.
No.141. Demachi, G. Trio Nr.1 für 3 Flöten oder 3 Violinen.
No.142. Schenk, J. Quartett für Flöte, 2 Englischhörner und Fagott.
No.143. Haydn, M. Sinfonia in C-dur.
No.144. Haydn, M. Intrada in G-dur für Orchester.
No.145. Haydn, M. Introduzione "Der büssende Sünder" für Orchester.
No.146. Pergolesi, G. B. Concerto a cinque.
No.147. Boccherini, L. Op.62/4. Quintetto in B-dur.
No.148. Hummel, J. N. Op.50. Sonate in D-dur für Flöte und Klavier.
No.149. Boccherini, L. Op.62/6. Quintetto in E-dur.
No.150–157. Boyce, W. Acht Symphonien:
No.150. Symphonie Nr.1.
No.151. Symphonie Nr.2.
No.152. Symphonie Nr.3.
No.153. Symphonie Nr.4.
No.154. Symphonie Nr.5.
No.155. Symphonie Nr.6.
No.156. Symphonie Nr.7.
No.157. Symphonie Nr.8.
No.158–163. Haibel, J. J. Aus der komischen Oper "Der Tiroler Wastel."
No.158. Lied der Marianne. Ein schöner Mann ist delikat.
No.159. Rezitativ und Arie der Luise. Du liebe Nachtigall.
No.160. Couplet des Wirtes. Schaffen Sie was Gut's, Ihr Gnaden.
No.161. Duett Liesel-Wastel. Die Tiroler sind often so lustig.
No.162. Duett Marianne-Jodel. Männer, wenn die Mädeln schmeicheln.
No.163. Arie des Josef. Wer nicht dem Bürgerstande.
No.164. Torelli, G. Sonata a cinque Nr.1 für Trompete und Streicher.
No.165. Torelli, G. Sonata a cinque Nr.2 für Trompete und Streicher.
No.166. Holzbauer, I. Sinfonia in D-dur.
No.167. Haydn, J. Sinfonia in B-dur. Hoboken I:107.
No.168. Haydn, J. Klavier-Sonate in Es-dur. Hoboken XVI:52.
No.169. Schubert, F. Atzenbrugger Tänze für Klavier (Racek).
No.201–249. Haydn, J. Die Sinfonien. Hoboken I:1–49.
No.201. Sinfonia Nr.1 in D-dur.
No.202. Sinfonia Nr.2 in C-dur.
No.203. Sinfonia Nr.3 in G-dur.
No.204. Sinfonia Nr.4 in D-dur.
No.205. Sinfonia Nr.5 in A-dur.
No.206. Sinfonia Nr.6 in D-dur. Le matin.
No.207. Sinfonia Nr.7 in C-dur. Le midi.
No.208. Sinfonia Nr.8 in G-dur. Le soir.
No.209. Sinfonia Nr.9 in C-dur.
No.210. Sinfonia Nr.10 in D-dur.
No.211. Sinfonia Nr.11 in Es-dur.
No.212. Sinfonia Nr.12 in E-dur.
No.213. Sinfonia Nr.13 in D-dur.
No.214. Sinfonia Nr.14 in A-dur.
No.215. Sinfonia Nr.15 in D-dur.
No.216. Sinfonia Nr.16 in B-dur.
No.217. Sinfonia Nr.17 in F-dur.
No.218. Sinfonia Nr.18 in G-dur.
No.219. Sinfonia Nr.19 in D-dur.
No.220. Sinfonia Nr.20 in C-dur.
No.221. Sinfonia Nr.21 in A-dur.
No.222. Sinfonia Nr.22 in Es-dur.
No.223. Sinfonia Nr.23 in G-dur.
No.224. Sinfonia Nr.24 in D-dur.
No.225. Sinfonia Nr.25 in C-dur.
No.226. Sinfonia Nr.26 in D-moll.
No.227. Sinfonia Nr.27 in G-dur.
No.228. Sinfonia Nr.28 in A-dur.
No.229. Sinfonia Nr.29 in E-dur.
No.230. Sinfonia Nr.30 in C-dur. Alleluja.
No.231. Sinfonia Nr.31 in D-dur. Hornsignal.
No.232. Sinfonia Nr.32 in C-dur.
No.233. Sinfonia Nr.33 in C-dur.
No.234. Sinfonia Nr.34 in D-moll.
No.235. Sinfonia Nr.35 in B-dur.
No.236. Sinfonia Nr.36 in Es-dur.
No.237. Sinfonia Nr.37 in C-dur.
No.238. Sinfonia Nr.38 in C-dur.
No.239. Sinfonia Nr.39 in G-moll.
No.240. Sinfonia Nr.40 in F-dur.
No.241. Sinfonia Nr.41 in C-dur.
No.242. Sinfonia Nr.42 in D-dur.
No.243. Sinfonia Nr.43 in Es-dur. Merkur.
No.244. Sinfonia Nr.44 in E-moll. Trauersymphonie.
No.245. Sinfonia Nr.45 in Fis-moll. Abschiedssymphonie.
No.246. Sinfonia Nr.46 in H-dur.
No.247. Sinfonia Nr.47 in G-dur.
No.248. Sinfonia Nr.48 in C-dur. Maria-Theresien-Symphonie.
No.249. Sinfonia Nr.49 in F-moll. La Passione.

Dirección de Cultura of the Ministerio de Educación Nacional in Caracas, *see* Archivo de música colonial venezolana.

DITTERS VON DITTERSDORF, KARL, 1739–1799.
Ausgewählte Orchesterwerke von Carl Ditters von Dittersdorf. Zur Centenarfeier des Todestages Dittersdorf 1799, 31 October, 1899, hrsg. von Josef Liebeskind. Abt.1–2, Bd.1–11 . . . Leipzig, Gebrüder Reinecke, [1899–1904].
11v.
Full score.
Portrait on title page.
Contents:

Abt.1.
Bd.1. Die vier Weltalter.
Bd.2. Der Sturz Phaëtons.
Bd.3. Verwandlung Actaeons in einen Hirsch.
Bd.4. Die Rettung der Andromeda durch Perseus.
Bd.5. Verwandlung der lycischen Bauern in Frösche.
Bd.6. Die Versteinerung des Phineus und seiner Freunde.
Abt.2.
Bd.7. Sinfonie, F dur.
Bd.8. Sinfonie, Es dur.
Bd.9. Ouverture zu dem Oratorium "Esther," und Musique pour un petit ballet en forme d'une contre danse, D dur.
Bd.10. Divertimento. Il combattimento dell' umane passione, D dur.
Neue Folge. Bd.11. Le carnaval ou la redoute. Grand symphonie.

DITTMER, LUTHER A.
. . . The Worcester fragments. A catalogue raisonné and transcription, by Luther A. Dittmer. With a foreword by Dom Anselm Hughes . . . [Rome], American Institute of Musicology, 1957.
185p. (Musicological studies and documents. No.2).

Dix-sept sonates et pièces anciennes d'auteurs espagnols, *see* Nin y Castellano, Joaquin. Dix-sept sonates et pièces anciennes d'auteurs espagnols.

Doblingers Reihe alter Musik, *see* Diletto musicale.

DOCUMENTA HISTORICA MUSICAE. Prague, Státní Nakladatelství Krásné Literatury, 1955– .
v.1– .
Contents:
Umění vokální polyfonie. Selectio artis musicae polyphonicae a XII.–XVI. saec. Anonymi, John of Fornsete, Giovanni da Cascia, Francesco Landino, Guillaume de Machaut, John Dunstable, Guillaume Dufay, Johannes Ockeghem, Jacob Obrecht, Josquin des Près, Heinrich Isaak, Jacob Gallus (Handl), Clément Jannequin, Giovanni Pierluigi da Palestrina, Orlandus Lassus, Luca Marenzio, Orazio Vecchi a jiní. Sestavil Jaroslav Vanický. 1955.
Kryštof Harant z Polžic a Bezdružic. Opera musica. Qui confidunt in Domino. Maria Kron. Missa quinis vocibus super Dolorosi martyr. Fragmenty. Editor Jiří Berkovec. 1956.
Madrigaly a chansony. Výběr polyfonních děl Skladatelů 16. a 17. století. J. Arcadelt, A. Banchieri, W. Byrd, G. Gabrieli, G. G. Gastoldi, D. C. Gesualdo, O. Gibbons, C. Jannequin, O. Lassus, L. Marenzio, C. Monteverdi, G. Pierluigi da Palestrina, C. de Rore, A. Striggio, O. Vecchi, T. Weelkes, A. Willaert. Sestavil Jaroslav Vanický. 1957.
Česká polyfinní tvorba. Musica polyphonica Bohemiae. Výběr vícehlasých děl českého původu z XVI. a XVII. století. Sestavila Jitka Snížková. 1958.
Minnesang. Středověký rytířský zpěv. 12.–15. století. Historické črty a výběr skladeb. Napsal a sestavil Jaroslav Vanický. 1958.
Pohanka, Jaroslav. Dějiny české hudby. V příkladech. 1958.
Tůma, František. Stabat Mater. Coro misto e organo. Editore Josef Plavec. 1959.
Kittl, Jan Bedřich. Symfonie Es dur. Lovecká Jagdsymphonie. Vydal. Hrsg. von Jarmil Burghauser. 1960.
Věnec ze Zpěvů Vlastenských. Sborník Obrozenských Písní. Vídal Josef Plavec. 1960.
Dušek, Jan Ladislav; Rösler, Josef; Voříšek, Jan Václav. Písně. Lieder. Songs. Výběr z vokální tvorby. Auswahl aus der Vokalmusik. Selection of vocal works. Canto e piano. 1961.
Staré české Fanfáry. Alte böhmische Fantaren. Old Czech fanfares. Editore Jarmil Burghauser. Score and parts. 1961.

DOCUMENTA LITURGIAE POLYCHORALIS SANCTAE ECCLESIAE ROMANAE. Ed. by R. D. Laurence Feininger. Rome, Societas Universalis Sanctae Ceciliae, 1957– .
No.1– .
Contents:
No.1. Benevoli, Orazio. Haec est Virgo sapiens. (4 altos). 1957.
No.2. Benevoli, Orazio. Regne terrae. (12 sopranos). 1957.
No.3. Benevoli, Orazio. Si quis mihi ministraverit. (3 sopranos). 1957.
No.4. Benevoli, Orazio. Haec est Virgo sapiens. (4 high and 4 low voices). 1957.
No.5. Benevoli, Orazio. Dirupisti Domine. (4 sopranos). 1958.
No.6. Pitoni, Giuseppe. Misericordia Domini. (4 voices, mixed). 1959.
No.7. Pitoni, Giuseppe. Beata es Virgo. (8 voices, mixed). 1959.
No.8. Pitoni, Giuseppe. Justorum animae. (8 voices, mixed). 1959.
No.9. Pitoni, Giuseppe. Introito, Kyrie, Offertorio. (4 voices). 1959.
No.10. Cannicciari, Pompeo. Christus factus est. (4 voices, mixed). 1961.
No.11. Cannicciari, Pompeo. Improperium exspectavit. (4 voices, mixed). 1961.
No.12. Giorgi, Giovanni. O sacrum convivium. (4 voices, mixed). 1961.
No.13. Giorgi, Giovanni. Et manducantibus illus. (4 voices, mixed). 1961.
No.14. Cannicciari, Pompeo. Confirma hoc Deus. (2 high voices and alto). 1962.
No.15. Cannicciari, Pompeo. Vidi turbam magnam. (9 voices, mixed). 1963.
No.16. Benevoli, Orazio. Collocet eum, a 4 bassi. 1964.
No.17. Benevoli, Orazio. Et ecce terremotus, a 4 bassi. 1964.
No.18. Carissimi, Giacomo. Christus factus est, a 9 voci. 1964.
No.19. Giorgi, Giovanni. Improperium exspectavit, a 4 voci. 1965.

DOCUMENTA MAIORA LITURGIAE POLYCHORALIS SANCTAE ECCLESIAE ROMANAE. Ed. R. D. Laurence Feininger. Rome, Societas

Universalis Sanctae Ceciliae, 1958– .
No.1– .
Contents:
No.1. Pitoni, Giuseppe Ottavio. Missa Cum clamarem. (4 voices, mixed). 1958.
No.2. Pitoni, Giuseppe Ottavio. Missa Sancta Maria. (4 voices, mixed). 1958.
No.3. Pitoni, Giuseppe Ottavio. Missa Sanctae Dei Genitrix. (4 voices, mixed). 1958.
No.4. Pitoni, Giuseppe Ottavio. Missa Virgo Virginum. (4 voices, mixed). 1958.
No.5. Pitoni, Giuseppe Ottavio. Missa Pro defunctis. (8 voices). 1959.
No.6. Giorgi, Giovanni. Missa. (4 voices, mixed). 1961.
No.7. Giorgi, Giovanni. Missa. (4 voices, mixed). 1724. 1961.
No.8. Giorgi, Giovanni. Missa. (4 voices, mixed). 1962.
No.9. Giorgi, Giovanni. Messa a 4 voci concertata. ca.1756. 1963.
No.10. Rossi, Giuseppe de. Graduale di S. Cecilia per soli, coro ed istrumenti. 1715. 1964.

DOCUMENTA MUSICOLOGICA. 2. Reihe: Handschriften-Faksimiles. Kassel, Bärenreiter-Verlag, 1955– .
v.1– . (facsim.). (Internationale Gesellschaft für Musikwissenschaft).
Contents:
Vol.1. Das Buxheimer Orgelbuch. 1955.
Vol.2. Codex Escorial. 1958.

DOCUMENTA POLYPHONIAE LITURGICAE SANCTAE ECCLESIAE ROMANAE. Ser.1. Roma, Societas Universalis Sanctae Ceciliae, 1947, cop.1948– .
No.1– .
Ser.1. A. Ordinarium missae.
Contents:
No.1. Dufay. Fragmentum missae. 1947.
No.2 Power. Missa super Alma redemptoris mater. 1947.
No.3. Dufay. Et in terra "Ad modum tube." 1949.
No.4. Dufay. Missa de Sanctissima Trinitate. 1949.
No.5. Binchois. Missa de angelis. 1949.
No.6. Standley. Missa Ad fugam reservatam. 1949.
No.7. Dufay. 2 Kyrie et 1 Gloria in Dominicis diebus. 1949.
No.8. Dunstable. Gloria e Credo. (Jesu Christi fili Dei vivi). 1950.
No.9. Leonel. Missa super Fuit homo missus. 1950.
No.10. Dufay. Et in terra de quaremiaux. 1951.
No.11. Franchoys (?). Gloria e Credo. 1952.

Ser.1. B. Ordinarium missae.
Contents:
No.1. De la Rue. Missa Ave sanctissima. 1950.

DOCUMENTA POLYPHONIAE LITURGICAE SANCTAE ECCLESIAE ROMANAE. Ser.2. Roma, Societas Universalis S. Ceciliae.
No.1– .
Ser.2. Proprium missae.
Proposed series.

DOCUMENTA POLYPHONIAE LITURGICAE SANCTAE ECCLESIAE ROMANAE. Ser.3. Roma, Societas Universalis S. Ceciliae.
No.1– .
Ser.3. Divinum officium.
Proposed series.

DOCUMENTA POLYPHONIAE LITURGICAE SANCTAE ECCLESIAE ROMANAE. Ser.4. Roma, Societas Universalis S. Ceciliae, 1950– .
No.1– .
Ser.4. Motecta.
Contents:
No.1. Standley. Quae est ista. (Fuga reservata). 1950.

Documents artistiques du XVe siècle. Tome 1, *see* Droz, Eugénie. Poètes et musiciens du XVe siècle.

Documents artistiques du XVe siècle. Tome 4, *see* [Droz, Eugénie]. Trois chansonniers français du XVe siècle.

DOCUMENTS OF THE MUSICAL PAST, ed. by Alfred Mann. [New Brunswick, N.J.], Rutgers University Press, [1953–].
v.1– .
On cover: G. Schirmer, New York, sole sales agents.
Contents:
Vol.1. Bach, Johann Christian. Concerto for piano. [1953].
Vol.2. Purcell, Henry. Christmas anthem; for three solo voices, choir, and instruments. [1953].
Vol.3. Gibbons, Orlando. Concerted anthems; for solo tenor, choir, and stringed instruments. Ed. in collaboration with Melvin Strauss. [1958].
Vol.4. Unpublished.
Vol.5. Unpublished.
Vol.6. Händel, Georg Friedrich. Messiah; an oratorio. Part I. [1962].
Part II. [1959].

DONOSTÍA, JOSÉ ANTONIO DE, 1886–1956.
Obras musicales. Edición preparada y anotada por Jorge de Riezu. Lecaroz, Navarra, Archivo P. Donostia, 1960– .
v.1– .
Contents:
Vol.1. Navidad. 1960.
Vol.6. Lili eder Bat. 1962.

Dörffel, Alfred, 1821–1905, ed. Musica sacra, *see* Musica sacra . . . hrsg. von Alfred Dörffel.

DOWNES, OLIN, 1886–1955. ed.
A treasury of American song; text by Olin Downes and Elie Siegmeister; music arranged by Elie Siegmeister. 2d ed., rev. and enl., with a new Introd. New York, A. A. Knopf, 1943.
408p., 3L.

"The music in this book was reproduced from handwritten originals . . . The book was printed in photo-offset."
Piano accompaniment.

Drei Werke pommerscher Komponisten, *see* Engel, Hans. Drei Werke pommerscher Komponisten.

DROZ, EUGÉNIE, 1893– . ed.
. . . Poètes et musiciens du XVe siècle. Paris, G. Jeanbin, 1924.
86p. front., plates. (Documents artistiques du XVe siècle. Tome 1).
French words; music for 2, 3, and 4 voices transcribed in modern notation; with piano reduction.
Illustrated by reproductions from manuscripts and tapestries.
300 copies printed.
Contents:
Andrieu, F. Première déploration sur la mort de Guillaume de Machaut; paroles de Eustache Deschamps. *Andrieu, F.* Seconde déploration sur la mort de Guillaume de Machaut. De ce que foul pense. *Binchois.* Deul angoisseux, rage des mesurée; paroles de Christine de Pisan. *Binchois.* Triste plaisir et douleureuse yoie; paroles d'Alain Chartier. Je ne prise point tels baysiers; paroles de Charles d'Orléans. Va tost mon amoreux désir; paroles de Charles d'Orléans. Quant jamés aultre bien n'auroye; paroles de Le Rousselet. *Mureau, G.* Grace attendant ou la mort pour tous mes; paroles et musique de Gilles Mureau. *Hayne.* Allez regret vuidés de ma présence; paroles de Jean de Bourbon. *Compère, L.* Vous me faittes morir d'envie; paroles de Jean de Bourbon. *Molinet, J.* Tart ara mon cueur sa plaisance; paroles et musique de Jean Molinet. Non mudera ma constance et firmesse. Epitaphe de l'amant vert; paroles de Jean Lemaire de Belges.

[DROZ, EUGÉNIE], 1893– . ed.
Trois chansonniers français du XVe siècle. Paris, [E. Droz], 1927– .
xviii, 125, [1]p. vii pl., facsims. (Half title: Documents artistiques du XVe siècle. Tome 4).
For 3 voices and/or instruments. French words.
300 copies printed.
"L'introduction a été rédigée par E. Droz et G. Thibault ainsi que la partie littéraire du commentaire, tandis que Y. Rokseth et G. Thibault se sont chargées de toute la partie musicale."–Note de l'éditeur.
"Nous donnerons la transcription du chansonnier de Dijon [ms. 517 de la Bibliothèque de la ville de Dijon (ancien 296)], puis celle des chansons qui ne se trouvent que dans les deux autres recueils [celui qui appartient actuellement au marquis de Laborde, et le ms. Extrav. 287 de la Bibl. de Wolfenbüttel]. Nous avons déjà publié dans la Revue de Musicologie (Février 1927) les quatre 'unica' [du ms. 291 du fonds Thott de la Bibliothèque royale] de Copenhague." – Introd.

The Dublin virginal manuscript, *see* The Wellesley edition. No.3.

DUFAY, GUILLAUME, ca.1400–1474.
Opera omnia. Edidit Guglielmus de Van and H. Besseler. Rome, American Institute of Musicology in Rome, 1947–66.
6v. (Corpus mensurabilis musicae. No.1).
Contents:
Vol.1. Pt.1. Motetti qui et cantiones vocantur. 1947.
Vol.1. Pt.2. Motetti qui et cantiones vocantur. 1948.
Vol.2. Pt.1. Missa sine nomine. 1949.
Vol.2. Pt.2. Missa Sancti Jacobi. 1949.
Vol.2. Pt.3 (includes pts.1–2). Missarum pars prior, 1–6. 1960.
Missa sine nomine. Missa Sancti Jacobi. Missa Sancti Antonii Viennensis. Alleluia veni Sancte Spiritus. (Fragmentum missae?). Missa Caput. Appendix. Missa La morte de Saint Gothard. 1960.
Vol.3. Missarum pars altera. 1951.
Missa Se la face ay pale. Missa L'homme armé. Missa Ecce ancilla Domini. Missa Ave Regina coelorum. 1951.
Vol.3. Suppl. Missarum pars altera, 7–10. Critical notes. 1962.
Vol.4. Fragmenta missarum. 1962.
Fragmenta tripartita. Fragmenta bipartita. Kyrie. Gloria. Appendix. Opus dobiose traditum. Contratenor Guillelmi Dufay in gloria anonymi. 1962.
Vol.5. Compositiones liturgicae minores. 1966.
Vol.6. Cantiones. 1964.

Dufay and his contemporaries, *see* Early Bodleian music: [I]. Dufay and his contemporaries.

DU MAGE, PIERRE, ca.1676–1751.
. . . Livre d'orgue, de Pierre Du Mage, 1676(?)–1751. Révision par Félix Raugel d'après l'exemplaire de la Bibliothèque Nationale (Vm 7 1831). Paris, Éditions Musicales de la Schola Cantorum, cop.1952.
1p.L., 20p. (Les grandes heures de l'orgue).

DU MONT, HENRI, 1610–1684.
. . . Meslanges divers, remis au jour et publiés par M. Henri Quittard, comme supplément musical à son étude sur Henry Du Mont, publiée par la Société du Mercure de France . . . Paris, Bureau d'Édition de la "Schola Cantorum," [ca.1906].
57p.
At head of title: Répertoire de la "Schola Cantorum." Documents pour servir à l'Histoire de la Musique.
Contents:
1. Cantica sacra: Ave gemma virginum, No.27.
2. Meslanges: Laisse moy soupirer, No.1.
3. Dialogus de anima; fragment.
4. Motets à deux choeurs: Que madmodum desirat cervus.

DUNAEVSKIĬ, ISAAK OSIPOVICH, 1900–1955.
Complete works. Moscow, State Music Publishers.

v.1– .
Proposed set about 12v.

Dunstable, John, ca.1370–1453, Complete works, *see* Musica Britannica. Vol.8.

DUPUIS, THOMAS SANDERS, 1733–1796.
Cathedral music in score, composed for the use of his Majesty's Royal Chapels, by the late T. S. Dupuis. Selected from the original manuscripts, and carefully revised by John Spencer. London, Published for the benefit of the New Musical Fund.
v.1– .
Contents:
Vol.1 and 2 contain the score.
Vol.3 is the organ part.

DUYSE, FLORIMOND VAN, 1843–1910. ed.
Het oude Nederlandsche lied; wereldlijke en geestelijke liederen uit vroegeren tijd, teksten en melodieën, verzameld en toegelicht door Fl. van Duyse . . . 'S-Gravenhage, M. Nijhoff, [etc., etc.], 1903–8.
4v.
Vols.1–3 paged continuously.
Issued in 44 parts, 1900–1908.
"Voornaamste bronnen voor de studie van het oude Nederlandsche lied": v.1, p.[ix]-xvi.
Contents:
1.–2. deel. Het wereldijk lied.
3. deel. Het geestelijk lied.
4. deel. Registers.

DUYSE, FLORIMOND VAN, 1843–1910. ed.
Het oude Nederlandsche lied. 1– . Vervolg. 'S-Gravenhage, M. Nijhoff, 1922– .
v.1– .
Contents:
1. Vervolg. [Zuylen van Nyevelt: Willem van] Souterliedekens . . . uitg. door Elizabeth Mincoff-Marriage. 1922.

DVOŘÁK, ANTONÍN, 1841–1904.
Kritische Gesamtausgabe. Nach Originalquellen zum Druck vorbereitet von der Kommission für die Herausgabe der Werke Antonín Dvořáks. Vorsitzender: Otakar Šourek. Leitender Redakteur: Jan Hanuš. Czechoslovakia, Artia, 1955– .
7 series. (in progress). (Volumes with dates are published).
Ser.I. Theatrical works.
Vol.1. Alfred.
Vol.2. The king and the charcoal-burner (version from the year 1871).
Vol.3. The king and the charcoal-burner (version from the year 1874 and 1887).
Vol.4. The stubborn lovers.
Vol.5. Vanda.
Vol.6. The cunning peasant.
Vol.7. Dimitri (version from the year 1883).
Vol.8. Dimitri (version from the year 1894).
Vol.9. Incidental music to Šamberk's "Josef Kajetán Tyl."
Vol.10. Pt.1–2. The Jacobin. Op.84. 1966.
Vol.11. Kate and the devil.
Vol.12. Rusalka. Op.114. 1960.
Vol.13. Armida.
Ser.II. Oratorios, cantatas, mass.
Vol.1. Stabat Mater. Op.58. 1958.
Vol.2. The spectre's bride.
Vol.3. Pt.1–2. St. Ludmilla. Op.71. 1964.
Vol.4. Requiem. Op.89. 1961.
Vol.5. Hymnus "The heirs of the White Mountain"; Hymn of the Czech peasants; Two evening songs (with orchestra acc.); The American flag; Ode Op.113.
Vol.6. The 149th psalm; Te deum; Biblical songs (with orchestra acc.).
Vol.7. Mass in D major (version I, with organ acc.).
Vol.8. Mass in D major (version II, with orchestra acc.).
Ser.III. Orchestral works.
Vol.1. Symphony in C minor ("The bells of Zlonice"). 1961.
Vol.2. Symphony in B flat major. Op.4. 1959.
Vol.3. Symphony in E flat major. Op.10. 1963.
Vol.4. Symphony in D minor (from the year 1874). Op.13. 1962.
Vol.5. Symphony in F major. Op.76. 1960.
Vol.6. Symphony in D major. Op.60. 1957.
Vol.7. Symphony in D minor (from the year 1884/5). Op.70. 1955.
Vol.8. Symphony in G major. Op.88. 1956.
Vol.9. Symphony in E minor. Op.95. 1955.
Vol.10. Piano concerto. Op.33. 1956.
Vol.11. Violin concerto. Op.53. 1955.
Vol.12. Cello concerto. Op.104. 1955.
Vol.13. The Hussite overture. Op.67. 1957; In nature's realm. Op.91. 1956; Carnival. Op.92. 1955; Othello. Op.93. 1957.
Vol.14. The water goblin. Op.107. 1958; The noon witch. Op.108. 1958; The golden spinning wheel. Op.109. 1958.
Vol.15. The wild dove. Op.110. 1955; A hero's song. Op.111. 1960.
Vol.16. Serenade in E major, Op.22. 1955; Serenade in D minor, Op.44. 1956.
Vol.17. Czech suite. Op.39. 1955; Suite in A major. Op.98b. 1957.
Vol.18. Rhapsody in A minor. Op.14. 1959; Three Slavonic rhapsodies. Op.45. 1959.
Vol.19. Slavonic dances. Op.46. 1955.
Vol.20. Slavonic dances. Op.72. 1955.
Vol.21. Legends.
Vol.22. Symphonic variations. Op.78. 1957; Scherzo capriccioso. Op.66. 1955.
Vol.23. Romance Op.11, for violin; Mazurek for violin Op.49; Silent woods for 'cello, Rondo for 'cello (all with orchestra acc.).
Vol.24. Entreacts from the year 1867; Notturno Op.40; Festival march Op.54, The vanda overture; Polonaise in E flat major; Prague valses; Polka in B flat major.
Ser.IV. Chamber music.
Vol.1. Romance for violin Op.11; Capriccio; Slavonic dance Op.46, No.2; Mazurek Op.49; Sonata in F major Op.57; Notturno in B major Op.40; Ballad Op.15; Romantic pieces Op.75; Sonatina Op.100.

Vol.2. Cello concerto in A major (with piano acc.).
Vol.3. Polonaise in A major for 'cello; Rondo for 'cello Op.94; Slavonic dance Op.46, No.8; Silent woods for 'cello (from Op.68).
Vol.4. Terzetto in C major Op.74; Miniatures Op.75a; Gavotta for three violins.
Vol.5. String quartets in A major Op.2; D major; E minor; B flat major; F minor Op.9; A minor Op.12.
Vol.6. String quartets in A minor Op.16; E major Op.80; D minor Op.34; E flat major Op.51; Two valses from Op.54; Quartet movement F major.
Vol.7. String quartet in C major Op.61; Cypresses; String quartets in F major Op.96; A flat major Op.105; G major Op.106.
Vol.8. String quintets in A minor Op.1; G major Op.77; E flat major Op.97; String sextet in A major Op.48.
Vol.9. Piano trios in B flat major Op.21. 1955; G minor Op.26. 1958; F minor Op.65. 1957; Dumkas Op.90. 1955.
Vol.10. Piano quartets in D major Op.23. 1958; Bagatelles Op.47. 1957; E flat major Op.87. 1955.
Vol.11. Piano quintets in A major Op.5. 1959; A major Op.81. 1955.
Ser.V. Piano works.
Vol.1. Polka in E major from the year 1860; Two minuets Op.28; Dumka Op.35; Tema con variazioni Op.36; Scotch dances Op.41; Two furiants Op.42; Silhouettes Op.8.
Vol.2. Valses Op.54; Eclogues Op.56; Album-leaves; Piano pieces Op.52; Mazurkas Op. 56.
Vol.3. Impromptu; Humoresque in F sharp major; Dumka and Furiant Op.12; Two little pearls; Poetic tone-pictures Op.85.
Vol.4. Suite in A major. Op.98. 1957; Humoresques Op.101. 1955; Lullaby and Capriccio. 1959.
Vol.5. Slavonic dances Op.46 and Op.72 (piano duet). 1955.
Vol.6. Legends Op.59 (piano duet). 1955; From the Bohemian forest Op.68 (piano duet). 1957.
Ser.VI. Vocal music.
Vol.1. Songs to words by E. Krásnohorská; The orphan Op.5; Four Serbian songs Op. 6; Six songs from the Dvůr Králové manu-script; Evening songs Op.3, 9, 11; Three songs to religious words (Ave Maria, Ave maris stella, Hymnus ad Laudes in festo SS. Trinitatis); Three modern Greek songs Op.50; Gipsy songs Op.55.
Vol.2. Four songs Op.2; Two songs to folk poetry; In folk style Op.73; Four songs Op.82; Love songs Op.83; Biblical songs Op.99; Lullaby; Song from "The black-smith of Lešetín."
Vol.3. Moravian duets. Op.20, 32, 38. 1962; O sanctissima for alto and baritone. Op.19A. 1962; Child's song without accompaniment. 1962.
Vol.4. Male choruses; From "Moravian duets" for female voices; Four mixed choruses Op.29; Mixed choruses "In nature's realm" Op.63.
Ser.VII. Supplement.

EARLY BODLEIAN MUSIC: [I]. Dufay and his contemporaries; 50 compositions (. . . from about AD. 1400 to 1440). Transcribed from Ms. Canonici misc. 213 in the Bodleian Library . . . by J. F. R. Stainer and C. Stainer. With an intro-duction by E. W. B. Nicholson, and a critical analysis of the music by Sir John Stainer. [With an appendix containing an index to the whole contents of Ms. Canonici misc. 213]. London, Novello & Co., 1898.
xix, 207, [1]p. 8 facs.

EARLY BODLEIAN MUSIC . . . Reprint. Irvington-on-Hudson, N.Y., Capitol Publishing Co., Inc.
p.1– .
Contents:
Introduction.
Eight facsimiles.
Chapter I. Biographical notice of Dufay and his contemporaries.
Chapter II. A key to mensurable music.
Chapter III. Critical and general remarks on the examples of music.
Fifty compositions (AD. 1400–1440). Trans-cribed into modern notation.
Glossary of old French words.
Appendix I. An index to the first lines of the whole ms.
Appendix II. List of composers whose works are included in ms.

EARLY BODLEIAN MUSIC . . . Reprint. Amsterdam. Frits A. M. Knuf, 1963.

EARLY BODLEIAN MUSIC: [II]. Sacred and secular songs, together with other ms. com-positions in the Bodleian Library, Oxford, ranging from about AD. 1185 to about AD. 1505; with an introduction by E. W. B. Nicholson . . . and transcriptions into modern musical notation by J. F. R. Stainer . . . and C. Stainer; ed. by Sir John Stainer . . . London, Novello & Co.; New York, Novello, Ewer & Co., 1901.
2v. cx pl. (facsim.).
Contents:
Vol.I. Facsimiles.
Vol.II. Transcriptions.

EARLY BODLEIAN MUSIC: [III]. Introduction to the study of some of the oldest Latin musical manuscripts in the Bodleian Library, Oxford; by Edward Williams Byron Nicholson . . . With 71 colletype facsimiles. London, Novello & Co.; New York, H. W. Gray Co., 1913.
xciv p., 2L. LXXI pl. (facsim.).
"This volume is the complement to . . . 'Early Bodleian music' produced by the late Sir John Stainer . . ." – Pref.

EARLY ENGLISH CHURCH MUSIC. General editor: Frank Llewellyn Harrison. London, Stainer and

Bell, Ltd., [cop.1963–].
v.1– .
Contents:
Vol.1. Early Tudor masses: I. Transcribed and ed. by John D. Bergsagel. 1963.
Vol.2. Mundy, William. Latin antiphons and psalms. Transcribed and ed. by Frank Ll. Harrison. 1963.
Vol.3. Gibbons, Orlando. Verse anthems. Transcribed and ed. by David Wulstan. 1964.
Vol.4. Early Tudor magnificats: I. Transcribed and ed. by Paul Doe. 1964.
Vol.5. Tomkins, Thomas. Musica deo sacra: I. Transcribed and ed. by Bernard Rose. 1965.
Subsequent volumes are planned to include fifteenth-century antiphons and mass music; early Tudor antiphons and magnificats; early Tudor liturgical organ music; the sacred works of John Sheppard, Robert Parsons, A. Ferrabosco I and II, John Ward, William Child, William and Henry Lawes; the sacred works in Thomas Myriell's Jacobean anthology; and the anthems of Thomas Tomkins.

Early English harmony from the 10th to the 15th century, Wooldridge, Harry Ellis, ed., *see* Plainsong and Mediaeval Music Society. Wooldridge, Harry Ellis. Early English harmony from the 10th to the 15th century.

Early English keyboard music, *see* Schott's anthology of early keyboard music.

Early English organ music (16th century). Glyn, Margaret Henrietta, ed., *see* Plainsong and Mediaeval Music Society. Glyn, Margaret Henrietta. Early English organ music (16th century).

Early fifteenth-century music, *see* Reaney, Gilbert. Early fifteenth-century music.

EARLY ITALIAN KEYBOARD MUSIC. Ed. and arr. by G. S. Bedbrook. London, Schott & Co., [cop.1955–].
No.1– .
Contents:
No.1. Merulo, Claudio. 4 Toccatas. [cop.1955].
No.2. Cavazzoni, Marco Antonio. 2 French chansons and a recercar. [1956].

Early Italian piano music, *see* Esposito, Michele. Early Italian piano music.

Early keyboard music, *see* Oesterle, Louis. Early keyboard music.

EARLY PSALMODY IN 17th CENTURY AMERICA. Ed. by Carleton Sprague Smith. New York, 1938– .
v.1– . (New York Public Library. Music publications).
Contents:
Ser.I. The Ainsworth psalter. (Plymouth). Vol.I. Psalm 65. 1938.

Early Spanish organ music, *see* Muset, Joseph. Early Spanish organ music.

EARLY SYMPHONIES AND CONCERTOS. Ed. by Sydney Beck. New York, Music Press, Inc., 1938– .
v.1– . (New York Public Library. Music publications).
Contents:
Vol.1. Gossec, F. J. Sinfonia in G major, Op.XII, No.2. For 2 oboes, 2 horns, and strings. Ed. by Sydney Beck. 1938.

Eastman School of Music. Publication. No.3, *see* Soderlund, Gustave Fredric. Examples illustrating the development of melodic line and contrapuntal style, from Greek melody to Mozart.

Eastman School of Music. Publication. No.4, *see* Soderlund, Gustave Fredric. Examples of Gregorian chant and works by Orlandus Lassus and Giovanni Pierluigi Palestrina.

Eastman School of Music. Publication. No.10, *see* Gleason, Harold. Examples of music before 1400.

ECCLESIASTICON. Eine Sammlung klassischer Kirchenmusik in Partitur. Wien, A. Diabelli & Co., [18?–].
78 nos.
Contents:
No.1–20. Michael Haydn. Graduales.
No.21. Horzalka. Missa solemnis. Op.27.
No.22. Stadler. Salvum fac.
No.23. Stadler. Magna et mirabilis.
No.24. Mozart. Regina coeli.
No.25. Cherubini, Luigi. Offertorium. (Pater noster, qui es in coelis) . . . [1830].
No.26. Cherubini, Luigi. Offertorium. (Ecce, panis angelorum) . . . [1830].
No.27. Cherubini, Luigi. Offertorium. (Ave, Maria, gratia plena) . . . [1830].
No.28. Cherubini, Luigi. Offertorium. (O Deus ego amo te) . . . [1830].
No.29. Cherubini, Luigi. Offertorium. (Lauda, anima mea, Dominum) . . . [1830].
No.30. Cherubini, Luigi. Offertorium. (Lauda, Sion! salvatorem) . . . [1830].
No.31. Cherubini, Luigi. Offertorium. (Laudate Dominum omnes gentes) . . . [1831?].
No.32. Cherubini, Luigi. Graduale to Mass No.4. (O salutaris hostia) . . . [183?].
No.33. Cherubini, Luigi. Regina coeli für 4 Singstimmen, 2 Violinen, [etc.]. [1831?].
No.34. Cherubini, Luigi. Tantum ergo und Genitori für Soprano, Alt, Tenor, Bass, [etc.]. [1831?].
No.35. Stadler. Delectare.
No.36. Stadler. Si Deus.
No.37. Bach, J. S. Chorus, Da pacem.
No.38. Winter. Dominus Israel.
No.39. Sechter. Mass, Graduale, etc.
No.40. Albrechtsberger. Offertorium.
No.41–62. Michael Haydn. Graduales.
No.63. Czerny. Six graduales. Op.318.
No.64. Reissiger. Grand mass in E flat.

No.65. Mozart. Tremendum.
No.66. Sechter. Salve Regina and Ave Maria.
No.67. Woržischek. Offertorium.
No.68. Geiger. Mass.
No.69–71. Assmayr. Offertoriums.
No.72. Mozart. Offertorium in F.
No.73. Seegner. Mass in F.
No.74. Sechter. Missa solemnis in C.
No.75. Mozart. Sancti et justi.
No.76. Seegner. Grand mass in E flat.
No.77. Seegner. Mass in D.
No.78. Beraneck. Offertorium.

ÉCHOS DE FRANCE. Paris, A. Durand & Fils, [1895?]–cop.1909.
4v.
Contents:
Vol.1–3. Recueil des plus célèbres airs, romances, duos, etc., de Lully, Rameau, Gluck, Piccini, Sacchini, Dalayrac, Grétry, Méhul, Monsigny, Guédron, Martini, Garat, Gaveaux, Mme. Gail, etc.
Vol.4. Recueil des plus célèbres airs de ballet de danses des Théâtres de la Foire, Opéra-comique, Comédie italienne, Marionnettes de Mgr. le Dauphin, Grands danseurs du Roy, Opéra-bouffon de 1698 à 1815. Recueillis et harmonisés par Léon Roques.

Échos du temps passé, *see* Weckerlin, Jean Baptiste Théodore. Échos du temps passé.

ECKARD, JOHANN GOTTFRIED, 1735–1809.
Oeuvres complètes pour le clavecin ou le piano-forte. Amsterdam, Ed. Heuwekemeijer; Kassel, Bärenreiter, [1956].
94p.

École classique de l'orgue, *see* Guilmant, Alexandre. École classique de l'orgue.

L'ÉCOLE DU VIOLON AU XVIIe ET XVIIIe SIÈCLE . . . Paris, B. Roudanez, cop.1905– .
No.1– .
This collection appeared originally as "Les maîtres français du violon au XVIIIe siècle," but beginning with number 1263 and continuing, with the exception of number 1264, on through the remainder of the collection, it is called L'école du violon au XVIIe et XVIIIe siècle.
Nos.1248 through 1296 were published by B. Roudanez, Paris. The numbers from then on were published by Henry Lemoine & Cie., Paris. The numbers used to indicate the different compositions are taken from the list of the collection printed on the back of the Lemoine publications only. They have been added to the Roudanez publications in order that there might be one system of numbering throughout the entire collection.
Beginning with No.1263 and, with the exception of No.1264, running through 1296, the imprint reads: M. Senart, B. Roudanez & Cie., Paris.
Contents:
No.1248. François Francoeur le cadet. Sonate en sol mineur.
No.1249. L'Abbé le fils. Sonate en ré majeur.
No.1250. Jean Baptiste Senaillié le fils. Sonate en mi majeur.
No.1251. François Du Val. Sonate en la majeur.
No.1252. Jean Pierre Guignon. Sonate en sol majeur.
No.1253. Jean Ferry-Rebel. Sonate en ré mineur.
No.1254. Branche. Sonate en sol mineur.
No.1255. Jacques Aubert. Sonate en fa majeur.
No.1256. Louis Aubert le fils. Sonate en la mineur.
No.1257. Antoine d'Auvergne. Sonate en sol majeur.
No.1258. Pagin. Sonate en ré majeur.
No.1259. Joseph Marchard le fils. Suite sonate.
No.1260. C. C. Mondonville le jeune. Sonate en fa mineur.
No.1261. Denis. Sonate en la mineur.
No.1262. François Francoeur le cadet. Sonate en mi mineur.
No.1263. Jean Baptiste Senallié le fils. Sonate en ut mineur.
No.1264. Le Blanc. Sonate en mi♭ majeur.
No.1265. Diogenio Bigaglia. Sonate en si♭ majeur.
No.1266. Carlo Tessarini. Sonate en ré majeur.
No.1267. Evaristo Felice Dall'Abaco. Sonate en fa majeur.
No.1268. Antonio Vivaldi. Sonate en la majeur.
No.1269. Jean François d'Andrieu. Sonate en sol majeur.
No.1270. Jean François d'Andrieu. Sonate en mi mineur. (2 violons et piano).
No.1271. François Bouvard. Sonate en fa majeur.
No.1272. Wenzel Pichl. 6 Fugues pour violon seul.
No.1273. John Humphries. Sonate en ut mineur.
No.1274. Michael Christian Festing. Sonate en si mineur.
No.1275. Gio. Battista Somis. Sonate en sol majeur.
No.1276. Arcangelo Corelli. La folia.
No.1277. Jean Baptiste Loeillet. Sonate en la majeur.
No.1278. Georg Friedr. Händel. Sonate en fa majeur.
No.1279. Johann Ernst Galliard. Sonate en mi mineur.
No.1280. Pietro Locatelli. Sonate en ré majeur.
No.1281. Arcangelo Corelli. Sonate en fa majeur.
No.1282. Brévio. Sonate en la majeur. (2 violons et piano).
No.1283. Georg Friedr. Händel. Sonate en sol mineur. (2 violons et piano).
No.1284. Jean Baptiste Dupuits. Sonate en ré majeur.
No.1285. Gioseppe Fedeli Saggione. Sonate en mi majeur.
No.1286. Nicolas Clérambault. (La félicité). Sonate en sol majeur. (2 violons et piano).
No.1287. Mangean. Sonate en fa majeur.
No.1288. Arcangelo Corelli. Sonate en ré majeur. (2 violons et piano).
No.1289. Joseph Exaudet. Sonate en ut mineur.
No.1290. Jacques Aubert. Suite, "Ma pinte et ma mie au gay." (2 violons et piano).
No.1291. 1er recueil. Louis Joseph Francoeur. Sarabande; Gaetano Pugnani. Andantino; Delin. Aria; Georg Friedr. Händel. Hornpipe.

No.1292. 2e recueil. Jean Joseph Mondonville. Sarabande; Giovanni Guido Antonio. La caccia; Francesco Geminiari. Allegretto; T. A. Arne. Hornpipe.
No.1293. 3e recueil. Jean Marie Leclair. Largo; Dauphin. Le coucou; François Du Val. La girouette; Jean Baptiste Senallié. Allegro.
No.1294. 4e recueil. Giovanni Chinzer. Andante; Johann Ernst Galliard. Hornpipe; (?) Rondo; Mondonville le jeune. Menuet et variations.
No.1295. 5e recueil. Jean François d'Andrieu. Gavotte; Jean Christian Schikhardt. Ciacona; Georg Friedr. Händel. Bourrée; Jean Pierre Guignon. Chasse.
No.1296. Campagnoli. 6 Fugues pour violon seul.

No.1333. 6e recueil. Jean Marie Leclair. Largo; (?) Les siflets ou les chaudronniers; Michele Mascitti. Forlana; Caix d'Hervelois. Moulinet.
No.1334. 7e recueil. Jean Paul von Westhoff. Aria; (?) La pie; Michele Mascitti. Sarabande; Chabran. La chasse.
No.1335. 8e recueil. Pietro Nardini. Adagio en ré; (?) Les tambourins; Pasqualli. Menuet de la 5e sonate; Mondonville. La chasse.
No.1336. 9e recueil. Blavet. Sarabande; Durand. Le retour du printemps; Jean Marie Leclair. Tambrin de la 10e sonate; Guillmain. La chasse.
No.1337. 10e recueil. De Lingy. Chanson à boire; De Chauvigny. La maladie de Monseigneur le Dauphin; (?) Les plaisirs de la campagne; Jean Marie Leclair. La chasse.
No.1338. 11e recueil. Jean Marie Leclair. Largo; Lully. Menuet du bourgeois gentilhomme; (?) Les papillons; Le Blanc. La chasse.
No.1339. 12e recueil. Michele Mascitti. Sarabande; Jacques Aubert. Les tambourins; Blavet. Les regrets; Antonio Vivaldi. Capriccio.
No.1340. 13e recueil. Jean Marie Leclair. Aria; Blavet. L'invincible; (?) Air gaulois; Gio. Battista Somis. Tambourin.
No.1341. 14e recueil. Michele Mascitti. Adagio religioso; Campra. Musette; Blavet. Tendres badinages; Jean Marie Leclair. Ciaconna.
No.1342. 15e recueil. Pietro Nardini. Adagio; Chédeville. La chicane; Jean Pierre Guignon. Tambourin; Jean Marie Leclair. Prestissimo.
No.1343. 16e recueil. Jean Marie Leclair. Sarabanda; Piffet le fils. Le choix d'un berger; Blavet. Les caquets; François Du Val. Papillon.
No.1344. 17e recueil. Blavet. Ciciliana; (?) La sauterelle; Jean Marie Leclair. Musette; Martini. Gavotte.
No.1345. 18e recueil. Anselme. Air sur la vendange; Huguenet. Air badin; Michele Mascitti. Les vents; Jean Marie Leclair. Presto.
No.1346. 19e recueil. Pietro Nardini. Adagio en mi; Piffet le fils. Le pastor fido; Jean Marie Leclair. Allegro; Fiorillo. 28e caprice.
No.1347. 20e recueil. Chédeville. Le tapage; Blavet. Le Marc-Antoine; Jean Marie Leclair. Allegro; Kreutzer. Étude marche.

Jacques Aubert. Les jolis airs ajustés pour 2 violons et accompagnement de piano. (Collection Joseph Debroux).
1e suite. Ma pinte et ma mye au gay.
2e suite. Ma femme fait un métier.
3e suite. Ma mye Margot.
4e suite. Aye, aye, aye Jeannette.
5e suite. Pierrot sur le bord d'un ruisseau.
6e suite. D'une main je tiens mon pot.
7e suite. Carillon de Dunkerque.
8e suite. Chère Lisette.
9e suite. La confession.
10e suite. Quoy my voisine.

ÉCORCHEVILLE, JULES ARMAND JOSEPH, 1872–1915. ed.
... Vingt suites d'orchestre du XVIIe siècle français. Publiées pour la première fois d'après un manuscrit de la Bibliothèque de Cassel et précédées d'une étude historique ... Paris, L.–M. Fortin & Cie., 1906.
2v. diagr., facsims. (music), illus. (music), plates.
"Les fac-similés du Manuscrit de Cassel, avec l'ancien et le nouveau Classement," tome 1, 47p., at end. "Partition d'orchestre et réduction pour le piano," tome 2.
Bibliography, tome 1, 1p., at end; also bibliographical footnotes.

Edwards music reprints. Ser.A. Complete works and monumenta, *see* Bach, Johann Sebastian. Werke. (Edwards music reprints, Ser.A, No.1); Beethoven, Ludwig van. Werke. (Edwards music reprints, Ser.A, No.2); Brahms, Johannes. Sämtliche Werke. (Edwards music reprints, Ser.A, No.3); Mozart, Wolfgang Amadeus. Sämtliche Werke. (Edwards music reprints, Ser.A, No.4).

Edwards music reprints. Ser.B. Individual and musicological works, *see* The Fitzwilliam virginal book. (Edwards music reprints, Ser.B, No.2).

EINSTEIN, ALFRED, 1880–1952. ed.
... Beispielsammlung zur älteren Musikgeschichte, von Alfred Einstein. Leipzig und Berlin, B. G. Teubner, 1917.
iv, 87p. (Aus Natur und Geisteswelt ... Bd.439).
Music supplement to his Geschichte der Musik.
Fourth edition, 1930. English edition, London, 1949.
Contents:
Anonym. Motetus des 13. Jahrhunderts; Dufay, W. Messesatz (um 1450); Pesenti, M. Ballata (1504); Senfl, L. Deutsches Lied (1534); Willaert, A. Niederländische Motette (1539); Certon, P. Chanson (1540); Nola, G. D. Mascherata (1541); Marenzio, L. Madrigal (1581); Gabrieli, G. Venezianische Motette (1587); Gastoldi, G. G. Tanslied (1591); Merulo, C. Ricercar (1567); Macque, G. de. Canzon alla francese (um 1600); Schütz, H. Konzertierende Motette (1647); Gabrieli, D. Kammerkantate (1691); Krieger, A. Deutsches Lied (1667); Caldara, A. Kirchensonate (1700); Somis, G. B. Kammersonate; Bach, J. S. Concerto grosso Form; Fischer,

J. K. F. Klavier-Suite (1696); Pachelbel, J. Orgelchoral; Haydn, J. Sonatenform (Quartettsatz); Ammerkungen.

EINSTEIN, ALFRED, 1880–1952. ed.
The golden age of the madrigal; 12 Italian madrigals for 5-part chorus of mixed voices never before published in a modern edition. Selected, ed., and annotated by Alfred Einstein, with English versions by Gustave Reese. New York, G. Schirmer, Inc., [cop. 1942].
95p.
Italian and English words.
Madrigals by Jacques Arcadelt, Andrea Gabrieli, Giovanni Gabrieli, Marco da Gagliano, Luzzasco Luzzaschi, Luca Marenzio, Claudio Merulo, Filippo di Monte, Costanzo Porta, Cipriano de Rore, Orazio Vecchi, and Giaches Wert.

Einstimmige Chor- und Sololieder des XVI. Jahrhunderts mit Instrumental-Begleitung, *see* Schering, Arnold. Einstimmige Chor- und Sololieder des XVI. Jahrhunderts mit Instrumental-Begleitung.

Einundneunzig gesammelte Tonsätze, *see* Hofhaimer, Paul. Einundneunzig gesammelte Tonsätze.

EISLER, HANNS, 1898–1962.
Lieder und Kantaten. Leipzig, Breitkopf & Härtel Musikverlag, [19?–].
v.1– .
Place of publication covered by label: Wiesbaden, Breitkopf & Härtel.
Consists of songs with piano, songs with instrumental ensemble, women's choruses in varying combinations, and cantatas (in full score).

Eitner, Robert, 1832–1905, ed. Buxheimer Orgelbuch. Das Buxheimer Orgelbuch, *see* Buxheimer Orgelbuch. Das Buxheimer Orgelbuch.

EITNER, ROBERT, 1832–1905. ed.
Cantaten des 17. und 18. Jahrhunderts, hrsg. von Robert Eitner . . . [Leipzig, Breitkopf & Härtel], 1884–86.
3 pts. in 1 v. (Beilage[n] zu den Monatsheften für Musikgeschichte [16.–18. Jahrg.]).
Paged continuously.
Contents:
Pt.1. Heinrich, Albert. Jst es unsrer salten Werk; Stoelzel, G. H. Die Rose bleibt der Blumen Königin; Keiser, Reinhard. Bei kühler Abenddämmerung. Mir wird bald heiss, bald kalt, begleitetes Recitative Deine Grossmut, deine Güte, Aria, Lieben, Leiden, Bitten, Flehen, Aria.
Pt.2. Schürmann, G. C. Pflüget ein neues und säet. Deine Krone samt dem Throne, Aria; Buxtehude, Dieterich. Auf! Salten. Nun freut euch, ihr Frommen.
Pt.3. Buxtehude, Dieterich. Con quassabit capita; Graun, K. H. Das Mitleid: Mitleid lebst du noch? ; Hasse, J. A. Che ti dirò, Regina? Vedrai che amore, aria.

Eitner, Robert, 1832–1905, ed. Publikationen älterer praktischer und theoretischer Musikwerke, *see* Publikationen älterer praktischer und theoretischer Musikwerke.

The elements of plainsong, *see* Plainsong and Mediaeval Music Society. The elements of plainsong (1895 ed.; 1909 ed.).

Elewyck, Xavier Victor Fidèle, *Chevalier*, van, 1825–1888, ed. Clavecinistes flamands, *see* Clavecinistes flamands.

Elf Orgelchoräle des siebzehnten Jahrhunderts, *see* Dietrich, Fritz. Elf Orgelchoräle des siebzehnten Jahrhunderts.

Elizabeth II, Queen of Great Britain, 1926– . The music with the form and order of the service to be performed at the coronation of her most excellent Majesty, Queen Elizabeth II, *see* The music with the form and order of the service to be performed at the coronation of her most excellent Majesty, Queen Elizabeth II.

ELIZABETHAN VIRGINAL COMPOSERS . . . ed. for the pianoforte from the mss. by Margaret H. Glyn. London, [etc.], Joseph Williams, Ltd., cop. 1922– .
v.1– .
Contents:
Vol.1. Orlando Gibbons. John Bull.

Elizondo, Hilarión Eslava y, *see* Eslava y Elizondo, Hilarión.

ELKAN-VOGEL ORGAN SERIES. H. William Hawke, ed. Philadelphia, Elkan-Vogel Co., Inc., [1947–48].
5v.
Contents:
Vol.1. Early Italian. (Bernardo Pasquini, Girolamo Cavazzoni, Girolamo A. Frescobaldi, G. B. Martini).
Vol.2. Early English. (Martin Peerson, T. A. Arne, Jonathan Battishill).
Vol.3. Early German. (J. L. Krebs, Johann Pachelbel, J. J. Froberger, J. K. F. Fischer).
Vol.4. Dietrich Buxtehude.
Vol.5. Early Spanish. (Antonius de Cabezón, Padre Rafael Anglès, Luis Milán, Fray Juan Bermudo, Miguel de Fuenllana).

Ellinwood, Leonard Webster, 1905– , ed. The works of Francesco Landino, *see* Landino, Francesco. The works of Francesco Landino.

ELÚSITIZA, JUAN B. DE. ed.
Antología musical; Siglo de oro de la música litúrgica de España; Polifonía vocal, siglos XV y XVI, por d. Juan B. de Elúsitiza . . . y d. Gonzalo Castrillo Hernández . . . Barcelona, R. Casulleras, 1933.
3p.L., [v]-lxxxviii, [2]p., 182p. (music), [2]p., 1L. col. pl.
"Prologo editorial" signed: José Noguer.
A collection of motets from two manuscripts, one

(signed "Diego Sanchez [clerigo] año 1616") preserved in the church of Santiago at Valladolid: the other (anonymous, early 16th century) in the Biblioteca Colombina, Seville.
"Biografías": p.[xxxii]-lxxxviii.
"Apéndice: 1. Antifona II del patrono de la Catedral, 4v., Juan B. de Elúsitiza; 2. Antifona III a la Stma. Virgen, 4v., Gonzalo Castrillo."
Contains compositions by Anchieta, R. Ceballos, Escobar, Eco. Guerrero, Pedro Guerrero, F. Montanos, C. Morales, J. Navarro, Peñalosa, Rivafiecha, Robledo, Villalar, and others unnamed.

ENGEL, CARL, 1883–1944. ed.
Music from the days of George Washington. Collected and provided with an introd. by Carl Engel . . . The music ed. by W. Oliver Strunk . . . With a preface by Hon. Sol Bloom . . . Washington, D.C., United States George Washington Bicentennial Commission, [cop. 1931].
ix, 61p.
Contains compositions by Samuel Arnold, William Brown, Henri Capron, Pierre Landrin Duport, James Hewitt, Francis Hopkinson, Philip Phile, Alexander Reinagle, William Shield, Stephen Storace, and Samuel Webbe.

Engel, Hans, 1894– , ed. Denkmäler der Musik in Pommern, *see* Denkmäler der Musik in Pommern.

ENGEL, HANS, 1894– . ed.
Drei Werke pommerscher Komponisten: Choralfantasien von Paul Luetkeman (1597); Lazarus, das erste deutsche Oratorium, von Andreas Fromm (1649); Der Herr hat seinen Ingeln befahlen (Psalm 91), geistliches Konzert von Johann Vierdanck (d.1646). Greifswald, L. Bamberg, 1931.
1p.L., 5–15p. illus. (music) facsims.
Signed: Hans Engel.
"Anlässlich der Aufführung am 18. Dezember 1931 im Stadttheater in Greifswald, veranstaltet zugensten der Greifswalder Notleidenden . . . vom Stadttheater, Medrowschen Madrigalchor und Collegium Musicum der Universität.– p.[2]. cf. cover.
"Die Texte des Actus Musicus [de divite et Lazaro] und des Geistlichen Konzertes," p.13–15.

ENGEL, LEHMAN, 1910– . ed.
Three centuries of choral music: Renaissance to Baroque, selected and ed., with historical and biographical notes, by Lehman Engel. Embellishments by Gibson Baker. New York, Harold Flammer, Inc., 1939–56.
5v. illus.
Part songs, with pianoforte accompaniment.
"Musical genealogy," 1300–1600, on cover.
Contents:
Vol.1. French-Netherland music. (Contains compositions by Binchois, Certon, Costeley, De la Rue, De Monte, Des Près, Dufay, Gombert, Goudimel, Janequin, Le Jeune, Machault, Mouton, Obrecht, Okeghem, and Sermisy).
Vol.2. Italian music. (Contains compositions by Felice Anerio, Emilio de Cavalieri, Andrea Gabrieli, Carlo Gesualdo, Francesco Landino, Claudio Monteverdi, Luca Marenzio, Giovanni Maria Nanino, Giovanni Pierluigi da Palestrina, Francesco Soriano, Orazio Vecchi, Tomás Luis de la Victoria, Adrian Willaert, and Gioseffe Zarlino).
Vol.3. English music. (Contains compositions by William Byrd, John Dowland, John Dunstable, John Farmer, Orlando Gibbons, King Henry VIII, Henry Lichfield, Thomas Morley, Peter Philips, Francis Pilkington, Thomas Ravenscroft, Thomas Tallis, John Taverner, Christopher Tye, Thomas Vautor, Thomas Weelkes, Thomas Whythorne).
Vol.4. German music. (Contains compositions by J. S. Bach, Dietrich Buxtehude, Melchior Franck, Hans Leo Hassler, Heinrich Isaak, Orlando di Lasso, Samuel Scheidt, Johann Hermann Schein, Heinrich Schütz, Ludwig Senfl, Jan Pieter Sweelinck, Johann Walther).
Vol.5. Spanish music. (Contains compositions by Juan de Anchieta, Brihuega, Joan Brudieu, Enrique, Juan del Ensina, Juan Escobar, Juan d'Espinosa, Matteo Flecha, Francisco Guerrero, Millán, Cristobal Morales, Juan Navarro, Juan Ponce, Antonio de Ribera, Francesco de la Torre, Juan Urrede, and Tomas Luis de Victoria).

The English dancing master, *see* Playford, John. The English dancing master.

ENGLISH INSTRUMENTAL MUSIC OF THE 16th AND 17th CENTURIES from manuscripts in the New York Public Library. [New York, New York Public Library, 1947– .
No.1– .
Contents:
No.2. Nine fantasias in 4 parts by Byrd, Bull, Ferrabosco, Jenkins, and Ives. For viola or modern string quartet. Ed. Sydney Beck. 1947.
No.7. Four suites made from consort music, by Matthew Locke. In 4 parts. For string quartet or string orchestra. Ed. Sydney Beck. 1947.

ENGLISH KEYBOARD MUSIC. London, Stainer & Bell, Ltd.
No.1– .
Contents:
[No.1]. Tomkins, Thomas. Nine organ pieces. Transcribed and ed. by Stephen D. Tuttle. Revised and selected by Thurston Dart. (Pieces selected from Vol.V of Musica Britannica). [cop.1955].
[No.2]. Tomkins, Thomas. Fifteen dances. Transcribed and ed. by Stephen D. Tuttle. Revised and selected by Thurston Dart. (Pieces selected from Vol.V of Musica Britannica). [cop.1955].
[No.3]. The Mulliner book. Eleven pieces for keyboard instruments. Ed. by Denis Stevens. [cop.1951].
[No.4]. Byrd, William. Fifteen pieces. Newly

transcribed and selected from the Fitzwilliam virginal book and Parthenia, by Thurston Dart. [cop.1956].
[No.5]. Purcell, Henry. Suites.
[No.6]. Locke, Matthew. Keyboard suites. Transcribed and ed. by Thurston Dart. [cop. 1959].
[No.7]. Locke, Matthew. Organ voluntaries. Transcribed and ed. by Thurston Dart. [cop. 1957].
[No.8]. Bull, John. Ten pieces. Transcribed and ed. by John Steele and Francis Cameron. (Pieces selected from Vol.XIV of Musica Britannica). [cop.1960].
[No.9]. Clement Matchett's virginal book. (1612).
[No.10]. The second part of Musick's Hand-maid. Revised and corrected by Henry Purcell. Transcribed and ed. by Thurston Dart. 2d rev. ed. (First pub. in 1689, reissued in 1705). [cop.1958].
(Compositions by John Blow, Henry Purcell, William Turner, [Moses] Snow, G. B. Draghi, Francis Forcer, Verdier, Richard Motley).
[No.11]. Farnaby, Giles. Seventeen pieces. Newly transcribed and selected from the Fitzwilliam virginal book by Thurston Dart. [cop.1957].
[No.12–13]. Morley, Thomas. Keyboard works. Transcribed by Thurston Dart. 2 v. [cop. 1959].
[No.14]. Tisdall, William. Complete keyboard works. Newly transcribed and ed. from the Fitzwilliam virginal book and the John Bull virginal book by Howard Ferguson. [cop. 1958].
[No.15]. Early Scottish keyboard music. Transcribed and ed. by Kenneth Elliott. Ten pieces by William Kinloch, Duncan Burnett, and others. [cop.1958].
[No.16]. Twenty-four pieces from the Fitzwilliam virginal book.
[No.17]. Gibbons, Orlando. A selection of short dances. [cop.1925, rev. ed. cop.1960].
[No.18]. Roseingrave, Thomas. Ten organ pieces. Transcribed and ed. by Peter Williams. [cop. 1961].
[No.19]. Parthenia. (William Byrd, John Bull, Orlando Gibbons). Transcribed and ed. by Thurston Dart. [cop.1960, rev. ed. cop.1962].

English lute music, *see* Schott's series of early lute music.

The English madrigal school, *see* Fellowes, Rev. Edmund Horace. The English madrigal school.

English organ music of the eighteenth century, *see* Butcher, Vernon. English organ music of the eighteenth century.

The English school of lutenist song writers, *see* Fellowes, Rev. Edmund Horace. The English school of lutenist song writers.

ENGLISH SONGS. London, Stainer & Bell, Ltd., [cop.1956–].
No.1– .
Contents:
No.1. Lawes, Henry. Ten ayres for contralto (or baritone) and keyboard. Selected and ed. by Thurston Dart. 1956.

DAS ERBE DEUTSCHER MUSIK. Hrsg. im Auftrage des Staatlichen Instituts für deutsche Musikforschung. 1. Reihe. Reichsdenkmale. Leipzig, Breitkopf & Härtel, 1935– .
v.1– .
Publishers vary with different volumes.
Contents:
Vol.1. Altbachisches Archiv aus Johann Sebastian Bachs Sammlung von Werken seiner Vorfahren Johann Heinrich, Georg Christoph, Johann Michael und Johann Christoph Bach. 1. Teil: Motetten und Chorlieder. 1935.
Vol.2. Altbachisches Archiv . . . 2. Teil: Kantaten. 1935.
Vol.3. Bach, Johann Christian. Sechs Quintette, Op.11. 1935.
Vol.4. Das Glogauer Liederbuch. 1. Teil: Deutsche Lieder und Spielstücke. 1936. (Note: A selection of these songs was published by Konrad Ameln under the title of "Das Glogauer Liederbuch," Kassel, Bärenreiter-Verlag, 1927).
Vol.5. Senfl, Ludwig. Sieben Messen zu vier bis sechs Stimmen. 1936.
Vol.6. Telemann, Georg Philipp. Pimpinone, oder Die ungleiche Heirat. 1936.
Vol.7. Trompeterfantaren, Sonaten und Feldstücke nach Aufzeichnungen deutscher Hoftrompeter des 16/17 Jahrhunderts. 1936.
Vol.8. Das Glogauer Liederbuch. 2. Teil: Ausgewählte lateinische Sätze. 1937.
Vol.9. Orgelchoräle um Johann Sebastian Bach, nach Handschriften und Drucken des 18. Jahrhunderts. 1937.
Composers: Ahle, Johann Rudolf; Alberti, Johann Friedrich; Armsdorff, Andreas; Bach, Johann Bernard; Bach, Johann Michael; Bach, Wilhelm Friedemann; Buttstedt, Johann Heinrich; Gerber, Heinrich Nicolaus; Kauffmann, Georg Friedrich; Keller, Heinrich Michael; Krebs, Johann Ludwig; Krebs, Johann Tobias; Krieger, Johann; Reichardt, Christian; Schiefferdecker, Johann Christian; Schneider, Johann; Vetter, Andreas; Volckmar, Tobias; Witte, Christian Friedrich.
Vol.10. Senfl, Ludwig. Deutsche Lieder. 1. Teil: Lieder aus handschriftlichen Quellen bis etwa 1533. 1938.
Vol.11. Gruppenkonzerte der Bachzeit. 1938.
Composers: Fasch, Johann Friedrich; Heinrichen, Johann David; Telemann, Georg Philipp.
Vol.12. Lautenmusik des 17/18 Jahrhunderts. Ausgewählte Werke von Essias Reusner und Silvius Leopold Weiss. 1939.
Vol.13. Senfl, Ludwig. Motetten. 1. Teil: Gelegenheitsmotetten und Psalmvertonungen. 1939.
Vol.14. Deutsche Bläsermusik vom Barock bis zur Klassik. 1941.

Vol.15. Senfl, Ludwig. Deutscher Lieder.
2. Teil: Lieder aus Hans Otts Liederbuch von 1534. 1940.
Vol.16. Othmayr, Caspar. Ausgewählte Werke.
1. Teil: Symbola. Leipzig, Peters, 1941.
Vol.17. Walther, J. J. Scherzi da Violino Solo con il Basso continuo (1676). 1941.
Vol.18. Bach, C. P. E. Vier Orchestersinfonien mit zwölf obligaten Stimmen. 1942.
Vol.19. (a). Rathegeber, V. Augsburger Tafelconfect. (b). Senfl, L. Motetten. 1943.
Vol.20. Forster, Georg. Frische teutsche Liedlein. (1539–56). Teil 1. 1942.
Vol.21. Rhaw, Georg. Sacrorum hymnorum Liber Primus. Teil 1. Proprium de tempore. 1942.
Vol.22. Stoltzer, Thomas. Ausgewählte Werke. Teil 1. 1942.
Vol.23. Dietrich, Sixt. Ausgewählte Werke. Teil 1. Hymnen, 1545. 1942.
Vol.24. Holzbauer, Ignaz. Ausgewählte Kammermusik. Kassel, 1953.
Vol.25. Rhaw, Georg. Sacrorum hymnorum Liber Primus. Teil 2. Proprium et commune sanctorum. 1943.
Vol.26. Othmayr, Caspar. Ausgewählte Werke. 2. Teil. 1956.
Vol.27. Hasse, Johann Adolf. Arminio. 1. Teil. 1 und 2 Akt. 1957.
Vol.28. Hasse, Johann Adolf. Arminio. 2. Teil. 3 Akt.
Vol.29. Jeep, Johann. Studentengärtlein, 1614. 1958.
Vol.30. Bach, Johann Christian. Sinfonien. 1956.
Vol.31. Werner, Gregor Joseph. Neuer und sehr Curios-musikalischer Instrumentalkalendar (1748) für zwei Violinen und Bass à Cembalo. Hrsg. von Fritz Stein. (Nagels Verlag, Kassel). 1956.
Vol.32/33/34. Der Codex des Magister Nicolaus Apel von Königshofen. Hrsg. von Rudolf Gerber. (Bärenreiter-Verlag, Kassel). 1956– .
Vol.35. Kirchhoff, Gottfried and Goldberg, Johann Gottlieb. Kantaten. Hrsg. von Alfred Dürr. (Bärenreiter-Verlag, Kassel). 1957.
Vol.36. Lüneburger Orgeltabulatur KN 208a. Hrsg. von Margarete Reiman. (Henry Litolff's Verlag, Frankfurt a/M). 1957.
Vol.37/38/39. Das Buxheimer Orgelbuch. Hrsg. von Bertha Antonia Wallner. (Bärenreiter-Verlag, Kassel). 1958.
Vol.40. Das Liederbuch des Dr. Hartmann Schedel. Hrsg. von Heinrich Besseler. (Bärenreiter-Verlag, Kassel).
Vol.41. Klarinettenkonzerte des 18. Jahrhunderts. Hrsg. von Heinz Becker. (Breitkopf & Härtel, Wiesbaden). 1957.
Vol.42. Coclico, Adrian Petit. Consolationes piae. Musica reservata. 1552. Hrsg. von Martin Ruhnke. (Kistner & Siegel & Co., Lippstadt). 1958.
Vol.43. Hammerschmidt, Andreas. Weltliche Oden. Hrsg. von Hans Joachim Moser. (B. Schott's Söhne, Mainz).
Vol.44. Schenk, Johann. Le nymphe di Rheno. Duette für Gamben. Hrsg. von Karl-Heinz Pauls. (Nagels Verlag, Kassel). 1956.
Vol.45/46. Geistliche Konzerte um 1700. Hrsg. von Hans Joachim Moser. (Bärenreiter-Verlag, Kassel).
Vol.47. Daser, Ludwig. Motetten. Hrsg. von Anton Schneiders. (Kistner & Siegel & Co., Lippstadt).
Vol.48. Geist, Christian. Ausgewählte Kirchenkonzerte. Hrsg. von B. Lundgren. (C. F. Peters, Frankfurt a/M). 1960.
Vol.49. Hammerschmidt, Andreas. Instrumentalwerke zu fünf und drei Stimmen. Hrsg. von Helmut Mönkemeyer. 1957.
Vol.50. Pfleger, Augustin. Geistliche Konzerte. Nr.1–11, aus dem Evangelien-Jahrgang. Hrsg. von Fritz Stein. 1961.
Vol.51. Lebermann, Walter, ed. Flöten-Konzerte des 18. Jahrhunderts.

Vol.57. Finck, Heinrich. Ausgewählte Werke. Hrsg. von Lothar Hoffmann-Erbrecht. 1. Teil: Messen und Motetten zum Proprium missae. 1962.
Vol.58. Reichardt, Johann Friedrich. Goethes Lieder, Oden, Balladen und Romanzen mit Musik.

DAS ERBE DEUTSCHER MUSIK. Hrsg. im Auftrage des Staatlichen Instituts für Deutsche Musikforschung. 2. Reihe. Landschaftsdenkmale. Alpen- und Donau Reichsgave. 1942.
1v.
Contents:
Vol.1. Wiener Lautenmusik im 18. Jahrhundert. 1942. (Same as Denkmäler der Tonkunst in Österreich, Vol.84).

DAS ERBE DEUTSCHER MUSIK. 2. Reihe. Landschaftsdenkmale. Bayern. Braunschweig, Henry Litolff's Verlag, 1936–38.
2v.
Bd.1–2 are also Denkmäler deutscher Tonkunst. Folge 2: Denkmäler der Tonkunst in Bayern. Veröffentliche durch Gesellschaft zur Herausgabe von Denkmälern der Tonkunst in Bayern. Jahrg.37/38.
Title also appears as: Landschaftsdenkmale der Musik. Bayern.
Contents:
Vol.1. Mayr, Rupert Ignaz. Ausgewählte Kirchenmusik. 1936.
Vol.2. Franck, Johann Wolfgang. Die drey Töchter Cecrops'. 1938.

DAS ERBE DEUTSCHER MUSIK. 2. Reihe. Landschaftsdenkmale. Kurhessen. Kassel, Bärenreiter Verlag, 1936–38.
1v.
Contains music.
Editor, Bd.1, Herbert Birtner.
Title also appears as: Landschaftsdenkmale der Musik. Kurhessen.
Contents:
Vol.1. Moritz, Landgraf von Hessen. Ausgewählte Werke.
1. Teil: 16 Pavanen, Gagliarden und Intraden. 1936.
2. Teil: Vier Fugen und fünf Madrigale. 1938.

DAS ERBE DEUTSCHER MUSIK. 2. Reihe. Landschaftsdenkmale. Mecklenburg und Pommern. Kassel, Bärenreiter Verlag, 1937–42.
2v.
Contains music.
Editors, Heft 1–2, Erich Schenk and Walther Vetter.
Title also appears as: Landschaftsdenkmale der Musik. Mecklenburg und Pommern.
Contents:
Vol.1. Hochzeitsarien und Kantaten stettiner Meister nach 1700. Friedrich Gottlieb Klingenberg und Michael Rohde. 1937.
Vol.2. Friderici, Daniel. Ausgewählte Kirchengesänge. 1942.

DAS ERBE DEUTSCHER MUSIK. 2. Reihe. Landschaftsdenkmale. Mitteldeutschland. Wolfenbüttel, [etc.], G. Kallmeyer Verlag, 1939.
1 v.
Contains music.
Title also appears as: Landschaftsdenkmale der Musik. Mitteldeutschland.
Editor, Bd.1, Max Schneider.
Contents:
Vol.1. Rust, Friedrich Wilhelm. Werke für Klavier und Streichinstrumente. 1939.

DAS ERBE DEUTSCHER MUSIK. 2. Reihe. Landschaftsdenkmale. Niedersachsen. Wolfenbüttel, G. Kallmeyer, 1937–42.
2v.
Contains music.
Editor, Bd.1–2, Hermann Zenck.
Title also appears as: Landschaftsdenkmale der Musik. Niedersachsen.
Contents:
Vol.1. Schultz, Johannes. Musikalischer Lüstgarte. 1937.
Vol.2. Crappius, Andreas. Werke. 1942.

DAS ERBE DEUTSCHER MUSIK. 2. Reihe. Landschaftsdenkmale. Ostpreussen und Danzig. Kassel, Bärenreiter Verlag, 1939.
1 v.
Editor, 1939, Hans Engel.
Title also appears as: Landschaftsdenkmale der Musik. Ostpreussen und Danzig.
Contents:
Vol.1. Preussische Festlieder. Zeitgenössische Kompositionen zu Dichtungen Simon Dachs. 1939.
Composers: Albert, Heinrich; Kaldenbach, Christoph; Kolb, Georg; Matthäi, Konrad; Sebastiani, Johann; Stobäus, Johann; Weichmann, Johann.

DAS ERBE DEUTSCHER MUSIK. 2. Reihe. Landschaftsdenkmale. Rhein-Main-Gebiet. Kassel, Bärenreiter Verlag, 1937.
1 v.
Contains music.
Editor: Bd.1, J. M. Müller-Blattau.
Title also appears as: Landschaftsdenkmale der Musik. Rhein-Main-Gebiet.
Contents:
Vol.1. Herbst, Johann Andreas. Drei mehrchörige Festkonzerte für die Freie Reichsstadt Frankfurt a.M. 1937.

DAS ERBE DEUTSCHER MUSIK. 2. Reihe. Landschaftsdenkmale. Schleswig-Holstein und Hansestädte. Braunschweig, H. Litolff, 1937–42.
4v.
Contains music.
Editor, Bd.1–4, Friedrich Blume.
Bd.1 pub. by the Staatliches Institut für Deutsche Musikforschung and the Gesellschaft für Schleswig-Holsteinische Geschichte.
Bd.2, 3 pub. by the Staatliches Institut für Deutsche Musikforschung.
Title also appears as: Landschaftsdenkmale der Musik. Schleswig-Holstein und Hansestädte.
Contents:
Vol.1. Bruhns, Nicolaus. Gesammelte Werke. 1. Teil: Kirchenkantaten Nr.1–7. 1937.
Vol.2. Bruhns, Nicolaus. Gesammelte Werke. 2. Teil: Kirchenkantaten Nr.8–12. Orgelwerke. 1939.
Vol.3. Kusser, Johann Sigismund. Arien, Duette und Chöre aus Erindo, oder Die unsträfliche Liebe. 1938.
Vol.4. Weckmann, Matthias. Ausgewählte Werke. 1942.

DAS ERBE DEUTSCHER MUSIK. 2. Reihe. Landschaftsdenkmale. Sudetenland, Böhmen und Mähren. Reichenberg, E. Ullmann Verlag, 1939.
1 v.
Editor, 1939, Gustav Becking.
Title also appears as: Landschaftsdenkmale der Musik. Sudetenland, Böhmen und Mähren.
Contents:
Vol.1. Demantius, Christoph. Neue teutsche weltliche Lieder, 1595. Convivalium concentuum farrago, 1609. 1939.

DAS ERBE DEUTSCHER MUSIK. Sonderreihe. v.1– .
Publishers vary.
Contents:
Vol.1. Demantius, Christoph. Neue teutsche weltliche Lieder. 1595. Kassel, Johann Philipp Hinnenthal Verlag, 1954.
Vol.2. Kugelmann, Johann. Concentus novi. 1540. Hrsg. von Hans Engel. Kassel und Basel, Bärenreiter-Verlag, 1955.
Vol.3. Widmann, Erasmus. Ausgewählte Werke. Hrsg. von Georg Reichert. Mainz, Verlag B. Schott's Söhne, 1959.
Vol.4. Schobert, Johann. Sechs Sinfonien für Cembalo mit Begleitung von Violine und Hörnern ad lib. Op.9 und Op.10. Bearb. von Gustav Becking. Aus dem Nachlass hrsg. von Walter Kramolisch. Kassel, Johann Philipp Hinnenthal Verlag, 1960.

DAS ERBE DEUTSCHER MUSIK. Reprint. Kiel, Das Erbe deutscher Musik, 1953– .
10 series (Proposed plan).
Publishers vary with series.
Reprint edition is in process of publication.
Contents:
I. Abt. Orchestermusik. (Wiesbaden, Brietkopf & Härtel).

II. Abt. Motetten und Messen. (Lippstadt, Kistner & Siegel & Co.).
III. Abt. Mehrstimmiges Lied. (Wolfenbüttel, Karl Heinrich Möseler Verlag).
IV. Abt. Oper und Sologesang. (Mainz, B. Schott's Söhne).
V. Abt. Kammermusik. (Kassel, Nagels Verlag).
VI. Abt. Orgel, Klavier und Laute. (Frankfurt, Henry Litolff's Verlag).
VII. Abt. Mittelalter. (Kassel, Bärenreiter Verlag).
VIII. Abt. Ausgewählte Werke einzelner Meister. (Frankfurt, C. F. Peters).
IX. Abt. Oratorium und Kantate. (Kassel, Bärenreiter Verlag).
X. Abt. Frühromantik. (München, G. Henle Verlag).
And the Sonderreihe (*see* preceding entry).

ESCUREL, JEHANNOT DE L', 14th century.
Collected works, ed. by Nigel E. Wilkins. [n.p.], American Institute of Musicology, 196? – . p.1– . (Corpus mensurabilis musicae. No.30).

ESLAVA Y ELIZONDO, HILARIÓN, 1807–1878. ed.
Lira sacro-hispana. Madrid, Salazar, 1869– . 10v.
Contents (from *Grove's Dictionary of music and musicians*, 1916, Vol.1, p.791–92):
Each century is represented by two *serias*; each *seria* is divided into two volumes or *tomos*. The number of the *seria* is indicated in Roman figures, that of the *tomo* in Arabic numerals.
16th century. i.1.
Ramos. Ave Regina. a 4 voices.
Anon. Magnificat. 4.
—— Domine Jesu. 4.
Fevin, A. Sanctus. 3.
—— Benedictus. 3.
—— Agnus. 4.
—— Agnus. 5.
—— Ascendens Christus. 6.
Peñalosa, F. Sancta Mater. 4.
—— Tribularer si nescirem. 4.
—— In passione positus. 4.
—— Memorare, piissima. 4.
—— Versa est in luctum. 4.
—— Precor te, Domine. 4.
Ribera, B. Magnificat. 4.
—— Virgo prudentissima. 5.
—— Rex autem David. 5.
Torrentes, A. de. Magnificat. 4.
Ceballos, F. Hortus conclusus. 4.
—— Inter vestibulum. 4.
—— Exaudiat Dominus. 4.
Morales, C. Emendemus. 5.
—— O vos omnes. 4.
—— Verbum iniquum. 5.
—— O crux ave. 5.
—— Lamentabatur Jacob. 5.
—— Kyrie; Christi; Gloria. 4.
Escobedo, B. Immutemur. 4.
—— Exurge. 4.
—— Erravi sicut ovis. 5.
Fernández, P. Dispersit, dedit. 4.
—— Heu mihi Domine. 4.
Bernal, A. Ave sanctissimum. 4.
Robledo, M. Domine Jesu. 4.
—— Regem cui omnia. 4.
—— Magna opera. 4 & 5.
—— Sumens illud ave. 4.

16th century. i.2.
Victoria, J. L. de. Mass, Ave maris stella. 4, solo.
—— Vere languores.
—— O Domine.
—— Jesu dulcis memoria.
—— O quam gloriosum.
—— Laudate.
—— Requiem mass, El canto Ilano.
Guerrero, F. Passio sec. Matthaeum. 2, 4, 5, 6.
—— Passio sec. Joannem. 4 & 5.
—— Ave Virgo. 5.
—— Trahe me post. 5.
—— Mass, Simile est regnum. 4.
Navarro, J. M. Lauda Jerusalem. 4.
—— Inexitu Israel. 4.
—— Magnificat 1mi toni. 4.
—— Magnificat 2di toni. 4.
—— Magnificat 8vi toni. 4.
Castillo, D. del. Quis enim cognovit. 5.
—— O altitudo. 5.
Las Infantas, F. de. Victimae paschali. 6.
Camargo, M. G. Defensor almae Hispanae. 4.
Ortiz, D. Pereat dies. 5.
Periañez, P. Maria Virgo. 5.

17th century. i.1.
Comes, J. B. Hodie nobis. 12.
Lobo, A. Versa est. 6.
—— Credo quod redemptor. 4.
—— Vivo ego. 4.
—— Ave Maria. 8.
Heredia, A. de. Magnificat (super tonos). 4.
Tafalla, P. Qui Lazarum. 5 & 8.
Romero, M. Libera me. 8.
Veana, M. Villaneico Asturiano. 8.
Vivanco, S. O Domine. 5.
Vargas, U. de. Magnificat. 8.
Babán, G. Voce mea. 8.
Juarez, A. Vulnerasti cor meum. 8.
—— Dum sacrum pignus. 9.
Caseda, D. Mass. 8.

17th century. ii.1.
Pontac, D. Mass, In exitu Israel. 4.
Patino, C. Mass, In devotione. 8.
Salazar, G. Heu mihi. 4 (soli).
—— O Rex gloriae. 8, col organo.
—— Quae est ista. 6, col organo.
—— Vida speciosam. 6, col organo.
—— Sancta Maria. 5, col organo.
—— Nativitas tua. 6, con organo.
—— Mater Dei. 5, con organo.
Ortells. Lamentatio. 12.
Montemayor, F. de. Requiem mass. 8.
Durón, S. O vos omnes. 4.

18th century. i.1.
Bravo, J. de T. M. Portions of a Misa de defuntos. 8.
—— J. de T. M. Parce mihi. 8.

—— Taedet animam meam. 8.
Dudoso. Dan, dan, don, don. 5.
Rabassa, P. Audite universi. 12.
Valls, F. Tota pulchra. 4.
Cabrera, F. V. Kyrie and Gloria. 8.
Roldan, J. P. Sepulto Domine. 4.
Sanjuan, N. Spiritus meus. 8.
Paez, J. Jesu redemptor. 4.
Muelas, D. O vos omnes. 8.
—— Dustus est Jesus. 4.
—— Dicebat Jesus. 4.
—— Erunt signa. 4.
—— Cum audisset Joannes. 4.
—— Vox clamantis. 3.
Caseda, J. de. Kyrie and Gloria. 4.
Literes, A. Vox saeculorum judices. 4.
—— Hi sunt quos fatue. 4.
Juliá, B. Dilexi quoniam. 4.
Fuentes, P. Beatus vir. 10.
Soler, F. A. Introito and offertoria de defuntos. 8.
Anon. Ecce sacerdos. 5.

18th century. ii.1.
Nebra, J. de. Requiem mass. 8. (strings and flutes).
Ripa, A. Mass. 8. (strings, trumpets, and organ).
—— Stabat Mater. (6 verses). 8. (organ).
Lidon, J. Ave maris stella. 4 and 8.

19th century. i.1.
Garcia, F. J. Lamentation. 8. (orch.).
—— Lamentation. 7. (orch.).
Aranaz, P. Ad te levavi. 4. (solos).
—— Laudate. 6. (viol. and trumpets).
Doyagüe, M. Miserere. 4. (wind).
Secanilla, F. Defensor almae Hispanae. 5. (strings, trumpets, and organ).
—— Pange lingua. 7.
Priento, J. Salve Regina. 4. (strings, trumpets, and organ).
Cuellar, R. Lauda Sion. 5. (strings, oboes, and trumpets).
Montesinor, A. Sancta et immaculata Virginitas. 8.
Pons, J. Letrida, O Madre. 8.
Cabo, F. J. Memento Domine. 7.

19th century. i.2.
Ledesma, N. Stabat Mater (12 verses). Accomp. by string quartet. 3.
Andrevi, F. Nunc dimittis. 4. (orch.).
—— Salve Regina. 6. (orch.).
Ledesma, M. R. Principes persecuti. 4. (orch.).
Bros, J. Benedictus. 4. (orch.).

19th century. ii.1.
Eslava, H. Te Deum. 4.
—— O sacrum convivium. 4.
—— Bone pastor. 4.
—— O salutaris hostia. 8.
—— Requiem mass. 8. (orch.).
—— Parce mihi. 8.
—— Taedet animam. 8.
—— Libera me. 8.

19th century. ii.2.
Perez y Alvarez, J. Salve Regina. 8.
—— O salutaris. 4. (bar. solo and orch.).
Hugalde, C. J. Bone pastor. Bass solo and organ.
Hugalde. O salutaris. 3. (organ).
Meton, V. O quonium suavis. 5.
—— Ecce panis. 5.
—— O salutaris. 5. (all with orch.).
Olleta, D. Salve Regina. 5. (organ and basses).
Garcia, M. Ave maris stella. 4. (strings, trumpets, and organ).
Prádanos, H. O quam suavis. 4. (strings).
Caballero, M. F. Ave maris stella. 4. (orch.).
Calahorra, R. O. Lauda Sion. 1.
—— Vere languores. 4. (orch.).

Appendix.
Secanilla, F. Hymn, Scripta sunt. 8, 3, 8, 4, 8. (orch.).
Doyagüe, M. Magnificat. 8. (strings, oboes, trumpets, and organ).
Durón, S. Fragmenta.

ESLAVA Y ELIZONDO, HILARIÓN, 1807–1878. ed.
Museo orgánico español. Madrid, Martin Salazar. v.1– .
Organ works of the 16th–19th centuries.

ESPOSITO, MICHELE, 1855–1930. ed.
Early Italian piano music; a collection of pieces written for the harpsichord and clavichord, ed. by M. Esposito . . . Boston, Oliver Ditson Co.; New York, C. H. Ditson & Co., [etc., etc., cop. 1906].
xiv p., 1L., 180p. 2pl. (The musicians library. [vol.XXII]).
"Italian composers for the harpsichord": p.[ix]-xiv.
Contains compositions by Muzio Clementi, Francesco Durante, Girolamo Frescobaldi, Baldassare Galuppi, G. B. Grazioli, Benedetto Marcello, Padre Giambattista Martini, P. D. Paradies, Bernardo Pasquini, Ercole Pasquini, C. F. Pollaroli, Niccolò Porpora, Michelangelo Rossi, Alessandro Scarlatti, Domenico Scarlatti, Ferdinando Turini, and Domenico Zipoli.

ÉTUDES DE PALÉOGRAPHIE MUSICALE BYZANTINE, ed. par J.-D. Petrescu; préface par M. A. Gastoué. [Tome 1–]. Paris, Librairie Orientaliste Paul Geuthner, 1932.
1 v. facsims., music.
Contents:
[Tome 1.] Petrescu, J. D. Les idiomèles et le canon de l'office de Noël (D'après des manuscrits grecs des XIe, XIIe, XIIIe, et XIVe siècle). 1932.

EUTERPE. A collection of madrigals and other music of the 16th and 17th centuries. Ed. by Charles Kennedy Scott, with a preface by J. A. Fuller-Maitland. London, Breitkopf, 1905–12. 13v.
Vol.1 and 2 were printed and published for the Oriana Madrigal Society by Alexander Moring, Ltd.

Contents:

Vol.1. Bateson. Down the hills Corina trips. (Madrigal, 1618).
Byrd. Come let us rejoice (Psalm, 1611). 1905.

Vol.2. Wilbye. Happy, oh, happy he. (Madrigal, 1609).
Vautor. Mother, I will have a husband. (Madrigal, 1619). Three rounds. 1905.

Vol.3. Dowland. If my complaints. (Ayre, 1597).
Lichfield. I always lov'd to call my lady 'Rose.' (Madrigal, 1613). Three rounds. 1906.

Vol.4. Rosseter and Campion. Eight songs for solo voice and lute. 1907.

Vol.5. Mundy. Hear my prayer, O Lord. (Psalm, 1594).
Dowland. Me, me, and none but me. (Ayre, 1603).
Ravenscroft. Four songs from Deuteromelia. 1609.
Three songs from Melismata . . . 1611. Three rounds. 1907.

Vol.6. Weelkes. Cease, sorrows, now. (Madrigal, 1597).
Morley. Hark! Alleluia . . . (Canzonet, 1597). Three rounds. 1907.

Vol.7. Weelkes. When Choralis delights to walk. (Madrigal, 1600).
Dowland. Flow my tears . . . (Ayre, 1600).
Campion. Three ayres . . . (1613), together with a preface by Janet Dodge. 1908.

Vol.8. White. O praise God in His holiness . . . (Psalm).
Pilkington. The messenger of the delightful spring. (Madrigal, 1613). Two rounds. 1909.

Vol.9. Vautor. Sweet Suffolk owl . . . (Madrigal, 1619).
Wilbye. Fly not so swift, my dear. (Madrigal, 1609).
Youll. Pipe, shepherds, pipe . . . (Canzonet, 1608). 1909.

Vol.10. Dowland. Fine knacks for ladies. (Ayre, 1600).
Dowland. Weep you no more, sad fountains. (Ayre, 1603).
Dowland. Sweet, stay awhile . . . (Ayre, 1612).
Dowland. Disdain me still . . . (Ayre, 1612).
Campion. Tune thy music . . . (Ayre, 1613).
Campion. O dear, that I with thee . . . (Ayre, 1613). Three rounds. 1910.

Vol.11. Morley. Clorinda false . . . (Madrigal, 1594).
Pilkington. Sweet Phillida . . . (Madrigal, 1613).
Bartlet. All my wits . . . (Ayre, 1606). 1910.

Vol.12. Morley. (a). Fire and lightning. (Canzonets, 1595).
Morley. (b). Flora wilt thou torment me. (Canzonets, 1595).
Jones, Robert. Though your strangeness . . . (Ayre, 1612).
Campion. Out of my soul's depths . . . (Ayre, 1613).
Dowland. Shall I strive . . . (Ayre, 1612).
Ford. What then is love . . . (Ayre, 1607).
Mundy. Sing ye unto the Lord . . . (Psalm), 1594).
Bateson. I heard a noise . . . (Madrigal, 1618). Three rounds. 1910. (double number).

Vol.13. Campion. Though your strangeness . . . (Ayre, 1613).
Dowland. Up, merry mates . . . (Ayre, 1612).
Dowland. Come away, come sweet love . . . (Ayre, 1597).
Dowland. Stay, time, awhile thy flying . . . (Ayre, 1612).
Wilbye. Happy streams . . . (Madrigal, 1609).
Pilkington. Have I found her . . . (Madrigal, 1613).
Byrd. This sweet and merry month of May. (Madrigal, 1590). 1912. (double number).

EUTERPE. A collection of madrigals and other music of the 16th and 17th centuries. Ed. by by Charles Kennedy Scott. London, Oxford University Press, 1929–36.
No.1– .
2d edition.

No.1. Bartlett, John. All my wits hath will enwrapped. (Ayre).
No.2. Bateson, Thomas. Down the hills Corina trips. (Madrigal).
No.3. Bateson, Thomas. I heard a noise. (Madrigal).
No.4. Byrd, William. Come, let us rejoice. (Psalm).
No.5. Byrd, William. This sweet and merry month of May. (Madrigal).
No.6. Byrd, William. Let not the sluggish sleep.
No.7. Campion, Thomas. Three ayres: (a) How eas'ly wert thou chained. (b) O what unhop'd for sweet supply. (c) Where she her sacred bow'r adorns.
No.8. Campion, Thomas. Two ayres: (a) Tune thy music to thy heart. (b) O, dear, that I with thee might live.
No.9. Campion, Thomas. Out of my soul's depths to Thee. (Ayre).
No.10. Campion, Thomas. Though your strangeness. (Ayre).
No.11. Campion, Thomas. Jack and Joan they think no ill. (Ayre).
No.12. Dowland, John. Flow, my tears. (Ayre).
No.13. Dowland, John. If my complaints. (Ayre).
No.14. Dowland, John. Me, me, and none but me. (Ayre).
No.15. Dowland, John. Fine knacks for ladies. (Ayre).

No.16. Dowland, John. Weep you no more, sad fountains! (Ayre).
No.17. Dowland, John. Sweet, stay awhile! (Ayre).
No.18. Dowland, John. Disdain me still. (Ayre).
No.19. Dowland, John. Shall I strive with words to move? (Ayre).
No.20. Dowland, John. Come away, come sweet love. (Ayre).
No.21. Dowland, John. Stay, time, awhile thy flying. (Ayre).
No.22. Dowland, John. Woeful heart with grief oppressed. (Ayre).
No.23. Dowland, John. Up, merry mates! (Ayre).
No.24. Ford, Thomas. What then is love, sings Coridon. (Ayre).
No.25. Gibbons, Orlando. Now each flow'ry bank. (Madrigal).
No.26. Jones, Robert. Though your strangeness. (Ayre).
No.27. Lichfield, Henry. I always lov'd to call my lady 'Rose.' (Madrigal).
No.28. Morley, Thomas. Hark! Alleluia. (Ayre).
No.29. Morley, Thomas. Clorinda false, adieu! (Madrigal).
No.30. Morley, Thomas. Two canzonets: (a) Fire and lightning from heav'n. (b) Flora, wilt thou torment me.
No.31. Morley, Thomas. Hark, jolly shepherds! (Madrigal).
No.32. Mundy, John. Hear my prayer, O Lord. (Psalm).
No.33. Mundy, John. Sing ye unto the Lord. (Psalm).
No.34. Mundy, John. Hey ho! chill go to plough no more. (Secular song).
No.35. Philips, Peter. The nightingale. (Madrigal).
No.36. Pilkington, Francis. The messenger of the delightful spring. (Madrigal).
No.37. Pilkington, Francis. Sweet Phillida! (Madrigal).
No.38. Pilkington, Francis. Have I found her? (Madrigal).
No.39. Ravenscroft, Thomas. (a) We be soldiers three. (b) We be three poor mariners. (from Deuteromelia).
No.40. Ravenscroft, Thomas. Willy, prithee go to bed. (from Deuteromelia).
No.41. Ravenscroft, Thomas. To-morrow the fox will come to town. (from Deuteromelia).
No.42. Ravenscroft, Thomas. It was the frog in the well. (from Melismata).
No.43. Ravenscroft, Thomas. There were three ravens. (from Melismata).
No.44. Ravenscroft, Thomas. A wooing song of a yeoman of Kent's son. (from Melismata).
No.45. Vautor, Thomas. Mother, I will have a husband. (Madrigal).
No.46. Vautor, Thomas. Sweet Suffolk owl. (Madrigal).
No.47. Weelkes, Thomas. Cease, sorrows, now. (Madrigal).
No.48. Weelkes, Thomas. When Thoralis delights to walk. (Madrigal).
No.49. Weelkes, Thomas. Those spots upon my lady's face. (Madrigal).
No.50. Whyte, Robert. O praise God in His holiness. (Psalm).
No.51. Wilbye, John. Happy, oh, happy he. (Madrigal).
No.52. Wilbye, John. Fly not so swift, my dear. (Madrigal).
No.53. Wilbye, John. Happy streams! whose trembling fall. (Madrigal).
No.54. Youll, Henry. Pipe, shepherds, pipe!
No.55. Rosseter, Philip. Eight songs from Rosseter's Book of ayres.
No.55a. Rosseter, Philip. When Laura smiles. (Unison).
No.56. The Euterpe round book. Containing fifty English rounds, catches, and canons of the 16th and 17th centuries.
No.57. Weelkes, Thomas. What have the gods.
No.58. Weelkes, Thomas. Methinks I hear.
No.59. Mundy, John. In deep distress.
No.60. Morley, Thomas. About the maypole.
No.61. Tomkins, Thomas. The fauns and satyrs tripping.
No.62. Apparently not published.
No.63. Mundy, John. In midst of woods.
No.64. Mundy, John. The blackbird.
No.65. Pilkington, Francis. O softly singing lute.
No.66. Weelkes, Thomas. Since Robin Hood.
No.67. Weelkes, Thomas. Ha ha, this world doth pass.
No.68. Weelkes, Thomas. Aye me, alas, hey ho.
No.69. Lichfield, Henry. All ye that sleep in pleasure.
No.70. Lichfield, Henry. Alas my Daphne, stay.

Der evangelische Kirchengesang, *see* Winterfeld, Carl Georg August Vivigens von. Der evangelische Kirchengesang.

Evening canticles. Church of England. Liturgy and ritual, *see* Plainsong and Mediaeval Music Society. Church of England. Liturgy and ritual. Evening canticles.

Ewerhart, Rudolf, ed., *see* Cantio sacra; Die Kantate; Die Motette.

Examples illustrating the development of melodic line and contrapuntal style, from Greek melody to Mozart, *see* Soderlund, Gustave Fredric. Examples illustrating the development of melodic line and contrapuntal style, from Greek melody to Mozart.

Examples of Gregorian chant, *see* Soderlund, Gustave Fredric. Examples of Gregorian chant.

Examples of music before 1400, *see* Gleason, Harold. Examples of music before 1400.

EXPERT, HENRY, 1863–1952. ed.
Anthologie de musique sacrée des maîtres anciens. Paris, 1926.
p.1– .

EXPERT, HENRY, 1863–1952. ed.
Chants de France et d'Italie. Paris.
2 series.
Contents:

Ser.1. Chansons mondaines des XVIIe et XVIIIe siècles français harmonisées par Emile Desportes.
Ser.2. Airs de cour d'Antoine Boësset, de Pierre Guédron, et airs et villanelles de Charles Tessier.

EXPERT, HENRY, 1863–1952. ed.
Collection d'ordre lyrique Expert-Pillard. Paris, 1922.
p.1– .
Contains compositions by Cherubini, Dalayrac, Méhul, Monsigny, Philidor, and others.

EXPERT, HENRY, 1863–1952. ed.
Florilège du concert vocal de la Renaissance. [No.] 1–8. Paris, A. la Cité des Livres, 1928–29.
8 nos. ports.
Editor, [No.] 1–8, H. Expert.
Contents:
No.1. Jannequin, C. Chantons, sonnons, trompétes . . . 1928.
No.2. Lasso, O. di. O temps divers . . . 1928.
No.3. Jannequin, C. Les cris de Paris . . . 1928.
No.4. Costeley, G. Arreste un peu, mon coeur . . . 1928.
No.5. Bonnet, P. . . . Airs et villanelles . . . 1929.
No.6. Le Jeune, C. . . . Las! ou vas-tu sans moy . . . 1929.
No.7. Mauduit, Jacques. Psaumes mesurés à l'antique de J.-A. de Baïf. 1928.
No.8. . . . Duos . . . (Claudin de Sermisy, Peletier, Guillaume le Heuteur, Antoine Gardane). 1928.

EXPERT, HENRY, 1863–1952. ed.
Florilège du concert vocal de la Renaissance. Reprint. New York, Broude Brothers, n.d.

EXPERT, HENRY, 1863–1952. ed.
Les maîtres musiciens de la Renaissance française; éditions publiées par M. Henry Expert sur les manuscrits les plus authentiques et les meilleurs imprimés du XVIe siècle, avec variantes, notes historiques et critiques, transcriptions en notation moderne, etc. [Sec.1. v.1–23]. Paris, Alphonse Leduc, 1894–1908.
23v. illus.
Contents:
Vol.1. Lasso, Orlando di. Les meslanges d'Orlande de Lassus. Fasc.1. [1894].
Vol. 2, 4, 6. Goudimel, Claude. Les 150 pseaumes de David. 3v. [1895–1897].
Vol.3, 18–19. Costeley, Guillaume. Musique de Guillaume Costeley. 3v. 1896–1904.
Vol.4. See Vol.2.
Vol.5. Attaingnant, Pierre. Trent et une chansons musicales. (Attaingnant 1529). 1897. (Contains compositions by Claudin de Sermisy, Consilium, Courtoys, Deslouges, Dulot, Gascongne, Hesdin, Jacotin, Jannequin, Lombart, Sohier, Vermont, et anonymes).
Vol.6. See Vol.2.
Vol.7. Jannequin, Clément. Chansons de maistre Clément Jannequin. [1898].
Vol.8, 9. [Antico, Andrea]. Liber quindecim missarum. [v.1– . 1898–].
Vol.10. Mauduit, Jacques. Chansonnettes mesurées de Jan Antoine de Baïf. 1899.
Vol.11. Le Jeune, Claude. Dodecacorde. Fasc.1. 1900.
Vol.12–14. Le Jeune, Claude. Le printemps. 3v. 1900–1901.
Vol.15. Regnard, François. Poésies de P. de Ronsard. 1902.
Vol.16. Le Jeune, Claude. Mélanges. Fasc.1. 1903.
Vol.17. Du Caurroy, Eustache, Sieur de St. Frémin. Mélanges. Fasc.1. 1903.
Vol.18–19. See Vol.3.
Vol.20–22. Le Jeune, Claude. Pseaumes en vers mezurez. 3v. 1905–6.
Vol.23. Gervaise, Claude. Danceriès. Vol.1. 1908.

EXPERT, HENRY, 1863–1952. ed.
Les maîtres musiciens de la Renaissance française. Reprint. New York, Broude Brothers, 195? – .

EXPERT, HENRY, 1863–1952. ed.
Les maîtres musiciens de la Renaissance française; éditions publiées par M. Henry Expert sur les manuscrits les plus authentiques et les meilleurs imprimés du XVIe siècle . . . [Sec.2]. Bibliographie thématique. [v.] 3, 8. Paris, A. Leduc, 1900.
2v.
Projected as a set of 15v.; only Vols.3 and 8 were published.
Contents:
Vol.3. Attaingnant, Pierre. Trent et une chansons musicales. (Attaingnant 1529).
Vol.8. Attaingnant, Pierre. Trent et sept chansons musicales. (Attaingnant 1528–30?). 1900.

EXPERT, HENRY, 1863–1952. ed.
Monuments de la musique française au temps de la Renaissance; éditions publiées par M. Henry Expert sur les manuscrits les plus authentiques et les meilleurs imprimés du XVIe siècle. Transcriptions en notation moderne. Paris, Éditions Maurice Senart, 1924–1929, 1958– .
v.1– .
Contents:
Vol.1. Le Jeune, C. Octonaires de la vanité et inconstance du monde. (I–VIII). 1924.
Vol.2. Certon, P. Messes à 4 voix. Sus le pont d'Avignon; Adiuva me; Regnum mundi. 1925.
Vol.3. Le Blanc, D. Airs de plusiers musiciens réduits à quatre parties. 1925.
Vol.4–5. Bertrand, A. de. Premier livre des amours de Pierre de Ronsard. (I–XXXV). 2v. 1926.
Vol.6. Bertrand. A. de. Second livre des amours de Pierre de Ronsard. 1927.
Vol.7. Bertrand, A. de. Troisième livre de chansons. 1927.

Vol.8. Le Jeune, Claude. Octonaires de la vanité et inconstance du monde. (IX–XII). Pseaumes des meslanges de 1612. Dialogue à sept parties. (1564). 1928.
Vol.9. Goudimel, Claude. Messes à 4 voix. Audi filia; Tant plus ie metz; De mes ennuys. 1928.
Vol.10. L'Estocart, P. de. Premier livre des octonaires de la vanité du monde. 1929.
Vol.11. L'Estocart, P. de. Second livre des octonaires de la vanité du monde. Rev. et introd. par J. Chailley et M. Honegger. [cop. 1958].

EXPERT, HENRY, 1863–1952. ed.
Monuments de la musique française au temps de la Renaissance. Reprint. New York, Broude Brothers, 19? – .

EXPERT, HENRY, 1863–1952. ed.
Psautier Huguenot du XVIe siècle. Textes poétiques de Clemént Marot et Théodore de Bèze. Paris, Fischbacher, 1902.
xii, 745p.

EXPERT, HENRY, 1863–1952. ed.
Répertoire classique de musique religieuse et spirituelle: Sér.A. (1re année). Musique d'église des XVIIe et XVIIIe siècles; Motets à une ou plusieurs voix, transcrits . . . par Charles Pineau. Paris, Senart, 1913–14.
No.1– .
Contains compositions by Giacomo Arigoni, Bernier, Caldara, Campra, Carissimi, Marc-Antoine Charpentier, Clérambault, F. Couperin, Henri Dumont, Durante, Alessandro Grandi, Lalande, Legrenzy, Leo, Lully, Le Père Martini, Monteverdi, and Rameau.

Fancies and ayres, by John Jenkins, *see* The Wellesley edition. No.1, 10.

FANTINI, GIROLAMO, fl.1638.
Modo per imparare a sonare di tromba tanto di guerra quanto musicalmente in organo, con tromba sordina, col cimbalo, e con ogn' altro strumento. Aggiuntovi molte sonate, come balletti, brandi, capriccio, sarabande, correnti, passaggi, e sonate con la tromba, & organo insieme. Di Girolamo Fantini da Spoleti . . . Francoforte, D. Vuastch, 1638. [Milano, Bollettino Bibliografico Musicale, 1934].
1p.L., facsim. (86, [2]p. illus. [port.]). (Added title page: Collezione di trattati e musiche antiche edite in Fac-simile).
Signatures: A–E^4.
Title within ornamental border: title vignette.
First edition pub. 1632.

Fareanu, A., ed. Die Kunst des Bachsen Geschlechts, *see* Bach Family. Die Kunst des Bachsen Geschlechts.

FARRENC, JACQUES HIPPOLYTE ARISTIDE, 1794–1865, and Farrenc, Jeanne Louise, née Dumont, 1804–1875. ed.
Le trésor des pianistes; collection des oeuvres choisies des maîtres de tous les pays et de toutes les époques depuis le XVIe siècle jusqu'à le moitié du XIXe. Accompagnées du notices biographiques, de renseignements bibliographiques et historiques . . . Recueillies et transcrites en notation moderne par Aristide Farrenc, avec le concours de Mme. Louise Farrenc . . . Paris, Farrenc, 1861–72.
23v.
Contents:
Vol.1. Préliminaries.
Vol.2. William Byrd, John Bull, et Orlando Gibbons: Parthenia; Divers auteurs anglais: Recueil de pièces de clavecin.
Claudio Merulo: Toccate.
Girolamo Frescobaldi: Trois fugues et six canzone, Diverses pièces.
Georges Muffat: Douze toccates.
J. de Chambonnières: Pièces de clavecin. 1st, 2d livre.
Vol.3. Henry d'Anglebert: Pièces de clavecin.
Jean Kuhnau: Sept sonates; Nouvel exercice pour le clavecin. 1st, 2d partie; Toccate.
Henri Purcell: Recueil de pièces.
Jacques Froberger: Cinq caprices; Six suites.
Louis Couperin, Antoine le Bègue, Bernard Pasquini, Gaspard de Kerl, Alexandre Scarlatti: Recueil de pièces de clavecin.
Vol.4. François Couperin: 1st, 2d, & 3d livre de pièces de clavecin.
Vol.5. François Couperin: 4th livre de pièces de clavecin.
Frédéric Haendel: Suites de pièces. 1st, 2d, & 3d livre. Six fugues.
Vol.6/7. Dominique Scarlatti: Pièces de clavecin, No.1–77; No.78–152.
Vol.8. Sebastien Bach: Exercices, diversés en six suites oeuv.1; Six grandes suites appelées Suites anglaises.
J. Philippe Rameau: 1st, 2d livre de pièces.
Nicolo Porpora: Six fugues.
Vol.9. François Durante: Six sonates.
François Dandrieu, Benoit Marcello, Philippe Telemann, Jean-Baptiste Pescetti: Recueil de pièces pour le clavecin.
Claude Daquin: Pièces de clavecin.
Le Père Martini: Douze sonates.
Louis Krebs: Trois fugues.
Vol.10. Friedemann Bach: Douze polonaises, sonate, huit fugues, une suite et quatre fantaisies.
Théophile Muffat: Recueil de pièces.
Christophe Nichelmann: Cinq sonates; Six sonates oeuv.2.
Vol.11. Théophile Goldberg: Prélude et fugue.
Ernest Eberlin: Six préludes et fugues.
Jean Matteson: Pièces diverses.
Dominique Zipoli: Pièces pour l'orgue et le clavecin.
Christophe Smith: Neuf suites de pièces.
Christophe Schaffrath: Deux sonates oeuv.2.
Vol.12. C.-P.-Emmanuel Bach: Six sonates 1st, 2d, 3d, 4th, 5th recueil.
Vol.13. C.-P.-Emmanuel Bach: Six sonates 1st, 6th, 7th, 8th, 9th recueil; Cinq sonates et quatre rondos 10th recueil; Six sonates 11th recueil.

Vol.14. Dominique Paradies: Six sonates.
Duphly: Pièces de clavecin.
Philippe Kirnberger: Six fugues; Diverses pièces 1st–3d recueil.
Vollrath Buttstedt: Deux sonates.
Georges Benda: Six sonates.
Vol.15. Christ.-Frédéric Bach: Sonates et diverses pièces.
Joseph Haydn: Cinq sonates 1st, 2d recueil.
J. G. Albrechtsberger: Douze fugues; Dix-huit fugues.
Chrétien Fasch: Deux sonates et une pièce.
Vol.16. Muzio Clementi: Trois sonates oeuv.2; Deux sonates oeuv.7; Trois sonates oeuv.8; Quatre sonates et une toccate tirées des oeuv.9, 10, et 14.
J.-Wilhelm Haessler: Deux fantaisies, six sonates, quatre solos, trois sonates.
O.-A. Lindemann: Pièces diverses.
Vol.17. W.-Amedée Mozart: Six sonates 1st, 2d, 3d, 4th recueil; Romance.
Vol.18. J.-Chrétien Bach: Sept sonates.
J.-Louis Dussek: Trois grandes sonates oeuv.5; Sonate oeuv.64.
J.-G. Wernicke: Cinq pièces.
Schwanenberg: Deux menuets.
Daniel Steibelt: Grande sonate oeuv.64.
J.-B. Cramer: Trois sonates.
Vol.19. Louis van Beethoven: Sonates oeuv.2, 7, 10, 13, 14, 22, 26, 27.
Vol.20. Louis van Beethoven: Sonates oeuv.28, 31, 49, 53, 54, 57, 78, 79, 81, 90.
Vol.21. Louis van Beethoven: Sonates oeuv.101, 106, 109, 110, 111; Six airs variés.
Vol.22. J.-N. Hummel: Chanson autrichienne, variée oeuv.8; Marche des deux journées, variée oeuv.9; God save the King, variée oeuv.10; Air des petits Savoyards, variée oeuv.15; Chansons hollandaise, variée oeuv.21; Marche de cendrillon, variée oeuv.40; Gavotte d'Armide, variée oeuv. 57; La belle Marie, Chansons anglaise, variée oeuv.75; Introduction et rondo oeuv.19; Rondo brillant oeuv.109; Sonate oeuv.13; Sonate oeuv.20; Adagio extrait de l'oeuv.38; Grande sonate oeuv. 81; Fantaisie oeuv.18.
Vol.23. Ferdinand Ries: L'infortunée grande sonate oeuv.26.
C.-Marie de Weber: Quatre grandes sonates oeuv.24, 39, 49, et 70.
F. Mendelssohn-Bartholdy: Rondo capriccioso oeuv.14; Trois fantaisies ou caprices oeuv.16.
Frédéric Chopin: Neuf nocturnes.

FASCH, KARL FRIEDRICH CHRISTIAN, 1736–1800.
Sämmtliche Werke, hrsg. von der Singakademie in Berlin. Berlin, 1839.
2v. in 7 parts.
Contents:
Bd.1.
Pt.1. 12 Chörale, 3–7 Stimmen.
Pt.2. Mendelssohniana. (Psalm 30), 3–7 Stimmen.
Pt.3: 1. Psalm "Inclina Domine," 4–6 Stimmen; 2. Requiem, 8 Stimmen; 3. Trauermotette "Selig sind die Toten" auf den Tod des Prinzen Louis von Preussen. 1797.
Pt.4. Davidiana. (Psalm nach Luthers Übersetzung, 8 Nummern, 4–8 Stimmen).
Pt.5. Der 119. Psalm "Heil dem Manne, der rechtschaffen lebt," 16 Nummern, bis zu 8 Stimmen.
Pt.6. Der 51. Psalm lateinisch "Miserere," 4–8 Stimmen.
Bd.2.
Pt.7. Missa a 16 Voci, 5 facher Kanon 25 Stimmen; Porträt des Komponisten; 12 [sic] Sonaten und La Cecchina (in Farrenc. Trésor des pianistes, Bd.15); "Ariette" und "Andantino" für Cembalo oder Klavier mit Variationen; Sonate G und La Cecchina für Klavier.

Faugues, Guillaume, 15th century. Collected works, *see* Institute of Mediaeval Music. Publications. Vol.7; Institute of Mediaeval Music. Collected works. Vol.1.

FAUVEL.
Le roman de Fauvel, par Gervais du Bus, publié d'après tous les manuscrits connus par Arthur Långfors. Paris, F. Didot et Cie., 1914–19.
3p.L., [iii]-cx, 220p. (Half title: Société des Anciens Textes Français).
In two *livres* composed in 1310 and 1314, respectively; the first anonymous, the second with the author's name given in form of a riddle. In the interpolated redaction of Chaillou de Pesstain the name "Gerües" is misspelled "de rues"; cf. Appendice: Notice et extraits de l'interpolation du ms. E. (Paris. Bibl. Nat. Fr. 146, p.[133]–95).

FAUVEL.
Le roman de Fauvel; reproduction photographique du manuscrit français 146 de la Bibliothèque Nationale de Paris; avec un index des interpolations lyriques par Pierre Aubrey. Paris, P. Guenthner, 1907.
vi, 7p., facsim.: 95 pl. (mounted photos) miniatures.
In two books: first *livre*, dated 1310, anonymous; second *livre*, 1314, by Gervais du Bus, with the author's name given in the enigmatic form "Gerues doi V boi V esse" in four lines at end, which in this manuscript (Bibl. Nat. Fr. 146) are omitted; the name appears instead in a line interpolated after 2886 (on verso of folio 23), where it is misspelled "de rues," from which an imaginary François de Rues was inferred and formerly accepted as author.
The Latin and French interpolated pieces (in part without relation to the subject Fauvel), accompanied by music, were added by Chaillou de Pesstain. They comprise motets, rondeaux, ballades, etc.; cf. Le roman de Fauvel . . . publié par Arthur Långfors. Paris, 1914–19 (Société des Anciens Textes Français), p.lxxi–lxxvii, and 135–38.
Bibliography: p.vi.

FAYRFAX, ROBERT, ca.1465–1521.
. . . Collected works. Ed. by Edwin B. Warren. [Rome], American Institute of Musicology, 1959– .
v.1– . (Corpus mensurabilis musicae. No.17).
Proposed set about 3v.
Contents:
Vol.1. The masses. O bone Jesu, Albanus, O quam glorifica, Regali, Tecum principium, and the incomplete Sponsus amat sponsam. 1959.
Vol.2. Magnificats and motets. Missa sponsus amat sponsam. 1964.

Federhofer, Hellmut, 1911– , ed. Musik alter Meister, *see* Musik alter Meister.

Feicht, Hieronim, 1894– , ed. Antiquitates musicae in Polonia, *see* Antiquitates musicae in Polonia.

Fellerer, Karl Gustav, 1902– , ed. Anthology of music, *see* Anthology of music.

FELLOWES, REV. EDMUND HORACE, 1870–1951. ed.
The English madrigal school, ed. by Rev. Edmund Horace Fellowes. London, Stainer & Bell, Ltd., 1913– .
v.1– . front. (v.6, facsim.).
Title varies slightly.
With reproduction of original title pages, etc.
Includes reduction for piano.
Contents:
Vol.1. Pt.I. Thomas Morley. Canzonets to 2 voices. (1595).
Vol.1. Pt.II. Thomas Morley. Canzonets to 3 voices. (1593).
Vol.2. Thomas Morley. Madrigals to 4 voices. (1594).
Vol.3. Thomas Morley. Canzonets to 5 and 6 voices. (1597).
Vol.4. Thomas Morley. Ballets to 5 voices. (1600).
Vol.5. Orlando Gibbons. Madrigals and motets of 5 parts. (1612).
Vol.6. John Wilbye. First set of madrigals. (1598).
Vol.7. John Wilbye. Second set of madrigals. (1609).
Vol.8. John Farmer. Madrigals to 4 voices. (1599).
Vol.9. Thomas Weelkes. Madrigals to 3, 4, 5, and 6 voices. (1597).
Vol.10. Thomas Weelkes. Ballets and madrigals to 5 voices. (1598).
Vol.11. Thomas Weelkes. Madrigals of 5 parts. (1600).
Vol.12. Thomas Weelkes. Madrigals of 6 parts. (1600).
Vol.13. Thomas Weelkes. Airs or fantastic spirits to 3 voices. (1608).
Vol.14. William Byrd. Psalms, sonnets, and songs for 5 voices. (1588).
Vol.15. William Byrd. Songs of sundry natures. (1589).
Vol.16. William Byrd. Psalms, songs, and sonnets. (1611).
Vol.17. Henry Lichfild [sic]. Madrigals of 5 parts. (1613).
Vol.18. Thomas Tomkins. Songs of 3, 4, 5, and 6 parts. (1622).
Vol.19. John Ward. Madrigals to 3, 4, 5, and 6 parts. (1613).
Vol.20. Giles Farnaby. Canzonets to 4 voices. (1598).
Vol.21. Thomas Bateson. First set of madrigals. (1604).
Vol.22. Thomas Bateson. Second set of madrigals. (1618).
Vol.23. John Bennet. Madrigals to 4 voices. (1599).
Vol.24. George Kirbye. Madrigals to 4, 5, and 6 voices. (1597).
Vol.25. Francis Pilkington. First set of madrigals. (1613).
Vol.26. Francis Pilkington. Second set of madrigals. (1624).
Vol.27. Richard Carlton. Madrigals to 5 voices. (1601).
Vol.28. Henry Youll. Canzonets to 3 voices. (1608).
Vol.29. Michael East. First set of madrigals. (1604).
Vol.30. Michael East. Second set of madrigals. (1606).
Vol.31. Michael East. The madrigals in his third and fourth books. (1610, 1618).
Vol.32. Thomas Morley. The triumphes of Oriana. (1601).
Vol.33. Richard Allison. An hour's recreation in music. (1606).
Vol.34. Thomas Vautor. Songs of divers airs and natures. (1619).
Vol.35. Pt.I. Robert Jones. Madrigals of 3, 4, 5, 6, 7, and 8 parts. (1607).
Vol.35. Pt.II. John Mundy. The madrigals in his songs and psalms composed into 3, 4, and 5 parts. (1594).
Vol.36. Madrigal writings of Michael Cavendish (1598); Thomas Greaves (1604); William Holborne (1597); Richard Edwards; etc.
In preparation:
Vol.37. Michael Cavendish. Madrigals. (1598); Thomas Greaves. Madrigals. (1604); Richard Edwards. In going to my naked bed.
Vol.38. Madrigals recovered from manuscript sources.

FELLOWES, REV. EDMUND HORACE, 1870–1951. ed.
The English madrigal school. Rev. ed. The English madrigalists. Ser.2. Rev. by Thurston Dart. London, Stainer & Bell, cop.1956– .
v.1– .

FELLOWES, REV. EDMUND HORACE, 1870–1951. ed.
The English school of lutenist song writers. Transcribed, scored and ed. from the original editions by Edmund Horace Fellowes . . . London, Stainer & Bell, Ltd., [cop.1920–1932, 1959– .

v.1– .
For 1 or 2 voices. Original accompaniment transcribed into modern notation for piano.
Contents:
Vol.1–2. Dowland, John. First book of airs. (1597).
Vol.3. Ford, Thomas. Airs to the lute from Musicke of sundrie kindes. (1607).
Vol.4, 13. Campian, Thomas. Songs from Rosseter's Book of airs. (1601).
Vol.5–6. Dowland, John. Second book of airs. (1600).
Vol.7, 15. Pilkington, Francis. First book of airs. (1605).
Vol.8–9. Rosseter, Philip. Songs from Rosseter's Book of airs. (1601).
Vol.10–11. Dowland, John. Third book of airs. (1603).
Vol.12, 14. Dowland, John. Fourth book of airs. (1612). (A pilgrimes solace).
Vol.16. Morley, Thomas. First book of airs. (1600).
Vol.17. Coperario, Giovanni. Funerall teares. (1606). 1959.

FELLOWES, REV. EDMUND HORACE, 1870–1951. ed.
The English school of lutenist song writers. 2d series. Transcribed, scored and ed. from the original editions by Edmund Horace Fellowes . . . London, Stainer & Bell, Ltd., [cop.1925–1927, 1961– .
v.1– .
For 1 or 2 voices. Original accompaniment transcribed into modern notation for piano.
Contents:
Vol.1. Campian, Thomas. First booke of ayres. (1613).
Vol.2. Campian, Thomas. Second booke of ayres. (1613).
Vol.3. Bartlett, John. A booke of ayres. (1606).
Vol.4. Jones, Robert. First booke of songes and ayres. (1600).
Vol.5. Jones, Robert. Second booke of ayres. (1601).
Vol.6. Jones, Robert. Ultimum vale. Third booke of ayres. (1608).
Vol.7. Cavendish, Michael. Songs included in [his] Booke of ayres and madrigalles. (1598).
Vol.8. Daniel, John. Songs for the lute, viol and voice. (1606).
Vol.9. Attey, John. First booke of ayres. (1622).
Vol.10. Campian, Thomas. Third booke of ayres. (1617).
Vol.11. Campian, Thomas. Fourth booke of ayres. (1617).
Vol.12. Corkine, William. First booke of ayres. (1610).
Vol.13. Corkine, William. Second booke of ayres. (1612).
Vol.14. Jones, Robert. A musicall dreame; or, Fourth booke of ayres. (1609).
Vol.15. Jones, Robert. The muses' gardin for delights; or, Fifth booke of ayres. (1610).
Vol.16. Ferrabosco, Alfonso. Ayres. (1609).
Vol.17. Johnson, Robert. Ayres, songs, and dialogues. 1961.
Vol.18. Greaves, Thomas. Songs of sundrie kindes. (1604); George Mason. Ayres. (1618); John Earsden. Ayres. (1618). 1962.

FELLOWES, REV. EDMUND HORACE, 1870–1951. ed.
The English school of lutenist song writers. Rev. ed. The English lute-songs. Ser.2. Rev. by Thurston Dart. London, Stainer & Bell, cop. 1956– .
v.1– .

Ferdinand III, Holy Roman Emperor, 1608–1657.
Werke, *see* Musikalische Werke der Kaiser Ferdinand III, Leopold I, und Joseph I.

FESTA, COSTANZO, d.1545.
Opera omnia. Edidit: Alexander Main. [n.p.], American Institute of Musicology, 1962– .
v.1– . (Corpus mensurabilis musicae, 25).
Proposed set about 10v.
Contents:
Vol.1. All the mass music, heretofore unpublished: Missa Et in terra pax; Missa Carminum; Missa de Domine Nostra; Missa Se congie pris; Credo solemnitas; Benedicamus Domino, I; Benedicamus Domino, II; Benedicamus Domino, III; Benedicamus Domino, IV. 1962.

Feste musicali della Firenze Medicea (1480–1589), *see* Ghisi, Federico. Feste musicali della Firenze Medicea (1480–1589).

FIBICH, ZDENĚK, 1850–1900.
[Works.] Souborné vydáni. Praha, Společnost Zdeňka Fibicha; Státní Nakl. Krásné Literatury Hudby a Umění, [1958–].
v.1– .
Contents:
Klavír na dvě ruce.
Op.2, Lístky do památníku (F. Vrána); Op.41/I, Nálady, dojmy a upominky, sešit I–4 (K. Šolc); Op.56, Malířské studie I. (V. Holzknecht) s reprodukcemi výtvarných předloh ke skladbám; Sonatina D moll; Dvě scherza (K. Šolc); Dětem; Cvičení a etudy (L. Láska); Album II. (R. Kurzová), výbor drobnějších skladeb; Poem, původní i zlehčené vydání.
Klavír na čtyři ruce.
Op.18, Smuteční pochod z opery Nevěsta messinská; Op.19, ř. I. Maličkosti; Op.22, Zlatý věk, výbor z cyklů; Op.26, Noc na Karlštejně, předehra. (1954); Op.37, Záboj, Slavoj a Luděk, symfonická báseň. (1962); Op.49, Toman a lesní panna, symfonická báseň. (1959); Op.52, Oldřich a Božena, předehra; Nálady, dojmy a upomínky; Skladbičky a cvičení.
Klavírní výtahy.
Op.18, Nevěsta messinská; Op.31, Námluvy Pelopovy; Op.32, Smir Tantalův; Op.33, Smrt Hippodamie; Op.39, V podvečer; Op.51, Šárka.
Zpěv a klavír.
Op.36, Jarní paprsky; Šest písní.

Housle a klavir.
Op.10, Romance B dur (S. Šorm); Koncertní polonéza (N. Kubát); Sonáta D dur (J. Zich); Nálady, dojmy a upomínky; Poem.
Komorní Hudba.
Op.42, Klavírní kvintet D dur, hlasy; Smyčcový kvartet A dur, hlasy; Trio F moll, hlasy.
Orchestrální Hudba. Partitury.
Op.6, Othello, symfonická báseň. (1960); Op.9, Štědrý den, melodram; Op.13, Vesna, symfonická báseň. (1961); Op.15, Vodník, melodram; Op.17, I. Symfonie. (1960); Op.23, Jarní romance, kantata. (1956); Op.26, Noc na Karlštejně, předehra. (1954); Op.38, II. Symphonie. (1955); Op.39, V podvečer, selanka pro orchestr. (1959); Op.49, Toman a lesní panna, symfonická báseň. (1959); Op.53, III. Symfonie. (1958); Pripravujeme: Op.37, Záboj, Slavoj a Luděk, symfonická báseň. (1962); Op.54, Dojmy z venkova. (1962); Op.34, Komenský, předehra. (1963).
Libreta.
Šárka (A. Schulzová); Nevěsta messinská (podle F. Schillera zpracoval O. Hostinský); Bouře (podle W. Shakespeara zpracoval J. Vrchlický).
Knihy o Zdeňku Fibichovi.
Z. Nejedlý, Milostný deník Zdeňka Fibicha; Fibichův sborník I–II; A. Schulzová, Zdeněk Fibich; J. Plavec, Z. Fibich, melodramatik; Dilo Zdeňka Fibicha, soupis skladeb; J. Teichman, Z českých luhů do světa; Připravujeme: Jaroslav Jiránek, Zdeněk Fibich.

58 English songs of the 17th and 18th century, *see* Hullah, John Pyke. 58 English songs of the 17th and 18th century.

Finck, Heinrich, 1445–1527. Ausgewählte Werke, *see* Das Erbe deutscher Musik. Erste Reihe. Vol. 57; Publikationen älterer praktischer und theoretischer Musikwerke. Jahrg. 7.

Fiori musicali di diverse compositioni, *see* Frescobaldi, Girolamo. Fiori musicali di diverse compositioni.

The first book of consort lessons, *see* Morley, Thomas. The first book of consort lessons.

The first four centuries of music for the organ from Dunstable to Bach (1370–1749), *see* Klein, John. The first four centuries of music for the organ from Dunstable to Bach (1370–1749).

FISCHER, JOHANN CASPAR FERDINAND, 1650–1746.
Sämtliche Werke für Klavier und Orgel, von Johann Kaspar Ferdinand Fischer; hrsg. von Ernst v. Werra. Leipzig, Breitkopf & Härtel, [1901].
xvi, 125p. incl. facsims.
Contents:
Les pièces de clavessin (Musical. Blumenbüschlein), Musicalischer Parnassus, Ariadne musica, Blumen-Strauss.

FISCHER, JOHANN CASPAR FERDINAND, 1650–1746.
Sämtliche Werke für Klavier und Orgel . . . Reprint. New York, Broude Brothers, 1965.

FISHER, WILLIAM ARMS, 1861–1948. ed.
The music that Washington knew. With an historical sketch by William Arms Fisher. A program of authentic music, vocal and instrumental, with historical and biographical data. Boston, New York, Oliver Ditson Co., Inc.; Chicago, Lyon & Healy, Inc., [cop.1931].
xxiv, 44p.
Contains compositions by Samuel Arnold, William Billings, William Boyce, Henry Carey (?), George F. Handel, Francis Hopkinson, Philip Phile, William Shield, and John Stafford Smith.

THE FITZWILLIAM MUSIC; being a collection of sacred pieces, selected from manuscripts of Italian composers in the Fitzwilliam Museum, now for the first time published by permission of the University of Cambridge, by Vincent Novello. . . London, Pub. for the Editor, 1825.
5v.
Contents:
Bd.1.
Leo: Sicut erat.
Carissimi: Surgamus eamus.
Durante: Cantate Domino.
Bononcini: In te Domine speravi.
Leo: Christus factus est.
Palestrina: Et incarnatus est.
Carissimi: Gaudeamus omnes.
Padre Martini: Sicut erat.
Leo: Tu es sacerdos.
Ferodi: Adoramus te.
Bononcini: Eterna fac.
Clari: Gloria Patri, Sicut erat, Amen.

Bd.2.
Pergolesi: Dominus ad dextris tuis, Gloria Patri, Sicut erat.
Clari: Stabat Mater, Cujus animam, O quam tristis, Quae maerabat.
Leo: Kyrie, Qui tollis.
Cafaro: Amen.
Clari: Domine Deus, Cum sancto.
Leo: Cum sancto spiritu.

Bd.3.
Jomelli: Confirma hoc Deus.
Clari: Kyrie, De profundis.
Pergolesi: Juravit Dominus.
Clari: Laetutus sum.
Bononcini: Te ergo quaesumus, Sanctus.
Clari: Tecum principium.
Leo: Te es sacerdos.
Perti: Adoramus te Christe.
Bonno: Cum sancto spiritu.
Leo: Qui tollis peccata.

Bd.4.
Leo: Te es sacerdos.
Carissimi: Dulce te. Et sic laudabimus.
Clari: Kyrie eleison. Qui tollis peccata, Cum sancto spiritus.
Durante: Protexisti me Deus.
Stradella: Dove Battista.
Orlando di Lasso: Sicut ablactatus est.
Padre Martini: Sicut erat.
Giuseppe Conti: Amen.
Clari: Gloria Patri.
Leo: Dixit Dominus.

Bd.5.
Clari: Sancta Mater.
Colonna: Domine ad adjuvandum, Gloria Patri, Sicut erat.
L. da Vittoria: Regina coeli.
Clari: Gratias agimus, Cum sancto.
Carissimi: O felix anima.
Colonna: Paratum cor ejus.
Clari: Quando corpus, Quando corpus morietur.
Edwardi Lupi: Audivi vocem de coelo.
Clari: Sicut erat.
Leo: Sicut erat. Amen.

THE FITZWILLIAM VIRGINAL BOOK. Ed. from the original manuscript, with an introd. and notes, by J. A. Fuller-Maitland and W. Barclay Squire. (Translated into German by John Bernhoff). Leipzig, Breitkopf & Härtel, 1899.
2v.
Contains compositions by William Blitheman, John Bull, William Byrd, Giles Farnaby, Richard Farnaby, Free, Galeazzo, Orlando Gibbons, Hooper, William Inglot, Edward Johnson, Robert Johnson, Marchant, Thomas Morley, John Munday, Thomas Oldfield, Jehan Oystermayre, Parsons, Martin Peerson, Peter Philips, Giovanni Pichi, Ferdinando Richardson, Nicholas Strogers, J. P. Sweelinck, Thomas Tallis, William Tisdall, Thomas Tomkins, and Thomas Warrock.

THE FITZWILLIAM VIRGINAL BOOK. Reprint. New York, Broude Brothers, 1949.
2v. facsims.
Introductory text and notes also in German, translated by John Bernhoff.
"List of books referred to in the notes": v.1, p.[xxii]; v.2, p.[v].

THE FITZWILLIAM VIRGINAL BOOK. Reprint. Ann Arbor, Mich., Edwards Brothers, 1949.
2v. (Edwards music reprints. Ser.B. Individual and musicological works. No.2).

THE FITZWILLIAM VIRGINAL BOOK.
Ausgewählte Stücke aus dem Fitzwilliam virginal book. Hrsg. von J. A. Fuller-Maitland and William Barclay Squire. Leipzig, Breitkopf & Härtel.
2v.
Vol.1 contains compositions by William Byrd and Thomas Morley.
Vol.2 contains compositions by John Bull, Giles Farnaby, Robert Johnson, John Munday, Martin Peerson, and Peter Philips.

Fitzwilliam virginal book, *see* Tisdall, William. Complete keyboard works.

Five sixteenth century Venetian lute books, *see* Lefkoff, Gerald. Five sixteenth century Venetian lute books.

Fleischer, Heinrich, ed. The parish organist, *see* The parish organist.

La flora, *see* Jeppesen, Knud. La flora.

FLORES MUSICAE; Oeuvres des musiciens des XVIIe et XVIIIe siècles, recueillies dans les manuscrits ou les éditions de l'époque et realisées par Claude Crussard. Lausanne, Foetisch, 1949– .
v.1– .
Contents:
Vol.1. Pt.1. Charpentier, M.-A. Pie Jesus. 1949.
Vol.1. Pt.2. Charpentier, M.-A. Magnificat. 1949.
Vol.2. Bach, J. S. Sonate en ut majeur, pour deux violons et continuo. 1949.
Vol.3. Telemann, G. P. Sonate à flûte, violon, alto et basse. 1949.
Vol.4. Leclair, J. M. Sonate en trio, pour deux violons et la basse continuo. 1955.
Vol.5. Leclair, J. M. Sonate à trois, avec une flûte allemande ou un violon, une viole et le clavecin. 1955.
Vol.6. Locatelli, P. A. Sonate à deux violons ou deux flûtes traversières. 1955.
Vol.7. Krieger, J. P. Sonate à trois, pour deux violons et le clavecin. 1958.
Vol.8. Geminiani, F. Sonate, pour deux violons, un violoncelle et la basse continue. 1958.
Vol.9. Scarlatti, A. Ariette a una voce, con e senza stromenti. 1958.

Flores musicales belgicae, *see* Société Belge de Musicologie. Publications. Flores musicales belgicae.

Florilège du concert vocal de la Renaissance, *see* Expert, Henry. Florilège du concert vocal de la Renaissance.

FLORILEGIUM MUSICAE ANTIQUAE. Kraków, Polskie Wydawnictwo Muzyczne, 19? – .
v.1– .
Contents:
Vol.1. Sieprawski, P. Fragment aus der Motette "Justus germinavit" (Sopran Solo, Violine, Violoncello und Orgel).
Vol.2. Zwierzchowski, M. Polonäse "Tuba mirum" aus "Requiem" (Bass Solo, 2 Trompeten, Violoncello und Orgel).
Vol.3. Milwid, A. Alla Polacca "Sub tuum praesidium" (Sopran und Bass Solo, Instrumenten-Ensemble und Orgel).
Vol.4. Koprzywnica, Hieronim von. Veni Sancte Spiritus (Männerchor).
Vol.5. Scarlatti, D. 2 Terzette und Duett aus der

Oper "Tetyde auf Skyros" (Singstimmen, Violoncello und Cembalo). 1963.
Vol.6. Scarlatti, D. 8 Arien der Tetyde aus der Oper "Tetyde auf Skyros" (Sopran Solo, Violine, Violoncello und Cembalo).
Vol.11. Telemann, G. Ph. Polnische Suite (Cembalo).
Vol.12. Janiewicz, F. Andante "Erhell' deinen Blick" (Rendi sereno il ciglio) (Streichorchester).

FLORILEGIUM MUSICUM. Ein Werkreihe alter Musik, hrsg. von Gustav Scheck & Hugo Ruf. Lörrach, Baden, Deutscher Ricordi-Verlag, [1954–].
v.1– .
Contents:
Vol.1. Bach, C. P. E. Sonate B-dur, 1738, für Flauto traverso und Basso Continuo. [1954].
Vol.2. Bach, C. P. E. Sonate G-dur, 1739, für Flauto traverso und Basso Continuo. [1954].
Vol.3. Bach, C. P. E. Sonate D-dur, 1747, für Flauto traverso und Cembalo obligato. [1954].
Vol.4. Händel, G. F. Sonate, C-moll, für Oboe (Flöte, Violine) und Basso Continuo. [1954].
Vol.5. Händel, G. F. Sonate, G-moll, für Oboe (Flöte, Violine) und Basso Continuo. [1954]
Vol.6. Leclair, J. M. Konzert, C-dur, Op.VII, 3, für Flöte oder Violine oder Oboe, Streicher und Generalbass. [1954].
Vol.7. Bach, C. P. E. Sonate, G-moll, für Oboe und Basso Continuo. [1954]
Vol.8. La Barre, Michel de. Suite, G-dur, für zwei Flöten oder andere Melodieinstrumente. [1954].
Vol.9. Platti, G. B. Sonate, D-dur, für Flauto traverso und Basso Continuo. [1955]

For connoisseurs and amateurs, *see* Für Kenner und Liebhaber.

Forty-five pieces for keyboard instruments, *see* Byrd, William. Forty-five pieces for keyboard instruments.

46 pieces pour orgue, *see* Raugel, Félix. Quarante-six pièces pour orgue.

FOSTER, STEPHEN COLLINS, 1826–1864.
. . . Songs, compositions and arrangements, by Stephen Collins Foster . . . Indianapolis, Ind., Privately printed by Josiah Kirby Lilly, 1933.
3v. (Foster Hall reproductions).
This set includes "two hundred and one original songs and compositions, to which are added all known arrangements of his own work and also his arrangements of the work of others."

Fourteen ancient fauxbourdons set to the song of the Blessed Virgin Mary, *see* Plainsong and Mediaeval Music Society. Fourteen ancient fauxbourdons set to the song of the Blessed Virgin Mary.

Fourteenth-century Italian cacce, *see* Marrocco, William Thomas. Fourteenth-century Italian cacce.

Fourteenth-century mass music in France, *see* Stäblein-Harder, Hanna. Fourteenth-century mass music in France.

FRANCISQUE, ANTOINE, fl.1600.
. . . Le trésor d'Orphée d'Antoine Francisque (1600). Transcrit pour piano par Henri Quittard. (1906). Paris, L. M. Fortin & Cie., [1906?].
80p. facsim. (Internationale Musikgesellschaft. Section de Paris. Publications).
Originally written for the lute.
Contains facsimiles of title page, dedication, and p.27 of original edition.
Cover title.

FRANCK, CÉSAR AUGUSTE, 1822–1890.
. . . Oeuvres complètes pour orgue. Édition originale. Paris, Durand & Cie., Éditeurs, n.d.
4v. (Édition Classique A. Durand & Fils. No.13791–13794).
Score for organ.
Contents:
Vol.1.
Fantaisie en ut majeur.
Grand pièce symphonique en fa♯ mineur.
Prélude, fugue et variation en si mineur.
Vol.2.
Pastorale en mi majeur.
Prière en ut♯ mineur.
Final en si♭ majeur.
Vol.3.
Fantaisie en la majeur.
Cantabile en si majeur.
Pièce héroïque en si mineur.
Vol.4.
Choral No.1 en mi majeur.
Choral No.2 en si mineur.
Choral No.3 en la mineur.

FRANCK, CÉSAR AUGUSTE, 1822–1890.
Oeuvres complètes pour orgue; revues, annotées et doigtées par Marcel Dupré. Paris, S. Bornemann, cop.1955– .
4v.
Contents:
Vol.1.
Fantaisie en ut majeur.
Grand pièce symphonique.
Prélude, fugue et variation.
Vol.2.
Pastorale.
Prière.
Final.
Vol.3.
Fantaisie en la majeur.
Cantabile.
Pièce héroïque.
Vol.4.
Trois chorals.

FRANCK, CÉSAR AUGUSTE, 1822–1890.
The organ works of César Franck. Ed. by Harvey Grace . . . London, Novello and Co., Ltd., n.d.
6v.
Contents:

Vol.1. Fantasy in C.
Vol.2. Grand pièce symphonique.
Vol.3. Prelude, fugue and variation.
Vol.4. Pastorale.
Vol.5. Prayer.
Vol.6. Finale.

FRANCK, CÉSAR AUGUSTE, 1822–1890.
. . . Orgelwerke . . . New York, London, C. F. Peters, cop.1919.
4v. (Edition Peters. No.3744a-d).
Contents:
Vol.1. Fantaisie, Grande pièce symphonique, Prélude, Fugue et variation.
Vol.2. Pastorale, Prière, Final.
Vol.3. Drei Choräle: E dur, H moll, A moll.
Vol.4. Fantaisie, Cantabile, Pièce héroïque.

Frederick II, the Great, King of Prussia, 1712–1786, *see* Friedrich II, der Grosse, King of Prussia.

The free organ compositions from the Lüneburg organ tablatures, *see* Shannon, John R. The free organ compositions from the Lüneburg organ tablatures.

The French organist, *see* Bedell, Robert Leech. The French organist.

French secular music of the late fourteenth century, *see* Apel, Willi. French secular music of the late fourteenth century.

FRESCOBALDI, GIROLAMO, 1583–1644.
. . . Ausgewählte Orgelsätze aus seinen gedruckten Werken. Hrsg. von F. X. Haberl. Neue Ausgabe revidiert von B. F. Richter. Leipzig, Breitkopf & Härtel, n.d.
2v. 30½cm. (On cover: Edition Breitkopf. Nr.4357–4358).

FRESCOBALDI, GIROLAMO, 1583–1644.
. . . Ausgewählte Orgelwerke in zwei Bänden; pezzi scelti per Organo in due Volumi. Hrsg. von Hermann Keller. Leipzig, New York, [etc.], C. F. Peters, [cop.1943, 1948].
2v. (On cover: Edition Peters. No.4514–4515).

FRESCOBALDI, GIROLAMO, 1583–1644.
Fiori musicali di diverse compositioni: toccate, Kirie, canzoni, capricci, e recercari in partitura a quattro utili per sonatori autori Girolamo Frescobaldi . . . Venetia, Appresso Alessandro Vincenti, 1635. Paris, Éditions Maurice Senart, 1922.
xxxii, 101p. front. (port.). (Édition Nationale de Musique Classique. No.5313).
Revision and notes by Jos. Bonnet. Biographical notes by M. A. Guilmant.

FRESCOBALDI, GIROLAMO, 1583–1644.
Orgel- und Klavierwerke; Gesamtausgabe nach dem Urtext hrsg. von Pierre Pidoux. Kassel, Bärenreiter, [1949–]. v.1, 1950.
v.1– .
Contents:
Vol.1. Fantasie (1608) und Canzoni alla Francese (1645).
Vol.2. Das erste Buch der Capricci, Ricercari, und Canzoni. (1626).
Vol.3–4. Toccaten: 1. Buch. Partituren usw. (1637); 2. Buch. Canzonen usw. (1637).
Vol.5. Fiori musicali. (1635).

FRIEDRICH II, DER GROSSE, KING OF PRUSSIA, 1712–1786.
Friedrichs des Grossen musikalische Werke. Erste kritisch durchgesehene Ausgabe . . . Leipzig, Breitkopf & Härtel, [1889].
7 parts in 4v.
"Vorwort," signed Philipp Spitta.
Contents:
Bd.1. Sonaten für Flöte und Klavier. Nr.1–12.
Bd.2. Sonaten für Flöte und Klavier. Nr.13–25.
Bd.3. I. Abt. Konzert für Flöte, Streichorchester und Generalbass. Partitur.
Bd.3. (4). 2. Abt. Konzerte für Flöte, Streichorchester und Generalbass. Bearb. für Flöte und Klavier.

Froberger, Johann Jakob, 1616–1667. Organ and clavier works, *see* Denkmäler der Tonkunst in Österreich. Vol.8, 13, 21.

FROIDEBISE, PIERRE, 1914– . ed.
Anthologie de l'orgue. Des primitifs à la Renaissance. Recueillie et interprétée par Pierre Froidebise . . . Paris, Les Nouvelles Éditions Méridian, [cop.1958–].
v.1– .
Contents (published):
Vol.1.
École Allemande. H. Buchner, L. Kieber, anonyme).
École Italienne. (M. Cavazzoni, G. Cavazzoni, A. Gabrieli).
École Flamande. (T. Susato).
École Française. (Pierre Attaingnant).

Frühmeister der deutschen Orgelkunst, *see* Moser, Hans Joachim. Frühmeister der deutschen Orgelkunst.

FRYE, WALTER, 15th century.
Opera omnia. Ed. by Sylvia W. Kenney. Rome, American Institute of Musicology, 1960.
83p. (Corpus mensurabilis musicae. No.19).
A single volume containing chansons, motets, masses, and a chanson and a motet in organ arrangement.

FULLER-MAITLAND, JOHN ALEXANDER, 1856–1936. ed.
The contemporaries of Purcell; harpsichord pieces, selected and ed. by J. A. Fuller-Maitland . . . London, J. & W. Chester, Ltd., cop.1921.
7v. (Chester Series. No.51–57).
Contents:
Vol.1–2. John Blow.
Vol.3–4. William Croft.
Vol.5. Jeremiah Clark.
Vol.6–7. Various composers: Benjamin Rogers,

Mark Coleman, Gerhard Diesner, Robert King, Daniel Purcell, John Eccles, Francis Piggott, William Turner, John Barrett.

Fuller-Maitland, John Alexander, 1856–1936.
Euterpe, *see* Euterpe.

Fuller-Maitland, John Alexander, 1856–1936, ed.
The Fitzwilliam virginal book, *see* The Fitzwilliam virginal book.

FULLER-MAITLAND, JOHN ALEXANDER, 1856–1936. ed.
Twenty-five pieces for keyed instruments from Benjamin Cosyn's Virginal book. Ed. by J. A. Fuller-Maitland and W. Barclay Squire. London, J. & W. Chester, Ltd., cop.1923.
3p.L., 61p. (On cover: Edition Chester. No.110).
Contains compositions by John Bull, William Byrd, Benjamin Cosyn, and Orlando Gibbons.

Fundamentbuch von Hans von Constanz, *see* Buchner, Hans (von Constanz). Fundamentbuch.

Fundamentum organisandi, by Conrad Paumann, *see* Das Locheimer Liederbuch. Locheimer Liederbuch und Fundamentum organisandi.

FÜR KENNER UND LIEBHABER. Pour connaisseurs et amateurs. For connoisseurs and amateurs. Basel, Switzerland, Editions Kneusslin; New York, C. F. Peters, 19? – .
No.1– .
Contents:
No.1. Mozart, Leopold. Trumpet concerto. Full score.
No.2. Bach, J. Christian. Sinfonia in E flat. Op.3, No.4. Full score.
No.3. Albinoni, Tomaso. Concerto a cinque. Op.7, No.5. 2 oboes, strings. Score.
No.4. Abel, C. F. Symphony No.12 in E. Full score.
No.5. Haydn, J. Symphony No.12 in E. Full score.
No.6. Rosetti, Anton. Parthia (Partita) for wind septet.
No.7. Albinoni, Tomaso. Concerto a cinque. Op.5, No.5. 2 violins, strings. Full score.
No.8. Danzi, Franz. Quintet for flute, oboe, clarinet, bassoon, horn. Op.67, No.2.
No.9. Albinoni, Tomaso. Concerto a cinque. Op.9, No.2. Oboe, strings. Full score.
No.10. Haydn, J. Symphony No.39 in F minor. Full score.
No.11. Mozart, W. A. Ombra felice (K.255) for alto voice and orchestra. Full score.
No.12. Stamitz, Carl. Sinfonia concertante. Violin, viola, and orchestra. Score.
No.13. Reicha, Anton. Woodwind quintet in D. Op.91, No.3.
No.14. Schubert, F. P. Salve Regina, for soprano and orchestra. Full score.
No.15. Haydn, J. Symphony No.63. Full score.
No.16. Abel, C. F. Symphony. Op.7, No.6. Full score.
No.17. Haydn, J. Symphony No.3. Full score.
No.18.
No.19. Devienne, François. Trio. Op.66, No.2. Flute, violin, and violoncello.
No.20. Reicha, Anton. Wind quintet. Op.100, No.4. Flute, oboe, clarinet, bassoon, and horn.
No.21. Stamitz, Carl. Symphonie concertante. (Violin, viola, piano).
No.22. Haydn, J. Symphony No.84. (Orchestra parts).
No.23. Danzi, Franz. Duos (2). Viola and violoncello.
No.24. Danzi, Franz. Quintet. Op.86, No.1. Parts.
No.25. Mozart, W. A. Adagio. K.580a. English horn, 2 horns, and bassoon.
No.26. Rosetti, Anton. Parthia. Score.
No.27. Crusell, Bernhard Henrik. Quatuor No.2, in E flat. Clarinet, violin, viola, and violoncello.
No.28. Reicha, Anton. Woodwind quartet. Op.91, No.1.
No.29. Devienne, François. Three duos concertantes. (2 violoncellos or bassoons).
No.30. Rosetti, Anton. Woodwind quintet, E flat.
No.31. Reicha, Anton. Quintet. Op.91, No.5 (A). Flute, oboe, clarinet, horn, and bassoon.
No.32. Hoffmeister, Franz Anton. Serenade in E flat. Parts.
No.33. Haydn, J. Symphony No.70.
No.34. Hoffmeister, Franz Anton. Serenade in E flat. Score.

FÜRSTLICHES INSTITUT FÜR MUSIKWISSENSCHAFTLICHE FORSCHUNG. Bückeburg.
Veröffentlichung. [No.] 1. Bückeburg, 1919.
1 no. 88 plates.
[No.] 1 in 2 parts: Text and plates (music).
[No.] 1 called Reihe Mozartscher Handschriften. [cf. Preface to No.1].
Contents:
[No.] 1. Mozart, W. A. W. A. Mozart's Handschrift in zeitlich geordneten Nachbildungen. Hrsg. von Ludwig Schiedermair. 1919.

FÜRSTLICHES INSTITUT FÜR MUSIKWISSENSCHAFTLICHE FORSCHUNG. Bückeburg.
Veröffentlichung. Zweite Reihe: Tafelwerke. [No.] 2–3. Bückeburg, 1923–24.
2v. facsims.
Contents:
[No.] 2. Wolf, Johannes. Musikalische Schrifttafeln. 100 facsims. 1923.
[No.] 3. Ganassi, S. Regola Rubertina. Facsimile ed. 1924.

FÜRSTLICHES INSTITUT FÜR MUSIKWISSENSCHAFTLICHE FORSCHUNG. Bückeburg.
Veröffentlichungen . . . Reihe 3: Alt-Bückeburger Musik. Bückeburg, [etc.], 1920–22.
3v. plus 1 no.
Contents:
Bach, J. C. F. Ausgewählte Werke. Bd.1^{1-2}, 5^{1-4}, 7^{1-4}, 1920–21.
Bd.1. Motetten: 1921.
No.1. Motette: Ich lieg und schlafe.
No.2. Motette a 4 voci sopra la cantilena: Wachet auf, ruft uns die Stimme.

Bd.5. Klaviersonaten: 1920.
No.1. A dur.
No.2. D dur.
No.3. A dur.
No.4. Sonate zu vier Händen, C dur.
Bd.7. Kammermusik. 1920.
No.1. Trio für Violine, Bratsche und Klavier, G-dur.
No.2. Trio für Flöte, Violine und Klavier, C-dur.
No.3. Septett für 2 Hörner, Oboe, Violine, Bratsche, Violoncell und Klavier, C-dur.
No.4. Sonate für Flöte und Klavier, mit Violoncell ad lib., D-dur.
... Musik am Hofe des Grafen Ernst (1601–22) ... 1922. 1 v.

FUSER, IRENEO, 1906– . ed.
... Classici Italiani dell'organo. Padova, Editore G. Zanibon, cop.1955.
176p.
Contains compositions by Giuseppe Aldrovandini, Andrea Antico, Andriano Banchieri, Giuseppe Bencini, Giov. Maria Casini, Girolamo Cavazzoni, Marcantonio Cavazzoni, Andrea Cima, Nicolò Corradine, Girolamo Diruta, Fabrizio Fontana, Girolamo Frescobaldi, Andrea Gabrieli, Giovanni Gabrieli, Giuseppe Guamo, Luzzasco Luzzaschi, Ascanio Majone, Cristoforo Malvezzi, Giov. Batt. Martini, Fiorenzo Maschera, Claudio Merulo, Annibale Padovano, Bernardo Pasquini, Vincenzo Pellegrini, Nicolò Porpora, Michelangelo Rossi, Agostino Soderini, Giov. Maria Trabaci, Antonio Valente, and Domenico Zipoli.

FUX, JOHANN JOSEPH, 1660–1741.
Sämtliche Werke. Hrsg. von der Johann-Joseph-Fux-Gesellschaft, Graz. Kassel, New York, Bärenreiter, 1959– .
8 series (v.1– .). facsims.
Proposed set about 40v.
Contents:
Ser.I. Messen und Requiem.
Vol.1. Missa corporis Christi. 1959.
Ser.II. Litaneien, Vespern, Kompletorien, Te Deum.
Vol.1. Te Deum. 1963.
Ser.III. Kleinere Kirchenmusikwerke.
Vol.1. Motetten und Antiphonen für Sopran mit Instrumentalbegleitung. 1961.
Ser.IV. Oratorien.
Vol.1. La Fede Sacrilega nella Morte del Precursor S. Giovanni Battista. K.291. 1959.
Ser.V. Opern.
Vol.1. Julio Ascanio Re d'Alba. 1962.
Ser.VI. Instrumentalmusik.
Vol.1. 1964.
Ser.VII. Theoretische Pädagogische Werke.
Ser.VIII. Supplement.

GABRIELI, GIOVANNI, 1557–1612.
Opera omnia, edidit Denis Arnold. Rome, American Institute of Musicology, 1956– .
v.1– . (Corpus mensurabilis musicae. No.12).
Vol.1– , for cantus, altus, tenor, and bassus and instruments in varying combinations of 6–12 parts.
Proposed set about 10v.
Contents:
Vol.1. Motetta: [From the] Concerti, 1587. [From the] Sacrae symphoniae, 1597. 1956.
Vol.2. Motetta: [From the] Sacrae symphoniae, 1597. 1959.
Vol.3. Motetta: [From the] Sacrae symphoniae, 1615. 1962.

GABRIELI, GIOVANNI, 1557–1612.
Music of Gabrieli and his time. Reissue of the musical part (Vol.III) of Carl von Winterfeld "Johannes Gabrieli und sein Zeitalter." Berlin, 1834; Ossining, N.Y., William Salloch, 1960.
157p.
Contains compositions by Giov. Gabrieli, Orlandus Lassus, Luca Marenzio, Claudio Merulo, Claudio Monteverdi, Palestrina, and Heinrich Schütz.

GAFFURIO, FRANCHINO, 1451–1522.
Collected musical works. Ed. by Lutz Finscher. Rome, American Institute of Musicology in Rome, 1955– .
v.1– . (Corpus mensurabilis musicae. No.10).
Contents:
Vol.1. Missa de carnival; Missa sexti toni irregularis. 1955.
Vol.2. Kyrie et Agnus Dei ad Missam sexti toni irregularis; Missa (in Nat. D.N.J.C.) Omnipotens genitor; Missa Sanctae Catherinae V. et M. quarti toni; Missa de tous biens pleine; Missa de O clara luce; Missa (sine nomine); Missa brevis primi toni. 1960.
Vol.3. Messe: Missa Sanctae Catharinae V. et M. quarti toni; Missa brevis et expedita; Alia missa brevis ejusdem toni; Missa de O clara luce; Missa brevis octavi toni; Messa a quattro. 1960.
Vol.4. Magnificat: I. Primi toni; II. Sexti toni; III. Octavi toni; IV. Primi toni; V. Primi toni; VI. Sexti toni; VII. Sexti toni; VIII. Sexti toni; IX. Octavi toni; X. Octavi toni; XI. Octavi toni. 1959.
Vol.5. Motetti: Stabat Mater. Adoramus Te Christe; Promissa mundo gaudia; O sacrum convivium; Accepta Christi munera; Virgo prudentissima; Beata progenies; Gloriosae Virginis Mariae; Sub tuam protectionem; Sponsa dei electa; Hortus conclusus; Descendi in hortum; Tota pulchra es; Quando venit ergo; Ave Corpus Jesu Christi; O sacrum convivium; Hoc gaudium; Gaude Virgo gloriosa; Produit puer. Res a saeculis; Joseph conturbatus est; Gaude Mater luminis. Te honorant superi; Ave mundi spes, Maria; Regina coeli laetare; Salve decus genetoris. Qui nepotes; Salve Mater salvatoris. Salve verbi sacra parens; Salve decus virginum. O convallis humilis; Tu thronus es. Salve Mater pietatis. Vox eclipsim nesciens; Imperatrix gloriosa. Florem ergo genuisti. Rex miranda; Beate Sebastiane; Omnipotens aeterne Deus; Virgo

Dei digna; Verbum sapientiae; Castra caeli; O res laeta; Imperatrix reginarum; Magnum nomen Domini; Audi benigne conditor; Salve Mater salvatoris. Inter natos mulierum. 1959.

Garre, Helmut Schmidt, *see* Schmidt-Garre, Helmut.

GASTOUÉ, AMÉDÉE, 1873–1943. ed.
Motets choisis des maîtres du XVe au XVIIIe siècle. Recueillis et annotés par Amédée Gastoué. Paris, Procure Générale, [1930].
p.1– .

Gay, Jesús Bal y, *see* Bal y Gay, Jesús.

GEIRINGER, KARL, 1899– . comp.
Music of the Bach family; an anthology. Cambridge, Harvard University Press, 1955.
viii, 248p.
Contains compositions by Carl Philipp Emanuel Bach, Georg Christoph Bach, Heinrich Bach, Johann Bach, Johann Bernhard Bach, Johann Christian Bach, Johann Christoph Bach, Johann Christoph Friedrich Bach, Johann Ernst Bach, Johann Ludwig Bach, Johann Michael Bach, Johann Nicolaus Bach, Wilhelm Friedemann Bach, and Wilhelm Friedrich Ernst Bach.

Geistliche und weltliche Lieder aus dem XVI.–XVII. Jahrhundert, *see* Commer, Franz. Geistliche und weltliche Lieder aus dem XVI.–XVII. Jahrhundert.

GENNRICH, FRIEDRICH, 1883– . ed.
Musikwissenschaftliche Studien-Bibliothek. Darmstadt, 19? – .
v.1– .
Contents:
Vol.1/2. Gennrich, F. Abriss der frankonischen Mensuralnotation nebst Uebertragungsmaterial.
Vol.3/4. Gennrich, F. Abriss der Mensuralnotation des XIV. und der ersten Hälfte des XV. Jahrhunderts nebst Uebertragungsmaterial.
Vol.5/6. Gennrich, F. Die Sankt Viktor-Clausulae und ihre Motetten.
Vol.7. Gennrich, F. Aus der Formenwelt des Mittelalters, 64 Beispiele zum Bestimmen musikalischer Formen.
Vol.8. Gennrich, F. Uebertragungsmaterial zur "Rhythmik der Ars antiqua."
Vol.9. Gennrich, F. Melodien altdeutscher Lieder. 47 Melodien in handschriftlicher Fassung.
Vol.10. Gennrich, F. Mittelhochdeutsche Liedkunst. 24 Melodien zu mittelhochdeutschen Liedern.
Vol.11. Gennrich, F. Lateinische Liedkontrafaktur. Eine Auswahl lateinischer Conductus mit ihren volkssprachigen Vorbildern.
Vol.12. Gennrich, F. Perotinus Magnus. Das Organum: Alleluia Nativitas gloriose Virginis Marie und seine Sippe.
Vol.13/14. Gennrich, F. Musica sine Littera. Notenzeichen und Rhythmik der Gruppennotation. Ein Abriss nebst Uebertragungsmaterial.
Vol.15/16. Gennrich, F. Magistri Franconis Ars cantus mensurabilis.
Vol.17. Gennrich, F. Exempla altfranzösischer Lyrik. 40 altfranzösische Lieder.
Vol.18/19. Gennrich, F. Lo Gai Saber. 50 Ausgewählte Troubadour-Lieder, Melodie, Text, Kommentar, Formenlehre und Glossar.
Vol.20. Gennrich, F. Adam de la Halle, Le jeu de Robin et de Marion. Li Rondel Adam.
Vol.21. Gennrich, F. Die autochthone Melodie. Uebungsmaterial zur musikalischen Textkritik.

Gennrich, Friedrich, 1883– , ed. Summa musicae medii aevi, *see* Summa musicae medii aevi.

GEORGII, WALTER. ed.
Keyboard music of the Baroque and Rococo. Ed. from early sources, with fingerings and commentary by Walter Georgii. Köln, Arno Volk, [1960].
3v.
Contents:
Vol.1. Music before Bach and Handel. (*England:* William Byrd, John Bull, Giles Farnaby, Henry Purcell; *Holland:* Jan Sweelinck; *Italy:* Girolamo Frescobaldi, Alessandro Poglietti, Bernardo Pasquini; *France:* Jacques Champion de Chambonnières, Louis Couperin, Nicolas Antoine Le Bègue; *Germany:* Johann Jakob Froberger, Georg Muffat, Johann Pachelbel, Ferdinand Tobias Richter, Johann Krieger, Joh. Kaspar Ferd. Fischer, Johann Kuhnau, Matthias Weckmann, Jan. A. Reinken, Dietrich Buxtehude, Georg Böhm).
Vol.2. Music of Bach's and Handel's contemporaries. (Domenico Scarlatti, François Couperin, Jean Philippe Rameau, Louis Claude Daquin, Jean François Dandrieu, Georg Philipp Telemann, Gottlieb Muffat).
Vol.3. Music after Bach and Handel. (B. Galuppi, Padre Martini, P. D. Paradisi, Etienne Nicolas Méhul, Georg Christoph Wagenseil, Johann Schobert, W. Friedemann Bach, Ph. E. Bach, Johann Christian Bach, Georg Benda, Johann Wilhelm Hässler).

GERHARDT, PAUL. ed.
. . . Album nordischer Komponisten für Orgel, hrsg. von Paul Gerhardt und Max Reger . . . Oslo, Norsk Musikforlag; Stockholm, A. B. Nordiska Musikförlaget, cop.1921.
2v. (Wilhelm Hansen Edition. No.2043–2044).
Contents:
Vol.1 contains compositions by Chr. Cappelen, J. P. E. Hartmann, Joh. Adam Krygell, Ludv. M. Lindemann, Otto Malling, G. Matthison-Hansen, P. Rasmussen, Emil Sjögren, and Johan Svendsen.
Vol.2 contains compositions by H. Amberg, Dietrich Buxtehude, Niels W. Gade, Edv. Greig, Joh. Adam Krygell, Otto Malling, G. Matthison-Hansen, Franz Neruda, Carl Nielsen, and Chr. Sinding.

Geschichte der Musik in Beispielen, *see* Schering, Arnold. Geschichte der Musik in Beispielen.

DIE GESCHICHTLICHEN DENKMÄLER DER JAPANISCHEN TONKUNST. Abt.I. Hofmusik. 1. Heft. Saibara. Im Auftrag der Nanki Musikbibliothek hrsg. v. Dr. Kanetune-Kiyoske und Dr. Syoiti Tudi. Tokio, Nanki Musik-Bibliothek, 1930.
vi, 16, 33, 10p.
In Japanese and German.
1. Heft is apparently all that was published.
Other proposed volumes (unpublished):
2. Heft. Rôei. (Alte Lieder).
3. Heft. Kume-Uta. (Altjapanische Kriegs- (Tan–) Lieder).
4. Heft. Aduma-Asobi, Kagura. (Kultgesänge).
5. Heft. Aduma-Asobi, Kagura. (Kultgesänge).
6. Heft. Chinesiche [sic] Orchestermusik.
7. Heft. Koreanische Orchestermusik.
(Bald erscheinen 2. und 3. Heft. Andere Hefte in Vorbereitung).
Contents 1. Heft:
p.1–16. Text in Japanese. Explanations of intervals, tuning of instruments, scales.
p.1–5. (pagination starts over). Ana Tôto (Sôdyô-Ryo). Music for Uta (voice), Syakubyôsi, Syô, Hitiriki, Huë, Koto, and Biwa in score.
p.6–8. Mushiroda (Sôdyô-Ryo). Music for Uta (voice), Syakubyôsi, Hitiriki, Huë, Koto, and Biwa in score.
p.9–15. Yamasiro (Sôdyô-Ryo). Music for Uta, Syakubyôsi, Syô, Hitiriki, Huë, Koto, and Biwa in score.
p.16–21. Minoyama (Sôdyô-Ryo). Music for Uta, Syakubyôsi, Syô, Hitiriki, Huë, Koto, and Biwa in score.
p.22–28. Ise No Umi (Hyôdyô-Ritu). Music for Uta, Syakubyôsi, Syô, Hitiriki, Huë, Koto, and Biwa in score.
p.29–33. Koromogae (Hyôdô-Ritu). Music for Uta, Syakubyôsi, Syô, Hitiriku, Huë, Koto, and Biwa in score.
p.I–II. (pagination starts over). Plates, showing the instruments of the court orchestra used in the pieces in main section.
p.III–VII. Anmerkungen in German, with German translations of the 6 song texts.
p.IX. Nachträge in German.
p.X. Nachträge in Japanese.

Gesellschaft für Herausgabe dänischer Musik, *see* Samfundet til Udgivelse af dansk Musik.

Gesellschaft für Musikforschung. Publikationen älterer praktischer und theoretischer Musikwerke, *see* Publikationen älterer praktischer und theoretischer Musikwerke.

Gesellschaft zur Herausgabe älterer Musik. Publikationen älterer Musik, *see* Publikationen älterer Musik.

GESUALDO, CARLO, PRINCIPE DI VENOSA, ca.1560–1613.
. . . Sämtliche Werke. Hrsg. von Wilhelm Weismann und Glenn E. Watkins. Hamburg, Ugrino Verlag, 1957– .
v.1– .
Contents:
Vol.1. Sämtliche Madrigale für fünf Stimmen. Nach dem Partiturdruck von 1613. 1962.
Vol.2. Sämtliche Madrigale für fünf Stimmen. Nach dem Partiturdruck von 1613. 1962.
Vol.3. Sämtliche Madrigale für fünf Stimmen. Nach dem Partiturdruck von 1613. 1960.
Vol.4. Sämtliche Madrigale für fünf Stimmen. Nach dem Partiturdruck von 1613. 1958.
Vol.5. Sämtliche Madrigale für fünf Stimmen. Nach dem Partiturdruck von 1613. 1958.
Vol.6. Sämtliche Madrigale für fünf Stimmen. Nach dem Partiturdruck von 1613. 1957.
Vol.7. Responsoria et alia ad officium Hebdomadae Sanctae Spectantis für sechs Stimmen. 1959.
Vol.8. Sacrae cantiones für fünf Stimmen. 1962.
Vol.9. Sacrae cantiones für sechs und sieben Stimmen. 1961.
Vol.10. Verschiedenes. (Psalmen, Instrumentalwerke).

GESUALDO, CARLO, PRINCIPE DI VENOSA, ca.1560–1613.
. . . Sämtliche Madrigale für fünf Stimmen. Nach dem Partiturdruck von 1613, hrsg. von Wilhelm Weismann. Hamburg, Ugrino Verlag, [cop.1957–62].
6v.
Same as Vol.1–6 of his Sämtliche Werke.

GEVAERT, FRANÇOIS AUGUSTE, 1828–1908. ed.
Les gloires de l'Italie; chefs-d'oeuvre anciens et inèdits de la musique vocale italienne aus XVIIe et XVIIIe siècles, recueillis, annotés, et transcrits pour piano et chant per F.-A. Gevaert, d'après les manuscrits originaux ou éditions primitives, avec basse chiffrée . . . Avec paroles italiennes originales et traduction française de Victor Wilder. Chaque volume composé de trente morceaux . . . Paris, Heugel et fils, [1868].
2v.
Dedication at head of title.
Italian and French words, with music.
Vol.1 contains compositions by Domenico Belli, Gio. Buononcini, Giulio Caccini, Giacomo Carissimi, Francesco Cavalli. Marcantonio Cesti, Domenico Cimarosa, Gioacchino Cocchi, Marco da Gagliano, Baldassare Galuppi, Christoforo Gluck, Adolfo Hasse, Niccolò Jommelli, Gio. Legrenzi, Leonardo Leo, Arcangelo del Leuto, Antonio Lotti, Giuseppe Manna, Benedetto Marcello, Gio. Paisiello, Giambattista Pergolese, Jacopo Peri, Niccolò Piccini, Luigi Rossi, Antonio Sacchini, Al. Scarlatti, Alessandro Stradella, Angelo Tarchi, Leonardo Vinco, and Filippo Vitali.
Vol.2 contains compositions by Gio. Buononcini, Giulio Caccini, Giacomo Carissimi, Francesco Cavalli, Marcantonio Cesti, Domenico Cimarosa, Marco da Gagliano, Baldassare Galuppi, Gluck, G. F. Haendel, Adolfo Hasse, Giuseppe Haydn, Incerto, Niccolo Jommelli, Gio. Legrenzi, Leonardo

Leo, P. Martini; Claudio Monteverdi, Gio. Paesiello, Giambattista Pergolese, Luigi Rossi, Antonio Sacchini, Giuseppe Sarti, and Leonardi Vinci.

GHISELIN-VERBONNET, JOHANNES, 15th–16th centuries.
Opera omnia, ed. by Clytus Gottwald. Rome, American Institute of Musicology, [1961–].
v.1– . (Corpus mensurabilis musicae. No.23).
Proposed set about 4v.
Contents:
Vol.1. All the motets. 1961.
Vol.2. Missa "La belle se siet"; Missa "De les armes"; Missa "Narayge." 1964.

GHISI, FEDERICO, 1901– . ed.
. . . Feste musicali della Firenze Medicea (1480–1589) a cura di Federico Ghisi. Firenze, Vallecchi, 1939.
2p.L., [iii]-xlviii, 94p., 1L. incl. facsims. (incl. music).
At head of title: Centro nazionale di studi sul rinascimento.
For 3–6 voices with reduction for piano.
Includes works by Alexander Coppinus, Francesco Corteccia, Orazio Vecchi, and Tiburzio Massaino.
Contents:
1.pte. Musiche per 1 canti carnascialeschi dei popolo. Musiche per 1 trionfi e la mascherate.
2.pte. Musiche per gli intermedi fatti in occasione di feste o nozze principesche alla corre medicea.

GIBBONS, ORLANDO, 1583–1625.
Complete keyboard works, in 5v. Transcribed and ed. from the Mss. by Margaret H. Glyn . . . London, Stainer & Bell, Ltd., [cop.1924–25].
5v.
Originally for harpsichord and organ.

GIBBONS, ORLANDO, 1583–1625.
Ten pieces arranged for modern organ from the Virginal book of Benjamin Cosyn. Composed by Orlando Gibbons. Ed. by J. A. Fuller-Maitland. London, J. & W. Chester, Ltd., [cop.1925].
2p.L., 36p.

GIEBUROWSKI, WACLAW, 1877–1943. ed.
Cantica selecta musices sacrae in Polonia saeculi XVI et XVII hodiernis choris accommodate editit Venceslaus Gieburowski. Posen, K. T. Barwicki, 1928–39.
p.1– .
Contains compositions by Wenzel von Samter, Nikolaus Gomolka, Nikolaus Zieleński, and Gregor Gerwazy Gorczyki.

GIESBERT, FRANZ JULIUS, 1896– . ed.
Altenglische Violenmusik zu drei Stimmen. Spielbar auch auf Blockflöten oder gemischten Instrumentenchor. Hrsg. und bearb. von F. J. Giesbert. Kassel, Nagels Verlag, [cop.1953–54].
2v. (Edition Nagel. 563, 565).
Score and parts.
Contents:
Vol.1. Orlando Gibbons, John Coperario (1648), and Thomas Lupo (1648).
Vol.2. Orlando Gibbons and Thomas Lupo.

Die Gitarre in der Haus- und Kammermusik vor 100 Jahren (1780–1820), *see* Albert, Heinrich. Die Gitarre in der Haus- und Kammermusik vor 100 Jahren (1780–1820).

GITARRE-KAMMERMUSIK. Hrsg. von Karl Scheit. Wien, Wiesbaden, Verlag Doblinger, 19? – .
No.1– .
Contents:
No.1. Corelli, Arcangelo. Sonata a tre, Op.4/3, für 2 Altblockflöten oder andere Melodieinstrumente und Gitarre.
No.2. Siegl, Otto. Sonatine D-moll für Violine und Gitarre.
No.3. Burkhart, Franz. Drei Adventlieder für mittlere-Singstimme, Oboe (Sopran-blockflöte) oder andere Melodieinstrumente und Gitarre.
No.4. Corelli, Arcangelo. Sonata a tre, Op.4/5, für 2 Altblockflöten oder andere Melodieinstrumente und Gitarre.
No.5. Peroni, Giuseppe. Concerto a tre für 2 Violinen und Gitarre.
No.6. Torelli, Giuseppe. Concerto für Solo-Violine, Streichquartett und Gitarre.
No.7. Reiter, Albert. Sonatine für Violine und Gitarre.
No.8. Lechthaler, Josef. Suite für 2 Gitarren.
No.9. Händel, Georg Friedrich. Sonata F-dur für Altblockflöte (Querflöte, Oboe, Violine) und Gitarre.
No.10. Pepusch, Johann Chr. Sonata D-moll für Altblockflöte (Querflöte, Oboe, Violine) und Gitarre.
No.11. Locatelli, Pietro. Sinfonia für Violine und Gitarre.
No.12. Pepusch, Johann Chr. Sonata G-dur für Altblockflöte (Querflöte, Oboe, Violine) und Gitarre.
No.13. Loeillet, Jean B. Sonata A-moll, Op.1/1, für Altblockflöte (Querflöte, Oboe, Violine) und Gitarre.
No.14. Burkhart, Franz. Toccata für 2 Gitarren.
No.15. Schickhardt, Johann Chr. Trio-Sonate F-dur für 2 Altblockflöten oder andere Melodieinstrumente und Gitarre.
No.16. Bloch, Waldemar. Sonate für Violine und Gitarre.
No.17. Telemann, Georg Ph. Sonate im Kanon für 2 Gitarren.
No.18. Pasquini, Bernardo. Sonate D-moll für 2 Gitarren oder Cembalo (Klavier) und Gitarre.
No.19. Corelli, Arcangelo. Sonate E-moll, Op. 5/8, für Violine und Gitarre.
No.20. Vivaldi, Antonio. Sonate G-moll für Violine und Gitarre.
No.21. Uray, Ernst Ludwig. Variationen und Fuge über ein Volkslied für 2 Gitarren.
No.22. Haydn, Joseph. Drei Lieder für mittlere Stimme und Gitarre: Eine sehr gewöhnliche Geschichte; Die Landlust; Die zu späte Ankunst der Mutter.

No.23. Händel, Georg Friedrich. Sonata A-moll für Altblockflöte (Querflöte, Oboe Violine) und Gitarre.
No.24. Händel, Georg Friedrich. Sonata D-moll für Altblockflöte (Querflöte, Oboe, Violine) und Gitarre, nach einem Autograph des Fitzwilliam-Museum, Cambridge.
No.25. Haydn, Joseph. Divertimento für Konzertante Gitarre (original: Baryton), Violine und Violoncello.
No.26. Händel, Georg Friedrich. Sonata C-moll für 2 Violinen (Altblockflöte und Violine) oder andere Melodieinstrumente und Gitarre.
No.27. Händel, Georg Friedrich. Zwei Gesänge aus dem deutschen Arien für Sopran, Violine (Flöte) und Gitarre.
No.28. Händel, Georg Friedrich. Nel dolce del oblio. Kantate für Sopran, Altblockflöte oder andere Melodieinstrumente und Gitarre.
No.29. Händel, Georg Friedrich. Sonata G-moll für Altblockflöte (Querflöte, Oboe, Violine) und Gitarre.
No.30. Kronsteiner, Josef. Partita für 2 Gitarren.
No.31. Haydn, Joseph. Cassation C-dur für Gitarre, Violine und Violoncello.
No.32. Haydn, Joseph. Quartett D-dur für Gitarre, Violine, Viola und Violoncello.
No.33. Kreutzer, Joseph. Trio D-dur, Op.9/3, für Flöte, Violine und Gitarre (2 Violinen und Gitarre).
No.34. Locatelli, Pietro. Sonata D-dur für Flöte (Oboe, Violine) und Gitarre.
No.35. Skorzeny, Fritz. Trio für Flöte, Viola und Gitarre.
No.36. Haydn, Joseph. Quartetto in G, Op.5/4, für Flöte (Violine), Violine, Viola und Gitarre.
No.37. Händel, Georg Friedrich. Sonata C-dur für Altblockflöte (Querflöte, Oboe, Violine) und Gitarre.
No.38. Bach, J. S. Arioso "Betrachte meine Seel" aus der Johannes-Passion für Bass, zwei Violinen (Viole d'amore) und Gitarre (doppelchörige Laute).

Burkhart-Scheit. Volksliederbuch zur Gitarre. Bd.1: Kinderlieder. Bd.2: Wander- und Abschiedslieder. Die Melodiestimme kamm auch instrumental ausgeführt werden.

GLEASON, HAROLD, 1892– . ed.
... Examples of music before 1400, selected and ed. by Harold Gleason ... Rochester, N.Y., Eastman School of Music of the University of Rochester, 1942.
xi, 117p. incl. facsim. (music). (Eastman School of Music. Publication. No.10).
Contains compositions by Adam de la Halle, Bernart de Ventadorn, Blondel de Nesle, Guido d'Arezzo, Ghirardello da Firenze, Guillaume d'Amiens, Jacopo da Bologna, Johannot de l'Escurel, Guillaume de Machaut, Francesco Landini, Moniot d'Arras, Neidhart von Reuental, Walter Odington, Magister Albertus Parisiensis, Perotin, Perrin d'Angincourt, Richard the Lion-Hearted, Reimbautz de Vaquieras, and Walter von der Vogelweide.

GLINKA, MICHAEL IVANOVITCH, 1803–1857.
Complete works. Moscow, State Music Publishers, 1955– .
v.1– .
Contents (asterisk indicates unpublished volumes):
Vol.1. Symphony on two Russian themes. Overtures. 1955.
Vol.2. Waltz-fantasy. Jota aragonesa. Night in Madrid.
Vol.3. Quartets and septet. Score and parts. 1957.
Vol.4. Sonata for viola and piano. 1958.
Vol.5. Compositions for piano. 1957.
Vol.6. Compositions for piano. 1958.
Vol.7. Moldavanka and the gypsy. 1958.
Vol.8. Vocal works with orchestra. Hymne. 1960.
Vol.9. Vocal works with piano accompaniment and a capella. 1960.
*Vol.10. Romances for voice and piano.
*Vol.11. Vocalises.
*Vol.12. Ivan Sussanin. Life for the Tzar.
*Vol.13. Ivan Sussanin. Vocal score.
*Vol.14. Russlan and Ludmilla. Score.
*Vol.15. Russlan and Ludmilla. Vocal score.
*Vol.16. Study works.
*Vol.17. Unfinished works.
*Vol.18. Transcriptions of works by other composers.

Literary writings and correspondence. 2v.
Romances and songs (not in Complete works).

GLINKA, MICHAEL IVANOVITCH, 1803–1857.
Complete works for piano solo and piano 4 hands. Moscow, State Music Publishers; New York, Leeds Music Corp., 1952.
xiv, [1], 442p. front. (port.).

Les gloires de l'Italie, *see* Gevaert, François Auguste. Les gloires de l'Italie.

GLUCK, CHRISTOPH WILLIBALD, *Ritter von,* 1714–1787.
Sämtliche Werke. Leipzig, Verlag der Gluckgesellschaft, 1931.
1 v.
Contents:
Vol.1. Die Pilger von Mecca. Partitur.

GLUCK, CHRISTOPH WILLIBALD, *Ritter von,* 1714–1787.
Werke. Kritisch durchgesehene Ausgabe seiner Hauptopern und anderer Werke. Hrsg. von J. Pelletan und B. Damcke, C. Saint-Saëns und Julien Tiersot. Partituren mit deutschem, französischem und italienischem Text. Leipzig, Breitkopf & Härtel, 1873–96.
v.1– .
Contains Alceste, Armida, Echo und Narziss, Iphigenie in Aulis, Iphigenie auf Tauris, Orpheus und Euridice, und Prolog für Sopran, Chor und Orchester.

GLUCK, CHRISTOPH WILLIBALD, *Ritter von,* 1714–1787.

. . . Sämtliche Werke. Hrsg. im Auftrag des Instituts für Musikforschung, Berlin, mit Unterstützung der Stadt Hannover von Rudolf Gerber . . . Kassel und Basel, Bärenreiter-Verlag, 1951– .
6 Abt. (in process).
Contents (asterisk indicates unpublished volumes):
1.Abt. Musikdramen.
1. Orfeo ed Euridice. 1963.
*2. Telemacco.
*3. Alceste.
4. Paride ed Elene. Paris und Helene. 1954.
*5. Iphigénie en Aulide.
*6. Orphée et Euridice.
7. Alceste. Alkestis. 1957.
*8. Armide.
*9. Iphigénie en Tauride.
10. Echo et Narcisse. Echo und Narziss. 1953.
*11. Iphigenie auf Tauris. (deutsch).
2.Abt. Tanzdramen.
*1. Don Juan, Semiramis.
*2. Alessandro, Orfano della China, Achille.
3.Abt. Italienische Opere serie und Operanserenaden.
*1. Ipermestra.
*2. Le nozze d'Ercole e d'Ebe.
*3. Semiramide riconosciuta.
*4. Ezio.
*5. La clemenza di Tito.
*6. L'innocenza giustificata.
*7. Antigono.
*8. Il re pastore.
*9. Il trionfo di Clelia.
*10. Le cinesi, La danza.
*11. Il parnaso confuso, La corona.
*12. La contesa dei numi.
*13. Tetide, Il prologo.
*14. Le feste d'Apollo.
15.
16.
17. Le cinesi. Die Chinesinnen. 1958.
4.Abt. Französische komische Opern.
1. L'ile de Merlin. Merlins Insel. 1956.
*2. La fausse esclave, Le diable à quatre.
*3. Cythère assiégée. (I).
*4. Cythère assiégée. (II).
5. L'ivrogne corrigé. (Der bekehrte Trunkenbold). 1951.
*6. Le cadi dupé.
7. La rencontre imprévue. 1964.
*8. L'arbre enchantée I und II.
5.Abt. Instrumental- und Vokalmusik.
1. Triosonaten. 1961.
*2. Einzelne Instrumentalstücke, Arien, Lieder, Kirchenmusik.
6.Abt. Ergänzungen und Fragmente.

Glyn, Margaret Henrietta, 1865–1946, ed. Early English organ music (16th century), *see* Plainsong and Mediaeval Music Society. Glyn, Margaret Henrietta. Early English organ music (16th century).

GLYN, MARGARET HENRIETTA, 1865–1946. ed. Twenty-one Old English compositions of the 16th and 17th centuries. Originally written for the virginal by William Byrd, Dr. John Bull and Orlando Gibbons and translated into modern notation for the piano, being "Parthenia." Newly ed. by careful comparison with the original text of 1611 by Margaret H. Glyn, with original barring, accidentals and ornaments, and freed from the many errors in previous editions. London, William Reeves, [1927].
5p.L., 30p.

Goethes Haus, Musik in, *see* Musik in Goethes Haus.

The golden age of the madrigal, *see* Einstein, Alfred. The golden age of the madrigal.

GOLDMAN, RICHARD FRANKO, 1910– . comp. and ed.
Landmarks of early American music, 1760–1800; a collection of 32 compositions compiled, arr., and ed. by Richard Franko Goldman and Roger Smith for orchestra or band or smaller instrumental groups, or mixed chorus . . . With or without accompaniment. Conductor's score . . . With historical and biographical notes and suggestions for performance . . . New York, G. Schirmer, Inc., [1943].
103p. illus. (facsims.).
"Bibliography": p.17–19.
Psalm tunes, humns and chorales, and patriotic and historical music, by Supply Belcher, Daniel Belknap, William Billings, Josiah Flagg, Jacob French, P. A. von Hagen, James Hewitt, Oliver Holden, Samuel Holyoke, Francis Hopkinson, G. K. Jackson, Simeon Jocelin, Jacob Kimball, Andrew Law, James Lyon, Justin Morgan, Daniel Read, Alexander Reinagle, Mr. Sicard, Timothy Swan, and William Tuckey.

Goldsmith, E. W. ed. A selection of communions with the musical notation from the Salisbury Gradual, *see* Plainsong and Mediaeval Music Society. A selection of communions with the musical notation from the Salisbury Gradual.

GOMBERT, NICOLAS, fl.1520–1552.
Opera omnia, edidit Joseph Schmidt-Görg. Rome, American Institute of Musicology, 1951– .
v.1– . (Corpus mensurabilis musicae. No.6).
Proposed set about 12v.
Contents:
Vol.1. Missa IV vocum. Missa da pacem. Missa Sancta Maria. Missa beati omnes. Missa Je suis desheritée. 1951.
Vol.2. Missae V vocum. Media vita. Sur tous regretz. Philomena. Forseulement. 1954.
Vol.3. Missae VI vocum. Credo (8 vocum). 1963.
Vol.4. Magnificat. 1957.
Vol.5. Cantiones sacrae. 1961.
Vol.6. Cantiones sacrae. 1964.

GOUDIMEL, CLAUDE, d.1572. Collected works, *see* Institute of Mediaeval Music. Collected works. (Gesamtausgaben). Vol.3.

Das Görlitzer Tabulaturbuch vom Jahre 1650, *see* Scheidt, Samuel. Das Görlitzer Tabulaturbuch vom Jahre 1650.

GOSTENA, GIOVANNI BATTISTA DALLA, d. before 1605.
Intavolatura di liuto; fantasie e canzoni. Trascritte in notazione moderna ed interpretate da Giuseppe Gullino. Firenze, Edizioni Musicali ditta R. Maurri, 1949.
ix p., 1L., 75p.
"La presente edizione consta di 300 esemplari numerati."

Graduale Sarisburiense. Catholic Church, Roman. Liturgy and ritual. Graduals. Salisbury, *see* Plainsong and Mediaeval Music Society. Catholic Church, Roman. Liturgy and ritual. Graduals. Salisbury. Graduale Sarisburiense.

GRAUPNER, CHRISTOPH, 1683–1760.
Ausgewählte Werke. Hrsg. in Verbindung mit der Stadt Darmstadt von Friedrich Noack. Kassel und Basel, Bärenreiter, 1955– .
v.1– .
Contents:
Vol.1. Sinfonia D-dur, für 2 Flöten, 2 Corni in D, Streicher und Cembalo.
Vol.2. Ouvertüre E-dur, für (Flöten), 2 Violinen, Viola und Cembalo.
Vol.3. Konzert C-moll, für Fag oder Violoncello, Streicher und Cembalo.
Vol.4. Konzert A-dur, für Violin, Streicher, und Cembalo.

The great Advent antiphons. Atkins, Ivor Algernon, *see* Plainsong and Mediaeval Music Society. Atkins, Ivor Algernon. The great Advent antiphons.

GREENE, MAURICE, 1695–1755.
Forty select anthems in score. Composed for 1, 2, 3, 4, 5, 6, 7, and 8 voices. London, Printed for and sold by J. Walsh, 1743.
2v.

GREFF, VALENTIN, 1507–1576.
Der Lautenist V. Barfark, 1507–1576, Leben und Werke, by Otto Gombosi. Budapest, Magyar Nemzeti Museum, 1935.
166p.; 32p. music examples. (Musicologia hungarica. II).
Hungarian text: p.1–69.
German text: p.71–145.
Letters and documents: p.147–66.
Music examples: 32 pages.

Greifswald, Universität, Musikwissenschaftliches Seminar, *see* Denkmäler der Musik in Pommern.

GRÉTRY, ANDRÉ ERNEST MODESTE, 1741–1813.
Collection complète des oeuvres de Grétry. Publiée par le Gouvernement Belge. (Erste vollständige, Kritisch durchgesehene Ausgabe. Hrsg. von der Kommission für Veröffentlichung der Kompositionen alter belgischer Meister: F. A. Gevaert, Th. Radoux, Édouard Fétis, Alfred Wotquenne, Ad. Wouters, E. Mathieu, und Lucien Solvay). Partituren mit unterlegtem Klavierauszug. Livr.1–49. Leipzig, Breitkopf & Härtel, [1884]–1936.
49v. facsims., fronts. (ports., v.1, 14).
Full score with piano reduction. French words.
The critical prefaces are by Édouard Fétis, F. A. Gevaert, Ad. Samuel, Victor Wilder, Alfred Wotquenne, and others.
Each volume contains reprint of original title page.
Contents:
Livr.1. Richard Coeur-de-Lion.
Livr.2. Lucile.
Livr.3. Céphale et Procris.
Livr.4. Céphale et Procris; morceaux inédits.
Livr.5. Les méprises par ressemblance.
Livr.6. L'épreuve villageoise.
Livr.7. Anacréon chez Polycrate.
Livr.8. Anacréon chez Polycrate; morceaux inédits.
Livr.9. Le tableau parlant.
Livr.10. Les événements imprévus.
Livr.11. L'embarras des richesses.
Livr.12. L'embarras des richesses; morceaux inédits.
Livr.13. Zémire et Azor.
Livr.14. Le Huron.
Livr.15. Colinette à la cour.
Livr.16. Colinette à la cour; morceaux inédits.
Livr.17. Le jugement de Midas.
Livr.18. Raoul Barbe-Bleue.
Livr.19. Panurge.
Livr.20. Les deux avares.
Livr.21. L'amant jaloux.
Livr.22. La caravane du Caire.
Livr.23. Panurge, et La caravane du Caire; morceaux inédits.
Livr.24. Guillaume Tell.
Livr.25. La fausse magie.
Livr.26. Le comte d'Albert.
Livr.27. Sylvain.
Livr.28. Denys le tyran, maître d'école à Corinthe.
Livr.29. La rosière républicaine.
Livr.30. La rosière de Salency.
Livr.31. Le magnifique.
Livr.32. Aucassin et Nicolette.
Livr.33–34. Amphitryon.
Livr.35. Les mariages samnites.
Livr.36–37. Andromaque.
Livr.38. L'ami de la maison.
Livr.39. Elisea.
Livr.40. Pierre le Grand.
Livr.41. Delphis et Mopsa.
Livr.42–43. L'amité à l'épreuve.
Livr.44. Lisbeth.
Livr.45. Le rival confident.
Livr.46. Les trois âges de l'opéra. Prologue.
Livr.47. Emilie. Comédie.
Livr.48. Le prisonnier anglais. Clarice et Belton I.
Livr.49. Le prisonnier anglais. Clarice et Belton II.

GRIEG, EDVARD HAGERUP, 1843–1907.
Sämtliche Klavierwerke. Leipzig, New York, [etc.], C. F. Peters, n.d.

3v. (Edition Peters. No.3100a–c).
Contents:
Vol.1. Lyrische Stücke. Op.12, 38, 43, 47, 54, 57, 62, 65, 68, 71.
Vol.2. Klavier-Werke. Op.1, 3, 6, 16, 19, 24, 28, 29, 41, 52, 73.
Vol.3. Klavier-Werke. Op.17, 34, 35, 37, 40, 46, 50, 53, 55, 56, 63, 66.

GRIGNY, NICOLAS DE, 1671–1703.
. . . Premier livre d'orgue de Nicolas de Grigny . . . publié, revisé et registré d'après l'édition princeps de 1699 par Nobert Dufourcq . . . et Noëlie Pierront . . . avec le concours de Marie-Madeleine Bourla . . . Paris, Éditions Musicales de la Schola Cantorum, cop.1953.
4p.L., 101p. front.
Score for organ.

GROVLEZ, GABRIEL MARIE, 1879–1944. ed.
Les plus belles pièces de clavessin de l'école française, transcrittes et mises en recueil par Gabriel Grovlez. London, J. & W. Chester, [1918].
2v.
Vol.1 contains compositions by D'Anglebert, J. C. de Chambonnières, François Couperin, J.-F. Dandrieu, L. C. Daquin, Antoine Dornel, N. A. Le Bègue, and Louis Marchand.
Vol.2 contains compositions by L. N. Clérambault, Michel Corrette, J. A. Dagincourt, J.-F. Dandrieu, L. C. Daquin, Duphly, and J.-P. Rameau.

GUENTHER, FELIX. ed.
Collection espagnole (Colección de obras españolas e iberoamericanas) from Albéniz to Villa-Lobos, for piano solo, ed. by Felix Guenther . . . New York, Edward B. Marks Music Corp., [1941].
96p.
Contains compositions by Albéniz, Chavarri, de Falla, O. L. Fernández, E. Granados, V. Granados, Isamitt, Lecuona, Longas, Robles, Sandoval, Suffern, Turina, and Villa-Lobos.

Guerrero, Francisco, 1527–1599. Opera omnia, *see* Monumentos de la música española. Vol. 16, 19.

GUILLAUME DE MACHAUT, d.1377.
Musikalische Werke. Hrsg. von Friedrich Ludwig. Leipzig, Breitkopf & Härtel, 1926– .
v.1– . tables. (Publikationen älterer Musik; veröffentlicht von der Abteilung zur Herausgabe älterer Musik bei Deutschen Musikgesellschaft. 1. Jahrg., 1.Teil; 3. Jahrg., 1.Teil; 4. Jahrg., 2.Teil).
Vols.2–3 "mit Unterstützung des Sächs. Staatl. Forschungsinstituts für Musikwissenschaft als Band 6 [und 8] der Publikationen des Instituts."
"Die Quellen der Werke G. de Machaut's": Vol.1, p.[7]–44.
Contents:
1.Bd. Balladen, Rondeaux, und Virelais.
2.Bd. Einleitung.
3.Bd. Motetten.
4.Bd. Messe und Lais.

GUILLAUME DE MACHAUT, d.1377.
Musikalische Werke. Reprint. Leipzig, Breitkopf & Härtel Musikverlag, 1954.
4v. tables.
First appeared in the series "Publikationen älterer Musik."

GUILLAUME DE MACHAUT, d.1377.
Opera. Edidit Guglielmus de Van. Rome, American Institute of Musicology in Rome, 1949.
30p. (Corpus mensurabilis musicae. No.2).
Contents:
Vol.1. Le messe de Nostre Dame. 1949.

GUILMANT, ALEXANDRE, 1837–1911. ed.
Archives des maîtres de l'orgue des XVIe et XVIIe et XVIIIe siècles, publiées d'après les manuscrits et éditions authentiques avec annotations et adaptations aux orgues modernes, par Alexandre Guilmant . . . avec la collaboration, pour les notices biographiques, de André Pirro. v.1–10. Paris, A. Durand & Fils, 1898–[1910].
10v. facsims. (incl. music), illus., pl., ports.
Vol.10 published in parts, with photostat title page reproduced from Vol.9.
Bibliographical footnotes.
Contents:
Vol.1. Titelouze, J. Oeuvres complètes. [1898].
Vol.2. Raison, A. Livre d'orgue. [1899].
Vol.3. Roberday, F. Fugues et caprices; Marchand, L. Pièces choisies pour l'orgue. [Livre 1.]; Clérambault, L. N. Premier livre d'orgue; Du Mage, P. Premier livre d'orgue; Daquin, L. C. Nouveau livre de Noëls. [1901].
Vol.4. Gigault, N. Livre de musique pour l'orgue. [1902].
Vol.5. Grigny, N. de. Livre d'orgue; Couperin, F. Pièces d'orgue; Marchand, L. Pièces choisies pour l'orgue. [Livre 2. 1904].
Vol.6. Boyvin, J. Oeuvres complètes d'orgue. [1905].
Vol.7. Dandrieu, J. F. Premier livre de pièces d'orgue; Guilain. Pièces d'orgue pour le Magnificat. [1906]. (Extrait: Mainz, B. Schott's Söhne, 1926).
Vol.8. Scherer, S. A. Oeuvres d'orgue. [1907].
Vol.9. Le Bègue, N. A. Oeuvres complètes d'orgue. [1909].
Vol.10. Liber Fratrum Cruciferorum Leodiensium. (pieces by A. Gabrieli, Pietro Philippi, J. P. Sweelinck, Cl. Merulo, unknown masters, Fr. G. Scronx, W. Brouno, P. Cornet, F. Fontana, G. M. Casini); Philips, P. Trios; Cornet, P. Pièces. [1910].

GUILMANT, ALEXANDRE, 1837–1911. ed.
. . . Concert historique d'orgue. Morceaux d'auteurs célèbres de différentes écoles du XVIe au XIXe siècle. Historical organ concert. Pieces by celebrated composers of different schools from the XVIth to the XIXth centuries. Mainz, G. Schott's Söhne;

London, Schott & Co., Ltd., [etc., etc.], n.d.
1p.L., 98p.
Contains compositions by J. S. Bach, Boëly, Buxtehude, Byrd, Clérambault, Dandrieu, Frescobaldi, Froberger, Gabrieli, Lemmens, Mendelssohn, Merulo, Muffat, Pachelbel, Palestrina, Scheidt, and Titelouze.

GUILMANT, ALEXANDRE, 1837–1911. ed.
École classique de l'orgue. Morceaux d'auteurs célèbres publiés. Paris, Durand & Fils, 1898–1903.
26 nos.
Contents:
No.1. Händel. 11 Fugues.
No.2. Buxtehude. Prélude et fugue G-moll.
No.3. Bruhns. Prélude-choral "Nun komm der Heiden Heiland."
No.4. J. G. Walther. Prélude et fugue A.
No.5. Pachelbel. Chant de Noël.
No.6. Sweelinck. Fantaisie D-moll.
No.7. Frescobaldi. Fugue G-moll.
No.8. W. F. Bach. Concert D-moll.
No.9. Zipoli. Canzona G-moll.
No.10. J. L. Krebs. 2 Trios.
No.11. Muffat. Toccata F.
No.12. Kerrl. Canzona G-moll.
No.13. J. Seeger. Fugue F-moll; C. Kopřiwa. Fugue As, F-moll.
No.14. Scheidt. Cantilena anglica fortuna.
No.15. J. L. Krebs. Fugue G.
No.16. Murschhauser. Praeambulum, arpeggiata, fuga.
No.17. Frescobaldi. 4 Courantes.
No.18. Roberday. Fugue D-moll; B. Czernohorsky. Fugue D-moll.
No.19. Kirnberger. 2 Caprices, fugue et choral.
No.20. C. P. E. Bach. Fantaisie et fugue C-moll.
No.21. Seeger. Prélude D.
No.22. Buxtehude. Fugue C.
No.23. J. L. Krebs und J. S. Bach. Prélude-Choral "Wir glauben all an einen Gott."
No.24. Père Martini. Sonata F-moll.
No.25. d'Anglebert. 5 Fugues et 1 Quatuor sur le Kyrie.
No.26. Frescobaldi. 4 Hymnes.

GUILMANT, ALEXANDRE, 1837–1911. ed.
Répertoire des concerts du Trocadéro. Paris, Brüssel, Schott, 1892–97.
4v.
Contents:
Vol.1. Händel. Concert D-moll; Martini. Gavotte F de la 12me sonata.
Vol.2. Couperin. Soeur Monique; Händel. Concert.
Vol.3. Bach. Sinfonia et sonatina; Corelli. Preludio; Couperin. Sarabande et fughette; Marcello. Psaume.
Vol.4. B. Schmid. Gagliarda; Händel. Sinfonia de Saul; Couperin. Sarabande grave; Rameau. Prélude musette et rondeau, air majestueux; Bach. Presto de la cantate Nr.35.

GURDJIEFF, GEORGES IVANOVITCH, 1872–1949.
The works of G. Gurdjieff. Paris, Janus, [1951–].
v.1– .
Cover title: Oeuvres musicales de Gurdjieff. Charts et rhythmes d'Orient.
Vol.1 for piano; in part for piano and tamburo orientale.
Contents:
Vol.1. Songs and rythms [sic] from Asia. 1951.
Vol.2. Chants et danses seïdes. 1952.
Vol.3. Chants et danses derviches. 1954.
Vol.4. Chants religieux. 1955.

HABERL, FRANZ XAVER, 1840–1910. ed.
Repertorium musicae sacrae ex auctoribus saeculi XVI et XVII, collectum et redactum à Franc. Xav. Haberl. Ratisbon, F. Pustet, 1885–1903.
2v. (22 Lfng.).

HABERT, JOHANNES EVANGELISTA, 1833–1896.
Johannes Evangelista Habert's Werke. Leipzig, Breitkopf & Härtel. 19? – .
v.1– .
Contents:
Ser.1. Messen.
Ser.2. Liber gradualis.
Ser.6. Orgelkompositionen.
Ser.9. Streichquartette.
Ser.10. Klavierkompositionen.
Ser.11. Klavierkompositionen zu vier Händen.
Ser.12. Orchesterwerke.
Ser.13. Theoretische Werke.
Ser.14. Zithercompositionen.

HAGEN, FRIEDRICH HEINRICH VON DER, 1780–1856. ed.
Minnesinger. Deutsche Liederdichter des zwölften, dreizehnten und vierzehnten Jahrhunderts, aus allen bekannten Handschriften und früheren drucken Gesammelt und Berichtigt, mit den Lesarten derselben, Geschichte des Lebens der Dichter und ihrer Werke, Sangweisen der Lieder, Reimverzeichnis der Anfänge, und abbildungen sämmtlicher Handschriften, von Friedrich Heinrich von der Hagen . . . Leipzig, J. A. Barth, 1838–61.
5v. in 4. illus. (music), pl. (music), 10 facsims. (part col., 1 double), and atlas of 54 pl.
Music: "Sangweisen der Jenaer Handscrift": v.4, p.[773]–852; "Über die Musik der Minnesinger": p.[853]–62; "Sangweisen der Meistersänger": p.[921]–36.

HAGEN, FRIEDRICH HEINRICH VON DER, 1780–1856. ed.
Minnesinger. Reprint. Aalen, Otto Zeller, 1963.

Halle, Adam de la, *see* Adam de la Halle.

HÄNDEL, GEORG FRIEDRICH, 1685–1759.
Georg Friedrich Händels Werke. Ausgabe der Deutschen Händelgesellschaft. Hrsg. von Friedrich Chrysander. Leipzig, Breitkopf & Härtel, 1858–94, 1902.
96v. and 6 supplements.
Vol.49 not published.
Vols.1–18 only were published by Breitkopf &

Härtel. The remaining volumes were published by Chrysander at Bergdorf bei Hamburg.

J. M. Coopersmith has collected and edited 10 volumes of unpublished material to complete the above edition, and has also completed a thematic index to the whole.

Contents:

Vol.1. Susanna. Oratorium. 1858.
Vol.2. Klavier-Stücke. 1859.
Vol.3. Acis und Galatea. Pastoral. 1859.
Vol.4. Herakles. Oratorium. 1859.
Vol.5. Athalia. Oratorium. 1859.
Vol.6. L'allegro, Il pensieroso, ed Il moderato. Oratorium. 1859.
Vol.7. Semele. Oratorium. 1860.
Vol.8. Theodore. Oratorium. 1860.
Vol.9. Passion nach dem Evang. Johannes. 1860.
Vol.10. Samson. Oratorium. 1861.
Vol.11. Trauerhymne auf den Tod der Königen Caroline. 1861.
Vol.12. Alexander's Fest. 1861.
Vol.13. Saul. Oratorium. 1862.
Vol.14. Krönungs Hymnen für König Georg II. 1863.
Vol.15. Passion, nach C. H. Brockes. 1863.
Vol.16. Israel in Aegypten. Oratorium. 1863.
Vol.17. Josua. Oratorium. 1864.
Vol.18. Die Wahl des Herakles. 1864.
Vol.19. Belsazar. Oratorium. 1864.
Vol.20. Sieg der Zeit und Wahrheit. Oratorium. 1865.
Vol.21. Instrumental-Concerte. 1865.
Vol.22. Judas Maccabaeus. Oratorium. 1866.
Vol.23. Caecilien-Ode. 1866.
Vol.24. Il trionfo del tempo e della verità. 1866.
Vol.25. Dettinger Te Deum. 1866.
Vol.26. Salomo. Oratorium. 1867.
Vol.27. Sonate da camera. 1879.
Vol.28. 12 Orgel-Concertos. 1881.
Vol.29. Debora. Oratorium. 1869.
Vol.30. 12 Grosse Concerte. 1869.
Vol.31. Te Deum und Jubilate for the Peace of Utrecht. 1869.
Vol.32. Italienische Duette und Trios. 1870.
Vol.32. 2. Ausg. Duette e terzetti. 1880.
Vol.33. Alexander Balus. Oratorium. 1870.
Vol.34, 35, 36. Psalmen. 1871, 1871, 1872.
Vol.37. 3 Te Deum. 1872.
Vol.38. Lateinische Kirchen-Musik. 1872.
Vol.39. La resurrezione. Oratorium. 1878.
Vol.40, 41. Esther. Oratorium. 1. und 2. Bearb. 1882.
Vol.42. Joseph. Oratorium. 1883.
Vol.43. Gelegenheits. Oratorium. 1884.
Vol.44. Jephtha. Oratorium. 1886.
Vol.45. Messias (Der). Oratorium. 1902.
Vol.46A. Ode für den Geburtstag der Königin Anna. 1887.
Vol.46B. Alceste. 1887.
Vol.47. Wassermusik. Feuerwerksmusik . . . 1886.
Vol.47. Suppl.: Concert III. Berichtigender Nachtrag. 1894.
Vol.48. Instrumental Musik. 1894.
Vol.49. (not published).
Vol.50. Cantate a voce sola a basso. 1887.
Vol.51. Cantate a voce sola a basso. 1887.
Vol.52A, 52B. Cantate con instrumenti. 1888, 1889.
Vol.53. Aci, Galatea, e Polifemo, serenata. 1892.
Vol.54. Il Parnasso in festa, serenata. 1878.
Vol.55. Almira. Opera. 1873.
Vol.56. Roderigo. Opera. 1873.
Vol.57. Agrippina. Opera. 1874.
Vol.58. Rinaldo. Opera. 1. & 2.versione. 1874, 1894. (2 editions).
Vol.59. Il pastor fido. Opera. 1.versione. 1876.
Vol.60. Teseo. Opera. 1874.
Vol.61. Silla. Opera. 1876.
Vol.62. Amidigi. Opera. 1875.
Vol.63. Radamisto. Opera. 1874.
Vol.64. Muzio Scevola. Opera atto terzo. 1875.
Vol.65. Floridante. Opera. 1875.
Vol.66. Ottone. Opera. 1881.
Vol.67. Flavio. Opera. 1875.
Vol.68. Giulio Cesare. Opera. 1875.
Vol.69. Tamerlane. Opera. 1876.
Vol.70. Rodelinda. Opera. 1876.
Vol.71. Scipione. Opera. 1877.
Vol.72. Alessandro. Opera. 1877.
Vol.73. Admeto. Opera. 1877.
Vol.74. Ricardo. Primo. Opera. 1877.
Vol.75. Siroe. Opera. 1878.
Vol.76. Tolomeo. Opera. 1878.
Vol.77. Lotario. Opera. 1879.
Vol.78. Partenope. Opera. 1879.
Vol.79. Poro. Opera. 1880.
Vol.80. Ezio. Opera. 1880.
Vol.81. Sosarme. Opera. 1880.
Vol.82. Orlando. Opera. 1881.
Vol.83. Arianna. Opera. 1881.
Vol.84. Terpsicore. Prologo, e la 2.versione dell opera Il pastor fido. 1890.
Vol.85. Ariodante. Opera. 1881.
Vol.86. Alcina. Opera. 1881. (2 issues; the 1st issue contained material from Händel Gesellschaft, v.28, p.133–40, inserted by error; the later issue omits these pages).
Vol.87. Atalanta. Opera. 1882.
Vol.88. Giustino. Opera. 1882.
Vol.89. Armino. Opera. 1883.
Vol.90. Berenice. Opera. 1883.
Vol.91. Faramondo. Opera. 1884.
Vol.92. Serse. Opera. 1884.
Vol.93. Imeneo. Opera. 1885.
Vol.94. Deidamia. Opera. 1885.
Vol.[95]. Das Autograph des Oratoriums "Jephta." 1885.
Vol.[96]. Das Autograph des "Messias." Hamburg, 1892.

Supplements:

1. Magnificat, by Dionigi Erba.
2. Te Deum, by Francesco Antonio Urio.
3. Serenata, by Alessandro Stradella.
4. Duetti, by Giovanni Carlo Maria Clari.
5. Componimenti musicali, by Gottlieb Muffat.
6. Octavio, by Reinhard Keiser.

HÄNDEL, GEORG FRIEDRICH, 1685–1759.

Georg Friedrich Händels Werke. Reprint. Ridgewood, New Jersey, Gregg Press, Inc., 1965.

HÄNDEL, GEORG FRIEDRICH, 1685–1759.
The works of Handel, in score; correct, uniform, and complete. Consisting of his oratorios, operas, duets, anthems, concertos, lessons, Te Deums, trios, fugues, etc., elegantly engraved, on large folio plates, under the immediate direction and inspection of Dr. Arnold, organist and composer to his Majesty. Printed for the Editor and sold by Longman and Co., 1787–97.
180 instalments.
(This list of contents is a copy of the list compiled by Dr. J. M. Coopersmith and printed in Music Library Association, Notes, September 1947, p.438–49).
Contents (HG indicates Händelgesellschaft, the term for the Breitkopf & Härtel edition of Händel):
1–4. Athalia, an oratorio or sacred drama in score, the music composed in the year 1733. 192p. HG 5.
5–8. Theodora, an oratorio, in score. Composed in the year 1737. 192p. HG 8.
9–13. Messiah. A sacred oratorio, in score, with all the additional alterations. Composed in the year 1741. 219p. HG 45.
13. [Te Deum I, D major]. A short Te Deum, in score, composed for her late Majesty, Queen Caroline, in the year 1737. 23p. HG 37.
14–15. [Te Deum II, B flat major]. Te Deum, in score, composed for His Grace the Duke of Chandos (in the year 1719). 88p. HG 37.
15–16. [Te Deum. "Utrecht"]. A grand Te Deum, composed in the year 1713 for the peace of Utrecht. 48p. HG 31.
16–17. [Jubilate, "Utrecht"]. A grand Jubilate, composed in the year 1713 for the peace of Utrecht. 44p. HG 31.
17–19. [Te Deum, "Dettingen"]. Te Deum, composed in the year 1743 for the victory at Dettingen. 104p. HG 25.
20. [Anthem I, O be joyful in the Lord: (Sonata)]. Symphony to the Jubilate. 3p. HG 34.
20. [Te Deum III, A major]. Te Deum, in score, composed for His Grace the Duke of Chandos (in the year 1720). 31p. HG 37.
20–23. Sosarme. Opera in tre atti. Rappresentata al teatro del re nel mercato del fieno a Londra nell' anno 1732. 116p. HG 81.
23–24. [Water Musik]. The celebrated water musick in score, composed in the year 1716. 56p. HG 47.
24. [Fireworks Musik]. The musick for the royal fireworks, performed in the year 1749. 20p. HG 47.
24–28. Semele, a dramatick performance in score, the words altered from Congreve, the musick composed in the year 1743. 191p. HG 7.
28–30. Acis and Galatea, a serenata composed for the Duke of Chandos in the year 1720. 103p. HG 3.
30–34. Tesco, opera in cinque atti rappresentata al teatro del re nel mercato del fieno a Londra nell' anno 1713. 159p. HG 60.
34–39. Hercules, an oratorio in score, composed in the year 1744. 248p. HG 4.
39–43. [Judas Maccabaeus]. Judas Macchabaeus, a sacred oratorio in score with all the additional alterations composed in the year 1746. 195p. HG 22.
43–47. Giulio Cesare, opera in tre atti rappresentata al teatro del re nel mercato del fieno a Londra nell' anno 1723. 170p. HG 68.
47–48. [Sonata, Op.2, No.1b, a, 4–7]. Six sonatas for two violins, two hautboys, or two German flutes and a violoncello. First published at Amsterdam, 1731. 60p. HG 27.
48–49. [Sonata, Op.5, No.1–2, 3a, 4–5, 6b, 7]. Seven sonatas or trios for two violins or two German flutes and a violoncello. Composed and published in the year 1739. 59p. HG 27.
49–54. Samson, a sacred oratorio, in score, the words taken from Milton, the musick composed in the year 1742. 216p. HG 10.
54. [Ode for Queen Anne's Birthday]. An ode or serenata for the birth day for Queen Ann composed in the year 1713. 44p. HG 46a.
55–56. The choice of Hercules. In score, composed in the year 1745. 80p. HG 18.
56–60. Joshua, a sacred oratorio, in score, composed in the year 1747. 169p. HG 17.
60–64. [Concerti grossi, Op.6, No.1–12]. Twelve grand concertos, in score, composed in the year 1737. 220p. HG 30.
64. [The Alchymist, pasticcio]. The music in the Alchymist. 8p. HG 56.
65–67. Alexander's feast, an ode on Saint Cecilia's day. The words by Dryden, the musick composed in the year 1736. 141p. HG 12.
68–72. Belshazzar. A sacred oratorio, in score, composed in the year 1743. 219p. HG 19.
72–73. [Anthem Va, I will magnify Thee]. Anthem, in score, composed at Cannons, for His Grace the Duke of Chandos between the years 1718 and 1720. Anthem 1st. 42p. HG 34.
73–74. [Anthem XIb, Let God arise]. Anthem II. 32p. HG 35.
74–75. [Anthem XIa, Let God arise]. Anthem III. 52p. HG 35.
75–76. [Anthem III, Have mercy upon me]. Anthem IV. 39p. HG 34.
76–77. [Anthem VIII, O come let us sing unto the Lord]. Anthem V. 59p. HG 35.
77. [Anthem IV, O sing unto the Lord a new song]. Anthem VI. 31p. HG 34.
78. [Anthem VII, My song shall be alway]. Anthem VII. 47p. HG 35.
79. [Anthem VIa, As pants the hart]. Anthem VIII. 40p. HG 34.
79–81. [Anthem X, The Lord is my light]. Anthem IX. 66p. HG 35.
81–82. [Anthem II, In the Lord put I my trust]. Anthem X. 48p. HG 34.
82–83. [Anthem IX, O praise the Lord with one consent]. Anthem XI. 60p. HG 35.
83–84. [Anthem XII, O praise the Lord ye Angels of His]. Anthem XII. 30p. HG 36.

84–85. [Alceste, musical scenes to the English drama]. Alcides, an English opera in score. 80p. HG 46b.
85–92. Solomon, a sacred oratorio in score composed in the year 1749. 344p. HG 26.
92–98. Israel in Egypt, a sacred oratorio, in score, composed in the year 1738. 282p. HG 16.
98–99. [Concerto grosso, C major, "Concertante"]. Concertante in nine parts for two violins and violoncello obligati, composed in the year 1738. 45p. HG 21.
99–105. [Occasional oratorio]. The occasional oratorio in score, composed in the year 1745. 270p. HG 43.
105–106. [Ode for Saint Cecilia's day]. Ode on St. Cecilia's day, the words by Dryden, set to musick in the year 1736. 74p. HG 23.
107–111. Joseph, a sacred oratorio in score, composed in the year 1746. 215p. HG 42.
111–116. Saul, a sacred oratorio, in score, composed in the year 1740. 253p. HG 13.
116–121. Jephtha, a sacred oratorio, in score, composed in the year 1751. 231p. HG 44.
121–124. [Concerto, organo e orchestra, Op.4, No.1, 2, 4, 3, 5, 6]. Six concertos, in score, for the organ or harpsichord, with accompanyments for two violins, two hautboys, viola & violoncello. Concerto I–[VI]. 52p., 23p., 30p., 16p., 11p., 13p. HG 28.
124–128. [Concerto, organo e orchestra, Op.7, No.1–6]. A second set of six concertos, in score, for the organ or harpsichord, with accompanyments for two violins, two hautboys, viola & violoncello. Concerto I–[VI]. 184p. HG 28.
128–129. [Suites, harpsichord, 1st collection, No.1–8]. Lessons for the harpsichord. First published in the year 1720. 60p. HG 2.
129–130. A second set of lessons for the harpsichord. 60p. HG 2.
130–131. A third set of lessons for the harpsichord. 20p. HG 2.
131. [Fugues, harpsichord, 4th coll. No.1–6]. Six fugues or voluntary's for the organ or harpsichord. 16p. HG 2.
131–135. Susanna, a sacred oratorio, in score, composed in the year 1743. 205p. HG 1.
135–139. Esther, a sacred oratorio, in score, composed in the year 1720. 185p. HG 40.
139–140. [Sonata, Op.1, No.1b, 2–9, 14, 11, 15]. Twelve sonatas or solo's for the German flute, hautboy and violin. Published about the year 1724. 44p. HG 27.
140–146. Deborah, a sacred oratorio, in score, composed in the year 1733. 275p. HG 29.
146–149. Agrippina, opera in tre atti rappresentata al teatro di Venizzia [sic] nell' anno 1709. 174p. HG 57.
150–153. L'allegro, Il pensieroso, ed Il moderato, the words taken from Milton; the musick composed in the year 1739. 149p. HG 6.
153–154. [Anthem XIV, Sing unto God, "Wedding Anthem B"]. Anthem. For the wedding of Frederick Prince of Wales, and the Princess of Saxa-Gotha. Composed in the year 1736. 87p. HG 36.
155–156. [Funeral anthem for Queen Caroline]. Anthem. For the funeral of Queen Caroline. Composed in the year 1737. 81p. HG 11.
156–157. [Anthem XV, "Dettingen," The King shall rejoice in Thy strength]. Anthem. For the victory at Dettingen. Composed in the year 1743. 44p. HG 36.
157. [Coronation anthem IV, Let thy hand be strengthened]. Anthem. For the coronation of George II. Composed in the year 1727. 18p. HG 14.
158. [Coronation anthem I, Zadok, the priest]. Anthem. For the coronation of George II. Composed in the year 1727. 28p. HG 14.
158–159. [Coronation anthem III, My heart is inditing]. Anthem. For the coronation of George II. Composed in the year 1727. 44p. HG 14.
159–160. Masque consisting of a prelude, airs, duettes, a chorus, and dances. 54p. HG 84, 83, 86, 67.
160–164. Alexander Balus, an oratorio, in score, composed in the year 1747. 210p. HG 33.
165–169. The triumph of time and truth, an oratorio in score, composed in the year 1751. 199p. HG 20.
169–171. La resurrezione, oratorio sacra in partizione. 105p. HG 39.
171–172. [Coronation anthem II, The king shall rejoice]. Anthem for the coronation of George II. Composed in the year 1727. 56p. HG 14.
172–174. [Concerti grossi, Op.3, No.1–6]. Concertos (commonly called the hautboy concertos) for two violins, two hautboys, two German flute, two tenors, two bassoons, two violoncellos, and a basso continuo, chiefly composed at Cannons, in the year 1720, and published about the year 1729. 100p. HG 21.
174–176. Two trios, and four cantatas, in score. 77p. HG 32, 52a, 52b.
176–179. Thirteen chamber duetto's [sic] and twelve cantatas. 92p, 58p. HG 32, 2.Ausg., 50, 51.
179–180. Concertos etc., for the organ in score, now first published 1797. 80p. HG 47, 48.

HÄNDEL, GEORG FRIEDRICH, 1685–1759.
The works of Handel. London, Printed for the members of the Handel Society [by Cramer, Beale & Co., 1843–58].
14v.
Full score with piano reductions. English words.
Contents:
Vol.[1]. Anthems for the coronation of King George II. Composed in the year 1727. 1844.
Vol.[2]. L'allegro, Il pensieroso, ed Il moderato. Composed in the year 1740; with the additional songs, composed in the year 1741. 1844.
Vol.[3]. Esther, an oratorio, composed in the year 1720; with additional pieces, composed at various periods. 1845.
Vol.[4]. Ode for St. Cecilia's day, composed in the year 1739. 1845.

Vol.[5]. Israel in Egypt. 1846.
Vol.[6]. The Dettingen Te Deum, composed in the year 1743. 1847.
Vol.[7]. Acis and Galatea, a masque, performed for the first time at Cannons in the year 1721. 1847.
Vol.[8]. Belshazzar, an oratorio, composed in the year 1744. 1848.
Vol.[9]. The Messiah, an oratorio, composed in the year 1741. 1850.
Vol.[10]. Chamber duets and trios. 1852.
Vol.[11]. Samson, an oratorio, composed in the year 1741. 1853.
Vol.[12]. Judas Maccabeus, an oratorio, composed in the year 1746 . . . with the additional pieces subsequently introduced by the composer. 1855.
Vol.[13]. Saul, an oratorio, composed in the year 1738. 1857.
Vol.[14]. Jephtha, an oratorio, composed in the year 1758. 1858.

HÄNDEL, GEORG FRIEDRICH, 1685–1759.
Veröffentlichungen der Händel-Gesellschaft. Leipzig, Breitkopf & Härtel, [1929–34].
10 nos.
Nos.2, 3, 5, 6, 8, 9 constitute Jahrg. I–VI of Händel-Jahrbuch, 1928–1933, [published 1929–34]. Jahrg.VII– , published by Georg Friedrich Händel-Gesellschaft, Halle an der Saale, 1955– .
Contents:
No.1. Trauerhymne auf den Tod der Königen Caroline. [Piano-vocal score]. 1928.
No.4. Hymne, O preist den Herrn mit einem Mund. [Piano-vocal score]. [1930].
No.7. Salve Regina. [Full score and parts]. 1932.
No.10. Ausgewählte Arien für Sopran mit Begleitung von Obligaten Instrumenten und Cembalo. Bearb. von Max Seiffert. Ausgewählt und Verdeutscht von Hans Joachim Moser. [Full score and parts]. 1934.

HÄNDEL, GEORG FRIEDRICH, 1865–1759.
Hallische Händel-Ausgabe im Auftrage der Georg Friedrich Händel-Gesellschaft. Hrsg. von Max Schneider und Rudolf Steglich. Kassel, Bärenreiter-Verlag, 1955– .
5 series (in progress).
A piano-vocal score and parts are also planned for each volume.
Contents (asterisk indicates unpublished volumes):
Ser.I: Oratorien und grosse Kantaten.
Vol.1. Alexander's Feast. Das Alexander-Fest. 1958.
*Vol.2. Passion nach dem Evangelisten Johannes.
*Vol.3. La resurrezione.
*Vol.4. Il trionfo del tempo e della verità.
*Vol.5. Aci, Galatea e Polifemo.
Vol.6. Ode for the birthday of Queen Anne. Ode für den Geburtstag der Königin Anna. 1962.
*Vol.7. Passion nach B. H. Brockes.
*Vol.8. Esther (1.Fassung. 1720).
*Vol.9. Acis and Galatea. Acis und Galatea.
*Vol.10. Esther (2.Fassung. 1732).
*Vol.11. Deborah.
*Vol.12. Athalia.
Vol.13. Saul. 1963.
*Vol.14. Israel in Egypt. Israel in Ägypten.
*Vol.15. Ode for St. Cecilia's Day. Cäcilien-Ode.
*Vol.16. L'allegro, Il pensieroso ed Il moderato.
*Vol.17. The Messiah. Der Messias.
*Vol.18. Samson.
*Vol.19. Semele.
*Vol.20. Joseph and his brethren. Joseph und seine Brüder.
*Vol.21. Belshazzar. Belsazar.
*Vol.22. Hercules. Herakles.
*Vol.23. Occasional oratorio. Gelegenheits-Oratorium.
*Vol.24. Judas Maccabaeus.
*Vol.25. Alexander Balus.
*Vol.26. Joshua. Josua.
*Vol.27. Solomon. Salomo.
*Vol.28. Susanna.
*Vol.29. Theodora.
*Vol.30. Alceste.
Vol.31. The choice of Hercules. Die Wahl des Herakles. 1964.
*Vol.32. Jephtha. Jephta.
*Vol.33. The triumph of time and truth. Der Triumph von Zeit und Wahrheit.
*Supplementbände.

Ser.II: Opern.
*Vol.1. Almira.
*Vol.2. Rodrigo.
*Vol.3. Agrippina.
*Vol.4. Rinaldo.
*Vol.5. Il pastor fido. (1.Fassung. 1712).
*Vol.6. Teseo.
*Vol.7. Silla.
*Vol.8. Amadigi di Gaula.
*Vol.9. Radamisto.
*Vol.10. Muzio Scevola.
*Vol.11. Floridante.
*Vol.12. Ottone.
*Vol.13. Flavio.
Vol.14. Giulio Cesare. 1962.
*Vol.15. Tamerlano.
*Vol.16. Rodelinda.
*Vol.17. Scipione.
*Vol.18. Alessandro.
*Vol.19. Admeto.
*Vol.20. Riccardo I.
*Vol.21. Siroe.
*Vol.22. Tolomeo.
*Vol.23. Lotario.
*Vol.24. Partenope.
*Vol.25. Poro.
Vol.26. Ezio. 1956.
*Vol.27. Sosarme.
*Vol.28. Orlando.
*Vol.29. Arianna in Creta.
*Vol.30. Il Parnasso in festa.
*Vol.31. Terpsicore (Il pastor fido. 2.Fassung. 1732).
*Vol.32. Ariodante.
*Vol.33. Alcina.
*Vol.34. Atalanta.

*Vol.35. Arminio.
*Vol.36. Giustino.
*Vol.37. Berenice.
*Vol.38. Faramondo.
Vol.39. Serse. 1959.
*Vol.40. Imeneo.
*Vol.41. Deidamia.
*Supplementbände.

Ser.III: Kirchenmusik.
*Vol.1–3: Lateinische Kirchenmusik. (Vol.1 published).
Vol.1. Dixit Dominus Domino meo. Psalm 109. 1960.
*Vol.4. Utrecht Te Deum und Jubilate.
*Vol.5. Dettingen Te Deum. Dettinger Te Deum.
*Vol.6–7. Chandos anthems.
*Vol.8. Coronation anthems. Krönungshymnen.
*Vol.9. Funeral anthem for Queen Caroline. Trauerhymne für Königin Caroline.
*Supplementbände.

Ser.IV: Instrumentalmusik.
Vol.1. Klaviermusik I: Die acht grossen Suiten. 1955.
Vol.2. Orgelwerke I: Sechs Konzerte, Op.4, Nr.1–6. 1956.
Vol.3. Elf Sonaten für Flöte und bezifferten Bass. 1955.
Vol.4. Sechs Sonaten für Violine und bezifferten Bass. 1956.
*Vol.5. Klaviermusik II.
*Vol.6. Klaviermusik III.
*Vol.7. Orgelwerke II: Sechs Konzerte.
*Vol.8. Orgelwerke III: Sechs Konzerte, Op.7, Nr.1–6.
*Vol.9/10. Trio Sonaten, Op.1, 2, und 5.
Vol.11. Sechs Concerti grossi, Op.3. 1959.
*Vol.12. Fünf Orchesterkonzerte.
Vol.13. Water music. Firework music. 1962.
Vol.14. Zwölf Concerti grossi, Op.6. 1961.
*Vol.15. Ouverturen, Sinfonien.
*Vol.16. Drei Concerti a due cori.
*Supplementbände.

Ser.V: Kleinere Gesangswerke.
*Vol.1–4. Italienische Kantaten.
*Vol.5–6. Sologesänge, Kammer-duerte und Trios.
*Supplementbände.

HÄNDEL, GEORG FRIEDRICH, 1685–1759.
Kompositionen für Klavier, von G. F. Händel . . . Hrsg. von Adolf Ruthardt. Leipzig, New York, [etc.], C. F. Peters, n.d.
4v. (Edition Peters. No.4).
Contents:
Vol.1. Suite I–VIII.
Vol.2. Suite IX–XVI.
Vol.3. Leçons, Chaconne, Pièces, Fugues.
Vol.4. Fughettes.

HÄNDEL, GEORG FRIEDRICH, 1685–1759.
The vocal works composed by G. F. Handel, arranged for the organ or pianoforte by Dr. John Clarke, of Cambridge. London, Button & Whitaker, [1809–].
v.1– .
Imprint varies.
Contents:
Vol.1. Messiah. Jephtha.
Vol.2. Judas Maccabaeus. Samson.
Vol.3. Acis & Galatea. Saul. Dettingen Te Deum.
Vol.4. Unavailable.
Vol.5. Theodora. Esther. Solomon.
Vol.6. Athalia. Israel in Egypt.

Handl, Jacob, 1550–1591. Opus musicum, *see* Denkmäler der Tonkunst in Österreich. Vol.12, 24, 30, 40, 48, 51–52.

Harmonia sacra, *see* Page, John. Harmonia sacra.

Harmonice musices Odhecaton A, *see* [Petrucci, Ottaviano dei]. Harmonice musices Odhecaton A.

Harrison, Frank Llewellyn, 1905– , ed. Early English church music, *see* Early English church music.

The Harrow replicas. No.3, *see* Parthenia; or The Maydenhead.

Hasse, Karl, 1883– , ed. Denkmäler der Tonkunst in Württemberg, *see* Denkmäler der Tonkunst in Württemberg.

HASSLER, HANS LEO, 1564–1612.
Sämtliche Werke. Hrsg. von C. Russell Crosby, Jr. Wiesbaden, Breitkopf & Härtel, 1961–
v.1– .
Proposed set about 12v.
At head of title: Veröffentlichungen der Gesellschaft für Bayerische Musikgeschichte.
Contents (asterisk indicates unpublished volumes):
Vol.1. Cantiones sacrae für 4 bis 12 Stimmen. 1961.
Vol.2. Canzonette von 1590 und Neue Teutsche Gesang von 1596. 1961.
Vol.3. Madrigale für 5 bis 6 Stimmen. 1961.
Vol.4. Messen zu 7 bis 8 Stimmen. 1961.
Vol.5/6. Sacri concentus für 4 bis 12 Stimmen. 1961.
Vol.7. Psalmen und Christliche Gesäng. (1607). 1965.
Vol.8. Psalmen und geistliche Lieder. (1608). 1966.
*Vol.9/10. Ungedruckte Vokalwerke.
*Vol.11. Lustgarten und ungedruckte Instrumentalwerke.
*Vol.12. Orgelwerke.

HAUSMUSIK. Wien, Österreichischer Bundesverlag, 1947– .
No.1– .
No.182, 183, 185, 186 also No.1–4 of series "Werke oberösterreichischer Komponisten."
Contents:
No.1. Wir spielen und singen. (Viktor Korda, Sigismund Schnabel). 1947.

No.2. Musik im Jahreskreis. (Viktor Korda, Sigismund Schnabel). 1947.
No.3. Aus klassischer Zeit; Wiener Musik aus der zweiten Hälfte des 18. Jahrhunderts. 1948, cop.1947.
No.4. Stücke aus der Romantic. (Viktor Korda). 1949.
No.5. Mozart, W. A. Duo für Violine und Viola. (Wilhelm Rohm). 1948.
No.6. Mozart, W. A. Sonate für Fagott und Violoncello, KV.292, auch für zwei Violoncelli. (Viktor Korda). 1948.
No.7. Mozart, W. A. Sieben Menuette mit Trio für zwei Violinen und Bass, KV.65a. (Wilhelm Rohm). 1948. 2.Aufl. 1950.
No.8. Mozart, W. A. Duo, Violine und Viola. (Wilhelm Rohm). 1949.
No.9. Mozart, W. A. Trio, KV.266. (Wilhelm Rohm). 1948.
No.10. Kleine Duos, Originalwerke für zwei Melodieinstrumente. (Viktor Korda). 1948.
No.11. Der Weg in die Gegenwart. (Viktor Korda). 1947.
No.12. Mozart, W. A. Serenade, Eine kleine Nachtmusik, KV.525. (Herbert Häfner). 1949.
No.13. Gál, Hans. Kleine Suite, für 2 Violinen und Violoncello, Klavier ad lib. Op.49a. cop. 1948.
No.14. Gál, Hans. Trio. Op.49b. 1949.
No.15. Scholz, A. J. 6 Quartettini, 1–3. 1949.
No.16. Schubert, F. P. Lieder der Liebe. (Erik Werba).
No.17. Donath, Gustav. Trio für zwei Violinen und Klavier, im alten Stil. 1949, cop.1948.
No.18. Gyrowetz, Adalbert. Quartett für zwei Violinen, Viola und Violoncello. (Louis Dité). 1949, cop.1948.
No.19. Sonnleithner, Christoph. Divertimento in Es dur. (Louis Dité). 1949, cop.1948.
No.20. Haager, Max. Spielmusik für drei Instrumente, Geigen, Flöten, usw. Werk 6a. 1949, cop.1948.
No.21. Mozart, W. A. 12 Waldhornduette, KV. 487. (Paul). 1949.
No.22. Fux, Johann Joseph. Drei Einzelstücke für Klavier. (Erich Schenk). cop.1949.
No.23. Fux, Johann Joseph. Zwölf Menuette für Klavier. (Erich Schenk). 1949, cop.1948.
No.24. Mozart, W. A. Sechs ländlerische Tänze, für zwei Violinen und Bass (Violoncello), KV.606. (Wilhelm Rohm). 1949.
No.25. Siderits, Joseph. Vom Schulgesang zur Hansmusik; kleine Stücke für drei Violinen. 1948.
No.26. Willfort, Egon Stuart. Waldsuite, für Klavier zu vier Händen. 1949, i.e., 1948.
No.27. Scholz, A. J. 6 Quartettini, 4–6. 1949.
No.28. Lechthaler, Josef. Weihnachtsbüchlein, zu besinnlichem Singen und Spielen für drei Melodieinstrumente, Op.62. 1950, cop.1948.
No.29. Beethoven, Ludwig van. Trio, für zwei Oboen und englisch Horn (zwei Violinen und Viola), Op.87. 1950.
No.30. Marckhl, Erich. Plomberger Haustänze, für Violine und Klavier. cop.1949.
No.31. Bach, C. Ph. E. La Xenophone. cop.1950.
No.32. Mayr, Anton. Kleine Suite. 1949.
No.33. Schaller, Erwin. Der Jahreskreis: Winterreise. 1948.
No.34. Schiske, Karl. Erstes Streichquartett, Op.4. 1949.
No.35. Bauernfeind, Hans. Heiteres Spiel, auf drei Instrumenten, Streicher oder Holzbläser. [1949, i.e., 1948].
No.36. Fuchs, Franz. Kleine Suite über Wie schön leuchtet der Morgenstern, für Flöte, zwei Geigen, und Bratsche. [1949].
No.37. Reiter, Albert. Kleine Suite für Streicher. [1949].
No.38. Harum, Günther. Fuge für Streichquartett, Op.31. [1948].
No.39. Tittel, Ernst. Sonate für drei gleiche oder ungleiche Stimmen, Op.30. [1949].
No.40. Scheidler, C. G. Sonàta, D-dur. 1949.
No.41. Beethoven, L. v. Drei Duos (C-dur, F-dur, B-dur) für Klarinette in B und Fagott. (Friedrich Wildgans). [1950].
No.42. Schollum, Robert. Im Frühtau zu Berge. [cop.1949].
No.43. Haydn, Michael. Duo Nr.1, C-dur, für Violine und Viola. (Joseph Siderits). [1950].
No.44. Haydn, Michael. Duo Nr.2, E-dur, für Violine und Viola. (Joseph Siderits). [1950].
No.45. Schaller, Erwin. Der Jahreskreis: Frühlingslieder.
No.46. Diabelli, Anton. Sonatine für Gitarre mit Klavier. 1951.
No.47. Weber, Karl M. F. E. Divertimento für Gitarre und Klavier, Op.38. (Karl Scheit). [cop.1952].
No.48. Wilhelmer, Ambros. Sonatine, für drei Trompeten. 2.Aufl. [cop.1949].
No.49. Eybler, Joseph. 3 Menuette (Nemetz-Fiedler). 1950.
No.50. Wagenseil, G. C. Das Glockengeläute. (Nemetz-Fiedler).
No.51. Vivaldi, Antonio. Sonata a tre, per due violini e basso continuo. (Erich Schenk). [1949].
No.52. Dostal, Viktor, comp. Der Weg zur Orgel. [1952].
No.53. Mozart, W. A. Sechs Kontretänze für zwei Violinen und Bass (Violoncello). KV.462. (Wilhelm Rohm). [1950].
No.54. Schaller, Erwin. Der Jahreskreis: Sommerlieder. 1949.
No.55. Schaller, Erwin. Der Jahreskreis: Herbstlieder. 1949.
No.56. Gál, Hans. Capriccio, für Mandolinenorchester. [1949].
No.57. Korda, Viktor. Serenade für Mandolinenorchester. 1949.
No.58. Korda, Viktor. Wir lernen Hausmusik, 1–8. 1949.
No.59. Caldara, Antonio. Sonata a tre per due violini, violoncello e basso continuo, Op.1/5. (Erich Schenk). [1949].
No.60. Haager, Max. Spielmusik, Op.6a. 1949.
No.61. Zeisl, Eric. Stücke für Barbara. 1949.
No.62. Diabelli, Anton. Trio für Flöte oder Violine, Viola (2.Violine) und Gitarre. (Otto Schindler). [1952].
No.63. Malzat, J. M. Quintett Nr.5, Es-dur. 1949.

No.64. Ruggieri, G. M. Sonata prima, aus Sonate da chiesa, Op.3, Venedig, 1693. (Leopold Nowak). [cop.1950].
No.65. Ruggieri, G. M. Sonata seconda, aus Sonate da chiesa, Op.3, Venedig, 1693. (Leopold Nowak). [cop.1950].
No.66. Ruggieri, G. M. Sonata terza, aus Sonate da chiesa, Op.3, Venedig, 1693. (Leopold Nowak). [cop.1949].
No.67. Ruggieri, G. M. Sonata quarta, aus Sonate da chiesa, Op.3, Venedig, 1693. (Leopold Nowak). cop.1949.
No.68. Telemann, G. Ph. Sonate in Kanonform. 1950.
No.69. Mozart, W. A. Acht Menuette mit Trio, für zwei Violinen und Bass, KV.585. (Wilhelm Rohm). 1954.
No.70. Staeps, H. U. Auf unserm Hof daheim; Spielmusik für drei Blockflöten, 2 F-Alt, 1 C-Tenor, über das böhmische Lied. cop. 1950.
No.71. Dawidowcz, Anton. Sechs Variationen über "Valet will ich der geben." cop.1951.
No.72. Steinbauer, Othmar. Die Ros' ist ohn' Warum. Tricinium. 1950.
No.73. Schaller, Erwin. Totenlieder; Volkslieder im Satz für zwei Knaben- oder Frauenstimmen. cop.1950.
No.74. Legrenzi, Giovanni. Sonata a tre, per due violini e basso continuo, Op.IV/1. [La Bernarda]. (Erich Schenk). cop.1951.
No.75. Siegl, Otto. Duo-sonatine, Op.138. 1949.
No.76. Eckhardt-Gramatté, S. C. Duo Nr.2. 1949.
No.77. Siegl, Otto. Trio in B-dur, Op.130. 1949.
No.78. Schaller, Erwin. Hirtenlieder aus dem oberösterreichischen Salzkammergut. cop. 1949.
No.79. Mayer, Rudolf. Kleine Stücke. 1949.
No.80. Siegl, Otto. Zwei Chöre zur Muttertagsfeier.
No.81. Reiter, Albert. Sonatine in einem Satz. 1949.
No.82. Kuntner, Leopold. Sonatine in D für Violine mit Klavier. 1949.
No.83. Püringer, Anton. Sonatine für Violine mit Klavier. 1949.
No.84. Michl, Artur. Sonatine für Violine und Klavier, Op.13. 1949.
No.85. Caldara, Antonio. Sonata da camera, Op.2/3. (Erich Schenk). 1951.
No.86. Siegl, Otto. Erstes Trio für zwei Violinen und Viola, Op.134a. 1950.
No.87. Werner, G. J. Instrumentalkalender. Der Mai. (Karl Halusa). [Continuo von Bruno Seidhofer]. 1950.
No.88. Schiske, Karl. Drei kleine Suiten, Op.15a–c. 1949.
No.89. Peter, H. A. Stücke für ein Melodieinstrument und Klavier. 1949.
No.90. Bach, J. S. Fantaisie, C-moll, für Klavier. (Wührer). 1949.
No.91. Siegl, Otto. Geigerstücke, Op.148, 1. 1949.
No.92. Siegl, Otto. Geigerstücke, Op.148, 2. 1949.
No.93. Czajanek, V. C. Klavierstücke. Nr.1, Ballett. Nr.2, Intermezzo. 1949.
No.94. Mixa, Franz. Sechs Lieder im Volkston. Nr.1–3, 4–6. 1949–50.
No.95. Salzburger Triosonate. (Erich Schenk). Klavier und Stimmen. 1950.
No.96. Kornauth, Egon. Kleine Hausmusik für Streichquartett, Op.41a. 1950.
No.97. Kölz, Ernst. Kleine Spielmusik für zwei Blockflöten. 1949.
No.98. Bach, W. Fr. Sechs Polonaisen. (Wilhelm Rohm). 1951.
No.99. Lerperger, Kurt. Andante für Violine mit Klavier. 1949.
No.100. Takacs, Jenö. Kleine Stücke, Op.50, 1–8. Für Violine mit Klavier. 1949.
No.101. Bermeiser, Viktor. Kleine Stücke, 1–3. Für Violine mit Klavier. 1949.
No.102. Sor, Fernando. [Stücke], Op.25, 35.
No.103. Dall'Abaco, E. F. Sonata da camera, 1–2.
No.104. Haydn, J. Variationen. (Wilhelm Rohm). 1950.
No.105. Beethoven, L. v. Präludium. (Wilhelm Rohm). 1950.
No.106. Beethoven, L. v. Andante, für Klavier zu zwei Händen. (Wilhelm Rohm). cop.1952.
No.107. Beethoven, L. v. Klavierstück, A-moll. (Wilhelm Rohm). 1951.
No.108. Beethoven, L. v. Rondo (A-dur; C-dur) für Klavier zu zwei Händen. (Wilhelm Rohm). cop.1951.
No.109. Haydn, Michael. Duo Nr.3, F-dur, für Violine und Viola. (Joseph Siderits). cop. 1952.
No.110. Frank, Marco. Drittes Streichquartett. cop.1951.
No.111. Albinoni, Tomaso. Sonata a tre, per due violini, violoncello e basso continuo, Op.I/6. (Erich Schenk). cop.1951.
No.112. Siegl, Otto. Lieder steirischer Komponisten, für eine Singstimme und Klavier. cop. 1951.
No.113. Siegl, Otto. Cellomappe II. 1950.
No.114. Siegl, Otto. Cellomappe I. 1950.
No.115. Mayer, Rudolf, Kleines Quartett für Violinen. cop.1950.
No.116. Kern, Frida. Tierbilder; fünf Stücke für Klavier, Op.54. cop.1951.
No.117a–b. Winter, Richard. Lieder für eine Singstimme und Klavier (mittel). cop.1950.
No.118.
No.119–120. Uhl, Alfred. Erstes Streichquartett, für zwei Violinen, Viola und Violoncello. 1950.
No.121. Caldara, Antonio. Sonata a tre per due violini, violoncello e basso continuo, Op.I/9. (Erich Schenk). cop.1951.
No.122. Ruggieri, G. M. Sonata quinta aus Sonate da chiesa, Op.3, Venedig, 1693. (Leopold Nowak). 1950, cop.1949.
No.123. Ruggieri, G. M. Sonata aus Sonate da chiesa, Op.3, Venedig, 1693. (Leopold Nowak). 1952.
No.124. Petyrek, Felix. Sonatine, C-dur, 1947. Klavier au zwei Händen. cop.1951.
No.125. Haydn, Michael. Duo Nr.4, D-dur, für Violine und Viola. (Joseph Siderits). cop.1952.

No.126. Schiske, Karl. Kleine Suite, für Klavier, Op.1. cop.1951.
No.127. Beethoven, L. v. 6 Ländlerische Tänze.
No.128a. Weiss, Silvius Leopold. Menuet, Sarabande, Menuet. Transcribed from the lute tablature and adapted for guitar by Karl Scheit. cop.1951.
No.128b. Weiss, Silvius Leopold. Tombeau sur la mort de Mr. Comte d'Logy arrivée 1721. Transcribed from the lute tablature and adapted for guitar by Karl Scheit. cop. 1951.
No.129. Ruggieri, G. M. Sonata aus Sonate da chiesa, Op.3/6. (Leopold Nowak). 1952.
No.130. Bononcini, G. M. Sonata a tre, per due violini e basso continuo, Op.I/6. (Erich Schenk). cop.1952.
No.131. Kornauth, Egon. Drei Canons. Klavier zu zwei Händen. cop.1951.
No.132. Schaller, Erwin. Lieder um Ostern; Volkslieder um Satz für eine Singstimme und zwei bis drei Instrumente. cop.1951.
No.133. Waldstein, Wilhelm. Variationen über ein Thema von Mozart, für Streichquintett, Op.11. cop.1951.
No.134. Schaller, Erwin. Lieder um Weihnacht. cop.1952.
No.135. Ruggieri, G. M. Sonata ottava, aus Sonate da chiesa, Op.3. (Leopold Nowak). 1952.
No.136. Porpora, Nicolo. Sinfonia da camera, Op.2/6. (Erich Schenk). cop.1951.
No.137. Pandion, Franz, ed. Lieder niederösterreichischer Komponisten. Singstimme (Mittel) und Klavier. cop.1953.
No.138. Vivaldi, Antonio. Sonata a tre, Op.5/5. (Erich Schenk).
No.139. Colista, Lelio. Sonata terza per due violini, violoncello e basso continuo. (Helene Kropik). cop.1952.
No.140. Kaufmann, Armin. Drei Stücke; Violoncello und Klavier. cop.1953.
No.141. Ruggieri, G. M. Sonata nona, aus Sonate da chiesa, Op.3, Venedig, 1693. (Leopold Nowak). 1952.
No.142. Ruggieri, G. M. Sonata decima, aus Sonate da chiesa, Op.3, Venedig, 1693. (Leopold Nowak). 1952.
No.143. Siegl, Otto. Orgelmusik steirischer Komponisten. 1952.
No.144. Albinoni, Tomaso. 2 Sonata da chiesa, Op.8. (Erich Schenk). cop.1952.
No.145. Cazzati, Maurizio. Capriccio a tre, per due violini e basso continuo, Op.50/29. "Il giustavilani." (Erich Schenk). cop.1952.
No.146. Uhl, Alfred. So ruhig . . . aus Frühlingsstimmen.
No.147. Vitali, G. B. Sonata a tre, per due violini e basso continuo, Op.II/6. (Erich Schenk). 1952.
No.148. Mazzaferrata, G. B. Sonata a tre, per due violini, violoncello e basso continuo, Op.V/6. (Erich Schenk). cop.1952.
No.149. Gabrielli, Domenico. Balletto a tre, per due violini e basso continuo, Op.I/9. (Erich Schenk). 1953.
No.150a–b. Mozart, W. A. Lieder und Gesänge, für eine Singstimme mit Klavierbegleitung. (Ernst Reichert). 1953–54, cop.1953.
No.151. Uccellini, Marco. Sinfonia a tre, per due violini e basso continuo, Op.9/7. (Erich Schenk). 1953.
No.152. Werba, Erik. Hochzeits-Spruch. (Richard Fritz). Gesang und Klavier, Mittel. cop.1952.
No.153–154. Willfort, Egon Stuart. Duos für Jedermann, für Klavier zu vier Händen. 1953.
No.155. Tůma, Franz. Partita a tre, Nr.7. (Erich Schenk). 1953.
No.156. Hoffmann. Divertimento a tre. (Erich Schenk). 1953.
No.157. Wagenseil, G. C. Sonata a tre per due violini e basso continuo, Op.I/3. (Erich Schenk). cop.1953.
No.158. Fux, J. J. Sonata pastorale a tre, per due violini e basso continuo. KV.397. (Erich Schenk). 1954.
No.159. Fux, J. J. Partita a tre, per due violini e basso continuo. KV.322. (Erich Schenk). 1954.
No.160. Korda, Viktor. Vier Feiermusiken. cop. 1954.
No.161. Gassmann, F. L. Divertimento a tre, per due violini e basso continuo, C-dur. (Erich Schenk). 1954.
No.162. Aspelmayr, Franz. Trio, per due violini e basso continuo, Op.I/4. (Erich Schenk). 1954.
No.163. Bauernfeind, Hans. Festliches Spiel, für zwei Klaviere. cop.1954.
No.164. Fux, J. J. Sinfonia a tre, per due violini e basso continuo. KV.330. (Erich Schenk). 1954.
No.165, 178, 181. Klavierwerke steiermärkischer Komponisten. 1954– . (Vol.1–2, Erich Marckhl).
No.166. Hasse, J. A. Sonata a tre, Op.3/6. (Erich Schenk). 1954.
No.167. Tartini, Giuseppe. Sonata a tre, per due violini e basso continuo, Op.VIII/6. (Erich Schenk). cop.1954.
No.168. Pergolesi, G. B. Sonata a tre, per due violini e basso continuo, Nr.11. (Erich Schenk). cop.1954.
No.169. Fontana, G. B. Sonata a tre, per due violini, fagotto e basso continuo, [Nr.14]. (Erich Schenk). cop.1954.
No.170. Höckh, Karl. Partita a tre, due violini e basso continuo, Nr.2. (Erich Schenk). cop. 1954.
No.171. Dandrieu, J. F. Sonata a tre, per due violini e basso continuo, Op.I/6. (Erich Schenk). 1955.
No.172. Pugnani, Gaetano. Sonata a tre, per due violini e basso continuo, Op.I/3. (Erich Schenk). cop.1955.
No.173. Krommer, Franz. Violinduett in A-dur. (Karl Nemeth). cop.1958.
No.174. Bonporti, F. A. Sonata a tre, per due violini e basso continuo. Op.IV/2. (Erich Schenk). cop.1955.
No.175. Sors, Fernando. Duo, für zwei Gitarren, Op.34. (Karl Scheit). cop.1958.

No.176. Bassani, G. B. Sonata a tre per due violini e basso continuo. Op.V/9. (Erich Schenk). cop.1955.
No.177. Mozart, Leopold. Sonata a tre, per due violini e basso continuo, Nr.4. (Erich Schenk). cop.1955.
No.178. See No.165.
No.179.
No.180. Reichert, Ernst. Lieder Salzburg Komponisten. 1955.
No.181. See No.165.
No.182. Schollum, Robert, ed. Klavierwerke oberösterreichischer Komponisten. (Kulturamt der Stadt Linz–Robert Schollum). cop.1956.
No.183. Kronsteiner, Joseph. Vier Rilke-Lieder, für Alt, Bratsche, Klavier. Zwei Hymnen, für Alt und Klavier, nach Gedichten von Karl Kleinschmidt. (Robert Schollum). cop.1956.
No.184. Reichert, Ernst. Sechs Gesänge, nach Texten von Hermann Hesse. Für hohe Stimme und Klavier. cop.1957.
No.185. Kubizek, K. M. Sonate für Oboe und Klavier. cop.1957.
No.186. Kittler, Richard. Sonate für Flöte und Klavier. cop.1957.

Hausmusik aus alter Zeit, *see* Riemann, Hugo. Hausmusik aus alter Zeit.

Hawke, H. William, ed. Elkan-Vogel organ series, *see* Elkan-Vogel organ series.

HAYDN, JOSEPH, 1732–1809.
Oeuvres complètes de Joseph Haydn. Cahier 1–12. Leipzig, Breitkopf & Härtel, [1802–43?].
12v.
Each cahier has special title page.
Title vignettes.
Contents:
Cahier 1. Contains piano sonatas Breitkopf & Härtel 52, 34, 49, 44–46, 19, and 18.
Cahier 2. Piano sonatas Breitkopf & Härtel 35–39 and 20, and Variations, Fantasia, Capriccio, Temo con variazioni, and Arietta con variazioni, all for piano.
Cahier 3. Contains 6 piano trios.
Cahier 4. Piano sonatas Breitkopf & Härtel 40–42, 48, and 47, and Arietta for piano.
Cahier 5. 5 Piano trios.
Cahier 6. 5 Piano trios.
Cahier 7. 6 Piano trios.
Cahier 8. Songs: Ein kleines Haus; Blick' hieher, du; O lass mich, Holder; Ja, Vetter, ja, ich fall euch bei; Freunde, Wasser macht stumme; Lebe, liebe, trinke, lärme; O wunderbare Harmonie; Der Jüngling hofft des greises Ziel; Du bists, dem Ruhm; Herr, der du mir das Leben; Ha! wie am scheindelnd hohen Mast; Der Umherirrende; Sympathie; Wie lieb' ich dich; Stets barg die Liebe sie; Heller Blick; Ob ich dich Liebe? ; Ariadne auf Naxos.
Cahier 9. Contains songs: Denkst du auch so innig meiner; Lob der Faulheit; Das Leben ist ein Traum; Auf meines Vaters Grab; Zufriedenheit; Eine sehr gewöhnliche Geschichte; Der erste Kuss; Trio: Daphnens einziger Fehler; Trio: An die Frauen; Quartetto: Der Greis; Quartetto: Der Augenblick; Quartetto: Die Warning; Quartetto: Wider den Uebermuth; Genügsamkeit; Gebet zu Gott; Dir nah' ich mich; Der Gleichsinn; Jeder meynt, das holde; Die Seejungfer; Rückerinnerung; Schäferlied; Die Verzweiflung; Ermunterung; Die Treue; Minna; Wünsche der Liebe; Liebeslied; Die Landlust; Die Verlassene; An Iris; Lachet nicht, Mädchen; An Thrysis; An die Geliebte; Die zu späte Ankunft der Mutter.
Cahier 10. Contains 5 piano trios and piano sonatas Breitkopf & Härtel 24–26.
Cahier 11. Piano sonatas Breitkopf & Härtel 27–32, 21–23, 51, 12–13.
Cahier 12. Piano sonatas Breitkopf & Härtel 33, 6, and 14; an adagio for piano; 2 violin and piano sonatas; and 3 piano trios.

HAYDN, JOSEPH, 1732–1809.
Joseph Haydns Werke. Erste kritische durchgesehene Gesamtausgabe. Ed. by Eusebius Mandyszewski and others. Ser.I, Bd.1–4; Ser.XIV, Bd.1–3; Ser.XVI, Bd.5, 6/7; Ser.XX, Bd.1. Leipzig, Breitkopf & Härtel, [1907–33].
11v. in 10.
"Vorwort" signed: Eusebius Mandyszewski.
Contents:
Ser.I. Bd.1. Symphonien Nr.1–12.
Ser.I. Bd.2. Symphonien Nr.13–27.
Ser.I. Bd.3. Symphonien Nr.28–40.
Ser.I. Bd.4. Symphonien Nr.41–49.
Ser.XIV. Bd.1. Klavierwerke. Sonaten. Nr.1–22.
Ser.XIV. Bd.2. Klavierwerke. Sonaten. Nr.23–38.
Ser.XIV. Bd.3. Klavierwerke. Sonaten. Nr.39–52.
Ser.XVI. Bd.5. Kantaten und Oratorien. Die Schöpfung.
Ser.XVI. Bd.6/7. Kantaten und Oratorien. Die Jahreszeiten.
Ser.XX. Bd.1. Einstimmige Lieder und Gesänge.

HAYDN, JOSEPH, 1732–1809.
Kritische Gesamtausgabe. Wissenschaftliche Leitung, Jens Peter Larsen. The complete works, critical edition. General editor: Jens Peter Larsen. Boston, Haydn Society in Zusammenarbeit mit Breitkopf & Härtel, Leipzig, cop.1950– .
v.1– .
Contents:
Ser.I.
Vol.5. Symphonies 50–57. Ed. by Helmut Schultz. 1952.
Vol.9. Symphonies 82–87. Ed. by H. C. Robbins Landon. 1950.
Vol.10. Symphonies 88–92. Ed. by H. C. Robbins Landon. 1951.
Ser.XXIII.
Vol.1. Masses 1–4. Ed. by Carl Maria Brand. 1951.
Missa brevis in F.

Missa in honorem B.V.M.
Missa Sanctae Caeciliae.
Missa Sancti Nicolai.

HAYDN, JOSEPH, 1732–1809.
... Werke. Hrsg. vom Joseph Haydn-Institut, Köln. Unter der Leitung von Jens Peter Larsen. München-Duisberg, G. Henle Verlag, 1958– .
v.1– .
Proposed set–34 series (approximately 60v.).
Contents (asterisk indicates unpublished volumes):
Reihe I. Symphonien.
Bd.4. Sinfonien 1764 und 1765. 1964.
Bd.6. Sinfonien 1767–1772. 1966.
Bd.17. Londoner Sinfonien. 3. Folge. 1966.
Bd.18. Londoner Sinfonien. 4. Folge.
*Reihe II. Ouvertüren.
*Reihe III. Märsche und Tänze für Orchester.
Reihe IV. Verschiedene Orchesterwerke. Die Sieben letzten Worte unseres Erlösers am Kreuze (Orchesterfassung).
*Reihe V. Konzerte für Klavier (Cembalo) und für Orgel.
*Reihe VI. Konzerte für Streichinstrumente.
*Reihe VII. Konzerte für Blasinstrumente.
*Reihe VIII. Divertimenti für gemischte Besetzung.
*Reihe IX. Divertimenti für Bläser.
*Reihe X. Divertimenti für Streicherbesetzung.
*Reihe XI. Streichquartette.
*Reihe XII. Streichtrios.
*Reihe XIII. Streichduos.
Reihe XIV. Barytontrios.
Bd.2. Barytontrios Nr.25–48.
Bd.3. Barytontrios Nr.49–72.
Bd.4. Barytontrios Nr.73–96.
*Reihe XV. Verschied. Barytonwerke.
*Reihe XVI. Kammermusik verschiedener Art ohne Klavier.
*Reihe XVII. Klavier-Divertimenti mit Begleitung.
Reihe XVIII. Klaviertrios.
Bd.3. Klaviersonaten. 3. Folge. 1966.
*Reihe XIX. Sonaten für Klavier mit Violine oder Flöte.
*Reihe XX. Klaviersonaten.
*Reihe XXI. Klavierstücke für zwei und vier Hände.
*Reihe XXII. Verschiedene Instrumentalmusik.
Reihe XXIII. Messen.
Bd.2. Messen. Nr.5–8.
Bd.3. Messen. Nr.9–10. 1965.
Bd.4. Messe. Nr.11. Schöpfungsmesse. 1801. 1967.
*Reihe XXIV. Kleinere Kirchenmusikwerke.
Reihe XXV. Opern.
Bd.2. La canterina. Intermezzo in musica.
Bd.3. Le speziale. Dramma giocoso.
Bd.5. L'infedeltà delusa. Burletta per musica in due atti. 1964.
Bd.6. Pt.1. L'incontro improvviso. Dramma giocoso per musica. Erster Halbband.
Bd.6. Pt.2. L'incontro improvviso. Dramma giocoso per musica. Zweiter Halbband.
Bd.12. Armida. Dramma eroica. 1783. 1965.
*Reihe XXVI. Arien, Duette, etc.
*Reihe XXVII. Kantaten.
Reihe XXVIII. Oratorien.
Bd.1. Pt.1. Il ritorno di Tobia. Oratorio. Erster Halbband.
Bd.1. Pt.2. Il ritorno di Tobia. Oratorio. Zweiter Halbband.
Bd.2. Die Sieben letzten Worte unseres Erlösers am Kreuze. (Vokalfassung).
Reihe XXIX. Einstimmige Lieder.
Bd.1. Lieder für eine Singstimme mit Begleitung des Klaviers. Hrsg. von Paul Mies. 1960.
*Reihe XXX. Mehrstimmige Gesänge.
*Reihe XXXI. Kanons.
Reihe XXXII. Bearbeitungen von Volksliedern.
Bd.1. Volksliedbearbeitungen. Schottische Lieder. Nr.1–100.
*Reihe XXXIII. Bearbeitungen verschiedener Art.
*Reihe XXXIV. Supplemente.

HAYDN, JOSEPH, 1732–1809.
Sämtliche Klavierwerke. Leipzig, New York, C. F. Peters, 193? – .
6v. (Edition Peters. No.4443, 713a–d, 4392).
Contents:
Vol.1. Leichte Divertimenti. (Carl Adolf Martienssen).
Vol.2–5. Sonaten. (Carl Adolf Martienssen).
Vol.6. Originalstücke. (Kurt Soldan and Max Marin Stein).

Haydn, Joseph, 1732–1809. Three divertimenti, *see* The Wellesley edition. No.4.

HEBRÄISCH-ORIENTALISCHER MELODIEN-SCHATZ. Zum ersten Male gesammelt, erläutet hrsg. von Abraham Zebi Idelsohn. Leipzig, Breitkopf & Härtel, 1914–32.
10v.
Contents:
Vol.1. Gesänge der jemenischen Juden. 1914.
Vol.2. Gesänge der babylonischen Juden. 1922.
Vol.3. Gesänge der persischen, bucharischen und daghestanischen Juden. 1922.
Vol.4. Gesänge der orientalischen Sefardim. 1923.
Vol.5. Gesänge der marokkanischen Juden. 1929.
Vol.6. Der Synagogengesang der deutschen Juden im 18. Jahrhundert. 1932.
Vol.7. Die traditionellen Gesänge der suddeutschen Juden. 1932.
Vol.8. Der Synagogengesang der osteuropäischen Juden. 1932.
Vol.9. Der Volkgesang der osteuropäischen Juden. 1932.
Vol.10. Gesänge der Chassidim. 1932.

HENRY VIII, KING OF ENGLAND, 1491–1547.
Songs, ballads and instrumental pieces, composed by King Henry the Eighth. Reproduced from the British Museum Ms.31922, collected and arranged by the Lady Mary Trefusis. To which is prefixed a list of the King's instruments, from the British Museum Ms. (Harl. Ms.1419).

Oxford, Privately printed for the Roxburghe Club, 1912.
xxx, 68p. front. (port.) plate.

Henry Bradshaw Society. Publications. Vol.VIII, *see* Catholic Church, Roman. Liturgy and ritual. Troper. The Winchester troper, from mss. of the Xth and XIth centuries.

Hernández, Gonzalo Castrillo, *see* Castrillo Hernández, Gonzalo.

HERRMANN, KURT. ed.
. . . Contemporaries of Purcell. Sixteen pieces for pianoforte by masters of the XVIIth century. Selected and ed. by Kurt Herrmann. London, Hinrichsen Edition, n.d.
2p.L., 20p. (Hinrichsen Edition. No.9).
Contains compositions by John Barrett, John Blow, Jeremiah Clarke, William Croft, John Eccles, Jean Baptiste Loeillet, Daniel Purcell, and Henry Purcell.

HERRMANN, KURT. ed.
Klaviermusik des 17. und 18. Jahrhunderts, ausgewählte und bearb. von Kurt Herrmann. Leipzig, Zürich, Gebrüder Hug & Co., cop. 1934.
3v.
Contains compositions by 41 different composers.
Contents:
Bd.I. Leicht.
Bd.II. Mittel.
Bd.III. Mittel bis Schwer.

HERRMANN, KURT. ed.
Lehrmeister und Schüler Joh. Seb. Bachs. Original-Kompositionen erstmalig neu veröffentlicht und bezeichnet von Kurt Herrmann . . . Leipzig, Zürich, Gebrüder Hug & Co., cop.1935.
2v.
Contents:
Vol.1 contains compositions by Georg Böhm, Dietrich Buxtehude, L. N. Clérambault, François Couperin, Charles Dieupart, J. K. F. Fischer, Girolamo Frescobaldi, J. J. Froberger, Nicolas Grigny, Johann Kuhnau, G. G. Nivers, Johann Pachelbel, J. A. Reinken, Gaspard le Roux.
Vol.2 contains compositions by J. F. Agricola, C. P. E. Bach, J. C. F. Bach, W. F. Bach, J. G. Goldberg, J. P. Kirnberger, J. L. Krebs, J. G. Müthel, and Christoph Nichelmann.

Hesbert, René Jean, 1899– , ed. Monumenta musicae sacrae, *see* Monumenta musicae sacrae.

Het oude Nederlandsche lied, *see* Duyse, Florimond van. Het oude Nederlandsche lied.

Hewitt, Helen Margaret, 1900– , ed. Harmonice musices Odhecaton A, *see* [Petrucci, Ottaviano dei]. Harmonice musices Odhecaton A, ed. by Helen Hewitt.

Heyden, Reinhold, ed. Musica practica, *see* Musica practica.

Heyden, Reinhold, ed. Volk Musiziert, *see* **Volk** Musiziert.

HIRSCH, PAUL ADOLF, 1881–1951.
Veröffentlichungen der Musik-Bibliothek Paul Hirsch. Frankfurt a.M. Unter Mitwirkung von Paul Hirsch; hrsg. von Johannes Wolf. [Reihe i, Bd.1–12]. Berlin, M. Breslauer, 1922–[40].
12v.
Vol.11 has imprint: Im Bärenreiter zu Kassel Verlag; Vol.12, London, Novello and Co.,Ltd.
Vol.12 has title: Publication of the Paul Hirsch Music Library (Cambridge), Volume 12.
Contents:
[Bd.] 1. Caza, F. Tractato vulgare de canto figurato. 1922.
[Bd.] 2. Conforto, G. L. Breue et facile maniera d'essercitarsi a far passagi. 1922.
[Bd.] 3. Friedlaender, M., editor. Neujahrsgrüsse empfindsamer Seelen. 1922.
[Bd.] 4. Telemann, G. P. Fantaisies pour le clavessin. 1923.
[Bd.] 5. Bottrigari, E. Il desiderio . . . 1924.
[Bd.] 6. Zelter, K. F. Fuenfzehn ausgewählte Lieder. 1924.
[Bd.] 7. Spataro, G. Dilucide et probatissime demonstratione de maestro Zoanne Spatario . . . 1925.
[Bd.] 8. Listenius, N. Musica Nicolai Listenii ab authore denuo recognita multisque novis regulis et exemplis adaucta. 1927.
[Bd.] 9. Bach, C. P. E. Zwölf zwei- und dreistimmige kleine Stücke für die Flöte oder Violine und das Klavier . . . 1928.
[Bd.] 10. Schultz, C. Das bittere Leiden und Sterben unsers Herren und Erlösers Jesu Christi. 1930.
[Bd.] 11. Luther, M. Deutsche Messe, 1526. 1934.
[Bd.] 12. Mozart, W. A. The ten celebrated quartets. [1940].

Hispaniae schola musica sacra, *see* Pedrell, Felipe. Hispaniae schola musica sacra.

Historical anthology of music, *see* Davison, Archibald Thompson. Historical anthology of music.

Historical organ-recitals, *see* Bonnet, Joseph. Historical organ-recitals.

Historical recital series for organ, *see* Dickinson, Clarence. Historical recital series for organ.

Hoffmann, Adolf, ed. Corona, *see* Corona.

HOFFMANN, ERNST THEODOR AMADEUS, 1776–1822.
E. T. A. Hoffmanns Musikalische Werke. Hrsg. von Gustav Becking. Bd.1, 2^1, 4^1. Leipzig, C. F. W. Siegel's Musikalienhandlung, [1922–27].
3 parts. facsims.
At head of title: E. Th. A. Hoffmann.
Imprint varies: Bd.2, No.1, and Bd.4, No.1, pub. by Fr. Kistner & C. F. W. Siegel.

Contents:
Bd.1. Klavierwerke: Vier Sonaten für Pianoforte.
Bd.2. Kammermusik: No.1. Quintett für Harfe od Pianoforte und Streichquartett (C moll). Score and 4 parts.
Bd.4. Chöre a cappella: No.1. Sechs geistliche Chore a cappella für gemischten Chor. Partitur. Latin words. 1927.

HOFHAIMER, PAUL, 1459–1537.
Einundneunzig gesammelte Tonsätze Paul Hofhaimer's und seines Kreises zum singen, für Orgel oder für Laute. Hrsg. von Hans Joachim Moser . . . Stuttgart, Berlin, J. G. Cotta'sche Buchhandlung Nachfolger, 1929.
1p.L., 194p.
"Sonderausgabe der Notenanhangs zu 'Paul Hofhaimer, ein Lied- und Orgelmeister des deutschen Humanismus' von H. J. Moser."

Hortênsia, Biblioteca Públia, *see* Joaquim, Manuel. O cancioneiro musical e poetico da Biblioteca Públia Hortênsia.

HORTUS MUSICUS. Kassel und Basel, Bärenreiter-Ausgabe, 1936– .
No.1–
A series of selected chamber music and music for home from the Middle Ages to the classical period.
Contents (f'-Blockflöte, indicates treble recorder; c'-Blockflöte, indicates tenor recorder):
No.1. Bach, J. S. Unschuld, kleinod Reiner Seelen. Arie für Sopran, Flauto traverso, Oboe, Viola und Violine. (Friedrich Smend). 1949.
No.2. Lasso, O. di. Bicinien, zum Singen und Spielen auf Streich- und Blasinstrumenten. (Gerhard Pinthus). 1949.
No.3. Händel, G. F. Sonate D-dur, für Flöte (Oboe, Violine) und Basso Continuo. (W. Hinnenthal). 1949.
No.4. Leichte Duette alter Meister des 16. Jahrhunderts, für gleiche Blockflöten oder andere Instrumente. (Walther Pudelko). n.d.
No.5. Leichte Duette alter Meister des 16. Jahrhunderts, für Sopran- und Altblockflöten oder andere Instrumente. (Walther Pudelko). n.d.
No.6. Telemann, G. P. Der getreue Musikmeister. Heft I: Vier Sonaten, für Blockflöte und Basso Continuo. (Dietz Degen). n.d.
No.7. Telemann, G. P. Der getreue Musikmeister. Heft 2: Sonaten und Spielstücke für ein Melodieinstrument (Geige, Flöte, Oboe) und Generalbass. (Dietz Degen). 1949.
No.8. Telemann, G. P. Der getreue Musikmeister. Heft 3: Spielstücke für Flöte (oder andere Melodieinstrumente) und Generalbass. (Dietz Degen). 1949.
No.9. Telemann, G. P. Der getreue Musikmeister. Heft 4: Spielstücke für Klavier oder andere Tasteninstrumente und Laute. (Dietz Degen). 1949.
No.10. Telemann, G. P. Der getreue Musikmeister. Heft 5: Triosonate für zwei Blockflöten (oder Geigen, Querflöten) und Generalbass. (Dietz Degen). 1949.
No.11. Telemann, G. P. Der getreue Musikmeister. Heft 6: Duette für zwei Melodieinstrumente (Blockflöten, Geigen, Querflöten, Gamben). (Dietz Degen). 1949.
No.12. Telemann, G. P. Der getreue Musikmeister. Heft 7: Lieder und Arien für Gesang und Klavier. (Dietz Degen). 1949.
No.13. Telemann, G. P. Der getreue Musikmeister. Heft 8: Sonate für Violoncello und Generalbass. (Dietz Degen). 1949.
No.14. Englische Fantasien für drei Streich- oder Blasinstrumente. Aus dem 17. Jahrhundert. (Ernst Hermann Meyer). 1949.
No.15. Händel, Georg Friedrich. Triosonate B dur für Oboe, Violine (oder 2 Violinen) und Basso Continuo. (W. Hinnenthal). 1949.
No.16. Bassani, Giovanni Battista. Sieben Trios für Violine/Viola/Viola da Gamba (oder andere Streich- oder Blasinstrumente). (Edith Kiwi). 1949.
No.17. Fischer, Johann. Tafelmusik Ouvertürensuite für vier Streichinstrumente mit oder ohne Basso Continuo. (Hans Engel). 1951.
No.18. Lasso, O. di. Sechs Fantasien für zwei Violinen oder andere Streich- oder Blasinstrumente besonders für Blockflöten. (Walther Pudelko). 1949.
No.19. Lasso, O. di. Sechs Fantasien für Violine und Viola oder andere Streich- oder Blasinstrumente besonders für Blockflöten. (Walther Pudelko). 1949.
No.20. Telemann, G. P. Konzert für vier Violinen ohne Basso Continuo. (Hans Engel). 1949.
No.21. Vierdanck, Johann. Capricci mit zwei oder drei Instrumenten. (Hans Engel). 1950.
No.22. Telemann, G. P. Konzert G-dur für Viola und Streichorchester mit Basso Continuo. (Hellmuth Christian Wolff). n.d.
No.23. Gastoldi, Giovanni Giacomo. Spielstücke für zwei gleiche Instrumente. (Edith Kiwi). 1949.
No.24. Gastoldi, Giovanni Giacomo. Spielstücke, für zwei ungleiche Instrumente. (Edith Kiwi). 1949.
No.25. Telemann, G. P. Triosonate E-moll für Altblockflöte (Querflöte/Violine), Oboe (Querflöte/Violine) und Basso Continuo. (Manfred Ruëtz). n.d.
No.26. Fasch, J. F. Sonate B-dur für Blockflöte, Oboe (Violine), Violine und Basso Continuo. (Waldemar Woehl). 1949.
No.27. Bicinien der Renaissance für zwei gleiche Instrumente. (Leopold Nowak). 1950.
No.28. Bicinien der Renaissance für zwei ungleiche Instrumente. (Leopold Nowak). 1949.
No.29. Isaac, Heinrich. Sechs Instrumentalsätze für vier Streich- oder Blasinstrumente. (Oskar Dischner). 1950.
No.30. Fux, Johann Joseph. Sonate (Kanon) für zwei Viola da Gamba (Bratschen) und Basso Continuo. (Hellmuth Christian Wolff). n.d.
No.31. Legrenzi, Giovanni. Triosonate G-dur für zwei Violinen und Basso Continuo. (Werner Danckert). 1949.

No.32. Telemann, G. P. Konzert A-moll für Violine und Streichorchester mit Basso Continuo. (Hellmuth Christian Wolff). 1950.

No.33. Anonymus um 1730. Drei Sonaten für Blockflöten und Basso Continuo. (Waldemar Woehl). 1949.

No.34. Cazzati, Mauritio. Triosonate D-moll für zwei Violinen und Basso Continuo. (Werner Danckert). n.d.

No.35. Locatelli da Bergamo, Pietro. Drei Sonaten für Querflöte und Basso Continuo. (Gustav Scheck). 1949.

No.36. Telemann, G. P. Triosonate B-dur für Blockflöte (Querflöte/Violine) konzertierender Cembalo (Klavier) und Basso Continuo. (Manfred Ruëtz). 1949.

No.37. Bach, J. Ch. Drei Streichtrios für zwei Violinen und Violoncello (Op.4, Nr.2, 4, und 6). (Walter Upmeyer). 1949.

No.38. Vitali, Tommaso Antonio. Sonate für Violine/Violoncello und Cembalo. (W. Hinnenthal). 1950.

No.39–40. Abel, Karl Friedrich. Sechs Sonaten für Viola da Gamba oder Geige (Querflöte) und Basso Continuo. (Joseph Bacher). 1949.

No.41. Haydn, Joseph. Zwölf deutsche Tänze für zwei Violinen und Violoncello. (Bernhard Paumgartner). 1949.

No.42. Bach, J. Ch. Quintett D-dur für Querflöte, Oboe, Violine, Violoncello und Obligates Cembalo. (Rolf Ermeler). 1944.

No.43. Loeillet, Jean Baptiste. Drei Sonaten für Flöte (Geige-Oboe) und Generalbass. (Philipp Hinnenthal). 1952.

No.44. Bonporti, Francesco Antonio. Inventionen für Violine und Basso Continuo, Op.10. (Franz Giegling). Heft I: Invenzione prima A-Dur, Invenzione seconda H-moll, Invenzione terza F-Dur. 1950.

No.45. Bonporti, Francesco Antonio. Inventionen für Violine und Basso Continuo. Op.10. (Franz Giegling). Heft II: Invenzione quarta G-moll. Invenzione quinta B-Dur. Invenzione sesta C-moll. 1949.

No.46. Bach, C. P. E. Sonate C-dur für Klavier, mit begleitung einer Violine und eines Violoncello. (Fritz Oberdörffer). 1949.

No.47. Telemann, G. P. Die kleine Kammermusik. Sechs Partiten für Violine (Querflöte/Oboe/Blockflöte/Diskantgambe u. A.) und Basso Continuo. (Waldemar Woehl). 1949.

No.48. Scarlatti, Alessandro. Sinfonien für Kammerorchester. (Raymond Meylan). Nr. IV, E-moll. 1950.

No.49. Hertel, Johann Wilhelm. Sonate in D-moll für Cembalo oder Klavier. (Hans Erdmann). 1950.

No.50, 58. Purcell, Henry. Spielmusik zum Sommernachtstraum für vier Streich- oder Blasinstrumente und Basso Continuo. (Hilmar Höckner). 1951.

No.51. Fux, Johann Joseph. Partiten, G-dur und F-dur für zwei Violinen und Bass. (Andreas Liess). 1950.

No.52. Telemann, G. P. Concerto D-dur, eine kleine Tanzsuite für Streichorchester mit Cembalo oder Streichquartett. (Walter Upmeyer). 1950.

No.53. Tartini, Giuseppe. Sinfonie oder Streichquartett in A. (Hans Erdmann). 1950.

No.54. Pachelbel, Johann. Triosuiten für zwei Geigen und Basso Continuo. (Fritz Zobeley). Heft I: Suiten F-dur und C-moll. 1950.

No.55. Pachelbel, Johann. Triosuiten für zwei Geigen und Basso Continuo. (Fritz Zobeley). Heft II.

No.56. Pachelbel, Johann. Triosuiten für zwei Geigen und Basso Continuo. (Fritz Zobeley). Heft III.

No.57. Bach, W. F. E. Trio G-dur für zwei Querflöten und Viola. (Rolf Ermeler). 1951.

No.58. See No.50.

No.59. Fischer, Johann Caspar Ferdinand. Vier Suiten für Blockflöte (Violine, Flöte, Oboe, Viola) mit Basso Continuo. (Waldemar Woehl). 1950.

No.60. Quantz, Johann Joachim. Trio-sonate C-dur für Blockflöte (oder Querflöte, Geige), Querflöte (oder Geige) und Basso Continuo. (Walter Birke). 1950.

No.61. Kindermann, Johann Erasmus. Tanzstücke für Klavier. (Cembalo, Clavichord oder andere Tasteninstrumente). (Richard Baum). 1950.

No.62. Binder, Christlieb Siegmund. Sonate G-dur, für Violine und Klavier (Cembalo). (Günter Hausswald). 1950.

No.63. Walter, J. Kanons in den Kirchentönen zu 2 und 3 Stimmen. (Ehmann).

No.64. Leichte Fantasien von Bassano, Lupo und Morley. Für drei Gamben oder andere Melodieinstrumente. (Joseph Bacher). 1950.

No.65. Haydn, Joseph. Divertimenti . . . für Baryton, Viola und Bass. (Waldemar Woehl). Nr.1–3. 1939.

No.66–68. Brescianello, G. A. Concerti a tre, für zwei Violinen und Bass. (Adelmo Damerini). 1950–51.

No.69. Torelli, Giuseppe. Sonate in G-dur für Violoncello und Klavier (Cembalo). (Franz Giegling). 1950.

No.70. Gabrieli, Giovanni. Sonate für drei Violinen und Basso Continuo. (Werner Danckert). 1950.

No.71–72. Bach, C. P. E. Sonaten für Flöten und Basso Continuo. (Kurt Walther). 1936–40.

No.73. Hassler, Hans Leo. Intraden aus dem "Lustgarten," für sechs Stimmen (Streich- oder Blasinstrumente). (Hilmar Hockner). 1937.

No.74. Rotenbucher, Erasmus. Schöne und liebliche Zweigesänge. (Diplona amoena et florida) für zwei Melodieinstrumente. (Dietz Degen). 1951.

No.75. Sweelinck, Jan Pieters. Rimes françaises et italiennes à deux parties. Duette zum Spielen und Singen. (Joh. Philipp Hinnenthal). 1951.

No.76. Quantz, Johann Joachim. Konzert ("Pour Potsdam") für Flöte und Streicher mit Cembalo (Klavier). (Walter Upmeyer). 1951.

No.77. Bonporti, F. A. Inventionen, Op.10. La pace, für Violinen und Basson Continuo. (Geigling). Heft 3: Invenzione 7–10.

No.78. Mozart, Johann Georg Leopold. Zwölf Duette für zwei Violinen. (Adolf Hoffmann). 1951.

No.79. Stamitz, Karl. Concerto in A für Violoncello und kleines Orchester. (Walter Upmeyer). 1951.

No.80. Bach, J. S. Virga Jesse floruit. Duett für Sopran, Bass und Continuo aus dem Magnificat. (1.Fassung). (Alfred Dürr). 1951.

No.81. Chédeville, Esprit Philippe. Sechs galante Duos für zwei gleiche Melodieinstrumente (besondere Blockflöten). (Arthur von Arx). 1951.

No.82. Ricciotti, Carlo. Concertini für vier Violinen, Viola Alta, Violoncello und Basso Continuo. (Joh. Philipp Hinnenthal). II. G dur. 1951.

No.83. Legrenzi, Giovanni. Sonate für vier Violinen mit Basso Continuo. Op.10, 3 Nr.1. (Karl Gustav). 1951.

No.84. Legrenzi, Giovanni. Sonate für Violine und Violoncello mit Basso Continuo. Op.10, 1 Nr.4. (Karl Gustav Fellerer). 1951.

No.85. Boismortier, Joseph Bodin de. Sonate à deux flûtes traversières sans basse. Oeuvre VI, No.6. (Felix Raugel). 1951.

No.86. Richter, Franz Xaver. Sechs Kammersonaten, Op.2. Für obligates Cembalo (Klavier), Flöte, (Violine), und Violoncello. Heft I: Sonate 1–3. (Walter Upmeyer). 1951.

No.87, 88. Platti, Giovanni. Ricercari für Violine und Violoncello. Nr.1–4. (Fritz Zobeley). 1951.

No.89. Römhild, Johann Theodor. Das neue Jahr ist kommen, Solokantete für Bass, zwei Violinen, Oboe (ad lib.) und Basso Continuo. (Hans Römhild). 1951.

No.90. Naumann, Johann Gottlieb. Sechs Leichte Duette für zwei Violinen. (Paul Bormann). 1951.

No.91. Pisandel, J. G. Sonate für Violine allein. (Hausswald). 1952.

No.92. Ditters von Dittersdorf, Karl. 6 Streichtrios für zwei Violinen, Violoncello. (Noack).

No.93. Stich, Johann Wenzel. Quartet für Horn, Geige, Bratsche und Violoncello. (Adam Bernhard Gottron). 1951.

No.94. Haydn, J. Divertimenti für Baryton (Violine, Viola), Viola, Violoncello. (Woehl). Heft 2: Nr.4–6. 1952.

No.95. Haydn, J. Divertimenti für Baryton (Violine, Viola), Viola, Violoncello. (Woehl). Heft 3: Nr.7–9. 1952.

No.96. Scheidt, S. Canzon Bergamasca für 3 Violine, Viola, Violoncello. (Garff). 1952.

No.97. Telemann, G. P. Sonate für 3 Violine und Basso Continuo. (Hoffmann). 1952.

No.98. Haydn, J. Streichquartett E-dur. (E. F. Schmid). 1936.

No.99. Witt, Chr. F. Suite in F-dur. Für drei Blockflöten (zwei f', eine c') oder andere Blas- oder Streichinstrumente und Basso Continuo. 1952.

No.100.

No.101. Roman, J. H. 2 Sonaten für Querflöte und Basso Continuo. (Senn). 1952.

No.102. Vivaldi, A. Sonate G-moll für Violine und Basso Continuo. (Upmeyer).

No.103. Strungk, N. A. Concerto I, G-dur, für Violoncello und Kammerorchester.

No.103. Strungk, N. A. Sonata für 3 Violinen, 2 Viola, Violoncello, Basso Continuo. (Stein).

No.104. Stamitz, C. Concert I, G-dur, für Violoncello und Kammerorchester. (Upmeyer).

No.105. Stamitz, C. Concerti III, C-dur, für Violoncello und Kammerorchester. (Upmeyer).

No.106. Stamitz, C. Trio G-dur für 2 Querflöte und Violoncello. (Schnapp).

No.107. Telemann, G. P. Kleine Suite D-dur für 2 Violinen, 2 Viola, Basso Continuo (oder 3 Violinen, Viola, Basso Continuo). (Höckner). 1953.

No.108. Telemann, G. P. Streichquartett A-dur. (Wolff). 1963.

No.109. Stamitz, C. Quartett D-dur für Querflöte, Violine, Viola (Horn in F), Violoncello. Op.VIII/1. (Upmeyer). 1954.

No.110. Rossi, S. Sonata detta la Moderna für 2 Violinen und Basso Continuo. (Danckert).

No.111. Wölfl, J. Sonate für Violoncello und Klavier, Op.31. (Längin). 1953.

No.112. Händel, G. F. Sonate für Gambe und obl. Cembalo. (Längin). 1960.

No.113. Mozart, W. A. Duo B-dur (K.V.424) für Violine und Viola. (Müller-Crailsheim).

No.114. Mozart, W. A. Duo G-dur (K.V.423) für Violine und Viola. (Müller-Crailsheim). 1953.

No.115. Mozart, W. A. 12 Duette für 2 Bassetthörner (K.V.487). Ausgabe für Violine und Viola. (Müller-Crailsheim).

No.116. Scarlatti, A. Sinfonie Violine D-moll für Kammerorchester. (Meylan). 1952.

No.117. Erlebach, Ph. H. Sonate 1, D-dur, für Violine, Gambe und Basso Continuo. (Zobeley). 1954.

No.118. Erlebach, Ph. H. Sonate III, A-dur, für Violine, Gambe und Basso Continuo. (Zobeley). 1954.

No.119. Bach, J. Chr. Quartett D-dur, Op.XX/2, für 2 Querflöte, Viola, Violoncello. (Ermeler). 1953.

No.120. Graupner, Chr. Sonata G-dur für Streichquartett oder Streichorchester. (Hoffmann). 1955.

No.121. Graupner, Chr. Zwei Sonaten für Cembalo (Klavier) und Violin oder Flöte. (Adolf Hoffmann). 1955.

No.122. Graf, Fr. K. zu Erbach. 6 Duos für 2 Violoncello (oder Fagott). (Noach). 1954.

No.123. Leichte Spielmusik für Gambe und Basso Continuo. (Bacher). 1954.

No.124. Telemann, G. P. Konzert E-moll für f'-Blockflöte, Querflöte, Streicher und Basso Continuo. (Kölbel).

No.125. Scarlatti, A. Sinfonie 1, F-dur, für Kammerorchester. (Meylan). 1954.

No.126. Zelenka, J. D. Sonate 1, F-dur, für 2 Oboen (Violinen), Fagott (Violoncello) und Basso Continuo. (Schönbaum).

No.127. Fesch, W. de. Sechs Sonaten für Violine und Basso Continuo. (Woehl). Heft 1: Nr.1–3. 1958.
No.128. Fesch, W. de. Sechs Sonaten für Violine und Basso Continuo. (Woehl). Heft 2: Nr.4–6.
No.129. Marini, B. Sonate D-moll für Violine und Basso Continuo. (Danckert). 1955.
No.130. Telemann, G. P. Konzert F-dur für f' f' -Blockflöte, Streich und Basso Continuo. (Ruetz).
No.131. Telemann, G. P. Konzert G-dur für Querflöte, 2 Violinen, Basso Continuo. (Upmeyer). 1955.
No.132. Zelenka, J. D. Sonate VI, C-moll, für 2 Oboen (Violinen), Fagott (Violoncello) und Basso Continuo. (Schönbaum).
No.133. Loeillet, J. Quintett H-moll für 2 f' -Blockflöte, Querflöte und Basso Continuo. (Ermelet). 1963.
No.134. In Nomine. Altenglische Kammermusik zu 4 und 5 Stimmen (Streichquartett und Streichquintett, bzw. Gamben oder Blockflöten). (Stevens).
No.135. Vivaldi, A. Il pastor fido. 6 Sonaten für ein Holzblasinstrumente oder Violine und Basso Continuo. (Upmeyer).
No.136. Morley, Th. 9 Fantasien für 2 Gamben. (Dolmetsch). 1964.
No.137. Carmina germanica et gallica. Ausgewählte Instrumentalstücke des 16. Jahrh. (Brennecke). Für Streicher und Bläser. Heft 1: Nr.1–17. 1956.
No.138. Carmina germanica et gallica. Ausgewählte Instrumentalstücke des 16. Jahrh. (Brennecke). Für Streicher und Bläser. Heft 2: Nr.18–32. 1957.
No.139. Danican-Philidor, A. Sonate D-moll für f' -Blockflöte (Querflöte, Oboe) und Basso Continuo. (Ruf). 1956.
No.140. Scheidt, S. Canzon super Intradem Aechiopicam für 3 Violinen, Viola, Violoncello. (Garff). 1956.
No.141. Purcell, H. Die Nacht. 3 Arien für hohe Stimme und Streichquartett. (Just). 1956.
No.142. Marcello, B. Sonaten für f' -Blockflöte und Basso Continuo. (Glode). Sonaten G-moll und E-moll, Op.II/3 und 4. 1963.
No.143. Marini, B. Sonate für 2 Violine und Basso Continuo. (Danckert). 1956.
No.144. Ricciotti, C. (Pergolesi?). Concertino IV, F-moll, für 4 Violinen, Viola, Violoncello, Basso Continuo. (Hinnenthal). 1957.
No.145. Zach, J. 2 Sinfonien für 2 Violinen und Basso Continuo. (Gottron). 1956.
No.146. Scarlatti, A. Sinfonie II, D-dur, für Kammerorchester. (Melyan). 1957.
No.147. Zelenka, J. D. Sonate IV, G-moll, für 2 Oboen (Violinen), Fagott (Violoncello) und Basso Continuo. (Schoenbaum). 1957.
No.148. Demantius, Chr. Deutsche Tänze für Streichquartett oder Streichorchester. (Degen). 1957.
No.149. Jenkins, J. 7 Fantasien für 3 Gamben. (Dolmetsch). 1957.
No.150. Albert, H. Duette für gleiche und gemischte Stimmen und Basso Continuo. (Noack). 1957.
No.151. Marcello, B. Sonaten für f' -Blockflöte und Basso Continuo. (Glode). Sonaten F-dur und D-moll, Op.II/1 und 2. 1958.
No.152. Marcello, B. Sonaten für f' -Blockflöte und Basso Continuo. (Glode). Sonaten C-dur und B-dur, Op.II/6 und 7. 1958.
No.153. Naudot, J. J. Konzert G-dur für f' -Blockflöte (Querflöte, Oboe), 2 Violinen und Basso Continuo. (Ruf). 1958.
No.154. Ricciotti, C. (Pergolesi?). Concertino V, B-dur, für 4 Violinen, Viola, Violoncello, Basso Continuo. (Hinnenthal). 1959.
No.155. Ricciotti, C. (Pergolesi?). Concertino VI, Es-dur, für 4 Violinen, Viola, Violoncello, Basso Continuo. (Hinnenthal). 1959.
No.156. Erbach, Chr. Canzona "La paglia" für 3 Violinen und 2 Violoncello. (Gottron). 1959.
No.157. Zelenka, J. D. Sonate V, F-dur, für 2 Oboen (Violinen), Fagott (Violoncello), und Basso Continuo. (Schoenbaum). 1959.
No.158. Ricciotti, C. (Pergolesi?). Concertino I, G-dur, für 4 Violinen, Viola, Violoncello, Basso Continuo. (Hinnenthal). 1959.
No.159. Ricciotti, C. (Pergolesi?). Concertino III, A-dur, für 4 Violinen, Viola, Violoncello, Basso Continuo. (Hinnenthal). 1959.
No.160. Boismortier, J. B. de. Sonate E-moll, Op.XXXVII/2, für Querflöte (Oboe, Violine), Gambe (Fagott, Violoncello), und Basso Continuo. (Ruf). 1959.
No.161. Pepusch, J. Chr. Triosonate D-moll für Querflöte (f' -Blockflöte, Violine), Viola (Gambe) und Basso Continuo. (Ruf). 1959.
No.162. Loeillet de Gant, J. B. Sonaten für Querflöte und Basso Continuo. (Hinnenthal). Heft 2: Sonaten, Op.III/9 und IV/9 und 10. 1960.
No.163. Purcell, H. "Herr, zu dir will ich schrein," für Bass, Streicher, und Basso Continuo. (Just). 1959.
No.164. Purcell, H. "Wie wonnig ist's auf blumigem Gefild," für Soprano, Tenor, 2 f' -Blockflöte, Basso Continuo. (Just). 1959.
No.165. Loeillet de Gant, J. B. Sonaten für Querflöte und Basso Continuo. (Hinnenthal). Heft 3: Sonaten, Op.III/12 und Op.IV/11 und 12. 1960.
No.166. Loeillet, J. B. Triosonate, Op.II/2, für f' -Blockflöte (Querflöte), Oboe (Violine) und Basso Continuo. (Ruf).
No.167. Locke, J. Duette für 2 Gamben. (Dolmetsch). 1960.
No.168. Scarlatti. Sinfonie XII C-moll für Kammerorchester. (Meylan). 1960.
No.169. Veracini, F. M. Konzert D-dur für Violine und Streicher. (Paumgartner). 1959.
No.170. Beecke, J. von. Streichquartett G-dur, Nr.6. (Gottron). 1960.
No.171. Stich, J. W. (Punto). Quartett, Op. XVIII/1, für Horn, Violine, Viola, Violoncello. (Gottron). 1960.

No.172. Colista, L. Triosonate A-dur für 2 Violinen, Violoncello und Basso Continuo. (Wessely). 1960.
No.173. Geminiani, Fr. Sonata A-dur, Op.I/1, für Violine und Basso Continuo. (Ruf).
No.174. Geminiani, Fr. Sonata D-dur, Op.I/4, für Violine und Basso Continuo. (Ruf).
No.175. Telemann, G. Ph. Suite G-moll ("Der getreue Musikmeister") für Violine (Oboe) und Basso Continuo. (Lebermann). 1961.
No.176. Loeillet, J. B. (John of London). Triosonate C-moll, Op.II/6, für f' -Blockflöte (Querflöte), Oboe (Violine) und Basso Continuo. (Ruf).
No.177. Zelenka, J. D. Sonata III, B-dur, für Violine, Oboe (Violine), Fagott (Violoncello) und Basso Continuo. (Schoenbaum). 1961.
No.178. Geminiani, Fr. Sonata E-moll für Oboe (Querflöte, Violine) und Basso Continuo. (Ruf). 1961.
No.179. Telemann, G. Ph. Triosonate B-dur für Oboe (Querflöte), Violine und Basso Continuo. (Ruf).

HOTHBY, JOHN, 1415–1487.
The musical works. Ed. by Albert Seay. Rome, American Institute of Musicology, 19? – .
v.1– . (Corpus mensurabilis musicae. No.33).
To be published.
Proposed set–1v.

Hughes, Anselm, *Father*, 1889– , ed. Anglo-French sequelae, *see* Plainsong and Mediaeval Music Society. Hughes, Anselm, *Father*. Anglo-French sequelae.

Hughes, Anselm, *Father*, 1889– , ed. Index to the facsimile edition of Ms. Wolfenbüttel 677. (St. Andrews music book), *see* Wolfenbüttel. Herzog-August-Bibliothek. Mss. (677 [Helmst. 628]). An old St. Andrews music book. Index.

Hughes, Anselm, *Father*, 1889– , ed. Old Hall manuscript, *see* Plainsong and Mediaeval Music Society. Old Hall manuscript.

Hughes, Anselm, *Father*, 1889– , ed. Worcester mediaeval harmony of the thirteenth and fourteenth centuries, *see* Plainsong and Mediaeval Music Society. Hughes, Anselm, *Father*. Worcester mediaeval harmony of the thirteenth and fourteenth centuries.

HULLAH, JOHN PYKE, 1812–1884. ed.
58 English songs of the 17th and 18th century, selected and arr. with pianoforte accompaniment by John Pyke Hullah. Offenbach, André, 1871.
p.1– .

HULLAH, JOHN PYKE, 1812–1884. ed.
Part music. A collection of vocal music by John Hullah. London, John W. Parker.
3 series.
Class A, for SATB. (Vol.i, 1842; Vol.ii, 1845). (was republished in 1868).
Class B, for voices of women and children. 1845.
Class B, for voices of men. 1845.
Each series contains sacred and secular pieces. Each was printed both in score and in separate parts, in royal 8vo, and the whole forms a collection unexampled at the time (at least in England) for extent, excellence, and variety, and for the clearness and accuracy of its production.–*Grove's Dicionary of music and musicians*, 1916, Vol.3, p.631.
Contents (from *Grove's, op. cit.*, Vol.3, p.631–32):
Class A. 1. Sacred.
Vol.I.
God save the Queen.
Farrant. Lord for Thy tender.
With one consent. (Ps.100).
Henry VIII. O Lord the maker.
Tallis. Sanctus and Responses.
O praise ye the Lord. (Ps.149).
Palestrina. I will give thanks.
Luther. Since on the cross. (Ein' feste Burg).
Croft. God is gone up.
When as we sat in Babylon. (Ps.137).
Palestrina. O be joyful.
Ye gates, lift up. (Ps.24).
Hullah. The day is past.
Haydn. Thou that from Thy throne.
Tallis. Venite.
Croce, G. Thou art beautiful.
Haydn, M. O Lord, another day.
Lawes, H. O Lord, I will. (Ps.34).
Clarke, Jer. Praise the Lord.
Purcell. Gloria Patri. (Canon).
Creyghton. Sanctus.
Palestrina. Be not Thou far.
Farrant. Hide not Thou Thy face.
LeJeune. O Jesu Lord.
Himmel. Give ear, O God.
Child. Praise the Lord.
Lotti. Blessed be Thou.
Rousseau. Forth from the dark.
Ford. Almighty God!
Creyghton. I will arise.
Tye. Sing to the Lord.
Haydn, M. Hear my prayer.
Croft. O King eternal. (Ps.8).
Rogers, B. O God of truth.
Rossini. O remember not.
Lvov. Give to us peace.
Purcell. Thou knowest, Lord.
Cooke. Amen.
Dumont, H. Sweet day, so cool.
Zingarelli. Go not far from me.
Richardson, V. O how amiable.
Clarke, Jer. To laud the heav'nly king. (Ps.148).
Gibbons. Almighty and everlasting.
Horsley, W. Awake, thou that sleepest. (Canon).
Boyce. Hallelujah.

Vol.II.
Kreutzer. O King of Kings.
Cooke. My soul doth magnify. (Chant).
Child. Responses.
O come all ye faithful. (Adeste fideles).
Berg. Hosanna. (Canon).
Neukomm. Amen.
Child. O Lord, grant the King.

Harrington. Ut queant. (Canon).
Rogers. Sanctus.
Palestrina. Why do the heathen.
Humphrey, P. I will magnify Thee. (Chant).
Croce, G. Plead Thou my cause.
Zingarelli. Ponder my words.
Clarke, Jer. Awake my soul.
—— Sleep, downy sleep.
Callcott. Thou shalt shew me. (Canon).
Reynolds. My God, my God.
Alcock. Wherewithal shall a young man.
Horsley, W. O Saviour!
Hullah. O most merciful.
Gossec. Praise the Lord.
Bassani. Sanctus.
Croft. We will rejoice.
Paxton. O Lord, in Thee. (Canon).
Nares. Try me, O God.
O Lord, teach us. (Canon).
Brassetti. Praise ye the Lord.
Croce, G. I will remember.
Haydn, M. Peace be to this habitation.
Bevin, E. Hallelujah. (Canon).
All people that on earth. (Old 100th).
Callcott. Praise the Lord (Canon).
Rogers. Behold now.
Blow. The Lord hear thee.
Walmisley, T. F. Hosanna. (Canon).
Durante. Help us, O God.
Decius, N. The day must come.
Horsley, W. Hear me when I call. (Canon).
Gibbons, O. Sanctus.
Palestrina. Let all the people.
Greene. Blessed be God.
Purcell. O God, Thou art.
Tye. Mock not God's name. (Canon).
Jannaconi. The voice of joy.

Class A. 2. Secular.
Vol.I.
Arne. Rule, Britannia.
Donato. All ye who music love.
Waelrent. Hard by a fountain.
Stevens. Ye spotted snakes.
Bennet, John. Flow, O my tears.
Saville. The waits.
Atterbury. Come let us all.
Long may life and health.
Purcell. Freeman, rejoice.
Mornington. Hail, hallowed fane.
Stevens. Crabbed age and youth.
Edwardes. In going to my lonely bed.
Anerio, F. Ah me! where is.
Horsley, W. Nymphs of the forest.
O never fear though rain be falling.
Neithart. May day.
Scarlatti. Solfeggio.
Marenzio. Lady see!
Cooke. How sleep the brave.
Cherubini. Hark, the village maids.
Lotti. All hail, Britannia.
Paxton. Upon the poplar bough.
Ford. Since first I saw.
Gluck. How glad with smiles.
Macfarren. Sing a song of sixpence.
Paxton. Happy are they.
Ruffo, V. See from his ocean bed.
Moscheles. Daybreak.
Pearsall. The hardy Norseman.
Dowland. Come again, sweet love.
Cooke. In paper case.
Harvest time.
Webbe. Thy voice, O harmony.
Danby. Awake, Aeolian lyre.
Bennet, J. My lady is as fair.
Gluck. Sing loud a joyful.
Morley. April is in my mistress' face.

Vol.II.
Spontone, B. The joyous birds.
Mornington. Here in cool grot.
Macfarren. Girls and boys.
Webbe. Swiftly from the mountain's brow.
Reichardt, G. Our native land.
Benedict. Like to the grass.
Paxton. Ode to spring.
Bennet, J. Come shepherds.
Cooke. Hark, hark, the lark.
Horsley, W. Come, my friends.
Rogers, Sir J. O how sweet 'tis.
Boyce. Long live the Queen. (Canon).
Grast. Come, shepherds.
Reading, J. Dulce domum.
Callcott. Thyrisis, when he left me.
Arne. Which is the properest day.
Cooke. Albion, thy sea-encircled isle.
Hullah. Pack clouds away.
Webbe. Breathe soft, ye winds.
Gluck. Amid the din.
Vert, G. de. Who will bring back.
Hark, hark, a merry note.
Bennet, J. Thyrisis, sleepest thou?
Unto the merry greenwood.
Schubert, F. Dance we so gaily.
Stevens. Blow, blow, thou winter wind.
Dowland. Awake, sweet love.
Hullah. 'Twas on a bank.
Stevens. From Oberon.
Wilbye. Thus saith my Chloris.
Dowland. Now, O now.
Webbe. Happy are we met.

Class B. 1. Sacred.
God save the Queen.
Boyce. Hallelujah.
Palestrina. Shew me Thy ways.
Salieri. Not unto us.
My shepherd is the Lord. (Ps.23).
Come let us strive to join.
It is a good and pleasant thing. (Ps.92).
Lord, dismiss us.
King, C. O Absalom my son.
Barbice, C. Servants of God.
Webbe. From everlasting.
Palestrina. Hear my crying.
Jehovah. Thou my maker art. (Ps.119).
Carafa. Prostrate before Thee.
O all ye works of the Lord.
Immler. Stand up and bless.
Palestrina. He hath put down.
Chant. Benedictus.
My voice went up. (Ps.57).
Christ whose glory fills the skies.
Luther. Great God, what do I.

Glasse. The midnight cry.
Jackson. Be merciful.
Hayes. Unto Thee, O God.
Pleyel. Great God of hosts.
Palestrina. And His mercy.
Hofmeister. Thee will I love.
O sing unto God.
I will always give thanks.
Be glad, O ye righteous.

Class B. 2. Secular.
Kreutzer. Child of the sun.
Danby. Come, follow me.
Hilton. Come, sprightly mirth.
Wilbye. Dear pity.
Fugato from Les solfèges d'Italie.
Gentle moon from Les solfèges d'Italie.
Go, gentle breezes from Les solfèges d'Italie.
Greene. Hail green fields and shady woods.
Byrd. Heigh ho, to the greenwood.
Atterbury. Hot cross buns.
Arne. Huntsman, rest.
Horsley, W. May-day.
Mozart. Prythee, do not chide me so.
Arne. Rule, Britannia.
Mozart. See, where the morning sun.
Solfeggio from Les solfèges d'Italie.
Mozart. The flowers their buds.
Shield. The load stars.
Pohlenz. The sunbeams streak.
Berg. Though I soon must leave.
Three blind mice.
Hayes. Weep o'er his tomb.
When the rosy morn appearing.
Bennett, J. Why do you sigh?

Class C. Sacred.
God save the Queen.
Byrd, W. Non nobis.
Cooke. Amen.
How blest the man. (Ps.1).
Roseingrave. Jerusalem.
Clarke, Jer. Sanctus.
Berner. And now the sun's.
My soul with patience. (Ps.130).
Boyce. Glory be to God on high.
Hullah. O God that madest.
Hayes. Hallelujah. (8v.).
Spaeth. Jehovah, O Jehovah.
Cantate (Chant).
Freck. In sleep's serene oblivion.
Gloria in excelsis.
O celebrate Jehovah's. (Ps.107).
Hiller. Soft slumbers now.
Cirri. Haste Thee, O God.
Heaven and earth.
Palestrina. He hath filled.
Lord, how are they increased.
Hayes. I will praise the Name.
Byrd, W. I will be glad.
O Thou, to whose all-searching.
Nägeli. Who are these all stars.
Palestrina. Draw nigh unto.
Hayes. Not unto us, O Lord.
Let hymns of praise.
Rolle. Lord, now we part.
Carissimi. Make a joyful noise.
Glory to Thee my God this night.

Class C. Secular.
Kreutzer. The smith.
Past twelve o'clock. Let's have a peal. Row the boat.
Lidarti. St. Martin's bells.
De Call, L. How exquisite the feeling.
Cooke. Halcyon days.
Atterbury. With horns and hounds.
Marella. Half an hour past twelve.
Werner. The war-cry is sounding.
Rogers, B. Come, come, all noble souls.
Purcell. Fairest isle.
Webbe. To the old, long life.
Clad in springtime beauty.
Mornington. When for the world's repose.
Hilton. Come let us all.
Harrington. How sweet in the woodlands.
Webbe. Would you know by Celia's charms?
Paxton. How sweet, how fresh!
Well done! Come let us sing! White sand! Hot mutton pies!
Stevens. The cloud-capt towers.
Callcott. You gentleman of England.
Arne. Rule, Britannia.
Harrington. Yawning catch.

Class A was republished in 1868 by Longmans. A few original pieces were omitted, and the following were added, chiefly from Hullah's Vocal scores:
Sacred.
Lotti. Credo.
Haeser. O remember.
McMurdie. Who is the King? (Canon).
Klein, B. Like as the hart.
Zingarelli. Haste Thee, O God.
Spohr. O magnify the Lord.
Vervoille, C. To Thee my God.
Crotch. Methinks I hear.
Walmisley, T. A. Praise the Lord. (Canon).
Rolle. The Lord is King.
Palestrina. O Saviour of the world.
Hopkins, E. J. For God is the King. (Canon).
Gibbons, O. O Lord, increase.
Homilius. Pater noster.

Secular.
Bennett, Sterndale. Come live with me.
Weber. Music, when soft voices.
Tieck. Softly, softly, blow ye breezes.
Hullah. Song should breathe.
Horsley. See the chariot at hand.
Rock, M. Slender's ghost.
May, O. Come follow me.
Paxton. Hail, blushing goddess.
Pilkington. Rest, sweet nymph.
Smith, J. S. Hark, the hollow woods.
Stevens, R. J. S. When the toil of day.
Mornington. As it fell upon a day.

HULLAH, JOHN PYKE, 1812–1884. ed.
Vocal scores. Collection of John Hullah. Pub. by John W. Parker in monthly numbers,

one sacred and one secular, beginning on Jan.1, 1846.

Contents (from *Grove's Dictionary of music and musicians*, 1916, Vol.5, p.359–60):

I. Sacred:

Crotch. Motet. Methinks I hear. a 5.
Telemann. Motet. Amen. Blessing and glory. 2 choirs.
McMurdie. Canon. Quis est Rex? 4 in 2.
Häser. Hymn. Oh! remember. a 5.
Walmisley, T. F. Hymn. Lord of all Lords. a 6.
Palestrina. Gloria in excelsis. a 6.
Klein. Anthem. Like as the hart. a 4.
Leisring. Hymn. Redeemer! now. 2 choirs.
Gabrieli, G. Hymn. Benedictus. 3 choirs.
Bach, J. C. Chorale. O sing unto God! a 5.
Anon. Anthem. O Lord, grant the King. a 4.
Palestrina. Sacred madrigal. Why art Thou? a 5.
Graun. Motet. Lift up your heads. a 4.
Callcott. Canon. Thou, Lord, hast been. 4 in 2.
Palestrina. Collect. O Saviour of the world. a 4.
Lotti. Credo. a 4.
Aldrich. Anthem. O give thanks. a 6.
Schneider, F. Motet. All thy works. a 5.
Rolle. Motet. The Lord is King. a 4.
Byrd. Anthem. Sing unto God. a 5.
Croce. Motet. O that I had wings! a 4.
Walmisley, T. A. Canon. Praise the Lord. 4 in 2.
Carissimi. Motet. O be joyful in God. a 3.
Walmisley, T. A. Hymn. Hail gladdening Light. a 5.
Palestrina. Hymn. I will call. a 4.
Marcello. Psalm. We have heard. a 4.
McMurdie. Canon. Agne Dei. 4 in 2.
Weelkes. Anthem. All people, clap. a 5.
Croft. Anthem. O give thanks. 2 choirs.
Zingarelli. Motet. Haste Thee, O God. a 4.
Anon. Canon. Sing, sing aloud unto God. 3 in 1.
McMurdie. Canon. Hallelujah. 4 in 2.
Gibbons, O. Anthem. Hosanna. a 6.
Nares. Anthem. Blessed is he. a 5.
Spohr. Fugue. O Magnify. a 4.
De Gouy. Psalm. O God of Jacob. a 4.
Homilius. Pater Noster. a 4.
Palestrina. Motet. Merciful Lord. a 4.
Ives. Canon. Si Deus nobiscum. 3 in 1.
Häser. Motet. Put me not to rebuke. a 5.
[Nares]. Anthem. O Lord grant. a 5.
Tye. Gloria in excelsis. a 6.
Graun. Chorus. Thou art the King. a 4.
Walmisley, T. F. Canon. I will praise. 4 in 2.
Arne. Canon. Help me, O Lord. 3 in 1.
Foggia. Motet. I will magnify Thee. a 4.
Gibbons, O. Anthem. O Lord, increase my faith. a 4.
Bishop, John. Hymn. When brightly shines. a 4.
Allison. Psalm. Ye children. a 4.
Tallis. Anthem. Hear the voice and prayer. a 4.
Farrant. Anthem. Call to remembrance. a 4.
Lawes, W. Psalm. Sing to the King of Kings. a 3.
Willaert. Canon. Amen. 4 in 2.
Byrd. Anthem. Sing joyfully. a 6.

II. Secular.

Wilbye. Madrigal. Sweet honey-sucking bees. a 5.
Horsley. Glee. Cold is Cadwallo's tongue. a 5.
Weelkes. Madrigal. Three woodland nymphs. a 4.
Stevens. Glee. Sigh no more, ladies. a 5.
Callcott. Glee. O snatch me swift. a 5.
Stevens. Glee. O mistress mine. a 5.
Mendelssohn. Part-song. For the woods. a 4.
Wilbye. Madrigal. Fly love aloft. a 3.
Bennet, J. Madrigal. All creatures now. a 5.
Webbe. Glee. When winds breathe soft. a 4.
Wilson. Part-song. From the fair Lavinian. a 3.
Horsley. Glee. See the chariot. a 4.
Morley. Ballet. Now is the month of Maying. a 5.
Smith, J. S. Part-song. Hark the hollow. a 4.
Croce. Madrigal. Cynthia, thy song. a 5.
McMurdie. Glee. By the dark rolling waters. a 4.
Smith, J. S. Glee. Blest pair of sirens. a 5.
Hullah. Madrigal. Wake now, my love. a 6.
Arne. Part-song. Where the bee sucks. a 4.
Morley. Ballet. Fire, fire! my heart. a 5.
Gibbons, O. Madrigal. O that the learned poets. a 5.
Webbe. Glee. Glorious Apollo. a 5.
Webbe. Glee. Glorious Apollo. a 3.
Rogers, Sir J. L. Part-song. Hears not my Phillis. a 6.
Cooke. Glee. As now the shades of eve. a 4.
Callcott. Glee. Who comes so dark. a 3.
Hilton. Madrigal. Gifts of feature. a 3.
Wilbye. Madrigal. Flora gave me. a 5.
Horsley. Ode. Daughter of faith. 2 choirs.
Battishill. Glee. Amidst the myrtles. a 5.
May, O. Part-song. Come follow me. a 4.
Gibbons. Madrigal. The silver swan. a 5.
Hayes. Round. May doth every. a 3.
Hutchinson. Madrigal. Return, my lonely maid. a 4.
Ward. Madrigal. Die not, fond man. a 6.
Mornington. Madrigal. As it fell. a 4.
Stevens. Glee. O nightingale. a 5.
Corfe. Part-song. The yellow-haired laddie. a 4.
MacFarren. Part-song. There was a man. a 4.
Converso. Madrigal. When all alone. a 5.
Corfe. Part-song. How blithe each morn. a 4.
Walmisley, T. F. Glee. From flower to flower. a 5.
Spofforth. Glee. Health to my dear. a 4.
Bennet, J. Madrigal. Sing out, ye nymphs. a 4.
Bennett, W. S. Part-song. Come live with me. a 4.
Wilbye. Madrigal. Lady, when I behold. a 6.
Webbe. Elegy. The death of fair Adonis. a 5.
Rock. Glee. Beneath a churchyard yew. a 4.
Anon. Canon. Summer is acoming in. a 6.
Smith, J. S. Canzonet. Stay, shepherd, stay. a 4.
Pilkington. Part-song. Rest, sweet nymphs. a 4.
Danby. Glee. When Sappho tuned. a 3.
Tieck. Part-song. Softly, softly. a 4.
McMurdie. Round. The daisies peep. a 3.
Dowland. Part-song. Rest awhile. a 5.
Mozart. Round. Come follow me. a 3.
Este. Madrigal. How merrily we live. a 3.
Walmisley, T. F. Round. O'er the glad waters. a 4.
Hullah. Part-song. Song should breathe. a 4.
Byrd. Part-song. My mind to me. a 5.
Cobbold. Madrigal. With wreaths of rose. a 5.
Morley. Ballet. Sing we and chant it. a 5.
Anon. Ode. Daughter of heaven. a 4.

Hymn melodies for the whole year from the Sarum service-books and other ancient English sources, *see* Plainsong and Mediaeval Music Society. Hymn melodies for the whole year from the Sarum service-books and other ancient English sources.

The hymner, *see* Plainsong and Mediaeval Music Society. The hymner.

Hymnus "Te Deum laudamus," *see* Plainsong and Mediaeval Music Society. Hymnus "Te Deum laudamus."

Idelsohn, Abraham Zebi, 1882–1938, ed. Hebräisch-orientalischer Melodienschatz, *see* Hebräisch-orientalischer Melodienschatz.

Institut d'Estudis Catalans, Barcelona. Biblioteca de Catalunya. Departámento de Música. Publicaciones, *see* Barcelona. Biblioteca Central. Sección de Música. Publicaciones.

INSTITUT FRANÇAIS D'ATHÈNES. Collection. Série musicale. Athènes, 194? – .
v.1– .
Contents:
Vol.2. Barbogles, Marios. Aye Varvara; prélude symphonique (Merlier). 1948.
Vol.3. Skalkottas, Nikos. Quatre danses grecques (Merlier). 1948.

Institut für Musikforschung Regensburg, *see* Monumenta monodica medii aevi; Musica divina.

Institut für Musikwissenschaftliche Forschung zu Bückeburg, *see* Fürstliches Institut für Musikwissenschaftliche Forschung. Bückeburg.

INSTITUTA ET MONUMENTA. Pubblicati della Biblioteca Governativa e Civita di Cremona con il concorso scientifico della Scuola Universitaria di Paleografia Musicale. Ser.1. Monumenta. Cremona, Athenaeum Cremonense, 1954, [cop. 1953–].
v.1– .
Contents:
Vol.1. Petrucci, Ottaviano dei, pub. Le frottole nell' edizione principe. 1954. [cop.1953].
Vol.2. Tintori, Giampiero, ed. Sacre rappresentazioni, nel manoscritto 201 della Bibliothèque Municipale di Orléans. Edizione Fototipica, 1958.
Vol.3. Vivaldi, Antonio. La fide ninfa.

INSTITUTE OF MEDIAEVAL MUSIC. Publications. Brooklyn, N.Y., Institute of Mediaeval Music, 1957– .
v.1– .
Contents:
Publications of mediaeval musical manuscripts. (Veröffentlichungen mittelalterlicher Musikhandschriften).
Vol.1. Dittmer, Luther A. Facsimile reproduction of the manuscript Madrid 20486. 1957.
Vol.2. Dittmer, Luther A. Wolfenbüttel 1099. 1960.
Vol.3. Dittmer, Luther A. A central source of Notre-Dame polyphony. 1959.
Vol.4. Dittmer, Luther A. Paris 13521 and 11411. Facsimile introduction, index, and transcriptions from the manuscripts Paris, Bibl. Nat. Nouv. Acq. Frç. 13521. 1959.
Vol.5. Dittmer, Luther A. Worcester Add.68; Westminster Abbey 33327; Madrid. Bibl. Nac. 192. 1959.
Vol.6. Dittmer, Luther A. Oxford, Latin liturgical d 20 and Chicago 654 app. 1960.
Vol.7. Schütze, George C., Jr. Opera omnia Faugues. Complete edition of facsimiles. 1961.
Vol.8. Plamenac, Dragan, ed. Sevilla 5–I–43 and Paris, Nouv. Acq. Frç. 4379. 1963.
Vol.9. Carmina burana.
Vol.10–11. Dittmer, Luther. Firenze Biblioteca Mediceo-Laurenziana, Pluteo 29, I. Pt.1–2. Fasc.1–262, 263–476.

Collected works. (Gesamtausgaben).
Vol.1. Faugues, Guillaume. Collected works. Transcriptions of all of the compositions. Ed. by George C. Schütze. 1961.
Vol.2. Rener, Adam. Collected works. (Pt.1: Motets). Ed. by Robert Parker. 1964. (To be completed in 1 or 2 more volumes: the mass settings, etc.).
Vol.3. Goudimel, Claude. Collected works. (Vol.1. Premier livre des psaumes en forme de motets d'après l'édition de 1557. Transcription de Henri Gagnebin. 1967. Vol.9. Les 150 psaumes d'après les éditions de 1564 et 1565. Transcription de Pierre Pidoux. 1967.).
Vol.4. Cabezón, Antonio de. Collected works. (Vol.1. Duos, Kyries, Variations, and Finales. Ed. by Charles Jacobs. 1967.).

Musicological studies. (Wissenschaftliche Abhandlungen).
Vol.1. Dittmer, Luther A. Auszug aus The Worcester music fragments. 1955.
Vol.2. Schütze, George C. An introduction to Faugues. 1961.
Vol.3. Trumble, Ernest. Fauxbourdon, an historical survey. I. 1961.
Vol.4. Spiess, Lincoln. Historical musicology. 1963.
Vol.5. Levarie, Sizmund. Fundamentals of music. 1963.
Vol.6. Southern, Eileen. The Buxheim organ book. 1963.
Vol.7. Ludwig, Friedrich. Repertorium organorum recentioris et motetorum vetustissimi stili. Vol.I, 1.ed. Luther A. Dittmer. 2d. ed.
Vol.8. Jacobs, Charles. Tempo notation in Renaissance Spain.
Vol.9. Thomson, E. An introduction to Caron.

Musical theorists in translation.
Vol.1. Dittmer, Luther A. Anonymous IV. 1959.

Vol.2. Dittmer, Luther A. Robert de Handlo. 1959.
Vol.3. Cohen, Albert. Guillaume Gabriel Nivers. Treatise on the composition of music. 1961.
Vol.4. Smit-Vanrotte, Ericka. Constantyn Huygens. Gebruyck of Ongebruyck van 't orgel in de kerken der Vereenighde Nederlanden. Use and nonuse of the organ in the churches of the United Netherlands. 1964.
Vol.5. Nelson, Philip. Nicolas Bernier. Principles of composition. 1964. (Vol.4: original language with parallel pages for the English translation; other volumes in English only).

Instituto Español de Musicología, *see* Monumentos de la música española; Música hispana.

INSTITUTO INTERAMERICANO DE MUSICOLOGIA. Editorial Cooperativa Interamericana de Compositores.
Publicaciónes. Montevideo, Uruguay, 1941– . No.1– .
Contents:
No.1. Suffern, Carlos. Cuentos de niños. (Suite para piano). 1941.
No.2. Cluzeau Mortet, Luis. Mar de luna. (Canto y piano). 1941.
No.3. Engelbrecht, Richard. Obra para violin solo. (En tres partes). 1941.
No.4. Estrada, Carlos. Caminos tristes. (Canto y piano). (Op.6, No.1). 1941.
No.5. Ponce, Manuel M. Cuatro danzas mexicanas. (Piano). 1941.
No.6. Sás, Andrés. Cuatro melodias. (Canto). 1941.
No.7. Letelier Llona, Alfonso. 8 Canciones corales. (Para cuatro voces mixtas, a capella). 1941.
No.8. Santoro, Claudio. Sonata. (Violin solo). 1941.
No.9. Graetzer, Guillermo. Tres tocatas. (Piano). 1941.
No.10. Paz, Juan Cárlos. Tercera sonatina. (Piano).
No.11. Ascone, V. Montes de mi Queguay. (Voz, cuarteto de cuerdas y piano).
No.12. Ginastera, Alberto Evaristo. Impresiones de la puna. (Para flauta y cuarteto de cuerdas). 1942.
No.13. Carpio Valdés, Roberto. Suite para piano. 1942.
No.14. Koellreutter, H.-J. Música 1941. (Piano). 1942.
No.15. Iglesias Villoud, Héctor. Catamarqueña, de la serie "Provincianas." 1942.
No.16. Santórsola, Guido. Agonia, para contralto y orquesta. (Piano y canto). 1942.
No.17. Garcia Morillo, Roberto. Conjuros. (Suite para piano). Op.3. 1942.
No.18. Cosme, Luiz. Canção do Tio Barnabé. (Piano). 1943.
No.19. Ponce, Manuel M. Seis canciones arcaicas. (Canto y piano). 1943.
No.20. Posada Amador, Carlos. Cinco canciones medioevales. (Coro mixto a cappella). 1943.
No.21. Negrete Woolcock, Samuel. Ritmica. (Piano). 1943.
No.22. Castro, Sergio Federico de. Dos canciones. (Canto y piano). 1943.
No.23. Ponce, Manuel M. Tres poemas de Enrique Gonzales Martinez. (Canto y piano). 1943.
No.24. Tosar Errecart, Héctor A. Seis canciones. (Sobre "El Barrio de Santa Cruz" de José María Pemán). (Canto y piano). 1943.
No.25. Melo Gorigoytía, Héctor. Manchas de color. (Piano). 1943.
No.26. Engelbrecht, Richard. Tres poemas de Rainer Maria Rilke. (Para voz intermedia y piano). I. Pont du carrousel; II. Hora grave; III. Dóis en la Edad Media. 1943.
No.27. Paz, Juan Cárlos. Cuarta composicion en los doce tonos. (Violin solo). Op.37. 1943.
No.28. Ardévol, Jośe. Dos sonatas a tres. Sonata No.1. (oboe, clarinete y violonchelo); Sonata No.2. (dos flautas y viola). 1943.
No.29. Caturla, Alejandro Garcia. Dos canciones corales cubanas. (Voces mixtas a capella). I. El caballo blanco; II. Canto de los cafetales. 1943.
No.30. Letelier Llona, Alfonso. Cuatro canciones de cuna. (Voz de mujer y orquesta de cámara). (Partitura). 1943.
No.31. Perle, George. Sonata. (Viola solo). Op.12. 1944.
No.32. Valcárcel, Theodoro. Danza del combate. (Kachampa). (Piano). 1944.
No.33. Holzmann, Rudolph. Pequeña suite. (Estilizaciones sobre motives del folklore del Perú). (Piano). 1944.
No.34. Mendoza, Vicente T. Canto funeral. (A la memoria de un poeta). Cuarteto de cuerdas. (Partitura). 1944.
No.35. Amengual, René. Sonatina. (Piano). 1945.
No.36. Pisk, Paul Amadeus. Sonatina. (Death valley). (Piano).
No.37. Villa-Lobos, Heitor. O pião. (El trompo). Sobre um antigo tema popular infantil brasileiro. (Partitura para banda). 1944.
No.38. Orbón, Julián. Tocata. (Piano). 1945.
No.39. Garcia Morillo, Roberto. Variaciones 1944. (Piano). Op.13. 1945.
No.40. Ardévol, José. Tercera sonata a tres. (Dos trompetas y trombón). 1945.
No.41. Bosmans, Arturo. Sonata en colores. (Piano). 1944.
No.42. Hernández Gonzalo, Gisela. Suitè coral. (Coro mixto a 4 voces). 1945.
No.43. Santoro, Claudio. Dos canciones. (Canto y piano). Extraidas de los poemas de Oneyda Alvarenga, "A menina Boba." 1. A menina exausta; 2. Asa ferida. 1945.
No.44. Cámara, Juan Antonio. Suite. (Flauta, clarinete y fagot). 1945.
No.45. Ardévol, José. Cuarta sonata a tres. (Dos oboes y corno inglés). 1945.
No.46. Fleites, Virginia. Pequeña suite. (Piano). 1946.

No.47. Ardévol, José. Sonata No.3. (Piano). 1946.
No.48. Gramatges, Harold. Dúo en la bemol. (Flauta y piano). 1946.
No.49. Fuchs, Arno. Tres canciones. (Canto y piano). 1945.
No.50. Revueltas, Silvestre. Dos canciones. (Canto y piano). 1946.

Instituto Interamericano de musicologia. Montevideo, *see* Archivo de música colonial venezolana.

Instrumentalsätze vom Ende des XVI. bis Ende des XVII. Jahrhunderts, *see* Wasielewski, Joseph Wilhelm von. Instrumentalsätze vom Ende des XVI. bis Ende des XVII. Jahrhunderts.

Intavolatura di balli per sonar di liuto, *see* Radino, Giovanni Maria. Intavolatura di balli per sonar di liuto.

Intavolatura di liuto, *see* Crema, Joan Maria da. Intavolatura di liuto.

Intavolatura di liuto, *see* Gostena, Giovanni Battista dalla. Intavolatura di liuto.

Intavolatura di liuto, *see* Molinaro, Simone. Intavolatura di liuto.

Internationale Gesellschaft für Musikwissenschaft, *see* Documenta musicologica. 2. Reihe: Handschriften-Faksimiles.

Internationale Musikgesellschaft. Section de Paris. Publications, *see* Francisque, Antoine. Le trésor d'Orphée d'Antoine Francisque. (1600).

Introduction to the Gregorian melodies. Wagner, Peter Josef, *see* Plainsong and Mediaeval Music Society. Wagner, Peter Josef. Introduction to the Gregorian melodies.

IRUARRÍZAGA, LUIS, 1891–1927.
Obras completas. 1.ed. de voces solas. Madrid, Editorial Coculsa, 1945.
xxxi, 431p.

ISAAC, HEINRICH, ca.1450–1517.
Choralis Constantinus. Book III. Transcribed from the Formschneider first edition (Nürnberg, 1555) by Louise Cuyler. Ann Arbor, University of Michigan Press, 1950.
xp., score (456p.). illus., facsims. (University of Michigan publications. Fine arts. Vol.2).
For discantus, altus, tenor, and bassus.
The original edition is in 3 vols., 1550–1555; Vol.3 finished by Ludwig Senfl after the death of Isaac. Vols.1–2 were later published in 1898–1909 in Denkmäler der Tonkunst in Österreich. Vol.10, 32.
Settings of texts from the Gradual. "The content of the third book seems to fall . . . into four groups: (1) commons of the Saints and of the Blessed Virgin; (2) tracts; (3) second musical versions for a number of the propers which appeared also in the second book . . .; (4) settings of portions of ten offices which do not occur in either of the two previous books."–p.16.
Critical and analytical commentary: p.[1]–49.
Bibliography: p.51–54.

ISTITUTO ITALIANO PER LA STORIA DELLA MUSICA. Pubblicazioni. Roma, Istituto Italiano per la Storia della Musica, 1941– .
v.1– .
Contents:
1. Monumenti I.
 Vol.1–2. Gesualdo. Madrigali. Vol.1–2. Ed. F. Vatielli. 1942/43.
 Vol.3. Gesualdo. Madrigali. Vol.3. 1957.
 Monumenti II.
 Vol.1. Pomponio Nenna. Madrigali. Vol.1. Ed. E. Dagnino. 1942.
 Monumenti III.
 Vol.1. Carissimi, Giacomo. Historie ed oratori. Vol.I. (Historia di Job. Historia di Ezechia). 1951.
 Vol.2. Carissimi, Giacomo. Oratori. Vol. II. (Historia di Abraham et Isaac. Vir frugi et pater familias). 1953.
 Vol.3. Carissimi, Giacomo. Oratori. Vol. III. (Historia di Baltazar). 1955.
 Vol.4. Carissimi, Giacomo. Oratori. Vol. IV. (Iudicium Extremum). 1956.
 Vol.5. Carissimi, Giacomo. Oratori. Vol. V. (Historia divitis. [Dives malus]). 1958.
 Vol.6. Carissimi, Giacomo. Messe e motetti.
 Vol.7. Carissimi, Giacomo. Daniele.
2. Antologie e raccolte.
 Vol.1. Villanelle alla Napolitana di compositori baresi del secolo XVI, raccolte da Giovanni de Antiquis, a cura di S. A. Luciani. 1941.

ISTITUZIONI E MONUMENTI DELL' ARTE MUSICALE ITALIANA. Vol.1–7. Milano, Edizioni Ricordi, 1931–41.
7v. facsims., plates.
Includes music.
Vol.1–2. Benvenuti, Giacomo, ed. Andrea e Giovanni Gabrieli e la musica strumentale in San Marco. Tomo 1–2. 1931–32.
Vol.3. Fedeli, Vito, ed. Le cappelle musicali di Novara, dal secolo XVI a primordi dell' ottocento. 1933.
Vol.4. Fano, Fabio, ed. La camerata fiorentina: Vicenzo Galilei, 1520?–1591, la sua opera d'artista e di teorico come espressione di nuove idealità musicali. 1934.
Vol.5. Pannain, Guido, ed. L'oratorio dei Filippini e la scuola musicale di Napoli. Tomo 1. 1934.
Vol.6. Cesari, Gaetano. La musica in Cremona, nella seconda metà del secolo XVI e I primordi dell' arte Monteverdiana. 1939.
Vol.7. Platti, G. B. Le sonate per tastiera. Ed. by Torrefranco. 1941.

ISTITUZIONI E MONUMENTI DELL' ARTE MUSICALE ITALIANA. Nuova serie. Milano, G. Ricordi & C., [cop.1956–].
v.1– . facsims., plates.
Contents:
Vol.1. La cappella musicale del duomo di Milano. Disegno generale di Gaetano Cesari. Parte prima. Fabio Fano. Le origini e il primo maestro di cappella: Matteo da Perugia. Con tre appendici, trascrizioni musicali e un supplemento. 1956.
Vol.2. Torrefranco, Fausto. Giovanni Benedetto Platti e la sonata moderna. [cop. 1963].
Vol.3. Bossinensis, Franciscus. Le frottole per canto e liuto intabulate. 1964.
Unnumbered:
a. Pannain, Guido. L'oratorio dei Filippini e la scuola musicale di Napoli. Tomo II.
b. Ronga, Luigi. Gerolamo Frescobaldi.

Italia sacra musica, *see* Jeppesen, Knud. Italia sacra musica.

Die italienische Orgelmusik am Anfang des Cinquecento, *see* Jeppesen, Knud. Die italienische Orgelmusik am Anfang des Cinquecento.

JACOPO DA BOLOGNA, 14th century.
The music of Jacopo da Bologna, by W. Thomas Marrocco. Berkeley, University of California Press, 1954.
xi, 162p. (University of California publications of music, v.5).
"The music in modern notation" (score for 2–4 voices): p.30–117.
Bibliography: p.161–62.

JENAER LIEDERHANDSCHRIFT.
Die Jenaer Liederhandschrift; mit Unterstützung der Königlich Sächsischen Gesellschaft der Wissenschaften, hrsg. von Dr. Georg Holz . . . Dr. Franz Saran . . . und Dr. Eduard Bernoulli . . . Leipzig, C. L. Hirschfeld, 1901.
2v.
Each volume has also special title page.
With music.
Contents:
Bd.1. Getreuer Abdruck des Textes, hrsg. von Georg Holz.
Bd.2. Übertragung, Rhythmik und Melodik, bearb. von Eduard Bernoulli und Franz Saran. Anhang: Melodien aus der Colmarer Handschrift in Übertragung.

JENAER LIEDERHANDSCHRIFT.
Die Jenaer Liederhandschrift. Reprint. Hildesheim, Georg Olms Verlagsbuchhandlung, 1966.

JENAER LIEDERHANDSCHRIFT.
Der Jenaer Liederhandschrift. [Jena, F. Strobel, 1896].
4p.L., facsim.: [266] p.
"Vorbericht" signed: K. K. Miller.
Issued in portfolio.
140 copies printed, of which 30 are printed on one side of leaf only.
"Photographische Aufnahme und Wiedergabe in Lichtdruck von der graphischen Kunstanstalt von Meisenbach, Reiffarth & Co., Berlin."

Jenkins, John, 1592–1678. Fancies and ayres, *see* The Wellesley edition. No.1, 10.

JEPPESEN, KNUD, 1892– . ed.
Balli antichi veneziani per cembalo. Copenhagen, Wilhelm Hansen, 1962.
27p.

JEPPESEN, KNUD, 1892– . ed.
La flora, arie & antiche italiane. Copenhagen, Hansen, 1949.
3v.
"Survey of . . . the Italian Belcanto from . . . about the year 1600 until . . . the middle of the 18th century."
For voice and piano; Vol.3 has also duets for unspecified voices.
Each volume has text consisting of notes on the composers and the compositions in Italian, English, and German and translations of the song texts into English by Evelyn Heepe and into German by Rita Ejlersen. Vol.1 has also a preface in Italian, English, and German.
Vol.1 contains compositions by Cherubino Busatti, Giovanni Buzzoleni, Giulio Caccini, Vincenzio Calestani, Francesco Cavalli, Giacomo Carissimi, Girolamo Frescobaldi, Marco da Gagliano, G. F. Händel, Luigi Manzia, Claudio Monteverdi, Nicolò Porpora, Bernardo Pasquini, Carlo Pietragrua, Alessandro Scarlatti, and Alessandro Stradella.
Vol.2 contains compositions by Tomasso Albinoni, Emanuele d'Astorga, G. P. Berti, Gerardo Biancosi, Cherubino Busatti, Giovanni Buzzoleni, Andrea Falconieri, Marco da Gagliano, G. F. Händel, G. da Gagliano, Francesco Mancini, Alessandro Melani, Claudio Monteverdi, Jacopo Peri, Martino Pesenti, Bernardo Pasquini, G. A. Perti, Nicolò Porpora, Rafaello Rontani, G. F. Sances, Barbara Strozzi, Alessandro Scarlatti, Filippo Vitali, and F. M. Zaneti.
Vol.3 contains compositions by Giulio Caccini, Vincenzio Calestani, Giacomo Carissimi, Francesco Cavalli, Antonio Cifra, G. P. Colonna, Francesco Durante, Andrea Falconieri, Girolamo Frescobaldi, G. da Gagliano, Marco da Gagliano, G. F. Händel, Benedetto Marcello, Claudio Monteverdi, G. F. Sances, Filippo Vitali, and Antonio Vivaldi.

JEPPESEN, KNUD, 1892– . ed.
Italia sacra musica. Musiche corali italiane sconoscuite della prima metà del cinquecento. Raccolte ed edite da Knud Jeppesen. Copenhagen, Wilhelm Hansen, [cop.1962–].
v.1– .
Contents:
Vol.1. Unknown Italian cathedral music of the

early 16th century. 1962. (Contains compositions by Gasparo Alberti, Giuliano Buonaugurio da Tivoli, Costanzo Festa, Iacopo Fogliano, Hieronimo Maffoni, Mutus, Laurus Patavus, Fra Petrus de Ostia, Franciscus Seraphin, Giovanni Spataro, and Philipp Verdelot).

Vol.2. Unknown Italian cathedral music of the early 16th century. 1962. (Contains compositions by Gasparo Alberti, Rufino Bartolucci da Assisi, Antonio Benincasa, Giuliano Buonaugurio da Tivoli, Marchetto Cara, Simon da Ferrara, Costanzo Festa, Sebastiano Festa, Ludovico Fogliano, Filippus de Lurano, Hieronimo Maffoni, and Don Michel).

JEPPESEN, KNUD, 1892– . ed.
Die italienische Orgelmusik am Anfang des Cinquecento. Die "Recerchari, Motetti, Canzoni, Libro primo" des Marco Antonio (Cavazzoni) da Bologna (1523) in Verbindung mit einer Auswahl aus den "Frottole Intabulate da Sonare Organi," des Andrea Antico da Montona (1517), eingeleitet und hrsg. von Knud Jeppesen. Kopenhagen, E. Munksgaard, 1943.
130, 82p. incl. facsims.
Music transcribed into modern notation, 82p.
6 numbers from "Frottole Intabulate da Sonare Organi" (organ transcriptions), and the complete reproduction of "Recerchari . . . ", which contains 8 pieces.

Jeppesen, Knud, 1892– , ed. Der kopenhagener Chansonnier, *see* Copenhagen Kongelige Bibliotek. Mss. (Thottske Samling 291[8]). Der kopenhagener Chansonnier. .

JEPPESEN, KNUD, 1892– . ed.
Die mehrstimmige italienische Laude um 1500; das 2. Laudenbuch des Ottaviano dei Petrucci (1507) in Verbindung mit einer Auswahl mehrstimmiger Lauden aus dem 1. Laudenbuch Petrucci's (1508) und aus verschiedenen gleichzeitigen Manuskripten, eingeleitet und hrsg. von dr. Knud Jeppesen . . . die Gedichte philologisch revidiert und mit einem Glossar versehen von dr. Viggo Brondal . . . Leipzig, Breitkopf & Härtel; Kopenhagen, Levin & Munksgaard, 1935.
xcviiip., 1L., incl. facsims. (music); 168p. (music).
Title vignette.
"Herausgegeben auf Kosten des Carlsbergfonds."
Transcriptions of 98 compositions, with words in Italian or Latin, chiefly from Laude, Libro secondo. Impressum Venetiis per Octauianum Petrutium, MDVII, and Laude, Libro primo/ In. Dam̃onis/ Curarum dulce lenimen. Impressum Venetiis per Octauianum Petrutium, MDVIII. Both books are preserved in the Biblioteca Colombina, Seville. (Catálogo, 1888, II, p.239; IV, p.229). cf. p.xxv, [lv] – lix.

Jeune, Claude le, *see* Le Jeune, Claude.

JOAQUIM, MANUEL. ed.
O cancioneiro musical e poetico da Biblioteca Públia Hortênsia. Com prólogo, transcrição e notas, de Manuel Joaquim. Coimbra, Edição Subsiciada pelo Instituto Para a Alta Cultura, 1940.
201p.
"A presente edição á de 500 exemplares."

The John Bull virginal book, *see* Tisdall, William. Complete keyboard works.

Joseph I, Holy Roman Emperor, 1678–1711. Werke, *see* Musikalische Werke der Kaiser Ferdinand III, Leopold I, und Joseph I.

Josquin de Près, *see* Deprès, Josquin.

Kaller, Ernst, ed. Liber organi, *see* Liber organi.

DER KAMMERCHOR. Hrsg. von Alfred Krings. Köln, Arno Volk Verlag, 195? – .
5v.
Vol.1 ed. by P. Wehrle and A. Krings.
Contents:
Vol.1. Französische Chansons. (Josquin des Prèz, Clément Jannequin, Claudin de Sermisy, Passereau, Pierre Certon, Guillaume Costeley, Orlando di Lasso). French words.
Vol.2. Deutsche Lieder. (Orlando di Lasso, Alexander Utendal, Antonius Scandellus, Leonhard Meldart, Leonhard Lechner, Hans Leo Hassler). German words.
Vol.3. Italienische Madrigale. (Luca Marenzio, Giovanni Pierluigi da Palestrina, Orlando di Lasso, Giovanni Gastoldi, Giovanni Gabrieli, Gesualdo da Venosa). Italian and German words.
Vol.4. Englische Madrigale. (Thomas Morley, John Wilbye, Thomas Weelkes, John Ward). English and German words.
Vol.5. Musik und Wien. (Matthäus le Maistre, Jacob Meiland, Johannes Eccard, Antonio Scandello, Christoph Demantius). German words.

KAMMERSONATEN. Ausgewählte Werke alter Musik für ein Soloinstrument mit Begleitung. Leipzig, Breitkopf & Härtel, 1928– .
No.1– .
Contents:
No.1. Abel, C. F. Sonate in B dur. Für Violine und Klavier. Hrsg. von Fritz Piersig.
No.2. Abel, C. F. Op.13, No.3. Sonate in A dur. Für Violine und Klavier. Hrsg. von Fritz Piersig.
No.3. Bach, Johann Christian. Op.10, No.4. Sonate in A dur. Für Violine und Klavier. Hrsg. von Fritz Piersig.
No.4. Bach, Johann Christian. Op.16, No.1. Sonate in D dur. Für Violine und Klavier. Hrsg. von Fritz Piersig.
No.5. Telemann, G. P. Sonate in H moll. (Tafelmusik 1733, I, Nr.5). Für Flöte mit Generalbass. Bearbeitung für Flöte und Cembalo (Klavier). Violoncell ad lib. von Max Seiffert.

No.6. Bach, C. Ph. Em. Sonate in C dur. Für Gambe und unbezifferten Bass. Bearbeitung für Violoncell (Violine) und Klavier von Paul Klengel. (Wotquenne-Katalog. No.136).
No.7. Bach, J. Ph. Em. Sonate in D dur. Für Gambe und unbezifferten Bass. Bearbeitung für Violoncell (Violine) und Klavier von Paul Klengel. (Wotquenne-Katalog. No.137).
No.8. Telemann, G. P. Sonate in G moll. (Tafelmusik 1733, III, Nr.5). Für Oboe mit Generalbass. Bearbeitung für Oboe und Cembalo (Klavier), Fagott (oder Violoncell) ad lib. von Max Seiffert.
No.9. Quantz, Joh. Joachim. Sonate in E moll. Für Flöte und Klavier. Bearb. von Heinz Schreiter.
No.10. Graun, Joh. Gottlieb. 1. Sonate in B dur. Für Viola und Cembalo (Klavier) mit Violoncell. Bearbeitung von Hellmuth Christian Wolff.
No.11. Graun, Joh. Gottlieb. 2. Sonate in F dur. Für Viola und Cembalo (Klavier) mit Violoncell. Bearbeitung von Hellmuth Christian Wolff.
No.12. Bach, Joh. Chr. Friedr. Sonata und Cembalo Concertate. Flöte und Violine. Hrsg. von W. Hinnenthal.
No.13. Telemann, G. P. Sonata in C moll. Violin (Oboe) Solo. Für Violine (Oboe) und Cembalo (Klavier) mit Violoncell ad lib. Bearb. von W. Hinnenthal.
No.14. Krebs, Johann Ludwig. Fantasie für Oboe und Orgel. (2 manual Cembalo mit Pedal) oder Klavier (Cembalo ohne Pedal). Klavier (Cembalo)- Übertragung und hrsg. von Joh. Nep. David.
No.15. Schraffrath, Christoph. Sonate in A dur. Für obligates Cembalo und Viola da Gamba (oder Klavier und Violoncell). Bearb. und hrsg. von Hans Neemann.
No.16. Vivaldi, Antonio. Drei Sonaten (D moll, C dur, F moll). Für Violine und Continuo (Klavier) mit Violoncell. Hrsg. von Willi Hillemann.
No.17. Vivaldi, Antonio. Sonate in G moll. Für Violine und Cembalo (Klavier) mit Violoncell ad lib. Hrsg. von Günther Hausswald.

Kammer-Sonaten für Violine und Pianoforte des 17. und 18. Jahrhunderts, *see* Moffat, Alfred Edward. Kammer-Sonaten für Violine und Pianoforte des 17. und 18. Jahrhunderts.

DIE KANTATE, hrsg. von Rudolf Ewerhart. Köln, Edmund Bieler, 1957– .
No.1– .
Contents:
No.1. Händel, Georg Friedrich. O qualis de coelo sonus. Sopran, 2 Violinen und Basso Continuo.
No.2. Händel, Georg Friedrich. Coelestis dum spirat aura. Sopran, 2 Violinen und B.C.
No.3. Campra, André, Domine, Dominus noster. Sopran, Flöte (Viol) und B.C.
No.4. Leo, Leonardo. Salve Regina. Sopran, 2 Violinen und B.C.
No.5. Scarlatti, Alessandro. Infirmata vulnerata. Alt, 2 Violinen und B.C.
No.6. Fiocco, Joseph Hector. Lamentatio secunda. Sopran, Violoncello (Viola da Gamba) und B.C.
No.7. Händel, Georg Friedrich. Ah, che troppo ineguali. Sopran, Streicher und B.C.
No.8. Werner, Gregor Joseph. Salve, Regina. Bass, 2 Violinen und B.C.
No.9. Bencini, Pietro Paolo. Jesu redemptor omnium. Sopran-Solo, gemischt Chor und B.C.
No.10. Couperin, François. Leçons de ténèbres. Troisième leçon. 2 Soprane und B.C.
No.11. Caldara, Antonio. Haec est regina virginum. Sopran, 2 Violinen und B.C.
No.12. Galuppi, Baldassare. Rapida cerva, fuge. Sopran, Streicher und B.C.
No.13. Fiocco, Joseph Hector. Lamentatio prima. Sopran, 2 Violoncelli (Viola da Gamba) und B.C.

Die Kantorei der Spätgotik, *see* Moser, Hans Joachim. Die Kantorei der Spätgotik.

KASTNER, MACÁRIO SANTIAGO. ed.
Alt-italienische Versetten. London, Schott & Co. p.1– .
Verses for keyboard in all church modes.

KASTNER, MACÁRIO SANTIAGO. ed.
Cravistas portuguezes. Les clavecinistes portugais. Old Portuguese keyboard music. Alte portugiesische Meister. Cembalo/Piano. Revus et édités par/ Revised and ed. by/ Bearb. und hrsg. von M. S. Kastner. Mainz, B. Schott's Söhne; London, Schott & Co., Ltd., [etc., etc., cop.1935].
2v. (Edition Schott 2382, 4050).
Contains compositions by Pedro de Araújo, de Sousa Carvalho, M. R. Coelho, Frei Jacinto, and Carlos Seixas.

KASTNER, MACÁRIO SANTIAGO. ed.
Silva iberica. De música para tecla de los siglos XVI, XVII y XVIII. Musik für Tasteninstrumente des XVI., XVII., und XVIII. Jahrhunderts aus Italien, Portugal, und Spanien. Easy keyboard music of the XVI., XVII., and XVIII. century from Italy, Portugal, and Spain. Bearb. und hrsg. von M. S. Kastner. Mainz, B. Schott's Söhne; London, Schott & Co., Ltd., [cop.1954].
3p.L., 29p.
Contains compositions by Antonio de Cabezón, João de Sousa Carvalho, Fr. Agostinho da Cruz, Fr. Manuel de Santo Elias, Freixanet, José Lidon, Alonso Mudarra, Fr. Berm. eu de Olagué, Bernardo Pasquini, Lucas Puxol, Antonio Valente, and Yepes.

Das katholische deutsche Kirchenlied, *see* Bäumker, Wilhelm. Das katholische deutsche Kirchenlied.

KELLER, HERMANN, 1885– . ed.
Achtzig Choralvorspiele deutscher Meister des

17. und 18. Jahrhunderts. Zum gottesdienstlichen Gebrauch. Hrsg. von Hermann Keller. Leipzig, C. F. Peters, 1937.
3p.L., 123p. (On cover: Edition Peters. No. 4448).
Contains compositions by J. F. Alberti, Andreas Armsdorf, Johann Christoph Bach, Johann Michael Bach, J. S. Bach, Georg Böhm, J. H. Buttstedt, Dietrich Buxtehude, J. K. F. Fischer, G. F. Kaufmann, J. E. Kindermann, J. L. Krebs, Johann Krieger, Johann Pachelbel, Michael Praetorius, Heinrich Scheidermann, Samuel Scheidt, A. N. Vetter, J. G. Walter, Matthias Weckmann, and F. W. Zachau.

KELLER, HERMANN, 1885– . ed.
Orgelvorspiele. Alter Meister in allen Tonarten. 32 Präludien, Präambeln, Toccaten von J. S. Bach, Händel, J. K. F. Fischer, Frescobaldi und anderen Meistern, zum Gebrauch im Gottesdienst und bei kirchlichen Feiern, hrsg. von Hermann Keller. Organ preludes by old masters in all keys . . . Basel, New York, [etc.], Bärenreiter, [1961].
49, [3] p. (Bärenteiter-Ausgabe. 668).
Contains compositions by J. S. Bach, L. Boyvin, J. F. Dandrieu, J. K. F. Fischer, G. Frescobaldi, G. F. Händel, J. L. Krebs, W. A. Mozart, A. Raison, M. Schildt, J. Titelouze, and J. G. Walther.

Keyboard music of the Baroque and Rococo, *see* Georgii, Walter. Keyboard music of the Baroque and Rococo.

Kirchengesänge der berühmtesten älteren italienischen Meister, *see* Tucher, Gottlieb, *Freiherr von.* Kirchengesänge der berühmtesten älteren italienischen Meister.

KIRCHENMUSIK DER DARMSTÄDTER MEISTER DES BAROCK. Berlin, C. Merseburger, [cop. 1955–].
v.1– .
Editor, v.1–4: Friedrich Noack; v.5–6: Elisabeth Noack.
Contents:
Vol.1. Graupner, Christoph. Jesu, führe meine Seele. 1955.
Vol.2. Graupner, Christoph. Wie bald hast du gelitten. 1955.
Vol.3. Briegel, Wolfgang Carl. Und es erhub sich ein Streit. 1955.
Vol.4. Briegel, Wolfgang Carl. Fahre auf die Höhe. 1955.
Vol.5. Briegel, Wolfgang Carl. Psalm 32. Wohl dem, dem die Übertretung vergeben ist. Kantate für Chor, Streicher und Basso Continuo. 1962.
Vol.6. Briegel, Wolfgang Carl. Mache dich auf, werde licht. Kantate für Chor, Streicher und Basso Continuo. 1962.

KIRCHENMUSIKALISCHES INSTITUT DER EVANGELISCH-LUTHERISCHEN LANDESKIRCHE IN SACHSEN am Landeskonservatorium der Musik, Leipzig. Veröffentlichungen . . . [Nr.] 1–3. Leipzig, Breitkopf & Härtel, [1927–32].
3 nos. facsims., illus., music.
Contents:
No.1, 3. Böhm, Georg. Sämtliche Werke. Bd.1–2. [1927–32]. Bd.1. Klavier- und Orgelwerke. Bd.2. Vokalwerke.
No.2. Martienssen, C. A. Die individuelle Klaviertechnik. 1930.

Klaviermusik des 17. und 18. Jahrhunderts, *see* Herrmann, Kurt. Klaviermusik des 17. und 18. Jahrhunderts.

De klaviersonate met vioolbegeleiding in het parijsche muziekleven ten tijde van Mozart, *see* Reeser, Eduard. De klaviersonate met vioolbegeleiding in het parijsche musiekleven ten tijde van Mozart.

KLEIN, JOHN, 1915– . ed.
The first four centuries of music for the organ from Dunstable to Bach (1370–1749), by John Klein. New York, Associated Music Publishers, Inc., [cop.1948].
2v.
Contains compositions by Johann Alberti, Jean Baptiste d'Anglebert, Andreas Armsdorff, Johann Christoph Bach, Johann Michael Bach, Adriano Banchieri, Georg Böhm, Nikolaus Bruhns, John Bull, Johann Heinrich Buttstedt, Dietrich Buxtehude, William Byrd, Antonio de Cabezón, Girolamo Cavazzoni, Louis Nicolas Clérambault, François Couperin, Jean Français Dandrieu, Josquin Des Près, Girolamo Diruta, Guillaume Dufay, John Dunstable, Fasolo, J. Caspar Ferdinand Fischer, Girolamo Frescobaldi, Jakob Froberger, Andrea Gabrieli, Giovanni Gabrieli, Orlando Gibbons, Nicolas Gigault, Nicolas de Grigny, Hans Leo Hassler, Paul Hofhaimer, Heinrich Isaac, George Friederich Kaufmann, Johann Kaspar Kerll, Johann Erasmus Kindermann, Johann Krieger, Nicolas Lebègue, Vincent Lübeck, Luzzasco Luzzaschi, Pierre du Mage, Louis Marchand, Claudio Merulo, Georg Muffat, G. Gabriel Nivers, Anthoni van Noordt, Jakob Obrecht, Joannes Okeghem, Johann Pachelbel, G. Pierluigi da Palestrina, Michael Praetorius, Henry Purcell, André Raison, John Redford, Jan Adams Reinken, François Roberday, Tomás de Santa María, Heinrich Scheidemann, Samuel Scheidt, Arnolt Schlick, Ludwig Senfl, Delphin Strungk, Jan Peeters Sweelinck, Jean Titelouze, Franz Tunder, Andreas Nikolaus Vetter, Johann Gottfried Walther, Matthias Weckmann, Adrian Willaert, Friedrich Zachau, and Domenico Zipoli.

KÖHLER, LOUIS, i.e., Christian Louis Heinrich, 1820–1886. ed.
Les maîtres du clavecin (Klavier-Musik aus alter Zeit), revus, doigtés et accentués. Bd.I (Heft 1–6); Bd.II (Heft 7–13). Braunschweig, Litolff, [187?].
2v.
Contents:

Heft 1.
Bach, W. Fr. Capriccio, Fugue, Sonate.
Bach, Phil. Em. Allegro, La xenophone.
Bach, Joh. Christ. Fr. Rondo.
Heft 2.
Bach, Joh. Christ. 2 Sonates.
Bach, Joh. Ernst. Fantaisie et Fugue.
Heft 3.
Graun, Carl Heinr. Gigue.
Krebs, Joh. Ludwig. Partita, No.2; Partita, No.6.
Nichelmann, Christoph. La gaillarde, La tendre, Sarabande, Gigue.
Wagenseil, Christoph. Sonate.
Heft 4.
Froberger, Joh. Fried. 2 Toccatas.
Haessler, Joh. Wilh. Sonate.
Kuhnau, Joh. Suite No.3, Sonate.
Muffat, Gottlieb. 2 Menuets et Courante, Gigue, Allegro spirituoso.
Heft 5.
Benda, Georg. Sonate No.5, Largo, Presto.
Eberlin, Joh. Ernst. Prélude et Fugue.
Mattheson, Joh. Suite No.5. 4 Gigues, Allemande, Courante, Gigue, Sarabande avec 3 Variations.
Murschhauser, Franz Xaver. Aria pastoralis variata.
Heft 6.
Hasse, Joh. Ad. Sonate Op.7, Allegro.
Kirnberger, Joh. Phil. Fugue à 2 voix, Fugue à 3 voix, Courante, Gavotte, Gigue, Allegro für die Singuhr.
Marpurg, Fried. Wilh. Capriccio Op.1, Prélude et Capriccio.
Rolle, Heinr. Joh. Sonate.
Heft 7.
Cherubini, Luigi. Sonate.
Durante, Francesco. Studio.
Frescobaldi, Girolamo. Correnti, Canzone.
Galuppi, Balthasar. Sonate.
Martini, *Padre* Giov. Battista. Gavotte, Ballet, Prélude, Fugue et Allegro.
Heft 8.
Grazioli, Giov. Battista. Sonate.
Lully, Giov. Battista. Allemande, Sarabande et Gigue.
Matielli, Giov. Ant. Gigue, Adagio, Allegro.
Paradisi, Pietro Dom. 2 Sonates.
Rossi, Michel Angelo. Andantino, Allegro.
Heft 9.
Porpora, Nicolò. 2 Fugues.
Sacchini, Ant. Sonate.
Sarti, Gius. Allegro.
Scarlatti, Aless. Fugue.
Turini, Ferd. Presto, Sonate No.6.
Zipoli, Dom. Prélude, Courante, Sarabande, Gigue.
Heft 10.
Couperin, Franç. La favorite, La fleurie ou la tendre Nanette, La ténébreuse, La bandoline, Les agréments, La bersan, L'Ausonienne, Les charmes, Le bavolet flottant, Les moissonneurs, Le réveil-matin, Les pavillons, Les bergeries.
Heft 11.
Rameau, Jean Phil. Deux gigues en rondeaux, Le rappel des oiseaux, Les tendres plaintes, 2 Menuets, L'Egyptienne, La poule, La livre, L'agacante, La timide, Gavotte et Variations, Musette, Tambourin.
Heft 12.
Chambonnières, J. Champion de. La rare, Courante, Sarabande, La lourense.
Dumont, Henri. Suite de pièces.
Loeilly, Jean Baptiste. Suite.
Méhul, Et. Henri. Sonate Op.1, No.3.
Schobert. Minuetto, Allegro molto.
Heft 13.
Arne, Thomas Aug. Sonate No.3.
Bull, John. The king's hunting jigg.
Bird, William. Prélude et The carman's whistle.

KOMITAS KEVORKIAN, *Vartabed*, 1869–1935.
Collected works. Moscow, State Music Publishers, 1960– .
v.1– .
Title page in Armenian. Added title page in Russian.
Contents:
Vol.1. Songs (Voice/Piano). Armenian Text. 1960.

Kompositionen für Orgel aus dem 16., 17., und 18. Jahrhundert, *see* Commer, Franz. Compositionen für Orgel aus dem 16., 17., und 18. Jahrhundert.

Königlich Sächsische Gesellschaft der Wissenschaften, *see* Jenaer Liederhandschrift. Die Jenaer Liederhandschrift.

KÖNIGLICHE AKADEMIE DER KÜNSTE. Berlin. Musicalische Section. Auswahl vorzüglicher Musik-Werke in gebundener Schreibart von Meistern alter und neuer Zeit . . . zur Beförderung des höhern Studiums der Musik . . . No.1–48. 1–16, Lief. Berlin, T. Trautwein, 1835–41.
48 nos. and appendix.
Contents (from *Grove's Dictionary of music and musicians*, 1916, Vol.1, p.132–33):
No.1. Graun. Fugue, Tu Rex.
No.2. Fasch. Fugue, Meine Zunge.
No.3. J. Haydn. Fugue from 4tet, F min.
No.4. Handel. Fugue, Halleluja.
No.5. Naumann. Fugue, Di l'alimenta.
No.6. W. F. Bach. Fugue for organ, G minor.
No.7. C. P. E. Bach. Fugue, Auf, dass wir.
No.8. Fesca. Fugue, Lobet seinen Namen.
No.9. Kirnberger. Fugue for piano, B flat.
No.10. Fux. Canon, Kyrie.
No.11. J. S. [J. C.] Bach. Fig. Choral. Ich lasse.
No.12. Clementi. Fugue for piano in F.
No.13. Keiser. Fugue, Gott ist offenbaret.
No.14. Keiser. Kyrie.
No.15. Marpurg. Fugue for piano, D minor.
No.16. J. C. Bach. Fugue. 2 choirs. Durch denselbigen.
No.17. Graun. Christe.
No.18. Telemann. Fugue for piano, A minor.
No.19. Hasse. Fugue, Christe.
No.20. M. Haydn. Fugue, Quam olim.
No.21. Mozart. Fugue for piano in C.
No.22. H. Schütz. Motet, Was betrübet.
No.23. Zelter. Fig. Choral, Ewiger Lob.

No.24. Pachelbel. Fugue for organ in C.
No.25. F. Schneider. Kyrie.
No.26. Spohr. Fugue, Lasst uns.
No.27. Kelz. Fugue for 4tet in C.
No.28. Palestrina. Motet (a 6), Tu es Petrus.
No.29. Horsley. Canon, Sanctus and Hosanna.
No.30. Pasterwitz. Fugue for organ in B flat.
No.31. Salieri. Benedictus, etc.
No.32. Rungenhagen. Fugue, Tu ad dexteram.
No.33. Albrechtsberger. Fugue for organ, B flat.
No.34. Homilius. Motet, Hilf Herr.
No.35. Jommelli. Fugue, Tune imponent.
No.36. Gassmann. Fugue for 4tet, A minor.
No.37. Marcello. Fugue, Mai non turbarsi.
No.38. Klein. Ave Maria.
No.39. Henning. Fugue for 4tet in C.
No.40. Vierling. Fugue, Timentibus.
No.41. Caldara. Fugue, Et in saecula.
No.42. Frescobaldi. Fugue for organ (4 subj.).
No.43. Astorga. Eja Mater.
No.44. Reissiger. Fughetta, Cum sancto.
No.45. M. G. Fischer. Introduction and Fugue for organ.
No.46. J. A. Perti. Motet, O d'immenso.
No.47. G. Harrer. Fugue, Halleluja.
No.48. Le Bégue. Fugue for piano, in F.
Some copies have an Appendix:
Durante. Aria, Ingemisco.
J. S. Bach. Aria, Agnus.
Steffani. Duet, Occhi perche.
Pergolesi. Salve Regina.
Handel. O my Irene. (Theodora).
C. P. E. Bach. Chorus and air. (Israeliten).
Reichardt. Duet and Chorus. (Morgengesang).
—— Solo and chorus. (Morgengesang).
Hasse. Aria, Pietà Signore.
Naumann. Scena. (Dividde pen).
Leo. Trio, Dominus.
F. Feo. Gratias and Deux Pater.

Konstanz, Hans von, *see* Buchner, Hans (von Constanz).

Der Kopenhagener Chansonnier, *see* Copenhagen Kongelige Bibliotek. Mss. (Thottske Samling 291[8]). Der Kopenhagener Chansonnier.

Kraus, Eberhard, ed. Cantantibus organis, *see* Cantantibus organis.

KREBS, JOHANN LUDWIG, 1713–1780.
Gesammt-Ausgabe der Tonstücke für Orgel von Carl Geissler. Magdeburg, Heinrichshofen, [18?–].
4 Abt.
Contents:
Abt.I. Grössere Praeludien und Fugen, Fantasien, Toccaten, etc. Heft 1, 2, 3, 4, 5, 6, 7, 8, 9, 10, 11.
Abt.II. Trios. Heft 1, 2, 3, 4, 5.
Abt.III. Kürzere Choral-Vorspiele. Übungesstücke, Fuguetten, Choräle, etc. Heft 1, 2, 3, 4, 5.
Abt.IV. Choräle für die Orgel und ein 2tes Instrument. Heft 1, 2.

KREBS, JOHANN LUDWIG, 1713–1780.
... Orgelwerke. Ausgewählte und hrsg. von Walter Zöllner. Leipzig, C. F. Peters, n.d.
2p.L., 70p. (On cover: Edition Peters. No.4179).

KRIEGER, JOHANN PHILIPPE, 1649–1725.
Ausgewählte Orgelstücke. Kritisch durchgesehen und für den praktischen Gebrauch bearb. von Max Seiffert. Leipzig, Kistner & Siegel, 1930.
p.1– .

Krings, Alfred, ed. Der Kammerchor, *see* Der Kammerchor.

Kroyer, Theodor, 1873–1945, ed. Publikationen älterer Musik, *see* Publikationen älterer Musik.

Kungliga Musikaliska Akademien. Monumenta musicae svecicae, *see* Monumenta musicae svecicae.

Die Kunst des Bachsen Geschlechts, *see* Bach Family. Die Kunst des Bachsen Geschlechts.

LALANDE, MICHEL RICHARD DE, 1657–1726.
Motets. Avec un discours sur la vie et les oeuvres de l'autheur. Gravé par L. Huë. Paris, Se vend chez Boivin, 1729.
20v.
For chorus and orchestra, principally SATBB. with 2 violins and figured bass.
Each volume contains an early and a late motet, with separate paginations.
Contents:
[1. Livre]. Benedictus Dominus, Deus meus. Confitebor Tibi.
2. Livre. O filii et filiae. Cantate Domino.
3. Livre. Regina coeli laetare. Miserere mei Deus.
4. Livre. Deus in adjutorium meum intende. Lauda Jerusalem Dominum.
5. Livre. Dixit Dominus Domino meo. Vsque quo Domine.
6. Livre. Te Deum laudamus. Beati omnes.
7. Livre. Confitemini Domino. Quemadmodum.
8. Livre. Dominus regnavit. Judica me, Deus.
9. Livre. Confitebimur Tibi Deus. De profundis clamavi.
10. Livre. Exaltabo Te Deus meus Rex. Deus noster refugium et virtus.
11. Livre. Notus in Judaea Deus. Dominus regit me.
12. Livre. Venite, exultemus Domino. Ad Te Domine clamabo.
13. Livre. Credidi propter quod locutus sum. In convertendo Dominus.
14. Livre. Exurgat Deus. Pangue lingua.
15. Livre. Exultate justi in Domino. Domine in virtute tua.
16. Livre. Nisi Dominus. Sacris solemniis.
17. Livre. Exaltabo Te Domine. Quare fremuerunt gentes.
18. Livre. Benedictus Dominus Deus Israel. Nisi quia Dominus.
19. Livre. Beatus vir, qui timet Dominum. Confitebor Tibi Domine.
20. Livre. Laudate Dominum. Magnus Dominus.

Lamb, Hubert. Six scenes from the Protevangelion, *see* The Wellesley edition. No.2.

LANDINO, FRANCESCO, ca.1325–1397.
The works of Francesco Landino. Ed. by Leonard Ellinwood. Cambridge, Mass., Mediaeval Society of America, 1939.
xliii, 316p. incl. front., illus. (music) pl., facsims. (music). (The Mediaeval Academy of America. Publication No.36. [Studies and documents. No.3]).
"Printed and lithoprinted."
2- and 3-part madrigals, a "pescha," a 2- and 3-part "ballate," and fragments.
Music in modern notation.
Bibliography: p.307–10.
"Cross-reference table of Francesco's works": p.311–16.

Landmarks of early American music, 1760–1800, *see* Goldman, Richard Franko. Landmarks of early American music, 1760–1800.

LANDSHOFF, LUDWIG, 1874–1941. ed.
Alte Meister des Bel Canto. Italienische Kammerduette des 17. und 18. Jahrhunderts. Für den praktischen Gebrauch hrsg. von Ludwig Landshoff. New York, London, [etc.], C. F. Peters, [cop.1955].
99p. (Edition Peters. No.3824).
Contains compositions by Marco da Gagliano, Alessandro Grandi, Hebreo, Marco Marazzoli, Claudio Monteverdi, and Salomone Rossi.

LANDSHOFF, LUDWIG, 1874–1941. ed.
Alte Meister des Bel Canto. Eine Sammlung von Arien aus Opern und Kantaten, von Kanzonen, Kanzonetten, Opern- und Kammerduetten, für den praktischen Gebrauch hrsg. von Ludwig Landshoff . . . Frankfurt, New York, C. F. Peters, 1912–27.
5v. (On cover: Edition Peters. No.3348).
Contents:
Vol.1–2. 50 Arien. 1912. Contains compositions by A. M. Abbattini, Attilio Ariosti, E. B. d'Astorga, Johann Christian Bach, G. B. Bononcini, Francesco Caccini, Antonio Caldara, Giacomo Carissimi, C. F. Cesarini, Marcantonio Cesti, Domenico Cimarosa, C. W. Gluck, K. H. Graun, J. A. Hasse, Giovanni Legrenzi, Leonardo Leo, C. A. Lonati, F. de Majo, Benedetto Marcello, Marco da Gagliano, Nicola Matteis, Domenico Mazzocchi, Jacopo Melani, Claudio Monteverdi, Giovanni Paisiello, Bernardo Pasquini, G. B. Pergolesi, Jacopo Perti, Nicola Piccinni, Nicolò Porpora, Francesco Provenzale, Paolo Quagliati, Raffaelle Rontani, Luigi Rossi, Domenico Sarri, Alessandro Scarlatti, and Alessandro Stradella.
Vol.3. 17 Arien für 1 Singstimme, 1 obligates Streichinstrument und Basso Continuo. 1915. Contains compositions by Aldovrandini, G. B. Bononcini, A. Caldara, C. F. Cesarini, M. Cesti, D. Gabrielli, B. Gaffi, G. F. Handel, F. Provenzale, A. Scarlatti, A. Steffani, A. Stradella, and G. Torelli.
Vol.4–5. 34 Kammerduette. 17. Jahrhunderts. 1927.

LANDSHOFF, LUDWIG, 1874–1941. ed.
I classici del Bel Canto. Duetti da camera italiani del secolo XVII e XVIII. Compilati ad uso practico da Ludwig Landshoff. Lipsia, C. F. Peters, cop.1927.
v.1– .

LANGE, FRANCISCO CURT, 1903– . ed.
Archivo de música religiosa de la Capitania Geral das Minas Gerais, Brasil, siglo XVIII. Mensoza, Universidad Nacional de Cuyo, Escuelo Superior de Música, Departamento de Musicología, 1951– .
p.1– .
Contains compositions by José Joaquim Emerico Lobo de Mezquita, Marcos Coelho Netto, and Francisco Gomes da Rocha.

LANNER, JOSEPH FRANZ KARL, 1801–1843.
Josef Lanners Werke. Neue Gesamtausgabe. Nach den Originalen. Hrsg. von Eduard Kremser. [für Klavier]. Leipzig, Breitkopf & Härtel, 1889–91.
8v.
Contents:
Bd.1–5. Walzer.
Bd.6. Ländler, Polkas und Mazurkas.
Bd.7. Galoppe.
Bd.8. Quadrillen, Märsche und andere Werke.

LA RUE, PIERRE DE, d.1518.
Liber missarum. Première transcription moderne, par le Docteur Tirabassi . . . Malines, Maison Dessain, 1943.
2p.L., 223p.
Deuxième partie de la thèse: La mesure dans La notation proportionnelle, Univ. of Bale, 1924.
" . . . 300 exemplaires numérotés . . . "

LA SABLONARA, CLAUDIO DE, fl.1599. comp.
Cancionero musical y poético del siglo XVII, recogido por Claudio de La Sablonara y transcrito en notación moderna por el maestro D. Jesús Aroca. Madrid, Imprenta de la "Rev. de Arch., Bibl. y Museos," 1916.
viii, 340p., 1L.
"Algunas palabras sobre el colector del presente cancionero y sobre los autores cuyas obras encierra": p.326–36.
Mss. in Biblioteca Nacional, Madrid.

LASSUS, ORLAND DE, d.1594.
Orlando di Lassus Sämtliche Werke. Hrsg. von F. X. Haberl und Adolf Sandberger. Leipzig, Breitkopf & Härtel, [1894–1926].
21v. ports.
Includes only about one third of Lassus' works.
Contents:
Bd.1. Magnum opus musicum. Lateinische Gesänge für 2, 3, 4, 5, 6, 7, 8, 9, 10 und 12 Stimmen. Theil I. Für 2, 3 und 4 Stimmen. 1904. 1894 (pref.).
Bd.2. Madrigale. Erster Theil. 1894.
Bd.3. Magnum opus musicum. Lateinische Gesänge für 2, 3, 4, 5, 6, 7, 8, 9, 10 und 12 Stimmen. Theil II. Für 4 und 5 Stimmen. 1895.

Bd.4. Madrigale. Zweiter Theil. 1895.
Bd.5. Magnum opus musicum. Lateinische Gesänge für 2, 3, 4, 5, 6, 7, 8, 9, 10 und 12 Stimmen. Theil III. Für 5 Stimmen. 1895.
Bd.6. Madrigale. Dritter Theil. 1896.
Bd.7. Magnum opus musicum. Lateinische Gesänge für 2, 3, 4, 5, 6, 7, 8, 9, 10 und 12 Stimmen. Theil IV. Für 5 Stimmen. 1896.
Bd.8. Madrigale. Vierter Theil. 1898.
Bd.9. Magnum opus musicum. Lateinische Gesänge für 2, 3, 4, 5, 6, 7, 8, 9, 10 und 12 Stimmen. Theil V. Für 5 Stimmen.
Bd.10. Madrigale. Fünfter Theil. 1898.
Bd.11. Magnum opus musicum. Lateinische Gesänge für 2, 3, 4, 5, 6, 7, 8, 9, 10 und 12 Stimmen. Theil VI. Für 5 und 6 Stimmen. 1900.
Bd.12. Kompositionen mit französischem Text. Erster Theil. (I. No.1–56).
Bd.13. Magnum opus musicum. Lateinische Gesänge für 2, 3, 4, 5, 6, 7, 8, 9, 10 und 12 Stimmen. Theil VII. Für 6 Stimmen. 1901.
Bd.14. Kompositionen mit französischem Text. Zweiter Theil. (I. No.57–93).
Bd.15. Magnum opus musicum. Lateinische Gesänge für 2, 3, 4, 5, 6, 7, 8, 9, 10 und 12 Stimmen. Theil VIII. Für 6 Stimmen. 1903.
Bd.16. Kompositionen mit französischem Text. Dritter Theil. (II. No.1–18; III. No.1–19; IV. No.1–5).
Bd.17. Magnum opus musicum. Lateinische Gesänge für 2, 3, 4, 5, 6, 7, 8, 9, 10 und 12 Stimmen. Theil IX. Für 6 Stimmen. 1905.
Bd.18. Kompositionen mit deutschem Text. Erster Theil. (I. No.1–15; II. No.1–15; III. No.1–11).
Bd.19. Magnum opus musicum. Lateinische Gesänge für 2, 3, 4, 5, 6, 7, 8, 9, 10 und 12 Stimmen. Theil X. Für 6, 7 und 8 Stimmen. 1908.
Bd.20. Kompositionen mit deutschem Text. Zweiter Theil. (IV. No.1–11; V. No.1–7; VI. No.1–25; VII. No.1–9). 1909.
Bd.21. Magnum opus musicum. Lateinische Gesänge für 2, 3, 4, 5, 6, 7, 8, 9, 10 und 12 Stimmen. Theil XI. Für 8, 9, 10 und 12 Stimmen. 1926.

LASSUS, ORLAND DE, d.1594.
Sämtliche Werke. Neue Reihe. Hrsg. von der Académie Royal de Belgique und der Bayerischen Akademie der Wissenschaften. Kassel, Bärenreiter Verlag, 1956– .
v.1– .
Contents:
Vol.1. Lateinische Motetten, Französische Chansons und Italienische Madrigale aus wieder aufgefundenen Drucken 1559–1588. Hrsg. von Wolfgang Boetticher. 1956.
Vol.2. Die vier Passionen. (Matthäus 1575. Markus 1582. Lukas 1582. Johannes 1580). 1961.
Vol.3. Messen 1–9. Hrsg. von Siegfried Hermelink. 1962.
Vol.4. Messen 10–17. Hrsg. von Siegfried Hermelink. 1964.
Vol.5. Messen 18–23. Hrsg. von Siegfried Hermelink. 1965.
Vol.6. Messen 24–29. Hrsg. von Siegfried Hermelink. 1966.
Vol.7. Messen 30–35. Hrsg. von Siegfried Hermelink. 1967.

László, Zsigmond, ed. The library of the Goldmark School, *see* The library of the Goldmark School.

LATROBE, CHRISTIAN IGNATIUS, 1758–1836. ed.
Selection of sacred music from the works of some of the most eminent composers of Germany & Italy . . . By C. I. Latrobe . . . The vocal parts in score, the instrumental parts adapted to the pianoforte. London, C. Lonsdale, 1806–[25].
6v.
Contains compositions by Abos, Alberti, Astorga, C. P. E. Bach, Bassani, Boccherini, Borri, Brassetti, Cafaro, Caldara, Ciampi, Danzi, Durante, Felici, Gaensbacher, Galuppi, Gluck, Gossec, Graun, Haeser, Hasse, J. Haydn, M. Haydn, Hummel, Jomelli, Leo, Lotti, Marcello, Morari, Moriari, Mozart, Naumann, Negri, Neukomm, Pergolesi, Ricci, Righini, Rolle, Sabbatini, Sala, Salvatore, Sarti, Serini, Siroli, Suidell, Telemann, Türck, Vögler, Winter, and Wolf.
The following work appears to be practically a reprint of this compilation.

LATROBE, JOHN ANTES, 1799–1878. ed.
The music of the church considered in its various branches, congregational and choral: an historical and practical treatise for the general reader. By John Antes La Trobe . . . London, R. B. Seeley and W. Burnside, 1831.
xvi, 454, [2] p.
Pieces are all in vocal score, with compressed accompaniments: some to the original text, some to translated words.
Contents (from *Grove's Dictionary of music and musicians*, 1916, Vol.2, p.650–51):
Abos. Stabat Mater. T. from Stabat.
Alberti, D. Salve Redemptor, C.
—— Salve.
—— O God, be not far, A.–Salve.
—— O Jesu, Salvator! C.–Salve.
Astorga. O quam tristis, T.–Stabat.
—— Quis est homo. D.–Stabat.
—— Blessed be the power, C.–Stabat.
—— Fac me penitentem, D.–Stabat.
—— Recordare, A.–Stabat.
—— Cum sitiam, C.–Stabat.
Bach, C. P. E. O come let us worship, C.–Anthem.
—— O Lord, hide not, A.–Israelites.
—— He opened the rock. C.–Israelites.
Bassani. Sanctus, C.–Requiem.
—— Recordare. C. & S.–Requiem.
Boccherini. Fac ut portem, A.–Stabat.
—— Stabat Mater, A.–Stabat.
—— Recordare, T.–Stabat.
—— Inflammatus, A.–Stabat.
Borri, B. Laudamus Te, A.–Mass.

—— Domine, T.–Mass.
—— Quoniam, T. from Mass.
—— Christe, C.–from Mass.
Brassetti. Praise the Lord, C.–Confitebor.
Cafaro, P. Stabat Mater, D. & C.–Stabat.
Caldara. Benedictus, T.–Mass.
—— Et incarnatus, A.–Mass.
—— Agnus, D.–Mass.
—— Et incarnatus, C.–Mass.
—— Crucifixus: D.–Mass.
—— Et resurrexit, C.–Mass.
—— Agnus, C.–Mass.
Ciampi, F. O my God, A.–Miserere.
—— Esse enim, D.–Miserere.
—— Cor mundum, D.–Miserere.
Danzi. Salve Redemptor, C.–Salve.
—— Agnus Dei, C.–Mass.
Durante. I will call, A.–Lamentatio.
—— O remember, C.–Lamentatio.
—— Omnis populus, C.–Service for Passion Week.
—— Quaerens me, D.–Requiem.
—— Agnus, C.–Litany.
Felice. Or che à nate, D.–Oratorio.
Galuppi. Sacre horrore, D.–Oratorio.
Gänsbacher. Quid sum miser, C. from Requiem.
Gluck. De profundis, C.–De profundis.
Gossec. Lachrymosa, D.–Requiem.
—— Pie Jesu, C.–Requiem.
Graun. Te Deum, C.–Te Deum.
—— Te gloriosus, C.–Te Deum.
—— Tu Rex gloriae, C.–Te Deum.
—— Tu ad liberandum, A.–Te Deum.
—— Tu ad dexteram, C.–Te Deum.
—— Te ergo quaesumus, D.–Te Deum.
—— Et rege, C.–Te Deum.
—— Dignare Domine, A.–Te Deum.
—— O Zion, mark, C.–Tod Jesu.
—— He was despised, C.–Tod Jesu.
—— Thou hast brought me, C.–Tod Jesu.
—— Sing to Jehovah, C.–Tod Jesu.
—— Astonish'd seraphim, R.–Tod Jesu.
—— Weep, Israel, Ch.–Tod Jesu.
—— Behold us here, C.–Tod Jesu.
—— Behold the Lamb of God, C.–Passione.
—— He was despised, C.–Passione.
—— God, my strength, D.–Passione.
—— Bless the Lord, A.–Passione.
—— Let us run, C.–Passione.
—— In songs of joy, Ch.–Passione.
—— Bow down, A.–Passione.
Häser. Against thee only, C.–Miserere.
Hasse. Inspiro O Deus, C.–Augustino.
—— Laudate coeli Patrem, C.–Augustino.
—— Uti furentibus, A.–Augustino.
—— Jesu mea pax, C.–Magdalena.
—— O portenta. A.–Magdalena.
—— Mea tormenta, A.–Magdalena.
—— Ad Te clamamus, A.–Salve.
—— O give thanks, C.–Caduta.
—— Finche solvo, A.–Caduta.
—— Blow the sacred trumpet. C.–Caduta.
—— Lauda. Qu. & C.–Pellegrini.
—— Viva fonte, A.–Pellegrini.
—— D'aspri legati, A.–Pellegrini.
—— Senti il mar, A.–Pellegrini.
—— Pellegrino e l'uomo, C.–Pellegrini.
—— Defende populum, C.–Giuseppe riconosciuto.
—— Dic quaeso, A.–Giuseppe riconosciuto.
—— Plebes inepte consitia, C.–Giuseppe riconosciuto.
—— Agnus Dei, D.–Litany.
—— O Lord, save thy people, A.–Depositione.
—— Rex tremendae, C. & A. Requiem.
—— Miserere mei Deus, C.–Miserere.
Haydn, J. Tu di grazia, C.–Passione.
—— Padre celeste, C.–Passione.
—— Kyrie, C.–Mass No.I in B flat.
—— Gloria, C.–Mass No.I in B flat.
—— Et incarnatus, C.–Mass No.I in B flat.
—— Sanctus, C.–Mass No.I in B flat.
—— Qui tollis, A. & C.–Mass No.II in C.
—— Gloria, C.–Mass No.III in D.
—— Et incarnatus, C. & C.–Mass No.III in D.
—— Quoniam, A.–Mass No.V.
—— Cum sancto, C.–Mass No.V.
—— Et incarnatus, S. & D.–Mass No.V.
—— Agnus, A.–Mass No.V.
—— Kyrie, C.–Mass No.VII in G.
—— Et incarnatus, S. & Qu.–Mass No.VII in G.
—— Sanctus, C.–Mass No.VII in G.
—— Benedictus, Q.–Mass No.VII in G.
—— Sanctus, C.–Mass No.VIII in B flat.
—— Benedictus, A.–Mass No.VIII in B flat.
—— Agnus Dei, C.–Mass No.VIII in B flat.
—— Kyrie, C.–Mass No.XII.
—— Stabat Mater, C.–Stabat.
—— Vidit suum, A.–Stabat.
—— Quis est homo, C.–Stabat.
—— Pro peccatis, A.–Stabat.
—— Flammis orci, A.–Stabat.
—— Fac me cruce, A.–Stabat.
—— Quando corpus, C.–Stabat.
—— Salve Redemptor, C.–Salve.
—— Pietà d'un infelice, C.–Tobia.
—— Non parmi, A. from Tobia.
—— O di le nostri, C.–Tobia.
—— My soul shall cry, Q.–Motetto.
Haydn, M. Lord, grant us thy, Ch.–Service for country church.
—— O full of all, Ch.–Service for country church.
—— While conscious, Ch.–Service for country church.
—— Blest Jesus, gracious, Ch.–Service for country church.
—— O love, all love excelling, Ch.–Service for country church.
—— While with her fragrant, Ch.–Service for country church.
—— Worship, honour, Ch.–Service for country church.
—— Tenebrae, C.–Tenebrae.
—— Sanctus, C.–Requiem.
—— Agnus, C.–Requiem.
—— Oro supplex, C.–Requiem.
—— Lauda Sion, Q.–Litany.
Hummel. Holy, Holy, C.–Mass.
Jommelli. Rex tremendae, D.–Requiem.
—— Kyrie, D.–Mass.
—— Agnus, D.–Mass.
Leo. Dal nuvoloso monte, A.–S. Elena.

—— Dal tuo soglio, D.–S. Elena.
—— Christus factus est, S.–Verse.
—— O Jesu, A.–Salve.
Lotti. Qui tollis, C.–Mass.
—— Gloria, C.–Mass.
—— Et in terra, Qu.–Mass.
—— Miserere mei, C.–Miserere.
Marcello. Save, o save, D.–Psalms.
Morari. Agnus Dei, T.–Mass.
Moriari. Cum sancto, C.–Mass.
Mozart. Recordare, Q.–Requiem.
—— Sanctus, C.–Mass No.I.
—— Benedictus, Q.–Mass No.I.
—— Agnus, A.–Mass No.I.
—— Gloria, C.–Mass No.II.
—— Benedictus, Q.–Mass No.III.
—— Agnus, C.–Mass No.III.
—— Agnus, D.–Mass No.VI.
—— Bless the Lord (Kyrie), D.–Mass No.X.
—— Benedictus, A. & C.–Mass No.X.
—— Agnus, C.–Mass No.X.
—— Benedictus, Q.–Mass No.XI.
—— O God, when Thou appearest, C.–Motetto I–II.
—— Ne purvis, C.–Motetto I–II.
—— Kyrie, D.–Litany I.
—— Jesu Domine, A.–Litany I.
—— Jesu Christe, D.–Litany II.
—— Verbum caro, C.–Litany II.
—— Enter unto his gates, A.–Litany II.
—— Kyrie, C.–Litany II.
—— Agnus, C.–Litany II.
—— Tho' by threatening storms, A.–Davidde.
Naumann. Christe, T.–Mass No.I.
—— Kyrie, C.–Mass No.I.
—— Et incarnatus, D.–Mass No.I.
—— Agnus, D.–Mass No.I.
—— Quoniam, D.–Mass No.II.
—— Cum sancto, C.–Mass No.II.
—— Benedictus, D. & C.–Mass No.II.
—— Agnus, C.–Mass No.II.
—— Qui tollis, C.–Mass No.III.
—— Et incarnatus, A.–Mass No.III.
—— Sanctus, C.–Mass No.III.
—— Et incarnatus, A.–Mass No.IV.
—— Agnus D. & C.–Mass No.IV.
—— Lauda Sion, C.–Offertorium.
—— Le porte a noi, Q.–Pellegrini.
—— O ye kindreds, C.–Psalm xcvi.
Negri. Qui sedes, A.–Mass.
Neukomm. Rex tremendae, C.–Requiem.
—— Sanctus, D.–Requiem.
Pergolesi. Kyrie, D.–Grand Mass.
—— Gloria, D.–Grand Mass.
—— Laudamus, D.–Grand Mass.
—— Gratias, C.–Grand Mass.
—— Domine, D.–Grand Mass.
—— Qui tollis, C.–Grand Mass.
—— Quoniam, A.–Grand Mass.
—— Cum sancto, C.–Grand Mass.
—— Hear my prayer, D.–Salve.
—— Ad Te suspiramus, C.–Salve.
—— O Jesu Salvator, D. from Salve.
—— Asperges, C.–Miserere I.
—— Redde mihi, D.–Miserere I.
—— Domine labia, A.–Miserere II.
—— Quoniam si voluisses, C.–Miserere II.
—— Sacraficium Deo, T.–Miserere II.
Ricci. Recordare, A.–Dies irae.
Righini. Qui tollis, C.–Mass.
—— Benedictus, Q.–Mass.
—— O Lord, who shall not, Q.–Gerus. lib.
Rolle. In Thee, O Lord, C.–Death of Abel.
—— Out of the deep, A.–Death of Abel.
—— Great God, to Thee, C.–Thirza.
—— O Lord, most holy, D.–Thirza.
Sabbatini. God be merciful, T. & C.–Dixit Dominus.
—— In my distress, D.–Dixit Dominus.
—— Dominus a dextris. A.–Dixit Dominus.
Sala. Qui tollis, A.–Mass.
Salvatore. Tenebrae, C.–Tenebrae.
—— Recessit pastor, C. from Responsorio.
—— In monte Oliveti, C.–from Responsorio.
Sarti. Miserere, D.–Miserere.
—— Amplius, T.–Miserere.
Serini. O fallaces, A.–Motetto.
—— Sum in demio, A.–Motetto.
Siroli. Praise the Lord, D.–Miserere.
Suidell. Crucifixus. D.–Mass.
Telemann. Mercy, Judgment, A.–Oratorio Passion.
Türck. Heavenly branch, D.–Christmas oratorio.
Vogler. Agnus Dei, C.–Requiem.
Winter. O quam tristis, C. & Q. Stabat Mater.
—— Quando corpus, C.–Stabat Mater.
—— Quid sum miser, A.–Requiem.
Wolf. Saints and angels, C.–Funeral anthem.
—— The Prince of life, D.–Easter anthem.
N. N. Tantum ergo, D.–Chorale.

La lauda, *see* Liuzzi, Fernando. La lauda.

Lautenspieler des XVI. Jahrhunderts, *see* Chilesotti, Oscar. Lautenspieler des XVI. Jahrhunderts.

LEA POCKET SCORES. New York, Lea Pocket Scores, 1950– .
No.1– .
Contents:
No.1a/b. Bach. The well-tempered clavier. Pts.I & II.
No.2. Bach. 6 Violin solo sonatas and 6 Cello solo suites.
No.3a/b. Beethoven. Violin sonatas 1–6, 7–10.
No.4. Bach. The 6 Violin-clavier sonatas.
No.5. Chopin. The 25 Preludes (Op.28, 45); 2 Piano sonatas (Op.35, 58); Fantasy in F (Op.49).
No.6. Brahms. The violin-piano sonatas. (complete).
No.7. Brahms. The 2 Cello-piano sonatas; The 2 Clarinet-piano sonatas.
No.8. Schumann. Carnaval, Op.9; Fantasiestücke, Op.12; Symphonic etudes, Op.13; Fantasy, Op.17.
No.9. Bach. The 6 English and 6 French suites.
No.10. Bach. The 3 Gamba (or Cello)-clavier sonatas; 7 Flute-clavier sonatas.
No.11–15. Beethoven. The 32 Piano sonatas. (No.1–6, 7–12, 13–20, 21–27, 28–32).
No.16a/b/c. Mozart. Violin-piano sonatas. Vols.I/II/III.
No.17. Schubert. Complete violin-piano works. (Op.70; Op.137/1–3; Op.159; Op.162).

No.18. Beethoven. The 5 Cello-piano sonatas.
No.19. Brahms. Piano variations; Op.9 (Schumann); Op.21; Op.24 (Händel); Op.35 (Paganini); Op.56b (Haydn).
No.20. Schumann. Humoresque, Op.20; Davidsbündler, Op.6; Kinderszenen, Op.15; Kreisleriana, Op.16; Toccata, Op.7.
No.21. Bach. Goldberg variations; Italian concerto; 15 2-part and 15 3-part inventions.
No.22. Bach. The 6 Partitas; French overture.
No.23. Schubert. Lieder. Vol.I: 2 Song cycles (Die schöne Müllerin and Schwanengesang).
No.24. Schubert. Lieder. Vol.II: Die Winterreise, Op.89.
No.25. Schumann. Lieder. Vol.I: 4 Song cycles (Dichterliebe; Frauenliebe und Leben; Liederkreis (Op.24, Heine); Liederkreis (Op.39. Eichendorff).
No.26. Bach. The musical offering; 3 Trio sonatas.
No.27/28. Bach. The 6 Brandenburg concerti. (1–3, 4–6).
No.29. Schubert. Wanderer fantasy, Op.15; 8 Impromptus, Op.90, 142; Moments musicaux, Op.94.
No.30. Beethoven. Variations: Op.34; Op.35 (Eroica); Op.76; Op.120 (Diabelli); Grove No.191 (C minor); Grove No.189.
No.31–38. Bach. The complete organ works.
- No.31. Organ mass.
- No.32. Orgelbüchlein and Chorale variations.
- No.33. Chorale preludes. (Kirnberger collection and others).
- No.34. 6 Trio sonatas; 6 Preludes and fugues. (531–36).
- No.35. 12 Preludes and fugues (537–48).
- No.36. 6 "Schübler" and 18 other chorales.
- No.37. Passacaglia, pastorale, 4 Organ concertos, 3 Toccatas, etc.
- No.38. Fantasies, 8 Little preludes and fugues, etc.

No.39/40. Mozart. The piano sonatas and fantasies, I and II.
No.41/42/43. Schubert. The piano sonatas. (1–8, 9–12, 13–15).
No.44. Chopin. Études complete. (Op.10, 25; Op.posth.).
No.45/46. Bach. Clavier works. Vols.VI and VII. (Suites, sonata, toccatas, fantasies/preludes and fugues, capriccios, aria variata, fantasies, fugues, preludes).
No.47. Mendelssohn. Songs without words. (complete).
No.48. Mendelssohn. Complete works for organ.
No.49/50. Mozart. The piano trios. (1–4, 5–8).
No.51/52/53. Schubert. All string quartets. (1–6, 7–11, 12–15).
No.54. Handel. 11 Concerti grossi. (Op.3, No.1–6; "Alexander's feast" Concerto; Oboe Concerti).
No.55. Bach. The 4 Suites (overtures) for orchestra.
No.56. Bach. The 2 Concerti for 3 claviers (D minor, C major).
No.57. Brahms. Piano sonatas. (complete). (Op.1, 2, 5).
No.58. Schubert. Piano pieces. (complete). Vol.II.
No.59. Mozart. Lieder for voice and piano. (complete).
No.60. Beethoven. Lieder for voice and piano. (incl. An die ferne Geliebte and others).
No.61–64. Beethoven. The 17 String quartets. (complete).
- No.61. Op.18, No.1–6.
- No.62. Op.59, No.1–3.
- No.63. Op.74, 95, 127, 130.
- No.64. Op.131, 132, 133, 135.

No.65. Beethoven. Piano pieces. (complete). (Bagatelles, rondos, fantasy, andante favori, minuets, etc.).
No.66. Brahms. Piano pieces, Op,76, 79, 116, 117, 118, 119. (Capricci, intermezzi, rhapsodies, ballades, romance).
No.67. Chopin. The 4 Ballades and The 4 Scherzi.
No.68. Bach. Clavier works. Vol.VIII. (2 Toccatas, fugues, concerto and fuga, scherzo, suites, etc.).
No.69. Bach. The 16 Concerti for harpsichord (after Vivaldi and others); also, Vivaldi. Violin concerto, Op,7/II/2.
No.70. Handel. 15 Sonatas, Op.1. (Flute, violin, oboe). 3 Early flute sonatas. Gamba sonata.
No.71/72. Handel. 12 Concerti grossi, Op.VI. (1–6, 7–12).
No.73. Bach. Die Kunst der Fuge. (The art of fugue).
No.74. Bach. Songs and arias. (Sacred and other). (complete).
No.75. Bach. 185 4-part chorales (C. P. E. Bach collection).
No.76/77. Bach. The motets. (Singen dem Herrn; Der Geist hilft; Jesu meine Freude; Fürchte dich nicht; Komm, Jesu; Lobet den Herrn; Ich lasse; Sei Lob and Preis).
No.78. Bach. Easter oratorio.
No.79. Bach. Cantatas 82, 83, 84, 85. (Ich habe genug; Erfreute Zeit; Ich bin vergnügt; Ich bin ein guter Hirt).
No.80. Bach. Cantatas 131, 132, 133. (Aus der Tiefe; Bereitet die Wege; Ich freue mich in dir).
No.81. Bach. Cantatas 168, 169, 170. (Thue Rechnung; Gott soll allein; Vergnügte Ruh', beliebte Seelenlust).
No.82. Bach. Cantatas 183, 184, 185. (Sie werden euch in den Bannthun; Erwünschtes Freudenlicht; Barmherziges Herze der eurigen Liebe).
No.83. Bach. Cantatas 188, 189, 190. (Ich habe meine Zuversicht; Meine Seele rühmt und preist; Singet dem Herrn).
No.84. Bach. (Secular) Cantata 201. (Phoebus und Pan).
No.85. Bach. (Secular) Cantatas 202, 203, 204. (Weichet nur; Amore traditore; Ich bin in mir vergnügt).
No.86. Handel. Works for clavier. (The 16 Harpsichord suites; 3 Leçons; Chaconne; 6 Fugues; Miscellaneous pieces).
No.87. Rameau. Pièces de clavecin. (complete). (Books of 1706, 1724, and 1731; La dauphone; 5 Pièces en concert).

No.88. Schumann. The 3 Piano sonatas. (Op.11, 14, 22).
No.89. Mozart. Piano variations. (complete).
No.90. Mozart. The 2 Quartets for piano and strings (K.478 in G; K.493 in E flat); Quintet for piano and winds, E flat. (K.452).
No.91/92. Mozart. Complete string quintets. (Vol.I: K.174, B flat; K.406, C; K.407, E flat (Horn quintet); K.515, C; K.516, G. Vol.II: K.581, A (Clarinet quintet); K.593, D; K.614, E flat; K.525, G (Kleine Nachtmusik).
No.93. Chopin. The complete nocturnes (19) and rondos (3).
No.94. Chopin. The complete waltzes (15) and impromptus (4).
No.95. Schumann. Album for the young, Op.68; 3 Sonatas for the young, Op.118; Forest scenes, Op.82.
No.96. Bach. Violin concerti: No.1 (A minor); No.2 (E major); Double concerto (D minor); Concerto movement (D major).
No.97. Bach. Harpsichord concerti. No.1 (D minor); No.2 (E major).
No.98. Bach. Harpsichord concerti. No.3 (D); No.4 (A); No.5 (F).
No.99. Beethoven. String trios. (complete). (Op.3; Op.9/1–3; Op.8 (Serenade).
No.100. Beethoven. Chamber music for winds (Octet, Op.103; Rondino, Grove No.146; Sextet, Op.71; Serenade, Op.25; Trio, Op.87; 3 Duos, Grove No.147).
No.101–104. Haydn. The 52 Piano sonatas.
No.101. No.1–18.
No.102. No.19–28.
No.103. No.29–41.
No.104. No.42–52.
No.105. Bach. Magnificat and appendix: Xmas interpolations.
No.106. Bach. Cantatas 69, 70. (Lobe den Herrn, Meine Seele; Wachet, betet).
No.107. Bach. Cantatas 137, 138, 139. (Lobe den Herren, den mächtigen König; Warum betrübst du dich; Wohl dem).
No.108. Bach. Cantatas 140, 141, 142. (Wachet auf; Das ist je gewisslich wahr; Uns ist ein Kind geboren).
No.109. Bach. Cantatas 151, 152, 153, 154. (Süsser Trost; Tritt auf; Schau, lieber Gott; Mein liebster Jesus).
No.110. Schubert. The piano trios. (Op.99, 100, 148).
No.111. Schubert. Piano quintet in A ("Trout"), Op.114; String quintet in C, Op.163.
No.112–116. Schubert. Lieder. Vols.III–VII. (1822–28).
No.117/118. Schumann. Lieder. Vols.II, III. (1840, 1840–42).
No.119/120. Chopin. The mazurkas and polonaises. (complete).
No.119. Mazurkas 1–41.
No.120. Mazurkas 42–56. Polonaises 1–12.
No.121–124. Haydn. The 31 Piano trios. (Hoboken 1–9, 10–16, 17–23, 24–31).
No.125–126. Handel. The 16 Organ concerti.
No.125. Op.IV/1–6 and Op.VII/1, 2.
No.126. Op.VII/3–6 and 13–16.

Lebègue, Nicolas Antoine le, *see* Bègue, Nicolas Antoine le.

LECHNER, LEONHARD, ca.1550–1606.
Werke. Kassel und Basel, Bärenreiter Verlag, 195? – .
15v. (in progress).
Contents (asterisk indicates unpublished volumes):
Vol.1. Motectae sacrae 4, 5 & 6 vocum. 1575. Herausgeber: Lutz Finscher. 1956.
*Vol.2. Newe teutsche Lieder zu 3 Stimmen nach art der Welschen Villanellen 1576/77. (Zwei Teile).
Vol.3. Newe teutsche Lieder mit vier und fünf Stimmen. 1577. Herausgeber: Uwe Martin. 1954.
Vol.4. Sanctissimae Virginis Mariae canticum (Magnificat) 1578 secundem octo vulgares Tonos, quatuor Vocibus. Herausgeber: Walther Lipphardt. 1960.
Vol.5. Vorabdruck: Italienische Madrigale 1579 und 1585 für 5 gemischte Stimmen (Come nave; Fato, fortuna/ Che più d'un giorno/ Fucco di sdegno). Herausgeber: Konrad Ameln.
*Vol.6. Sacrarum cantionem 5 & 6 vocum Liber secundem. 1581.
*Vol.7. Newe teutsche Lieder mit 5 und 4 Stimmen 1582. Herausgeber: Ernst Fritz Schmid.
*Vol.8. Liber missarum 6 & 5 vocum 1584. Herausgeber: Ernst Fritz Schmid.
Vol.9. Newe lustige teutsche Lieder nach art der Welschen Canzonen mit 4 und 5 Stimmen 1586 und 1588. Herausgeber: Ernst Fritz Schmid.
*Vol.10. 7 Psalmi poenitentiales 6 vocibus compositi 1587. Herausgeber: Walther Lipphardt.
*Vol.11. Newe geistliche und weltliche teutsche Lieder mit 5 und 4 Stimmen. 1589. Herausgeber: Konrad Ameln.
Vol.12. Historia der Passion und Leidens unsers einigen Erlösers und Seligmachers Jesu Christi 1593, für vier gemischte Stimmen. Herausgeber: Konrad Ameln. 1960.
*Vol.13. Newe geistliche von weltliche teutsche Gesanng, sampt zwayen lateinischen . . . mit 4 und 5 Stimmen. (Posthome Handschrift der Landesbibl. Kassel). 1606. Herausgeber: Walther Lipphardt.
*Vol.14–15. Werke aus besonderem Anlass 1575–1604.

LEFKOFF, GERALD, 1930– . ed.
Five sixteenth century Venetian lute books. Washington, D.C., Catholic University of America Press, 1960.
xv, 208p.
Transcriptions into modern notation of the following lute tablatures; Intabolatura de lauto de diversi autori, 1563; Intabolatura de lauto di Bernardino Balletti, 1554; La intabolatura de lauto dell' Eccellente P. Pauolo Borrono da Milano; Intabolatura di liuto di Iulio Abundante, 1563; Libro primo da Leuto de M. Antonio di Becchi Parmegiano, 1568.

"The commentary": p.1–41.
"Critical notes": p.168–80.
Thesis–Catholic University of America.

Lehrmeister und Schüler Joh. Seb. Bachs, *see* Herrmann, Kurt. Lehrmeister und Schüler Joh. Seb. Bachs.

LEICHTENTRITT, HUGO, 1874–1951. ed.
Deutsche Hausmusik aus vier Jahrhunderten. Ausgewählte und zum Vortrag eingerichtet nebst erläuterndem Text. Die Musik hrsg. von Richard Strauss. Berlin, Bord Marquardt & Co., 1907. [Berlin, Max Hesses Verlag, 1905].
110p. (music, p.61–110).
Contains compositions by Heinrich Albert, J. K. Ferd. Fischer, J. J. Froberger, Hans Leo Hassler, Paul Hofhaimer, Reinhard Keiser, Adam Krieger, Orlando di Lasso, Jacob Regnart, Neidhart von Reuenthal, Wizlaw Fürst von Rugen, Joh. Herm. Schein, Georg Phil. Telemann, Oswald von Wolkenstein.

LE JEUNE, CLAUDE, d.1600.
Airs. (1608). Ed. by D. P. Walker, in 4v., introd. by François Lesure and D. P. Walker. Rome, American Institute of Musicology in Rome, 1951–59.
4v. (Miscellanea. No.1).
Contents:
Vol.1. Pt.I of the Premier livre. 1951.
Vol.2. Pt.II of the Premier livre. 1959.
Vol.3–4. Second livre. 1959.

LEMMENS, NICOLAS JACQUES, 1823–1881.
Oeuvres inédites de J.-N. Lemmens. Leipzig et Bruxelles, Breitkopf & Härtel, 1883–87.
4v.
Contents:
Tome 1. Musique d'orgue. 1883.
Tome 2. Chants liturgiques. 1884.
Tome 3. Messes et motets. 1886.
Tome 4. Varia. 1887.

Leopold I, Holy Roman Emperor, 1640–1705. Die ältesten musikalischen Denkmäler, *see* Zagiba, František. Die ältesten musikalischen Denkmäler.

Leopold I, Holy Roman Emperor, 1640–1705. Werke, *see* Musikalische Werke der Kaiser Ferdinand III, Leopold I, und Joseph I.

Le Roux, Gaspard, *see* Roux, Gaspard le.

L'Escurel, Jehannot de, *see* Escurel, Jehannot de l'.

LESURE, FRANÇOIS. ed.
Anthologie de la chanson parisienne au XVIe siècle. Réunie par François Lesure, avec le collaboration de N. Bridgman, I. Cazeaux, M. Levin, K. J. Levy, et D. P. Walker. Monaco, Éditions de l'Oiseau Lyre, [cop.1953].
xp., score (146p.).
For 3–7 voices.
Contains compositions by Boni, Bonnet, Boyvin, Certon, Clêreau, Costeley, Courville, De Bussy, Du Caurroy, Gardane, Goudimel, Hesdin, Jacotin, Janequin, La Grotte, Le Jeune, Millot, Passereau, Planson, Rore, Sandrin, Sermisy, Tessier, and Anonymes.

Leuckartiana, *see* Alte Musik. (Reihe "Leuckartiana").

Liber missarum, *see* La Rue, Pierre de. Liber missarum.

LIBER ORGANI. Mainz und Leipzig, B. Schott's Söhne; New York, Associated Music Publishers, Inc., [etc., etc., cop.1931–cop.1958].
10v.
Editor Bd.1–4, 6–7: Ernst Kaller.
Editor Bd.5: Ernst Kaller and Dr. Erich Valentin.
Editor Bd.8: Hans Klotz.
Editor Bd.9: Gregor Klaus.
Editor Bd.10: Gordon Phillips.
Contents:
Bd.1. Altfranzösische Orgelmeister. I. Edition Schott No.1343. (Compositions by J. Titelouze, J. d'Anglebert, N. Gigault, F. Couperin, N. Lebègue, and L. Marchand). [cop.1931].
Bd.2. Altfranzösische Orgelmeister. II. Edition Schott No.1344. (Compositions by J. Titelouze, F. Roberday, F. Couperin, Guilain, N. de Grigny, L. N. Clérambault, and L. Cl. d'Aquin.). [cop.1931].
Bd.3. Altspanische Orgelmeister. Edition Schott No.1621. (Compositions by Antonio de Cabezón and Tomás de Santa María). [cop. 1933].
Bd.4. Altitalienische Orgelmeister. Edition Schott No.1674. (Compositions by Girolamo Frescobaldi, G. B. Fasolo, Adriano Banchieri, and Domenico Zipoli). [cop.1933].
Bd.5. Toccaten des 17. und 18. Jahrhunderts. Edition Schott No.1675. (Compositions by G. Frescobaldi, J. J. Froberger, J. Pachelbel, W. H. Pachelbel, Georg Muffat, and Gottlieb Muffat). [cop.1933].
Bd.6. Deutsche Meister des 16. und 17. Jahrhunderts. I. Edition Schott No.2266. (Compositions by Christian Erbach, Samuel Scheidt, Dietrich Buxtehude, Johann Pachelbel, and Gottlieb Muffat). [cop.1935].
Bd.7. Deutsche Meister des 16. und 17. Jahrhunderts. II. Edition Schott No.2267. (Contains Ariadne musica, by J. K. F. Fischer). [cop.1935].
Bd.8. Orgelmeister der Gotik. Edition Schott No.2556. (Compositions by Guillaume Dufay, Heinrich Isaac, Josquin des Près, Paul Hofhaimer, and Ludwig Senfl). [cop.1958].
Bd.9. Süddentsche Orgelmeister: Joh. Speth. Edition Schott No.4537. [cop.1954].
Bd.10. Alte Englische Orgelmeister. Hrsg. von Gordon Phillips. Edition Schott No.4786. (Compositions by John Redford, William Byrd, Richard Alwoode, Thomas Tomkins, Orlando Gibbons, John Blow, Henry Purcell, Maurice Greene, William Boyce, Charles John Stanley, and Samuel Wesley.

THE LIBRARY OF THE GOLDMARK SCHOOL, ed. by Bence Szabolsci and Zsigmond László. Budapest, Cserépfalvi, 1949?.

3v.
A series devoted to the music of the ancient civilizations, especially Jewish.
Contents:
Vol.1. Jewish choruses.
Vol.2. Collection of piano works. (The music of ancient peoples).
Vol.3. 100 Ancient Jewish liturgical melodies.

Das Lied der Völker, *see* Möller, Heinrich. Das Lied der Völker.

Das Liederbuch des Arnt von Aich, *see* Aich, Arnt von. Das Liederbuch des Arnt von Aich.

Lira sacro-hispana, *see* Eslava y Elizondo, Hilarión. Lira sacro-hispana.

Lissa, Zofia, 1908– , ed. Music of the Polish Renaissance, *see* Chomiński, Józef Michal. Music of the Polish Renaissance.

LISZT, FRANZ, 1811–1886.
Musikalische Werke. Hrsg. von der Franz Liszt-Stiftung durch Ferruccio Busoni, Peter Raabe, August Stradal, J. V. da Motta, Berth. Kellermann, Bernh. Stavenhagen, Béla Bartók, Otto Taubmann, Philipp Wolfrum und Andere. Leipzig, Breitkopf & Härtel, 1907–36.
v.1– .
Contents:
Part I. Für Orchester.
Bd.I. Symphonische Dichtungen. (Nr.1 und 2).
Bd.II. Symphonische Dichtungen. (Nr.2a–4).
Bd.III. Symphonische Dichtungen. (Nr.5 und 6).
Bd.IV. Symphonische Dichtungen. (Nr.7 und 8).
Bd.V. Symphonische Dichtungen. (Nr.9 und 10).
Bd.VI. Symphonische Dichtungen. (Nr.11 und 12).
Bd.VII. Eine Symphonie zu Dantes Divina commedia.
Bd.VIII und IX. Eine Faustsinfonie.
Bd.X. Kleinere Orchesterwerke. Nr.1/4.
Bd.XI. Kleinere Orchesterwerke. Nr.5/8.
Bd.XII. Kleinere Orchesterwerke. Nr.9/13.
Bd.XIII. Werke für Pianoforte und Orchester.
Part II. Pianoforte-Werke.
Bd.I. Etüden. 1. Band.
Bd.II. Etüden. 2. Band.
Bd.III. Etüden. 3. Band.
Bd.IV. Tagebuch eines Wanderers. (Album d'un voyageur).
Bd.V. Aus der Wanderzeit.
Bd.VI. Wanderjahre. (Années de pélerinage).
Bd.VII–IX. Verschiedene Werke.
Bd.X. Tänze.
Bd.XII. Ungarische Rhapsodien.
Part V. Kirchliche und geistliche Gesangwerke.
Bd.I. Missa solennis. (Graner Festmesse).
Bd.II. Ungarische Krönungsmesse.
Bd.III. Messen und Requiem mit Orgel.
Bd.IV. Psalmen.
Bd.V. Hymne, sowie sonstige Chorgesänge mit Orchester.
Bd.VI. Kleine Chor- und Einzelgesänge mit Orgel.
Bd.VII. Letzte zyklische Chorgesänge mit Orgel nebst Bearbeitungen.
Part VI. Weltliche mehrstimmige Gesangwerke.
Bd.III. Männerchöre ohne Begleitung. Männergesang mit Klavierbegleitung, Männergesang und Blasinstrumente, 2 Soprane und Alt oder 2 Tënore und Bass. Frauen- und Kinderchor.
Part VII. Einstimmige Lieder und Gesänge.
Bd.I. 25 Einstimmige Lieder und Gesänge.
Bd.II. 44 Einstimmige Lieder und Gesänge.
Bd.III. 38 Einstimmige Lieder und Gesänge.
Bearbeitungen.
Bd.I. Bearbeitungen und Transkriptionen für Pianoforte zu 2 Händen von Werken Richard Wagners.
Bd.II. Bearbeitungen für Pianoforte zu 2 Händen von Beethovens Symphonien Nr.1–5.
Bd.III. Bearbeitungen für Pianoforte zu 2 Händen von Beethovens Symphonien Nr.6–9.

LISZT, FRANZ, 1811–1886.
Liszt society publications. London, Schott, [1950?–].
v.1– .
Contents:
Vol.1. Late piano works.
(Czárdás macabre. En rêve–Nocturne. Nuages gris. La lugubre gondola I–II. Richard Wagner–Venezia. Vier kleine Klavierstücke. Trauer- Vorspiel und Marsch. Unstern! Dritter Mephisto Walzer).
Vol.2. Early and late piano works.
(Harmonies poétiques et religieuses. Apparitions, No.1–2. Lyon. Reminiscences de Boccanegra. Am Grabe Richard Wagners. Vierter Mephisto Walzer).
Vol.3. Hungarian and late piano works.
(2 Pieces in the Hungarian style. Funeral music to Mosonyi's death. To the memory of Petöfi. 5 Hungarian folksongs. Csárdás Obstiné. Elegy, No.1–2. Schlaflos, Frage und Antwort.
Vol.4. Dances for piano.
(Valse mélancolique. Valse de concert. Sur deux motifs de Lucia et Parisina. Valse oubliée, No.2, 3. Galop in A minor).

LISZT, FRANZ, 1811–1886.
Orgelkompositionen, von Franz Liszt. Hrsg. von Karl Straube. Neue Ausgabe. Leipzig, C. F. Peters, n.d.
2v. (Edition Peters. No.3628a–b).
Contents:
Vol.1: 1. Variationen; 2. Evocation à la Chapelle Sixtine; 3. Ora pro nobis, Litanei; 4. Der Papst–Hymnus; 5. Ave Maria von Arcadelt; 6. Angelus. Prière aux anges gardiens; 7. Introitus; 8. Trauerode.
Vol.2: 1. Phantasie und Fuge; 2. Praeludium und Fuge über BACH; 3. Adagio; 4. Kirchen-Hymne: Salve Regina; 5. Kirchen-Hymne: Ave Maris Stella; 6. Messe; 7. Requiem; 8. Zur Trauung.

LISZT, FRANZ, 1811–1886.
Werke für Klavier zu 2 Händen, von Franz Liszt. Hrsg. von Emil von Sauer. Leipzig, C. F. Peters, [cop.1917].
12v. (Edition Peters. No.3600a–d, 3601a–d, 3602a–d).
Contents:
Vol.1. Rhapsodien. No.1–8.
Vol.2. Rhapsodien. No.9–16.
Vol.3. Etüden. Etudes d'exécution transcendante.
Vol.4. Etüden. Paganini; Etüden. Drei Konzert; Etüden. Zwei Konzert; Etüden.
Vol.5–6. Original Kompositionen.
Vol.7–8. Bearbeitungen aus Opern.
Vol.9. Lieder-Bearbeitungen.
Vol.10. Bearbeitungen. Schubert. Soirées de Vienne; Bach. Seche Präludien und Fugen für Orgel; Bach. Weinen und Klaven; Bach. Orgelphantasie und Fuge; Rossini. Soirées Nr.2 und 9.
Vol.11. Konzerte und andere Werke mit Orchester.
Vol.12. Supplement. Wagner. Tannhäuser. Overture; Meyerbeer. Prophet. Die Schlittschuhläufer; Liszt. Faust. Symphonie: Gretchen; Schubert. Drei Märsche; Liszt. Scherzo und Märsche; Liszt. Phantasie und Fuge über BACH.

Litaniae solemnes seu laudes in die Paschae, *see* Plainsong and Mediaeval Music Society. Litaniae solemnes seu laudes in die Paschae.

The litany and suffrages from the Book of Common Prayer, *see* Plainsong and Mediaeval Music Society. The litany and suffrages from the Book of Common Prayer.

LITURGICAL CHOIR BOOKS. Ed. by Francis Burgess . . . London, Plainchant Publications Committee, n.d.
26v.
Contents:
Vol.1. Mass and office responses.
Vol.2. The Benedicamus melodies for the year.
Vol.3. The anthems of the BVM.
Vol.4. A tenor tonale. (Gregorian tones).
Vol.5. Vespers of the Blessed Sacrament.
Vol.6. Vespers of the Blessed Virgin Mary.
Vol.7. Vespers of the dead.
Vol.7a. Vespers of the dead. (Small edition in plainsong notation).
Vol.8. Sunday compline.
Vol.9. A simple plainchant requiem.
Vol.10. A polyphonic requiem. (Anerio, Viadana, and Casciolini).
Vol.11. Casciolini's missa brevissima.
Vol.12. An English kyriale. (Ninefold settings).
Vol.13. Solemn reception of a bishop.
Vol.14. An English benediction manual.
Vol.15. The Candlemas and Ash Wednesday rites.
Vol.16. The Palm Sunday rite (with short Passion).
Vol.17. The Palm Sunday passion (complete form).
Vol.18. The Maundy Thursday rite.
Vol.19. Maundy Thursday rite.
Vol.20. The Good Friday rite (with short Passion).
Vol.21. The Good Friday passion (complete form).
Vol.22. Good Friday tenebrae.
Vol.23. The Holy Saturday rite.
Vol.24. Holy Saturday tenebrae.
Vol.25. Missa seraphica (with plainsong Credo).
Vol.26. Missa angelica (with plainsong Credo and Gloria).

THE LITURGICAL MUSIC PRESS, INC.
Commemoration folio. Music for Victory day, Armistice day, Memorial day, Thanksgiving day. New York, Liturgical Music Press, Inc., cop.1944.
4 parts in 1 v.
Organ score.
Contents:
Buxtehude. A mighty fortress is our God; Walther. All glory be to God on high; Kreiger. Battaglia; Byrd. The battell, a suite.

THE LITURGICAL MUSIC PRESS, INC.
Masterpieces of organ music. Selected compositions of the old masters, Norman Hennefield, editor. New York, Liturgical Music Press, Inc., cop.1944– .
Folio 1– .
Organ score.
Contents:
Folio 1. Pachelbel: Fugue; Toccata in E minor; Blessed be Thou, Lord Jesus Christ; Lord Christ, God's only son; Magnificat . . . My soul doth magnify the Lord; When in the hour of utmost need. 1945.
Folio 2. Buxtehude. Suite on chorale "Upon my loving God"; We thank Thee, Lord Jesus Christ; Our Father who art in Heaven; Salvation now is come to us; Come now, Saviour of the Gentiles. 1944.
Folio 3. Walther: Concerto del Sig. Torelli; Help, God maker of all things; Lord keep us steadfast in Thy word; God be merciful unto us; O God and Lord. 1944.
Folio 4. Scheidt: When Jesus on the cross was found; We all believe in one true God, the creator; Courante. 1944.
Folio 5. Walther. Christ whose all saving light; Pachelbel. My heart is filled with yearning; Telemann. O lamb of God spotless and pure; Scheidt. Lord Christ, Thou art the Heavenly light. 1944.
Folio 6. Böhm: Christ lay in bonds of death; Lord Jesus Christ, be present now; Our Father who art in Heaven; Prelude and fugue in A minor. 1944.
Folio 7. Fischer: Prelude and fugue No.1 in C major; Prelude and fugue No.2 in C sharp minor; Prelude and fugue No.3 in D minor; Prelude and fugue No.4 in D major; Prelude and fugue No.5 in E flat major; Prelude and fugue No.7 in E major; Recercare on Ave Maria Klare; Recercare on Come Holy Ghost with thy grace. 1944.
Folio 8. Zachau: Prelude and fugue No.4 in G major; Prelude and fugue No.5 in G major;

O God, who lookest down from Heaven; O Lord, we poor sinners; All glory be to God on high; When Adam fell. 1944.

Folio 9. Krebs: From God will naught divide me; O eternity, thou terrifying word; I cry to Thee, Lord Jesus Christ; Fugue on B–A–C–H. 1944.

Folio 10. Voluntaries: Purcell. Voluntary on the 100th Psalm tune; Stanley. Voluntary No.5; Kerll. Capriccio Cucu; Sweelinck. Toccata. 1944.

Folio 11. Telemann: Concerto No.5; Deck thyself, my soul, with gladness; Lord Jesus Christ, reveal thy face. 1944.

Folio 12. The Bach family: Bach, C. P. E. Adagio. Sonata for organ; Bach, J. B. From Heavens high above to earth I come; Bach, W. F. Jesus, priceless treasure; Bach, J. M. These are the Holy ten commandments; Bach, J. B. Rejoice, good Christian folk; Bach, J. C. Fugue. 1944.

Folio 13. Lübeck: Prelude and fugue in C major; Prelude and fugue in C major; Now let us come before Him. 1944.

Folio 14. Buxtehude: This day so full of joy; In dulci jubilo; Blessed be Thou, Lord Jesus Christ; Prelude and fugue in E minor. 1944.

Folio 15. Scheidt. Come, now Saviour of the Gentiles; Gronau. A mighty fortress is our God; Krieger. Lord Christ, God's only son. 1944.

Folio 16. Travers: Voluntary No.1; Voluntary No.3; Voluntary No.4. 1944.

Folio 17. The Lord's prayer: Buxtehude. Our Father who art in Heaven; Schneider. Our Father who art in Heaven; Kauffmann. Our Father who art in Heaven; Krieger. Our Father who art in Heaven; Scheidt. Our Father who art in Heaven; Pachelbel. Our Father who art in Heaven; Steigleder. Our Father who art in Heaven. 1944.

Folio 18. Lent and Communion: Krebs. O Lord, hear my suffering; Kauffman. Farewell, henceforth forever; Walther. O God and Lord; Krebs. Jesus mine, I'll not leave; Krebs. Oh God who lookest down from Heaven. 1945.

Folio 19. Easter music: Scheidt. Christ lay in bonds of death; Böhm. Christ lay in bonds of death; Volckmar. Christ lay in bonds of death; Walther. The Holy day is arrived; Bach, J. H. Christ is risen; Walther. To Christ the little Easter lamb. 1945.

Folio 20. Toccatas: Buxtehude. Toccata in F major; Ahle. Toccata; Krieger. Toccata in F major. 1945.

Folio 21. Gibbons: Voluntary No.1; Voluntary No.2; Voluntary No.3; Pavan to the Lord of Salisbury; Cornet voluntary. 1945.

Folio 22. Palestrina: Ricercare on the 2d tone; Ricercare on the 3d tone; Ricercare on the 4th tone; Ricercare on the 5th tone; Ricercare on the 6th tone. 1945.

Folio 23. Titelouze: Magnificat on 6th tone; Ave Maris Stella; Ut queant laxis. 1945.

Folio 24. Frescobaldi: Kyrie; Christ; Kyrie; Toccata for elevation; Fugue; Toccata. 1945.

Folio 25. Sonatas: Bassani. Sonata; Ritter. Sonatine; Zipoli. Sonata. 1945.

Folio 26. Buttstett: Christ lay in bonds of death; God's son is coming; From Heaven high above to earth I come; This day so full of joy; How brightly shines the morning star. 1945.

Folio 27. Pachelbel: My heart, why are you so sorrowful? ; Fugue No.2; Except the Lord build a house, I; Except the Lord build a house, II; Toccata No.2 in F; Toccata No.3 in F. 1945.

Folio 28. Böhm: O how cheating, o how fleeting; Prelude and fugue, No.2; Christ, that Thou art day and night. 1945.

Folio 29. Couperin: From the mass for use of convents. 1st Kyrie; Solemn mass. Part 1. For use of parishes; Gloria in excelsis Deo. 1945.

Folio 30. Fugues: Bach, C. P. E. Fugue; Telemann. Fugue X; Telemann. Double-fugue; Fux. Fugue 3; Buxtehude. Fugue in C. 1945.

Folio 31. Clérambault. Suite. 1st tone. 1945.

Folio 32. Sweelinck: Fantasia, in the manner of an echo; Psalm 140. Deliver me, O Lord, from the evil man. 1945.

Folio 33. Couperin. From the mass for the use of convents. 4th–8th couplet; Solemn mass. Part 2. For the use of parishes. 1944.

Folio 34. Hassler: Ricercare. 5th tone; Canzona; Ricercare. 8th tone. 1946.

Folio 35. Fantasias: Krieger. Fantasia; Gibbons. A fancy; Weckmann. Fantasia; Froberger. Fantasia. 1946.

Folio 36. Praetorius: The life of the blessed; Bless the Lord, O my soul; O light of blessed Trinity; Christ, we praise in duty bound. 1946.

Folio 37. Couperin: Solemn mass. Part III. For the use of parishes. Gloria; Sanctus. 2d couplet; Benedictus elevation; Agnus Dei; Agnus Dei. 3d couplet; Thanks be to God; Mass for the use of convents; Agnus Dei. 1st couplet. 1946.

Folio 38. Mage: Full organ. Fugue; Trio; Mixture in tenor; Lower register of the trumpet; Solo; Duet. 1946.

Folio 39. Walther: Prepare thyself, o my spirit; Concerto del Sig. Albinoni; Blessed Jesus at thy word. 1946.

Folio 40. Toccatas: Reincken. Toccata in G; Krieger. Toccata in D. 1946.

Folio 41. Bach, Johann Christoph: 11 Choral preludes. 1946.

Folio 42. Barthélemon: Sonata No.1; Sonata No.3; Sonata No.4; Sonata No.6. 1946.

Folio 43. Krebs: Come enter into thy dwelling; We all believe in one true God, the Creator; Rejoice, good Christian folk. 1946.

Folio 44. Erbach: Versetten; Introit. 5th tone; Ricercare. 1946.

Folio 45. Preludes: Flor. Prelude; Kolb. Prelude; Krieger. Prelude; Praetorius. Prelude; Pachelbel. Prelude; Tunder. Prelude; Schildt. Prelude. 1946.

Folio 46. Stanley: Voluntary No.7; Voluntary No.8. 1946.

Folio 47. Krieger: Toccata in C; In Thee, O Lord, have I placed my trust. 1946.

Folio 48. Marchand: Fugue; Mixture in tenor I; Duet; Solo; Low register trumpet, II; Foundation spots; Dialogue. 1947.
Folio 48, Suppl. Beethoven: Prelude through all major keys No.1; Prelude through all major keys No.2; Fugue in D. 1947.
Folio 49 and 50. Handel: Fugue No.1, G minor; Fugue No.2, G; Fugue No.3, B flat; Fugue No.4, B minor; Fugue No.5, A minor; Fugue No.6, C minor. 1947.
Folio 51. Schlick: Salve Regina. 1947.
Folio 52. Lübeck: Prelude and fugue in G minor; Now let us come before Him. 1947.
Folio 53. Scheidt: Magnificat. 9th tone; Pedaliter I, II; Christ that Thou art day and light. 1947.
Folio 54. Walther: In all my deeds, I and II; In Thee, O Lord, have I placed my trust; Lord God, now open wide Thy heaven, II; Lord Jesus Christ, true man and God, I and II. 1947.
Folio 55. Ricercari: Palestrina. Ricercare. 7th tone; Palestrina. Ricercare. 8th tone; Fischer. Ricercare on Christ is risen; Fischer. Ricercare on When Jesus on the cross was found; Pachelbel. Ricercare. 1947.
Folio 56. Böhm. Lord, Jesus Christ, be present now. Verses I, II, IV, V, VI; Our Father, who art in Heaven, II. 1947.
Folio 57. Krieger: Suite in D minor; Prelude in C major. 1947.
Folio 58. Muffat: Toccata with 6 versets or fugues: I in D minor; Toccata with 6 versets or fugues: VII in D; Toccata: VIII in G. 1947.
Folio 59. Telemann: Fugues, No.I, V, VII, VIII, IX, XIII, and XIV. 1947.
Folio 60. Pieces for manuals: Burney. Cornet, IV; Kerll. Canzona, IV; Michael. Toccata for 2 parts in F; Stanley. Voluntary, I. 1947.
Folio 61. Hanff: O God, from Heaven looking forth; From my dear God; A might fortress is our God; Hear my cry, O God; Aid for the praise of God's goodness; If God had not been on our side. 1949.
Folio 62. Froberger: Toccata; Capriccio; Fantasia; Ricercare. 1949.
Folio 63. Tunder: Praeludium in G; Praeludium in F; Praeludium in G. 1949.
Folio 64. Strungk, D. Let me be yours; My soul is raised by the Lord; Strungk, N. A. Ricercare. 1949.
Folio 65. Josquin des Près. Canzone benedictus qui venit benedicta es; Hofhaimer. Ave Maris Stella; Senfl. Bright and shining is the day. 1949.
Folio 66. Gabrieli, Andrea. Toccata del 2d tono; Toccata del 10th tono; Pass'e mezzo antico. 1952.
Folio 67. Early German masters, 16th century: Fridolin Sicher's Tabulaturbuch, Ave Maris Stella, In dulci jubilo, Resonet in laudibus, Es geieng ein man den berg off, Trio, In patrientia vestra; Meyer, Gregor. Kyries No.1–2.
Folio 68.
Folio 69/70. Handel, G. F. Fugue No.7, G major; Fugue No.8, B flat; Fugue No.9, A minor; Fugue No.10, A minor; Fugue No.11, C minor. 1952.
Folio 71. Music for Lent. Ed. by Ernest White. (Johann Christoph Bach, Dietrich Buxtehude, Girolamo Frescobaldi, Frederick W. Marpurg, and Johann Gottfried Walther). 1953.
Folio 72. Music for Easter. Offertory for Easter. Ed. by Ernest White. Dandrieu, Jean François. O filii et filiae; Dialogue; Offertory. 1953.
Folio 73. Old English album. Ed. by Ernest White. (Richard Alwood, Orlando Gibbons, John Redford, and Christopher Tye). 1953.

LIUZZI, FERNANDO, 1884–1940. ed.
. . . La lauda e i primordi della melodia italiana . . . [Roma], La Libreria dello stato, anno XIII E.F., [1935].
2v. col. fronts., plates (part col.), facsims. (music).
Each plate accompanied by guard sheet with descriptive letterpress. Plates are reproductions of miniatures from the original manuscripts.
"Di questa opera . . . sono stati stampati . . . 500 esemplari numerati da 1 a 500."
Includes bibliographies.
Contents:
Vol.1. Albori della lirica musicale in Italia. Le melodie del Laudario 91 di Cortona. Le melodie del Laudario II, I, 122 di Firenze. Laude di Garzo, di Jacopone, di Ugo Panziera. Notazione e trascrizione. La melodia italiana fino all' "ars nova." Monumenti: Il Laudario 91 di Cortona; facsimili, trascrizioni, testi e note.
Vol.2. Monumenti: Il Laudario magliabechiano II, I, 122 di Firenze; facsimili, trascrizioni, testi e note.

LOBO, DUARTE, 1540–1643.
Composições polifónicas. Transcritas em partitura por Manuel Joaquin. Lisboa, Instituto Para a Alta Cultura, 1945– .
v.1– . port., facsims.
Contents:
T.1. Magnificats.

DAS LOCHEIMER LIEDERBUCH.
Das Locheimer Liederbuch nebst der Ars organisandi von Conrad Paumann, als Documente des deutschen Liedes sowie des frühesten geregelten Contrapunktes und der ältesten Instrumentalmusik aus den Urschriften kritisch bearb. von Friedrich Wilhelm Arnold.
p.1–234.
In: Jahrbücher für Musikalische Wissenschaft, hrsg. von Friedrich Chrysander. Bd. 2. Leipzig, Breitkopf & Härtel, 1867.
Contents:
A. Einleitung. p.1–90.
B. Das Locheimer Liederbuch, nach dem Tode des Herausgebers bearb. und mit Erläuterungen versehen von Heinrich Bellermann. p.91–157.
Verzeichniss der Lieder und Melodien.
1. Mein Mut ist mir wetrübet gar. p.91.
2. Wach auf mein Hort der leucht dort her. p.94.
3. Köm mir ein Trost zu diser Zeyt. p.95.
4. Mein Hercz in hohen frewden ist. p.97.

5. Ellend du hast umbfanden mich. p.97.
6. Der Winder wil hin weichen (3stg.). p.98.
7. Mein Frewd möcht ich wol meren. p.101.
8. Ich var dohin, wann es muss sein. p.103.
9. Ich het mir aufzerkoren. p.104.
10. Eine Melodie ohne Text. p.106.
11. Ach meyden du Vil sene Pein. p.107.
12. Mein Hercz das ist bekümert sere. p.108.
13. Von Meyden pin ich dich werarbt. p.110.
14. Dein alleyn was ich eyn Zeit. p.111.
15. Des Klaffers neyden tut mich Mayden (3stg.). p.112.
16. Möcht ich dein wegeren, zarte Lieb. p.116.
17. Der Wald hat sich entlaubet (3stg.). p.118.
18. Ein Vrouleen edel von Naturen (3stg.). p.121.
19. Frau hör und merk. p.122.
20. Ich bin pey jr. p.123.
21. Kan ich nit über werden. p.124.
22. Ich sach ein Pild in plaben Hosen. p.126.
23. Myniglich zartleich geczyret. p.127.
24. Was ich begynne mit Schimpf. p.128.
25. Mein Hercz hat lange Zeit gewellt. p.129.
26. Act got was meyden Tut. p.130.
27. Wollhyn es muess geschaiden sein. p.131.
28. Mir ist mein Pferd vernagelt gar. p.133.
29. Ein gut selige Jar, gelück und alles Heyl (mit Facsimile der Melodie). p.134.
30. Verslossen jn das Hercze mein (ohne Melodie). p.135.
31. Mit ganczem Willen wünsch ich dir. p.136.
32. Lassz fraw mein Laid. p.137.
33. Sollt mich nit pilleich Wunder han. p.138.
34. Almechtger got her Jesu Crist. p.139.
35. Verlangen tut mich krencken. p.140.
36. Mein Hercz das ist verwundet. p.141.
37. Mein Hertz jn Freuden erquicket. p.143.
38. Unmut hat mir beladen. p.144.
39. All mein Gedencken dy ich hab (mit Facsimile, Schriftprobe, Datum und Namen). p.145.
40. Mein trawt Geselle (3stg.). p.147.
41. Der Summer (2stg. Satz ohne Text). p.149.
42. Ich spring an disem Ringe (mit Facsimile, Schriftprobe, Datum und Namen). p.150.
43. Mocht Gedencken bringen mich dohin. p.151.
44. Czart lip wie süfz dein Anfanck ist. p.153.
45. Es für ein Pawr ven Holcz. p.154.

Drei Frohnleichnamsgesänge:
I. Ave dulce instrumentum. p.155.
II. Vale cibus salutaris. p.156.
III. Virginalis flos vernalis. p.157.

Anmerkungen Arnold's zu einigen der vorstehenden Lieder. p.158–76.

C. Conrad Paumann's Fundamentum organisandi. p.177–224.
Abhandlung über Mensuralnotation, übersetzt und erläutert von H. Bellermann. p.178.
32 gröfstentheils 2stg. Orgelstücke. p.182–224.

D. Nachwort der Herausgeber Fr. Chrysander und H. Bellermann. p.225–34.

DAS LOCHEIMER LIEDERBUCH.
Locheimer Liederbuch und Fundamentum organisandi des Conrad Paumann, in Faksimiledruck hrsg. von Konrad Ameln. Berlin, Wölbing-Verlag, 1925.
2p.L., facsim. ([2], 92, [2] p.), 24p., 1L. illus., pl.
"Der kodex Z b.14 der Fürstlich Stolbergschen Bibliothek."
"Es wurde eine einmalige Vorzugsausgabe von 300 numerierten Exemplaren in Lederband, dir übrige Auflage, von 700 Exemplaren in Halbpergament angefertigt."
"Literatur-nachweis": p.16.

DAS LOCHEIMER LIEDERBUCH . . . Neudeutsche Fassung von Karl Escher. Bearbeitung der Melodien von Walter Lott. Berlin, Wölbing-Verlag, 1926.
94p.

DAS LOCHEIMER LIEDERBUCH. Die mehrstimmigen Sätze, hrsg. von Konrad Ameln.
I.Teil. Augsburg, Bärenreiter, 1926.
32p.
This appears to be Vol.1 of the following work:
Deutsche Liedsätze des fünfzehnten Jahrhunderts für Singstimmen und Melodieinstrumente, hrsg. von Konrad Ameln. Kassel, Bärenreiter, [cop.1927–33].
2v.
Contents:
Vol.2. Glogauer Liederbuch. [cop.1927].
Vol.3. Münchener Liederbuch. Das Schedelsche Liederbuch. [1933].

LOEWE, KARL, 1796–1869.
Carl Loewes Werke. Gesamtausgabe der Balladen, Legenden, Lieder und Gesänge für eine Singstimme, im Auftrage der Loeweschen Familie, hrsg. von Dr. Max Runze. Leipzig, Breitkopf & Härtel, [1899–1904].
17v. front. (port.).
Contents:
Bd.1. Lieder aus der Jugendzeit und Kinderlieder.
Bd.2. Bisher unveröffentlichte und vergessene Lieder, Gesänge, Romanzen und Balladen.
Bd.3. Balladen nationalen Gepräges.
Bd.4. Die deutschen Kaiserballaden.
Bd.5. Hohenzollern-Gesänge und vaterländische Lieder.
Bd.6. Französische, spanische und orientalische Balladen und Gesänge.
Bd.7. Die polnischen Balladen.
Bd.8. Geisterballaden und Gesichte, Todes- und Kirchhofsbilder.
Bd.9. Sagen, Märchen, Fabeln. Aus Tier- und Blumenwelt.
Bd.10. Romantische Balladen aus dem Höfischen und Bürgerlichen Leben. Bilder aus Land und See.
Bd.11. Goethe und Loewe. 1.Abt. Lieder und Balladen.
Bd.12. Goethe und Loewe. 2.Abt. Gesänge im grossen Stil, Oden, Grosslegenden und Grossballaden.
Bd.13/14. Legenden I. 2.Abt. 1. Die eigentlich Legendenperiode; 2. Vereinzelte Legenden, später Legendenperioden.

Bd.15. Lyrische Phantasien, Allegorien, Hymnen, Gesänge, hebräische Gesänge.
Bd.16. Das Loewesche Lied.
Bd.17. Liederkreise.

LOUIS FERDINAND, PRINCE OF PRUSSIA, 1772–1806.
Musikalische Werke; hrsg. von Hermann Kretzschmar . . . Nr.1–6, 8. Leipzig, Breitkopf & Härtel, [1915–17].
7v.
No.1, 4, 8, 1915; No.5, 1916; No.2–3, 6, 1917. No.7 (Rondo in B dur, Op.9) not published in this edition; appeared in 1926 (with plate number L.F.7) as No.3089 of Breitkopf & Härtels Partitur-Bibliothek.
Contents:
Nr.1. Quintett für Pianoforte, zwei Violinen, Viola und Violoncell, Op.1. [score and 4 string parts].
Nr.2. Trio in As dur für Pianoforte, Violine, und Violoncell, Op.2. [score and 2 string parts].
Nr.3. Trio in Es dur für Pianoforte, Violine und Violoncell, Op.3. [score and 2 string parts].
Nr.4. Andante mit Variationen in B dur für Pianoforte, Violine, Viola und Violoncell, Op.4. [score and 3 string parts].
Nr.5. Quartett für Pianoforte, Violine, Viola und Violoncell, Op.5. [score and 3 string parts].
Nr.6. Quartett in F moll, für Pianoforte, Violin, Viola und Violoncell.
Nr.8. Grosses Trio in Es dur für Pianoforte, Violine und Violoncell, Op.10. [score and 2 string parts].

LÜBECK, VINCENT, 1654–1740.
Musikalische Werke; hrsg. im Auftrage der Oberleitung der Glaubensgemeinde Ugrino von Gottlieb Harms. Klecken, Ugrino Abt. Verlag, 1921.
122p.
Contents:
Werke für Orgel: Praeambulum et fuga ex G flat. Praeambulum et fuga ex C. Praeambulum et fuga ex E. Praeambulum et fuga ex C flat. Praeambulum et fuga ex D flat. Praeambulum et fuga ex F. Ich rufzu dir Herr Jesu Christ. Nun lasst uns Gott dem Herren (Fragment). Klavierübung: Praeludium, fuga, allemande, courante, sarabande, gigue. Lobt Gott Ihr Christen allzugleich in einer Chaconne. Kantaten: Gott wie dein name. Willhommen süsser Bräutigam. Hilf deinem Volk. Nachweise.

LÜBECK, VINCENT, 1654–1740.
. . . Orgelwerke, hrsg. von Hermann Keller. Leipzig, C. F. Peters, [cop.1941].
3p.L., 51p. (On cover: Edition Peters. No.4437).
Contents:
Pt.1. Praeludien und Fugen.
Pt.2. Choralbearbeitungen.

LUDFORD, NICHOLAS, ca.1485–ca.1557.
Collected works. Ed. by John D. Bergsagel. [n.p.], American Institute of Musicology, 1963– .
3v. (in progress). (Corpus mensurabilis musicae. No.27).
Contents:
Vol.1. Seven Lady masses. 1963.

LULLY, JEAN BAPTISTE DE, 1632–1687.
Oeuvres complètes de J.-B. Lully, 1632–1687, publiées sous la direction de Henry Prunières. Paris, Éditions de la Revue Musicale; Londres et New York, Stainer and Bell, Ltd., 1930–39.
10v. facsims. (incl. music), front. (port.), plates.
325 copies printed.
25 Exemplaires sur Papier pur fil vergé Lafuma. Numérotés de 1 à 25.
300 Exemplaires sur Papier alfa satiné Lafuma. Numérotés de 26 à 325.
Contents:
[Vol.1]. Les opéras. Tome 1. Cadmus et Hermione. 1930.
[Vol.2]. Les ballets. Tome 1. Ballet du temps. Ballet des plaisirs. Ballet de l'amour malade. 1931.
[Vol.3]. Les motets. Tome 1. Miserere mei Deus. 1931.
[Vol.4]. Les comédies-ballets. Tome 1. Le mariage forcé. L'amour Médecin. 1931.
[Vol.5]. Les opéras. Tome 2. Alceste. 1932.
[Vol.6]. Les ballets. Tome 2. Ballet d'Alcidiane. Ballet des gardes. Ballet de Xerxes. 1933.
[Vol.7]. Les comédies-ballets. Tome 2. Les plaisirs de l'île enchantée. La pastorale comique. Le sicilien. Le grand divertissement royal de Versailles. 1933.
[Vol.8]. Les motets. Tome 2. Plaude, laetare, Gallia. Te Deum laudamus. Dies irae, Dies illa . . . 1935.
[Vol.9]. Les comédies-ballets. Tome 3. Monsieur de Pourceaugnac. Le bourgeois gentilhomme. Les amants magnifiques. 1938.
[Vol.10]. Les opéras. Tome 3. Amadis. 1939.

Lüneburg organ tablatures, *see* Shannon, John R. The free organ compositions from the Lüneburg organ tablatures.

Les luthistes espagnols du XVIe siècle, *see* Morphy, Guillermo, *Conde de*. Les luthistes espagnols du XVIe siècle.

LUTTENBERGER, WILHELM, 1900–1933.
Gesamtausgabe (1926–1933). Hrsg. von Karl Luttenberger. Stuttgart, Im Kommission: Verlag der Christengemeinschaft, 19? – .
v.1– .
Vol.3 includes part for violin and for violoncello for the composer's Sonatine für Geige (Cello) und Klavier.
Contents:
Heft 2. Sologesänge. 1933.
Heft 3. Instrumentalmusik. 1933.

Maatschapij tot bevordering der toonkunst, *see* Vereniging voor Nederlandsche muziekgeschiedenis. Uitgave.

Machaut, Guillaume de, *see* Guillaume de Machaut.

Madrigales y canciones polifónicas, *see* Oller, Maria Teresa. Madrigales y canciones polifónicas.

MADRIGALISTI ITALIANI. Kassel und Basel, Bärenreiter Verlag, 1952– .
v.1– .
Contents:
Vol.1. Marenzio, Luca. Madrigali a 4 e 5 voci. Fascicolo 1. (6 Madrigale). 1952.

Madrigals by English composers of the close of the 15th century, *see* Plainsong and Mediaeval Music Society. Madrigals by English composers of the close of the 15th century.

MAESTRI BOLOGNESI. Pubblicazioni della Biblioteca del Conservatorio G(iovanni) B(attista) Martini in Bologna, 1953– .
v.1– .
Contents:
Vol.1. Giacobbi, Girolamo. L'aurora ingannata (1605). Canti rappresentativi del Conte Ridolfo Campeggio. A cura di Giuseppe Vecchi. 1954.
Vol.2. Azzaiolo, Filippo. Il secondo libro de villotte del Fiore alla padovana (1559). A cura di Giuseppe Vecchi. 1953.
Vol.3. Dattari, Ghinolfo. Le villanelle (1568). A cura di Giuseppe Vecchi. 1955.
Vol.4. Trombetti, Ascanio. Il primo libro delle Napolitane (1573). A cura di Giuseppe Vecchi. 1955.

Mage, Pierre du, *see* Du Mage, Pierre.

Magnificat for double chorus and organ, *see* Pachelbel, Carl Theodorus. Magnificat for double chorus and organ.

MAHLER, GUSTAV, 1860–1911.
Sämtliche Werke; kritische Gesamtausgabe. Hrsg. von der Internationalen Gustav Mahler Gesellschaft. Wien, 1960– .
v.1– .
Contents:
Bd.4. Symphonie Nr.4. Erstausgabe der endgültigen Fassung. Wien, Universal Edition, 1963.
Bd.6. Symphonie Nr.6. Berlin, Wiesbaden, Bote & Bock, 1963.
Bd.7. Symphonie Nr.7. Berlin, Wiesbaden, Bote & Bock, 1960.
(Presumably, Vols.1–3, 5 will be the Symphonies No.1–3, 5).

Les maîtres du chant, *see* Prunières, Henry. Les maîtres du chant.

Les maîtres du clavecin, *see* Köhler, Louis. Les maîtres du clavecin.

Les maîtres français de l'orgue aux XVIIème et XVIIIème siècles, *see* Raugel, Félix. Les maîtres français de l'orgue aux XVIIème et XVIIIème siècles.

Les maîtres musiciens de la Renaissance française, *see* Expert, Henry. Les maîtres musiciens de la Renaissance française.

MALDÉGHEM, ROBERT JULLIEN VAN, 1810–1893. ed.
Trésor musical. Collection authentique de musique sacrée & profane des anciens maîtres belges, recueillie et transcrite en notation moderne par R. J. van Maldéghem. Année 1–29 (1865–1893). Brussels, C. Muquardt, [1865–93].
29v.
Score; parts for année 11–29.
Each année issued in 2 parts: Musique profane; Musique religieuse.
For annotated index see "Maldéghem and his buried treasure," by Gustave Reese, in Music Library Association, Notes. Ser.2, Vol.6, Dec.1948, p.87–117, with corrections of incorrect attributions made by Maldéghem.
Contains compositions by Alexander Agricola, Benedictus Appenzeller, Jacob Arcadelt, Josquin Baston, Jacob van Berchem, Antoine Brumel, Jacobus Bultel, Cabilliau, Clemens non Papa, Joannes de Cleve, Loyset Compère, Francesco Corteccia, Jean Courtois, Thomas Crecquillon, Pierre des Cronets, Josquin des Près, Ludovicus Episcopius, Noel Faignient, Costanzo Festa, Arnoldus Feys, Joannes de Fossa, Gheerkin, Hayne van Ghizeghem, Nicolas Gombert, Claude Goudimel, Benedictus Hertoghs, Jean de Hollande, Hutinet, Jachet de Mantua, Jacotin, Clément Janequin, Gossen Junckers, Jacob de Kerle, Philippe Lapperdey, Pierre de La Rue, Orlando di Lasso, Claudin Le Jeune, Mattheus Le Maistre, Jean Longueval, Joannes de Macque, Joannes de Martelaere, Rinaldo del Mel, Leonard van Meldert, Lambertus de Monte, Philippe de Monte, Jacob Obrecht, Johannes Ockeghem, Van Ongueval, Andrea Pevernage, Matthaeus Pipelare, Jacob van Ponte, Jean Richafort, Philippe Rogier, Maitre Rogier-Pathie, Cipriano de Rore, Barthelemy van Roy, Franciscus Sale, D'Oude Scheure, Claudin de Sermisy, Jacob Vaet, Philippe Verdelot, Cornelius Verdonck, Hubert Waelrant, Adrian Willaert, and A. Yver.

Mannheim symphonists, *see* Riemann, Hugo. Mannheim symphonists.

MANTICA, FRANCESCO. ed.
Prime fioriture del melodramma italiano, collezione diretta da Francesco Mantica . . . Roma, Casa Editrice Claudio Monteverdi, 1912–30.
2v. facsims.
Editor: Vol.1–2, F. Mantica.
Contents:
Vol.1. Cavalieri, E. de'. Dalla rappresentatione di anima, et di corpo. 1912.
Vol.2. Caccini, G. Le nuove musiche. 1930.

MARCKHL, ERICH. ed.
Klavierwerke steiermärkischer Komponisten . . . Works for the piano by Styrian composers.

Wien, Österreichischer Bundesverlag, [cop. 1954–56].
3v. (Hausmusik ÖBV 6781, 165/6781, 178/6781, 181).
Contents:
Vol.1.
Bloch, Waldemar. Sonatine in E.
Haager, Max. Fünf Klavierstücke. Werk 2b.
Aigner, H. F. Vier kleine Klavierstücke, Op.9.
Vol.2.
Haidmayer, Karl. VII. Sonate für Klavier.
Eisel, Günther. Klaviersonate.
Kainz, Walter. Sonatine in E.
Vol.3.
Marckhl, Erich. Klaviersonate in F.
Mixa, Franz. Klaviersonate.

Marenzio, Luca, ca.1553–1599. Sämtliche Werke, *see* Publikationen älterer Musik. Jahrg.4[1], 6.

MARIX, JEANNE, 1896–1939. ed.
Les musiciens de la cour de Bourgogne au XVe siècle (1420–1467) . . . Messes, motets, chansons. Publiés par J. Marix. Paris, Éditions de l'Oiseau-Lyre, [cop.1937].
xxviii, 240p. incl. front. (facsim.).
Open score: 2 to 4 mixed voices. French or Latin words.
300 copies printed.
Bibliography included in "Notes" (p.xxiii–xxvi).
Contains compositions by Gilles de Binche, Pierre Fontaine, Jacques Vide, Nicole Grenon, Gilles Joye, Hayne de Ghizeghem, and Robert Morton.

MARROCCO, WILLIAM THOMAS, 1909– . ed.
Fourteenth-century Italian cacce, ed. by W. Thomas Marrocco. Cambridge, Mass., Mediaeval Academy of America, 1942.
xx, 84p. incl. front., illus. (music), facsims. (music). (Half title: The Mediaeval Academy of America. Publication No.39. [Studies and documents. No.4]).
"Lithoprinted."
Includes 20 transcriptions of 2- and 3-part cacce.
Cacce by Lorenzo da Firenze, Zaccaria, Magister Piero, Giovanni da Firenze, Francesco Landini, Niccolò da Perugia, Vincentius de Arimino, Jacopo da Bologna, and Ghirardello da Firenze.

MARROCCO, WILLIAM THOMAS, 1909– . ed.
Fourteenth-century Italian cacce. 2d ed., rev. Cambridge, Mass., Mediaeval Academy of America, 1961.
xxii, 114p. facsims., music. (The Mediaeval Academy of America. Publication No.39).
"Lithoprinted."
Includes 26 transcriptions, in score, of 2- and 3-part cacce.
Bibliography: p.99.

MARROCCO, WILLIAM THOMAS, 1909– . ed.
Music in America, an anthology from the landing of the pilgrims to the close of the Civil War, 1620–1865. Compiled and ed., with historical and analytical notes, by W. Thomas Marrocco and Harold Gleason. New York, W. W. Norton, [1964].
371p. facsims.
"Biographical notes": p.355–61.

Martens, Heinrich, 1876– , ed. Musikalische Formen in historischen Reihen, *see* Musikalische Formen in historischen Reihen.

MARTÍNEZ TORNER, EDUARDO, 1888– . ed.
. . . Colección de vihuelistas españoles del siglo XVI; estudio y transcripción de las ediciones originales, por Eduardo M. Torner . . . Cuad.1. Madrid, Orfeo Tracio, S.A., [1923].
1 v. to date. facsims., table.
At head of title: Junta para Ampliación de Estudios e Investigaciones Científicas. Centro de Estudios Históricos.
Contents:
Cuad.1. Narváez. El delphin de música, 1538. 1923.

MARTÍNEZ TORNER, EDUARDO, 1888– . ed.
. . . Colección de vihuelistas españoles del siglo XVI. Composiciones escogidas de El delphin de música (1538), de Narváez, arregladas para piano y para canto y piano, por Eduardo M. Torner. Madrid, Centro de Estudios Históricos, [pref.1923].
19p.
At head of title: Junta para Ampliación de Estudios e Investigaciones Científicas. Centro de Estudios Históricos.
Arranged for piano or piano and voice.

MARTINI, GIOVANNI BATTISTA, 1706–1784.
. . . 20 Composizioni originali per organo. A cura di Ireneo Fuser. Padova, Editori G. Zanibon, cop.1956.
55p. (N.4135).

Marx, Josef, ed. Music for wind instruments by 18th century masters, *see* Music for wind instruments by 18th century masters.

Mascaudio, Guglielmi de, *see* Guillaume de Machaut.

Mass for Ascension Day, *see* Plainsong and Mediaeval Music Society. Mass for Ascension Day.

Mass for the dead. Church of England. Liturgy and ritual, *see* Plainsong and Mediaeval Music Society. Church of England. Liturgy and ritual. Mass for the dead.

Masterpieces of music before 1750, *see* Parrish, Carl. Masterpieces of music before 1750.

Masterpieces of organ music, *see* The Liturgical Music Press, Inc. Masterpieces of organ music.

The Mediaeval Academy of America. Publication No.36. (Studies and documents. No.3), *see* Landino, Francesco. The works of Francesco Landino.

The Mediaeval Academy of America. Publication No.39. (Studies and documents. No.4), *see* Marrocco, William Thomas. Fourteenth-century Italian cacce.

The Mediaeval Academy of America. Publication No.42. (Studies and documents. No.5), *see* [Petrucci, Ottaviano dei]. Harmonice musices Odhecaton A, ed. by Helen Hewitt.

The Mediaeval Academy of America. Publication No.55, *see* Apel, Willi. French secular music of the late fourteenth century.

MEDTNER, NIKOLAI KARLOVITCH, 1880–1951.
Collected works. Moscow, State Music Publishers, 1959– .
v.1– .
Title page in Russian.
Contents:
Vol.1. Piano works. Op.1, 2, 4, 5, 7, 8, 9, 10, 11, 14.
Vol.2. Piano works. Op.17, 20, 22, 23, 25, 26, 27, 30, 31.
Vol.3. Piano works. Op.34, 35, 38, 39, 40, 42, 47.
Vol.4. Piano works. Op.48, 49, 51, 53, 54, 55, 56, 59.
Vol.5. Works for voice and piano. Op.3, 6, 12, 13, 15, 16, 18, 24, 28, 29.
Vol.6. Works for voice and piano. Op.32, 36, 37, 41, 45, 46, 52, 61.
Vol.7. Works for violin and piano. Op.16, 21, 43, 44, 57.
Vol.8. Chamber ensembles. Quintet for piano and strings.
Vol.9. Works and arrangements for 2 pianos. Op.33, 50, 58, 60.
Vol.10. Works for piano and orchestra. (Orch. score). Concerto No.1.
Vol.11. Works for piano and orchestra. (Orch. score). Concerto No.2.
Vol.12. Works for piano and orchestra. (Orch. score). Concerto No.3.
Vol.13. Unpublished works for piano.

Die mehrstimmige italienische Laude um 1500, *see* Jeppesen, Knud. Die mehrstimmige italienische Laude um 1500.

Meister-Schule der alten Zeit. Sammlung klassischer Violin-Sonaten, *see* Moffat, Alfred Edward. Meister-Schule der alten Zeit. Sammlung klassischer Violin-Sonaten.

Meister-Schule der alten Zeit. Sammlung klassischer Violoncello-Sonaten, *see* Moffat, Alfred Edward. Meister-Schule der alten Zeit. Sammlung klassischer Violoncello-Sonaten.

MÉLANGES DE MUSICOLOGIE CRITIQUE, publiés par Pierre Aubry. Paris, H. Welter, 1900–1905.
4v.
Contents:
Vol.1. Aubry, Pierre. La musicologie médiévale. 1900.
Vol.2. Adam de Saint-Victor. Les proses d'Adam de Saint-Victor. 1900.
Vol.3. Jeanroy, A. Lais et descorts français du XIIIe siècle. 1901.
Vol.4. Aubry, Pierre. Les plus anciens monuments de la musique française. 1905.

Mellor, Hugh, ed. The English dancing master, *see* Playford, John. The English dancing master.

MELODIARIUM HUNGARIAE MEDII AEVI. Hrsg. von Benjamin Rajeczky. 1956– .
v.1– .
Contents:
Vol.1. Hymnen und Sequenzen. Beschreibung der Quellen von Polikárp Radó. 1956.

Die Melodien der deutschen evangelischen Kirchenlieder, *see* Zahn, Johannes. Die Melodien der deutschen evangelischen Kirchenlieder.

MENDELSSOHN-BARTHOLDY, FELIX, 1809–1847.
Werke. Kritisch durchgesehene Ausgabe von Julius Rietz. Ser.1–19. Leipzig, Breitkopf & Härtel, 1874–77.
19 series.
Contents:
Ser.I. Symphonien. Nr.1–4.
Ser.II. Ouvertüren. Nr.1–10.
Ser.III. Marsch für Orchester. Op.108.
Ser.IV. Violinkonzert mit Orchester.
Ser.V. Oktett und 2 Quintette.
Ser.VI. Streichquartette. Nr.1–7.
Ser.VII. Für Blasinstrumente. Op.24, 103, 113, 114.
Ser.VIII. Für Pianoforte und Orchester. Op.25, 40, 22, 29, 43.
Ser.IX. Für Pianoforte und Saiteninstrumente. Nr.1–11.
Sextett. Op.110.
Drei Quartette. Op.1, 2, 3.
Zwei Trios. Op.49, 66.
Fünf Duos. Op.4, 17, 45, 58, 109.
Ser.X. Für Pianoforte zu 4 Händen. Nr.1, 2.
Ser.XI. Für Pianoforte allein. 4 Bände.
Ser.XII. Für Orgel. Op.37, 65.
Ser.XIII. Oratorien.
1. Paulus.
2. Elias.
3. Christus.
Ser.XIV. Geistliche Gesangwerke.
Abt.A. Für Solostimmen Chor und Orchester.
1.Bd. Psalm 115, 42, 95, 114, 98.
2.Bd. Lobgesang, Symphonie-Kantate.
3.Bd. Lauda Sion: Hymne für Altstimme; Tu es Petrus; Verleih uns Frieden.
Abt.B. Für Solostimme, Chor und Orgel.
Abt.C. Für Solostimme und Chor ohne Begleitung.
Ser.XV. Grössere weltliche Gesangwerke.
1.Bd. Antigone.
2.Bd. Athalia.
3.Bd. Oedipus in Kolonos.
4.Bd. Sommernachtstraum.
5.Bd. Walpurgisnacht.

6.Bd. Festgesang "An die Künstler" und Festgesang zur 4. Säkularfeier der Erfindung der Buchdruckerkunst.
7.Bd. Die Hochzeit des Camacho.
8.Bd. Heimkehr aus der Fremde.
9.Bd. Loreley.
10.Bd. Konzertarie.
Ser.XVI. Lieder für Sopran, Alt, Tenor, und Bass.
Ser.XVII. Lieder und Gesänge für 4 Männerstimmen.
Ser.XVIII. Lieder und Gesänge für 2 Stimmen mit Pianoforte-Begleitung.
Ser.XIX. Lieder und Gesänge für 1 Singstimme mit Pianoforte.

MENDELSSOHN-BARTHOLDY, FELIX, 1809–1847.
Leipziger Ausgabe der Werke Felix Mendelssohn Bartholdys. Hrsg. von der Internationalen Felix-Mendelssohn-Gesellschaft. Leipzig, Deutscher Verlag für Musik, 1960– .
v.1– .
Contents:
Unveröffentlichte Werke.
Konzert für zwei Klaviere und Orchester E-dur. 1960.
Konzert für zwei Klaviere und Orchester As-dur. 1961.
Sinfonie in D. 1965.
Ser.V. Bühnenwerke, Musik zu Schauspielen.
Bd.1. Die beiden Pädagogen. Singspiel in einem Aufzug. Hrsg. von Karl-Heinz Köhler. 1966.

MENDELSSOHN-BARTHOLDY, FELIX, 1809–1847.
Complete organ works. New York, C. F. Peters, n.d.
p.1– .
Contents: .
Op.37. 3 Preludes and fugues.
Op.65. 6 Sonatas.

MENDELSSOHN-BARTHOLDY, FELIX, 1809–1847.
. . . Complete piano works . . . London, Augener Ltd., [1909].
5v. (Augener's Edition. No.8237, 5076–5077, 8235, 5078).
Contents:
Vol.1. Songs without words.
Vol.2. Op.5, 7, 14, 72, 16, 33 No.1–3, and Andante cantabile.
Vol.3. Op.28, 35, 54, 82, 104, Book 1–2; Scherzo; Scherzo à capriccio; Etude in F minor.
Vol.4. Op.25, 40, 22, 29, 43.
Vol.5. Op.6, 15, 105, 106, 117–119; Prelude and fugue in E minor; Two musical sketches; Gondellied in A.

MENDELSSOHN-BARTHOLDY, FELIX, 1809–1847.
Sämtliche Klavierwerke. Hrsg. von Theodor Kullak. Leipzig, C. F. Peters, 19? – .
5v. (Edition Peters. 1704a–e).
Contents:
Vol.1. Lieder ohne Worte.
Vol.2. Op.5, Capriccio. Op.7, Charakterstücke. Op.14, Rondo. Op.16, Fantaisies. Op.33, Caprices. Op.72, Kinderstücke. Andante cantabile e presto agitato.
Vol.3. Op.28, Phantasie. Op.35, Präludien und Fugen. Op.54, Variations sérieuses. Op.82, Andante con variazioni. Op.83, Variationen. Op.104, Etüden. Scherzi. Etude F moll.
Vol.4. Zwei Konzerte. Op.22, Capriccio brillante. Op.29, Rondo brillante. Op.43, Serenade.
Vol.5. Supplement: Sonaten, Präludien und Stücke.

Meslanges divers, *see* Du Mont, Henri. Meslanges divers.

Messe du XIIIe siècle, *see* Coussemaker, Edmond de. Messe du XIIIe siècle.

MESSNER, JOSEPH. ed.
Alte salzburger Meister der kirchlichen Tonkunst. Für den liturgischen und konzertanten Gebrauch hrsg. von Joseph Messner. Die Einleitung schreib der salzburgische Musikhistoriker Dr. Erich Schenk. Augsburg und Wien, Anton Böhm & Sohn, [1927–].
13v.
Contents:
Heft 1. Bernardi, Steffano. O sacrum convivium.
Heft 2. Caldara, Antonio. Lauda anima mea.
Heft 3. Haydn, Michael. Tenebrae factae sunt.
Heft 4. Bonamico, Pedro. Laudate Dominum.
Heft 5. Mozart, Leopold. Du wahrer Mensch und Gott!
Heft 6. Mozart, Leopold. Parasti mensam.
Heft 7. Mozart, Wolfgang Amadeus. Sub tuum praesidium.
Heft 8. Biber, H. F. Oelberg-Sonate.
Heft 9. Mozart, Wolfgang Amadeus. Alma Dei creatoris.
Heft 10. Bernardi, Steffano. Missa "Il bianco e dolce cigno."
Heft 11. Haydn, Michael. Gott, ich falle Dir zu füssen.
Heft 12. Mozart, Wolfgang Amadeus. Adagio für Violinsolo und Orgel. Nach K.V.261.
Heft 13. Bernardi, Steffano. Missa "Praeparate corda vestra."

MESTRES DE L'ESCOLANIA DE MONTSERRAT; obres musicals dels monjos del Monestir de Montserrat 1500–1800. [Montserrat], Monestir de Montserrat, 1930–36.
5v. music.
Contents:
Pujol, David, ed. Joan Cererols. [v.] 1–3. 1930–1932.
Pujol, David, ed. Musica instrumental. v. 1–2. 1934–1936.
(Vol.1. Miquel López. Narcis Casanoves.
Vol.2. Anselm Viola. Felip Rodríguez. Josep Vinyals).

MIASKOVSKY, NIKOLAI, 1881–1950.
Collected works. Moscow, State Music Publishers, 1953– .
v.1– .

Contents:
Vol.1. Symphonies No.4 and 5.
Vol.2. Symphony No.6.
Vol.3. Symphonies No.15 and 16.
Vol.4. Symphonies No.18 and 21.
Vol.5. Symphonies No.24 and 25.
Vol.6. Symphonies No.26 and 27.
Vol.7. Works for orchestra:
Sinfonietta for orchestra, Op.10; Sinfonietta for string orchestra, Op.32, No.2; Sinfonietta for string orchestra, Op.68, No.2; Divertissment, Op.80; Triumphal march for band; Dramatic overture for band, Op.60.
Vol.8. String quartets No.1–13.
Vol.9. Sonata No.1, Op.12. (Violoncello and piano); Sonata No.2, Op.81. (Violoncello and piano); Concerto, Op.44, Violin and orchestra. (Violin and piano); Concerto, Op.66, Violoncello and orchestra. (Violoncello and piano).
Vol.10. Piano works.
Vol.11. Vocal works.
Vol.12. Cantata: Kirov is with us.

Michigan. University. Publications. Fine arts. Vol.2, *see* Isaac, Heinrich. Choralis Constantinus. Book III.

Migot, Georges, 1891– , ed. Musiques françaises, *see* Musiques françaises.

Milán, Luis, 16th century. Libro de musica de vihuela de mano, *see* Publikationen älterer Musik. Jahrg.2.

Minnesinger, *see* Hagen, Friedrich Heinrich von der. Minnesinger.

Miscellanea. No.1, *see* Le Jeune, Claude. Airs.

Mischiati, Oscar, ed. Monumenti di musica italiana, *see* Monumenti di musica italiana.

Missa "O quam suavis" for 5 voices, *see* Plainsong and Mediaeval Music Society. Missa "O quam suavis" for 5 voices.

Missa "Rex Splendens," *see* Plainsong and Mediaeval Music Society. Missa "Rex Splendens."

Missa Tornacensis, *see* Catholic Church, Roman. Liturgy and ritual. Missal. Missa Tornacensis.

MITTELDEUTSCHES MUSIKARCHIV. Veröffentlichungen des Musikwissenschaftlichen Seminars der Friedrich-Schiller-Universität Jena. 2.Reihen. Leipzig, Breitkopf & Härtel, 1955– .
v.1– .
Contents:
Reihe I: Klaviermusik.
Bd.1. Mattheson, Johann. Die wohlklingende Fingersprache. Fugen und Suitensätze für Cembalo oder Klavier. Hrsg. von Lothar Hoffmann-Erbrecht. 1957.
Bd.2. Graupner, Johann Christoph. Acht Partiten für Cembalo oder Klavier. Hrsg. von Lothar Hoffmann-Erbrecht. 1957.
Bd.3. Platti, Giovanni Benedetto. Zwölf Sonaten für Cembalo oder Klavier. 1.Teil: Nr.1–6. Hrsg. von Lothar Hoffmann-Erbrecht. 1957.
Bd.4. Platti, Giovanni Benedetto. Zwölf Sonaten für Cembalo oder Klavier. 2.Teil: Nr.7–12. Hrsg. von Lothar Hoffmann-Erbrecht. 1957.
Bd.5. Martini, Giovanni Battista. Sechs Sonaten für Cembalo oder Klavier. Hrsg. von Lothar Hoffmann-Erbrecht. 1957.
Bd.6. Müthel, Johann Gottfried. Drei Sonaten für Klavier. Hrsg. von Lothar Hoffmann-Erbrecht. 1957.
Bd.7. Müthel, Johann Gottfried. Zwei Ariosi mit zwölf Variationen für Klavier. Hrsg. von Lothar Hoffmann-Erbrecht. 1957.
Reihe II: Kammermusik.
Bd.1. Pepusch, Johann Christoph. Sechs Triosonaten für Violine, Oboe und Basso Continuo. 1.Teil: Sonaten I–III. Hrsg. von Lothar Hoffmann-Erbrecht. 1957.
Bd.2. Pepusch, Johann Christoph. Sechs Triosonaten für Violine, Oboe und Basso Continuo. 2.Teil: Sonaten IV–VI. Hrsg. von Lothar Hoffmann-Erbrecht. 1957.

Mocquereau, Dom André, 1849–1930, ed. Paléographie musicale, *see* Paléographie musicale.

Modo per imparare a sonare di tromba tanto di guerra quanto musicalmente in organo, *see* Fantini, Girolamo. Modo per imparare a sonare di tromba tanto di guerra quanto musicalmente in organo.

MOECKS GELBE MUSIKHEFTE. Celle, Hermann Moeck, 19? – .
v.1– .
Contents:
Vol.1. Mönkemeyer, Helmut. Hohe Schule des Blockflötenspiels. Advanced school of recorder playing. L'art de la flute douce. 51 Übungen für die Alt-Blockflöte.
Vol.3. Erlebach, Philipp Heinrich. 3 Arien für mittlere Singstimme, 2 Alt-Blockflöten und Basso Continuo. (Mühlen).
Vol.4. Sambeth, Heinrich. Das Blockflötchen. Bunte Liedbilder als Anweisung für die Grundschule.
Vol.5. Bauer, Franz. Suite Nr.1 für Alt-Blockflöte und Tasteninstrumente. (leicht).
Vol.6. Mönkemeyer, Helmut. Das Spiel auf der Blockflote in C-moll.
Vol.7. Von Beckerath, Alfred. Sonate in einem Satz für Alt-Blockflöte und Klavier.
Vol.8. Märsche und Tänze zu spielen auf 1 oder 2 Blockflöten oder anderen Melodieinstrumenten, gesetzt von Willi Wolter. Grosse Ausgabe mit Klavier- oder Gitarrenbegleitung ad lib. (einschliesslich Flötenstimme).
Vol.9. Bauer, Franz. Suite Nr.2 für Alt-Blockflöte und Tasteninstrumente. (leicht).
Vol.10. Fecker, Adolf. Das dreistimmige Blockflötenspiel aus dem Stegreif. Anleitung zu Improvisation und Zusammenspiel im Gruppenunterricht.
Vol.11. Händel, Georg Friedrich. Sonate G-moll

für Alt-Blockflöte und Basso Continuo. (Mönkemeyer).

Vol.12. Händel, Georg Friedrich. Sonate F-dur für Alt-Blockflöte und Basso Continuo.

Vol.13. Händel, Georg Friedrich. Sonate C-dur für Alt-Blockflöte und Basso Continuo.

Vol.14. Händel, Georg Friedrich. Sonate A-moll für Alt-Blockflöte und Basso Continuo.

Vol.15. Lorenz, Karl. Orchesterausgabe. (Schnitzler). Klavierauszug (mit Akkordeonbezifferung) und 7 Stimmen.

Vol.16. Bach, J. S. Doch Jesus will . . . Arie aus Kantate 46 für 2 Alt-Blockflöten, Alt-Singstimme und Basso Continuo. (Hillemann).

Vol.17. Händel, G. Fr. Herz, der Liebe susser Born . . . Arie aus "Acis und Galatea" für 2 Alt-Blockflöten, Sopran-Singstimme und Basso Continuo. (Hillemann).

Vol.22. Advent- und Weihnachtslieder und -gesänge, 1–4 Stimmig für gleiche und gemischte Stimmen. (Mönkemeyer).

Vol.23. Bach, J. S. Höchster, was ich habe . . . Arie aus Kantate 39 für Alt-Blockflöte, Sopran-Singstimme und Basso Continuo.

Vol.24. Bach, J. S. Die Obrigkeit ist Gottes Gabe . . . Arie aus Kantate 119 für Alt-Blockflöte, Alt-Singstimme und Basso Continuo.

Vol.25. Bach, J. S. Leget euch dem Heiland unter . . . Arie aus Kantate 182 für Alt-Blockflöte, Alt-Singstimme und Basso Continuo.

Vol.26. Bach, J. S. Jesu, Dir sie Preis . . . Arie aus Kantate 142 für 2 Alt-Blockflöten, Alt-Singstimme und Basso Continuo.

Vol.27. Bach, J. S. Schafe können sicher weiden . . . Arie aus Kantate 208 für 2 Alt-Blockflöten, Sopran-Singstimme und Basso Continuo.

Vol.28. Bach, J. S. Komm, du süsse Todesstunde . . . Arie aus Kantate 161 für Alt- und Tenor-Blockflöte, Alt-Singstimme und Basso Continuo.

Vol.29. Bach, J. S. Komm, leite mich . . . Arie aus Kantate 175 für 3 Alt-Blockflöten, Alt-Singstimme und Basso Continuo.

Vol.30. Allerlei Volkslieder zum Singen und Spielen auf 1 oder 2 Blockflöten oder anderen Melodieinstrumenten, gesetzt von Willi Wolter.

Vol.31. Von Beckerath, Alfred. Sonatine für Alt-Blockflöte und Tasteninstrument.

Vol.32. Hausmusik zur Weihnacht. Vokalsätze und Choralvorspiele von Meistern des 16.–18. Jahrhunderts für 2 Melodieinstrumente und Tasteninstrument.

Vol.33. Mönkemeyer, Helmut. Handleitung für das Spiel der Alt-Blockflöte in F.

Vol.34. Die Markus-Passion aus Grundigs Handschrift der Historienreihe von Heinrich Schütz für Einzelstimmen und 4-stimmigen Chor. (Fritz Schmidt). Score.

Vol.35. Same as Vol.34. Parts.

Vol.36. Allerlei Volkslieder zum Singen und Spielen auf 1 oder 2 Blockflöten oder anderen Melodieinstrumenten (kleine Ausgabe), gesetzt von Willi Wolter.

Vol.37. Märsche und Tänze zu spielen auf 1 oder 2 Blockflöten oder anderen Melodieinstrumenten (kleine Ausgabe), gesetzt von Willi Wolter.

Vol.38. Mönkemeyer, Helmut. Das Spiel aus der Bass-Blockflöte. Playing the bass recorder. Introduction au maniement de la flute douce basse.

Vol.39. Ambrosius, Hermann. Sonatine für 2 Geigen oder andere Melodieinstrumente.

Vol.40. Pekiel, Bartolomäus. 40 Stücke für Laute (oder Gitarre) (Ochs).

Vol.41. Berger, Gregor. Sonate in G für Alt-Blockflöte und Tasteninstrument.

Vol.42. Mönkemeyer, Helmut. Schule für Sopran-Gambe oder 6-saitige Sopran-Fidel in Quart-Terz-Stimmung.

Vol.43. Mönkemeyer, Helmut. Schule für Alt-Tenor-Gambe oder -Fidel.

Vol.44. Mönkemeyer, Helmut. Schule für Tenor-Bass-Gambe oder -Fidel.

Vol.45. Mönkemeyer, Helmut. Die Quintfidel. Heft I. Spielanleitung für das Sopran- Alt-Instrument.

Vol.46. Mönkemeyer, Helmut. Die Quintfidel. Heft II. Spielanleitung für das Tenor- Bass-Instrument.

Vol.47. Mönkemeyer, Helmut. Die Quintfidel. Heft III. 10 Übungen für das Tenor- Bass-Instrument.

Vol.48. Mönkemeyer, Helmut. Die Quinfidel. Heft IV. Spielanleitung für das Sopran- Alt-Instrument.

Vol.49. Fernandez-Lavie, Fernand. Gitarrespiel im Überblick Einführung in die Spielweise nach klassisch-spanischer Schule.

Vol.50. Schulz, Johann Abraham Peter. Serenata im Walde zu singen. Für 4-stimmigen Chor, 3 Blockflöten oder andere Blasinstrumente und Streichorchester eingerichtet von Helmut Mönkemeyer.

Vol.51. Mönkemeyer, Helmut. Das Spiel auf der Blockflöte in C-moll.

Vol.52. Mönkemeyer, Helmut. Dänisch-schwedisch-norwegische Ausgabe.

Vol.53. Mönkemeyer, Helmut. Flämisch-holländische Ausgabe.

Vol.54. Miedlar, Marian. Schule für Violoncello. Heft I.

Vol.55. Miedlar, Marian. Schule für Violoncello. Heft II.

Vol.56. Miedlar, Marian. Schule für Violoncello. Heft III.

Vol.57. Wilkomirski, Kasimir. 12 Etuden für Violoncello.

Vol.60. 9 Pastoralen alter Meister für 2 Melodieinstrumente (Violinen, Sopran- und Alt-Blockflöte, etc.) und Klavier oder Gitarre; Violoncello (Gambe) ad lib. (Ochs), mit 3 farbigem Kunstdruck-Umschlag.

Vol.61. Am Weihnachtsbaum. 40 Lieder für die Advent- und Weihnachtszeit zum Klavier ein- oder zweistimmig zu singen oder auf Instrumenten (2 Sopran-Blockflöten oder Geigen) zu spielen.

Vol.62. Am Weihnachtsbaum. 40 Lieder für die Advent- und Weihnachtszeit zweistimmig zu

singen oder auf Instrumenten (2 Sopran-Blockflöten oder Geigen) zu spielen.
Vol.63. Kommt, pfeift und trombt! Spielstücke für die Weihnachtszeit für Blockflöten- oder andere Instrumentalgruppen, drei- und vierstimmig.
Vol.65. Klassische Tanzweisen von Haydn bis Schubert für 2 Melodieinstrumente (2 Sopran- oder Sopran- und Alt-Blockflöten) mit Klavier oder Gitarre ad lib. (Grosse Ausgabe).
Vol.66. Klassische Tanzweisen von Haydn bis Schubert für 2 Melodieinstrumente (2 Sopran- oder Sopran- und Alt-Blockflöten) mit Klavier oder Gitarre ad lib. Heft II. (Grosse Ausgabe).
Vol.67. Klassische Tanzweisen von Haydn bis Schubert für 2 Melodieinstrumente. (2 Sopran- oder Sopran- und Alt-Blockflöten). Heft I. (Kleine Ausgabe).
Vol.68. Klassische Tanzweisen von Haydn bis Schubert für 2 Melodieinstrumente (2 Sopran- oder Sopran- und Alt-Blockflöten). Heft II. (Kleine Ausgabe).
Vol.69. Zweistimmige Spielstücke alter Meister, für Gitarre zusammengestellt und hrsg. von Josef Rentmeister. Heft I.
Vol.70. Zweistimmige Spielstücke alter Meister, für Gitarre zusammengestellt und hrsg. von Josef Rentmeister. Heft II.
Vol.71. Duett-Buch für Alt-Blockflöten. (Hechler). (mit Hinweisen für den Unterricht). Heft I. Meister des 17. und 18. Jahrhunderts.

MOECKS KAMMERMUSIK. Celle, Hermann Moeck, 1939– .
v.1– .
Contents:
Vol.1. Telemann, G. P. Sonata a tre in F moll für Alt-Blockflöte (Querflöte), Violine und Basso Continuo. (Rodemann). 1939.
Vol.2. Dieupart, Charles. Suite I für Tenor-Blockflöte (Sopran-Blockflöte, Querflöte) und Basso Continuo. 1939. Alto reprint 1947.
Vol.3. Dieupart, Charles. Suite II for the same. 1939. Reprint 1947.
Vol.4. Van Konink, Servaas. Sonata IX für Alt-Blockflöte (Querflöte, Oboe, Violine) und Basso Continuo. (Friedrich).
Vol.5. Telemann, G. P. Trio-Sonate F-dur für Alt-Blockflöte (Querflöte), Violine (2 Alt-Blockflöte) und Basso Continuo. (Rodemann). 1939.
Vol.6. Schultze, Johann Christoph. Ouvertüre (Suite) I, F-dur, für 2 Alt-Blockflöten (Querflöten, Violinen) und Basso Continuo. (Friedrich).
Vol.7. Finger, Gottfried. 2 Sonaten für 2 Alt-Blockflöten oder Querflöten. (Rodemann).
Vol.8. Van Konink, Servaas. Sonata VII und X.
Vol.9. Bononcini, Giovanni Battista. Divertimento da Camera für Alt-Blockflöte (Querflöte, Oboe, Violine) und Basso Continuo. (Rodemann).
Vol.10. Telemann, G. P. Sonate F-dur für Alt-Blockflöte (Querflöte) und Oboe (Violine, Tenor-Blockflöte) und Basso Continuo. (Rodemann).
Vol.11. Pepusch, Johann Christoph. Sonata I und II für Alt-Blockflöte (Querflöte, Oboe, Violine) und Basso Continuo. (Dancker-Langner). 1939.
Vol.12. Paisible, Jacques. Sonata prima für 2 Alt-Blockflöten (Querflöten, Oboen, Violinen) und Basso Continuo. (Friedrich).
Vol.13. Paisible, Jacques. Sonata seconda und Sonata terza for the same.
Vol.14. Paisible, Jacques. Sonata quarta for the same.
Vol.15. Paisible, Jacques. Sonata quinta for the same.
Vol.16. Prowo, P. Sonata Nr.5 a tre für 2 Alt-Blockflöten (Querflöten, Oboen, Violinen) und Basso Continuo. (Friedrich).
Vol.17. Prowo, P. Sonata Nr.6 a tre für 2 Alt-Blockflöten (Querflöten, Oboen, Violinen) und Basso Continuo. (Friedrich). 1940.
Vol.18. Von Beckerath, Alfred. Sonatine für 2 Blas- oder Streichinstrumente (Alt-Blockflöten, Querflöten, Oboen, Klarinetten, Violinen) und Klavier. 1939.
Vol.19. Fesch, Willem de. 3 Sonaten für 2 Violoncelli (Gamben), Op.8, Nr.7–9. (Schäffler). 1940.
Vol.20. Fesch, Willem de. 3 Sonaten für 2 Violoncelli (Gamben). Op.8, Nr.10–12. 1940.
Vol.21. Pepusch, Johann Christoph. Sonata III und IV für Alt-Blockflöte (Querflöte, Oboe, Violine) und Basso Continuo. (Dancker-Langner).
Vol.22. Pepusch, Johann Christoph. Sonata V und VI für Alt-Blockflöte (Querflöte, Oboe, Violine) und Basso Continuo.
Vol.23. Pepusch, Johann Christoph. Sonata VII und VIII für Alt-Blockflöte (Querflöte, Oboe, Violine) und Basso Continuo.
Vol.24. Hammerschmidt, Andreas. Ballet & Canzone in 3 parts, etc. 1942.
Vol.25. Hammerschmidt, Andreas. Ballet & Canzone in 3 parts, etc. 1942.
Vol.26. Hammerschmidt, Andreas. Ballet & Canzone Nr.2, 3 parts, for 2 C Recorders (Flute, Oboe and Violin) and Piano. 1942.
Vol.27. Hammerschmidt, Andreas. Ballet & Cansone, etc. 1942.
Vol.28. Loeillet, Jean Baptiste. Sonate A-moll, Op.1, Nr.1 für Alt-Blockflöte (Querflöte, Oboe, Violine) und Basso Continuo. (Mönkemeyer).
Vol.29. Loeillet, Jean Baptiste. Sonate F-dur, Op.1, Nr.4 for the same.
Vol.30. Loeillet, Jean Baptiste. Sonate C-dur, Op.1, Nr.6 for the same.
Vol.31. Loeillet, Jean Baptiste. Sonate D-moll, Op.1, Nr.8 for the same.
Vol.32. Loeillet, Jean Baptiste. Sonate C-moll, Op.2, Nr.5 und Sonate G-moll, Op.4, Nr.6 for the same.
Vol.33. Buxtehude, Dietrich. Choralvorspiele für Alt-Blockflöte (Querflöte, Violine, Oboe) und Orgel oder Klavier. (Jöde).
Vol.34. Händel, Georg Friedrich. 9 Sätze aus der Oper "Almira" für Sopran-Blockflöte oder Violine und Basso Continuo.
Vol.35. Scarlatti, Alessandro. Concerto A-moll

für Alt-Blockflöte (Querflöte), 2 Violinen und Basso Continuo. (Frotscher).

Vol.36. Scarlatti, Alessandro. Sonate für 3 Alt-Blockflöten (Querflöten, Oboen, Violinen) und Basso Continuo. (Roy).

Vol.37. Scarlatti, Alessandro. Sonate A-dur für 2 Querflöten (Blockflöten, Oboen), 2 Violinen und Basso Continuo. (Roy).

Vol.38. Corelli, Arcangelo. Sonate II nach den Concerti grossi für 2 Alt-Blockflöten (Violinen) und Basso Continuo. (Moeck/Callenberg).

Vol.39. Rokoko-Duette für 2 Violoncelli, Gamben, Fideln oder Fagotte (Edelstein). Heft I. Josef Bodin de Boismortier. 3 Sonaten.

Vol.40. Fasch, Johann Friedrich. Sonate G-dur für Querflöte, 2 Alt-Blockflöten und Basso Continuo. (Moeck/Callenberg).

Vol.41. Scheibe, Johann Adolf. Concerto a 4 für Alt-Blockflöte (Querflöte), 2 Violinen und Basso Continuo. (Moeck/Callenberg).

Vol.42. Telemann, Georg Philipp. Quadro G-moll für Alt-Blockflöte (Querflöte), Violine, Viola (2 Violine) und Basso Continuo. (Moeck/Callenberg).

Vol.43. Bodinus, Sebastian. Sonate E für 2 Querflöten oder Violinen. (Birkner).

Vol.44. Geuss. 8 Duette für 2 Querflöten oder Violinen. (Birkner).

Vol.45. Rokoko-Duette für 2 Violincelli, Gamben, Fideln oder Fagotte (Edelstein). Heft II. Josef Bodin de Boismortier, 2 Sonaten und Michel Corrette, Sonate.

Vol.46. Fasch, Joh. Friedr. Canon/Sonata a 3, F-dur, für Alt-Blockflöte, Violine (Querflöte, Viola, Violoncello) und Basso Continuo. (Moeck/Callenberg).

Vol.47. Vivaldi, Antonio. Trio für Alt-Blockflöte (Querflöte, Violine, Oboe), Violine (2 Alt-Blockflöte, Querflöte, Oboe) und Basso Continuo. (Kolneder).

Vol.48. Reinagle, Joseph. 12 leichte Violoncello-Duette "for the use of beginners." (Huttenbach). Heft I. Duette Nr.1–7.

Vol.49. Reinagle, Joseph. For the same. Heft II. Nr.8–12.

Vol.50. Fux, Johann Joseph. Tänze für 2 Violinen, Viola (3 Violine) bzw. Sopran- und Alt-Blockflöten oder Streichorchester und Basso Continuo. (Juntner).

Vol.54. Abel, Karl Friedrich. Trio-Sonate C-dur für Flöte, Violine und Basso Continuo. (Möbius).

Vol.55. Bach, Johann Christian. 3 Trios für 2 Violinen und Viola (Violoncello) in B-dur, Es-dur, D-dur. (Möbius).

Vol.56. Marcello, Benedetto. Sonaten II und V für 2 Violoncelli (Gamben) und Basso Continuo. (Glode).

Vol.61. Schultze, Johann Christoph. Ouvertüre (Suite) II B-dur. (Moeck-Callenberg). Für 2 Alt-Blockflöten (Querflöten, Violinen) und Basso Continuo.

Vol.62. Schultze, Johann Christoph. Ouvertüre (Suite) III A-moll für 2 Alt-Blockflöten (Querflöten, Violinen) und Basso Continuo.

Vol.63. Bach, Johann Christian. Sonate F-dur für Flöte (Alt-Blockflöte) und Cembalo oder für Flöte, Violine und Violoncello oder Viola. (Marguerre).

Vol.64. Telemann, Georg Philipp. Concerto A-moll für Alt-Blockflöte, Gambe (Violoncello), Streicher und Basso Continuo. (Haendler). Studienausgabe für Alt-Blockflöte, Gambe (Violoncello) und Klavier.

Vol.65. Telemann, Georg Philipp. Concerto C-dur für Alt-Blockflöte, Streicher und Basso Continuo. (Hechler). Studienausgabe für Alt-Blockflöte und Klavier.

Vol.66. Telemann, Georg Philipp. Concerto a 4 (A-moll) für Alt-Blockflöte, Oboe (Tenor-Blockflöte, Violine), Violine und Basso Continuo. (Hechler).

Vol.67. Telemann, Georg Philipp. Sonata a 3 (D-moll für Alt-Blockflöte, Violine und Basso Continuo. (Hechler).

Vol.68. Graun, Johann Gottlieb. Concerto C-dur für Alt-Blockflöte, Violine und Streicher. (Hechler). Studienausgabe für Alt-Blockflöte, Violine und Klavier.

Vol.69. Heinichen, Johann David. Concerto a 8, C-dur, für 4 Alt-Blockflöten, Streicher und Basso Continuo. (Hechler).

Vol.70. Schetky, Christoph. 12 Violoncello-Duette. Heft I.

Vol.71. Schetky, Christoph. 12 Violoncello-Duette. Heft II.

Vol.72. Bach, Carl Philipp Emanuel. Trio-Sonate A-moll für Flöte, Violine und Basso Continuo. (Dürr).

Vol.73. Bach, Carl Philipp Emanuel. Trio-Sonate A-dur für Flöte, Violine und Basso Continuo.

Vol.74. Bach, Carl Philipp Emanuel. Trio-Sonate D-moll für Flöte, Violine und Basso Continuo.

Vol.75. Prowo, P. Concerto a 6 für 2 Alt-Blockflöten, 2 Oboen (Violinen), 2 Violoncelli (Fagotte) und Cembalo (Klavier) ad lib. (Ochs).

Vol.101. Telemann, G. Ph. Sonate I und II für Violine und Basso Continuo. (Baum).

Vol.102. Telemann, G. Ph. Sonate III und IV für Violine und Basso Continuo.

Vol.103. Telemann, G. Ph. Sonate V und VI für Violine und Basso Continuo.

Vol.104. Von Beckerath, Alfred. Weisensonate für Violine und Klavier.

Vol.105. Pepusch, Joh. Chr. 3 Sonaten für Violine (Flöte, Oboe) und Basso Continuo.

Vol.106. Furloni, Gaetano. Sonata I und II für 2 Violinen, Gambe (Violoncello).

Vol.107. Furloni, Gaetano. Sonata III und IV für 2 Violinen, Gambe (Violoncello).

Vol.108. Albinoni, Tomaso. Sonate A-moll für Violine (Alt-Blockflöte, Querflöte, Oboe) und Basso Continuo. (mit der Bassaussetzung von Heinrich Nikolaus Gerber und deren Korrektur von Johann Sebastian Bach).

Vol.201. Gröning, Herbert. Kleine Stücke für 1 Streichinstrument allein oder zum Unisonospiel von Geige, Bratsche und Cello. (Höckner).

Vol.202. Lerich, Rudolf. Spiele zu zweien. Leopold Mozart. Kleine Stücke für 2 gleiche Streichinstrumente. (Höckner).

Vol.203. Mann, Alfred. Kleine Schulmusik. Franz Bauer. Sätze für 3 gleiche Streichinstrumente. (Höckner).

Abt.Klavier.
Vol.251. Aus einem Klavierbuch des Henricus Jacobus Rosen. (Mönkemeyer).

Abt.Musica nova.
Vol.501. Aulich, Bruno. Divertimento für Flauto dolce, Violine und Viola.
Vol.502. Schilling, Hans Ludwig. Suite für Sopran-Blockflöten oder Oboe und Klavier.
Vol.503. Jacobi, Wolfgang. 5 Studien für Flauto dolce und Klavier oder Cembalo.
Vol.504. Roeseling, Kaspar. 2 Sonaten für Flauto dolce solo.
Vol.505. Martelli, Henri. Melodien für Flauto dolce und Klavier.
Vol.506. Poletzky, Erwin. Fünf Inventionen für Flauto dolce und Klavier.
Vol.507.
Vol.508. Martelli, Henri. Melodien für Flauto dolce und Klavier.

MOFFAT, ALFRED EDWARD, 1866–1950. ed.
Kammer-Sonaten für Violine und Pianoforte des 17. und 18. Jahrhunderts. Nach den Original-Ausgaben für Violine mit beziffertem Bass bearbt. Mainz, Schott.
29 nos.
Contents:
No.1. Tarini. (A).
No.2. Geminiani. (Dm).
No.3. Tessarini. (G).
No.4. Händel. (F).
No.5. Leclair, J. M. (A).
No.6. Veracini. (Hm).
No.7. Mascitti. (Em).
No.8. Corelli. (Dm).
No.9. De Giardini. (G).
No.10. Vivaldi. (Dm).
No.11. Senaillié. (A).
No.12. Albinoni. (Dm).
No.13. Veracini. (Am).
No.14. Francoeur. (Dm).
No.15. Nardini. (G).
No.16. Sammartini. (Am).
No.17. Telemann. (E).
No.18. Locatelli. (B).
No.19. Porpora. (D).
No.20. Dall'Abaco. (Hm).
No.21. Tartini. (Hm).
No.22. Leclair, J. M. (F).
No.23. Valentini. (Hm).
No.24. Tessarini. (D).
No.25. Senaillié. (Dm).
No.26. Francoeur. (B).
No.27. Collett, John. Sonata C dur für Violine und Pianoforte bearb. von A. Moffat. 1926.
No.28. Eccles, Henry. Sonate E-moll (La Guitate) für Violine und Pianoforte bearb. von A. Moffat. 1926.
No.29. Stanley, John. Sonata G dur für Violine und Pianoforte bearb. von A. Moffat. 1926.

MOFFAT, ALFRED EDWARD, 1866–1950. ed.
Meister-Schule der alten Zeit. Sammlung klassischer Violin-Sonaten berühmter Komponisten des 17. und 18. Jahrhunderts. Nach den Original-Ausgabe für "Violine mit beziffertem Bass" mit Pianoforte Bearbeitung, mit Vortragszeichen versehen und hrsg. Berlin, Simrock.
36 nos.
Contents:
No.1. Purcell, Henry. Sonate (Gm).
No.2. Händel, G. F. Sonate (A).
No.3. Veracini, F. A. Sonate (Dm).
No.4. Leclair, J. M. Sonate (D).
No.5. Mossi, Giovanni. Sonate (Cm).
No.6. Francoeur, François. Sonate (Em).
No.7. Locatelli, Pietro. Sonate (G).
No.8. Melande, Georgio. Sonate (Am).
No.9. Aubert, Louis. Sonate (G).
No.10. Vivaldi, Antonio. Sonate (Gm).
No.11. Tessarini, Carlo. Sonate (C).
No.12. Jones, Richard. Sonate (Am).
No.13. Corelli, Arcangelo. Sonate (Em).
No.14. Nardini, Pietro. Sonate (D).
No.15. Porpora, Niccolò. Sonate (Gm).
No.16. Somis, Lorenzo. Sonate (G).
No.17. Valentino, Robert. Sonate (Am).
No.18. Tartini, Giuseppe. Sonate (A).
No.19. Barbella, Emanuele. Sonate (Gm).
No.20. Senaillié, J. B. Sonate (G).
No.21. Loeillet, J. B. Sonate (Em).
No.22. Benda, Franz. Sonate (A).
No.23. Geminiani, Francesco. Sonate (Hm).
No.24. Mascitti, Michele. Sonate (A).
No.25. Nardini, Pietro. Sonate No.5. (D).
No.26. Senaillié, J. B. Sonate (Dm).
No.27. Porpora, N. Sonate (D).
No.28. Abaco, E. F. dall'. Sonate. (Gm).
No.29. Giardini, Felice de. Sonate (Em).
No.30. Senaillié, J. B. Sonate (Gm).
No.31. Schickhard, J. Chr. Sonate (Dm).
No.32. Leclair, J. M. Sonate (Gm).
No.33. Corelli, A. Sonate (F).
No.34. Collett, J. Sonate (B).
No.35. Castrucci, P. Sonate (D).
No.36. Vivaldi, A. Sonate (G).

MOFFAT, ALFRED EDWARD, 1866–1950. ed.
Meister-Schule der alten Zeit. Sammlung klassischer Violoncello-Sonaten berühmter Komponisten des 17. und 18. Jahrhunderts. Nach den Original-Ausgabe für Violoncello mit beziffertem Bass, mit Pianoforte Bearbeitung, mit Vortragszeichen versehen und hrsg. Berlin, Simrock.
12 nos. (later combined into 3v.).
Contents:
Vol.1.
No.1. Boccherini, L. Sonate (G).
No.2. Duport, J. P. Sonate (Am).
No.3. Birkenstock, J. A. (Sonate (Em).
No.4. Breval, J. B. Sonate (G).
Vol.2.
No.5. Galliard, J. E. Sonate (F).
No.6. Galeotti, St. Sonate (Cm).
No.7. Eccles, Henry. Sonate (Fm).
No.8. Fesch, Willem de. Sonate (F).

Vol.3.
No.9. Hervelois, Caix de. Sonate (Am).
No.10. Cervetto, G. B. Sonate (G).
No.11. Caporale, A. Sonate (Dm).
No.12. Visconti, Gasp. Sonate (A).

MOFFAT, ALFRED EDWARD, 1866–1950. ed.
Trio-Sonaten alter Meister für 2 Violinen und Violoncello (ad lib.) mit hinzugefügter Klavierbegleitung nach der Originalausgabe für 2 Violinen mit beziffertem Bass bearbt. Berlin, Simrock.
28 nos.
Contents:
No.1. Corelli, Arcangelo. Trio-Sonate (Dm).
No.2. Locatelli, Pietro. Trio-Sonate (Dm).
No.3. Telemann, G. Ph. Trio-Sonate (Em).
No.4. Vivaldi, Antonio. Trio-Sonate (Dm).
No.5–10. Corelli, A. 6 Sonaten: No.1 (D), No.2 (Dm), No.3 (C), No.4 (Em), No.5 (B), No.6 (Gm).
No.11. Gluck, Chr. W. v. Sonate (F).
No.12. Sammartini, G. Sonate (Gm).
No.13. Boccherini, L. Sonate (Cm).
No.14. Vivaldi, A. Sonate (Em).
No.15. Pugnani, G. Sonate (C).
No.16. Avison, Ch. Sonate (Em).
No.17.
No.18. Schickhard, J. Chr. Sonate (Cm).
No.19. Tessarini, C. Sonate (G).
No.20. Valentini, G. Sonate (G).
No.21. Bonporti, F. A. Sonate (C).
No.22. Locatelli, P. Sonate (G).
No.23. Händel, G. F. Sonate (B).
No.24. Boyce, W. Sonate (Cm).
No.25. Stamitz, Joh. Sonate (G).
No.26. Campioni, C. A. Sonate (Gm).
No.27. Valentini, Gius. Sonate (D).
No.28. Boccherini, L. Sonate (Es).

MOLINARO, SIMONE, fl.1600.
. . . Intavolatura di liuto . . . trascritto in notazione moderna ed interpretate da Giuseppe Gullino, con presentazione di Piero Jahier. Firenze, Edizioni Musicali Ditta R. Maurri di E. Stanta, 1940.
2p.L., vii–x, [2], 115, [1]p., 2L. facsims. (incl. music).
With facsimile of original title page: Intavolatura di liuto di Simone Molinaro . . . Libro primo, nel quale si contengono saltarelli, pass'e mezi, gagliarde, e fantasie. Nouamente, composto, & dato in luce. In Venetia, Appresso Ricciardo Amadino, 1599.
300 copies printed.
The arrangements are from the works by T. Crequillon, Clemens non Papa, and G. Guami.

MÖLLER, HEINRICH. ed.
Das Lied der Völker; eine Sammlung von fremdländischen Volksliedern, ausgewählt, übersetzt und mit Benutzung der besten ausländischen Quellen und Bearbeitungen. Hrsg. von Dr. Heinrich Möller. Mainz, New York, [etc.], B. Schott's Sohne, n.d.
13v.
Contents:
Vol.1. Russische Volkslieder.
Vol.2. Skandinavische Volkslieder.
Vol.3. Englische und nordamerikanische Volkslieder.
Vol.4. Keltische (bretonische, kymrische, schottische, irische) Volkslieder.
Vol.5. Französische Volkslieder.
Vol.6. Spanische, portugiesische, katalanische, baskische Volkslieder.
Vol.7. Italienische Volkslieder.
Vol.8. Südslawische Volkslieder.
Vol.9. Griechische, albanische und rumänische Volkslieder.
Vol.10. Westslawische (böhmische, mährische und slowakische) Volkslieder.
Vol.11. Westslawische (polnische und wendische) Volkslieder.
Vol.12. Ungarische Volkslieder.
Vol.13. Volkslieder baltischer Länder.

Monatshefte für Musikgeschichte. Beilagen. Jahrg. 16.–18. Jahrg., *see* Eitner, Robert, ed. Cantaten des 17. und 18. Jahrhunderts; 19.–20. Jahrg., *see* Buxheimer Orgelbuch. Das Buxheimer Orgelbuch.

Mönkemeyer, Helmut, ed. Antiqua Chorbuch, *see* Antiqua Chorbuch.

Mont, Henri du, *see* Du Mont, Henri.

MONTE, PHILIPPE DE, 1521–1603.
Complete works. Ed. by Ch. Van den Borren and J. van Nuffel. Düsseldorf, Sumptibus L. Schwann, 1927–39.
32v.
Imprint varies.
Contents:
Vol.1. Missa Inclina cor meum. 1927.
Vol.2. Motettum O bone Jesu. 1927.
Vol.3. Missa sine nomine. No.2. 1927.
Vol.4. Missa O altitudo divitiarum. 1930.
Vol.5. Missa Ultimi miei sospiri. 1928.
Vol.6. Madrigalium spiritualium liber primus. 1928.
Vol.7. Missa sine nomine. 1929.
Vol.8. Missa Anchor che col partire. 1929.
Vol.9. Missa Reviens vers moy. 1929.
Vol.10. Missa Nasce la pena mia. 1929.
Vol.11. Missa sine nomine. No.1. 1930.
Vol.12. VIII Magnificat. 1930.
Vol.13. Missa Requiem. 1930.
Vol.14. Missa La dolce vista. 1930.
Vol.15. Collectio decem motettorum. 1930.
Vol.16. Missa quaternis vocibus. 1931.
Vol.17. Liber septimus motettorum quinque vocibus. 1931.
Vol.18. Missa sex vocum (ex codex Bibl. Municipalis Norimbergensis). 1931.
Vol.19. Liber quartus madrigalium. 1931.
Vol.20. Collectio decem carminum gallicorum. 1932.
Vol.21. Missa Super cara la vita mia. 1932.
Vol.22. Liber quartus motettorum. 1932.
Vol.23. Missa Quando lieta sperai. 1933.
Vol.24. Missa Super cum sit omnipotens rector Olympi. 1933.

Vol.25. Cantiones ad testudinis usum accommodatae. 1934.
Vol.26. Missa Aspice Domine. 1935.
Vol.27. Missa Quomodo dilexi. 1936.
Vol.28. Missa quinque vocum sine nomine. 1936.
Vol.29. Missa sine nomine, 8 voices. 1937.
Vol.30. Missa sine nomine, 6 voices. 1938.
Vol.31. Missa sine nomine, 6 voices. 1939.
Vol.32. Missa sine nomine, 6 voices. 1939.

MONTEVERDI, CLAUDIO, 1567–1643.
Tutte de opere, di Claudio Monteverdi, gia' maestro di cappella della serenissima republica. Nuovamente date in luce da G. Francesco Malipiero. Asolo, G. Francesco Malipiero; Vienna, Universal Edition, 1926–42.
16v.
Contents:
Vol.1. Primo libro de madrigali a cinque voci.
A che tormi il ben mio.
All'hora i pastori tutti.
Almo divino raggio.
Amor per tua mercè.
Amor s'il tuo ferire.
Ardi o gela; Arsi e alsi.
Ardo si ma non t'amo.
Arsie e alsi.
Baci soavi e cari.
Ch'io ami la mia vita.
Donna s'il miro voi.
Filli cara e amata.
Fumia la pastorella; Almo divino raggio; All'hora i pastor.
Poi che del mio dolore.
Questa ordi il laccio.
Se nel partir da voi.
Se per havervi oimè.
Se pur non mi consenti.
Tra mille fiamme.
Uscian ninfe homai.
La vaga pastorella.
Vol.2. Secondo libro de madrigali a cinque voci.
Bevea Fillide mia.
La bocca onde.
Cantai un tempo.
Crudel perchè mi fuggi.
Dolcemente dormiva.
Dolcissimi legami.
Donna nel mio ritorno.
Ecco mormorar l'onde.
E dicea l'una sospirando.
Intorno a due vermiglie.
Mentre io mirova fiso.
Non giacinti o nascisi.
Non mi è grave.
Non si levava ancor; E dicea l'una sospirando.
Non sono in queste rive.
Quell'ombra esser.
Questo specchio ti dono.
S'andasse amor a caccia.
Se tu mi lassi.
Ti spontò l'ali amor.
Tutte le bocche belle.
Vol.3. Terzo libro de madrigali a cinque voci.
Ch'io non t'ami
La giovinetta pianta.
Io pur verrò.
Là tra'l sangue.
Lumi miei cari.
Ma dove o lasso.
O come è gran martire.
O dolce anima mia.
O primavera.
O rossignuol.
Occhi un temp mia vita.
Ond'ei di morte.
Perfidissimo volto.
Poi ch'ella.
Rimanti in pace; Ond'ei di morte.
Se per estremo ardore.
Sovra tenere herbette.
Stracciami pur il core.
Vallene pur crudel; Là tra'l sangue; Poi ch'ella.
Vivrò fra i miei; Ma dove o lasso; Io pur verrò.
Vol.4. Quattro libro de madrigali a cinque voci.
Ah dolente partita.
Anima del cor mio.
Anima dolorosa.
Anima mia perdona; Che se tu se'il cor mio.
A un giro sol de bell' occhi.
Che se tu se'il cor mio.
Cor mio mentre vi miro.
Cor mio non mori.
Io mi son giovinetta.
Longe da te cor mio.
Luci serene e chiare.
Non più guerra pietate.
Ohimè se tanto amate.
La piaga c'ho nel core.
Piagne e sospira.
Quel augellin che canta.
Sfogava con le stelle.
Si ch'io vorrei morire.
Voi pur da me partite.
Volgea l'anima mia.
Vol.5. Quinto libro de madrigali a cinque voci.
Ahi come a un vago sol.
Amor se guisto sei.
Che dar più vi poss'io.
Ch'io t'ami; Deh bella e cara; Ma tu più che mai.
Cruda Amarilli.
Deh bella e cara.
Dorinda, ah dirò.
E così a poco a poco.
Ecco piegando.
Ecco Silvio; Ma se con la pietà; Dorinda, ah dirò; Ecco piegando; Ferir quel petto.
Era l'anima mia.
Ferir quel petto.
Ma se con la pietà.
Ma tu più che mai.
M'è più dolce il penar.
O Mirtillo anima mia.
Questi vaghi.
T'amo mia vita.
Troppo ben può.
Vol.6. Sesto libro de madrigali a cinque voci.
A Dio florida bella.
Ahi ch'ei non pur risponde.
Batto qui pianse.

Darà la notte il sol.
Ditelo voi.
Dove, dove è la fede.
Dunque amate reliquie.
Incenerite spoglie.
Lagrime d'amante al sepolcro dell' amata (Sestina).
1. Incenerite spoglie.
2. Ditelo voi.
3. Darà la notte il sol.
4. Ma te raccoglie.
5. O chiome d'or.
6. Dunque amate religuie.
Lamento d'Ariana.
1. Lasciatemi morire.
2. O Teseo, Teseo mio.
3. Dove, dove è la fede.
4. Ahi ch'ei non pur.
Lasciatemi morire.
Ma te raccoglie.
Misero Alceo.
O chiome d'or.
O Teseo, Teseo mio.
Ohimè il bel viso.
Presso un fiume tranquillo.
Qui rise Tirsi.
Una donna fra l'altre.
Zefiro torna e'bel tempo rimena.

Vol.7. Settimo libro de madrigali a 1, 2, 3, 4, and 6 voci. Concerto.
Ah, che non si conviene.
Ahi, sciocco mondo.
Al lume della stella.
Amor che deggio far.
A quest' olmo.
Augellin.
Chiome d'oro.
Con che soavità.
Dice la mia bellissima. Licori.
Dunque ha potuto in me.
Dunque ha potuto sol.
Ecco vicine o bella Tigre.
Eccomi pronta aibaci.
Interrotte speranze.
Io son pur vezzosetta.
Lettera amorosa.
Non è di gentil core.
Non vedrò mai le stelle.
O come sei gentile.
O viva fiamma.
Ohimé dov'è il mio ben; Dunque ha potuto sol; Dunque ha potuto in me; Ahi, sciocco mondo.
Parlo misero taccio.
Partenza amorosa.
Perchè fuggi.
Per monti e per valli.
Se i languidi miei sguardi.
S'el vostro cor Madonna.
Se pur destina.
Soave libertate.
Tempro la cetra.
Tirsi e Clori.
Tornate.
Tu dormi.
Vaga su spina ascoasa.
Vorrei baciarti.

Vol.8. Ottavo libro. Madrigali guerrieri et amorosi.
Altri canti d'amor.
Altri canti di Marte; Due belli occhi.
Amor dove.
Ardo avvampo.
Armi false non son.
Ballo (a 5 voci con doi violini).
Ballo delle ingrate.
Canti amorosi.
Canti guerrieri.
Chi vol haver felice.
Combattimento di Tancredi e Clorinda.
Cor mio non val fuggir.
Così sol d'una chiara fonte.
Dell'usate mie corde.
Dolcissimo uscignolo.
Due belli occhi.
Gira il nemico insidiosa; Nol lasciamo accostar; Armi false non son; Vuol degli occhi; Non è più tempo; Cor mio.
Hor ch'el ciel e la terra; Cosi sol d'una chiara.
Io che nel'otio naqui.
Ma per quel ampio.
Mentre vaga angioletta.
Movete al mio.
Ninfa che scalza il piede; Qui deh meco; Dell'usate mie corde.
Nol lasciamo accostar.
Non è più tempo.
Non haveo Feva ancora; Amor; Si tra sdegnosi.
Non partir ritrosetta.
Ogni amante è guerrier; Io che nel'otio; Ma per quel ampio.
Perchè t'en fuggi o Fillide.
Qui deh meco t'arresta.
Riedi ch'al nostr'ardir.
Si tra sdegnosi.
Su su pastorelli vezzosi.
Vago augelletto.
Volgendo il ciel.
Vuol degli occhi.

Vol.9. Nono libro. Madrigali e canzonette a due tre voci.
Alcun non mi consigli.
Alle danze, alle danze.
Ardo e scoprir.
Armato il cor.
Bel pastor.
Come dolce hoggi l'auretta.
Di far sempre gioire.
La mia turca.
Non voglio amare.
O come vaghi.
O mio bene.
O sia tranquillo il mare.
Ohimé ch'io cado.
Perchè se m'odiavi.
Quando dentro al tuo seno.
Se vittorie si belle.
Si dolce è il tormento.
Si si ch'io v'amo.
Su su su partorelli vezzosi.
Taci Armelin.
Zefiro torna e di soavi.

Vol.10. Canzonette a tre voci. Scherzi musicali a tre voci. Scherzi musicali coie arie e madrigali a 1 e 2 voci.
Amarilli onde m'assale.
Amorosa pupilletta.
Canzonette d'amore.
Chi vuol veder d'inverno.
Chi vuol veder un bosco.
Come farò cuor mio.
Corse a la morte.
Damigella tutta bella.
Deh chi tace il bel pensero.
De la bellezza le dovute lodi.
Dispiegate guance amate.
Dolci miei sospiri.
Ecco di dolci raggi.
Eri già tutta mia.
Et è pur dunque vero.
La fiera vista.
Fugge il verno dei dolori.
Già mi credea.
Giovinetta ritrosettsa.
Giù li a quel petto.
Glori amorosa.
Gode pur del bel sen.
Hor care canzonette.
I bei legami.
Il mio martir.
Io che armato sin hor.
Io mi vivea.
Io son fenice.
Lidia spina del mio core.
Maledetto sia l'aspetto.
Non così.
O rosetta che rosetta.
La pastorella mia spietata.
Qual si può dir.
Quando l'Alba in oriente.
Quando sperai.
Quel sguardo sdegnosetto.
Raggi dov'è il mio bene.
Si come crescon.
Son questi i crespi crini.
Su su su ch'el giorno.
Tu ridi sempre mai.
Vaghi rai de cigli ardenti.
La violetta.
Vita de l'alma mia.
Vol.11. Orfeo. Favola in musica.
Lamento d'Arianna.
Musiche de Alcuni.
Vol.12. Il ritorno d'Ulisse in patria. Drama in musica.
Vol.13. L'incoronazione di Poppea. Drama in musica.
Vol.14. Sacrae cantiunculae tribus vocibus.
Sanctissimae Virgini missa senis vocibus.
Vespro della beata Vergine.
Sonata sopra Sancta Maria.
Ave Maria stella.
Magnificat a 7.
Magnificat a 6.
Vol.15. Selva morale e spirituale. (Messe, Motetti, Concerti, etc.).
Vol.16. Messa et salmi a 1, 2, 3, 4, 5, 6, 7 e 8 voci. Concertati, e parte da cappella, e con le letanie della B.V.
Frammenti pubblicati in varie raccolte.
Appendice: Madrigali spirituali a quattro voci. (Bass parts only).

MONTEVERDI, CLAUDIO, 1567–1643.
Tutte de opere. Reprint edition in progress.

MONTPELLIER, FRANCE. UNIVERSITÉ. FACULTÉ DE MÉDICINE. Bibliothèque. Mss. (H 196).
Polyphonies du XIIIe siècle. Le manuscrit H 196 de la Faculté de Médicine de Montpellier, publié par Yvonne Rokseth . . . Paris, Éditions de l'Oiseau Lyre, Louise B. M. Dyer, 1935–[39].
4v. plates, facsims.
Vol.1: Il a été tiré de cet ouvrage cent exemplaires sur papier velin Muller relies en bois "Blackwood" d'Australie . . . numérotés de 1 à 100, deux cents exemplaires sur papier velin Muller, numérotés de 101 à 300, et quinze exemplaires hors commerce, numérotés de I à XV.
"Bibliographie sommaire": v.4, p.[15]–16.
Contents:
Vol.1. Reproduction phototypique du manuscrit. 1935.
Vol.2. Transcription intégrale du manuscrit. Fasc.I–V. 1936.
Vol.3. Transcription intégrale du manuscrit. Fasc.VI–VIII. 1936.
Vol.4. Études et commentaires. Appendice: Table des compositions et remarques particulières. [1939].

Montpellier, France. Université. Faculté de Médicine. Bibliothèque. Mss. (H 196), *see* Coussemaker, Edmond de. L'art harmonique aux XIIe et XIIIe siècles.

Montserrat (Benedictine Abbey). Mestres de l'escolania de Montserrat, *see* Mestres de l'escolania de Montserrat.

MONUMENTA HUNGARIAE MUSICA. Graz, Akademische Druck- und Verlagsanstalt; Budapest, Akadémiai Kiadó, 1963– .
v.1– .

MONUMENTA LEODIENSIUM MUSICORUM. v.1. Liège, Belgium, Les Éditions Dynamo, 1939.
1 v.
Contents:
Vol.1. Chaumont. Livre d'orgue. 1695.

MONUMENTA LITURGIAE POLYCHORALIS SANCTAE ECCLESIAE ROMANAE. Ser.I. Ordinarium missae cum quatuor choris. No.1– . Rome, Societas Universalis Sanctae Cecilae, 1950– .
No.1– .
Contents:
No.1. Benevoli, O. Missa. Tu es Petrus. XVI vocum. 1950.
No.2. Benevoli, O. Missa. Maria prodigio celeste (Benevola). XVI vocum. 1950.

No.3. Benevoli, O. Missa. Tira corda. XVI vocum. 1951.
No.4. Benevoli, O. Missa. Si Deus pro nobis quis contra nos.XVI vocum. 1953.
No.5. Pitoni, G. O. Missa. Albana. 1719. XVI vocum. 1955.
No.6. Petti, Paolo. Missa in honorem S. Ceciliae 1670. XVI vocum. 1956.
No.7. Pitoni, G. O. Missa. S. Pietro. 1720. XVI vocum. 1960.
No.8. Benevoli, O. Missa in augustia pestilentiae. XVI vocum. 1963.

MONUMENTA LITURGIAE POLYCHORALIS SANCTAE ECCLESIAE ROMANAE. Ser.II. Psalmodia cum duobus choris. No.1– . Rome, Societas Universalis Sanctae Ceciliae, 1953– .
No.1– .
Contents:
No.1. Benevoli, O. Magnificat sexti toni I. Octo vocum. 1953.

MONUMENTA LITURGIAE POLYCHORALIS SANCTAE ECCLESIAE ROMANAE. Ser.III. Psalmodia cum tribus choris concertata. No.1– Rome, Societas Universalis Sanctae Ceciliae, 195? – .
No.1– .
Contents:
No.1. Benevoli, O. Canticum Magnificat secundi toni. XIV vocum. 1955.

MONUMENTA LITURGIAE POLYCHORALIS SANCTAE ECCLESIAE ROMANAE. Ser.IV. Psalmodia cum quatuor choris. No.1– . Rome, Societas Universalis Sanctae Ceciliae, 1951– .
No.1– .
Contents:
No.1. Benevoli, O. Dixit Dominus I. Toni detto Il bello. XVI vocum. 1951.
No.2. Benevoli, O. Dixit Dominus VIII. Toni detto Bello carioso. XVI vocum. 1951.
No.3. Benevoli, O. Confitebor tibi Domine. Tertii toni. Concertato e piano. XVI vocum. 1954.
No.4. Benevoli, O. Laudate pueri Dominum. Sexti toni. XVI vocum. 1954.
No.5. Pitoni, G. O. Dixit Dominus. No.5. XVI vocum. 1959.
No.6. Pitoni, G. O. Dixit Dominus II. No.6. XVI vocum. 1960.
No.7. Pitoni, G. O. Dixit Dominus III. No.7. XVI vocum. 1960.
No.8. Pisari, P. Dixit Dominus. No.8. XVI vocum. 1961.
Ser.4.
No.9. Benevoli, O. Magnificat III toni. XVI vocum. 1964.
No.11. Fabris, Stephani. Magnificat VIII toni. XVI vocum. 1965.
No.12. Fabris, Stephani. Psalmus. Confitebor II toni. XVI vocum. 1965.

MONUMENTA LITURGIAE POLYCHORALIS SANCTAE ECCLESIAE ROMANAE. Ser.V. Psalmodia cum sex choris. No.1– . Rome, Societas Universalis Sanctae Ceciliae, 1950– .
No.1– .
Contents:
No.1. Benevoli, O. Psalmus. Dixit Dominus. XXIV vocum. 1950.

MONUMENTA LITURGIAE POLYCHORALIS SANCTAE ECCLESIAE ROMANAE. Ser.VI. Ordinarium missae cum duobis choris. No.1– . Rome, Societas Universalis Sanctae Ceciliae, 19? – .
No.1– .
Contents:
No.1. Benevoli, O. Missa pastoralis. VIII vocum. 1957.
No.2. Georgi, G. Two masses; V. Tozzi. Missa octo vocum. 1963.

MONUMENTA LITURGIAE POLYCHORALIS SANCTAE ECCLESIAE ROMANAE. Ser.VII. Ordinarium missae cum tribus choris. No.1– . Rome, Societas Universalis Sanctae Ceciliae, 19? – .
No.1– .
Contents:
No.1. Benevoli, O. Missa. Angelus Domini. XII vocum. 1958.

MONUMENTA LITURGIAE POLYCHORALIS SANCTAE ECCLESIAE ROMANAE. Ser.VIII. Proprium de tempore (for varying numbers of voices). No.1– . Rome, Societas Universalis Sanctae Ceciliae, 19? – .
No.1– .
Contents:
No.1. Giorgi, G. Liturgia paschalis (sections for 2, 4, 8 voices). 1960.
No.2. Giorgi, G. Liturgia pentecostes (sections for 1, 2, 4, 8 voices). 1961.

MONUMENTA LITURGIAE POLYCHORALIS SANCTAE ECCLESIAE ROMANAE. Ser.IX. Proprium de sanctis (for varying numbers of voices). No.1– . Rome, Societas Universalis Sanctae Ceciliae, 19? – .
No.1– .
Contents:
No.1. Pt.1. Giorgi, G. Officium de Beata Virgine (sections for 2, 3, 4, 8 voices). 1962.
No.1. Pt.2. Giorgi, G. Officium de Beata Virgine (mixed voices). 1962.

MONUMENTA LITURGIAE POLYCHORALIS SANCTAE ECCLESIAE ROMANAE. Ser.X. Catalogi thematici et bibliographici. No.1– Rome, Societas Universalis Sanctae Ceciliae, 19? – .
No.1– .
Contents:
No.1. Catalogus thematicus et bibliographicus Joannis de Georgiis operum sacrarum omnium. Ed. by Feininger.

Monumenta liturgiae polychoralis sanctae ecclesiae romanae. Horatii Benevoli. Opera omnia, *see* Benevoli, Orazio. Opera omnia.

MONUMENTA MONODICA MEDII AEVI. Hrsg. im Auftrag des Instituts für Musikforschung Regensburg mit Unterstützung der Musikgeschichtlichen Kommission von Bruno Stäblein. Kassel, Bärenreiter-Verlag, 1956– .
v.1– . facsims.
Plainsong notation.
"Addenda et corrigenda" (leaf) inserted in v.1.
"Kritischer Bericht" at end of each volume.
Contents:
Vol.1. Hymnen I. Die mittelalterlichen Hymnenmelodien des Abendlandes. Hrsg. von Bruno Stäblein. 1956.
Vol.2. Altrömischer Choralgesang. Hrsg. von Bruno Stäblein.

MONUMENTA MUSICA NEERLANDICA. Amsterdam, Nederlandse Muziekgeschiedenis, 1959– .
v.1– .
Proposed set about 12v.
Contents:
Vol.1. Hellendaal, Pieter. Concerti grossi. Op.3. Hans Brandts Buys. 1959.
Vol.2. Klavier-boek Anna Maria Van Eijl. Ed. Frits Noske. 1959.
Vol.3. Nederlandse klaviermuziek uit de 16e en 17e eewu. Ed. Alan Curtis. 1961.
Vol.4. Locatelli, Pietro. Opera quarta prima parte. Ed. Arend Koole. 1961.
Vol.5. Padbrué, Cornelis Thymanszoon. Nederlandse madrigalen. Ed. Frits Noske. 1962.

MONUMENTA MUSICAE BELGICAE. Uitgegeven door de Vereeniging voor Muziekgeschiedenis te Antwerpen. Berchem-Antwerpen, "De Ring," 1932–51, 1960– .
v.1– .
"Uitgegeven door de Vereeniging voor Muziekgeschiedenis te Antwerpen."
Contents:
Vol.1. Loeillet, Jean Baptiste. Werken voor clavecimbel. Ed. by Jos. Watelet. 1932.
Vol.2. Kerckhoven, A. van den. Werken voor orgel. Ed. by Jos. Watelet. 1933.
Vol.3. Fiocco, Joseph Hector. Werken voor clavecimbel. Ed. by Jos. Watelet with a short biography by Christiane Stellfeld. 1936. Second ed. 1955.
Vol.4. Charles Guillet/Giovanni (de) Macque/ Carolus Luython. Werken voor orgel of vier speeltuigen. Ed. by Jos. Watelet. With a short biography by Anny Pisaer.
Vol.5. Boutmy, Josse. Werken voor klavecimbel. Ed. by Jos. Watelet. With a short biography by Suzanne Clercx. 1943.
Vol.6. Raick, Dieudonné/ van Helmont, Charles Joseph. Werken voor orgel en/ of clavecimbel. Ed. by Jos. Watelet. With a short biography by Suzanne Clercx. 1948.
Vol.7. Havigha, Gerhardus. Werken voor clavecimbel. Ed. by Jos. Watelet. With a short biography by Edgard Lemaire. 1951.
Vol.8. De la Rue, Pierre. Drei Missen. 1. Missa de Beata Virgine. 2. Missa de virginibus "O quam pulchra est." 3. Missa de Sancta Anna. 1960.
Vol.9. Nederlandse polyfonie uit spaanse bronnen. (1. Noë Bauldewijn. Missa en douleur et tristesse. 2. Matheus Gascongne. Missa es hat ein sin. 3. Theo Verelst. Missa quatuor vocum. Appendix: Noë Bauldewijn. Chanson en douleur en tristesse.). Ed. by René Bernard Lenaerts. 1963.
Contents (proposed):
Vol.10. 16th century lute music from the Netherlands. (Hortus musarum [Phalesius, 1552–1553] and Pratum musicum by Emmanuel Adriaensen, 1594).
Vol.11. Concerting motets by Joseph Hector Fiocco, from the Fonds Ste. Gudule in Brussels.
Vol.12. Sonatas, concertos, and symphonies from 18th century composers at the Brussels court.

MONUMENTA MUSICAE BYZANTINAE . . . Série-principale. [v.] 1– . Copenhague, Levin & Munksgaard, Eljar Munksgaard, 1935– .
v.1– .
Facsimile reproductions.
At head of title: Union Académique Internationale.
Editors: v.1–2, Carsten Høeg, H. J. W. Tillyard, and Egon Wellesz.
Contents:
[Vol.] 1. Sticherarium. (Réproduction intégrale du Codex Vindobonensis Theol. Gr.181). 1935.
[Vol.] 2. Hirmologium athoum. (Réproduction intégrale du Codex Monasterii Hiberorum 470). Ed. Carsten Høeg. 1938.
[Vol.] 3. Pt.1–2. Hirmologium cryptense. Réproduction intégrale du Codex Cryptensis E, Gamma, II). Ed. Lautentius Tardo. Rome, Libreria dello Stato, 1950–51.
[Vol.] 4. Contacarium ashburnhamense. Codex Bibl. Laurentianae Ashburnhamensis. 1956.
[Vol.] 5. Pt.1–2. Fragmenta Chiliandorica palaeoslavica. 2v. 1957.
[Vol.] 6. Contacarium palaeoslavicum. Mosquense. 1960.
[Vol.] 7. Jerusalem Hirmologion Saba 83. Edendum curavit Jorgen Raasted. 1963.

MONUMENTA MUSICAE BYZANTINAE. Lectionaria. v.1– . Copenhague, Eljar Munksgaard, 1939– .
v.1– .
At head of title: Union Académique Internationale.
Editors: Carsten Høeg, Silva Lake, and Günther Zuntz.
Contents:
Vol.1. Fasc.1. Prophetologium. Lectiones nativitatis et Epiphaniae. 1939.
Vol.1. Fasc.2. Prophetologium. Lectiones hebdomadarum 1ae et 2ae quadragesimae. 1940.
Vol.1. Fasc.3. Prophetologium. Lectiones hebdomadarum 3ae et 4ae quadragesimae. 1952.
Vol.1. Fasc.4. Prophetologium. Lectiones hebdomadae 5ae quadragesimae et habdomadae in palmis et maioris. 1960.

Vol.1. Fasc.5. Prophetologium. Lectiones Sabbati Sancti. 1962.
Vol.2. Fasc.1. Evangeliarium. Ed. Silva Lake.

MONUMENTA MUSICAE BYZANTINAE. . . . Subsidia . . . v.1– . Copenhague, Levin & Munksgaard, Eljar Munksgaard, 1935– .
v.1– .
At head of title: Union Académique Internationale . . .
Contents:
Vol.1. Fasc.1. Tillyard, H. J. W. Handbook of the middle Byzantine musical notation. 1935.
Vol.1. Fasc.2. Høeg, Carsten. La notation ekphonétique. 1935.
Vol.2. (Also: American series, No.1). Wellesz, Egon. Eastern elements in western chant. Boston, Printed at the University Press, Oxford, for the Byzantine Institute, Inc., 1947.
Vol.3. Verdeil, R. Palikarova. La musique byzantine chez les Bulgares et les Russes (en collaboration avec l'Institut Byzantin de Boston). Copenhague, 1953.
Vol.4. Pt.1–2. Byzantine elements in early Slavic chant. The hirmologion: 1. Main volume; 2. Volume of appendices. 1960.

MONUMENTA MUSICAE BYZANTINAE. Transcripta . . . v.1– . Copenhague, Levin & Munksgaard, Eljar Munksgaard, 1936– .
v.1– .
At head of title: Union Académique Internationale.
Contents:
Vol.1. The hymns of the Sticherarium for September. Transcribed by Egon Wellesz. 1936.
Vol.2. The hymns of the Sticherarium for November. Transcribed by H. J. W. Tillyard. 1938.
Vol.3. The hymns of the Octoechus, Part I. Transcribed by H. J. W. Tillyard. 1940.
Vol.4. (Also: American series, No.2). Twenty canons from the Trinity Hirmologium. Transcribed by H. J. W. Tillyard. Boston, Byzantine Institute, 1952.
Vol.5. The hymns of the Octoechus, Part II. Transcribed by H. J. W. Tillyard. 1949.
Vol.6. The hymns of the Hirmologium, Part I. Transcribed by A. Ayoutanti and M. Stöhr, rev. and annotated by Carsten Høeg. 1952.
Vol.7. The hymns of the Pentecostarium. Transcribed by H. J. W. Tillyard. 1960.
Vol.8. The hymns of the Hirmologium. Part III. The third plagel mode. Barys. Transcribed by A. Ayoutanti, rev. and annotated by H. J. W. Tillyard. 1956.
Vol.9. Orthodox Eastern Church. Liturgy and ritual. Akathistoi. The Akathistos hymn. Introduced and transcribed by Egon Wellesz. 1957.
Vol.10. The hymns of the Sticherarium for January. Transcribed by H. J. W. Tillyard.

MONUMENTA MUSICAE IN POLONIA. The Polish Academy of Sciences and the State Institute of Fine Arts. Warsaw, Polskie Wydawnictwo Muzyczne, 1964– .
v.1– .
Contents:
Ser.B. 1. Tabulatura Oranowa Jana z Lublina. 1964.

MONUMENTA MUSICAE SACRAE. Collection de manuscrits et d'études publiée sous la direction de Dom Hesbert. Mâcon, Protat Frères, 1952– .
v.1– .
Contents:
Vol.1. Le prosaire de la Sainte-Chapelle, manuscrit du Chapitre de Saint-Nicolas de Bari (vers 1250). 1952.
Vol.2. Les manuscrits musicaux de Jumièges. 1954.
Vol.3. Le prosaire d'Aix-la-Chapelle. 1961.

Monumenta musicae sacrae in Polonia, *see* Surzyński, Joseph. Monumenta musicae sacrae in Polonia.

MONUMENTA MUSICAE SVECICAE. Under the auspices of Kungliga Musikaliska Akademien. Pub. by Svenska Samfundet för Musikforskning. (Swedish Society for Music Research). Stockholm, Almqvist & Wiksell, 1958– .
v.1– .
Contents:
Vol.1. Roman, Johan Helmich. Assaggi a violino solo, I. Ed. by Ingmar Bengtsson and Lars Frydén. 1958.
Vol.2. Kraus, Joseph Martin. Sinfonie C-moll/ C-minor. Ed. by Richard Engländer. 1960.
Vol.3. Johannespassion/ St. John's Passion. Ed. by Lennart Reimers. 1962.
In preparation:
Albrici, Vincenzo. Fader wår (Vater unser) für Streicher und vierstimmigen Chor mit Basso Continuo (Orgel). 1654.
Düben, Gustaf. Odae svecicae, gedruckt 1674, für 1 Singstimme und Basso Continuo.
—— Sinfonia a 4 con cembalo e spinetta. 1654.
—— Veni Sancte Spiritus, für Streicher und vierstimmigen Chor mit Basso Continuo (Orgel). 1650.
Kraus, Joseph Martin. Stella caeli. Motette für Soli, Chor und Orchester, 1783.
Roman, Johan Helmich. Sinfonien 1–3 in G– , F– , und B-dur.
Rudbeck, Olof d. Ä. Trauer- und Klagegesang zur Beerdigung Axel Oxenstiernas, für 2 (gleiche) Singstimmen mit Basso Continuo (Orgel).
Wikmanson, Johan. Streichquartett Nr.1, D-moll (1800).
—— Streichquartett Nr.2, E-moll (1800).

MONUMENTA POLYPHONIAE ITALICAE. Roma, Pontif. Instituto Musicae Sacrae, 1930–36, 1958– .
v.1– .
"A Pontif. Instituto Musicae Sacrae edita."
Contents:
Vol.1. Casimiri, R. C., ed. Missa: Cantantibus organis, Caecilia, 12 vocibus. (von Stabile, Soriano, Palestrina). 1930.

Vol.2. Festa, Costanzo . . . Sacrae cantiones 3, 4, 5, 6 vocibus . . . Ed. by Dagnino. 1936.
Vol.3. Festa, Costanzo. Hymni per totum annum. 3, 4, 5, 6 vocibus. Transcripsit et curavit: Glen Haydon. 1958.

MONUMENTA POLYPHONIAE LITURGICAE SANCTAE ECCLESIAE ROMANAE. Ser.I. Ordinary of the mass. Roma, Societas Universalis Sanctae Ceciliae, 1948– .
v.1– .
Contents:
Tomus I.
Fasc.1. Dufay, Gulielmus. Missa super l'homme armé. 1948.
Fasc.2. Busnois, Antonius. Missa super l'homme armé. 1948.
Fasc.3. Caron, Firminus. Missa super l'homme armé. 1948.
Fasc.4. Faugues, G.· Missa super l'homme armé. 1948.
Fasc.5. Regis, Johannes. Missa super l'homme armé. 1948.
Fasc.6. Ockeghem, Johannes. Missa super l'homme armé. 1948.
Fasc.7. De Orto. Missa super l'homme armé. 1948.
Fasc.8. Basiron, Philippus. Missa super l'homme armé. 1948.
Fasc.9. Tinctoris, Johannes. Missa super l'homme arme. 1948.
Fasc.10. Vaqueras. Missa super l'homme armé. 1948.

Tomus II.
Fasc.1. Dufay. Missa Caput. Anonymous. Veterem hominem et Christus surrexit. 1951.
Fasc.2. Dufay. Missa Se in face ay pale. Anonymous. Sine nomine et Pax vobis ego sum. 1952.
Fasc.3. Dufay. Missa Ave Regina caelorum. 1963.
Fasc.4. Dufay. Missa Ecce ancilla Domini. Anonymous. Puisque ie vis. 1952.

Tomus III.
Fasc.I. Anonymous. Missa I super l'homme armé. (Codicem Neapolitanum. Ms.VI.E.40). 1957.
Fasc.2. Anonymous. Missa II super l'homme armé. (Codicem Neapolitanum. Ms.VI.E.40). 1957.
Fasc.3. Anonymous. Missa III super l'homme armé. 1965.
Fasc.4. Anonymous. Missa IV super l'homme armé. 1965.

MONUMENTA POLYPHONIAE LITURGICAE SANCTAE ECCLESIAE ROMANAE. Ser.II. Proper of the mass. Roma, Societas Universalis Sanctae Ceciliae, 1947– .
v.1– .
Contents:
Vol.1. 16 Anonymous propers (early 15th century).

MONUMENTI DI MUSICA ITALIANA. Editi a cura di Oscar Mischiati, Giuseppe Scarpat, (e) Luigi Ferdinando Tagliavini. Kassel, Bärenreiter, 1961– .
v.1– .
Contents:
Ser.I: Organo e cembalo.
Vol.1. Merula, Tarquinio. Compozioni per organo e cembalo. Edite a cura di Alan Curtis. 1961.
Vol.2. Frescobaldi, Girolamo. Nove toccate inedite. A cura di Sandro Dalla Libera. 1962.

Monumenti Vaticani di paleografia musicale latina, *see* Bannister, Henry Marriott. Monumenti Vaticani di paleografia musicale latina.

MONUMENTOS DE LA MÚSICA ESPAÑOLA. [t.] 1– . Barcelona, Consejo Superior de Investigaciones Científicas, Instituto Español de Musicología, 1941– .
v.1– .
Vol.1 published in Madrid.
Vol.1. Anglés, Higini. La música en la corte de los reyes católicos. 1. Polifonía religiosa. [Treatise (144p.) and 6 masses in score by Alonso de Alba, Juan de Anchieta, Pedro (?) de Escobar, and Francisco de Peñalosa]. 1941.
Vol.2. Anglés, Higini. Le música en la corte de Carlos V. Con la transcripción del "Libro de cifra nueva para tecla, harpa y vilhuela" de Luys Venegas de Henestrosa. (Alcalá de Henares. 1557). 1944.
Vol.3. Narvaez, Luys de. Los seys libros del Delphin de música de cifra para Tañer Vihuela. (Valladolid, 1538). Transcripción y estudio por E. Pujol. 1945.
Vol.4. Vásquez, Juan. Recopilación de sonetos y villancicos a quatro y a cinco. (Sevilla, 1560). Transcripción y estudio por H. Anglés. 1946.
Vol.5. Anglés, Higini. La música en la corte de los reyes católicos. I. Cancionero musical de palacio. (siglos XV–XVI). II. Polifonía profana. 1947.
Vol.6, 12. Correa de Arauxo, Francisco. Libro de tientos y discursos de musica practica y theorica de organo intitulado Facultad organica. (Alcalá, 1626). Vol.I. Transcripción y estudio por S. Kastner. Vol.II. Transcripción y estudio por S. Kastner. 1948. 1952.
Vol.7. Mudarra, Alonso. Tres libros de música en cifra para Vihuela. (Sevilla, 1546). Transcripción y estudio por E. Pujol. 1949.
Vol.8–9. Querol Gavaldá, Miguel. Cancionero musical de la casa de Medinaceli. I–II. Polifonía profana. (Ms. Bibl. Medinaceli, sign. No.13230). 1949–1950. (*See* another edition under Asenjo y Barbieri).
Vol.10. Anglés, Higini. La música en la corte de los reyes católicos. III. Polifonía profana. Cancionero musical de palacio. (siglos XV–XVI). 1951.
Vol.11, 13, 15, 17, 20, 21. Morales, Cristóbal de. Opera omnia. Transcripción y estudio por

Mons. Higinio Anglés. Vol.I. Missarum liber primus. Vol.II. Motetes I–XXV. Vol.III. Missarum liber secundus. Vol.IV. XVI Magnificat. Vol.V. Motetes XXVI–L. Vol.VI. Missarum liber secundus (Roma, 1544). Segunda parte. 1952, 1953, 1954, 1956, 1959, 1962.
Vol.12. *See* Vol.6.
Vol.13. *See* Vol.11.
Vol.14.
Vol.15. *See* Vol.11.
Vol.16, 19. Guerrero, Francisco. Opera omnia. Transcripción por Vicente García. Introducción y estudio por Miguel Querol Gavaldá. Vol.I. Canciones y villanescas espirituales, primera parte, a cinco voces. Vol.II. Canciones y villanescas espirituales, segunda parte, a cuatro y a tres voces. 1955, 1957.
Vol.17. *See* Vol.11.
Vol.18. Querol Gavaldá, Miguel, ed. Romances y letras a tres voces. Siglo XVII. Vol.I. 1956.
Vol.19. *See* Vol.16.
Vol.20, 21. *See* Vol.11.

Les monuments de l'Ars nova, *see* Van, Guillaume de. Les monuments de l'Ars nova.

Monuments de la musique française au temps de la Renaissance, *see* Expert, Henry. Monuments de la musique française au temps de la Renaissance.

Monuments de la notation ekphonétique et neumatic de l'église latine, *see* Thibaut, Jean Baptiste. Monuments de la notation ekphonétique et neumatic de l'église latine.

MONUMENTS OF MUSIC AND MUSIC LITERATURE IN FACSIMILE. First series: Music. New York, Broude Brothers, 1965– .
No.1– .
Contents:
No.1. Purcell, Henry. Orpheus britannicus. (1698 and 1702).
No.2. Blow, John. Amphion anglicus. (1700).
No.3. Chambonnières, J. C. de. Les pièces de clavecin. (1670).
No.4. Anglebert, J. H. d'. Pièces de clavecin. (1689).
No.5. Mattheson, Johann. Pièces de clavecin. (1714).
No.6. Bickham, George. The musical entertainer. (1740).
No.7. Rameau, J. P. Pièces de clavecin. (1731).
No.8. Muffat, Gottlieb. Componimenti musicale. (1739?).
No.9. Couperin, François. Pièces de clavecin. (1713–1730).
No.10. Petrucci, O. dei. Harmonice musices odhecaton. (1501).
No.11. Parthenia. (Byrd, Blow, Gibbons). (1612–1613).
No.12. The musical miscellany. (1729–1731).
No.13. Rameau, J. P. Nouvelles suites de pièces de clavecin. (1727).

Morales, Cristóbal, ca.1500–1553. Opera omnia, *see* Monumentos de la música española. Vol.11, 13, 15, 17, 20, 21.

Moritz, Landgraf of Hesse-Cassel, 1572–1632. Ausgewählte Werke, *see* Das Erbe deutscher Musik. Zweite Reihe. Landschaftsdenkmale. Kurhessen. Vol.1. 1. and 2. Teil.

MORLEY, THOMAS, 1557–ca.1603. comp.
The first book of consort lessons. Collected by Thomas Morley, 1599 and 1611. Reconstructed and ed. with an introd. and critical notes by Sydney Beck. Foreword by Carleton Sprague Smith. New York, Pub. for the New York Public Library by C. F. Peters, [cop. 1959].
xix, 194p. (Edition Peters).
For treble viol, flute, bass viol, lute, cittern, and pandora.

MOROCCO. SERVICE DES ARTS INDIGÈNES.
. . . Corpus de musique marocaine, publié sous la direction de M. Prosper Ricard, chef du Service des Arts Indigènes . . . Paris, Heugel, [1931–33].
2v.
At head of title: Gouvernement chérifien. Protectoral de la République française au Maroc. Direction générale de l'instruction publique, des beaux-arts et des antiquités. Service des arts indigènes.
Contents:
Fasc.1. Nouba de ochchâk (prelude et première phase rythmique: bsīt); transcription, traduction et notes par Alexis Chottin [transliterated Moroccan words with tunes]; Moroccan and French words of each song on page preceding music.
Fasc.2. Musique et danses berbères du pays Chleuh.

MORPHY, GUILLERMO, *Conde de*, 1836–1899. ed.
Les luthistes espagnols du XVIe siècle. (Die spanischen Lautenmeister des 16. Jahrhunderts), von G. Morphy . . . Mit . . . einem Vorwort von F. A. Gevaert. Französischer Text revidiert von Charles Malherbe. Deutsche Übersetzung von Hugo Riemann . . . Leipzig, Breitkopf & Härtel, 1902.
2v. in 1. facsims., illus.
Text in French and German. Spanish words of songs.
Contents:
Vol.1. Préface. F. A. Gevaert. I. Notes biographiques pour servir à l'histoire de Luis Milan; II. Explication de la tablature; III. Exemples de tablature pour le luth et la guitare, tirés des livres espagnols de 1536 à 1677; IV. Observations générals. G. Morphy. Essai d'une bibliographie des livres de tablature pour le luth et la guitare, G. Morphy. [Music by] Luis Milan, 1536; Luis de Narvaez, 1538.
Vol.2. [Music by] Alonso de Mudarra, 1546; Enriquez de Valderrábano, 1547; Diego

Pisador, 1552; Miguel de Fuenllana, 1554; Venagas de Henestrosa, 1557; Estaban Daza, 1576.

MOSCHELES, IGNAZ, 1794–1870.
Collection complète des oeuvres composes pour le piano par J. Moscheles. Paris, Société pour la Publication de Musique Classique et Moderne.
5v. with parts.
Contents:
Vol.1. Ouvrages pour piano seul.
Vol.2. Piano seul; Piano et violon.
Vol.3. Musique à 4 mains.
Vol.4. Septeur, sextuor, trio et divers.
Vol.5. Musique pour piano seul.

MOSER, HANS JOACHIM, 1889– . ed.
Alte Meister des deutschen Liedes. 30 Gesänge des 17. und 18. Jahrhunderts für 1 Singst. mit Pianoforte ausgewählt und bearb. von Hans Joachim Moser. Leipzig, Edition Peters, 1912.
30 nos.
Contents:
No.1. Selle, Th. Vom 30 Jähr. Kriege: Beso las manos.
No.2, 3. Albert, H. Die Jungfrau mit dem Rosenstock: Du vormals grüner Stock; Herbstlied: Jetzung heben Wald und Feld.
No.4, 5. Hammerschmidt, A. Der Verführer: Ich lieb' an allen Ort' und Enden; Kunst des Küssens: Nirgends hin als auf den Mund.
No.6, 7. Voigtländer, G. Ach böses Herz; Zum Lobe der Musik: Als Orpheus schlug sein Instrument.
No.8–10. Dedekind, Chr. Schäfers Totenlied: Was soll ich armer Schäfer doch; Von der Modenarrheit: Jeder Schneider Lobt die Kleider; Wandel der Zeit: Wir sind ein Traum der Zeiten.
No.11–13. Krieger, Adam. Abendlied: Non sich der Tag geendet hat; Verhasstes Liebesjoch: Weicht, ihr Gedanken; Junggesellenfreunden: Ich will es nicht achten.
No.14, 15. Franck, J. W. Vergänglichkeit: In Eitelkeit war's nur gelebet; Weihnachtslied: Uns ist ein Kind zu Nutz gebor'n.
No.16. Ratheber, Val. Von der edlen Musik: Der hat vergeben das ewig Leben.
No.17, 18. Scholtze, J. S. Blaustrumpflied: Ihr Schönen, höret an; Absage an das Gluck: Kirre mich nur immer.
No.19, 20. Hurlebusch, C. F. Dieb Amor: Wer raubt mir Freiheit; Schäferlied: Angenehme grüne Zweige.
No.21. Graun, K. H. Abschiedsode an Phyllis: Endlich muss ich mich entschliessen.
No.22. Sach, J. Ph. Ode von Zachariae: Denk ihn nur aus.
No.23, 24. Neefe, J. G. Serenade: Düster liegt die Nacht umher; Die Wassernymphe: Flattre, flattr' um deine Quelle.
No.25. Rheineck, Chr. Hinterm Ofen zu singen: Der Winter ist ein rechter Mann.
No.26. Schubart, D. Weihnachtslied der Hirten: Schlaf wohl, du Himmelsknabe du.
No.27. Bach, C. Ph. Em. Nonnelied: 's ist kein verdrüsslicher Lebe.
No.28, 29. Reichardt, J. Fr. Mailied: Freude jubelt, Liebe waltet; Rhapsodie aus Goethes Winterreise: Ach wer heilet die Schmerzen.
No.30. Zelter, K. Fr. Rastlose Liebe: Dem Schnee, dem Regen.

MOSER, HANS JOACHIM, 1889– . ed.
Alte Meister des deutschen Liedes. 46 Gesänge des 17. und 18. Jahrhunderts. Ausgewählt und bearb. von Hans Joachim Moser. Neue durchgesehene und erweiterte Ausgabe. Leipzig, C. F. Peters, [1931].
81p. (Edition Peters. No.3495).
Contents:
No.1. Unbekannt. (Fliegendes Blatt. 1623). Kipp-, Wipp- und Münzerlied.
No.2. Selle, Thomas. Vom dreissigjährigen Kreige.
No.3. Selle, Thomas. An die Musikanten.
No.4. Albert, Heinrich. Treues Gedenken.
No.5. Albert, Heinrich. Die Jungfrau mit dem Rosenstock.
No.6. Albert, Heinrich. Herbstlied.
No.7. Hammerschmidt. Andreas. An die Geliebte.
No.8. Hammerschmidt, Andreas. Kunst des Küssens.
No.9. Hammerschmidt, Andreas. Der Verführer.
No.10. Voigtlaender, Gabriel. Ach böses Herz.
No.11. Voigtlaender, Gabriel. Zum Lobe der Musik.
No.12. Dedekind, K. Ch. An den Tadler.
No.13. Dedekind, K. Ch. Schäfers Totenlied.
No.14. Dedekind, K. Ch. Von der Modenarrheit.
No.15. Dedekind, K. Ch. Wandel der Zeit.
No.16. Kreiger, Adam. Die Leipziger Schönen.
No.17. Kreiger, Adam. Abendlied.
No.18. Krieger, Adam. Verhasstes Liebesjoch.
No.19. Krieger, Adam. Der Augen Schein sein Scherz und Pein.
No.20. Krieger, Adam. Junggesellenfreuden.
No.21. Krieger, Adam. Der Rhein'sche Wein tanzt gar zu fein.
No.22. Franck, Johann Wolfgang. Vergänglichkeit.
No.23. Franck, Johann Wolfgang. Weihnachtslied.
No.24. Bach, J. S. Erbauliche Gedanken eines Tabakrauchers.
No.25. Görner, Johann Valentin. Des Heidelberger Fass.
No.26. Rathgeber, Valentin. Von der edlen Music.
No.27. Rathgeber, Valentin. Modicum, ein wenig.
No.28. Scholtze, Johann Sigismund. Blaustrumpflied.
No.29. Scholtze, Johann Sigismund. Absage an das Glück.
No.30. Hurlebusch, Konrad Friedrich. Dieb Amor.
No.31. Hurlebusch, Konrad Friedrich. Schäferlied.
No.32. Graun, Carl Heinrich. Abschiedsode an Phyllis.

No.33. Telemann, Georg Ph. Das Glück kommt nicht per Eilpost.
No.34. Herbing, August Bernhard Valentin. Die Haushaltung.
No.35. Sack, Johann Philipp. Ode.
No.36. Hiller, Johann Adam. Ariette.
No.37. Hiller, Johann Adam. Das alten, lahmen Invaliden Görgels Neujahrswunsch.
No.38. Neefe, Johann Gottlob. Serenate.
No.39. Neefe, Johann Gottlob. Die Wassernymphe.
No.40. Schultz, Johann Abraham Peter. Liebeszauber.
No.41. Rheineck, Christof. Ein Lied, hintern Ofen zu singen.
No.42. Schubart, Christof Friedrich Daniel. Weihnachtslied der Hirten.
No.43. Bach, Carl Philipp Emanuel. Nonnelied.
No.44. Reichardt, Johann Friedrich. Mailied.
No.45. Reichardt, Johann Friedrich. Rhapsodie.
No.46. Zelter, Carl Friedrich. Rastlose Liebe.

MOSER, HANS JOACHIM, 1889– . ed.
Frühmeister der deutschen Orgelkunst. Leipzig, [pref.1930].
72p.
Contains compositions by Konrad Brumann, Hans Buchner, Paul Hofhaimer, Heinrich Isaac, Leonhard Kleber, Hans Kotter, Othmar Nachtigall, Bernhard von Salem, Joh. Schrem, Fridolin Sicher, and 6 anonymous composers.

MOSER, HANS JOACHIM, 1889– . ed.
Die Kantorei der Spätgotik. Alte Meistersätze deutscher Vierstimmigkeit für die heutige Chorpraxis, hrsg. von Hans Joachim Moser. Berlin, W. Sulzbach, 1928.
iv, 32p.
Contains compositions by Mathias Eckel, Heinrich Finck, Michael Gass, Konrad Rupsch, Ludwig Senfl, and anonymous.

MOSER, HANS JOACHIM, 1889– . ed.
Das Musikkränzlein. Meisterwerken der Vergangenheit und Gegenwart. Lippstadt, Kistner & Siegel & Co., 19? – .
No.1– .
Contents:
No.4. Haydn, Joseph. Zwölf deutsche Tänze für Orchester.
No.5. Rein, Walter. "Dreikönigsmusik" zum Spielen und Singen in der Weihnachtszeit.
No.7. Bach, Johann Sebastian. Vier Stücke aus dem Klavierbuche der Anna Magdalena Bach.
No.8. Geminiani, Francesco. Op.2, No.4. Concerto grosso D-dur für Streicher und Cembalo (Klavier).
No.9. Geminiani, Francesco. Op.2, No.5. Concerto grosso D-moll für Streicher und Cembalo (Klavier).
No.10. Geminiani, Francesco. Op.2, No.6. Concerto grosso A-dur für Streicher und Cembalo (Klavier).
No.11. Schubert, Franz. Siebzehn Valses sentimentales. Op.50a. (1824).
No.11a. Lully, J. Baptiste. Des Königs Musikanten. Orchester Suite bearb. von Fritz Koschinsky.

Motets choisis des maîtres du XVe au XVIIIe siècle, *see* Gastoué, Amédée. Motets choisis des maîtres du XVe au XVIIIe siècle.

MOTETT SOCIETY.
[Collection of ancient church music]. London, J. Alfred Novello, [1842–43].
3v.
Contents (from *Grove's Dictionary of music and musicians*, 1916, Vol.3, p.277):
Division 1. Anthems for festivals.
Redford. Rejoice in the Lord. 4 voices.
Lupa. Now it is high time. 6v.
Vittoria. Behold I bring you. 5 voices.
Palestrina. If Thou shalt confess. 4v.
—— Almighty and everlasting. 4v.
—— O Jerusalem. 4v.
—— These things have I. 4v.
—— These are they. 4v.
—— This shall be. 5v.
—— Break forth. 5v.
Della Porta, F. I have appeared. 4v.
Lasso. Behold I will send. 4v.
Vittoria. Come unto me. 4v.
Lasso. And the angel. 4v.
—— If ye keep my. 4v.
Masera. Blessed is the man. 4v. [Maschera?].
Lasso. For he was a good. 4v.
—— The voice of him. 4v.
—— He saith unto them. 4v.
—— Are ye able to drink. 4v.
Croce. And they went forth. 4v.
—— Charge them that are. 4v.
Byrd. Bless the Lord ye. 5v.
Lasso. But watch thou. 4v.
Croce. Now unto Him. 4v.
Nanini, G. M. All thy works. 5v.
Lasso. Miserere. 5v.
Palestrina. Behold the Lamb of God. 5v.
—— How beautiful. 4v.
Tallis. If ye love me. 4v.
Palestrina. Holy, Holy. 5v.

Division 2. Services.
Vittoria. Communion service. 4v.
Colonna. Magnificat and Nunc dimittis. 8v.
Gabrieli. Magnificat. 8v.
Barcroft. Te Deum and Benedicite. 4v.
Stonard. Magnificat and Nunc dimittis. 5v.
Palestrina. Magnificat and Nunc dimittis. 4v.
Blow. Sanctus and Gloria. 4v.

Division 3. Miscellaneous anthems.
Barcroft. O Almighty God. 4v.
Gibbons, O. Why art thou so heavy. 4v.
Lasso. O praise the Lord. 5v.
—— Not unto us. 5v.
Certon, P. I will alway give. 3v.
Byrd. Prevent us, O Lord. 4v.
Tallis. Hear the voice. 4v.
Palestrina. O God, Thou art. 4v.
Tallis. All people that on earth. 4v.
Farrant. Unto Thee, O Lord. 4v.
Palestrina. I will magnify Thee. 5v.
Della Porta, F. Be merciful. 4v.
—— Righteous art Thou. 4v.
Palestrina. O Lord my God. 4v.

Gibbons, O. O Lord, increase. 4v.
Vittoria. I will give thanks. 4v.
—— It is a good thing. 4v.
—— Teach me, O Lord. 4v.
—— How long wilt Thou. 4v.
—— My God, my God. 4v.
—— Unto Thee, O God. 4v.
—— Behold, now praise. 4v.
Palestrina. O Lord God of our salvation. 5v.
Tallis. Great and marvellous. 5v.
Lasso. Hear my prayer. 4v.
Byrd. Save me, O God. 4v.
Tye. From the depth. 4v.
Lasso. I will love Thee. 4v.
Vittoria. Save me, O God. 4v.
Mel. O praise the Lord. 4v.
Tallis. Blessed are those. 5v.
Shepherd. Haste Thee, O God. 4v.
Croce. Behold now, praise. 4v.
—— O praise the Lord. 4v.
—— O give thanks. 4v.
—— Teach me Thy way. 4v.
—— Give ear, Lord. 4v.
—— Behold, I bring you. 4v.
Lasso. Save me, O God. 4v.
Vittoria. O God, wherefore. 4v.
Hooper. Teach me Thy way. 4v.

DIE MOTETTE, hrsg. von Rudolf Ewerhart. Köln, Edmund Bieler, 19? – .
No.1– .
Contents:
No.1. Giorgi, Giovanni. Laetentur coeli. 4 gemischten Stimmen und Basso Continuo.
No.2. Gasparini, Quirino. Adoramus Te, Christe. 4 gemischten Stimmen und Basso Continuo.
No.3. Calvi, Lorenzo. Victimae paschali laudes. 4 gemischten Stimmen und Basso Continuo, alternatim mit Greg. Choral.
No.4. Scarlatti, Alessandro. Domine, refugium factus es. 5 gemischten Stimmen.

Moussorgskiĭ, Modest Petrovich, *see* Musorgskiĭ, Modest Petrovich.

MOZART, WOLFGANG AMADEUS, 1756–1791.
W. A. Mozarts Sämtliche Werke. Kritisch durchgesehene Gesamtausgabe. Hrsg. von Johannes Brahms, Franz Espagne, Otto Goldschmidt, Joseph Joachim, Ludwig Ritter von Köchel, Gustav Nottebohm, Carl Reinecke, Ernst Rudorff, Philipp Spitta, Paul Graf Waldersee, Franz Wüller. Ser.I–XXIV and Revisionsberichte in 8 parts. Leipzig, Breitkopf & Härtel, 1876–1905.
24 series.
Contents:
Ser.1. Messen.
Erster Band.
1. Missa brevis, G dur.
2. Missa brevis, D moll.
3. Missa, C dur.
4. Missa, C moll.
5. Missa in honorem S. Smae Trinitatis, C dur.
6. Missa brevis, F dur.
7. Missa brevis, D dur.
8. Missa brevis, C dur.
Zweiter Band.
9. Missa, C dur.
10. Missa, C dur.
11. Missa brevis, C dur.
12. Missa, C dur.
13. Missa brevis, B dur.
14. Missa, C dur.
15. Missa, C dur.
Ser.2. Litaneien und Vespern.
1. Litaniae Lauretanae, B dur.
2. Litaniae de venerabili altaris sacramento, B dur.
3. Litaniae Lauretanae, D dur.
4. Litaniae de venerabili altaris sacramento, Es dur.
5. Dixit et Magnificat, C dur.
6. Vesperae de Dominica, C dur.
7. Vesperae solennes de confessore, C dur.
Ser.3. Kleinere geistliche Gesangwerke.
Erster Band.
1–5. Kyrie.
6. Spruch. God is our refuge.
7. Veni Sancte Spiritus.
8. Miserere.
9. Antiphone.
10–12. Regina coeli.
13. Te Deum.
14–15. Tantum ergo.
16. Zwei deutsche Kirchenlieder.
Zweiter Band.
17–18. Offertorium.
19. Psalm. De profundis.
20. Offertorium.
21. Recitativ und Arie.
22. Motette.
23–26. Offertorium.
27. Graduale ad festum B.M.V.
28. Offertorium de B.M.V.
29–30. Hymnus.
31. Motette. Ave verum corpus.
Ser.4. Cantaten und Oratorien.
Erste Abtheilung. Cantaten.
1. Grabmusik. (Passions-Cantate).
2. Die Maurerfreude. Cantate für Solo-Tenor, Männerchor und Orchester.
3. Eine kleine Freimaurer Cantate. Laut verkünde uns're Freude.
Zweite Abtheilung. Oratorien.
4. Betulia liberata. Italiänisches Oratorium in 2 Theilen.
5. Davidde penitente. Oratorium.
Ser.5. Opern.
1. Die Schuldigkeit des eraten Gebotes.
2. Apollo et Hyacinthus.
3. Bastien und Bastienne.
4. La finta semplice.
5. Mitridate, Re di Ponto.
6. Ascanio in Alba.
7. Il sogno di Scipione.
8. Lucio Silla.
9. La finta giardiniera.
10. Il re pastore.
11. Zaide.
12. Thamos, König in Aegypten.
13. Idomeneo, Re di Creta, ossia Ilia e Adamante.

14. Balletmusik zur oper Idomeneo.
15. Die Entführung aus dem Serail.
16. Der Schauspieldirector.
17. Le nozze di Figaro.
18. Il dissoluto punito, ossia il Don Giovanni.
19. Cosi fan tutte.
20. Die Zauberflöte.
21. La clemenza di Tito.

Ser.6. Arien, Duette, Terzette und Quartette mit Begleitung des Orchesters.

Erster Band.

1. Arie für Tenor. Va dal furor portata. K.V.21.
2. Arie für Sopran. Conservati fedele. K.V.23.
3. Recitativ und Arie (Licenza) für Tenor. Or che il dover. K.V.36.
4. Recitativ und Arie (Licenza) für Sopran. A Berenice e Vologeso. K.V.70.
5. Recitativ und Arie für Sopran. Misero me. Misero pargoletto. K.V.77.
6. Arie für Sopran. Per pietà, bell' idol mio. K.V.78.
7. Recitativ und Arie für Sopran. O temerario Arbace. K.V.79.
8. Arie für Sopran. Se tutti i mali miei. K.V.83.
9. Arie für Sopran. Fra cento affanni. K.V.88.
10. Arie für Sopran (Passionslied). Kommt her, ihr frechen Sünder. K.V.146.
11. Arie für Tenor. Si mostra la sorte. K.V.209.
12. Arie für Tenor. Con ossequio, con rispetto. K.V.210.
13. Arie für Sopran. Voi avete un cor fedele. K.V.217.
14. Recitativ und Arie (Rondo) für Alt. Ombra felice. K.V.255.
15. Arie für Tenor. Clarice, cara mia sposa. K.V.256.
16. Scene für Sopran. Ah lo previdi.
17. Recitativ und Arie für Sopran. Alcandro lo confesso.
18. Arie für Tenor. Se al labbro mio non credi.
19. Recitativ und Arie für Sopran. Popoli di Tessaglia.
20. Recitativ und Arie für Sopran. Ma che vi fece o stelle.
21. Scene und Arie für Sopran. Misera, dove son?
22. Recitativ und Arie für Sopran. A questo seno.
23. Arie für Sopran. Nehmt meinen Dank.

Zweiter Band.

24. Recitativ und Rondo für Sopran. Mis speranza adorata. K.V.416.
25. Arie für Sopran. Vorrei spiegarvi, oh Dio. K.V.418.
26. Arie für Sopran. No, no, che non sei capace. K.V.419.
27. Rondo für Tenor. Per pietà, non ricercate. K.V.420.
28. Recitativ und Arie für Tenor. Misero! O sogno, o son desto? K.V.431.
29. Recitativ und Arie für Bass. Cosi dunque tradisci. K.V.432.
30. Terzett. Ecco, quel fiero. K.V.436.
31. Terzett. Mi lagnerò tacendo. K.V.437.
32. Quartett. Dite almeno in che mancai. K.V.479.
33. Terzett. Mandina amabile. K.V.480.
34. Recitativ und Rondo für Sopran mit obligatem Klavier. Ch'io mi scordi. K.V.505.
35. Recitativ und Arie für Bass. Alcandro, lo confesso. K.V.512.
36. Arie für Bass. Mentre ti lascio, o figlia. K.V.513.
37. Recitativ und Arie für Sopran. Bella mia fiamma. K.V.528.
38. Arie für Sopran. Ah se in ciel, benigne stelle. K.V.538.
39. Ein deutsches Kriegslied. Ich möchte wohl der Kaiser sein. Für Bass. K.V.539.
40. Ariette für Bass. Un bacio di mano. K.V.541.
41. Canzonette. Più non si trovano. K.V.549.
42. Arie für Sopran. Alma grande e nobil core. K.V.578.
43. Arie für Sopran. Chi sà, chi sà, qual sia. K.V.582.
44. Arie für Sopran. Vado, ma dove? Oh Dio! K.V.583.
45. Arie für Bass. Rivolgete a lui lo sguardo. K.V.584.
46. Arie für Bass. Per questa bella mano. K.V.612.
47. Komisches Duett. Nun liebes Weibchen, ziehst mit mir. K.V.625.

Ser.7.

Erste Abtheilung. Lieder und Gesänge mit Begleitung des Pianoforte.

1. Daphne, deine Rosenwangen. K.V.52.
2. An die Freude. K.V.53.
3. Wie unglücklich bin ich nit. K.V.147.
4. O heiliges Band. K.V.148.
5. Die grossmüthige Gelassenheit. K.V.149.
6. Geheime Liebe. K.V.150.
7. Die Zufriedenheit im niedrigen Stande. K.V.151.
8. Canzonetta. Ridente la calma. K.V.152.
9. Arietta. Oiseaux, si tous les ans. K.V.307.
10. Arietta. Dans un bois. K.V.308.

11a. Die Zufriedenheit. K.V.349.

11b. Die Zufriedenheit. Andere Bearbeitung. K.V.349.

12. Wiegenlied. K.V.350.
13. Komm, liebe Zither. K.V.351.
14. Ich würd' auf meinem Pfad'. K.V.390.
15. An die Einsamkeit. K.V.391.
16. Verdankt sei es dem Glanz. K.V.392.
17. Das Bändchen. K.V.441.
18. Gesellenreise. K.V.468.
19. Der Zauberer. K.V.472.
20. Die Zufriedenheit. K.V.473.
21. Die betrogene Welt. K.V.474.
22. Das Veilchen. K.V.476.
23. Zur Eröffnung der . . . K.V.483.
24. Zum Schluss der . . . K.V.484.

25. Lied der Freiheit. K.V.506.
26. Die Alte. K.V.517.
27. Die Verschweigung. K.V.518.
28. Das Lied der Trennung. K.V.519.
29. Als Luise die Briefe ihres ungetreuen Liebhabers Verbrannte. K.V.520.
30. Abendempfindung. K.V.523.
31. An Chloe. K.V.524.
32. Des kleinen Friedrichs Geburtstag. K.V.529.
33. Das Traumbild. K.V.530.
34. Die kleine Spinnerin. K.V.531.
35. Grazie agl' inganni tuoi. K.V.532.
36. Un moto di gioja. K.V.579.
37. Sehnsucht nach dem Frühlinge. K.V.596.
38. Im Frühlingsanfang. K.V.597.
39. Das Kinderspiel. K.V.598.
40. Cantate. Die ihre des unermesslichen Weltalls. K.V.619.

Zweite Abtheilung. Kanons.

41. Doppel-Kanon für vier Stimmen. K.V.228.
42. Kanon für drei Stimmen. K.V.229.
43. Kanon für zwei Stimmen. K.V.230.
44. Kanon für sechs Stimmen. K.V.231.
45. Kanon für vier Stimmen. K.V.232.
46. Kanon für drei Stimmen. K.V.233.
47. Kanon für drei Stimmen. K.V.234.
48. Kanon für sechs Stimmen. K.V.347.
49. Kanon. V'amo di core, für drei vierstimmige Chöre. K.V.348.
50. Kanon für drei Stimmen. K.V.507.
51. Kanon für drei Stimmen. K.V.508.
52. Kanon. Alleluja, für vier Stimmen. K.V.553.
53. Kanon. Ave Maria, für vier Stimmen. K.V.554.
54. Kanon. Lacrimoso son io, für vier Stimmen. K.V.555.
55. Kanon. Grechtelts enk, für vier Stimmen. K.V.556.
56. Kanon. Nascoso è il mio sol, für vier Stimmen. K.V.557.
57. Kanon. Gehn wir im Prater, für vier Stimmen. K.V.558.
58. Kanon. Difficile lectu, für drei Stimmen. K.V.559.
59a. Kanon. O du eselhafter Martin, für vier Stimmen. K.V.560b.
59b. Kanon. O du eselhafter Peierl, für vier Stimmen. K.V.560a.
60. Kanon. Bona nox, für vier Stimmen. K.V.561.
61. Kanon. Caro bell' idol mio, für drei Stimmen. K.V.562.

Ser.8. Symphonien.

Erster Band.

1. Symphonie, Es dur. K.V.16.
2. Symphonie, B dur. K.V.17.
3. Symphonie, Es dur. K.V.18.
4. Symphonie, D dur. K.V.19.
5. Symphonie, B dur. K.V.22.
6. Symphonie, F dur. K.V.43.
7. Symphonie, D dur. K.V.45.
8. Symphonie, D dur. K.V.48.
9. Symphonie, C dur. K.V.73.
10. Symphonie, G dur. K.V.74.
11. Symphonie, D dur. K.V.84.
12. Symphonie, G dur. K.V.110.
13. Symphonie, F dur. K.V.112.
14. Symphonie, A dur. K.V.114.
15. Symphonie, G dur. K.V.124.
16. Symphonie, C dur. K.V.128.
17. Symphonie, G dur. K.V.129.
18. Symphonie, F dur. K.V.130.
19. Symphonie, Es dur. K.V.132.
20. Symphonie, D dur. K.V.133.
21. Symphonie, A dur. K.V.134.

Zweiter Band.

22. Symphonie, C dur. K.V.162.
23. Symphonie, D dur. K.V.181.
24. Symphonie, B dur. K.V.182.
25. Symphonie, G moll. K.V.183.
26. Symphonie, Es dur. K.V.184.
27. Symphonie, G dur. K.V.199.
28. Symphonie, C dur. K.V.200.
29. Symphonie, A dur. K.V.201.
30. Symphonie, D dur. K.V.202.
31. Symphonie, D dur. K.V.297.
32. Symphonie, G dur. K.V.318.
33. Symphonie, B dur. K.V.319.
34. Symphonie, C dur. K.V.338.

Dritter Band.

35. Symphonie, D dur. K.V.385.
36. Symphonie, C dur. K.V.425.
37. Symphonie, G dur. K.V.444.
38. Symphonie, D dur. K.V.504.
39. Symphonie, Es dur. K.V.543.
40. Symphonie, G moll. K.V.550.
41. Symphonie, C dur. K.V.551.

Ser.9.

Erste Abtheilung. Cassationen und Serenaden für Orchester.

1. Cassation. No.1, G dur. K.V.63.
2. Cassation. No.2, B dur. K.V.99.
3. Serenade. No.1, D dur. K.V.100.
4. Serenade. No.2, F dur. K.V.101.
5. Serenade. No.3, D dur. K.V.185.
6. Serenade. No.4, D dur. K.V.203.
7. Serenade. No.5, D dur. K.V.204.
8. Serenade. No.6, D dur. K.V.239.
9. Serenade. No.7, D dur. K.V.250.
10. Notturno (Serenade No.8), D dur. K.V.286.
11. Serenade. No.9, D dur. K.V.320.
12. Serenade. No.10, B dur. K.V.361.
13. Serenade. No.11, Es dur. K.V.375.
14. Serenade. No.12, C moll. K.V.388.

Zweite Abtheilung. Divertimenti für Orchester.

15. Divertimento. No.1, Es dur. K.V.113.
16. Divertimento. No.2, D dur. K.V.131.
17. Divertimento. No.3, Es dur. K.V.166.
18. Divertimento. No.4, B dur. K.V.186.
19. Zehn Stücke (Divertimento No.5). K.V.187.
20. Divertimento. No.6, C dur. K.V.188.
21. Divertimento. No.7, D dur. K.V.205.
22. Divertimento. No.8, F dur. K.V.213.
23. Divertimento. No.9, B dur. K.V.240.
24. Divertimento. No.10, F dur. K.V.247.
25. Divertimento. No.11, D dur. K.V.251.
26. Divertimento. No.12, Es dur. K.V.252.
27. Divertimento. No.13, F dur. K.V.253.

28. Divertimento. No.14, B dur. K.V.270.
29. Divertimento. No.15, B dur. K.V.287.
30. Divertimento. No.16, Es dur. K.V.289.
31. Divertimento. No.17, D dur. K.V.334.

Ser.10. Märsche und kleinere Stücke für Orchester (auch für Harmonika und Orgelwalze).
1. Marsch, D dur. K.V.189.
2. Marsch, C dur. K.V.214.
3. Marsch, D dur. K.V.215.
4. Marsch, D dur. K.V.237.
5. Marsch, F dur. K.V.248.
6. Marsch, D dur. K.V.249.
7. Marsch, D dur. K.V.290.
8. Zwei Märsche, D dur, D dur. K.V.335.
9. Drei Märsche, C dur, D dur, C dur. K.V.408.
10. Allegro (Schlusssatz einer Symphonie), D dur. K.V.121.
11. Menuett (Mittelsatz einer Symphonie), C dur. K.V.409.
12. Maurerische Trauermusik, C moll. K.V.477.
13. Ein musikalischer Spass, F dur. K.V.522.
14. Sonate für Fagott und Violoncell, B dur. K.V.292.
15. Kanonisches Adagio für 2 Bassethörner und Fagott, F dur. K.V.410.
16. Adagio für 2 Clarinetten und 3 Bassethörner, B dur. K.V.411.
17. Adagio für Harmonika, C dur. K.V.356.
18. Adagio und Rondo für Harmonika mit Begleitung, C moll. K.V.617.
19. Phantasie für eine Orgelwalze, F moll. K.V.608.
20. Andante für eine Walze in eine kleine Orgel, F dur. K.V.616.
21. Marsch für 2 Violinen, Viola, Bass und 2 Hörner, D dur. K.V.445.

Ser.11. Tänze für Orchester.
1. Zwölf Menuette. K.V.568.
2. Zwölf Menuette. K.V.585.
3. Sechs Menuette. K.V.599.
4. Vier Menuette. K.V.601.
5. Zwei Menuette. K.V.604.
6. Sechs deutsche Tänze. K.V.509.
7. Sechs deutsche Tänze. K.V.536.
8. Sechs deutsche Tänze. K.V.567.
9. Sechs deutsche Tänze. K.V.571.
10. Zwölf deutsche Tänze. K.V.586.
11. Sechs deutsche Tänze. K.V.600.
12. Vier deutsche Tänze. K.V.602.
13. Drei deutsche Tänze. K.V.605.
14. Contretanz. K.V.123.
15. Vier Contretänze. K.V.267.
16. Fünf Menuette. K.V.461.
17. Sechs Contretänze. K.V.462.
18. Zwei Menuette mit eingefügten Contretänzen. K.V.463.
19. Neun Contretänze oder Quadrillen. K.V.510.
20. Contretanz. (La bataille). K.V.535.
21. Contretanz. (Der Sieg vom Helden Koburg). K.V.587.
22. Zwei Contretänze. K.V.603.
23. Fünf Contretänze. K.V.609.
24. Contretanz. (Les filles malicieuses). K.V.610.

Ser.12.

Erste Abtheilung. Concerte für Violine und Orchester.
1. Concert für Violine, B dur. K.V.207.
2. Concert für Violine, D dur. K.V.211.
3. Concert für Violine, G dur. K.V.216.
4. Concert für Violine, D dur. K.V.218.
5. Concert für Violine, A dur. K.V.219.
6. Adagio für Violine, E dur. K.V.261.
7. Rondo concertant für Violine, B dur. K.V.269.
8. Rondo für Violine, C dur. K.V.373.
9. Concertone für 2 Solo-Violinen, C dur. K.V.190.
10. Concertante Symphonie für Violine und Viola, Es dur. K.V.364.

Zweite Abtheilung. Concerte für ein Blasinstrument und Orchester.
11. Concert für Fagott, B dur. K.V.191.
12. Concert für Flöte und Harfe, C dur. K.V.299.
13. Concert für Flöte, G dur. K.V.313.
14. Concert für Flöte, D dur. K.V.314.
15. Andante für Flöte, C dur. K.V.315.
16. Concert für Horn, D dur. K.V.412.
17. Concert für Horn, Es dur. K.V.417.
18. Concert für Horn, Es dur. K.V.447.
19. Concert für Horn, Es dur. K.V.495.
20. Concert für Clarinette, A dur. K.V.622.

Ser.13. Quintette für Streichinstrumente.
1. Quintett für 2 Violinen, 2 Violen und Violoncell, B dur. K.V.174.
2. Quintett für 2 Violinen, 2 Violen und Violoncell, C moll. K.V.406.
3. Quintett für 1 Violine, 2 Violen, 1 Horn, 1 Violoncell (oder statt des Horns ein 2 Violoncell), Es dur. K.V.407.
4. Quintett für 2 Violinen, 2 Violen und Violoncell, C dur. K.V.515.
5. Quintett für 2 Violinen, 2 Violen und Violoncell, G moll. K.V.516.
6. Quintett für 1 Clarinette, 2 Violinen, Viola, Violoncell, A dur. K.V.581.
7. Quintett für 2 Violinen, 2 Violen, Violoncell, D dur. K.V.593.
8. Quintett für 2 Violinen, 2 Violen, Violoncell, Es dur. K.V.614.
9. Eine kleine Nachtmusik für 2 Violinen, Viola, Violoncell, Contrabass, G dur. K.V.525.

Ser.14. Quartette für Streichinstrumente.
1. Quartett, G dur. Für 2 Violinen, Viola und Violoncell. K.V.80.
2. Quartett, D dur. Für 2 Violinen, Viola und Violoncell. K.V.155.
3. Quartett, G dur. Für 2 Violinen, Viola und Violoncell. K.V.156.
4. Quartett, C dur. Für 2 Violinen, Viola und Violoncell. K.V.157.
5. Quartett, F dur. Für 2 Violinen, Viola und Violoncell. K.V.158.
6. Quartett, B dur. Für 2 Violinen, Viola und Violoncell. K.V.159.
7. Quartett, Es dur. Für 2 Violinen, Viola und Violoncell. K.V.160.

8. Quartett, F dur. Für 2 Violinen, Viola und Violoncell. K.V.168.
9. Quartett, A dur. Für 2 Violinen, Viola und Violoncell. K.V.169.
10. Quartett, C dur. Für 2 Violinen, Viola und Violoncell. K.V.170.
11. Quartett, Es dur. Für 2 Violinen, Viola und Violoncell. K.V.171.
12. Quartett, B dur. Für 2 Violinen, Viola und Violoncell. K.V.172.
13. Quartett, D moll. Für 2 Violinen, Viola und Violoncell. K.V.173.
14. Quartett, G dur. Für 2 Violinen, Viola und Violoncell. K.V.387.
15. Quartett, D moll. Für 2 Violinen, Viola und Violoncell. K.V.421.
16. Quartett, Es dur. Für 2 Violinen, Viola und Violoncell. K.V.428.
17. Quartett, B dur. Für 2 Violinen, Viola und Violoncell. K.V.458.
18. Quartett, A dur. Für 2 Violinen, Viola und Violoncell. K.V.464.
19. Quartett, C dur. Für 2 Violinen, Viola und Violoncell. K.V.465.
20. Quartett, D dur. Für 2 Violinen, Viola und Violoncell. K.V.499.
21. Quartett, D dur. Für 2 Violinen, Viola und Violoncell. K.V.575.
22. Quartett, B dur. Für 2 Violinen, Viola und Violoncell. K.V.589.
23. Quartett, F dur. Für 2 Violinen, Viola und Violoncell. K.V.590.
24. Divertimento für 2 Violinen, Viola und Bass, D dur. K.V.136.
25. Divertimento für 2 Violinen, Viola und Bass, B dur. K.V.137.
26. Divertimento für 2 Violinen, Viola und Bass, F dur. K.V.138.
27. Adagio und Fuge für 2 Violinen, Viola und Violoncell, C moll. K.V.546.
28. Quartett für Flöte, Violine, Viola, Violoncell, D dur. K.V.285.
29. Quartett für Flöte, Violine, Viola, Violoncell, A dur. K.V.298.
30. Quartett für Oboe, Violine, Viola, Violoncell, F dur. K.V.370.

Ser.15. Duos und Trio für Streichinstrumente.
1. Duo für Violine und Viola, G dur. K.V.423.
2. Duo für Violine und Viola, B dur. K.V.424.
3. Duo (für 2 Violinen), C dur. K.V.487.
4. Divertimento für Violine, Viola und Violoncell, Es dur. K.V.563.

Ser.16. Concerte für das Pianoforte.

Erster Band.
1. Concert, F dur. K.V.37.
2. Concert, B dur. K.V.39.
3. Concert, D dur. K.V.40.
4. Concert, G dur. K.V.41.
5. Concert, D dur. K.V.175.
6. Concert, B dur. K.V.238.
7. Concert für 3 Pianoforte, F dur. K.V.242.
8. Concert, C dur. K.V.246.

Zweiter Band.
9. Concert, Es dur. K.V.271.
10. Concert für 2 Pianoforte, Es dur. K.V.365.
11. Concert, F dur. K.V.413.
12. Concert, A dur. K.V.414.
13. Concert, C dur. K.V.415.
14. Concert, Es dur. K.V.449.
15. Concert, B dur. K.V.450.
16. Concert, D dur. K.V.451.

Dritter Band.
17. Concert, G dur. K.V.453.
18. Concert, B dur. K.V.456.
19. Concert, F dur. K.V.459.
20. Concert, D moll. K.V.466.
21. Concert, C dur. K.V.467.

Vierter Band.
22. Concert, Es dur. K.V.482.
23. Concert, A dur. K.V.488.
24. Concert, C moll. K.V.491.
25. Concert, C dur. K.V.503.
26. Concert, D dur. K.V.537.
27. Concert, B dur. K.V.595.
28. Concert-Rondo, D dur. K.V.382.

Ser.17.

Erste Abtheilung. Pianoforte-Quintett und zwei Quartette für Pianoforte mit Begleitung.
1. Quintett für Pianoforte, Oboe, Clarinette, Horn und Fagott, Es dur. K.V.452.
2. Quartett No.1 für Pianoforte, Violine, Viola und Violoncell, G moll. K.V.478.
3. Quartett No.2 für Pianoforte, Violine, Viola und Violoncell, Es dur. K.V.493.

Zweite Abtheilung. Trios für Pianoforte, Violine und Violoncell.
4. Trio No.1 für Pianoforte, Violine und Violoncell, B dur. K.V.254.
5. Trio No.2 für Pianoforte, Violine und Violoncell, D moll. K.V.442.
6. Trio No.3 für Pianoforte, Violine und Violoncell, G dur. K.V.496.
7. Trio No.4 für Pianoforte, Clarinette und Viola, Es dur. K.V.498.
8. Trio No.5 für Pianoforte, Violine und Violoncell, B dur. K.V.502.
9. Trio No.6 für Pianoforte, Violine und Violoncell, E dur. K.V.542.
10. Trio No.7 für Pianoforte, Violine und Violoncell, C dur. K.V.548.
11. Trio No.8 für Pianoforte, Violine und Violoncell, G dur. K.V.564.

Ser.18. Sonaten und Variationen für Pianoforte und Violine.

Erster Band.
1. Sonate, C dur. K.V.6.
2. Sonate, D dur. K.V.7.
3. Sonate, B dur. K.V.8.
4. Sonate, G dur. K.V.9.
5. Sonate, B dur. K.V.10.
6. Sonate, G dur. K.V.11.
7. Sonate, A dur. K.V.12.
8. Sonate, F dur. K.V.13.
9. Sonate, C dur. K.V.14.
10. Sonate, B dur. K.V.15.
11. Sonate, Es dur. K.V.26.
12. Sonate, G dur. K.V.27.
13. Sonate, C dur. K.V.28.
14. Sonate, D dur. K.V.29.
15. Sonate, F dur. K.V.30.

16. Sonate, B dur. K.V.31.
17. Sonate, F dur. K.V.55.
18. Sonate, C dur. K.V.56.
19. Sonate, F dur. K.V.57.
20. Sonate, Es dur. K.V.58.
21. Sonate, C moll. K.V.59.
22. Sonate, E moll. K.V.60.
23. Sonate, A dur. K.V.61.

Zweiter Band.

24. Sonate, C dur. K.V.296.
25. Sonate, G dur. K.V.301.
26. Sonate, Es dur. K.V.302.
27. Sonate, C dur. K.V.303.
28. Sonate, E moll. K.V.304.
29. Sonate, A dur. K.V.305.
30. Sonate, D dur. K.V.306.
31. Allegro einer Sonate, B dur. K.V.372.
32. Sonate, F dur. K.V.376.
33. Sonate, F dur. K.V.377.
34. Sonate, B dur. K.V.378.
35. Sonate, G dur. K.V.379.
36. Sonate, Es dur. K.V.380.
37. Sonate, A dur. K.V.402.
38. Sonate, C dur. K.V.403.
39. Sonate, C dur. K.V.404.
40. Sonate, B dur. K.V.454.
41. Sonate, Es dur. K.V.481.
42. Sonate, A dur. K.V.526.
43. Sonate, F dur. K.V.547.
44. 12 Variationen über "La bergère Silimène," G dur. K.V.359.
45. 6 Variationen über "Hèlas, j'ai perdu mon amant," G moll. K.V.360.

Ser.19. Für ein und zwei Pianoforte zu vier Händen.

1. Sonate, G dur. K.V.357.
2. Sonate, B dur. K.V.358.
3. Sonate, D dur. K.V.381.
4. Sonate, F dur. K.V.497.
5. Sonate, C dur. K.V.521.
6. Andante mit fünf Variationen, G dur. K.V.501.
7. Fuge für zwei Pianoforte, C moll. K.V.426.
8. Sonate für zwei Pianoforte, D dur. K.V.448.

Ser.20. Sonaten und Phantasien für das Pianoforte.

1. Sonate, C dur. K.V.279.
2. Sonate, F dur. K.V.280.
3. Sonate, B dur. K.V.281.
4. Sonate, Es dur. K.V.282.
5. Sonate, G dur. K.V.283.
6. Sonate, D dur. K.V.284.
7. Sonate, C dur. K.V.309.
8. Sonate, A moll. K.V.310.
9. Sonate, D dur. K.V.311.
10. Sonate, C dur. K.V.330.
11. Sonate, A dur. K.V.331.
12. Sonate, F dur. K.V.332.
13. Sonate, B dur. K.V.333.
14. Sonate, C moll. K.V.457.
15. Sonate, C dur. K.V.545.
16. Sonate, B dur. K.V.570.
17. Sonate, D dur. K.V.576.
18. Phantasie mit einer Fuge, C dur. K.V.394.
19. Phantasie, C moll. K.V.396.
20. Phantasie, D moll. K.V.397.
21. Phantasie, C moll. K.V.475.

Ser.21. Variationen für das Pianoforte.

1. Acht Variationen über ein Allegretto. K.V.24.
2. Sieben Variationen über "Wilhelm von Nassau." K.V.25.
3. Zwölf Variationen über ein Minuett von Fischer. K.V.179.
4. Sechs Variationen über "Mio caro Adone" von Salieri. K.V.180.
5. Neun Variationen über "Lison dormait." K.V.264.
6. Zwölf Variationen über "Ah vous dirais-je, Maman." K.V.265.
7. Acht Variationen über den Marsch der "Mariages Samnites" von Grétry. K.V.352.
8. Zwölf Variationen über "La belle Françoise." K.V.353.
9. Zwölf Variationen über "Je suis Lindor." K.V.354.
10. Fünf Variationen über "Salve tu Domine" von Paisiello. K.V.398.
11. Zehn Variationen über "Unser dummer Pöbel meint." K.V.455.
12. Acht Variationen über "Come un agnello" von Sarti. K.V.460.
13. Zwölf Variationen über ein Allegretto. K.V.500.
14. Neun Variationen über ein Minuett von Duport. K.V.573.
15. Acht Variationen über das Lied "Ein Weib ist das herrlichste Ding." K.V.613.

Ser.22. Kleinere Stücke für das Pianoforte.

1. Menuett. No.1 mit Trio, G dur. K.V.1.
2. Menuett. No.2, F dur. K.V.2.
3. Menuett. No.3, F dur. K.V.4.
4. Menuett. No.4, F dur. K.V.5.
5. Menuett. No.5, D dur. K.V.94.
6. Menuett. No.6, D dur. K.V.355.
7. Rondo, D dur. K.V.485.
8. Kleines Rondo, F dur. K.V.494.
9. Rondo, A moll. K.V.511.
10. Claviersuite (Ouverture, Allemande, Courante, Sarabande), C dur. K.V.399.
11. Fuge, G moll. K.V.401.
12. Allegro, B dur. K.V.3.
13. Allegro einer Sonate, G moll. K.V.312.
14. Allegro und Andante, F dur. K.V.533.
15. Andantino, Es dur. K.V.236.
16. Adagio, H moll. K.V.540.
17. Eine kleine Gigue, G dur. K.V.574.
18. 36 Cadenzen. K.V.624.

Ser.23. Sonaten für mehrere Instrumente mit Orgel.

1. Sonate für 2 Violinen, Bass und Orgel, Es dur. K.V.67.
2. Sonate für 2 Violinen, Bass und Orgel, B dur. K.V.68.
3. Sonate für 2 Violinen, Bass und Orgel, D dur. K.V.69.
4. Sonate für 2 Violinen und Orgel oder Bass, D dur. K.V.144.
5. Sonate für 2 Violinen und Orgel oder Bass, F dur. K.V.145.
6. Sonate für 2 Violinen, Bass und Orgel, B dur. K.V.212.
7. Sonate für 2 Violinen, Bass und Orgel, F dur. K.V.224.

8. Sonate für 2 Violinen, Bass und Orgel, D dur. K.V.225.
9. Sonate für 2 Violinen, Bass und Orgel, F dur. K.V.244.
10. Sonate für 2 Violinen, Bass und Orgel, D dur. K.V.245.
11. Sonate für 2 Violinen, Bass und Orgel, G dur. K.V.274.
12. Sonate für 2 Violinen, Violoncell, Bass, 2 Oboen, Trompeten, Pauken und Orgel, C dur. K.V.278.
13. Sonate für 2 Violinen, Bass und Orgel, C dur. K.V.328.
14. Sonate für 2 Violinen, Bass, 2 Oboen, 2 Hörner, Violoncell, Trompeten, Pauken und Orgel, C dur. K.V.329.
15. Sonate für 2 Violinen, Bass und Orgel, C dur. K.V.336.

Ser.24. Supplement.
No.1. Requiem. K.V.626.
No.2–7. Symphonien.
No.2. Symphonie, F dur. K.V.75.
No.3. Symphonie, F dur. K.V.76.
No.4. Symphonie, D dur. K.V.81.
No.5. Symphonie, D dur. K.V.95.
No.6. Symphonie, C dur. K.V.96.
No.7. Symphonie, F dur. K.V.97.
No.7a–18. Kleinere Orchesterstücke. (Ser. 8–11).
No.7a. Concertantes Quartett für Oboe, Clarinette, Horn und Fagott mit Begleitung. K.V. Anh.9.
No.8. Letzter Satz einer Symphonie. K.V.102.
No.9. Letzter Satz einer Symphonie. K.V.120.
No.10. Letzter Satz einer Symphonie. K.V.163.
No.10a. Balletmusik zur Pantomime: Les petits riens. K.V. Anh.10.
No.11. Fuge für Orchester: (Fragment). K.V.291.
No.12. Galimathias Musicum für Clavier und Orchester: (Partiturentwurf). K.V.32.
No.13. Sieben Menuette mit Trio. K.V.65a.
No.13a. Menuett (ohne Trio). K.V.122.
No.14. Drei Menuette. K.V.363.
No.14a. Zwei Menuette.
No.15. Ouverture und drei Contretänze. K.V.106.
No.16. Sechs ländlerische Tänze für Orchester. Übertragung für 2 Violinen und Bass. K.V.606.
No.17. Contretanz. Il trionfo delle donne. (Fragment). K.V.607.
No.18. Musik zu einer Pantomime für 2 Violinen, Viola und Bass. (Fragment). K.V.446.
No.19–21. Concerte. (Ser.12).
No.19. Concert für die Violine, Es dur. K.V.268.
No.20. Concert für Oboe, F dur. K.V.293.
No.21. Concert-Rondo für Horn, Es dur. K.V.371.
No.21a–27a. Concert, Kammermusik- und Clavierwerke. (Ser.13–15). (Ser.22).
No.21a. Concert für Clavier und Violine mit Begleitung. (Fragment). K.V. Anh.56.
No.22. Quintett für 2 Violinen, 2 Violen und Violoncell. K.V.46.
No.22a. Quintett für Clarinette, 2 Violinen, Viola und Violoncell. (Fragment). K.V. Anh.91.
No.23. Quartett für 2 Violinen, Viola und Violoncell. (Fragment). K.V. Anh.72.
No.23a. Trio für 2 Violinen und Bass. K.V.266.
No.24. Kleine Phantasie für Clavier. K.V.395.
No.25. Zwei Fugen für Clavier. K.V.153, 154.
No.26. Erster Satz einer Sonate für Clavier. K.V.400.
No.27. Contretanz "Das Donnerwetter" für Orchester. Übertragung für Clavier. K.V.534.
No.27a. Adagio und Allegro für eine Orgelwalze. Übertragung für Clavier zu vier Händen. K.V.594.
No.28, 48a. Geistliche und weltliche Gesangwerke. (Ser.1 und 6).
No.28. Missa brevis für 4 Singstimmen und Orgel. K.V.115.
No.48a. Arie für Sopran "Se ardire, e speranza" mit Begleitung. K.V.82.
No.29. Messe, in C moll. K.V.427.
No.30–53. Kleinere geistliche und weltliche Gesangwerke. (Ser.3, 6 und 7).
No.30. Lacrymosa für 4 Singstimmen, Bass und Orgel. K.V. Anh.21.
No.31. Antiphone "Cibavit eos" für 4 Singstimmen und Orgel. K.V.44.
No.32. Kyrie für 4 Singstimmen (mit Begleitung). K.V.91.
No.33. Kyrie für 4 Singstimmen (mit Begleitung). K.V.116.
No.34. Kyrie für 4 Singstimmen und Orgel. K.V.221.
No.35. Credo für 4 Singstimmen (mit Begleitung). (Fragment). K.V.337.
No.36a/b. Cantata. Dir, Seele des Weltalls. K.V.429.
No.39. Arie für Tenor. Ah, più tremar non voglio. (Fragment). K.V.71.
No.40. Arie für Sopran. Der Liebe himmlisches Gefühl. (mit Clavier). K.V.119.
No.41. Arie für Sopran. Ah spiegarti, Oh Dio. (mit Clavier). K.V.178.
No.42. Duett für 2 Tenors. Welch ängstliches Beben. (Fragment). K.V.389.
No.43. Arie für Bass. Männer suchen stets zu naschen. (Fragment). K.V.433.
No.44. Terzett für Tenor und 2 Bässe. Del gran regno delle amazoni. (Fragment). K.V.434.
No.45. Arie für Tenor. Müsst ich auch durch tausend Drachen. (Fragment). K.V.435.
No.46. Terzett für 2 Soprane und Bass. Se lontan, ben mio, tu sei. (Fragment). K.V.438.

No.47. Arie für Sopran. In te spero, O sposo amato. K.V.440.
No.48. Arie für Sopran. Schon lacht der holde Frühling. K.V.580.
No.49. Solfeggien für Sopran mit und ohne Begleitung. (Fragment). K.V.393.
No.50. Scherzhaftes Quartett für Sopran, 2 Tenore und Bass. Caro mio, Druck und Schluck. (Fragment). K.V. Anh.5.
No.51. Kanon für 4 Stimmen. Anhang, K.V.191.
No.52. Kanon für 4 Stimmen. K.V.232.
No.53. Kanon für 5 Stimmen. K.V.89a.I.
No.37–38. Opern. (Ser.5).
No.37. L'oca del Cairo. Komische Oper. K.V.422.
No.38. Lo sposo deluso. Opera buffa in due atti. K.V.430.
No.54. Arie "Conservati fedele" für Sopran mit Begleitung von Streichinstrumenten. K.V.23. Neue Ausgabe.
No.55. Quintett für 2 Violinen, 2 Violen und Violoncell. K.V. Anh.II.80.
No.56. Symphonie für 2 Violinen, Viola, Bass, 2 Oboen und 2 Hörner. K.V.98.
No.57. 6 Menuette für 2 Violinen, Bass, 2 Oboen (Flöte) und 2 Trompeten (2 Hörner). K.V.164.
No.58. Zwölf Duette für 2 Bassethörner. K.V.487.
No.59. Skisse zum Quintett für Pianoforte, Oboe, Clarinette, Horn und Fagott. K.V.452.
No.60. Sonate für 2 Claviere. Fragment. K.V. Anh.II.42.
No.61. Recitativ und Arie "Basta, vincesti, eccoti il foglio" . . . "Ah non lasciarmi, no." Für Sopran mit Begleitung des Orchesters. K.V.486a.
No.62. Fünf Divertimenti für 2 Klarinetten und Fagott. K.V. Anh.229, 229a.
Revisionsbericht.

MOZART, WOLFGANG AMADEUS, 1756–1791.
W. A. Mozarts Sämtliche Werke. Another issue. Ann Arbor, Mich., J. W. Edwards, 1951–56.
24 series. (Edwards music reprints. Ser.A. Complete works and monumenta, No.4).
"Photolithographischer Neudruck."

MOZART, WOLFGANG AMADEUS, 1756–1791.
Oeuvres complettes de Wolfgang Amadeus Mozart. Leipzig, Breitkopf & Härtel, [1798–1804?].
17v.
Engraved title page and title vignettes.
Contents:
Cahier 1. VII Sonates pour le pianoforte.
Cahier 2. XII Thèmes variés pour le pianoforte.
Cahier 3. VII Sonates pour le pianoforte.
Cahier 4. VI Sonates pour le pianoforte avec l'accompagnement d'un violin. [piano and violin parts].
Cahier 5. XXX Pièces avec l'accompagnement d'un pianoforte.
Cahier 6. XIV Différentes pièces pour le pianoforte.
Cahier 7. IV Sonates pour le pianoforte à quatre mains.
Cahier 8. VI Pièces pour le pianoforte à deux et à quatre mains.
Cahier 9. V Sonates pour le pianoforte avec l'accompagnement d'un violon. [piano and violin parts].
Cahier 10. IV Sonates pour le pianoforte avec l'accompagnement d'un violon et violoncelle. [piano and 2 string parts].
Cahier 11. V Sonates et II Airs variés pour le pianoforte avec l'accompagnement d'un violon. [piano and violin parts].
Cashier 12. III Trios et I quintetto pour le pianoforte. [piano and 7 string and wind parts].
Cahier 13. II Quatuors et I Sonate pour le pianoforte.
Cahier 14. I Sonate pour 2 pianofortes. [piano I and II parts]. I Quintetto pour le pianoforte avec l'accompagnement de hautbois, clarinette, cor et basson [full score]; le même arrangé en quartetto pour le pianoforte avec l'accompagnement de violon, alto, et violoncelle. [piano and 3 string parts].
Cahier 15. XII Sonatines pour le pianoforte avec l'accompagnement de violon [piano and violin parts] et VI Canons [with German, and Italian and German, words].
Cahier 16. VI Sonatines pour le pianoforte avec l'accompagnement de violon [piano and violin parts] et XVI Canons [with German words].
Cahier 17. I Sonate, 2 Fantaisies, 3 Airs variés, 1 Menuetto et 1 Allegretto varié pour le pianoforte seul, et 4 Sonates pour le pianoforte avec l'accompagnement d'un violon. [piano and violin parts].

MOZART, WOLFGANG AMADEUS, 1756–1791.
Neue Ausgabe Sämtliche Werke. Hrsg. von der Internationalen Stiftung Mozarteum. Salzburg, International Mozarteum Foundation, 1956– .
10 series. (approximately 110v.). (in progress).
To be published over a period of approximately 15 years.
A "Kritische Bericht" is planned with most of the volumes.
Contents (published volumes are listed in German; unpublished are listed in English, preceded by an asterisk):
Ser.I. Geistliche Gesangswerke.
1. Messen und Requiem.
Bd.2. Requiem. Teil 1–2. 1965.
2. Litaneien, Vespern.
Bd.2. Vespern und Vesperpsalmen. 1959.
3. Kleinere Kirchenwerke. 1963.
4. Oratorien, geistliche Singspiele und Kantaten.
Bd.1. Die Schuldigkeit des ersten Gebots. 1958.
Bd.2. Betulia liberata. 1960.
Bd.4. Kantaten. 1957.
Ser.II. Bühnenwerke.
5. Opern und Singspiele.
Bd.1. Apollo und Hyacinth. 1959.

Bd.4. Mitridate, Re di Ponte. 1966.
Bd.5. Ascanio in Alba. (Luigi Ferdinando Tagliavini). 1956.
Bd.10. Zaide. (Das Serail). 1957.
Bd.13. L'oca del Cairo. 1960.
Bd.15. Der Schauspieldirektor. 1958.
6. Musik zu Schauspielen, Pantomimen und Balletten.
Bd.1. Chöre und Zwischenaktmusiken zu Thamos, König in Ägypten. 1956.
Bd.2. Musik zu Pantomimen und Balletten. 1963.
*7. Scenes, ensembles, arias, and choruses with orchestra.
Ser.III. Lieder, mehrstimmige Gesänge, Kanons.
8. Lieder. 1963.
*9. Part-songs with piano, with wind instruments and a cappella.
*10. Canons.
Ser.IV. Orchesterwerke.
11. Symphonien.
Bd.3. K.V.128, 129, 130, 132, 133, 134, 141, 126, 161/163. 1956.
Bd.4. K.V.162, 184, 199, 181, 182, 183, 200. 1960.
Bd.5. K.V.201, 202, 196, 121/207, 297, 208, 102/213. 1957.
Bd.7. K.V.204, 250, 320. 1959.
Bd.9. K.V.543, 550, 551. 1957.
12. Kassationen, Serenaden und Divertimenti für Orchester.
Bd.2. K.V.113, 131, 189, 185. 1961.
Bd.3. K.V.237, 203, 215, 204, 239. 1962.
Bd.6. K.V.136–138, 525. Anh.223c, 525a. 1964.
13. Tänze und Märsche.
Abt.1. Tänze.
Bd.1. K.V.65, 123, 122, 103, 104, 105, 61, 164, 176, 101, 267, 94, 315. 1961.
Ser.V. Konzerte.
*14. Concertos for one or more string, wind or plucked instruments and orchestra.
15. Konzerte für ein oder mehrere Klaviere und Orchester mit Kadenzen.
Bd.5. K.V.453, 456, 459, 624. 1965.
Bd.6. K.V.466, 467, 482. 1961.
Bd.7. K.V.488, 491, 503. 1959.
Bd.8. K.V.537, 595, 386. Anh.65, 59, 58, 63, 64, 62, 60, 57, 61. 1960.
Ser.VI. Kirchensonaten.
16. Sonaten für Orgel und Orchester. 1957.
Ser.VII. Ensemble music. For larger groups of performers.
*17. Divertimenti and Serenades for 6 to 13 wind instruments.
*18. Divertimenti for 6 and 7 string and wind instruments.
Ser.VIII. Kammermusik.
19. Streichquintette und Quintette mit Bläsern.
Abt.2. Quintett mit Bläsern. 1958.
20. Streichquartette und Quartette mit einem Blasinstrument.
Abt.1. Streichquartette.
Bd.1. K.V.80, 155–160 (159a), 168–173. 1966.
Bd.2. K.V.387, 421, 458, 428, 464, 465. 1962.
Bd.3. K.V.499, 575, 589, 590. Anh.77, 76, 84, 75, 71, 72, 74, 68, 73. 1961.
Abt.2. Quartette mit einem Blasinstrument. 1962.
*21. Trios and Duos for strings and winds.
22. Quintette, Quartette und Trios mit Klavier und mit Glasharmonika.
Abt.1. Quartette und Quintette mit Klavier und mit Glasharmonika. 1957.
Abt.2. Klaviertrios. 1966.
23. Sonaten und Variationen für Klavier und Violine.
Bd.1. 1964.
Bd.2. 1965.
Ser.IX. Klaviermusik.
24. Werke für 2 Klaviere und für Klavier zu 4 Händen.
Abt.1. Werke für 2 Klaviere. 1955.
Abt.2. Werke für Klavier zu 4 Händen. 1955.
*25. Sonatas, fantasies and rondos for piano.
26. Variationen für Klavier. 1961.
*27. Single pieces for piano, for Glasharmonika and for the Orgelwalze.
Ser.X. Supplement.
28. Bearbeitungen, Ergänzungen und Übertragungen Fremder Werke.
Abt.1. Bearbeitungen von Werken Georg Friedrich Händels.
Bd.2. Der Messias. 1961.
Bd.3. Das Alexander-Fest. 1962.
Abt.2. Bearbeitungen von Werken verschiedener Komponisten Klavierkonzerte und Kadenzen. 1964.
*29. Works of doubtful authenticity.
30. Studien, Skizzen. Entwürfe, Fragmente, Varia.
Bd.1. Thomas Attwoods Theorie- und Kompositionsstudien bei Mozart, 1965.
31. Nachträge zu allen Serien und Werkgruppen. 1964.
32. Mozart und seine Welt in zeitgenössischen Bildern. 1961.
*33. Selected documents in Mozart's hand, arranged chronologically.
34. Mozart. Die Dokumente seines Lebens. 1961.
*35. Index and Concordance.

MOZART, WOLFGANG AMADEUS, 1756–1791.
Werke für Klavier. Leipzig, C. F. Peters, 19? – . 5v. (Edition Peters. No.1800a–b, 6, 273, 765).
Contents:
Vol.1–2. Sonaten. Neuausgabe nach dem Urtext. (Martienssen/Weismann).
Vol.3. Stücke: Phantasien, Rondos, usw.
Vol.4. Variationen.
Vol.5. Acht berühmte Konzerte.

MUFFAT, GEORG, d.1704.
... Apparatus musico-organisticus. Rev. and ed. from the original edition of the year 1690 with preface and hints concerning the use of the pedal and the art of registration, by S. de

Lange. Leipzig, New York, [etc.], C. F. Peters, [pref.1888].
3p.L., 75p. (On cover: Peters Edition. No.6020).

MÜLLER-BLATTAU, JOSEPH MARIA, 1895– . ed.
Musica reservata. Meisterwerke der Musik des 16. und 17. Jahrhunderts. Kassel, Bärenreiter, cop.1952– .
v.1– .
Vol.1–2 also published in the series, Chor-Archiv.
Contents:
Vol.1. Vier- bis sechstimmige Motetten von Senfl, Orlando di Lasso und Stobäus.
Vol.2. Vier- bis sechstimmige Motetten von Josquin, Senfl und Orlando di Lasso.

Müller-Blattau, Josef Maria, 1895– , ed. Das Rostocker Liederbuch, *see* Das Rostocker Liederbuch.

Museo orgánico español, *see* Eslava y Elizondo, Hilarión. Museo orgánico español.

MUSET, JOSEPH. ed.
Early Spanish organ music. Collected, transcribed, and ed. by Joseph Muset . . . New York, G. Schirmer, Inc., [cop.1948].
4p.L., 92p.
Contains compositions by Pau Bruna, Joan Cabanílles, Antonio de Cabezón, Narcis Casanovas, Joseph Elias, Cándido Eznarriága, Sebastián Aguiléra de Herédia, Miquel Lopez, Francesco Llusá, Gabriel Menalt, Juan Moreno, Joaquin Oxinagas, Francisco Fernandez Paléro, Francisco Peraza, Tomás de Santa Mariá, Pedro de Soto, Diego de Torrijos, Pedro Alberto Vila, and Anselm Viola.

MUSIC FOR WIND INSTRUMENTS BY 18th CENTURY MASTERS, ed. by Josef Marx. New York, McGinnis & Marx, 1946– .
No.1– .
Contents:
No.1. Vivaldi, Antonio. Il pastor fido. Sonata No.VI in G minor for flute, or oboe, or violin, and piano. 1946.
No.2. Galliard, Johann Ernest. Six sonatas for bassoon or cello and piano. 2v. 1946.
No.3. Stamitz, Karl. Two quartets for clarinet or flute or oboe, violin, viola, and cello or string quartet. 1947.
No.4. Mozart, Wolfgang Amadeus. Twelve duos for 2 French horns, K.487. 1947.
No.5. Kraft, Anton. Sonata, Op.2, No.2, for cello and piano or two celli alone. 1948. (Music for string instruments, No.5).
No.6. Wanhal, Johann Baptist. Sonate for clarinet (violin, flute, or oboe) and piano. 1948. (was mistakenly marked as No.5).
No.7. Stamitz, Johann Wenzel Anton. Two divertimenti in two parts for one unaccompanied violin. 1949. (Music for string instruments, No.7).
No.8. Bach, Johann Sebastian. Canonic trio for oboe, violin (or two tenor recorders) and piano. 1957.
No.9. Corelli, Arcangelo. Variations on La follia, Op.5, No.12, for alto recorder (flute, oboe) and piano. 1957.
No.10. Porpora, Nicola. Sinfonia for recorder (flute, oboe, violin) and piano. 1963.
No.11. Fasch, Johann Friedrich. Sonata for bassoon (cello) and figured bass. 1963.
No.12. Cambini, Giuseppe. Quintet No.3 for flute, oboe, clarinet, bassoon, and horn.
No.13. Pla, José. Trio No.6 for two oboes or flutes and figured bass.

Music from the days of George Washington, *see* Engel, Carl. Music from the days of George Washington.

Music in America, *see* Marrocco, William Thomas. Music in America.

Music of earlier times, *see* Wolf, Johannes. Music of earlier times. Vocal and instrumental examples. (13th century to Bach).

Music of early times for piano, *see* Apel, Willi. Musik aus früher Zeit für Klavier.

The music of fourteenth-century Italy, *see* Pirrotta, Nino. The music of fourteenth-century Italy.

Music of Gabrieli and his time, *see* Gabrieli, Giovanni. Music of Gabrieli and his time.

Music of the Bach family, *see* Geiringer, Karl. Music of the Bach family.

The music of the church considered in its various branches, *see* Latrobe, John Antes. The music of the church considered in its various branches.

MUSIC OF THE MORAVIANS IN AMERICA from the archives of the Moravian Church at Bethlehem, Pennsylvania. Ed. by Hans T. David. New York, C. F. Peters, cop.1947, 1954– .
v.1– . (New York Public Library. Music publications).
Contents:
Vol.1. Ten sacred songs for soprano, strings, and organ (two flutes ad lib. for No.8) by J. Dencke, J. F. Peter, S. Peter, J. Herbst, G. G. Müller, and J. Antes. cop.1946, 1954.
Vol.2. Six quintets by John Frederick Peter. 1955.

Music of the Polish Renaissance, *see* Chomiński, Józef Michal. Music of the Polish Renaissance.

MUSIC PRESS, INC., New York.
[Choral series]. New York, Music Press, Inc., 1944–49.
126v.
Title supplied by the University of California Library.
A collection of both sacred and secular choral works for various combinations of voices, both accompanied and unaccompanied.
Vols.94–100 have added title: Ballads and folk

songs of America from the repertoire of the Margaret Dodd Singers.
Vols.125–126 have added title: Grinnell College choral series.
Vols.104–107, 109–114, 118–122 have added title: Contemporary choral series.
Vols.1–48 are evidently the same as Vols.1–48 of the Dessoff choir series (q.v.).
Vol.49 was evidently never published.
Contents:
Vol.50. Marenzio, Luca. Hodie Christus natus est.
Vol.51. Byrd, William. Two sacred songs in 4 parts.
Vol.52. Purcell, Henry. No, no, resistance is but vain.
Vol.53. Morley, Thomas. Three motets in 4 parts.
Vol.54. David, Hans T., ed. French chansons of the sixteenth century.
Vol.55. Early American hymn tunes, 1800–1860.
Vol.56. Le Jeune, Claude. 3-part psalms.
Vol.57. Cowell, Henry. American muse.
Vol.58. Palestrina, G. P. da. Two madrigals. I. Amor, quando fioria. II. Gioia m'abond' al cor.
Vol.59. Ten Christmas carols from ancient sources for unison or mixed voices.
Vol.60. Tallis, Thomas. Magnificat and Nunc dimittis.
Vol.61. Classic anthems, ed. by Ernest White. [Aldrich, Rogers, and Child].
Vol.62. Billings, William. Three fuguing tunes.
Vol.63. Billings, William. Hark! Hark! Hear you not?
Vol.64. Billings, William. A Virgin unspotted.
Vol.65. Reichenbach, Herman, ed. Classic canons.
Vol.66. Reichenbach, Herman, ed. Easy canons.
Vol.67. Handl, Jacob. O admirabile commercium.
Vol.68. Handl, Jacob. Jesu dulcis memoria.
Vol.69. Victoria, Tomás Luis da. Tantum ergo. (For 5 mixed voices).
Vol.70. Victoria, Tomás Luis da. Tantum ergo. (For 4 mixed voices).
Vol.71. Scarlatti, Alessandro. Exultate Deo.
Vol.72. Practical polyphony. Five easy anthems of the 16th century. [by Lassus, Arcadelt, Ruffo, and Rosselli].
Vol.73. Lassus, Orlandus. Salve Regina.
Vol.74. Berchem, Jachet van. O Jesu Christe.
Vol.75. Palestrina, G. P. da. Sicut cervus.
Vol.76. Lassus, Orlandus. Adoramus Te.
Vol.77. Marenzio, Luca. O sacrum convivium.
Vol.78. Ruffo, Vincenzo. Adoramus Te.
Vol.79. Victoria, Tomás Luis da. Ave Maria.
Vol.80. Lassus, Orlandus. Jubilate Deo.
Vol.81. Arcadelt, Jacques. Deh come trista.
Vol.82. Arcadelt, Jacques. Ecco d'oro l'eta.
Vol.83. Haydn, Joseph. Harmony in marriage.
Vol.84. Haydn, Joseph. 'Tis Thou to whom all honor.
Vol.85. Reichenbach, Herman, ed. Modern canons.
Vol.86. Four folk songs from Switzerland. (For 4 mixed voices).
Vol.87. Four folk songs from Switzerland. (For 4 equal voices).
Vol.88. Billings, William. Modern music.
Vol.89. Billings, William. Consonance.
Vol.90. Whythorne, Thomas. Three songs, ed. by Manfred F. Bukofzer.
Vol.91. Mouton, Jean. Iocundare Ierusalem.
Vol.92. Byrd, William. Two sacred songs in 5 parts.
Vol.93. Josquin des Prez. Salve Regina.
Vol.94. He's gone away. Folk song from the Southern Appalachians. Arr. by A. Lief.
Vol.95. Old bang 'am. Folk song from Virginia. Arr. by M. Dodd.
Vol.96. Schuckin' of the corn. Folk song from Tennessee. Arr. by W. Preston.
Vol.97. Per Spelmann. Norwegian folk song from Minnesota. Arr. by M. Dodd.
Vol.98. The wee cooper of Fife. Folk song from North Carolina. Arr. by A. Lief.
Vol.99. Sourwood Mountain. Folk song from the Appalachians. Arr. by A. Lief.
Vol.100. A la puerta del cielo. Arr. by M. Dodd.
Vol.101. Billings, William. Be glad then, America.
Vol.102. Billings, William. When Jesus wept.
Vol.103. Ginastera, Alberto. The lamentations of Jeremiah.
Vol.104. Donovan, Richard. How should I love?
Vol.105. Diamond, David. Young Joseph.
Vol.106. Shepherd, Arthur. Jolly Wat.
Vol.107. Sanders, Robert. An American psalm.
Vol.108. Lawton, Edward, ed. Catches for 3, 4, and 5 voices.
Vol.109. Guarnieri. Egbegi.
Vol.110. Guarnieri. Coco de major.
Vol.111. Guarnieri. Vamus Aloanda.
Vol.112. Guarnieri. Sinhor lau.
Vol.113. Chávez. Arbolucu.
Vol.114. Bacon, Ernst. Seven canons.
Vol.115. Belcher, Supply. Choruses from The harmony of Maine.
Vol.116. Dufay, Guillaume. Ave Regina coelorum, ed. by Manfred F. Bukofzer.
Vol.117. Krebs, Johann Ludwig. Eight chorale preludes for unison chorus and organ.
Vol.118. Rorem, Ned. Four madrigals.
Vol.119. Carter, Elliott. Musicians wrestle everywhere.
Vol.120. Carter, Elliott. Emblems.
Vol.121. Ten glees, madrigals, and airs [1600–1765], ed. by M. Bartholomew.
Vol.122. Kimball, Jacob. Down East spirituals.
Vol.123. Billings, William. Lamentation over Boston and Jargon.
Vol.124. Billings, William. Retrospect.
Vol.125. Bacon, Ernst. The Lord star.
Vol.126. Clément, Jacques. Adoramus Te.

The music that Washington knew, *see* Fisher, William Arms. The music that Washington knew.

THE MUSIC WITH THE FORM AND ORDER OF THE SERVICE TO BE PERFORMED AT THE CORONATION OF HER MOST EXCELLENT MAJESTY, QUEEN ELIZABETH II, in the Abbey Church of Westminster on Tuesday the 2nd day of June 1953. London, Novello and Co., Ltd., 1953.
viii, 183p.
Contains compositions by William Byrd, George Dyson, Orlando Gibbons, G. F. Handel,

William H. Harris, Herbert Howells, C. Hubert H. Parry, attributed to John Redford, C. V. Stanford, R. Vaughan Williams, William Walton, S. S. Wesley, and Healey Willan.

Musica, *see* Reale Accademia d'Italia, Rome. Musica.

La música andaluza medieval en las canciones de trovadores, troveros y minnesinger, *see* Ribera y Tarragó, Julián. La música andaluza medieval en las canciones de trovadores, troveros y minnesinger.

Musica antiqua, *see* Smith, John Stafford. Musica antiqua.

MUSICA ANTIQUA BATAVA. Quam edendam curavit Vereniging voor Nederlandse Muziekgeschiedenis. The Hague, Editio Musico, 195? – .
v.1– .
Contents:
MA–1. Belle, Jan. Laet ons nu al verblijden./ Lasst sich das Herz erfreuen./ Now let there be rejoicing. Dr. R. Lagas. 1954.
MA–2. Belle, Jan. Cherry red lips.
MA–3. Auctoris incerti. Wij comen hier gheloopen./ Wir kommen hier gelaufen./ The beggar's song. Dr. R. Lagas. 1954.
MA–4. Episcopius, Lu. Laet varen alle fantasie./ Lass fahren Alles was dich drücket./ All fancies from your mind. 1954.
MA–5. Episcopius, Lu. More ale, more cake.
MA–6. Hellinck, Lupus. Janne moye, al claer!/ Lustig Hanne, nur zu!/ Tom the tiddler, all clear! Dr. R. Lagas.
MA–7. Des Prez, Josquin. Petite camusette. Prof. Dr. A. Smijers.
MA–8. Wintelroy, Joan. Al is den tijt nu doloreus./ Und ist die Zeit auch noch so schlecht./ What though the times be dolorous. Dr. R. Lagas.
MA–9. Sweelinck, Jan P. Psalmus 134. 1954.
MA–10. Sweelinck, Jan P. Psalmus 90: Tu es été./ Thou art, O Lord./ Gij zijt, O Heer! B. van den Sigtenhorst Meyer. 1952.
MA–11. Sweelinck, Jan P. Psalmus 122: Incontinent que j'eus nui./ How greatly did my heart rejoice./ Ik ben verblijd wanneer men mij. Dr. R. Lagas. 1954.
MA–12. Sweelinck, Jan P. Hodie Christus natus est, noe Hodie Salvator apparuit./ Hodie Christus natus est, Noel!/ Behold now our Saviour comes. Dr. R. Lagas. 1954.
MA–13. Sweelinck, Jan P. Psalm 114.

MUSICA ANTIQUA BOHEMICA. Prague, Editio Artia, 1949– .
v.1– .
Introductory material in Czech, English, French, German, Italian, and Russian.
Contents:
Vol.1. Voříšek, Jan Hugo. Impromptus. Op.7. Pour le pianoforte.
Vol.2. Benda, Jiří. Sonata per 2 violini e clavicembalo.
Vol.3. Černohorský, Bohuslav. Varhanní skladby. (organ).
Vol.4. Voříšek, Jan Hugo. Sonata. Op.20. Pour le pianoforte.
Vol.5. Krommer, František Vincenc (registered at birth Kramář). Quartetto. Op.5, No.1. Per 2 violini, viola e violoncello.
Vol.6. Míča, František Adam. II. Quartetto do maggiore. Per 2 violini, viola e violoncello.
Vol.7. Pichl, Václav. Sei fughe con un preludio fugato. Per un violino solo.
Vol.8. Dušek, František Xaver. Sonate per il clavicembalo.
Vol.9. Zach, Jan. Sonata a 3 stromenti. Per 2 violini e basso.
Vol.10. Benda, Jiří. Concerto sol minore. Per il cembalo obbligato con accompagnamento a 2 violini, viola e violoncello (contrabasso).
Vol.11. Čeští klasikové. (The Czech classics). (František Benda, Jiří Benda, Jan Benda, Jan Křtitel Vanhal, Josef Mysliveček, Jan Hugo [Václav] Voříšek, and Jan Ladislav Dusík.) Violino e Piano.
Vol.12. Čeští klasikové. (The Czech classics). (Bohuslav Matěj Černohorský, Jan Zach, Josef Ferd. Norbert Seger, Jiří Ignác Linek, František Xaver Brixi, Jan Křtitel Vaňhal, Jan Křtitel Kuchař, Karel Blazej Kopřiva, Antonín Josef Rejcha, and Karel František Píč [Pitsch].) Organo.
Vol.13. Krommer, František Vincenc (registered at birth Kramář). Concerto Mi♭ maggiore. Clarinetto e piano.
Vol.14. Čeští klasikové. (The Czech classics). (Jiří Benda, Františék Xaver Brixi. Josef Antonín Štěpán, František Xaver Dušek, Leopold Koželuh, Antonín Felix Bečvařovský, Pavel Vranický, Matouš Alois Cibulka, Vojtěch Jírovec, Jan Theobald Held, and Jan Augustin Vitásek.) Piano.
Vol.15. Koželuh, Leopold Antonín. Op.32/I. Quartetto d'archi. Si♭ maggiore.
Vol.16. Vranický, Antonín. Concerto Si♭ maggiore. Violino e piano.
Vol.17. České sonatiny. (Sonatinas by old Czech composers). (Jiří A. Benda, Frant. X. Dušek, Jan Ladislav Dusík, Leopold Ant. Koželuh, Josef Mysliveček, Jan Křtitel Vaňhal, and Jan Václav [Hugo] Voříšek.) Piano.
Vol.18. Fils, Antonín. Concerto Re maggiore. Flauto e piano.
Vol.19. Míča, Jan Adam František. Concertino notturno in dis. a violino principale, 2 violini, 2 oboi, 2 corni, 2 fagotti, 2 viole e basso.
Vol.20. Čeští klasikové. (The Czech classics). (Jan Ladislav Dusík, Antonín Rejcha, Václav Jan Tomášek, Jan Václav [Hugo] Voříšek, and František Škroup.) Piano.
Vol.21. Dusík, Jan Ladislav. Dvanáct melodických etud. (Douze études mélodiques). Piano.
Vol.22. Dusík, Jan Ladislav. 6 Sonatines pour la harpe.
Vol.23. České vánoční pastorely. Pastorelle boemiche. (Daniel Alois František Milčinský, Tomáš Norbert Koutník, Jiří Ignác Linek, and Jan Michalička.)

Vol.24. Benda, Jiří Antonín. Sonate I–XVI. Piano.
Vol.25. Vranický, Pavel. Op.15–III. Quartetto d'archi Si^{b} maggiore.
Vol.26. Brixi, František Xaver. Concerto Fa maggiore per organo principale, 2 corni, 2 violini, viola, basse e cembalo.
Vol.27. Krommer, František Vincenc (registered at birth Kramář). Concerto, Op.36, Fa maggiore, oboe e piano.
Vol.28. Stamic, Jan Václav. Op.6a. Sonata Sol maggiore. Violino e continuo (cembalo-piano).
Vol.29. Tomášek, Václav Jan. Op.65. 3 Ditirambi. Piano.
Vol.30. Voříšek, Jan Hugo. Sonata. Op.5. Violino e piano.
Vol.31. Mysliveček, Josef. 3 Quintetti d'archi.
Vol.32. Rössler-Rosetti, František Antonín. Notturno in D per flauto traverso, violino, viola, violoncello, corni in D.
Vol.33. Rejcha, Antonín. 3 Quintetti per stromenti da fiato. Op.88, No.3, Sol maggiore. Op.91, No.9, Re maggiore. Op.91, No.11, La maggiore. Per flauto, oboe, clarinetto, corno e fagotto.
Vol.34. Voříšek, Jan Hugo. Sinfonia re maggiore.
Vol.35. Serenate Boeme, partite e notturni. (E. Kammel, J. Druzecký, F. X. Dusek, V. Mašek.)
Vol.36. Vejvanovský, Pavel Josef. Serenate e sonate per orchestra.
Vol.37. Benda, Jiří Antonín. Sonatine I–XXXIV. Piano.
Vol.38. Losy z Losimtálu, Jan Antonín. Pièces de guitarre.
Vol.39. Štěpán, Josef Antonín. Concerto in D per il clavicembalo, flauto traverso, violino, corni e contrabasso.
Vol.40. Tolar, Jan Křtitel. Balletti e sonate.
Vol.41. Dusík, Jan Ladislav. Sonate. Op.69, No.1, 2. Violino e piano.
Vol.42. Krommer, František Vincenc (registered at birth Kramář). Il quartetti per oboe, violino, viola e violoncello.
Vol.43. Zach, Jan. 5 Sinfonie d'archi per 2 violini, viola e basso.
Vol.44. Fils, Antonín. 6 Sinfonie per orchestra. Op.2.
Vol.45. Benda, Jiří Antonín. 3 Concerti per cembalo con accompagnamento di 2 violini, viola e basso.
Vol.46. Dusík, Jan Ladislav. Sonate I–VII. Piano. Volume primo. 1960.
Vol.47–49. Veljvanovsky. Composizioni per orchestra. Pt.I–III.
Vol.50. Rejcha, A. L'art de varier. Op.57. Piano.
Vol.51. Seger, J. Composizioni per organo. Preludi, toccata e fughe. Pt.I. (1–36).
Vol.52. Voříšek, J. V. Composizioni. Piano.
Vol.53. Dusík, J. L. Sonate. Pt.II. Piano.
Vol.54. Vodicka, V. 6 Sonate. Violino e piano.
Vol.55. Mysliveček, J. 3 Octets. Oboe, 2 clarinets, 2 trumpets, 2 bassoons.
Vol.56. Seger, J. Composizioni per organo. Preludi e fughe. Pt.II.
Vol.57. Benda, J. A. 4 Sonatas. Violino e quartetto d'archi.
Vol.58. Benda, J. A. Sinfonie 1–3. Pt.I.
Vol.59. Dusík, J. L. Sonate. Pt.III. Piano.
Vol.60. Benda, F. Sonata. Flauto, violoncello e cembalo.

MUSICA BRITANNICA; a national collection of music. Pub. for the Royal Musical Association with the support of the Arts Council of Great Britain. London, Stainer & Bell, Ltd., 1951– . v.1– . facsims.
General editor: 1951– , Anthony Lewis.
Contents:
Vol.1. The Mulliner book. Ed. by Denis Stevens. Comprises some 120 pieces. 1951. Rev. ed. 1962.
Vol.2. Cupid and Death, by Matthew Locke and Christopher Gibbons. Ed. by Edward J. Dent. 1951.
Vol.3. Comus, by Thomas Augustine Arne. Ed. by Julian Herbage. 1951.
Vol.4. Mediaeval carols. Ed. by John Stevens. 1952. A complete collection of all extant pieces in this form written between 1400 and 1500.
Vol.5. The keyboard music of Thomas Tomkins. Ed. by Stephen D. Tuttle. 1955.
Vol.6. Dowland, John. Ayres for 4 voices. Transcribed by Edmund H. Fellowes. Ed. by Thurston Dart and Nigel Fortune. 1953.
Vol.7. Blow, John. Coronation anthems. Anthems with strings. Ed. by Anthony Lewis and Harold Watkins Shaw. 1953.
Vol.8. Dunstable, John. Complete works. Ed. by Manfred F. Bukofzer. 1953. (American Musicological Society. Studies and documents. No.2).
Vol.9. Jacobean consort music. Ed. by Thurston Dart and William Coates. 1955. Rev. ed. 1962.
Vol.10, 11, 12. The Eton choir book. Transcribed and ed. by Frank Llewellyn Harrison. 1956, 1958, 1961.
Vol.13. Boyce, William. Overtures. Ed. by Gerald Finzi. 1957.
Vol.14, 19. Bull, John. Keyboard music. I–II. Vol.14 ed. by John Steele and Francis Cameron with introductory material by Thurston Dart. 1960. Vol.19 transcribed and ed. by Thurston Dart. 1963.
Vol.15. Elliott, Kenneth, ed. Music of Scotland, 1500–1700. Song texts ed. by Helena Mennie Shire. 1957.
Vol.16. Storace, Stephen. No song, no supper. A comic opera in two acts. The words by Prince Hoare. Ed. by Roger Fiske. 1959.
Vol.17. Field, John. Piano concertos. Ed. by Frank Merrick. 1961.
Vol.18. Henry VIII's book. Music at the court of Henry VIII. Transcribed and ed. by John Stevens. 1962.
Vol.19. *See* Vol.14.
Vol.20. Gibbons, Orlando. Keyboard music. Transcribed and ed. by Gerald Hendrie. 1962.
Vol.21. Lawes, William. Select consort music. Transcribed and ed. by Murray Lefkowitz. 1963.
Vol.22. Elizabethan consort songs. Ed. by Philip Brett.

Other volumes in process include editions of sacred music by Thomas Weelkes, madrigals by Peter Philips and Richard Dering, and further volumes in the series of collected keyboard works.

MUSICA DIVINA. Kirchenmusikalische Werke für Praxis und Forschung. Hrsg. im Auftrag des Instituts für Musikforschung Regensburg von Bruno Stäblein, Regensburg, Verlag Friedrich Pustet, 1950– .
v.1– .
Contents:
Vol.1. Cavalli, Francesco. Vier Marianische Antiphonen (1656) für 2 bis 5 Singstimmen und Orgel. (Generalbass). Hrsg. von Bruno Stäblein. 1: Ave Regina, zweistimmig für Sopran und Alt, oder Tenor und Bass. 1950.
Vol.2. Cavalli, Francesco. Vier Marianische Antiphonen. Hrsg. von Bruno Stäblein. 2: Regina caeli, dreistimmig für Alt, Tenor und Bass. 1950.
Vol.3. Cavalli, Francesco. Vier Marianische Antiphonen. Hrsg. von Bruno Stäblein. 3: Salve Regina, vierstimmig für Sopran, Alt, Tenor und Bass. 1950.
Vol.4. Cavalli, Francesco. Vier Marianische Antiphonen. Hrsg. von Bruno Stäblein. 4: Alma redemptoris Mater, fünfstimmig für zwei Soprane, Alt, Tenor und Bass. 1950.
Vol.5. Porta, Costanzo. Missa tertii Toni (1578) für 4 Stimmen a cappella. Hrsg. von Joseph Schmidt-Görg. 1950.
Vol.6. Gindele, Corbinian. Orgelintonationen in den acht Kirchentonarten. 2. Aufl. 1958.
Vol.7. Gindele, Corbinian. Gregorianische Choralvorspiele für die Orgel. 1: Proprium de tempore. 1959.
Vol.8. Gindele, Corbinian. Gregorianische Choralvorspiele für die Orgel. 2: Proprium sanctorum. 1951, 1959.
Vol.9. Lasso, Orlando di. Missa Beschaffens Glück. (Il me suffit) (1581) für 4 Stimmen a cappella. Hrsg. von Wilhelm Leuger. 1953, 1962.
Vol.10. Grossi da Viadana, Ludovico. Missa Dominicalis (1609) für 1 Stimme mit Orgel. Hrsg. von August Scharnagl. 1954, 1964.
Vol.11. Anerio, Giovanni Francesco. Missa Della Battaglia (1605) für 4 gemischte Stimmen und Orgel ad lib. Hrsg. von Karl Gustav Fellerer. 1955.
Vol.12. Fux, Johann Josef. Missa Sancti Ioannis (1727) für 4 gemischte Stimmen. Orgel ad lib. Hrsg. von (Andreas Liess und) J. H. Van der Meer. 1956.
Vol.13. Fossa, Johannes de. Missa super theutonicam cantionem "Ich segge â Dieu" für 4 gemischte Stimmen a cappella. Hrsg. von August Scharnagl. 1956.
Vol.14. Gindele, Corbinian. Kleine Orgelstücke. 1957.
Vol.15. Victoria, Tomás Luis de. Missa pro defunctis cum responsorio, Libera me Domine, 1605. Hrsg. von Rudolf Walter. 1962.
Vol.16. Allardo, Jacobus. Missa, 1580. (for 4 mixed voices a cappella). 1962.

Musica divina, *see* Proske, Karl. Musica divina.

MÚSICA HISPANA. Barcelona, Instituto Español de Musicología, Consejo Superior de Investigationes Científicas, 1952– .
v.1– .
Contents:
Ser.A: Canción popular.
No.1. Doce canciones populares españolas, con acompañamiento de piano, par J. Rodrigo. 1952.
Ser.B: Polifonía.
No.1. Morales, Cristóbal de. Misa De Beata Virgine, a 4 voces mixtas. Transcripción por H. Anglés. 1953.
No.2. Morales, Cristóbal de. Misa Quaeramus cum pastoribus, a 5 voces mixtas. Transcripción por H. Anglés. 1953.
No.3. Morales, Cristóbal de. Selección de motetes. Transcripción por H. Anglés. 1953.
Ser.C: Música de cámara.
No.1. Soler, P. Antonio. III. Concierto para dos instrumentos de tecla. Transcripción por Santiago Kastner. 1952.
No.2. Manalt, Francisco. Sonatas, no.I y II, para violin y piano. Transcripción y realización por el P. J. A. de Donostia. 1953.
No.3. Soler, P. Antonio. I. Concierto para dos instrumentos de tecla. Transcripción por Santiago Kastner. 1956.
No.4. Soler, P. Antonio. II. Concierto para dos instrumentos de tecla. Transcripción por Santiago Kastner. 1957.
No.5. Soler, P. Antonio. IV. Concierto para dos instrumentos de tecla. Transcripción por Santiago Kastner. 1958.
No.6. Soler, P. Antonio. V. Concierto para instrumentos de tecla. Transcripción por Santiago Kastner. 1959.
No.7. Manalt, Francisco. Sonatas III–IV para violin y piano. Transcripción por el P. José A. de Conostia. 1960.
No.8. Soler, P. Antonio. VI. Concierto para dos instrumentos de tecla. Transcripción por Santiago Kastner. 1962.

MUSICA HUNGARICA. Klavierstücke ungarischer Komponisten. Piano pieces of Hungarian composers. Budapest, Editio Musica, 1958.
86p.
Contains compositions by Béla Bartók, Ernö Dohnányi, Zoltán Kodály, Ferenc Liszt, and Leo Weiner.

MUSICA INSTRUMENTALIS; eine neue Werkreihe für Melodieinstrumente, hrsg. von Egon Kraus. Zürich, Musikverlag zum Pelikan, 1954– .
v.1– .
Contents:
Vol.1. Kraus, Egon, ed. Sechs Fugen, von J. K. F. Fischer [et al]. [1954].
Vol.2. Kraus, Egon, ed. Vier Fugen, von J. Pachelbel, F. Tunder, J. S. Bach. [1954].
Vol.3. Frescobaldi, Girolamo. Capriccio G moll. 1955.

Vol.4. Mönkemeyer, Helmut, ed. Meister des 16. und 17. Jahrhunderts; Spielstücke zu zwei Stimmen im Quintabstand. [cop.1960].
Vol.5. Mönkemeyer, Helmut, ed. Instrumentale Liedsätze um 1500, zu drei Stimmen. [cop. 1960].
Vol.6. Mönkemeyer, Helmut, ed. Italienische Meister um 1600; ricercari e canzoni a quattro voci. [cop.1960].
Vol.7. Telemann, G. P. Zwei Suiten. [cop.1961].

MUSICA LITURGICA. Cincinnati, Ohio, World Library of Sacred Music, 1958– .
v.1– .
Contents:
Vol.1. Fasc.1. Ruffo, Vincenzo. Missa sine nomine, for 5 equal voices (missa a voci pari). Ed. by Robert J. Snow. 1958.
Vol.1. Fasc.2. Sermisy, Claude de. Missa pro defunctis. Ed. by Robert J. Snow. 1958.
Vol.1. Fasc.3. Porta, Costanzo. Musica in introitus missarum. (No.1–4). Ed. by Robert J. Snow. 1958.
Vol.1. Fasc.4. Corteccia, Francesco di Bernardo. Hinnario secondo l'vso della chiesa romana et fiorentina. (No.1–5). Ed. by Glen Haydon. 1958.
Vol.1. Fasc.5. Isnardi, Paolo. Missa angelus Domini. Ed. by Carol MacClintock. 1959.
Vol.1. Fasc.6. Aretino, Paolo. Passio Jesu Christi. Secundum Joannem. Ed. by Kurt von Fischer. 1960.
Vol.2. Fasc.1. Anonymous, Valladolid Codex. Missa pro defunctis. Ed. by Sister Marie Sagués. 1960.
Vol.2. Fasc.2. Corteccia, Francesco di Bernardo. Hinnario secondo l'vso della chiesa romana et fiorentina. (No.6–10). Ed. by Glen Haydon. 1960.
Vol.2. Fasc.3. Porta, Costanzo. Musica in introitus missarum. (No.5–8). Ed. by Robert J. Snow. 1961.

MUSICA PRACTICA. Hannover, A. Nagel, [193?–].
No.1– .
Choral and instrumental music in score. German or Latin words.
Editors: R. Heyden and W. Twittenhoff.
Contents:
No.3. Melchior Franck. Zwei Galliarden für vier und fünf Blockflöten.
No.4. Valentin Hausmann. Drei deutsche Tänze für vier Instrumente (Streicher oder Blockflöten).
No.7. Altflämische Weise "Der Winter ist vergangen." Alte Weise "Es steht ein Baum im Odenwald." Im Satz von Reinhold Heyden für zwei Frauen- und eine Männerstimme (einzeln oder chorisch) oder drei Streichinstrumente oder drei Blockflöten mit oder ohne Singstimme.
No.9. Heinrich Isaac. Zwei Instrumentalsätze zu drei Stimmen für Streich- oder Bläser-Trio.
No.13. Anonym. Partie für Altblockflöte und drei Streichinstrumente (2 Geigen und Cello).
No.14. Joh. Chr. Witt. Drei Märsche für vier Streichinstrumente oder Blockflöten (einfach oder chorisch).
No.17a. Theodor Stoltzer. Zwei Liedsätze "Ich klag den Tag" und "Entlaubet ist der Walde" für 4 stimmigen gemischten Chor oder Blockflöten- oder Streichquartett.
No.17b. "Ich klag den Tag" und "Entlaubet ist der Walde" in Instrumentalbearbeitungen (Intavolierungen) des 16. Jahrhunderts (Newsidler, Gerle) für Laute (oder ein hohes und tiefes Streich- oder Blasinstrument) mit oder ohne Singstimme (Blockflöte) oder für vier Streichinstrumente.
No.18. Melchior Franck. Zwei deutsche Tänze für vier Instrumente. (Streicher oder Blockflöten).
No 19. Samuel Scheidt. Zwei Paduanen für drei Blockflöten, Gambe (Laute, Cello) und Basso Continuo.
No.26. Gottfried Finger. Sonate für zwei F-Blockflöten oder Blockflöte und Violine (Oboe) und Basso Continuo.
No.27. Anonym. Drei kleine Terzette für Blockflöten (aus einem Manuskript von 1709).
No.43. Erasmus Kindermann. Sonetta und zwei Arien für drei Blockflöten.
No.44. Tanzsätze des 16. Jahrhunderts für Blockflöten- oder Streichquartett, I. (Susalo, Attaingnant, Phalèse, Gervaise).
No.45. Tanzsätze des 16. Jahrhunderts für Blockflöten- oder Streichquartett, II. (Attaingnant, Phalèse).
No.46. Tanzsätze des 16. Jahrhunderts für Blockflöten- oder Streichquartett, III. (Phalèse, Gervaise).
No.53. Albert Barkhausen. Kleine Stücke für drei Blockflöten.
No.60. Gerd. Watkinson. Vier musikantische Spielstücke für Melodieinstrumente, Schlagwerk und Zupfbass.
No.61. Gerd. Watkinson. Aufzug und Abendmusik für Singstimmen, Melodieinstrumente, Schlagzeug und Zupfbass. (bzw. Bordunbass).

Musica reservata, *see* Müller-Blattau, Joseph Maria, ed. Musica reservata.

MUSICA SACRA. Sammlung der besten Meisterwerke des 16., 17., und 18. Jahrhunderts. Berlin, Bote & Bock, 1839– .
v.1– .
Contents:
Vol.1. Sammlung . . . für die Orgel. (new ed. by F. Redlich under the title "Meister des Orgelbarock").
Vol.2, 3. Choral music. (Caldara, Carnazzi, Cordans, Durante, Giovanni Gabrieli, Lotti, Palestrina, and others).
Vol.4. Solo songs with piano accompaniment. (Durante, Hasse, Jommelli, and others).
Vol.5–12. Lasso.
Vol.13, 14. Hasler, etc.
Vol.15. Croce, Molinari, Steffanini, Tonsor, Varoti, Nuceti, Gabrieli, Anerio, Gallus, Ingegneri, Dressler, Scandellus, Walliser.
Vol.16. G. Aichinger, R. del Mel, S. Molinari, A. Rota, M. Varoti, J. Gabrieli, O. Vecchio,

St. Venturi, J. Croce, L. Marenzio, C. Merulo, A. Stabile.
Vol.17, 18. Mahu, etc.
Beginning with Vol.5 there appeared under the same name a parallel publication by A. H. Neithardt and others (Vols.5–16), containing also 19th-century German church music by Bortnianski, Grell, Homilius, and others (*see* next entry).

MUSICA SACRA. Sammlung religiöser Gesänge älterer und neuester Zeit zum bestimmten Gebrauch für den königlich preussischen Berliner Domchor. Berlin, Bote & Bock, ca.1842–96.
v.5–16.
Bd.5, 7, 12 ed. by A. H. Neithardt; Bd.6 by A. H. Neithardt, Seyler und C. J. A. H. Hoffmann; Bd.8–10 by Emil Naumann; Bd.11 and 13 by G. Rebling; Bd.14 by R. von Hertzberg; Bd.15 by A. E. A. Becker.
Contents:
Vol.5–7. Sammlung religiöser Gesänge älterer und neuester Zeit.
Vol.8–10. Psalmen auf Sonn- und Festtage des evangelischen Kirchenjahres. (A. Neithardt, E. Naumann, Mendelssohn, Hiller, Kästner, O. Nicolai, Dupuis, Engel, Meyerbeer, Grell, Reissiger, Ferd. Schultz, Stahlknecht, E. F. Richter, und Reinthaler).
Vol.11. Sammlung deutschevangelischer Kirchenmusik des XVI. und XVII. Jahrhunderts. (32 Gesänge aus den Jahren 1566–97 von Dressler, Burek, Gumpeltzhaimer).
Vol.12. Sammlung religiöser Gesänge älterer und neuester Zeit zum bestimmten Gebrauch für den Königlichen Berliner Domchor für Männerstimmen. (20 Gesänge von Palestrina, Lasso, Hassler, Prätorius, Gallus).
Vol.13. Sammlung deutsch-evangelischer Kirchenmusik des XVI. und XVII. Jahrhunderts. (45 Gesänge aus den Jahren 1607–1614 von Prätorius, Gesius, Hassler).
Vol.14. Sammlung religiöser Gesänge älterer und neuester Zeit.
Vol.15. Sammlung religiöser Gesänge älterer Zeit. (29 compositions for 4–9 voices).
Vol.16. Sammlung geistlicher Gesänge. (12 compositions, Psalms, and motets for 4–8 voices).

MUSICA SACRA, hrsg. von F. Commer. Neue Folge hrsg. von Heinrich Reimann und F. Volbach. Berlin, Rühle & Hunger, between 1892–97.
8 nos.
Published later, ca.1900, by Wernthal in Berlin.
Contents:
No.1. Raselius, Andreas. Vater unser im Himmelreich. 5stimm. Choralsatz.
No.2. Raselius, Andreas. Christ unser Herr zum Jordan kam. 4stimm. Choralsatz.
No.3. Asola, G. M. Pange lingua, für S.A.T.B.
No.4. Franck, Melchior. Geistliches Lied: Jesu, du zartes Kindelein, für S.A.2T.B.
No.5. Leisring. Geistliches Lied: Parvus pu ellus prodiit; Uns ist geboren ein Kindelein, für 2 gemischte Chöre.
No.6. Scandellus, Antonius. Geistliches Lied: Lobet den Herren, denn er ist sehr freundlich, für S.A.T.B.
No.7. Gabrieli, Andreas. Magnificat octavi toni.
No.8. Magni, Benedetto. Motetto: Giligam te Domine, für S.A.T.

MUSICA SACRA. Ed. by Hans Ferdinand Redlich. Berlin, Ed. Bote & G. Bock, [cop.1931–32].
2v.
Reedition of Vol.1–2 of Franz Commer's Musica sacra, 1839 edition.
Contents:
Vol.1. Meister des Orgelbarock. Sammlung der besten Meisterwerke des 16. bis 18. Jahrhunderts für die Orgel. Zum Gebrauch beim Gottesdienst und zum Studium gesammelt und hrsg. von Franz Commer. Neurevision und Neuausgabe von H. F. Redlich.
Vol.2. Sammlung der besten Meisterwerke des 16., 17., und 18. Jahrhunderts für zwei, drei und vier Männerstimmen hrsg. von Franz Commer (mit einer deutschen Übersetzung von W. von Waldbrühl).

MUSICA SACRA. Sammlung berühmter Kirchenchöre hrsg. von Alfred Dörffel, mit Vortragsbezeichnungen von Carl Riedel. Leipzig, Peters, [1886?].
2v.
Contents:
Vol.1. Lateinische Texte.
Vol.2. Deutsche Texte.

MUSICA SPIRITUALIS. Eine Auswahl altklassischer kirchlicher a cappella Gesänge und Messen, in Verbindung mit Dr. F. Haberl, H. Hübsch, Prof. Th. B. Rehmann, Prof. Dr. Th. Schrems, Prof. H. Schroeder, hrsg. von Dr. K. Roeseling. Regensburg, Verlag Franz Feuchtinger, [1950–].
v.1– .
Contents:
Ser.IA.
No.1. Gabrieli, G. Missa brevis. [1950].
No.2. Palestrina, G. B. P. Missa aeterna Christi munera. [1952].
No.3. Hasler, H. L. Missa et motettum dixit Maria. [1952].
No.4. Vittoria, T. L. de. Missa quarti toni. [1951].
Ser.IB.
No.5. Palestrina, G. B. P. Sicut cervus. Sitivit anima mea. [1950].
No.6. Lassus, O. de. Jubilate–Factus est. Tibi laus. [1950].
No.7. Vittoria, T. L. de. Ave Maria. [1952]. Hasler, H. L. Ave maris stella.
No.8. Vittoria, T. L. de. O magnum mysterium. Handl, Jacob. Natus est nobis.
Ser.IIA.
No.9. Vittoria, T. L. de. Missa Ave maris stella. [1956].
No.10. Lassus, O. de. Missa octavi toni. [1956].
No.11. Lassus, O. de. Missa puisque j'ay perdu. [1957].
No.12. Lassus, O. de. Missa on me l'a dit. [1960].

Ser.IIB.
No.13. Fevin, A. de. Descende in hortum meum.
Vittoria, T. L. de. Veni sponsa Christi. [1952].
No.14. Hasler, H. L. Beata es Virgo Maria.
Vittoria, T. L. de. Ne timeas Maria. [1954].
No.15. Aichinger, Gregor. In lectulo meo. Viderunt eam. [1956].
Ser.III.
No.21/22. Cantiones sacrae, I.
No.23/24. Cantiones sacrae, II, ex auctoribus saeculi XVI et XVII ad 2–4 voces aequales. [1959].

MUSICA VIVA HISTORICA. Prague, Státní Hudební Vydavatelství, 1961– .
v.1– .
Contents:
Vol.1. Haydn, J. Divertimento B-dur für Violine, Violoncello und Klavier. (Hoboken XV:38).
Vol.2. Kraft, A. Violoncello-Konzert C-dur. (Piano reduction).
Vol.3. Kuttenberger Menuett-Büchlein für Klavier. (Jitka Snížková, ed.).
Vol.4. Vitàsek, J. A. Drei Vortragsstücke für Klavier.
Vol.5. Sonatinen alter tschechischer Meister für Klavier.
Vol.6. Jelinek, J. Klaviertrio Es-dur.
Vol.7. Kramer-Krommer, F. Klarinetten-konzert Es-dur, Op.36. (Piano reduction).
Vol.8. Kompositionen für Cembalo.
Vol.9. Štěpán, J. A. Menuette für Klavier.
Vol.10. Vanhal, J. B. Bratschenkonzert C-dur. (Piano reduction).
Vol.11. Filcik, J. N. J. Duette für 2 Violinen.
Vol.12. Haydn, J. Violoncellokonzert C-dur. (Hoboken VIIb:1). (Piano reduction).
Vol.14. Vodicka, V. Sinfonia für Streichquartett (Cembalo ad lib.).

MUSICAL ANTIQUARIAN SOCIETY. London.
Publications of the Musical Antiquarian Society. [London, Printed for Members of the Musical Antiquarian Society by Chappell, 1840–48].
19v. front. (v.18, facsim.), illus. (incl. coat of arms).
With reproductions of original title pages, dedications, and prefaces.
List of members in Vols.3, 8, 12, 15, 17; also reports of the society.
List of publications in Vol.3.
Reports in Vol.3, 8, 12, 15, 17.
Contents:
Vol.1. Byrd, William. A mass for 5 voices.
Vol.2. Wilbye, John. The first set of madrigals.
Vol.3. Gibbons, Orlando. Madrigals and motets for 5 voices.
Vol.4. Purcell, Henry. Dido and Aeneas.
Vol.5. Morley, Thomas. The first set of ballets for 5 voices.
Vol.6. Byrd, William. Book 1 of Cantiones sacrae for 5 voices.
Vol.7. Purcell, Henry. Bonduca.
Vol.8. Weelkes, Thomas. The first set of madrigals.
Vol.9. Gibbons, Orlando. Fantasies in 3 parts, composed for viols.
Vol.10. Purcell, Henry. King Arthur.
Vol.11. The whole book of psalms . . . in 4 parts . . . published by Thomas Este.
Vol.12. Dowland, John. The first set of songs.
Vol.13. Hilton, John. Ayres or fa las.
Vol.14. Rimbault, E. F., ed. A collection of anthems [by M. Este, T. Ford, Weelkes, and Bateson].
Vol.15. Bennet, John. Madrigals for 4 voices.
Vol.16. Wilbye, John. The second set of madrigals.
Vol.17. Bateson, Thomas. The first set of madrigals.
Vol.18. Parthenia; or, The first musick ever printed for the virginals . . . by William Byrd, John Bull, and Orlando Gibbons. Translated into modern notation and ed. by Edward F. Rimbault. 1847.
Vol.19. Purcell, Henry. Ode, composed for the anniversary of St. Cecilia's Day. 1692.

The musical notation of the Middle Ages, *see* Plainsong and Mediaeval Music Society. The musical notation of the Middle Ages.

Musiche vocali e strumentali sacre e profane, sec. XVII–XVIII–XIX, *see* Somma, Bonaventura. Musiche vocali e strumentali sacre e profane, sec. XVII–XVIII–XIX.

Les musiciens de la cour de Bourgogne au XVe siècle, *see* Marix, Jeanne. Les musiciens de la cour de Bourgogne au XVe siècle.

The musick of the Mass for the dead, Church of England. Liturgy and ritual, *see* Plainsong and Mediaeval Music Society. Church of England. Liturgy and ritual. The musick of the Mass for the dead.

Musicologia hungarica. II, *see* Greff, Valentin. Der Lautenist V. Barfark, 1507–1576.

Musicological studies and documents. No.2, *see* Dittmer, Luther A. The Worcester fragments.

Musicological studies and documents. No.7, *see* Stäblein-Harder, Hanna. Fourteenth-century mass music in France.

MUSICOLOGISCH ONDERZOEK . . . (Oudheidkundige dienst in Ned.-Indië). [Batavia], Uitgegeven door het Koninklijk Bataviaasch Genootschap van Kunsten en Wetenschappen, 1931– .
2v. illus. (music), plates (incl. music).
At head of title: Oudheidkundige dienst in Ned.-Indië.
Contents:
[No.] 1. Kunst, J. Over zelzame fluiten en veelstemmige musiek in het Ngada- en Nahehgebied (West Flores). 1931.
[No.] 2. Kunst, J. . . . Songs of North New Guinea. 1931.

MUSIK ALTER MEISTER. Beiträge zur Musik- und Kulturgeschichte Innerösterreichs. Hrsg. von Hellmut Federhofer. Graz, Akademische Druck- und Verlagsanstalt, 1954– .
v.1– .
Contents:
Heft 1. Cleve, Johannes de. Missa, Vous perdes temps. 1960. Sermisy, Claude de. Chanson, Vous perdes temps. 1960.
Heft 2. Brassicanus, Johannes. Sechs Choralbearbeitungen und das Quodlibet "Was wölln wir aber heben am? " 1954.
Heft 3. Begräbnisgesänge Nürnberger Meister für Exulanten aus der Steiermark. 1955.
Heft 4. Herold, Johannes. Historia des Liedens und Sterbens unsers Herrn und Heilands. (Matthäuspassion). 1955.
Heft 5. Jelich, Vincenz. Sechs Motetten aus Arion Primus (1628). 1957.
Heft 6. Ducis, Benedictus. Zwei Psalmmotetten. 1957.
Heft 7. Homberger, Paul. Brautgesänge für vier- bzw. fünfstimmigen gemischten Chor. 1959.
Heft 8. Vaet, Jacobus. Zwei Hymnen. 1958.
Heft 9. Senfl, Ludwig. Anonymus. Zwei Orgelstücke aus einer Kärntner Orgeltabulatur des 16. Jahrhunderts. 1958.
Heft 10. Ausgewählte Werke aus der Ausseer Gitarretabulatur des 18. Jahrhunderts. 1958.
Heft 11. Ducis, Benedictus. Missa de Beata Virgine. 1959.
Heft 12. De Cleve, Johannes. Missa, Rex Babylonis venit ad lacum. Vaet, Jacobus. Motette, Rex Babylonis venit ad lacum. 1960.
Heft 13. Brassart, Johannes. Sechs Motetten. Hrsg. von Keith E. Mixter. 1960.
Heft 14.
Heft 15. Poss, Georg. Drei Motetten für zwei vierstimmige gemischte Chöre.

Musik alter Polnischer Meister, *see* Denkmäler altpolnischer Musik.

Musik am preussischen Hofe, *see* Thouret, Georg. Musik am preussischen Hofe.

Musik am Sächsischen Hofe, *see* Schmid, Otto. Musik am Sächsischen Hofe.

Musik aus früher Zeit für Klavier, *see* Apel, Willi. Musik aus früher Zeit für Klavier.

MUSIK IN GOETHES HAUS. Wolfenbüttel, Verlag für Musikalische Kultur und Wissenschaft, 1949–
v.1– .
Contents:
Vol.1. Reichardt, Johann Friedrich. Stücke für Klavier. Hrsg. von Albert Küster. 1949.

Musik-Institut der Universität Tübingen. Denkmäler der Tonkunst in Württemberg, *see* Denkmäler der Tonkunst in Württemberg.

MUSIKALISCHE DENKMÄLER. Bd.1– . Mainz, B. Schott's Söhne, [1955–].
v.1–
At head of title: Akademie der Wissenschaften.
Contents:
Bd.1. Schmitz, Arnold, ed. Oberitalienische Figuralpassionen des 16. Jahrhunderts. 1955.
Bd.2. Binchois, Egidius. Die Chansons von Gillis Binchois (1400–1460). Hrsg. von Wolfgang Rehm. 1957.
Bd.3. Sweelinck, Jan Pieters. 46 Chörale für Orgel von J. P. Sweelinck und seinen deutschen Schülern. Nach den Handschriften hrsg. von Gisela Gerdes. 1957.
Bd.4. Frescobaldi, Girolamo. Arie musicali. (Florenz 1630). Eingeleitet und hrsg. von Helga Spohr. 1960.
Bd.5. Mainerio, Giorgio. Il primo libro de balli, Venedig, 1578. Hrsg. von Manfred Schuler. 1961.

MUSIKALISCHE FORMEN IN HISTORISCHEN REIHEN; Spiel- und Singmusik für den Musikunterricht und für das häusliche Musizieren. Bd.1–20. Berlin-Lichterfelde, C. F. Vieweg, G.m.b.H., [1930–37?].
20 nos. illus.
Editor: Bd.1–20, H. Martens.
Contains music.
Ceased publication with Bd.20.
Contents:
Bd.1. Martens, H. Das Menuett. [1930].
Bd.2. Fischer, H. Die Variation. [1930].
Bd.3. Moser, H. J. Die Ballade. [1931].
Bd.4. Piersig, F. Das Rondo. [1931].
Bd.5. Halbig, H. Geistliche Musik bis zum Ausgang des 16. Jahrhunderts. [1930].
Bd.6. Spitta, H. Der Marsch. [1931].
Bd.7. Roy, Otto. Die Fuge. [1930].
Bd.8. Herrmann, W. Der Walzer. [1931].
Bd.9. Münnich, R. Die Suite. [1931].
Bd.10. Wetzel, J. H. Die Liedformen. [1931].
Bd.11. Martens, H. Das Melodram. [1932].
Bd.12. Bodky, E. Das Charakterstück. [1933].
Bd.13. Schubert, Kurt. Die Programm-Musik. [1933].
Bd.14. Roy, Otto. Der Volkstanz. [1935].
Bd.15. Schmidt, H. Märsche und Signale der deutschen Wehrmacht. [1934].
Bd.16. Halbig, Hermann. Die Ouverture. [1935].
Bd.17. Jöde, F. Der Kanon. [1934].
Bd.18. Fischer, H. Die Sonate. [1936].
Bd.19. Martens, H., ed. . ... Polonaise und Mazurka. [1936].
Bd.20. Göttsching, R., ed. Das Soldatenlied. [1937].

MUSIKALISCHE SELTENHEITEN; Wiener Liebhaberdrucke. Geleitet von O. E. Deutsch. Wien, Universal-Edition A.-G., cop.1921–23.
6v. facsims.
Contents:
Bd.1. Beethoven, L. van. Sonate Op.27, Nr.2. cop.1921.
Bd.2. Haydn, F. J. [Selection of Scots airs]. cop.1921.
Bd.3. Brahms, J. Drei Lieder. cop.1921.
Bd.4. Schubert, F. P. [Songs. Collection. (Universal)]. Fünf erste Lieder. cop.1922.
Bd.5. Mozart, W. A. Zwei Rondos, D-dur und A-moll. cop.1923.

Bd.6. Bach, J. S. Praeludium und Fuge H-moll für Orgel. cop.1923.

MUSIKALISCHE STUNDENBÜCHER. Eine Sammlung erlesener, kleiner Tonschöpfungen, hrsg. und mit Einleitungen versehen von hervorragenden Künstlern. Jeder Band enthält das Bildnis des Komponisten als Titelbild. München, Drei Masken Verlag, 192? – .
v.1– .
Contents (partial):
Bach, J. S. Capriccio in B-dur, sopra la lontananza del suo fratello dilettissimo. Nebst einer Sonate aus Johann Kuhnaus. Eingeleitet und hrsg. von Herman Roth.
—— Sechzig Choralgesänge. Ausgewählt und eingeleitet von Herman Roth.
Beethoven, Ludwig van. Bagatellen. Hrsg. und eingeleitet von Paul Bekker.
Berlioz, Hector. Ausgewählte Lieder. Eingeleitet und hrsg. von Dr. Karl Blessinger.
Cornelius, Peter. Weihnachtslieder und Trauer und Trost. Hrsg. und eingeleitet von G. von Westermann.
Händel, G. F. Neun deutsche Arien. Hrsg., gesetzt und eingeleitet von Herman Roth.
Lanner, Josef. Ausgewählte Walzer. Ausgewählt und eingeleitet von Prof. Dr. Oskar Bie.
Mendelssohn-Bartholdy, Felix. Lieder ohne Worte. Ausgewählte und mit einem Vorwort von H. W. von Waltershausen.
Mozart, W. A. Gesellige Lieder. Hrsg. und eingeleitet von Dr. B. Paumgartner.
Palestrina, G. P. Missa Papae Marcelli. Eingeleitet und hrsg. von Dr. Alfred Einstein.
Wagner, Richard. Zehn Lieder aus den Jahren 1838–1858. Hrsg. und eingeleitet von Prof. Dr. Wolfgang Golther.
Weber, Karl Maria von. Dritte grosse Sonate D-moll. Hrsg. und eingeleitet von Dr. W. Georgii.

MUSIKALISCHE WERKE DER KAISER FERDINAND III, LEOPOLD I, UND JOSEPH I. Im Auftrage des K.K. Ministeriums für Cultus und Unterricht hrsg. von Guido Adler. Wien, Artaria & Co., [pref.1892–93].
2v.
Contents:
Bd.1. Kirchenwerke.
Bd.2. Gesänge aus Oratorien und Opera. Instrumentalkompositionen.

Musikalische Werke schweizerischer Komponisten des XVI. XVII. und XVIII. Jahrhunderts, *see* Verein schweizerischer Tonkünstler. Musikalische Werke schweizerischer Komponisten des XVI. XVII. und XVIII. Jahrhunderts.

MUSIKALISCHER SPIELPLATZ. Wiesbaden, Breitkopf & Härtel, 1963– .
v.1– .
Contents:
Vol.1. Strohbach, Siegfried. Unser Metronom: Kommet all herbei. Kleine Kantate für 2 stimmigen Kammer-Chor, 3 Melodien-Instrumente, Bass und Schlagwerk. 1963.

MUSIKALISKA KONSTFÖRENINGEN. Stockholm, Swedish "Society of Musical Art," 1860– .
v.1– .
The Swedish Society of Musical Art was founded in 1859.
Publications issued annually.
Contents:
1860. Hallström, I. Blommornas undran. Idyll for solo voices, chorus, and piano.
Söderman, J. S. Tannhäuser. Ballad for baritone and orchestra.
1861. Boom, J. van. Grand sonata for piano.
Stenhammar, P. U. Four songs with piano.
1862. Wennerberg, G. Jesu födelse. Oratorio. Piano score.
1863. Gille, E. J. Mass No.7, A major.
Gille, E. J. Trio for violin, violoncello, and piano.
Bauch, C. W. String quartet, G major.
1865. Andrée, Elfrida. Piano quintet, E minor.
Lindroth, A. F. Five studies for violin solo.
1866. Söderman, J. A. Qvanriomem. Ballad for baritone and orchestra.
Lindegren, J. Fugue in free style for piano.
1867. Grieg, E. I host. Op.11. Fantasy for piano duet.
Lindegren, J. Grand sonata, canon, for piano, Op.2.
1870. Hylén, O. W. String quartet, D major.
1871. Heintze, G. W. Grand sonata for piano.
1873. Norman, L. Symphony, No.2, E flat major, Op.40. Score.
Norman, L. Symphony, No.2, E flat major, Op.40. Arr. for piano, 4 hands.
1874. Berwald, F. Symphony, G minor (sérieuse). Score.
Berwald, F. Symphony, G minor (sérieuse). Arr. for piano, 4 hands.
1875. Dannström, I. Three songs for tenor and mixed chorus.
1876. Andersen, A. J. Sonata for violoncello and piano, D minor.
1877. Arlberg, E. I skogen. Op.10. Tone poem for orchestra. Score.
Arlberg, E. I skogen. Op.10. Tone poem for orchestra. Arr. for piano, 4 hands.
1878. Maier, A. E. Violin sonata, B minor.
1880. Sjögren, E. Seven songs for voice and piano. Op.3.
1881. Söderman, J. A. Catholic mass.
1882. Klint, F. W. String quartet, Op.25, No.2, A major.
1883. Berwald, F. Estrella de Soria. Opera. Piano score.
1884. Andrée, Elfrida. Snöfrid. Ballad.
Lindroth, A. F. Andante and Bolero for violin and piano.
1885. Norman, I. Symphony, No.3, D minor, Op.58. Score.
Norman, I. Symphony, No.3, D minor, Op.58. Arr. for piano, 4 hands.
Lindblad, A. F. Quintet for 2 violins, 2 violas, and violoncello. Score.
Lindblad, A. F. Quintet for 2 violins, 2 violas, and violoncello. Arr. for piano. 4 hands.

1886. Valentin, K. Eight songs for voice and piano, Op.7.
1887. Andrée, Elfrida. Trio for violin, violoncello, and piano, G major.
Rubenson, A. En nott bland fjellen. Operetta.
1888. Aulin, Valberg. String quartet, F major.
Jacobson, J. Cavatina. For tenor and orchestra.
1889. Andersson, R. Sonata for piano, Op.11.
Åkerberg, E. Piano quintet, Op.18.
1890. Dente, J. Symphony, D minor. Score.
Dente, J. Symphony, D minor. Arr. for piano, 4 hands.
1891. Lundh, L. A. Requiem.
Söderman, J. A. Ode till glädjen. Men's chorus and orchestra.
1892. Söderman, J. A. Signe lill's färd. Concert poem.
Lindblad, A. F. Allegro, Andante, Scherzo. For violin and piano.
Hallén, J. A. En sommarsaga. Op.36. Symphonic concert piece.
1893. Beckman, B. Sonata for violin and piano, Op.1, A minor.
Berwald, F. Grand septet.
1894. Wennerberg, G. Stabat Mater.
1895. Bäck, K. Theme and variations for piano, Op.2.
Norman, L. Concert overture, Op.21. Arr. for piano, 4 hands.
1896. Jacobsson, J. Three pieces for clarinet, viola, and piano, Op.45.
Körling, A. Hatunaleken.
1897. Byström, O. Symphony, D minor. Arr. for piano, 4 hands.
Hallström, I. Cantata for the 25 years' jubilee of the reign of King Oskar II.
1898. Berwald, F. Duo for violin and piano, D major.
Hallén, J. A. Skogsrået. Op.33.
1899. Sjöberg, S. Sonata for violin and piano, A minor, Op.2.
1899–1900. Stenhammar, P. U. David och Saul. Oratorio.
1900. Bäck, K. Tomten. Op.5.
1902. Rubenson, A. Selection from the music to Halte-Hulda.
Rubenson, A. Symphonic intermezzo, No.1.
1903. Andersen, A. J. Symphony, D major.
1904. Sjögren, E. Sonata for piano, No.2, A major, Op.44.
Backman, B. Om lyckan. Op.10. Tone poem.
1905. Hallén, A. A Christmas oratorio.
Berwald, F. Symphonie singulière.
1906. Stenhammar, W. Ithaka. Op.21.
Alfvén, H. Vid sekelskiftet. Op.12.
1908. Sjögren, E. Six hymns and psalms.
Lindegren, J. Quintet for 2 violins, 2 violas, and violoncello.
1910. Fryklöf, H. Fugue for piano.
Alfvén, H. Herrans Bön. Op.15.
1911. Norman, L. Trio, No.2, B minor, Op.38.
Norman, L. Three overtures for orchestra.
1912. Olsson, O. Te Deum. Op.25.
Olsson, O. String quartet, No.2, G major, Op.27.
1914. Sjögren, E. Violin sonata, No.5, A minor, Op.61.
Sjögren, E. Five poems for voice and piano, Op.63.
1915. Lundberg, L. Piano sonata, D minor, Op.33.
Alfvén, H. Uppenbarelsekantat. Op.31.
1916. Rangström, T. Six songs.
Hallén, A. Den unge herr Sten Sture. Op.35. Melodrama.
Henneberg, R. Serenade. Octet.
1917. Attenberg, K. String quartet, Op.11.
Olsson, O. Six Latin hymns for chorus a cappella.
1919. Jonsson, J. Korallrevet. Op.10. Symphonic poem.
Fryklöf, H. Sonata à la legenda.
1921. Alfvén, H. Cantata for the Reformation Festival at Uppsala. Op.36.
Berwald, F. Alvlek. Tone picture.
1923. Bratt, L. Six intimate songs for voice and piano.
1924. Stenhammar, W. Sången. Op.44. Symphonic cantata.
1925. Sjögren, E. Islandsfärd. Op.18. Men's chorus and orchestra.
1926. Berg, N. Höga Visan.
Fryklöf, H. Symphonic piece for organ.
1927. Sköld, Y. Sonatina for violin and piano, Op.23.
Sköld, Y. Preludio e fuga. Op.20. For piano.
1928. Stenhammar, W. String quartet, No.6, D minor, Op.35.
Stenhammar, W. Five songs for voice and piano.
1929. Lindberg, O. Requiem.
Fryklöf, H. Passacaglia for organ.
1930. Håkanson, K. Ten variations and fugue for piano, Op.37.
Atterberg, K. Sonata for a string instrument, violoncello, viola, violin, and piano, Op.27.
Rangström, T. Four poems (songs).
1931. Haquinius, A. String quartet, A minor.
Nordqvist, G. Dryaden. Three songs.
1932. Sorgemusik med anledning av Gustaf II Adolfs död. (T. Bolzius. Threnodier. 1632; A. Düben. Pugna troumphalis. 1634) Melchers, H. M. Sonata for violin and piano, Op.22, G major.
1933. Alfvén, H. Unge herr Sten Sture. Op.30. Men's chorus and orchestra.
1934. Lindberg, O. Jungfru Maria.
Ohlsson, R. String quartet, No.3.
1935. Frumerie, G. de. Sonata for violin and piano.
Frumerie, G. de. Four Chinese poems.
1936. Alfvén, H. Cantata in celebration of the quincentenary of the Swedish Riksdag.
Mankell, H. Barcarolle for piano, Op.60, No.1.
1937. Byström, O. String quartet, No.2.
Rangström, T. Trolltyg. Two ballads.
Rangström, T. Hennes ord. Three songs.

1938. Jonsson, J. Missa solemnis. Op.37.
1939. Rangström, T. Den Utvalda. Lyrical scene.
1940. Melchers, H. M. Sonata for violoncello and piano, Op.20.
Lilja, B. Andante religiosa for organ.
1941. Sköld, Y. Fantasy for viola and organ, Op.12.
Larsson, L. E. Förklädd. Op.24.
1942. Peterson-Berger, W. Cantata for the 150 years' jubilee of the Royal Theatre, Stockholm.
1943. Mankell, H. Andante and variations for piano, Op.57.
1944. Heintze, G. Piano trio, Op.17.
1945. Hallnäs, H. Sonata for viola and piano, Op.19.
1946. Koch, E. von. String quartet, No.2, Op.28.
1947. Pergament, M. Duo for violin and violoncello, Op.28.
Wikander, D. Mass for mixed choir, a cappella.
1948. Frumerie, G. de. Piano quartet.
1949. Rangström, T. Un notturno. String quartet.
Wirén, D. Sonatina for violin and piano, Op.15.
1950. Frumerie, G. de. Violin sonata, No.2.
1952. Uddén, A. String trio.
1953. Rosenberg, W. Fantasia and fugue for organ.
1954. Olsson, O. Six Latin hymns for mixed chorus, a cappella.
1955. Frumerie, G. de. Piano trio, No.2.
1956. Larsson, L. E. String quartet, No.1, Op.31.
1957. Bäck, S. E. String quartet, No.2.
1958. Nystroem, G. String quartet. 1956.
1959. Wirén, D. Triptyk. For orchestra.

Musikdrucke aus den Jahren 1538 bis 1545 in praktischer Neuausgabe, *see* Rhaw, Georg. Musikdrucke aus den Jahren 1538 bis 1545 in praktischer Neuausgabe.

Musikgeschichte in Beispielen, *see* Riemann, Hugo. Musikgeschichte in Beispielen.

Musikgeschichtlicher Atlas, *see* Steinitzer, Max. Musikgeschichtlicher Atlas.

Das Musikkränzlein, *see* Moser, Hans Joachim. Das Musikkränzlein.

MUSIKSCHÄTZE DER VERGANGENHEIT. Berlin, Chr. Friedrich Verlag, 1928– . v.1– .

Contents:

Abel, K. F. Kleine Sinfonie in F-dur. Für Streicher und nach belieben mit Bläsern.
Albicastro, H. de B. Dritte Sonate für 2 Violinen und Violoncello mit Cembalo.
Albinoni, Tommaso. Konzert für Violine mit Streichorchester und Cembalo oder Orgel.
Amalia, Anna Amalia, Princess of Prussia. Sonate für Flöte in F-dur (Violine) und Cembalo.
Bach, J. S. Acht Canons aus dem "Musikalischen Opfer" für Streichinstrumente (2 Violinen, Viola, Cello-bass).
—— Fünf Stücke für kleines Orchester aus den Kirchenkantaten.
—— Ricercare aus dem "Musikalischen Opfer" für Streichinstrumente (2 Violinen, 2 Violen, 2 Cell-basse).
—— Sarabanden und andere Suitensätze. Für drei oder vier Streichinstrumente zum Solo- wie zum Chorspiel.
Boccherini, L. Quintettino "The military nightwatch in Madrid" für 2 Violinen, Viola, und 2 Violoncelli.
Bodinus, S. Trio Sonate für 2 Oboen oder Violinen und Basso Continuo.
Call, Leonard von. Notturno, Op.93, für Flöte, Viola und Gitarre.
Carrassi-Matteo. Op.17. Variationen auf "Le songe de Rousseau" für Laute oder Gitarre.
Corelli, Arcangelo. Op.2 Zwölf Kammersonaten für zwei Violinen und Violoncello in ein- oder mehr- facher besetzung mit Klavier (Cembalo).
Friedrich der Grosse. 1. Symphonie, G-dur, für Streicher und Basso Continuo. Score and parts.
—— 2. Symphonie, G-dur, für Streicher und Basso Continuo. Score and parts.
—— 4. Symphonie, A-dur, für Streicher und Basso Continuo. Score and parts.
—— Andante für 2. Symphonie für 2 Flöten und Violinen oder 3 Violinen.
—— Recitative und Aria "Nota v'e quesya Dea" aus Il re pastore für Sopran, Streichorchester und Basso Continuo. Score and parts.
Fux, J. J. Suite in D-moll, aus dem "Concertus Musico-Instrumentalis" für kleines Streichorchester und Cembalo (Klavier). 1937.
Gibbons, Orlando. 2 Fantasias für 2 Violinen und Cello.
Gluck, Chr. W. 3 "Festival marches" für Streicher, 2 Oboen, 2 Hörner, 2 Trompeten, Trommeln.
Händel, G. F. Concerto für Harfe (Orgel, Pianoforte) und Streicher. Score and parts.
—— Tanz- und Spielmusik für Violine (Oboe, Flöte ad lib.), Viola (Violine II), Violoncello und Cembalo (Klavier).
—— Ouvertüre zu Esther für Streichorchester, ad lib. 2 Oboen und Fagott, mit Cembalo.
—— Kleine Stück für Streichinstrumente und Continuo (Klavier).
Hasse, J. A. Concerto in G-dur (original) für Mandolin-Solo und 2 Violinen (Mandolinen) und Basso Continuo (Piano und Laute, Gitarre, Cello, Bass oder Mandobass).
Haydn, Joseph. Eine Abendmusik. (Tassatio in Es) für Streichorchester und 2 Hörner in Es. 1936.
—— Cassatio in C-dur für Laute obligat, Violine und Cello.
—— Op.31, Nr.3. Divertimento für Streichorchester, Flöte und zwei Hörner. 1937.
—— Sechstes Konzert in F-dur für Cembalo und Orchestra (Streicher und 2 Flöten).
—— Drei Trios für 2 Flöten (oder 2 Violinen) und Violoncello (bei Ausführung durch

Streicher auch in mehrfacher besetzung).
1. Trio in C-dur; 2. Trio in G-dur; 3. Trio in G-dur.
Heinichen, Johann David. Konzert in G-dur für Flöte oder Oboe, zwei Violinen und Continuo. 1938.
Jacchini, Giuseppe. Op.5, Nr.3. Triosonate G-dur für 2 Violinen, Violoncello und Cembalo (Klavier). 1936.
Kohaut, Carl. Concerto in F-dur für Laute, 2 Violinen, und Violoncello.
Leo, Leonardo. Konzert für 4 Violinen und Bass (Violoncell, Kontrabass und Cembalo oder Orgel).
Locatelli da Bergamo, Pietro. Op.1, Nr.6. Concerto grosso. Für Streichorchester mit Klavier.
Mozart, Leopold. Drei Divertimenti für 2 Violinen und Violoncello, auch in mehrfacher besetzung.
1. Divertimento in D-dur.
Mozart, W. A. Fünf Contretänze für zwei Violinen, Violincello, Kontrabass, Flöte und Trommel. (K.V.609).
—— Trio für 2 Violinen und Cello. K.V.266.
Muffat, George. Respectable wedding. Suite. Ansehnliche Hochzeit). Für Streichorchester.
Pez, Johann Christoph. Concerto pastorale in Einfacher oder Chorischer besetzung mit Cembalo (Klavier). 1937.
Richter, F. X. Concerto in E-moll für Cembalo (Klavier) und Streichorchester.
—— Symphonie in G-dur für Streichorchester.
Rust, Fr. W. Sonate in D-moll für Laute und Violine.
Scarlatti, Alessandro. Sechs Concerti grossi für Streichorchester mit Cembalo. Erstes und zweites Konzert.
—— Drittes Konzert in F-dur für Streichorchester mit Cembalo.
Scheiffelhut, Jakob. Siebente Suite aus dem "Lieblichen frühlings Anfang" für 2 Violinen, Bratsche und Violoncello mit Cembalo.
Schiassi, Gaetano Maria. Weihnachts-Symphonie für Streichorchester und (nach belieben) Orgel oder Cembalo.
Schneider, Lorenz. 3 Duos für 2 Violinen.
Schwindl, Friedrich. Quartett in G-dur für Flöte, Violine (oder für zwei Violinen), Viola und Violoncello.
Selle, Thos. O Jesulein. Concerto Nr.3 für Sopran oder Tenor, 2-Teile Chor (S.S. oder T.T.) und Pianoforte.
—— Wenn Trübsal da ist. Concerto Nr.4 für Chor S.S.A.B. und Basso Continuo (Piano mit Cello oder Fagott oder Orgel allein).
Stamitz, Johann Wenzel Anton. Sinfonia pastorale D-dur. Op.4, Nr.2. Für Streichinstrumente, Oboen (Flöten), Hörner und (nach belieben) Cembalo.
Stamitz, Karl. Sinfonie Es-dur für Streichorchester, zwei Flöten und zwei Hörner.
—— Sonate in F-dur für zwei Violinen und Violoncello.
Starzer, J. Divertimento für Streichquartett oder Streichorchester.
Telemann, G. P. Concerto Nr.1 in G-dur für 4 Violinen allein.
—— Concerto Nr.2 in D-dur für 4 Violinen allein.
—— Don-Quichotte Suite. (Ouverture) für Streichorchester und Cembalo.
—— Zwei Divertimenti für Streichorchester und Cembalo (Klavier) (statt Viola auch dritte Violine). Nr.1. A-dur. 1936.
—— Zwei Divertimenti für Streichorchester und Cembalo (Klavier) (statt Viola auch dritte Violine). Nr.2. B-dur. 1937.
—— Konzert in B-dur für zwei Block- oder Querflöten, Streichquartett in einfacher oder Chorischer besetzung (Viola oder Violine 3), Brassblockflöte oder Fagott nach belieben und Cembalo (Klavier). 1938.
—— Ouvertüre (Suite) G-dur für Streichorchester und Cembalo.
—— Sinfonia melodica C-dur für Streichorchester (statt Viola auch dritte Violine), 2 Oboen (oder Flöten) und Cembalo (Klavier). 1936.
Uccellini, Marco. The wedding of the hen and the cuckoo. 2 Oboen und Basso Continuo.
Vivaldi, Antonio. Concerto grosso für Streichorchester mit soli (Violine und Violoncello) und Pianoforte (Cembalo). Op.3, Nr.3.
Vogler, Georg Joseph. Konzert für Cembalo (Klavier), 2 Violinen und Cello-Bass.
Wagenseil, G. Chr. Concerto in C-dur für Cembalo (Klavier) mit 2 Violinen und Cello.
Werner, J. G. "October" aus dem "Musical instrumental calendar" für 2 Violinen und Basso Continuo (Soli oder Violine Ensemble).
—— "December" aus dem "Musical instrumental calendar" für 2 Violinen und Basso Continuo.
Zachow, F. W. Fantasia für Streichorchester, arr. G. Lenzewski.
—— 2 Stücke für 2 Violinen und Cello (Soli oder Ensemble); Präludium und Fuge und Choral "Allein Gott in der Hoh."

Das Musikwerk, *see* Anthology of music.

Musikwissenschaftliche Studien-Bibliothek, *see* Gennrich, Friedrich, ed. Musikwissenschaftliche Studien-Bibliothek.

Musikwissenschaftliches Seminar der Universität Greifswald. Denkmäler der Musik in Pommern, *see* Denkmäler der Musik in Pommern.

Musique du moyen âge pour piano, *see* Apel, Willi. Musik aus früher Zeit für Klavier.

MUSIQUES FRANÇAISES. Old French music. Collection publiée sous la direction de Georges Migot. Genève, Editions du Siècle Musical, 1948–
22v.
Contents:
Vol.1. Corrette, Michel. Airs pour flûte et clavier. (violon ou hautbois et clavier). 1948.
Vol.2. Lefèvre, Jean Xavier. 5ème sonate pour clarinette et clavier. Réalization de la basse par Renée Viollier. 1949.
Vol.3. Ainé, Pierre Chédeville l'. Troisième sonatille. Extraite des "Sonatilles galantes." Op.VI, pour hautbois et basse continue (flûte ou violon). 1949.

Vol.4. Naudot, Jean-Jacques. Première fête rustique. Extraite des "Six fêtes rustiques." Op.VIII, pour hautbois et basse continue (flûte ou violon). Réalization de la basse par Georges Favre. 1949.
Vol.5. Borrel, Eugène, ed. Au jardin de la flûte de France (1er cahier). Pièces pour flûte (violon ou hautbois) et basse continue de Michel Blavet, Jean-Jacques Naudot, Joseph Bodin de Boismortier et F. Philidor. 1949.
Vol.6. Hotteterre, Jacques de. Sonate en ré majeur pour hautbois (flûte ou violon) et basse continue (1715). Réalisation de la basse par Renée Viollier. 1949.
Vol.7. Ozi, Étienne. Adagio et rondo (1787). Pour basson (ou violoncello) et clavier. Réalisation de la basse continue par Georges Favre. 1949.
Vol.8. Charpentier, Marc Antoine. Nuit. Interlude instrumental pour cordes et clavecin (ou piano) extrait de "In nativitatem Domini." Canticum à 4 voix. Tome IX des "Meslanges." 1949.
Vol.9. Dornel, Antoine. Première suite pour la flûte traversière (violon ou hautbois) avec la basse (1709). Réalisation de la basse par Pauline Aubert. 1950.
Vol.10. Corrette, Michel. Noël allemand. (Lobt Gott ihr allzugleich). 5ème concerto pour la flûte (ou violon) avec la basse continue (ou flûte [ou violon] solo, 2d violon concertant, 3ème violon et cello ad lib. et clavier). 1949.
Vol.11. Mouret, Jean Joseph. Deux divertissements. Extraits des divertissements pour la comédie italienne pour cor (en fa) et clavier. 1950.
Vol.12. Boismortier, Joseph Bodin de. Sonate No.5 pour basson (ou violoncelle) et clavier. Réalisée par Fernand Oubradous. 1950.
Vol.13. Gaultier de Marseille, Pierre. Suite en sol pour flûte à bec ou traversière (flûte douce alto en fa, violon ou hautbois) et clavier. Réalisation de la basse continue par Georges Favre. 1950.
Vol.14. Chédeville, Nicolas, le Cadet. Sixtième sonate. Extraite des six sonates pour hautbois (flûte ou violon) avec la basse (Oeuvre VII). Réalisation de la basse continue par Georges Favre. 1951.
Vol.15. Lefèvre, Jean Xavier. Sonate III pour clarinette et basse. Op.XII. Réalisation de la basse par Eugène Borrel. 1951.
Vol.16. Charpentier, Marc Antoine. Concert pour quatre parties de violes. Quatuor ou orchestre à cordes. Réalisation de la basse continue par Guy Lambert. 1952.
Vol.17. Barre, Michel de la. Sonate dite L'inconnue en sol majeur pour flûte (ou hautbois ou violin), clavier et basse. 1952.
Vol.18. Anet, J. B. Sonate No.10 pour violon (ou 2 flûtes) et clavier. Réalisation par Guy Lambert. 1953.
Vol.19. Leclair, J. M. Sonate No.XI pour flûte (violon ou hautbois) et clavier. Réalisation par Paule Druilhe. 1954.
Vol.20. Lefèvre, J. X. Sonate No.2 pour clarinette, cello et clavier.
Vol.21. Ozi, E. Grande sonate pour basson et clavier.
Vol.22. D'Andrieu, J. F. Sonate pour 2 violons, violoncelle et clavier.

MUSORGSKIĬ, MODEST PETROVICH, 1839–1881.
. . . Sämtliche Werke. Bd.1– . Hrsg. von Paul Lamm. Moskau, Staatsmusikverlag, 1928/34 .
v.1– .
Pub. jointly by Musiksektion des Staatsverlages, and Universal-Edition A. G., Wien.
Title pages in Russian and German. Title page of Vol.8 in Russian and French.
Contents:
Vol.1. Ser.1. Boris Godunov. 1st act, 2d scene. (An inn on the Lithuanian border). Orchestra score. Russian-German texts. 1933.
Vol.1. Ser.2. Boris Godunov. 4th act, 2d scene. (A forest glade at Kromy). Orchestra score. Russian-German texts. 1933.
Vol.1. Ser.3. Boris Godunov. Vocal score. Russian-German texts. 1931.
Vol.1. Ser.4. Boris Godunov. Full orchestra score of the complete opera in 4v. Folio size. Russian text. 1928.
Vol.2. Khovantschina. Vocal score. Russian-German texts. 1931. Reprint 1932.
Vol.3. Ser.1. The fair at Sorotschinsk. Vocal score. Russian-German texts. 1933.
Vol.3. Ser.2. The fair at Sorotschinsk. Full orchestra score of the complete opera. Russian-German texts. 1934.
Vol.4. Ser.2. The marriage. Vocal score. Russian-German texts. 1933.
Vol.4. Ser.3, 1. Mlada. Market scene, for voices and piano, 4 hands. Russian-German texts. 1931.
Vol.4. Ser.3, 2. Mlada. Procession of the princes and priests, for voices and piano, 4 hands. Russian-German texts. 1931.
Vol.5. Ser.1, 2. Songs of youth. 1st and 2d versions. Russian-German texts. 1931.
Vol.5. Ser.3. Songs and arias. 1st and 2d versions. Russian-German texts. 1933.
Vol.5. Ser.4. Songs and arias. 1st and 2d versions. Russian-German texts. 1931.
Vol.5. Ser.5. Musician's peep show. 1st and 2d versions. Russian-German texts. 1931.
Vol.5. Ser.6. The nursery. 1st and 2d versions. Russian-German texts. 1931.
Vol.5. Ser.7. Without sun. 1st and 2d versions. Russian-German texts. 1931.
Vol.5. Ser.8. Songs and arias. 1st and 2d versions. Russian-German texts. 1934.
Vol.5. Ser.9. Songs and dances of death. 1st and 2d versions. Russian-German texts. 1931.
Vol.5. Ser.10. Folk song notes and other material. Russian text.
Vol.6. Choral works (three choruses) for voices and piano. Russian text.
Vol.7. Ser.1. Mlada. Triumphant march. Orchestra score. 1931.
Vol.7. Ser.2. Khovantschina. Marfa's song, for voice and orchestra. Russian-German texts. Orchestra score. 1931.
Vol.7. Ser.3. Night. Voice and orchestra. Russian-German texts. Orchestra score. 1931.

Vol.7. Ser.4. Scherzo in B flat major. Orchestra score. 1931.
Vol.7. Ser.5. Intermezzo. Orchestra score. 1931.
Vol.7. Ser.6. Hopak. Voice and orchestra. Russian-German texts. Orchestra score. 1931.
Vol.8. Ser.1. Triumphant march, arranged for piano, 4 hands, by Lamm. 1931.
Vol.8. Ser.2. Pictures at an exhibition, for piano. Titles and descriptive material in Russian-German. 1931.
Vol.8. Ser.3. Scherzo in B flat major, arranged for piano, 4 hands, by D. Kabalevsky. 1931.
Vol.8. Ser.4. Intermezzo, arranged for piano, 4 hands, by D. Kabalevsky. 1931.

MUSORGSKIĬ, MODEST PETROVICH, 1839–1881.
Complete works. Russian State Edition, 1939– .
v.1– .
2v. appeared in 1940.
Includes some unpublished piano pieces and choruses.

MUSORGSKIĬ, MODEST PETROVICH, 1839–1881.
Complete romances and songs. Moscow, State Music Publishers, 1960.
387, [1]p.

MUZIEK VOOR DE EREDIENST. Orgelkoralen van oude meesters. Voor orgel . . . Goes, Holland, Ars Nova, [cop.1952].
2v.
Score for organ.
Contents:
Vol.1 contains compositions by Joh. Chr. Bach, Georg Böhm, Joh. Heinrich Buttstedt, W. Dyckerhoff, Georg Friedrich Kaufmann, Joh. Ludw. Krebs, and F. W. Zachau.
Vol.2 contains compositions by Joh. Chr. Bach, Wolfgang Carl Briegel, Heinrich Buttstedt, Fried. Gradehand, Joh. Christoph Conrad, Joh. Krieger, J. L. Krebs, and Joh. Christoph Oley.

My Ladye Nevells booke, *see* Byrd, William. My Ladye Nevells booke.

NAGELS MÄNNERCHOR-BLÄTTER. Kassel, Nagels Verlag, 19? – .
No.1– .
Contents:
No.1. K. Marx. Die Gedanken sind frei; G. Maasz. Vo Luzern uf Wäggis aue. 4stg.
No.2. W. Rein. Der Winter ist vergangen; K. Marx. Wie schön blünt uns. 4stg. (vierseitig).
No.3. H. L. Hassler. Tanzen und Springen; F. Neumeyer. Auf, auf zum fröhlichen Jagen. 4stg. (vierseitig).
No.4. H. Beuerle. Es kommt ein Schiff. 4stg.; J. S. Bach. Welt ade. 5stg. (vierseitig).
No.5. E. L. von Knorr. Erstanden ist der heil'ge Christ. 4stg.
No.6. W. Maler. Ich hört ein Sichelein. 3stg.; H. Distler. Der Tag hat sich geneiget. 4stg. (vierseitig).
No.7. B. Weber. Jagdfest. 4stg.
No.8. R. Schwarz-Schilling. Grenzen der Menschheit. (Wenn der uralte, heilige Vater). 3stg.
No.9. D. Frederici. Wir lieben sehr; J. Bender. Wir gehn noch nicht nach Haus. 3stg.
No.10. K. Marx. Erhebt euch, Brüder; Jeden Morgen geht die Sonne auf; J. S. Bach. Wach auf, mein Herz. 4stg. (vierseitig).
No.11. M. Praetorius. Es ist ein Ros entsprungen; In dulce jubilo; S. Calvisius. Ein Kindelein so löbelich. 4stg. (vierseitig).
No.12. H. Beuerle. O Heiland, reiss die Himmel auf; Chr. Lahusen. Es lagen im Felde; Mit Schall von Zungen. 4stg. (vierseitig).
No.13. E. L. von Knorr. Wahre Freundschaft; C. F. Zelter. In allen guten Stunden. 4stg.
No.14. K. Marx. Weiss mit ein Blümlein. 4stg.
No.15. H. Bornefeld. Ade zur guten Nacht; Nun ade, du mein lieb Heimatland. 4stg.
No.16. J. R. Ahle. Was mag doch diese Welt. 4stg.
No.17. G. Gastoldi. In maienhellen Tagen; An hellen Tagen. 4stg.
No.18. J. Brahms. In stiller Nacht. 4stg.; W. Rein. Das Weinlaub (Kanon). 3stg.
No.19. J. S. Bach. Komm, O Tod; Ach wie flüchtig. 4stg.
No.20. G. Maasz. Und in dem Schneegebirge; J. Bender. Es gingen zwei Gespielen; J. Dreissler. Es geht ein dunkle Wolk herein. 4stg. (vierseitig).
No.21. G. Maasz. Hin über die Almen. 3stg.; Fein sein, beinander bleibn. 4stg.
No.22. K. Marx. Heut will ich zu mein Schätzlein gehen; G. Maasz. Rosestock, Holderblüh. 4stg. (vierseitig).
No.23. K. Marx. Kein schöner Land; E. L. von Knorr. Da drunten im Tale; H. Beuerle. Es dunkelt schon in der Heide. 4stg. (vierseitig).
No.24. S. Borris. Feiger Gedanken. 4stg.
No.25. B. Donati. Wenn wir hinausziehn. 4stg. (vierseitig).
No.26. W. Rein. Der Mai, der lustige Mai. 4stg.
No.27. K. Marx. Herfür, herfür. 4stg.
No.28. E. L. von Knorr. Auf der Ofenbank; Der Apfel ist nicht gleich am Baum. 4stg.
No.29. K. Marx. Da kommt die liebe Sonne wieder; Der Mond ist aufgegangen. 4stg.
No.30. K. Marx. Skifahrerlied; Kläffer. 3stg.
No.31. B. Stürmer. Die strassburger Münster-Engelchen. (Gib dir weiter keine Mühe). 4stg.; Joh. H. E. Koch. Orpheus Laute. 5stg.

NAGELS MUSIK-ARCHIV. Nr.1– . Hannover, Adolph Nagel, 1927– .
v.1– .
No.1. Bach, J. Christian. Zwei Sonaten (Op.XVI, Nr.1 und 2), 1779, für Klavier, Flöte oder Violine. Hrsg. von Albert Huster. 1927.
No.2. Bach, J. Ernst. Sonate D-dur für Klavier und Geige. 1927.
No.3. Deutsche Klaviermusik, aus dem Beginne des 18. Jahrhunderts. Suiten- und Sonatensätze von Gottfried Kirchhoff und anderen Meistern. Hrsg. von Th. W. Werner. 1927, 1938.
No.4. Bach, J. Christian. Sonate C-dur für Klavier zu vier Händen. Hrsg. von Albert Küster. 1927, 1938.
No.5. Caldara, Antonio. Triosonate, Op.1, Nr.4,

B-dur, für zwei Violinen, Violoncell und Orgel (oder Cembalo). Hrsg. von Prof. Dr. Walter Upmeyer. 1927.

No.6. Bach, C. Ph. Em. Die preussischen Sonaten für Klavier. Nr.1–3. Hrsg. von Rudolf Steglich. 1927.

No.7. Haydn, Michael. Divertimento D-dur für zwei Violinen, Viola und Bass (Violoncello). Neu hrsg. von Walter Upmeyer. 1928.

No.8. Telemann, G. P. Sonate in F-dur für Alt-Blockflöte und Klavier. 1927.

No.9. Albinoni, Tommaso. Op.6, Zwei Kammersonaten für Violine mit beziffertem Bass (Klavier). Hrsg. von Walter Upmeyer. 1928.

No.10. Telemann, G. P. Quartett in E-moll für Flöte, Violine, Violoncello und Basso Continuo. (Nr.6 aus "Nouveaux quatuors en six suites," Paris). Hrsg. von Ellinor Dohrn. 1928.

No.11. Hässler, J. W. Zwei Sonaten für Klavier und Flöte oder Violine. Neuausgabe von Martin Glöder. 1928.

No.12. Caldara, Antonio. Triosonate C-moll für zwei Violinen, Violoncello, und Basso Continuo. Hrsg. von Walter Upmeyer. 1928.

No.13. Telemann, G. P. XX Kleine Fugen, So wohl auf der Orgel. Hrsg. von Walter Upmeyer. 1928.

No.14. Weiland, J. J. Jauchzet Gott, alle Lande. Für eine Singstimme, zwei Violinen und Basso Continuo (Orgel oder Klavier mit Streichbass). Hrsg. von Ferdinand Saffe. 1928.

No.15. Bach, C. Ph. Em. Die preussischen Sonaten. (1714–1788). Für Klavier. Nr.4–6. Hrsg. von Rudolf Steglich. 1928, 1937.

No.16. Telemann, G. P. Duett G-dur für Flöte und Violine. Hrsg. von Rolf Ermeler. 1928.

No.17. Schütz, Heinrich. Psalm 18, Herzlich lieb hab ich dich, O Herr. Für Alt mit zwei Violinen und beziffertem Bass (Orgel oder Cembalo). Hrsg. von Walter Upmeyer. 1928.

No.18. Vivaldi, Antonio. Pastorale für Flöte (Violine, Oboe), obligates Violoncello und Orgel (Cembalo), aus Op.13, Nr.4 (1773). Hrsg. von Prof. Dr. Walter Upmeyer. 1931.

No.19. Hässler, J. W. Zwei Sonaten für Klavier zu drei und zu vier Händen. 1928.

No.20. Hässler, J. W. Drei leichte Sonaten für Klavier, mit einem selbstverfassten Lebenslauf des Komponisten. 1928.

No.21–22. Bach, C. Ph. Em. Die württembergischen Sonaten. (1714–1788). Für Klavier. Nr.1–6. Hrsg. von Rudolf Steglich. 1928.

No.23. Telemann, G. P. Sonate D-dur für Violoncello und Basso Continuo. Hrsg. von Prof. Dr. Walter Upmeyer. 1928.

No.24. Telemann, G. P. Quartett in H-moll für Flöte, Violine, Violoncello und Basso Continuo, aus "Six nouveaux quatuors en six suites," Paris. Hrsg. von Dr. Ellinor Dohrn. 1928.

No.25. Birckenstock, J. A. Sonate B-dur, Op.1, Nr.2, für Violine und Basso Continuo. Hrsg. von Waldemar Woehl. 1928.

No.26. Chédeville, Nicholas. Zwei Pastoral-Sonaten, für zwei Quer- oder Blockflöten (auch zwei Violinen oder Oboen). Hrsg. von Walter Upmeyer. 1928.

No.27–28. Rosenmüller, Johann. Lamentationes Jeremiae prophetae. Hrsg. von Fred Hamel. 2v. 1929.

No.29. Rosenmüller, Johann. Sonate G-moll für zwei Violinen mit beziffertem Bass (zwei Violinen und Violoncello, bzw. Dreistimmiges Streichorchester, mit Cembalo). Hrsg. von Ferdinand Saffe. 1928.

No.30. Rosenmüller, Johann. Sonate E-moll (Nr.2 aus den "XII Sonaten à 2, 3, 4, e 5 Stromenti da Arco et Altri . . ." vom Jahre 1682) für zwei Violinen mit beziffertem Bass (zwei Violinen und Violoncello, bzw. dreistimmiges Streichorchester, mit Cembalo). Hrsg. von Ferdinand Saffe. 1928.

No.31. Fürstenau, Kaspar. 12 Original-Kompositionen, für Flöte und Guitarre, Op.35. Revidiert von O. Homann. 1928.

No.32. Loewe, J. J. Neuen Arien mit Ritornellen. (1682). 1929.

No.33. Stamitz, Karl. Trio für Flöte, Violine (oder zwei Violinen) und beziffertem Bass (Klavier), Op.14, Nr.1. Hrsg. von Prof. Dr. Walter Upmeyer. 1928.

No.34. Albinoni, Tommaso. Sonata a tre, zwei Violini e Violoncello col Basso per l'Organo, Op.1, Nr.3. Hrsg. von Walter Upmeyer. 1929.

No.35. Bach, C. Ph. Em. Zwei Duos, ohne Generalbass, für Flöte und Violine oder zwei Violinen oder andere Melodieinstrumente. Hrsg. von Wolfgang Stephan. 1929.

No.36. Wagenseil, G. C. Vier Divertimenti. 1929.

No.37. Reichardt, J. F. Lieder und Oden in Auswahl. Hrsg. von F. Jöde. 1929.

No.38. Fasch, K. F. C. Ariette mit 14 Variationen. Andantino mit 7 Variationen. Für Cembalo oder Klavier. Neu hrsg. von Ludwig Landshoff. 1929.

No.39. Bach, W. F. Sonate Es-dur für zwei Flöten (oder Violinen). Hrsg. von Martin Glöder. 1929.

No.40. Praetorius, Michael. Fantasie über "Ein feste Burg ist unser Gott" für Orgel. 1929.

No.41. Dittersdorf, K. D. von. Konzert A-dur für Cembalo, zwei Violinen und Violoncello. Hrsg. von Prof. Dr. Walter Upmeyer. 1929.

No.42. Corelli, Arcangelo. Concerto grosso in D, Op.6, Nr.1. Für zwei Solo-Violinen und -Violoncello, Streicher und Basso Continuo. Hrsg. von Th. W. Werner. 1929.

No.43. Dedekind, C. C. Vier geistliche Konzerte, für eine Altstimme mit Basso Continuo. Hrsg. von Albert Rodemann. 1929.

No.44. Vulpius, Melchior. Von der Geburt Jesu Christ. (1609). 1929.

No.45. Geistliche Abendlieder in Sätzen zu vier Stimmen von Meistern des 17. Jahrhunderts. 1929.

No.46. Heyden, Reinhold. Geistliche Morgenlieder. 1931.

No.47. Telemann, G. P. Triosonate E-dur für Flöte, Violine und Continuo (aus "Essercizii musici" Trio, Nr.9). Hrsg. von Rolf Ermeler. Aussetzen des beziffertem Basses Prof. Dr. Karl Päsler. 1930.

No.48. Hotteterre, Louis. Suite D dur. 1929.

No.49. Bach, J. S. Triosonate D-moll für zwei

Violinen, Klavier oder Orgel, Violoncello ad lib. Hrsg. von Hermann Keller. 1929.

No.50. Telemann, G. P. Sonata polonese (Nr.1) für Violine, Viola und Basso Continuo. Hrsg. von Dr. Alicja Simon. 1929.

No.51. Telemann, G. P. Sonate polonoise (Nr.2) für zwei Violinen und Basso Continuo. Hrsg. von Dr. Alicja Simon. 1930.

No.52. Haydn, Joseph. Divertimento für Viola d'Amour, Violine und Violoncello. Hrsg. von Clemens Meyer. 1930.

No.53. Carmina. Ausgewählte Instrumentalsätze des XVI. Jahrhunderts. (Heinrich Finck, Heinrich Isaac, Ludwig Senfl). Hrsg. von Hans Joachim Moser und Fritz Piersig. 1929.

No.54. Beyer, J. S. Weihnachtskantate für Sopran- oder Tenorsolo, Gemischten Chor (Soloquartett), Streichinstrumente und Orgel oder Klavier. Hrsg. von Richard Fricke. 1929.

No.55. Boccherini, Luigi. Trio. Op.54, Nr.2.

No.56. Fasch, J. F. Triosonate. Nr.1. 1930.

No.57. Böddecker, P. F. Weihnachtskonzert für eine Singstimme und Basso Continuo. Hrsg. von Albert Rodemann. 1929.

No.58, 113. Purcell, Henry. Fantasien für Streichinstrumente. Hrsg. von Herbert Just. 1930.

No.59. Rosenmüller, Johann. Der 138. Psalm (Psalmus 137). 1930.

No.60. Zelter, K. F. Lieder, Balladen und Romanzen in Auswahl. 1930.

No.61. Rosenmüller, Johann. Studenten-Music. Darinnen zu befinden Allerhand Sachen, mit drey und funff Violen/ oder auch andern Instrumenten zu spielen. 1654. In praktischer Neuausgabe für zwei Violinen, Violoncello und Klavier (zwei Violen oder dritte Violine und Viola, sowie Kontrabass ad lib.) von Fred Hamel. Suite I bis X in vier Heften. 1929.

No.62. Stamitz, Karl. Drei Duette, Op.27, Nr.1–3, für zwei Flöten (oder Violinen). Hrsg. von Martin Glöder. 1930.

No.63. Bach, W. F. Sämtliche Klaviersonaten. Heft I: Nr.1–3. Hrsg. von Friedrich Blume. 1930.

No.64. Reichardt, J. F. Sonaten. 1930.

No.65. Bach, C. Ph. Em. Kleine Stücke für Klavier. Hrsg. von Otto Vrieslander. 1940.

No.66. Mozart, W. A. Fünf Lieder für eine Singstimme mit Klavierbegleitung. 1930.

No.67. Loewe, J. J. Zwei Suiten für Streichorchester und Basso Continuo. Hrsg. von Albert Rodemann. 1930.

No.68. Keiser, Reinhard. Sonata a tre, Flauto traverso, Violino con Cembalo, Nr.1. Hrsg. von Erich Schenk. 1930.

No.69. Schop, Johann. Vom Himmel hoch, da komm ich her. Geistliches Konzert für Sopran, Tenor, Bass, und Basso Continuo (Orgel oder Cembalo). Hrsg. von Adolf Strube. 1930.

No.70. Torelli, Giuseppe. Konzert, Op.6, Nr.10, für vier Streichinstrumente und Orgel oder Cembalo. Hrsg. von Prof. Dr. Hans Engel. 1931.

No.71. Haydn, Joseph. Die Londoner Trios für zwei Flöten und Violoncello. Hrsg. von Dr. Leo Balet. 1931.

No.72. Richter, F. X. Sinfonia da Camera für vierstimmiges Streichorchester und Continuo. Hrsg. von Prof. Dr. Walter Upmeyer. 1930.

No.73. Bach, C. Ph. Em. Sinfonie Nr.3 für vierstimmiges Streichorchester und Cembalo. Hrsg. von Dr. Ernst Fritz Schmid. 1931.

No.74. Albinoni, Tommaso. Sonate für Flöte (Oboe oder Violine) und Basso Continuo. Hrsg. von Ludwig Schäffler. 1931.

No.75. Riccio, Gio. Jubilent omnes (1620), geistliches Konzert für eine Singstimme (Sopran oder Tenor), Flöte, Violine (oder zwei Violinen), Fagott (oder Violoncello) und Basso Continuo (Orgel oder Klavier). Hrsg. von Prof. Dr. Adam Adrio. 1931.

No.76. Kraus, J. M. Sonata a Flauto traverso e Viola. Hrsg. von Jos. St. Winter. 1931.

No.77. Bach, J. S. Sonate in G-moll für obligates Cembalo und Flöte. Hrsg. von Dr. Leo Balet. 1931.

No.78. Bach, W. F. Sämtliche Klaviersonaten. Heft II: Nr.4–6. Hrsg. von Friedrich Blume. 1930.

No.79. Pfeiffer, Johann. Konzert für Cembalo, zwei Violinen und Violoncello ad lib. Hrsg. von Rudolf Steglich. 1932.

No.80. 22 Altdeutsche Tanzsätze, von Valentin Hausmann, Melchior Franck, Johann Staden und Georg Vintz. Für vier Instrumentalstimmen. Hrsg. von Rudolf Steglich. 1932.

No.81. Rosenmüller, Johann. Der 134. Psalm (Psalmus 133). "Auf, nun lobet Gott" für Alt-Solo (oder Mezzo, oder Bariton), zwei Violinen und Generalbass. Hrsg. von Fred Hamel. 1932.

No.82. Zumsteeg, J. R. Kleine Balladen und Lieder in Auswahl. 1932.

No.83. Bella, Domenico. Sonate für Violoncello und unbezifferten Bass (Cembalo oder Orgel). Hrsg. von Walter Upmeyer. 1931.

No.84. Haydn, Joseph. Divertimento Es-dur für vier Streichinstrumente. Hrsg. von Karl Geiringer. 1931.

No.85. Neubaur, F. Duetten.

No.86. Haydn, Joseph. Konzert in G-dur für Cembalo oder Pianoforte mit Begleitung von Streichern und Blasern ad lib. Hrsg. von Kurt Schubert. 1932.

No.87. Recercare, Canzonen und Fugen des 17. und 18. Jahrhunderts für Orgel oder Klavier. Hrsg. von Willi Hillemann. 1932.

No.88. Faber, J. C. Partita für drei Blockflöten oder andere Melodieinstrumente. Hrsg. von Ruth Brachvogel. 1932.

No.89. Walther, J. J. Sonate C-dur für Violine und Basso Continuo. Hrsg. von Erna Bethan. 1932.

No.90. Bach, C. Ph. Em. Leichte Sonaten für Klavier. Hrsg. von Otto Vrieslander. 1935.

No.91. Zelter, K. F. Johanna Sebus (Goethe) für Singstimmen am Pianoforte. 1932.

No.92. Zelter, K. F. Die Gunst des Augenblicks. Hrsg. von Schiller. 1932.

No.93. Türk, D. G. Kleine Handstücke für angehende Klavierspieler. Hrsg. von Dr. Cornelia Auerbach. 1933.

No.94. Couperin, François. Musik für Cembalo. Hrsg. von Otto Vrieslander. 1933.

No.95. Alte deutsche Weihnachtsmusik, von S. Scheidt, J. Pachelbel, Fr. W. Zachow, V. Lübeck, Fr. X. A. Murschhauser, G. Muffat und V. Rathgeber. Für Klavier oder Orgel. Hrsg. von Rudolf Steglich. 1932.
No.96. Bach, C. Ph. Em. Sinfonie Nr.2 für vierstimmiges Streichorchester und Basso Continuo. Hrsg. von Ernst Fritz Schmid. 1933.
No.97. Alte Liedsätze. Aus Peter Schöffers Liederbuch (1513) mit vier Singstimmen oder Instrumenten. Hrsg. von Carl Gerhardt. 1933.
No.98. Krumpholtz, J. B. Sonate für Flöte (oder Violine) und Harfe (oder Klavier). Hrsg. von Hans Joachim Zingel. 1933.
No.99. Hasse, J. A. Sonate Nr.1, D-dur, für Flöte und bezitterten Bass. Hrsg. von Kurt Walther. 1933.
No.100. Kusser, J. S. Ouverture IV aus "Composition de musique" (1682) für Streicher und Basso Continuo. Hrsg. von Dr. Helmuth Osthoff. 1933.
No.101. Schiassi, G. M. Concerto. 1933.
No.102. Schütz, Heinrich. Deutsches Konzert. Der Herr ist mein Licht. Für zwei Männerstimmen (Tenor und Bariton), zwei Instrumente (Bläser oder Streicher) und Generalbass (Cembalo oder Orgel). (Aus: Symphoniae Sacrae II. Teil. Dresden 1647). Hrsg. von Hans Hoffmann. 1933.
No.103. Bach, J. Christian. Sonate A-dur für Violine oder Flöte und Klavier. Hrsg. von Albert Küster. 1933.
No.104. Händel, G. F. Weihnachtsarie. Und siehe! Der Engel des Herrn kam über sie. Für Sopran und Basso Continuo. Hrsg. von Rudolf Steglich. 1933.
No.105. Rathgeber, Valentin. Musikalischer Zeitvertreib aus dem Klavier. 19 Ausgewählte Stücke. Hrsg. von Prof. Dr. Rudolf Steglich. 1933.
No.106. Vivaldi, Antonio. Konzert für Violine mit Streichorchester und Basso Continuo. Op.6, Nr.1, G-moll. 1934.
No.107. Pergolesi, G. B. Zwei Triosonaten für zwei Violinen und Basso Continuo. Hrsg. von Th. W. Werner. [Nr.5 und 10.] 1934.
No.108. Händel, G. F. Zwölf Märsche für Streichorchester mit Blasern nach Belieben. Klavier Partitur. Hrsg. von Rudolf Steglich. 1933.
No.109. Krebs, J. L. Sonate A-moll für zwei Violinen mit ausgesetzten Generalbass. 1934.
No.110. Friedrich der Grosse. Sinfonie D-dur für zwei Flöten, zwei Oboen, zwei Hörner, Streicher und Cembalo (Oboen und Hörner nach Belieben). 1934.
No.111. Pez, J. C. Triosonate für zwei Blockflöten und Basso Continuo. Hrsg. von Waldemar Woehl. 1934.
No.112. Biber, H. I. Serenade für fünf Streichinstrumente (Nachwächter-Bass) und Cembalo. Hrsg. von Paul Nettl. 1934.
No.113. *See* No.58.
No.114. Keiser, Reinhard. Sonate a tre, Flauto traverso, Violino con Cembalo, Nr.2, G-dur. Hrsg. von Prof. Dr. Erich Schenk. 1931.
No.115. Bach, J. Christian. Sonate Nr.2, A-dur, für Klavier zu vier Händen, Op.XVIII, Nr.5. Hrsg. von Albert Küster. 1935.
No.116. Quantz, J. J. Sonate für drei Flöten (oder Violinen und andere Instrumente) ohne Bass. Hrsg. von Erich Doflein.
No.117. Buxtehude, Dietrich. Sonate E-dur, Op.2, Nr.6, für Violine, Viola da Gamba (oder Violoncello) und Cembalo (oder Klavier). Hrsg. von Christian Döbereiner. 1935.
No.118. Fürstenau, Kaspar. Zwölf Originalkompositionen für Flöte und Gitarre, Op.34.
No.119. Staden, Johann. Fünfzehn vier- und fünfstimmige Instrumentalsätze aus dem "Venus-Kraentzlein" (1610). 1936.
No.120. Bach, W. F. Zwei Sonaten für zwei Flöten (Violinen) allein.
No.121. Drei Sonaten für Block- oder Querflöte und Cembalo eines unbekannten Meisters, vom Ende des 17. Jahrhunderts. Hrsg. von Albert Rodemann. 1935.
No.122. Händel, G. F. Vier Original-Sonaten, für Alt-Blockflöte und Cembalo (Klavier). Hrsg. von Albert Rodemann. 1935.
No.123. Bach, J. Christian. Quintett Es-dur, Op.11, Nr.4, für Querflöte (Violine), Oboe (Violine), Violine, Viola, Violoncell und Generalbass (Cembalo). Hrsg. von Rudolf Steglich. Einzeldruck aus "Das Erbe deutsche Musik." Reichsdenkmale Bd.3. Abt. Kammermusik. Bd.1. 1936.
No.124. Bach, J. Christian. Quintett D-dur für Querflöte (Violine), Oboe (Violine), Violine, Viola, Violoncello und Generalbass (Cembalo). Op.11, Nr.6. Hrsg. von Rudolf Steglich. 1935.
No.125. Eichner, Ernst. Sechs Duette für Violine und Bratsche, Op.10. Heft I. Neu hrsg. von Prof. Dr. Wilhelm Altmann. 1929.
No.126. Bach, J. Christian. Sechs Duette für zwei Violinen.
No.127. Bach, J. Christian. Quartett in F-dur, Op.8, Nr.4, für Flöte, Violine, Viola, Violoncello oder Streichquartett.
No.128. Eichner, Ernst. Sechs Duette für Violine und Bratsche, Op.10.
No.129. Haydn, Joseph. Op.5, Nr.IV. Quartett G-dur für Flöte (Violine), Violine, Viola und bezifferten Bass. Hrsg. von Prof. Dr. Walter Upmeyer. 1937.
No.130. Bach, C. Ph. Em. Sinfonie Nr.4 für vierstimmiges Streichorchester und ausgesetzten Generalbass. 1937.
No.131. Telemann, G. P. Trio F-dur für Flauto dolce (oder Traverso), Viola da Gamba (oder Violoncello oder Bratsche) und Basso Continuo (Cembalo mit Violoncello ad lib.). Hrsg. von Walter Upmeyer. 1937.
No.132. Keiser, Reinhard. Sonata a tre, Flauto traverso, Violino con Cembalo, Nr.3, D-dur. Hrsg. von Prof. Dr. Erich Schenk. 1937.
No.133. Stölzel, G. H. Triosonate F-moll für zwei Violinen oder Oboen und Basso Continuo. Hrsg. von Helmuth Osthoff. 1937.
No.134. Schobert, Johann. Klaviertrio F-dur, Op.16, Nr.4. Hrsg. von Maria Schumacher. 1937.
No.135. Krieger, J. P. Triosonate A-moll für

Violine, Viola da Gamba und Cembalo. Hrsg. von Helmuth Osthoff. 1937.
No.136. Händel, G. F. Konzert B-dur, Op.4, Nr.6, für Klavier (Cembalo oder Orgel), zwei Violinen und Violoncello oder kleines Orchester. Hrsg. von Willi Hillemann. 1937.
No.137. Scheidt, Samuel. Suite für fünf Streicher oder Bläser und Generalbass. Hrsg. von Gerd Ochs. 1937.
No.138. Henkel, Michael. Sonate für Flöte oder Violine und Gitarre, Op.9.
No.139. Gelli, Vincenzo. Drei Divertimenti für Flöte oder Violine und Gitarre, Op.2. Hrsg. von Otto Schindler. 1938.
No.140. Bach, J. Christian. Sechs Duette für zwei Violinen. Heft II: Duette IV–VI. Hrsg. von Wilhelm Friedrich.
No.141. Zwei feierliche Vorspiele: Antonio Sartorio. Sinfonia zur Oper "L'Adelaide"; Agostino Steffani. Ouverture zu Oper "Enrico Leone" für Streichorchester und ausgesetzten Generalbass. 1938.
No.142. Pfeiffer, Johann. Sonate D-dur für Viola da Gamba (Violine. 1. Lage) und Konzertierendes Cembalo (Klavier). Hrsg. von Ludwig Schäffler.
No.143. Boismortier, J. B. de. Trio D-dur, Op.50, Nr.6, für Violine, Violoncello und Basso Continuo. Hrsg. von Pierre Ruyssen. 1938, 1960.
No.144. Benda, Georg. Konzert für Cembalo und Streichorchester in G-dur.
No.145. Nichelmann, Christoph. Konzert für Cembalo und Streichorchester. Hrsg. von Carl Bittner. 1938.
No.146. Fux, J. J. Sinfonia für Flauto, Hautbois et Basso (Cembalo) (auch für zwei Altblockflöten und Cembalo). Hrsg. von Leo Kuntner. 1938.
No.147. Vivaldi, Antonio. Triosonate, Op.1, Nr.2, E-moll, für zwei Violinen und Basso Continuo. Hrsg. von Erich Schenk. 1939.
No.148. Fasch, J. F. Sonata a 4, für Altblockflöte, Oboe und Violine, Violoncello und ausgesetzten Generalbass.
No.149. Valentino, Roberto. Drei Sonaten für Block- oder Querflöte und Basso Continuo. Hrsg. von Albert Rodemann. 1940.
No.150. Händel, G. F. Trio für Altblockflöte, Violine und Cembalo. Hrsg. von Albert Rodemann. 1940.
No.151. Telemann, G. P. Das Darmstädter Trio für Violine, Viola (Gamba) und Basso Continuo. 1940.
No.152. Boccherini, Luigi. Trio, Op.54, Nr.3, für zwei Violinen und Violoncello. Hrsg. von Walter Upmeyer.
No.153. Manfredini, Francesco. Concerto grosso, Op.3, Nr.11, für zwei Solo-Violinen und Streichorchester mit Cembalo oder Orgel. Hrsg. von Walter Upmeyer. 1941.
No.154. Benda, Georg. Sonate für Querflöte und obligates Cembalo. Hrsg. von Manfred Ruetz.
No.155.
No.156. Bach, W. F. Sonaten für Klavier. Nr.7–9. Hrsg. von Friedrich Blume.
No.157. Giordani, Giuseppe. Konzert für Klavier und Streichorchester. Hrsg. von Carl Bittner. 1941.
No.158. Gluck, C. W. Triosonate G-moll für zwei Violinen und Cembalo (Klavier). 1942.
No.159. Hasse, J. A. Triosonate D-dur für zwei Flöten (oder Violinen) mit Fagott oder Violoncello (ad lib.) und Generalbass. 1941.
No.160. Banner, Filippo. Sonate für Violoncello und Klavier (Cembalo). Hrsg. von Walter Upmeyer. 1942.
No.161. Picinetti, F. M. Sonate für Violoncello und Klavier (Cembalo). Hrsg. von Walter Upmeyer. 1941.
No.162. Vivaldi, Antonio. Vier Sonaten für Violine und Basso Continuo, Op.V, Nr.1–4. Hrsg. von Walter Upmeyer.
No.163. Telemann, G. P. Sonate D-dur für Flöte und Basso Continuo. Hrsg. von Walter Upmeyer. 1953.
No.164. Mayer, Martin. Das Weihnachtsevangelium. Dialog für Sopran und Alt mit zwei Violinen und Orgel. Hrsg. von Fritz Koschinsky. 1952.
No.165. Zach, Johann. Konzert für Cembalo mit begleitung von Streichorchester. Hrsg. von Adam Bernhard Gottron. 1947.
No.166. Vivaldi, Antonio. Konzert A-moll für Violoncello und Streichorchester. Hrsg. von Walter Upmeyer. 1952.
No.167. Telemann, G. P. Konzert A-moll für zwei Soloflöten, Streichorchester und Basso Continuo. Hrsg. von Fritz Stein. 1953.
No.168. Graupner, Christoph. Konzert für Oboe, Streicher, und Cembalo. Hrsg. von Alfred Kreutz. 1952.
No.169. Fasch, J. F. Sonate für zwei Violinen und Basso Continuo. Hrsg. von Günter Hausswald. 1954.
No.170. Bach, J. Christian. Konzert in F-moll für Klavier (Cembalo) mit Streichorchester. Hrsg. von Eduard Martini. 1954.
No.171. Vivaldi, Antonio. Zwei Sonaten für zwei Violinen und Basso Continuo (Cembalo und Violoncello), Op.V, Nr.5–6. Hrsg. von Walter Upmeyer. 1954.
No.172. Boccherini, Luigi. Konzert für Flöte und kleines Streichorchester. Hrsg. von Walter Upmeyer. 1954.
No.173. Dowland, John. Lachrimae oder sieber Tränen. Dargestellt in sieben tief empfundenen Pavanen, für fünfstimmigen Violen- oder Blockflötenchor und Laute ad lib. Hrsg. von F. H. Giesbert. 1954.
No.174. Krieger, J. P. Vierundzwanzig Lieder und Arien für eine Singstimme und Basso Continuo. Heft I: Nr.1–12. Hrsg. von Hans Joachim Moser. 1930.
No.175. Krieger, J. P. Vierundzwanzig Lieder und Arien für eine Singstimme und Basso Continuo. Heft II: Nr.13–24. Hrsg. von Hans Joachim Moser. 1930.
No.176. Müthel, J. G. Sonate (Duett). Zwei Klaviere. 1954.
No.177. Telemann, G. P. Konzertsuite für Altblockflöte, Streicher und Basso Continuo (Klavier). Hrsg. von Adolf Hoffmann. 1954.
No.178. Stamitz, Karl. Sechs Duette für zwei Flöten oder Violinen, Op.27. Hrsg. von Paul Bormann. Heft II, Book 2. 1954.

No.179. Scheidt, Samuel. Spielmusik. Heft I. Fünf Stücke aus der "Tabulatura nova" für vier Instrumentalstimmen. Hrsg. von Gerd Ochs. 1954.
No.180. Scheidt, Samuel. Spielmusik. Heft II. Suite für vier Streichinstrumenten.
No.181. Reichardt, J. F. Konzert in Es-dur für Violine und Streichorchester. Hrsg. von Hellmuth Lungershausen. 1955.
No.182. Konzertante Weihnachtsmusik von Händel, Corelli, Manfredini, Schiassi für Streichorchester und Generalbass meist mit Solo-Instrumenten (Violine, Flöte, Oboe). Hrsg. von Adolf Hoffmann. 1954.
No.183. Beethoven, L. von. Zwölf Menuette für Orchester. Hrsg. von Willy Hess. 1955.
No.184. Leffloth, Matthias. Konzert D-dur für obligates Cembalo und Flöte oder Violine. Hrsg. von Hugo Ruf. 1955.
No.185. Goldberg, J. G. Trio in A-moll für zwei Violinen und Basso Continuo. Hrsg. von Alfred Dürr. 1956.
No.186. Beethoven, L. von. Präludium und Fuge in C-dur für Streichquartette. Hrsg. von Willy Hess. 1955.
No.187. Beethoven, L. von. Präludium und Fuge in F-dur für Streichquartette. Hrsg. von Willy Hess.
No.188. Beethoven, L. von. Präludium und Fuge in E-moll für Streichtrio. Hrsg. von Willy Hess. 1955.
No.189. Albinoni, Tommaso. Sonate G-moll, Op.2, Nr.6, für zwei Violinen, zwei Violen, Violoncello und Basso Continuo. Hrsg. von Franz Giegling. 1956.
No.190. Pepusch, J. C. Sonate A-moll für Violine, Viola da Gamba (Viola) und Basso Continuo. Hrsg. von Lothar Hoffmann-Erbrecht. Continuoaussetzung Peter Benary. 1955.
No.191. Wendling, J. B. Quartett G-dur, Op.10, Nr.4, für Flöte, Violine, Viola und Violoncello. Hrsg. von Joseph Bopp. 1957.
No.192. Bach, J. C. F. Sonate D-dur für Konzertierendes Cembalo (Klavier), Flöte oder Violine und Violoncello. Hrsg. von Hugo Ruf. 1957.
No.193. Beck, Franz. Sinfonia D-moll für Streichorchester und Basso Continuo, Op.III, Nr.5. Hrsg. von H. C. Robbins Landon. 1958.
No.194. Hasse, J. A. Konzert G-dur für Flöte, Streicher und Basso Continuo. Hrsg. von Richard Engländer. 1957.
No.195. Fesch, W. de. Konzert D-dur für Querflöte, Streicher und Basso Continuo, Op.X, Nr.7. Hrsg. von Hugo Ruf. 1958.
No.196. Pisendel, J. G. Konzert Es-dur für Violine, Streichorchester und Basso Continuo. Hrsg. von Günter Hauswald. 1958.
No.197. Schobert, Johann. Klaviertrio Es-dur für Klavier, Violine und Violoncello, Op.6, Nr.1. Hrsg. von Albert Karsch. 1958.
No.198. Goldberg, J. G. Trio in G-moll für zwei Violinen und Basso Continuo (oder für obligates Cembalo und Violine). Hrsg. von Alfred Fürr. 1958.
No.199. Schobert, Johann. Sonata A-dur für Konzertierendes Cembalo und Violine, Op.9, Nr.2. Hrsg. von Walter Kramolisch. 1962.
No.200. Haydn, Joseph. Konzert C-dur für Klavier (Cembalo) und Streicher. Hrsg. von Horst Heussner. 1959.
No.201. Corrette, Michel. Konzert D-moll, Op. XXVI, Nr.6, für Cembalo oder Orgel, Querflöte ad lib. und Streicher. Hrsg. von Hugo Ruf. 1959.
No.202. Geminiari, Francesco. Concerto grosso, Op.VII, Nr.1, für zwei Violinen, Viola und Violoncello. Hrsg. von Emil Platen. 1960.
No.203. Festing, M. C. Concerto a 7, D-dur, für zwei Flöten, Streicher und Basso Continuo, Op.3, Nr.10. Hrsg. von Hugo Ruf. 1960.
No.204. Caesar, J. M. Ballett-Suite für Streichquartett (Streichorchester) und Basso Continuo. Hrsg. von Ernst Fritz Schmid. 1962.
No.205. Gluck, C. W. Triosonaten C-dur und G-moll für zwei Violinen und Basso Continuo oder Streichorchester. Hrsg. von Croll.
No.206. Gluck, C. W. Triosonaten A-dur und Bs-dur für zwei Violinen und Basso Continuo oder Streichorchester. Hrsg. von Croll.
No.207. Gluck, C. W. Triosonaten Es-dur und F-dur für zwei Violinen und Basso Continuo oder Streichorchester. Hrsg. von Croll.
No.208. Gluck, C. W. Triosonaten E-dur und F-dur für zwei Violinen und Basso Continuo oder Streichorchester. Hrsg. von Croll.
No.209. Leclair, J. M. Konzert A-moll für Violine, Streichorchester und Basso Continuo, Op.VII, Nr.5. Hrsg. von Hugo Ruf. 1963.
No.210. Arne, T. A. Concerto V, G-moll, für Orgel, Cembalo oder Klavier mit Instrumenten. Hrsg. von Albert de Klerk. 1962.
No.211. Geminiari, Francesco. Concerto grosso C-dur aus Sonate Op.5, Nr.8, von Corelli für Violine, Violoncello, Streicher und Basso Continuo.

NAGELS MUSIK-ARCHIV. Sonderausgabe. Hannover, Adolph Nagel, 1931– .
No.1– .
Contents:
No.1. Haydn, J. Werke für das Laufwerk (Flötenuhr). Für Klavier zu zwei Händen übertragen und erstmalig hrsg. von Ernst Fritz Schmid. 1931.

Neithardt, August Heinrich, 1793–1861, ed. Musica sacra, *see* Musica sacra. Sammlung religiöser Gesänge älterer und neuester Zeit . . .

NEW MUSIC. New York, American Music Center, 1927–57, 1958– .
v.1– .
In June, 1958, the Theodore Presser Co. became selling agent and publisher for the New Music Edition.
Contents:
Vol.1. No.1. Oct.1927. Ruggles, Carl. Symphonic ensemble. Men and mountains. 1927.
Vol.1. No.2. Jan.1928. Rudhyar, Dane. 3 Paeans for piano. 1927.
Vol.1. No.3. Apr.1928. Ornstein, Leo. The

corpse, for voice and piano. 1928; Weisshaus, Imre. 6 Pieces for solo voice. Unacc.

Vol.1. No.4. July 1928. Chávez, Carlos. Sonatina; violin and piano. 1928.

Vol.2. No.1. Oct.1928. Seeger, Ruth Porter (Crawford). 4 Preludes for piano. 1928.

Vol.2. No.2. Ives, Charles Edward. Fourth symphony. (Second movement). Full score. 1929. (*see also* Orchestra series, below, No.15).

Vol.2. No.3. Apr.1929. Weiss, Adolph. 6 Preludes for piano. 1929.

Vol.2. No.4. Oct.1929. Copland, Aaron. As it fell upon a day; Song for soprano, with flute and clarinet acc. 1929.

Vol.3. No.1. Oct.1929. Slonimsky, Nicolas. Studies in black and white. Piano. 1929.

Vol.3. No.2. Jan.1930. Becker, John Joseph. Symphonia brevis; Symphony No.3. Arr. for the piano by the composer. 1930; McPhee, Colin. Kinesis, Invention. Piano. (To be reprinted).

Vol.3. No.3. Apr.1930. Ruggles, Carl. Portals, for full string orchestra. Full score. 1930.

Vol.3. No.4. July 1930. Riegger, Wallingford. Suite for flute alone.

Vol.4. No.1. Oct.1930. Chávez, Carlos. 36, for piano.

Vol.4. No.1a. Oct.1930. Weiss, Adolph. Sonata for flute and viola.

Vol.4. No.1b. Oct.1930. Webern, Anton. Geistlicher Volkstext. Voice, clarinet, and bass clarinet.

Vol.4. No.2. Jan.1931. McPhee, Colin. Concerto for piano with wind octette acc. Full score. 1931.

Vol.4. No.3. Apr.1931. Antheil, George. Second sonata "The airplane" for piano solo. 1931.

Vol.4. No.4. July 1931. Brant, Henry Dreyfuss. "Variations" for 4 instruments and "Two sarabandes" for keyboard instrument. 1931.

Vol.5. No.1. Oct.1931. Achron, Joseph. "Statuettes" for piano. 1931.

Vol.5. No.2. Jan.1932. Ives, Charles Edward. A set of pieces for theater or chamber orchestra. Full score. Arrangement of Part I (for voice with pianoforte acc., 1 leaf) and of Part II (for pianoforte, 8p.). 1932.

Vol.5. No.3. Apr.1932. Schönberg, Arnold. Klavierstück. For piano. 1932.

Vol.5. No.4. July 1932. Riegger, Wallingford. 3 Canons for woodwinds, Op.9. 1931; Strang, Gerald. Mirrorrorrim. Piano. 1932.

Vol.6. No.1. Oct.1932. Seeger, Ruth Porter (Crawford). Piano study in mixed accents. 1932; Engel, Lehman. 4 Excerpts from "Job," Op.3. Voice and piano. 1932.

Vol.6. No.2. Jan.1933. Chávez, Carlos. Sonata for piano. 1933.

Vol.6. No.3. Apr.1933. Donovan, Richard Frank. Suite for piano. 1933; Hardcastle, Arthur E. Prelude, No.4. Piano. 1933.

Vol.6. No.4. July 1933. Piston, Walter. 3 Pieces for flute, clarinet, and bassoon. 1933; Fine, Vivian. 4 Songs. 1933.

Vol.7. No.1. Oct.1933. Ives, Charles Edward. 34 Songs. 1933. (Reprint 1963; order of songs slightly altered).

Vol.7. No.2. Jan.1934. Roldán, Amadee. Motivos de son. Voice and piano. 1934; Ruyneman, Daniel. Sonata for chamber choir. 1934. (To be reprinted).

Vol.7. No.3. Apr.1934. Green, Ray. Compositions. 2 Madrigals. Sonatina for piano. 2 Songs. 1934.

Vol.7. No.4. July 1934. Ardévol, José. Sonatina. Piano. 1934; Caturla, Alejandro Garcia. Preludio corte. Sonata corta. Piano. 1934; Strang, Gerald. 11. 15. Piano. 1934.

Vol.8. No.1. Oct.1934. Contemporary Russian composers. 1934; Davidenko, A. Song of a shepherd perishing in the mountains. Chorus, a cappella; Khachaturian, A. Dance, No.3. Piano; Mossolov, A. A Turkmenian lullaby. Chorus, a cappella; Polovinkin, L. A. Humoresque philosophique. Piano; Veprik, A. Stalinstan. Chorus with piano acc.

Vol.8. No.2. Jan.1935. Creston, Paul. 7 Theses for piano. 1935.

Vol.8. No.3. Apr.1935. Chávez, Carlos. Spiral movement for violin and piano. 1935; Bowles, Paul Frederic: Cafe sin nombre. Piano. 1935; Danger de mort, Letter to Freddy, Scènes d'Anabase. Voice with piano acc. 1935.

Vol.8. No.4. July 1935. Rudhyar, Dane. Granites. Piano. 1935; Luening, Otto. Only themselves understand themselves. Voice and piano. 1935; Heilner, Irwin. Second rhapsody for tenor and piano (4 hands). 1935.

Vol.9. No.1. Oct.1935. Ives, Charles Edward. 18 [i.e., 19] Songs. 1935. (Reprint 1964; order of songs slightly altered).

Vol.9. No.2. Jan.1936. Rózsa, Béla. Sonata for piano. 1936.

Vol.9. No.3. Apr.1936. Harris, Roy. Trio for piano, violin, and violoncello. 1936.

Vol.9. No.4. July 1936. Siegmeister, Elie. The strange funeral, for baritone and piano. 1936; Brooks, Ernest. Toccata, from Third piano sonata. 1936.

Vol.10. No.1. Oct.1936. Chávez, Carlos. 7 Pieces for piano: Paligonos; Solo; 36; Blues; Fox; Paisaje; Unidad. 1936.

Vol.10. No.2. Jan.1937. Bailey, William H. Idless, for piano and violin. 1937; Couper, Mildred. Dirge, for 2 pianos. Second piano tuned one quarter tone higher than the first. 1937.

Vol.10. No.3. Apr.1937. Caturla, Alejandro Garcia: Comparsa (Negro dance). From the Second suite of Cuban dances. Piano. 1937; Yambambó. Canto negro para voz y piano. 1937; Stocker, Clara. 2 Little pieces. Piano. 1937.

Vol.10. No.4. July 1937. Luening, Otto. Fantasia brevis, for clarinet and piano. 1937; Strang, Gerald: Sonatina for clarinet alone. 1937; 3 Pieces for flute and piano. 1937.

Vol.11. No.1. Oct.1937. Finney, Ross Lee. Piano sonata. 1937.

Vol.11. No.2. Jan.1938. Nancarrow, Conlon: Toccata for violin and piano. 1938; Prelude, for piano. 1938; Blues, for piano. 1938.

Vol.11. No.3. Apr.1938. Creston, Paul. Suite, for E alto saxophone or B clarinet and piano. 1938.

Vol.11. No.4. July 1938. Cleghorn, James. How do you like this? Three ironies for piano. 1938; Harrison, Lou. Sarabande and prelude. Piano. 1938.
Vol.12. No.1. Oct.1938. Ficher, Jacobo. Sonatina. Piano, trumpet, alto saxophone. 1938.
Vol.12. No.2. Jan.1939. Tremblay, George. 2 Piano sonatas, Op.8, No.1 and 2. 1939.
Vol.12. No.3. Apr.1939. Santa Cruz, Domingo. 3 Pieces for violin and piano. 1939.
Vol.12. No.4. July 1939. Carvajal, Armando. 3 Pieces for children. Piano. 1939; Uribe-Holguín, Guilermo. Preludio, Op.49, No.1, Op.56, No.1. 1939.
Vol.13. No.1. Oct.1939. Diamond, David Leo. Sonata for violoncello and piano. 1939.
Vol.13. No.2. Jan.1940. Cazden, Norman. Sonatina, Op.7. Piano. 1940; McKay, George Frederick. Dance suite No.2. Piano 1940; Creston, Paul. 7 Theses for piano. 1940.
Vol.13. No.3. Apr.1940. Kerr, Harrison. Trio, for clarinet, violoncello, and piano. Full score. 1940.
Vol.13. No.4. July 1940. Weber, Ben. 5 Bagatelles for piano. 1940.
Vol.14. No.1. Oct.1940. Cowell, Henry Dixon. Maestoso, for piano. 1940.
Vol.14. No.2. Jan.1941. Seeger, Ruth Porter (Crawford). String quartet 1931. 1941.
Vol.14. No.3. Apr.1941. Donovan, Richard Frank. Serenade for oboe, violin, viola, and violoncello. 1941; Kerr, Harrison. Study for violoncello (unacc.). 1941.
Vol.14. No.4. July 1941. Strang, Gerald. Intermezzo (second movement of a symphony). 1941.
Vol.15. No.1. Oct.1941. Goldman, Richard Franko. Hymn for brass choir. 1941; Jemnitz, Alexander. Second sonata for violin alone, Op.37. 1941.
Vol.15. No.2. Jan.1942. Bacon, Ernst. 6 Songs. 1942.
Vol.15. No.3. Apr.1942. Luening, Otto. 8 Preludes for piano. 1942; Pisk, Paul Amadeus. 5 Sketches for piano, Op.39. 1942.
Vol.15. No.4. July 1942. Achron, Joseph. Sextet for flute, oboe, clarinet, bassoon, French horn, and trumpet, Op.73. 1942.
Vol.16. No.1. Oct.1942. Piano music of Brazil. 1942: Fernandez, Oscar Lorenzo. Moda; Guarnieri, Camargo. Valsa; Gnattali, Radames. Chôro; Villa-Lobos, Heitor. Melodia da Montanha; Villa-Lobos, Heitor. New York sky-line; Mignone, Francisco. Lenda sertaeja No.9.
Vol.16. No.2. Jan.1943. Paz, Juan Cárlos. 3[a] composicion en los 12 tonos, for clarinet in B and piano. Score with clarinet part. 1943.
Vol.16. No.3. Apr.1943. Ruggles, Carl: Evocations. 3 Chants for piano. 1943; Angels, for brass or strings. 1943.
Vol.16. No.4. July 1943. Cage, John. Amores, for piano and percussion. 1943.
Vol.17. No.1. Oct.1943. Harrison, Lou. 6 Sonatas for cembalo or pianoforte. 1943. (To be reprinted).
Vol.17. No.2. Jan.1944. Van Vactor, David. Vocal works. 1944.
Vol.17. No.3. Apr.1944. Carillo, Julián. Preludio a Cristobal Colón (in 16th tones). For flute, violin, soprano, guitar, and harp. 1944.
Vol.17. No.4. July 1944. Riegger, Wallingford. Op.35. Duos for 3 woodwinds. 1944.
Vol.18. No.1. Oct.1944. Thomson, Virgil. Sonata da chiesa. Clarinet, trumpet, viola, horn, and trombone. 1945.
Vol.18. No.2. Jan.1945. Ruggles, Carl. Evocation No.4. Chant for piano. 1945.
Vol.18. No.3. Apr.1945. Carter, Elliott. Pastoral, for piano and viola [or] English horn or clarinet. 1945.
Vol.18. No.4. July 1945. McPhee, Colin. 4 Iroquois dances. 1945.
Vol.19. No.1. Oct.1945. Cowell, Henry Dixon. Hilarious curtain opener, and Ritournelle. From incidental music for "Les Maries de la Tour Eiffel." Piano. 1945.
Vol.19. No.2. Jan.1946. Brown, Merton. Cantabile, for string orchestra. 1946.
Vol.19. No.3. Apr.1946. Hovaness, Alan. Mihr (Ancient Armenian fire god), for 2 pianos. 1946.
Vol.19. No.4. July 1946. Dahl, Ingolf. Variations on a Swedish folktune. For flute solo. 1946 (rev. ed. published August 1962); Varèse, Edgard. Density 21.5. For flute solo. 1946.
Vol.20. No.1. Oct.1946. Wolpe, Stefan. Passacaglia. For piano solo. 1947. (To be published in rev. ed.).
Vol.20. No.2. Jan.1947. Gideon, Miriam. Canzona. For piano solo. 1947.
Vol.20. No.3. Apr.1947. Thomson, Virgil. Capital, capitals. For 4 men and a piano. 1947.
Vol.20. No.4. July 1947. Sessions, Roger. Duo, for violin and piano. 1947.
Vol.21. No.1. Oct.1947. Piano works by Charles Ives, Henry Cowell, and Carl Ruggles. 1947: Ives, Charles Edward. Three protests; Cowell, Henry Dixon. Two`woofs; Ruggles, Carl. Organum.
Vol.21. No.2. Jan.1948. Harrison, Lou. Alleluia. For orchestra. 1948.
Vol.21. No.3. Apr.1948. Fine, Vivian. The Great Wall of China. For voice and flute. 1948; Strongin, Theodore. 4 Duos for 2 flutes. 1948.
Vol.21. No.4. July 1948. Haines, Edmund Thomas. Slow dance, for organ. 1948; Bradley, Will: The deep quarry. 1948; Honeysuckle and clover. For brass choir. 1948.
Vol.22. No.1. Oct.1948. Becker, John J. Soundpiece No.4, second string quartet. 1948.
Vol.22. No.2. Jan.1949. Weber, Ben. Dance, for unacc. violoncello, Op.28. 1949; Prausnitz, Frederick. Episode. 1949; Perle, George. Hebrew melodies, for unacc. violoncello, Op.19. 1949.
Vol.22. No.3. Apr.1949. Kauder, Hugo. Quartet for oboe, clarinet, horn, and bassoon. 1949.
Vol.22. No.4. July 1949. Babbitt, Milton. Composition for 4 instruments (flute, violin, clarinet, and violoncello). 1949.

Vol.23. No.1. Oct.1949. Perle, George. Quartet No.3. Strings 1949.
Vol.23. No.2. Jan.1950. Toch, Ernst. Fugue from the Geographie. Vocal score. S.A.T.B. 1950.
Vol.23. No.3. Apr.1950. Woronoff, Wladimir. Sonnet, for dallapiccolo. Piano. 1950.
Vol.23. No.4. July 1950. Feldman, Morton. Illusions for piano. 1950; Shifrin, Seymour. 4 Canons, for piano. 1950.
Vol.24. No.1. Oct.1950. Berger, Arthur. 3 Poems of Yeats, from "Words for music, perhaps." For flute, clarinet, voice, and violoncello. 1950.
Vol.24. No.2. Jan.1951. Ives, Charles Edward. Sonata No.3 for piano and violin. [Ed. by Ingolf Dahl and Sol Babitz]. 1951. (To be reprinted, ed. by Ingolf Dahl).
Vol.24. No.3. Apr.1951. Wolff, Christian. For prepared piano. 1951.
Vol.24. No.4. July 1951. Wilkinson, Marc. 3 Pieces for violoncello and piano. 1952.
Vol.25. No.1. Oct.1951. Nancarrow, Conlon. Rhythm study No.1, for player piano. 1952.
Vol.25. No.2. Jan.1952. Monod, Jacques Louis. Passacaile, for soprano and 7 instruments, Op.1. 1952.
Vol.25. No.3. Apr.1952. Nowak, Lionel. Sonata for solo violin. 1952.
Vol.25. No.4. July 1952. Chou Wen-Chung. 7 Poems of T'ang dynasty. 1952.
Vol.26. No.1. Oct.1952. Cowell, Henry Dixon. Ostinato pianissimo (for percussion band). 1953.
Vol.26. No.2. Jan.1953. Ives, Charles Edward. Lincoln, the great commoner. 1953. (*see also* Orchestra series, below, No.1).
Vol.26. No.3. Apr.1953. Seeger, Ruth Porter (Crawford). Diaphonic suite (1930) for solo flute or oboe. 1954; Seeger, Charles. The letter, song for solo voice; Psalm 137. Recitation for solo voice. 1954.
Vol.26. No.4. July 1953. Ives, Charles Edward. Calcium light, for orchestra. 1953. (Same as The gong on the hook and ladder, by C. E. Ives. Pub. by Peer International, 1960).
Vol.27. No.1. Oct.1953. Avshalomoff, Jacob. Tom O'Bedlam. For mixed chorus, solo oboe, tabor, and jingles. 1953.
Vol.27. No.2. Jan.1954. Weber, Ben. 4 Songs. For soprano or tenor with solo violoncello. Op.40. 1954.
Vol.27. No.3. Apr.1954. Macero, Teo. Canzona No.1. For 4 saxophones and 1 trumpet. 1954.
Vol.27. No.4. July 1954. Brant, Henry Dreyfuss. Ice age, for clarinet, glockenspiel, and piano. 1954.
Vol.28. No.1. Oct.1954. Weber, Ben. Closing piece, for organ, Op.36. 1955.
Vol.28. No.2. Jan.1955. Pisk, Paul Amadeus. Meadow-saffrons. For contralto, clarinet, and bass clarinet. 1956.
Vol.28. No.3. Apr.1955. Russell, William. 3 Dance movements. For piano and percussion instruments. Score. cop.1936. (*see also* Orchestra series, below, No.18).
Vol.28. No.4. July 1955. Spinner, Leopold. Trio for violin, violoncello, and piano. Score. cop.1957.
Vol.29. No.1.
Vol.29. No.2.
Vol.29. No.3.
Vol.29. No.4. July 1956. Wuorinen, Charles. Sonatina for woodwind quartet. cop.1957.
Vol.30. No.1.
Vol.30. No.2. Jan.1957. Wuorinen, Charles. Into the organ pipes and steeples. For antiphonal orchestra. cop.1957.
Vol.30. No.3. 1957. Hiller, Lejaren A., Jr. and Isaacson, Leonard M. Illiac suite for string quartet.

Orchestra series. No.1. Ives, Charles Edward. Lincoln, the great commoner. For chorus and orchestra. Score. n.d. (*see also* Vol.26. No.2).
—— No.2. Weiss, Adolph. American life. Scherzaso jazzoso for large orchestra (1929). 1943.
—— No.3. Ives, Charles Edward. The Fourth of July. Orchestra.
—— No.4. Riegger, Wallingford. Dichotomy, Op.12. For chamber orchestra. 1932.
—— No.5. Ives, Charles Edward. A set of pieces, for theatre or chamber orchestra. (No.1, "The cage," for voice and piano; No.2, "In the inn," arr. for piano inserted). n.d.
—— No.6. Russell, William. Fugue. 8 percussion instruments.
—— No.7. Becker, John J. Concerto arabesque, for piano and orchestra. n.d.
—— No.8. Moross, Jerome. Paeans. Orchestra. 1933.
—— No.9. Moross, Jerome. Biguine. 1935.
—— No.10. Caturla, Alejandro Garcia. Primero suite cubana. Winds and piano.
—— No.11. Varèse, Edgard. Ionisation, for percussion ensemble of 13 players. 1934.
—— No.12. Miaskovsky, Nikolai. Fragment lyrique. Orchestra. 1934.
—— No.13. Rudhyar, Dane. Sinfonietta. 1934.
—— No.14. Ruggles, Carl. Sun treader. Orchestra.
—— No.15. Ives, Charles Edward. Fourth symphony (second movement). Full score. 1929. (*see also* Vol.2. No.2).
—— No.16. Roldán, Amadeo. Motivos de son. 8 Cuban songs for voice and small orchestra. 1935.
—— No.17. Becker, John J. Concerto for horn in F and orchestra. 1936.
—— No.18. Beyer, Johanna M. IV; Davidson, Harold G. Auto accident; Green, Roy. Three inventories of Casey Jones; Humphrey, Doris. Dance rhythms; Russell, William. 3 Dance movements. (*see also* Vol.28. No.3). (Separate reprint, Nov.1962); Strang, Gerald. Percussion music.
—— No.19. Hermann, Bernard. Sinfonietta for string orchestra. 1936.
—— No.20. Ives, Charles Edward. Symphony "Holidays." First movement. Orchestra.

—— No.21. Still, William Grant. Dismal swamp. 1937.
—— No.22. Rudhyar, Dane. 5 Stanzas for strings' ensemble. 1938.
—— No.23. Becker, John J. Soundpiece No.2. (Homage to Haydn). 1938.
—— No.24. Levant, Oscar. Nocturne. 1938.
—— No.25. Kerr, Harrison. Notations on a sensitized plate, for voice, clarinet, string quartet, and piano. 1939.
—— No.26. Fernandez, Oscar Lorenzo. Batuque. Negro dance from the opera "Malazarte." 1939.
—— No.27. Moross, Jerome. Suite for chamber orchestra.

Special edition. Becker, John J. Soundpiece No.5. A short sonata for piano. 1938.
—— Brown, Merton. Arioso for piano. 1950.
—— Brown, Merton. Choral for strings.
—— Cowell, Henry Dixon. Sunset; Rest. Two songs for low voice.
—— Cowell, Henry Dixon. United quartet; for string art. n.d.
—— Ruggles, Carl. Organum. Large orchestra.
—— Slonimsky, Nicolas. Suite. Arr. of studies in black and white for small ensemble.

Subsequent numbers published by Theodore Presser Co. (perhaps intended as Vol.29, No.1–3; Vol.30, No.1):
Jan.1961. Wuorinen, Charles. Movement for wind quintet.
Aug.1962. Weber, Ben. Nocturne for flute, violoncello, and celeste.
Oct.1963. Nemiroff, Isaac. Sonata, No.2, for violin and piano.
1962. Lee, Noël. Dialogues for violin and piano. [cop.1958].

Other publications issued by Theodore Presser Co. since 1958 under the New Music Edition imprint:
Aug.1963. Tokunaga, Hidenori. 3 Interludes for piano.
Mar.1964. Gaburo, Kenneth. Ideas and transformations for violin and viola.

Other publications scheduled for publication in the New Music Edition:
Harrison, Lou. Spring in Nak Yang for mixed chorus and orchestra.
Wigglesworth, Frank. Duo for oboe and viola. (alternate version for oboe and B flat clarinet).
Hiller, Lejaren A., Jr. and Baker, Robert. Computer cantata.

New York Public Library. Music publications, *see* Early psalmody in 17th century America; Early symphonies and concertos; English instrumental music of the 16th and 17th centuries; Morley, Thomas. The first book of consort lessons; Music of the Moravians in America; Pachelbel, Carl Theodorus. Magnificat for double chorus and organ; Parthenia-in-Violata.

NEWMAN, WILLIAM S., 1912– . ed.
Thirteen keyboard sonatas of the 18th and 19th centuries, ed. with critical commentaries by William S. Newman. Chapel Hill, University of North Carolina Press, [cop.1947].
vii, 175p.
Contains compositions by J. J. Agrell, Domenico Alberti, Jean Barrière, Georg Benda, K. V. von Dittersdorf, E. T. A. Hoffmann, Karl Loewe, Ignaz Moscheles, M. B. de Nebra, C. G. Neefe, Giovanni Platti, J. F. Reichardt, and Joseph Wölfl.

NIETZSCHE, FRIEDRICH WILHELM, 1844–1900.
Musikalische Werke, von Friedrich Nietzsche. Hrsg. im Auftrage des Nietzsche Archives von Georg Göhler. Bd.1. Leipzig, R. Kistner, 1924.
1v.
No more published.
Contents:
Vol.1. Lieder für eine Singstimme mit Klavierbegleitung. 1924.

NIN Y CASTELLANO, JOAQUIN, 1879–1949. ed.
Dix-sept sonates et pièces anciennes d'auteurs espagnols. Deuxième recueil . . . Publiées pour la première fois par Joaquin Nin. Paris, Éditions Max Eschig, 1928.
1p.L., iii, 75p. (Classiques espagnols du piano).
Score for piano.
Contains compositions by Padre Rafael Anglès, Padre Narciso Casanovas, Freixanet, Padre José Gallés, Padre Felipe Rodriguez, Padre Vincente Rodriguez, and Padre Antonio Soler.

NIN Y CASTELLANO, JOAQUIN, 1879–1949. ed.
Seize sonates anciennes d'auteurs espagnols . . . Publiées pour la première fois par Joaquin Nin . . . Paris, Éditions Max Eschig, 1925.
vi, 73p. (Classiques espagnols du piano).
Score for piano.
Contains compositions by Mateo Albeniz, Cantallos, Mateo Ferrer, Blas Serrano, and Padre Antonio Soler.

Noord-Nederlandsche meesterwerken. Uitgave, *see* Vereniging voor Nederlandsche Muziekgeschiedenis.

NORDRAAK, RIKAR, 1842–1866.
Samlede verker. Oslo, Musikk-huset, 19? – .
v.1– .

Norsk musikksamling, *see* Oslo. Universitet. Bibliotek. Norsk musikksamling.

OBERDÖRFFER, FRITZ, 1895– . ed.
Deutsche Klaviermusik des 17. und 18. Jahrhunderts. New York, C. F. Peters, 19? – .
9v.
Contents:
Vol.1. Easy pieces of both centuries.
Vol.2/3. Composers of the 17th century. Composers of the 18th century.
Vol.4/5. Telemann. Overtures. No.1–3, 4–6.
Vol.6. Benda. 12 Sonatinas. 1 Sonata.
Vol.7. C. P. E. Bach. 3 Sonatas. (violin or violoncello ad lib.).

Vol.8/9. Music in Berlin at the time of Frederick the Great.

OBRECHT, JACOB, ca.1430–1505.
Werken, van Jacob Obrecht, uitgegeven door Prof. Dr. Johannes Wolf. Vereeniging voor Noord-Nederlands Muziekgeschiedenis. Amsterdam, Alsbach, Leipzig, Breitkopf & Härtel, 1908–21.
30v.
Contents:
Lief.1. Missa Je ne demande.
Lief.2. Motetten I.
Lief.3. Missa Graecorum. Missa Fortuna desperata (Kyrie-Gloria).
Lief.4. Motetten II.
Lief.5/6. Missa Fortuna desperata (Credo-Agnus III). Missa Malheur me bat.
Lief.7. Missa Salve diva parens.
Lief.8. Motetten III.
Lief.9/10. Missa super Sub tuum praesidium. Missa super Maria zart.
Lief.11. Missa de sancto Martino.
Lief.12. Missa Si dedero.
Lief.13. Missa O quam suavis est.
Lief.14. Missa Sicut spina rosam.
Lief.15/16. Weltliche Werke.
Lief.17. Missa Ave Regina coelorum.
Lief.18. Missa super Petrus Apostolus.
Lief.19. Missa Adieu mes amours, I.
Lief.20/21. Missa sine nomine. Missa carminum.
Lief.22. Missa Schoen Lief.
Lief.23/24. Missa Caput.
Lief.25. Missa sine nomine.
Lief.26. Missa L'homme armé.
Lief.27. Missa Beata viscera.
Lief.28. Passio Domini nostri Jesu Christi secundum Matthaeum.
Lief.29. Missa Forseulement. Missa sine nomine.
Lief.30. Motetten IV.

OBRECHT, JACOB, ca.1430–1505.
. . . Opera omnia. Editio altera quam edendam curavit Vereniging voor Nederlandse Muziekgeschiedenis. Amsterdam, Prostat apud G. Alsbach & Co., 1953– .
v.1– .
Editor: Dr. A. Smijers.
Contents:
Vol.1. Fasc.1. Missa Je ne demande. 1953.
Vol.1. Fasc.2. Missa Graecorum. 1954.
Vol.1. Fasc.3. Missa Fortuna desperata. 1954.
Vol.1. Fasc.4. Missa Malheur me bat. 1955.
Vol.1. Fasc.5. Missa Salve diva parens. 1957.
Vol.2. Fasc.1. Motetti. 1956.
Vol.2. Fasc.2. Motetti. 1958.
Vol.6. Sub tuum presidium. Edidit M. Van Crevel. 1959.

OCKEGHEM, JEAN DE, d. ca.1496.
Collected works, ed. by Dragan Plamenac . . . New York, Pub. for the American Musicological Society by Columbia University Press, 1947– .
v.1– . facsims. (American Musicological Society. Studies and documents. No.3, 1).
For Vol.1, 1st edition, *see* Publikationen älterer Musik, Jahrg.1^2.
Contents:
Vol.1. 2d. ed. Masses I–VIII. 1959.
Vol.2. Masses and mass sections IX–XVI. 1947.

OESTERLE, LOUIS. ed.
. . . Early keyboard music. A collection of pieces written for the virginal, spinet, harpsichord, and clavichord. Ed. by Louis Oesterle. With an introd. by Richard Aldrich . . . New York, G. Schirmer, Inc., cop.1932.
2v. (Schirmer's Library of musical classics. Vol.1559, 1560).
Contents:
Vol.1 contains compositions by J. H. D'Anglebert, John Blow, John Bull, Dietrich Buxtehude, William Byrd, J. C. de Chambonnières, Louis Couperin, Henri Dumont, Girolamo Frescobaldi, J. J. Froberger, Orlando Gibbons, J. C. Kerll, Johann Kuhnau, J.-B. Loeillet, J.-B. Lully, Johann Pachelbel, Bernardo Pasquini, Henry Purcell, Padre M. A. Rossi, and Alessandro Scarlatti.
Vol.2 contains compositions by François Couperin, Johann Mattheson, Gottlieb Muffat, F. X. Murschhauser, J.-P. Rameau, and Domenico Scarlatti.

Office de Pierre de Corbeil, *see* Pierre de Corbeil. Office de Pierre de Corbeil.

The offices, or introits for Sundays and festivals, *see* Plainsong and Mediaeval Music Society. The offices, or introits for Sundays and festivals.

Ohl, John F., joint ed. Masterpieces of music before 1750, *see* Parrish, Carl. Masterpieces of music before 1750.

Okeghem, Jean de, *see* Ockeghem, Jean de.

Old chamber music, *see* Riemann, Hugo. Old chamber music.

Old English composers for the virginals and harpsichord, *see* Pauer, Ernst. Old English composers for the virginals and harpsichord.

Old English dance tunes, 17th century, *see* Playford, John. Old English dance tunes, 17th century.

The old English edition, *see* Arkwright, Godfrey Edward Pellew. The old English edition.

Old English organ music, *see* West, John Ebenezer. Old English organ music.

Old English popular music, *see* Chappell, William. Old English popular music.

Old English viol music, *see* Giesbert, Franz Julius. Altenglische Violenmusik zu drei Stimmen.

Old Hall manuscript. The Old Hall manuscript, *see* Plainsong and Mediaeval Music Society. Old Hall manuscript. The Old Hall manuscript.

An old St. Andrews music book. (Cod. Helmst.628), *see* Wolfenbüttel. Herzog-August-Bibliothek. Mss. (677 [Helmst.628]). An old St. Andrews music book.

OLLER, MARIA TERESA. ed.
Madrigales y canciones polifónicas; autores anónimos de los siglos XVI y XVII. [Valencia], Instituto Valenciano de Musicología, Institución Alfonso el Magnánimo, 1958.
24p., score (25–119p.), facsims.
"Estudio sobre morfología, historia y estética del Madrigal y la canción polifónica, por Manuel Palau": p.[5]–23.
"Bibliografía": p.24.

An order for compline. Church of England. Liturgy and ritual, *see* Plainsong and Mediaeval Music Society. Church of England. Liturgy and ritual. An order for compline.

The order for 'Placebo,' *see* Plainsong and Mediaeval Music Society. The order for 'Placebo.'

The order for the burial of the dead, *see* Plainsong and Mediaeval Music Society. The order for the burial of the dead.

The order of compline, *see* Plainsong and Mediaeval Music Society. The order of compline.

The ordinary of the mass, *see* Plainsong and Mediaeval Music Society. The ordinary of the mass.

ORGAN ALBUM OF TEN PIECES BY SPANISH COMPOSERS. Boston, Boston Music Co.; New York, G. Schirmer, [etc., etc.,], cop.1922.
42p. (No.37).
Score for organ.
Contains compositions by P. Tomás de Elduayen, José Antonio de Erauzquin, N. Otaño, P. Nicolás de Tolesa, Eduardo Torres, Luis Urteaga.

ORGAN MASTERS OF THE BAROQUE PERIOD . . . Rev. by Gerard Alphenaar. New York, Edward B. Marks Music Corp., n.d.
3v. (Marks organ library. No.79–81).
Contents:
Vol.1. Johann Pachelbel.
Vol.2. Nikolaus Bruhns, Girolamo Frescobaldi, Johann Jacob Froberger, Claudio Merulo, Georg Muffat, and Johann Gottfried Walther.
Vol.3. Johann Sebastian Bach, Dietrich Buxtehude, Johann Ernst Eberlin, Wilhelm Hieronymus Pachelbel, and Friedrich Wilhelm Zachow.

Organ series, *see* Buszin, Walter Edwin. Organ series.

ORGANUM. Ausgewählte älterer vokale und instrumentale Meisterwerke kritisch durchgesehen und zum praktischen Gebrauch hrsg. unter Leitung von Max Seiffert. 1. Reihe: Geistliche Gesangmusik für Solo- oder Chorstimmen mit oder ohne Begleitung. Nr.1– . Leipzig, F. Kistner & C. F. W. Siegel, [1924–].
No.1– .
Editor: Nr.1–24, M. Seiffert.
Contents:
Nr.1. Weckmann, M. Wie liegt die Stadt so wüste. [1924].
Nr.2. Weckmann, J. Wenn der Herr die Gefangenen zu Zion. [1924].
Nr.3. Krieger, J. P. Wo wilt du hin, weil's Abend ist. [1924].
Nr.4. Tunder, F. Ein kleines Kindelein. [1929].
Nr.5. Zachow, F. W. Herr, wenn ich nur dich habe. [1924].
Nr.6. Krieger, J. P. Die Gerechten werden weggerafft. [1924].
Nr.7. Tunder, F. Arie: Ach Herr, lass deine lieben Engelein. [1924].
Nr.8. Schütz, H. Vom reichen Manne und armen Lazarus. [1924].
Nr.9. Ritter, C. Gott hat Jesum erwecket. [1925].
Nr.10. Krieger, J. P. Rufet nicht die Weischeit. [1925].
Nr.11. Sweelinck, J. P. Hodie Christus natus est. [1924].
Nr.12. Händel, G. F. Ach Herr, mich armen Sünder. [1928].
Nr.13. Tunder, F. Wachet auf! Ruft uns die Stimme. [1928].
Nr.14. Kuhnau, J. Ich habe Lust abzuscheiden. [1928].
Nr.15. Tunder, F. Ein' feste Burg ist unser Gott. [1929].
Nr.16. Buxtehude, D. Ihr lieben Christen, freut euch nun. [1929].
Nr.17. Weckmann, M. Zion spricht: der Herr hat mich verlassen. [1929].
Nr.18. Weckmann, M. Weine nicht! es hat überwunden. [1929].
Nr.19–20. Niederländische Bild-Motetten vom Ende des 16. Jahrhundert. Heft 1–2. [1929].
Nr.21. Rosenmüller, Johann. Dialog von Tobias und Raguel. [1930].
Nr.22. Buxtehude, D. Alles, was ihr tut mit Worten oder mit Werken. [1935].
Nr.23. Ebart, Samuel. Miserere, Christe, mei. [1931].
Nr.24. Rosenmüller, Johann. In hac misera valle. [1933?].
Nr.25. Vierstimmige Choräle aus dem Melodeyen-Gesangbuch. Hamburg, 1604. No.1–12. [1951].
Nr.26. The same. No.13–23.
Nr.27. The same. No.24–35.
Nr.28. Stölzel, Gottfried Heinrich. Weihnachtskantate. Kündlich gross ist das Gottselige Geheimnis. [1953].
Nr.29. Stölzel, G. H. Lob und Dank. Kantate. [1954].
Nr.30. Frauenholtz, Johann Christoph. Verbirg nicht deine Holden Strahlen. Kantate. [1954].
Nr.31. Frauenholtz, J. Chr. Der Herr Gedenkt an uns. Kantate. [1954].
Nr.32. Benda, Georg. Erschallet ihr Himmel. Kantate. [1961].
Nr.33. Erlebach, Philipp Heinrich. Der Herr hat offenbaret. Kantate. [1962].

ORGANUM. 2. Reihe. Weltliche Gesangmusik für Solo- oder Chorstimmen mit oder ohne Begleitung. Nr.1– . Leipzig, F. Kistner & C. F. W. Siegel, [1924–39].
No.1– .
Editor: Nr.1–20, M. Seiffert.
Contents:
Nr.1. Sweelinck, J. P. Chanson. Vom Jan, der alles hat. [1924].
Nr.2. Sweelinck, J. P. Chanson. Von der Liebe Sehnsucht. [1924]..
Nr.3. Sweelinck, J. P. Chanson. Die spröde Schöne. [1924].
Nr.4. Händel, G. F. Deutsche Arie für Sopran. Flammende Rose. [1924].
Nr.5. Händel, G. F. Deutsche Arie für Sopran (Tenor). Süsse Stille. [1924].
Nr.6. Albert, H. Ausgewählte Arien für 1 oder 2 Singstimmen. [1929].
Nr.7. Krieger, A. Ausgewählte Arien für Sopran. [1929].
Nr.8. Erlebach, P. H. Ausgewählte Arien und Duette. [1929].
Nr.9. Franck, J. W. and others. Ausgewählte "geistreiche" Lieder Heinrich Elmenhorsts. [1929].
Nr.10. Händel, G. F. Deutsche Arie für Sopran. Das zitternde Glänzen der spielenden Wellen. [1929].
Nr.11. Händel, G. F. Konzert-Arie für Sopran (Tenor). Preis der Tonkunst. [1929].
Nr.12. Telemann, G. P. Ausgewählte Lieder für eine Singstimme und Generalbass. [1929].
Nr.13–14. [Scholze, J. S.] . . . Sperontes. [Pseud.]. Singende Muse an der Pleisse . . . Heft 1–2. [1930].
Nr.15. Goerner, J. V. . . . Ausgewählte Neue Oden und Lieder für eine Singstimme und Generalbass . . . [1930].
Nr.16. Schütz, H. [Madrigali Lib.1, No.17, 13]. Zwei fünfstimmige Madrigale. [1930?].
Nr.17. Schütz, H. [Liebster, sagt in süssen Schmerzen]. Liebster. [1930].
Nr.18. Händel, G. F. Pastorella, vagha bella. [1933?].
Nr.19. Gletle, J. M. . . . Wer da will frisch und gesund auf Erden länger elben. [1939].
Nr.20. Händel, G. F. Meine Selle hört in Sehen. [1939].

ORGANUM. 3. Reihe. Kammermusik. Nr.1– . Leipzig, F. Kistner & C. F. W. Siegel, [cop. 1924–].
No.1– .
Vol.35– , ed. by Hans Albrecht.
Contents:
Nr.1. Corelli, A. Sonata da chiesa a tre. Op.III, Nr.4, H-moll (1689) für 2 Violinen, Violoncello, und Cembalo. [1924].
Nr.2. Corelli, A. Kammersonate. Op.V, Nr.11, E-dur (1700), für Violine und Cembalo. [1924].
Nr.3. Graff, J. Violinsonate. Op.1, Nr.3, D-dur (1718). [1924].
Nr.4. Vierdanck, J. Triosuite (1641) für 2 Violinen, Violoncello und Klavizimbel. [1924].
Nr.5. Erlebach, P. H. Sonate (E-moll) (1694) für Violine, Gambe (oder Violoncello) und Cembalo. [1924].
Nr.6. Buxtehude, D. Sonate (D-dur). Op.2 (1696), Nr.2, für Violine, Gambe (Violoncello) und Cembalo. [1924].
Nr.7. Telemann, G. P. Sonate (C-moll) für Flöte oder Violine mit Cembalobegleitung. (Forsetzung der "Methodischen Sonaten." 1732, Nr.2). [1924].
Nr.8. Telemann, G. P. Sonate (B-dur) für Flöte oder Violine mit Cembalobegleitung. (Forsetzung der "Methodischen Sonaten." 1732, Nr.4). [1924].
Nr.9. Krieger, J. P. Partie F-dur ["Feldmusik" 1704, No.III] für Bläser oder Streicher, bzw. Bläser und Streicher mit Cembalo [1925].
Nr.10. Krieger, J. P. Sonate (D-moll) für Violine, Gambe (Violoncello) und Cembalo. (Op.II, 1693, Nr.2). [1925].
Nr.11. Krieger, J. P. Sonate [F-dur] für 2 Violinen und Generalbass (Op.1, Nr.3. 1688). [1926].
Nr.12. Gebel, G. Triosonate für 2 Violinen (Flöten), Violoncell und Cembalo. [1926].
Nr.13. Gebel, G. Triosonate für 2 Violinen (Flöten), Violoncell und Cembalo. [1926].
Nr.14. Förster, C. Trio für 2 Violinen (Flöten), Violoncell und Cembalo. [1926].
Nr.15. Erlebach, P. H. Ouvertüren-Suite [C-dur] für Streicher (Ouvertüren, 1693, Nr.3). [1926].
Nr.16. Erlebach, P. H. Ouvertüren-Suite [D-moll] für Streicher (Ouvertüren, 1693, Nr.4). [1926].
Nr.17. Schnittelbach, N. Suite für Streicher und Cembalo. [1929].
Nr.18. Strungk, N. A. Triosonate für 2 Violinen, Gambe (Violoncell) und Orgel. [1929].
Nr.19. Theile, J. Suite für Violine, 2 Violen, Violoncell und Cembalo. [1929].
Nr.20. Reinken, J. A. Triosuite für 2 Violinen, Gambe (Violoncell) und Cembalo. [1929].
Nr.21. Buxtehude, D, Sonate [E-moll] (1696) für Violine, Gambe (Violoncell) und Cembalo. Op.1, Nr.7. [1924].
Nr.22. Pachelbel, J. Partie für 5 Streicher und Generalbass. [1929].
Nr.23. Sidow, S. P. Sonate mit Suite für Violine und Generalbass. [1929?].
Nr.24. Pachelbel, J. Kanon und Gigue für drei Violinen mit Generalbass. [1929].
Nr.25. Zachow, F. W. Kammertrio für Flöte (Oboe), Fagott und Generalbass. [1929].
Nr.26. Furchheim, J. W. . . . Suite für 5 Streicher und Generalbass . . . [1930].
Nr.27. Bleyer, N. . . . Variationen über "Est ce Mars" . . . [1930].
Nr.28. Walther, J. J. . . . Sonate mit Suite für Violine und Generalbass . . . [1930].
Nr.29. Mozart, L. . . . Konzert in D-dur . . . [1930].
Nr.30. Mozart, L. . . . Drei Divertimenti für zwei Violinen und Violoncello . . . [1930].
Nr.31. Schmierer, J. A. [Zodiacus musicus No.4] . . . Ouvertüren-Suite für Streicher und Cembalo. [1934].
Nr.32. Quantz, J. J. [Sonatas. Flöte (Oboe),

Violine und Klavier. D-dur. Trio-Sonate]. [1933?].
Nr.33. Böddecker, P. F. Sonata sopra "La monica." Für Violine, Bassoon und Violoncello. [1934].
Nr.34. Funck, David. Sonaten-Suite für vier Gamben. [193?].
Nr.35. Pleyel, Ignaz. Op.16, Nr.1. Sonate für Klavier, Flöte (Violine) und Violoncello. [1949].
Nr.36. Pleyel, Ignaz. Op.16, Nr.2. Sonate für Klavier, Flöte (Violine) und Violoncello. [1949].
Nr.37. Pleyel, Ignaz. Op.16, Nr.5. Sonate für Klavier, Flöte (Violine) und Violoncello. [1949].
Nr.38. Haydn, Michael. Quintett C-dur für 2 Violinen, 2 Violen und Violoncello. [1952].
Nr.39. Pleyel, Ignaz. Op.20, Nr.1. Quartett für Flöte, Violine, Viola und Violoncello. [1951].
Nr.40. Haydn, Michael. Quintett G-dur für 2 Violinen, 2 Violen und Violoncello. [1952].
Nr.41. Kozeluch, Leopold Anton. Klavier-Trio, G-moll. Op.12, Nr.3. [1952].
Nr.42. Haydn, Michael. Quintett F-dur für 2 Violinen, 2 Violen und Violoncello. [1952].
Nr.43. Gyrowetz, Adalbert. Divertissement für Klavier, Violine und Cello. Op.50. [1950].
Nr.44. Pleyel, Ignaz. Op.20, Nr.2. Quartett für Flöte, Violine, Viola und Violoncello. [1951].
Nr.45. Gassmann, Florian. Trio (Sonate) B-dur, für Flöte, Violine (ou 2 Violinen) und Viola. [1950].
Nr.46. Locatelli, Pietro. Trio-Sonate C-dur, Op.V, Nr.4, für 2 Violinen (2 Flöten) und Violoncello. [1951].
Nr.47. Pleyel, Ignaz. Op.20, Nr.3. Quartett für Flöte, Violine, Viola und Violoncello. [1951].
Nr.48. Gassmann, Florian. Trio (Sonate) G-dur für Flöte, Violine und Viola. [1951].
Nr.49. Eler, Andreas. Quartett. Streicher. Op.2, Nr.3. [1953].
Nr.50. Locatelli, Pietro. Trio-Sonate D-moll für 2 Violinen oder 2 Flöten und Generalbass. Op.V, Nr.5. [1952].
Nr.51. Gassmann, Florian. Trio (Sonate) Es-dur für Flöte (Violine), Violine und Viola. [1953].
Nr.52. Locatelli, Pietro. Trio Sonate G-dur für 2 Violinen oder 2 Flöten und Generalbass. Op.V, Nr.1. [1954].
Nr.53. Gassmann, Florian. (Trio (Sonate) C-dur für Flöte (Violine), Violine und Viola. [1954].
Nr.54. Kozeluch, L. A. Trio (Sonate), Op.12, Nr.2, für Violine, Violoncello und Cembalo.
Nr.55. Gassmann, Florian. Trio (Sonate) D-dur für Flöte (Violone), Violine und Viola. [1954].
Nr.56. Pepusch, Johann Christoph. Triosonate F-dur für 2 Violinen (2 Oboen oder 2 Querflöten) und Generalbass. [1960].
Nr.57. Pepusch, Johann Christoph. Triosonate D-dur für 2 Violinen oder 2 Oboen und Generalbass. [1960].
Nr.58. Gassmann, Florian. Trio (Sonate) A-dur für Flöte, Violine (oder 2 Violinen) und Viola. [1957].
Nr.59. Kozeluch, Leopold Anton. Op.12, Nr.1. Sonate für Klavier, Violine und Violoncello.
Nr.60. Erbach, Friedrich Karl, *Graf zu.* Divertissement melodieux D-dur für 2 Violinen und Generalbass. [1961].
Nr.61. Pepusch, Johann Christoph. Triosonate G-dur für 2 Violinen (2 Oboen oder 2 Querflöten) und Generalbass. [1961].
Nr.62. Krebs, Johann Ludwig. Triosonate H-moll für 2 Querflöten (oder 2 Violinen) und Generalbass. [1961].
Nr.63. Bach, Johann Christian. Quartett C-dur für zwei Querflöten (Violinen), Viola und Violoncello. [1961].
Nr.64. Bach, Johann Christian. Quartett D-dur für Querflöte I (Violine), Querflöte II (Oboe oder Violine), Viola und Violoncello. [1962].
Nr.65. Quantz, Johann Joachim. Triosonate A-moll für 2 Querflöten (Violinen) und Generalbass.
Nr.66. Bach, Johann Christian. Quartett G-dur für zwei Querflöten (Violinen), Viola und Violoncello.
Nr.67. Pepusch, Johann Christoph. Sonata da camera G-moll für Querflöte (Blockflöte, Violine oder Oboe), Violine (Oboe) und Generalbass.
Nr.68. Bach, Johann Christian. Quartett C-dur für zwei Querflöten, Violine und Violoncello.

ORGANUM. 4. Reihe. Orgelmusik. Nr.1– Leipzig, F. Kistner & C. F. W. Siegel, [1925–]. No.1– .
Contents:
Nr.1. Scheidemann, H. 15 Praeludien und Fugen. [1925].
Nr.2. Orgelmeister, I. [1925].
(a) Praetorius, Jakob. 3 Praeambeln.
(b) Schildt, Melchior. 2 Praeambeln.
(c) Decker, Johann. Praeambulum.
(d) Meyer, D. Praeludium.
(e) Olter, Marcus. 1 Canzon.
(f) Flor, Christian. 2 Praeludien.
Nr.3. Weckmann, M. 14 Praeludium, Fugen und Toccaten. [1925].
Nr.4. Böhm, G. 5 Praeludium, Fugen und Toccaten. [1925].
Nr.5. Orgelmeister, II. [1925].
(a) Reinken, Jean Adam. Toccata.
(b) Ritter, Christian. Sonatina.
Nr.6. Tunder, F. 4 Praeludien. [1925].
Nr.7. Orgelmeister, III. [1925].
(a) Brunckhorst, Arnold M. Praeludium.
(b) Kneller, Andreas. Praeludium und Fuge.
(c) Leyding, Georg Dietrich. 2 Praeludien.
Nr.8. Bruhns, N. 3 Praeludien und Fugen. [1925].
Nr.9. Lübeck, V. 4 Praeludien und Fugen. [1925].
Nr.10. Anonymi der Norddeutschen Schule. 6 Praeludium und Fugen. [1925].
Nr.11. Froberger, J. J. 10 Orgelwerke. [1929].
Nr.12. Pachelbel, J. Praeludien, Fantasien und Toccaten. [1929].
Nr.13. Pachelbel, J. Ciaconen, Fugen und Ricercari. [1929].
Nr.14. Pachelbel, J. Magnificat, Fugen. [1929].
Nr.15. Walther, J. G. Fünf ausgewählte Orgelstücke. [1930].

Nr.16. Zachow, F. W. . . . Drei Fugen für Orgel. [1930].
Nr.17. Krieger, J. . . . Ausgewählte Orgelstücke. [1930].
Nr.18. Strungk, N. A. Zwei Doppelfugen. [1938].
Nr.19. Kuhnau, Johann. 2 Praeludien und Fugen und 1 Toccata.
Nr.20. Siefert, Paul. 13 Fantasien a 3.
Nr.21. Orgelmeister, IV.
(a) Scheidt, Samuel. Toccata.
(b) Düben, Andreas. Praeambulum.
(c) Düben, Andreas. Praeludium.
(d) Abel, David. Praeludium.
(e) Abel, David. Praeludium pedaliter.
(f) Hasse, Peter. Praeambulum.
(g) Karges, Wilhelm. Capriccio.
(h) Karges, Wilhelm. Praeludium.
(i) Karges, Wilhelm. Fantasia.
(k) Hasse, Peter. Praeludium.
Nr.22. Seeger, Joseph. 8 Toccaten und Fugen für Orgel. [1949].

ORGANUM. 5. Reihe. Klaviermusik. Nr.1– . Leipzig, F. Kistner & C. F. W. Siegel, 1950– . No.1– .
Nr.1. Clementi, Muzio. Sonate C-dur. [1950].
Nr.2. Bach, Carl Philipp Emanuel. Sonate G-dur. [1951].
Nr.3. Dussek, Johann Ladislaus. Sonate G-moll, Op.10, Nr.2. [1950].
Nr.4. Clementi, Muzio. Sonate B-dur, Op.10. Nr.3. [1950].
Nr.5. Kozeluch, Leopold Anton. Sonate Es-dur, Op.51, Nr.2. [1950].
Nr.6. Dussek, Johann Ladislaus. Sonate Es-dur (The farewell), Op.44. [1951].
Nr.7. Wolf, Ernst Wilhelm. Zwei leichte Klaviersonaten D-moll und E-dur. [1951].
Nr.8. Hummel, Johann Nepomuk. Variationen über ein Thema aus Glucks "Armida." [1951].
Nr.9. Türk, Daniel Gottlob. Sonate E-moll für Klavier. [1951].
Nr.10. Cramer, Johann Baptist. Les menus plaisirs. [1951].
Nr.11. Forkel, Johann Nikolaus. Sonate D-dur für Klavier. [1952].
Nr.12. Dussek, Johann Ladislaus. Sonate B-dur Op.45, Nr.1. [1952].
Nr.13. Türk, Daniel Gottlob. Sonate C-dur für Klavier. [1952].
Nr.14. Steibelt, Daniel. Rondo C-dur für Klavier. [1953].
Nr.15. Clementi, Muzio. Sonate G-moll, Op,7, Nr.3. [1953].
Nr.16. Clementi, Muzio. Sonate F-moll, Op.14, Nr.3. [1953].
Nr.17. Forkel, Johann Nikolaus. Sonate D-moll für Klavier. [1953].
Nr.18. Clementi, Muzio. Sonate B-dur, Op.14, Nr.1. [1954].
Nr.19. Türk, Daniel Gottlob. Sonate A-moll für Klavier. [1954].
Nr.20. Clementi, Muzio. Sonate H-moll, Op.40, Nr.2. [1954].
Nr.21. Wolf, Ernst Wilhelm. Zwei leichte Sonaten in G-dur und F-dur. [1954].
Nr.22. Dussek, Johann Ladislaus. Sonate C-moll, Op.35, Nr.3. [1954].
Nr.23. Kozeluch, Leopold Anton. Sonate D-moll, Op.51, Nr.3. [1958].
Nr.24. Türk, Daniel Gottlob. Sonate D-dur. [1958].
Nr.25. Wolf, Ernst Wilhelm. Zwei leichte Klaviersonaten C-moll. [1958].
Nr.26. Hässler, Johann Wilhelm. Zwei leichte Klaviersonaten. [1960].
Nr.27. Bach, Wilhelm Friedemann. Solo-Konzert G-dur. [1960].
Nr.28. Hässler, Johann Wilhelm. Zwei leichte Klaviersonaten. Neue Folge. [1960].
Nr.29. Müthel, Johann Gottfried. Sonate B-dur mit sechs Variationen. [1961].
Nr.30. Hässler, Johann Wilhelm. Zwei leichte Klaviersonaten. Dritte Folge. [1961].
Nr.31. Bach, Wilhelm Friedemann. Fantasie C-dur.

DIE ORGEL. Ausgewählte Werke zum praktischen Gebrauch erscheint in zwei Reihen. Leipzig, F. Kistner & C. F. W. Siegel, 1957– . No.1– .
Contents:
Reihe I: Werke des 20. Jahrhunderts.
Nr.1. Schindler, Walter. Kleine Toccata für die Orgel über den Choral "Ein feste Burg ist unser Gott."
Nr.2. Grabner, Hermann. Media vita in morte sumus. Präludium, Passacaglia und Fuge über die gleichnamige Antiphon für Orgel. Op.24.
Nr.3. Schindler, Walter. Präludium und Ricercare für Orgel über den 3. Psalmton. Gross ist der Herr und hochberühmt in dei Stadt unseres Gottes auf seinem heiligen Berge.
Nr.4. Schindler, Walter. Partita über den Choral "Nun ruhen alle Wälder."
Nr.5. Grabner, Hermann. Der 66. Psalm, "Jauchzt, alle Lande, Gott zu Ehren," für Orgel.
Nr.6. Bossler, Kurt. Heut singt die liebe Christenheit. Choralpartita für Orgel.
Nr.7. Grabner, Hermann. Meditationen für Orgel über ein geistliches Lied von J. S. Bach.
Reihe II: Werke alter Meister.
Nr.1. Homilius, Gottfr. August. Fünf Choralbearbeitungen. Hrsg. von Georg Feder.
Nr.2. Homilius, Gottfr. August. Sechs Choralvorspiele. Hrsg. von Georg Feder.
Nr.3. Krieger, Johann. Präludiem und Fugen. Hrsg. von Friedr. Wilhelm Riedel.
Nr.4. Bölsche, Jakob. Präambulum; Heidorn, Peter. Fuga (um 1683). Hrsg. von Friedr. Wilhelm Riedel.
Nr.5. Poglietti, Alessandro. Zwölf Ricercare. 1. Folge. Nr.1–6. Hrsg. von Friedr. Wilhelm Riedel.
Nr.6. Poglietti, Alessandro. Zwölf Ricercare. 2. Folge. Nr.7–12. Hrsg. von Friedr. Wilhelm Riedel.
Nr.7. Kellner, Johann Peter. Ausgewählte Orgelwerke. Hrsg. von Georg Feder.
Nr.8. Muffat, Gottlieb. Toccata, Fuge und

Capriccio. Hrsg. von Friedr. Wilhelm Riedel.
Nr.9. Italienische und süddeutsche Orgelstücke des frühen 17. Jahrhunderts. Hrsg. von Lydia Schierning.
Nr.10. Muffat, Gottlieb. Drei Toccaten. Hrsg. von Friedr. Wilhelm Riedel.
Nr.11. Erbach, Christian. Drei Introitus mit Versus. Hrsg. von Wilhelm Krumbach.
Nr.12. Strungk, Delphin. Zwei Choralfantasien. Hrsg. von Wilhelm Krumbach.
Nr.13. Muffat, Gottlieb. Drei Toccaten und Capriccios. Neue Folge. Hrsg. von Friedr. Wilhelm Riedel.
Nr.14. Kirnberger, Johann Philipp. Orgelchoräle. Hrsg. von Friedr. Wilhelm Reidel.
Nr.15. Leiding, Georg Dietrich. Präludium in B. Hrsg. von Friedr. Wilhelm Riedel.
Nr.16. Muffat, Gottlieb. Zwölf kleine Präludien. Hrsg. von Friedr. Wilhelm Riedel.
Nr.17. Muffat, Gottlieb. Sechs Fugen. Hrsg. von Friedr. Wilhelm Riedel.
Nr.18. Krebs, Joh. Ludw. Ausgewählte Orgelwerke. 1. Folge. Hrsg. von Karl Tittel.
Nr.19. Briegel, Wolfgang Carl. Acht Fugen durch die Kirchentöne und Fuga super "Dies sind die heiligen zehn Gebot." Hrsg. von Wilhelm Krumbach.
Nr.20. Krebs, Joh. Ludw. Ausgewählte Orgelwerke. 2. Folge. Hrsg. von Karl Tittel.

ORGELMUSIK STEIRISCHER KOMPONISTEN. Hrsg. von Otto Siegl. Wien, Österreichischer Bundesverlag.
v.1– .
Contents:
Bloch, Woldemar. Ricercar über den Namen Bach.
Eisel, Günther. Kleine Fuge.
Kögler, Walter. Choralfantasie über "O Haupt voll Blut und Wunden."
Marckhl, Erich. Zwei kleine Choraltrios über: 1. Puer natus in Bethlehem; 2. Vom Himmel hoch.
Michl, Artur. Choralvorspiel über "Wie schön leuchtet uns der Morgenstern."
Siegl, Otto. Toccata.

Orgelspiel im Kirchenjahr, *see* Rohr, Heinrich. Orgelspiel im Kirchenjahr.

Orgelvorspiele, *see* Keller, Hermann. Orgelvorspiele.

. . . ORGELWERKE. ALTBÖHMISCHER MEISTER. Hrsg. von Rudolf Quoika . . . Wiesbaden, Breitkopf & Härtel, G.m.b.H., [cop.1949].
3v. (Edition Breitkopf. No.5925–5927).
Score for organ.
Contents:
Vol.1. Gottlob Czernozorsky.
Vol.2. Josef Seeger.
Vol.3. Johann Zach; Franz Xavier Brixi.

ORGUE ET LITURGIE. Paris, Les Éditions Musicales de la Schola Cantorum et de la Procure Générale de Musique, [192?–].
v.1– .
Editors: 192? : N. Dufourcq, F. Raugel, and J. de Valois.
A collection of organ music, some for organ with various other instruments.
Contents:
Vol.1. Langlais, Jean. Pâques [de Pachelbel]. Établi par N. Dufourcq et F. Raugel.
Vol.2. Schlick, A. [et al.]. L'orgue en Europe aus XVIe et XVIIe siècles. Établi par N. Pierront [et al.].
Vol.3. Palestrina. 8 Ricercari dans les 8 tons.
Vol.4. Grunenwald, J. J. Noël [de Scheidt].
Vol.5. Reboulot, Antoine. Ricercari de Luzzaschi.
Vol.6. Couperin, Louis. L'oeuvre d'orgue.
Vol.7. Bach, J. S. [Paraphrases extraites du recueil intitule l'Autograph de Leipzig].
Vol.8. Hymnes et antiennes. Établi par N. Pierront et N. Dufourcq.
Vol.9. Orgue et cuivres: G. Litaize, Cortège [et] H. Gagnebin. Sonata. Score and 2 parts: trumpets and trombones.
Vol.10. Muffat, Georg [et al.]. Toccata. Établi par N. Pierront [et al.].
Vol.11. Notre Dame. Établi par J. de Valois et J. Pagot.
Vol.12. Fauchard, A. Le mystère de Noël.
Vol.13. Campion, F. Pièces pour le luth.
Vol.14. À la Vierge.
Vol.15. Bruhns, N. [et al.]. La fugue au XVIIIe siècle.
Vol.16. Lebègue, N. A. Noëls variés.
Vol.17. Lübeck, V. 6 Préludes et fugues.
Vol.18. Au Saint-Sacrement: Boulnois, M. 3 Pièces sur des thèmes de la Fête du Saint-Sacrement; Girod, M. L. Triptyque sur l'hymne sacris solemnis.
Vol.19. Viens Sauveur des paiens.
Vol.20. Litaize, G. [et al.]. La fugue au XXe siècle.
Vol.21. Brahms, J. 12 Préludes de chorals.
Vol.22. Chacones et passacailles.
Vol.23. Pièces funèbres.
Vol.24. Notre Père.
Vol.25. Varia I.
Vol.26. Frescobaldi, G. 12 Toccatas.
Vol.27–28. Daquin, L. C. Nouveau livre de Noëls.
Vol.29. Deux grand-messes: N. Le Begue and G. Litaize.
Vol.30, 34. Cabezon, A. de. [Oeuvres]. 2v.
Vol.31. Agincourt, F. d'. [Pièces d'orgue].
Vol.32, 35. Frescobaldi, G. A. 12 Fantaisies.
Vol.33. L'orgue néo-classique.
Vol.34. *See* Vol.30.
Vol.35. *See* Vol.32.
Vol.36. Lalande, M. R. de. Suite factice.
Vol.37. Bach, W. F. Les oeuvres pour orgue.
Vol.38. Le tombeau de González.
Vol.39. Le Jeune, C. 3 Fantaisies instrumentales.
Vol.40. Noëls variés.
Vol.41. Frescobaldi, G. Toccatas. IIe fasc.
Vol.42. Litaize, Gaston. Messe basse pour tous les temps.
Vol.43. Babou. 13 Pièces.
Vol.44. Tournemire, C. Symphonie sacrée pour orgue.
Vol.45. Bach, W. F. 8 Fugues sans pedale.

Vol.46. Varia II.
Vol.47. Bermudo, J. Oeuvres d'orgue.
Vol.48. Préludes à l'introit.
Vol.49. Tomás de Santa Maria, Father. Oeuvres.
Vol.50–51. Corrette, G. Messe du 8e ton pour l'orgue.
Vol.52. Offertories.
Vol.53. Charpentier, M. A. Transcriptions pour orgue.
Vol.54. Tournemire, C. Triple choral.
Vol.55–56, 58–59. Raison, A. Premier livre d'orgue. 2v.
Vol.57. Elévations.
Vol.58–59. *See* Vol.55–56.

Oriana, The triumphs of, *see* The triumphs of Oriana.

Orlando de Lassus, *see* Lassus, Orland de.

OSLO. UNIVERSITET. BIBLIOTEK.
Norsk musikksamling. Oslo, Universitetsbiblioteket, 1953– .
No.1– .
Contents:
Nr.1. Berlin, Johan Daniel. Sonatina for Klaver. Utgitt av Magne Elvestrand. 1953. (Sonatina for piano. Ed. by Magne Elvestrand).
Nr.2. Bjercke, Ole. Romeriks-svite. Fem danser. Arrangert av Magne Elvestrand. 1955. (Suite from Romerike. Five dances. Arr. by Magne Elvestrand).
Nr.3. Lindeman, Ludvig Mathias. Aeldre og nyere fjeldmelodier. Samlede og bearbeidede for pianoforte. Faksimileutgave. Med etterord og merknader av O. M. Sandvik og register av Øystein Gaukstad. 1962.

Othmayr, Kaspar, 1515–1553. Ausgewählte Werke, *see* Das Erbe deutscher Musik. Erste Reihe. Vol.16, 26.

Oudnederlandse meesters, voor het orgel, *see* Peeters, Flor. Oudnederlandse meesters, voor het orgel.

PACELLI, ASPRILIO, ca.1570–1623.
Opera omnia. Studio e cura di Matteo Glinski. Roma, Edizioni de Santis, [cop.1946–].
v.1– .
Contents:
Vol.1. Madrigali. Trascritti in notazione moderna e messi in partitura a cura di Matteo Glinski. [cop.1946].

PACHELBEL, CARL THEODORUS, 1690–1750.
Magnificat for double chorus and organ. Ed. by Hans T. David. New York, New York Public Library, 1937.
p.1– .

Padovano, Annibale, *see* Annibale Padovano.

Paesler, Karl, 1863–1942, ed. Fundamentbuch von Hans von Constanz, *see* Buchner, Hans (von Constanz). Fundamentbuch.

PAGE, JOHN, ca.1750–1812. ed.
Harmonia sacra; a collection of anthems in score, selected for cathedral and parochial churches, from the most eminent masters of the 16., 17., and 18. centuries. London, 1800.
3v.
Suppl. to the collections of Boyce and Arnold.
Contents (from *Grove's Dictionary of music and musicians*, 1916, Vol.3, p.596):
Vol.1.
Verse anthems.
Croft. Blessed is the people.
Croft. Deliver us, O Lord.
Weldon. I will lift up mine eyes.
Boyce. Let my complaint.
Purcell. Out of the deep.
Kent. O Lord our governor.
Croft. Praise the Lord.
Greene. Ponder my words.
Clark. The Lord is my strength.
Dupuis. The Lord, even the most.
Kent. The Lord is my shepherd.
Arnold. Who is this that cometh.

Full anthems with verse.
Battishill. Call to remembrance.
Aldrich. God is our hope.
Stroud. Hear my prayer.
Dupuis. I cried unto the Lord.
Goldwin. I will sing.
Mason. Lord of all power.
Reynolds. My God, my God.
King. O be joyful.
Attwood. Teach me, O Lord.

Full anthems.
Boyce. Burial service.
Farrant. Lord for thy tender.
Tucker. O give thanks.
Richardson. O how amiable.
King. Unto Thee, O Lord.

Vol.2.
Verse anthems.
Handel. As pants the heart.
Purcell. Blessed is he.
Clark. Bow down thine ear.
Battishill. How long wilt Thou.
Greene. Hear my crying.
Purcell. I was glad.
S. Wesley. I said, I will take heed.
King. I will always give thanks.
C. Wesley. My soul hath patiently.
Croft. O Lord, Thou hast searched.
Marcello. O Lord our governer.
Goldwin. O praise God.
Hine. Rejoice in the Lord.
Greene. Save me, O God.
Croft. The Lord is king.
Greene. The Lord is my strength.

Full anthems with verse.
Nares. Blessed be the Lord God.
Blake. I have set God.
Baildon. Behold, how good.
Travers. Keep, we beseech Thee.
Wood. Lord of all power.
Clark. O Lord God of my salvation.
Blow. Sing we merrily.

Croft. Sing praises to the Lord.
King. The Lord is full.

Vol.3.
Verse anthems.
Holmes. Arise and shine.
Handel. Behold, I tell you.
Linley. Bow down thine ear.
Henley. Hear my prayer.
Greene. I will alway give thanks.
Boyce. I will magnify Thee.
Hine. I will magnify Thee.
Greene. O look down from Heaven.
Handel. There were shepherds.
Croft. The Lord is my light.
Handel. Thou art gone up on high.

Full anthems with verse.
Battishill. Behold, how good.
Handel. Behold the Lamb of God.
Battishill. I will magnify Thee.
Handel. Moses and the children.
Busby. O God, Thou art my God.
Banks. O Lord, grant the King.

Full anthems.
Greene. Bow down thine ear.
Battishill. Deliver us, O God.
Tye. From the depth, I called.
Rogers. Lord, who shall dwell.
Marsh. O Lord, who hast taught.
Marenzio. Save Lord, hear us.

PALÉOGRAPHIE MUSICALE. Les principaux manuscrits de Chant-Grégorien, Ambrosien, Mozarabe, Gallican, publiés en fac-similés phototypiques par les Bénédictins de Solesmes. (VIII ff. sous la direction de Dom André Mocquereau; XIV sous la direction de Dom Joseph Gajard). Solesmes, Imprimerie St. Pierre (Tournay Société Saint-Jean l'Évangéliste), 1889– .
v.1– . facsims., music.
Quarterly; publication suspended July 1914–Nov. 1921. (Tome 11, No.103 (July/Oct.1914) published Dec.1921).
Tome 1–14 also called Année [1]–39.
Tome 1–16 numbered 1–192.
1901–date, imprint reads: Soc. de Saint-Jean l'Évangéliste; Desclée, Lefebure & Cie., Tournai, Belgium (Oct.1907–date: . . .Desclée & Cie . . .).
Editors: July 1904–30, A. Mocquereau; 1931–date, J. Gajard.
Contents:
Bd.I. Le Codex 339 de la Bibliothèque de Saint-Gall. Antiphonale missarum Sancti Gregorii. 1889.
Bd.II/III. Le répons-graduel Justus ut Palma. 1891–92.
Bd.IV. Codex 121 de la Bibl. d'Einsiedeln. Antiphonale missarum Sancti Gregorii. 1894.
Bd.V/VI. Antiphonarium Ambrosianum du Musée Britannique. 1896, 1900.
Bd.VII/VIII. Antiphonarium tonale missarum. Codex H. 159 de la Bibl. de l'École de Médecine de Montpellier. 1907, 1901–1905.
Bd.IX. Antiphonaire monastique. Codex 601 de la Bibl. Capitulaire de Lucques. 1906.
Bd.X. Antiphonale missarum Sancti Gregorii. Codex 239 de la Bibl. de Laon. 1909.
Bd.XI. Antiphonale missarum Sancti Gregorii. Codex 47 de la Bibl. de Chartres. 1912.
Bd.XII. Antiphonaire monastique. Codex F 160 de la Bibl. de la Cathédrale de Worcester. 1922.
Bd.XIII. Graduel de Saint-Yrieix. Codex 903 de la Bibl. Nationale de Paris. 1925.
Bd.XIV. Graduel Bénéventain. Codex 10673 de la Bibl. Vaticana. 1931.
Bd.XV. Le Codex VI-34 de la Bibl. Capitulaire de Bénévent, XI–XIIe siècle, Graduel Bénéventain avec Prosaire et Tropaire. 1953.
Bd.XVI. Le manuscrit du Mont-Renaud. Xe siècle. Graduel et Antiphonaire de Noyen. 1955–1956.
Bd.XVII. Fragments des manuscrits de Chartres. 1958.

PALÉOGRAPHIE MUSICALE. Sér.2. (Monumentale). [Tome] 1–2.
Tournay (Belgique): Société de Saint-Jean l'Évangéliste, Desclée & Cie., 1900–1924.
2v.
Editor: [Tome] 2, André Mocquereau.
Contents:
Tome 1. Antiphonale du B. Hartker. 1900.
Tome 2. Cantatorium de Saint-Gall. Codex 359. Bibl. de Saint-Gall. 1924.

PALESTRINA, GIOVANNI BATTISTA PIERLUIGI DA, d.1594.
Giovanni Pierluigi da Palestrinas Werke. Erste kritisch durchgesehene Gesammtausgabe. Hrsg. von Th. de Witt, J. N. Rauch, Fr. Espagne, Fr. Commer, F. X. Haberl. Leipzig, Breitkopf & Härtel, [1862–1907].
33v.
Vol.1–6 of the Motetten are not designated as part of the Werke, being originally a separate publication.
The 27 Responsoria included in Bd.32 as doubtful works were composed by Ingegneri.
Contents:
Bd.1. 33 Fünf- , sechs- und siebenstimmige Motetten.
Fünfstimmige Motetten.
1. O admirabile commercium.
2. Stella quam viderant magi.
3. O Antoni eremita.
4. Senex puerum portabat. (prima pars).
Hodie beata Virgo Maria. (secunda pars)
5. Suscipe verbum Virgo Maria. (prima pars).
Paries quidem filium. (secunda pars).
6. Alleluja! tulerunt Dominum.
7. Crucem sanctam subiit.
8. O beata et gloriosa Trinitas. (prima pars).
O verra summa sempiterna Trinitas. (secunda pars).
9. Ego sum panis vivus. (prima pars).
Panis quem ego dabo. (secunda pars).
10. Puer qui natus est.

11. Beatae Mariae Magdalenae.
12. Sancte Paule apostole.
13. Beatus Laurentius orabat.
14. Hodie nata est beata Virgo.
15. O beatum virum.
16. Venit Michael archangelus.
17. O beatum pontificem.
18. Deux qui dedisti legem.
19. Lapidabant Stephanum.
20. Hic est discipulus ille.
21. Sicut lilium inter spinas.
22. Quam pulchri sunt gressus.
23. Unus ex duobus.
24. Cum pervenisset beatus Andreas.

Sechsstimmige Motetten.

25. Viri Galilaei quid statis. (prima pars).
    Ascendit Deus in jubilatione. (secunda pars).
26. Dum complerentur dies pentecostes. (prima pars).
    Dum ergo essent in unum discipuli. (secunda pars).
27. Pulchra es, O Maria Virgo.
28. Solve jubente Deo. (prima pars).
    Quodcumque ligaveris. (secunda pars).
29. Vidi turbam magnam. (prima pars).
    Et mones angeli stabant. (secunda pars).
30. O magnum mysterium. (prima pars).
    Quem vidistis pastores. (secunda pars).
31. O Domine Jesu Christi.

Siebenstimmige Motetten.

32. Tu es Petrus.
33. Virgo prudentissima. (prima pars).
    Maria Virgo. (secunda pars).

Bd.2. 29 Fünf- , sechs- und achtstimmige Motetten.

Fünfstimmige Motetten

1. O Virgo simul et mater.
2. Memor esto verbi tui servo tuo.
3. Corona aurea. (prima pars).
   Domine praevenisti eum. (secunda pars).
4. In illo tempore egressus.
5. O sacrum convivium.
6. Coenantibus illis accepit Jesus.
7. Derelinquat impius viam.
8. Ascendo ad patrem meum. (prima pars).
   Ego rogabo patrem. (secunda pars).
9. Homo quidam fuit.
10. Canite tuba in Sion. (prima pars).
    Rorate coeli. (secunda pars).
11. Exi cito in plateas.
12. Circuire. (prima pars). (Angeli Petraloysii).
    In hac cruce te invenit. (secunda pars).
13. Gaude Barbara beata. (prima pars).
    Gaude quia meruisti. (secunda pars).
14. Domine Pater. (Syllae Petraloysii).
15. Confitebor tibi Domine. (Rodulfi Petraloysii).
16. Peccantem me quotidie.
17. Dominus Jesus in qua nocte.

Sechsstimmige Motetten.

18. Tribularer si nescirem. (prima pars).
    Secundum multitudinem dolorum. (secunda pars).
19. Veni Domine et noli tardare. (prima pars).
    Excita Domine. (secunda pars).
20. Hierusalem, cito veniet salus tua. prima pars).
    Ego enim sum Dominus. (secunda pars).
21. Beata Barbara. (prima pars).
    Gloriosam mortem. (secunda pars).
22. Sancta et immaculata Virginitas. (prima pars).
    Benedicta tu. (secunda pars).
23. Cantabo Domino in vita mea. (prima pars).
    Deficiant peccatores. (secunda pars).
24. Tu es Petrus et super hanc petram. (prima pars).
    Quodcumque ligaveris. (secunda pars).
25. Nunc dimittis servum tuum. (Syllae Petraloysii).

Achtstimmige Motetten.

26. Confitebor tibi Domine. (prima pars).
    Notas facite in populis. (secunda pars).
27. Laudate pueri Dominum. (prima pars).
    Quis sicut Dominus Deus. (secunda pars).
28. Domine in virtute tua. (prima pars).
    Magna est gloria ejus. (secunda pars).
29. Laudate Dominum omnes gentes.

Bd.3. 33 Fünf- , sechs- und achtstimmige Motetten.

Fünfstimmige Motetten.

1. Pater noster.
2. Ave Maria.
3. Cantantibus organis. (prima pars).
   Biduanis ac triduanis. (secunda pars).
4. Caro mea vere est cibus.
5. Angelus Domini descendit de coelo. (prima pars).
   Et introeuntes in momentum. (secunda pars).
6. Congrega, Domine. (prima pars).
   Afflige opprimentes nos. (secunda pars).
7. Inclytae sanctae virginis Catherinae.
8. Fuit homo missus a Deo. (prima pars).
   Erat Joannes in deserto. (secunda pars).
9. O lux et decus. (prima pars).
   O singulare praesidium. (secunda pars).
10. Quid habes Hester. (prima pars).
    Vidi te Domine (secunda pars).
11. Tradent enim vos.
12. Sanctificavit Dominus.
13. O quam metuendus.
14. Jubilate Deo, omnis terra. (prima pars).
    Laudate nomen ejus. (secunda pars).
15. Omnipotens sempiterne Deus.
16. O sancte praesul Nicolae. (prima pars).
    Gaude praesul optime. (secunda pars).
17. Domine Deus, qui conteris. (prima pars).
    Tu Domine. (secunda pars).
18. Manifesto vobis veritatem. (prima pars).
    Pax vobis, noli timere. (secunda pars).

Sechsstimmige Motetten.

19. Susanna ab improbis. (prima pars).
    Postquam autem. (secunda pars).
20. Cum ortus fuerit.

21. Rex pacificus.
22. Haec dies, quam fecit Dominus.
23. Columna es immobilis.
24. Judica me Deus, et discerne.
25. Accepit Jesus calicem.
26. O bone Jesu.
27. Deus qui ecclesiam tuam.

Achtstimmige Motetten.

28. Surge illuminare Hierusalem.
29. Lauda Sion.
30. Veni Sancte Spiritus.
31. Ave Regina coelorum.
32. Hodie Christus natus est.
33. Jubilate Deo.

Bd.4. 50 Fünfstimmige Motetten.

1. Osculetur me osculo oris sui.
2. Trahe me post Te.
3. Nigra sum, sed formosa.
4. Vineam meam non custodivi.
5. Si ignoras te, o pulchra inter mulieres.
6. Pulchrae sunt genae tuae.
7. Fasciculus myrrhae.
8. Ecce tu pulcher es, dilecte mi.
9. Tota pulchra es amica mea.
10. Vulnerasti cor meum.
11. Sicut lilium inter spinas.
12. Introduxit me Rex in cellam.
13. Laeva ejus sub capite meo.
14. Vox dilecti mei.
15. Surge, propera amica mea.
16. Surge amica mea, speciosa mea.
17. Dilectus meus mihi et ego illi.
18. Surgem et circuibo civitatem.
19. Adjuro vos, filiae Hierusalem.
20. Caput ejus aurum optimum.
21. Dilectus meus descendit in hortum suum.
22. Pulchra es amica mea.
23. Quae est ista.
24. Descendi in hortum meum.
25. Quam pulchri sunt gressus tui.
26. Duo ubera tua.
27. Quam pulchra es et quam decora.
28. Guttur tuum sicut.
29. Veni, veni dilecte mi.

Liber Quintus.

1. Laetus Hyperboream.
   O patruo pariterque.
2. Paucitas dierum meorum.
   Manus tuae Domine.
3. Tempus est, ut revertar.
   Nisi ego abiero.
4. Domine secundum actum meum.
5. Ave Trinitatis sanctuarium.
6. Parce mihi Domine.
   Peccavi, peccavi.
7. Orietur stella.
8. Aegipte noli flere.
9. Ardena est cor meum.
10. Sic Deus dilexit mundum.
11. Surge Petre.
12. Apparuit caro suo.
13. Ecce merces Sanctorum.
14. Videns secundus.
15. Pex Melchior.
16. Ave Regina coelorum.
17. Gaude gloriosa.
18. Exultate Deo.
19. Tribulationes civitatum. Peccavimus.
20. Surge sancte Dei.
    Ambula sancte Dei.
21. Salve Regina.
    Eia ergo advocata.

Bd.5. 57 Vierstimmige Motetten.

1. In Festo Nativitatis Domini. Dies sanctificatus.
2. In Festo S. Stephani. Lapidabant Stephanum.
3. In Festo S. Joannis Evang. Valde honorandus est.
4. In Die Circumcisionis Domini. Magnum haer ditatis mysterium.
5. In Epiphania Domini. Tribus miraculis.
6. In Festo Purificationis B. Mariae. Hodie beata Virgo Maria.
7. In Festo Annuntiationis B. Mariae. Ave Maria gratia plena.
8. In Festo Resurrectionis Domini. Jesus junxit se discipulis.
9. In Festo Ascensionis Domini. O Rex gloriae.
10. In Die Pentecostes. Loquebantur variis linguis.
11. In Festo S.S. Trinitatis. Benedicta sit Sancta Trinitas.
12. In Festo Corporis Christi. Lauda Sion Salvatorem.
13. In Festo S. Joannis Baptistae. Fuit homo missus a Deo.
14. In Festo S. Petri Apostoli. Tu es pastor ovium.
15. In Festo S. Pauli Apostoli. Magnus Sanctus Paulus.
16. In Festo visitationis B. Mariae. Surge, propera amica mea.
17. In Festo S. Mariae Magdalenae. In diebus illis.
18. In Festo S. Laurentii. Beatus Laurentius.
19. In Festo Assumptionis B. Mariae. Quae est ista.
20. In Decollatione S. Joannis Baptistae. Misso Herodes spiculatore.
21. In Festo Nativitatis B. Mariae. Nativitas tua.
22. In Festo S. Crucis. Nos autem gloriari.
23. In Festo Omnium Sanctorum. Salvator mundi salva nos.
24 In Festo S. Martini. O quantus luctus.
25. In Festo Praesentationis B. Mariae. Congratulamini mihi omnes.
26. In Festo S. Caeciliae. Dum aurora finem daret.
27. In Festo S. Andreae. Doctor bonus.
28. In Festo Conceptionis B. Mariae. Quam pulchri sunt.

Commune Sanctorum.

29. In Festo Apostolorum. Tollite jugum meum.
30. In Festo Evangelistarum. Isti sunt viri sancti.
31. In Festo unius Martyris. Hic est vere Martyr.
32. In Festo plurimorum Martyrum. Gaudent in coelis.
33. In Festo Confess. Pontificum. Iste est qui ante Deum.

34. In Festo Confess. Pontificum. Beatus vir qui suffert.
35. In Festo Virginum. Veni sponsa Christ.
36. In dedicatione templi. Exaudi Domine.

Liber Secundus.

1. Domine quando veneris.
   Commissa mea.
2. Heu mihi Domine.
   Anima mea turbata.
3. Super flumina Babilonis.
4. Ecce nunc benedicite Dominum.
5. Ad Te levavi oculos meos.
   Miserere nostri Domine.
6. Ad Dominum cum tribularer.
   Sagittae potentis.
7. Fundamenta ejus.
   Numquid Sion dicet.
8. Quid vidistime Thoma.
9. Ego sum panis vivus.
10. Sicut cervus desiderat.
    Sitivit anima mea.
11. Ave Regina cóelorum.
    Gaude gloriosa.
12. Alma redemptoris mater.
    Tu quae genuisti natura mirante.
13. Salve Regina. Eja ergo advocata nostra.
14. Ave Maria gratia plena.
15. Haec dies quam fecit.
16. Confitemini Domino.
17. Pueri Hebraeorum.
18. Sub tuum praesidium.
19. Adoramus Te Christe.
20. Surrexit pastor bonus.
21. Gloriosi principes.

Bd.6. 36 Fünf- , sechs- und achtstimmige Motetten.

Achtstimmige Motetten.

1. Sub tuum praesidium.
2. Fratres ego enim accepa.
3. Caro mea vere est cibus.
4. Hic est panis. (secunda pars).

Fünfstimmige Motetten.

5. Tu es pastor ovium.
6. Quodcumque ligaveris. (secunda pars).

Sechsstimmige Motetten.

7. Assumpta est Maria.
8. Quae est ista. (secunda pars).
9. Cum autem esset Stephanus.
10. Positis autem genibus. (secunda pars).
11. Hic est beatissimus Evangelista.
12. Hic est discipulus ille. (secunda pars).
13. Responsum accepit Simeon.
14. Cum inducerent puerum Jesum. (secunda pars).
15. Tradent enum vos in conciliis.

Achtstimmige Motetten.

16. Surrexit pastor bonus.
17. Stenim pascha nostrum. (secunda pars).
18. Jesus junxit se discipulis.
19. Et increpavit eos dicens. (secunda pars).
20. Spiritus Sanctus replevit.
21. Hodie gloriosa semper Virgo Maria.
22. Regina mundim hodie. (secunda pars).
23. Et ambulabunt gentes in lumine.
24. Stabat Mater dolorosa.
25. Ave mundi spes, Maria.
26. Beata es, Virgo Maria.
27. Ave Maria, gratia plena.
28. O quam suavis est, Domine, spiritus tuus.
29. Disciplinam et sapientiam docuit eos Dominus.
30. O bone Jesu, exaudi me.
31. O Domine Jesu Christe.
32. Expurgate vetus fermentum.
33. Pater noster, qui es in coelis.
34. Salve Regina, mater misericordiae.
35. Alma redemptoris Mater.
36. Regina coeli, laetare.

Bd.7. 36 Vier- , sechs- , acht- und zwölfstimmige Motetten.

Sechsstimmige Motetten.

1. Salve Regina, mater misericordiae.
2. Eja ergo, advocata nostra. (secunda pars).

Achtstimmige Motetten.

3. O pretiosum et admirandum convivium.
4. O admirabile commercium.
5. Videntes stellam Magi.

Zwölfstimmige Motetten.

6. Laudate Dominum in tympanis.
7. Ecce nunc benedicite Dominum.
8. Nunc dimittis servum tuum, Domine.

Vierstimmige Motetten.

9. Ascendens Christus in altum.
10. Domine secundum actum meum.
11. Ne recorderis peccata mea, Domine.
12. Ecce nunc benedicite Dominum.
13. Deus, qui animae famuli tui Gregorii.
14. Innocentes pro Christo intantes.
15. Princeps gloriosissime, Michael Archangele.
16. Gaude, Barbara beata.

Achtstimmige Motetten.

17. Alma redemptoris Mater.
18. Tria sunt munera pretiosa.
19. Fili, non te frangant labores.
20. Ecce veniet dies illa. (secunda pars).
21. Haec dies, quam fecit Dominus.
22. Lauda Sion Salvatorem.
23. Victimae paschali laudes.
24. Victimae paschali laudes.
25. Veni Sancte Spiritus.
26. Ave Regina coelorum.

Zwölfstimmige Motetten.

27. Stabat Mater dolorosa.

Achtstimmige Motetten.

28. Apparuit gratia Dei.
29. Dies sanctificatus illuxit nobis.
30. Haec est, dies praeclara.
31. Congratulamini mihi omnes.
32. Magnus Sanctus Paulus.
33. Sancte Paule Apostole. (secunda pars).
34. Nunc dimittis servum tuum.
35. Omnes gentes plaudite.
36. Victimae paschali laudes.

Bd.8. 45 Hymnen, hrsg. von F. Espagne.

1. In Adventu Domini. Conditor alme siderum.
2. In Nativitate et Circumcisione Domini. Christe redemptor omnium.
3. In Nativitate. Ad Laudes. A solis ortus cardine.

4. In Festo Ss. Innocentium. Salvete flores martyrum.
5. In Epiphania Domini. Hostis Herodes impie.
6. In Dominicis per annum. Lucis creator optime.
7. In Sabbatis. O lux beata, Trinitas.
8. In Dominicis Quadragesimae. Ad preces nostras.
9. In Dominica passionis et exaltatione S. Crucis. Vexilla regis prodeunt.
10. In Dominicis Tempore Paschali. Ad coenam agni providi.
11. In Ascensione Domini. Jesu, nostra redemptio.
12. In Festo Pentecostes. Veni Creator Spiritus.
13. In Festo Corporis Christi. Pange lingua gloriosi.
14. In Festo Cathedrae S. Petri. Quodcumque vinclis.
15. In Conversione et Commemoratione S. Pauli. Doctor egregie.
16. In Festo Beatae Virginis. Ave maris stella.
17. In Inventione S. Crucis. Vexilla regis prodeunt.
18. In Festo S. Joannis Baptistae. Ut queant laxis.
19. In Festa Apostolorum Petri et Pauli. Aurea luce.
20. In Festo S. Mariae Magdalenae. Lauda mater ecclesiae.
21. In Festo S. Petri ad Vincula. Petrus beatus.
22. In Festo Transfigurationis Domini. Quicumque Christum quaecitis.
23. In Festo S. Michaelis Archangeli. Tibi Christe, splendor patris.
24. In Festo Omnium Sanctorum. Christe redemptor omnium.
25. In Communi Apostolorum et Evangelistarum. Exultet coelum laudibus.
26. In Festo Apostolorum et Evangelistorum Tempore Paschali. Tristes erant Apostoli.
27. In Communi Unius Martyris. Deus tuorum militum.
28. In Festo Unius Martyris Tempore Paschali. Deus tuorum militum.
29. In Communi Plurimorum Martyrum. Sanctorum meritis.
30. In Festo Plurimorum Martyrum Tempore Paschali. Rex gloriose martyrum.
31. In Natali Confessorum. Iste confessor.
32. In Natalitiis Virginum et Martyrum. Jesu corona virginum.
33. In Festo Virginum et Martyrum Tempore Paschali. Jesu corona virginum.
34. In Festo Sanctarum Mulierum. Hujus obtentu.
35. In Festo Dedicationis Ecclesiae. Urbs beata Jerusalem.
36. In Festo S. Augustini. Magne pater Augustine.
37. In Festo S. Nicolai de Tolentino. Laudibus summis.
38. In Festo S. Antonii de Padua. En gratulemur hodie.
39. In Festo S. Francisci in primis vesperis. Proles de coelo prodiit.
40. In Festo S. Francisci in secundis vesperis. Decus morum, dux minorum.
41. In Quadragesima ad Completorium. Christe, qui lux es et dies.
42. In Festo S. Elisaei. Prima lux surgens.
43. In Festo S. Eliae. Nunc juvat celsi.
44. In Festo S. Alberti. Mensis Augusti.
45. In Festo S. Jacobi. Hymnus canoris personet.

Bd.9. 68 Offertorien, hrsg. von F. Commer.

1. Ad Te levavi animam meam.
2. Deus tu conversus vivificabis nos.
3. Benedixisti Domini terram tuam.
4. Ave Maria gratia plena Dominus tecum.
5. Tui sunt coeli et tua est terra.
6. Elegerunt Apostoli Stephanum levitam.
7. Justus ut palma florebit.
8. Anima nostra sicut passer erepta est.
9. Posuisti Domine in capite eius.
10. Deus enim firmavit orbem terrae.
11. Inveni David servum meum.
12. Reges Tarsis et insulae munera offerent.
13. Iubilate Deo omnis terra.
14. Iubilate Deo universa terra.
15. Dextera Domini fecit virtutem.
16. Bonum est confiteri Domino.
17. Perfice gressus meos in semitis tuis.
18. Benedictus Domine doce me iustificationes tuas.
19. Scapulis suis obumbrabit tibi Dominus.
20. Meditabor in mandatis tuis.
21. Iustitiae Domini rectae.
22. Laudate Dominum quia benignus est.
23. Confitebor tibi Domine in toto corde meo.
24. Improperium expectavit cor meum.
25. Terra tremuit et quievit.
26. Angelus Domini descendit de coelo.
27. Deus Deus meus ad Te de luce vigilo.
28. Lauda anima mea Dominum.
29. Benedicite gentes Dominum nostrum.
30. Ascendit Deus in iubilatione.
31. Confirma hoc Deus quod operatus es.
32. Benedictus sit Deus Pater.
33. Sacerdotes Domini incensum et panes offerunt.
34. Domine convertere et eripe animam meam.
35. Sperent in Te omnes qui noverunt nomen tuum.
36. Illumina oculos meos.
37. Benedicam Dominum qui tribuit mihi intellectum.
38. Sicut in holocaustis arietum et taurorum.
39. Populum humilem salvum facies Domine.
40. Iustitiae Domini rectae.

Secunda pars.

41. Exaltabo Te, Domine.
42. Precatus est Moyses.
43. In Te speravi Domine.
44. Immittet Angelus Domini.
45. Expectans expectavi Dominum.
46. Domine, in auxilium meum.
47. Oravi ad Dominum Deum meum.
48. Sanctificavit Moyses altare Domino.
49. Si ambulavero in medio.
50. Super flumina Babylonis.
51. Vir erat in terra Hus.

52. Recordare mei, Domine.
53. De profundis clamavi.
54. Justus ut palma florebit.
55. Mihi autem nimis.
56. Confessio et pulchritudo.
57. Assympta est Maria.
58. Stetit angelus juxta aram.
59. Constitues eos principes.
60. Confitebuntur coeli.
61. In omnem terram exivit.
62. Justorum animae in manu.
63. Veritas mea, et misericordia.
64. Laetamini in Domino.
65. Afferentur regi virgines.
66. Domine Deus, in simplicitate.
67. Diffusa est gratia.
68. Tu es Petrus.

Bd.10. Erstes Buch der Messen.
Cum quatuor vocibus.
Missa Ecce sacerdos magnus.
Missa Oregem celi.
Missa Virtute magna.
Missa Gabriel Arcangelus.
Cum quinque vocibus.
Missa Ad cenam agni providi.
Missa Pro defunctis.
Cum sex vocibus.
Missa sine nomine.

Bd.11. Zweites Buch der Messen.
Cum quatuor vocibus.
Missa De Beata Virgine.
Missa Inviolata.
Missa sine nomine.
Missa Ad Fugam.
Cum quinque vocibus.
Missa Aspice Domine.
Missa Salvum me fac.
Cum sex vocibus.
Missa Papae Marcelli.

Bd.12. Drittes Buch der Messen.
Quatuor vocum.
Missa Spem in alium.
Missa. Primi toni.
Missa. Brevis.
Missa. De feria.
Quinque vocum.
Missa. L'homme arme.
Missa. Repleatur os meum.
Sex vocum.
Missa. De Beata Virgine.
Missa. Ut re mi fa sol la.

Bd.13. Viertes Buch der Messen.
Quatuor vocum.
Missa prima.
Missa secunda.
Missa tertia.
Missa quarta.
Quinque vocum.
Missa prima.
Missa secunda.
Missa tertia.

Bd.14. Fünftes Buch der Messen.
Quatuor vocum.
Aeterna Christi munera.
Jam Christus astra ascenderat.
Panis quem ego dabo.
Iste confessor.
Quinque vocum.
Nigra sum.
Sicut lilium inter spinas.
Sex vocum.
Nasce la gioia mia.
Missa sine nomine.

Bd.15. Sechstes Buch der Messen.
(Juxte Editionem Secundam 1596).
Missa. Dies sanctificatus.
Missa. In Te Domine speravi.
Missa. Sine nomine.
Missa. Quam pulchra es.
Missa. Dilexi quoniam. 5 voc.
Missa. Ave Maria. 6 voc.

Bd.16. Siebentes Buch der Messen.
Quatuor vocibus.
Missa Ave Maria.
Missa Sanctorum meritis.
Missa Emendemus.
Quinque vocibus.
Missa Sacerdos et pontifex.
Missa Tu es pastor ovium.

Bd.17. Achtes Buch der Messen.
Missa. Quem dicunt homines. 4 voc.
Missa. Dum esset Summus Pontifex. 4 voc.
Missa. O admirabile commercium. 5 voc.
Missa. Memor esto. 5 voc.
Missa. Dum complerentur. 6 voc.
Missa. Sacerdotes Domini. 6 voc.

Bd.18. Neuntes Buch der Messen.
Missa. Ave Regina coelorum. 4 voc.
Missa. Veni sponsa Christi. 4 voc.
Missa. Vestiva i coeli. 5 voc.
Missa. Sine nomine. 5 voc.
Missa. In Te Domine speravi. 6 voc.
Missa. Te Deum laudamus. 6 voc.

Bd.19. Zehntes Buch der Messen.
Missa. In illo tempore. 4 voc.
Missa. Già fu chi m'hebbe cara. 4 voc.
Missa. Petra Sancta. 5 voc.
Missa. O Virgo simul et mater. 5 voc.
Missa. Quinti toni. 6 voc.
Missa. Illumina oculos meos. 6 voc.

Bd.20. Elftes Buch der Messen.
Missa. Descendit angelus Domini. 4 voc.
Missa. Regina coeli. 5 voc.
Missa. Quando lieta sperai. 5 voc.
Missa. Octavi toni. 6 voc.
Missa. Alma redemptoris. 6 voc.

Bd.21. Zwölftes Buch der Messen.
Missa. Regina coeli. 4 voc.
Missa. O Rex gloriae. 4 voc.
Missa. Ascendo ad Patrem. 5 voc.
Missa. Qual e il piu grand' Amor. 5 voc.
Missa. Tu es Petrus. 6 voc.
Missa. Viri Galilaei. 6 voc.

Bd.22. Dreizehntes Buch der Messen.
Missa. Laudate Dominum omnes Gentes.
Missa. Hodie Christus natus est.
Missa. Fratres ego enim accepi.
Missa. Confitebor tibi Domine.

Bd.23. Vierzehntes Buch der Messen.
Missa. In majoribus duplicibus. 4 voc.
Missa. In minoribus duplicibus. 4 voc.
Missa. Beatus Lautentius. 5 voc.
Missa. O sacrum convivium. 5 voc.
Missa. Assumpta est Maria. 6 voc.

Missa. Veni Creator Spiritus. 6 voc.
Bd.24. Fünfzehntes Buch der Messen.
1. Missa. Pater noster. 4 voc.
2. Missa. Panem nostrum. 5 voc.
3. Missa. Salve Regina. 5 voc.
4. Missa. Sine titulo. 6 voc.
5. Missa. Tu es Petrus. 6 voc.
6. Missa. Ecce ego Joannes. 6 voc.
Bd.25. Vier Bücher Lamentationen zu vier, fünf und sechs Stimmen.
Lamentationum Hieremiae Prophetae.
Liber primus.
Liber secundus.
Liber tertius.
Liber quartus.
Bd.26. Drei Bücher Litaneien zu vier, fünf, sechs und acht Stimmen, und sechs zwölfstimmige Motetten und Psalmen.
Litaniae Deiparae Virginis.
Liber primus.
Liber secundus.
Liber tertius.
Bd.27. 35 Magnificat (Lobgesang Mariens).
Magnificat octo tonum.
Liber primus.
Quaternis vocibus.
Liber secundus.
Quinis et senis vocibus.
Liber tertius.
Bd.28. Erstes und zweites Buch der vierstimmigen und drittes Buch (aus Sammelwerke) dreibis sechsstimmiger Madrigale.
Il primo libro de madrigali a 4 voci.
Il secondo libro de madrigali a 4 voci.
Libro terzo di madrigali a 3, 4, 5 e 6 voci.
Ahi che quest' occhi.
Ahi! letizia fugace. (Rid. Pierluigi).
Alla riva del tebro.
Amor, ben puoi.
Amor, che meco.
Amor, fortuna.
Amor, quando fioria.
Ardo lungi.
Beltà, se com'.
Che debbo far.
Che non fia.
Chiara, si chiaro.
Chi dunque fia.
Chi estinguera.
Com' in piu negre.
Cosi la fama.
Cosi le chiome.
Da cosi dotta man sei.
Deh! fuss'or.
Deh or foss'io.
Dido, chi giace.
Dolor non fu.
Donna bell'e gentil.
Donna gentil.
Donna, vostra mercede.
Ecc' oscurati.
Ecc' ove ginnse.
Eran le vostre lagrime.
Febbre, ond'or.
Fu l'ardor grave.
Già fu chi m'ebbe cara.
Gioia m'abond!
Gitene liete rime.
Godete dunque.
Il dolce sonno.
Il tempo vola.
Io dovea ben.
Io felice sarei.
Io sento qui d'intorno.
Io son ferito.
I vaghi fiori.
Ivi vedrai.
La cruda mia.
La ver l'aurora.
Le sely' avea.
Lontan dalla mia diva.
Mai fu più cruda.
Ma vio fioriti.
Mentre a le dolci.
Mentre ch'al mar.
Mirate altrove.
Mori quasi il mio.
Ne spero.
Nessun visse giammai.
Non son le vostre mani.
O bella ninfa.
O che splendor.
Ogni beltà.
Ogni loco.
Oh! felici ore.
O me felice.
Onde seguendo.
Ovver de sensi.
Partomi donna.
Perche s'annida.
Per mostrar gioia.
Però contento.
Placide l'acqu'.
Poscia che.
Pose un gran foco.
Prima vedransi.
Prima vedrassi.
Privo di fede.
Quando dal terzo cielo.
Quando fe'.
Quai rime.
Queste saranno.
Questo doglioso.
Rare beltà.
Rime, da i sospir.
Saggio e santo pastor.
Se ben non veggon.
Se di pianti.
Se fra quest' erbe.
Se lamentar.
Se 'l pensier.
Se non fuss' il pensier.
Si è debile il filo.
S'i' 'l dissi mai.
Soave fia il morir.
S'un sguardo.
Struggomi.
Vaghi pensier.
Vedrassi prima.
Veramente in amore.
Vestiva i coeli.
Bd.29. Erstes und zweites Buch der fünfstimmigen geistlichen Madrigale.
Il primo libro de madrigali a 5 voci.

Delli madrigali spirituali a 5 voci.
- Al fin, madre di Dio.
- Amor, senza il tuo dono.
- Anzi, se foco e ferro.
- Cedro gentil.
- Città di Dio.
- Dammi, scala del ciel.
- Dammi, vermiglia Rosa.
- Dunque divin spiracolo.
- E con i raggi tuoi.
- E dal letto.
- Ed arda ognor.
- Eletta mirra.
- E quella corta speme.
- E questo spirto.
- E, se fur già.
- E, se il pensier.
- E se mai voci.
- E, se nel foco.
- E tua mercè.
- E tu, anima mia.
- E tu Signor.
- Fa, che con l'acque tue.
- Figlio immortal.
- Giammai non resti.
- Ma so ben Signor.
- Non basta ch' una volta.
- Novella aurora.
- O cibo di dolcezza.
- O Jesu dolce.
- O manna saporito.
- O refrigerio acceso.
- Or tu sol, che.
- O sole incoronato.
- Orto che sei si chiuso.
- Paraclito amoroso.
- Per questo, Signor mio.
- Quanto più t'offend' io.
- Regina delle Vergini.
- Santo Altare.
- Se amarissimo fiele.
- Signor dammi scienza.
- S'io non ti conoscessi.
- Specchio che fosti.
- Spirito Santo, amore.
- Tu di fortezza torre.
- Tu sei soave fiume.
- Vello di Gedeon.
- Vergine bella.
- Vergine chiara.
- Vergine pura.
- Vergine quante lagrime.
- Vergine saggia.
- Vergine santa.
- Vergine sola al mondo.
- Vergine tale è terra.
- Vincitrice de l'empia idra.

Bd.30. Erster Nachtrag zu Gesammtausgabe der Werke.
- A. Ex collectionibus impressis saeculi XVI et XVII.
  - I. Cantiones sacrae.
  - II. Cantiones profanae.
- B. Ex archive capellae Juliae ad S. Petrum.
  - Amo, e non nacque.
  - Amore, non volendo io.
  - Amor, se pur sei Dio.
  - Anima, dove sei.
  - Ave Maria.
  - Beata es, Virgo.
  - Benedictus Dominus Deus.
  - Che se tanto a voi piace.
  - Chiare, fresche, e dolce acque.
  - Con dolce, altiero, ed amoroso cenno.
  - Da' be' rami.
  - Da fuoco cosi bel.
  - Da l'empia gelosia.
  - Deus, tuorum militum.
  - Donna, presso al cui viso.
  - Dunque perfido amante.
  - E di voi non mi doglio.
  - Exultet coelum laudibus.
  - Fuggir dovriasi.
  - Gloria, laus et honor.
  - Gloria tibi Domine.
  - Jesu, flos matris.
  - Jesu, Rex admirabilis.
  - Il caro è morto.
  - Illumina.
  - In Domino laetabitur.
  - Io non ho lingua.
  - L'alta cagion.
  - Laudate Dominum de coelis.
  - Laudate Dominum in sanctis.
  - Miserere mei Deus.
  - Misero stato.
  - Missa Papae Marcelli.
  - Missa sine titulo.
  - Monstra te esse matrem.
  - Non fu già suon di trombe.
  - Non mi sferra.
  - O effetto rio.
  - O gloriosa Domina.
  - O quam suavis est.
  - Or che la nobil lungua.
  - O Redemptor.
  - Pange lingua.
  - Però che da l'ardore.
  - Poi che la vista.
  - Pueri Hebraeorum.
  - Quod Heva tristis.
  - Quand', ecco, donna.
  - Quante volte diss' io.
  - Rapace ingorda.
  - Regina coeli.
  - Sazio di tormentormi.
  - Se da' soavi accenti.
  - S'egli è pur.
  - Si mi vince.
  - Tantum ergo.
  - Tempo verrà.
  - Tua Jesu dilectio.
  - Tu regis alti janua.
  - Veni Creator Spiritus.
  - Vexilla regis prodeunt.
  - Voi mi poneste in foco.
  - Vos amici mei estis.

Bd.31. Zweiter Nachtrag zur Gesammtausgabe der Werke.
- Audi benigne conditor. 4 voc.
- Benedictus Dominus Deus. 2 chori. 4 voc.
- Benedictus Dominus Deus. 5 voc.
- Coeli Deus sanctissime. 4 voc.
- Creator alme siderum. 4 voc.

Crux fidelis. (cf. Populе meus).
Cum descendisset (? op.dub.) 4 voc.
De lamentatione Jeremiae Prophetae. Heth. Cogitavit. 4 voc.
De lamentatione Jeremiae Prophetae. Heth. Cogitavit. 4 voc.
Dexteram meam. (?) 5 voc).
Dum complerentur c.II.p.(?). 4 voc.
Ecce nunc benedicite. (Falsob. 4 et 5 voc.).
Ecce sacerdos magnus. c.II.p.(?). 6 voc.
Esercizi (XI) sopra la scala.
Estote fortes in bello. 6 voc.
Et repleti sunt. (cf. Dum complerentur ?). 4 voc.
Gloria, laus et honor. 4 voc.
Gloria Patri. 4 voc.
Heth. Peccatum peccavit. 4 voc.
Hodie Christus natus est. 4 voc.
Ideo jurejurando. (cf. Ecce sacerdos?). 6 voc.
Immense coeli conditor. 4 voc.
Improperia vide "Populе meus."
Incipit oratio Jeremiae. 6 voc.
Ingrediente Domino. (?) 4 voc.
Lamed. Matribus suis. 4 voc.
Laudate coeli. (?) 5 voc.
Libera me Domine. 4 voc.
Libera me Domine.
Magnae Deus potentiae. 4 voc.
Miserere mei Deus. 4 et 5 voc.
Miserere mei Deus. 4, 5 et 9 voc.
Miserere mei Deus. (Falsob.). 5 voc.
Misit rex incredulus. (?) 4 voc.
Ne reminiscaris. (?) 5 voc.
Nunc dimittis. 4 et 5 voc.
O bone Jesu. 4 voc.
O Doctor optime. (?) 4 voc.
O Redemptor, sume carmen. 4 voc.
Para mea Dominus. (Fragment). 4 voc.
Per lignum salvi. (?) 5 voc.
Plasmator hominis Deus. 4 voc.
Populе meus. 2 chori. 4 voc.
Populе meus.
Quem dicunt homines. (?) 5 voc.
Qui manducat. (?) 5 voc.
Quodcumque ligaveris. (cf. Tu es pastor). 5 voc.
Salvatorem exspectamus. c.II.p. 6 voc.
Salve Regina. 4 voc.
Salvum me fac. (?) 5 voc.
Sobrie et juste. (cf. Salvatorem). 6 voc.
Telluris ingens conditor. 4 voc.
Teth. (Fragment). 4 voc.
Tristes erant Apostoli. (?) 4 voc.
Tu es pastor. c.II.p. 5 voc.

Bd.32. Dritter Nachtrag zur Gesammtausgabe der Werke.
Aestimatus sum. (Resp.) (?) (op.dub.) 4 voc.
Amicus meus. (Resp.) (?) 4 voc.
Animam meam. (Resp.) (?) 4 voc.
Asperges me. (Ant.) (?) 4 voc.
Astiterunt reges. (Resp.) (?) 4 voc.
Audi benigne. (Hymnus) (?) 4 voc.
Ave Maria. (cf. Beata es) (?) 6 voc.
Beata es, cum 2.p. (?) 6 voc.
Benedictus Dominus. (Cant. Zach.). 4, 5, et 9 voc.
Benedictus Dominus. ("Er erexit"). 4 voc.
Caligaverunt. (Resp.) (?) 4 voc.
Ecce quomodo moritur. (Resp.) (?) 4 voc.
Ecce vidimus eum. (Resp.) (?) 4 voc.
Eram quasi agnus. (Resp.) (?) 4 voc.
Jerusalem surge. (Resp.) (?) 4 voc.
Jesum tradidit. (Resp.) (?) 4 voc.
Incipit lamentatio. (Fer.V., I. Lectio) (?) 8 voc.
In manus tuas. (Resp.br.) 4 voc.
In monte Oliveti. (Resp.) (?) 4 voc.
Jod. Manum suam. (Fragment) (?) 8 voc.
Judas mercator. (Resp.) (?) 7 voc.
Libera me Domine. (Resp.) (?) 5 voc.
Lumen. (Ant. cum Cant. Nunc dimittis) (?) 4 et 5 voc.
Miserere mei. (Ps.) Falsob. (?) 5 voc.
Miserere mei. (Ps.) Falsob. (?) 6 voc.
Miserere mei. (Ps.) 12 voc. in 3 choris.
Missa sine titulo. (?) 6 voc.
Nunc dimittis. (Cant. Sim.). 4 voc.
O bone Jesu. (?) 4 voc.
O Domine Jesu. (?) 4 voc.
Omnes amici mei. (Resp.) (?) 4 voc.
O vos omnes. (Resp.) (?) 4 voc.
Plange quasi virgo. (Resp.) (?) 4 voc.
Regina coeli. (Ant.) 4 voc.
Recessit pastor noster. (Resp.) (?) 4 voc.
Ricercari (VIII) super 8 modos. (?) 4 voc.
Seniores populi. (Resp.) (?) 4 voc.
Sepulto Domino. (Resp.) (?) 4 voc.
Sicut ovis. (Resp.) (?) 4 voc.
Stabat Mater. (Sequ.) (?) 4 et 8 voc.
Tamquam ad latronem. (Resp.) (?) 4 voc.
Te lucis. (Hymn 1) 4 voc.
Tenebrae factae sunt. (Resp.) (?) 4 voc.
Thomas unus ex duodecim. 4 voc.
Tradiderunt me. (Resp.) (?) 4 voc.
Tristis est. (Resp.) (?) 4 voc.
Una hora non potuistis. (Resp.) (?) 4 voc.
Unus ex discipulis. (Resp.) (?) 4 voc.
Vau. Et egressus est. (Lect. II in Fer.V.) (?) 8 voc.
Velum templi. (Resp.) (?) 4 voc.
Veni Sancte Spiritus. (Sequ.) (?) 4 voc.
Venite exsultemus. (Ps. Invit.) 5 voc.
Victimae paschali laudes. (Sequ.) 4 et 8 voc.
Vinea mea. (Resp.) (?) 4 voc.

Bd.33. Vierter Nachtrag zur Gesammtausgabe der Werke.
Ave Maria. diminuito. 4 voc. (Cantus).
Ave verum corpus. diminuito dal madrigal Io son ferito.
Benedicta sit. diminuito. (Cantus et Bassus).
Così le chiome. diminuito.
Così le chiome. (I.p.Vestiva). (intavolatura per liuto).
Da poi ch'io viddi. 4 voc. Madrigal. (Tenor et Bass).
Donna presso al cui. integrum. 5 voc.
Fuit homo missus a Deo. diminuito. (Bassus).
Hodie beata Virgo. diminuito. (Cantus).
Il dolce sonno. (Intavolatura per luito).
Index alphabeticus verborum a quibus moduli operum Praenestini initium faciunt.
Index musicus omnium operum Joannis Petraloysii Praenestini.

Introduxit me rex. diminuito. (Cantus et Bassus).
Io son ferito. diminuito. (Cantus). ex Libro Gio. Bassano.
Io son ferito. diminuito. (Cantus). ex Libro Giov. Bovicelli.
Io son ferito. diminuito. (Cantus). (Intavolatura per liuto).
Misit me vivens Pater. (Resp.) 5 voc.
Missa dominicalis. 5 voc. integra.
O bone Jesu, exaudi me. 8 voc. (op.dub.).
O Domine Jesu. 8 voc. (op.dub.).
Opem nobis, O Thoma. 5 voc. Mvt.
Perchè al viso. Madrigal. 4 voc. (Tenor et Bass).
Plange quasi virgo. 5 voc. in Paolocci.II, 149.
Pulchra es, amica. diminuito. (Cantus et Bassus).
Qual più crudel. Madrigal. 4 voc. (Tenor et Bass).
Quanti mercenarii. Io son ferito. 5 voc.
Se fra quest' erb'. 5 voc. Intavolatura per liuto.
Surge propera, amica mea, columba mea. (II.p. Veni dilecto mi. Così le chiome). Vestiva in colli.
Tota pulchra es. diminuito. 5 voc. (Cantus et Bassus).
Veni dilecti mi, *vide* Veni, veni, dilecte mi.
Veni dilecti mi. Così le chiome. (I.p. Surge propera, amica mea, columba mea). 5 voc. Mvt.
Veni, veni, dilecte mi. diminuito. (Cantus et Bassus).
Vestiva i colli. diminuito. (Cantus) II.p. Così chiome.
Vestiva i colli. diminuito. da Girolamo da Udine. II.p. Così le chiome.
Vestiva i colli. diminuito. (Intavolatura per luito). II.p. Così le chiome.

ALESTRINA, GIOVANNI BATTISTA PIERLUIGI DA, d.1594.
Le opere complete, di Giovanni Pierluigi da Palestrina. Roma, Edizione Fratelli Scalera, 1939– .
v.1– . facsims. (incl. music).
Each volume has special title page; Vol.1 has also facsimile reproduction of original title page: Missarum liber primus.
"Per cura e studio di Raffaele Casimiri."
Contents:
Vol.1. Il libro primo delle messe a 4, 5 et 6 voci. 1939.
A 4 voci.
Missa. Ecce sacerdos magnus.
Missa. O Regem coeli.
Missa. Virtute magna.
Missa. Gabriel Archangelus.
A 5 voci.
Missa. Ad coenam agni providi.
Missa. Pro defunctis.
A 6 voci.
Missa. Sine nomine.
Vol.2. Il libro primo de madrigal a 4 voci. Secondo la ristampa del 1590. Con altri madrigali a 4 e 5 voci pubblicati in raccolte dal 1554 al 1561. 1939.
Madrigali a 4 voci.
Amare non volendo.
Amo, e non nacque.
Amore, amor che meco.
Amor, fortuna.
Che debbo far.
Che non fia che giammai.
Che se tant'a voi piace.
Chiaro, sì chiare.
Chiare, fresche e dolci acque.
Chi estinguera.
Con dolce, altiero.
Da' be' rami scendea.
Da fuoco sì bel.
Da l'empia gelosia.
Deh, or foss'io.
Donna, vostra mercè.
Ecc'oscurati.
Ecco ove quinse.
E di voi non mi doglio.
Fuggir dovriasi.
Già fu chi m'ebbe cara.
Gitene liete rime.
Io non ho lingua.
L'alta cagion.
Là vêr l'aurora.
Lontan dalla mia diva.
Mai fu più cruda.
Ma voi fioriti.
Mentre a le dolci.
Mentre ch'al mar.
Misero stato.
Nè spero i dolci dì.
Nessun visse giammai.
Non mi sferra.
O effetto rio.
Ovver de' sensi è priva.
Però che da l'ardore.
Poi che la vista.
Privo di fede.
Quai rime fur si chiare.
Quante volte.
Queste saranno.
Questo doglioso stil.
Rapace, ingorda.
Rara beltà.
Rime, dai sospir miei.
Sazio di tormentarmi.
Se da' soavi accenti.
S'egli è pur mio.
S'il dissi mai.
Sì mi vince talor.
Tempo verrà.
Vaghi pensier.
Voi mi poneste.
Madrigali a 5 voci.
Dolor non fu.
Donna bell'e gentil.
Il dolce sonno.
Io son ferito.
Ogni loco mi porge.
Poscia che per mio mal.
Se ben non veggon.
Se fra quest' erbe.

Se lamentor augelli.
Struggomi e mi disfaccio.

Vol.3. Il libro primo dei motetti a 4 voci. 1939.
- Ave Maria.
- Beatus Laurentuis.
- Beatus vir qui suffert.
- Benedicta sit.
- Congratulamini mihi.
- Dies sanctificatus.
- Doctor bonus.
- Dum aurora finem daret.
- Exaudi, Domine.
- Fuit homo.
- Gaudent in coelis.
- Hic est vere martyr.
- Hodie Beata Virgo.
- In diebus illis.
- Iste est qui ante Deum.
- Isti sunt.
- Jesus junxit se.
- Lapidabant Stephanum.
- Lauda Sion.
- Loquebantur.
- Magnum haereditatis mysterium.
- Magnus Sanctus Paulus.
- Misso Herodes spiculatore.
- Nativitas tua.
- Nos autem gloriari.
- O quantus luctus.
- O Rex gloriae.
- Quae est ista.
- Quam pulchri sunt.
- Salvator mundi.
- Surge, propera.
- Tollite jugum meum.
- Tribus miraculis.
- Tu es pastor ovium.
- Valde honorandus est.
- Veni sponsa Christi.

Vol.4. Il libro secondo delle messe a 4, 5 e 6 voci. 1939.
- A 4 voci.
  - Missa. De Beata.
  - Missa. Inviolata.
  - Missa. Sine nomine.
  - Missa. Ad fugam.
- A 5 voci.
  - Missa. Aspice Domine.
  - Missa. Salvum me fac.
- A 6 voci.
  - Missa. Papae Marcelli.
- Appendix: Gloria ex missa "De Beata," edition anno 1600.

Vol.5. Il libro primo dei motetti a 5, 6 e 7 voci. 1939.
1. Alleluja; Tulerunt Dominum. 5 voc.
2. Ascendit Deus. 6 voc.
3. Beatae Mariae Magdalenae. 5 voc.
4. Beatus Laurentius. 5 voc.
5. Crucem sanctam. 5 voc.
6. Cum pervenisset beatus Andreas. 5 voc.
7. Deus qui dedisti legem. 5 voc.
8. Dum complerentur. 6 voc.
9. Dum ergo essent. 6 voc.
10. Ego sum panis vivus. 5 voc.
11. Et omnis angeli. 6 voc.
12. Hic est discipulus ille. 5 voc.
13. Hodie Beata Virgo. 5 voc.
14. Hodie nata est. 5 voc.
15. Lapidabant Stephanum. 5 voc.
16. Maria Virgo. 7 voc.
17. O admirabile commercium. 5 voc.
18. O Antoni eremita. 5 voc.
19. O beata et benedicta . . . Trinitas. 5 voc.
20. O beatum pontificem. 5 voc.
21. O beatum virum. 5 voc.
22. O Domine Jesu Christi. 6 voc.
23. O magnum mysterium. 6 voc.
24. O vera, summa, sempiterna Trinitas. 5 voc.
25. Panis quem ego dabo. 5 voc.
26. Paries quidem filium. 5 voc.
27. Puer qui natus est. 5 voc.
28. Pulchra es, O Maria. 6 voc.
29. Quam pulchri sunt. 5 voc.
30. Quem vidistis, pastores. 6 voc.
31. Quodcumque ligaveris. 6 voc.
32. Sancti Paule apostole. 5 voc.
33. Senex puerum portabat. 5 voc.
34. Sicut lilium. 5 voc.
35. Solve, jubente Deo. 6 voc.
36. Stellam quam viderant Magi. 5 voc.
37. Suscipe verbum. 5 voc.
38. Tu es Petrus. 7 voc.
39. Unus ex duobus. 5 voc.
40. Venit Michael Archangelus. 5 voc.
41. Vidi turbam magnam. 6 voc.
42. Virgo prudentissima. 7 voc.
43. Viri Galilaei. 6 voc.

Vol.6. Il libro terzo delle messe a 4, 5 e 6 voci. 1939.
- A 4 voci.
  - Missa. Spem in alium.
  - Missa. Primi toni.
  - Missa. Brevis.
  - Missa. De feria.
- A 5 voci.
  - Missa. L'homme armé.
  - Missa. Repleatur os meum.
- A 6 voci.
  - Missa. De Beata Virgine.
  - Missa. Ut, re, mi, fa, sol, la.

Vol.7. Il libro secondo dei motetti a 5, 6 ed 8 voci. 1940.
1. Ascendo ad Patrem. 5 voc.
2. Beata Barbara. 6 voc.
3. Benedicta tu. 6 voc.
4. Canite tuba in Sion. 5 voc.
5. Cantabo Domine. 6 voc.
6. Circuire possum. 5 voc. di Angelo Pierluigi.
7. Coenantibus illis. 5 voc.
8. Confitebor tibi Domine. 8 voc.
9. Confitebor tibi, Domine. 5 voc. di Rodolfo Pierluigi.
10. Corona aurea. 5 voc.
11. Deficiant peccatores. 6 voc.
12. Derelinquat impius. 5 voc.
13. Domine, in virtute tua. 8 voc.
14. Domine Pater. 5 voc. di Silla Pierluigi.
15. Domine, praevenisti. 5 voc.
16. Dominus Jesus. 5 voc.
17. Ego enim sum Dominus. 6 voc.
18. Ego rogabo Patrem. 5 voc.
19. Excita, Domine. 6 voc.

20. Exi cito. 5 voc.
21. Gaude, Barbara. 5 voc.
22. Gaude, quia meruisti. 5 voc.
23. Gloriosam mortem. 6 voc.
24. Hierusalem, cito veniet. 6 voc.
25. Homo quidam. 5 voc.
26. In hac cruce. 5 voc. di Angelo Pierluigi.
27. In illo tempore. 5 voc.
28. Laudate Dominum omnes gentes. 8 voc.
29. Laudate pueri. 8 voc.
30. Magna est gloria ejus. 8 voc.
31. Memor esto. 5 voc.
32. Notas facite in populis. 8 voc.
33. Nunc dimittis. 6 voc. di Silla Pierluigi.
34. O sacrum convivium. 5 voc.
35. O Virgo simul et Mater. 5 voc.
36. Peccantem me quotidie. 5 voc.
37. Quis sicut Dominus. 8 voc.
38. Quodcumque ligaveris. 6 voc.
39. Rorate coeli. 5 voc.
40. Sancta et immaculata. 6 voc.
41. Secundum multitudinem. 6 voc.
42. Tribularer, si nescirem. 6 voc.
43. Tu es Petrus. 6 voc.
44. Veni, Domine. 6 voc.

Vol.8. Il libro terzo dei motetti a 5, 6 ed 8 voci. 1940.

1. Accepit Jesus calicem. 6 voc.
2. Afflige apprimentes nos. 5 voc.
3. Angelus Domini descendit. 5 voc.
4. Ave Maria. 5 voc.
5. Ave, Regina coelorum. 8 voc.
6. Beduanis ac treduanis. 5 voc.
7. Cantantibus organis. 5 voc.
8. Caro mea. 5 voc.
9. Columna es immobilis. 6 voc.
10. Congrega, Domine. 5 voc.
11. Cum ortus fuerit sol. 6 voc.
12. Deus, qui ecclesiam tuam. 6 voc.
13. Domine Deus, qui conteris bella. 5 voc.
14. Erat Joannes in deserto. 5 voc.
15. Et introeuntes in monumentum. 5 voc.
16. Fuit homo missus a Deo. 5 voc.
17. Gaude, praesul optime. 5 voc.
18. Haec dies. 6 voc.
19. Hodie Christus natus est. 8 voc.
20. Inclytae sanctae virginis Catherinae. 5 voc.
21. Jubilate Deo. 5 voc.
22. Jubilate Deo. 8 voc.
23. Judica me, Deus. 6 voc.
24. Laudate nomen ejus. 5 voc.
25. Lauda, Sion, Salvatorem. 8 voc.
26. Manifesto vobis veritatem. 5 voc.
27. O bone Jesu. 6 voc.
28. O lux et decus Hispaniae. 5 voc.
29. Omnipotens sempiterne Deus. 5 voc.
30. O quam metuendus est. 5 voc.
31. O singulare praesidium. 5 voc.
32. Pater noster. 5 voc.
33. Pax vobis. 5 voc.
34. Postquam autem. 6 voc.
35. Quid habes, Hester. 5 voc.
36. Rex pacificus. 6 voc.
37. Sancte praesul Nicolae. 5 voc.
38. Santificavit Dominus. 5 voc.
39. Surge, illuminare, Hierusalem. 8 voc.
40. Susanna, ab improbis. 6 voc.
41. Tradent enim vos. 5 voc.
42. Tu, Domine. 5 voc.
43. Veni, Sancte Spiritus. 8 voc.
44. Vidi Te, Domine. 5 voc.

Vol.9. Il libro primo dei madrigal (spirituali) a 5 voci con appendice di madrigali pubblicati in raccolte dal 1566 al 1576. 1940.

1. Amor, senza il tuo dono.
2. Dunque, divin spiracolo.
3. E tu, anima mia.
4. Giammai non resti.
5. Ma so ben, signo mio.
6. Non basta ch'una volta.
7. O cibo di dolcezza.
8. O Jesu dolce.
9. O manna saporito.
10. O refrigerio accesso.
11. O sol' incoronato.
12. Paraclito amoroso.
13. Per questo, Signor mio.
14. Quanto più T' offend' io.
15. Signor, dammi scienza.
16. S'io non Ti conoscessi.
17. Spirito Santo, amor.
18. Tu sei soave fiume.
19. Vergine bella.
20. Vergine chiara.
21. Vergine pura.
22. Vergine, quante lagrime.
23. Vergine saggia.
24. Vergine santa.
25. Vergine sola al mondo.
26. Vergine, tale è terra.

Appendice. (Madrigali profani a 5 voci).

27. Ahi letizia fugace.
28. Così le chiome mie.
29. Il tempo vola.
30. Io felice sarei.
31. Ivi vedrai la gloria.
32. Le selv' avea d'intorno.
33. Onde seguendo l'onorata impresa.
34. Placide l'acque.
35. Quando fe' loro impallidir.
36. Saggio e santo pastor.
37. Se di pianti e di stridi.
38. Soave fia il morir.
39. Vestiva i colli.

Vol.10. Il libro quarto delle messe a 4 e 5 voci. 1940.

A 4 voci.
- Missa prima. Lauda Sion.
- Missa secunda. [2 primi toni].
- Missa tertia. Jesu nostra redemptio.
- Missa quarta. L'homme armé.

A 5 voci.
- Missa prima. Eripe me de inimicis meis.
- Missa secunda. [2 primi toni].
- Missa tertia. O magnum mysterium.

Vol.11. Il libro secondo dei motetti a 4 voci. 1941.

1. Ad Dominum cum tribularer.
2. Adoramus Te, Christi.
3. Ad Te levavi oculos meos.
4. Alma redemptoris mater.
5. Anima mea turbata est.
6. Ave Maria.
7. Ave Regina coelorum.

8. Commissa mea pavesco.
9. Confitemini Domini.
10. Domine, quando veneris.
11. Ecce nunc benedicite Dominum.
12. Ego sum panis vivus.
13. Eja ergo.
14. Fundamenta ejus.
15. Gaude, Virgo gloriosa.
16. Gloriosi principes.
17. Haec dies.
18. Heu mihi.
19. Miserere nostri, Domine.
20. Numquid Sion dicet.
21. Pueri Hebraeorum.
22. Quia vidiste me, Thoma.
23. Salve, Regina.
24. Sagittae potentis acutae.
25. Sicut cervus.
26. Sitivit anima mea.
27. Sub tuum praesidium.
28. Super flumina Babylonis.
29. Surrexit pastor bonus.
30. Tu quae genuisti.

Il libro quarto dei mottetti a 5 voci.

1. Adjuro vos.
2. Caput ejus.
3. Descendi in hortum meum.
4. Dilectus meus descendit.
5. Dilectus meus mihi.
6. Duo ubera tua.
7. Ecce tu pulcher es.
8. Fasciculus myrrae.
9. Guttur tuum.
10. Introduxit me rex.
11. Laeva ejus.
12. Nigra sum, sed formosa.
13. Osculetur me.
14. Pulchra es.
15. Puchrae sunt genae tuae.
16. Quae est ista.
17. Quam pulchra es.
18. Quam pulchri sunt.
19. Sicut lilium inter spinas.
20. Si ignoras te.
21. Surgam et circuibo civitatem.
22. Surge, amica mea.
23. Surge, propera.
24. Tota pulchra es.
25. Trahe me: post Te.
26. Veni, dilecte mi.
27. Vineam meam non custodivi.
28. Vox dilecti mei.
29. Vulnerasti cor meum.

Vol.12. Il libro quinto dei mottetti a 5 voci. 1941.

1. Aegypte, noli flere.
2. Ambula, sancte Dei.
3. Apparuit caro suo Joanni.
4. Ardens est cor meum.
5. Ave Regina coelorum.
6. Ave, Trinitatis Sacrarium.
7. Domine, secundum actum meum.
8. Ecce merces sanctorum.
9. Eja ergo.
10. Exsultate Deo.
11. Gaude Virgo gloriosa.
12. Laetus Hyperboream.
13. Manus tuae.
14. Nisi ego abiero.
15. O patruo.
16. Orietur stella.
17. Parce mihi, Domine.
18. Paucitas dierum.
19. Peccavimus.
20. Peccavi, quid faciam tibi.
21. Rex Melchior.
22. Salve Regina.
23. Sic Deus dilexit mundum.
24. Surge, Petre.
25. Surge, sancte Dei.
26. Tempus est.
27. Tribulationes civitatum.
28. Videns secundus.

Vol.13. Le lamentazioni a 4, 5, 6 ed 8 voci. 1941.

Vol.14. Inni di tutto l'anno a 4, 5 e 6 voci. 1942.

1. Ad coenam agni providi.
2. Ad preces nostras.
3. A solis ortus cardine.
4. Aurea luce.
5. Ave, maris stella.
6. Christe, qui lux es et dies.
7. Christe Redemptor . . . ex Patre.
8. Christe Redemptor . . . conserva.
9. Conditor alme siderum.
10. Decus morum, dux minorum.
11. Deus tuorum militum.
12. Deus tuorum militum.
13. Doctor egregie Paule.
14. En gratulemur hodie.
15. Exaultet coelum laudibus.
16. Hostis Herodes impie.
17. Hymnus canoris personet.
18. Hujus obtentu.
19. Iste confessor.
20. Jesu, corona virginum.
21. Jesu, corona virginum.
22. Jesu nostra redemptio.
23. Lauda mater ecclesia.
24. Laudibus summis.
25. Lucis Creator optime.
26. Magne pater Augustine.
27. Mensis Augusti.
28. Nunc juvat celsi.
29. O lux beata Trinitas.
30. Pange lingua gloriosi
31. Petrus beatus.
32. Prima lux surgens.
33. Proles coelo prodiit.
34. Quicumque Christum quaeritis.
35. Quodcumque vinclis.
36. Rex gloriose martyrum.
37. Salvete flores martyrum.
38. Sanctorum merites.
39. Tibi, Christe, splendor Patris.
40. Tristes erant Apostoli.
41. Urbs beata Jerusalem.
42. Ut queant laxis.
43. Veni Creator Spiritus.
44. Vexilla regis prodeunt.
45. Vexilla regis prodeunt.

Vol.15. Il libro quinto delle messe a 4, 5 e 6 voci. 1941.

A 4 voci.

Missa. Aeterna Christi munera.
Missa. Jam Christus astra ascenderat.

Missa. Panis quem ego dabo.
Missa. Iste confessor.
A 5 voci.
Missa. Nigra sum.
Missa. Sicut lilium inter spinas.
A 6 voci.
Missa. Nasce la gioia mia.
Missa. Sine nomine.
Vol.16. I magnificat a 4, 5, 6 e 8 voci. 1943.
Vol.17. Offertori di tutto l'anno a 5 voci. 1952.
1. Ad Te levavi.
2. Afferentur regi.
3. Angelus Domini.
4. Anima nostra.
5. Ascendit Deus.
6. Assumpta est.
7. Ave Maria.
8. Benedicam Dominum.
9. Benedicite, gentes.
10. Benedictus es.
11. Benedictus sit Deus.
12. Benedixisti, Domine.
13. Bonum est confiteri.
14. Confessio et pulchritudo.
15. Confirma hoc, Deus.
16. Confitebor tibi.
17. Confitebuntur coeli.
18. Constitues eos.
19. De profundis.
20. Deus, Deus meus.
21. Deus enim firmavit.
22. Deus tu convertens.
23. Dextera Domini.
24. Diffusa est gratia.
25. Domine, convertere.
26. Domine Deus.
27. Domine, in auxilium.
28. Elegerunt Apostoli.
29. Exaltabo te.
30. Exspectans exspectavi.
31. Illumina oculos meos.
32. Immittet Angelus.
33. Improperium.
34. In omnem terram.
35. In Te speravi.
36. Inveni David.
37. Jubilate Deo omnis terra.
38. Jubilate Deo universa terra.
39. Justitiae Domine.
40. Justitiae Domine.
41. Justorum animae.
42. Justus ut palma.
43. Justus ut palma.
44. Laetamini in Domino.
45. Lauda anima mea.
46. Laudate Dominum.
47. Meditabor.
48. Mihi autem.
49. Oravi ad Dominum.
50. Perfice gressus meos.
51. Populum humilem.
52. Posiusti Domine.
53. Precatus est Moyses.
54. Recordare mei.
55. Reges Tharsis.
56. Sacerdotes Domini.
57. Sanctificat Moyses.
58. Scapulis suis.
59. Si ambulavero.
60. Sicut in olocaustis.
61. Sperent in Te.
62. Stetit Angelus.
63. Super flumina Babylonis.
64. Terra tremuit.
65. Tu es Petrus.
66. Tui sunt coeli.
67. Veritas mea.
68. Vir erat in terra Hus.
Vol.18. Le messe di Mantova. (Vol.I) 1954.
1. Missa in duplicibus (Minoribus I).
2. Missa in duplicibus (Minoribus II).
3. Missa Beatae Mariae Virg(inis I).
4. Missa Beatae Mariae Virg(inis II).
5. Missa Beatae Mariae Virg(inis III).
Vol.19. Le messe di Mantova. (Vol.II) 1954.
1. Missa in Festis Apostolor(um I).
2. Missa in Festis Apostolor(um II).
3. Missa in semidupl(icibus) maior(ibus I).
4. Missa in semidupl(icibus) maior(ibus II).
5. Missa (sine nomine).
Vol.20. Le litanie a (3), 4, 5, 6 e 8 voci. 1955.
Litaniae Deiparae Virginis.
Litaniae liber secundus.
Appendix.
Litaniae de Beata Virgine Maria.
Litaniae Domini.
Litaniae Sacrosanctae Evcharistiae.
Vol.21. Il libro sesto delle messe a 4, 5 e 6 voci. 1956.
A 4 voci.
Missa. Dies sanctificatus.
Missa. In Te Domine speravi.
Missa. Sine nomine.
Missa. Quam pulchra es.
A 5 voci.
Missa. Dilexi quoniam.
A 6 voci.
Missa. Ave Maria.
Vol.22. Il libro secondo dei madrigali spirituali a 5 voci. 1957.
Figlio immortal d'immortal Padre, e figlio.
E se mai voci di qua giù son grate.
Hor tu sol, che di vivi almi splendori.
Dammi, scala del ciel e del ciel porta.
E se fur già de le mie mani immonde.
Dammi, vermiglia rosa e bianco e puro.
E se 'l pensier de la futura morte.
Eletta Mirra, che soave odore.
Cedro gentil, da gli amorosi vermi.
Fa che con l'acque tue splendenti e vive.
S'amarissimo fele e mortal tosco.
Horto che sei sì chiuso e sì serrato.
E, se nel foco di lascivi ardendo.
Vincitrice de l'empia hidra infernale.
Città di Dio, cui fan tempi e fortezze.
Santo Altare, d'odor più veri e degni.
Tu di fortezza torre e torre eburna.
Specchio che fosti sì polito e terso.
Vello di Gedeon, cui Dio sì largo.
Novella Aurora, che nascend' allegri.
E questo spirto, de la propria sede.
E dal letto di mille e mille colpe.
Et arda ogn'hor sopra 'l lapideo altare.
E tua mercè da così cieca e folta.

E quella certa speme e quella fede.
Anzi, se foco e ferro e se veleno.
E con i raggi tuoi splendenti e chiari.
Regina de le Vergini e di tutte.
Al fin, Madre di Dio, che né più bella.
E tu Signor, tu la tua grazia infondi.

Vol.23. Il libro settimo delle messe a 4 e 5 voci. 1957.
A 4 voci.
Missa. Ave Maria.
Missa. Sanctorum meritis.
Missa. Emendemus.
A 5 voci.
Missa. Sacerdos et pontifex.
Missa. Tu es pastor ovium.
Appendix.
A 4 voci.
Missa. In majoribus duplicibus.
Missa. In minoribus duplicibus.

Vol.24. Il libro ottavo delle messe a 4, 5 e 6 voci. 1958.
A 4 voci.
Missa. Quem dicunt homines.
Missa. Dum esset summis pontifex.
A 5 voci.
Missa. O admirabile commercium.
Missa. Memor esto.
A 6 voci.
Missa. Dum complerentur.
Missa. Sacerdotes Domini.
Appendix.
A 5 voci.
Missa. Beatus Laurentius.
Missa. O sacrum convivium.

Vol.25. Il libro nono delle messe a 4, 5 e 6 voci. 1958.
A 4 voci.
Missa. Ave Regina coelorum.
Missa. Veni sponsa Christi.
A 5 voci.
Missa. Vestiva i colli.
Missa. Sine nomine.
A 6 voci.
Missa. In Te Domine speravi.
Missa. Te Deum laudamus.
Appendix.
A 6 voci.
Missa. Assumpta est Maria.
Missa. Veni Creator Spiritus.

Vol.26. Messa Tu es Petrus a 18 voci, in 3 cori. 1959.
Kyrie.
Gloria.
Credo.
Sanctus.
Agnus Dei.

Vol.27. Il libro decimo delle messe a 4, 5 e 6 voci. 1959.
A 4 voci.
Missa. In illo tempore.
Missa. Già fu chi m'effe cara.
A 5 voci.
Missa. Petra Sancta.
Missa. O Virgo simul et Mater.
A 6 voci.
Missa. Quinti toni.
Missa. Illumina oculos meos.
Appendix.
A 4 voci.
Missa. Pater noster.
A 5 voci.
Missa. Panem nostrum.

Vol.28. Il libro decimoprimo delle messe a 4, 5 e 6 voci. 1960.
A 4 voci.
Missa. Descendit Angelus Domini.
A 5 voci.
Missa. Regina coeli.
Missa. Quando lieta sperai.
A 6 voci.
Missa. Octavi toni.
Missa. Alma Redemptoris.
Appendix.
A 5 voci.
Missa. Salve Regina.
A 6 voci.
Missa. Sine titulo.
Missa. Tu es Petrus.

Vol.29. Il libro decimosecondo delle messe a 4, 5 e 6 voci. 1961.
A 4 voci.
Missa. Regina coeli.
Missa. O Rex gloriae.
A 5 voci.
Missa. Ascendo ad Patrem.
Missa. Qual' è il più grande amor.
A 6 voci.
Missa. Tu es Petrus.
Missa. Viri Galilaei.
Appendix.
A 5 voci.
Missa. Ecce ego Joannes.

Vol.30. Le messe a 8 voci. 1961.
Missa. Laudate Dominum omnes gentes.
Missa. Hodie Christus natus est.
Missa. Fratres ego enim accepi.
Missa. Confitebor tibi Domine.

Vol.31. Il libro secondo dei madrigali a 4 voci. 1965.
1. Così la fama scriva.
2. S'un sguardo un fa beato.
3. Amor, ben puoi tu hormai.
4. Partomi, donna, e teco.
5. Veramente in amore.
6. Gioia m'abond'al cor.
7. Donna gentil.
8. Io dovea ben pensarmi.
9. Se'l pensier che mi strugge.
10. Chi dunque fia.
11. Mirate altrove.
12. Si è debile il filo.
13. I vaghi fiori.
14. Morì quasi il mio core.
15. Alla riva del Tebro.
16. Amor, quando fioriva.
17. Beltà se come in ment'.
18. La cruda mia nemica.
19. O che splendor.
20. Io sento qui d'intorno.
21. Deh, fuss'hor qui madonna.
22. Se non fusse il pensier.
23. Perchè s'annida amor.
24. Ogni beltà, madonna.
25. Ardo lungi e dapresso.

PALESTRINA, GIOVANNI BATTISTA PIERLUIGI DA, d.1594.
Raccolta di musica sacra in cui contengonsi i capi lavori de' più celebri compositori italiani consistente in messe, sequenze, offertori, mottetti, salmi, inni, responsori, ec. opera di Pietro Alfieri.
7v.
"Catalogo di tutte le opere del Palestrina": v.7, p.361–73.
Contents:
Vol.1. Messe scelte.
Vol.2. Mottetti, a 5 voci.
Vol.3. Inni, a 4 voci.
Vol.4. Lamentazioni.
Vol.5. Offertori, a 5 voci.
Vol.6–7. Mottetti, responsori, antifons, salmi, sequenze, a 6, 7, e 8 voci.

PAŃSTWOWA WYŻSZA SZKOLA MUZYCZNA W KATOWICACH. Biblioteka. Katowice, Poland, 1963– .
No.1– .
Contents:
Faksymilia Nr.1. Szymanowski, Karol. Études pour piano, Op.33. 1963.

PAOLI, DOMENICO DE. ed.
Sonate italiane del secolo XVIII per cembalo o pianoforte novamente date in luce, da Domenico de Paoli. London, J. & W. Chester, Ltd., 1939.
2p.L., 36p.
Contains compositions by Baldassare Galuppi, Padre G. B. Martini, P. D. Paradies, G. M. Rutini, and Domenico Scarlatti.

PAOLO TENORISTA, *Don*, 15th century.
Paolo Tenorista in a new fragment of the Italian Ars nova. A facsim. edition of an early fifteenth-century ms. now in the library of Edward E. Lowinsky, Berkeley, Calif., with an introd. by Nino Pirrotta. Palm Springs, [Calif.], E. E. Gottlieb, 1961.
83p. 3 plates (1 col.) facsims.
For 2–3 voices.
"500 copies printed at the Cole-Holmquist Press, Los Angeles."
"Inventory of the Lowinsky Fragment": p.49.
"Catalogue of Paolo's work": p.53–56.
Transcription in score format (modern notation) of the composer's S'amor in cor gentil; Dolce mie donna; Doglia continua; Amor, tu solo 'l sai; and Amor, de' dimmi: p.69–83.

Papa, Clemens non, *see* Clément, Jacques.

PARIS, BIBLIOTHÈQUE DE L'ARSENAL. Mss. (No.5198).
. . . Le chansonnier de l'Arsenal. (Trouvères du XIIe–XIIIe siècle). Reproduction phototypique du manuscrit 5198 de la Bibliothèque de l'Arsenal. Transcription du texte musical en notation moderne, par Pierre Aubry . . . Introd. et notices par A. Jeanroy . . . Paris, Paul Geuthner; Leipzig, Otto Harrassowitz, [etc., etc.], n.d.
64p., 384 numbered pl. (Publications de la Société Internationale de Musique. [Section de Paris]).

THE PARISH ORGANIST. One hundred twenty chorale preludes, voluntaries, and postludes by older masters and contemporary composers, ed. by Heinrich Fleischer. St. Louis, M., Concordia Publishing House, cop.1953.
8v. and suppl.
Contents:
Vol.1–4. One hundred twenty chorale preludes, voluntaries, and postludes by older masters and contemporary composers. Contain compositions by Yury Arbatsky, Johann Christoph Bach, Johann Michael Bach, Johann Sebastian Bach, Jan Bender, M. Alfred Bichsel, Paul Bouman, Johannes Brahms, Paul Bunjes, Johann Heinrich Buttstedt, Dietrich Buxtehude, Thomas Canning, Heinrich Fleischer, Girolamo Frescobaldi, Hugo Gehrke, Nicolas Gigault, Georg Frederic Handel, Friedrich Hark, Victor Hildner, Theodore Hoelty-Nickel, Sigvart A. Hofland, Camil van Hulse, Georg Friedrich Kaufmann, Johann Erasmus Kindermann, Hans Klotz, Paul Kretzshmar, Johann Krieger, Johann Kuhnau, Orlando di Lasso, Ludwig Lenel, Henry J. Markworth, Hans Arnold Metzger, George Th. Miles, Rudolf Moser, Gottfried Mueller, Gottlieb Muffat, Franz Xaver Anton Murschhauser, Johann Christoph Oley, Johann Pachelbel, Newman W. Powell, Michael Praetorius, André Raison, Max Reger, Samuel Scheidt, Martin Stellhorn, Theodore G. Stelzer, Georg Philipp Telemann, Rolf Unkel, Johann Gottfried Walther, Richard Weinhorst, Healey Willan, and Friedrich Wilhelm Zachau.
Vol.5. Advent and Christmas music.
Vol.6. Christmas and Epiphany music.
Vol.5–6 contain compositions by Johann Sebastian Bach, Jan Bender, Georg Boehm, Johannes Brahms, Dietrich Buxtehude, Louis Claude d'Aquin, Jean François d'Andrieu, Hugo Distler, Johann Kaspar Ferdinand, César Franck, Hugo Gehrke, Friedrich Hoegner, Georg Friedrich Kaufmann, Paul Kickstat, Antoine Nicolas Lebègue, Ludwig Lenel, Hans Arnold Metzger, Georg Th. Miles, Rudolf Moser, Franz Xaver Anton Murschhauser, Kaspar Othmayr, Johann Pachelbel, Bernhard Reichel, Samuel Scheidt, Fridolin Sicher, Albert Thate, Johann Gottfried Walther, and Friedrich Wilhelm Zachau.
Vol.7. Music for Lent, Palm Sunday, and Holy Week.
Vol.8. Music for Easter, Ascension, Pentecost, and Trinity.
Vol.7–8 contain compositions by Johann Sebastian Bach, Jan Bender, Johannes Brahms, François Couperin, Jean François d'Andrieu, Johann Kaspar Ferdinand Fischer, César Franck, Girolamo Frescobaldi, Johann Jakob Froberger, Wolfgang Hiltscher, Ludwig Lenel, Hans Arnold Metzger, George Th. Miles, Rudolf Moser, Gottfried Mueller, Robert Noehren, Johann Pachelbel, Andre Raison,

Guenter Raphael, Bernhard Reichel, Heinrich Scheidemann, Samuel Scheidt, Hermann Schroeder, Jean Titelouze, Tobias Volckmar, Johann Gottfried Walther, Matthias Weckmann, Wilhelm Weismann, Healey Willan, and Friedrich Wilhelm Zachau.
Suppl. Accompanying manuel.
A list of offertories for the Sundays and festivals of the church year.
Classified index.
Suggested Hammond registration. Prepared by Lawrence Cain.

PARISOTTI, ALESSANDRO, 1853–1913. ed.
. . . Arie antiche, raccolte per cura di Alessandro Parisotti . . . Milano, Ricordi, [Introd.1885–ca.1898].
3v.
Italian words; music for 1 voice with piano acc.
At head of title: Edizione Ricordi . . .
Contents:
Bd.1. G. M. Bononconi, A. Caldara, G. G. Carissimi, M. A. Cesti, W. C. Gluck, G. F. Händel, N. Jommelli, G. Legrenzi, L. Leo, A. Lotti, B. Marcello, G. Martini, G. Paisiello, G. B. Pergolesi, N. Piccinni, A. Scarlatti, D. Scarlatti, T. Traetta, and A. Vivaldi.
Bd.2. G. B. Bassani, G. B. Bononcini, G. Caccini, F. Cavalli, M. A. Cesti, F. Durante, A. Falconieri, G. B. Fasolo, F. Gasparini, G. Giordani, A. del Leuto, S. de Luca, B. Marcello, C. Monteverdi, P. D. Paradies, N. Piccinni, R. Rontani, D. Sarri, A. Scarlatti, A. Stradella, and A. F. Tenaglia.
Bd.3. "Anonimo," G. M. F. Blangini, G. Caccini, G. G. Carissimi, F. Cavalli, L. Cherubini, D. Cimarosa, N. Dalayrac, A. Falconieri, G. B. Fasolo, F. Gasparini, G. F. Händel, C. Monteverdi, G. P. Pergolesi, J. Peri, R. Rontani, S. Rosa, A. Sartorio, A. Scarlatti, G. Spontini, A. Stradella, A. F. Tenaglia, T. Traetta, and L. Vinci.

PARISOTTI, ALESSANDRO, 1853–1913. ed.
. . . Arie antiche. Milano, New York, [etc.], G. Ricordi & Co., 1947.
3v.
Reprint.

PARRISH, CARL, 1904– . ed.
Masterpieces of music before 1750; an anthology of musical examples from Gregorian chant to J. S. Bach, compiled and ed. with historical and analytical notes by Carl Parrish and John F. Ohl. [1st ed.]. New York, Norton, [1951].
x, 235p.
Contents:
1. Antiphon: Laus Deo Patri, and Psalm 113: Laudate pueri.
2. Alleluia: Vidimus stellam.
3. Sequence: Victimae Paschali. (11th century).
4. Trouvère song, Virelai: Or la truix. (12–13th century).
5. Minnelied: Neidhart von Reuenthal. Willekommen mayenschein. (13th century).
6. Parallel organum, sequence: Rex caeli, Domine. (9th century).
7. Free organum, trope: Agnus Dei. (12th century).
8. Melismatic organum: Benedicamus Domino. (12th century).
9. Organum: Perotin. Alleluya. (12th century).
10. Motet: En non Diu! Quant voi; Eius in Oriente. (13th century).
11. Conductus: De castitatis thalamo. (13th century).
12. Estampie. Instrumental dance. (13th century).
13. Guillaume de Machaut. Agnus Dei (I) from the Mass.
14. Ballata: Landino, Francesco. Chi più le vuol sapere.
15. Dufay, Guillaume. Kyrie (I) from the Mass "Se la face ay pale."
16. Chanson: Binchois, Gilles. Adieu m'amour.
17. Ockeghem, Johannes. Sanctus from the "Missa Prolationum."
18. Motet: Obrecht, Jacob. Parce, Domine.
19. Motet: Prèz, Josquin des. Ave Maria.
20. Chanson: Crequillon, Thomas. Pour ung plaisir.
21. Gabrieli, Andrea. Canzone francese deta "Pour ung plaisir."
22. Lute dances: Der Prinzen-Tanz; Proportz.
23. Motet: Lassus, Orlandus. Tristis est anima mea.
24. Palestrina, G. P. da. Agnus Dei (I) from the Mass "Veni sponsa Christi."
25. Motet: Byrd, William. Ego sum panis vivus.
26. Canzona: Canzona per l'epistola. (early 17th century).
27. Madrigal: Marenzio, Luca. S'io parto, i' moro.
28. Madrigal: Bennet, John. Thyrsis, sleepest thou?
29. Variations: Farnaby, Giles. Loth to depart.
30. Madrigal: Caccini, Giulio. Dovrò dunque morire.
31. Recitative: Monteverdi, Claudio. Tu se' morta, from "Orfeo."
32. Scene: Carissimi, Giacomo. Afferte gladium, from "Judicium Salomonis."
33. Cantata: Schütz, Heinrich. O Herr, hilf.
34. Frescobaldi, Girolamo. Ricercar.
35. Froberger, J. J. Suite in E minor.
36. Lully, J. B. Overture to "Armide."
37. Pachelbel, Johann. Toccata in E minor.
38. Ground: Purcell, Henry. A new ground.
39. Corelli, Arcangelo. Sonata da chiesa in E minor.
40. Clavecin piece: Couperin, François. La galante.
41. Rameau, Jean-Philippe. Scene from "Castor et Pollux."
42. Scarlatti, Domenico. Sonata in C minor.
43. Händel, G. F. Concerto grosso in C major. First movement.
44. Recitative, Sinfonia, and Aria: Händel, G. F. Cara sposa, from "Rinaldo."
45. Chorus: Händel, G. F. Draw the tear, from "Solomon."
46. Chorale: Bach, J. S. Christ lag in Todesbanden, from Cantata No.4.
47. Chorale prelude: Bach, J. S. Christ lag in Todesbanden.

48. Chorus: Bach, J. S. Es war ein wunderlicher Krieg, from Cantata No.4.
49. Arioso: Bach, J. S. Ach Golgatha, from the "St. Matthew Passion."
50. Fugue: Bach, J. S. Contrapunctus III, from "Die Kunst der Fuge."

PARRISH, CARL, 1904– . ed.
A treasury of early music; an anthology of masterworks of the Middle Ages, with Renaissance, and the Baroque era. Compiled and ed. with notes. [1st ed.]. New York, W. W. Norton, [cop.1958].
x, 331p.
Contents:
1. Ambrosian psalmellus for Quadragesima: Redde mihi.
2. Gallican improperia for Good Friday: Popule meus.
3. Mozarabic antiphon for Easter: Gaudete populi.
4. Gregorian hymn for Whitsunday: Veni Creator Spiritus.
5. Liturgical drama: Infantem vidimus. (11th–12th century).
6. Troubadour canso: Bernart de Ventadorn. Be m'an perdut.
7. Cantiga: Alfonso El Sabio. Gran dereit'.
8. Lauda: Ogne homo. (13–14th century).
9. Organum duplum: Leonin. Viderunt omnes.
10. Motet: Ave gloriosa mater, Ave Virgo, Domino. (13th century).
11. Instrumental motet (Hocket): In seculum longum. (13th century).
12. Vocal motet: Je n'amerai autre, In seculum. (13th century).
13. Agnus Dei from the Mass of Tournai. (14th century).
14. Polyphonic trope: Fronciaco. Kyrie Jhesu dulcissime. (14th century).
15. Organ paraphrase of a Kyrie. (14th century).
16. Caccia: Giovanni da Firenze. Con brachi assai. (14th century).
17. Ballade: Anthonello de Caserta. Notes pour moi. (14th century).
18. Isorhythmic motet: Dunstable, John. Veni Sancte Spiritus.
19. Villancico: Encina, Juan del. Soy contento y vos servido.
20. Frottola: Cara, Marchetto. O mia cieca e dura sorte.
21. Lute transcription: Capirola, Vincenzo. O mia cieca e dura sorte. (16th century).
22. Meistersinger melody: Sachs, Hans. Gesangweise.
23. Morales, Cristobal. Magnificat octavi toni.
24. Chorale: Walter, Johann. Komm, Gott Schöpfer, heiliger Geist.
25. Psalm setting, French psalter of 1564: Goudimel, Claude. Mon Dieu me paist.
26. Psalm setting, French psalter of 1565: Goudimel, Claude. Mon Dieu me paist.
27. Anthem: Tallis, Thomas. Heare the voyce and prayer of thy servaunts.
28. Polychoral motet: Hassler, Hans Leo. Laudate Dominum.
29. Organ toccata: Merulo, Claudio. Toccata quinta, secondo tuono.
30. Bull, John. Pavana for the virginal.
31. Quodlibet: Fricassée. (16th century).
32. Lied: Senfl, Ludwig. Oho, so geb' der Mann ein'n Pfenning.
33. Madrigal: Gesualdo, Carlo. Moro lasso.
34. Lute ayre: Dowland, John. My thoughts are wing'd with hope.
35. Instrumental dance: Passamezzo d'Italie. (16th century).
36. Viol consort: Gibbons, Orlando. In nomine.
37. Oratorio scene: Cavalieri, Emilio de. Rappresentatione di anima e di corpo.
38. Chorale concerto: Schein, Johann Hermann. Erschienen ist der herrlichte Tag.
39. Lute piece: Gaultier, Denis. Tombeau de Mademoiselle Gaultier.
40. Harpsichord piece: Poglietti, Alessandro. Capriccio über dass Hennengeschrey.
41. Organ chorale prelude: Buxtehude, Dietrich. Nun komm, der Heiden Heiland.
42. Oratorio scene: Charpentier, Marc-Antoine. Le reniement de St. Pierre.
43. Anglican canticle: Blow, John. Jubilate Deo.
44. Scarlatti, Alessandro. Sinfonia to the opera "Le caduta de decem viri."
45. Campra, André. Chaconne from the opera-ballet "Les fêtes vénitiennes."
46. Opera seria: Keiser, Reinhard. Aria from Croesus, "Hoffe noch."
47. Concerto: Vivaldi, Antonio. La primavera. (Allegro).
48. Telemann, Georg Philipp. Fantasie for violin solo.
49. Cantata da camera: Marcello, Benedetto. Recitative and Aria from Stravaganze d'amore, "Amor tu sei."
50. Opera buffa: Pergolesi, Giovanni Battista. Recitative and Aria from Livietta e Tracollo, "Misero."

Pars antiphonarii, *see* Plainsong and Mediaeval Music Society. Pars antiphonarii.

Part music, *see* Hullah, John Pyke. Part music.

Parthenia, *see* Glyn, Margaret Henrietta. Twenty-one Old English compositions of the 16th and 17th centuries.

PARTHENIA; or The Maydenhead of the first musicke that ever was printed for the virginals. Composed by three famous masters, William Byrd, Dr. John Bull, and Orlando Gibbons . . . Ingraven by William Holo. London, Print. for M. Dor. Emans, n.d.
[34]p. (The Harrow replicas. No.3).
"This, the third in a series of facsimiles of memorable autographs and documents, was printed in the autumn of 1942 by the Chiswick Press in London for a group of music-lovers."

PARTHENIA-IN-VIOLATA; or Mayden-Musicke for the virginalls and bass-viol. Selected by Robert Hole. Facsimile of the unique copy of the

New York Public Library. Historical introd. by Thurston Dart. Bibliographical note by Richard J. Wolfe. Foreword by Sydney Beck. New York, New York Public Library, 1961.
103p. (p.49–95 facsim.).
20 duets for virginal and bass viol.
Reproduction of the original ed.
"Foreword": p.11–16. "Historical introduction": p.17–46.
"Watermarks": p.94–95.
"A bibliographical note": p.97–103.

Patrocinium musices, *see* Berg, Adam. Patrocinium musices.

PAUER, ERNST, 1826–1905. ed.
Alte Klavier-Musik. Leipzig, Senff, between 1860–1867.
2 series.
Contents (from *Grove's Dictionary of music and musiciens,* 1916, Vol.2, p.584):
1st series.
Part 1.
Frescobaldi. Corrente and Canzona.
Lully. Sonata in E minor.
Porpora. 2 Fugues.
Part 2.
Galuppi. Sonata in D.
Padre Martini. Gavotte and Ballet.
Paradies. Sonata in A.
Part 3.
Kerl. Toccata in C.
Froberger. Toccata in A minor.
Kuhnau. Suite in E minor.
Part 4.
Mattheson. Suite in A.
Muffat. Courante and 2 Minuets.
Hasse. Sonata in D.
Part 5.
J. L. Krebs. Fugue in F.
Marpurg. Preludium and Capriccio.
Kirnberger. Gigue, Gavotte, Courante, and Allegro for a musical clock.
Part 6.
Dumont. Allemande in D minor.
Chambonnières. Allemande, Courante, Sarabande, and La lourense.
Couperin. La favorite, La tendre Nanette, La ténébreuse.
2d series.
Part 1.
A. Scarlatti. Fugue in F minor.
D. Scarlatti. 3 Studies.
Durante. Study in A.
Part 2.
Murschhauser. Aria pastoralis variata.
W. Fr. Bach. Capriccio in D minor.
Eberlin. Prelude and Fugue in A minor.
Part 3.
Nichelmann. La guillarde et La tendre (Sarabande and Gigue) in G.
Benda. Sonata in G minor.
J. E. Bach. Fantasia and Fugue in F.
Part 4.
J. C. F. Bach. Rondeau in C.
J. Ch. Bach. Sonata in B♭. Op.17.
Part 5.
Rameau. Deux gigues en rondeau, Le rappel des oiseaux, Les tendres plaintes, Deux menuets, L'égyptienne, La poule.
Part 6.
Byrd. Praeludium and Carman's whistle.
Bull. The King's hunting jigg.
O. Gibbons. Praeludium and Galliard.
Arne. Sonata No.3 in G.

PAUER, ERNST, 1826–1905. ed.
Alte Klavier-Musik. A new edition, ed. by Arthur Bliss, appears to have been brought out between 1919–23 by Simrock, Berlin.

PAUER, ERNST, 1826–1905. ed.
Alte Meister. Sammlung werthvoller Klavierstücke des 17. und 18. Jahrhunderts, hrsg. von E. Pauer. Leipzig, Breitkopf & Härtel, between 1868–91.
67 nos. (3 Bd.).
Contents:
No.1. Rameau, J. Ph. Gavotte und Variationen. (A minor).
No.2. Kirnberger, J. Ph. Dreistimmige Fuge. (D minor).
No.3. Kirnberger, J. Ph. Zweistimmige Fuge. (D).
No.4. Marpurg, F. W. Op.1. Capriccio. (F).
No.5. Méhul, E. H. Op.1, No.3. Sonate (A).
No.6. Bach, J. Christian. Sonate (C minor).
No.7. Bach, C. Ph. Em. Allegro. (A).
No.8. Bach, W. Fr. Fuge. (C minor).
No.9. Kuhnau, Joh. Sonate No.2. (D).
No.10. Martini, Padre G. B. Präludium, Fuge und Allegro (E minor).
No.11. Krebs, J. L. Partita No.2. (B flat).
No.12. Krebs, J. L. Partita No.6. (E flat).
No.13. Mattheson, Joh. Vier Giguen.
No.14. Couperin, Fr. La bandoline. Les agrémens.
No.15. Paradies, P. Dom. Sonate No.10. (D).
No.16. Zipoli, Dom. Preludio, Corrente, Sarabanda und Giga. (G minor).
No.17. Cherubini, L. Sonate No.3. (B flat).
No.18. Hässler, J. W. Sonate (A minor).
No.19. Wagenseil, Chr. Op.4. Sonate. (F).
No.20. Benda, G. Largo und Presto. (F).
No.21. Frohberger, J. J. Toccata. (D minor).
No.22. Sacchini, Ant. Sonate (F).
No.23. Hasse, Joh. Ad. Allegro. (B flat).
No.24. Bach, W. Fr. Sonate (C).
No.25. Rolle, J. H. Sonate (Es).
No.26. Händel, G. F. Capriccio (G).
No.27. Rameau, J. Ph. La livri, L'agaçante, La timide.
No.28. Loeilly, J. B. Suite (G minor).
No.29. Rossi, M. A. Andantino und Allegro. (G).
No.30. Turini, F. Presto. (G minor). Sonate. (D flat).
No.31. Bach, C. Ph. Em. La xenophone, Sybille, La complaisante, Les langueurs tendres.
No.32. Graun, C. H. Gigue. (B flat minor).
No.33. Matielli, G. A. Gigue, Adagio und Allegro.
No.34. Sarti, G. Allegro. (G).
No.35. Grazioli, G. B. Sonate No.5 (G).
No.36. Scarlatti, Dom. 2 Studien.

No.37. Mattheson, Joh. Suite No.5 (C minor).
No.38. Couperin, Fr. La bersan, L'ausonienne (allemande), Les charmes, Le bavolet flottant.
No.39. Schobert. Minuetto und Allegro molto. (E flat).
No.40. Muffat, Gottlieb. Gigue (B flat) und Allegro spirituoso. (D).
No.41. Couperin, Fr. Suite (G minor). (Allemande. Courante I, II. Sarabande. Gavotte. Gigue).
No.42. Couperin, Fr. La florentine, La Terpsichore, La garnière, La tendre Fanchon, La lugubre, Passepied.
No.43. Rameau, J. P. Suite (A minor). (Allemande. Courante. Sarabande. Les trois mains. Fanfarinette. La triomphante).
No.44. Rameau, J. P. Les troubillons (rondeau). L'indifférente. La villageoise (rondeau). L'entretien des muses. Les soupirs.
No.45. Marcello, Benedetto. Sonata (B).
No.46. Zipoli, Domenico. Suite (Hm). (Preludio. Corrente. Aria. Gavotte).
No.47. Zipoli, Domenico. Partita (A minor). (Arie mit 12 Variationen).
No.48. Galuppi, Baldassare. Sonate (C minor).
No.49. Galuppi, Baldassare. Sonate (A).
No.50. Paganelli, Giuseppe Antonio. Sonate (F).
No.51. Pescetti, G. B. Sonate (C minor).
No.52. Martini, G. B. Sonate (F).
No.53. Paradies, Pietro D. Sonate (G).
No.54. Paradies, Pietro D. Sonate (F).
No.55. Paradies, Pietro D. Sonate (C).
No.56. Rutini, G. P. Sonate (C).
No.57. Rutini, G. P. Sonate (A).
No.58. Rutini, G. P. Sonate (C).
No.59. Martinez, M. A. Sonate (E).
No.60. Martinez, M. A. Sonate (A).
No.61. Frescobaldi, Girolamo. Toccata No.1 und 2. (G minor).
No.62. Frescobaldi, Girolamo. Toccata No.3 und 4. (G minor).
No.63. Frescobaldi, Girolamo. Toccata No.5 und 6. (E minor).
No.64. Frescobaldi, Girolamo. Toccata No.7 und 8. (D minor, F).
No.65. Frescobaldi, Girolamo. Toccata No.9 und 10. (A minor, F).
No.66. Frescobaldi, Girolamo. Toccata No.11 und 12. (C, C).
No.67. Bach, C. Ph. Em. Concerto (C) per il cembalo solo.

PAUER, ERNST, 1826–1905. ed.
Alte Meister. Reprint. Leipzig, Breitkopf & Härtel, n.d.
6v. (Edition Peters. No.111a–b, 112a–b, 411a–b).

PAUER, ERNST, 1826–1905. ed.
Old English composers for the virginals and harpsichord. A collection of preludes, galliards, pavanes, grounds, chaconnes, suites, overtures, sonates, etc., etc., selected from the works of William Byrd, John Bull, Orlando Gibbons, John Blow, Henry Purcell, and Thomas Aug. Arne, rev. and enl. London, Augener & Co., 1879.
p.1– .

Paumann, Conrad, ca.1410–1473. Fundamentum organisandi, *see* Das Locheimer Liederbuch.

Paumgartner, Bernhard, 1887– , ed. Das Taghorn, *see* Das Taghorn.

Pease, Edward, ed. Pixérécourt manuscript, *see* Pixérécourt manuscript. Music from the Pixérécourt manuscript.

PEDRELL, FELIPE, 1841–1922. ed.
Antología de organistas clásicos españoles (siglos XVI, XVII y XVIII); coleccionada y comentada con juicios y datos biográfico-bibliográficos, par Felipe Pedrell. Madrid, I. Alier, [1908].
2v. in 1.
Contains compositions by Fr. C. de Arauxo, J. Cabanilles, A. Cabezon, Fr. A. Soler, and others.

PEDRELL, FELIPE, 1841–1922. ed.
Hispaniae schola musica sacra. Opera varia (saecul XV, XVI, XVII, et XVIII). Diligenter excerpta, accurate revisa, secula concinnata, a Philippe Pedrell . . . Barcelona, Juan Bta. Pujol; Leipzig, Breitkopf & Härtel, 1894–98.
8v.
Text in Spanish and French.
Contents:
Bd.1. Christophorus Moıales. Composiciones.
Bd.2. Franciscus Guerrero. Composiciones.
Bd.3–4. Antonius a Cabezón. Composiciones, Fabordones, Salmodia, Intermedios, Tiento.
Bd.5. Joannes Ginesius Pérez. Composiciones.
Bd.6. Fray Tomás de Santa Maria. Psalmodia variata; Auctore ignoto. Falsum bordonem; Franciscus Guerrero. Falsum bordonem in IV tono; Tomás Luis de Victoria. Falsum bordonem; Ceuallos (Ceballos). Psalmodia modulata; Auctore incerto. Aliqui psalmi modulata, ut agunt, ad falsum bordonem. Psalmodia modulata (vulgo fabordones).
Bd.7–8. Antonius a Cabezón. Composiciones a cinco y seis partes I, II.

PEDRELL, FELIPE, 1841–1922. ed.
Teatro lirico español anterior al siglo XIX. Ed. Filipe Pedrell. Madrid, 1897–98.
5v.
Contents:
Bd.1. La decantada vica y muerte del General Malbru (Leben und Tod des Generals Marlborough), eine "Tonadilla" von Jacinto Valledor (1785). Mit Betrachtungen über das Werk.
Bd.2. Bruchstücke aus Opern (Tonadillas) des 18. Jahrhunderts von Literes, Esteve, Laserna, Ferrer.
Bd.3. Proben aus Opern des 17. Jahrhunderts das heisst aus Zarzuelas (Schauspielen, Komödien, Balletten, Cuatros und Tonadas)

von Bassa, Correa, Durón, Ferrer, Hidalgo, Latorre, Marin, Navas, Patiño, Peyró, Romero.
Bd.4/5. Weitere Proben aus Werken von Asturiano, Berxes, Duran, Hidalgo, Juato, Literes, Machado, Marin, Marti, Monjo, Navarro, Navas, Patiño, Serqueyra, Valenciano, Villaflor.

PEETERS, FLOR, 1903– . ed.
Altniederländische Meister für Orgel oder Harmonium. Maîtres anciens néerlandais. Early Flemish masters. Hrsg. von Flor Peeters. Mainz, B. Schott's Söhne, [1958].
40p.
Contains compositions by Cornet, Guillet, van Helmont, van den Kerckhoven, Luython, J. de Macque, and J. P. Sweelinck.

PEETERS, FLOR, 1903– . ed.
Anthologia pro organo. Oeuvres choisies de la musique d'orgue du 13me au 18me siècle. Selected pieces of the organ music from 13th to 18th century. Bruxelles, Schott, [1949–50, cop.1949].
4v.
Preface in French, English, and German.
Contents:
Vol.1 contains compositions by J. Bull, W. Byrd, A. de Cabezon, P. Cornet, J. Des Près, G. Dufay, G. Frescobaldi, J. Froberger, A. Gabrieli, Perotin Le Grand, S. Scheidt, J. P. Sweelinck, J. Titelouze, Tomás de Santa Maria, and A. Van den Kerckhoven.
Vol.2 contains compositions by G. Boehm, D. Buxtehude, J. Cabanilles, L. N. Clerambault, F. Couperin, B. Czernohorský, N. De Grigny, V. Lübeck, G. B. Martini, J. Pachelbel, H. Purcell, J. Stanley, M. Van den Gheyn, and J. G. Walther.
Vol.3 contains compositions by G. Brignoli, J. Bull, W. Byrd, A. de Cabezon, G. Cavazzoni, P. Cornet, G. Dufay, G. Frescobaldi, J. Froberger, H. Isaac, G. P. da Palestrina, V. Pellegrini, Perotin Le Grand, M. Praetorius, S. Scheidt, J. P. Sweelinck, J. Titelouze, Thomas de Sancta Maria, and A. Van den Kerckhoven.
Vol.4 contains compositions by G. Boehm, D. Buxtehude, J. Cabanilles, L. N. Clerambault, A. Corelli, Fr. Couperin, N. De Grigny, M. Green, V. Lübeck, G. B. Martini, J. Pachelbel, J. Stanley, M. Van den Gheyn, and J. G. Walther.

PEETERS, FLOR, 1903– . ed.
. . . Oudnederlandse meesters, voor het orgel. Les maîtres anciens néerlandais. Pour grand orgue. 3eme édition. Paris et Bruxelles, Henry Lemoine et Cie., Éditeurs, cop.1938–45.
3v.
Score for organ.
Contents:
Vol.1 contains compositions by J. T. Baustetter, Pieter Cornet, Jozef Hector Fiocco, Hendrik Isaac, Josquin des Près, A. van den Kerckhoven, Jan. Baptist Loeillet, Jan de Macque, Filip de Monte, Jacob Obrecht, Jan Ockeghem, Dieudonné Raick, Jan Pieterszoon Sweelinck, and Adriaan Willaert.
Vol.2 contains compositions by Anton Brumel, Pieter Cornet, Guillaume Dufay, J. H. Fiocco, Mathias van den Gheyn, Charles Guillet, Hendrik Isaac, Josquin des Près, A. van den Kerckhoven, Orlandus Lassus, J. B. Loeillet, Carolus Luython, Jan de Macque, Anthony van Noordt, Jacob Obrecht, Peter Philips, D. Raick, Gherardus Scronx, J. P. Sweelinck, and Adriaan Willaert.
Vol.3 contains compositions by Antoine Brumel, Pieter Cornet, Guillaume Dufay, Mathias van den Ghein, Charles Guillet, Hendrik Isaac, Josquin des Près, A. van den Kerckhoven, Orlandus Lassus, J. B. Loeillet, Carolus Luyton, Jan de Macque, C. F. van Meert, Jacob Obrecht, Peter Philips, Dieudónne Raick, Gherardus Scronx, J. P. Sweelinck, and Adriaan Willaert.

THE PENN STATE MUSIC SERIES. University Park, Pa., Pennsylvania State University Press, 1963– .
No.1– .
Contents:
No.1. Händel, G. F. Look down, harmonious Saint. Cantata for solo tenor and strings. Ed. by Denis Stevens. 1963.
No.2. Roseingrave, Thomas. Compositions for organ and harpsichord. Ed. by Denis Stevens. 1964.
No.3. Lawes, William. Dialogues, for 2 voices and continuo, by William and Henry Lawes. Ed. by Roy Jesson. 1964.
No.4. Gamble, Edwin, ed. Renaissance Lieder [by] Thomas Stolzer, Heinrich Finck, [and] Erasmus Lapicida. 1964.
No.5. Dering, Richard. The cries of London. Ed. by Denis Stevens. 1964.
No.6. Dandrieu, François. Music for harpsichord. Ed. by John White. 1965.
No.7. Monteverdi, Claudio. Hor ch'el ciel e la terra. Ed. by Denis Stevens. 1965.
No.8. La Rue, Pierre de. Magnificat, quinti toni. Ed. by Nigel Davison. 1965.
No.9. Paglietti, Alessandro. Harpsichord music. Ed. by William Earle Nettles. 1966.
No.10. Perti, Giacomo Antonio. Laudate pueri. Ed. by Jean Berger. 1966.
No.11. Hassler, Hans Leo. Mass Dixit Maria. Ed. by Peter Gano. 1966.
No.12. Sixteenth century Italian dances. From British Museum Royal Appendix Ms.59–62. Ed. by Joel Newman. 1966.
No.13. Marenzio, Luca. Giovane Donna. Ed. by Denis Arnold. 1967.

PERGOLESI, GIOVANNI BATTISTA, 1710–1736.
Opera omnia di Giov. Batt. Pergolesi . . . Opere liriche, giocose, cantate, concerti, sonate, oratori, messe, motetti integralmente riprodotti e riumiti in XXV volumi . . . Roma, [Gli Amici della Musica da Camera, 1939–42].
25 (26)v. facsims. (music).

The vocal works are in vocal score with instrumental cues. The instrumental ensemble works include realized basso continuo. One choral part (16p.) in pocket of Vol.23; one part for instrumental solos (15p.) in pocket of Vol.21.
Thirty-one volumes published separately and issued in 3 portfolios with mounted label. On spine of each portfolio: Opera omnia Pergolesiana, Vol.I–VIII (IX–XVI, and XVII–XXV [i.e., XXVI]).
Ed. by Francesco Caffarelli.
Contents:
[Vol.1]. La morte di S. Giuseppe.
[Vol.2]. Lo frate 'nnamorato.
[Vol.3]. Il geloso schernito.
[Vol.4]. Guglielmo d'Aquitania.
[Vol.5]. Sonate a tre per 2 violini e basso continuo.
[Vol.6]. Messa in fa maggiore per 10 voci, 2 cori, 2 orchestre e 2 organi.
[Vol.7]. Sei concertini per stumenti ad arco.
[Vol.8]. Salmi.
[Vol.9]. Salustia.
[Vol.10]. Cantate per soprano: Lontananza. L'addio. Amor fedele. Segreto tormento. Il canto del pastere. Contrasti crudeli. [2 voices] Orfeo.
[Vol.11, No.1]. La serva padrona.
[Vol.11, No.2]. La contadina astuta.
[Vol.11, No.3]. Livietta e Tracollo.
[Vol.12]. Flaminio.
[Vol.13]. "Miserere" Psalmus 50 [2 settings].
[Vol.14]. Adriano in Siria.
[Vol.15, No.1]. Salve Regina. [No.1, 2, and 4 for soprano; No.3 for 2 sopranos].
[Vol.15, No.2]. Messa in re maggiore.
[Vol.16]. Requiem.
[Vol.17, No.1]. Motetti: Adorate devote. Ave verum. Domine ad adiuvandum. Dormo, benigne Jesu. In coelestibus regnis. In hac die. Magnificat. O sacrum convivium. Pro Jesu dum vivo. Siste, superbe fragor. Vexilla regis.
[Vol.17, No.2]. Super flumina.
[Vol.18]. Messa in fa maggiore.
[Vol.19]. Frammenti di opere teatrali: Due sinfonie; Tre arie; Due frammenti dal dramma di P. Metastasio "Artaseres"; Due frammenti dal dramma di P. Metastasio "Catone in Utica"; Aria nel dramma di P. Metastasio "Ciro Riconosciuto"; Recitativo nel dramma di P. Metastasio "Demofoonte"; Due frammenti di una primitiva stesura de l'"Olimpiade"; Aria nel dramma "Semiramide"; Cinque duetti di opere non conosciute.
[Vol.20]. Il prigioniero superbo, opera seria.
[Vol.21]. Sonate e concerti: Sei sonate per clavicembalo. Tre "Suites" per clavicembalo. Sonata per organo. Sinfonia per violoncello e basso continuo. Sonata per violino "in stile di concerto" con accompagnamento di due violini, viola e basso continuo. Due concerti per flauto traverso con accompagnamento di violini e basso continuo. Concerto a cinque per 3 violini, violetta e basso con accompagnamento di 2 corni e organo.
[Vol.22]. Arie da camera: Arie per soprano con accomp. di quartetto d'archi. Arie per contralto con accomp. di quartetto d'archi. Ariette per contralto (basso realizzato). Canzoni per soprano con accomp. di quartetto d'archi. Cantate per soprano con accomp. di quartetto d'archi. Arie buffe con accomp. di quartetto d'archi. Canone a 3 voci.
[Vol.23]. Due messe per 4 voci con accomp. di strumenti e organo. Messa solenne. Messe estense. Frammenti [di messa] (1727–1730).
[Vol.24]. Olimpiade.
[Vol.25]. Il maestro di musica.
[Vol.26]. Sequenze: Stabat Mater. Dies irae.

PERGOLESI, GIOVANNI BATTISTA, 1710–1736.
Opera omnia. This set was republished by F. Caffarelli in 1943 in another arrangement, 5v., as follows:
Vol.1: Vol.21, 5, 7, 10, 22.
Vol.2: Vol.9, 20, 14, 24, 19.
Vol.3: Vol.3, 25, 2, 11, 12.
Vol.4: Vol.1, 4, 23, 16, 6, 15, 18.
Vol.5: Vol.8, 13, 26, 15, 17.

Perlen alter Kammermusik deutscher und italienischer Meister, *see* Schering, Arnold. Perlen alter Kammermusik deutscher und italienischer Meister.

PESSL, YELLA, 1906– . ed.
The art of the suite; eight suites of dances for piano or harpsichord, by masters of the 17th and 18th centuries. Selected and ed. by Yella Pessl. New York, Marks Edition, cop.1947. 80p.
Contains compositions by L. C. d'Aquin, J. C. de Chambonnières, François Couperin, Charles Dieupart, J. C. F. Fischer, J. J. Froberger, Gottlieb Muffat, and Henry Purcell.

Petrescu, Joan D., 1884– , ed. Études de paléographie musicale byzantine, *see* Études de paléographie musicale byzantine.

[PETRUCCI, OTTAVIANO DEI], 1466–1539. pub.
Harmonice musices Odhecaton A. [Milano, Bollettino Bibliografico Musicale, 1932].
103 numbered L., 1L. (Collezione di trattati e musiche antiche edite in fac-simile).
Errors in foliation: p.25 and 31 transposed in numbering; p.84 numbered 48.
Facsimile reprint of the Treviso copy of the Odhecaton, the original of which was first published in Venice probably either January 14, 1503 or May 25, 1504. Folio with colophon wanting in Treviso copy. cf. [Petrucci, Ottaviano dei], pub. Harmonice musices Odhecaton A, ed. by Helen Hewitt . . . Cambridge, Mass., 1942.
Contains 96 three- and four-part compositions with the *incipits* of song texts, mostly secular, underneath the parts. Parts on confronting pages.

[PETRUCCI, OTTAVIANO DEI], 1466–1539. pub.
Harmonice musices Odhecaton A, ed. by Helen

Hewitt; edition of the literary texts by Isabel Pope. Cambridge, Mass., Mediaeval Academy of America, 1942.
ix, [2], 421p. incl. front., facsims. (music), illus. (music). (Half title: The Mediaeval Academy of America. Publication No.42. [Studies and documents. No.5]).
"Lithoprinted."
The original work was published in Venice by Petrucci in 1501.
96 three- and four-part compositions with all available French, Latin, Flemish, Italian, German, and Spanish texts supplied from contemporary sources. Music (in score) in modern transcription (p.219–421).
"List of sources with abbreviations": p.105–28. "Concordance": p.128–67. "Index of text incipits": p.211–13. "Index of composers": p.215–18.

Petrucci, Ottaviano dei, 1466–1539, pub. Laudenbuch, *see* Jeppesen, Knud. Die mehrstimmige italienische Laude um 1500.

Piae cantiones. Ruuta, Theodoricus Petri, comp., *see* Plainsong and Mediaeval Music Society. Ruuta, Theodoricus Petri. Piae cantiones.

PIDOUX, PIERRE. ed.
Le psautier Huguenot du XVIe siècle. Mélodies et documents. Bâle, Bärenreiter, 1962.
2v.

Pièces de clavecin des XVIIme et XVIIIme siècles, *see* Selva, Blanche. Pièces de clavecin des XVIIme et XVIIIme siècles.

PIEDELIEVRE, PAULE.
Les anciens maîtres espagnols. Pièces pour orgue (ou harmonium) XVIe–XVIIIe siècles. Annotation et registration par Paule Piedelievre. Paris, Éditions Musicales de la Schola Cantorum, cop.1952.
1p.L., 46p.
Score for organ.
Contains compositions by Juan Cabanilles, Antonio de Cabezón, Jimenez, Francisco Llissá, Fray Miguel López, Joaquin Oxinagas, F. Fernández Palero, and Fray Antonio Soler.

PIERRE DE CORBEIL, d.1222.
. . . Office de Pierre de Corbeil. (Office de la circoncision) improprement appelé "Office des fous." Texte et chant pub. d'après le Manuscrit de Sens (XIIIe siècle) avec introd. et notes par l'abbé Henri Villetard. Paris, A. Picard & Fils, 1907.
xii, 244p. 2 pl., 4 facsims. (Bibliothèque Musicologique. IV).
"Bibliographie": p.23–37.

PIERRONT, NOËLIE. ed.
Cent versets de Magnificat des XVIème, XVIIème et XVIIIème siècles pour orgue. Recueillis, annotés et registrés par Noëlie Pierront . . . et Norbert Dufourcq . . . Paris, S. Bornemann, cop.1949.
6p.L., 147p.
Score for organ.
Contains compositions by Attaingnant, Bach, Buxtehude, Cabezon, Caldara, Carissimi, Cavazzoni, Dandrieu, Fasolo, Frescobaldi, Guilain, Kerl, Lebègue, Lopez, Pachelbel, Scheidt, Strungk, and Titelouze.

PIPELARE, MATTHAEUS, ca.1500.
Opera omnia. Ed. by Ronald Cross. Rome, American Institute of Musicology, 19? – .
3v.(proposed). (Corpus mensurabilis musicae. No.34).
Contents:
Vol.1. Chansons and motets.

PIRROTTA, NINO, 1908– . ed.
The music of fourteenth-century Italy. Amsterdam, American Institute of Musicology, 1954– .
v.1– . (Corpus mensurabilis musicae. No.8).
Contents:
Vol.1. Bartholus de Florentia, Johannes de Florentia, Gherardellus de Florentia. 1954.
Vol.2. Maestro Piero. Codex Vatican Rossi 215. Anonymous madrigals and cacce from other manuscripts. 1960.
Vol.3. Laurentius Masii de Florentia, Donatus de Florentia, Rosso da Collegrano, and Nine anonymous pieces. 1962.
Vol.4. Jacobus de Bononia, Vincentius de Arimino. 1963.
Vol.5. Andreas de Florentia, Guilielmus de Francia, Bonaiutus Corsini, Andrea Stefani, Ser Feo, Jacopo Pianelaio, Gian Toscano. 1964.

Pirrotta, Nino, 1908– , ed. Paolo Tenorista, *see* Paolo Tenorista, *Don.* Paolo Tenorista in a new fragment of the Italian Ars nova.

PISANO, BERNARDO.
Opera omnia. Ed. by Frank D'Accone. Rome, American Institute of Musicology, 19? – .
v.1– . (Corpus mensurabilis musicae. No.32).
To be published.
Proposed set 2v.

PISTONE, PIER GIOVANNI. ed.
Capalavori della polifonia italiana (sec.XVI). Canzoni e madrigali inediti a 5 voci. Torino, S. Tempia, 1929– .
v.1– . (Repertorio dell' Accademia di Canto Corale Stefano Tempia).

PIXÉRÉCOURT MANUSCRIPT.
Music from the Pixérécourt manuscript. A modern edition of 12 compositions from Paris, Bibliothèque Nationale ms. Fonds Français 15123. Ed. by Edward Pease. Ann Arbor, Mich., University Microfilms, 1960.
95p.
For 3–4 voices: French words.
"A thematic index to the entire manuscript": p.67–87.
"A complete index of textual incipits": p.89–93.

The plainchant of the ordinary of the mass. Catholic Church, Roman. Liturgy and ritual. Graduals. Salisbury, *see* Plainsong and Mediaeval Music Society. Catholic Church, Roman. Liturgy and ritual. Graduals. Salisbury. The plainchant of the ordinary of the mass.

PLAINSONG AND MEDIAEVAL MUSIC SOCIETY.
Publications. Nashdom Abbey, Burnham, Bucks, and [London], Plainsong and Mediaeval Music Society, cop.1890– .
v.1– .
Contents:

Additional settings of certain of the canticles at mattins and evensong adapted from the Sarum service-books by G. H. Palmer. Wantage, Imprinted at the Convent of S. Mary, 1908.
27p.

The anthems of the Blessed Virgin Mary according to the season. Nashdom Abbey, Burnham, Bucks, Plainsong and Mediaeval Music Society, [1931?].
8p.

Antiphonae Beatae Mariae Virginis. Nashdom Abbey, Burnham, Bucks, Plainsong and Mediaeval Music Society, [1931?].
8p.
See also preceding entry, The anthems of the Blessed Virgin Mary.

Antiphons for the Psalms. Part 1 . . . [London], Plainsong and Mediaeval Music Society, 1922.
1v.
Contents:
Part 1. Ferial antiphons.

The antiphons upon the Magnificat and Nunc dimittis from the Salisbury antiphoner. Words translated and the musick adapted by G. H. Palmer. New and revised ed. Wantage, Imprinted at the Convent of S. Mary, 1911.
p.1– .

Atkins, Ivor Algernon, 1869–1953. ed.
The great Advent antiphons. The English translation revised by T. A. Lacey . . . The music adapted from the Worcester antiphoner (Ms. F.160), by Ivor Atkins. Burnham, Bucks, Plainsong and Mediaeval Music Society, 1928.
8p.

Bibliotheca musico-liturgica. A descriptive handlist of the musical and Latin-liturgical mss. of the Middle Ages preserved in the libraries of Great Britain and Ireland. Drawn up by Walter Howard Frere . . . and printed for the members of the Plainsong and Mediaeval Music Society . . . London, Bernard Quaritch, 15, Piccadilly, W., 1901–32.
2v. 17 facsims. (incl. music) on 15 L.

Borren, Charles van den, 1874– . ed.
Polyphonia sacra; a Continental miscellany of the fifteenth century, ed. by Ch. van den Borren. Nashdom Abbey, Burnham, Bucks, and [London], Plainsong and Mediaeval Music Society, 1932.
2p.L., lv p.; 294p. (music), illus. (music).
Caption title: Latin compositions of the Bodleian ms. Canonici misc., transcribed by Charles van den Borren.
"These transcriptions are designed as a completion to those of Sir John Stainer published in 1898 under the title of Dufay and his Contemporaries." Introd.
Includes compositions by Antonius de Civitate, Ar. de Ructis, Arnoldus de Lantins, Bartholomaeus de Bononia, Bartholomeus, Brollo, Baltrame Feragu, Billart, Binchois, Carmen, Cesaris, Chierisy, Franchoys Lebertoul, Gilet Velut, Johannes Brasart, Johannes Ciconia, Johannes de Quatris, Johannes de Sarto, Johannes Franchoys, Guillaume Legrant, Nicolas Grenon, Nicolaus Zacharias, Richardus Loqueville, Ubertus de Psalinis, Ugo de Lantins, Presbyter P. del Zocholo, and anonymous composers.

Briggs, H. B.
Recent research in plainsong. A paper read to the members of the Plainsong and Mediaeval Music Society, by H. B. Briggs. London, Messrs. Vincent, 1898.
31, [1]p. illus.

Catholic Church, Roman. Liturgy and ritual. Antiphonary. Salisbury.
Antiphonale Sarisburiense; a reproduction in facsimile of a manuscript of the thirteenth century, with a dissertation and analytical index, by Walter Howard Frere . . . Prepared for members of the Plainsong and Mediaeval Music Society. [London, The Society, 1901–25].
vi, 101, [1]p. facsim. (668p.).
Facsimile issued in 24 parts, 1901–1915. The following parts are issued combined: fasc. 3 and 4, 5 and 6, 7 and 8, 9 and 10, 11 and 12, 13 and 14, 15 and 16, 17 and 18, 19 and 20, 21 and 22, 23 and 24. Introd. issued in 2 parts, 1923–1925.
Issued in portfolios.
"Three mss. and a printed edition of the Sarum Antiphonal have been utilised, and are represented in this facsimile. [The main part . . . is from the late XIIIth century ms. at the University library at Cambridge, called Ms.ii.9]."
"Description of the . . . authorities which have been consulted as representing the text of the Sarum Antiphonal": p.77–82.

Catholic Church, Roman. Liturgy and ritual. Graduals. Salisbury.
Graduale Sarisburiense. A reproduction in facsimile of a manuscript of the thirteenth century, with a dissertation and historical index illustrating its development from the Gregorian antiphonale missarum. By Walter Howard Frere . . . Prepared for the members of the Plainsong and Mediaeval Music Society.

London, B. Quaritch, 1894.
cii p., 1 L. facsims.

Catholic Church, Roman. Liturgy and ritual. Graduals. Salisbury.
The plainchant of the ordinary of the Mass, adapted from the Sarum Gradual to the English text. 10th ed. Westminster, [London], Plainsong and Mediaeval Music Society, 1937.
1p.L., 67, [1] p.
First edition, 1896, published under title "The plainsong of the Mass. Adapted from the Sarum Gradual . . . Part I." No more published.
7th edition, 1919.

Choir responses. [London, Plainsong and Mediaeval Music Society, 1913?].
4p.

Church of England. Liturgy and ritual.
Evening canticles. Nashdom Abbey, Burnham Bucks, Plainsong and Mediaeval Music Society, 1929.
22p.

Church of England. Liturgy and ritual.
Mass for the dead; arranged to English words by the late Rev. G. H. Palmer . . . 2d. ed. Nashdom Abbey, Burnham, Bucks, Plainsong and Mediaeval Music Society, 1930.
16p.

Church of England. Liturgy and ritual.
The musick of the Mass for the dead; adapted to the English text from the Sarum Manuale by the Rev. G. H. Palmer . . . [London], Plainsong and Mediaeval Music Society, 1902.
16p.

Church of England. Liturgy and ritual.
An order for compline. Nashdom Abbey, Burnham, Bucks, Plainsong and Mediaeval Music Society, 1929.
13p.
See also Plainsong and Mediaeval Music Society. The order of compline.

Church of England. Liturgy and ritual.
Services in Holy Week; being a Palm Sunday procession, a Maundy service, the solemn prayers, reproaches and other devotions of Good Friday, blessing the Paschal and the great vigil service of Easter Eve. Nashdom Abbey, Burnham, Bucks, Plainsong and Mediaeval Music Society, [1933].
68p.

A collection of songs and madrigals by English composers of the close of the 15th century. Prepared for the members of the Plainsong and Mediaeval Music Society [from mss. in the British Museum, with accomp. written by C. W. Pearce]. London, B. Quaritch, 1891.
3p.L., xviii p., 2L., 10p., 1L., 31p.
Half title and binder's title: Songs and madrigals of the fifteenth century.
Accompanied by 8 sheets of music (ancient notation) in portfolio.
300 copies printed.
Sections of introduction are variously signed: "C. W. P." (i.e., C. W. Pearce), "H. B. B." (i.e., H. B. Briggs), and "A. H. H." (i.e., Hughes-Hughes).
"The accompaniments to the songs have been written specially for this work by C. W. Pearce."—Pref.
Songs: Kitt hath lost her kye. Alone I live, by Dr. Cooper. To live alone, by John Cole. In May, that lusty season, by Thos. Forthing. The little pretty nightingale. Though that she cannot redress. Ah! the signs, by Wm. Cornish, Jr.
Madrigals: Jolly Rutterkin, by Wm. Cornish, Jr. Margaret Meek, by Browne. This day day dawns. The farther I go, by Wm. Newark. I love, loved, and loved would I be, by Rob. Fairfax. I love, I love, and whom love ye, by Sir Thos. Phillips. If love now reigned (instrumental) by King Henry VIII.

Cook, Edgar Thomas, 1880–1953.
The use of plainsong, by Edgar T. Cook . . . Nashdom Abbey, Burnham, Bucks, Plainsong and Mediaeval Music Society, 1928.
4p.L., 56p.
Includes music.
"Publishers' lists": p.49–56.

The elements of plainsong; comp. from a series of lectures delivered before the members of the Plainsong and Mediaeval Music Society, 1895. Ed. H. B. Briggs.
p.1– .

The elements of plainsong; comp. from a series of lectures delivered before the members of the Plainsong and Mediaeval Music Society. New ed., curtailed and rearranged. London, Plainsong and Mediaeval Music Society, 1909.
2p.L., vii–x p., 1L., 83p., 1L., 6p.
First ed., 1895, ed. by H. B. Briggs.
Appendix: The psalm-tones from the Sarum Tonale. (6)p.

Fourteen ancient fauxbourdons set to the song of the Blessed Virgin Mary in English, together with the eight tones (in solemn form as to I, II, IV, VI & VII) with the majority of their endings as given in the Sarum Tonale. Selected and arr. by E. W. Goldsmith. 5 parts. (Plainsong and Mediaeval Music Society. Fauxbourdons, Ser.1).

Glyn, Margaret Henrietta, 1865–1946. ed.
Early English organ music (16th century) . . . Transcribed and ed. from the mss. by Margaret Glyn. v.1– . London, Plainsong and Mediaeval Music Society, 1939– .
v.1– .

Hughes, Anselm, *Father*, 1889– . ed.
Anglo-French sequelae; ed. from the papers of the late Dr. Henry Marriott Bannister by Anselm Hughes . . . Nashdom Abbey, Burnham, Bucks, [etc.], Plainsong and Mediaeval Music Society, 1934.
142p.

Hughes, Anselm, *Father*, 1889– . ed.
Worcester mediaeval harmony of the thirteenth and fourteenth centuries. Transcribed, with general introd., fifteen facsimiles, and notes, by Dom Anselm Hughes . . . With a preface by Sir Ivor Atkins . . . Nashdom Abbey, Burnham, Bucks, Plainsong and Mediaeval Music Society, 1928.
x, 11–149p. incl. front. (facsim.), illus. (music), facsims. (music).
Fragments assembled from 15th-century bindings, wrappers to bundles of old accounts in the library of Worcester Cathedral, fly-leaves of books in the Bodleian and the British Museum, etc. The editor believes that the fragments formed portions of at least three Worcester choirbooks, now lost. cf. p.viii.

Hymn melodies for the whole year from the Sarum service-books and other ancient English sources together with sequences for the principal Seasons and Festivals. [London], The Society, 1896.
xxiii, 22, 23p.

The hymner, containing translations of the hymns from the Sarum Breviary together with sundry sequences and processions. 2d. ed. London, 1905.
164p.

Hymnus "Te Deum laudamus," secundum usum Sarisburiensem. London, J. Masters & Co., 1892.
1 sheet.

Litaniae solemnes seu laudes in die Paschae (necnon in fexto Domini Nostri Jesu Christi Regis) e codice F.160, Bibliothecae Ecclesiae Cathedralis Wigorniensis, opere et studio Landelotti Long . . . ac Domini Anselmi Hughes . . . sumptae et recognitae. Nashdom Abbey, Burnham, Bucks, Plainsong and Mediaeval Music Society, 1928.
8p.

The litany and suffrages from the Book of Common Prayer, with the musick from the Sarum Processional. [London], C. Vincent, [1901?].
10p.

The litany and suffrages from the Book of Common Prayer, with the music from the Sarum Processional. Organ accomp. by Francis Burgess. [London], 1904.
(1), 6p.

Madrigals by English composers of the close of the 15th century [from mss. in the British Museum]. London, Novello, Ewer & Co., 1893.
[39]p.
250 copies printed.

Mass for Ascension Day. n.d.
sheet.

Missa "O quam suavis" for 5 voices, by an anonymous English composer, circa 1500 A.D. (Cambridge, University Library, Ms. Nn vi 46). Transcribed and ed., with introd. and explanatory notes, by H. B. Collins . . . Nashdom Abbey, Burnham, Buckinghamshire, Plainsong and Mediaeval Music Society, 1927.
xxxvi, 83p. facsimile plate.

Missa "Rex splendens," e graduali anglicano [Latin text]. London, J. Masters & Co., 1891.
7p.

Missa "Rex splendens," e graduali anglicano. [Same] adapted to the English Communion Service. [English text]. London, J. Masters & Co., 1891.
1L., 9p.

Missa "Rex splendens," e graduali anglicano. [Same] composed by Saint Dunstan (as to the Kyrie) and adapted to the English Communion Service from early manuscripts by the Plainsong and Mediaeval Music Society, with accompanying harmonies by Ch. W. Pearce. [English text]. London, Novello, Ewer & Co., [1892?].
2L., 7p.

The musical notation of the Middle Ages exemplified by facsimiles of mss. written between the 10th and 16th centuries inclusive. London, J. Masters & Co., 1890.
p.1– .
245 copies printed.
Consists of 20 facsimile plates and 1 explanatory plate.

The offices, or introits for Sundays and Festivals, with the musical notation from the Sarum Graduale adapted by G. H. Palmer. Wantage, Imprinted at the Convent of S. Mary the Virgin, 1904.
(6), 80p.

Old Hall manuscript.
The Old Hall manuscript, transcribed and ed. by the Rev. A. Ramsbotham. [Compiled by H. B. Collins and Dom Anselm Hughes]. Nashdom Abbey, Burnham, Bucks, Plainsong and Mediaeval Music Society, 1933–38.
3v.
Issued in parts. Fasc.1 (p.1–120) was issued in 1931 as the Society's annual volume for 1930.

A collection of 15th-century English music containing compositions by Chirbury, Aleyn, Lambe, Typp, Oliver, Leonel, Cooke, Damett, Sturgeon, and others. "The manuscript . . . rests in the Library of St. Edmund's College, Old Hall, near Ware."–cf. Introd.

The order for "Placebo" or vespers of the dead with the musical notation from the Salisbury Antiphoner. Adapted by G. H. Palmer, 2d. ed. rev. Wantage, Imprinted at the Convent of S. Mary, 1903.
12p.

The order for the burial of the dead, adapted to plainchant from the Sarum Antiphoner by G. H. Palmer. Wantage, Imprinted at the Convent of S. Mary, 1903.
(2), 9p.

The order of compline throughout the year with the musical notation from the Salisbury Antiphoner, adapted by G. H. Palmer. 2d. ed. rev. Wantage, Imprinted at the Convent of S. Mary, 1899.
(4), 35p.
See also Plainsong and Mediaeval Music Society. Church of England. Liturgy and ritual. An order for compline.

The ordinary of the Mass. Organ accompaniments. London, The Society, 1910.
61 (1)p., 2L.

Pars antiphonarii. A reproduction in facsimile of a manuscript of the eleventh century in the Chapter Library at Durham (Ms. B. iii. II). London, Plainsong and Mediaeval Music Society, 1923.
p.136–59.

The plainsong of the Holy Communion. [London], 1912.
2 parts.
Pt.ii has title: The plainsong of the Holy Communion adapted from the Sarum Gradual.

The plainsong of the Mass, adapted from the Sarum Gradual to the English text. Pt.1. The ordinary, containing Kyrie, Creed, Sanctus, Agnus Dei and Gloria in Excelsis. London, 1896.
p.1– .
5th ed., 1906.
See also Plainsong and Mediaeval Music Society. Catholic Church, Roman. Liturgy and ritual. Graduals. Salisbury. The plainchant of the ordinary of the Mass.

The Psalm tones. [London], 19?– .
13p.

The Psalm tones from the Sarum Tonale, with organ accompaniment. London, Plainsong and Mediaeval Music Society, [19?–].
2p.L., 2–13p., [4]p.
"The object of this work is to provide organists with a manual of accompaniments for use with the Sarum Psalter.–Pref.

Psalms of David pointed to the eight Gregorian tones as given in the Sarum Tonale by G. H. Palmer. 1908.
p.1– .

The reproaches. [an ancient service of the Holy Week]. London, The Society, [1903?].
[7]p.

Requiem services, containing the musick for Vespers and Mass together with the Order for the Burial of the Dead. [London, Plainsong and Mediaeval Music Society, 1903.
3 parts in 1 v.

Ruuta, Theodoricus Petri, fl.1581–1625. comp.
Piae cantiones; a collection of church and school song, chiefly ancient Swedish, originally published in AD. 1582 by Theodoric Petri of Nyland. Rev. and re-edited with preface and explanatory notes, by the Rev. G. R. Woodward M.A. and printed at the Chiswick Press for the Plainsong and Mediaeval Music Society. London, 1910.
xxxiv, 281p. front., illus. (facsims.).

Salve Rex. [Words adapted from the Primer of 1542 in St. Paul's Cathedral Library]. [London], n.d.
(3)p.

A selection of communions with the musical notation from the Salisbury Graduale. Ed. and in part adapted by E. W. Goldsmith. London, 1907.
16p.

A selection of grails, alleluyas and tracts for Sundays and Holy-Days from the Sarum Graduale. Adapted to the English Text by G. M. Palmer. Wantage, Imprinted at the Convent of S. Mary, 1908.
iv, 74p.

A selection of offices, grails and alleluyas for Sundays and Festivals from the Sarum Graduale, adapted by G. H. Palmer. Wantage, Imprinted at the Convent of S. Mary, 1900.
p.1– .

The service of Tenebrae or Mattins and Lauds of the last three days of Holy Week from the Sarum Breviary. Newly done into English and adapted to the original note by G. H. Palmer. Wantage, Imprinted at the Convent of S. Mary, [1906–8].
Pt.I, III.

Simple music for the Holy Communion. n.d.
(8)p.

Songs of Syon; a collection of hymns and sacred poems mostly translated from ancient Greek, Latin and German services. [pref.1904].
p.1– .

Te Deum laudamus. [English words]. [London, The Society, 18?–].
2L.

Three plainsong masses from early manuscripts, adapted to the English Communion Service. 2d. ed. rev. London, J. Masters & Co., 1890.
7p.

Wagner, Peter Josef, 1865–1931.
Introduction to the Gregorian melodies; a handbook of plainsong by Prof. Peter Wagner, Ph.D. 2d ed., completely rev. and enl. . . . London, Plainsong and Mediaeval Music Society, [1901]– .
v.1– .
Contents:
Vol.1. Origin and development of the forms of the liturgical chant up to the end of the Middle Ages.

Wooldridge, Harry Ellis, 1845–1917. ed.
Early English harmony from the 10th to the 15th century, illustrated by facsimiles of mss. with a translation into modern notation; ed. by H. E. Wooldridge . . . Prepared for the members of the Plainsong and Mediaeval Music Society. London, B. Quaritch, 1897–1913.
2v.
Contents:
Vol.1. Facsimiles. Ed. by H. E. Wooldridge.
Vol.2. Transcriptions and notes. Ed. by H. V. Hughes.

Wyatt, Edward Gerald Penfold, 1869– .
St. Gregory and the Gregorian music. [London, Sprague & Co.], 1904.
40p., 8L. plates, ports.
"Sources": p.[3].

The plainsong of the Holy Communion, *see* Plainsong and Mediaeval Music Society. The plainsong of the Holy Communion.

The plainsong of the Mass, *see* Plainsong and Mediaeval Music Society. The plainsong of the Mass.

PLATZMUSIK. Originalwerke und Bearbeitung für Blasorchester hrsg. von Walter Lott. Lippstadt, F. Kistner & C. F. W. Siegel & Co., 19? – .
No.1– .
Contents:
Nr.1. Grabner. Op.44. Burgmusik: I. Einzug; II. Ständchen; III. Tanz im Burghof.
Nr.2. Höffner. Fliegermusik.
Nr.3. Höffner. Musik zu einem Volkspiel.
Nr.4. Grabner. Firlefei. Variationen zum Spielen und Tanzen.
Nr.5. Herrmann. Süddeutsche Dorfmusiken: I. Bauernmarsch; II. Kleines Tanzliederspiel; III. Ländlicher Reigen; IV. Dorfabend; V. Weckruf.
Nr.6. Reuter. Sudetendeutsche Suite.
Nr.7. Höffer. Fliegermorgen. Fantasiestück für Blasorchester.
Nr.8. Händel. Ouverture aus der Feuerwerksmusik (Concerto grosso Nr.20) bearb. von R. Kröber.
Nr.9. Genzmer. Musik für Flieger-Orchester.
Nr.10. Höffer. Heitere Bläser-Sinfonie.
Nr.11. Walter. Kleine Suite für Bläser und Pauken.
Nr.12. Aschenbrenner. Ländlicher Festtag.

PLAYFORD, JOHN, 1623–1686. comp.
The English dancing master. Ed. by Hugh Mellor. London, Hugh Mellor, pref. 1933.
104p.
With reproduction of the original title page: The English dancing master: or, Plaine and easie rules for the dancing of country dances, with the tune to each dance. London, Printed by Thomas Harper, and are to be sold by John Playford at his shop in the Inner Temple neere the church doore. 1651.

PLAYFORD, JOHN, 1623–1686. comp.
Old English dance tunes, 17th century, from Playford's "The dancing master." For pianoforte, by Adam Carse. London, Augener, Ltd., [cop.1922].
15p. (Album series. No.178).

Les plus belles pièces de clavessin de l'école française, *see* Grovlez, Gabriel Marie. Les plus belles pièces de clavessin de l'école française.

Poètes et musiciens du XVe siècles, *see* Droz, Eugénie. Poètes et musiciens du XVe siècles.

A polifonia clássica portuguesa, *see* Santos, Julio Eduardo. A polifonia clássica portuguesa.

POLIFONÍA ESPAÑOLA. Madrid, Union Musical Española, cop.1952– .
v.1– .
Vol.1. Morales, Cristobal. Cuatro motetes (Benois). cop.1952.
Vol.2. Rubio, Samuel. Canciones espirituales polifónicas. 2v. cop.1955–1956.
Vol.3. Pérez, Juan Ginés. Miseremini fideles animarum; motete a 5 voces a capella (Benois). cop.1958.
Vol.4. Pérez, Juan Ginés. Parce mihi, Domine; motete a 5 voces a capella (Benois). cop.1958.
Vol.5. Tomás de Santa María. Fabordon del i tono, a 4 voces a capella (Benois). cop.1958.
Vol.6. Robledo, Melchor. Ave maris stella, a 4 voces a capella (Benois). cop.1958.
Vol.7. Castillo, Diego del. O altitudo divitiarum; motete a 5 voces a capella (Benois). cop.1958.
Vol.8. Ortiz, Diego. Pereat dies; motete a 5 voces a capella (Benois). cop.1958.
Vol.9. Infantas, Fernando de las. Victimae paschali; secuencia de resurrección para 6 voces a capella (Benois). cop.1958.
Vol.10. Fernández de Castilleja, Pedro. Dispersit; motete a 4 voces a capella (Benois). cop. 1958.

Vol.11. Fernández de Castilleja, Pedro. Heu mihi; motete a 5 voces a capella (Benois). cop.1958.
Vol.12. Ribera, Bernardino de. Rex autem David; motete a 5 voces a capella (Benois). cop.1958.
Vol.13. Escobedo, Bartolomé. Exsurge, quare obdormis; motete a 4 voces a capella (Benois). cop.1958.
Vol.14. Escobedo, Bartolomé. Immutemur (Benois). cop.1958.
Vol.15. Cevallos, Francisco. Exaudiat; motete a 4 voces a capella (Benois). cop.1958.
Vol.16. Gómez Camargo, Miguel. Himno de Santiago apostol, a 4 voces a capella (Benois). cop.1958.
Vol.17. Pérez, Juan Ginés. Domine Deus; motete a 5 voces a capella. cop.1958.
Vol.18. Victoria, Tomás Luis de. Ave Maria. cop.1953.
Vol.19. Navarro, Juan. Lauda Jerusalem; salmo a 4 voces a capella. cop.1956.
Vol.20. Pérez, Juan Ginés. Gloria, laus et honor; himno a 5 voces a capella. cop.1958.
Vol.21. Guerrero, Francisco. Ave Virgo sanctissima; motete a 5 voces a capella. cop.1958.
Vol.22. Guerrero, Francisco. Trahe me post Te, Virgo Maria; motete a 5 voces a capella. cop. 1956.
Vol.23. Vietoria, Tomás Luis de. O quam gloriosum; motete a 4 voces a capella. cop.1956.
Vol.24. Victoria, Tomás Luis de. Jesu dulcis memoria; motete a 4 voces a capella. cop. 1956.
Vol.25. Victoria, Tomás Luis de. O vox omnes, motete a 4 voces. cop.1958.
Vol.26. Victoria, Tomás Luis de. O! Domine; motete a 6 voces a capella (O Domine Jesu Christe). cop.1956.
Vol.27. Victoria, Tomás Luis de. Vere languores; motete a 4 voces a capella. cop.1956.
Vol.28. Peñalosa, Francisco de. Sancta Mater; motete a 4 voces a capella. cop.1956.

Polifonia vocale sacra e profana. Sec.XVI, *see* Somma, Bonaventura. Polifonia vocale sacra e profana. Sec.XVI.

Polish Academy of Sciences and the State Institute of Fine Arts. Monumenta musicae in Polonia, *see* Monumenta musicae in Polonia.

Polyphonia sacra. Borren, Charles van den, *see* Plainsong and Mediaeval Music Society. Borren, Charles van den. Polyphonia sacra.

Polyphonic music of the fourteenth century, *see* Schrade, Leo, ed. Polyphonic music of the fourteenth century.

Polyphonies du XIIIe siècle, *see* Montpellier, France. Université. Faculté de Médicine. Bibliothèque. Mss. (H 196). Polyphonies du XIIIe siècle.

The polyphony in the Manuscript J.II.9, *see* Turin. Biblioteca Nazionale. Mss. (J.II.9). The Cypriot-French repertory.

Popular music of the olden time, *see* Chappell, William. Old English popular music.

PORTUGALIAE MUSICA. Lisboa, Fundação Calouste Gulbenkian, 1959– .
v.1– .
Contents:
Sér.A. Vol.1. Coelho, Manuel Rodrigues. Flores de musica. Pera o instrumento de tecla y harpa. Vol.1. Transcrição e estudo de Macario Santiago Kastner. 1959.
Sér.B. Vol.2. Carvalho, João de Sousa. L'amore industrioso. Revisão e estudo de Filipe de Sousa. 1960. Score and parts.
Sér.A. Vol.3. Coelho, Manuel Rodrigues. Flores de musica. Pera o instrumento de tecla y harpa. Vol.2. Transcrição e estudo de Macario Santiago Kastner. 1961.
Sér.A. Vol.4. Lopes Morago, Estêvão. Várias obras de música religiosa "a cappella." Edição preparada, ante os textos originais, por Manuel Joaquim. 1961.
Sér.A. Vol.5. Cardoso, Frei Manuel. Liber primus missarum. Vol.1. Transcrição e estudo de José Augusto Alegria. 1962.
Sér.A. Vol.6. Cardoso, Frei Manuel. Liber primus missarum. Vol.2. Transcricão e estudo de José Augusto Alegria. 1962. [cop.1963].
Sér.A. Vol.7. João da Costa de Lisboa. Tenção. Selecção e transcrição de Cremilde Rosado Fernandes. 1963.
Sér.B. Vol.8. Bontempo, João Domingos. Sinfonia, No.1/Op.11. Revisão e estudo de Filipe de Sousa. 1963. Score and parts.
Sér.B. Vol.9. Portugal, Marcos. Il duca di foix. Revisão e marcação de Mário de Sampayo Ribeiro. 1964. Score and parts.
Sér.A. Vol.10. Seixas, Carlos. 80 Sonatas para instrumentos de tecla. Transcrição e estudo de Macario Santiago Kastner. 1965.

Portuguese old masters, *see* Kastner, Macário Santiago. Cravistas Portuguezes.

POTTER, FRANK HUNTER. ed.
Reliquary of English song. Collected and ed., with an historical introd. and notes, by Frank Hunter Potter. The accompaniments harmonized and arranged by Charles Vincent . . . and T. Tertius Noble . . . New York, G. Schirmer, Inc., [cop. 1915–16].
2v.
Piano-vocal score.
Contents:
Vol.1. 1250–1700. Contains compositions by John Blow, John Dowland, Pelham Humphrey, Henry Lawes, William Lawes, Thomas Morley, Henry Purcell, J. Wilson.
Vol.2. 1700–1800. Contains compositions by Michael Arne, T. A. Arne, Thomas Attwood, William Boyce, Henry Carey, John Davy, William Defesch, Charles Dibdin, J. E. Galliard, G. F. Händel, James Hook, Samuel Howard, Richard Leveridge, Thomas Linley, George Monro, James Oswald, Mrs. Plowden, William Reeve, William Shield, R. J. S. Stevens, Stephen Storace, John Weldon.

Pour connaisseurs et amateurs, *see* Für Kenner und Liebhaber.

Practical harmony, Selection of, *see* Clementi, Muzio. Clementi's Selection of practical harmony.

PRAETORIUS, MICHAEL, 1571–1621.
Gesamtausgabe der musikalischen Werke von Michael Praetorius. In Vergindung mit Arnold Mendelssohn und Willibald Gurlitt. Hrsg. von Friedrich Blume. Wolfenbüttel-Berlin, Georg Kallmeyer Verlag, 1928–41, 1960.
21v. in 22.
Published in Lieferungen.
Contents:
Bd.1–9. Musae Sioniae I–IX. (1605– 1610).
Bd.10. Musarum Sioniarum Motectae et Psalmi latini. (1607).
Bd.11. Missodia Sionia. (1611).
Bd.12. Hymnodia Sionia. (1611).
Bd.13. Eulogodia Sionia. (1611).
Bd.14. Megalynodia Sionia. (1611).
Bd.15. Terpsichore. (1612).
Bd.16. Urania. (1613).
Bd.17. I. und II. Polyhymnia caduceatrix et Panegyrica. (1619).
Bd.18. Polyhymnia exercitatrix. (1620).
Bd.19. Puericinium. (1621).
Bd.20. Gesammelte kleinere Werke. Gesamtbericht Register.
Bd.21. Generalregister. Bearb. von Walther Engelhardt. 1960.

PRAETORIUS, MICHAEL, 1571–1621.
Sämtliche Orgelwerke. Hrsg. von Karl Matthaei. Eingeleitet von Willibald Gurlitt. Wolfenbüttel, Georg Kallmeyer, 1930.
105p.

Près, Josquin de, *see* Deprès, Josquin.

Prime fioriture del melodramma italiano, *see* Mantica, Francesco. Prime fioriture del melodramma italiano.

Il primo libro d'intavolatura di balli d'arpicordo, *see* Radino, Giovanni Maria. Il primo libro d'intavolatura di balli d'arpicordo.

PROKOFIEFF, SERGE, 1891–1953.
Complete works. Moscow, State Music Publishers, 1955– .
v.1– .
Contents:
Vol.1. Piano pieces, Op.2, 3, 4, 11, 12, 17, 22, 31, 32, 59, 65.
Vol.2. Piano sonatas.
Vol.3. Orchestral works, arr. for piano by the composer, Op.25, 36b, 52, 75, 77, 95, 96, 97, 102. Organ prelude and fugue (Buxtehude). Schubert waltzes.
Vol.4. Piano concerti No.1, 2, 3 (arr. for 2 pianos).
Vol.5. Piano concerti No.1, 2, 3 (orchestra score).
Vol.6a/b/c. War and peace. (orchestra score).
Vol.7a/b. War and peace. (vocal score).
Vol.8a/b. Romeo and Juliet. (orchestra score).
Vol.9. Romeo and Juliet. (piano score).
Vol.10a/b. Cinderella. (orchestra score).
Vol.11. Cinderella. (piano score).
Vol.12a/b. Tale of the stone flower. (orchestra score).
Vol.13. Tale of the stone flower. (piano score).
Vol.14a. Symphonies No.1 and 3. (orchestra score).
Vol.14b. Symphonies No.5 and 7. (orchestra score).

PROSKE, KARL, 1794–1861. ed.
Musica divina. Sive thesaurus consentuum selectissimorum omni cultui divino totius anni juxta ritum Sanctae Ecclesiae Catholicae inservientium: Ab excellentissimis superioris aevi musicis muneris harmonicis compositoram. Quos e codicibus originalibus tam editis quam ineditis accuratissime in partitionem redactos. Ad instaurandam polyphoniam vere ecclesiasticam publice offert Carolus Proske. Annus 1–2. Ratisbonae, Friderici Pustet, 1853–between 1874–1878.
8v. in 2 years.
Contents (from *Grove's Dictionary of music and musicians*, 1916, Vol.3, p.329–30):
Annus primus.
Tom 1. Liber missarum. 1853.
1. Palestrina. Missa brevis.
2. Palestrina. Missa brevis. Iste confessor.
3. Palestrina. Missa brevis. Dies sanctificatus.
4. Lasso, O. Missa brevis. Octavi toni.
5. Lasso. Missa brevis. Puisque j'ay perdu.
6. Vittoria. Missa brevis. Quarti toni.
7. Gabrieli, A. Missa brevis.
8. Hasler. Missa brevis. Dixit Maria.
9. Pitoni. Missa brevis. In Nat. Domini.
10. Lotti. Missa brevis.
11. Asola. Missa brevis. Pro defunctis.
12. Pitoni. Missa brevis. Pro defunctis.

Tom 2. Liber motettorum. 1854.
Advent.
Fux, J. J. Domine.
Handl, J. Ecce concipies. Pt.2. Super solium David.
—— Obsecro domine.
Cardoso, M. Cum audisset.
Fux, J. J. Dicite pusillanimes.
Handl, J. Egredietur virga. Pt.2. Radix Jesse.
—— De coelo veniet.
Canniciari, P. Ave Maria.
Nativity of Christ.
Palestrina. Dies sanctificatus.
Nanini, G. M. Hodie Christus.
Vittoria. O magnum mysterium.
Porta, C. Hodie nobis de coelo.
Handl, J. Natus est nobis Deus.
Turini, Fr. Hodie Christus.
St. Stephen.
Nanini, G. M. Lapidabunt Stephanum.
Marenzio, L. Sepelierunt Stephanum.
St. John.
Nanini, G. M. Hic est beatissimus.
Palestrina. Valde honorandus.
Innocents.
Clemens non Papa. Vox in Rama.
Circumcision.
Constantini, F. O admirabile commercium.

Lasso, Rud. Ecce Maria genuit.
Epiphany.
Marenzio, L. Tribus miraculis.
Handl, J. Ab oriente.
Sundays after Epiphany.
Lasso, O. Jubilate.
—— Dextera Domini.
Septuagesima.
Aichinger, G. Ubi est Abel?
Sexagesima.
Kerle, J. de. Exurge. Pt.2. Exurge.
Quinquagesima.
Lasso, O. Benedictus es.
Quadragesima.
Croce, G. Exaltabo te.
Cardoso, M. Angelis suis.
Lasso, O. Meditabor.
Vecchi, Orazio. Erat Jesus.
Scarlatti, A. Laetatus sum.
Passion Sunday.
Lasso, O. Eripe me de inimicis. Pt.2. Confitebor tibi.
Palm Sunday.
Palestrina. Pueri Hebraeorum.
Lasso, O. Improperium.
Coena Domini.
Asola. Christus factus est.
Good Friday.
Vittoria. Popule meus.
Aichinger. Adoramus.
Easter Eve.
Handl, J. Vespere autem.
Easter Day.
Palestrina. Haec dies.
Anerio, F. Angelus autem.
—— Alleluja Christus.
Gabrieli, A. Maria Magdalenae.
Lasso, O. Christus resurgens.
Marenzio. Et respicientes.
Sundays after Easter.
Palestrina. Surrexit pastor.
Croce, G. Virtute magna.
Aichinger, G. Laude anima mea.
Turini, G. Cantate Domino.
Lasso, O. Benedicite gentes.
Marenzio. O rex gloriae.
Handl, J. Ascendens Christus.
Casini, G. M. Omnes gentes.
Whitsunday.
Palestrina. Loquebantur.
Allegri, G. Veni Sancti Spiritus.
Aichinger, G. Factus est repente. Pt.2. Confirma hoc Deus.
Trinity Sunday.
Gabrieli, A. Te Deum Patrem.
Lasso, O. Tibi laus.
Agazzari. Benedicta sit.
Corpus Christi.
Croce, G. O sacrum convivium.
Bernabei, G. A. O sacrum convivium.
Gabrieli, A. Caro mea.
Constantini, A. Ego sum panis.
Agostini, P. Ego sum panis.
Pitoni. In voce exultationis.
—— Ex altari tuo.
—— Qui terrena triumphat.
Biordi, G. Transfige.
Vittoria. Domine non sum dignus. Pt.2. Miserere mei.
—— Duo seraphini. Pt.2. Tres sunt qui.
Lasso, O. Domine convertere.
—— Sperent in te omnes.
—— Illumina.
—— Benedicam.
—— In te speravi.
—— Expectans.
—— Domine in auxilium.
—— Super flumina.
St. Andrew.
Vittoria. Doctor bonus.
St. Nicholas.
Anon. Beatus Nicolas.
Conception.
Palestrina. Quam pulchri.
Marenzio. Conceptio tua.
Porta, C. Conceptio tua.
St. Thomas.
Hasler. Quia vidisti.
Name of Jesus.
Handl, J. In nomine.
Lasso, Rud. O Jesu benignissime.
Purification.
Vittoria. Senex puerum.
Constantini, F. Hodie puerum.
Annunciation.
Marenzio. Gabriel Angelus.
Vittoria. Ne timeas.
Hasler. Dixit Maria.
Invention of the Cross.
Anerio, F. Nos autem.
St. John Baptist.
Palestrina. Fuit homo.
Lasso, L. Joannes est nomen.
St. Peter and Paul.
Clemens non Papa. Tu es Petrus.
Marenzio. Quem dicunt.
—— Hodie Paulus.
Visitation B.V.M.
Hasler. Beata es.
Mary Magdalene.
Gabrieli, A. Mulier quae erat.
St. Lawrence.
Gabrieli, A. Levita Laurentius.
Assumption.
Palestrina. Quae est ista.
Anerio, F. Vidi speciosam.
—— Sicut cedras.
Aichinger, G. Assumpta est, a 3.
Beheading of St. John Baptist.
Palestrina. Missa Herodes.
Nativity of B.V.M.
Marenzio. Nativitas gloriosae.
Handl, J. Regali ex progenie.
Bai. Cum jucunditate.
Pitoni. Felix namque.
Exaltation of the Cross.
Palestrina. Adoramus.
Anerio, F. Crux fidelis.
—— Factum est.
Guardian Angels.
Aichinger. Omnes sancti angeli.
All Saints.
Palestrina. Salvator mundi.
Gabrieli, A. Angeli, archangeli.

Porta, C. Vidi turbam.
Vittoria. O quam gloriosum.
Marenzio. O quam gloriosum.
St. Martin.
Palestrina. O quantus luctus.
Marenzio. O Beatum.
Presentation of B.V.M.
Palestrina. Congratulamini.
St. Cecilia.
Palestrina. Dum aurora.
Marenzio. Cantantibus organis.
Bai. Triduanas.

Palestrina. Isti sunt viri.
Vittoria. Estote fortes.
Gabrieli, A. Tolite jugum.
Croce, G. Beati eritis.
Gabrieli, A. Beatus vir.
Vittoria. Iste Sanctus.
Anerio, F. Honestum fecit.
—— Desiderium animae.
Vittoria. Gaudent in coelis.
Nanini, G. M. Laetamini, a 3.
Casciolini, C. Istorum est enim.
Gabrieli, A. Filiae Jerusalem.
Vittoria. Ecce sacerdos.
Gabrieli, A. Sacerdos et pontifex.
Marenzio. Dum esset summus.
Brissio, G. F. In medio ecclesiae, a 3.
Vittoria. Hic vir despiciens.
Marenzio. Similabo eum.
Vecchi, Orazio. Euge serve.
Bai. Serve bone.
Anon. Intercessio nos.
Palestrina. Veni sponsa Christi.
Vittoria. Veni sponsa Christi.
Gabrieli, A. Veni sponsa Christi.
Anerio, F. Regnum mundi.
Palestrina. Exaudi Domine.
Vittoria. O quam metuendus.
Handl, J. Domum tuam.

Appendix.
Preface, tables of contents, clefs, etc.
Palestrina. Sicut cervus. Pt.2. Sitivit anima.
Lasso, O. Factus est Dominus.
Vittoria. Benedicam.
Anerio, F. Ego dixi.
Hasler, J. L. Cantate Domino.
—— Domine Deus.
—— Gratias agimus.
Vecchi, Orazio. Cantabo Domino.
—— Velociter exaudi.
Croce, G. Exaude Deus.
—— Voce mea.
—— Ego sum pauper.
—— Benedicam.
Constantini, A. Confitemini.
Pitoni. Cantate Domino.
—— Laudate Dominum.
Scarlatti, A. Exultate Deo.

Tom 3. Liber vesperarum. 1859.
Falsibordoni, by Vittoria, Bernabei, C. de Zachariis, L. Viadana.
Psalmodia modulata, by Demantius, C. de Zachariis.
Psalmi ad vesperas, by Ortiz, G. Turini.
Anerio, F. 6 Psalmi.
Nanini, B. 4 Psalmi.
Anon. 4 Psalmi.
Psalmi.
Giovanelli, R. Dixit.
Pitoni, O. Laudate.
Anon. Laudate.
Fux, J. J. Nisi Dominus.
—— Beati.
—— De profundis.
Suriano. Magnificat. 8 tonorum.
Lasso, O. Magnificat. 8 tonorum.
Palestrina. Magnificat. 8th tone.
Lasso, O. Magnificat. 1st tone.
Morales. Magnificat. 8th tone.
Ortiz. Magnificat. 5th tone.
Anerio, F. Magnificat. 5th tone.
Marenzio. Magnificat. 4th tone.
Pitoni. Magnificat. 4th tone.
Fux. Magnificat. 4th tone.
Hymns for vespers.
Anerio, F. Christi redemptor.
Palestrina. Hostis Herodes.
—— Vexilla regis.
Vittoria. Jesu nostra redemptio.
Palestrina. Veni Creator.
Vittoria. O lux beata.
—— Pange lingua.
Pitoni. Pange lingua.
Casini. Pange lingua.
Ortiz. Nuntius celso.
—— Junctor coeli.
Anon. Collaudamus.
Ortiz. Christe redemptor.
Vittoria. Urbs beata.
—— Ave maris stella.
Suriano. Ave maris stella.
Hasler. Ave maris stella.
Biordi. Ave maris stella.
Antiphons of the B.V.M.
Suriano, F. Alma Redemptoris.
—— Ave Regina.
—— Regina coeli.
—— Salve Regina.
—— Salve Regina.
Anerio, F. Alma Redemptoris.
—— Ave Regina.
—— Regina coeli.
—— Salve Regina.
Aichinger, G. Alma Redemptoris.
—— Ave Regina.
—— Regina coeli.
—— Salve Regina.
—— Alma Redemptoris.
—— Ave Regina.
—— Regina coeli. Pt.2. Resurrexit.
—— Salve Regina.
Palestrina. Alma Redemptoris. Pt.2. Tu quae genuisti.
Anerio, F. Alma Redemptoris.
Aichinger. Alma Redemptoris.
Lasso, O. Ave Regina.
Porta, C. Ave Regina.
Aichinger. Ave Regina.
Fux. Ave Regina.
Ortiz. Regina coeli. Pt.2. Resurrexit.

Porta, C. Regina coeli.
Lotti. Regina coeli.
Lasso, L. Salve Regina. Pt.2. Et Jesum.
Anerio, F. Salve Regina.
Aichinger. Salve Regina.

Tom 4. Liber vespertinus. 1862.
Suriano. Passio Christi.
Matthew.
Mark.
Luke.
John.
Palestrina. Lamentationes.
In coena Domini.
Parasceve.
Sabbato sancto.
Responsoria.
Croce, G. In monte Oliveti.
—— Tristis est anima.
Viadana, L. Ecce vidimus.
—— Amicus meus.
Zoilo, A. Judas mercator.
Croce, G. Unus ex discipulis.
Viadana, L. Eram quasi agnus.
Ferrario. Una hora.
Viadana, L. Seniores populi.
—— Omnes amici.
Croce, G. Velum templi.
Viadana, L. Vinea mea.
Croce, G. Tenebrae factae.
Zoilo, A. Tradiderunt.
—— Caligaverunt.
Viadana, L. Sicut ovis.
—— Jerusalem surge.
—— Plange quasi virgo.
Handl, J. Recepti pastor. Pt.2. Ante cujus conspectum.
Croce, G. O vos omnes.
Handl, J. Ecce quomodo moritur. Pt.2. In pace factus.
Zoilo, A. Aestimatus.
Handl, J. Sepulto Domino. Pt.2. Ne forte veniant.
18 Selectissimae modulationes.
Vittoria. For Thursday, Friday, and Saturday in Holy Week.
Supplementum harmoniarum for Holy Week.
Miserere in falso bordone, by Palestrina, F. Dentice, S. M. Nanini, Lud. Viadana. (3).
Miserere, by Handl, Turini, Uttendal.
Guidelli. Benedictus in falso bordone. (3).
Palestrina. Benedictus.
Vittoria. Benedictus.
Handl, J. Benedictus.
Ortiz, Did. Benedictus.
Handl, J. Christus factus est.
Pitoni. Christus factus est.
Palestrina. Improperia.
Bernabei, G. A. Improperia.
Rosselli. Adoramus.
Lasso, O. Adoramus.
Agostini, P. Adoramus.
Anon. Adoramus.
Selection of litanies.
Aichinger, G. Litany of B.V.M. a 3.
Lasso, O. Litany of B.V.M. a 3.
Fossa, J. de. Litany of B.V.M. a 3.
Finetti, J. Litany of B.V.M. a 3.
Agazzari, A. Litany of B.V.M. a 3.
Biordi, G. Litany of B.V.M. a 3.
Zuchino, G. Litany of B.V.M. a 3.
Palestrina. Litany of B.V.M. a 3.
Victorinus, S. Litany of Name of Jesus.
Lasso, O. Litany of All Saints.
Aichinger, G. Stabat Mater. a 3.
Agazzari, Ant. Stabat Mater. a 3.
Vittoria. Asperges me.
—— Vidi aquam.
Paminger, L. Pater noster.
Vittoria. Ave Maria.
Anerio. Te Deum.
Ortiz, Did. Te Deum.
Handl, J. Te Deum.

Annus secundus.
Tom 1. between 1852–1879.
Fasc.1. Ascola, Jo. Matth. Missa octavi toni.
Fasc.2. Anerio, Fr. (Romano). Missa. Pro defunctis.
Fasc.3. Hassler, J. L. Missa.
Fasc.4. Praenestinus, J. P. A. Missa. Tu es Petrus. 6 vocum. Part.
Fasc.5. Vittoria, T. L. da. Missa. Pro defunctis. 6 vocum. Part.
Fasc.6. Praenestinus, J. P. A. Missa. Ascendo ad Patrem. 5 vocum. Part.
Fasc.7. Praenestinus, J. P. A. Missa. Papae Marcelli. 6 vocum. Part.
Fasc.8. Praenestinus, J. P. A. Missa. Aeterna Christi munera. 4 vocum. Part.

Tom 2.
Fasc.1. Sex motetta 4, 5, 6 et 8 vocum, auctores Casciolini, Anerio, Orlando de Lasso, Jovanelli, Vittoria. Part.
Fasc.2. Decem motetta 4, 5 et 6 vocum, auctorum C. Porta, A. Gabrieli, J. Handl, J. Clodiensi, J. P. A. Praenestinus, C. Verdonck, L. Marenzio, B. Nanini, P. Nenna et T. L. da Vittoria. Part.
Fasc.3. Octo motetta 5 et 6 vocum, auctorum L. Vittoria, G. Croce, A. Gabrieli, J. Reiner, Orlando de Lasso, Giovanelli, G. Aichinger, et J. P. A. Praenestinus. Part.

Tom 3.
Fasc.1. Quatuor litaniae Lauretanae, 4 et 5 vocum, auctore ignoto, Orlando de Lasso, Rinaldo de Mel et Felino Cornazzano. Part.
Fasc.2. Vesperas de communi unius martyris extra tempus Paschale, 4, 5 et 6 vocum in falso bordone, auctorum G. A. Bernabei, Fr. C. Andreae, L. Viadana, E. G. Stemmelio, Incerto et B. Ratti. Part.

Tom 4.
Fasc.1. Quinque psalmi vespertini 5 et 6 vocum in falso bordone. Variorum auctorum unacum cantico "Magnificat" 8 vocum, auctoris Ioanne Gabrieli, pro festo Dedicationis B.V.M. ad Nives, necnon in Communi B.V.M. Part.

PROSKE, KARL, 1794–1861. ed. .
Selectus novus missarum praestantissimorum superioris aevi auctorum, juxta codices originales tum manuscriptos tum impressos editarum a Carolo Proske. Ratisbonae, Pustet, 1853–61.
2v.
Contents (from *Grove's Dictionary of music and musicians*. 1916, Vol.3, p.330):
Annus primus.
Tom 1. 1857.
Palestrina. Veni sponsa Christi, a 4.
Anerio, F. Hor le tue forze adopra, a 4.
Lasso, O. Quai donna attende a gloriosa fama, a 5.
Palestrina. Assumpta est Maria, a 6.
Vittoria. Simile est regnum coelorum, a 4.
—— Vidi speciosum, a 6.
Soriano, F. Super voces musicales, a 6.
Hasler, Leo. Missa, a 8.

Tom 2. 1861.
Vittoria. O quam gloriosum, a 4.
Paciotti. Si bona suscepimus, a 5.
Lasso, O. In die tribulationis, a 5.
Palestrina. Dum complerentur, a 6.
Soriano, F. Nos autem gloriari, a 4.
Vittoria. Trahe me post Te, a 5.
Gabrieli, A. Pater peccavi, a 6.
Vecchi, Orazio. Pro defunctis, a 8.

Annus secundus.
Tom 1. Liber missarum.
Asola, G. M. Octavi toni, a 4.
Anerio, F. Pro defunctis, a 4.
Hasler, J. L. Quatuor vocum.
Palestrina. Tu es Petrus, a 6.
Vittoria. Pro defunctis, a 6.
Palestrina. Ascendo ad Patrem, a 5.
—— Papae Marcelli, a 6.
—— Aeterna Christi, a 4.

Tom 2. Liber motettorum.
Casciolini, Claudio. Angelus Domini.
Anerio. Laudemus Domini.
Lasso, O. Justorum animae.
Giovanelli, R. Benedicta.
Lasso, O. Ave Maria.
Vittoria. Taedet animam meam.
Porta, Constanzo. Ecce sacerdos.
Gabrieli, A. O sacrum convivium.
Handl, J. Beatus vir.
Clodiensi, J. a Cruce. Diligam Te.
Palestrina. Diffusa est gratia.
Verdonck, C. Ave Maria.
Marenzio, L. Hodie Christus.
Nanini, G. B. Hodie nobis coelorum.
Nenna, Pomponio. Veni Creator.
Vittoria. Pange lingua.
Vittoria. Ecce Domine venerit.
Clodiensi, J. a C. (Giov. Croce). Dies sanctificatus.
Gabrieli, A. De profundis.
Reiner, Jac. Cum transisset.
Lasso, O. Confirma hoc Deus.
Giovanelli, R. O quam suavis est.
Aichinger, G. Domine non sum.
Palestrina. Vidi turbam magnam.

Tom 3. Liber litaniarum.
Auctore ignoto. Litaniae Lauretanae.
Lasso, O. Litaniae Lauretanae.
Mel, Rinaldo del. Litaniae Lauretanae.
Cornazzono. Litaniae Lauretanae.
Vesperas de communi unius martyris.
Vittoria; G.A. Bernabei; F. C. Andreae; L. Viadana; E. G. Stemmelio; Auctore incerto; B. Ratti; C. de Zachariis.

Tom 4. Liber vespertinus.
Variorum auctorum. Psalmi vespertini.
Gabrieli, G. Magnificat, a 6.

PRUNIÈRES, HENRY, 1886– . ed.
Les maîtres du chant; répertoire de musique vocal ancienne publiée d'après les textes originaux, par Henry Prunières . . . Transcription et réalisation de la basso continuo, par G. Tailleferre . . . Paris, Heugel, [cop.1924–27].
6v. in 1.
French, or Italian and French, words; music for 1 voice with piano acc.
Recueil 1, cop.1925.
Contents:
Recueil 1. Airs italiens, v.1: A. and D. Scarlatti, F. Mancini, E. d'Astorga, A. Vivaldi, Pergolesi, L. Leo, G. Latilla, and G. A. Hasse.
Recueil 2. Airs de Lully.
Recueil 3. Airs italiens, v.2: C. Monteverdi, G. Caccini, D. Brunetti, S. d'India, S. P. de Negri, G. H. Kapsperger, D. Mazzocchi, M. A. Rossi, and L. Rossi.
Recueil 4. Airs français, v.1: P. Guédron, A. Boësset, E. Moulinié, D. Macé, G. Michel, L. de Mollier, Chancy, M. Lambert, H. Dumont, J. de Cambeforte, M. Charpentier, L'Affilard.
Recueil 5. Airs italiens, v.3: Carissimi, L. Rossi, M. A. Cesti, G. Bononcini, Bassani, Ballarini, A. Scarlatti, and F. Lanciani.
Recueil 6. Airs français, v.2: Campra, Destouches, Clérambault, Montéclair, Mouret, S. B. Matho, Mondonville, and Philidor.

The Psalm tones, *see* Plainsong and Mediaeval Music Society. The Psalm tones.

Psalmody in 17th century America. Ed. by Carleton Sprague Smith, *see* Early psalmody in 17th century America.

Psalms of David, *see* Plainsong and Mediaeval Music Society. Psalms of David.

Psautier Huguenot du XVIe siècle, *see* Expert, Henry. Psautier Huguenot du XVIe siècle.

Le psautier Huguenot du XVIe siècle, *see* Pidoux, Pierre. Le psautier Huguenot du XVIe siècle.

Publicacions Catalunya. Publicacions del Departáment de Música de la Biblioteca de Catalunya. Barcelona, Institut d'Estudis Catalans, *see* Barcelona. Biblioteca Central. Sección de Música. Publicaciones.

Publications de musique ancienne polonaise, *see* Denkmäler altpolnischer Musik.

Publications of mediaeval musical manuscripts, *see* Institute of Mediaeval Music. Publications.

Publications of the Institute of Mediaeval Music, *see* Institute of Mediaeval Music. Publications.

PUBLIKATIONEN ÄLTERER MUSIK; veröffentlicht von der Abteilung zur Herausgabe älterer Musik bei der Deutschen Musikgesellschaft. Unter der Leitung von Theodor Kroyer. Leipzig, Breitkopf & Härtel, 1926–40.
11v. illus.
Consists chiefly of music.
Editor: Jahrg.1–10, T. Kroyer; Jahrg.11, Helmut Schultz.
1926–1932, "Veröffentlicht von der Abteilung zur Herausgabe älterer Musik bei der Deutschen Musikgesellschaft"; 1935, 37 "veröffentlicht von der Abteilung zur Herausgabe älterer Musik bei der Deutschen Gesellschaft für Musikwissenschaft."
Jahrg.3, Teil 2, title reads: Publikationen der Abteilung zur Herausgabe älterer Musik bei der Deutschen Musikgesellschaft . . . Abhandlungen [Nr.] 1.
Jahrg.3^2, 5, 9^{11} are also Bd.7, 9, 12^{14} of: Staatliche Forschungsinstitute in Leipzig. Forschungsinstitut für Musikwissenschaft. Publikationen (Jahrg.5 "mit Unterstützung der Deutschen Akademie in Munchen").
Contents:
Jahrg.1^1, 3^1, 4^2. Guillaume de Machaut. Musikalische Werke, hrsg. von Fr. Ludwig. Bd.1–3. 1926–1929.
Jahrg.1^2. Ockeghem, J. Sämtliche Werke. Bd.1. Messen 1–8, hrsg. von Dragan Plamenac. 1927.
Jahrg.2. Milán, L. Libro de musica de vihuela de mano, hrsg. von L. Schrader. 1927.
Jahrg.3^1. *See* Jahrg.1^1.
Jahrg.3^2. Zenck, H. Sixtus Dietrich. 1928.
Jahrg.4^1, 6. Marenzio, L. Sämtliche Werke, hrsg. von A. Einstein. 6 books of 5-part madrigals. Bd.1–2. 1929–1931.
Jahrg.4^2. *See* Jahrg.1^1.
Jahrg.5, 7. Catholic Church, Roman. Liturgy and ritual. Gradual. Das Graduale der St. Thomaskirche zu Leipzig, hrsg. von P. Wagner. Bd.1–2. 1930–1932.
Jahrg.6. *See* Jahrg.4^1.
Jahrg.7. *See* Jahrg.5.
Jahrg.8. Petrucci, Ottaviano dei. Frottole, Buch I und IV, hrsg. von R. Schwartz. 1935.
Jahrg.9. Willaert, Adrian. Sämtliche Werke, hrsg. von H. Zenck. 4-voice motets. 1539 and 1545. Bd.1. 1937
Jahrg.10. Schultz, Helmut. Das Madrigal als Formideal.
Jahrg.11. Husmann, H., ed. Die drei- und vierstimmigen Notre-Dame-Organa. 1940.

PUBLIKATIONEN ÄLTERER PRAKTISCHER UND THEORETISCHER MUSIKWERKE, vorzugsweise des XV. und XVI. Jahrhunderts. Hrsg. von der Gesellschaft für Musikforschung. (Hrsg. Robert Eitner). Berlin (Leipzig), Bahn (Liepmannssohn, Trautwein, Breitkopf & Härtel), 1873–1905.
29v. (33 Jahrg.).
Ceased publication with Bd.29.
Contents:
Jahrg.1–3. Joh. Ott's Mehrstimmiges deutsches Liederbuch von 1544. [Matthias Eckel, Heinr. Isaac, Johann Müller, Osw. Reytter, Ludw. Senfl, Thomas Stoltzer, Wilh. Breytengraser, Arnold van Bruck, Thom. Creyquillon, Sixtus Dietrich, Nic. Gombert, Lupus Hellinck, Steffan Mahu, Leonhard Paminger, Jean Richafort, Bruyer, Robert Naich, Andreas de Silva, Phil. Verdelot, Joh. Wannenmacher].
Jahrg.4, I. Zu Ott's Liederbuch die Einleitung, Biographien, Texte und Melodien.
Jahrg.4, II. P. Anselm Schubiger: Musikalische Spizilegien . . .
Jahrg.5. Josquin Deprès: Ausgewählte Kompositionen.
Jahrg.6. Joh. Walther's Wittenbergisch Gesangbuch von 1524 . . .
Jahrg.7. Heinr. Finck (und Herm. Finck): Ausgewählte Kompositionen.
Jahrg.8. Erhart Oeglin's Liederbuch zu 4 Stimmen. Augsburg 1512. [Paul Hofhaimer, Heinr. Isaac, Machinger (Malchinger), Ad. Rener, Ludw. Senfl].
Jahrg.9. Die Oper von ihren ersten Anfängen bis zur Mitte des 18. Jahrg.I.Teil: Einleitung (Marienklabe u.A.): Caccini, Euridice; Gagliano, Dafne; Monteverdi, Orfeo.
Jahrg.10. Sebast. Virdung's Musica Getutscht. Basel 1511. Facs. (Facs. ed. by L. Schrade, Bärenreiter, 1930).
Jahrg.11. Die Oper. II.Teil: Cavalli, Il giasone; Marc. Ant. Cesti, La dori.
Jahrg.12. Mich. Praetorius' Syntagma Musici, Tomus 2.
Jahrg.13. Jean Bapt. Lully's Oper Armide.
Jahrg.14. Alessandro Scarlatti's La rosaura. Opera.
Jahrg.15. Hans Leo Hassler's Lustgarten. 1601.
Jahrg.16–18. Glarean's Dodecachord in deutscher Übersetzung.
Jahrg.19–20. Georg Casp. Schürmann's Oper Ludovicus Pius oder Ludwig der Fromme. 1726.
Jahrg.21–22. Reinhard Keiser's Oper Der lächerliche Prinz Jodelet, 1726.
Jahrg.23. Jac. Regnart's Dreistimmige deutsche Lieder nebst Leonh. Lechner's Bearbeitung.
Jahrg.24. Martin Agricola's Musica instrumentalis deutsch.
Jahrg.25. Joh. Eccard's Neue geistliche und weltliche Lieder.
Jahrg.26. Joachim von Burck: Lieder und Passionen.
Jahrg.27. 60 Chansons zu 4 Stimmen aus der ersten Hälfte des 16. Jahrhunderts von französischen und niederländischen Meistern. [Jacques Archadelt, Jacques Berchem, Bon Voisin, Bourguignon, Pierre Cadéac, Pierre Certon, Clemens non Papa, Pierre Colin, Jean Courtois, Garnier, Gentian, Godard, Grenier, Pierre Hesdin, Heurteur, Jacques Jacotin, Clement Jannequin, Pierre de la Rue, Le Gendre, Lupi (Hellinck), Magdelain, Maillard, Nicolas de Marle, Mittantier, Clement Morel,

Antoine Mornable, Pagnier (Paignier), Passereau, H. René, Rogier (Pathie), Sandrin, Claudin (Sermisy), P. Symon, du Tertre, Pierre de Villiers (Vuillers].
Jahrg.28. Gallus Dressler: XVII Motetten.
Jahrg.29. Gregor Langius: Sammlung von Motetten.
Jahrg.30. Orazio Vecchi: L'amfiparnasso.
Jahrg.31. Jean Marie Leclair d'aîné: 12 Sonaten und 1 Trio.
Jahrg.32. Martin Zeuner: 82 Geistliche Kirchenlieder.
Jahrg.33. Georg Forster: Kurtzweilige . . . Liedlein. 2.Teil. (1540).

Pujol, Joan, 1573–1626. Opera omnia, *see* Barcelona. Biblioteca Central. Sección de Música. Publicaciones. Vol.3, 7.

PURCELL, HENRY, 1658 (or 9)–1695.
Complete works. Pub. by the Purcell Society. London, Novello & Co., Ltd., 1878– .
v.1– .
Contents:
Bd.1. The Yorkshire feast song. Ode for voices and orchestra. 1878.
Bd.2. The masque in Timon of Athens. For voices and orchestra. 1882.
Bd.3. Dido and Aeneas. Opera. 1889.
Bd.4. The Duke of Gloucester's birthday ode. For voices and orchestra. 1891.
Bd.5. 12 Sonatas of 3 parts. For stringed instruments and pianoforte. 1893.
Bd.6. Harpsichord and organ music. 1895.
Bd.7. 10 Sonatas of 4 parts. For stringed instruments and pianoforte. 1896.
Bd.8. Ode on St. Cecilia's Day, 1692. For voices and orchestra. 1897.
Bd.9. Dioclesian. Opera. 1900.
Bd.10. 3 Odes for St. Cecilia's Day. For voices and orchestra. 1899.
Bd.11. Birthday odes for Queen Mary, Pt.I. For voices and orchestra. 1902.
Bd.12. The fairy queen. Opera. 1903.
Bd.13. Sacred Music, Pt.I. 9 Anthems with orchestral accompaniment. 1921.
Bd.14. Sacred music, Pt.II. 9 Anthems with orchestral accompaniment. 1904.
Bd.15. Welcome songs for Charles II and James II, Pt.I. For voices and orchestra. 1905.
Bd.16. Dramatic music, Pt.I. For stringed instruments, voices and pianoforte, and voices and orchestra. 1906.
Bd.17. Sacred music, Pt.III. 7 Anthems with orchestral accompaniment. 1907.
Bd.18. Welcome songs for Charles II and James II, Pt.II. For voices and orchestra. 1910.
Bd.19. The Indian queen and The tempest. 2 Operas. 1912.
Bd.20. Dramatic music, Pt.II. For stringed instruments, voices and pianoforte, and voices and orchestra. 1916.
Bd.21. Dramatic music, Pt.III. For stringed instruments, voices and pianoforte, and voices and orchestra. 1917.
Bd.22. Catches, rounds, 2-part and 3-part songs. 1922
Bd.23. Services. 1923.
Bd.24. Birthday odes for Queen Mary, Pt.II. For voices and orchestra. 1926.
Bd.25. Secular songs and cantatas. For a single voice. 1928.
Bd.26. King Arthur. 1928.
Bd.27. Miscellaneous odes and cantatas. 1957.
Bd.28. Sacred music, Pt.IV. Anthems. 1959.
Bd.29. Sacred music, Pt.V. Anthems. 1960.
Bd.30. Sacred music, Pt.VI. Anthems.
Bd.31. Fantasias and other instrumental music. 1959.
Bd.32. Sacred music, Pt.VII. Anthems and miscellaneous church music. 1962.

PURCELL, HENRY, 1658 (or 9)–1695.
. . . Organ works. Ed. by Hugh McLean. London, Novello & Co., Ltd., [cop.1957].
4p.L., 20p. (Original compositions. [New series]. No.294).

PURCELL, HENRY, 1658 (or 9)–1695.
Suites, lessons, and pieces for the harpsichord, by Henry Purcell . . . Ed. by William Barclay Squire . . . London, J. & W. Chester, Ltd., cop.1918.
4v. (On cover: Edition Chester. No.36–39. Original works for the harpsichord).

Queen Elizabeth's virginal book, *see* The Fitzwilliam virginal book.

Quinze chansons françaises du XVIe siècle à quatre et cinq voix, *see* Cauchie, Maurice. Quinze chansons françaises du XVIe siècle à quatre et cinq voix.

Quittard, Henri, 1864–1919, ed. Meslanges divers, *see* Du Mont, Henri. Meslanges divers.

Quoika, Rudolf, 1897– , ed. Orgelwerke. Altböhmischer Meister, *see* Orgelwerke. Altböhmischer Meister.

Raccolta di musica sacra, *see* Alfieri, Pietro. Raccolta di musica sacra.

Raccolta di musica sacra, *see* Palestrina, Giovanni Battista Pierluigi da. Raccolta di musica sacra.

Raccolta nazionale delle musiche italiane, *see* I classici della musica italiana.

RADINO, GIOVANNI MARIA, fl.1579–1598.
. . . Intavolatura di balli per sonar di liuto. Trascritti in notazione moderna ed interpretati, da Giuseppe Gullino. Firenze, Edizioni Musicali ditta R. Maurri, 1949.
v [1]p., 1L., 20p.
Transcriptions for lute in modern notation from the tablature of the original ed. (Venetia, G. Vincenti, 1592).
"La presente edizione consta di 300 esemplari numerati."

RADINO, GIOVANNI MARIA, fl.1579–1598.
Il primo libro d'intavolatura di balli d'arpicordo, di Gio. Maria Radino . . . Facsimile with

transcription by Rosamond E. M. Harding . . . Cambridge, W. Heffer & Sons, Ltd.; New York, Broude Bros., [1949].
v p., facsim. (28p.) 31–75p.
Facsimile of the original edition of an Italian lute tablature (Venetia, G. Vincenti, 1592) and transcription in modern notation.
"Seruiranno a due sorti di Stromenti Grauecembalo & Liuto."

RAHTER'S KAMMER-ORCHESTER; eine Sammlung von Instrumental- und Vokalwerken für Schule und Haus. No.1–4. Leipzig, D. Rahter, [1932].
14 nos. music.
Full title: D. Rahter's Kammer-Orchester . . .
Editors: No.1–14, H. Erdlen and others.
Contents:
No.1. Maurice, the Learned, Landgrave of Hesse-Cassel. [Fugues] . . . Vier Fugen (vierstimmig) auszuführen auf allerlei Instrumenten. [1932].
No.2–2a. Maurice, the Learned, Landgrave of Hesse-Cassel. . . . Pavanen, Gaillarden, Intraden, auszuführen auf allerlei Instrumenten. Heft 1–2. [1932].
No.3–3a. Altenburg, M. . . . Choral-Intraden. Heft 1–2. [1932].
No.4. Otto, V. . . . Intrada. [1932].
No.5. Becker, D. [Musicalische Frülings-Fruchte. Sonata a 3. G major] . . . Sonata a 3 aus der Sammlung "Musikalische Frühlingsfrüchte." [1932].
No.6. Becker, D. [Musicalische Frülings-Fruchte. Sonata a 4. E minor] . . . Sonata a 4 aus der Sammlung "Musikalische Frühlingsfrüchte." [1932].
No.7. Becker, D. [Musicalische Frülings-Fruchte. Sonata a 5. G minor] . . . Sonata a 5 aus der Sammlung "Musikalische Frühlingsfrüchte." [1932].
No.8.
No.9. Telemann, G. P. . . . Presto, Flauto (Violino Solo), 2 Violinen, Viola (3d Violino), Violoncello e Continuo. [1932].
No.10. Telemann, G. P. [Concertos. Violin, strings, and pianoforte. A minor] . . . Concerto per Violino, Orchestra di Strumenti ad Arco e Continuo." [1932].
No.11.
No.12. Bach, J. S. [Canzone. Organ. D minor. Arr. for string orchestra] . . . Canzone für Streichorchester. [1932].
No.13. Bach, J. S. [Fugues. Organ. C minor. Arr. for orchestra] . . . Fuge über ein Thema von Corelli für Streichorchester. [1932].
No.14. Holzbauer, I. J. [Symphonies. E major] . . . Sinfonia, Mi majeur . . . für Streichorchester. [1932].

Rajeczky, Benjamin, 1901– , ed. Melodiarium Hungariae medii aevi, *see* Melodiarium Hungariae medii aevi.

RAMEAU, JEAN PHILIPPE, 1693–1764.
. . . Oeuvres complètes, publiées sous la direction de C. Saint-Saëns. Paris, A. Durand et Fils, 1895–1913.
18v. and portfolio of 8 instrumental parts in tome 2. diagrs., facsims., fronts., plates, ports., tables.
"Notice biographique," tome 1, p.[ix]–xxvii, signed Ch. Malherbe.
Each volume contains a "Commentaire bibliographique"; also facsims. of original title pages.
"Publication [was begun] under the editorship of C. Saint-Saëns and Ch. Malherbe; after the latter's death his part of the work was divided between M. Emmanuel and M. Teneo."–Baker. 5th ed.
Contents:
Bd.1. Pièces de clavecin.
Bd.2. Musique instrumentale.
Bd.3. Cantates à 1 et 2 voix.
Bd.4. Motets 1e sèrie.
Bd.5. Motets 2e sèrie.
Bd.6. Hippolyte et Aricie.
Bd.7. Les Indes galantes.
Bd.8. Castor et Pollux.
Bd.9. Les fêtes d'Hébé ou Les talents lyriques.
Bd.10. Dardanus.
Bd.11. La princesse de Navarre; Les fêtes de Ramile; Nêlée et Myrthis; Zéphire.
Bd.12. Platée.
Bd.13. Les fêtes de Polymnie.
Bd.14. Le temple de la gloire.
Bd.15. Les fêtes de l'Hymen et l'amour ou Les dieux d'Égypte.
Bd.16. Zaïs.
Bd.17. 1. Pygmalion; Les surprises de l'amour.
Bd.17. 2. Anacréon; Les sybarites.
Bd.18. Naïs.

RAMEAU, JEAN PHILIPPE, 1693–1764.
. . . Pièces de clavecin . . . with the composer's original appended texts unabridged and with several facsimile reproductions. Ed. by Erwin R. Jacobi. Basel, London, [etc.], Bärenreiter, [1958–59].
3v. (Bärenreiter-Ausgabe. No.3800–3802).

Ramsbotham, Alexander, 1870–1932, ed. Old Hall manuscript, *see* Plainsong and Mediaeval Music Society. Old Hall manuscript.

Ranke, Friedrich, ed. Das Rostocker Liederbuch, *see* Das Rostocker Liederbuch.

RAUGEL, FÉLIX, 1881– . ed.
46 Pièces pour orgue . . . d'anciens auteurs français et étrangers. Paris, n.d.
p.1– .

RAUGEL, FÉLIX, 1881– . ed.
Les maîtres français de l'orgue aux XVIIème et XVIIIème siècles. Recueil de 50 pièces d'orgue ou harmonium choisies et publiées avec des indications de registration, par Félix Raugel . . . Paris Éditions de la Schola Cantorum, [1925?].
2p.L., 97, [2]p.
Contains compositions by L.-C. d'Aquin, Claude Balbastre, Nicolas Le Bègue, Jacques Boyvin, Chambonnières, J.-F. Dandrieu, Henry Du Mont, Nicolas Gigault, Nicolas de Grigny, Gilles Jullien, Guillaume Lasceux, Mésangeau,

Monard, G.-G. Nivers, André Raison, Étienne Richard, Louis Séjan, and Nicolas Siret.

RAUGEL, FÉLIX, 1881– . ed.
... Les maîtres français de l'orgue aux XVIIe et XVIIIe siècles. 100 pièces pour orgue ou harmonium choisies et registrées par Félix Raugel. Préface de Ch.-M. Widor. Paris, Éditions Musicales de la Schola Cantorum, [cop.1951].
2v. (Les maîtres anciens de l'orgue).
Contents:
Vol.1 contains compositions by Louis Claude d'Aquin, Claude Balbastre, Jacques Boyvin, Chambonnières, Jean François Dandrieu, Henry Du Mont, Nicolas Gigault, Nicolas de Grigny, Gilles Jullien, Guillaume Lasceux, Nicolas Lebègue, Mésangeau, Monard, Guillaume Gabriel Nivers, André Raison, Étienne Richard, Louis Séjan, and Nicolas Siret.
Vol.2 contains compositions by François d'Agincour, J. B. Henry d'Angelbert, Pierre Attaingnant, Nicolas Le Bègue, Joseph de la Barre, Jacques Boyvin, Pierre François Boëly, François Benoist, Louis Couperin, Gaspard Corrette, Nicolas Clérambault, Michel Corrette, Jean Jacques Beauvarlet-Charpentier, Eustache Du Caurroy, Jean Denis, Henry Du Mont, Pierre Dandrieu, Jean François Dandrieu, Louis Antoine Dornel, Dufour, Nicolas Gigault, Jean Nicolas Geoffroy, Nicolas de Grigny, Pierre Février, Pierre du Mage, Louis Marchand, Gullaume Lasceux, Jean Nicolas Marrigues, Guillaume Gabriel Nivers, Charles Piroye, Charles Racquet, François Roberday, André Raison, Nicolas Séjan, and Jean Titelouze.

RAUGEL, FÉLIX, 1881– . ed.
Quarante-six pièces pour orgue ou harmonium d'anciens auteurs. Français et étrangers. Choises et publiés avec indications de registration par Félix Raugel. Paris, Les Éditions de Musique Henri Hérelle, n.d.
107 [2] p.
Score for organ.
Contains compositions by J. G. Albrechtsberger, Pierre Attaingnant, Floriano Arresti, William Byrd, Antonio de Cabezon, Eustache du Caurroy, Antoine de Cousu, C. Bohuslaw Czernohorský, Pierre Dandrieu, Johann Ernest Eberlin, Giovanni Frescobaldi, Jacob Froberger, Ferdinand Fischer, Giovanni Gabrieli, Orlando Gibbons, Matthias van den Gheyn, Johann Krieger, Francesco Landino, P. Antonio Mortaro, Ant. Murschhauser, W. A. Mozart, G. P. da Palestrina, G. Nivers, J. Pachelbel, Nicolo Porpora, Luigi Rossi, Étienne Richard, Michel Angelo Rossi, Thomas Roseingrave, Anton Reicha, Georg Schapf, Bernhard Schmid, G. P. Telemann, F. W. Zachow, and Domenico Zipoli.

REALE ACCADEMIA D'ITALIA, ROME.
... Musica. Roma, Reale Accademia d'Italia, 1934–41.
6 nos. facsims. (incl. music).
Contents:
Vol.1. Gaffurio. Theorica musical. 1934.
Vol.2. Galilei. Dialogo della musica. 1934.
Vol.3. Peri. Euridice. 1934.
Vol.4. Caccini, Giulio. Le nuove musiche. 1934.
Vol.5. Bellini. Norma. 2v. 1935.
Vol.6. Bellini. Compozioni giovanili inedite. 1941.

REANEY, GILBERT. ed.
Early fifteenth-century music. [Rome], American Institute of Musicology, 1955 [cop.1956]– .
v.1– . (Corpus mensurabilis musicae. No.11).
"Complete edition of the works of Cordier, Cesaris, Carmen, and Tapissier."–Pref. v.1, p.i.
Vol.1– , for 2–5 partly unspecified voices; part of the words in Latin, part in French.
Contents:
Vol.1. B. Cordier, J. Cesaris, J. Carmen, J. Tapissier. Collected works, complete with introd., critical notes, poetical texts, 1955.
Vol.2 contains compositions by Adam, Bosquet, Briquet, Cameraco, Cardot, de Bellengues. Charité, Coutreman, Francus de Insula, R. Gallo and Francus de Insula, Johannes Simon de Haspre, Johannes de Alte Curie (Haucourt), La Beausse, Franchois Lebertoul, Guillaume Le Grant, Johannes Le Grant, Gautier Libert, Guillermus Malbecque, Passet de Tornaco, Paullet, Raulin de Vaux, Johannes Reson, and Gilet Velut. 1959.
Vol.3 contains compositions by Benoit, Estienne Grossin, R. Libert, and Richard Loqueville. 1966.

Recent research in plainsong. Briggs, H. B., *see* Plainsong and Mediaeval Music Society. Briggs, H. B. Recent research in plainsong.

RECENT RESEARCHES IN THE MUSIC OF THE BAROQUE ERA. New Haven, Conn., A–R Editions, Inc., 1964– .
v.1– .
Contents:
Vol.1. Charpentier, Marc Antoine. Judicium Salomonis. Ed. by H. Wiley Hitchcock. 1964.
Vol.2. Telemann, Georg Philipp. 48 Chorale preludes for organ. Ed. by Alan Thaler. 1965.
Vol.3. Kerll, Johann Caspar. Missa superba. Ed. by Albert C. Giebler. 1967.

RECENT RESEARCHES IN THE MUSIC OF THE RENAISSANCE. New Haven, Conn., A–R Editions, Inc., 1964– .
v.1– .
Contents:
Vol.1. Asola, Giovanni Matteo. 16 Liturgical works. Ed. by Donald M. Fouse. 1964.
Vol.2. Rogier, Philippe. 11 Motets. Ed. by Lavern J. Wagner. 1966.
Vol.3. Tye, Christopher. The instrumental music. Ed. by Robert W. Weidner. 1967.

RECUEIL DE MUSIQUE ANCIENNE.
Recueil des morceaux de musique ancienne, exécutés aux concerts de la Société de Musique Vocale, Religieuse et Classique, fondée à Paris en 1843 . . . sous la direction de M. Le Prince de la Moskowa. Publié par la Société. Paris, Pacini, 1843? .
11v.
Contents:
Bd.1.
Palestrina. Messe du Pape Marcel.
—— Messe Aeterna Christi munera.
—— Stabat Mater.
—— Fratres ego enim.
—— Adoramus.
—— Pleni sunt coeli.
—— Alla riva del Tebro.
Bd.2.
Allegri. De lamentatione Jeremiae.
—— Miserere.
Lassus, Orlando de. Regina coeli.
—— Salve Regina.
—— Miserere.
Auteur inconnu. Chants des Frères Moraves.
—— Alla Trinita beata.
Arcadelt. Ave Maria.
Vittoria. Jesus dulcis memoria.
—— Pueri Hebraeorum.
Leisring. Filii et filiae.
Scarlatti. Cor mio.
Bach, Sebastien. Tantum ergo.
Bd.3.
Stradella. Pieta Signore.
L'Abbé Clari. Cantando un di.
—— Non ti sdegnar.
—— Addio compagne amene.
Marcello. Donde cotanto fremito.
—— I cieli immensi narrano.
Handel. Lascia ch'io pianga.
—— Air d'Alcina. Ah! mio cor.
—— Tutta raccolta ancor.
—— Che vai cercando.
—— Alleluya.
Gluck (sic). Scène d'Orphèe.
Bd.4.
Bach. Qui presse al mio Gesù.
Haydn. E Dio disse . . . Création.
—— Trio et choeur. Création.
—— Insane et vanae curae.
—— Vidit suum.
—— Fac me vere.
—— Virgo virginum.
—— Quando corpus morietur.
Bd.5.
Josquin des Près. La déploration de Jéhan Ockeghem.
Jannequin. Clément. La bataille de Marignan.
Lassus, Orlando de. Scain tu dir d'avé.
—— Si le long tems.
—— Ce faux amour.
—— Fuyons tous l'amour le jeu.
—— Bonjour mon coeur.
—— Le tems peut bien.
—— Je l'ayme bien.
—— Si vous n'êtes en bon point.
—— Per pianto la mia carne.
Inconnu. Belle qui tient ma vie.
Palestrina. Vaghi pensier.
—— Là ver l'aurora.
Arcadelt. Il bianco e dolce cigno.
Don Carlo Gesualdo, Prince de Venosa. Gelo ha madonna il seno.
—— Come esser suo.
Marcello. Ei fuor dell' acque.
Lotti. Spiritu di Dio.
Bd.6.
Gabrieli. Magnificat.
—— Benedictus.
Nanini. Diffusa est gratia. Motet.
Lassus, Orlando de. Quia cinerem. Fragment.
Anerio. Ave Regina coelorum. Antienne.
—— Adoramus. Motet.
Talys. Kyrie eleison.
Gallus. Media vita. Motet.
—— Adoramus. Motet.
—— Ecce quomodo moritur. Motet.
Lupus. Audivi vocem.
Vulpius. Exultate justi. Motet.
Vittoria. O vox omnes. Motet.
—— Gloria Patria.
Don Juan IV. Crux fidelis.
Carissimi. O felix anima. Motet.
Barbieri. Veni de libano sponsa. Motet.
Durante. Christe eleison.
Bd.7.
Palestrina. Tribularer si nescirem.
—— Agnus Dei.
—— Popule meus.
—— Canite tuba.
—— Vinea mea electa.
—— Una hora non potuisti.
—— Tantum ergo.
—— Tristis est anima. In monte Oliveti.
—— Esurientes.
—— Corporis misterium.
—— O Bone Jesu.
—— Sicut erat.
—— Dei mater alma.
—— Lauda anima mea.
—— Hodie Christus natus est.
—— Gloria Patri.
Bd.8.
Carissimi. Gaudeamus.
—— Surgamus! eamus.
Buononcini. In Te Domine speravi.
Giov. Paolo Colonna. Domine ad adjuvandum.
Leo, Leonardo. Sicut erat.
Clari. Gratias agimus tibi.
Bd.9.
Palestrina. Messe canonique.
—— Messe de Requiem.
Gabrieli, Giov. Magnificat.
—— Miserere.
—— Beata es Virgo.
Lassus, Orlando de. De psalmis penitentialibus.
Bd.10.
Palestrina. Dies sanctificatus. Motet.
—— Sicut cervus. Motet.
—— Même morceau en la bémol.
—— Laus honor virtus gloria. Motet.
—— Veni sponsa Christi. Motet.
Vittoria. O quam gloriosum. Motet.
—— Vere languores. Motet.
Lotti, Antonio. Miserere.

—— Benedictus.
Auteur inconnu. Fragment d'un ancien Noël français.
Cauroy, Eustache du. Noël, Noël. Choeur.
Auteur inconnu. Se questa valle di miseria. Lodi spirituali du 16me siècle.
Donato, Baldassare. Villote napolitaine.
Gastoldi. Viver lieto voglio. Ballet.
Bd.11.
Benevoli. Sanctus.
Lotti, A. Christi eleison.
Carissimi. Le rudiment ou la déclinaison du pronom hie [sic] haec, hoc.
Jannequin, Clément. Le chant des oiseaux.
Gibbons, Orlando. Le vieux chasseur. Madrigal.
—— Le croisé captif. Madrigal.
Maillart. Tout au rebours. Canon par mouvement contraire.
Gabrieli, Andrea. Sento un rumor. Choeur.
Auteur inconnu. A chi more per Dio. Fragment d'un madrigal spirituel.
Marenzio, Luca. Ahi dispietata morte. Madrigal.

Redlich, Hans Ferdinand, 1903– , ed. Musica sacra, *see* Musica sacra. Ed. by Hans Ferdinand Redlich.

REESER, EDUARD, 1908– . comp.
De klaviersonate met vioolbegeleiding in het parijsche muziekleven ten tijde van Mozart, door dr. Eduard Reeser. Met negentig muziekvoorbeelden en een bijvoegsel van twaalf sonates. Rotterdam, W. L. & J. Brusse's Uitgeversmaatschappij n.v., 1939.
178p., 1L.: 102p. (music), illus. (music).
"Dit boek is ontstaan als profschrift . . . aan de Rijksuniversiteit te Utrecht." – Voorbericht.
Includes biographies of composers.
"Bibliographie": p.[168]–71.
The sonatas in the appendix are by J. J. Mondonville (Op.III, No.3); L. G. Guillemain (Op.XIII, No.2); C. F. Clément (Op.I, No.6); Johann Schobert (Op.I, No.2; Op.XVII, No.2); Leontzi Honauer (Op.III, No.4); A. L. Couperin (Op.II, No.3); J. J. Beauvarlet-Charpentier (Op.II, No.6); N. J. Hüllmandel (Op.I, No.2; Op.VI, No.3); J. F. Edelmann (Op.VIII, No.1); and M. A. Guénin (Op.V, No.3).

REGER, MAX, 1873–1916.
. . . Sämtliche Werke. Unter Mitarbeit des Max Reger-Institutes (Elsa-Reger-Stiftung), Bonn. Wiesbaden, Breitkopf & Härtel, 1954– .
35v. (in progress). (Asterisk indicates unpublished volumes).
Contents:
Orchesterwerke.
Bd.1. Sinfonietta A-dur, Op.90. 1958.
Bd.2. Serenade, Op.95. 1956.
Bd.3. Variationen und Fuge über ein Thema von Joh. Ad. Hiller, Op.100; Symphonischer Prolog zu einer Tragödie, Op.108. 1959.
Bd.4. Eine Lustspielouvertüre, Op.120; Konzert im alten Stil, Op.123; Eine romantische Suite, Op.125. 1962.
Bd.5. Böcklin-Suite, Op.128; Eine Ballet-Suite, Op.130; Pantalon, Op.130, IV (ungedruckter Nachlass); Mozart-Variationen, Op.132. 1958.
*Bd.6. Eine vaterländische Ouvertüre, Op.140; Beethoven-Variationen, Op.86; Suite im alten Stil, Op.93; Heroide und Elegie, E-moll (ungedruckter Nachlass).

Werke für Soloinstrumente mit Orchester.
Bd.7. Zwei Romanzen für Violine mit Begleitung von kleinem Orchester, Op.50; Konzert A-dur für Violine mit Begleitung des Orchesters, Op.101; Aria A-dur für Solo-Violine mit Begleitung von kleinem Orchester, Op.103, 3. [1964].

Werke für Klavier Zweihändig.
Bd.9. Sieben Walzer, Op.11; Lose Blätter, Op.13; Aus der Jugendzeit, Op.17; Improvisationen, Op.18; Fünf humoresken, Op.20; Sechs Stücke, Op.24; Aquarellen, Op.25; Sieben Fantasiestücke, Op.26; Sieben Charakterstücke, Op.32; Bunte Blätter, Op.36; Zehn kleine Vorstragsstücke, Op.44. 1957.
Bd.10. Sechs Intermezzi, Op.45; Silhouetten, Op.53; Kompositionen für Pianoforte, Op.79a; Bach-Variationen, Op.81; Aus meinem Tagebuch, Op.82. 1959.
*Bd.11. Vier Sonatinen, Op.89; Sechs Präludien und Fugen, Op.99; Episoden, Op.115; Telemann-Variationen, Op.134; Träume am Kamin, Op.143.
Bd.12. Kanons durch alle Moll-Tonarten; Sechs Klavierstücke aus A. Lindners Reger-Archiv (1898); Blätter und Blüten; Perpetuum mobile; Grüsse an die Jugend und Humoreske in D-dur (ungedruckter Nachlass) und weitere Klavierstücke ohne Opuszahl. 1963.

Werke für Klavier Vierhändig.
Bd.13. Walzer-Capricen, Op.9; Deutsche Tanze, Op.10; Seche Walzer, Op.22; Cinq pièces pittoresques, Op.34; Seche Burlesken, Op.58; Seche Stücke, Op.94. 1956.

Werke für Zwei Klaviers Vierhändig.
Bd.14. Beethoven-Variationen, Op.86; Introduction, Passacaglia und Fuge, Op.96; Klavierkonzert, F-moll, Op.114; Mozart-Variationen, Op.132a. 1954.

Werke für Orgel.
Bd.15. Drei Orgelstücke, Op.7; Suite, E-moll, Op.16; Acht Fantasien über Choräle, Op.27, 29, 30, 40 (I–11), 52 (I–III); Sonate, Fis-moll, Op.33; Fantasie und Fuge über B–A–C–H, Op.46; Sechs Trios, Op.47. 1956.
Bd.16. Fünf leicht ausführbare Präludien und Fugen, Op.56; Symphonische Fantasie und Fuge, Op.57; Zwölf Stücke, Op.59; Zweite Sonate, D-moll, Op.60; Monologe, Op.63; Zwölf Stücke, Op.65. 1959.
*Bd.17. Zwölf Stücke, Op.65; 52 leicht ausführbare Stücke, Op.67; Zehn Stücke, Op.69; Variationen und Fuge, Fis-moll, Op.73; Dreizehn Vorspiele, Op.79b.

*Bd.18. Zwölf Stücke, Op.80; Vier Präludien und Fugen, Op.85; Suite, G-moll, Op.92; Introduction, Passacaglia und Fuge, E-moll, Op.127; Neun Stücke, Op.129; Dreissig kleine Choralvorspiele, Op.135a; Fantasie und Fuge, D-moll, Op.135b; Sieben Stücke, Op.145; Präludium, C-moll (ungedruckter Nachlass); Introduction and Passacaglia, D-moll, und weitere Stücke ohne Opuszahl).

Werke für Klavier und Streichinstrumente.
Bd.19. Fünf Sonaten für Violine und Klavier, Op.1, 3, 41, 72 und Op.84; Drei Stücke, Op.79d; Zwei Kompositione, Op.87. 1958.
Bd.20. Suite im alten Stil, Op.93; Sechs Vortragsstücke, Op.103a; Zwei kleine Sonaten, Op.103b; Zwölf kleine Stücke nach eigenen Liedern, Op.103c; Zwei Sonaten für Violine und Klavier, Op.122, 139; Romanze G-dur; Petite caprice, G-moll. 1963.
*Bd.21. Vier Sonaten für Violoncello und Klavier, Op.5, 28, 78, 116; Kompositionen für Violoncello und Klavier, Op.79e; Caprice, A-moll.

Werke für Klavier und ein Blasinstrument.
*Bd.21. Drei Sonaten für Klarinette und Klavier, Op.49 und Op.107; Allegretto grazioso für Flöte und Klavier; Albumblatt und Tarantella.

Klaviertrios, -Quartette und -Quintette.
Bd.22. Zwei Klaviertrios, Op.2, 102; Largo, D-dur, für Klaviertrio (ungedruckter Nachlass); Zwei Klavierquartette, Op.113, 133. 1958.
Bd.23. Klavierquintett. Erstes Quintett, C-moll, Op.21; Zweites Quintett, C-moll, Op.64. 1960.

Werke für Streicher Solo, *Duo und *Trio.
Bd.24. Sonaten, Präludien, Fugen und Suiten für Violine, Bratsche, Violoncello Solo, Op.42, 91, 117, 131a, c, d; Drei Duos im alten Stil, Op.131b; Streichtrio, A-moll, Op.77b; Streichtrio, D-moll, Op.141b. 1957.

Streichquartette.
Bd.25. Streichquartette, Op.54 (Nr.1–2), 74, 109, 121; Streichquartett, D-moll (1889). 1960.

Streichquintettsatz und Streichsextette.
Bd.26. Serenade, D-dur, für Flöte, Violine und Viola, Op.77a; Sextett, F-dur, für zwei Violinen, zwei Violen und zwei Violoncelli, Op.118; Serenade, G-dur, für Flöte, Violinen und Viola (oder zwei Violinen und Viola), Op.141a; Quintett, A-dur, für Klarinette, zwei Violinen, Viola und Violoncello, Op.146. 1963.

Chorwerke a cappella.
Bd.27. I. Werke für gemischten Chor a cappella: Drei sechsstimmige Chöre, Op.39; Acht "Tantum ergo," Op.61a; Acht Marienlieder, Op.61d; Sechs Trauergesänge, Op.61g; Drei Motetten, Op.110; Acht geistliche Gesänge, Op.138; Tantum ergo sacramentum; Gloriabunter; "Maria Himmelsfreud!"; Palmsonntagmorgan; Oster-Motette "Lasset uns den Herren preisen"; Zwanzig Responsorien; Abschiedslied. 1961.

Werke für Soli, Chor und Orchester.
*Bd.28. Die Weihe der Nacht, Op.119; Der Einsiedler, Op.144a; Requiem, Op.144b; Totenfeier, Op.145a; Weihegesang.

Werke für Chor und Orchester.
*Bd.29. Hymne an den Gesang, Op.21; Gesang der Verklärten, Op.71; Der 100. Psalm, Op.106; Die Nonnen, Op.112; Römischer Triumphgesang, Op.126.

Chöre oder Duette mit Klavier oder anderen Instrumenten.
*Bd.30. Op.6, 14, 61b, c, e, f; Drei Duette für Sopran und Alt mit Klavier, Op.111a; Fünf Choralkantaten; Trauungslied für Sopran und Alt mit Orgel.

Sologesänge mit Klavier.
Bd.31. Op.4, 8, 12, 14b, 15, 23, 31, 35, 37, 43, 48, 51, 55. 1955.
Bd.32. Op.62, 66, 68, 70, 75. 1958.
Bd.33. Schlichte Weisen, Op.76. 1959.
*Bd.34. Op.79c, 88, 97, 98, 104, 142; Bitte, Zwei Lieder und Schelmenlied (ungedruckter Nachlass) und weitere Lieder ohne Opuszahl.

Sologesänge mit Orgel oder Harmonium.
*Bd.34. Zwei geistliche Gesänge mit Orgel, Op.19; Zwei geistliche Lieder, Op.105; Zwölf geistliche Lieder für eine Stimme und Klavier oder Orgel, Op.137; Zwei geistliche Lieder für mittl. Stimme und Orgel; "Ehre sei Gott"; Geistliches Lied "Wohl denen"; Trauungsgesang mit Orgel.

*Bd.35. An die Hoffnung, Op.124; Hymnus der Liebe, Op.136; Sechs Lieder für eine Stimme mit Orchester (vom Komponisten instrumentiert, 1914); Aus den Himmelsaugen (Instrumentation von Op.98, 1); Fünf Lieder für eine Stimme mit Orchester (vom Komponisten instrumentiert, 1916).

REGIS, JOHANNES, 15th century.
... Opera omnia. Edidit Cornelis Lindenburg. Rome, American Institute of Musicology, 1956.
2v. (Corpus mensurabilis musicae. No.9).
Contents:
Vol.1. Missae: Dum sacrum mysterium. (L'homme armé). Ecce ancilla Domini. Fragmentum missae. Patrem Vilayge. 1956.
Vol.2. Motets and chansons. 1956.

REHBERG, WILLY, 1863–1937. ed.
Alte Hausmusik für Klavier (1550–1780) ... Harpsichord works of old masters. Original pieces of masters of the 16th–18th century. Selected and ed. by Willy Rehberg. Mainz und Leipzig, B. Schott's Söhne; London, Schott & Co., Ltd., [cop.1934].
2v. (Edition Schott. Nr.2347–2348).
Contains compositions by 32 composers.

Rehm, Wolfgang, 1929– , ed. Codex Escorial, *see* Codex Escorial.

REIMANN, HEINRICH, 1850–1906. ed.
Das deutsche geistliche Lied von der ältesten bis aus unsere Zeit für 1 Singstimme mit Pianoforte (oder Orgel). Nach den Quellen bearbeitet und hrsg. [Fortsetzung und Ergänzung von "Das deutsche Lied"]. Berlin, Simrock, between 1892–97.
6v.

REIMANN, HEINRICH, 1850–1906. ed.
Das deutsche Lied. Eine Auswahl aus den Programmen der historischen Lieder-Abende der Frau Amalie Joachim, mit deutschem und englischem Text. Berlin, Simrock, 1892–93.
4v.
Contents:
Vol.1. Contains folk songs. Compositions by H. Albert, Beethoven [one of the Scottish songs], Melch. Franck, Hans Leo Hassler, Jos. Haydn, F. H. Himmel, H. Isaac, Reinh. Keiser, Adam Krieger, Wolfg. Amadeus Mozart [The spurious lullaby], J. A. P. Schultz, Hans Sommer, B. A. Weber, C. M. von Weber, and Pet. von Winter.
Vol.2. Contains folk songs. Compositions by Joh. Rud. Ahle, C. Ph. Em. Bach, Joh. Seb. Bach, Friedrich Curschmann, Al. Fesca, Carl H. Graun, Jos. Haydn, J. Ph. Kirnberger, B. Klein, Conr. Kreutzer, Wolfg. Amadeus Mozart, Chr. Gottl. Neefe, J. F. Reichardt, C. Friedrich Rungenhagen, L. Spohr, Carl F. Zelter, and J. R. Zumsteeg.
Vol.3. Contains folk songs. Compositions by Joh. Seb. Bach, C. W. Gluck, Hans Leo Hassler, F. H. Himmel, Fr. W. Rust, J. A. P. Schultz, W. Weiss, and Carl F. Zelter.
Vol.4. Contains folk songs. Compositions by Joh. Seb. Bach, Gräfe (1741), Jos. Haydn, Joh. Adam Hiller, F. H. Himmel, H. G. Nägeli, J. F. Reichardt, Luise Reichardt, J. A. P. Schultz, G. P. Telemann, Chr. Weinlich, and Carl F. Zelter.

Reimann, Heinrich, 1850–1906, ed. Musica sacra, *see* Musica sacra, hrsg. von F. Commer.

Reliquary of English song, *see* Potter, Frank Hunter. Reliquary of English song.

Renaissance to Baroque, *see* Engel, Lehman. Three centuries of choral music: Renaissance to Baroque.

Rener, Adam, ca.1485–ca.1520. Collected works, *see* Institute of Mediaeval Music. Collected works. Vol.2.

Répertoire classique de musique religieuse et spirituelle, *see* Expert, Henry. Répertoire classique de musique religieuse et spirituelle.

RÉPERTOIRE DES CLAVECINISTES.
Répertoire des clavecinistes. A. Zuric chez Jean George Naigueli. Lale Script. F. Hegi ft. [Vortitel]. [Haupttitel]: A. Zuric chez Jean George Naigueli (Heft 16. Jean George Naigueli et Comp.; Heft 17. J. George Naigueli & Comp.), 1803–11?.
17 Hefte.
Contents:
Heft 1. Muzio Clementi. 3 Sonates. 1803.
Heft 2. J. B. Cramer. 3 Sonates. 1803.
Heft 3. J. L. Dussek. 3 Sonates. 1803.
Heft 4. D. Steibelt. 2 Sonates.
Heft 5. Louis van Beethoven. 2 Sonates. Op.31, Nr.1 und 2.
Heft 6. C. G. Haak. Caprice et variations.
Heft 7. [Ch. E. F.] Weyse. Allegri di bravura.
Heft 8. Maximilien Stadler. 2 Sonates suivies d'une fugue. 1804.
Heft 9. Antoine Liste. 2 Sonates. 1804.
Heft 10. Muzio Clementi. 3 Sonates.
Heft 11. Louis van Beethoven. 2 Sonates. Op.13, Pathétique. Op.31, Nr.3.
Heft 12. Joseph Woelfl. Sonate précédée d'une introduction et fugue.
Heft 13. François Pollini. Variations et rondeaux.
Heft 14. W. J. Tomascheck. Sonate et rondeau. 1805.
Heft 15. Louis van Beethoven. Grande sonate. Op.53. Waldstein–Sonate. 1805.
Heft 16. [Ch. E. F.] Weyse. Allegri di bravura. 1809.
Heft 17. Antoine Liste. Grande sonate. 1811.

Répertoire des concerts du Trocadéro, *see* Guilmant, Alexandre. Répertoire des concerts du Trocadéro.

Repertorio dell' Accademia di Canto Corale Stefano Tempia, *see* Pistone, Pier Giovanni. Capalavori della polifonia italiana.

Repertorium, *see* Societas Polyphonica Romanae. Repertorium.

Repertorium musicae sacrae ex auctoribus saeculi XVI et XVII, *see* Haberl, Franz Xaver. Repertorium musicae sacrae ex auctoribus saeculi XVI et XVII.

The reproaches, *see* Plainsong and Mediaeval Music Society. The reproaches.

Requiem services, *see* Plainsong and Mediaeval Music Society. Requiem services.

RHAW, GEORG, 1488–1548. pub.
Musikdrucke aus den Jahren 1538 bis 1545 in praktischer Neuausgabe. Bd.1– . Kassel, Bärenreiter-Verlag; St. Louis, Concordia Pub. House, [1955–].
12v. (in progress).
Contents:
Vol.1. Balthasar Resinarius. Responsoriorum numero octoginta. Erster Band: De Christo et regno eius, doctrina, vita, passione, resurrectione et ascensione. Hrsg. von Inge-Maria Schröder. 1955.
Vol.2. Balthasar Resinarius. Responsoriorum numero octoginta. Zweiter Band: De

sanctis et illorum in Christum fide et cruce. Hrsg. von Inge-Maria Schröder. 1957.
Vol.3. Symphoniae jucundae, atque adeo breves 4 vocum, ab optimis quibusque musicis compositae. 1538. Hrsg. von Hans Albrecht. 1959.
Vol.4. Vesperarum precum officia. (Wittenberg 1540). Hrsg. von Hans Joachim Moser. 1960.
Vol.7. Dietrich, Sixtus. Novum ac insigne opus musicum 36 antiphonarum. 1541. Hrsg. von Walter E. Buszin. 1964.

Other volumes to be published:
Selectae harmoniae 4 vocum de passione Domini. 1538.
Officia paschalis, de resurrectione et ascensione Domini. 1539.
Opus decem missarum 4 vocum. 1541.
Tricinia. Tum veterum, tum recentiorum in arte musica symphonistarum latina, germanica, brabantica et gallica. 1542.
Novum ac insigne opus musicum 36 antiphonarum. 1543.
Postremum vespertini officii opus. 1544.
Neue deutsche geistliche Gesänge. 1544.
Officiorum (ut vocant) de nativitate, circumcisione, epiphania Domini et purificatione. 1545.
Bicinia gallica, latina, germanica. Tomus I et II. 1545.

Rheinischer Musik, Denkmäler, *see* Denkmäler rheinischer Musik.

RIBERA Y TARRAGÓ, JULIÁN, 1858–1936. ed.
La música andaluza medieval en las canciones de trovadores, troveros y minnesinger, por Julián Ribera . . . Fasc.1–3 . . . Madrid, Topografía de la "Revista de Archivos," 1923–25.
3v. in 1.
Fasc.2–3 has imprint: Madrid, Imprenta de Estanistao Maestre.
Each fascicle has a historical and critical introduction.
Bibliographical footnotes.
Contents:
Fasc.1. 130 Canciones transcritas (12 armonizadas) de El Cancionero del Arsenal, el de Saint Germain de Prés y el del núm. 844 de la Biblioteca Nacional de Paris.
Fasc.2. 136 Canciones transcritas (14 armonizadas) de El Cancionero núm. 846 de la Biblioteca Nacional de Paris.
Fasc.3. 90 Canciones de los minnesinger del Códice de Jena (25 armonizadas).

RIEMANN, HUGO, 1849–1919. ed.
Collegium musicum. Auswahl älterer Kammermusikwerke für den praktischen Gebrauch, bearb. und hrsg. von Hugo Riemann und Anderen. No.1– . Leipzig, Breitkopf & Härtel, 1903– .
No.1– .
Contents:
No.1. Stamitz, Johann. Orchestertrio. Op.1, Nr.1, in C dur. Für 2 Violinen, Violoncell und Klavier.
No.2. Stamitz, Johann. Orchestertrio. Op.1, Nr.2, in A dur. Für 2 Violinen, Violoncell und Klavier.
No.3. Stamitz, Johann. Orchestertrio. Op.1, Nr.3, in F dur. Für 2 Violinen, Violoncell und Klavier.
No.4. Stamitz, Johann. Orchestertrio. Op.1, Nr.4, in D dur. Für 2 Violinen, Violoncell und Klavier.
No.5. Stamitz, Johann. Orchestertrio. Op.1, Nr.5, in B dur. Für 2 Violinen, Violoncell und Klavier.
No.6. Stamitz, Johann. Orchestertrio. Op.1, Nr.6, in G dur. Für 2 Violinen, Violoncell und Klavier.
No.7. Stamitz, Johann. Orchestertrio. Op.5, Nr.3, in E dur. Für 2 Violinen, Violoncell und Klavier.
No.8. Fasch, Joh. Friedr. Trio in D moll. Kanon für Violine und Viola mit Violoncell und Klavier.
No.9. Fasch, Joh. Friedr. Trio in D dur. Kanon für Violine und Viola mit Violoncell und Klavier.
No.10. Fasch, Joh. Friedr. Trio in A moll. Für 2 Violinen, Violoncell und Klavier.
No.11. Fasch, Joh. Friedr. Trio in F dur. Für 2 Violinen, Violoncell und Klavier.
No.12. Fasch, Joh. Friedr. Trio in G dur. Für 2 Violinen, Violoncell und Klavier.
No.13. Fasch, Joh. Friedr. Sonata a 4 in D moll. Für 2 Violinen, Viola und Violoncell. Partitur und Stimmen.
No.14. Telemann, G. Phil. Trio in Es dur. Für 2 Violinen, Violoncell und Klavier.
No.15. Jiránek, Anton. Trio in A dur. Für 2 Violinen, Violoncell und Klavier.
No.16. Bach, K. Ph. Em. Trio in G dur. Für 2 Violinen, Violoncell und Klavier.
No.17. Filtz, Anton. Trio in Es dur. Op.3, Nr.5. Für 2 Violinen, Violoncell und Klavier.
No.18. Richter, Franz Xaver. Sonata da camera in A dur. Für Violine (Flöte), Violoncell und obligates Klavier.
No.19. Bach, Joh. Chr. Trio in D dur. Für Klavier, Violine und Violoncell.
No.20. Mysliwecek, Jos. Trio in B dur. Op.1, Nr.4. Für Flöte (1. Violine), Violine, Violoncell und Klavier.
No.21. Locatelli, Pietro. Trio in G dur. Op.3, Nr.1. Für 2 Violinen (Flöten), Violoncell und Klavier.
No.22. Förster, Christ. Suite (mit Ouvertüre) in G dur. Für 2 Violinen, Viola, Violoncell. (Streichorchester). Partitur und Stimmen.
No.23. Porpora, Nicola. Trio in D dur. (Op.2, Concerto IV). Für 2 Violinen, Violoncell und Klavier.
No.24. Graun, J. G. Trio in F dur. Für Oboe (1. Violine), Violine, Violoncell und Klavier.
No.25. Graun, J. G. Trio in G dur. Für 2 Violinen, Violoncell und Klavier.
No.26. Graun, J. G. Trio in C moll. Für 2 Violinen, Violoncell und Klavier.
No.27. Sammartini, G. B. Trio in A moll. Op.3, Nr.9. Für 2 Violinen, Violoncell und Klavier. (1743).

No.28. Sammartini, G. B. Trio in Es dur. Op.1, Nr.3. Für 2 Violinen, Violoncell und Klavier.
No.29. Pergolesi, G. B. Trio Nr.1 in G dur. Für 2 Violinen, Violoncell und Klavier.
No.30. Pergolesi, G. B. Trio Nr.2 in B dur. Für 2 Violinen, Violoncell und Klavier.
No.31. Krebs, Joh. Ludwig. Trio (Suite mit Ouvertüre) in D dur. Für Flöte (1. Violine), Violine, Violoncell und Klavier. Gluck, Chr. W. von. Sechs Triosonaten. Für 2 Violinen, Violoncell und Klavier (1746).
No.32. Gluck, Chr. W. von. Trio Nr.1 in C dur.
No.33. Gluck, Chr. W. von. Trio Nr.2 in G moll.
No.34. Gluck, Chr. W. von. Trio Nr.3 in A dur.
No.35. Gluck, Chr. W. von. Trio Nr.4 in B dur.
No.36. Gluck, Chr. W. von. Trio Nr.5 in Es dur. (G. Beckmann).
No.37. Gluck, Chr. W. von. Trio Nr.6 in F dur.
No.38. Gluck, Chr. W. von. Trio Nr.7 in E dur. Für 2 Violinen, Violoncell und Klavier. (G. Beckmann).
No.39. Asplmayr, Franz. Trio in F dur. Op.5, Nr.1. Für 2 Violinen, Violoncell, und Klavier.
No.40. Asplmayr, Franz. Quartett in D dur. Op.2, Nr.2. Für 2 Violinen, Viola und Violoncell.
No.41. Abaco, Everisto Felice dall'. Sonata a tre. Op.3, Nr.4, G dur (da chiesa). Für 2 Violinen, Violoncell und Klavier.
No.42. Abaco, Everisto Felice dall'. Sonata a tre. Op.3, Nr.5, D dur (da chiesa). Für 2 Violinen, Violoncell und Klavier.
No.43. Abaco, Everisto Felice dall'. Sonata a tre. Op.3, Nr.9, A moll (da camera). Für 2 Violinen, Violoncell und Klavier.
No.44. Ravenscroft, John. Trio da chiesa in H moll. Für 2 Violinen, Violoncell und Klavier. Op.1, Nr.2 (Früher unter Antonio Caldara veröffentlicht).
No.45. Bach, W. Friedemann. Trio in B dur. Für 2 Violinen, Violoncell und Klavier.
No.46. Sacchini, Antonio. Triosonate in G dur aus Op.1. Für 2 Violinen, Violoncell und Klavier.
No.47. Gossec, Fr. J. Trio in Es dur. Op.9, Nr.1. Für 2 Violinen und Violoncell.
No.48. Stamitz, Johann. Orchestertrio in C moll. Op.4, Nr.3. Für 2 Violinen, Violoncell. (orchestration by P. H. Láng).
No.49. Stamitz, Johann. Orchestertrio in C dur. Op.9, Nr.6. Für 2 Violinen, Violoncell und Klavier.
No.50. Schobert, Johann. Op.7, Nr.2. Quartett in F moll. Für 2 Violinen, Violoncell und Klavier.
No.51. Richter, Franz Xaver. Streichquartett in C dur. Op.5, Nr.1. Für 2 Violinen, Viola und Violoncell. (Paul Mies).
No.52. Reichardt, Joh. Fr. Trio in Es dur. Für 2 Violinen, Violoncell und Klavier. (Paul Klengel). 1926.
No.53. Buxtehude, Dietrich. Sonate in D dur. Für Violine, Viola da Gamba (oder Violoncell) und Klavier. (Christian Döbereiner). 1926.
No.54. Corelli, Arcangelo. Sonate da chiesa in E moll. Op.3, Nr.7. Für 2 Violinen, Violoncell und Klavier. (Paul Klengel).
No.55. Telemann, G. Phil. Trio für Flöte, Oboe, Violoncell und Klavier. (Max Seiffert).
No.56. Telemann, G. Phil. Quartett für Violine, Flöte, Violoncell obligat und Klavier. (Max Seiffert).
No.57. Arne, Thomas Augustine. Triosonate für 2 Violine, Violoncell und Klavier. Op.3, Nr.1. (Max Seiffert). 1928.
No.58. Guillemain, L. G. Conversation galante et amusante entre une flûte, un violon, une basse de viole et basse continue. Op.12, Nr.1. Für Flöte, Violine, Viola (oder Violoncell) und Klavier. (Paul Klengel).
No.59. Telemann, G. Phil. Quartett in D moll für Flauto dolce (oder Fagott, oder Violoncell), zwei Querflöten, Cembalo und Violoncell. Tafelmusik 1733, II, Nr.2. (Max Seiffert).
No.60. Furchheim, Johann Wilhelm. Dritte Sonate in A dur und Sechste Sonate in B dur aus der "Musikalischen Taffel-Befienung" 1674. Für 2 Violinen, 2 Violen, Violon und Basso Continuo. (Paul Rubardt).
No.61. Abel, Karl Friedrich. Op.8, Nr.3. Streichquartett Es dur. Für 2 Violinen, Viola und Violoncell. (W. Hillemann). [1935].
No.62. Haydn, Joseph. Trio. Für 2 Violinen und Violoncell. (W. Hinnenthal).
No.63/65. Nardini, Pietro. Sechs Streichquartette. Erstes Heft: Quartette Nr.1/2; Zweites Heft: Quartette Nr.3/4; Drittes Heft: Quartette Nr.5/6. (Wilhelm Altmann).
No.66. Telemann, G. P. Trio-Sonate in F dur für 2 Blockflöten (F-alt) und Cembalo (Klavier). Score, Blockflöte I, Blockflöte II und Violoncell.
No.67. Telemann, G. P. Trio-Sonate in C dur für Blockflöte, Violine (Blockflöte II) und Cembalo (Klavier). Score, Violin, Blockflöte II und Violoncell.
No.68. Janitsch, Joh. Gottl. Kammersonate "Echo" für Flauto traverso, Oboe (Violine oder 2 Flauto), Viola da Braccio (oder da Gamba) und Cembalo und Violoncell. (Hellmuth Christian Wolff).
No.69. Telemann, G. Phil. Sonate für 2 Flöten und Cembalo. (Heinz Schreiter).
No.70. Stamitz, Karl. Trio-Sonate für Flöte, Violine (oder zwei Violinen), Violoncell und Klavier. (W. Hillemann).
No.71. Schaffrath, Christoph. Trio in Do maggiore per 3 Violini.
No.72. Stölzel, G. H. Sonata a 3.
No.73–75. Telemann, G. Phil. Tre trietti melodiche e tre scherzi (1948).
No.76. Stölzel, G. H. Sonate für Oboe, Violine und Generalbass.
No.77. Reinken, Joh. Adam. Hortus musicus: Sonata 6, A dur. 1952.
No.78. Heinichen, Joh. Sonate. 1951.
No.79. Stölzel, G. H. Sonate F dur.
No.80–100.
No.101. Dittersdorf, K. D. v. Drei Partiten für Bläser, 2 Oboen, 2 Hörner und Fagott oder 3 Violinen, Viola und Cello. 1948.
No.102. Purcell, Henry. Sonate, G moll. 1952.
No.103. Bach, C. Ph. Em. Sonate G moll für

Oboe, Cembalo (Klavier) und Violoncello (Fagott) ad lib. 1953.
No.106. Becker, Heinrich. Klarinetten Duette. 1954.

RIEMANN, HUGO, 1849–1919. ed.
Hausmusik aus alter Zeit; intime Gesänge mit Instrumental-Begleitung aus dem 14. bis 15. Jahrhundert, in ihrer Originalgestalt in die heutige Notenschrift übertragen und mit Vortragsbezeichnung versehen von Prof. Dr. Hugo Riemann. Mit Originaltext und deutscher Übersetzung. Leipzig, Breitkopf & Härtel, [pref.1906].
3v. in 1.
Words in original language with German translation. Music for 1 to 3 voices, with instruments.
Contains compositions by Adam von Fulda, Binchois, Cordier, Domenico di Ferrara, Dufay, Grenon, Guillaume de Machaut, Landino, Paolo da Firenze, and others.

RIEMANN, HUGO, 1849–1919. ed.
Mannheim symphonists. A collection of 24 orchestral works. Ed. by Hugo Riemann . . . New York, Broude Brothers, n.d.
2v.
Contents:
Vol.1 contains compositions by Anton Filtz, Franz Xaver Richter, and Johann Stamitz.
Vol.2 contains compositions by Franz Beck, Christian Cannabich, Ernst Eichner, Anton Filtz, Ignaz Holzbauer, Carl Stamitz, and Joseph Toeschi.

RIEMANN, HUGO, 1849–1919. ed.
Musikgeschichte in Beispielen; eine Auswahl von 150 Tonsätzen, geistliche und weltliche Gesänge und Instrumentalkompositionen zur Veranschaulichung der Entwicklung der Musik im 13.–18. Jahrhundert, in Notierung auf 2 Systemen von Dr. Hugo Riemann . . . Mit Erläuterungen von Dr. Arnold Schering. Leipzig, E. A. Seemann, 1912.
4p.L., 16p., 2L., 334p.
Issued in 3 parts, 1911–12; Pt.1 has special title page and index.
2d. ed. 1921; 3d. ed. 1925; 4th. ed. 1929.

RIEMANN, HUGO, 1849–1919. ed.
. . . Old chamber music. (Alte Kammermusik). A selection of canzones, sonates, etc. (da chiesa and da camera). For strings alone, or with a thoroughbass, by composers of the 17th and 18th centuries. Ed. and arr. by Dr. Hugo Riemann . . . London, Augener, Ltd., [1898–1902].
4v.
Contents:
Vol.1. No.1–8. Contains compositions by Gregor Aichinger, G. Frescobaldi, Andrea Gabrieli, Giovanni Gabrieli, Landgraf Moritz von Hessen, and L. Viadana.
Vol.2. No.9–18. Contains compositions by Georg Engelmann, Carlo Farina, Melchior Franck, Johann Naubauer, Valerius Otto, Paul Peurl, Samuel Scheidt, Johann Hermann Schein, Thomas Simpson, and Erasmus Widmann.
Vol.3. No.19–25. Contains compositions by Carlo Farina, Biagio Marini, Tarquinio Merula, Salomone Rossi, and Giovanni Valentini.
Vol.4. No.26–31. Contains compositions by G. B. Buonamenti, Nicolaus à Kempis, Giovanni Legrenzi, Marco Uccellini, and Giovanni Battista Vitali.

RIMBAULT, EDWARD FRANCIS, 1816–1876. ed
The rounds, catches and canons of England; a collection of specimens of the sixteenth, seventeenth, and eighteenth centuries, adapted to modern use; The words revised, adapted, or rewritten by the Rev. J. Powell Metcalfe. The music selected and revised, and an introductory essay On the rise and progress of the round, catch and canon; also, biographical notices of the composers, written by Edward F. Rimbault . . . London, Cramer, Wood & Co., [ca.1863].
lxxii, 208p.

RIMSKIĬ-KORSAKOV, NIKOLAĬ ANDREEVICH, 1844–1908.
[Works]. Moscow, State Music Publishers, 1948– .
v.1– .
Contents:
Vol.2A–B. May night. Full score.
Vol.3A–B. Snowmaiden. Full score.
Vol.4A–B. Mlada. Full score.
Vol.4. Suppl. Mlada. Act 3. (Night on the Three-headed mountain). Full score.
Vol.5A–B. Christmas Eve. Full score.
Vol.6. Sadko. Orchestra score.
Vol.7. Mozart and Salieri. Full score.
Vol.8. Vera Sheloga. Full score.
Vol.9A–B. The Tzar's bride. Full score.
Vol.10A–B. Tzar Saltan. Full score.
Vol.11. Servilia. Opera in 5 acts. Full score.
Vol.12. Kaschei the immortal. Full score.
Vol.13A–B. Pan Voyevode. Full score.
Vol.14A–B. Tale of the invisible city of Kitezh and the maid of Fevronia. Full score.
Vol.14. Suppl. Tale of the invisible city of Kitezh and the maid of Fevronia. Commentaries.
Vol.15A–B. Le coq d'or. Full score.
Vol.16. Symphony, No.1. Full score.
Vol.17A–B. Antar. Op.9. (Symphony, No.2). Original version and second version (1903).
Vol.18. Symphony, No.3. Full score.
Vol.19A. Sadko. (Musical tone picture). (3 versions: 1867, 1870, 1892). Full score.
Vol.19B. Fantasy on Servian themes. (2 versions). 5 Selections from "Pskovityanka."
Vol.20. Works for orchestra: Overture on a Russian theme; Fairy tale; Sinfonetta. Full score.
Vol.21. Capriccio espagnol.
Vol.22. Sheherazade. Full score.
Vol.24. Cantatas. Full score.
Vol.25. Works for solo instruments and band.
Vol.27. Works for chamber ensemble. (Strings, woodwinds, brass).

Vol.28A. Chamber works: Quintet for piano and winds. Score and parts.
Vol.30. May night. Vocal score.
Vol.31A–B. Snowmaiden. Vocal score.
Vol.32. Mlada. Vocal score.
Vol.33. Night before Christmas. Vocal score.
Vol.34. Sadko. Vocal score.
Vol.35. Mozart and Salieri. Vocal score.
Vol.36. Vera Sheloga. Vocal score.
Vol.37. The Tzar's bride. Vocal score.
Vol.38. Tzar Saltan. Vocal score.
Vol.39. Servilia. Vocal score.
Vol.40. Kashchei the immortal. Vocal score.
Vol.41. Pan Voyevode. Vocal score.
Vol.42. The invisible city of Kitezh. Vocal score.
Vol.43. Le coq d'or. Vocal score.
Vol.44. Cantatas. Vocal score.
Vol.45. Complete collection of songs. Voice and piano. Op.2–4, 7–8, 25–27, 39–43, 45–46, 49–51, 55–56.
Vol.46A. Duets and trios. Voice and piano; voice and orchestra.
Vol.46B. Choruses without accompaniment.
Vol.47. Russian folk songs. (100 songs [Op.24] and 40 songs. Harmonized for voice and piano).
Vol.49A. Piano works.

Literary works and correspondence.
Vol.2. Criticisms; materials pertaining to his work with the Russian Navy orchestra, the Court chorus, and the St. Petersburg Conservatory; Articles for the press.
Vol.4. Textbook of harmony.
Vol.5–6. Letters.

Rochester, N.Y. University. Eastman School of Music. Publication. No.10, *see* Gleason, Harold. Examples of music before 1400.

ROCHLITZ, FRIEDRICH, 1769–1842. ed.
Sammlung vorzüglicher Gesangstücke der anerkanntgrössten zugleich für die Geschichte der Tonkunst wichtegsten die eigene höhere Ausbildung für diese Kunst und den würdigsten Genuss an derselben förderndsten Meister die für Musik entscheidendsten Nationen gewählt, nach der Zeitfolge geordnet, und mit den nöthigsten historischen und andern Nachweisungen hrsg. von F. Rochlitz, Erster (bis dritter) Band. Mainz, Paris, Antwerpen, Schott, 1838–40.
3v.
Latin words for most of the selections; German or Italian for the others.
Prefaces in Bd.1, Abt.2, and Bd.2 and 3 in German and French.
Contents (from *Grove's Dictionary of music and musicians*, 1916, Vol.4, p.115):
First period. (1380–1550). (Bd.1. Pt.1).
1. Dufay. Kyrie, a 4. Se la face ay pale.
2. Dufay. Kyrie, a 4. L'homme armé.
3. Okeghem. Kyrie and Christe, a 4.
4. Josquin de Près. Hymnus, a 4. Tu pauperum refugium.
5. Josquin de Près. Zwischengesang einer der grössten messen des meisters, Et incarnatus, a 4.
6. Josquin de Près. Motet. Misericordias Domini. a 4.
7. Lasso, O. Regina coeli, a 4.
8. Lasso, O. Salve Regina, a 4.
9. Lasso, O. Angelus pastores, a 5.
10. Lasso, O. Miserere. Amplius, Cor mundum, Ne proficeas, Redde mihi, etc., a 5.
11. Goudimel, C. Domine quid multiplicati, a 4.
12. Morales, Ch. de. Kyrie et Christe, a 4.
13. Morales, Ch. de. Gloria.
14. Tallis, T. Verba mea, a 4.
15. Senfl, L. Motet on a choral, "Mag ich ungluck," a 4.
16. Senfl, L. Deus propitius esto, a 5.
17. Senfl, L. Nunc dimittis, a 4.

Second period. (1550–1630). 1838. (Bd.1. Pt.2).
1. Palestrina. Adoramus, a 4.
2. Palestrina. Gloria, 2 choirs, a 4.
3. Palestrina. Pleni sunt, a 3.
4. Palestrina. O bone Jesu, a 4.
5. Palestrina. Popule meus, 2 choirs, a 4.
6. Palestrina. Madrigal. Cedro gentil, a 5.
7. Palestrina. Lauda anima mea, a 4.
8. Nanini, G. M. Stabat Mater, a 4.
9. Nanini, G. M. Exaudi nos, a 4.
10. Nanini, G. M. Haec dies, a 5.
11. Vittoria. Jesu dulcis, a 4.
12. Vittoria. O quam gloriosum, a 4.
13. Anerio, F. Adoramus. a 4.
14. Anerio, F. Christus factus est, a 4.
15. Allegri. Miserere, 2 choirs, a 5.
16. Gabrieli. In excelsis. Soprano solo, tenor solo, and chorus, a 4, with 3 horns, 2 trombones, and violins.
17. Gabrieli. Benedictus, 3 choirs, a 4.
18. Böhm, Brüder. 2 Lieder, a 4: Der Tag vertreibt; Die Nacht ist kommen.
19. Böhm, Brüder. 2 Lieder, a 4: Vieleih' uns Frieden; Nimm' von uns.
20. Walther. Aeterno gratias, a 4.
21. Gesänge Martin Luthers, a 4: Mit Fried und Freud; Es woll' uns Gott; Nun komm der Heiden Heiland; Christ lag; Jesus Christus.
22. Gallus. Ecce quomodo moritur justus, a 4.
23. Gallus. Adoramus, a 6.
24. Gallus. Media vitae, 2 choirs, a 4.
25. Vulpius. Exultate justi, a 4.
26. Vulpius. Surrexit Christus, 2 choirs, a 4.
27. Walliser. Gaudent in coelis, 2 choirs, a 4.
28. Praetorius. Ecce Dominus, a 8.

Appendix.
Palestrina. Et incarnatus, etc. (from mass "Assumpta est"). a 6.
Praetorius. O vos omnes.

Third period. (1600–1700). 1840. (Bd.2).
1. Caccini. Solo and chorus. Funeste piaggie.
2. Caccini. Chorus. Biondo arcier.
3. Carissimi. Recitative and chorus. Turbabuntur (from cantata "Plaintes des réprouvés").
4. Carissimi. Ardens est cor, 4 solos and chorus.
5. Carissimi. O sacrum convivium. 3 solo voices.
6. Carissimi. Cantemus omnes, chorus and scena. (Jeita). Plorate, a 6.

7. Benevoli. Sanctus, 4 choirs, a 4.
8. Benevoli. Christe, a 4.
9. Bernabei. Alleluja, a 4.
10. Bernabei. Salve Regina, a 4.
11. Scarlatti, A. Kyrie, a 4.
12. Scarlatti, A. Gloria, a 5.
13. Scarlatti, A. Vacuum est. Canto solo and chorus, with violins.
14. Scarlatti, A. Sanctus, a 4, and Agnus, a 7.
15. Caldara, Salve Regina, a 3.
16. Caldara. Agnus, alto and tenor.
17. Caldara. Qui tollis, a 4.
18. Astorga. Stabat.
19. Astorga. Fac me.
20. Astorga. O quam.
21. Durante. Kyrie.
22. Durante. Regina angelorum.
23. Durante. Requiem aeternam.
24. Durante. Domine Jesu.
25. Lotti. Crucifixus, a 6.
26. Lotti. Qui tollis, a 4.
27. Lotti. Crucifixus, a 8.
28. Marcello. Udir' le orecchie, Psalm xliv, a 4.
29. Marcello. Et incarnatus, a 4.
30. Hasler. Pater noster, a 7.
31. Schütz, H. Selig sind die Todten, a 4.
32. Schütz, H. Chorus. Christus ist hier, a 4.
33. Schütz, H. Psalm. Was betrübst du?
34. Schütz, H. Vater unser.
35. Leisring, V. Trotz sey dem Teufel, 2 choirs, a 4.
36. Grimm. Gloria, a 5.
37. Fux, J. J. Domine Jesu, a 4.
38. Fux, J. J. Trema la terra. Chorus from oratorio "La deposizione."

Fourth period. (1700–1760). (Bd.3).

1. Handel. Te Deum, in D, Gloriae tuae.
2. Handel. He sent a thick darkness.
3. Handel. He rebuked the Red Sea.
4. Handel. And Israel saw.
5. Handel. Behold the Lamb of God.
6. Handel. He was despised.
7. Handel. Thy rebuke.
8. Handel. Lift up your hands.
9. Handel. Hear, Jacob's God.
10. Handel. Zadok the priest.
11. Bach, Christoph. Ich lasse dich nicht.
12. Bach, J. S. Nimm' von uns Herr.
13. Bach, J. S. Mache dich mein Geist.
14. Bach, J. S. Wir setzen uns mit Thränen nieder.
15. Bach, J. S. Wie sich ein Vater. Lobet den Herrn.
16. Zelenka. Credo.
17. Telemann. Amen. Lob und Ehre, a 8.
18. Stölzel. Gloria.
19. Homilius. Vater unser, a 4.
20. Pasterwitz. Requiem.
21. Hasse. Duet and chorus. Le porte a noi.
22. Hasse. Alto solo. Ad Te clamamus.
23. Hasse. Miserere and Benigni.
24. Hasse. Te Deum, a 4.
25. Graun. Machet die Thür weit.
26. Graun. Tu rex gloriae, a 4.
27. Graun. Freuet euch. (Tod Jesu).
28. Graun. Wir hier liegen. (Tod Jesu).
29. Rolle. Der Herr ist König.
30. Rolle. Welt-Richter. (Tod Abel).
31. Wolf. Laus et perennis gloria, a 4.
32. Wolf. De Lebens Fürsten.
33. Bach, C. Ph. Em. Et misericordia, a 6, from Magnificat.
34. Bach, C. Ph. Em. Heilig, 2 choirs, a 4.
35. Haydn, M. Salvos fac nos.
36. Haydn, M. Tenebrae factae.
37. Haydn, M. Miserere.
38. Leo. Chorus. Di quanta pena. (S. Elena).
39. Leo. Et incarnatus.
40. Leo. Miserere; Ecce enim, a 8.
41. Jommelli. Confirma hoc Deus, 5 solos and chorus.
42. Jommelli. Miserere.
43. Pergolesi. Eja ergo (Salve Regina).
44. Pergolesi. Qui tollis, a 6.
45. Pergolesi. Stabat Mater.

ROHR, HEINRICH. ed.
... Orgelspiel im Kirchenjahr. 62 leichte Choralvorspiele alter Meister für Orgel (ohne Pedal), auch Harmonium oder Klavier. Hrsg. von Heinrich Rohr. Mainz, B. Schott's Söhne, [cop.1951].
63 [1] p. (Edition Schott 4336).
Contains compositions by Andreas Armsdorf, Johann Christoph Bach, Johann Sebastian Bach, Johann Heinrich Buttstedt, Dietrich Buxtehude, Johann Kaspar Ferdinand Fischer, Johann Philipp Kirnberger, Johann Krieger, Johann Pachelbel, Michael Praetorius, Samuel Scheidt, Johann Gottfried Walther, and Friedrich Wilhelm Zachau.

ROITZSCH, FERD. AUGUST, 1805–1889. ed.
Alte Klavier-Musik. Leipzig, Peters.
3 Hefte.
Contents:
Bach, J. Ernst. Fantasie and fugue in F.
Kirnberger. Prelude and fugue in C sharp minor.
Bach, C. Ph. Em. Solfeggio in C minor.
—— Sonata in F minor.
Couperin. March in A flat.
—— Le réveille-matin in F.
Rameau. Tambourin in E minor.
Scarlatti, D. Allegro in G minor.
—— Sonata in A.
—— The cat's fugue in G minor.
Clementi. Toccata in B flat.
Field. Rondo in E.
Cherubini. Fugue in C.
Bach, W. F. Sonata in D.
Eberlin. Prelude and fugue in E minor.
Hässler. Fantasie in C minor.
Cramer, J. B. Toccatina in A flat.

Rokseth, Yvonne, 1890–1948, ed. Polyphonies du XIIIe siècle, *see* Montpellier, France. Université. Faculté de Médicine. Bibliothèque. Mss. (H 196). Polyphonies du XIIIe siècle.

Rokseth, Yvonne, 1890–1948, ed. Trois chansonniers français du XVe siècle, *see* [Droz, Eugénie]. Trois chansonniers français du XVe siècle.

Le roman de Fauvel, *see* Fauvel. Le roman de Fauvel.

Romances y villancicos españoles del signo XVI, *see* Bal y Gay, Jesús. Romances y villancicos españoles del signo XVI.

RORE, CIPRIANO DE, 1516–1565.
Opera omnia. Edidit Bernhardus Meier. [Rome], American Institute of Musicology, 1959– .
v.1– . (Corpus mensurabilis musicae. No.14).
Proposed set about 9 or 10v.
Contents:
Vol.1. Motets. (29 of them). 1959.
Vol.2. Madrigalia 5 vocum. 1963.
Vol.3. Madrigalia 5 vocum. 1961.
Vol.7. Missae. 1966.

ROSEINGRAVE, THOMAS, 1690–1766.
Fifteen voluntaries & fugues for the organ. Ed. by A. V. Butcher . . . London, Hinrichsen Edition, [1938?].
42p.

ROSSINI, GIOACCHINO ANTONIO, 1792–1868.
Quaderni Rossiniani, a cura della Fondazione Rossini. Pesaro, [Italy], Fondazione Rossini, 1954– .
v.1– .
Contents (published):
Vol.1. Sei sonate a quattro. 1954.
Vol.2. Prima scelta di pezzi per pianoforte. 1954.
Vol.3. Prélude thème et variations pour cor. 1954.
Vol.4. Melodie italiane per canto e pianoforte. 1955.
Vol.5. Melodie francesi per canto e pianoforte. 1956.
Vol.6. Musica da camera. 1957.
Vol.7. Cori a voci. Pari o dispari. 1958.
Vol.8. Sinfonia [di Bologna]. Sinfonia [di Odense]. Le chant des Titans. 1959.
Vol.9. Variazioni a più strumenti obbligati. Grande fanfare par Rossini. Scena da "Il viaggio a Reims." 1959.
Vol.10. Seconda scelta di pezzi per pianoforte. 1960.

DAS ROSTOCKER LIEDERBUCH.
. . . Das Rostocker Liederbuch, nach den Fragmenten der Handscrift neu hrsg. von Friedrich Ranke und J. M. Müller-Blattau. Halle (Salle), Max Niemeyer Verlag, 1927.
2p.L., p.[193]–306. v facsim. (incl. music). (Schriften der Königsberger Gelehrten Gesellschaft. Geisteswissenschaftliche Klasse. 4.Jahr., Heft 5).
With music.
"1.Auflage."

Rottauscher, Alfred, ed. Das Taghorn, *see* Das Taghorn.

The rounds, catches and canons of England, *see* Rimbault, Edward Francis. The rounds, catches and canons of England.

ROUX, GASPARD LE, 1660–1705.
. . . Pieces for harpsichord. Ed. with a pref. by Albert Fuller. New York, London, [etc.], C. F. Peters, [1956].
AA xxxi [1] p., 1L., 77p.
Contents:
Suite I–VII.
Pièces pour 2 clavecins.

Royal Musical Association. Musica Britannica, *see* Musica Britannica.

RUBIO, SAMUEL. ed.
Antología polifónica sacra. 71 piezas, a cuatro voces mixtas, de autores espagñoles del siglo XVI, recogidas, ordenadas y transcritas por Samuel Rubio . . . Madrid, Editorial Coculsa, 1954– .
v.1– .
Vocal score.
Contents:
Vol.1. Proprium de tempore. (Contains compositions by Joseph Bernal, Emmanuel Cardoso, Joannes de Castro, Rodericus Ceballos, Raphael Coloma, Joannes Esquivel, Michael Guerau, Franciscus Guerrero, Orlandus Lassus, Ildephonsus Lobo, Christophorus Morales, Bernardinus Nanini, Didacus Ortiz, J. Petraloysius Praenestinus, Joannes Ginesius Pérez, Melchior Robledo, Michael Sanchez, Thomas Ludovicus de Victoria, Fr. Martinus de Villaneuva, Sebastianus Vivanco, and Nicasius Zorita).

Rue, Pierre de la, *see* La Rue, Pierre de.

RUNGE, PAUL, 1848–1911. ed.
Die Sangesweisen der Colmarer Handschrift und die Liederhandschrift Donaueschingen. Hrsg. von Paul Runge. Leipzig, Breitkopf & Härtel, 1896.
xx, 199p. col. facsims. (incl. music).
German words, with tunes.

Russischer Romanzen, Sammlung, *see* Sammlung russischer Romanzen.

Ruuta, Theodoricus Petri, comp. Piae cantiones, *see* Plainsong and Mediaeval Music Society. Ruuta, Theodoricus Petri. Piae cantiones.

Sablonara, Claudio de la, *see* La Sablonara, Claudio de.

St. Andrews University Publications. No.XXX, *see* Wolfenbüttel. Herzog-August-Bibliothek. Mss. (677 [Helmst.628]). An old St. Andrews music book.

Saint-Gervais, Chanteurs de, *see* Bordes, Charles. Chansonnier du XVe siècle.

St. Gregory and the Gregorian music. Wyatt, Edward Gerald Penfold, *see* Plainsong and Mediaeval Music Society. Wyatt, Edward Gerald Penfold. St. Gregory and the Gregorian music.

Sainte-Chapelle, Chants de la, *see* Clément, Félix. Chants de la Sainte-Chapelle.

Salve Rex, *see* Plainsong and Mediaeval Music Society. Salve Rex.

SAMFUNDET TIL UDGIVELSE AF DANSK MUSIK. Copenhagen, Danish "Society for the Publication of Danish Music," 1872– .
v.1– .
The Society was founded in 1871.
Contents (language of each volume is taken from the volume):
Ser.I.
No.1. Kunzen, F. L. Ae. Gyrithe. Drama. Vocal score. 1872.
No.2. Hartmann, J. P. E. Syvsoverdag. Comedy. Op.30. Vocal score. 1872.
No.3. Kuhlau, Fr. William Shakespeare. Op.74. Drama. Vocal score. 1873.
No.4. Hartmann, J. P. E. Hakon Jarl. Op.40. Tragedy. Overture and entr'acte music. Piano solo. 1873.
No.5. Heise, P. Tornerose. Choral work. Vocal score. 1874.
No.6. Løvenskiold, H. S. Fra Skoven ved Furesø. Concert-ouverture. Op.29. Piano duet. 1874.
No.7. Weyse, C. E. F. Festen paa Kenilworth. Opera. Vocal score. 1877.
No.8. Hansen, C. J. Koncert-ouverture (E-dur). Piano duet. 1875.
No.9. Hartmann, Johan. Balders Død. Singspiel. Vocal score. 1876.
No.10. Kuhlau, Fr. Ouverture til "Euridice i Tartarus." Op.47. Piano duet. 1877.
No.11. Hartmann, J. P. E. Undine. Fairy play. Op.33. Vocal score. 1878.
No.12. Lange-Müller, P. E. Tove. Singspiel. Op.7. Vocal score. 1879.
No.13. Schultz, J. A. P. Christi Død. Oratorium. Vocal score. 1879.
No.14. Heise, P. Musik til "Palnatoke." Tragedy. Piano duet. 1880.
No.15. Fröhlich, J. F. Erik Menveds Barndom. Ballet. Op.51. Piano solo. 1880.
No.16. Hartmann, J. P. E. Korsarerne. Opera. Op.16. Vocal score. 1883.
No.17. Bendix, Victor. Fjeldstigning. Symphoni. Op.16. Piano duet. 1882.
No.18. Kuhlau, Fr. Ouverture til "Trillingbrødrene fra Damask." Op.115. Piano duet. 1883.
No.19. Weyse, C. E. F. Reformations-Kantate. Vocal score. 1884.
No.20. Malling, Otto. Symfoni, D-moll, Op.17. Piano duet. 1884.
No.21. Hartmann, Johan. Musik til "Fiskerne." Singspiel. Vocal score. 1886.
No.22. Winding, Aug. Konzert-Ouverture (D-moll). Op.14. Piano duet. 1885.
No.23. Rosenfeld, Leop. Henrik og Else. Op.25. Choral work. Vocal score. 1886.
No.24. Hartmann, J. P. E. Cantate ved Universitetets Fest. Op.84. (8 April 1888). Vocal score. 1888.

Ser.II.
No.1. Lange-Müller, P. E. Industri,-Landbrugs-og Kunst-Udstillings. (18 Maj 1888). Op.37. 1889.
No.2. Hartmann, Emil. Symphoni Nr.3 (D-dur). Op.42. Piano duet. 1889.
No.3. Bendix, Victor. Sommerklange fra Syd-Rusland. Symfoni Nr.2. Op.20. Piano duet. 1890.
No.4. Malling, Otto. Prolog til "Den gyldne Legende." Op.25. Choral work. Vocal score. 1890.
No.5. Hartmann, J. P. E. La légende de Thrym. Ballet by Bournonville. Op.67. Piano duet. 1891.
No.6. Horneman, C. F. E. Aladdin. Opera. Vocal score. 1893.
No.7. Winding, Aug. Symphonie (C–moll). Op.39. Piano duet. 1894.
No.8. Gade, Niels W. and Hartmann, J. P. E. Et Folkesagn. Ballet by Bournonville. Piano duet. 1896.
No.9. Malling, Otto. Det heilige Land. (Das heilige Land). Op.46. Choral work. Vocal score. 1897.
No.10. Gade, Niels W. Baldurs Drøm. Choral work. Vocal score. 1897.
No.11. Rung, Frederik. Den trekantede Hat. Opera. Vocal score. 1898.
No.12. Glass, Louis. Sommerliv. Suite for orchestra. Op.27. Piano duet. 1899.
No.13. Heise, P. Ouverture til "Marsk Stig." Piano duet. 1899.
No.14. Hartmann, J. P. E. Valkyrien. Ballet by Bournonville. Op.62. Piano duet. 1900.
No.15. Malling, Jørgen. Küwala. Choral work. Vocal score. [1902].
No.16. Lange-Müller, P. E. Middelalderlig. Op.55. Melodrama. Vocal score. [1902].
No.17. Heise, P. Rus-Kantate. Vocal score. [1903].
No.18. Hartmann, J. P. E. Koncert-Indledning. Choral work. Vocal score. 1903.
No.19. Bendix, Victor. Symphoni Nr.3 (A-moll). Op.25. Piano duet. 1904.
No.20. Horneman, C. F. E. Kalanus. Tragedy. Vocal score. 1904.
No.21. Nielsen, Carl. Helios. Ouverture. Op.17. Piano duet. 1905.
No.22. Lange-Müller, P. E. H. C. Andersen-Kantàte. Op.71. Vocal score. [1906].
No.23. Glass, Louis. Symfoni Nr.3, D-dur. (Skovsymfoni). Op.30. Piano duet. 1906.
No.24. Malling, Otto. Oktet for Strygeinstrumenter. Op.50. Piano duet. 1907.
No.25. Horneman, C. F. E. Kampen med Muserne. Drama. Vocal score. 1907–10.
No.26. Barnekow, Christian. Kvintet for 2 Violiner, Bratsch og 2 Violonceller. Op.20. Piano duet. [1908].
No.27. Scalabrini, P. Kaerlighed uden Strømper. Tragedy. Vocal score. 1909.
No.28. Lange-Müller, P. E. Agnete og Havmanden. Op.73. Choral work. Vocal score. 1910.
No.29. Lange-Müller, P. E. Stavnsbaandskantate. Op.36. Vocal score. 1911.
No.30. Nielsen, Ludolf. Symfoni Nr.2, E-dur. Op.19. Piano duet. 1911.
No.31. Buxtehude, D. Udvalgte Kompositioner. Arr. by Chr. Carnekow. Piano duet. [1912].
No.32. Barnekow, Christian. Idyller for Strygeorkester. Op.29. Piano duet. 1913.
No.33. Henrichsen, Roger. Sct. Hans Hymne. Op.9. Choral work. Vocal score. 1913.
No.34. Glass, Louis. Symfoni Nr.4, E-moll. Op.43. Piano duet. 1914.

No.35. Helsted, Gustav. Vort Land. Op.30. Choral work. Vocal score. 1915.
No.36. Matthison-Hansen, Gottfred. Drapa. For Orkester. Piano solo. 1915.
No.37. Gade, Niels W. Snact Hansaften-Spil. Choral work. Vocal score. 1916.
No.38. Rosenfeld, Leopold. Bjergpigen. Choral work. Vocal score. 1916.
No.39. Nielsen, Carl. Symfoni Nr.2. "The four temperaments." Op.16. Piano duet. 1917.
No.40. Hartmann, J. P. E. Orla Lehmann. Choral work. Vocal score. 1917.

Ser.III.
No.1. Helsted, Gustav. Koncert for Violin og Orkester. Op.27. Violin/Piano. 1918.
No.2. Lange-Müller, P. E. "1848." Kantate. Op.60. Vocal score. 1919.
No.3. Glass, Louis. Fantasi for Klaver. Op.35. Piano solo. 1919.
No.4. Børresen, Hadon. Kaddara. Opera. Vocal score. 1921.
No.5. Nielsen, Ludolf. Dronning Margrethe. Op.50. Choral work. Vocal score. 1922.
No.6. Tofft, Alfred. Vifandaka. Opera. Vocal score. [1922].
No.7. Helsted, Gustav. Strygekvartet 1, F-mol. Op.33. [1922].
No.8. Gram, Peder. Koncert for Violin og Orkester. Op.20. Full score and Violin/Piano. 1922–23.
No.9. Raasted, N. O. Orgelsonate Nr.3. Op.33. Organ. 1922–23.
No.10. Nielsen, Ludolf. Lackschmi oder Ein indisches Liebesmärchen. Ballet. Piano score. [1923].
No.11. Kuhlau, Fr. Elverhøj. Ouverture. Score and parts. 1922–23.
No.12. Glass, Louis. Fantasi for Pianoforte og Orkester. Op.47. 2 pianos, 4 hands. 1923–24.
No.13. Helsted, Gustav. Sonate (D-dur) for Orgel. Op.29. Organ. 1923–24.
No.14. Riisager, Knudåge. Sonate pour violon et piano. Violin/Piano. 1925.
No.15. Tofft, Alfred. Ouverture til "Vifandaka." Full score. 1924–25.
No.16. Raasted, N. O. Serenade für Flöte, Oboe, Viola und Violoncell. Op.40. Study score. 1924–25.
No.17. Henrichsen, Roger. 4 Klaverstykker. Op.23. Piano solo. 1924–25.
No.18. Nielsen, Carl. Synfoni No.5. Op.50. Study score. 1925–26.
No.19. Glass, Louis. Skovsymfoni, D-dur, No.3. Op.30. Study score. 1925–26.
No.20. Emborg, J. L. Concerto for Orgel med Strygere og Klaver. Op.49. Full score and parts. Piano score. 1926.
No.21. Gram, Peder. Symphonie Nr.2. Op.25. Score and parts. 1927.
No.22. Tofft, Alfred. 10 Danske Sange for blandet Kor. Op.64. Choral score. 1929.
No.23. Riisager, Knudåge. Ouverture "Erasmus Montanus." Full score. 1929.
No.24. Nielsen, Ludolf. Ouverture "Isbella." Op.10. Full score. 1929.
No.25. Crome, Fritz. Zwei Lieder. Op.29. (mit dänischen und deutschen Text). No.1, Tre Soldater. No.2, Für Dag. Voice and piano. 1929.
No.26. Bangert, Emilius. Kantate ved K.F.U.M.s 50 Aars Fest 16 September 1928. Vocal score. [1930].
No.27. Nielsen, Carl. Ouverture til "Maskerade." Full score. [1930].
No.28. Weis, Flemming. Musik for Fløjte, Clarinet og Fagot. Study score and parts. 1930.
No.29. Nielsen, Ludolf. Strygekvartet Nr.3, C-dur. For 2 Violiner, Viola og Violoncel. Study score and parts. 1930.
No.30. Bentzon, J. Symfonisk Trio. (Kammerkoncert). Op.18. For tre Instrumentgrupper: Violiner, Horn og Violonceller med Bas. Study score. 1930.
No.31. Raasted, N. O. Kuvia suomesta. (Billeder fra Finland). Symfonisk Suite for Orkester. Op.56. Score and parts. 1931.
No.32. Nielsen, Carl. Koncert for Klarinet og Orkester. Op.57. Score and parts. Clarinet/Piano. [1931].
No.33. Glass, Louis. Klaverstykker. Op.66. Piano solo. 1931.
No.34. Langgaard, Rud. Strygekvartet, Nr.3. Study score and parts. 1931.
No.35. Strandquist, Alfred. Davids 84. Psalme. (Vers 1–5). Sopran, Violin og Orgel. 1931.
No.36. Høffding, Finn. Symphonie Nr.3. Op.12. For Orkester. Full score. 1931.
No.37. Børresen, Hakon. Symphonie Nr.3, C-dur. Op.21. Full score. 1931.
No.38. Godske-Nielsen, Sv. Strygekvartet. Op.14. Study score and parts. [1931].
No.39. Hartmann, J. F. E. Ouverture "Hakon Jarl." Op.40. Score and parts. 1932.
No.40. Nielsen, Carl. Commotio. Op.58. Organ. [1932].
No.41. Schierbeck, P. Kantate. Op.16. Akademisk Festmusik. Op.17. Score and parts. 1933.
No.42. Tarp, Svend Erik. Serenade for Fløjte, Klarinet, Violin, Viola og Violoncel. Study score and parts. 1933.
No.43. Henriques, Fini. Strygekvartet. Study score and parts. [1933].
No.44. Hamerik, Ebbe. Orkester Variationer. Over et gammel-dansk Motiv. Full score. 1934.
No.45. Emborg, J. L. Concerto for Stygere og Piano. Op.72. Score and parts. 1934.
No.46. Senstius, Kai. Concertino for Fløjte og Orkester. Op.5. Full score. 1934. (cf.No. 59).
No.47. Koppel, Herm. D. Suite for Klaver. Op.21. Piano solo. 1935.
No.48. Weis, Flemming. Sonate for Clarinet og Klaver. Clarinet/Piano. 1935.
No.49. Grøndahl, Launy. Koncert for Violin og Orkester. Violin/Piano. 1935.
No.50. Gram, Peder. Ouverture i C-dur. Op.21. Score and parts. 1935.
No.51. Raasted, N. O. Kriste Fødsel. Op.67. Cantata. Score and parts. Vocal score. 1935.
No.52. Bangert, Emilius. Jeg Vaelger mig April. Koncertouverture. Op.7. Score and parts. 1936.

No.53. Brene, Erling. To Gange tre smaa Klaverstykker. Piano solo. 1936.
No.54. Holmboe, Vagn. Sonate for Violin og Klaver. Violin/Piano. 1936.
No.55. Schierbeck, Poul. Tre italienske Duetter. Op.28. Vocal duet/Piano. 1936.
No.56. Børresen, Hakon. Mod Døden. For Strygere. Score and parts. 1936.
No.57. Kuhlau, Fr. Ouverture til "William Shakespeare." Op.74. 1826. Score and parts. 1936.
No.58. Sandberg Nielsen, Otto. Praeludium, Trio, Ciacona. Op.11. Organ. 1937.
No.59. Senstius, Kai. Concertino for Fløjte og Orkester. Op.5. Flute/Piano. 1937. (cf. No.46).
No.60. Nielsen, Carl. Symphonie Nr.6 for Orkester. "Sinfonia semplice." Score and parts. 1937.
No.61. Gram, Peder. Prolog. Til et Drama af Shakespeare. Op.27. Score and parts. 1938.
No.62. Høffding, Finn. Sinfonia Concertante for Kammerorkester. Op.23. Full score. 1938.
No.63. Riisager, Knudåge. Tre danske Peblingeviser for Orkester. Score and parts. 1938.
No.64. Mortensen, Otto. Strygekvartet. 1937. For 2 Violiner, Viola og Violoncel. Study score and parts. 1938.
No.65. Raasted, N. O. Sangen om København. Op.60. Chorus. Vocal score. 1939.
No.66. Schultz, Svend S. Sonate for Klaver. Piano solo. 1939.
No.67. Agersnap, Harald. Interludium. Trio for Fløjte, Violin og Violoncel. Study score and parts. 1939.
No.68. Tarp, Svend Erik. Concertino for Fløjte og Orkester. Op.30. Score and parts. Flute/Piano. 1940.
No.69. Reesen, Emil. Variationer for Orkester. Over et Tema af Fr. Schubert. Full score. 1940.
No.70. Børresen, Hakon. Strygekvartet. For 2 Violiner, Viola og Violoncel. Study score and parts. 1940.
No.71. (Parts for above No.67).
No.72. Koppel, Herm. D. Strygekvartet No.2. Op.34. (1939). Study score and parts. 1941.
No.73. Schierbeck, Poul. Ouverture "Fête galante." Op.25. Full score. 1941.
No.74. Holmboe, Vagn. Kammerkoncert. Nr.2. Score and parts. 1942.
No.75. Gram, Peder. Strygekvartet. Nr.3. Op.30. Study score and parts. 1942.
No.76. Tarp, Svend Erik. Lystspilouverture. Score and parts. 1942.
No.77. Bentzon, Jørgen. Kammerkoncert. No.3. Op.39. Clarinet/Piano. 1943.
No.78. Børrensen, Hakon. Serenade for Horn, Strygeorkester og Pauker. Horn/Piano. 1943.
No.79. Hamerik, Ebbe. Kvintet for Fløjte, Obo, Clarinet, Horn og Fagot. Study score and parts. 1943.
No.80. Høffding, Finn. "Det er Ganske Vist." "En Lille Fjer Kan Nok Blive til Fem Høns." Symfonisk Fantasi for Orkester. Op.37. Score and parts. 1944.
No.81. Horneman, C. F. E. Strygekvartet. No.1, G-moll. Study score. 1945.
No.82. Grøndahl, Launy. Koncert for Fagot og Orkester. Bassoon/Piano. 1944.
No.83. Emborg, J. L. Kammer-Koncert for Violin, Fløjte og Klaver, med Viola I, Viola II, Violoncel og Kontrabas. Op.57. Score and parts. 1945.
No.84. Brene, Erling. Sonatine for Klaver. Piano solo. 1945.
No.85. Senstius, Kai. Fantasia i D-mol for Orgel. Organ. [1946].
No.86. Tarp, Svend Erik. Te Deum. Op.33. Vocal score. 1946.
No.87. Langgaard, Rud. Symfoni Nr.6. Det Himmelrivende. Full score. 1946.
No.88. Riisager, Knudåge. Finalegalop for Orkester. Score and parts. 1946.
No.89. Buxtehude, D. Min Gud er med Mig. Der Herr ist mir. Cantata. Score and parts. [1946].
No.90. Hartmann, J. P. E. Ouverture til Adam Oehlenschlägers Heltedigt. "Yrsa." Score and parts. 1946.
No.91. Lumbye, H. C. Champagner Galop. Op.14. Orchester. Score and parts. 1946.
No.92. Schultz, Svend S. "Job." Symfonisk Oratorium. For Kor, Blaesere og Harper. Vocal score. 1947.
No.93. Bentzon, Niels Viggo. Sonate for Violoncel og Klaver. Op.43. Violoncello/Piano. [1947].
No.94. Koppel, Herm. D. Fest-Orkester. Op.33. Score and parts. [1947].
No.95. Riisager, Knudåge. Primavera. Koncertouverture. Score and parts. [1947].
No.96. Raasted, N. O. Sinfonia da chiesa. Op.76. Score and parts. 1947.
No.97. Høffding, Finn. Evolution. Fantasi for Orkester. Op.31. Score and parts. 1947.
No.98. The two Danish national anthems. Orchestra. Score and parts. [1948]; Harmony orchestra. Score; Piano edition. Piano solo.
No.99. Emborg, J. L. De Tolv Masker. Op.50. Orchestra. Score and parts. 1948.
No.100. Bentzon, Jørgen. Mikrofoni Nr.1. Op.44. Score and parts. 1948.
No.101. Kuhlau, Fr. Ouverture til Syngestykket "Røverborgen." Score and parts. 1948.
No.102. Reesen, Emil. Gaucho-Suite. Orchestra. Score and parts. 1948.
No.103. Tarp, Svend Erik. Symfoni i Es. Op.50. Score and parts. 1949.
No.104. Schierbeck, Poul. "Adrienne Lecouvreur." Radio-Rapsodi. Op.49. Score and parts. 1949.
No.105. Du Puy, Edouard. Ouverture til Syngestykket "Ungdom og Galskab." Score and parts. 1949.
No.106. Møller, Svend-Ove. Orgel Te Deum. Op.56. Organ. 1949.
No.107. Senstius, Kai. Strygekvartet 1, A-mol. Op.28. Score and parts. 1949.
No.108. Gram, Peder. Poème lyrique for Orkester. Op.9. Score and parts. [1949].
No.109. Horneman, C. F. E. Aladdin. En Eventyr-Ouverture for Orkester. Score and parts. 1950.
No.110. Schultz, Svend S. Storstrømsbroen. The Storstroem bridge. Orchestra. Score and parts. 1951.

No.111. Christensen, Bernhard. Karneval. Af Balletten den Evige Trio. Orchestra. Score and parts. 1951.
No.112. Riisager, Knudåge. Kvartet for Fløjte, Obo, Clarinet og Fagot. Op.40a. Score and parts. 1951.
No.113. Høgenhaven Jensen, Knud. Lamento for Strygeorkester. Op.9. Score and parts. 1951.
No.114. Kayser, Leif. Kong Kristien Stod. Koncertouverture. Op.5. Full score. 1951.
No.115. Raasted, N. O. Passionsmusik. Oratorio. Op.86. Score and parts. 1951.
No.116. Børresen, H. Nordiske Folketoner. Fra Island og Faerøerne. For Strygeorkester. Score and parts. 1951.
No.117. Nielsen, Carl. Koncert for Fløjte og Orkester. Score and parts. Flute/Piano. 1952.
No.118. Schierbeck, Poul. Fête galante. Op.25. Opera. Vocal score. 1954.
No.119. Bjerre, Jens. Mosaïque musicale. Trio for Fløjte, Violin og Violoncel. Study score and parts. 1953.
No.120. Hartmann, J. P. E. Ouverture til Correggio. Op.59. Score and parts. 1953.
No.121. Riisager, Knudåge. Darduse. Suite for Orkester. Dances from "The fairy-tale play" by Johannes V. Jensen. Score and parts. 1954.
No.122. Møller, Svend-Ove. Gak under Jesu Kors at Stå. Op.40. Passionskantate. Full score. 1953.
No.123. Maegaard, Jan. Trio for Obo, Clarinet og Fagot. Study score and parts. [1953].
No.124. Grøndahl, Launy. Koncert for Trombone og Orkester. Score and parts. Trombone/Piano. 1954.
No.125. Senstius, Kai. Serenade for Obo, Viola og Fagot. Op.36. Score and parts. 1954.
No.126. Lumbye, H. C. Danse. Suite Nr.1. For Orkester. Score and parts. Pianodirektion. [1956].
No.127. Lumbye, H. C. Concert-Polka for 2 Violiner. Score and parts. [1956].
No.128. Rovsing Olsen, Poul. Variations symphoniques. Op.27. Score and parts. 1958.
No.129. Høffding, Finn. Fantasia sinfonica. "The arsenal at Springfield." (H. W. Longfellow). Op.54. Full score and vocal score. [1958].
No.130. Frøhlich, J. F. Majgildet. Ouverture. Score and parts. [1958].
No.131. Koppel, Herm. D. Divertimento pastorale. For Obo, Viola og Violoncel. Op.61. Score and parts. 1955.
No.132. Thybo, Leif. Concerto per organo. Organ. 1955.
No.133. Nielsen, Carl. Symfoni Nr.6. "Sinfonia semplice." Rev. ed. (cf. No.60). Score and parts. 1957.
No.134. Høgenhaven, Knud. Danse triomphale. Orchestra. Score and parts. 1957.
No.135. Frøhlich, J. F. Riberhus march. Orchestra. Score and parts. [1958].
No.136. Kuhlau, Fr. Concerto for Klaver og Orkester. Oeuvre 7. Score and parts. 2 pianos, 4 hands. 1958.
No.137. Kayser, Leif. 3 Salmi per contralto solo e organo. Voice and organ. 1956.
No.138. Buxtehude, Diderich. 4 Latinske Kantater. Score and parts. 1957.
No.139. Schierbeck, Poul. Natten. Symfonish Scene for Klaver og Orkester. Op.41. Score and parts. [1958].
No.140. Jersild, Jörgen. Alice in Wonderland. A musical fairy-tale by Flemming Geill. Full score and vocal score. [1958].
No.141. Bjerre, Jens. Sonate for Violoncel. Cello solo. [1958].
No.142. Raasted, N. O. Primavera. Trio for Violin, Viola og Violoncel. Op.96. Study score and parts. [1959].
No.143. Kuhlau, Fr. Kvintet. Op.51. Nr.1. For Fløjte, Violin, Viola I–II og Violoncel. Study score and parts. [1961].
No.144. Maegaard, Jan. 5 Preludes for solo violin. Violin solo. 1961.
No.145. Høffding, Finn. Kammermusik. For Sopran, Obo og Piano. Op.11. Study score and parts. [1960].
No.146. Wellejus, Henning. "Det har Slet ingen Hast for Den, Som Tror." "Haste is not for him that believeth." Freedom overture. Op.13. Written to commemorate the liberation of Denmark in 1945. Score and parts. [1960].
No.147. Rovsing Olsen, Poul. Schickalslieder für Singstimme mit Instrumentalgruppe. Op.28. Score and parts. 1961.
No.148. Schierbeck, Poul. Häxa. For Sopran Solo og Orkester med Orgel. Op.48. Score and parts. [1961].
No.149. Weis, Flemming. Concertino for Orgel. Organ. 1961.
No.150. Borup-Jørgensen, Axel. Musik for Slagtoj og Viola. Music for percussion and viola. Op.18. Score and parts. [1961].
No.151. Koppel, Herm. D. Concertino No.2 for Strygeorkester. Op.66. Score and parts. [1962].
No.152. Thybo, Leif. Concerto per archi. Score and parts. [1962].
No.153. Nørholm, Ib. Trio for Klaver, Violin og Violoncel. Op.22. Score and parts. 1962.
No.154. Gudmundsen-Holmgreen, Pelle. 2 Improvisations. Op.9. Score and parts. 1962.
No.155. Berg, Gunnar. For Clarinet og Violin. Score. 1962.
No.156. Riisager, Knudåge. Månerenen. Ballet.
No.157. Rovsing Olsen, Poul. Prolana. Op.33. For Clarinet, Violin og Klaver. Score and parts. [1963].
No.158. Schultz, Svend S. Strygekvartet. Nr.4. [1963].
No.159. Weis, Flemming. Concertino for Strygeorkester. 1960. [1963].
No.160. Møller, Svend-Ove. 22 Sange. Op.18. 1963.
No.161a. Maegaard, Jan. Kammerkonzert Nr.2 (1962). For 3 Traeblaesere, Strygere og Klaver ad lib. Score and parts. 1964.
No.161b. Maegaard, Jan. Oktomeri (1962). For Violin og Klaver. Score and part. 1964.
No.162. Raasted, N. O. Sonate for Klaver. Op.109.

No.163. Kuhlau, Friederich. Elverhøj. 4.–5. Akt. Score.
No.164. Borup-Jørgensen, Axel. To Sange. Op. 49. Voice and piano. 1964.
No.165. Nørhom, Ib. Kenotafium for Sopran, Kor og Orkester. Op.23. 1960–61. (Tekst: Asger Pedersen. "Genesis"). Full score. 1964.
No.166. Gudmundsen-Holmgreen, Pelle. Chronos (22–24 musicians). Full score. 1964.
No.167. Nielsen, Carl. Kvintet for Stygere, G-dur 1888. Miniature score. 1965.
No.168. Nielsen, Carl. Tre Klaverstykker. Op. posth. 59. Komponeret 1928.
No.169. Nielsen, Carl. Preludio e presto per violino solo, Op.52. 1965.
No.170.
No.171. Koppel, Thomas. Quartetto d'archi No.2, Op.12. Miniature score. 1965.
No.172. Westergaard, Svend. Sinfonia, Op.21. Full score. 1966.
No.173. Christiansen, Henning. Sonate, Op.13. For Violin og Klavier. Score and part. 1965.
No.174. Nørgaard, Helmer. Serenade to young man with a horn. For clarinet, trumpet, trombone, vibraphone, double-bass and singers, 1959. Score. 1966.
No.175. Jørgensen, Erik. Figure in tempo per violoncello e piano. Score and part. 1965.
No.176. Holm, Mogens Winkel. Concerto Piccolo for Orkester (1961). Full score. 1965.

Extra:
Tofft, Alfred. Airs melancoliques. Quatre pièces pour piano. Op.36. London, Augener & Co., cop.1902.
Liebmann, Axel. Humoreske (Elskov en Jaegerdreng) til Text af Thomas Moore; Sang ved Endymions og Hermiones Bryllupsfest; Planternes LIV. Kjöbenhavn, C. C. Loses Bog og Musikhandel.

Supplementary volumes:
1895. I. Barnekow, C. Eight Finnish folk poems. (R. Hertzberg); Six songs by Finnish poets, for soprano with piano, Op.11.
II. Matthison-Hansen, G. Album for piano.
1897. I. Bechgaard, J. Selected characteristic pieces. Piano.
II. Malling, J. Eight Scottish folksongs, Op.2.
1898. Hartmann, Emil. Selected songs.
1899. I. Dupont-Hansen, G. Pieces for piano, Op.1.
II. Lerche, C. A. Six songs. (Bondeliv i Norge).
1900. I. Winding, A. Genrebilleder for piano. (from Op.15).
II. Winding, A. Songs (Klaus Groth) from Op.2 and Op.14.
1901. Lembcke, G. A. Selected songs.
1902. I. Ravnkilde, N. Four pieces for piano, Op.2.
II. Ravnkilde, N. Four songs.
1905. I. Barnekow, C. Four folksongs from the Russian (Thor Lange), for soprano or tenor with piano, Op.14.
II. Barnekow, C. Nocturnes (T. Lange), for baritone with piano, Op.19.
1906. I. Bartholdy, J. Solomons Sang i Vingaarden, Op.15.
II. Bartholdy, J. Tannhäuser, song cycle (H. Drachmann), for baritone or mezzo-soprano.
1918. Fabricus, J. Brogede Blade, eight pieces for piano.
1925–26. Otte nye danske Sange. Voice and piano. (Harald Agersnap, Johannes Andersen, Jørgen Bentzon, Christian Christiansen, N. O. Raasted, Knudåge Riisager, Ad. Riis-Magnussen, Poul Schierbeck).
1930. Børresen, Hakon. Raadhus-Intrade, for Lurer og Orkester. Piano.

Ser.IV. Dania sonans; Kilder til Musikens Historie i Danmark. København, Levin & Munksgaard, 1933– .
No.1. Vaerker, af. M. Pedersøn; kritisk udgivne og forsynede med Indledning af K. Jeppesen. 1. Pratum spirituale (1620); 2. Madrigali a cinque voci, libro primo (1608). 1933.

Sammlung älterer Musik aus dem XVI. und XVII. Jahrhundert, *see* Dehn, Siegfried Wilhelm. Sammlung älterer Musik aus dem XVI. und XVII. Jahrhundert.

SAMMLUNG RUSSISCHER ROMANZEN, für eine und zwei Singstimmen mit Begleitung des Pianoforte. Übersetzung von Bruno. Bearbeitung und Übersetzung Eigentum des Verlegers. Leipzig, Fritz Schuberth, Jr., n.d.
313 nos.
Contents:
No.1. Warlamoff. Kummer.
No.2. Lvoff. Volkshymne.
No.3. Warlamoff. Der Engel.
No.4. Paschkoff. Er liebt mich nicht mehr.
No.5. Alabieff. Die Nachtigall.
No.6. Dreigespann. Volkslied.
No.7. Warlamoff. Rothe Sarafan.
No.8. Alabieff. Der Verlassene.
No.9. Alabieff. Hoffnungsstrahl.
No.10. Warlamoff. Heimliches Bangen.
No.11. Warlamoff. Hoffnungslos.
No.12. Warlamoff. Die schwarzen Augen.
No.13. Glinka. An Molly.
No.14. Glinka. Liebesgluck.
No.15. Glinka. Erinnerung.
No.16. Glinka. Zweifel.
No.17. Glinka. Unvergängliche Liebe.
No.18. Bulachoff. Zigeunerlied.
No.19. Dargomijsky. Ewige Liebe.
No.20. Warlamoff. Herzeleid.
No.21. Gurileff. Der Liebe erwachen.
No.22. Gurileff. Das Herz.
No.23. Dübüque. Das Vöglein.
No.24. Dargomijsky. Liebesqual.
No.25. Warlamoff. Erscheinung.
No.26. Bulachoff. Wiegenlied.
No.27. Warlamoff Warum erscheinst Du wieder.
No.28. Warlamoff. Unvergleichlicher.
No.29. Lvoff. Zigeunerlied.

No.30. Warlamoff. Morgenroth.
No.31. Titoff. Talisman.
No.32. Russisches Zigeunerlied.
No.33. Werstowski, A. Lied der Nadäschda.
No.34. Warlamoff. Junges Vöglein.
No.35. Glinka. Die Lerche.
No.36. Titoff. Schwermuth.
No.37. Warlamoff. Nachtgedanken.
No.38. Warlamoff. Bleibe.
No.39. Warlamoff. Nachtigall, mein Bote.
No.40. Warlamoff. Weile, O Weile.
No.41. Warlamoff. Lied eines Räubers.
No.42. Warlamoff. Trost in Ruhe.
No.43. Warlamoff. Thränen.
No.44. Warlamoff. Am Fenster.
No.45. Warlamoff. Entschwunden.
No.46. Warlamoff. O kehrt zurück.
No.47. Warlamoff. Trennungsschmerz.
No.48. Dargomijsky. Hersensmädchen.
No.49. Pauffer. Vision.
No.50. Kotschubei. Sagt's ihr.h.
No.50a. Kotschubei. Sagt's ihr.t.
No.51. Bulachoff. Sie ist nicht mehr.
No.52. Bulachoff. Ich will nicht.
No.53. Bachmetieff. Klage eines Jämschick.
No.54. Bachmetieff. Der Kosackin Wiegenlied.
No.55. Derfeldt. Freundschaft.
No.56. Markewitsch. Bitte.
No.57. Werstowski, A. Lied des Unbekaunten.
No.58. Werstowski, A. Lied des Tarob.
No.59. Werstowski, A. Ballade.
No.60. Glinka. Waisenlied. Aus: Das Leben für den Czaar.
No.61. Glinka. Barcarole.
No.62. Bachmetieff. Drei Rosen.
No.63. Bachmetieff. Der graue Bart.
No.64. Dmitrieff. Erinnerung.
No.65. Dmitrieff. Gebet.
No.66. Dübüque. Der Winter.
No.67. Dübüque. Dreigespann.
No.68. Glinka. Liebliche Rose.
No.69. Glinka. Die Unbekannte.
No.70. Gurileff. Sie sie schön ist.
No.71. Gurileff. Sie ist nicht hier.
No.72. Jewsejeff. Des Lebens Frühling ist dahin.
No.73. Nowikoff. Stets denk ich dein.
No.74. Schiff. Er liebt mich noch.
No.75. Stutzmann. Iwans Lied.
No.76. Tolstoy. Mein Schwert.
No.77. Titoff. Trugvoller Freund.
No.78. Titoff. Heimliche Liebe.
No.79. Warlamoff. Gesang der Ophelia. Aus: Hamlet.
No.80. Warlamoff. Sei glücklich.
No.81. Warlamoff. Die Schiffer.
No.82. Warlamoff. Einsamkeit.
No.83. Warlamoff. Der leuchtende Stern.
No.84. Warlamoff. Der Nachen.
No.85. Wielhorsky. Ich liebte.
No.86. Wielhorsky. Verloren.
No.87. Christianowitsch. Erstarrung.
No.88. Dargomijsky. Resignation.
No.89. Dargomijsky. Abschied.
No.90. Dargomijsky. Verschwiegen.
No.91. Dübüque. Tiefes Lied.
No.92. Dübüque. Trimklied.
No.93. Dübüque. Die Liebe der Zigeunerin.
No.94. Dübüque. Die Wahrsagerin. t.
No.94a. Dübüque. Die Wahrsagerin. h.
No.95. Dübüque. Lass ab.
No.96. Dübüque. Zweierlei Scheiden.
No.97. Dübüque. Das Füsschen.
No.98. Dübüque. Marie.
No.99. Dür. Wiedersehn.
No.100. Glinka. Gretchen am Spinnrade.
No.101. Glinka. Israels Sehnsucht.
No.102. Glinka. Beim Wein.
No.103. Klimoffsky. Das Hüttchen. h.
No.103a. Klimoffsky. Das hüttchen. t.
No.104. Paschkoff. O sei mir gut.
No.105. P——koy. Mein Lieben.
No.106. Stutzmann. Liebe mich.
No.107. Warlamoff. Barcarole.
No.108. Warlamoff. Neuer Schmerz.
No.109. Wassileff. Zigeunersinn.
No.110. Wassileff. Der Zigeunerin Heimkehr.
No.111. Zigeunerlied. Entschwundener Frühling.
No.112. Balakireff. Traure nicht.
No.113. Dargomijsky. Nur lieben.
No.114. Dargomijsky. Werd ich dich wiedersehn?
No.115. Dargomijsky. Du.
No.116. Dargomijsky. Du. 2 Sgst.
No.117. Glinka. Liebespein.
No.118. Glinka. Wenn's immer so bliebe.
No.119. Glinka. Er kehrt nicht wieder.
No.120. Kontsky. Arm und reich.
No.121. Kontsky. O Zauberin.
No.122. Kotschubei. Eifersucht.
No.123. Kotschubei. Selife Lust.
No.124. Manei. O bleib.
No.125. Moniuschko. Die Spinnerin.
No.126. Moniuschko. Am Abend.
No.127. Romberg. Das einsame Mädchen.
No.128. Trubetzkoy. Verlorne Jugend.
No.129. Werstowski, A. Der schwarze Schleier.
No.130. Villebois. Im Sturm.
No.131. Villebois. Am Seegestade.
No.132. Villebois. Dämmerungszauber.
No.133. A——. N. Wann kehrt er wieder?
No.134. Bulachoff. Des Herzens Wiegenlied.
No.135. Bulachoff. O eile! Romanze.
No.136. Bunakoff. Vergiss sie nicht. Duett.
No.137. Eugenieff. Verlass mich nicht.
No.138. Gurileff. Heimkehr. Romanze.
No.139. Gurileff. Leuchte meiner stillen Nächte.
No.140. Gurileff. Der treulose Hirt. Romanze.
No.141. Gurileff. Auf der Wolga. Volkslied.
No.142. Kuscheleff-Besbarodko. Vergieb. Romanze.
No.143. Petroff. Die Spinnerin.
No.144. Rubinstein. Wünsche. Romanze.
No.145. Rubinstein. Das fallende Sternlein.
No.146. Rubinstein. Willst Du mein sein?
No.147. Schaschin. Sehnsucht nach Ruhe.
No.148. Schwarze Farbe. Volkslied.
No.149. Stutzmann. Die Kokette.
No.150. Selesneff. Der arme Trödler.
No.151. Sokoloff. Aufforderung zur Freude.
No.152. Zigeunerlied. Die Werbung.
No.153. Zigeunerlied. Der Trauernde Postillon.
No.154. Zigeunerlied. Lied das Mähers.
No.155. Zigeunerlied. Mir gilt es gleich.
No.156. Dargomijsky. Der Eifersüchtige.
No.157. N. A——. Warum. Romanze.

No.158. Tarnoffsky. Ich denke stets.
No.159. Lvoff. Das verlassene Vöglein.
No.160. Fitinghoff. Du bist es nicht.
No.161. Zigeunerlied. Des Postillons Kläge.
No.162. Dübüque. Dich nur liebe ich.
No.163. Paschkoff. Die zwei Zigeunerinnen.
No.164. Sokoloff. Meine Augen.
No.165. Zigeunerlied. Mein Lieb.
No.166. Schiloffsky. Wir sind getrennt.
No.167. Warlamoff. Leben ohne Liebe.
No.168. Bulachoff. Thränen der Freude.
No.169. Donaüroff. Einsam.
No.170. Derwis. Vielleicht.
No.171. Sokoloff. Der Hoffnungsstrahl.
No.172. Schaschin. Drei Worte.
No.173. Sokoloff. Er kehrt nicht wieder.
No.174. Sokoloff. Er kommt.
No.175. Genischta. Elegie.
No.176. Rupini. Freundschaft.
No.177. Sideroff. Verzweiflung.
No.178. Sideroff. Einerlei.
No.179. Sokoloff. Die Trauernde.
No.180. Sokoloff. Mein Liebster.
No.181. Bachmetieff. Liebes Mädchen. Zigeunerlied.
No.182. Bachmetieff. Ahnung.
No.183. Warlamoff. Namenloser Schmerz.
No.184. Warlamoff. Die Lerche.
No.185. Warlamoff. Das treue Ross.
No.186. Warlamoff. Das weisse Segel.
No.187. Warlamoff. Das Meteor.
No.188. Werstowski, A. Entr'Act und Chor aus der Oper: Ascolds Grab.
No.189. Glinka. Erstes Begegnen.
No.190. Glinka. Der Sieger.
No.191. Glinka. Trost in Thränen.
No.192. Glinka. Bekenntniss.
No.193. Moniuschko. Glockenstimmen.
No.194. Moniuschko. Kukuk und Mädchen.
No.195. Moniuschko. Der Morgen.
No.196. Pauffer. Die Nacht.
No.197. Pauffer. Lebewohl.
No.198. Sokoloff. Die blauen Augen.
No.199. Sokoloff. Ich erwarte Dich.
No.200. Sokoloff. Meide mich.
No.201. Die Bärtnerin. Russisches Volkslied.
No.202. Der Kosack vom Don. Volkslied.
No.203. Zigeunerlied. Horch!
No.204. Zigeunerlied. Sarafanschik.
No.205. Zigeunerlied. Die Gänsehüterin.
No.206. Zigeunerlied. Liebesgruss.
No.207. Borodin. Verschmäht.
No.208. Borodin. Misston.
No.209. Borodin. Sage vom schlafenden Mädchen.
No.210. Brasch. Wehmuth
No.211. Brasch. Sonnenschein.
No.212. Donaüroff. Getäuscht.
No.213. Dübüque. Zigeunerlied.
No.214. Dübüque. Ich denke Dein.
No.215. Glinka. Das Leben für den Czaar. Terzett.
No.216. Glinka. Das Leben für den Czaar. Waisenlied.
No.217. Glinka. Das Leben für den Czaar. Duett.
No.218. Glinka. Ruslan und Ludmilla. Arie: Die Glut des heissen "Tages."
No.219. Glinka. Ruslan und Ludmilla. Arie: Du trauter Stern. h.
No.220. Glinka. Ruslan und Ludmilla. Arie: Ihr sanfter Gruss. t.
No.221. Gurileff. Das Ringlein.
No.222. Kotschubei. Die Augensterne.
No.223. Moniuschko. Erwartung.
No.224. Moniuschko. Der sterbende Kosak.
No.225. Anna R——. Bin ich schuld daran?
No.226. Rubinstein. Ständchen.
No.227. Rubinstein. Hergstgedanken.
No.228. Schtscherbatscheff. Mein Alles.
No.229. Sokoloff. Heiss mich nicht gehen.
No.230. Warlamoff. Verwelktes Grün.
No.231. Woronzoff. Glück der Liebe.
No.232. Petroff. Lüftchen.
No.233. Donaüroff. Sie lieb ich ewiglich.
No.234. Kozlow. Wenn ich nur wüsste.
No.235. Machotin. Bete für mich.
No.236. Glinka. Lass mich allein. 2 Sgst.
No.237. Glinka. An den Sturmwind.
No.238. Gurileff. Trennung.
No.239. Gurileff. An die Schwalbe.
No.240. Cavos. Komm mit mir.
No.241. Jakowieff-Glinka. O Lieder schweigt.
No.242. Dargomijsky. Elegie.
No.243. Dargomijsky. Spanische Romanze.
No.244. Dargomijsky. Romanze aus: Der steinerne Gast.
No.245. Dargomijsky. Bezauberung.
No.246. Dargomijsky. Erwartung.
No.247. Dargomijsky. Wolken wohin?
No.248. Dargomijsky. Fischleins Geheimniss. Aus der Oper: Russalka.
No.249. Tschaikowsky. Vergieb.
No.250. Tschaikowsky. Sei still, O Herz.
No.251. Tschaikowsky. Wie schmerzvoll beglückend.
No.252. Tschaikowsky. Warum.
No.253. Tschaikowsky. Nur wer die Sehnsucht kennt.
No.254. Tschaikowsky. Vögleins Rath.
No.255. Tschaikowsky. Dennoch.
No.256. Ssjeroff. Ballade aus: Rogneda.
No.257. Ssjeroff. Kriegslied aus: Judith.
No.258. Pomasanski. Grusisches Lied.
No.259. Balakireff. Wiegenlied.
No.260. Dütsch. Vergiss mein nicht.
No.261. Glinka. Zweifel. t.
No.262. Warlamoff. Die Schiffer. 2 Sgst.
No.263. Bachmetieff. Der graue Bart. t.
No.264. Machotin. Bete für mich. t.
No.265. Kozlow. Wenn ich nur wüsste. t.
No.266. Tarnoffsky. Ich denk stets. t.
No.267. Cuy. Die blauen Augen.
No.268. Cuy. Verhaltenes Wehe.
No.269. Cuy. Du liebst mich nicht.
No.270. Naprawnik. Gebet.
No.271. Naprawnik. Lauschen und Küssen.
No.272. Tschaikowsky. Gieb mir Gewissheit.
No.273. Ssjeroff. Jagdlied.
No.274. Balakireff. O komm zu mir.
No.275. Dargomijsky. Mein Sehnen.
No.276. Dargomijsky. Cavatine aus der Oper: Russalka.
No.277. Klemm. Freudvoll und leidvoll. h.
No.278. Warlamoff. Gedenkst Du noch?

No.279. Glinka. Sei wieder gut. 2 Sgst.
No.280. Dargomijsky. Die Birkenruthe.
No.281. Glinka. Das Leben für den Czaar. Höher steigt der Sonne Licht.
No.282. Klemm. Freudvoll und leidvoll. t.
No.283. Dargomijsky. Stiller Gram. Terzett.
No.284. Warlamoff. Nachtigallensang.
No.285. Kalabin. Verlassen.
No.286. Rschewsky. Ahnst Du nicht?
No.287. Derfeldt. Der Bettler.
No.288. Samoiloff. Der Sterbende.
No.289. Jakowieff. Traumbild.
No.290. Dargomijsky. Das Mädchen und die Rose. 2 Sgst.
No.291. Dargomijsky. Verschwundener Tage Herrlichkeit. 2 Sgst.
No.292. Dargomijsky. Die beiden Ritter. 2 Sgst.
No.293. Dargomijsky. Liebesspiel. 2 Sgst.
No.294. Gurileff. Klaga. 2 Sgst.
No.295. Gurileff. Schöne Jugendzeit. 2 Sgst.
No.296. Glinka. Sehnsucht. 2 Sgst.
No.297. Glinka. Zweifel. 2 Sgst.
No.298. Bulachoff. Geschwundenes Glück. 2 Sgst.
No.299. Bulachoff. Barcarole. 2 Sgst.
No.300. Bulachoff. Banges Sehnen. 2 Sgst.
No.301. Warlamoff. Wach auf. 2 Sgst.
No.302. Warlamoff. Hoffnungslos. 2 Sgst.
No.303. Warlamoff. Nachtgedanken. 2 Sgst.
No.304. Warlamoff. Frühlingsnacht. 2 Sgst.
No.305. Warlamoff. Nachtigall, mein Bote. 2 Sgst.
No.306. Sokoloff. Frage nicht. 2 Sgst.
No.307. Sokoloff. Liebeshoffen. 2 Sgst.
No.308. Dutsch-Warlamoff. Herzeleid. 2 Sgst.
No.309. Imbert. Trost. 2 Sgst.
No.310. Rschewsky. Küsse mich. 2 Sgst.
No.311. Bulachoff. Ständchen. 2 Sgst.
No.312. Scheremetieff. Ich liebte Dich.
No.313. Alabieff. Die Nachtigall. t.

Sammlung von Stücken alter italienischer Meister für die moderne Orgel, *see* Bossi, Marco Enrico. Sammlung von Stücken alter italienischer Meister für die moderne Orgel.

Sammlung vorzüglicher Gesangstücke, *see* Rochlitz, Friedrich. Sammlung vorzüglicher Gesangstücke.

Sang und Klang aus alter Zeit, *see* Tappert, Wilhelm. Sang und Klang aus alter Zeit.

Die Sangesweisen der Colmarer Handschrift und die Liederhandschrift Donaueschingen, *see* Runge, Paul. Die Sangesweisen der Colmarer Handschrift und die Liederhandschrift Donaueschingen.

SANTOS, JÚLIO EDUARDO. ed.
A polifonia clássica portuguesa. Transcrições, em notação moderno de trechos dos mestres mais notáveis dos séculos XVIe e XVIIe. Estudo critico por Júlio Eduardo dos Santos. Lisbon, Emprêsa Nacional de Publicidade, 1938.
122p. folio.
Contains compositions by F. M. Cardosa, Don João IV, and Duarte Lobo.

SCARLATTI, ALESSANDRO, 1660–1725.
Gli oratorii di Alessandro Scarlatti, a cura e studio di Lino Bianchi. Roma, Edizioni de Santis, 1964– .
v.1– .
Contents:
Vol.1. La giuditta. 1964.
Vol.2. Agar et Ismaele Esiliati. 1965.
Vol.3. La giuditta di "Cambridge." 1966.

SCARLATTI, DOMENICO, 1685–1757.
. . . Opere complete per clavicembalo . . . (Alessandro Longo). Milano, G. Ricordi & Co.; New York, G. Ricordi & Co., [etc., etc.], 1947–51. (E.R. 541–551).
10v. and Suppl.
Contents:
Vol.1–10. 10 Suites in each volume.
Suppl. Quarantacinque pezzi disposti per ordine di tonalità.

SCARLATTI, DOMENICO, 1685–1757.
. . . Opere complete per clavicembalo . . . Indice tematico delle sonate per clavicembalo. Contenute nella raccolta completa riveduta da A. Longa . . . Thematic index of the harpsichord, sonatas included in the complete collection edited by A. Longo. Milano, G. Ricordi & Co., 1952. (E.R. 1912).
1p.L., 36[1]p.

Scarpat, Giuseppe, ed. Monumenti di musica italiana, *see* Monumenti di musica italiana.

Scenes from the Protevangelion, by Hubert Lamb, *see* The Wellesley edition. No.2.

Schatz des evangelischen Kirchengesanges, *see* Tucher, Gottlieb, Freiherr von. Schatz des evangelischen Kirchengesanges.

Schatz des liturgischer Chor- und Gemeindegesanges, *see* Schöberlein, Ludwig. Schatz des liturgischer Chor- und Gemeindegesanges.

SCHEIDT, SAMUEL, 1587–1654.
Samuel Scheidt's Werke; hrsg. von der Oberleitung der Glaubens-Gemeinde Ugrino durch Gottlieb Harms . . . Bd.1– . Klecken-Ugrino Abtlg. Verlag, 1923– .
v.1– . illus. (facsims.).
Facsimiles include title page and dedication of original editions.
Imprint varies: Bd.2–7 published at Hamburg.
Contents:
Bd.1. Tabulaturbuch vom Jahre 1650. 1923.
Bd.2/3. Paduana, Galliarda, Couranta, Alemande, Intrada, Canzonetto. Hamburg, 1621. 1928.
Bd.4. Cantiones sacrae zu 8 Stimmen von Jahre 1620. 1933.
Bd.5. Unedierte Kompositionen für Tasteninstrumente. 1937.
Bd.6 Tabulatura nova. Teil I und II. Hamburg, 1624. 1953.
Bd.7. Tabulatura nova. Teil III für die Orgel. Hamburg, 1624. 1953.
Bd.8. Geistliche Konzerte. Teil I. Hamburg, 1631. 1957.

Bd.9. Geistliche Konzerte. Teil II. Halle, 1634. 1960.
Bd.10/11. Geistliche Konzerte. Teil III. Halle, 1635.
Bd.12. Geistliche Konzerte. Teil IV. Leipzig, 1640.
Bd.13. Siebzig Symphonien auf Concerten-Manier mit drei Instrumentalstimmen (zwei Diskante, Bass) und Generalbass. Breslau, 1645. 1962.
Bd.14/15. Pars prima concertium sacrorum (lateinische geistliche Konzerte, I.Teil). Hamburg, 1622.
Bd.16. Liebliche Kraftblümlein für zwei Vokalstimmen (Cantus und Tenor) mit Generalbass. Halle, 1635.

SCHEIDT, SAMUEL, 1587–1654.
. . . Ausgewählte Werke für Orgel und Klavier. Hrsg. von Hermann Keller. Leipzig, C. F. Peters, [cop.1939].
3p.L., 145p. (On cover: Edition Peters. No.4393b).

SCHEIDT, SAMUEL, 1587–1654.
. . . Das Görlitzer Tabulaturbuch vom Jahre 1650. Für den Praktischen Gebrauch eingerichtet von Christhard Mahrenholz. Leipzig, C. F. Peters, [cop.1941].
2p.L., 81p. (On cover: Edition Peters. No.4494).

SCHEIN, JOHANN HERMANN, 1586–1630.
Johann Hermann Scheins Sämtliche Werke. Hrsg. von Arthur Prüfer. Bd.1–7. Leipzig, Breitkopf & Härtel, [1901–23].
7v. facsims., front. (Bd.1), ports.
Includes facsimile title pages of original editions.
Contents:
Bd.1. Venuskränzlein und Banchetto musicale.
Bd.2. Musica boscareccia oder Waldliederlein in 3 Teilen.
Bd.3. Diletti pastoriali (Hirten-Lust) 1624 mit Begleitung des Generalbasses und Studentenschmaus für 5 Stimmen (1626).
Bd.4. Cymbalum sionium (Cantiones sacrae) [Leipzig, 1615] zu 5, 6, 8, 10 und 12 Stimmen.
1.Abt.: 5– und 6 stimmige Motetten.
2.Abt.: 8– , 10– und 12 stimmige Motetten.
Bd.5. Opella nova. Geistliche Konzerte. [Leipzig, 1626]. 1.Abt.
Bd.6. Opella nova. 2.Abt.
Bd.7. Opella nova. 3.Abt.

SCHEIN, JOHANN HERMANN, 1586–1630.
Neue Ausgabe sämtlicher Werke. Kassel und Basel, Bärenreiter Verlag, 1963– .
v.1– .
Contents:
Bd.1. Israelsbrünnlein, 1623, geistliche Madrigale für 5–6 Stimmen mit Bass Continuo. 1963.
Bd.2. Cantionae oder Gesangbuch Augsburgischer Confession 1627 und 1645.

Scheit, Karl, 1909– , ed. Gitarre-Kammermusik, *see* Gitarre-Kammermusik.

SCHERING, ARNOLD, 1877–1941. ed.
Alte Meister aus der Frühzeit des Orgelspiels. 12 Kompositionen für Orgel des 15. und 16. Jahrhunderts. Hrsg. von Arnold Schering. Leipzig, Breitkopf & Härtel, [pref.1913].
40p.
Contains compositions by Anton Brumel, Johann Buchner, De Orto, Josquin de Près, Heinrich Finck, Jakob Hobrecht, Heinrich Isaak, Johannes Martini, and Gregor Meyer.

SCHERING, ARNOLD, 1877–1941. ed.
Alte Meister des Violinspiels für den praktischen Gebrauch zum ersten Mal, hrsg. von Arnold Schering. Leipzig, C. F. Peters, [cop.1909].
Score (87p.) and 1 part. (On cover: Edition Peters. No.8226).
Score for violin and piano; part for violin.
Contains compositions by Franz Benda, Joh. Adam Birckenstock, Archangelo Corelli, Pietro Locatelli, Joh. Georg Pisendal, Niccolo Porpora, Jean Ferry Rebel, Giuseppe Tartini, Tremais, Pierre Vachon, Francesco Veracini, Antonio Vivaldi, and Joh, Jakob Walther.

SCHERING, ARNOLD, 1877–1941. ed.
Einstimmige Chor- und Sololieder des XVI. Jahrhunderts mit Instrumental-Begleitung. Mit untergelegtem Klavierauszug, hrsg. von Arnold Schering . . . Leipzig, Breitkopf & Härtel, [cop.1912–13].
2v. in 1.
Score. German words.
Contents:
Teil 1. 10 Geistliche Gesänge.
Teil 2. 12 Weltliche Gesänge.

SCHERING, ARNOLD, 1877–1941. ed.
Geschichte der Musik in Beispielen; dreihunderfünfzig Tonsätze aus Neun Jehrhunderten, gesammelt, mit quellenhinweisen versehen und hrsg. von Arnold Schering. Leipzig, Breitkopf & Härtel, 1931.
viii, 481p. (music).
The detachable "Textteil" (35, [1]p.) has subtitle: Quellennachweis und Revisionsbemerkungen, Verzeichnis der Tonsätze nach Komponisten geordnet, Namen- und Sachregister.

SCHERING, ARNOLD, 1877–1941. ed.
Geschichte der Musik in Beispielen. Reprint. [New York, Broude Bros., 1950].
[1]L., reprint: viiip., music (481p.).
Added title page in English.

SCHERING, ARNOLD, 1877–1941. ed.
Geschichte der Musik in Beispielen. Reprint. Quellennachweis und Revisionsbemerkungen, Verzeichnis der Tonsätze, Namen- und Sachregister. [New York, Broude Bros., 1950].
[1]L., reprint: 35p.
Added title page in English.

SCHERING, ARNOLD, 1877–1941. ed.
Perlen alter Kammermusik deutscher und italienischer Meister. Nach dem Originalen bearb. und zum ersten Mal hrsg. von Arnold

Schering. Leipzig, C. F. Kahnt Nachf, 19? – .
No.1– .
Contents:
Ouvertüren.
Händel, G. F. Festliche Ouvertüre in B-dur (zum Oratorium "Salomo"). Zwei Oboen (auch ohne Oboen aufführbar), Fagott ad lib. nach Violoncellstimme, zwei Violinen, Viola, Violoncello (Kontrabass), Cembalo (Klavier).
—— Ouvertüre zum Oratorium "Herakles." Zwei Oboen, zwei Violinen, Viola, Violoncello (Kontrabass), Cembalo (Klavier).
—— Ouvertüre zu "Theodora." Zwei Violinen, Viola, Violoncello (Kontrabass), Cembalo (Klavier).
Hasse, J. A. Ouvertüre zur Oper "Euristeo." Zwei Violinen, Viola (statt Viola auch dritte Violine lieferbar), Violoncello (Kontrabass), Cembalo (Klavier).

Intraden.
Frank, Melchior. Zwei Intraden aus "Neue musicalische Intraden auff allerhand Instrumenten." Nürnberg 1608.
Hassler, Hans Leo. Zwei Intraden aus "Lustgarten neuer teutscher Gesäng, Balletti," usw. Nürnberg, 1601. Drei Violinen, zwei Violen, Violoncello (Kontrabass).

Sinfonien.
Locatelli, Pietro. Trauersymphonie. Zwei Violinen, Viola (statt Viola auch dritte Violine lieferbar), Violoncello (Kontrabass), Orgel (Cembalo, Klavier).
Manfredini, Francesco. Weihnachtssymphonie (Pastorale aus dem Weihnachtskonzert). Zwei Soloviolinen, zwei Violinen, Viola, Violoncello (Kontrabass). Cembalo (Klavier, Orgel, Harmonium).
Tartini, Giuseppe. Sinfonia pastorale. Eine Soloviolinе oder zwei Soloviolinen, Solo-Violoncello, zwei Tuttiviolinen, Viola (statt Viola auch dritte Violine lieferbar), Violoncello (Kontrabass), Cembalo (Klavier).
Torelli, Giuseppe. Sinfonia E-moll (Nr.6 aus "Concerti musicali," Op.6, Bologna 1698). Zwei Violinen, Viola (statt Viola auch dritte Violine lieferbar), Violoncello (Kontrabass), Cembalo (Klavier).

Suiten.
Fischer, Johann Kasper Ferdinand. Festliche Suite in B-dur (aus "Tafel-Musik," 1702). Zwei Oboen, Fagott ad lib., zwei Trompeten (auch ohne Trompeten ausführbar, Trompeten auch durch Oboen ersetzbar), zwei Violinen, zwei Violen, Violoncello, Kontrabass, Cembalo (Klavier).
Händel, G. F. Mirtillo-Suite. Eine Flöte, zwei Oboen (oder Soloviolinen), Fagott ad lib., zwei Violinen, Viola, Violoncello (Kontrabass), Cembalo (Klavier).
Krieger, J. P. Suite F-dur aus "Lustige Feldmusik." Zwei Violinen, Viola (statt Viola auch dritte Violine lieferbar), Violoncello (Kontrabass).
Pezel, Johann. Suite G-moll aus "Delitiae musicales oder Lust-Music." Zwei Violinen, zwei Violen, Violoncello (oder Fagotto), Kontrabass, Cembalo (Klavier).
Rosenmüller, Johann. Suite C-moll aus "Studenten-Musik." Zwei Violinen, zwei Violen, Violoncello, Kontrabass, Cembalo (Klavier).
Schein, J. H. Suite aus "Banchetto musicale." Zwei Violinen, zwei Violen, Violoncello (Kontrabass).
Telemann, G. P. Suite A-moll. Zwei Violinen, Viola (statt Viola auch dritte Violine lieferbar), Violoncello (Kontrabass), Cembalo (Klavier).
—— Suite G-moll. Zwei Violinen, Viola (statt Viola auch dritte Violine lieferbar), Violoncello (Kontrabass), Cembalo (Klavier).

Concerti grossi.
Corelli, Arcangelo. Concerto grosso C-moll, Nr.III. (Op.6, Nr.3, 1712). Zwei Soloviolinen, Solo-Violoncell; zwei Violinen, Viola (statt Viola auch dritte Violine lieferbar), Violoncello (Kontrabass), Cembalo (Klavier).
—— Weihnachtskonzert. (Concerto grosso, Nr.8. Fatto per la notte di natale, 1712). Zwei Soloviolinen, Solo-Violoncello; zwei Violinen, Viola (statt Viola auch dritte Violine lieferbar), Violoncello (Kontrabass), Cembalo (Klavier).
—— Pastorale aus der Weihnachtsmusik (Concerto grosso, Nr.8). Zwei Soloviolinе, Solo-Violoncello; zwei Violinen, Viola, Violoncello (Kontrabass), Cembalo (Klavier).
Geminiani, Francesco. Concerto grosso B-dur, Op.3, Nr.5, um 1735. Zwei Soloviolinen, Solo-Viola, Solo-Violoncello; zwei Violinen, Viola (statt Viola auch dritte Violine lieferbar), Violoncello (Kontrabass), Cembalo (Klavier).
Händel, G. F. Konzert F-dur in zwei Sätzen. Zwei Oboen, Fagott, zwei Hörner, zwei Violinen, Viola (statt Viola auch dritte Violine lieferbar), Violoncello (Kontrabass), Cembalo (Klavier).
Locatelli, Pietro. Concerto grosso F-moll mit Pastorale (Nr.8 aus Op.1, 1721). Zwei Soloviolinen, zwei Solo-Violen, ein Solo-Violoncello; zwei Violinen, zwei Violen, Violoncello (Kontrabass), Cembalo (Klavier).
Manfredini, Francesco. Weihnachtskonzert. (Concerto grosso per il santissimo natale). Zwei Soloviolinen; zwei Violinen, Viola (statt Viola auch dritte Violine lieferbar), Violoncello (Kontrabass), Cembalo (Klavier, Orgel, Harmonium).
—— Weihnachtssymphonie (Pastorale aus dem Weihnachtskonzert). Zwei Soloviolinen; zwei Violinen, Viola, Violoncello (Kontrabass), Cembalo (Klavier, Orgel, Harmonium).
Scarlatti, Alessandro. Concerto grosso F-moll. Zwei Violinen, Viola (statt Viola auch dritte Violine lieferbar), Violoncello (Kontrabass), Cembalo (Klavier).
Torelli, Giuseppe. Weihnachtskonzert. Concerto a 4, in forma di Pastorale per il santissimo natale. Aus Op.8, Bologna 1709. Zwei Soloviolinen; zwei Violinen, Viola (statt Viola auch dritte Violine lieferbar), Violoncello (Kontrabass), Cembalo (Klavier, Orgel, Harmonium).

Einzelne Werke verschiedener Art.
Corelli, Arcangelo. Pastorale aus der Weihnachtsmusik (Concerto grosso Nr.8). Zwei Soloviolinen, Solo-Violoncello; zwei Violinen, Viola, Violoncello (Kontrabass), Cembalo (Klavier).
Händel, G. F. Weihnachts-Pastorale aus dem "Messias." Drei Violinen, Viola, Violoncello (Kontrabass), Cembalo (Klavier, Orgel). (Zwei Violinen, Violoncello und Cembalo [Klavier, Orgel]).
Marcello, Alessandro. Largo aus einem Concerto grosso. Einstimmiger Violinenchor und Cembalo (Klavier, Orgel, Harmonium).
Valentini, Giuseppe. Weihnachts-Pastorale. Zwei Violinen, Violoncello, Cembalo (Klavier, Orgel).
Vivaldi, Antonio. Largo aus einer Violinsonate. Violine und Klavier (Cembalo, Orgel).
—— Largo aus einem Violinkonzert. Violine und Klavier (Cembalo).

SCHLICK, ARNOLD, fl.1512.
Spiegel der Orgelmacher und Organisten, allen Stiften und Kirchen, so Orgeln halten oder machen lassen, hochnützlich; durch den hochberühmten und kunstreichen Meister Arnold Schlick, Pfalzgräflichen Organisten, gewissenhaft verfasst . . . Heidelberg, 1511. Neudruck in moderner Sprache übertragen und hrsg. von Ernst Flade. Mainz, P. Smets, 1932.
49p. facsim.

SCHLICK, ARNOLD, fl.1512.
Spiegel der Orgelmacher und Organisten, allen Stifften und Kirchen so Orgel halten oder machen lassen, hochnützlich, durch den hochbreümpten [sic] und künstreichen Meyster Arnold Schlicken, Pfaltzgrauischen Organisten, artlich verfasst . . . [Mainz, Der Rheingold-Verlag, 1937].
39p. incl. facsims.
"300 numerierte exemplare . . ."
"Wortgetreuer neudruck, den Paul Smets . . . herausgegeben hat . . . 1511 erschien die erstausgabe, die Peter Schöffer in Mainz gedruckt hat . . . Die abweichungen vom satz des originales beschränken sich ausschliesslich auf das aussetzen der damals verwendeten abbreviaturen."–p.[4]–5.

SCHLICK, ARNOLD, fl.1512.
Spiegel der Orgelmacher und Organisten, allen Stiften und Kirchen, so Orgeln halten oder machen lassen, hochnützlich; durch den hochberühmten und kunstreichen Meister Arnold Schlick, Pfalzgräflichen Organisten, gewissenhaft verfasst . . . 1511. Neudruck übertragen und hrsg. von Ernst Flade, 1951. Kassel, Bärenreiter Verlag, [1951].
47p. facsim.

SCHLICK, ARNOLD, fl.1512.
. . . Tabulaturen etlicher Lobgesang und Lidlein uff die Orgeln und Lauten etc./ Hrsg. im Auftrage der Oberleitung der Glaubensgemeinde Ugrino von Gottlieb Harms. Klecken, Ugrino/ Abt. Verlag, 1924.
61p., 1L.
With reproduction (p.5–15) of title page and text of the original edition, Mainz, P. Schöffer, 1512. Music (p.[18]–56) in modern notation.

SCHLICK, ARNOLD, fl.1512.
. . . Tabulaturen etlicher Lobgesang und Lidlein. Facsimile edition. Hamburg, Ugrino Verlag, 1957.
61p.

SCHMID, OTTO, 1858–1931. ed.
Musik am sächsischen Hofe . . . Hrsg. von Otto Schmid . . . Bd.1–9. Leipzig, [etc.], Breitkopf & Härtel, cop.1898– .
v.1– .
Preface to each volume in German and English.
Contents:
Bd.1. [Ausgewählte Werke (arrangiert) für Klavier]. Walther, Johann: Herr Christ, der einig Gotts sohn; Wol dem, der in Gottes furchte steht. Schütz, Heinrich: Bringt her dem Herren. Lotti, Antonio: Arie des Evander, Arie der Silvia, aus der Oper "Ascanio." Hasse, J. A.: Triumph-Marsch aus der Oper "Ezio"; Arie des Ezio aus der Oper "Ezio"; Te Deum laudamus. Naumann, J. G.: Kyrie aus der As-dur-Messe; Agnus Dei aus der D-moll-(Pastoral-) Messe. Schuster, Joseph: Ave Maria. Morlacchi, Francesco: Agnus Dei aus der E-dur-Messe. Weber, C. M. von: Schlusschor aus der Jubel-Cantate (Op.58); Sanctus aus der Es-dur-Messe; Benedictus aus der G-dur-(Jubel-) Messe. Reissiger, C. G.: Credo aus der As-dur-Messe. Wagner, Richard: Eingamschor aus dem "Liebesmal der Apostel."
Bd.2. [Ausgewählte Werke von J. A. Hasse (arrangiert) für Klavier]. Ouverture zur Oper "Siroë." Zwei Märsche: Aus der Oper "Cleofide"; Aus der Oper "Artaserse." Arie aus der Oper "Il re pastore." Duett aus der Oper "Il re pastore." Chor aus der Oper "Olimpiade." Ouverture zum Oratorium "I pellegrini al sepolcro di Nostro Salvatore." "Domine Deus" aus der D-moll-Messe. Chor aus dem Oratorium "La conversione di Sant' Agostino." "Recordare Jesus" aus dem Requiem in C-dur.
Bd.3. Ausgewählte Werke von Mitgliedern des sächsischen Königshauses.
Bd.4. Ausgewählte Original-Kompositionen für Pianoforte von Peter August und Christlieb Siegmund Binder. Revidiert und hrsg. von Otto Schmid.
Bd.5. Anton, König von Sachsen. 2 Märsche (Erzherzog Karl-Marsch-Marsch). Für Pianoforte bearb. von Otto Schmid.
Bd.6. Ausgewählte Werke der Instrumentalmusik von Joh. Christoph Schmidt, Christian Petzold, Joh. Dismas Zelenka, Joh. David Heinichen, Joh. Adolph Hasse, Christlieb Siegmund Binder, Joh. Gottlieb Naumann, für Pianoforte bearb. von Otto Schmid.
Bd.7. [Ausgewählte geistliche Gesänge für Sopran und Sopran und Alt mit Orgel- oder

Klavierbegleitung von J. A. Hasse]: "Nel mirar quel sasso amato" (Arie aus dem Oratorium "Sant' Elena al calvario"). "Quoniam, si voluisses sacrificium" (Aus einem Miserere). Benedictus (Aus einer Messe in F-dur). Agnus Dei (Aus dem Requiem in Es-dur). Domine Deus (Aus der D-moll-Messe). Aus einer Messe in G-dur: Benedictus; Crucifixus.

Bd.8. [Ausgewählte geistliche Gesänge für Alt und Alt und Sopran mit Orgel- oder Klavierbegleitung von J. A. Hasse]: "Un guardo è bastante" (Arie aus dem Oratorium "La deposizione dalla croce di Gesù Cristo"). "In Te s'affida e spera" (Arie aus dem Oratorium "Sant' Elena al calvario"). "Ad Te clamamus" (Aus einem Salve Regina). Agnus Dei (Aus der D-moll-Messe). Crucifixus (Aus einer Messe in G-dur). Crucifixus (Duett aus einer Messe in G-dur).

Bd.9. Altsächsische Fantaren- und Armeemärsche, Zapfenstreich und Abtrupp für Pianoforte bearb. und hrsg. von Otto Schmid.

SCHMIDT-GARRE, HELMUT. ed.
Benedicamus Domino. Drei dreistimmige Organa aus der Zeit um 1200. Mainz, Schott, 1934.
v.1– .

SCHÖBERLEIN, LUDWIG, 1813–1881. ed.
Schatz des liturgischer Chor- und Gemeindegesanges, nebst den Altargesängen in der deutschen evangelischen Kirche. Göttingen, Vandenhoeck, 1865–72.
3v.

Schola Cantorum, *see* Antologie des maîtres religieux primitifs des XVe, XVIe et XVIIe siècles; Bordes, Charles. Chansonnier du XVe siècle; Du Mont, Henri. Meslanges divers.

SCHÖNBERG, ARNOLD, 1874–1951.
The complete works of Arnold Schoenberg. Mainz, B. Schott's Söhne; Vienna, Universal Edition, 196? – .
29v.
Contents (proposed):
Sec.I. Songs.
Vol.1. Songs with piano: Op.1, 2, 3, 6, 12, 14, 15, 48. Appendix: Sketches.
Vol.2. Songs with instrumental accompaniment: 6 Songs with orchestra Op.8; Herzgewächse Op.20; 4 Songs with orchestra Op.22; Appendix: Sketches.
Sec.II. Piano and organ music.
Vol.3. 3 Piano pieces Op.11; 6 Little piano pieces Op.19; 5 Piano pieces Op.23; Suite for piano Op.25; Klavierstück Op.33a; Variations on a recitative for organ Op.40; Appendix: Sketches.
Sec.III. Stage works.
Vol.4. Erwartung Op.17; Die glückliche Hand Op.18; Appendix: Sketches and vocal score to Op.17.
Vol.5. Von heute auf Morgen Op.32.
Vol.6. Moses and Aaron, Act 1; Appendix: Performance directions and sketches.
Vol.7. Moses and Aaron, Act 2.
Sec.IV. Orchestral works.
Vol.8. Pelleas and Melisande Op.5; Appendix: Sketches.
Vol.9. Chamber symphony E major Op.9; The same for full orchestra Op.9B; The same for piano 4 hands; Appendix: Sketches.
Vol.10. 5 Orchestral pieces Op.16; The same for reduced orchestra; Suite for strings; Appendix: Sketches.
Vol.11. Variations for orchestra Op.31; Music to a motion picture scene Op.34; Appendix: Sketches.
Vol.12. Second chamber symphony Op.38; The same for 2 pianos Op.38B; Theme and variations for band Op.43A; The same for orchestra Op.43B; Appendix: Sketches.
Sec.V. Choral works.
a. With soloists and orchestra.
Vol.13. Gurrelieder; Appendix: Sketches.
Vol.14. Die Jakobsleiter, Oratorio (Particello and Sketches).
b. Choral works a capella and with instrumental accompaniment.
Vol.15. Friede auf Erden (Peace on earth) Op.13; 4 Pieces for mixed chorus Op.27; 3 Satiren for mixed chorus (with appendix) Op.28; 6 Pieces for men's chorus Op.35; Appendix: Drafts and sketches.
Vol.16. Kol Nidre Op.39; Prelude Op.44; A survivor from Warsaw Op.46; 3 Folk songs Op.49; The same in an earlier version; Choruses Op.50 A, B, and C; Appendix: Sketches.
Sec.VI. Concertos for various instruments.
Vol.17. Concerto for violin and orchestra Op.36; Concerto for piano and orchestra Op.42; Appendix: Sketches.
Vol.18. Concerto for cello and orchestra (after G. M. Monn); Concerto for string quartet and orchestra (after Handel); Appendix: Sketches.
Sec.VII. Chamber music.
Vol.19. String sextet Verklaerte Nacht Op.4; The same for string orchestra (rev. version of 1943); Appendix: String quartet D major (1897).
Vol.20. First string quartet Op.7 D minor; Second string quartet Op.10 F sharp minor; The same for string orchestra; Appendix: Sketches.
Vol.21. Third string quartet Op.30; Fourth string quartet Op.37; String trio Op.45; Appendix: Sketches.
Vol.22. 3 Little pieces for chamber combinations; Pierrot Lunaire Op.21; Serenade Op.24; Appendix: Sketches.
Vol.23. Woodwind quintet Op.26; Suite Op.29; Appendix: Sketches.
Vol.24. Ode to Napoleon Op.41; Fantasy for violin and piano Op.47; 30 Canons; Appendix: Sketches.
Sec.VIII. Arrangements.
a. For large orchestra.
Vol.25. J. S. Bach. 2 Choral preludes; J. S. Bach. Prelude and fugue E flat

major; J. Brahms. Piano quartet G minor, Op.25.
b. For smaller combinations.
Vol.26. Song of the dove from Gurrelieder for voice and chamber orchestra; works by F. Busoni, G. Mahler, Johann Strauss, C. Loewe, G. M. Monn, Fr. Tuma; 4 German folksongs for voice and piano.
Sec.IX. Early and uncompleted works.
Vol.27. Early songs with piano accompaniment.
Vol.28. Early works.
Vol.29. Early and uncompleted works.

Schott, B., pub. Antiqua Edition, *see* Antiqua Edition.

SCHOTT'S ANTHOLOGY OF EARLY KEYBOARD MUSIC. English virginalists. London, Schott & Co., Ltd., [cop.1951].
5v.
Editor: Frank Dawes.
Vol.1. 10 Pieces by Hugh Aston and others. [cop.1951].
Vol.2. 12 Pieces from Mulliner's book. (ca.1555). [cop.1951]. (Contains compositions by Richard Allwood, William Blitheman, John Redford, and Thomas Tallis).
Vol.3. 7 Virginal pieces (from British Museum. Add. 30486). [cop.1951].
Vol.4. Pieces from the Tomkins manuscript. [cop.1951]. (Contains compositions by Nicholas Carleton, Orlando Gibbons, Arthur Phillips. John Tomkins, and Thomas Tomkins).
Vol.5. 15 Pieces from Elizabeth Roger's virginal book (1656). [cop.1951].

SCHOTT'S SERIES OF EARLY LUTE MUSIC. London, Schott & Co., Ltd., [cop.1954–].
v.1– .
Contents:
Vol.1. Dowland, Robert, comp. Varietie of lute lessons (1610). Transcribed and ed. by Edgar Hunt. (Edition Schott 10310). [cop.1957].
Vol.2. An anthology of English lute music (16th century). Selected, transcribed and ed. by David Lumsden. Foreword by Thurston Dart. (Edition Schott 10311). [cop.1954].
Vol.3. Byrd, William. Compositions for the lute. Transcribed and ed. by David Lumsden. (Edition Schott 10312).

SCHRADE, LEO, 1903– . ed.
Polyphonic music of the fourteenth century. Ed. by Leo Schrade. Monaco, Éditions de l'Oiseau-Lyre, [cop.1956–].
v.1– .
The edition consists of 330 copies on Oiseau-Lyre paper numbered 1 to 300, with 25 copies numbered I to XXV for presentation and 5 copies A to E reserved for the publishers.
Vol.1–4 are accompanied by a separate editorial commentary.
Contents:
Vol.1. The roman de Fauvel; The works of Philippe de Vitry; French cycles of the Ordinarium Missae. cop.1956.
Vol.2. The works of Guillaume de Machaut. First part. cop.1956.
Vol.3. The works of Guillaume de Machaut. Second part. cop.1956.
Vol.4. The works of Francesco Landini. cop.1958.

SCHUBERT, FRANZ PETER, 1797–1828.
Werke. Franz Schubert's Sämmtliche Compositionen. Erste vollständige und rechtmässige Gesamtausgabe, revidirt und corrigirt von L. Winkler und H. Sattler. Wolfenbüttel, L. Holle, [18–].
10v.
Contents:
Vol.1–5. Lieder für eine [höhere] Singstimme mit Pianoforte Begleitung. (Op.1–131, Nachlass. Lief.1–50).
Portrait of Schubert in Vol.4.
Vol.6. [87] Lieder für eine Contra-Alt-Bass-Stimme mit Pianoforte Begleitung.
Vol.7. Compositionen für das Pianoforte Solo. Revidirt . . . von F. W. Markull. (Op.9–91).
Vol.8. Compositionen für das Pianoforte Solo. Revidirt, corrigirt und theilweise mit Applicatur versehen von F. W. Markull. (Op.94–164, 3 Sonaten [Allerletzte Compositionen], Marsch und Trio, 5 Clavierstücke).
Vol.9 und 10. Compositionen für das Pianoforte zu vier Händen, revidirt und corrigirt von F. W. Markull. (Op.10–66, Op.69–152, Fuge, Grazer Galopp, Trauerwalzer aus Op.9).

SCHUBERT, FRANZ PETER, 1797–1828.
Franz Schuberts Werke. Kritische durchgesehene Gesammtausgabe. Ser.1–21. Hrsg. von Johannes Brahms, Ignaz Brüll, Anton Door, Jul. Epstein, J. N. Fuchs, J. Gänsbacher, J. Hellmesberger, Eusebius Mandyczewski. Leipzig, Breitkopf & Härtel, 1884–97.
21v. and Revisionsbericht.
"Vorwort" to Lieder und Gesänge, by Eusebius Mandyczewski. Ser.20, Bd.1.
Contents:
Ser.1. Symphonien. 2 Bde. No.1–8.
Ser.2. Ouvertüren und andere Orchesterwerke. No.1–10.
Ser.3. Oktette. No.1–3.
Ser.4. Streichquintett. Op.163.
Ser.5. Streichquartette. No.1–15.
Ser.6. Trio (für Streichinstrumente).
Ser.7. 1 Bd. Pianoforte Quintett und Quartett. Partitur und Stimmen; 2 Bd. Pianoforte-Trios. Partitur und Stimmen.
Ser.8. Für Pianoforte und 1 Instrument. 2 Bde. Partitur und Stimmen.
Ser.9. Für Pianoforte zu 4 Händen. No.1–32.
1 Bd. Märsche.
2 Bd. Ouvertüren, Sonaten, Rondos, Variationen.
3 Bd. Divertissements, Polonaisen, Fantasien usw.
Ser.10. Sonaten für Pianoforte. No.1–15.
Ser.11. Fantasie, Impromptus und andere Stücke für Pianoforte. No.1–16.
Ser.12. Tänze für Pianoforte. No.1–31.
Ser.13. Messen. 2 Bde. No.1–7.
Ser.14. Kleinere Kirchenmusikwerke. No.1–22.

Ser.15. Dramatische Musik.
1 Bd. Des Teufels Lustschloss.
2 Bd. Der vierjährige Posten. Fernando. Die beiden Freunde von Salamanka.
3 Bd. Die Zwillingbrüder. Die Verschworenen (Der Häusliche Krieg).
4 Bd. I, Die Zauberharfe. II, Rosamunde.
5 Bd. Alfonso und Estrella.
6 Bd. Fierrabras.
7 Bd. Claudine von Villa Bella. Der Spiegelritter. Die Bürgschaft. Adrast Einlagen zu Hérolds Oper "Das Zauberflöckchen."
Ser.16. Für Mannerchor. No.1–46.
Ser.17. Für gemischten Chor. No.1–19.
Ser.18. Für drei und mehr Frauenstimmen mit Pianoforte-Begleitung. No.1–6.
Ser.19. Kleine Gesängwerke. No.1–36.
Ser.20. Sämtliche einstimmige Lieder und Gesänge. No.1–603.
Ser.21. Supplement: Instrumentalmusik. Gesängmusik.
Revisionsbericht. 1 Bd.

SCHUBERT, FRANZ PETER, 1797–1828.
Franz Schuberts Werke. Reprint. New York, Dover Publications, [1965–].

SCHUBERT, FRANZ PETER, 1797–1828.
Neue Ausgabe sämtlicher Werke. Hrsg. von der Internationalen Schubert-Gesellschaft. Kassel, Bärenreiter, 1964– .
8 series.
Contents (proposed):
Ser.I: Kirchenmusik.
1. Messen.
2. Kleinere kirchenmusikalische Werke.
Ser.II: Bühnenwerke.
Ser.III: Mehrstimmige Gesänge.
1. für gemischte Stimmen.
a) mit Orchesterbegleitung.
b) mit Klavierbegleitung (dazu Stimmen).
c) ohne Begleitung.
2. für Männerstimmen.
a) mit Begleitung mehrerer Instrumente.
b) mit Klavierbegleitung (dazu Stimmen).
3. für Frauenstimmen mit Klavierbegleitung (dazu Stimmen).
Ser.IV: Lieder.
Ser.V: Orchesterwerke.
1. Sinfonien.
2. Ouvertüren und andere Orchesterwerke.
Ser.VI: Kammermusik.
1. Nonette. Oktette.
2. Streichquintette.
3. Streichquartette.
4. Streichtrios.
5. Kammermusik mit Klavier (dazu Stimmen).
a) Quintett, Quartett und Trios.
b) für Klavier und ein Instrument.
Ser.VII: Klaviermusik.
1. zu vier Händen.
2. zu zwei Händen.
a) Sonaten.
b) Fantasien, Impromptus und Verwandtes.
c) Tänze.
Ser.VIII: Supplement.
1. Bearbeitungen, Incerta.
2. Studien.
3. Nachträge.
4. Liedertexte.
5. Schubert. Die Dokumente seines Leben.
6. Schubert und seine Welt in zeitgenössischen Bildern.
7. Register.
8. Thematisches Verzeichnis.

SCHUBERT, FRANZ PETER, 1797–1828.
. . . Klavier-Werke. Pianoforte works. Oeuvres de piano. Hrsg. von Max Pauer . . . Leipzig, Breitkopf & Härtel, [cop.1928].
7v.
Contents:
Vol.1–2. Sonaten.
Vol.3. Sonaten und Stücke.
Vol.4. Phantasien, Impromptus, Moments musicaux.
Vol.5–6. Tänze.
Vol.7. Kleinere Stücke.

SCHUBERT, FRANZ PETER, 1797–1828.
Werke für Klavier. Leipzig, C. F. Peters, 19? – .
5v. (Edition Peters. No.488a–b, 716, 150, 718).
Contents:
Vol.1–2. Sonaten.
Vol.3. Wanderer-Phantasie; Impromptus; Moments musicaux. (Niemann).
Vol.4. Tänze: Walzer, Ländler, Deutsche Tänze usw.
Vol.5. Supplement: Sonaten. Adagios, Scherzi.

Schuh, Willi, 1900– , ed. Schweizer Sing- und Spielmusik, *see* Schweizer Sing- und Spielmusik.

SCHUMANN, ROBERT ALEXANDER, 1810–1856.
Robert Schumann's Werke. Hrsg. von Clara Schumann. Ser.1–14. Leipzig, Breitkopf & Härtel, 1881–93.
14v.
Clara Schumann began publishing Schumann's works in 1879 with Lief.1 of Series 7, Piano works, Op.9, 12, 17, 21. Later, new serial numbering, complete for each series and not running through the whole edition, was used.
Contents:
Ser.1. Symphonien für Orchester. Partitur. No.1–4.
Ser.2. Ouvertüren für Orchester. Partitur. No.1–8.
Ser.3. Concerte und Concertstücke für Orchester. 1, Partitur. 2, Pianoforte allein. (Op.131, 129, 86, 54, 92, 134).
Ser.4. Für Streichinstrumente. Partitur. Op.41.
Ser.5. Für Pianoforte und andere Instrumente. 1–3 Bd. No.1–14.
Ser.6. Für ein oder zwei Pianoforte, zu vier Händen. No.1–5.
Ser.7. Für Pianoforte zu zwei Händen. Bd.1–6. No.1–38.
Ser.8. Sechs Fugen über den Namen Bach für Orgel (oder Pianoforte mit Pedal).
Ser.9. Grössere Gesängwerke mit Orchester oder mehreren Instrumenten. Partitur 1–7. Bd., No.1–18.
Bd.1. Das Paradies und die Peri. Adventlied.

Bd.2. Genoveva: Oper in vier Acten.
Bd.3. Beim Abschied zu Singen, Verzweifle nicht in Schmerzensthal. Requiem für Mignon. Nachtlied. Der Rose Pilgerfahrt.
Bd.4. Manfred, dramatisches Gedicht in drei Abt. . . . Der Königssohn.
Bd.5. Vom Pagen und der Königstocher. Das Glück von Edenhall. Neujahrslied.
Bd.6. Messe. Requiem.
Bd.7. Scenen aus Goethes Faust.
Ser.10. Mehrstimmige Gesängwerke mit Pianoforte. Partitur. 1–2 Bd. No.1–12.
Ser.11. Für Männerchor [ohne Begleitung]. Partitur.
Ser.12. Für Sopran, Alt, Tenor, und Bass. [Ohne Begleitung]. Partitur.
Ser.13. Für eine Singstimme, mit Begleitung des Pianoforte. 1–4 Bd., No.1–38.
Ser.14. Supplement. (July 18, 1912).

SCHUMANN, ROBERT ALEXANDER, 1810–1856.
. . . Complete works for piano solo, in 6v. . . . Edited according to manuscripts and from her personal recollections by Clara Schumann. Scarsdale, N.Y., Edwin F. Kalmus, n.d.
7v. (Kalmus piano series).
Contents:
Vol.1. Op.1–8.
Vol.2. Op.9–13.
Vol.3. Op.14–19.
Vol.4. Op.20–23, 26, 28, 32.
Vol.5. Op.56, 58, 68, 72, 76, 82.
Vol.6. Op.99, 111, 118, 124, 126, 133.
Vol.7. Op.54, 92, 134.

SCHUMANN, ROBERT ALEXANDER, 1810–1856.
Sämtliche Werke für Klavier. Hrsg. von Emil von Sauer. Leipzig, C. F. Peters, 19? – .
5v. (Edition Peters. No.2300a–e).
Contents:
Vol.1. Op.68, Album für die Jugend. Op.15, Kinderszenen. Op.124, Albumblätter. Op.99, Bunte Blätter. Op.18, Arabeski. Op.19, Blumenstück. Op.82, Waldszenen. Op.28, Romanzen.
Vol.2. Op.6, Davidsbündlertänze. Op.9, Carnaval. Op.21, Novelletten. Op.12, Phantasiestücke. Op.16, Kreisleriana.
Vol.3. Op.20, Humoreske. Op.26, Faschingsschwank. Op.13, Études symphoniques. Op.17, Phantasie C dur. Op.1, Abegg-Variationen. Op.2, Papillons. Op.7, Toccata. Op.8, Allegro. Op.4, Intermezzi. Op.5, Impromptus.
Vol.4. Op.32, Klavierstücke. Op.72, 4 Fugen. Op.23, Nachtstücke. Op.111, Phantasiestücke. Op.76, Märsche. Op.126, Fughetten. Op.133, Gesänge der Frühe. Op.3, Paganini-Studien. Op.10, Études d'après Paganini. Op.118, Jugend-Sonaten.
Vol.5. Op.11, Sonate Fis moll. Op.22, Sonate G moll. Op.11, Sonate F moll. Op.54, Konzert A moll. Op.92, Konzertstück. Op.134, Konzert-Allegro. Nachlass: Scherzo F moll. Presto G moll.

SCHÜTZ, HEINRICH, 1585–1672.
Heinrich Schütz's Sämtliche Werke. Hrsg. von Philipp Spitta, Arnold Schering, Heinrich Spitta. Leipzig, Breitkopf & Härtel, [1885–1927].
18v. facsims. (incl. music), pl., port.
Bd.17, ed. by Arnold Schering; Bd.18, by Heinrich Spitta.
Contents:
Bd.1. Die evangelischen Historien und die Sieben Worte Jesu Christi am Kreuz. 1885.
Bd.2–3. Mehrchörize Psalmen mit Instrumental Abt.1 und 2. 1886–87.
Bd.4. Cantiones sacrae für 4 Singstimmen mit Generalbass. 1887.
Bd.5. Symphoniae sacrae. 1.Teil. 1887.
Bd.6. Kleine geistliche Konzerte. 1. und 2.Teil. 1887.
Bd.7. Symphoniae sacrae. 2.Teil. 1888.
Bd.8. Geistliche Chormusik. 1889.
Bd.9. Italienische Madrigale. 1890.
Bd.10–11. Symphoniae sacrae. 3.Teil. 1. und 2.Abt. 1891.
Bd.12–15. Gesammelte Motetten, Konzerte, Madrigale und Arien. 1.–4. Abt. 1892–93.
Bd.16. Die Psalmen Davids nach Cornelius Beckers Dichtungen. 1894.
Bd.17. Suppl.: Historia von der Geburt Jesu Christi 1664. 1909.
Bd.18. Suppl.2: Gesammelte Motetten, Konzerte, Madrigale und Arien. 5.Abt. 1927.

SCHÜTZ, HEINRICH, 1585–1672.
Neue Ausgabe Sämtlicher Werke. Hrsg. von der Neuen Schütz-Gesellschaft. Kassel und Basel, Bärenreiter-Verlag, 1955– .
30v. (in progress). (Asterisk indicates unpublished volume):
Contents:
Vol.1. Historia der Geburt Jesu Christi. 1955.
Vol.2. Die Sieben Worte Jesu Christi am Kreuz. Die Lukas-Passion. Die Johannes-Passion. Die Matthäus-Passion. 1957.
Vol.3. Historia der Auferstehung Jesu Christi. 1956.
Vol.4. Musikalische Exequien. 1956.
Vol.5. Geistliche Chormusik, 1648. 1955.
Vol.6. Der Psalter in vierstimmigen Liedsätzen nach Cornelius Beckers Dichtungen. 1957.

Vol.8. Cantiones sacrae I–XX. 1960.
Vol.9. Cantiones sacrae XXI–XL. 1960.
Vol.10. Kleine geistliche Konzerte I. 1963.
Vol.11. Kleine geistliche Konzerte II. 1963.
Vol.12. Kleine geistliche Konzerte III. 1963.
Vol.13. Symphoniae sacrae I, Nr.1–10. 1957.
*Vol.14. Symphoniae sacrae I, Nr.11–20.

Vol.22. Italienischer Madrigale. (Venedig 1611). 1962.

Schweich, C., ed. Caecilia, *see* Caecilia; eine Sammlung von Tonstücken verschiedensten Charakters für die Orgel.

SCHWEIGER, HERTHA, 1909– . ed.
A brief compendium of early organ music. (ca.

1600–ca.1850), compiled and provided with biographical, analytical, and technical comments by Hertha Schweiger. New York, G. Schirmer, Inc., cop.1943.
xv, [1], 86p. illus. (incl. music).
Contains compositions by Jean Baptiste Henri d'Anglebert, Johann Christian Bach, William Friedemann Bach, Dietrich Buxtehude, Johann Kaspar Ferdinand Fischer, Girolamo Frescobaldi, George Frederic Handel, Hans Leo Hasler, Nicolas Antoine Lebègue, Samuel Scheidt, Robert Schumann, Nicolas Adam Strungk, Jan Pieters Sweelinck, and Johann Gottfried Walther.

SCHWEIZER SING- UND SPIELMUSIK.
Heft 1–12. Zürich, Hug, [1928–36].
12 nos.
Editors: Heft 1–12, Alfred Stern and Willi Schuh.
Contents:
Heft 1. Stern, Alfred. 6 Alte schweizer Lieder. [1928].
Heft 2. Stern, Alfred. 10 Alte schweizer Lieder... [1928].
Heft 3. Senfl, L. Weltliche Lieder für vierstimmigen gemischten Chor. [1929].
Heft 4. Stern, Alfred. 8 Alte schweizer Lieder für 2 und 3 gleiche Stimmen in Polyphonem Satz. [1929].
Heft 5. Stern, Alfred. 8 Alte schweizer Lieder für 2 bis 4 gemischte Stimmen in Polyphonem Satz. [1929].
Heft 6. Gletle, J. M. [Trompeterstücklein. Selections] ... 12 Kleine Duos ... auf Blockflöten. [1932].
Heft 7. Glutz-Blotzheim, A. [Waltzes. Voice and piano. Op.10. Arr. for 2 violins] ... 6 Walzer-Melodien. [1932].
Heft 8. Stern, Alfred and Leeb, H. Schweizer Volkslieder mit Gitarre-(Lauten). Satz versehen. [1933].
Heft 9. Wehrli, W. Tafelmusik. [1932].
Heft 10. Gletle, J. M. ... Wein und Musik; [und] Neu und Alt. [1933].
Heft 11. Stern, Alfred, arr. Alte Wiegenlieder. [1934?].
Heft 12. Stern, Alfred, arr. 3 Kleine Kantaten nach Liedern aus dem 17. Jahrhundert. [1936].

SCHWEIZERISCHE MUSIKDENKMÄLER, Hrsg. von der Schweizerischen Musikforschenden Gesellschaft. Kassel und Basel, Bärenreiter-Verlag, 1955– .
v.1– .
Contents:
Vol.1. Albicastro, Henricus. 12 Concerti a 4, Op.7. Hrsg. von Max Zulauf.
Vol.2. Gletle, Joh. Melchior. Ausgewählte Kirchenmusik. Hrsg. von Hans Peter Schanzlin und Max Zulauf.
Vol.3. Bourgeois, Loys. 24 Psaumes a 4 voix. Publié par Paul André Gaillard.
Vol.4. Benn, Johannes. Missae concertatae, 3 vocum, adiuncto secundo choro, et una Missa ab octo. Hrsg. von Max Zulauf.
Vol.5. Das Liederbuch des Hans Heer. Hrsg. von Arnold Geering.

Scott, Charles Kennedy, 1876– , ed. Euterpe, *see* Euterpe.

Scriabin, Alexander, *see* Skriabin, Aleksandr Nikolaevich.

Seay, Albert, ed. Transcriptions of chansons for keyboard, *see* Attaingnant, Pierre. Transcriptions of chansons for keyboard.

Die sechs Sammlungen von Sonaten, *see* Bach, Carl Philipp Emanuel. Die sechs Sammlungen von Sonaten.

Seiffert, Max, 1868–1948, ed. Organum, *see* Organum.

Seize sonates anciennes d'auteurs espagnols, *see* Nin y Castellano, Joaquin. Seize sonates anciennes d'auteurs espagnols.

Selecta musices sacrae in Polonia, *see* Gieburowski, Waclaw. Cantica selecta musices sacrae in Polonia.

A selection of communions, *see* Plainsong and Mediaeval Music Society. A selection of communions.

A selection of grails, alleluyas and tracts for Sundays and Holy-Days, *see* Plainsong and Mediaeval Music Society. A selection of grails, alleluyas and tracts for Sundays and Holy-Days.

A selection of offices, grails and alleluyas for Sundays and Festivals, *see* Plainsong and Mediaeval Music Society. A selection of offices, grails and alleluyas for Sundays and Festivals.

Selection of practical harmony, *see* Clementi, Muzio. Clementi's Selection of practical harmony.

Selection of sacred music from the works of some of the most eminent composers of Germany & Italy, *see* Latrobe, Christian Ignatius. Selection of sacred music from the works of some of the most eminent composers of Germany & Italy.

Selectus novus missarum, *see* Proske, Karl. Selectus novus missarum.

Seltenheiten aus Süddeutschen Bibliotheken in getreuen Nachbildungen, hrsg. unter Leitung von Ernst Freys, Otto Glauning, Erich Petzet. Bd.3, *see* Attaingnant, Pierre. Chansons und Tänze.

SELVA, BLANCHE. ed.
... Pièces de clavecin des XVIIme et XVIIIme siècles. Révision par Blanche Selva. Paris, Éditions Maurice Senart, n.d.
43p. (Édition Nationale. No.5147).
Contains compositions by J. C. de Chambonnières, J. Dagincourt, Girolamo Frescobaldi, J. J. Froberger, Balthazar Galuppi, J. B. Lully, Gottlieb Muffat, and P. D. Paradies.

SENFL, LUDWIG, ca.1492–1555.
Sämtliche Werke. Hrsg. von der Schweizerischen Musikforschenden Gesellschaft in Verbindung mit dem Staatlichen Institut für Deutsche Musikforschung und dem Schweizerischen Tonkünstlerverein. Basel, Kommissionsverlag Hug & Co.; Wolfenbüttel, Möseler Verlag, 1937– .
v.1– .
Vol.1–4 were published in the series Das Erbe deutscher Musik, Series 1, Vol.5, 10, 13, 15.
Contents:
Vol.1. Sieben Messen zu vier bis sechs Stimmen. Hrsg. von Edwin Löhrer und Otto Ursprung. 1937. (1962).
Vol.2. Deutsche Lieder zu vier bis sechs Stimmen. I.Teil: Lieder aus handschriftlichen Quellen. Hrsg. von Arnold Geering und Wilhelm Altwegg. 1937. (1962).
Vol.3. Motetten. I.Teil: Gelegenheitemotetten und Psalmvertonungen. Hrsg. von Walter Gerstenberg. 1939. (1962).
Vol.4. Deutsche Lieder zu vier bis sieben Stimmen. II.Teil: Lieder aus Johannes Otts Liederbuch von 1534. Hrsg. von Arnold Geering und Wilhelm Altwegg. 1940. (1962).
Vol.5. Deutsche Lieder zu vier bis sechs Stimmen. III.Teil: Lieder aus den gedruckten Liederbüchern von Egenoff 1535, Finck 1536, Schöffer und Apiarius 1536, Forster 1539–1540, Salblinger 1540 und Ott 1544. Hrsg. von Arnold Geering und Wilhelm Altwegg. 1949.
Vol.6: A. Deutsche Lieder. IV.Teil: Lieder aus den gedruckten Liederbüchern von Rhaw 1544, Forster 1549 und 1556. Einzelne Stimmen-Möglicherweise von Ludwig Senfl stammende Lieder; B. Italienische, Französische und Lateinische Lieder und Gesänge; C. Lateinische Oden aus den Drucken von Formschneyder 1534, Petrejus 1539 und Egenolf 1552. Hrsg. von Arnold Geering und Wilhelm Altwegg. 1961.
Vol.7. Instrumental-Carmina aus handschriftlichen und gedruckten Quellen. Lieder in Bearbeitungen für Geigen, Orgel und Laute von Kleber, Sicher, Judenkünig, Gerle H. und M. Newsidler, Heckel, Ochsenkuhn, Ammerbach, Waissel und Paix. Hrsg. von Arnold Geering und Wilhelm Altwegg. 1960.

The service of Tenebrae or Mattins and Lauds, *see* Plainsong and Mediaeval Music Society. The service of Tenebrae or Mattins and Lauds.

Services in Holy Week. Church of England. Liturgy and ritual, *see* Plainsong and Mediaeval Music Society. Church of England. Liturgy and ritual. Services in Holy Week.

SEVENTEENTH-CENTURY CHAMBER MUSIC.
London, Stainer & Bell, Ltd.
No.1– .
Contents:
I. For 2 violins, bass viol (or cello), and organ (or harpsichord or piano).
No.1. Purcell, Henry. Sonata I (1683) in G minor.
No.2. Purcell, Henry. Sonata X (1683) in A major.
No.3. Lawes, William. Fantasy suite No.5 in D minor.
No.4. Jenkins, John. Fantasy suite No.5 in C major.
No.5. Colista, Lelio. Sonata IV in D major.
No.6. Vitali, G. B. Sonata in F major, Op.5, No.8. (La Guidoni).
II. For violin, bass viol (or cello), and organ (or harpsichord or piano).
No.20. Lawes, William. Fantasy suite No.5 in D minor.
No.21. Jenkins, John. Fantasy suite No.4 in G major.

SHANNON, JOHN R., tr. and ed.
The free organ compositions from the Lüneberg organ tablatures. Transcribed and ed. by John R. Shannon. St. Louis, Concordia Publishing House, [cop.1958].
2v.

Siegl, Otto, 1896– , ed. Orgelmusik steirischer Komponisten, *see* Orgelmusik steirischer Komponisten.

SIEGMEISTER, ELIE, 1909– . arr.
Songs of early America, 1620–1830, compiled and arr. by Elie Siegmeister. Radio City, N.Y., Edward B. Marks Music Corporation, cop.1944.
56p.
Score: principally 3–4 voices, and piano reduction.
Contains compositions by William Billings, Jezeniah Sumner, and Cool White.

Las siete canciones de amor, *see* Codax, Martin. Las siete canciones de amor.

Sievers, Heinrich, 1908– , ed. Das Wienhäuser Liederbuch, *see* Wienhäuser Liederbuch. Das Wienhäuser Liederbuch.

SILCHER, FRIEDRICH, 1789–1860.
Ausgewählte Werke. Kritische Neuausgabe, im Auftrag des Schwäbischen Sängerbundes, hrsg. von Hermann Josef Dahmen. Kassel, Nagels Verlag, [1960].
10v. (Edition Nagel, 1211–1220).
Contents:
Vol.1–5. Volkslieder.
Vol.6. Chöre und Quartette für Mannerstimmen e cappella und mit Klavierbegleitung.
Vol.7. Kinderlieder und dreistimmige Kanons.
Vol.8. Sologesänge und Gesangsvariationen mit Klavier begleitung und anderen Instrumenten.
Vol.9. Variationen für Klavier über "Gib mir die Blumen."
Vol.10. Variationen über "Nel cor più non mio sento," für Flöte und Klavier. [score and part].

Silva iberica, *see* Kastner, Macário Santiago. Silva iberica

Simple music for the Holy Communion, *see* Plainsong and Mediaeval Music Society. Simple music for the Holy Communion.

Sing- und Spielmusik aus älterer Zeit, *see* Wolf, Johannes. Sing- und Spielmusik aus älterer Zeit.

Six scenes from the Protevangelion, by Hubert Lamb, *see* The Wellesley edition. No.2.

The Skene manuscript, *see* Dauney, William. Ancient Scotish melodies, from a manuscript of the reign of King James VI.

SKRIABIN, ALEKSANDR NIKOLAEVICH, 1872–1915.
Complete piano works. Moscow, State Music Publishers, 195? – .
v.1– .
Contents:
Vol.1. Op.1, Waltz; Op.2, 3 Pieces; Op.3, 10 Mazurkas; Op.4, Allegro appassionato; Op.5, 2 Nocturnes; Op.6, Sonate in F minor; Op.7, 2 Impromptus in the form of mazurkas; Op.8, 12 Études; Op.9, Prelude and Nocturne for left hand; Op.10, 2 Impromptus; Op.11, 24 Preludes, 12 Youthful compositions.
Vol.2. Op.12–19, 21–23, 25, 27, 28, 30–42.

SLOVENSKA AKADEMIJA ZNANOSTI IN UMETNOSTI. Razred za umetnosti. Serija za glasbeno umetnost. Ljubljana, 19? – .
v.1– .
Contents:
Vol.1. Lajovic, Anton. Tri pesmi za visoli glas s spremlijevanjam klavirja. 1952.
Vol.2. Škerjanc, Lucijan. Šest klavirskih skladb za eno roko. 1952.
Vol.3. Škerjanc, Lucijan. Koncert za klavir in orkester; partitura. 1954.
Vol.4. Lajovic, Anton. Caprice. 1955.
Vol.5. Kozina, Marjan. Bela krajina. 1955.
Vol.6. Škerjanc, Lucijan. Kvintet. 1955.
Vol.7. Škerjanc, Lucijan. IV.Simfonija. 1955.
Vol.8. Lajovic, Anton. Album samospevov. 1956.
Vol.9. Škerjanc, Lucijan. Koncert za violino. 1956.
Vol.10. Kozina, Marjan. Proti morju. 1956.
Vol.11. Kozina, Marjan. Padlim; zalna glasba za veliki orkester. 1956.
Vol.12. Lajovic, Anton. Pesem jeseni; simfonična lirska pesnitev. 1956.
Vol.13. Škerjanc, Lucijan. Gazele; sedem orkestrskih pesnitev, partitura. 1957.
Vol.14. Lajovic, Anton. Pesmi mladosti. 1958.
Vol.15.
Vol.16. Kozina, Marjan. Balada Petrice Kerempuha, za bas in orkester. 1959.
Vol.17. Kozina, Marjan. Baletna suite. 1959.
Vol.18. Škerjanc, Lucijan. Sonetni venec Dr. Franceta Prešerna; kantata v treh delih za soliste, zbor in orkester. 3v. 1959–60.
Vol.19.
Vol.20. Kozina, Marjan. Davnina; simfonična pesnitev 1. del cikla Novo mesto. 1961.
Vol.21. Škerjanc, Lucijan. II.Simfonija. 1961.
Vol.22. Kozina, Marjan. Izbrane pesmi, za glas in klavir. 1964.
Vol.23. Lajovic, Anton. Zbori. Zbral in uredil L. M. Škerjanc. 1963.
Vol.24. Škerjanc, Lucijan. III.Simfonija. 1963.

SMETANA, BEDŘICH, 1824–1884.
Souborná dila Bedricha Smetany; rediguje Zdenek Nejedlý. Svazek 1–4 . . . Vajadání Sboru pro postavení pomniku B. Smetanovi. [V Praze, Státní Nakladatelstvi, 1924–36].
4v. facsims., ports.
Contents:
Svazek 1. Skadby z mládí do r. 1843
Svazek 2–4. Prodaná nevésta I–[III]. Vydal Otakal Ostrčil.

SMIJERS, ALBERT, 1888– . ed.
Van Ockeghem tot Sweelinck; Nederlandse muziekgeschiedenis in voorbeelden, uitgegeven door Prof. Dr. A. Smijers. 2d. ed. Aflg.1–7. Amsterdam, G. Alsbach & Co., 1949–56.
7v.
Open score: 3 to 5 voices.
At head of title: Vereniging voor Nederlandse Muziekgeschiedenis.
Contents:
Aflg.1. Ockeghem, Johannes. Kyrie uit de Missa L'homme armé. Intemerata Dei mater. D'ung aultre amer; Busnoys, Antonius. Kyrie uit de Missa L'homme armé. Regina coeli laetare. Anima mea liquifacta est. Corps digne (Dieu quel mariage); Basiron, Philippe. D'un aultre amer. 1952.
Aflg.2. Caron. Agnus Dei uit de Missa L'homme armé; Barbireau, Jacob. Osculeter me osculo oris sui; Hobrecht, Jacob. Kyrie uit de Missa Libenter gloriabor. Kyrie uit de Missa Adieu mes amours. Kyrie uit de Missa Rose playsante; Phillipon? . Rosa playsant. 1952.
Aflg.3. Hobrecht, Jacob. Salve Regina. Laet u ghenoughen, liever Johan. Waer sij di han. Lacen adieu, wel zoete partye. Den haghel ende die calde snee. Weet ghij wat mynder jonghen herten deert. Ic hoerde de clocskins luden. Als al de weerelt in vruechden leeft. Ic draghe de mutse clutse. Ic en hebbe gheen ghelt in myn bewelt. Ic weinsche alle scoene vrouwen eere. 1952.
Aflg.4. Tinctoris, Johannes. Agnus Dei uit de Missa Cunctorum plasmator; Agricola, Alexander. D'ung aultre amer (3 sections). Tout a par moy; Craen, Nicolas. Si ascendero in caelum; Compère, Loyset. Kyrie uit de Missa L'homme armé. O bone Jesu, illumina oculos meos. Lourdault, lourdault, lourdault. Se mieulx ne vient d'amours; La Rue, Pierre de. Kyrie uit de Missa Incessament. Vexilla regis prodeunt. Passio Domini nostri Jesu Christi. 1952.
Aflg.5. La Rue, Pierre de. Mijn hert altiji heeft verlanghen; Prez, Josquin des. Kyrie uit de Missa L'homme armé super voces musicales. Kyrie uit de Missa Mater patris; Brumel,

Antoine. Mater patris et filia; Prez, Josquin des. Victimae paschali laudes; Ghizeghem, Hayne van. De tous biens playne; Prez, Josquin des. Benedicta es coelorum Regina. L'homme armé. Adieu mes amours. Petite camusette. 1949.

Aflg.6. Brumel, Antonius. Lauda, Sion, salvatorem; Weerbecke, Gaspar van. Kyrie uit de Missa Princesse d'Amourette. Verbum caro factum est. Tenebrae factae sunt; Isaac, Henricus. Kyrie uit de Missa Quant j'ay au Cueur; Busnoys, Antonius. Quant j'ay au Cueur; Isaac, Henricus. Puer natus est nobis. Ich stund an einem Morgen; Isbruck, Ich muss dich lassen. Donna, di dentro dalla tua casa. Dammene un pocho. Fortuna d'un gran tempo. Par ung jour de matinee. E qui la dira; Stappen, Crispinus van. Ave Maria, gratia plena. 1951.

Aflg.7. Mouton, Joannes. Quaeramus cum pastoribus. Salve, Mater salvatoris. Gaude, virgo Katherina; Richafort, Jean. Christus resurgens ex mortuis; Hellinck, Lupus. Missa Christus resurgens; Arcadelt, Jacobus. Io mi rivolgo indietro; Gombert, Nicolas. Homo erat in Jerusalem. 1956.

SMIJERS, ALBERT, 1888– . ed.
Van Ockeghem tot Sweelinck. A new series of 7v. is planned.

Smith, Carleton Sprague, 1905– , ed. Early psalmody in 17th century America, *see* Early psalmody in 17th century America.

SMITH, JOHN STAFFORD, 1750–1836. comp. and ed.
Musica antiqua. A selection of music of this and other countries from the commencement of the twelfth to the beginning of the eighteenth century; comprising some of the earliest & most curious motetts, madrigals, hymns, anthems, songs, lessons & dance tunes, some of them now first published from manuscripts and printed works of great rarity & value. The whole calculated to shew the original sources of the melody & harmony of this country, & to exhibit the different styles and degrees of improvement of the several periods. Selected and arr. by John Stafford Smith. London, Preston, [1812].
2v. in 1.
Each volume has separate title page.
Paging continuous.
Contains compositions by John Ambrose, Hugh Aston, Thibaut de Blason, Dr. John Blow, Gaces Brulez, William Byrd, Dr. Thomas Campion, Peter Certon, Dr. William Child, Clemens non Papa, John Cole, Raoul de Coucy, Perrin Dangecourt, John Dowland, John Earsden, Jehan Erars, Thomas Erars, Francesco Geminiani, Jhan Gero, Orlando Gibbons, Heath, Henry VIII, Pelham Humfrey, Simon Ives, John Jenkins, Robert Johnson, Robert Jones, Nicholas Laniere, Orlando di Lasso, Jehan de Latre, William Lawes, Matthew Locke, George Mason, Tiburtio Massaino, Christofero Morales, Jacob Obrecht, Johannes Okeghem, Parker (monk of Stratford), Francis Pilkington, Jodocus Pratensis, Daniel Purcell, Henry Purcell, Richafort, Dr. Nicholas Staggins, Thomas Tallis, Thibaut King of Navarre, Thierres, Orazio Vecchi, Thomas Weelkes, Giaches Wert, Adrian Willaert, and Gioseffo Zarlino.

SMITH COLLEGE MUSIC ARCHIVES. No.1– .
Northampton, Mass., Smith College, [1935–].
v.1– . illus. (facsims.).
Contains music.
Contents:
No.1. Geminiani, Francesco. Twelve sonatas for violin and piano. Ed. by Ross Lee Finney. 1935.
No.2. Fux, Johann Josef. Costanza e Fortezza. Ed. by Gertrude Parker Smith. 1936.
No.3. Boccherini, Luigi. Concerto for violoncello and string orchestra. Ed. by Marion DeRonde. 1937.
No.4. Canzoni, sonetti, strambotti et frottole. Libro tertio. (Andrea Antico, 1517). Ed. by Alfred Einstein. 1941.
No.5. Arcadelt, Jacques. Chansons. Ed. by Everett B. Helm. 1942.
No.6. Rore, Cipriano de. Madrigals for 3 and 4 voices. Ed. by Gertrude Parker Smith. 1945.
No.7. Caccini, Francesca. La liberazione di Ruggiero dall' isola d'Alcina. Ed. by Doris Silbert. 1945.
No.8. Galilei, Vincenzo. Contrapunti a due voci. Ed. by Louise Rood. 1947.
No.9. Tartini, Giuseppe. Concerto in A minor. Concerto in F major. Two concertos for violin and string orchestra. Ed. and provided with cadenzas by Gilbert Ross. 1948.
No.10. Haydn, Joseph. Symphony No.87 in A major. Ed. by Alfred Einstein. 1949.
No.11. Steffani, Agostino. Eight songs for solo voice with one or two woodwinds (flute, recorder or oboe) and continuo. Ed. by Gertrude Parker Smith. 1950.
No.12. Vitali, Tommaso Antonio. Concerto di sonate, Op.4, for violin, violoncello, and continuo. Ed. by Doris Silbert, Gertrude Parker Smith, and Louise Rood. 1954.
No.13. Quagliati, Paolo. La sfera armoniosa (1623) and Il carro di fedeltà d'amore (1611). Ed. by Vernon D. Gotwals and Philip Keppler. 1957.
No.14. Vitali, Giovanni Battista. Artifici musicali. Opus XIII. 1689. Ed. by Louise Rood and Gertrude Parker Smith. 1959.

SOCIETAS POLYPHONICA ROMANAE.
. . . Repertorium; cura et studio Raph. Casimiri. v.1–6. Roma, Edizioni "Psalterium," 1925–34.
6v.
Cover title.
Contents:
Vol.1. Palestrina, G. P. da. Laudate Dominum, a 5 voci. Vox diletti mei, a 5 voci. Improperium, a 5 voci; Vittoria, T. L. da. Caligaverunt, a 4 voci; Le Bel, F. Puer natus est,

a 6 voci; Palestrina, G. P. da. Ad Te levavi, a 5 voci. O quantus Iustus, a 4 voci; Lasso, O. Velociter exaudi me, a 5 voci; Vittoria, T. L. da. Tenebrae factae sunt, a 4 voci; Palestrina, G. P. da. Exultate Deo, a 5 voci.

Vol.2. Palestrina, G. P. da. Bonum est, a 5 voci; Lasso, O. Justorum animae, a 5 voci; Des Près, J. Ave Maria, a 4 voci; Marenzio, L. Innocentes, a 4 voci; Palestrina, G. P. da. Alleluja, tulerunt Dominum, a 5 voci. Adjuro vos, a 5 voci. Paucitas dierum meorum et Manus tuae, a 5 voci. Credo della "Missa Papae Marcelli, a 6 voci.

Vol.3. Palestrina, G. P. da. Exaltabo Te, a 5 voci. Nigra sum, a 5 voci. Tribulationes and Peccavimus, a 5 voci; Vittoria, T. L. da. Ave, Maria, a 4 voci; Palestrina, G. P. da. Tota pulchra es, a 5 voci. Dextera Domini, a 5 voci; Vittoria, T. L. da. Animam meam, a 4 voci; Palestrina, G. P. da. Super flumina Babylonis, a 4 voci. Introduxit me Rex, a 5 voci. Incipit oratio Hieremiae, a 6 ed. 8 voci.

Vol.4. Viadana, L. Exultate justi, 4 vocibus; Palestrina, G. P. da. Dilextus meus, 5 vocibus; Ingegnerius, M. A. Vines mea, 4 vocibus. Velum templi, 4 vocibus; Marentius, L. Estote fortes, 4 vocibus; Palestrina, G. P. da. Sicut cervus, 4 vocibus; Carissimi, J. O felix anima, 3 vocibus; Marentius, L. O rex gloriae, 4 vocibus; Benevoli, H. Laudate coeli, 5 vocibus.

Vol.5. Palestrina, G. P. da. Surge amica mea, 5 vocibus; Marentius, L. Puer qui natus est, 4 vocibus; Palestrina, G. P. da. Hodie Christus, 4 vocibus; Lassus, O. Quem vidistis, pastores, 5 vocibus; Palestrina, G. P. da. Confitebor, 5 vocibus; Goudimel, C. Videntes stellam, 4 vocibus; Lassus, O. Tristis est anima mea, 5 vocibus; Victoria, T. L. de. O Domine Jesu, 6 vocibus.

Vol.6. Palestrina, G. P. da. Peccantem me quotidie, 5 vocibus; Gabrieli, A. [Ps.129] De profundis. Sustinuit, 6 vocibus; Marenzio, L. Dum aurora finem daret, 6 vocibus; Croce, G. In spiritu humilitatis, 8 vocibus; Palestrina, G. P. da. Stabat Mater, 8 vocibus.

Societas Universalis Sanctae Ceciliae, Rome, *see* Documenta liturgiae polychoralis sanctae ecclesiae romanae; Documenta maiora liturgiae polychoralis sanctae ecclesiae romanae; Documenta polyphoniae liturgicae sanctae ecclesiae romanae; Monumenta liturgiae polychoralis sanctae ecclesiae romanae; Monumenta polyphoniae liturgicae sanctae ecclesiae romanae.

SOCIÉTÉ BELGE DE MUSICOLOGIE.
Publications. Flores musicales belgicae. Bruxelles, Éditions de la Librairie Encyclopédique, 1950– .
1 v. to date.
Contents:
Vol.1. Pièces polyphoniques profanes de provenance Liégeoise (XVe siècle) transcrites et commentées per Charles van den Borren. 1950.

LA SOCIÉTÉ DE MUSIQUE D'AUTREFOIS.
Publications. Neuilly-sur-Seine, Société de Musique d'Autrefois. 1955– .
v.1– .
Contents:
Textes musicaux.
Tome 1. Capirola, Vincenzo. Compositione. Lute-book (circa 1517). 1955.

Société des Anciens Textes Français, *see* Fauvel. Le roman de Fauvel.

Société des Bibliophiles et Iconophiles de Belgique. Publication. No.4, *see* Basses danses. Le manuscrit dit des basses danses de la Bibliothèque de Bourgogne.

Société du Mercure de France. Meslanges divers, *see* Du Mont, Henri. Meslanges divers.

SOCIÉTÉ FRANÇAISE DE MUSICOLOGIE, PARIS.
Publications. Sér.1, tome 1– ; Sér.2, tome 1– ; Sér.3, tome 1– . Paris, E. Droz, 1925– .
v.1– . illus., plates.
Contents:
Sér.I. Monuments de la musique ancienne:
Bd.1. Deux livres d'orgue édités par Pierre Attaingnant (1531). Transcrits et publiés par Yvonne Rokseth. 1925.
Bd.2. Oeuvres inédites de Beethoven. Recueilles et publiés par G. de Saint-Foix. 1926.
Bd.3–4. Chansons au luth et airs de cour français du XVIe siècle. Recueils originaux transcrits et publiés par Adrienne Mairy, avec une introduction de Lionel de la Laurencie et une étude des sources par G. Thibault. 1927–29.
Bd.5. Treize motets et un prélude réduits en la tablature des orgues. Transcription du 3e livre d'orgue édité par Attaingnant (1531), publié d'après l'exemplaire unique de la Bibliothèque d'Etat de Munich, avec l'adjonction des versions vocales originales des motets, par Yvonne Rokseth. 1930.
Bd.6. La rhétorique des dieux et autres pièces de luth de Denis Gaultier. Publiées dans le texte original de tablature avec la reproduction ès dessins d'Abr. Bosse, R. Nanteuil et E. Lesueur du manuscrit du Cab. des Estampes de Berlin, par André Tessier. Étude artistique du manuscrit par Jean Cordey. 1931.
Bd.7. La rhétorique des dieux. Transcription du texte par André Tessier. 1932–33.
Bd.8. Pièces de clavecin, composées par J. Henry d'Anglebert. Publiées par Marguerite Roesgen-Champion. 1934.
Bd.9. Pièces de clavecin en sonates, de J. J. C. de Mondonville. Publiées par M. Pincherle. 1935.
Bd.10. Le manuscrit de musique polyphonique de Trésor d'Apt (XIVe–XVe siècles). Transcrit en notation moderne, avec introductions, notes, fac-similés, par A. Gastoué. 1936.

Bd.11–12. Boieldieu, François Adrien. Sonates pour piano. Choix publié par G. Favre. 1944–48.
Bd.13. Jullien, Gilles. Premier livre d'orgue. Publié avec une introduction de N. Dufourcq. 1952.
Bd.14. Nivers, Guillaume Gabriel. Troisième livre d'orgue. Publié par N. Dufourcq. 1958.
Bd.15. Les chansons à la Vierge de Gautier de Coinci (1177[78]–1236). Édition musicale critique avec introduction et commentaires de Jacques Chailley. 1959.
Bd.16. Airs de cour pour voix et luth (1603–1643). Transcription avec une introduction et des commentaires par A. Verchaly. 1961.
Bd.17. Anthologie du motet latin polyphonique en France (1609–61). Transcription avec une introduction et des commentaires par D. Launay. 1963.

Sér.II. Documents, inventaires et catalogues:
Bd.1–2. Inventaire du Fonds Blancheton de la Bibliothèque du Conservatoire de Musique de Paris (Symphonies du milieu du XVIIIe siècle). Publié avec l'incipit et le tableau de la composition thématique de chaque symphonie, par Lionel de la Laurencie. 1930–31.
Bd.3–4. Mélanges offerts à M. L. de la Laurencie. 1932–33.
Bd.5–6. Documents inédits relatifs à l'orgue français. Extraits des archives et des bibliothèques (XIVe–XVIIIe siècles). Publiés avec une introduction et des notes par N. Dufourcq. 1934–35.
Bd.7. Catalogue des livres de musique (manuscrits et imprimés) de la Bibliothèque de l'Arsenal, à Paris, par L. de la Laurencie et A. Gastoué. 1936.
Bd.8. Bibliographie des poésies de P. de Ronsard mises en musique au XVIe siècle, par G. Thibault et L. Perceau. 1942.
Bd.9. Bibliographie des éditions d'Adrian Le Roy et Robert Ballard (1551–1598), par F. Lesure et G. Thibault. 1955.
Bd.10. La musique dans les Congrès Internationaux (1835–1939), par M. Briquet. 1961.

Sér.III. Études.
Bd.1. Les chansons de Clément Marot, étude historique et bibliographique, par Jean Rollin. 1951.

Société Internationale de Musique. Section de Paris. Publications, *see* Aubry, Pierre. Cent motets du XIIe siècle publiés d'après le Manuscrit Ed. IV. 6 de Bamberg; Paris. Bibliothèque de l'Arsenal. Mss. (No.5198). Le chansonnier de l'Arsenal.

SOCIETY FOR THE PUBLICATION OF AMERICAN MUSIC.
Publications. 1st– season. ([No.1]– . 1919/20–). New York, G. Schirmer, Inc., [cop.1920–].
v.1– .
Contents:

1st season. 1919–20.
D. G. Mason. Sonata for clarinet (or violin) and piano. Op.14.
Alois Reiser. String quartet. Op.16.
2d season. 1920–21.
H. H. Huss. String quartet.
Leo Sowerby. String quartet. Serenade in G major.
3d season. 1921–22.
D. S. Smith. String quartet. Op.46.
Tadeuz Jarecki. String quartet.
4th season. 1922–23.
W. C. Heilman. Piano trio.
C. M. Loeffler. Music for four stringed instruments.
D. G. Mason. Three pieces for flute, harp, and string quartet. Op.13.
5th season. 1923–24.
D. S. Smith. Sonata. Piano and violin. Op.51.
Albert Stoessel. Suite antique. Two violins and piano.
6th season. 1924–25.
Frederic Ayres. Piano trio.
Aurelio Giorni. Sonata for violoncello (or viola) and piano.
Carlos Salzedo. Sonata for harp and piano.
7th season. 1925–26.
D. S. Smith. Sonata for piano and oboe. Op.43.
Frederic Jacobi. String quartet, No.1 (on Indian themes).
8th season. 1926–27.
Arthur Shepherd. Triptych. Soprano and string quartet.
E. B. Hill. Sonata. Piano and clarinet (or violin).
9th season. 1927–28.
Bernard Wagenaar. Sonata. Violin and piano.
10th season. 1928–29.
J. G. Heller. Three aquatints for string quartet.
Parker Bailey. Sonata for flute and piano.
11th season. 1929–30.
Ulric Cole. Sonata. Violin and piano.
D. G. Mason. String quartet on Negro themes. Op.19.
12th season. 1930–31.
Leo Sowerby. Quintet for flute, oboe, clarinet, horn, and bassoon.
Frances Terry. Sonata. Violin and piano. Op.15.
13th season. 1931–32.
Vittorio Giannini. Quintet for piano and strings.
14th season. 1932–33.
Quincy Porter. Sonata, No.2. Violin and piano.
Wallingford Riegger. Trio for piano and strings in B minor.
15th season. 1933–34.
D. G. Mason. Serenade for string quartet. Op.31.
F. P. Search. Sextet in F minor for strings.
16th season. 1934–35.
Arthur Shepherd. String quartet in E minor.
Frederic Jacobi. String quartet, No.2.
17th season. 1935–36.
Leroy Robertson. Quintet in A minor for piano and strings.
Quincy Porter. String quartet, No.3.
18th season. 1936–37.
D. S. Smith. String quartet, No.6 in C major.

19th season. 1937–38.
Douglas Moore. String quartet.
E. B. Hill. Sextet for flute, oboe, clarinet, horn, bassoon, and piano. Op.39.
20th season. 1938–39.
David Holden. Music for piano and strings.
21st season. 1939–40.
Bernard Wagenaar. String quartet, No.3.
22d season. 1940–41.
Ulric Cole. Quintet for piano and strings.
David Van Vactor. Quintet for flute and strings.
23d season. 1941–42.
David Diamond. Quintet in B minor. Flute, string trio, and piano.
Quincy Porter. Sixth string quartet.
24th season. 1942–43.
Gail Kubik. Sonatina. Violin and piano.
Leo Sowerby. Sonata for clarinet (or viola) and piano.
25th season. 1943–44.
Isadore Freed. Triptych. Violin, viola, violoncello, and piano.
Boris Koutzen. String quartet, No.2.
26th season. 1944–45.
William Bergsma. First string quartet.
Charles Jones. Sonatina for violin and piano.
27th season. 1945–46.
Normand Lockwood. String quartet, No.3.
Lehman Engel. Sonata for violoncello and piano.
28th season. 1946–47.
Anthony Donato. Quartet in E minor.
Douglas Moore. Quintet for winds.
29th season. 1947–48.
Lukas Foss. String quartet in G.
Halsey Stevens. Quintet for flute, strings, and piano.
30th season. 1948–49.
Ross Lee Finney. String quartet, No.4.
Robert Palmer. Piano quartet.
31st season. 1949–50.
Marion Bauer. Sonata. Viola and piano. Op.22.
Ingolf Dahl. Divertimento. Viola and piano.
32d season. 1950–51.
Harold Morris. Trio No.2 for violin, violoncello, and piano.
33d season. 1951–52.
George Balch Wilson. String quartet in G.
34th season. 1952–53.
Elliott Cartet. Sonata for violoncello and piano.
Paul Fetler. Three pieces for violin and piano.
35th season. 1953–54.
Irving Gifford Fine. String quartet.
36th season. 1954–55.
Karol Rathaus. Fourth string quartet.
37th season. 1956.
George Rochberg. String quartet.
Ernest Gold. String quartet, No.1.
38th season. 1957.
Mel Powell. Divertimento for five winds: flute, oboe, clarinet in B flat, trumpet in B flat, bassoon.
39th season. 1958.
Easley Blackwood. String quartet, No.1. [Op.4].
40th season. 1959–60.
William Bergsma. Quartet, No.3, for strings.
41st season. 1960–61.
Leslie Raymond Bassett. Five pieces for string quartet.
Hall Overton. Second string quartet.
42d season. 1961–62.
Howard Boatwright. Quartet for clarinet and strings.
43d season. 1963.
Wilson Coker. Woodwind quintet in three movements.
44th season. 1963–64.
Arthur Custer. Colloquy for string quartet.
Lester Trimble. String quartet, No.1.
45th season. 1965.
Philip Bezanson. String quartet, No.1.

Society for the Publication of Danish Music, *see* Samfundet til Udgivelse af dansk Musik.

Society for the Publication of Polish Music, *see* Denkmäler altpolnischer Musik.

SODERLUND, GUSTAVE FREDRIC, 1881– . comp.
Examples illustrating the development of melodic line and contrapuntal style, from Greek melody to Mozart. For use in classes of counterpoint and history of music, comp. by Gustave Fredric Soderlund . . . Rochester, N.Y., Eastman School of Music, Univ. of Rochester, [cop.1932].
52p. (Eastman School of Music. Publication. No.3).

SODERLUND, GUSTAVE FREDRIC, 1881– . comp.
Examples illustrating the development of melodic line . . . New York, Appleton-Century-Crofts, 1945.
52p.
Reproduced from ms.

SODERLUND, GUSTAVE FREDRIC, 1881– . comp.
. . . Examples of Gregorian chant and works by Orlandus Lassus and Giovanni Pierluigi Palestrina, for use in classes of counterpoint; comp. by Gustave Fredric Soderlund . . . Rochester, N.Y., Eastman School of Music of the University of Rochester, 1937.
4p.L., 171p. incl. facsims. (music). (Eastman School of Music. Publication. No.4).
"Planographed."

SODERLUND, GUSTAVE FREDRIC, 1881– . comp.
Examples of Gregorian chant and works by Orlandus Lassus, Giovanni Pierluigi Palestrina and Marc Antonio Ingegneri, for use in classes of counterpoint. 3d ed. New York, F. S. Crofts, 1946.
244p. facsims. (Eastman School of Music series).
With English translations of Latin texts.

SOLER, ANTONIO, *Padre*, 1729–1783.
Sonatas para instrumentos de tecla. Edicion e introduccion del Padre Samuel Rubio . . . Madrid, Union Musical Española, [cop.1957]–1962.
6v.
Contents:
Vol.1. Sonata. No.1–20. 1957.
Vol.2. Sonata. No.21–40. 1958.
Vol.3. Sonata. No.41–60. 1958.
Vol.4. Sonata. No.61–68. 1958.

Vol.5. Sonata. No.69–90. 1959.
Vol.6. Sonata. No.91–99. 1962.

Solesmes, Benedictines of. Paléographie musicale, *see* Paléographie musicale.

SOMMA, BONAVENTURA, 1893– . ed.
Capolavori polifonici del secolo XVI. v.1– . Rome, Edizioni de Santis, [cop.1939–].
v.1– .
Contents:
Vol.1. Banchieri, A. Festino nella sera . . . 1608. 1939.
Vol.2. Vecchi, O. Le veglie di Siena, 1604. 1940.
Vol.3. Croce, G. Triaca musicale, 1596. 1943.
Vol.4. Striggio, A. Il cicalamento delle Donne al Bucato. 1947.
Vol.5. Vecchi, O. L'Amphiparnasso. 1953.
Vol.6. Banchieri, A. La pazzia senile.
Vol.7. Torelli, G. I fidi amanti.
Vol.8. Vecchi, O. Convito musicale, a 3, 4, 5, 6, 7 e 8 voci.

SOMMA, BONAVENTURA, 1893– . ed.
Musiche vocali e strumentali sacre e profane, Sec. XVII–XVIII–XIX. Roma, Edizioni de Santis, 1941– .
v.1– .
Contents:
Vol.1. Scarlatti, D. Stabat Mater. 1941.
Vol.2. Scarlatti, A. Toccata No.11. 1941.
Vol.3. Scarlatti, D. 4 Sonate. 1941.
Vol.4. Pasquini, B. Introduzione e pastorale. 1941.
Vol.5. Pasquini, B. Toccata con lo scherzo . . . 1941.
Vol.6. Monteverdi, C. Salmo. 1951.
Vol.7. Pergolesi, G. B. Stabat Mater. 1946.
Vol.8. Pergolesi, G. B. Stabat Mater. 1947.
Vol.9. Monteverdi, C. Messa a 4 voci da cappella. 1948.
Vol.10. Vivaldi, A. Juditha triumphans. 1949.
Vol.11–21. Manfredini, Francesco. Il sinfonie dell' Op.2 a 2 violini (violoncello) col basso per l'organo et 1 viola a beneplacito. Revisione e realizzazione del continuo di Riccardo Nielsen.
Vol.22. Manfredini, Francesco. 12a Sinfonia pastorale a 2 violini col basso per l'organo et 1 viola a beneplacito, Op.2. Revisione e realizzazione del continuo: Riccardo Nielsen. (Partitur). 1949.
Vol.23. Torelli, Giuseppe. Concerti musicali Op.VI, No.1. (per archi e cembalo). Realizzazione di Giuseppe Piccioli. (Partitur). 1952.
Vol.24. Albinoni, Tomaso. Concerti a 5 con violino concertante, Op.V, No.1. Realizzazione di Giuseppe Piccioli. (Partitur). 1952.
Vol.25. Castrucci, Pietro. Sonate a violino, violine e cembalo: Sonata in sol minore, Op.1. Elaborazione per violino e pianoforte di Aldo Priano. (1952).
Vol.26. Ariosti, Attilio. 6 Sonate per viola d'amore o violino o viola. Fascicolo I: Sonate No.1 e 2. Revisione, realizzazione e trascrizione di Renzo Sabatini. Editione per viola d'amore. 1957.
Vol.27. Ariosti, Attilio. 6 Sonate per viola d'amore o violino o viola. Fascicolo I: Sonate No.1 e 2. Edizione per viola. 1957.
Vol.28. Ariosti, Attilio. 6 Sonate per viola d'amore o violino o viola. Fascicolo I: Sonate No.1 e 2. Edizione per violino. 1957.

SOMMA, BONAVENTURA, 1893– . ed.
Polifonia vocale sacra e profana. Sec.XVI. A cura di Bonaventura Somma. Roma, Edizioni De Santis, 1940– .
v.1– .
Contents:
Vol.1. Animuccia, Giovanni. Missa "Ave maris stella," 4 vocum inaequalium (1567). Transcripsit et curavit Bonaventura Somma. 1940.
Vol.2. Nanino, Giovanni Maria. Il primo libro delle canzonette a 3 voci miste (1593). Trascrizione e interpretazione di Achille Schinelli e Bonaventura Somma. 1955.
Vol.3. Palestrina, Giovanni Pierluigi da. Missa Papae Marcelli 6 vocum (1567). Cura et studio Bonaventura Somma. 1949.
Vol.4. Palestrina, Giovanni Pierluigi da. Missa brevis 4 vocum (1570). Transcripsit et curavit Bonaventura Somma. 1947.

Sonatas para instrumentos de tecla, *see* Soler, Antonio, *Padre*. Sonatas para instrumentos de tecla.

Sonate italiane del secolo XVIII per cembalo o pianoforte novamente date in luce, *see* Paoli, Domenico de. Sonate italiane del secolo XVIII per cembalo o pianoforte novamente date in luce.

SONDHEIMER, ROBERT, 1881– . ed.
Werke aus dem 18. Jahrhundert. Sammlung Sondheimer. Hrsg. von Dr. Robert Sondheimer. Berlin, Basel (u.A.): Edition Bernoulli, (1922–39).
52 Hefte.
Contents:
Nr.1. Luigi Boccherini. Sinfonie C-dur, Op.16, Nr.3, Part.
Nr.2. Johann Stamitz. Quartett B-dur, Part. und St.
Nr.3. Luigi Boccherini. Streichquintett Es-dur, Op.12, Nr.2, Part. und St.
Nr.4. Luigi Boccherini. Largo aus Op.12, Nr.1, für Streichquintett, St.
Nr.5. H. J. Rigel. Sinfonie in D-dur, Part.
Nr.6. Polaci. Sinfonie in D-dur, Part.
Nr.7. J. G. Naumann. 10 Stücke für Klavier.
Nr.8. Joh. Christian Bach. 2 Stücke für Klavier.
Nr.9. Luigi Boccherini. 3 Stücke für Klavier.
Nr.10. Johann Stamitz. 2 Stücke für Violine und Klavier.
Nr.11. Luigi Boccherini. Menuett für Violine und Klavier.
Nr.12. H. J. Rigel. Adagio für Violine und Klavier.
Nr.13. Giov. Battista Sammartini. Introduzione, D dur, [aus einer Sinfonie von ca.1730] für Violine und Klavier. [1923].
Nr.14. H. J. Rigel. Andante G-dur, Nr.1, für Violine und Klavier. [1923].
Nr.15. Ernst Eichner. Sonata F-dur für Violine und Klavier.
Nr.16. J. G. Naumann. 2 Lieder für eine Singstimme mit Klavierbegleitung. 1923.
Nr.17. J. G. Naumann und Joh. Christian Bach. Sonaten für Klavier.
Nr.18. H. J. Rigel. Andante G-dur, Nr.2, für Violine und Klavier.

Nr.19. Jos. Haydn. Einleitung zu "Die sieben letzten Worte unserers Erlösers am Kreuz," Part.
Nr.20/21. Franz Beck. Sinfonie, Nr.1, G-moll; Nr.2, Es-dur, Part. 1927.
Nr.22. Georg Chr. Wagenseil. Sinfonie in D-dur, Part. 1927.
Nr.23. Anton Filz. Böhmische Sinfonie, A-dur. Part.
Nr.24. Georg Benda. Sinfonie B-dur für Streicher, Part.
Nr.25. Franz Xaver Richter. Sinfonie C-moll, Part.
Nr.26. Antonio Vivaldi. Concerto G-dur, Part.
Nr.27/28. Johann Stamitz. Sinfonie A-dur (Frühlingssinfonie); Sinfonie D-dur (Reitersinfonie), Part.
Nr.29. Joh. Baptist Vanhall. Sinfonie C-dur, Part.
Nr.30/31. J. G. Naumann. Ballet-Suite aus der Oper "Protesilao," Part.; Medea-Suite, Part.
Nr.32. Luigi Boccherini. Sinfonie D-moll, Part.
Nr.33. Anton Hoffmeister. Sinfonie C-dur, Part.
Nr.34. Joh. Christian Bach. Sinfonie G-dur, Part.
Nr.35. Christian Cannabich. Sinfonie G-dur, Part.
Nr.36. Luigi Boccherini. Sinfonie D-dur, Part.
Nr.37/38. Giov. Battista Sammartini. Trio C-dur, Part.; Trio Es-dur, Part.
Nr.39/41. A. Corelli. Sonate E-moll; A-dur; F-dur für Violine und Klavier, Op.5, Nr.8–10.
Nr.42. F. J. Gossec. Sinfonie C-dur, Part.
Nr.43. Franz Beck. Sinfonie Grande, Nr.3, G-moll, Part.
Nr.44/45. Luigi Boccherini. Sinfonie A-dur, Part.; Sinfonia funèbre B-dur, Part.
Nr.46/47. Leonardo Leo. Sinfonie D-dur zu "Amor vuol sofferenze," Part.; Sinfonie G-moll zu "S. Elena al Calvario," Part.
Nr.48. Johann Stamitz. Sinfonie B-dur, Part.
Nr.49. Giov. Battista Sammartini. Sinfonie D-dur, Part.
Nr.50. H. J. Rigel. Sinfonie C-moll, Op.12, Nr.4, Part.
Nr.51. H. J. Rigel. Sinfonie G major, Op.12, Nr.2, Part.
Nr.52. H. J. Rigel. Overture in F major to "Le savatier et le financier," Part.
Another series entitled: Orchesterwerke aus dem 19. Jahrhundert.
Nr.350. Carl Loewe. Ouverture zu "Die Zerstörung von Jerusalem," Op.30, Part. Berlin: Edition Bernoulli, (1925). 1 Heft. (No more published in this series).

Songs of early America, 1620–1830, *see* Siegmeister, Elie. Songs of early America, 1620–1830.

Songs of Syon, *see* Plainsong and Mediaeval Music Society. Songs of Syon.

Specimens of various styles of music, *see* Crotch, William. Specimens of various styles of music.

SPENDIAROV, ALEKSANDR AFANAS'EVICH, 1871–1928.
[Works]. Polnoe sobranie sochineniĭ. Moscow, State Music Publishers, 1950– .
v.1– .
Added title page in Armenian.
Contents:
Vol.2. Vocal ensembles, choruses, recitations, arrangements of Russian and Ukrainian folk songs. (Text in Armenian and original language).
Vol.3. Instrumental works (piano, violin and piano, violoncello and piano, ensembles).
Vol.4. Songs and romances for low and medium voices with orchestra. (Armenian and Russian). Orchestra score.
Vol.5. Vocal quartets, choruses (S.A.T.B.), and recitations with orchestra. (Armenian and Russian). Orchestra score.
Vol.6. Symphonic works (Op.3, No.1, 2; Op.12; Op.4; Op.9; Op.10). Orchestra score.

Vol.9. Symphonic works arranged for piano, 4 hands.

Spiegel der Orgelmacher und Organisten, *see* Schlick, Arnold. Spiegel der Orgelmacher und Organisten.

Spielbuch für Kleinorgel, oder andere Tasteninstrumente, *see* Auler, Wolfgang. Spielbuch für Kleinorgel, oder andere Tasteninstrumente.

SPIELSTÜCKE FÜR BLOCKFLÖTEN, GEIGEN, LAUTEN ODER ANDERE INSTRUMENTE.
Heft 1–9. Kassel, Im Bärenreiter-Verlag, 1930–33. 9 nos.
Contains music.
Contents:
Heft 1. Pudelko, W., ed. Zehn leichte Duette. 1930.
Heft 2. Pudelko, W., ed. Zwölf leichte Duette. 1930.
Heft 3. Nowak, L., ed. Bicinien der Renaissance für gleiche Stimmlagen. 1931.
Heft 4. Nowak, L., ed. Bicinien der Renaissance für verschiedene Stimmlagen. 1931.
Heft 5. Walther, J. [Fugues. (1542). Collection]. . . . Acht Kanons. 1933.
Heft 6. Pudelko, W., ed. Alte Musik. 1931.
Heft 7. Bornefeld, H. Neue Musik. [1931].
Heft 8. Walther, J. [Fugues. (1542). Collection]. . . . Acht Kanons. 1933.
Heft 9. Pudelko, W., ed. Aus dem Baltischen Lautenbuch. 1933.

SPOHR, LOUIS, 1784–1859.
Ausgewählte Werke. In Verbindung mit der Stadt Braunschweig und der Stadt Kassel hrsg. von Friedrich Otto Leinert. Kassel und Basel, Bärenreiter, 195? – .
v.1– .
Contents:
Doppel-Quartett, Nr.1, D moll, Op.65, für 4 Violinen, 2 Violen und 2 Violoncelli. Hrsg. von Eugen Schmitz.
Dritte Sinfonie C-moll, Op.78. Hrsg. von Heussner.
Duo, Op.13. Hrsg. von Doflein.
Fantasie C-moll, Op.35, für Violine und Harfe. Hrsg. von Hans Joachim Zingel.
Klaviertrio, Nr.4, B-dur, Op.133. Hrsg. von Leinert.
Konzert A-dur (1804), für Violine und Orchestra. Hrsg. von Göthel.
Konzert C-moll, Op.26, für Klarinette und Orchestra. Hrsg. von Leinert.

Nonett, Op.31, Querflöte, Oboe, Klarinette, Horn, Fagott, Streicher. Hrsg. von Schmitz.
Oktett in E, Op.32, Klarinette, 2 Hörner, Violin, 2 Viola, Violoncelle, Kontrabass. Hrsg. von Uhlendorf.
Quintett C-moll, Op.52, für Klavier, Querflöte, Klarinette, Horn, Fagott. Hrsg. von Schmitz.
Sechs deutsche Lieder, Op.103, für Singstimme, Klarinette und Klavier. Hrsg. von Friedrich Otto Leinert.
Sechs Lieder, Op.25, für Singstimme und Klavier. Hrsg. von Friedrich Otto Leinert.
Sonate C-moll, für Violine und Harfe. Hrsg. von Hans Joachim Zingel.
Streichquartette, Op.15, Nr.1 und 2. (Es-dur und D-dur). Hrsg. von Friedrich Otto Leinert.
Streichquartette, Op.29, Nr.1. (Es-dur). Hrsg. von Friedrich Otto Leinert.

SPOHR, LOUIS, 1784–1859.
Neue Auswahl der Werke. Published by the Louis Spohr Gesellschaft. Kassel.
v.1– .
To be published in several 10v. series.

SPORER, THOMAS, ca.1534.
Die erhaltenen Tonwerke des Alt-Strassburger Meisters Thomas Sporer, 1534, eingeleitet und hrsg. im Auftrag des Wissenschaftlichen Instituts der Elsass- Lothinger im Reich (Frankfurt a.M.) von Hans Joachim Moser. Kassel, Bärenreiter-Verlag, 1929.
24p. illus. (facsims., ports.). (Bärenreiter Ausgabe [No.] 295).
German words; music for 3 to 5 voices.

SQUARCIALUPI CODEX.
Der Squarcialupi-Codex, Pal.87 der Biblioteca Medicea Laurenziana zu Florenz. Zwei- und dreistimmige italienische weltliche Lieder, Ballate, Madrigali und Cacce des vierzehnten Jahrhunderts. Lipstadt, Fr. Kistner & C. F. W. Siegel, cop.1955.
359p.
Ed. by Johannes Wolf.
2- and 3-voice Italian secular songs, ballads, madrigals, and *cacce* from the 14th century.

SQUIRE, WILLIAM BARCLAY, 1855–1927. ed.
Ausgewählte Madrigale und mehrstimmige Gesänge berühmter Meister des 16., 17. Jahrhundert. Ed. by W. Barclay Squire. Leipzig, Breitkopf & Härtel, [19?–].
50 nos.
50 madrigals of the 16th and 17th centuries.
The original texts are given and supplemented with a translation into German.
Contents:
No.1. Sweelinck, J. P. Poi che voi non volete.
No.2. Sweelinck, J. P. Madonna con questi occhi.
No.3. Dowland, J. Shall I seek?
No.4. Ward, J. Hope of my heart.
No.5. Gastoldi, G. Al mormorar.
No.6. Bateson, T. Have I found her?
No.7. Bateson, T. Sister, awake.
No.8. Haiden, H. C. Mach mir ein lustige Liedelein.
No.9. Lasso, O. di. Quand mon mari; Jeune, Claude Le. O Vilanella quand a l'aqua vai.
No.10. Tomkins, T. See, the shepherds' queen.
No.11. Hassler, H. L. Luce negl' occhi.
No.12. Dowland, J. Say, Love, if ever thou didst find; Byrd, W. I thought that Love had been a boy.
No.13. Wilbye, J. Down in a valley.
No.14. Waelrant, H. Musiciens qui chantez.
No.15. Morley, T. I will no more come to thee.
No.16. Marenzio, L. Scendi dal Paradiso venere.
No.17. Morley, T. Come, lovers, follow me.
No.18. Jannequin, C. Petite nymphe folastre; Jeune, Claude Le. O occhi manza mia.
No.19. Wert, Giaches de. Chi salira per me.
No.20. Tomkins, T. Fusca, in thy starry eyes.
No.21. Gibbons, O. What is our life?
No.22. Archadelt, J. Il bianco e dolce cigno.
No.23. Vecchi, O. Il bianco e dolce cigno.
No.24. Marenzio, L. Scaldava il sol.
No.25. Gibbons, O. I feign not friendship where I hate.
No.26. Nanino, G. M. Vienn' Himeneo.
No.27. Byrd, W. In fields abroad.
No.28. Fabrianese, Tiberio. La canzon della Gallina; Pizzoni, G. Duo begl'occhi lucenti.
No.29. Lichfild, Henry. I always loved to call my lady Rose.
No.30. Lichfild, Henry. Injurious hours.
No.31. Philips, Peter. Dispiegate guancie amate.
No.32. Spontone, B. Vieni soave e dilettoso Maggio.
No.33. Wilbye, J. What needeth all this travail.
No.34. Vecchi, O. Pastorella, graziosella.
No.35. Vautor, T. Shepherds and nymphs.
No.36. Valenzuela, P. La Verginella.
No.37. Wilbye, J. Thou art but young, thou say'st.
No.38. Gastoldi, G. G. Un nuovo cacciator.
No.39. Farmer, J. Fair Phyllis I saw sitting all alone.
No.40. Wert, Giaches de. Un jour de m'en allai.
No.41. Weelkes, T. Mars in a fury.
No.42. Utendal, A. Petite nymphe folastre.
No.43. Weelkes, T. Thule, the period of cosmographie.
No.44. Greaves, T. Come away sweet love.
No.45. Tomkins, T. O yes, has any found a lad.
No.46. Gesualdo, C. Felice primavera.
No.47. Coversi, G. Sola soletta.
No.48. Croce, G. Cinthia il tuo dolce canto.
No.49. Utendal, A. Ich weiss ein hübsches Frewelein.
No.50. Regnart, J. Herzlich tut mich erfreuen.

Squire, William Barclay, 1855–1927, ed. The Fitzwilliam virginal book, *see* The Fitzwilliam virginal book. Ausgewählte Stücke . . .

STAATLICHE AKADEMIE FÜR KIRCHEN- UND SCHULMUSIK. Berlin. Veröffentlichungen.
[Nr] 1–2. Leipzig, Breitkopf & Härtel, [1930–31].
2 nos. music.
Nr.1–2, cover title and text in English, French, and German.
Contents:

[Nr.] 1. Moser, H. J. Frühmeister der deutschen Orgelkunst. [1930].
[Nr.] 2. Moser, H. J. Die mehrstimmige Vertonung des Evangeliums. 1931.

Staatlichen Instituts für deutsche Musikforschung. Das Erbe deutscher Musik, *see* Das Erbe deutscher Musik.

Stäblein, Bruno, 1895– , ed., *see* Monumenta monodica medii aevi; Musica divina.

STÄBLEIN-HARDER, HANNA. ed.
Fourteenth-century Mass music in France. Companion volume to Musicological studies and documents, 7. [n.p.], American Institute of Musicology, 1962.
144p. facsims. (Corpus mensurabilis musicae. No.29).
Transcriptions of the music into modern notation.

STÄBLEIN-HARDER, HANNA. ed.
Fourteenth-century Mass music in France. Critical text. Companion volume to Corpus mensurabilis musicae, 29. [n.p.], American Institute of Musicology, 1962.
182p. (Musicological studies and documents. No.7).

Stainer, Sir John, 1840–1901, ed. Early Bodleian music, *see* Early Bodleian music.

Stainer, John Frederick Randall, ed. Early Bodleian music, *see* Early Bodleian music.

STANDARD SERIES OF ORGAN COMPOSITIONS.
New York, H. W. Gray Co., 19? – .
No.1– .
Contents:
No.1. Karg-Elert, S. Harmonies du soir.
No.2. Purcell, H. Voluntary on 100th Psalm tune.
No.3. Karg-Elert, S. Clair de lune.
No.4. Hollins, A. Spring song.
No.5. Hollins, A. Intermezzo.
No.6. Brahms, J. 11 Chorale preludes.
No.7. Karg-Elert, S. La nuit.
No.8. Schumann, R. 4 Sketches.
No.9. Bach, J. S. Chorale prelude "Kyrie, Gott heiliger Geist."
No.10. Karg-Elert, S. Choral improvisation on "Now thank we all."
No.11. Malling, O. Easter morning.
No.12. Handel, G. F. I know that my redeemer liveth. Hallelujah chorus.
No.13. Bach, J. S. Toccata and fugue in D minor.
No.14. Wesley, Samuel. 3 Short pieces.
No.15. Huré-Bedell. Communion on a Noël.
No.16. Bridge, F. Adagio in E major.
No.17. Bach, J. S. Chorale prelude "O God, be merciful."
No.18. West, J. E. Old Easter melody "O Filii."
No.19. Wagner-Bennett. Good Friday music from "Parsifal."
No.20. Bach, J. S. Chorale prelude "In Thee is joy."
No.21. Bruch-Reimann-Bedell. Kol nidrei.
No.22. Commette-Bedell. Offertoire (Sur des Noëls).
No.23. Fletcher, P. Festival toccata.
No.24. Fletcher, P. Fountain reverie.
No.25. Wesley, S. S. Choral song.
No.26. West, J. E. Fantasy on two well-known Christmas carols.
No.27. Karg-Elert, S. Choral improvisation on "In dulci jubilo."
No.28. Marcello-Dubois-Bedell. Psalm XVIII.
No.29. Bach, J. S. Chorale prelude "We all believe in one God."
No.30. d'Evry, E. Meditation and toccata.
No.31. Olsson-Bedell. Choral prelude on "How brightly shines."
No.32. Bach, J. S. Prelude and fugue in A minor. (Great).
No.33. Bach, J. S. Little fugue in G minor.
No.34. Bach-Best. Pastoral symphony (from the Christmas oratorio).
No.35. Bach, J. S. Fugue in G major (Fugue à la Gigue).
No.36. Handel, G. F. 2 Pieces (1. Pastoral symphony; 2. March).
No.37. Buxtehude, D. Fugue à la Gigue.
No.38. Bach, J. S. Fantasia and fugue in G minor. (Great).
No.39. Bach, J. S. Toccata, adagio and fugue in C major.
No.40. Bach, J. S. Prelude and fugue in C major.
No.41. Bach, J. S. Prelude and fugue in E minor. (The wedge).
No.42. Buxtehude, D. 2 Chorale preludes. (1. In dulci jubilo; 2. Puer natus).
No.43. Reger-Bedell. Introduction and passacaglia in D minor.
No.44. Bach, J. S. Toccata in F.
No.45. Bach, J. S. Fugue in E flat. (St. Ann's).
No.46. Koch-Bedell. Prelude and fugue on "Christ is risen."
No.47. Buxtehude-Bedell. 2 Preludes and fugues. (1. E major; 2. A minor).
No.48. Reger-Bedell. Benedictus.
No.49. Elgar, E. Andante espressivo. (Sonata I).
No.50. Mulet-Bedell, S. Carillon-sortie.
No.51. Bach, J. S. Prelude and fugue in G major.
No.52. Bach, J. S. Allabreve in D major.
No.53. Bossi-Bedell. An Easter alleluia.
No.54. Vierne-Bedell. Finale from Symphony I.
No.55. Mendelssohn, F. 4 Slow movements from the sonatas.
No.56. Schumann, R. Canon in B minor.
No.57. Bach, J. S. Prelude and fugue in E minor. (The cathedral).
No.58. Handel-Guilmant-Dickinson. Aria. (Tenth concerto for strings).
No.59. Bach, J. S. Fugue in B minor. (Subject by Corelli).
No.60. Bach, J. S. Aria in F.
No.61. Andriessen-Nevins. Choral No.1.
No.62. Bach, J. S. Canzona in D minor.
No.63. Buxtehude, D. Chaconne in E minor.
No.64. Bach, J. S. Chorale prelude on "Sleepers, Wake!"
No.65. Hollins, A. Wedding benediction.
No.66. Bach, J. S. Chorale prelude on "Abide with us."
No.67. Bach, J. S. Prelude and fugue in A major.

STANLEY, CHARLES JOHN, 1713–1786.
... Voluntaries for the organ. A facsimile reproduction of the eighteenth-century edition of thirty voluntaries. With an introd. by Denis Vaughan. [London], Oxford University Press, [1957].
3v.

STASOV, VLADIMIR VASILIEVITCH, 1824–1906.
[Collected works]. St. Petersburg, Tip. M. M. Stasiulevicha, 1894–1906.
3v. (4th v. added in 1905).

Steiermärkischer Komponisten, *see* Marckhl, Erich. Klavierwerke steiermärkischer Komponisten.

STEIN, EDWIN, ed.
Twelve Franco-Flemish masses of the early 16th century. Rochester, N.Y., Eastman School of Music, 1941.
p.1– .
This is Vol.II, Pts.1–4, of the author's Ph.D. dissertation entitled: The polyphonic Mass in France and the Netherlands, c.1525 to c.1560. Rochester, N.Y., Eastman School of Music, 1941. 2v. in 5.
Contains compositions by Pierre Cadeac, Thomas Crecquillon, Mattheus Gascongne, Nicolas Gombert, Jean Herissant, Guillaume Le Heurteur, "Lupus," Jean Maillard, Pierre de Manchicourt, Clemens non Papa, Jean Richafort, Vulfran Samin, Claudin de Sermisy.

Stein, Fritz Wilhelm, 1879– , ed. Das weltliche Konzert im 18. Jahrhundert, *see* Das weltliche Konzert im 18. Jahrhundert.

STEINITZER, MAX, 1864–1936. ed.
Musikgeschichtlicher Atlas; eine Beispielsammlung zu jeder Musikgeschichte, mit erlaüterndem Text. Von Dr. Max Steinitzer ... Freiburg im Breisgau, C. Ruckmich, [1908].
v, 120p.
Choral and instrumental music in close score. With biographical and explanatory notes.
"Verzeichnis von Sammelwerken usw. zum Nachschlagen," p.[vii].
Contains 114 examples illustrating the history of music from the 15th to the early-19th centuries.

Stern, Alfred, ed. Schweizer Sing- und Spielmusik, *see* Schweizer Sing- und Spielmusik.

STETSENKO, KYRYLO HRYHOROVYCH, 1882–1922.
[Works]. Zibrannia tvoriv. Kiev, Mistetstvo, 1963– .
v.1– .
Contents:
Vol.1. Pt.1. Khorovi tvori.

Stradella, Alessandro, 1642–1682. Cantata, *see* The Wellesley edition. No.7.

STRAUBE, KARL, 1873–1950. ed.
... Alte Meister; eine Sammlung deutscher Orgelkompositionen aus dem XVII und XVIII Jahrhundert für den praktischen Gebrauch bearb., von Karl Straube. Leipzig, C. F. Peters, [pref.1904].
107p. (On cover: Edition Peters. No.3065).
Contains compositions by Joh. Seb. Bach, Georg Böhm, Dietrich Buxtehude, Johann Kaspar Kerll, Georg Muffat, Johann Pachelbel, Samuel Scheidt, Delphin Strungk, and Johann Gottfried Walther.

STRAUBE, KARL, 1873–1950. ed.
Alte Meister des Orgelspiels, hrsg. von Karl Straube. Neue Folge. Leipzig, C. F. Peters, [pref.1929].
2v. (On cover: Edition Peters. No.4301a–b).
Contains compositions by Georg Böhm, Nikolaus Bruhns, Dietrich Buxtehude, Antonius A. Cabezón, Girolamo Frescobaldi, Johann Jakob Froberger, Johann Kaspar Kerll, Georg Muffat, Johann Pachelbel, Michael Praetorius, Samuel Scheidt, Arnold Schlick, Jan Pieters Sweelinck, Jean Titelouze, and Franz Tunder.

STRAUBE, KARL, 1873–1950. ed.
... Choralvorspiele alter Meister für den praktischen Gebrauch bearb., von Karl Straube. Leipzig, C. F. Peters, [pref.1907].
170p. (On cover: Edition Peters. No.3048).
Contains compositions by Johann Friedrich Alberti, Johann Bernhard Bach, Johann Michael Bach, Wilhelm Friedemann Bach, Georg Böhm, Johann Heinrich Buttstedt, Dietrich Buxtehude, Daniel Erich, Johann Nicolaus Hanff, Johann Peter Kellner, Anton Kniller, Johann Ludwig Krebs, Johann Kuhnau, Vincent Lübeck, Johann Pachelbel, Heinrich Scheidemann, Samuel Scheidt, Delphin Strungk, Franz Tunder, Johann Caspar Vogler, Johann Gottfried Walther, Matthias Weckmann, and Friedrich Wilhelm Zachau.

STRAUSS, JOHANN, Sr., 1804–1849.
Johann Strauss Sämtliche Werke. Hrsg. von seinem Sohne Johann Strauss. [für Klavier]. Leipzig, Breitkopf & Härtel, [1889].
7 Bde.
Contents:
Bd.1–5. Walzer.
Bd.6. Polkas, Galoppe und Märsche.
Bd.7. Quadrillen, Tempete, Polstertanz und Galopade, Op.10 [und] Palatinal-Tanz nach ungarischen. Nationalmelodien, Op.214.

STRAUSS, RICHARD, 1864–1949.
... Lieder. Gesamtausgabe. Complete edition. Édition complète. Hrsg. von/ Edited by/ Édité par Dr. Franz Trenner. Fürstner, Boosey & Hawkes, 1964– .
4v.
Contents:
Vol.1. Lieder für eine Singstimme und Klavier. Op.10. Op.14. 1964.
Vol.2. Lieder für eine Singstimme und Klavier. Op.43. Op.68. 1964.
Vol.3. Lieder für eine Singstimme und Klavier. Op.69. Op.88. Lieder ohne Opuszahl. Jugendlieder. 1964.
Vol.4. Lieder für eine Singstimme und Orchester. Full scores.

Strickland, William, 1914– , ed. Contemporary organ series, *see* Contemporary organ series.

Strunk, William Oliver, 1901– , ed. Music from the days of George Washington, *see* Engel, Carl. Music from the days of George Washington.

SUMMA MUSICAE MEDII AEVI. Hrsg. von Friedrich Gennrich. Darmstadt, 1957– .
v.1– .
Publisher, v.7– : Frankfurt, Langen.
Contents:
Vol.1. Guillaume de Machaut. La Messe de Nostre Dame. 1957.
Vol.2. Gennrich, Friedrich, ed. Bibliographie der ältesten französischen und lateinischen Motetten. 1957.
Vol.3–4. Gennrich, Friedrich, ed. Die musikalische Nachlass der Troubadours. 1958–60.
Vol.5. Gennrich, Friedrich, ed. Die Wimpfener Fragmente. Der Hessischen Landesbibliothek Darmstadt. Faksimile-Ausgabe der Handscrift 3471. 1958.
Vol.6. Gennrich, Friedrich, ed. Ein altfranzösischer Motettenkodex. Faksimile-Ausgabe der Handscrift La Clayette. Paris, Bibl. Nat. Nouv. Acq. Frç. 13521. 1958.
Vol.7. Ludwig, Friedrich. Repertorium organorum recentioris et motetorum vetustissimi stili. Band 1. Catalogue raisonné der Quellen. Abt.II. Handschriften in Mensuralnotation. Die Quellen der Motetten ältesten Stile. 1961.
Vol.8. Ludwig, Friedrich. Repertorium organorum recentioris et motetorum vetustissimi stili. Band 2. Musikalisches Anfangs-Verzeichnis des nach Tenores geordneten Repertorium, besorgt von Friedrich Gennrich. 1962.
Vol.9. Gennrich, Friedrich, ed. Neidhart-Lieder. Kritische Ausgabe der Neidhart von Reuenthal zugeschriebenen Melodien. 1962.
Vol.10. Das altfranzösische Rondeau und Virelai im 12. und 13. Jahrhundert. 1963.
Vol.11. Die Jenaer Liederhandschrift. Faksimile-Ausgabe ihrer Melodien. 1963.
Vol.12. Die Kontrafaktur im Liedschaffen des Mittelalters. 1965.

SURZYŃSKI, JOSEPH, 1851–1919. ed.
Monumenta musicae sacrae in Polonia. (Kompozyce Kóscielne Wzorowych Mistrzów Muzycznych z epoki klasyczéj w Polsce). Poznán, between 1885–1896.
4v.
The works are all for 4-part choirs except where indicated as for 5-part.
Contents:
Vol.1. 1885.
Historical preface.
Szadek, Tomasz. Missa in melodiam moteti Pisneme (1580).
Zieleński, Mikolaj. Adoramus Te Christe (1611).
Vol.2. 1887.
Gorczycki, Grzegórz G. Ave Maria (Offertorium toni peregrini).
Zieleński, M. In Nativitate Domini.
Gorczycki, G. G. Sepulto Domini.
Zieleński, M. In Monte Oliveti. (5-pt.).
Szamotulski, Wachaw. Ego sum pastor bonus.
Zieleński, M. In festo Inventionis S. Crucis.
Felsztyński, Sebastian. Prosa ad rorate. Tempore Paschali.
Zieleński, M. In festo SS. Trinitatis. Benedicimus Deum coeli. (5-pt).
Vol.3. 1889.
Leopolita, Martinus. (Marcin ze Lwowa). Missa Paschalis. (5-pt.).
Vol.4. 1896.
Pekiel, Bartlomiej. Missa Pulcherrima ad instar Pracnestini. (1669).

SVENSK SANGLYRIK. Stockholm, Nordiska Musikförlaget, [1950].
2v.
Swedish words.
Contents:
Vol.1 contains compositions by Viking Dahl, Josef Eriksson, John Fernström, Gunnar de Frumerie, Harold Fryklöf, Knut Håkansson, Algot Haquinius, Josef Jonsson, Edvin Kallstenius, and Sigurd von Koch.
Vol.2 contains compositions by Erland von Koch, Ingvar Lidholm, Bernhard Lilja, Ingemar Liljefors, Oskar Lindberg, H. M. Melchers, John Norrman, Gösta Nystroem, Gustaf Paulson, Moses Pergament, Hilding Rosenberg, Yngve Sköld, Åke Uddén, Henry Weman, David Wikander, Adolf Wiklund, and Dag Wirén.

SVENSKA SAMFUNDET FÖR MUSIKFORSKNING.
Äldre svensk musik. 1935–45.
9 nos.
No.1–4, distributed through A. B. Nordiska Musikförlaget. No.5–9, through Gehrmans Musikverlag, Stockholm.
No.1, Utgiven av Gunnar Wennerbergs Sällskapet.
No.5, 8. Utgiven av Svenska Samfundet för Musikforskning.
Contents:
No.1. Roman, J. H. Sonata a tre. 1935.
No.2. Roman, J. H. Violinkonzert in D. 1935.
No.3. Roman, J. H. Violinkonzert mit Klavier.
No.4. Roman, J. H. Sinfonia per la chiesa. 1935. Sämtlich bearb. von Hilding Rosenberg.
No.5. Roman, J. H. Jubilate. Psalm 100, bearb. von S. E. Svensson. 1938.
No.6. Ron, Martin de. Streichquartett in F. 1941, bearb. von Sven Kjellström.
No.7. Wesström, Anders. Streichquartett in E, bearb. von Sven Kjellström.
No.8. Roman, J. H. Besinner doch. (Ps.4, V.4) 1944, bearb. von V. Söderholm.
No.9. Roman, J. H. Herre, Hjälp. (Ps.12, V.2) 1945, bearb. von V. Söderholm.

Svenska Samfundet för Musikforskning. Monumenta musicae svecicae, *see* Monumenta musicae svecicae.

Swedish Society for Music Research. Monumenta musicae svecicae, *see* Monumenta musicae svecicae.

Swedish "Society of Musical Art," *see* Musikaliska Konstföreningen.

SWEELINCK, JAN PIETERS, 1562–1621.
Werken van Jan Pieterszn. Sweelinck; uitgegeven door de Vereeniging voor Noord-Nederlands Muziekgeschiedenis . . . s'Gravenhage, M. Nijhoff; Leipzig, Breitkopf & Härtel, 1894–1901.
12v. in 10. facsims. (part mounted, incl. music), port. (v.2).
Issued (1894–1901) as 10v. in 12.
Edited by Max Seiffert. Vol.10 edited by Hermann Gehrmann.
Introductions to Vol.1–9 in Dutch and German; Vol.10 in German only.
Title index to first nine volumes, Vol.9, p.[86]–89.
Contents:
Deel 1. Werken voor orgel en clavecimbel: Fantasieën. Fantasieën op de manier van een echo. Toccata's. Praeludium en koraalbewerkingen. Wereljlijke liederen. Danswijzen; Aanhangsel: Capriccio. Fantazia op de fuga van M: Jan Pietersn. fecit Dr. Bull 1621, 15. Decemb. Toccata (onvolledig). Praeludium pedaliter (andere lezing).
Deel 2. Pt.1–2. Psalmen voor 4, 5, 6 en 7 stemmen, eerste boek [50 Psalms, French words, and Cantique de Simeon].
Deel 3. Pt.1–2. Psalmen voor 4, 5, 6, 7 en 8 stemmen, tweede boek [30 Psalms, French words].
Deel 4. Psalmen voor 4, 5, 6, 7 en 8 stemmen, derde boek [30 Psalms, French words, and Oraison dominicale à 3].
Deel 5. Psalmen voor 4, 5, 6, 7 en 8 stemmen, vierde boek [43 Psalms, French words].
Deel 6. Cantiones sacrae voor 5 stemmen. [1619].
Deel 7. Chansons voor 5 stemmen. [1594].
Deel 8. Rimes françaises et italiennes voor 2, 3 en 4 stemmen. [1612].
Deel 9. Vershillende gelegenheids-compositiën: Ricercar; Pavana hispanica, 8 variatiën voor klavier; Pseaume 10: D'ou vient cela, Seigneur [5 voices]; Pseaume 3: O Seigneur que de gents [6 voices]; Canticum nuptiale in honorem Jacopi Praetorii [5 voices]; Melos sancto quondam thalamo dicatum, nuns vero sensu verborum immutato studio et cura Joh. Stobaei [5 voices]; Canticum in honorem nuptiarum Joh. Stobaei [8 voices]; Tes beaux yeux causent mon amour [4 voices]; Tu es tout seul, Jan [5 voices]; Je ne fay rien que requerir [4 voices]; Poi che voi non volete [5 voices]; Madonna con quest' occhi [6 voices]; Chi vuol veder quantumque può natura [6 voices]; Ave maris stella, canon; Vanitas vanitatum, canon; Miserere mei Domine, canon; Sine Cerere et Baccho friget Venus, canon; Vanitas vanitatum, canon; Beatus qui soli Deo confidit, canon.
Deel 10. Composition regeln.

SWEELINCK, JAN PIETERS, 1562–1621.
Werken. Amsterdam, G. Alsbach & Co., 1943– .
v.1– .
Published volumes:
Vol.1. Werken voor orgel en clavecimbel. (Max Seiffert). 1943.
Vol.1. Suppl. Werken voor orgel en clavecimbel. (Alfons Annegarn). 1958.
Vol.6. Cantiones sacrae. (B. Van den Sigten Horst Meyer). 1957.

SWEELINCK, JAN PIETERS, 1562–1621.
. . . Ausgewählte Werke für Orgel und Klavier. Hrsg. von Diethard Hellmann . . . New York, London, [etc.], C. F. Peters, 1957.
2v.
Contents:
Vol.1. Werke für Orgel oder Klavier (Cembalo).
Vol.2. Werke für Orgel (Cembalo).

Szabolsci, Bence, ed. The library of the Goldmark School, *see* The library of the Goldmark School.

Tabulaturen etlicher Lobgesang und Lidlein uff die Orgeln und Lauten, *see* Schlick, Arnold. Tabulaturen etlicher Lobgesang und Lidlein uff die Orgeln und Lauten.

DAS TAGHORN. Dichtungen und Melodien des Bayrisch-Österreichischen Minnesangs. Eine Neuausgabe der alten Weisen für die Künstlerische wiedergabe in unserer Zeit. Mit beigefügter Klavierbegleitung. Buchschmuck nach zeitgenössischen Werken. In drei Bänden: Dichtungsgeschichtlicher Teil und neuhochdeutsche Übertragungen von Alfred Rottauscher, Musikalischer Teil von Dr. Bernhard Paumgartner. Wien, C. Stephenson, [1923].
3v. illus., plates. (part col.).
"Literatur": Vol.I, p.79–80.
Contents:
Vol.I. Allgemeiner Teil.
Vol.II. Die Dichtungen.
Vol.III. Die Sangesweisen.

TAGLIAPIETRA, GINO, 1887– . ed.
. . . Antologia di musica antica e moderna per pianoforte . . . Milano, [etc.], G. Ricordi & Co., 1931–32.
18v. facsims. (music). port.
Includes bio-bibliographical notes in Italian, French, English, and Spanish.
Contents:
Bd.1. F. Verdelotto, A. Willaert, L. Molan, G. Cavazzoni, A. de Mudarra, M. de Fuenllana, G. Bermudo, C. de Rore, A. Gabrieli, A. de Cabezon, A. Padovano.
Bd.2. C. Merulo, L. Luzzaschi, W. Byrd, T. Morley, G. Gabrieli, F. Richardson, P. Philips, G. Farnaby.
Bd.3. J. P. Sweelinck, J. Mundy, J. Bull, J. Titelouze, H. L. Hassler, A. Banchieri, C. Erbach, B. Praetorius, O. Gibbons.
Bd.4. Girolamo Frescobaldi: Fiori musicali, Il primo libro de' capricci.
Bd.5. G. Frescobaldi, G. M. Trabani, G. Picchi, A. Gabrieli.
Bd.6. S. Scheidt, H. Scheidemann, G. B. Fasolo, M. A. Rossi, T. Merula, F. Fontana, J. J. Froberger.
Bd.7. D. Strungk, W. Ebner, J. E. Kindermann,

F. Roberday, J. C. de Chambonnières, H. Dumont, J. A. Reinken, N. Gigault, J. K. von Kerll, J. d'Anglebert, G. B. de Lully, J. Gaultier (le "Vieux").
Bd.8. A. Poglietti, A. Le Bègue, L. Couperin, G. Muffat, D. Buxtehude, B. Pasquini.
Bd.9. J. C. Bach, J. Krieger, C. F. Pollaroli, A. Corelli, J. Pachelbel, H. Purcell, A. Scarlatti.
Bd.10. J. Kuhnau, F. X. A. Murschhauser, J. K. F. Fischer, J. B. Loeillet, F. Couperin, L. Marchand, A. B. Della Ciaja, D. Zipoli, A. Vivaldi, G. Ph. Telemann, J. Mattheson.
Bd.11. J. Ph. Rameau, J. F. Dandrieu, F. Durante, C. F. Händel, J. S. Bach, D. Scarlatti, B. Marcello, N. Porpora.
Bd.12. G. Muffat, L. C. Daquin, L. Leo, J. A. Hasse, G. B. Sammartini, G. A. Paganelli, G. B. Pescetti, G. B. Martini, B. Galuppi, W. F. Bach, P. D. Paradies, J. L. Krebs.
Bd.13. K. P. E. Bach, F. W. Marpurg, J. P. Kirnberger, G. Benda, J. E. Bach, F. Bertoni, G. P. Rutini, J. Haydn, A. Sacchini, J. C. Bach, J. W. Hässler, F. Turini, G. B. Grazioli, M. Clementi, W. A. Mozart.
Bd.14. L. Cherubini, J. L. Dussek, F. Pollini, D. Steibelt, L. von Beethoven, J. B. Cramer, J. N. Humel, J. Field, F. Ries, K. M. von Weber.
Bd.15. F. W. M. Kalkbrenner, K. Czerny, I. Moscheles, F. P. Schubert, J. C. Kessler, F. Mendelssohn, F. F. Chopin.
Bd.16. R. Schumann, F. Liszt, S. Thalberg, H. Kjerulf, S. Golinelli.
Bd.17. J. Raff, A. Fumagalli, A. Rubinstein, J. Brahms, G. Sgambati, M. Esposito, G. Martucci, C. Albanesi, N. von Westerhout, A. Longo, G. Orefice.
Bd.18. F. Busoni, F. Cilèa, A. Zanella, A. Savasta, D. Alageona, R. Pick-Mangiagalli, L. Perrachio, A. Casella, F. Santoliquido, P. Coppola, A. Veretti, M. Castelnuovo-Tedesco, S. Musella, E. Masetti, M. Pilati.

Tagliavini, Luigi Ferdinando, 1929– , ed. Monumenti di musica italiana, *see* Monumenti di musica italiana.

TALLIS, THOMAS, ca.1505–1585.
. . . Complete keyboard works. Ed. by Denis Stevens . . . New York, London, [etc.], Peters Edition & Hinrichsen Edition, [cop.1953].
42p. (Hinrichsen Edition. No.1585).

TALLIS TO WESLEY. A new series of original English organ music, partly on two staves, from the sixteenth to the nineteenth century. New York, London, [Frankfurt], Hinrichsen Edition, [cop.1953–].
v.1– .
Contents:
Vol.1. John Stanley, William Walond, William Boyce. Voluntaries for the organ or harpsichord in D minor, E, and G; Thomas Tallis. 2-stave keyboard works associated with the organ rather than with the harpsichord. 1956.
Vol.2. Thomas Tallis. 3 Organ hymn verses and 4 Antiphons. 1953.
Vol.3. Thomas Tallis. 4 Pieces, partly from the Mulliner book. Antiphon: Natus est nobis; Hymn: Iam lucis orto sidere; A point; Fantasy. 1953.
Vol.4. Maurice Greene. 3 Voluntaries for organ or harpsichord. 1958.
Vol.5. The Wesleys: Charles, Samuel, Samuel Sebastian. 1960.
Vol.6. Matthew Locke. 7 Organ voluntaries from "Melothesia." 1957.
Vol.7. Samuel Wesley. 12 Short pieces for the organ or harpsichord. I/II. 1957.
Vol.8. William Byrd. Album.
Vol.9. Orlando Gibbons. Fantasia for a double organ, Voluntary in A minor. 4-part fantasia from "Parthenia." 1957.
Vol.10. Henry Purcell. Voluntary in A on "The Old Hundredth." Voluntary in D minor. Voluntary in C for cornet. 1961.
Vol.11. John Stanley. 3 Voluntaries from "Opera quinta." 1959.
Vol.12. G. F. Händel. 6 Fugues or voluntaries. 1960.
Vol.13. S. S. Wesley. Andante. 1958.
Vol.14. Samuel Wesley and Dr. Mendelssohn. 3 Organ fugues. 1962.
Vol.15. Maurice Greene. 4 Voluntaries. Second set. 1960.
Vol.17. Thomas Tomkins. 3 hitherto unpublished voluntaries. 1959.
Vol.18. Samuel Wesley. Air and gavotte. (from Vol.7). 1957.
Vol.19. G. F. Händel. 4 Voluntaries. Second set. 1961.
Vol.20. William Walond. 3 Cornet voluntaries. 1961.
Vol.21. John Blow and his pupils: Reading and Barrett. 3 Voluntaries. 1962.
Vol.22. Preludes and fugues by Dupuis, Keeble, and Travers. 1961.
Vol.23. John Alcock. 4 Voluntaries. 1961.
Vol.24. The Wesleys. (Charles, Samuel, Samuel Sebastian). 3 Pieces. Second set. 1961.
Vol.26. William Boyce. 4 Voluntaries. 1966.
Vol.32. William Walond. 3 Voluntaries. Second set. 1962.
Vol.33. G. F. Händel. Cuckoo and the nightingale. (Concerto No.13).
Vol.34. John Stanley. Twelve diapason movements from the Voluntaries. 1966.

TAPPERT, WILHELM, 1830–1907. ed.
Sang und Klang aus alter Zeit. Hundert Musikstücke aus Tabulaturen des XVI bis XVIII. Jahrhunderts. Gesammelt und übersetzt von Wilhelm Tappert. Mit dem Portrait des letzten Lautenisten Christian Gottlieb Scheidler und zahlreichen Nachbildungen alter Notenschriftproben. Berlin, Leo Liepmannssohn, [pref.1906].
xvi, 129p.
Published in an edition of 525 numbered copies.
Contains preludes, dances, and arrangements of vocal works (some with solo voice part) from tablatures for organ, lute, mandora, calichon, angelica, guitar, cither, violin, and flageolet.

Tarragó, Julián Ribera y, *see* Ribera y Tarragó, Julián.

TCHAIKOVSKIĬ, PETER ILICH, 1840–1893.
[Complete works]. Moscow, State Music Publishers, 1940– .
v.1– .
Russian text.
Contents:
Vol.1. Voevode. Full score.
Vol.1 Suppl. Voevode. Vocal score.
Vol.2. Excerpts from "Ondine" and "Mandragore." Full score and vocal-piano score.
Vol.3A–B. Oprichnik. Full score.
Vol.4. Eugen Onegin. Full score.
Vol.5A–B. Maid of Orleans. Vocal score.
Vol.7A–B. Cherevichki. (Les caprices d'Oxane). Full score.
Vol.8A–B. Charodeika. (The enchantress). Full score.
Vol.9A–C. Pique dame. Full score.
Vol.10. Iolanthe. Full score.
Vol.11A–B. Swan Lake. (Complete ballet). Full score.
Vol.12A–D. Sleeping beauty. Full score.
Vol.13A–B. The nutcracker. (Complete ballet). Full score.
Vol.14. Music for plays. Full score.
Vol.15A. Symphony No.1. Full score.
Vol.15B. Symphony No.2. (Two versions). Full score.
Vol.16A. Symphony No.3. Full score.
Vol.16B. Symphony No.4. Full score.
Vol.17A. Symphony No.5. Full score.
Vol.17B. Symphony No.6. Full score.
Vol.18. Manfred symphony, Op.58. Full score.
Vol.19A. Suite No.1, Op.43. Full score.
Vol.19B. Suite No.2, Op.53. Full score.
Vol.20. Suite No.3, Op.55. Full score; Suite No.4, Op.61. (Mozartiana). Full score; Serenade for strings, Op.48. Full score.
Vol.21. Overtures: The storm; Overture in F (1st version); Overture in F (2d version); Overture in C minor. Full score.
Vol.22. Overture on the Danish national hymn, Op.15; "Fatum" (Fantasy), Op.77.
Vol.23. Romeo and Juliet. (Two versions). Full score.
Vol.24. Serenade to the Name-Day of Rubinstein; Marche slave; The tempest; Francesca da Rimini. Full score.
Vol.25. Capriccio italien; Overture 1812; Festive march. Orchestra score.
Vol.26. Elegy to the memory of Samarin (for string orchestra); March solennelle (dedicated to the law students); Hamlet (Overture-fantasy); Voyevoda (Symphonic ballad).
Vol.27. Vocal works with orchestra. Orchestra score.
Vol.28. Piano concerto, No.1, Op.23. Full score; Piano concerto, No.2, Op.44. Full score.
Vol.29. Concert fantasy, Op.56. Full score; Piano concerto, No.3, Op.75. Full score.
Vol.30A. Works for violin and orchestra. Full score.
Serenade melancholique, Op.26.
Waltz-scherzo, Op.34.
Violin concerto, Op.35.
Vol.30B. Works for violoncello and orchestra. Full score.
Variations on a rococo theme.
Pezzo capriccioso.
Andante cantabile.
Nocturne.
Vol.31. Complete chamber works. Score and parts.
Quartet in B "Unfinished".
Quartet No.1, Op.11.
Quartet No.2, Op.22.
Quartet No.3, Op.30.
Vol.32A. Trio, Op.50, for piano, violin, violoncello.
Vol.32B. Souvenir de Florence, Op.70. (Sextet for 2 violins, 2 violas, 2 violoncellos).
Vol.34. Oprichnik. Piano-vocal score.
Vol.35. Vakula the blacksmith. Piano-vocal score.
Vol.36. Eugen Onegin. Vocal score.
Vol.37. Maid of Orleans. Full score.
Vol.39. Cherevichki. (Les caprices d'Oxane). Vocal score.
Vol.40A–B. Charodeika. (The enchantress). Vocal score.
Vol.41. Pique dame. Vocal score.
Vol.42. Iolanthe. Vocal score.
Vol.43. Chorus works.
Vol.44–45. Songs.
Vol.46A. Piano concerto, No.1; Piano concerto, No.2. 2-piano reduction.
Vol.46B. Concert fantasy; Concerto No.3, Op.75. 2-piano reduction.
Vol.47. Symphony No.2. Piano, 4 hands.
Vol.49. Suites No.1, Op.43; No.2, Op.53; No.3, Op.55. Piano, 4 hands.
Vol.51A. Piano works: Theme and variations in A minor; Sonate in C sharp minor (Posthumous); 2 Pieces, Op.1; 3 Pieces, Op.2.
Vol.51B. Piano works: Waltz-caprice, Op.4; Romance, Op.5; Waltz-scherzo, Op.7; Capriccio, Op.8; 3 Pieces, Op.9. 2 Pieces, Op.10; 6 Pieces, Op.19; 6 Pieces on one theme, Op.21; 3 Transcriptions of romances; Potpourri from the opera "Voyevoda."
Vol.52. Piano works: The seasons, Op.37 bis (12 numbers); March; 21 Pieces of medium difficulty, Op.40; Children's album, Op.39 (24 numbers); Grand sonata, Op.37, in G major.
Vol.53. Piano works: 6 Pieces, Op.51; Impromptu-caprice; Dumka; Waltz-scherzo; Impromptu-march; 18 Pieces, Op.72; Aveu passione, Waltz (1st version of Op.40, No.9).
Vol.54. The nutcracker. Piano score.
Vol.55A. Violin works (violin and piano): Serenade melancholique, Op.26; Waltz-scherzo, Op.34; Concerto, Op.35; 3 Pieces, Op.42 (Meditation, Scherzo, and Melody); 2 Pieces (Humoresque, Op.10, No.2, and Andante from String quartet, Op.30).
Vol.55B. Works for violoncello and orchestra. Reduction for violoncello and piano.
Vol.56. Swan Lake. Complete piano score.
Vol.57. Sleeping beauty. Complete piano score transcribed by Siloti.
Vol.61. Arrangements and transcriptions of folk songs.
50 Russian folk songs (for piano, 4 hands).

Russian folk songs for voice and piano.
Children's songs on Russian and Ukrainian folk melodies.
Vol.62. Works completed by S. I. Taneyev.
Andante and finale, Op.79. Full score.
Andante and finale. 2-piano reduction.
Romeo and Juliet (Duet for tenor and soprano with orchestra).
Romeo and Juliet (Duet for soprano and tenor with voice and piano).
Impromptu (Momento lirico). Piano.

Literary writings and correspondence.
Vol.3B. Translations.
Vol.7. Letters.
Vol.8. Letters.
Vol.9. Letters.

TCHAIKOVSKIĬ, PETER ILICH, 1840–1893.
Ausgewählte Klavierwerke in drei Bänden. Hrsg. von Ftitz Weitzmann. Leipzig, C. F. Peters, n.d.
3v. (Edition Peters. No.4652–4654).
Contents:
Vol.1. Scherzo à la Russe; Capriccio; Thema und Variationen; Sechs Stücke über ein Thema; Doumka.
Vol.2. Romanze. Op.5; Valse; Scherzo. Op.7; Stücke aus Op.2, 9, 10, 19, 40; Werke ohne Opuszahl.
Vol.3. 14 Stücke aus Op.51 und 72.

TCHAIKOVSKIĬ, PETER ILICH, 1840–1893.
Werke für Klavier. Leipzig, C. F. Peters, 19? – .
3v. (Edition Peters. No.3066, 3781, 3782).
Contents:
Vol.1. Auswahl: Aus Op.2. Chant sans paroles; Op.5. Romance; Op.9. Polka de salon, Mazurka de salon; Op.10. Zwei Nocturnes, Humoresque; Op.37a. Barcarolle, Chant d'automne, Troïka, Noël; Op.40. Chanson triste, Chant sans paroles, Danse russe.
Vol.2. Op.37a. Die Jahreszeiten. (Niemann).
Vol.3. Op.39. Jugendalbum, 24 kleine Stücken. (Niemann).

Te Deum laudamus, *see* Plainsong and Mediaeval Music Society. Te Deum laudamus.

Teatro lirico espanol anterior al siglo XIX, *see* Pedrell, Felipe. Teatro lirico espanol anterior al siglo XIX.

TELEMANN, GEORG PHILIPP, 1681–1767.
. . . Musikalische Werke. Hrsg. im Auftrag der Gesellschaft für Musikforschung. Kassel und Basel, Bärenreiter-Verlag, 1950– .
v.1– .
Contents:
Vol.1. Zwölf methodische Sonaten für Querflöte (Violine und Basso Continuo). Hamburg 1728 und 1732. Score and part. 1950.
Vol.2. Der harmonische Gottesdienst. 72 Solokantaten für 1 Singstimme, 1 Instrument und Basso Continuo. Hamburg 1725/26. Teil I: Neujahr bis Reminiscere. Cantatas 1–15. Score and parts. 1953.
Vol.3. Der harmonische Gottesdienst. 72 Solokantaten für 1 Singstimme, 1 Instrument und Basso Continuo. Hamburg 1725/26. Teil II: Oculi bis 1.Pfingsttag. Cantatas 16–31. Score and parts. 1953.
Vol.4. Der harmonische Gottesdienst. Teil III. Cantatas 32–50. Score and parts. 1957.
Vol.5. Der harmonische Gottesdienst. Teil IV. Cantatas 51–72. Score and parts. 1957.
Vol.6. Kammermusik ohne Generalbass. Zwölf Fantasien für Querflöte. Zwölf Fantasien für Violine. 1735. Drei Konzerte für vier Violinen, C-dur, G-dur, D-dur. 1955.
Vol.7. Kammermusik ohne Generalbass. Sechs Sonaten für zwei Querflöten. Folge 1–2. 1955.
Vol.8. Kammermusik ohne Generalbass. Sechs Sonaten, Op.2 (1727) für zwei Querflöten oder Violinen. Sechs Sonaten im Kanon, Op.5 (1738) für zwei Querflöten oder Violinen. 1955.
Vol.9. Sechs Suiten für Querflöte, Violine und Basso Continuo. Score and parts. 1955.
Vol.10. Sechs ausgewählte Ouvertüren für Orchester mit vorwiegend programmatischen Überschriften. Hrsg. von Friedrich Noach. 1955.
Vol.11. Sechs Konzerte für Querflöte mit konzertierendem Cembalo, oder Querflöte mit konzertierendem Cembalo und Violoncello, oder Querflöte, Violine und Violoncello, oder Querflöte, Violine und Generalbass. Hrsg. von Joh. Philipp Hinnenthal. Score and parts. 1957.
Vol.12. Tafelmusik. Teil I. Hrsg. von Joh. Philipp Hinnenthal. 1959.
Vol.13. Tafelmusik. Teil II. Hrsg. von Joh. Philipp Hinnenthal. 1962.
Vol.14. Tafelmusik. Teil III. Hrsg. von Joh. Philipp Hinnenthal. 1963.
Vol.15. Lukaspassion 1728. Hrsg. von Hans Hörner und Martin Ruhnke. 1964.

Vol.18. Zwölf Pariser Quartette. Nr.1–6. Hrsg. von Walter Bergmann. 1965.
Vol.19. Zwölf Pariser Quartette. Nr.7–12; Hrsg. von Walter Bergmann. 1965.

TELEMANN, GEORG PHILIPP, 1681–1767.
. . . Zwölf leichte Choralvorspiele, für Orgel manualiter oder Klavier (Harmonium). Hrsg. von Hermann Keller. Leipzig, C. F. Peters, [cop.1936].
2p.L., 24p. (Edition Peters. No.4239).

Tenorista, *Don* Paolo, *see* Paolo Tenorista, *Don.*

Theatrical chansons of the 15th and early 16th centuries, *see* Brown, Howard Mayer. Theatrical chansons of the 15th and early 16th centuries.

Thibault, G., ed. Trois chansonniers français du XVe siècle, *see* [Droz, Eugénie]. Trois chansonniers français du XVe siècle.

THIBAUT, JEAN BAPTISTE, 1872–1937.
Monuments de la notation ekphonétique et neumatic de l'église latine. Exposé documentaire

des manuscrits de Corbie, St. Germain-des-Prés et de Pologne, conservés à la Bibliothèque Impériale de Saint-Pétersbourg. Par Jean-Baptiste Thibaut . . . Saint-Pétersbourg, [Impr. Kügelgen, Glitsch & Cie.], 1912.
xviip., 2L., [3]–104p., 1L. illus. (facsims.), XCIV pl. (376 facsim. on 47L.).

Thirteen keyboard sonatas of the 18th and 19th centuries, *see* Newman, William S. Thirteen keyboard sonatas of the 18th and 19th centuries.

THOURET, GEORG, 1855–1924. ed.
Musik am preussischen Hofe. Mit Genehmiging des Kaisers Wilhelm II aus dem Musikschätzen der Königl. Hausbibliothek zu Berlin, hrsg. von Georg Thouret. Leipzig, Breitkopf & Härtel, 1892/97– .
No.1– .
Contents:
No.1. Friedrich der Grosse. Arioso aus der Flöten-Sonate (Gm) für Harmonika und Pianoforte, bearb. von Waldemar Waege.
No.2. Quantz, Joh. Joachim. Arioso aus dem Flöten-Konzert (F) für Harmonika und Pianoforte, bearb. von Waldemar Waege.
No.3. Lieblingswalzer der Königin Luise von Preussen für grosse Orchester bearb. von C. Frese; für Infanteriemusik instrumentirt von C. Frese; für Pianoforte zu 4 Händen bearb. von Waldemar Waege; zu 2 Händen neu bearb. von Waldemar Waege.
No.4. Boccherini, Luigi. Pastorale, Menuett und Trio aus der Sinfonia (Cm) für Violine, Harmonika und Pianoforte, bearb. von Waldemar Waege.
No.5. Stamitz, Carl. Andantino aus der Symphonie (Es) für 2 Orchester, für Pianoforte, Violine und Violoncello, bearb. von Waldemar Waege; für Pianoforte zu 4 Händen bearb. von Waldemar Waege.
No.6. Quantz, Joh. Joachim. Arioso und Presto aus der Flöten-Sonate (D). Die Klavierbegleitung ausbearbeitet von Waldemar Waege.
No.7. Altpreussische Kriegslieder für 4 Männderstimmen bearb. von Carl te Peerdt. (No.1–3 ohne Begleitung. No.4–7 auch Begleitung).
No.8. Zwei altpreussische Kriegsmärsche. (No.1. Marsch des Regiments von Schönfeld; No.2. Walch. Marsch aus den Befreiungskriegen 1813–1815) neu instrumentirt von Carl Frese und Rud. Britzke für grosse Orchester; für Infanteriemusik.
No.9. Zwei altenglische Militärmärsche (No.1. Quick-March, "The Duke" of York's favourite; No.2. Marsch aus der Oper "The Siege of Belgrad" von Storace. 1798) neu instrumentirt von Carl Arnold und Otto Brinkmann für grosse Orchester; für Infanteriemusik; für Kavalleriemusik neu instrumentirt von Th. Kewitsch.
No.10. Zwei altenglische "short Troops" neu instrumentirt von Aug. Kalkbrenner und Adolph Reckzeh für grosse Orchester; für Infanteriemusik.
No.11. Himmel, Fr. Hr. Wiegenlied (zum Andenken an Kaiser Wilhelm der Grossen) für Orchester instrumentirt von Ad. Schinck und R. Britzke; für Infanteriemusik instrumentirt von R. Britzke; für Kavalleriemusik instrumentirt von A. Schinck.
No.12. Grosser Tusch und Fantaren beim Vorzeigen der Schilde aus der Musik zum Turnier auf dem Hoffeste "Der Zauber der weissen Rose" für Kavalleriemusik neu instrumentirt von Adolph Schinck.
No.13.
No.14. Musik auf dem Kostümball am 27. Februar 1897 im Königl. Schlosse zu Berlin. Klavierauszug der alten Märsche und Tänze nebst Tanzbeschreibungen.
No.15. Alter Reitermarsch "Prinz von Coburg" für 3 Trompeten und Pauken eingraviert von G. Thouret.
No.16. Altpreussischer Kavalleriemarsch "Backhoff-Kürassier" 1783, für Kavalleriemusik neu instrument, von E. Ruth.
No.17. Cavos. Preussischer Armeemarsch No.20 (im langsamen Schrift) für Infanteriemusik neu instrument, von Theodor Kewitsch; für Kavalleriemusik neu instrument, von Theodor Kewitsch.
No.18. Händel, G. Fr. Das grosse Halleluja aus "Messias" für Militärmusik bearb. und eingraviert von Theodor Kewitsch.
No.19.
No.20. Abendmusik. Ein Strauss alter Tänze. Klavierbearbeitet von Georg Thouret.

Three centuries of choral music: Renaissance to Baroque, *see* Engel, Lehman. Three centuries of choral music: Renaissance to Baroque.

Three plainsong masses from early manuscripts, *see* Plainsong and Mediaeval Music Society. Three plainsong masses from early manuscripts.

TINCTORIS, JOHANNES, ca.1435–1511.
Opera omnia, ed. by Fritz Feldmann. Rome, American Institute of Musicology, 1960– .
v.1– . (Corpus mensurabilis musicae. No.18).
Contents:
Vol.1. Mass dedicated to Ferdinand, King of Sicily and Aragon.

TISDALL, WILLIAM, 16th century.
Complete keyboard works, newly transcribed and ed. from The Fitzwilliam virginal book and The John Bull virginal book by Howard Ferguson. London, Stainer & Bell, [cop. 1958].
12p. (English keyboard music).
"The titles of nos.6 and 7 have been added by the editor . . . It is by no means certain they were composed by the Tisdall who wrote the pieces from the F.W.V.B."

TORCHI, LUIGI, 1858–1920. ed.
L'arte musicale in Italia. Pubblicazione nazionale delle più importanti opere musicali italiane

dal secolo XIV al XVIII, tratte da codici, antichi manoscritti ed edizioni primitive, scelte, transcritte in notazione moderna, messe in partitura, armonizate ed annotate da Luigi Torchi . . . Milano, Roma, [etc.], G. Ricordi & Co., [1897–1908?].
7v.
Contents:
Bd.1. Composizioni sacre e profane a più voci, secoli XIV, XV e XVI: Jacopo da Bologna, Alessandro Demophon, Francesco d'Ana, Bartolomeo Tromboncino, Giovanni Spataro, Costanzo Festa, Simon Ferrarese, Giuseppe Zarlino, Jan Gero, Francesco Corteccia, Domenico da Nola, Nicola Vicentino, Giovanni Animuccia, Baldassare Donato, Vincenzo Ruffo, Annibale Padovano, Constanzo Porta, Annibale Zoilo, Pietro Vinci, Alessandro Striggio, Claudio Merulo, Vincenzo Bell'Haver, Andrea Rota, Ascanio Trombetti.
Bd.2. Composizioni sacre e profane a più voci, secolo XVI: Gio. M. Nanini da Valerano, Bartolomeo Spontone, Giacomo Gastoldi, Andrea Gabrieli, Giovanni Gabrieli, Andrea e Giov. Gabrieli, Luca Marenzio, Orazio Vecchi, Benedetto Pallavicino, Giovanni Croce, Matteo Asola, Achille Falcone, Leone Leoni, Ruggero Giovanelli.
Bd.3. Composizioni per organo e cembalo, secoli XVI, XVII e XVIII: Gerolamo Cavazzoni, Antonio Valento, Vincenzo Pellegrini, Bertoldo Sperindio, Andrea Gabrieli, Annibale Padovano, Claudio Merulo, Giovanni Gabrieli, Giovan Paolo Cima, Ascanio Majone, Luzzasco Luzzaschi, Costanzo Antegnati, Gabriel Fatorini, Girolamo Diruta, Antonio Romanini, Paolo Quagliati, Vincenzo Bell'Haver, Gioseffo Guami, Agostino Soderini, Giovanni Cavaccio, Fabrizio Fontana, Girolamo Frescobaldi, Ercole Pasquini, Bernardo Pasquini, Michelangelo Rossi, Pollaroli, Tarquinio Merula, Adriano Banchieri, Gio. Maria Trabaci, Domenico Zipoli, Floriano Arresti, Giuseppe Bencini, Giovan Maria Casini, Nicolo Porpora, Bernardo Sabadini.
Bd.4. Composizioni a più voci, secolo XVII: Principe Gesualdo di Venosa, Marco da Gagliano, Pietro Eredia, Claudio Monteverdi, Gaspare Torelli, Orazio Vecchi, Adriano Banchieri.
Bd.5. Composizioni ad una e più voci, secolo XVII: Giacomo Carissimi, Francesco Nigetti, Stefano Landi, Jacopo Peri, Virgilio Mazzocchi, Orazio dell'Arpa, Autore anonimo sel seçolo XVII, Luigi Rossi, Carlo Mannelli, Francesca Caccini, Alessandro Costantini, Carlo Caprioli, Giacomo Carissimi, Alessandro Scarlatti.
Bd.6. La musica scenica, secolo XVII: Jacopo Peri, Claudio Monteverdi.
Bd.7. Musica istrumentale, secolo XVII: Biagio Marini, Gio. Battista Fontana, Martino Pesenti, Andr. Falconiero, Gio. Battista Vitali, Gio. Battista Bassani, Marco Uccellinini.

Torner, Eduardo Martínez, *see* Martínez Torner, Eduardo.

Toulouze, Michel. L'art et instruction de bien dancer, *see* The Wellesley edition. No.6.

Tournai Mass, *see* Catholic Church, Roman. Liturgy and ritual. Missal. Missa Tornacensis.

Transcriptions of chansons for keyboard, *see* Attaingnant, Pierre. Transcriptions of chansons for keyboard.

A treasury of American song, *see* Downes, Olin. A treasury of American song.

A treasury of early music, *see* Parrish, Carl. A treasury of early music.

Treasury of early organ music, *see* Biggs, Edward Power. Treasury of early organ music.

A treasury of shorter organ classics, *see* Biggs, Edward Power. A treasury of shorter organ classics.

Treize livres de motets, *see* Attaingnant, Pierre. Treize livres de motets.

Le trésor d'Orphée, *see* Francisque, Antoine. Le trésor d'Orphée.

Trésor de musique byzantine, *see* Wellesz, Egon. Trésor de musique byzantine.

Le trésor des pianistes, *see* Farrenc, Jacques Hippolyte Aristide. Le trésor des pianistes.

Trésor musical, *see* Maldéghem, Robert Jullien van. Trésor musical.

Trio-Sonaten alter Meister für 2 Violinen und Violoncello, *see* Moffat, Alfred Edward. Trio-Sonaten alter Meister für 2 Violinen und Violoncello.

THE TRIUMPHS OF ORIANA. 1601. [i.e., 1603].
A reprint by William Hawes appeared in London in 1814.
Between Aug. 1905 and Oct. 1907, Novello & Co., London, published the first 21 numbers as No.1–21 of "The Oriana," each as a separate publication. The editor was Lionel Benson.
Contents:
Michael Este. Hence stars, a 5 (printed at the back of the dedication, with a note explaining that it was sent in too late for inclusion in the proper place).
Daniel Norcome. With angel's face, a 5.
John Mundy. Lightly she tripped, a 5.
Ellis Gibbons. Long live fair Oriana, a 5.
John Benet. All creatures now are merry-minded, a 5.
John Hilton. Fair Oriana, beauty's queen, a 5.
George Marson. The nymphs and shepherds danced Lavolto's, a 5.
Richard Carlton. Calm was the air, a 5.
John Holmes. Thus Bonny-boots, a 5.
Richard Nicolson. Sing shepherds all, a 5.

Thomas Tomkins. The fauns and satyrs tripping, a 5.
Michael Cavendish. Come gentle swains, a 5.
William Cobbold. The wreaths of rose and laurel, a 5.
Thomas Morley. Arise, awake, a 5.
John Farmer. Fair nymphs, a 6.
John Wilbye. The Lady Oriana, a 6.
Thomas Hunt. Hark, did ye ever hear so sweet a singing? a 6.
Thomas Weelkes. As Vesta was from Latmos hill descending, a 6.
John Milton. Fair Orian, a 6.
Ellis Gibbons. Round about her chariot, a 6.
G. Kirbye. Bright Phoebus, a 6. (With angel's face).
Robert Jones. Fair Oriana, a 6.
John Lisley. Fair Citherea, a 6.
Thomas Morley. Hard by a crystal fountain, a 6.
Edward Johnson. Come blessed bird, a 6.
Giovanni Croce. Hard by a crystal fountain, a 6.
Thomas Bateson. When Oriana walked to take the air, a 6. (First printed in Bateson's first set, in 1604).
Francis Pilkington. When Oriana walked to take the air, a 5. (First printed in Pilkington's first set, 1613).
Thomas Bateson. Hark, hear you not? (Oriana's farewell), a 5. (First printed in Bateson's first set, in 1604).

Trois chansonniers français du XVe siècle, *see* [Droz, Eugénie]. Trois chansonniers français du XVe siècle.

Tübingen. Universität. Musik-Institut, *see* Denkmäler der Tonkunst in Württemberg.

TUCHER, GOTTLIEB, *Freiherr von*, 1798–1877. ed.
Kirchengesänge der berühmtesten älteren italienischen Meister. Wien, 1827.
2v.
Contains compositions by Anerio, Nanino, Palestrina, and Vittoria.

TUCHER, GOTTLIEB, *Freiherr von*. ed.
Schatz des evangelischen Kirchengesänges. 1848.
2v.

TUDOR CHURCH MUSIC. Editorial Committee: P. C. Buck, A. Ramsbotham, E. H. Fellowes, R. R. Terry (Bd.1–3), S. Townsend Warner. London, New York, Pub. for the Carnegie United Kingdom Trust by the Oxford University Press, 1922–29. [v.1, 1923].
10v. port., facsims.
Contents:
Vol.1. John Taverner. Part I. 1923.
Vol.2. William Byrd: English church music. Part I. 1922.
Vol.3. John Taverner. Part II. 1924.
Vol.4. Orlando Gibbons. 1925.
Vol.5. Robert White. 1926.
Vol.6. Thomas Tallis. 1928.
Vol.7. William Byrd: Gradualia I, II. 1927.
Vol.8. Thomas Tomkins. Part I: Services. 1928.
Vol.9. William Byrd: Masses, cantiones, and motets. 1928.
Vol.10. Hugh Aston; John Marbeck; Osbert Parsley. 1929.

TUDOR CHURCH MUSIC. Appendix with supplementary notes by Edmond H. Fellowes. London, New York, Oxford University Press, 1948.
55p.
"Additional manuscripts": p.5–12.
Music supplements to Vol.2–6, 9–10: p.32–55.

THE TUDOR EDITION OF OLD MUSIC, transcribed and ed. by Gerald M. Cooper. Ser.A and B. London, J. & W. Chester, Ltd., cop.1924.
4 nos.
Contents:
Ser.A.
No.1. Dowland. Lachrimae. 1924.
Ser.B.
No.1. Greaves, T. 3 Songs. 5 parts. cop.1924.
No.2. Caccini, G. 2 Songs. 2 parts. cop.1924.
No.3. Jones, R. 4 Duets. 2 parts. cop.1924.

TURIN. BIBLIOTECA NAZIONALE. Mss. (J.II.9).
The Cypriot-French repertory of the Manuscript Torino, Biblioteca Nazionale, J.II.9. Ed. by Richard H. Hoppin. Rome, American Institute of Musicology, 1960–63.
4v. facsims. (Corpus mensurabilis musicae. No.21).
Transcriptions of the music into modern notation.
Contents:
Vol.1. Polyphonic mass movements. 1960.
Vol.2. Motets. 1961.
Vol.3. Ballades. 1963.
Vol.4. Virelais and rondeaux. 1963.

Twelve Franco-Flemish masses of the early 16th century, *see* Stein, Edwin. Twelve Franco-Flemish masses of the early 16th century.

Twenty-five pieces for keyed instruments from Benjamin Cosyn's Virginal book, *see* Fuller-Maitland, John Alexander. Twenty-five pieces for keyed instruments from Benjamin Cosyn's Virginal book.

Twenty-one Old English compositions of the 16th and 17th centuries, *see* Glyn, Margaret Henrietta. Twenty-one Old English compositions of the 16th and 17th centuries.

Twittenhoff, W., ed. Musica practica, *see* Musica practica.

U.N.E.S.C.O. Conseil International de la Musique. Classici italiani della musica, *see* Classici italiani della musica.

Uitgave van oudere Noord-Nederlandsche meesterwerken, *see* Vereniging voor Nederlandsche Muziekgeschiedenis.

The use of plainsong. Cook, Edgar Thomas, *see* Plainsong and Mediaeval Music Society. Cook, Edgar Thomas. The use of plainsong.

Vaet, Jacobus, 1529–1567. Sämtliche Werke, *see* Denkmäler der Tonkunst in Österreich. Vol.98, 100, 103/104, 108/109.

VAN, GUILLAUME DE. ed.
Les monuments de l'Ars nova. La musique polyphonique de 1320 à 1400 environ, transcrite par Guillaume de Van. Fasc.I. Paris, Éditions de l'Oiseau Lyre, [cop.1938].
1 v. (vi p., 1L., 41p.).
No more published.
Contents:
I. Les morceaux liturgiques de P [Paris, Bib. Nat. ital. 568].
1. Ser Gherardello. Gloria.
2. Bartolino da Padova. Credo.
3. Lorenzo da Firenze. Sanctus.
4. Ser Gherardello. Agnus Dei.
5. Benedicamus Domino. (Anonymous).
II. Les morceaux liturgiques de Pad_1 et Pad_2 [Padua, Bib. dell' Univ. 1475 et 687].
6. Gratiosus de Padua. Gloria.
7. Gratiosus de Padua. Sanctus.
8. Gloria "Clementie pax baiula." (Anonymous).

VAN, GUILLAUME DE. ed.
Les monuments de l'Ars nova . . . transcrite par Guillaume de Van. Paris, Éditions de l'Oiseau Lyre, [1938].
6 nos.
Published in modern notation to accompany Oiseau Lyre recordings of the music.
Contents:
Guillaume de Machaut. Double hoquet.
Jacopo de Bologna. Lux purpurata radiis.
A vous, vierge de doucour.
Or sus, vour dormès trop.
Jacopo da Bologna. Non al suo amante.
Matheus de Perusio. Gloria in excelsis.

Van den Borren, Charles, *see* Borren, Charles van den.

Van Duyse, Florimond, *see* Duyse, Florimond van.

Van Elewyck, Xavier Victor Fidèle, *Chevalier, see* Elewyck, Xavier Victor Fidèle, *Chevalier*, van.

Van Maldéghem, Robert Jullien, *see* Maldéghem, Robert Jullien van.

Van Ockeghem tot Sweelinck, *see* Smijers, Albert. Van Ockeghem tot Sweelinck.

VEGA CARPIO, LOPE FÉLIX DE, 1562–1635.
Treinta canciones de Lope de Vega, puestas in música por Guerrero, Orlando de Lasso, Palomares, Romero, Compañy, etc., y transcritas por Jesús Bal. Con unas páginas inéditas de Ramón Menéndez Pidal y Juan Ramón Jiménez. (1635–1935) . . . Madrid, [Residencia de Estudiantes], 1935.
xi p., 2L., 109p., 1L., xvii–xxvi, [2] p. incl. illus., ports., facsims.
"Residencia, revista de la Residencia de Estudiantes. Número extraordinario en homenaje a Lope."
"Edicion de 2.100 ejemplares, 100 en papel especial numerados."
For reduced chorus or solo ensemble. One of the parts may be taken by viola or violoncello (cf.p.101).
Entre dos àlamos verdos, por Juan Blas de Castro; Entre dos mansos arroyos, por Mateo Romero, "Maestro capitan"; Gigante cristalino, anónimo; Si tus penas no pruebo, Jesús mío, por Francisco Guerrero; Hermosas alamedas, anónimo; En el más soberbío monte, anónimo; En dos partes del cielo, por Compañy; Cómo retumban los remos! anónimo; En el campo florido, por Juan de Palomares; En una playa amena, por Mateo Romero, "Maestro capitan"; Al humilde Manzanares, anónimo; En esta larga ausencia, anónimo; Mañanicas Floridas, anónimo; De pechos sobre una torre, anónimo; Encontrándose dos arroyuelos, anónimo; La verde primavera, anónimo; A quién contaré mis Quejas? por Mateo Romero, "Maestro capitan"; Ay amargas soledades! anónimo; Al son de los arroyuelos, por Joseph Marin; Diferencias sobre el canto llano del caballero, por Antonio de Cabezón; Siendo de amor Susana requerida, por Orlando de Lasso; Otras veces me habéis visto, anónimo; Rio de Sevilla, anónimo; Oh qué bien que baila Gil! anónimo; Madre, la mi madre, anónimo; Madre, la mi madre, por Pedro Rimonte; Molinillo que muelas amores, por Juan del Vado; Arrojóme las naranjicas, anónimo; Por la puente, Juana, anónimo; Por la puente, Juana, por Laserna; Comentario del transcriptor.

Verbonnet, Johannes Ghiselin, *see* Ghiselin-Verbonnet, Johannes.

VERDELOT, PHILIPPE, d. ca.1565.
Opera omnia. Edidit Anne Marie Bragard. [n.p.]. American Institute of Musicology, 1966– .
v.1– . (Corpus mensurabilis musicae. No.28).

Vereeniging voor Muziekgeschiedenis te Antwerpen, *see* Monumenta musicae belgicae.

Vereeniging voor Nederlandsche Muziekgeschiedenis, *see* Vereniging voor Nederlandsche Muziekgeschiedenis.

VEREIN SCHWEIZERISCHER TONKÜNSTLER.
. . . Musikalische Werke schweizerischer Komponisten des XVI., XVII. und XVIII. Jahrhunderts, veröffentlicht unter der Leitung von Karl Nef. Genève, Édition Henn, cop. 1927–34.
5 nos.
Contains music.
Title and text in French and German; French title reads: Oeuvres musicales de compositeurs suisses des XVIe, XVIIe et XVIIIe siècles (with slight variations. Some numbers have title in French only).
At head of title: Édition nationale suisse publiée par l'Association des Musiciens Suisses (slight variations).
Contents:

Heft 1. Merian, W., ed. Geistliche Werke des XVI. Jahrhunderts. 1927.
Heft 2. Fritz, G. Sonata, violin and piano, Op.2, No.4; Albicastro, H. Sonata, violin and piano, Op.5, No.2–3. 1931.
Heft 3. Wannenmacher, J. Psaumes et cantiques; Alderinus. Chöre. Hrsg. von A. Geering. 1934.
Heft 4. Gletle, J. M. Werke.
Heft 5. Albicastro, H. Konzerte. Hrsg. von Zulauf.

VERENIGING VOOR NEDERLANDSCHE MUZIEKGESCHIEDENIS. Uitgave. [deel] 1–45. Amsterdam, G. Alsbach & Co., [etc., etc.], 1869–1938, 1955– .
v.1– . ports., facsims.
No.1–18 were published as: Maatschapij tot bevordering der toonkunst. Uitgave van oudere Noord-Nederlandsche meesterwerken.
Title varies: Vol.1–20, 1869–1897, Uitgave van oudere Noord-Nederlandsche meesterwerken.
Vol.18–31 issued by the society under an earlier name: Vereeniging voor Noord-Nederlands Muziekgeschiedenis; Vol.1–17, 32– , issued under the old spelling of the name: Vereeniging voor Nederlandsche Muziekgeschiedenis.
Contents:
No.1. Sweelinck's Regina coeli. (ed. H. A. Viotta, 1869).
No.2. Old Dutch songs, from the lute-book of Adrianus Valerius. (ed. A. D. Loman, 1871).
No.3. Organ compositions, by Sweelinck and Scheidt. (ed. R. Eitner, 1871).
No.4. 12 Geuzeliedjes, songs of the Gueux during the Spanish oppression. (ed. A. D. Loman, 1872).
No.5. 3 Madrigals, by Schuijt, and 2 Chansons by Sweelinck. (ed. R. Eitner, 1873).
No.6. 8 Psalms by Sweelinck (ed. R. Eitner), with Life by F. H. L. Tiedeman. (1876).
No.7. Chanson by Sweelinck. (ed. R. Eitner, 1877).
No.8. Selections from Johannes Wanning's LII Sententiae. (ed. R. Eitner, 1878).
No.9. Mass, Fortuna desperata, by Jacob Obrecht. (ed. R. Eitner, 1880).
No.10. Old Dutch dances arranged for piano (4 hands) by J. C. M. van Reimsdijk. (1882).
No.11. Const. Huygens. Correspondance et oeuvres musicales. Pathodia sacra et profana. (ed. W. J. A. Jonckbloet and J. P. N. Land). 1882.
No.12. 6 Psalms by Sweelinck, in 4 parts. (ed. R. Eitner, 1884).
No.13. J. A. Reinken's Hortus musicus. (ed. J. C. M. van Riemsdijk, 1886).
No.14. J. A. Reinken. Partite diverse sopra l'aria: Schweiget mir von Weiber nehmen. (1887).
(Without No.) J. P. Sweelinck. O sacrum convivium, 5-part motet.
No.15. J. P. Sweelinck. Cantio sacra, Hodie Christus natus est, 5 parts.
No.16. 24 Songs of the 15th and 16th centuries, for 1 voice with accompaniment. (ed. J. C. M. van Riemsdijk). 1890.
No.17. J. P. Sweelinck's Psalm CL, for 8 voices.
No.18. Obrecht's Passio Domini (St. Matthew), for 4 voices.
No.19. A. van Noordt's Tabulaturbuch. Psalms and fantasias. (1659). (ed. Max Seiffert).
No.20. Old Dutch boerenliedjes and contradanses, for violin with piano accompaniment. (ed. Julius Röntgen), first set.
No.21. Marches used in Holland during the War of the Spanish Succession, 1702–1713, collected by J. W. Enschedé, arranged for piano duet by A. Averkamp.
No.22. 50 Psalms by Cornelis Boskoop (1568). (ed. Max Seiffert).
No.23. Old Dutch boerenliedjes and contradanses (ed. piano and violin by Julius Röntgen), second set.
No.24. 6-part madrigals by Jan Tollius (1597). (ed. Max Seiffert).
No.25. Netherlandish dances of the 16th century (arranged for piano duet by J. Röntgen), first set.
No.26. A Dutch music book. (1572). (ed. Fl. van H. Duyse).
No.27. Netherlandish dances of the 16th century (arranged for piano duet by J. Röntgen), second set.
No.28. Scherzi musicali per la viola da gamba, by Johan Schenk. (ed. by Dr. Hugo Leichentritt).
No.29. First music-book of Tielman (Tylman) Susato after the edition of 1551. (ed. Fl. van Duyse).
No.30. 25 3-voiced old Dutch songs. 15th century. (ed. Julius Wolf).
No.31. 2 Sonatas for violin with piano accompaniment, by Pietro Locatelli da Bergamo. (ed. Julius Röntgen).
No.32. Compositioni musicali per il cembalo. Divisi in due parti di Corrado Federigo Hurlebusch. (ed. Max Seiffert).
No.33. Old Dutch boerenliedjes and contradanses (ed. Julius Röntgen), third and fourth sets, cf. No.20, 23.
No.34. Orchestral compositions by Dutch masters of the early 17th century. "Paduanen" and "Galliarden" by Melchior Borchgreving, Benedictus Grep, and Nicolaus Gistow. (ed. H. F. Wirth).
No.35. Missa super benedicta, by Adrian Willaert, for 5-voiced mixed choir. (ed. Ant. Averkamp).
No.36. Old Dutch boerenliedjes and contradanses (ed. J. Röntgen), fifth set.
No.37. Old Dutch clavier music from the Music-book of Anna Maria van Eyl. (1671). (ed. Julius Röntgen).
No.38. Missa ad modulum benedicta. (6v.); Philippo de Monte. (ed. A. Smijers). 1920.
No.39. Wat leeren ons de schilderijen en prenten der zestiende eeuw over de instrumentale begelieding van den zang en den oorsprong van de muziekgravure, ed. by Max Seiffert. 1920.
No.40. Lente-film composities Nederlandsche boerendansen . . . by J. Röntgen. 1923.
No.41. Hillendaal, P. 4 Sonates voor violoncel en becijferde bas . . . 1926.
No.42. I. von Vondels Kruisbergh, op musijck gebraght door Cornelis Padbrué. 1931.

No.43. Reeser, Eduard, ed. De muzikale handschriften van Alphons Diepenbrock. 1933.
No.44. Reeser, Eduard, ed. 3 Oud-Nederlandsche motetten. (Jacob Obrecht, Josquin des Prez, Jacobus Clemens non Papa). 1936.
No.45. Schuyt, Cornelis. Vijfstemmige madrigalen. Bunden 1–2. (A. Smijers). 1938.
No.46. 6 Suites voor klavier van Rynoldus Popma van Oevering. (1692–1782). Op.1. (Ed. H. B. Buys). 1955.
No.47. Sweelinck, Jan Pieter. Supplement zu Teil I der Gesamtausgabe Werke für Orgel und Cembalo.

Vereniging voor Nederlandse Muziekgeschiedenis, *see* Musica antiqua batava; Smijers, Albert. Van Ockeghem tot Sweelinck.

Veröffentlichungen. Berlin. Institut für Musikforschung, *see* Berlin. Institut für Musikforschung. Veröffentlichungen.

Veröffentlichungen der Beethovenhauses Bonn, *see* Beethoven, Ludwig van. Veröffentlichungen der Beethovenhauses Bonn.

Veröffentlichungen der Händel-Gesellschaft, *see* Händel, Georg Friedrich. Veröffentlichungen der Händel-Gesellschaft.

Veröffentlichungen der Musik-Bibliothek Paul Hirsch, *see* Hirsch, Paul Adolf. Veröffentlichungen der Musik-Bibliothek Paul Hirsch.

Veröffentlichungen der neuen Bachgesellschaft, *see* Bach, Johann Sebastian. Veröffentlichungen der neuen Bachgesellschaft.

Veröffentlichungen der Staatlichen Akademie für Kirchen- und Schulmusik, *see* Staatliche Akademie für Kirchen- und Schulmusik. Berlin. Veröffentlichungen.

Veröffentlichungen des Fürstlichen Institutes für Musikwissenschaftliche Forschung. Bückeburg, *see* Fürstliches Institut für Musikwissenschaftliche Forschung. Bückeburg. Veröffentlichungen.

Veröffentlichungen des Kirchenmusikalischen Institutes des Evangelisch-Lutherischen Landeskirche in Sachsen am Landeskonservatorium der Musik, Leipzig, *see* Kirchenmusikalisches Institut der Evangelisch-Lutherischen Landeskirche in Sachsen am Landeskonservatorium der Musik, Leipzig. Veröffentlichungen.

VICENTINO, NICOLA, 1511–1572.
Collected works, ed. by Henry W. Kaufmann. Rome, American Institute of Musicology, 1963.
163p. (Corpus mensurabilis musicae. No.26).
Contains 5-voice madrigals of 1546, 5-voice madrigals of 1572, a 7-voice Dialogo, a Capitolo de la Passione di Christo, a 3-voice sonnet, a 6-voice sonnet, a 6-voice motet, an incomplete motet, and the Quintus of the Fourth book of 5-voice motets of 1571.

VICTORIA, TOMÁS LUIS DE, d.1611.
Thomas Ludovici Victoria Abulensis Opera omnia, ex antiquissimus iisdemque rarissimus, hactenus cognitis editionibus in unum collecta, atque adnotationibus, tum bibliographicis, tum interpretatoriis ornata a Philippo Pedrell. Leipzig, Breitkopf & Härtel, 1902–13.
8v.
Music in score. Latin words.
Contents:
Bd.1. Motetten.
Bd.2. Messen, 1. Buch.
Bd.3. Magnificat und Canticum Simeonis.
Bd.4. Messen, 2. Buch.
Bd.5. Hymnen.
Bd.6. Messen, 3. Buch.
Bd.7. Psalmi; Antiphonae Marianae; Antiphonae; Asperges me et Vidi aquam; Sequentiae; Litaniae de B. Virgine.
Bd.8. Documenta biographica et bibliographica; Appendicis; Cantiones sacrae ex collectionibus non impressis et aliè.

VICTORIA, TOMÁS LUIS DE, d.1611.
Thomas Ludovici Victoria Abulensis Opera omnia. Reprint. Ridgewood, N. J., Gregg Press, Inc., 1965.

VILLANCICOS DE DIUERSOS AUTORES.
Cancionero de Upsala. Introducción, notas y commentarios de Rafael Mitjana. Transcripción musical en notación moderna de Jesús Bal y Gay. Con un estudio sobre "El villancico polifónico" de Isabel Pope. [Mexico], El Colegio de México, [1944].
2p.L., 7–71p., 1L., 155, [1]p., 1L.
With reduced reproduction of original title page (Venetiis 1556) on cover.
"Edición Mitjana, Upsala, 1909. Primera edición moderna completa, 1944."
"Música" (p.1–152); 2–5 voices, with Spanish, Catalan, or Gallegan words.
"Colecciones de poesía con música polifónica de autores españoles entre los siglos XV y XVII": p.11.

Vingt suites d'orchestre du XVIIe siècle français, *see* Écorcheville, Jules Armand Joseph. Vingt suites d'orchestre du XVIIe siècle français.

VIVALDI, ANTONIO, ca.1675–1743.
Le opere di Antonio Vivaldi. Rome, Edizioni Ricordi, 1947– .
v.1– . (Istituto Italiano Antonio Vivaldi. Direzione artistica di Gian Francesco Malipiero).
General plan ("F." stands for Antonio Fanna who made listing used; "n." stands for number):
F.I. Concerti per violino.
F.II. Concerti per viola.
F.III. Concerti per violoncello.
F.IV. Concerti per violino con altri archi solisti.
F.V. Concerti per mandolino.
F.VI. Concerti per flauto.
F.VII. Concerti per oboe.
F.VIII. Concerti per fagotto.
F.IX. Concerti per tromba.

F.X. Concerti per corno.
F.XI. Concerti per archi.
F.XII. Concerti per complessi vari.
F.XIII. Sonate per violino.
F.XIV. Sonate per violoncello.
F.XV. Sonate per fiati.
F.XVI. Sonate per complesse vari.
Contents:
Vol.1.
Tomo 1. Concerto in Si ♭ maggiore per violino, archi e cembalo. (F.I, n.1). 1947.
Tomo 2. Concerto in Re minore per oboe, archi e cembalo. (F.VII, n.1). 1947.
Tomo 3. Concerto in Do maggiore per 2 oboi, 2 clarinetti, archi e cembalo. (F.XII, n.1). 1947.
Tomo 4. Concerto in Do minore per violino, archi e cembalo. (F.I, n.2). Il sospetto. 1947.
Tomo 5. Concerto in La maggiore per archi e cembalo. (F.XI, n.1). 1947.
Tomo 6. Concerto in Fa maggiore per archi e cembalo (F.XI, n.2). 1947.
Tomo 7. Concerto in Si ♭ maggiore per archi e cembalo. (F.XI, n.3). 1947.
Tomo 8. Concerto in La maggiore per archi e cembalo. (F.XI, n.4). 1947.
Tomo 9. Concerto in Si ♭ maggiore per archi e cembalo. (F.XI, n.5). 1947.
Tomo 10. Concerto in Do maggiore per 2 oboi, 2 clarinetti, archi e cembalo. (F.XII, n.2). 1947.
Tomo 11. Concerto in Sol minore per archi e cembalo. (F.XI, n.6). 1947.
Tomo 12. Concerto in Si ♭ maggiore per fagotto, archi e cembalo. La notte. (F.VIII, n.1). 1947.

Vol.2.
Tomo 13. Concerto in Do maggiore per violino, archi e cembalo. (F.I, n.3). 1947.
Tomo 14. Concerto in Fa maggiore per oboe, archi e cembalo. (F.VII, n.2). 1947.
Tomo 15. Concerto in Mi maggiore per violino e archi. Il riposo. (F.I, n.4). 1947.
Tomo 16. Concerto in La maggiore per violino, archi e cembalo (F.I, n.5). 1947.
Tomo 17. Sonata in Sol maggiore per 2 violini e basso continuo. (F.XIII, n.1). 1947.
Tomo 18. Sonata in La minore per flauto, fagotto e basso continuo. (F.XV, n.1). 1947.
Tomo 19. Concerto in Do minore per violoncello, archi e cembalo. (F.III, n.1). 1947.
Tomo 20. Sonata in Do minore per violino, violoncello e basso continuo. (F.XVI, n.1). 1947.
Tomo 21. Sonata A 4 in Mi ♭ maggiore per 2 violini, viola e basso continuo. Al santo sepolcro. (F.XVI, n.2). 1947.
Tomo 22. Sinfonia in Si minore per archi. Al santo sepolcro. (F.XI, n.7). 1947.
Tomo 23. Concerto in Sol minore per flauto, oboe e fagotto. (F.XII, n.4). 1947.
Tomo 24. Concerto in Si ♭ maggiore per 2 violini e basso continuo. (F.XIII, n.2). 1947.
Tomo 25. Concerto in Sol minore. Per l'orchestra di Dresda, per violino, 2 flauti, 2 oboi, 2 fagotti, archi e cembalo. (F.XII, n.3). 1947.

Vol.3.
Tomo 26. Concerto in Sol maggiore per 2 violini, 2 violoncelli, archi e cembalo. (F.IV, n.1). 1949.
Tomo 27. Concerto in Sol maggiore per 2 violini, archi e cembalo. (F.I, n.6). 1949.
Tomo 28. Concerto in La minore per fagotto, archi e cembalo. (F.VIII, n.2). 1949.
Tomo 29. Concerto in Mi maggiore per violino, archi e cembalo. (F.I, n.7). 1949.
Tomo 30. Concerto in Do minore per archi e cembalo. (F.XI, n.8). 1949.
Tomo 31. Concerto in Re maggiore per violino, archi e cembalo. (F.I, n.8). 1949.
Tomo 32. Concerto in Do minore per archi e cembalo. (F.XI, n.9). 1949.
Tomo 33. Concerto in Sol minore per flauto, fagotto, archi e cembalo. La notte. (F.XII, n.5). 1949.
Tomo 34. Concerto in Do maggiore per fagotto, archi e cembalo. (F.VIII, n.3). 1949.
Tomo 35. Concerto in Si ♭ maggiore per violino, violoncello, archi e cembalo. (F.IV, n.2). 1949.
Tomo 36. Concerto in Re minore per archi e cembalo. Madrigalesco. (F.XI, n.10). 1949.
Tomo 37. Concerto in Re maggiore per violino, archi e cembalo. L'inquietudine. (F.I, n.10). 1949.

Vol.4.
Tomo 38. Concerto in Mi ♭ maggiore per violino, archi e cembalo. (F.I, n.9). 1949.
Tomo 39. Concerto in Re maggiore per flauto, violino, fagotto o violoncello. (F.XII, n.7). 1949.
Tomo 40. Concerto in Sol minore per flauto, oboe, violino, fagotto e basso continuo. (F.XII, n.6). 1949.
Tomo 41. Concerto in Sol minore per flauto, violino, fagotto e basso continuo. (F.XII, n.8). 1949.
Tomo 42. Concerto in Re maggiore per flauto, oboe, violino, fagotto e basso continuo. Del gardellino. (F.XII, n.9). 1949.
Tomo 43. Concerto in Fa maggiore per 2 oboi, fagotto, 2 corni, violino, archi e cembalo. (F.XII, n.10). 1949.
Tomo 44. Concerto in La minore per flauto, 2 violini e basso continuo. (F.XII, n.11). 1949.
Tomo 45. Concerto in Re minore per violino "senza cantin," archi e cembalo. (F.I, n.11). 1949.
Tomo 46. Concerto in Fa maggiore per flauto, archi e cembalo. (F.VI, n.1). 1949.
Tomo 47. Concerto in Do maggiore per fagotto, archi e cembalo. (F.VIII, n.4). 1949.
Tomo 48. Concerto in Do minore per 2 violini, archi e cembalo. (F.I, n.12). 1949.
Tomo 49. Concerto in Sol maggiore per archi e cembalo, Alla rustica. (F.XI, n.11). 1949.
Tomo 50. Concerto in Si ♭ maggiore per archi e cembalo. (F.XI, n.12). 1949.

Vol.5.
Tomo 51. Concerto funebre in Si ♭ maggiore

per oboe, corno inglese, violino, 2 viole, violoncello, archi e cembalo. (F.XII, n.12). 1949.
Tomo 52. Concerto in Sol maggiore per flauto, oboe, violino, fagotto e basso continuo. (F.XII, n.13). 1949.
Tomo 53. Concerto in Do maggiore per violino, 2 violoncelli, archi e cembalo. (F.IV, n.3). 1949.
Tomo 54. Concerto in Do maggiore per 2 flauti, 2 oboi, 2 clarinetti, fagotto, 2 violini, archi e cembalo. Per la solennita' di S. Lorenzo. (F.XII, n.14). 1949.
Tomo 55. Concerto in Do maggiore per violino, archi "in due cori" e 2 cembali. Per la SS. Assunzione di Maria Vergine. (F.I, n.13). 1949.
Tomo 56. Concerto in Mi minore per archi e cembalo. (F.XI, n.13). 1949.
Tomo 57. Sonate in Fa maggiore per 2 violini e basso continuo. (F.XIII, n.3). 1949.
Tomo 58. Sonata in Fa maggiore per 2 violini e basso continuo. (F.XIII, n.4). 1949.
Tomo 59. Concerto in Fa maggiore per archi e cembalo. (F.XI, n.14). 1949.
Tomo 60. Concerto in Do minore per 2 violini, archi e cembalo. (F.I, n.14). 1949.
Tomo 61. Concerto in Sol minore per 2 violoncelli, archi e cembalo. (F.III, n.2). 1949.
Tomo 62. Concerto in Re maggiore per 2 violini, liuto e basso continuo. (F.XII, n.15). 1949.

Vol.6.
Tomo 63. Trio in Do maggiore per violino, liuto e basso continuo. (F.XVI, n.3). 1949.
Tomo 64. Concerto in Si ♭ maggiore per violino, archi e cembalo. (F.I, n.15). 1949.
Tomo 65. Concerto in Sol minore per violino, archi e cembalo. (F.I, n.16). 1949.
Tomo 66. Concerto in Fa maggiore per violino, archi e cembalo. (F.I, n.17). 1949.
Tomo 67. Concerto in Re minore per fagotto, archi e cembalo. (F.VIII, n.5). 1949.
Tomo 68. Concerto in Re maggiore per violino, archi e cembalo. (F.I, n.18). 1949.
Tomo 69. Concerto in Re maggiore per violino, archi e cembalo. (F.I, n.19). 1949.
Tomo 70. Concerto in Fa maggiore per violino, archi e cembalo. Per la solennita' di S. Lorenzo. (F.I, n.20). 1949.
Tomo 71. Concerto in Mi minore per fagotto, archi e cembalo. (F.VIII, n.6). 1949.
Tomo 72. Concerto in La minore per fagotto, archi e cembalo. (F.VIII, n.7). 1949.
Tomo 73. Concerto in Si ♭ maggiore per oboe, violino, archi e cembalo. (F.XII, n.16). 1949.
Tomo 74. Concerto in Re minore per violino, archi e cembalo. (F.I, n.21). 1949.
Tomo 75. Trio in Sol minore per violino, liuto e basso continuo. (F.XVI, n.4). 1949.

Vol.7.
Tomo 76. Concerto in Mi maggiore per violino, archi e organo (o cembalo). La primavera. (F.I, n.22). 1950.
Tomo 77. Concerto in Sol minore per violino, archi e organo (o cembalo). L'estate. (F.I, n.23). 1950.
Tomo 78. Concerto in Fa maggiore per violino, archi e organo (o cembalo). L'autunno. (F.I, n.24). 1950.
Tomo 79. Concerto in Fa minore per violino, archi e organo (o cembalo). L'inverno. (F.I, n.25). 1950.
Tomo 80. Concerto in Mi ♭ maggiore per violino, archi e organo (o cembalo). La tempesta di mare. (F.I, n.26). 1950.
Tomo 81. Concerto in Do maggiore per violino, archi e organo (o cembalo). Il piacere. (F.I, n.27). 1950.
Tomo 82. Concerto in Re minore per violino, archi e organo (o cembalo). (F.I, n.28). 1950.
Tomo 83. Concerto in Si ♭ maggiore per violino, archi e organo (o cembalo). La caccia. (F.I, n.29). 1950.
Tomo 84. Concerto in Re maggiore per violino, archi e organo (o cembalo). F.I, n.30). 1950.
Tomo 85. Concerto in Do maggiore per violino, archi e organo (o cembalo). F.I, n.31). 1950.
Tomo 86. Concerto in Si ♭ maggiore per violino, archi e cembalo. (F.I, n.32). 1950.
Tomo 87. Concerto in Fa maggiore per violino, archi e cembalo. (F.I, n.33). 1950.
Tomo 88. Concerto in Fa maggiore per 3 violini, archi e cembalo. (F.I, n.34). 1950.
Tomo 89. Concerto in Re maggiore per 2 violini, archi e cembalo. (F.I, n.35). 1950.

Vol.8.
Tomo 90. Concerto in Do maggiore per 2 flauti, 2 oboi, fagotto, 2 violini, archi e cembalo. (F.XII, n.17). 1950.
Tomo 91. Concerto in Fa maggiore per 2 corni, archi e cembalo. (F.X, n.1). 1950.
Tomo 92. Concerto in Sol minore per violino, archi e cembalo. (F.I, n.36). 1950.
Tomo 93. Concerto in Mi minore per violino, archi e cembalo. (F.I, n.37). 1950.
Tomo 94. Concerto in Fa maggiore per 2 oboi, fagotto, 2 corni, violino, archi e organo. (F.XII, n.18). 1950.
Tomo 95. Concerto in Re minore per violino, organo, archi e cembalo. (F.XII, n.19). 1950.
Tomo 96. Concerto in Si minore per violino, archi e cembalo. (F.I, n.38). 1950.
Tomo 97. Concerto in Do maggiore per 2 trombe, archi e cembalo. (F.IX, n.1). 1950.
Tomo 98. Concerto in Do maggiore per mandolino, archi e cembalo. (F.V, n.1). 1950.
Tomo 99. Concerto in Re maggiore per 2 violini, 2 violoncelli, archi e cembalo. (F.IV, n.4). 1950.
Tomo 100. Concerto in La maggiore per violino, archi e cembalo. (F.I, n.39). 1950.

Vol.9.
Tomo 101. Concerto in Do maggiore per 2 flauti, archi e cembalo. (F.XI, n.2). 1951.
Tomo 102. Concerto in Re maggiore per flauto, archi e cembalo. (F.VI, n.3). 1951.
Tomo 103. Concerto in Sol minore per flauto, oboe, violino, fagotto e basso continuo. (F.XII, n.20). 1951.
Tomo 104. Concerto in Sol maggiore per 2 mandolini, archi e organo. (F.V, n.2). 1951.

Tomo 105. Concerto in Do maggiore per ottavino, archi e cembalo. (F.VI, n.4). 1951.
Tomo 106. Concerto in Fa maggiore per flauto, violino, fagotto e basso continuo. (F.XII, n.21). 1951.
Tomo 107. Concerto in Si ♭ maggiore per 2 violini, archi e cembalo. (F.I, n.40). 1951.
Tomo 108. Concerto in Re maggiore per 2 violini, archi e cembalo. (F.I, n.41). 1951.
Tomo 109. Concerto in Fa maggiore per fagotto, archi e cembalo. (F.VIII, n.8). 1951.
Tomo 110. Concerto in Do maggiore per ottavino, archi e cembalo. (F.VI, n.5). 1951.
Tomo 111. Concerto in Si ♭ maggiore per 2 violini, archi e cembalo. (F.I, n.42). 1951.
Tomo 112. Concerto in Do maggiore per 2 violini, archi e cembalo. (F.I, n.43). 1951.
Tomo 113. Concerto in Re maggiore per archi e cembalo. (F.XI, n.15). 1951.
Tomo 114. Concerto in Re maggiore per archi e cembalo. (F.XI, n.16). 1951.

Vol.10.
Tomo 115. Concerto in Sol minore per archi e cembalo. (F.XI, n.17). 1951.
Tomo 116. Concerto in Do maggiore per 2 violini, archi e cembalo. (F.I, n.44). 1951.
Tomo 117. Concerto in Re maggiore per violino, archi e cembalo. (F.I, n.45). 1951.
Tomo 118. Concerto in Do maggiore per fagotto, archi e cembalo. (F.VIII, n.9). 1951.
Tomo 119. Concerto in La minore per fagotto, archi e cembalo. (F.VIII, n.10). 1951.
Tomo 120. Concerto in Do maggiore per violino, archi e cembalo. (F.I, n.46). 1951.
Tomo 121. Concerto in Fa maggiore per 2 corni, archi e cembalo. (F.X, n.2). 1951.
Tomó 122. Concerto in Do maggiore per violino, archi e organo (o cembalo). (F.I, n.47). 1951.
Tomo 123. Concerto in Mi maggiore per violino, archi e organo (o cembalo). (F.I, n.48). 1951.
Tomo 124. Concerto in Sol maggiore per violino, archi e organo (o cembalo. (F.I, n.49). 1951.
Tomo 125. Concerto in Si minore per violino, archi e organo (o cembalo). (F.I, n.50). 1951.

Vol.11.
Tomo 126. Concerto in La maggiore per violino, archi e organo (o cembalo). (F.I, n.51). 1952.
Tomo 127. Concerto in Sol minore per violino, archi e organo (o cembalo). (F.I, n.52). 1952.
Tomo 128. Concerto in La minore per violino, archi e organo (o cembalo). (F.I, n.53). 1952.
Tomo 129. Concerto in La maggiore per violino, archi e organo (o cembalo. (F.I, n.54). 1952.
Tomo 130. Concerto in Si ♭ maggiore per violino, archi e organo (o cembalo). (F.I, n.55). 1952.
Tomo 131. Concerto in Re minore per violino, archi e organo (o cembalo). (F.I, n.56). 1952.
Tomo 132. Concerto in Si ♭ maggiore per 2 violini, archi e organo (o cembalo). (F.I, n.57). 1952.
Tomo 133. Concerto in Do minore per violino, archi e organo (o cembalo). (F.I, n.58). 1952.
Tomo 134. Concerto in Si ♭ maggiore per 4 violini, viole, violoncelli e cembalo. (F.I, n.59). 1952.
Tomo 135. Concerto in Fa maggiore per violino, violoncello, archi e cembalo. Il proteo o sia il mondo al Rovescio. (F.IV, n.5). 1952.
Tomo 136. Concerto in Si ♭ maggiore per violino, archi "in due cori" e 2 cembalo. (F.I, n.60). 1952.
Tomo 137. Concerto in Mi minore per violoncello, fagotto, archi e cembalo. (F.XII, n.22). 1952.
Tomo 138. Concerto in Sol maggiore per flauto, archi e cembalo. (F.VI, n.6). 1952.
Tomo 139. Concerto in Do maggiore per 2 oboi, archi e cembalo. (F.VII, n.3). 1952.

Vol.12.
Tomo 140. Concerto in La minore per 2 violini, archi e cembalo. (F.I, n.61). 1952.
Tomo 141. Concerto in Re maggiore. Per la SS. assunzione di Maria Vergine, per violino, archi "in due cori" e 2 cembali. (F.I, n.62). 1952.
Tomo 142. Concerto in Do maggiore per 2 flauti, oboe, corno inglese, 2 trombe, violino, 2 viole, archi e 2 cembali. (F.XII, n.23). 1952.
Tomo 143. Concerto in Do maggiore per flauto, oboe, violino, fagotto e basso continuo. (F.XII, n.24). 1952.
Tomo 144. Concerto in Re maggiore per flauto, oboe, violino, fagotto e basso continuo. (F.XII, n.25). 1952.
Tomo 145. Concerto in Si ♭ maggiore per 2 violini, archi e cembalo. (F.I, n.63). 1952.
Tomo 146. Concerto in La maggiore per violino, violoncello, archi e cembalo. (F.IV, n.6). 1952.
Tomo 147. Concerto in Fa maggiore per flauto, oboe, violino, fagotto e basso continuo. (F.XII, n.26). 1952.
Tomo 148. Concerto in La minore per flauto, archi e cembalo. (F.VI, n.7). 1952.
Tomo 149. Concerto in Re maggiore per flauto, violino, fagotto e basso continuo. (F.XII, n.27). 1952.
Tomo 150. Concerto in Fa maggiore per flauto, oboe, fagotto, violini, viole e cembalo. La tempesta di mare. (F.XII, n.28). 1952.

Vol.13.
Tomo 151. Concerto in Sol maggiore per flauto, archi e cembalo. (F.VI, n.8). 1953.
Tomo 152. Concerto in La minore per ottavino, archi e cembalo. (F.VI, n.9). 1953.
Tomo 153. Concerto in Re maggiore per flauto, archi e cembalo. (F.VI, n.10). 1953.
Tomo 154. Concerto in Re maggiore per flauto, oboe, violino, fagotto e basso continuo. La pastorella. (F.XII, n.29). 1953.
Tomo 155. Concerto in Do maggiore per flauto, oboe, 2 violini e basso continuo. (F.XII, n.30). 1953.
Tomo 156. Concerto in Sol maggiore per violino, archi e cembalo. (F.I, n.64). 1953.
Tomo 157. Concerto in Si ♭ maggiore per violino, archi e cembalo. (F.I, n.65). 1953.
Tomo 158. Concerto in Fa maggiore per violino, archi e cembalo. (F.I, n.66). 1953.
Tomo 159. Concerto in Do minore per flauto, archi e cembalo. (F.VI, n.11). 1953.

Tomo 160. Concerto in Do maggiore per violino, archi e cembalo. (F.I, n.67). 1953.
Tomo 161. Concerto in Mi maggiore per archi e cembalo. (F.XI, n.18). 1953.
Tomo 162. Concerto in Do maggiore per violino, archi e cembalo. (F.I, n.68). 1953.
Tomo 163. Concerto in Si ♭ maggiore per violino, archi e cembalo. (F.I, n.69). 1953.

Vol.14.
Tomo 164. Concerto in Mi minore per violino, archi e cembalo. (F.I, n.70). 1953.
Tomo 165. Concerto in Fa maggiore per violino, archi e cembalo. (F.I, n.71). 1953.
Tomo 166. Concerto in Mi maggiore per violino, archi e cembalo. (F.I, n.72). 1953.
Tomo 167. Concerto in Do maggiore per violino, archi e cembalo. (F.I, n.73). 1953.
Tomo 168. Concerto in Mi minore per violino, archi e cembalo. (F.I, n.74). 1953.
Tomo 169. Concerto in Mi ♭ maggiore per violino, archi e cembalo. (F.I, n.75). 1953.
Tomo 170. Concerto in Si ♭ maggiore per violino, archi e cembalo. (F.I, n.76). 1953.
Tomo 171. Concerto in Si minore per violino, archi e cembalo. (F.I, n.77). 1953.
Tomo 172. Concerto in Si ♭ maggiore per violino, archi e cembalo. (F.I, n.78). 1953.
Tomo 173. Concerto in Do minore per violino, archi e cembalo. (F.I, n.79). 1953.
Tomo 174. Concerto in Re maggiore per violino, archi e cembalo. (F.I, n.80). 1953.
Tomo 175. Concerto in Sol minore per violino, archi e cembalo. (F.I, n.81). 1953.

Vol.15.
Tomo 176. Concerto in Re minore per archi e cembalo. (F.XI, n.19). 1954.
Tomo 177. Concerto in Do minore per archi e cembalo. (F.XI, n.20). 1954.
Tomo 178. Concerto in Sol minore per violino, archi e cembalo. (F.I, n.82). 1954.
Tomo 179. Concerto in Si minore per violino, archi e cembalo. (F.I, n.83). 1954.
Tomo 180. Concerto in Mi maggiore per violino, archi e cembalo. (F.I, n.84). 1954.
Tomo 181. Concerto in Do maggiore per 2 violini, archi e cembalo. (F.I, n.85). 1954.
Tomo 182. Concerto in Sol minore per archi e cembalo. (F.XI, n.21). 1954.
Tomo 183. Concerto in Si maggiore per violino, archi e cembalo. (F.I, n.86). 1954.
Tomo 184. Concerto in La maggiore per archi e cembalo. (F.XI, n.22). 1954.
Tomo 185. Concerto in Do maggiore per archi e cembalo. (F.XI, n.23). 1954.
Tomo 186. Concerto in Sol maggiore per violino, archi e cembalo. (F.I, n.87). 1954.
Tomo 187. Concerto in Fa maggiore per violino, archi e cembalo. (F.I, n.88). 1954.
Tomo 188. Concerto in Re maggiore per violino, archi e cembalo. (F.I, n.89). 1954.

Vol.16.
Tomo 189. Concerto in La maggiore per viola d'amore, archi e cembalo. (F.II, n.1). 1954.
Tomo 190. Concerto in Si ♭ maggiore per archi e cembalo. (F.XI, n.24). 1954.
Tomo 191. Concerto in La maggiore per violino, archi e cembalo. (F.I, n.90). 1954.
Tomo 192. Concerto in Sol maggiore per violino, archi e cembalo. (F.I, n.91). 1954.
Tomo 193. Concerto in Mi ♭ maggiore per violino, archi e cembalo. (F.I, n.92). 1954.
Tomo 194. Concerto in Do maggiore per violino, archi e cembalo. (F.I, n.93). 1954.
Tomo 195. Concerto in Do maggiore per violino, archi e cembalo. (F.I, n.94). 1954.
Tomo 196. Concerto in Re minore per viola d'amore, archi e cembalo. (F.II, n.2). 1954.
Tomo 197. Concerto in Re minore per viola d'amore, archi e cembalo. (F.II, n.3). 1954.
Tomo 198. Concerto in Re minore per viola d'amore, archi e cembalo. (F.II, n.4). 1954.
Tomo 199. Concerto in Si ♭ maggiore per violino, archi e cembalo. (F.I, n.95). 1954.
Tomo 200. Concerto in Do maggiore per archi e cembalo. (F.XI, n.25). 1954.

Vol.17.
Tomo 201. Concerto in La minore per archi e cembalo. (F.XI, n.26). 1955.
Tomo 202. Concerto in Sol maggiore per violino, archi e cembalo. (F.I, n.96). 1955.
Tomo 203. Concerto in Re maggiore per violino, archi e cembalo. (F.I, n.97). 1955.
Tomo 204. Concerto in Do maggiore per violoncello, archi e cembalo. (F.III, n.3). 1955.
Tomo 205. Concerto in La minore per violoncello, archi e cembalo. (F.III, n.4). 1955.
Tomo 206. Concerto in Mi ♭ maggiore per violoncello, archi e cembalo. (F.III, n.5). 1955.
Tomo 207. Concerto in Sol minore per 2 violini, archi e cembalo. (F.I, n.98). 1955.
Tomo 208. Concerto in Si ♭ maggiore per 2 violini, archi e cembalo. (F.I, n.99). 1955.
Tomo 209. Concerto in Re minore per 2 violini, archi e cembalo. (F.I, n.100). 1955.
Tomo 210. Concerto in Mi ♭ maggiore per 2 violini, archi e cembalo. (F.I, n.101). 1955.
Tomo 211. Concerto in Do maggiore per violoncello, archi e cembalo. (F.III, n.6). 1955.
Tomo 212. Concerto in Re minore per violoncello, archi e cembalo. (F.III, n.7). 1955.
Tomo 213. Concerto in Re minore per 2 flauto, 2 oboi, fagotto, 2 violini, archi e cembalo. (F.XII, n.31). 1955.

Vol.18.
Tomo 214. Concerto in Sol minore per fagotto, archi e cembalo. (F.VIII, n.11). 1955.
Tomo 215. Concerto in La minore per oboe, archi e cembalo. (F.VII, n.5). 1955.
Tomo 216. Concerto in Do maggiore per oboe, archi e cembalo. (F.VII, n.6). 1955.
Tomo 217. Concerto in Do maggiore per oboe, archi e cembalo. (F.VII, n.7). 1955.
Tomo 218. Concerto in Do maggiore per violoncello, archi e cembalo. (F.III, n.8). 1955.
Tomo 219. Concerto in Si minore per violoncello, archi e cembalo. (F.III, n.9). 1955.
Tomo 220. Concerto in La minore per violoncello, archi e cembalo. (F.III, n.10). 1955.

Tomo 221. Concerto in Fa maggiore per violoncello, archi e cembalo. (F.III, n.11). 1955.
Tomo 222. Concerto in Do maggiore per oboe, archi e cembalo. (F.VII, n.4). 1955.
Tomo 223. Concerto in La minore per fagotto, archi e cembalo. (F.VIII, n.12). 1955.
Tomo 224. Concerto in Do maggiore per fagotto, archi e cembalo. (F.VIII, n.13). 1955.
Tomo 225. Concerto in Do minore per fagotto, archi e cembalo. (F.VIII, n.14). 1955.

Vol.19.
Tomo 226. Concerto in Sol minore per archi e cembalo. (F.XI, n.27). 1956.
Tomo 227. Concerto in Mi ♭ maggiore per violino, archi e cembalo. (F.I, n.102). 1956.
Tomo 228. Concerto in Sol maggiore per violino, archi e cembalo. (F.I, n.103). 1956.
Tomo 229. Concerto in La maggiore per violino, archi e cembalo. (F.I, n.104). 1956.
Tomo 230. Concerto in Do minore per violino, archi e cembalo. (F.I, n.105). 1956.
Tomo 231. Concerto in Sol maggiore per violoncello, archi e cembalo. (F.III, n.12). 1956.
Tomo 232. Concerto in La minore per violoncello, archi e cembalo. (F.III, n.13). 1956.
Tomo 233. Concerto in Fa maggiore per violoncello, archi e cembalo. (F.III, n.14). 1956.
Tomo 234. Concerto in Sol minore per violoncello, archi e cembalo. (F.III, n.15). 1956.
Tomo 235. Concerto in Re maggiore per violoncello, archi e cembalo. (F.III, n.16). 1956.
Tomo 236. Concerto in Fa maggiore per fagotto, archi e cembalo. (F.VIII, n.15). 1956.
Tomo 237. Concerto in Do maggiore per fagotto, archi e cembalo. (F.VIII, n.16). 1956.

Vol.20.
Tomo 238. Concerto in Do maggiore per fagotto, archi e cembalo. (F.VIII, n.17). 1956.
Tomo 239. Concerto in Do maggiore per fagotto, archi e cembalo. (F.VIII, n.18). 1956.
Tomo 240. Concerto in Fa maggiore per fagotto, archi e cembalo. (F.VIII, n.19). 1956.
Tomo 241. Concerto in Fa maggiore per archi e cembalo. (F.XI, n.28). 1956.
Tomo 242. Concerto in Fa maggiore per archi e cembalo. (F.XI, n.29). 1956.
Tomo 243. Concerto in Fa maggiore per violoncello, archi e cembalo. (F.III, n.17). 1956.
Tomo 244. Concerto in La minore per violoncello, archi e cembalo. (F.III, n.18). 1956.
Tomo 245. Concerto in La maggiore per violino, archi e cembalo. (F.I, n.106). 1956.
Tomo 246. Concerto in Re maggiore per archi e cembalo. (F.XI, n.30). 1956.
Tomo 247. Concerto in Sol maggiore per violino, archi e cembalo. (F.I, n.107). 1956.
Tomo 248. Concerto in Fa maggiore per viola d'amore, 2 oboi, fagotto, 2 corni e basso continuo. (F.XII, n.32). 1956.
Tomo 249. Concerto in Sol minore per 3 oboi, fagotto, 2 corni, violino, archi e cembalo. "Per S.A.R. di Sassonia." (F.XII, n.33). 1956.
Tomo 250. Concerto in Do maggiore per oboe, 2 violini, archi e cembalo. (F.XII, n.34). 1956.

Vol.21.
Tomo 251. Concerto in Re minore per archi e cembalo. (F.XI, n.31). 1957.
Tomo 252. Concerto in Sol maggiore per archi e cembalo. (F.XI, n.32). 1957.
Tomo 253. Concerto in Sol minore per violino, archi e cembalo. (F.I, n.108). 1957.
Tomo 254. Concerto in Mi ♭ maggiore per violino, archi e cembalo. (F.I, n.109). 1957.
Tomo 255. Concerto in Sol maggiore per violino, archi e cembalo. (F.I, n.110). 1957.
Tomo 256. Concerto in Do maggiore per violino, archi e cembalo. (F.I, n.111). 1957.
Tomo 257. Concerto in Sol minore per violino, archi e cembalo. (F.I, n.112). 1957.
Tomo 258. Concerto in Re minore per violino, archi e cembalo. (F.I, n.113). 1957.
Tomo 259. Concerto in Do maggiore per violino, archi e cembalo. (F.I, n.114). 1957.
Tomo 260. Concerto in Si minore per violino, archi e cembalo. (F.I, n.115). 1957.
Tomo 261. Concerto in Re maggiore per violino, archi e cembalo. (F.I, n.116). 1957.
Tomo 262. Concerto in Si ♭ maggiore per violino, archi e cembalo. (F.I, n.117). 1957.

Vol.22.
Tomo 263. Concerto in La minore per 2 oboi, archi e cembalo. (F.VII, n.8). 1957.
Tomo 264. Concerto in Re minore per 2 oboi, archi e cembalo. (F.VII, n.9). 1957.
Tomo 265. Concerto in Fa maggiore per oboe, violino, archi e cembalo. (F.XII, n.35). 1957.
Tomo 266. Concerto in Fa maggiore per fagotto, archi e cembalo. (F.VIII, n.20). 1957.
Tomo 267. Concerto in Do maggiore per fagotto, archi e cembalo. (F.VIII, n.21). 1957.
Tomo 268. Concerto in Fa maggiore per fagotto, archi e cembalo. (F.VIII, n.22). 1957.
Tomo 269. Concerto in Sol minore per fagotto, archi e cembalo. (F.VIII, n.23). 1957.
Tomo 270. Concerto in Si ♭ maggiore per fagotto, archi e cembalo. (F.VIII, n.24). 1957.
Tomo 271. Concerto in Fa maggiore per fagotto, archi e cembalo. (F.VIII, n.25). 1957.
Tomo 272. Concerto in Do maggiore per fagotto, archi e cembalo. (F.VIII, n.26). 1957.
Tomo 273. Concerto in Mi ♭ maggiore per fagotto, archi e cembalo. (F.VIII, n.27). 1957.
Tomo 274. Concerto in Do maggiore per fagotto, archi e cembalo. (F.VIII. n.28). 1957.
Tomo 275. Concerto in Sol maggiore per fagotto, archi e cembalo. (F.VIII, n.29). 1957.

Vol.23.
Tomo 276. Concerto in Sol maggiore per fagotto, archi, e cembalo. (F.VIII, n.30). 1958.
Tomo 277. Concerto in Do maggiore per fagotto, archi e cembalo. (F.VIII, n.31). 1958.
Tomo 278. Concerto in Fa maggiore per fagotto, archi e cembalo. (F.VIII, n.32). 1958.
Tomo 279. Concerto in Re maggiore per oboe, archi e cembalo. (F.VII, n.10). 1958.
Tomo 280. Concerto in Sol maggiore per oboe, fagotto, archi e cembalo. (F.XII, n.36). 1958.
Tomo 281. Concerto in Do maggiore per fagotto, archi e cembalo. (F.VIII, n.33). 1958.

Tomo 282. Concerto in Do maggiore per fagotto, archi e cembalo. (F.VIII, n.34). 1958.
Tomo 283. Concerto in Do maggiore per oboe, archi e cembalo. (F.VII, n.11). 1958.
Tomo 284. Concerto in Si ♭ maggiore per violino, archi e cembalo. (F.I, n.118). 1958.
Tomo 285. Concerto in Re minore per violino, archi e cembalo. (F.I, n.119). 1958.
Tomo 286. Concerto in Re maggiore per violino, archi e cembalo. (F.I, n.120). 1958.
Tomo 287. Concerto in Sol minore per archi e cembalo. (F.XI, n.33). 1958.

Vol.24.
Tomo 288. Concerto in Fa maggiore per archi e cembalo. (F.XI, n.34). 1958.
Tomo 289. Concerto in Fa minore per archi e cembalo. (F.XI, n.35). 1958.
Tomo 290. Concerto in Sol maggiore per archi e cembalo. (F.XI, n.36). 1958.
Tomo 291. Concerto in Si ♭ maggiore per violino, archi e cembalo. (F.I, n.121). 1958.
Tomo 292. Concerto in Sol minore per violino, archi e cembalo. (F.I, n.122). 1958.
Tomo 293. Concerto in La maggiore per violino, archi e cembalo. (F.I, n.123). 1958.
Tomo 294. Concerto in Re maggiore per violino, archi e cembalo. (F.I, n.124). 1958.
Tomo 295. Concerto in Sol minore per violino, archi e cembalo. (F.I, n.125). 1958.
Tomo 296. Concerto in Re minore per violino, archi e cembalo. (F.I, n.126). 1958.
Tomo 297. Concerto in Mi maggiore per violino, archi e cembalo. L'amoroso. (F.I, n.127). 1958.
Tomo 298. Concerto in Si ♭ maggiore per fagotto, archi e cembalo. (F.VIII, n.35). 1958.
Tomo 299. Concerto in Si ♭ maggiore per fagotto, archi e cembalo. (F.VIII, n.36). 1958.
Tomo 300. Concerto in Col maggiore per fagotto, archi e cembalo. (F.VIII, n.37). 1958.

Vol.25.
Tomo 301. Concerto in Fa maggiore per violino, archi e cembalo. (F.I, n.128). 1960.
Tomo 302. Concerto in Re maggiore per violino, archi e cembalo. (F.I, n.129). 1960.
Tomo 303. Concerto in Fa maggiore per violino, archi e cembalo. (F.I, n.130). 1960.
Tomo 304. Concerto in Mi ♭ maggiore per violino, archi e cembalo. (F.I, n.131). 1960.
Tomo 305. Concerto in Re maggiore per violino, archi e cembalo. (F.I, n.132). 1960.
Tomo 306. Concerto in Re maggiore per violino, archi e cembalo. (F.I, n.133). 1960.
Tomo 307. Concerto in Re maggiore per violino, archi e cembalo. (F.I, n.134). 1960.
Tomo 308. Concerto in Do maggiore per archi e cembalo. (F.XI, n.37). 1960.
Tomo 309. Concerto in Do maggiore per archi e cembalo. (F.XI, n.38). 1960.
Tomo 310. Concerto in Sol minore per archi e cembalo. (F.XI, n.39). 1960.
Tomo 311. Concerto in Do maggiore per violino, archi e cembalo. (F.I, n.135). 1960.
Tomo 312. Concerto in Re maggiore per violino, archi e cembalo. (F.I, n.136). 1960.
Tomo 313. Concerto in La maggiore per violino, archi e cembalo. (F.I, n.137). 1960.
Tomo 314. Concerto in Re maggiore per violino, archi e cembalo. (F.I, n.138). 1960.

Vol.26.
Tomo 315. Concerto in Fa maggiore per oboe, archi e cembalo. (F.VII, n.12). 1960.
Tomo 316. Concerto in La minore per oboe, archi e cembalo. (F.VII, n.13). 1960.
Tomo 317. Concerto in Sol maggiore per violoncello, archi e cembalo. (F.III, n.19). 1960.
Tomo 318. Concerto in Do maggiore per 2 flauti, 2 salmò, 2 trombe, 2 mandolini, 2 tiorbe violoncello, archi e cembalo. (F.XII, n.37). 1960.
Tomo 319. Concerto in La maggiore per violino, 3 violini "per eco," archi e cembalo. (F.I, n.139). 1960.
Tomo 320. Concerto in Re minore per viola d'amore, liuto, archi e cembalo. (F.XII, n.38). 1960.
Tomo 321. Sinfonia in Sol maggiore per archi e cembalo. (F.XI, n.40). 1960.
Tomo 322. Concerto in Do maggiore per violino, archi e cembalo. (F.I, n.140). 1960.
Tomo 323. Concerto in La maggiore per violino, archi e cembalo. (F.I, n.141). 1960.
Tomo 324. Concerto in Re minore per violino, archi e cembalo. (F.I, n.142). 1960.
Tomo 325. Concerto in Re minore per violino, archi e cembalo. (F.I, n.143). 1960.

Vol.27.
Tomo 326. Concerto in Si minore per violino, archi e cembalo. (F.I, n.144). 1961.
Tomo 327. Concerto in Mi maggiore per violino, archi e cembalo. (F.I, n.145). 1961.
Tomo 328. Concerto in Do maggiore per violono, archi e cembalo. (F.I, n.146). 1961.
Tomo 329. Concerto in Sol minore per violino, archi e cembalo. (F.I, n.147). 1961.
Tomo 330. Concerto in La maggiore per violino, archi e cembalo. (F.I, n.148). 1961.
Tomo 331. Concerto in Re maggiore per violino, archi e cembalo. (F.I, n.149). 1961.
Tomo 332. Concerto in Si ♭ maggiore per violino, archi e cembalo. (F.I, n.150). 1961.
Tomo 333. Concerto in Re minore per violino, archi e cembalo. (F.I, n.151). 1961.
Tomo 334. Concerto in Sol minore per violino, archi e cembalo. (F.I, n.152). 1961.
Tomo 335. Concerto in Re maggiore per violino, archi e cembalo. (F.I, n.153). 1961.
Tomo 336. Concerto in Re minore per violino, archi e cembalo. (F.I, n.154). 1961.
Tomo 337. Concerto in Re maggiore per viola d'amore, archi e cembalo. (F.II, n.5). 1961.
Tomo 338. Concerto in Fa maggiore per 2 oboi, fagotto, 2 corni, violino, archi e cembalo. (F.XII, n.39). 1961.

Vol.28.
Tomo 339. Concerto in La maggiore per violino, archi e cembalo. (F.I, n.155). 1961.
Tomo 340. Concerto in Mi ♭ maggiore per violino, archi e cembalo. (F.I, n.156). 1961.

Tomo 341. Concerto in La minore per viola d'amore, archi e cembalo. (F.II, n.6). 1961.
Tomo 342. Concerto in Do maggiore per 2 violini, archi e cembalo. (F.I, n.157). 1961.
Tomo 343. Concerto in Re maggiore per violino, archi e cembalo. (F.I, n.158). 1961.
Tomo 344. Concerto in La maggiore per 2 violini, archi e cembalo. (F.I, n.159). 1961.
Tomo 345. Concerto in Re maggiore per violino, archi e cembalo. (F.I, n.160). 1961.
Tomo 346. Concerto in Fa maggiore per violino, archi e cembalo. (F.I, n.161). 1961.
Tomo 347. Concerto in Re maggiore per violino, archi e cembalo. (F.I, n.162). 1961.
Tomo 348. Concerto in Si ♭ maggiore O sia il corneto da posta per violino, archi e cembalo. (F.I, n.163). 1961.
Tomo 349. Concerto in Mi ♭ maggiore per violino, archi e cembalo. (F.I, n.164). 1961.
Tomo 350. Concerto in Fa maggiore per 2 oboi, fagotto, 2 corni, violino, archi e organo. (F.XII, n.40). 1961.

Vol.29.
Tomo 351. Concerto in Sol minore per violino, archi e cembalo. (F.I, n.165). 1962.
Tomo 352. Concerto in Mi ♭ maggiore per violino, archi e cembalo. (F.I, n.166). 1962.
Tomo 353. Concerto in Fa maggiore per violino, organo e archi. (F.XII, n.41). 1962.
Tomo 354. Concerto in Re minore per violino, flauto, fagotto e basso continuo. (F.XII, n.42). 1962.
Tomo 355. Concerto in Re maggiore per violino, flauto e basso continuo. (F.XII, n.43). 1962.
Tomo 356. Sonata in Sol minore per violino e basso continuo. (F.XIII, n.5). 1962.
Tomo 357. Concerto in Fa maggiore per violino, archi e cembalo. (F.I, n.167). 1962.
Tomo 358. Concerto in Sol maggiore per violino, archi e cembalo. (F.I, n.168). 1962.
Tomo 359. Concerto in Si ♭ maggiore per 2 flauti, 2 oboi, fagotto, archi e cembalo. (F.XII, n.44). 1962.
Tomo 360. Concerto in Sol maggiore per flauto, archi e cembalo. (F.VI, n.12). 1962.

Vol.30.
Tomo 361. Concerto in Sol maggiore per archi e cembalo. (F.XI, n.41). 1962.
Tomo 362. Concerto in Re maggiore per 2 oboi, fagotto, archi e cembalo. (F.XII, n.45). 1962.
Tomo 363. Concerto in Fa maggiore per 2 corni, fagotto, archi e cembalo. (F.XII, n.46). 1962.
Tomo 364. Sonata in Re maggiore per violino e basso continuo. (F.XIII, n.6). 1962.
Tomo 365. Sonata in Re minore per violino e basso continuo. (F.XIII, n.7). 1962.
Tomo 366. Sonata in Do maggiore per violino e basso continuo. (F.XIII, n.8). 1962.
Tomo 367. Sonata in Re minore per violino e basso continuo. (F.XIII, n.9). 1962.
Tomo 368. Sonata in Do minore per violino e basso continuo. (F.XIII, n.10). 1962.
Tomo 369. Sonata in Do maggiore per violino e basso continuo. (F.XIII, n.11). 1962.
Tomo 370. Sonata in La maggiore per violino e basso continuo. (F.XIII, n.12). 1962.
Tomo 371. Sonata in Sol maggiore per violino e basso continuo. (F.XIII, n.13). 1962.
Tomo 372. Sonata in Do minore per violino e basso continuo. (F.XIII, n.14). 1962.
Tomo 373. Sonata in Sol minore per violino e basso continuo. (F.XIII, n.15). 1962.
Tomo 374. Sonata in Si ♭ maggiore per violino e basso continuo. (F.XIII, n.16). 1962.
Tomo 375. Sonata in Do minore per oboe e basso continuo. (F.XV, n.2). 1962.

Vol.31.
Tomo 376. Concerto in Do maggiore per violino, archi e cembalo. (F.I, n.169). 1963.
Tomo 377. Concerto in Si ♭ maggiore per violino, archi e cembalo. (F.I, n.170). 1963.
Tomo 378. Concerto in Si minore per violino, archi e cembalo. (F.I, n.171). 1963.
Tomo 379. Concerto in Do maggiore per violino, archi e cembalo. (F.I, n.172). 1963.
Tomo 380. Concerto in Re maggiore per 2 oboi, 2 corni, violino, archi e 2 organi. (F.XII, n.47). 1963.
Tomo 381. Concerto in La maggiore "in due cori cori" per 4 flauti, 4 violini, 2 violoncelli, 2 organi e archi. (F.XII, n.48). 1963.
Tomo 382. Sonata in Sol minore per 2 violini e violoncello o cembalo. (F.XIII, n.17). 1963.
Tomo 383. Sonata in Mi minore per 2 violini e violoncello o cembalo. (F.XIII, n.18). 1963.
Tomo 384. Sonata in Do maggiore per 2 violini e violoncello o cembalo. (F.XIII, n.19). 1963.
Tomo 385. Sonata in Mi maggiore per 2 violini e violoncello o cembalo. (F.XIII, n.20). 1963.

Vol.32.
Tomo 386. Sonata in Fa maggiore per 2 violini e violoncello o cembalo. (F.XIII, n.21). 1963.
Tomo 387. Sonata in Re maggiore per 2 violini e violoncello o cembalo. (F.XIII, n.22). 1963.
Tomo 388. Sonata in Mi ♭ maggiore per 2 violini e violoncello o cembalo. (F.XIII, n.23). 1963.
Tomo 389. Sonata in Re minore per 2 violini e violoncello o cembalo. (F.XIII, n.24). 1963.
Tomo 390. Sonata in La maggiore per 2 violini e violoncello o cembalo. (F.XIII, n.25). 1963.
Tomo 391. Sonata in Si ♭ maggiore per 2 violini e violoncello o cembalo. (F.XIII, n.26). 1963.
Tomo 392. Sonata in Si minore per 2 violini e violoncello o cembalo. (F.XIII, n.27). 1963.
Tomo 393. Sonata in Re minore "La follia" per 2 violini e violoncello o cembalo. (F.XIII, n.28). 1963.
Tomo 394. Sonata in Sol minore per violino e basso continuo. (F.XIII, n.29). 1963.
Tomo 395. Sonata in La maggiore per violino e basso continuo. (F.XIII, n.30). 1963.
Tomo 396. Sonata in Re minore per violino e basso continuo. (F.XIII, n.31). 1963.
Tomo 397. Sonata in Fa maggiore per violino e basso continuo. (F.XIII, n.32). 1963.
Tomo 398. Sonata in S minore per violino e basso continuo. (F.XIII, n.33). 1963.
Tomo 399. Sonata in Do maggiore per violino e basso continuo. (F.XIII, n.34). 1963.
Tomo 400. Sonata in Do minore per violino e basso continuo. (F.XIII, n.35). 1963.

Vocal scores, *see* Hullah, John Pyke. Vocal scores.

Volbach, Fritz, 1861–1940, ed. Musica sacra, *see* Musica sacra, hrsg. von F. Commer.

VOLK MUSIZIERT. Heft 1– . Hannover, A. Nagel, 1936– .
v.1– . (Werkreihe des Kulturamtes der Reichsjugendführung).
Scored in 4 parts for various instruments ad lib.
Editor: 1936– , Reinhold Heyden.
Contents:
Heft 1. Nordische Volkmärsche. Sechzehn Bauermärsche aus Schweden und Norwegen. Bearb. von Reinhold Heyden. Edition Nagel 1001.
Heft 2. Spielmusik aus Altösterreich. Märsche, Ländler, "Deutsche," Walzer und eine Hochzeitsmusik. Bearb. von Viktor Korda. Edition Nagel 1003.
Heft 3. Appenzeller Volkstänze. Acht Volkstänze und Ländler. Bearb. von Carl Aeschbacher. Edition Nagel 1006.
Heft 4. Lieder und Tänze aus Franken. Zwölf Lieder und Tänze. Bearb. von Karl Schäger. Edition Nagel 1009.
Heft 5. Alte hessische Märsche. Bearb. von Edgar Stahmer. Edition Nagel 1011.
Heft 6. Tänze aus Niederbayern. Bearb. von Wilh. Twittenhoff. Edition Nagel 1013.
Heft 7. Pommersche Tänze und Märsche. Bearb. von August Kremser. Edition Nagel 1016.
Heft 8. Spielmusik aus Mähren. (Hochzeitmusik). Bear. von Viktor Korda. Edition Nagel 1017.
Heft 9. Thüringer Volkstänze. Bearb. von Curt Rücker. Edition Nagel 1018.
Heft 10. Tänze aus der Lüneburger Heide. Bearb. von Fritz Jöde. Edition Nagel 1019.
Heft 11. Sudentenländlische Volksmusik. Nach den Aufzeichnungen Karl M. Kliers. Bearb. von Viktor Korda. Edition Nagel 1021.
Heft 12. Tänze aus der Steiermark. Bearb. von Walter Kolneder. Edition Nagel 1022.
Heft 13. Tänze und Märsche vom Niederrhein. Bearb. von Herbert Napiersky. Edition Nagel 1025.
Heft 14.
Heft 15. Alte grazer Kontratänze. Bearb. von Walter Kolneder. Edition Nagel 1027.
Heft 16.
Heft 17. Schwäbische Tanzweisen. Bearb. von Luis Steiner. Edition Nagel 1029.

Voluntaries for the organ, *see* Stanley, Charles John. Voluntaries for the organ.

Von Aich, Arnt, *see* Aich, Arnt von.

Wagner, Peter Josef, 1865–1931. Introduction to the Gregorian melodies, *see* Plainsong and Mediaeval Music Society. Wagner, Peter Josef. Introduction to the Gregorian melodies.

WAGNER, RICHARD, 1813–1883.
Richard Wagners Musikalische Werke, hrsg. von Michael Balling. Leipzig, Breitkopf & Härtel, 1912–22.
10v.
Contents:
Musikdramen:
Bd.3. Tannhäuser. In 3 Aufzügen.
Bd.4. Lohengrin. Oper in 3 Akten.
Bd.5. Tristan und Isolde. Handlung in 3 Aufzügen.
Jugendopern:
Bd.12. Die Hochzeit. Introduktion, Chor, und Septett.
Bd.13. Die Feen. Romantische Oper in 3 Akten.
Bd.14. Das Liebesverbot oder die Novize von Palermo. Grosse komische Oper in 2 Akten.
Musikalische Werke:
Bd.15. Lieder und Gesänge.
Bd.16. Chorgesänge.
Bd.18. Orchesterwerke.
Bd.20. Orchesterwerke.

WALTHER, JOHANN, 1496–1570.
Sämtliche Werke. Hrsg. von Otto Schröder.
Bd.1– . Kassel, Bärenreiter; St. Louis, Mo., Concordia Publishing House, 1953– .
v.1– .
Contents (asterisk indicates unpublished volumes):
Bd.1. Geistliches Gesangbüchlein. Wittenberg, 1551. Teil 1. Deutsche Gesänge. 1953.
Bd.2. Geistliches Gesangbüchlein. Wittenberg, 1551. Teil 2. Cantiones latinae. 1953.
Bd.3. Geistliches Gesangbüchlein. Wittenberg, 1551. Teil 3. Lieder und Motetten, die nur 1524, 1525 und 1544 im Wittenbergischen Gesangbüchlein enthalten oder in Handschriften und Drucken verstreut sind. 1955.
*Bd.4. Das Christlich Kinderlied D. Martin Lutheri "Erhalt uns, Herr." 1566.
Bd.5. Cantiones 7 vocum (1544). 1545. Magnificat 8 tonorum, 4, 5 et 6 vocibus. Jenae, 1557. 1961.
*Bd.6. Zwei Passionen nach Matthaeus und Johannes. Composed between 1525 and 1530; Psalmen und Magnificat 8 tonorum. 1540; 26 Fugen auf 8 tonos. 1542.

Ward, John, 1917– , ed. The Dublin virginal manuscript, *see* The Wellesley edition. No.3.

WASHINGTON (STATE) UNIVERSITY.
Music series. Seattle, Wash., University of Washington Press, 1953– .
No.1– .
Contents:
No.1. Wood, Carl Paige. Winter winds; for women's voices and strings. Arr. for women's voices and piano. 1953.
No.2. Cadzow, Dorothy. Prelude for strings. [score] 1953.
No.3. Beale, James. Second piano sonata. Op.8. 1953.
No.4. Verrall, John. 4 Pieces for piano. 1954.
No.5a/b. McKay, George Frederick. String quartet, No.2. [score and parts] 1955.

WASIELEWSKI, JOSEPH WILHELM VON, 1822–1896. ed.
Instrumentalsätze vom Ende des XVI. bis Ende

des XVII. Jahrhunderts. (als Musikbeilagen zu "Die Violine im XVII. Jahrhundert"). Gesammelt und hrsg. von Jos. Wilh. von Wasielewski. Bonn, Max Cohen & Sohn, 1874.
80p.
Contains compositions by Mont. Albano, Gregorio Allegri, Adriano Banchieri, Giov. B. Bassani, Giov. Battista Fontana, Giov. Gabrieli, Giovanni Legrenzi, Gioan Battista Magni, Biagio Marini, Florentio Maschera, Maxxaferrata, Tarquinio Merulo, Massimiliano Neri, Giuseppe Torelli, Marco Uccellini, Antonio Veracini, and Giov. Batt. Vitali.

WASIELEWSKI, JOSEPH WILHELM VON, 1822–1896. ed.
Instrumentalsätze vom Ende des XVI. bis Ende des XVII. Jahrhunderts. Neuer mit einem Inhaltsverzeichnis versehener Abdruck. Berlin, L. Liepmannssohn, [1888–?].
2p.L., 80p.

THE WA-WAN SERIES OF AMERICAN COMPOSITIONS. Newton Centre, Mass., Wa-Wan Press, cop.1901– .
v.1– .
A collection of vocal and instrumental compositions published in serial form.
Contents: (taken from article, "The Wa-Wan Press: An Adventure in Musical Idealism," by Edward N. Waters, in *A birthday offering to Carl Engel* [New York, G. Schirmer, Inc., 1943]).
(Those compositions without volume number appeared only as sheet music, not in the periodical series).
(Abbreviations: Spa., Song, piano acc.; Ps., Piano solo).
Andersen, Arthur Olaf. Kinderwacht (A slumber song). Spa. German and English text. 1909.
Avery, Stanley R. Eskimo love song. Spa. 1906. (Vol.5, No.33c).
—— On a balcony. Spa. 1907. (Vol.6, No.48a).
Ayres, Frederic. Come unto these yellow sands (The tempest). Op.3, No.3. Spa. 1907.
—— Fugue. Op.12, No.1. Ps. 1910.
—— Hesper. Op.6, No.2. Spa. 1911.
—— Sea dirge, from The tempest. Op.4, No.2. Spa. 1907. (Vol.6, No.42a).
—— Take, O, take those lips away. Op.3, No.1. Spa. 1906. (Vol.5, No.33b2).
—— Where the bee sucks, from The tempest. Op.3, No.2. Spa.1907. (Vol.6, No.47a).
Beach, John Parsons. Autumn song. Spa. 1904. (Vol.3, No.17b).
—— A garden fancy. Ps. 1907. (Vol.6, No.49b).
—— Ici-bas. Spa. French and English text. 1903. (Vol.2, No.15b).
—— In a gondola. (Dramatic monologue for baritone or tenor). Spa. 1905. (Vol.4, No.25).
—— Intermezzo. Ps. 1905. (Vol.4, No.30b).
—— Is she not pure gold? Spa. 1907. (Vol.6, No.45a).
—— 'Twas in a world of living leaves. Spa. 1903.
—— The kings. Spa. 1904. (Vol.3, No.17a).
—— Monologue. Ps. 1907. (Vol.6, No.41b).
—— Nay, but you who do not love her. Spa. (Apparently not published; announced on verso of p.9 of Farwell's "The farewell").
—— New Orleans miniatures. Ps. 1906. (Vol.5, No.36). Contents: Esplanade (Promenade). In an Ursuline court (Cloud reverie). Balcony lyric. Place d'Orléans (St. Louis Cathedral). Masques (Mardi Gras). Envoi.
—— Rhapsody. Ps. 1907. (Vol.6, No.43b).
—— A Song of the lilac. Spa. 1904. (Vol.3, No.17c).
—— Take, O, take those lips away. Spa. 1906. (Vol.5, No.33b1).
—— A Woman's last words. Spa. 1903. (Vol.2, No.15a).
Bergh, Arthur. The raven. A melodrama. Op.20. Recitation, piano acc. 1910. (Orchestra score and parts for hire).
Branscombe, Gena. (Mrs. John Ferguson Tenney). Serenade. Spa. 1905. (Vol.4, No.29c).
—— Sleep, then, ah sleep! Spa. 1906.
—— What are we two? Spa. 1905. (Vol.4, No.29d).
Burlin, Natalie Curtis. Songs from A child's garden of verses by Robert Louis Stevenson. Spa. 1902. (Vol.2, No.9). Contents: Time to rise. Rain. The wind. At the seashore. The swing. System. Farewell to the farm.
Damon, Julia. The valley of lovers. Spa. 1906.
Farwell, Arthur. American Indian melodies. Ps.1901. (Vol.1, No.2). Contents: Approach of the Thunder God. The old man's love song. Song of the deathless voice. Ichibuzzhi. The mother's vow. Inketunga's thunder song. Song of the ghost dance. Song of the spirit. Song of the leader. Choral.
—— Dawn. Op.12. Ps. 1902. (Vol.1, No.4b). (Revised for orchestra; score and parts available on loan).
—— The domain of Hurakan. Op.15. Ps. 1902. (Vol.2, No.10). (A revised orchestral version announced on verso of back cover of Kreider's "Six preludes").
—— Drake's drum. Spa. 1907. (Vol.6, No.41a).
—— The farewell. Spa. 1911.
—— Folk-songs of the west and south. Negro, Cowboy, and Spanish-California. Harmonized. Spa. 1905. (Vol.4, No.27). Contents: Two negro spirituals (De rocks arenderin'; Moanin' dove). The lone prairee. The hours of grief (Las horas de luto). The black face (La cara negra). Bird dance song (Cahuilla tribe). (Spanish songs with Spanish and English texts).
—— From mesa and plain. Indian, cowboy, and Negro sketches. Ps. 1905. (Vol.4, No.28). Contents: Navajo war dance. Pawnee horses. Prairie miniature. Wa-Wan choral. Plantation melody.
—— Ichibuzzhi. Op.13. Ps. 1902. (Vol.1, No.6c).
—— Impressions of the Wa-Wan ceremony of the Omahas. Op.21. Ps. 1906. (Vol.5, No.38). Contents: Receiving the messenger. Nearing the village. Song of approach. Laying down the pipes. Raising the pipes. Invocation. Song of peace. Choral.
—— Love's secret. Spa. 1903. (Vol.2, No.13a).
—— Owasco memories. Op.8. Ps. 1907. (Vol.6,

No.50b). Contents: Spring moods. By moonlight. By quiet waters. Waltz. Autumn comes.

—— Requiescat. Spa. 1904. (Vol.3, No.21c).

—— A ruined garden. Op.14. Spa. 1904. (Vol.3, No.21b).

—— To Morfydd. Oboe and piano. 1903. (Vol.2, No.14c).

—— Toward the dream. Op.16. Ps. 1904. (Vol.3, No.20a). (Pub. in sheet form as "Symbolistic study No.1").

Freer, Eleanor Everest. To a painter. (Ode LVII, Anacreon-Moore). Spa. 1907. (Vol.6, No.49a).

—— A valentine. Op.21. Spa. 1909.

Getty, Alice. J'ai cherché trente ans mes soeurs. Spa. French and English text. 1903. (Vol.2, No.11b).

Gilbert, Henry Franklin Belknap. Celtic studies. Spa. 1905. (Vol.4, No.31). Contents: Bring from the craggy haunts of birch and pine. O would I were the cool wind. My heart is heavy night and day. One night when one o' the Irish kings. (Titles from first lines).

—— Two episodes for orchestra. Op.2. Orchestra scores. 1897. Contents: Legend. Negro episode. (Taken over, but not published, by Wa-Wan Press; announced in 1907 catalog).

—— Faery song. Spa. 1905. (Vol.4, No.29a).

—— Fish wharf rhapsody. Spa. 1909.

—— The island of the fay. Ps. 1904. (Vol.3, No.22).

—— The lament of Deirdré. Spa. 1903. (Vol.2, No.13a).

—— Mazurka. Ps. 1902. (Vol.1, No.8a).

—— Negro episode. Op.2, No.2. Ps. 1902. (Vol.1, No.6b). (cf. Two episodes for orchestra).

—— Orlamonde. Spa. 1907. (Vol.6, No.51a).

—— The owl. Spa. 1910.

—— Pirate song. Spa. 1902. (Vol.1, No.7b).

—— Salammbo's invocation to Tänith. Spa. 1902. (Vol.1, No.5c). (Orchestra parts for rent).

—— Scherzo. Ps. 1902. (Vol.1, No.8b).

—— Two South American gypsy songs. Spa., violin obbligato. 1906. (Vol.5, No.35). Contents: La montonéra. La zambulidora.

—— Tell me where is fancy bred? Spa. (Evidently not published, although announced in 1907 catalog).

—— Two Verlaine moods. Ps. 1903. (Vol.2, No.16b).

—— Zephyrus. Spa. 1903. (Vol.2, No.11a).

Gilman, Lawrence. The curlew. Recitation, piano acc. 1904. (Vol.3, No.21a).

—— A dream of death. Recitation, piano acc. 1903. (Vol.2, No.16a).

—— The heart of the woman. Spa. 1903. (Vol.2. No.15c).

Goldmark, Rubin. I have done, put by the lute. Op.19, No.4. Spa. 1908.

Gott, Rudolph. Landscape. Oboe and piano. 1903. (Vol.2, No.14b).

Heyman, Katherine Ruth Willoughby. Lament for Adonis. Spa. 1903. (Vol.2, No.11c).

Hill, Edward Burlingame. At the grave of a hero. Ps. 1903. (Vol.2, No.14a).

Ide, Chester Edward. Lovers of the wild. Spa. 1907. (Vol.6, No.43a).

—— Names. Spa. 1907. (Vol.6, No.52a).

—— Waltz– To Margaret. Ps. 1907. (Vol.6, No.47b).

Kelley, Edgar Stillman. Eldorado. Op.8, No.1. Spa. 1901. (Vol.1, No.1a).

—— Israfel. Op.8, No.2. Spa. 1901. (Vol.1, No.1b).

Knowlton, Fanny Snow. Portuguese love song. Spa. (Evidently not published, although announced in 1907 catalog).

Kreider, Noble W. Ballad. Op.3. Ps. 1906. (Vol.5, No.40).

—— Impromptu for pianoforte. Op.5. Ps. 1907. (Vol.6, No.42b).

—— Nocturn. Op.4, No.2. Ps. 1907. (Vol.6, No.46b).

—— Preludes. No.II, III, V from Op.7. Ps. 1908.

—— Six preludes. Op.7. Ps. 1910.

—— Study. Op.6, No.1. Ps. 1908.

—— Study. Op.6, No.2. Ps. 1908.

Kroeger, Ernest Richard. Memory. A song cycle. Op.66. Spa. 1906. (Vol.5, No.39). Contents: Grey skies and leafless trees. Bird notes are hushed. O memory! Our joy art Thou, and pain. Life! Thou art fair, Thou art young. A stretch of burning sand. Life! Thou art fair, Thou art sweet. What mocks the garish light of summer day? What mocks the garish light but solitude? Could I in crowded street.

Lambord, Benjamin. Valse fantastique. Op.6. Ps. 1905. (Vol.4, No.26).

Little, Alfred E. I look into my glass. Spa. 1903. (Vol.2, No.13b).

Little, Arthur Reginald. The city of sleep. Spa. 1906. (Vol.5, No.33a).

—— Drink to me only with thine eyes. Spa. 1902. (Vol.1, No.5b).

—— Helen. Spa. 1902. (Vol.1, No.5a).

—— Ulalume. Ps. 1902. (Vol.1, No.6a).

Loomis, Harvey Worthington. After the lesson. Op.75. Piano duet. 1902. (Published in conjunction with Birchard).

—— Hark! hark! the lark. Spa. 1902. (Vol.1, No.3a).

—— The hour of the whippoorwill. Spa. 1906. (Published, under arrangement, by Birchard).

—— In the moon-shower. Op.70, No.4. Recitation, obbligato for piano, violin, and voice. 1902. (Vol.1, No.3c).

—— Intermezzo from "The tragedy of death." Op.72. Ps. 1902. (Vol.1, No.4a). (Arranged from orchestra version).

—— Lyrics of the red-man. Op.76, Book 1. Ps. 1903. (Vol.2, No.12). Contents: Music of the Calumet. A song of sorrow. Around the wigwam. The silent conqueror. Warriors' dance.

—— Lyrics of the red-man. Op.76, Book 2. Ps. 1904. (Vol.3, No.24). Contents: Prayer to Wakonda (Offering of the sacred pipe). On the war path. Ripe corn dance (Harvest ceremonial). Evening at the lodge. The chattering squaw. Scalp dance. The thunder

god and the rainbow. The warrior's last word.
—— Morning song. Spa. 1907. (Vol.6, No.44a).
—— My mammy's voice. Spa. (Evidently not published, although announced in 1907 catalog).
—— O'er the sea. Spa. 1902. (Vol.1, No.3b).
—— Star rays. Ps. 1902. (Vol.1, No.8c).
McCoy, William J. The only voice (Ihre Stimme). Op.51, No.1. Spa. English and German text. 1905. (Vol.4, No.29b).
Oldberg, Arne. Badinage. (From "Three miniatures." Op.27). Ps. 1907. (Vol.6, No.52b).
—— Carillon. (From "Three miniatures." Op.27). Ps. 1907. (Vol.6, No.51b).
—— Concerto, G minor, for piano and orchestra. Op.17. Edition for 2 pianos. 1907. (Listed in 1907 catalog as "Symphonic concerto." Orchestra parts for hire).
—— Intermezzo. (From "Three miniatures." Op.27). Ps. 1908.
—— A legend. Op.26. Ps. 1907. (Vol.6, No.48b).
Roper, Virginia. In Venezia. Serenade. Ps. 1906.
Schneider, Edward Faber. A midwinter idyl. Violin and piano. 1906. (Vol.5, No.34b).
—— A romantic fantasy. Op.11. Violin and piano. 1907.
Schuyler, William. In the golden fullness. Spa., with 'cello obbligato ad lib. 1906. (Vol.5, No.37a).
Shepherd, Arthur. The lost child. Op.7, No.4. Spa. 1909.
—— Mazurka. Op.2, No.1. Ps. 1905. (Vol.4, No.30a).
—— Prelude. Op.2, No.2. Ps. 1906. (Vol.5, No.34a).
—— Five songs. Op.7. Spa. 1909. Contents: Lift up the curtains of thine eyes. Nocturn. There is a light in thy blue eyes. The lost child. Rhapsody.
—— A star in the night. Spa. 1906. (Vol.5, No.37c).
—— Theme and variations. Op.1. Ps. 1905. (Vol.4, No.32).
Tipton, Louis Campbell–. Four sea lyrics. Quatre poèmes lyriques de la mer. A cycle. Spa. English and French text. 1907. Contents: After sunset (Après le coucher du soleil). Darkness (Ténèbres). The crying of water (Le cri des eaux). Requies.
—— Sonata heroic. Ps. 1904. (Vol.3, No.18).
Troyer, Carlos. Ghost dance of the Zuñis. Ps. 1904. (Vol.3, No.20b). (Also announced in 1907 catalog in arrangement for violin and piano, a version evidently not published).
—— Hymn to the sun. An ancient jubilee song of the sun-worshippers. With historic account of the ceremony and the derivation of music from the sun's rays. Spa. 1909.
—— Indian fire-drill song. "Uru Kuru." (As sung by the Mojave-Apaches, while revolving the fire-stick). Spa. 1907. (Vol.6, No.46a).
—— Kiowa-Apache war-dance. Ps. 1907. (Vol. 6, No.45b).
—— Traditional songs of the Zuñis. Spa. English and Indian text. 1904. (Vol.3, No.19). Contents: Zuñian lullaby and incantation. The lover's wooing, or Blanket song. The sunrise call. The coming of Montezuma.
—— Traditional songs of the Zuñis. Second series. Spa. English text. 1904. (Vol.3, No.23). Contents: The festive sun dance of the Zuñis. The great rain dance of the Zuñis.
Walker, Caroline Holme. The lonely garden (Wanderlied). Spa. 1907. (Vol.6, No.50a).
—— When the dew is falling. Spa. 1906. (Vol.5, No.37b).
Waller, Henry. The spirit of wine. Spa. 1902. (Vol.1, No.7a).
Wright, Louise Drake. The shadow rose. Spa. 1903. (Vol.2, No.15d).

WEBER, CARL MARIA FRIEDRICH ERNST, *Freiherr von*, 1786–1826.
Carl Maria von Weber Musikalische Werke. Erste kritische Gesamtausgabe unter Leitung von Hans Joachim Moser. Augsburg und Cöln, Benno Filser Verlag, G.m.b.H., 1926–33.
3v. (Akademie zur Erforschung und zur Pflege des Deutschtums [Deutsche Akademie]. Abt.III B: Musik. Geschäftsführender Sekretär: Adolf Sandberger).
Contents:
2.Reihe: Dramatische Werke.
Vol.1. Jugendopern. Eingeleitet und revidiert von Alfred Lorenz. 1926.
A. Das stumme Waldmädchen. (Bruchstücke).
B. Peter Schmoll und seine Nachbarn.
Vol.2. Eingeleitet und revidiert von Willibald Kaehler. 1928.
A. Rübezahl. (Bruchstücke).
B. Silvana.
Vol.3. Salzburger Jugendmesse. Eingeleitet und revidiert von Const. Schneider. 1933.

WEBER, CARL MARIA FRIEDRICH ERNST, *Freiherr von*, 1786–1826.
Compositionen von Carl Maria von Weber. Erste rechtmässige Gesamtausgabe, revidirt und corrigirt von H. W. Stolze . . . Bd.1– . Wolfenbüttel, [L. Holle, 1857–].
v.1– . front. (port., v.2).
Various paging.
Each opus has separate title page.
"Carl Maria von Weber's Biographie und Characteristik. Von Dr. Heinrich Döring, Bd.1, p.[1]–24; "Verzeichniss von Weber's Sämmtlichen Compositionen, von ihn selbst bis zum Jahre 1823 ausgesetzt," Bd.1, p.[25]–26.
Contents:
Bd.1. Compositionen für das Pianoforte solo: Op.2. 6 Variationen über ein Thema von Saromi; Op.3. Leichte Stücke; Op.5. 8 Variationen über eine Melodie aus Castor und Pollux; Op.7. 7 Variationen über ein italienisches Thema: "Vien qua Dorina bella"; Op.12. Capriccio; Op.21. Grosse Polonaise (in Es); Op.24. Erste grosse Sonate (in C-dur); Op.28. Variationen über die Romanze: "A peine au sortir de l'enfance"; Op.37, oder 40. Variationen über eine russische Arie: "Schöne Minka"; Op.39. Zweite grosse Sonate (in

As-dur); Op.49. Dritte grosse Sonate (in D-moll); Op.55. 7 Variationen über ein Zigeunerlied; Op.62. Rondo brillante (in Es-dur); Op.65. Aufforderung zum Tanz: Rondo brillante (in Des-dur); Op.70. Vierte grosse Sonate (in G-dur); Op.72. Pollacca brillante (in E-dur); Op.79. Concertstück; Op.81. Lebewohl, Fantasie. Letztes Walzer. Ouvertüre zu Sylvana. Ouvertüre zu Turandot. Ouvertüre zu Preciosa. Jubel-Ouvertüre zu Abu Hassan. Ouvertüre zu Euryanthe. Ouvertüre zu Beherrscher der Geister (Rübezahl).

Bd.2. Compositionen für das Pianoforte zu 4 Händen: Op.3, Nr.1. 6 Leichte Stücke; Op.3, No.2. 6 Leichte Stücke; Op.10. 6 Progressive und angenehme Sonaten; Op.60. 8 Stücke. Ouvertüre zu Sylvana. Ouvertüre zu Turandot. Ouvertüre zu Preciosa. Jubel-Ouvertüre. Ouvertüre zu Freischütz. Ouvertüre zu Oberon. Ouvertüre zu Peter Schmoll. Ouvertüre zu Abu Hassan. Ouvertüre zu Euryanthe. Ouvertüre zu Beherrscher der Geister (Rübezahl).

WEBER, CARL MARIA FRIEDRICH ERNST, *Freiherr von*, 1786–1826.
Sämtliche Werke für Pianoforte, von C. M. von Weber. Hrsg. von Louis Köhler und Adolf Ruthardt . . . Revidierte Ausgabe. Leipzig, C. F. Peters, n.d.
3v. (Edition Peters. No.717a–c).
Title pages of volumes vary.
Contents:
Vol.1. Sonaten; C-dur. As-dur. D-moll. E-moll.
Vol.2. Stücke. Polonaise. Rondo brillante. Polacca, usw.
Vol.3. Variationen und Konzerte.

WECKERLIN, JEAN BAPTISTE THÉODORE, 1821–1910. ed.
. . . Échos du temps passé; recueil de chansons, Noëls, madrigaux, brunettes, musettes, airs à boire et à danser, menuets, chansons populaires, etc., du XIIme au XVIIIme siècle. Transcrits avec accompagnement de piano par J. B. Weckerlin . . . Paris, A. Durand & Fils, [189?].
3v.
For 1 voice with piano acc. A few numbers for 4 mixed voices.
Vol.2 reprinted from plates of G. Flaxland, 1855; Vol.3 from plates of Durand, Schoenewerk et Cie., 1878?.

Weckmann, Matthias, 1619–1674. Ausgewählte Werke, *see* Das Erbe deutscher Musik. Zweite Reihe. Landschaftsdenkmale. Schleswig-Holstein und Hansestädte. Vol.4.

THE WELLESLEY EDITION. Jan La Rue, director. Wellesley, Mass., Wellesley College, 1950– .
v.1– .
Contents (asterisk indicates unpublished volumes):
No.1. Jenkins, John. Fancies and ayres. Ed. by Helen Joy Sleeper. 1950.
No.2. Lamb, Hubert. Six scenes from the Protevangelion. 1951.
No.3. Ward, John, ed. The Dublin virginal manuscript. 1954. 2d edition, corrected, revised, and augmented. Ed. by John Ward. 196?.
*No.4. Haydn, Joseph. Three divertimenti. Ed. by Jan La Rue.
No.5. The Italian cantata, I. Antonio Cesti (1623–1669). Ed. by David Burrows. 1963.
No.6. Fifteenth century basse dances. Brussels Bibl. Roy. MS.9085. Collated with Michel Toulouze's "L'art et instruction de bien dancer." Ed. by James L. Jackman. 1964.
*No.7. The Italian cantata, II. Stradella, Alessandro. Ed. by Owen Jander.
No.8. The Bottegari lutebook. Ed. by Carol MacClintock. 1965.
*No.9. The Italian cantata, III. (to be announced).
No.10. Jenkins, John. Three-part fancy and ayre divisions for two trebles and a bass to the organ. Ed. by Robert Austin Warner. 1966.

WELLESZ, EGON, 1885– . ed.
Trésor de musique byzantine . . . Par Egon Wellesz . . . Paris, Éditions de l'Oiseau Lyre, Chez L. B. M. Dyer, [cop.1934].
1 v.
"Il a été tiré de cet ouvrage trois cent trents exemplaires sur papier d'Orient, numérotés de 1 à 300, et trent exemplaires hors de commerce numérotés de I à XXX."
Introductory text in German and French; words of hymns in Greek, with French translation.
Transcription, in modern notation, of liturgical melodies, chiefly from manuscripts of the thirteenth century.
"Sources": Vol.I, pt.1, p.[23].
Contents:
Bd.I. 1.pt. Notes explicatives.
2.pt. Mélodies dans le premier mode.

DAS WELTLICHE KONZERT IM 18. JAHRHUNDERT. Heft 1– . Braunschweig, H. Litolff, [1932–].
No.1– . music.
Editor: Heft 1– , Fritz Wilhelm Stein.
Contents:
Heft 1. Telemann, G. P. Konzert F-moll für Solo-Oboe mit Begleitung von Streichorchester und Cembalo (Klavier). [1932].
Heft 2. Mozart, W. A. [Concertos. Bassoon. B flat major. (Bückenburg). Arr. for bassoon and pianoforte] . . . Konzert B-dur für Fagott . . . [1934].
Heft 4. Händel, G. F. [Concertos. Oboe. E major] . . . Konzert Es-dur für Solo-Oboe, Streichorchester und Cembalo. [1935].

Werke aus dem 18. Jahrhundert, *see* Sondheimer, Robert. Werke aus dem 18. Jahrhundert.

Werke oberösterreichischer Komponisten. No.1–4, *see* Hausmusik. No.182, 183, 185, 186.

Werkreihe des Kulturamtes der Reichsjugendführung, *see* Volk Musiziert.

WERT, GIACHES DE, 1535–1596.
Opera omnia. Ed. by Carol MacClintock (secular

music); assisted by Melvin Bernstein (sacred music). Rome, American Institute of Musicology, 1961– .
v.1– . (Corpus mensurabilis musicae. No.24).
Proposed set more than a dozen volumes.
Contents:
Vol.1. Madrigals of 1558. 1961.
Vol.2. Madrigals of 1561. 1962.
Vol.3. Madrigals of 1563. 1962.
Vol.4. Madrigals of 1567. 1965.
Vol.5. Madrigals of 1571. 1966.
Vol.6. Madrigals. Il sesto libro di madrigali a cinque voci (1577). 1966.
Vol.7. Madrigals. Il settimo libro de madrigali a cinque voci, 1581. 1967.

WEST, JOHN EBENEZER, 1863–1929. ed.
Old English organ music. London, Novello & Co., [cop.1906].
2p.L., 36p.
Twelve selected pieces.

Widmann, Erasmus, 1572–1634. Ausgewählte Werke, *see* Das Erbe deutscher Musik. Sonderreihe. Vol.3.

WIENHÄUSER LIEDERBUCH.
Das Wienhäuser Liederbuch, hrsg. von Heinrich Sievers. Wolfenbüttel, Möseler, 1954.
2v. illus., facsims., music.
"Von Paul Alpers Text kritisch bearbeitet."
"Die Handschrift trägt heute die Signatur Hs. Nr.9 und wird im Kosterarchiv zu Wienhausen aufbewahrt."
Vol.1 contains introductory material and partial transcription of the manuscript, the facsimile of which forms Vol.2.
Bibliography: Vol.[1], p.27–28.

WIENIAWSKI, HENRI, 1835–1880.
Oeuvres. (Comité de rédaction: Irena Dubiska, Eugenia Umińska, Secrétaire du Comité: Adam Walaciński). Krakow, Polskie Wydawnictwo Muzyczne, [1962–].
9v. (in progress).
Contents:
Vol.1. Ier concerto pour violon en fa dièse mineur, Op.14. 1962.
Vol.2. IIe concerto pour violon en ré mineur, Op.22. 1962.

WILLAERT, ADRIAN, ca.1480–1562.
Opera omnia. Edidit Hermannus Zenck und W. Gerstenberg. Rome, American Institute of Musicology in Rome, 1950– .
15v. (in progress). (Corpus mensurabilis musicae. No.3).
Continued after the death of Hermann Zenck by W. Gerstenberg of Der Freien Universität, Berlin.
Vol.1 appeared previously as Vol.9 of *Publikationen älterer Musik*. 1937.
Contents (asterisk indicates unpublished volumes):
Vol.1. Motetta IV vocum, Liber primus, 1539 et 1545. 1950.
Vol.2. Motetta IV vocum, Liber secundus, 1539 et 1545. 1950.
Vol.3. Motetta V vocum 1539 et 1550. 1950.
Vol.4. Motetta VI vocum 1542. 1952.
Vol.5. Motetta. Musica nuova, 1559. 1957.
*Vol.6. Supplementum Mt. 1519–69.
Vol.7. Hymnorum musica, 1542. 1959.
*Vol.8. Psalmi IV et VIII vocum. 1555, 1565, 1571, 1550, 1557.
*Vol.9. Missae IV vocum. 1536.
*Vol.10. Missae V et VI vocum.
*Vol.11. Cantilenae italicae I. (Verdelot 1536).
*Vol.12. Cantilenae italicae II. 1537/63.
Vol.13. Musica nova. 1559. Madrigalia. 1966.
*Vol.14. Cantilenae galicae et Opera instr. 1520–93.
*Vol.15. Critical appendix to Vol.1–14.

Williams, Alberto, 1862–1952, ed. Antologia de compositores argentinos, *see* Antologia de compositores argentinos.

The Winchester troper, *see* Catholic Church, Roman. Liturgy and ritual. Troper. The Winchester troper.

WINTERFELD, CARL GEORG AUGUST VIVIGENS VON, 1784–1852. ed.
Der evangelische Kirchengesang und sein verhältniss zur Kunst des Tonsatzes, dargestellt von Carl von Winterfeld . . . Leipzig, Breitkopf & Härtel, 1843–47.
3v.
Musikbeilagen: Vol.1, 161p.; Vol.2, 204p.; Vol.3, 276p.
Contents:
Vol.1. Der evangelische Kirchengesang im ersten Jahrhunderts der Kirchenverbesserung.
Vol.2. Der evangelische Kirchengesang im siebzehnten Jahrhunderts.
Vol.3. Der evangelische Kirchengesang im achtzehnten Jahrhunderts.

Winterfeld, Carl Georg August Vivigens von, 1784–1852. Johannes Gabrieli und sein Zeitalter. Vol.III, *see* Gabrieli, Giovanni. Music of Gabrieli and his time.

WOLF, HUGO, 1860–1903.
Nachgelassene Werke, vorgelegt von Robert Haas und Helmut Schultz. Leipzig, Musikwissenschaftlicher Verlag, [cop.1936–].
v.1– .
With English translations of the songs by A. H. Fox-Strangways.
Contents:
1.Folge. Lieder mit Klavierbegleitung.
Heft 1. Elf Jugendlieder.
Heft 2. Elf Lieder nach Gedichten von Heine und Lenau.
Heft 3. Acht Lieder nach Gedichten von Mörike und Eichendorff.
Heft 4. Sieben Lieder nach Gedichten von Robert Reinick.
2.Folge.
Heft 1. Zwei Orchesterlieder aus dem Spanischen Liederbuch.
3.Folge. Instrumentalwerke.
Heft 2. Penthesilea.
Heft 3. Scherzo und Finale.

WOLF, HUGO, 1860–1903.
Sämtliche Werke. Kritische Gesamtausgabe, hrsg. von der Internationalen Hugo Wolf-Gesellschaft unter Leitung von Hans Jancik. Wien, Musikwissenschaftlicher Verlag, 1960– .
v.1– .
Contents:
Vol.1. Gedichte von E. Mörike für eine Singstimme und Klavier.
Vol.15. Kammermusik: Streichquartett D moll; Intermezzo für Streichquartett: Italienische Serenade für Streichquartett.

WOLF, JOHANNES, 1869–1947. ed.
Chor- und Hausmusik aus älter Zeit. Hrsg. von Prof. Dr. Johannes Wolf. Berlin, Wolbing-Verlag, 1926–27.
2v.
Contents:
Vol.1. Gesänge für gemischten Chor. 17p. Contains works by Ulrich Brätels, Jodocus von Brandts, Arnold von Bruck, Otto Siegfr. Harnisch, Senfl, and Stoltzer. 1926.
Vol.2. Gesänge für gemischten Chor. 23p. Contains works by Valentin Haussmann and Paul Sartorius. 1927.

WOLF, JOHANNES, 1869–1947. ed.
Music of earlier times. Vocal and instrumental examples (13th century to Bach). New York, Carl Fischer, 1946.
158p.

WOLF, JOHANNES, 1869–1947. ed.
... Sing- und Spielmusik aus älterer Zeit; hrsg. als Beispielband zur Allgemeinen Musikgeschichte von Dr. Johannes Wolf ... Leipzig, Quelle & Meyer, 1926.
viii, 158p. (Wissenschaft und Bildung. [v].218).
2d ed. 1931.
Contains 66 examples illustrating the history of music from about 1400 to 1650.

Wolf, Johannes, 1869–1947, ed. Squarcialupi Codex, *see* Squarcialupi Codex. Der Squarcialupi-Codex.

WOLFENBÜTTEL. HERZOG-AUGUST-BIBLIOTHEK. Mss. (677 [Helmst.628]).
... An old St. Andrews music book (Codex Helmst.628) published in facsimile, with an introd. by J. H. Baxter ... London, Pub. for St. Andrews University by H. Milford, Oxford University Press; [etc., etc.], 1931.
xix, [1]p., facsim.: [394]p. (St. Andrews University publications. No.XXX).

WOLFENBÜTTEL. HERZOG-AUGUST-BIBLIOTHEK. Mss. (677 [Helmst.628]).
Index to the facsimile edition of Ms. Wolfenbüttel 677, prepared by Dom Anselm Hughes ... Edinburgh & London, W. Blackwood & Sons, Ltd., 1939.
41p.

Wooldridge, Harry Ellis, 1845–1917, ed. Early English harmony from the 10th to the 15th century, *see* Plainsong and Mediaeval Music Society. Wooldridge, Harry Ellis. Early English harmony from the 10th to the 15th century.

The Worcester fragments, *see* Dittmer, Luther A. The Worcester fragments.

Worcester mediaeval harmony of the thirteenth and fourteenth centuries. Hughes, Anselm, *Father*, *see* Plainsong and Mediaeval Music Society. Hughes, Anselm, *Father*. Worcester mediaeval harmony of the thirteenth and fourteenth centuries.

WORK, HENRY CLAY, 1832–1884.
Songs of Henry Clay Work, poet and composer. Compiled by Bertram G. Work, nephew of the author, and presented with his compliments. No imprint, "Press of J. J. Little & Ives Co., New York," [1920].
180p.

Wyatt, Edward Gerald Penfold, 1869– . St. Gregory and the Gregorian music, *see* Plainsong and Mediaeval Music Society. Wyatt, Edward Gerald Penfold. St. Gregory and the Gregorian music.

Wydawnictwo Dawnej Muzyki Polskiej, *see* Denkmäler altpolnischer Musik.

Zachau, Friedrich Wilhelm, 1663–1712. Selected compositions, *see* Denkmäler deutscher Tonkunst. [1.Folge]. Vol.21–22.

ZAGIBA, FRANTIŠEK, 1912– . ed.
Die ältesten musikalischen Denkmäler zu Ehren des heiligen Leopold, Herzog und Patron von Österreich. Ein Beitrag zur Choralpflege in Österreich am Ausgange des Mittelalters. Zürich, Amalthea-Verlag, [1954].
41p. col. front., 45 facsims., music.
Bibliographical footnotes.
Contents:
Untersuchungen.
Die musikalischen Denkmäler: 1. Das Melker Offizium zu Ehren des heiligen Leopold. 2. Das Klosterneuburger Offizium zu Ehren des heiligen Leopold.

ZAHN, JOHANNES, 1817–1895. ed.
Die Melodien der deutschen evangelischen Kirchenlieder, aus den quellen Geschöpft und Mitgeteilt, von Johannes Zahn. Gütersloh, C. Bertelsmann, 1889–93.
6v.
Contents:
Vol.1. Zweizeilige bis fünfzeilige Melodien. 1889.
Vol.2. Sechszeilige Melodien. 1890.
Vol.3. Die siebenzeiligen und die jambischen achtzeiligen Melodien. 1890.
Vol.4. Die Melodien von den achtzeiligen Trochäischen bis zu den zehnzeiligen inklusive enthaltend. 1891.
Vol.5. Die übrigen Melodien von den Elkzeiligen an, nebst Anhang und Nachlese, sowie das Chronologisch Verzeichnis der ersinder von

Melodien und das alphabetische Register der Melodien. 1892.
Vol.6. Chronologisches Verzeichnis der benutzten Gesang– , Melodien- und Choralbücher, und die letzten Nachträge. 1893.

ZEITSCHRIFT FÜR SPIELMUSIK. Celle, Hermann Moeck, Verlag.
No.1– .
Contents:
No.1. Altniederländische Tänze um 1550.
No.2. Agricola, Martin. Choralkanons.
No.3. Erde singe- Lied- und Tanzsätze. (Jöde).
No.4. Der Waldjäger. Volkstänze aus dem Böhmerwald. (Kuntz).
No.5. Mattheson, Johann. Tanzsätze.
No.6. Regnart, Jacob. Kurtzweilige teutsche Lieder, zu singen oder zu spielen. 1.Heft.
No.7. Schüler, Karl. "Es waren zwei Königskinder." Volksliederspiel nach verschiedenen Weisen für 2 Singstimmen und 2 Blockflöten oder andere Instrumente.
No.8. Hense, Alfred. Thema mit Variationen für Sopran- oder Tenor-Blockflöte.
No.9. Isaac, Heinrich. Vierstimmige Instrumentalsätze.
No.10. 10 Leichte Volksliedsätze von Victor Korda.
No.11. Gervaise, Claude. Tänze.
No.12. Telemann, G. Ph. 7 Menuette von Melante für 1 Melodieinstrumente und Bass (mit freier Mittelstimme ad lib.).
No.13. Schlensog, Martin. Der Jahreskreis.
No.14. Bach, Johann Sebastian. 4-Stimmige Choräle.
No.15. Weihnacht. 8 Alte Lieder in 3-stimmigen Sätzen mit Gitarre ad lib. von Erich Scharff.
No.16. Bauer, Franz. Sätze für 3 Sopran-Blockflöten oder andere Instrumente.
No.17. Regnart, Jacob. Kurtzweilige teutsche Lieder, zu singen oder zu spielen. 2.Heft.
No.18. Lasso, Orlando di. Bicinien.
No.19. Ein Bündel bekannter Kernlieder in Sätzen von Helmut Mönkemeyer.
No.20. Deutsche Volkstänze. 1.Teil.
No.21. Kugelmann, Hans. Kleine Messe.
No.22. Schlensog, Martin. 7 Tanzweisen für Sopran-Blockflöte und Klavier.
No.23. Müller, Friedrich Ewald. Thema mit Variationen.
No.24. Peuerl, Paul. 2 Suiten.
No.25. Schlensog, Martin. 3 Stücke für 2 Blockflöten und Klavier.
No.26. Neue bayerische Tänze von Franz Biebl.
No.27. Der Weihnachtsmann in neuen und alten Weisen zu 2–3 Stimmen.
No.28. Franck, Melchior. Deutsche weltliche Gesänge und Täntze.
No.29. Mozart, W. A. Kontratänze und Menuette.
No.30. Bekannte Volkslieder. 1.Teil. Für das anfangende Zusammenspiel auf 2 oder 3 Blockflöten, gesetzt von Eilli Wolter.
No.31. Deutsche Volkstänze. 2.Teil.
No.32. Franck, Melchior. 4-stimmige Suite. (1614).
No.33. Gastoldi, Giovanni. 7 Ballette; Marenzio, Luca. 2 Villanellen, zu singen oder zu spielen.
No.34. 12 Tanzlieder und Spiele für Kinder mit Instrumentalsätzen für 2 Blockflöten oder Geigen und Gitarre ad lib., gesetzt von Adolf Hoffmann (mit Tanz- und Spielbeschreibung).
No.35. Bauer, Franz. 7 Variationen über ein Thema von J. Ph. Krieger für ein Melodieinstrument und Klavier.
No.36. Korda, Victor. Suite im alten Stil.
No.37. Hohn, Wilhelm. Stücke für 3 Blockflöten.
No.38. Telemann, G. Ph. 11 Stücke.
No.39. Alte Weihnachtsmusik. Eine Folge von Spielstücken und Liedern für 2 Sopran-Blockflöten oder andere Instrumente; Singstimme und Gitarre ad lib. Zusammengestellt von Martin Schlensog.
No.40. "Lieber Herrgott, sing mit!" 15 schöne Gsangl vom Alpenland (Wastl Fanderl). Neuausgabe.
No.41. Schlensog, Martin. Bei Schäfern und Hirten. Romantische Suite.
No.42. "Alle Vögel sind schon da." Bekannte Volkslieder. 2.Teil. Für das anfangende Zusammenspiel auf 2–4 Blockflöten.
No.43. Schein, Johann Hermann. 2 Fünfstimmige Suiten.
No.44. Telemann, G. Ph. Tänze.
No.45. Purcell, Henry. Fröhliche Kanons.
No.46. Jeep, Johann. Dreistimmige Lieder, au singen oder zu spielen.
No.47. 3 Suiten aus einem Flötenbuch von Anfang des 18. Jahrhunderts.
No.48. Nordische Weisen. Volksmelodien aus Skandinavien. (Schlensog).
No.49. Schein, Johann Hermann. 4-stimmige Suitensätze.
No.50. Faber, Frank. Eine kleine Weihnachtskantate für 2 Singstimmen und 3 Blockflöten.
No.51. Schreyer, Wilhelm. Kleine Weihnachtsmusik für 3 gleiche Singstimmen, Sprecher und 2 Blockflöten.
No.52. Beckerath, Alfred von. Kleine Stücke für Sopran-Blockflöte und Tasteninstrument.
No.53. Hochzeitsarien und -tänze aus dem Mühlviertel in Oberösterreich.
No.54. Lange, G., Regnart, J., Schaerer, M. Newe deudsche Lieder.
No.55. Meyer, Otto. "Herzlich tut mich erfreuen die fröhlich Sommerzeit." Eine Sommerkantate für 1–3 gleiche Singstimmen und 3 Blockflöten oder andere Instrumente.
No.56. Haussmann, Valentin. Neue artige und liebliche Tänze.
No.57. Beckerath, Alfred von. Tag für Tag. Kleine Spielmusiken.
No.58. Isaac, Heinrich. Dreistimmige Instrumentalstücke.
No.59. Mann, Alfred. Kleine Schulmusik.
No.60. Mozart, Leopold. 12 Spielstücke.
No.61. Altenglische Stücke.
No.62. Glötzner, Karl Hermann. Vetter Florian. Eine Herbst- und Winterkantate für 2 gleiche Singstimmen und 2 Melodieinstrumente.
No.63. Bauer, Franz. Variationen über "Im Märzen der Bauer die Rosslein einspannt."
No.64. Schlüter, Gustav. Ein niederdeutscher Tageskreis (z.T. Volkslieder), zu singen und zu spielen.

No.65. Girgensohn, Arend. Variationen über "Schwesterlein, Schwesterlein, wann geh'n wir nach Haus."
No.66. "Im Maien." Alte Lieder in Sätzen von Erich Scharff.
No.67. Eizenberger, Josef. Österreichische Tanzsuite.
No.68. Kuntner, Leo. 2 Suiten für 2 Blockflöten oder andere Instrumente.
No.69. Duette alter Meister (Corelli, Fasch, J. S. Bach, Telemann, Händel, Keiser, Vivaldi, Hasse). Neuausgabe.
No.70. Schreyer, Wilhelm. Kleine Abendkantate für 2–3 Melodieinstrumente und 1–2 Singstimmen (Worte von Chr. Morgenstern).
No.71. Forck, Wilhelm. Introduktion und Doppelfuge in der lydischen Tonart.
No.72. Blunck, Adolf. Keine Hausmusik für Sopran- oder Tenor-Blockflöte und Klavier.
No.73. Hörschelmann, Ottmar. Weihnachtsliederspiel für eine Singstimme und 3 Instrumente.
No.74. Glötzner, Karl Hermann. Spielmusik.
No.75. Französische Volkslieder. (Lemit).
No.76. Händel, G. F. 9 Duette nach den "Pieces for Harpsichord." Neuausgabe.
No.77. Beckerath, Alfred von. Ambacher Quartett.
No.78. Häfner, Wolfgang Erich. 2 Präludien mit Fugen/ Karl Heinrich Mösler: s1 Duo.
No.79. "Tra-ri-ra, der Sommer, der ist da." Alte Lieder in Sätzen von Erich Scharff.
No.80. Faber, Frank. "Ein neuer Tag ist angebrochen." Kleine Morgenmusik für 3 Melodieinstrumente und Singstimme.
No.81. Napiersky, Herbert. Fröhliche Musik. Sonatine für 2 Blockflöten und Tasteninstrument.
No.82. Hark, Friedrich. Erntedank-Kantate aus Texte von Conrad Ferdinand Meyer, Georg Trakl und Matthias Claudius, für 3 gleiche Instrumente und 3 gleiche Singstimmen.
No.83. "Wenn alle Brünnlein fliessen." Bekannte Volkslieder, 3.Teil. Für das anfangende Zusammenspiel auf 2 oder 3 Blockflöten, gesetzt von Fritz Jöde.
No.84. Deutsche Tänze aus der Zeit Schuberts. (Jöde).
No.85. "Zünde an die Kerzen." Neue Weihnachtsweisen in 3-stimmigen Sätzen mit Gitarre ad lib. von Ftitz Jöde.
No.86. Demantius, Christoph. 4 Galliarden.
No.87. Hilton, John. Tricinien.
No.88. Alte deutsche Volksmärsche. (Jöde).
No.89. Schein, Johann Hermann. Waldliederlein, zu singen oder zu spielen.
No.90. Klingender Norden. Einstimmige Volksweisen der nordischen Völker.
No.91. Bischoff, Heinz. Salzburger Sonatine in F für 1 Blas- oder Streichinstrument und Gitarre.
No.92. Englische Lieder und Kanons. (Schultz).
No.93. Bresgen, Cesar. Tagesmusik für den Morgen, den Mittag und den Abend.
No.94. Altitalienische Kanonkunst für 2–3 gleiche Instrumente.
No.95. Alte Lothringer Lieder in 3-stimmigen Instrumentalsätzen von Heinz Haag.
No.96. Sweelinck, Jan Pieterszoon. Zwiegesänge.
No.97. Deutsche Zwiefache. (Jöde).
No.98. Haydn, Joseph. Divertimento C-dur.
No.99. Mozart, Wolfgang Amadeus. 3 Terzette, zu singen oder zu spielen.
No.100. Kuntz, Michael. Kleine Passacaglia auf ein altdeutsches Volkslied.
No.101. Die schönsten Weisen aus Sperontes' "Singender Muse." (1751).
No.102. Alpenländische Jodler für 2–3 Singstimmen oder Instrumente. (Jöde).
No.103. Lerich, Rudolf. Spiele zu zweien.
No.104. Weiss, Helmut. Serenade.
No.105. Die triumphierende Liebe. Ballatt-Tänze um 1650.
No.106. Jacobsen, Karsten. Niederdeutsche Präludien.
No.107. Schubert, Franz. Wiener Tänze für 2 Melodieinstrumente und Gitarre, gesetzt von Fritz Jöde.
No.108. Deutsche Oden um 1750.
No.109. Volkstanzweisen aus dem Schönhengstgau. (Gregor).
No.110. Schüler, Karl. Klänge von unterwegs.
No.111. Jöde, Fritz. Kleine Ulfiaden, Stundenblätter aus meinen Sohn Ulf.
No.112. Rhau, Georg. Bicinia Germanica.
No.113. Ehrhardt-Pitsch, Else. 5 Flötensprünge.
No.114. Rosenmüller, Johann. Kammersonate für 3 Melodieinstrumente allein oder 2 mit Basso Continuo.
No.115. Schüler, Karl. Klänge von unterwegs.
No.116. Hermann, Paul. Flötenmusik über ein Nachtigallenlied.
No.117. "Flieg her, flieg hin." Volkslieder für Singstimme und Alt-Blockflöte oder ein anderes Melodieinstrument, gesetzt von Victor Korda.
No.118. Beckerath, Alfred von. Neue Tänze.
No.119. Mozart, Wolfgang Amadeus. Serenade in C.
No.120. Teuscher, Hans. Sonate G-moll für 2 Blockflöten oder andere Instrumente.
No.121. Korda, Victor. Variationen über ein altes Dragonerlied.
No.122. Tisch, Lustig vor. Altmärkische Volkstänze. (Horenburg).
No.123. Jöde, Fritz. Männerloten. Der kleine Ulfiaden anderer Teil.
No.124. Schöne deutsche Liebeslieder, zu singen oder zu spielen, gesetzt von Werner Ochs.
No.125. Schwarzwälder Bauerntänze. 1.Teil. (Pfeil).
No.126. Breuer, Franz Josef. Blockflötenbüchlein für Wolfgang und Angelica.
No.127. Bauer, Franz. 6 Variationen über ein eigenes Thema für 1 Melodieinstrument und Klavier.
No.128. Telemann, G. Ph. Sonate 1 für 2 Alt-Blockflöten.
No.129. 9 Stücke aus dem Notenbüchlein für Anna Magdalena Bach.
No.130. Gröning, Herbert. Kleine Stücke für eine Blockflöte allein.

No.131. Hainlein, Paul. 12 Monatslieder, zu singen und zu spielen.
No.132. Oberborbeck, Felix. Kirchlintler Weihnachtsgeschichte. 10 Weihnachtslieder zum Weihnachtsevangelium des Lukas, 3-stimmig zu singen und zu spielen.
No.133. "Nun ruhen alle Wälder." 8 Abendlieder auf 4 Instrumenten zu spielen, gesetzt von Felix Oberborbeck.
No.134. Heyden, Reinhold. Variationen über "Grün sind alle meine Kleider" für 2 Blockflöten.
No.135. Hausmusik mit Johann Sebastian Bach, 2- oder 3-stimmige zu spielen.
No.136. Twittenhoff, Wilhelm. Kleine Tanzstücke.
No.137. Bach, Johann Sebastian. 8 Choräle.
No.138. Pfannenstiel, Ekkehart. Altstädler Suite für 4 gleiche Instrumente.
No.139. Bach, Johann Sebastian. 2 Fugen aus der "Kunst der Fuge."
No.140. Berger, Gregor. Aus sommerlichen Tagen.
No.141. 8 Tänze aus Leopold Mozarts Notenbuch dür Wolfgang (1762).
No.142. Aus Johann Sebastian Bachs Notenbüchlein für Anna Magdalena und andere Spielstücke.
No.143. Bauer, Franz. 7 Variationen über ein bretonisches Volkslied.
No.144. Ein kleines Weihnachtsoratorium mit Liedern, Chorälen und Instrumentalstücken von Johann Sebastian Bach, 3–4 stimmig zu singen und zu spielen. (Oberborbeck).
No.145. Ein kleines Weihnachtsoratorium mit Liedern, Chorälen und Instrumentalstücken von Johann Sebastian Bach, 3–4 stimmig zu singen und zu spielen. Englische Ausgabe: The Christmas story with instrumental pieces, songs and chorales by Johann Sebastian Bach.
No.146. Fux, Johann Joseph. 8 Menuette für ein Melodieinstrument und ein Tasteninstrument.
No.147. Aus dem "Musikalischen Lustgarten" des Johannes Schultz für 2 gleiche Stimmen zu singen oder zu spielen.
No.148. Deutsche Volkslieder mit Begleitung eines Instrumentes zu singen oder zweistimmig zu spielen, gesetzt von Gelicitas Kukuck.
No.149. Tänze aus den Alpenländern für 2 Melodieinstrumente und Gitarre ad lib. (Kolneder).
No.150. Oberborbeck, Felix. "Ich ging durch einen grasgrönen Wald." Kleine Kantate, 3–4 stimmig zu singen und zu spielen.
No.151. Werdin, Eberhard. 4 Tanzstücke für 1–3 Sopran-Blockflöten, 2 Streicher, Glockenspiel, Trommel und Triangel.
No.152. Ungarische Volksweisen aus den Sammlungen von Béla Bartók und Zoltán Kodály, gesetzt von Walter Unger. Neuausgabe.
No.153. Schöne Menuette aus alter Zeit für 1, 2 oder 3 Melodieinstrumente.
No.154. Schwarzwälder Bauerntänze. (Pfeil). 2.Teil.
No.155. Bossler, Kurt. Sonatine für Alt-Blockflöte und Violine.
No.156. Alte Kontratänze, gesetzt von Theodor Warner.
No.157. Volksmusik aus Steiermark für 2 Melodieinstrumente und Gitarre ad lib.
No.158. Rosenmüller, Johann. Studentenmusik.
No.159. Teuscher, Hans. Sonate A-moll für 2 Blockflöten oder andere Instrumente.
No.160. Bach, Johann Sebastian. 2 Fugen für 4 Instrumente (aus den Orgelfugen).
No.161. Sachs, Ilse. Berliner Sonatine in G für Sopran- oder Tenor-Blockflöte und Klavier.
No.162. Fecker, Adolf. Lustige Hamburger Flötenstücke.
No.163. Oberborbeck, Felix. Variationen über "Der Mai, der lustige Mai."
No.164. Mozart, W. A. 5 Spielstücke.
No.165. Alte französische Duette.
No.166. Werdin, Eberhard. Muntere Runde. 5 Tanzweisen für Glockenspiel, 3 Blockflöten, Handtrommel und Triangel.
No.167. Cox, Harry. 2 Flämische Suiten für Sopran- und Alt-Blockflöte.
No.168. Sydow, Kurt. Jagdliedvariationen.
No.169. Choralvorspiele von Joh. Gottfried Walther, Friedrich Wilh. Zachow und Dietrich Buxtehude.
No.170. "Lobt Gott, ihr Christen . . . " Alte Weihnachtslieder für Singstimme und Instrument gesetzt von Hans Siebert.
No.171. Lorenz, Karl. Herzdame. 3 Barsbüttler und 2 französische Tanzweisen in 3-stimmigen Sätzen und für vielerlei Besetzungen möglich. (Blockflöten, Geigen, Fideln, etc.).
No.172. "Non dieser Tag ist vergangen." Lieder zur Nacht, zu singen oder zu spielen, gesetzt von Felix Oberborbeck.
No.173. Bach, Johann Sebastian. Passionschoräle.
No.174. Purcell, Henry. Frühlingslied für 4 Instrumente oder 3 Instrumente mit Singstimme.
No.175. Maasz, Gerhard. Maienzeit. Variationen über eine alte Weise für 2 Sopran- und 1 Alt-Blockflöte.
No.176. Europäische Volkslieder, zu singen oder zu spielen, gesetzt von F. Oberborbeck.
No.177. Weber, Hanns Joachim. "Einem jeden gefällt seine Art wohl." Sing- und Spielstücke zu 2 Stimmen.
No.178. Altspanische Liedsätze, zu singen oder zu spielen.
No.179. Schäfer, Fuhrmann und andere Leute. 8 Kinderlieder mit Vorspielen für 2 Melodieinstrumente und Gitarre oder Streichinstrument, gesetzt von Hermann Dick.
No.180. Coenen, Hans. Das Märchen vom Dicken, fetten Pfannkunchen für 2 Einzelsänger, 2-stimmigen Chor, 2 Blockflöten, Stabspiel und Triangel.
No.181. 3 Instrumentalstücke des Mittelalters.
No.182. Oberborbeck, Felix. Vechtaer Adventkantate, 3-stimmig zu singen und zu spielen.
No.183. Sabel, Hans. Kleine Musik für Sopran-Blockflöte und Klavier.
No.184. Scheidt, Samuel. Fünfstimmige Tänze.
No.185. "Der Morgenstern ist aufgegangen." 8 Morgenlieder für Singstimme und

2 Instrumente oder 3-stimmig zu spielen in Sätzen von Cesar Bresgen, Karl Marx, Walter Rein und Jena Rohwer.

No.186. Bialas, Günter. Rhythmische Miniaturen für 2 Melodieinstrumente (mit ostinatem Bass und Schlagwerk nach Belieben).

No.187. Aus einem obersteirischen Flötenbuch von 1813.

No.188. Altniederländische Abschiedslieder, zu singen oder zu spielen.

No.189. Schlensog, Martin. Festliche Musik.

No.190. Uns in dem Schneegebirge. Kleine Instrumentalmusiken zu schlesischen Volksliedern von Alois Heiduczek.

No.191. Beckerath, Alfred von. Kuckucks im Duett und andere Bicinien.

No.192. 2 Passamezzi aus Elias Nikolaus Ammerbachs "Orgel- oder Instrument-Tabulatur." (1571).

No.193. "Ich wollt gern singen. "Alte Weisen zu singen oder zu spielen in Sätzen von Helmut Mönkemeyer.

No.194. Weber, Hanns Joachim. Marienauer Weihnachtsmusik für 4 Instrumente mit oder ohne Singstimme.

No.195. Praetorius, Michael. Choräle.

No.196. Knapp, Arno. Suite zu dritt.

No.197. "Hänsel und Gretel." Bekannte Kinderlieder für Sopran- Blockflöte und Klavier, gesetzt von Hanns Hübsch.

No.198. "Zwischen Berg und tiefen Tal." Volkslieder für Singstimme und Sopran-Blockflöte oder 2 Instrumente, gesetzt von Heinrich Lemacher.

No.199. Coenen, Hans. Kinderzirkus Bum. Szenische Spielmusik für Kinderstimmen, 1–2 Melodieinstrumente, Stabspiel und Schlagwerk.

No.200. Oberborbeck, Felix. Steinbacher Tageskreis. 3– und 4–stimmig zu singen und zu spielen.

No.201. Praag, Henri C. van. Kleine Dialoge.

No.202. "Von fremden Küsten." Musik aus 3 Erdteilen für 2 Melodieinstrumente und Gitarre, Schlagzeug ad lib.

No.203. Bach, Johann Sebastian. 2 Spielgelfugen aus der "Kunst der Fuge."

No.204. Keller, Wilhelm. Kleine Vogelpredigt für 3 Blockflöten oder andere hohe Blasinstrumente.

No.205. 2 Katalanische Sardanas für 2 Chorische Instrumentalstimmen (Blockflöten, Streich- oder Zupfinstrumente) oder einzelne Instrumente, mit Schlagzeug ad lib.

No.206. "Es ist für uns eine Zeit angekommen." Alte Adventlieder in 3-stimmigen Sätzen zu singen oder zu spielen mit 2 instrumentalen Überstimmen ad lib. oder 3 Singstimmen mit Instrumenten und 2 Sopran-Blockflöten, gesetzt von Bernward Beyerle.

No.207. Mozart, Wolfgang Amadeus. Fuge G-moll (K.V.401).

No.208. Mozart, Wolfgang Amadeus. Aus den Londoner Skizzenbuch.

No.209. Rumänische Volksweisen für 3 Blockflöten oder andere Instrumente, gesetzt von Cesar Bresgen.

No.210. Demantius, Christoph. Polnischer und teutscher art Täntze, für 4 oder 5 Instrumente.

No.211. Koch, Johannes H. E. Capriccio für 3 Blockflöten oder andere Instrumente.

No.212. "Die vier Sprünge." Französische Volkstänze für 2 oder 3 Melodieinstrumente, Gitarre ad lib. 1.Teil.

No.213. Maasz, Gerhard. O musica. Quartettmusik nach einem Motiv von Paul Peuerl.

No.214. Poser, Hans. Tanzbüchlein. Zehn rhythmische Spielstücke.

No.215. "Aus meines Herzens Grunde." Sieben Choräle, zu singen und auf Instrumenten zu spielen, gesetzt von Friedrich Grünke.

No.216. "Lieb Nachtigall, wach auf!" Zwei Weihnachtliche Lieder für 3 Singstimmen, Sopran-Blockflöte und Bassinstrument, gesetzt von Hinrich Luchterhandt.

No.217. Badings, Henk. Divertimento für 3 Blockflöten oder Geigen (mit Streichergezeichnungen).

No.218. Mozart, Leopold. 12 Hochzeitsmenuette.

No.219. Frotscher, Gotthold. Der Volksliedvogel. Eine seltsame Geschichte zu erzählen und 3-stimmig zu singen oder zu spielen.

No.220. Quartettstücke nach W. A. Mozarts Duetten für 2 Hörner, gesetzt von Eberhard Werdin. Teil I.

No.221. Kirmsse, Herbert. Divertimento zu 3 Stimmen.

No.222. Baumann, Herbert. Kleines Quartett.

No.223. Hirtenlieder und Tänze aus dem Südosten, in Musizierfolgen für Sopran-Blockflöte und allerlei Begleitinstrumente (Blockflöten, Zupf- oder Streichinstrumente) mit Schlagzeug ad lib. Zusammengestellt von Walter Wünsch.

No.224. Stolte, Siegfried. Kleines Konzert für 2 Blockflöten und Klavier.

No.225. Wölke, Konrad. Reinickendorfer Flötenmusik.

No.226. Steiner, Luis. Kleine Hirtenkantate, zu singen und zu spielen auf Blockflöten, Stabspielen oder allerlei anderen Begleitinstrumenten.

No.227. Hartmann, Peter. Rhythmische Szenen.

No.228. Albert, Heinrich. Weltliche und geistliche Arien.

No.229. Beethoven, Ludwig van. Deutsche Tänze. (Schaller).

No.230. Genzmer, Harald. Fünf Bagatellen.

No.231. Spanische Romanzen für 2 Melodieinstrumente.

No.232. Klein, Richard Rudolf. Tänze und Spielweisen für mehrere Sopran-Blockflöten und Violine; Schlaginstrumente ad lib.

No.233. Kammeier, Hans. Quartettino.

No.234. Desprez, Josquin. La plus des plus. 5 Chansons für 3 Instrumente.

No.235. Roeseling, Kaspar. Tänzerische Suite in A-moll.

No.236. Weihnachtspastoralen von Antonio Vivaldi, Reinhard Keiser, Felice Giardini, Georg Friedrich Händel. (Gerd Ochs).

No.237. Poser, Hans. Weihnachtspartita. "Fröhlich soll mein Herze springen" zu 3 Stimmen.

No.238. Quartettstücke nach W. A. Mozart's

Duetten für 2 Hörner, gesetzt von Eberhard Serdin. II.Teil. .
No.239. Peuerl, Paul. Tänze.
No.240. Poletzky, Erwin. Tanzporträts.
No.241. Händel, Georg Friedrich. Aus der "Wassermusik."
No.242. Haydn, Joseph. Sechs Menuette und Trios.
No.243. Purcell, Henry. Trio-Stücke.
No.244. Szeligowski, Tadeusz. Polnische Liebeslieder.
No.245. Killmayer, Wilhelm. Balletto für verschiedene Blockflöten und Rhythmusinstrumente.
No.246. Scheidt, Samuel. Gelobet seist du, Jesu Christ, hrsg. von Ilse Hechler.
No.247. Barthel, Rudolf. Weihnachtsweisen mit Variationen für ein Instrument allein.
No.248. Witte, Gerd. Sieben kanonische Sätze über alte Weihnachtsweisen.
No.249. Händel, Georg Friedrich. Aus der "Feuerwerksmusik."
No.250. Poser, Hans. Dreizehn Kanons.
No.251. Gümbel, Martin. Fünf kurze Stücke für Blockflöten-Quartett oder andere Instrumente.
No.252. Pergolesi, Giovanni Battista. Tänze.
No.253. Njiric, Niksa. Die schöne Jana. Südslawische Tanzsuiten.
No.254. Thiele, Alfred. Die Vogelhochzeit. Variationen für 3 Blockflöten.
No.255. Serocki, Kazimierz. Improvisationen für Blockflöten-Quartett.
No.256. "Blues and Spirituals" für 3 Melodieinstrumente und Gitarre ad lib. gesetzt von Erwin Poletzky.
No.257. "Der Felsenquell." Französische Volkstänze für 2 oder 3 Melodieinstrumente, Gitarre ad lib. 2.Teil.
No.258. Rathegeber, Valentin. Pastorellen vor die Weynacht-Zeit.
No.259. Lutoslawski, Witold. Sechs polnische Weihnachtslieder.
No.260. Schöndlinger, Anton. Partita über "O Heiland, reiss die Himmel auf."
No.261. Händel, Georg Friedrich. Sieben Spielstücke, dreistimmig (S.A.B.) oder zweistimmig (S.A.) mit Basso Continuo. (Mönkemeyer).
No.262. Altenglische Tänze und Lieder (S.A.). (Danckert).
No.263. Salomon, Karel. Drei Miniaturen (S.S.A.).
No.264. Schubert, Franz. Tänze (S.AS.T.).
No.265. Maasz, Gerhard. Scherzo für Blockflöten-Quartett (S.A.T.B.).
No.266. Gadsch, Herbert. Die undankbare Flunder. Nach einem Text von James Krüss für 1–3 gleiche Stimmen, Sopran- und Alt-Blockflöten, 2 Violinen, Sopran-Glockenspiel und Schlaginstrumente.
No.267. Tschechische und slowakische Volkslieder (S.SA.AT.). (Jeletz).
No.268. Fünf ungarische Tänze nach überlieferten Originalmelodien (S.SA.AT.T.). (Unger).
No.269. Purcell, Henry. Sechs Instrumentalstücke aus Opern- und Schauspielmusiken (S.S.AT.TB.). (Unger).
No.270. Kirnberger, J. Ph. Recueil d'Airs de Danse caractéristiques (S.SA.AB.). (Ochs).
No.271. Baumann, Max. Divertimento (ST.ST.AB.).
No.272. Weihnachts-Choräle in vierstimmigen Sätzen von J. S. Bach. (S.A.T.B.).
No.273. "Allerhand lustige musicalische Sachen." Stücke unbekannter Meister aus Simpsons "Taffel Consort," 1621. (S.S.A.B., Cembalo ad lib.). (Mönkemeyer).
No.274. Poser, Hans. Kleine Serenade für Alt-Blockflöte und Gitarre.
No.275. Flämische Lieder und Tänze (S.SA.AT.; Gitarre ad lib.). (Tanner).
No.276. Sweelinck, J. P. Weltliche Lieder und Tänze (S.A.T.B.). (Ochs).
No.277. Rosenstengel, A. Der Rätselzoo. Eine lustige Kantate für Solostimmen, Kinderchor und Instrumente ad lib. nach einem Text von Markus Polder.
No.278. Knapp, Arno. Neue Suite zu dritt (S.A.TA.).
No.279. Beethoven, Ludwig van. Allegro und Menuett für eine Flötenuhr (S.A.T.TB.). (Altemark).
No.280. Staeps, Hans Ulrich. Rondelli (S.S.A.A.A.).
No.281. Haydn, Joseph. Schottische Volkslieder. (S.A. Klavier; B. ad lib.). (Ochs).
No.282. Marx, Karl. Es liegt ein Schloss in Österreich. Kleine Kantate nach einer alten Volksballade für Solostimmen, gemischter Chor. und Instrumente.
No.283. Weihnachtsmusik. (Titel noch unbestimmt).
No.284. Französische Weihnachtslieder und -tänze (S.A.T.). (Martelli).
No.285. Fritsch, Balthasar. Vierstimmige Tänze aus "Primitia musicales" (1606). S.A.T.B. (Mönkemeyer).
No.286. Rosenstengel, Albrecht. Vater und Sohn. Fünf Bildergeschichten nach E. O. Plauen für Kinderchor und Instrumente.
No.287. Wallonische Volkstänze in dreistimmigen Sätzen von Rose Thisse-Derouette. S.A.T.B.
No.288. Buschmann, Rainer Glen. Vier Stücke für Blockflöten-Quartett (S.S.A.T.).
No.289. Gadsch, Herbert. Spatzenlügen. Eine kleine Kantate nach Texten von James Krüss für Chor und Instrumente (S.S.A.).
No.290. "American favorite ballads" in zwei- oder dreistimmigen Sätzen mit Gitarre ad lib. von Erwin Poletzky.
No.291. Oettingen-Wallersteinische Kontratänze (S.A.B.). (Mönkemeyer).
No.292. Rosenstengel, Albrecht. Klingende Miniaturen (S.S.A., Schlaginstrumente ad lib.).
No.293. Provençalische Lieder und Tänze in zwei- oder dreistimmigen Sätzen mit Gitarre ad lib. von Henri Martelli.
No.294. Banchieri, Adriano. Aus den "Canzoni alla Francese" (S.A.T.B.). (Vierendeels).
No.295. Weihnachtsheft. Titel steht noch nicht fest.
No.296. Europäische Weihnachtslieder in

zweistimmigen Sätzen mit Gitarre oder Klavier von Gerd Ochs.

Zenck, Hermann, 1898–1950, ed., *see* Dietrich, Sixtus. Hymnen.

ŹRÓDŁA DO HISTORII MUZYKI POLSKIEJ. Krakow, Polskie Wydawnictwo Muzyczne, 19? – .
v.1– .
Contents:
Vol.1. Polnische Tänze aus Vietoris-Kodex (Cembalo).
Vol.2. Polnische Tänze aus den Lautentabulaturen. [1962].
Vol.3. Gołąbek, J. Sinfonien. [cop.1963].
Vol.4. Gołąbek, J. Partita (Blasinstrumenten-Ensemble). [cop.1961].
Vol.5. Wanski, J. Zwei Sinfonien. [cop.1962].
Vol.6. Polnische Tänze aus der Sammlung der Anna Szirmay-Keczer. [cop.1963].
Vol.7. Gorczycki, G. G. Completorium (gemischter Chor, 2 Violinen, 2 Clarini und Basso Continuo). [cop.1963].

Zwei- und dreistimmige Solostücke für die Laute, *see* Attaingnant, Pierre. Zwei- und dreistimmige Solostücke für die Laute.

Index

A LA PUERTA DEL CIELO.
Arr. by M. Dodd.
In: Music Press, Inc. [Choral series]. Vol.100.
ABACO, EVARISTO FELICE DALL', 1675–1742.
Selected works.
In: Denkmäler deutscher Tonkunst. [2. Folge]. Vol.1, 9 (i).
Kammer-Sonaten für Violine und Pianoforte.
In: Moffat. Kammer-Sonaten für Violine und Pianoforte. No.20.
Sonate (Gm). Violin and piano.
In: Moffat. Meister-Schule der alten Zeit. Violin-Sonaten. No.28.
Sonata, Op.3, No.3, for organ, strings.
In: Antica musica strumentale italiana. In preparation.
Sonata a tre. Op.3. Nr.4, 5, 9.
In: Riemann. Collegium musicum. No.41–43.
Sonata da camera, 1–2.
In: Hausmusik. No.103.
Sonata en fa majeur.
In: L'école du violon au XVIIe et XVIIIe siècle. No.1267.
ABBATINI, ANTONIO MARIA, ca.1595–1680.
(var. sp.: A. M. Abbattini).
Arias.
In: Landshoff. Alte Meister des Bel Canto. Eine Sammlung von Arien. Vol.1–2.
ABBÉ LE FILS, *see* L'ABBÉ, JOSEPH BARNABÉ SAINT-SEVIN.
ÄBEL, DAVID, fl.1639.
Organ music.
In: Organum. 4.Reihe. Nr.21.
ABEL, KARL FRIEDRICH, 1723–1787.
(var. sp.: Chr. Fr. Abel; C. F. Abel).
Kompositionen. v.1– .
Streichquartett Es dur. Op.8. Nr.3. Für 2 Violinen, Viola, und Violoncell.
In: Riemann. Collegium musicum. No.61.
Sechs Sonaten, für Viola da Gamba oder Geige (Querflöte) und Basso Continuo.
In: Hortus musicus. No.39–40.
Sonate E-moll für Viola da Gamba, Cembalo (Klavier) und Bass-Instrument ad lib.; Ausgabe für Violoncello und Klavier.
In: Antiqua Edition.
Sonate in A dur, Op.13, No.3. Violine und Klavier.
In: Kammersonaten. No.2.
Sonate in B dur. Violine und Klavier.
In: Kammersonaten. No.1.
Kleine Sinfonie in F-dur.
In: Musikschätze der Vergangenheit.
Symphony. Op.7. No.6.
In: Für Kenner und Liebhaber. No.16.
Symphony No.12 in E.
In: Für Kenner und Liebhaber. No.4.
Trio-Sonate C-dur für Flöte, Violine und Basso Continuo.
In: Moecks Kammermusik. Vol.54.
ABERT, ANNA AMALIE, 1906– . ed.
Opera from its beginnings to the beginning of the nineteenth century.
In: Anthology of music. Vol.5.
ABONDANTE, GIULIO, 16th CENTURY.
(var. sp.: Iulio Abundante).
Intabolatura di liuto.
In: Lefkoff. Five sixteenth century Venetian lute books.
ABOS, GIROLAMO, 1715–1760.
Sacred music.
In: Latrobe, C. I. Selection of sacred music.
In: Latrobe, J. A. The music of the church.
ABUNDANTE, IULIO, *see* ABONDANTE, GIULIO.
ACHRON, JOSEPH, 1886–1943.
Sextet for flute, oboe, clarinet, bassoon, French horn, and trumpet. Op.73.
In: New music. Vol.15. No.4. July 1942.
"Statuettes" for piano.
In: New music. Vol.5. No.1. Oct.1931.
ADAM, 15th CENTURY.
Selections.
In: Reaney. Early fifteenth-century music. Vol.2.
ADAM DE LA HALLE, ca.1235–ca.1288.
Oeuvres complètes. 440p.
Selections.
In: Gleason. Examples of music before 1400.
ADAM DE SAINT-VICTOR, d.1192.
Les proses.
In: Mélanges de musicologie critique. Vol.2.
ADAM VON FULDA, ca.1440–1550.
Hymnen.
In: Das Chorwerk. No.32.
Songs.
In: Aich. Das Liederbuch.
In: Riemann. Hausmusik aus alter Zeit.
ADLGASSER, ANTON CAJETAN, 1729–1777.
Church music.
In: Denkmäler der Tonkunst in Österreich. Vol.80. (Jg.XLIII/1).
ADRIAENSEN, EMMANUEL, 16th CENTURY.
Pratum musicum.
In: Monumenta musicae belgicae. Vol.10.
ADRIO, ADAM, 1901– . ed.
The fugue. Vol.1.
In: Anthology of music. Vol.19.
AFFILARD, MICHEL L', 17th CENTURY.
Songs.
In: Prunières. Les maîtres du chant. Recueil 4.
AGAZZARI, AGOSTINO, 1578–1640.
Sacred music.
In: Proske. Musica divina. Annus primus. Tom 2, 4.
AGERSNAP, HARALD, 1899– .
Interludium. Trio for fløjte, violin og violoncel.

In: Samfundet til Udgivelse af dansk Musik. Serie III. No.67; parts: Serie III. No.71.
Songs.
In: Samfundet til Udgivelse af dansk Musik. Suppl. 1925–26.
AGINCOURT, FRANÇOIS D', *see* DAGINCOURT, FRANÇOIS.
AGOSTINI, PAOLO, 1593–1629.
Sacred music.
In: Proske. Musica divina. Annus primus. Tom 2, 4.
AGRELL, JOHAN JOACHIM, 1701–1765.
Keyboard sonatas.
In: Newman. Thirteen keyboard sonatas of the 18th and 19th centuries.
AGRICOLA, ALEXANDER, 1446–1506.
Opera omnia. 5v. (in progress).
Selections.
In: Ambros. Auserwählte Tonwerke.
In: Maldéghem. Trésor musical.
Choral music.
In: Smijers. Van Ockeghem tot Sweelinck. Aflg.4.
AGRICOLA, JOHANN FRIEDRICH, 1720–1774.
Keyboard music.
In: Herrmann. Lehrmeister und Schüler Joh. Seb. Bachs. Vol.2.
AGRICOLA, MARTIN, 1486–1556.
Choral music.
In: Antiqua Chorbuch. Vol.1. Heft 1.
Choralkanons.
In: Zeitschrift für Spielmusik. No.2.
Musica instrumentalis deutsch.
In: Publikationen älterer praktischer und theoretischer Musikwerke. Jahrg.24..
AGUILÉRA DE HERÉDIA, SEBASTIÁN, b.ca.1570.
Organ music.
In: Bonnet. Historical organ-recitals. Vol.6.
In: Muset. Early Spanish organ music.
Sacred music.
In: Eslava y Elizondo. Lira sacro-hispana. 17th century. i.1.
AHLE, JOHANN RUDOLF, 1625–1673.
Choral music.
In: Antiqua Chorbuch. Vol.1. Heft 5; Vol.2. Heft 5.
In: Nagels Männerchor-Blätter. No.16.
Lied.
In: Reimann. Das deutsche Lied. Vol.2.
Organ music.
In: Das Erbe deutscher Musik. 1.Reihe. Vol.9.
In: The Liturgical Music Press, Inc. Masterpieces of organ music. Folio 20.
Selected vocal works.
In: Denkmäler deutscher Tonkunst. [1.Folge]. Vol.5.
AICH, ARNT VON, d.1530.
Das Liederbuch des Arnt von Aich. (Köln um 1510). 133p.
AICHINGER, GREGOR, 1564–1628.
Selected works.
In: Denkmäler deutscher Tonkunst. [2.Folge]. Vol.10 (i).
In: Musica sacra. 1839– . Vol.16.
Chamber music.
In: Riemann. Old chamber music. Vol.1.
Choral music.
In: Antiqua Chorbuch. Vol.1. Heft 4.
In lectulo meo. Viderunt eam.
In: Musica spiritualis. Ser.IIB. No.15.
Organ music.
In: Cantantibus organis. Vol.7.
Sacred music.
In: Proske. Musica divina. Annus primus. Tom 2, 3, 4. Annus secundus. Tom 2.
In: Proske. Selectus novus missarum. Annus secundus. Tom 2.
AIGNER, H. F.
Vier kleine Klavierstücke, Op.9.
In: Marckhl. Klavierwerke steiermärkischer Komponisten. Vol.1.
AINÉ, PIERRE CHÉDEVILLE L', 1694–1724.
Troisième sonatille. Extraite des "Sonatilles galantes." Op.VI.
In: Musiques françaises. Vol.3.
THE AINSWORTH PSALTER (PLYMOUTH).
Psalm 65.
In: Early psalmody in 17th century America. Ser.I. Vol.1.
AIX-LA-CHAPELLE, LE PROSAIRE D'.
In: Monumenta musicae sacrae. Vol.3.
THE AKATHISTOS HYMN. (ORTHODOX EASTERN CHURCH. LITURGY AND RITUAL. AKATHISTOI).
In: Monumenta musicae byzantinae. Transcripta. Vol.9.
ÅKERBERG, CARL ERIK EMANUEL, 1860–1938.
Piano quintet, Op.18.
In: Musikaliska konstföreningen. 1889.
AKUTAGAWA, YASUSHI, 1925– .
Music for strings. No.1.
In: Contemporary Japanese music series. No.12.
ALABIEFF, *see* ALJABJEW, ALEXANDER ALEXANDROWITSCH.
ALAGEONA, D.
Piano music.
In: Tagliapietra. Antologia di musica antica e moderna per pianoforte. Bd.18.
ALAIN, JEHAN, 1911–1940.
L'oeuvre d'orgue. 3v.
ALBA, ALONSO DE, *see* ALONSO DE ALBA.
ALBANESI, CARLO, 1856–1926.
Piano music.
In: Tagliapietra. Antologia di musica antica e moderna per pianoforte. Bd.17.
ALBANO, MONT.
Instrumental music.
In: Wasielewski. Instrumentalsätze vom Ende des XVI. bis Ende des XVII. Jahrhunderts.
ALBÉNIZ, MATEO PÉREZ DE, ca.1755–1831.
Keyboard music.
In: Guenther. Collection espagnole.
Sonatas. Piano.
In: Nin y Castellano. Seize sonates anciennes d'auteurs espagnols.
ALBERDI, J. B.
Selections.
In: Antologia de compositores argentinos.
ALBERT, PRINCE CONSORT OF QUEEN VICTORIA, 1819–1861.
The collected compositions. 221p.
ALBERT, HEINRICH, 1604–1651.
Selections.

In: Leichtentritt. Deutsche Hausmusik aus vier Jahrhunderten.
Arien.
In: Denkmäler deutscher Tonkunst. [1.Folge]. Vol.12–13.
In: Organum. 2.Reihe. Nr.6.
In: Zeitschrift für Spielmusik. No.228.
Choral music.
In: Antiqua Chorbuch. Vol.2. Heft 5.
Duette für gleiche und gemischte Stimmen und Basso Continuo.
In: Hortus musicus. No.150.
Hasten hither.
In: Arion. Vol.3.
Lieder.
In: Moser. Alte Meister des deutschen Liedes. 30 Gesänge. No.2, 3.
In: Moser. Alte Meister des deutschen Liedes. 46 Gesänge. No.4, 5, 6.
In: Reimann. Das deutsche Lied. Vol.1.
Preussische Festlieder.
In: Das Erbe deutscher Musik. 2.Reihe. Ostpreussen und Danzig. Vol.1.
ALBERTI, DOMENICO, ca.1710–1740.
Keyboard sonatas.
In: Newman. Thirteen keyboard sonatas of the 18th and 19th centuries.
Sacred music.
In: Latrobe, C. I. Selection of sacred music.
In: Latrobe, J. A. The music of the church.
ALBERTI, GASPARO, ca.1480–ca.1560.
Sacred music.
In: Jeppesen. Italia sacra musica. Vol.1, 2.
ALBERTI, JOHANN FRIEDRICH, 1642–1710.
Organ music.
In: Buszin. Organ series. Vol.1.
In: Dietrich. Elf Orgelchörale des siebzehnten Jahrhunderts.
In: Das Erbe deutscher Musik. 1.Reihe. Vol.9.
In: Keller. Achtzig Choralvorspiele deutscher Meister des 17. und 18. Jahrhunderts.
In: Klein. The first four centuries of music for the organ from Dunstable to Bach (1370–1749).
In: Straube. Choralvorspiele alter Meister.
ALBICASTRO, HENRICO DEL BISWANG, ca.1680–ca.1730.
(var. sp.: Henricus Albicastro).
Zwölf Concerti a 4, Op.7.
In: Schweizerische Musikdenkmäler. Vol.1.
Sonata, violin and piano, Op.5, No.2–3; Konzerte.
In: Verein schweizerischer Tonkünstler. Musikalische Werke. Heft 2, 5.
Dritte Sonate für 2 Violinen und Violoncello mit Cembalo.
In: Musikschätze der Vergangenheit.
ALBINONI, TOMMASO, 1671–1750.
(var. sp.: Tomaso Albinoni).
Concerto a cinque, Op.5, No.5.
In: Für Kenner und Liebhaber. No.7.
Concerto a cinque, Op.7, No.5.
In: Für Kenner und Liebhaber. No.3.
Concerto a cinque, Op.9, No.2.
In: Für Kenner und Liebhaber. No.9.
Concerti a cinque.
In: Somma. Musiche vocali e strumentali sacre e profane, Sec.XVII–XVIII–XIX. Vol.24.
Concerto in C, Op.9, No.9. (2 oboes, strings, cembalo).
In: Antica musica strumentale italiana. Ser.I. Vol.1.
Concerto in F, Op.9, No.10. (violin solo, strings, cembalo).
In: Antica musica strumentale italiana. Ser.I. Vol.2.
Concerto in G for 7 strings, basso continuo.
In: Antica musica strumentale italiana. In preparation.
Kammer-Sonaten für Violine und Pianoforte.
In: Moffat. Kammer-Sonaten für Violine und Pianoforte. No.12.
Zwei Kammersonaten für Violine und Klavier. Op.6.
In: Nagels Musik-Archiv. No.9.
Konzert für Violine mit Streichorchester und Cembalo oder Orgel.
In: Musikschätze der Vergangenheit.
Organ music.
In: The Liturgical Music Press, Inc. Masterpieces of organ music. Folio 39.
Sinfonia No.3 in G (strings).
In: Antica musica strumentale italiana. Ser.II. Vol.11.
Sinfonia No.5 in D (strings).
In: Antica musica strumentale italiana. Ser.I. Vol.3.
Sinfonia a 4 für Streichorchester.
In: Concertino.
Sinfonia G-dur für Streichorchester und Bläser ad lib.
In: Concertino.
Sonata für Flöte (Oboe oder Violine und Basso Continuo).
In: Nagels Musik-Archiv. No.74.
Sonata A-moll für Violine und Basso Continuo.
In: Moecks Kammermusik. Vol.108.
Sonata in A, Op.2, No.3 (strings, cembalo).
In: Antica musica strumentale italiana. Ser.I. Vol.4.
Sonate G-moll, Op.2, Nr.6, für zwei Violinen, zwei Violen, Violoncello und Basso Continuo.
In: Nagels Musik-Archiv. No.189.
Sonata in G minor, Op.6, No.2, for strings, cembalo.
In: Antica musica strumentale italiana. In preparation.
Sonata a tre, zwei Violini e Violoncello col Basso per l'Organo, Op.1, Nr.3.
In: Nagels Musik-Archiv. No.34.
Sonata a tre, per due violini, violoncello e basso continuo, Op.I/6.
In: Hausmusik. No.111.
2 Sonata da chiesa, Op.8.
In: Hausmusik. No.144.
Songs.
In: Jeppesen. La flora. Vol.2.
ALBRECHTSBERGER, JOHANN GEORG, 1736–1809.
Fugue for organ, B flat.
In: Königliche Akademie der Künste. Auswahl vorzüglicher Musik-Werke. No.33.
Instrumental works.
In: Denkmäler der Tonkunst in Österreich. Vol.33. (Jg.XVI/2).
Keyboard music.

In: Clementi. Clementi's Selection of practical harmony. Vol.1, 2, 4.
In: Farrenc. Le trésor des pianistes. Vol.15.
Offertorium.
In: Ecclesiasticon. No.40.
Organ music.
In: Caecilia; Sammlung von Choralvorspielen.
In: Raugel. Quarante-six pièces pour orgue ou harmonium.
ALBRICI, VINZENZIO, 1631–1696.
Fader wår. (Vater unser).
In: Monumenta musicae svecicae.
ALCALÁ DE HENARES, *see* VENEGAS DE HENESTROSA, LUYS.
ALCOCK, JOHN, SR., 1715–1806.
Organ music.
In: Tallis to Wesley. Vol.23.
Part music.
In: Hullah. Part music. Class A.1. Vol.2.
ALCORTA, A.
Selections.
In: Antologia de compositores argentinos.
ALDERINUS, COSMAS, ca.1497–1550.
Chöre.
In: Verein schweizerischer Tonkünstler. Musikalische Werke. Heft 3.
ALDOVRANDINI, GIUSEPPE, *see* ALDROVANDINI, GIUSEPPE ANTONIO VINCENZO.
ALDRICH, HENRY, 1647–1710.
Selections.
In: Crotch. Specimens of various styles of music. Vol.2.
Anthems.
In: Music Press, Inc. [Choral series]. No.61.
Sacred music.
In: Arnold. Cathedral music. Vol.1, 3.
In: Boyce. Cathedral music. Vol.1, 2; 1894, Vol.1, 2, 3.
In: Page. Harmonia sacra. Vol.1.
Vocal music.
In: Hullah. Vocal scores. I. Sacred.
ALDROVANDINI, GIUSEPPE ANTONIO VINCENZO, 1665–1707.
(var. sp.: Aldovrandini).
Arias.
In: Landshoff. Alte Meister des Bel Canto. Eine Sammlung von Arien. Vol.3.
Organ music.
In: Fuser. Classici italiani dell'organo.
ALEXANDER, FLORENTINUS.
Selections.
In: Ambros. Auserwählte Tonwerke.
ALEYN.
Selections.
In: Plainsong and Mediaeval Music Society. Publications. (Old Hall manuscript).
ALFONSO X, EL SABIO, KING OF CASTILE AND LEON, 1221–1284.
Las cantigas de Santa María del Rey. 3v.
In: Barcelona. Biblioteca Central. Sección de Música. Publicaciones. Vol.15.
Gran dereit'.
In: Parrish. A treasury of early music. No.7.
ALFVÉN, HUGO, 1872– .
Cantata for the Reformation Festival at Uppsala. Op.36.
In: Musikaliska konstföreningen. 1921.
Cantata in celebration of the quincentenary of the Swedish Riksdag.
In: Musikaliska konstföreningen. 1936.
Herrans Bön. Op.15.
In: Musikaliska konstföreningen. 1910.
Unge herr Sten Sture. Op.30.
In: Musikaliska konstföreningen. 1933.
Uppenbarelsekantat. Op.31.
In: Musikaliska konstföreningen. 1915.
Vid sekelskiftet. Op.12.
In: Musikaliska konstföreningen. 1906.
ALISON, RICHARD, *see* ALLISON, RICHARD.
ALJABJEW, ALEXANDER ALEXANDROWITSCH, 1787–1851.
(var. sp.: Alabieff).
Vocal music.
In: Sammlung russischer Romanzen. No.5, 8, 9, 313.
ALLARDO, JACOBUS.
Missa, 1580.
In: Musica divina. Vol.16.
ALLEGRI, GREGORIO, ca.1582–1652.
Choral music.
In: Recueil de musique ancienne. Recueil des morceaux de musique ancienne. Bd.2.
In: Rochlitz. Sammlung vorzüglicher Gesantstücke. Bd.1. Pt.2.
Instrumental music.
In: Wasielewski. Instrumentalsätze vom Ende des XVI. bis Ende XVII. Jahrhunderts.
Sacred music.
In: Proske. Musica divina. Annus primus. Tom 2.
ALLENDA, PEDRO HUMBERTO, 1885– .
Songs.
In: Boletín latino-americano de música. Vol.1.
ALLISON, RICHARD, 16th–17th CENTURIES.
(var. sp.: Richard Alison).
An hour's recreation in music.
In: Fellowes. The English madrigal school. Vol.33.
Vocal music.
In: Hullah. Vocal scores. I. Sacred.
ALLWOOD, RICHARD, *see* ALWOOD, RICHARD.
ALONSO DE ALBA.
Selections.
In: Monumentos de la música espagñola. Vol.1.
ALONSO DE MUDARRA, *see* MUDARRA, ALONSO DE.
ALTENBURG, MICHAEL, 1584–1640.
Choral-Intraden. Heft 1–2.
In: Rahter's Kammer-Orchester. No.3–3a.
ALVAREZ, J. PEREZ Y, *see* PEREZ Y ALVAREZ, J.
ALWOOD, RICHARD, 16th CENTURY.
(var. sp.: Richard Allwood; Richard Alwoode).
Keyboard music.
In: Schott's Anthology of early keyboard music. Vol.2.
Organ music.
In: Liber organi. Bd.10.
In: The Liturgical Music Press, Inc. Masterpieces of organ music. Folio 73.
AMADOR, CARLOS POSADA, *see* POSADA AMADOR, CARLOS.
AMALIA, ANNA AMALIA, PRINCESS OF PRUSSIA, *see* ANNA AMALIA, PRINCESS OF PRUSSIA.

AMBERG, H.
Organ music.
In: Gerhardt. Album nordischer Komponisten für Orgel. Vol.2.
AMBROSE, JOHN.
Selections.
In: Smith. Musica antiqua.
AMBROSE, SAINT, 340–397.
(var. sp.: Saint Ambroise).
Vocal music.
In: Delsarte. Archives du chant. Livr.1, No.1; Livr.6, No.1; Livr.10, No.1.
AMBROSIUS, HERMANN, 1897– .
Sonatine für 2 Geigen oder andere Melodieinstrumente.
In: Moecks gelbe Musikhefte. Vol.39.
AMENGUAL, RENÉ, 1911– .
Sonatina. (Piano).
In: Instituto Interamericano de Musicologia. Publicaciónes. No.35.
AMERICAN HYMN TUNES, 1800–1860.
In: Music Press, Inc. [Choral series]. No.55.
AMERICAN MUSIC, *see* FOLKSONGS, U.S.; U.S.–MUSIC.
AMIENS, GUILLAUME D'.
Selections.
In: Gleason. Examples of music before 1400.
AMMERBACH, ELIAS NIKOLAUS, ca.1530–1597.
(var. sp.: Elias Nic. Ammerbach).
Keyboard music.
In: Apel. Musik aus früher Zeit für Klavier. Bd.1.
Organ music.
In: Cantantibus organis. Vol.11.
2 Passamezzi aus "Orgel- oder Instrument-Tabulatur."
In: Zeitschrift für Spielmusik. No.192.
AMMON, BLASIUS, *see* AMON, BLASIUS.
AMON, BLASIUS, ca.1560–1590.
(var. sp.: Blasius Ammon).
Church music.
In: Denkmäler der Tonkunst in Österreich. Vol.73. (Jg.XXXVIII/1).
Masses.
In: Berg. Patrocinium musices. Vol.10.
AMPHION ANGLICUS (1700). FACSIMILE. (BLOW).
In: Monuments of music and music literature. First series. No.2.
ANA, FRANCESCO D', d.ca.1502.
Selections.
In: Ambros. Auserwählte Tonwerke.
In: Torchi. L'arte musicale in Italia. Bd.1.
ANCHIETA, JUAN DE, d.1523.
Selections.
In: Monumentos de la música española. Vol.1.
Choral music.
In: Engel. Three centuries of choral music. Vol.5.
Motets.
In: Elúsitiza. Antología musical.
ANDALUSIA–MUSIC.
In: Ribera y Tarragó. La música andalusa medieval en las canciones de trovadores, troveros y minnesinger.
ANDERSEN, ANTON JORGEN, 1845–1926.
Sonata for violoncello and piano, D minor.
In: Musikaliska konstföreningen. 1876.
Symphony, D major.
In: Musikaliska konstföreningen. 1903.
ANDERSEN, ARTHUR OLAF, 1880– .
Song.
In: The Wa-Wan series of American compositions.
ANDERSEN, JOHANNES.
Songs.
In: Samfundet til Udgivelse af dansk Musik. Suppl. 1925–26.
ANDERSSON, RICHARD, 1851–1918.
Sonata for piano, Op.11.
In: Musikaliska konstföreningen. 1889.
ANDREAE, FR. C.
Sacred music.
In: Proske. Musica divina. Annus secundus. Tom 3.
In: Proske. Selectus novus missarum. Annus secundus. Tom 3.
ANDREAS DE FLORENTIA.
Selections.
In: Pirrotta. The music of fourteenth-century Italy. Vol.5.
ANDRÉE, ELFRIDA, 1841–1929.
Piano quintet, E minor.
In: Musikaliska konstföreningen. 1865.
Snöfrid. Ballad.
In: Musikaliska konstföreningen. 1884.
Trio for violin, violoncello, and piano, G major.
In: Musikaliska konstföreningen. 1887.
ANDREVI, FRANCISCO, 1786–1853.
Sacred music.
In: Eslava y Elizondo. Lira sacro-hispana. 19th century. i.2.
ANDRIESSEN, HENDRIK, 1892– .
Organ music.
In: Standard series of organ compositions. No.61.
ANDRIEU, JEAN FRANÇOIS D', *see* DANDRIEU, JEAN FRANÇOIS.
ANDRIEU, PIERRE D', *see* DANDRIEU, PIERRE.
ANERIO, FELICE, ca.1560–1614.
Selections.
In: Musica sacra. 1839– . Vol.15.
Choral music.
In: Engel. Three centuries of choral music. Vol.2.
In: Recueil de musique ancienne. Recueil des morceaux de musique ancienne. Bd.6.
In: Rochlitz. Sammlung vorzüglicher Gesangstücke. Bd.1. Pt.2.
Kirchengesänge.
In: Tucher. Kirchengesänge der berühmtesten älteren italienischen Meister.
Part music.
In: Hullah. Part music. Class A.2. Vol.1.
Sacred music.
In: Proske. Musica divina. Annus primus. Tom 2, 3, 4; Annus secundus. Tom 1, 2.
In: Proske. Selectus novus missarum. Annus primus. Tom 1; Annus secundus. Tom 1, 2.
ANERIO, GIOVANNI FRANCESCO, ca.1567–1630.
Drei geistliche Konzerte. Bass und B.C.
In: Cantio sacra. No.14.
Missa Della Battaglia.
In: Musica divina. Vol.11.

ANET, JEAN BAPTISTE, ca.1661–1755.
Sonate No.10 pour violon (ou 2 flûtes) et clavier.
In: Musiques françaises. Vol.18.
ANGINCOURT, PERRIN D', *see* DAGINCOURT, FRANÇOIS.
ANGLEBERT, JEAN HENRI D', 1635–1691.
5 Fugues et 1 Quatuor sur le Kyrie. Organ.
In: Guilmant. École classique de l'orgue. No.25.
Keyboard music.
In: Farrenc. Le trésor des pianistes. Vol.3.
In: Grovlez. Les plus belles pièces de clavessin de l'école française. Vol.1.
In: Monuments of music and music literature. First series. No.4.
In: Oesterle. Early keyboard music. Vol.1.
In: Société Française de Musicologie, Paris. Publications. Ser.I. Bd.8.
In: Tagliapietra. Antologia di musica antica e moderna per pianoforte. Bd.7.
Organ music.
In: Klein. The first four centuries of music for the organ from Dunstable to Bach (1370–1749).
In: Liber organi. Bd.1.
In: Raugel. Les maîtres français de l'orgue. Vol.2.
In: Schweiger. A brief compendium of early organ music.
ANGLÈS, HIGINI, 1888– . ed.
Las cantigas de Santa María del Rey D. Alfonso el Sabio. (1252–1284).
In: Barcelona. Biblioteca Central. Sección de música. Publicaciones. Vol.15.
Els madrigals i la missa de difunts d'en Brudieu.
In: Barcelona. Biblioteca Central. Sección de música. Publicaciones. Vol.1.
La música a Catalunya fins al segle XIII.
In: Barcelona. Biblioteca Central. Sección de música. Publicaciones. Vol.10.
Spanish music.
In: Monumentos de la música española.
ANGLÈS, PADRE RAFAEL, 1731–1816.
Keyboard music.
In: Nin y Castellano. Dix-sept sonates et pièces anciennes d'auteurs espagnols.
Organ music.
In: Elkan-Vogel organ series. Vol.5.
ANIMUCCIA, GIOVANNI, ca.1500–1571.
Selections.
In: Torchi. L'arte musicale in Italia. Bd.1.
Missa "Ave Maris Stella."
In: Somma. Polifonia vocale sacra e profana. Sec.XVI. Vol.1.
ANNA AMALIA, PRINCESS OF PRUSSIA, 1723–1787.
Sonate für Flöte in F-dur (Violine) und Cembalo.
In: Musikschätze der Vergangenheit.
ANNA VON KÖLN, LIEDERBUCH DER.
In: Denkmäler rheinischer Musik. Vol.4.
ANNIBALE PADOVANO, 1527–1575.
Ricercari. 104p.
Selections.
In: Denkmäler der Tonkunst in Österreich. Vol.77. (Jg.XLI), 90.
In: Torchi. L'arte musicale in Italia. Bd.1, 3.
Keyboard music.
In: Tagliapietra. Antologia di musica antica e moderna per pianoforte. Bd.1.
Organ music.
In: Fuser. Classici italiani dell'organo.
ANSELME.
Air sur la vendange.
In: L'école du violon au XVIIe et XVIIIe siècle. No.1345.
ANTEGNATI, COSTANZO, 1549–1624.
Selections.
In: Torchi. L'arte misicale in Italia. Bd.3.
L'antegnata intavolatura de ricercari d'organo. 1608.
In: Corpus of early keyboard music. Vol.9.
ANTES, JOHN, 1740–1811.
Sacred songs.
In: Music of the Moravians in America. Vol.1.
ANTHEIL, GEORGE, 1900– .
Second sonata "The airplane" for piano solo.
In: New music. Vol.4, No.3. April 1931.
ANTHEMS
In: Arkwright. The Old English edition. Vol.21, 22.
In: Billings. The continental harmony.
In: Chor-Archiv.
In: Early English church music. Vol.3, 6.
In: Greene. Forty select anthems in score.
In: Music Press, Inc. [Choral series]. Vol.61, 72.
In: Musica Britannica. Vol.7.
In: Musical Antiquarian Society. Publications. Vol.14.
In: Page. Harmonia sacra.
In: Plainsong and Mediaeval Music Society. Publications.
In: Recent researches in the music of the Renaissance. Vol.3.
ANTHONELLO DA CASERTA, *see* CASERTA, ANTHONELLO DA.
ANTICO, ANDREA, *see* ANTIQUUS, ANDREAS.
ANTIPHONALS.
In: Paléographie musicale.
ANTIPHONS.
In: Early English church music. Vol.2.
In: Plainsong and Mediaeval Music Society. Publications.
ANTIQUUS, ANDREAS, 15th CENTURY.
(var. sp.: Andrea Antico).
Liber quindecim missarum.
In: Expert. Les maîtres musiciens de la Renaissance française. Vol.8, 9.
Organ music.
In: Fuser. Classici italiani dell'organo.
In: Jeppesen. Die italienische Orgelmusik am Anfang des Cinquecento.
ANTON, KING OF SAXONY.
(var. sp.: Anton, König von Sachsen).
Piano compositions.
In: Schmid. Musik am sächsischen Hofe. Bd.5.
ANTONELLI, ABONDIO DI FABRICA, 17th CENTURY.
Missa brevis. S.A.T.B.
In: Basilica. 1953.
ANTONIO, GIOVANNI GUIDO.
La caccia.
In: L'école du violon au XVIIe et XVIIIe siècle. No.1292.

ANTONIUS DE CIVITATE, 15th CENTURY.
Sacred music.
In: Plainsong and Mediaeval Music Society. Publications. (Borren).
APEL, NICOLAUS, d.1537.
Der Codex des Magister Nicolaus Apel von Königshofen.
In: Das Erbe deutscher Musik. 1.Reihe. Vol.32/33/34.
Organ music.
In: Cantantibus organis. Vol.8.
APEL, WILLI, 1893– . ed.
Keyboard music of the fourteenth and fifteenth centuries.
In: Corpus of early keyboard music. Vol.1.
APPENZELLER, BENEDICTUS, 16th CENTURY.
(var. sp.: Benedictus).
Selections.
In: Maldéghem. Trésor musical.
Chanson.
In: Brown. Theatrical chansons of the 15th and early 16th centuries.
APT, LE MANUSCRIT DE MUSIQUE POLYPHONIQUE DE TRÉSOR D'.
In: Société Française de Musicologie, Paris. Ser.I. Bd.10.
AQUIN, LOUIS CLAUDE D', *see* DAQUIN, LOUIS CLAUDE.
AQUINAS, THOMAS, *see* THOMAS AQUINAS.
ARANAZ Y VIDES, PEDRO, 1742–1821.
Sacred music.
In: Eslava y Elizondo. Lira sacro-hispana. 18th century. i.1.
ARAÚJO, PEDRO DE, *see* CORREA DE ARAUXO, FRANCISCO.
ARAUXO, FRANCISCO CORREA DE, *see* CORREA DE ARAUXO, FRANCISCO.
ARBATSKY, YURY, 1911– .
Organ music.
In: The parish organist. Vol.1–4.
ARCADELT, JACOB, ca.1514–ca.1575.
(var. sp.: Jacques Arcadelt; Jakob Arcadelt).
Opera omnia. v.1– .
Selections.
In: Documenta historica musicae.
In: Maldéghem. Trésor musical.
Anthems.
In: Music Press, Inc. [Choral series]. No.72.
Ave Maria. Organ.
In: Dickinson. Historical recital series for organ. Vol.2. No.37.
Il bianco e dolce cigno.
In: Squire. Ausgewählte Madrigale und mehrstimmige Gesänge. No.22.
Chansons.
In: Cauchie. Quinze chansons françaises du XVIe siècle.
In: Publikationen älterer praktischer und theoretischer Musikwerke. Jahrg.27.
In: Smith College music archives. No.5.
Choral music.
In: Commer. Collectio operum musicorum batavorum saeculi XVI. Bd.8, 12.
In: Music Press, Inc. [Choral series]. Vol.81, 82.
In: Recueil de musique ancienne. Recueil des morceaux de musique ancienne. Bd.2, 5.
In: Smijers. Van Ockeghem tot Sweelinck. Aflg.7.
Madrigals.
In: Das Chorwerk. No.58.
In: Einstein. The golden age of the madrigal.
Motet.
In: Das Chorwerk. No.54.
Organ music.
In: Cantantibus organis. Vol.6.
ARDÉVOL, JOSÉ, 1911– .
Sonatas a tres.
In: Instituto Interamericano de Musicologia. Publicaciónes. No.28, 40, 45.
Sonata No.3. (Piano).
In: Instituto Interamericano de Musicologia. Publicaciónes. No.47.
Sonatina. Piano.
In: New music. Vol.7. No.4. July 1934.
ARETINO, PAOLO.
Passio Jesu Christi.
In: Musica liturgica. Vol.1. Fasc.6.
AREZZO, GUIDO D', *see* GUIDO D'AREZZO.
ARGENTINA–MUSIC
In: Antologia de compositores argentinos.
ARIADNE MUSICA. (J. C. F. FISCHER).
In: Liber organi. Bd.7.
ARIAS.
In: Landshoff. Alte Meister des Bel Canto. Eine Sammlung von Arien.
ARIAS, GERMAN *(see also* DARMSTADT–MUSIC; FOLKSONGS, GERMAN; GERMANY–MUSIC; SONGS, GERMAN).
In: Denkmäler der Tonkunst in Österreich. Vol.64. (Jg.XXXIII/2).
ARIGONI, GIOVANNI GIACOMO, *see* ARRIGONI, GIOVANNI GIACOMO.
ARIMINO, VINCENTIUS DE, *see* VINCENTIUS DE ARIMINO.
ARIOSTI, ATTILIO, 1666–ca.1740.
Arias.
In: Landshoff. Alte Meister des Bel Canto. Eine Sammlung von Arien. Vol.1–2.
6 sonate per viola d'amore o violino o viola.
Fasc.I: Sonate No.1 e 2.
In: Somma. Musiche vocali e strumentali sacre e profane, Sec.XVII–XVIII–XIX. Vol.26, 27, 28.
ARLBERG, GEORG EFRAIM FRITZ, 1830–1896.
I skogen. Op.10. Tone poem for orchestra. Score.
In: Musikaliska konstföreningen. 1877.
I skogen. Op.10. Tone poem for orchestra. Arr. piano, 4 hands.
In: Musikaliska konstföreningen. 1877.
ARMSDORF, ANDREAS, 1670–1699.
(var. sp.: Andreas Armsdorff).
Organ music.
In: Buszin. Organ series. Vol.1.
In: Dietrich. Elf Orgelchörale des siebzehnten Jahrhunderts.
In: Das Erbe deutscher Musik. 1.Reihe. Vol.9.
In: Keller. Achtzig Choralvorspiele deutscher Meister des 17. und 18. Jahrhunderts.
In: Klein. The first four centuries of music for the organ from Dunstable to Bach (1370–1749).
In: Rohr. Orgelspiel im Kirchjahr.

ARNE, MICHAEL, 1741–1786.
Songs.
In: Potter. Reliquary of English song. Vol.2.
ARNE, THOMAS AUGUSTINE, 1710–1778.
Comus.
In: Musica Britannica. Vol.3.
Concerto V, G-moll, für Orgel, Cembalo oder Klavier mit Instrumenten.
In: Nagels Musik-Archiv. No.210.
Hornpipe.
In: L'école du violon au XVIIe et XVIIIe siècle. No.1292.
Keyboard music.
In: Pauer. Alte Klavier-Musik. 2d series. Part 6.
In: Pauer. Old English composers for the virginals and harpsichord.
Organ music.
In: Butcher. English organ music of the eighteenth century. Vol.2.
In: Elkan-Vogel organ series. Vol.2.
Part music.
In: Hullah. Part music. Class A.2. Vol.1; Class A.2. Vol.2; Class B.2; Class C. Secular.
Sonate No.3. Piano.
In: Köhler. Les maîtres du clavecin. Heft 13.
Songs.
In: Arkwright. The Old English edition. Vol.2.
In: Potter. Reliquary of English song. Vol.2.
Triosonate für 2 Violine, Violoncell und Klavier. Op.3. Nr.1.
In: Riemann. Collegium musicum. No.57.
Vocal music.
In: Hullah. Vocal scores. I. Sacred; II. Secular.
ARNELL, RICHARD ANTHONY SAYER, 1917– .
Baroque prelude and fantasia. Organ.
In: Contemporary organ series. No.20.
ARNOLD, SAMUEL, 1740–1802.
Selections.
In: Engel. Music from the days of George Washington.
In: Fisher. The music that Washington knew.
Sacred music.
In: Page. Harmonia sacra. Vol.1.
ARNOLDUS DE BRUCK, *see* BRUCK, ARNOLD VON.
ARNOLDUS DE LANTINS, *see* LANTINS, ARNOLD DE.
ARNT VON AICH, *see* AICH, ARNT VON.
ARPA, ORAZIO DELL'.
Selections.
In: Torchi. L'arte musicale in Italia. Bd.5.
ARRAŜ, MONIOT D'.
Selections.
In: Gleason. Examples of music before 1400.
ARRESTI, FLORIANO, ca.1650–1719.
Selections.
In: Torchi. L'arte musicale in Italia. Bd.3.
Organ music.
In: Raugel. Quarante-six pièces pour orgue ou harmonium.
ARRIGONI, GIOVANNI GIACOMO, 17th CENTURY.
(var. sp.: Giacomo Arigoni).
Selections.
In: Expert. Répertoire classique de musique. 1re année.
ARSENAL, BIBLIOTHÈQUE DE L'.
Catalogue des livres de musique.
In: Société Française de Musicologie, Paris. Publications. Ser.II. Bd.7.
ARSENAL À PARIS. BIBLIOTHÈQUE DE, *see* BIBLIOTHÈQUE DE L'ARSENAL À PARIS.
ASCHENBRENNER, CHRISTIAN HEINRICH, 1654–1732.
Ländlicher Festtag.
In: Platzmusik. Nr.12.
ASCONE, V.
Selections.
In: Boletín latino-americano de música. Vol.3.
In: Instituto Interamericano de Musicologia. Publicaciónes. No.11.
ASENJO Y BARBIERI, FRANCISCO, 1823–1894.
Choral music.
In: Recueil de musique ancienne. Recueil des morceaux de musique ancienne. Bd.6.
ASOLA, GIOVANNI MATTEO, d.1609.
Selections.
In: Torchi. L'arte musicale in Italia. Bd.2.
Sixteen liturgical works.
In: Recent researches in the music of the Renaissance. Vol.1.
Organ music.
In: Cantantibus organis. Vol.8.
Pange lingua.
In: Musica sacra, between 1892–1897. No.3.
Sacred music.
In: Proske. Musica divina. Annus primus. Tom 1, 2; Annus secundus. Tom 1.
In: Proske. Selectus novus missarum. Annus secundus. Tom 1.
ASPLMAYR, FRANZ, 1728–1786.
(var. sp.: Franz Aspelmayr).
Quartett in D dur. Op.2. Nr.2.
In: Riemann. Collegium musicum. No.40.
Trio in F dur. Op.5. Nr.1.
In: Riemann. Collegium musicum. No.39.
Trio, per due violini e basso continuo. Op.I/4.
In: Hausmusik. No.162.
ASSISI, RUFINO BARTOLUCCI DA.
Sacred music.
In: Jeppesen. Italia sacra musica. Vol.2.
ASSMAYER, IGNAZ, 1790–1862.
(var. sp.: Assmayr).
Offertoriums.
In: Ecclesiasticon. No.69–71.
ASTON, HUGH, ca.1480–1522.
Selections.
In: Smith. Musica antiqua.
Church music.
In: Tudor church music. Vol.10.
Keyboard music.
In: Apel. Musik aus früher Zeit für Klavier. Bd.2.
In: Schott's Anthology of early keyboard music. Vol.1.
ASTORGA, EMANUELE GIOACCHINO CESARE RINCÓN, BARON D', 1680–ca.1757.
Airs.
In: Prunières. Les maîtres du chant. Recueil 1.

Arias.
In: Landshoff. Alte Meister des Bel Canto. Eine Sammlung von Arien. Vol.1–2.
Choral music.
In: Commer. Cantica sacra. Vol.1, No.9; Vol.2, No.2.
In: Rochlitz. Sammlung vorzüglicher Gesangstücke. Bd.2.
Eja Mater.
In: Königliche Akademie der Künste. Auswahl vorzüglicher Musik-Werke. No.43.
Sacred music.
In: Latrobe, C. I. Selection of sacred music.
In: Latrobe, J. A. The music of the church.
Songs.
In: Jeppesen. La flora. Vol.2.
Vocal music.
In: Delsarte. Archives du chant. Livr.17. No.1.

ASTURIANO.
Selections.
In: Pedrell. Teatro lirico español anterior al siglo XIX. Bd.4/5.

ATTAINGNANT, PIERRE, fl.1528–1549.
Chansons und Tänze. 5v.
Transcriptions of chansons for keyboard. 3v. in 1. (204p.).
Chansons.
In: Collegium musicum. Vol.2.
Chansons musicales.
In: Expert. Les maîtres musiciens de la Renaissance française. [Sec.2]. Vol.3, 8.
Trent et une chansons musicales.
In: Expert. Les maîtres musiciens de la Renaissance française. Vol.5.
Treize livres de motets. v.1– .
Treize motets et un prélude.
In: Société Française de Musicologie, Paris. Publications. Ser.I. Bd.5.
Deux livres d'orgue.
In: Société Française de Musicologie, Paris. Publications. Ser.I. Bd.1.
Organ music.
In: Froidebise. Anthologie de l'orgue. Vol.1.
In: Pierront. Cent versets de Magnificat.
In: Raugel. Les maîtres français de l'orgue. Vol.2.
In: Raugel. Quarante-six pièces pour orgue ou harmonium.
Tanzsätze.
In: Musica practica. No.44, 45.
Zwei- und dreistimmige Solostücke für die Laute. 35p.

ATTERBERG, KURT, 1887– .
Part music.
In: Hullah. Part music. Class A.2. Vol.1; Class B.2; Class C. Secular.
Sonata for a string instrument, violoncello, viola, violin, and piano, Op.27.
In: Musikaliska konstföreningen. 1930.
String quartet, Op.11.
In: Musikaliska konstföreningen. 1917.
Suite pastorale in modo antico, Op.34.
In: Collegium musicae novae. No.13.

ATTEY, JOHN, d.ca.1640.
Book of ayres.
In: Fellowes. The English school of lutenist song writers. 2d series. Vol.9.

ATTWOOD, THOMAS, 1765–1838.
Sacred music.
In: Page. Harmonia sacra. Vol.1.
Songs.
In: Potter. Reliquary of English song. Vol.2.

AUBERT, JACQUES, 1689–1753.
Forlane. (La reine des peris). Organ.
In: Dickinson. Historical recital series for organ. Vol.1, No.20.
Les jolis airs ajustés pour 2 violons et accompagnement de piano.
In: L'école du violon au XVIIe et XVIIIe siècle.
Sonate en fa majeur.
In: L'école du violon au XVIIe et XVIIIe siècle. No.1255.
Suite, "Ma pinte et ma mie au gay." (2 violons et piano).
In: L'école du violon au XVIIe et XVIIIe siècle. No.1290.
Les tambourins.
In: L'école du violon au XVIIe et XVIIIe siècle. No.1339.

AUBERT, LOUIS, 1720–ca.1800.
Sonate (G). Violin and piano.
In: Moffat. Meister-Schule der alten Zeit. Violin-Sonaten. No.9.
Sonate en la mineur.
In: L'école du violon au XVIIe et XVIIIe siècle. No.1256.

AUBRY, PIERRE, 1874–1910.
La musicologie médiévale.
In: Mélanges de musicologie critique. Vol.1.
Les plus anciens monuments de la musique française.
In: Mélanges de musicologie critique. Vol.4.

AUGUST, PETER, d. after 1781.
Piano compositions.
In: Schmid. Musik am sächsischen Hofe. Bd.4.

AULEN, JOHANNES, 15th CENTURY.
Missa zu 3 Stimmen.
In: Das Chorwerk. No.31.

AULICH, BRUNO.
Divertimento für Flauto dolce, Violine und Viola.
In: Moecks Kammermusik. Vol.501.

AULIN, LAURA VALBORG, 1860–1928.
String quartet, F major.
In: Musikaliska konstföreningen. 1888.

AUSTRIA–MUSIC.
In: Denkmäler der Tonkunst in Österreich.
In: Hausmusik.
In: Zeitschrift für Spielmusik. No.53, 67, 282.

AUSTRIAN LUTE MUSIC.
In: Denkmäler der Tonkunst in Österreich. Vol.37. (Jg.XVIII/2); Vol.50. (Jg.XXV/2).

AUVERGNE, ANTOINE D', *see* DAUVERGNE, ANTOINE.

AVERY, STANLEY R., 1879– .
Songs.
In: The Wa-Wan series of American compositions.

AVISON, CHARLES, 1710–1770.
Concerto grosso. Op.3/1.
In: Diletto musicale. No.133.
Sonate (Em).
In: Moffat. Trio-Sonaten alter Meister. No.16.

AVSHALOMOV, JACOB, 1919– .
(var. sp.: Jacob Avshalomoff).
Tom O'Bedlam. For mixed chorus, solo oboe, tabor, and jingles.
In: New music. Vol.27. No.1. Oct.1953.
AYRES, FREDERIC, 1876–1926.
Piano trio.
In: Society for the Publication of American Music. Publications. 6th season. 1924–25.
Songs; Piano music.
In: The Wa-Wan series of American compositions.
AYRTON, WILLIAM, 1777–1858.
Sacred music.
In: Arnold. Cathedral music. Vol.3.
AZZAIOLO, FILIPPO, 16th CENTURY.
Il secondo libro de villotte del fiore alla padovana.
In: Maestri bolognesi. Vol.2.

BABÁN, GRACIÁN, 17th CENTURY.
Sacred music.
In: Eslava y Elizondo. Liro sacro-hispana. 17th century. i.1.
BABBITT, MILTON, 1916– .
Composition for 4 instruments (flute, violin, clarinet, and violoncello).
In: New music. Vol.22. No.4. July 1949.
BABOU.
Treize pièces. Organ.
In: Orgue et liturgie. Vol.43.
BACH, CARL PHILIPP EMANUEL, 1714–1788.
Die sechs Sammlungen von Sonaten, freien Fantasien und Rondos für Kenner und Liebhaber. 6v.
Selections.
In: Crotch. Specimens of various styles of music. Vol.3.
In: Geiringer. Music of the Bach family.
Allegro. (A).
In: Pauer. Alte Meister. No.7.
Allegro, La xenophone.
In: Köhler. Les maîtres du clavecin. Heft 1.
Choral music.
In: Commer. Cantica sacra. Vol.1, No.17, 19, 22.
In: Rochlitz. Sammlung vorzüglicher Gesangstücke. Bd.3.
Chorus and air. (Israeliten)
In: Königliche Akademie der Künste. Auswahl vorzüglicher Musik-Werke. Appendix.
Concerto (C) per il cembalo solo.
In: Pauer. Alte Meister. No.67.
Zwei Duos, ohne Generalbass, für Flöte und Violine.
In: Nagels Musik-Archiv. No.35.
Fantasie and fugue. Organ.
In: Dickinson. Historical recital series for organ. Vol.1. No.14.
Fantaisie et fugue C-moll. Organ.
In: Guilmant. École classique de l'orgue. No.20.
Fugue. Auf, dass wir.
In: Königliche Akademie der Künste. Auswahl vorzüglicher Musik-Werke. No.7.
Instrumental concertos.
In: Denkmäler deutscher Tonkunst. [1.Folge]. Vol.29–30.
Keyboard music.
In: Clementi. Clementi's Selection of practical harmony. Vol.1, 2, 3.
In: Farrenc. Le trésor des pianistes. Vol.12, 13.
In: Georgii. Keyboard music of the Baroque and Rococo. Vol.3.
In: Herrmann. Lehrmeister und Schüler Joh. Seb. Bachs. Vol.2.
In: Roitzsch. Alte Klavier-Musik.
In: Tagliapietra. Antologia di musica antica e moderna per pianoforte. Bd.13.
Lieder.
In: Moser. Alte Meister des deutschen Liedes. 30 Gesänge. No.27.
In: Moser. Alte Meister des deutschen Liedes. 46 Gesänge. No.43.
In: Reimann. Das deutsche Lied. Vol.2.
Vier Orchestersinfonien.
In: Das Erbe deutscher Musik. 1.Reihe. Vol.18.
Organ music.
In: The Liturgical Music Press, Inc. Masterpieces of organ music. Folio 12, 30.
Die preussischen Sonaten. Nr.1–3, 4–6, für Klavier.
In: Nagels Musik-Archiv. No.6, 15.
Sacred music.
In: Latrobe, C. I. Selection of sacred music.
In: Latrobe, J. A. The music of the church.
Sinfonie Nr.2 für vierstimmiges Streichorchester und Basso Continuo; Sinfonie Nr.3 für vierstimmiges Streichorchester und Cembalo; Sinfonie Nr.4 für vierstimmiges Streichorchester und Basso Continuo.
In: Nagels Musik-Archiv. No.96, 73, 130.
Sonaten für Flöten und Basso Continuo.
In: Hortus musicus. No.71–72.
Sonate. Flauto traverso und Basso Continuo.
In: Florilegium musicum. Vol.1, 2, 3.
Sonaten für Klavier.
In: Nagels Musik-Archiv. No.90.
Sonate G moll für Oboe, Cembalo (Klavier) und Violoncello (Fagott) ad lib.
In: Riemann. Collegium musicum. No.103.
Sonate G-moll, für Oboe und Basso Continuo.
In: Florilegium musicum. Vol.7.
3 Sonatas. Piano. (Violin or violoncello ad lib.).
In: Oberdörffer. Deutsche Klaviermusik des 17. und 18. Jahrhunderts. Vol.7.
Sonate C-dur für Klavier, mit begleitung einer Violine und eines Violoncello.
In: Hortus musicus. No.46.
Sonate in C dur (Gamba und Bass. Arr. Cello und Klavier); Sonate in D dur. (Gamba und Bass. Arr. Violoncell und Klavier).
In: Kammersonaten. No.6, 7.
Sonate G-dur. Piano.
In: Organum. 5.Reihe. Nr.2.
Kleine Stücke für Klavier.
In: Nagels Musik-Archiv. No.65.
Trio in G dur. Für 2 Violinen, Violoncell und Klavier.
In: Riemann. Collegium musicum. No.16.
Trio-Sonate A-moll, A-dur, D-moll für Flöte, Violine und Basso Continuo.
In: Moecks Kammermusik. Vol.72, 73, 74.

Die württembergischen Sonaten. Für Klavier. No.1–6.
In: Nagels Musik-Archiv. No.21/22.
La xenophone.
In: Hausmusik. No.31.
La xenophone, Sybille, La complaisante, Les langueurs tendres.
In: Pauer. Alte Meister. No.31.
Zwölf zwei- und drei- stimmige kleine Stücke für die Flöte oder Violine und das Klavier.
In: Hirsch. Veröffentlichungen. [Bd.] 9.
BACH, GEORG CHRISTOPH, 1642–1697.
Selections.
In: Geiringer. Music of the Bach family.
Altbachisches Archiv.
In: Das Erbe deutscher Musik. 1.Reihe. Vol.1–2.
BACH, JOHANN.
Selections.
In: Geiringer. Music of the Bach family.
BACH, JOHANN BERNHARD, 1676–1749.
Selections.
In: Geiringer. Music of the Bach family.
Erste Ouvertüre für Sologeige und Streichorchester.
In: Bach Family. Die Kunst des Bachsen Geschlechts. No.1.
Organ music.
In: Das Erbe deutscher Musik. 1.Reihe. Vol.9.
In: The Liturgical Music Press, Inc. Masterpieces of organ music. Folio 12.
In: Straube. Choralvorspiele alter Meister.
Variations on the chorale, Thou Prince of Peace. Organ.
In: Dickinson. Historical recital series for organ. Vol.1. No.11.
BACH, JOHANN CHRISTIAN, 1735–1782.
Selections.
In: Geiringer. Music of the Bach family.
Arias.
In: Landshoff. Alte Meister des Bel Canto. Eine Sammlung von Arien. Vol.1–2.
Concerto for piano.
In: Documents of the musical past. Vol.1.
Concerto II, A-dur, für Cembalo (Klavier) und Streichorchester; Konzert G-dur für Klavier und Streichorchester.
In: Antiqua Edition. Solo-Instrument mit Begleitung.
Konzert A-dur für Cembalo.
In: Corona. Vol.73.
Konzert in F-moll für Klavier (Cembalo) mit Streichorchester.
In: Nagels Musik-Archiv. No.170.
Sechs Duette für zwei Violinen.
In: Nagels Musik-Archiv. No.126, 140.
Fugue. 2 choirs. Durch denselbigen.
In: Königliche Akademie der Künste. Auswahl vorzüglicher Musik-Werke. No.16.
Keyboard music.
In: Farrenc. Le trésor des pianistes. Vol.18.
In: Georgii. Keyboard music of the Baroque and Rococo. Vol.3.
In: Pauer. Alte Klavier-Musik. 2d series. Part 4.
In: Tagliapietra. Antologia di musica antica e moderna per pianoforte. Bd.9, 13.
2 Stücke für Klavier.
In: Sondheimer. Werke aus dem 18. Jahrhundert. Nr.8.
Organ music.
In: Caecilia; Sammlung von Choralvorspielen.
In: Muziek voor de eredienst. Vol.1, 2.
In: Schweiger. A brief compendium of early organ music.
Overture. La clemenza di Scipione.
In: Diletto musicale. No.96.
Prelude and fugue. Organ.
In: Dickinson. Historical recital series for organ. Vol.1. No.9.
Quartett für Violine, Viola, Violoncello und Klavier (Cembalo).
In: Antiqua Edition. Von 4 Instrumenten an.
Quartett, für zwei Querflöten (Violinen), Viola und Violoncello.
In: Organum. 3.Reihe. Nr.63, 64, 66, 68.
In: Hortus musicus. No.119.
Quartett in F-dur, Op.8, Nr.4. Für Flöte, Violine, Viola, Violoncell oder Streichquartett.
In: Nagels Musik-Archiv. No.127.
Sechs Quintette, Op.11.
In: Das Erbe deutscher Musik. 1.Reihe. Vol.3.
Quintett D-dur für Querflöte, Oboe, Violine, Violoncello und Obligates Cembalo.
In: Hortus musicus. No.42.
Quintett D-dur, Op.11, Nr.6, für Querflöte, (Violine), Oboe (Violine), Violine, Viola, Violoncello und ausgesetzten Generalbass.
In: Nagels Musik-Archiv. No.124.
Quintett Es-dur, Op.11, Nr.4.
In: Nagels Musik-Archiv. No.123.
Rondo; 2 Sonates.
In: Köhler. Les maîtres du clavecin. Heft 1, Heft 2.
Sinfonien.
In: Das Erbe deutscher Musik. 1.Reihe. Vol.30.
Drei Sinfonietten.
In: Corona. Vol.69.
Sinfonia in E flat, Op.3, No.4.
In: Für Kenner und Liebhaber. No.2.
Sinfonie G-dur.
In: Sondheimer. Werke aus dem 18. Jahrhundert. Nr.34.
Sonaten für Klavier.
In: Sondheimer. Werke aus dem 18. Jahrhundert. Nr.17.
Sonate (Cm).
In: Pauer. Alte Meister. No.6.
Sonate Nr.2, A-dur, für Klavier zu vier Händen.
In: Nagels Musik-Archiv. No.115.
Sonate C-dur für Klavier zu vier Händen.
In: Nagels Musik-Archiv. No.4.
Zwei Sonaten für Klavier und Flöte oder Violine.
In: Nagels Musik-Archiv. No.1.
Sonate F-dur für Flöte und Cembalo.
In: Moecks Kammermusik. Vol.63.
Sonate D-dur für Konzertierendes Cembalo (Klavier), Flöte oder Violine und Violoncello.
In: Nagels Musik-Archiv. No.192.
Sonate A-dur für Violine oder Flöte und Klavier.
In: Nagels Musik-Archiv. No.103.

Sonate in A dur, Op.10, No.4. Für Violine und Klavier.
In: Kammersonaten. No.3.
Sonate in D dur, Op.16, No.1. Für Violine und Klavier.
In: Kammersonaten. No.4.
Sonate Es-dur für Violine und Cembalo (Klavier).
In: Antiqua Edition. Von 2 Instrumenten an.
Drei Streichtrios für zwei Violinen und Violoncello (Op.4, Nr.2, 4 und 6).
In: Hortus musicus. No.37.
3 Trios für 2 Violinen und Viola (Violoncello) in B-dur, Es-dur, D-dur.
In: Moecks Kammermusik. Vol.55.
Trio in D dur. Für Klavier, Violine und Violoncell.
In: Riemann. Collegium musicum. No.19.
BACH, JOHANN CHRISTOPH, 1642–1703.
Selections.
In: Geiringer. Music of the Bach family.
Altbachisches Archiv.
In: Das Erbe deutscher Musik. 1.Reihe. Vol.1–2.
Choral music.
In: Rochlitz. Sammlung vorzüglicher Gesangstücke. Bd.3.
Motetten. No.1–3.
In: Bach Family. Die Kunst des Bachsen Geschlechts. No.4.
Organ music.
In: Buszin. Organ series. Vol.1.
In: Keller. Achtzig Choralvorspiele deutscher Meister des 17. und 18. Jahrhunderts.
In: Klein. The first four centuries of music for the organ from Dunstable to Bach (1370–1749).
In: Liturgical Music Press, Inc. Masterpieces of organ music. Folio 12, 41, 71.
In: The parish organist. Vol.1–4.
In: Rohr. Orgelspiel im Kirchenjahr.
Vocal music.
?In: Hullah. Vocal scores. I. Sacred.
BACH, JOHANN CHRISTOPH FRIEDRICH, 1732–1795.
Selections.
In: Geiringer. Music of the Bach family.
Ausgewählte Werke.
In: Fürstliches Institut für musikwissenschaftliche Forschung. Veröffentlichungen. 3.Reihe. Bd.1, No.1–2; Bd.5, No.1–4; Bd.7, No.1–4.
Die kindheit Jesu. Die auferweckung Lazarus.
In: Denkmäler deutscher Tonkunst. [1.Folge]. Vol.56.
Keyboard music.
In: Clementi. Clementi's Selection of practical harmony. Vol.3.
In: Farrenc. Le trésor des pianistes. Vol.15.
In: Herrmann. Lehrmeister und Schüler Joh. Seb. Bachs. Vol.2.
In: Pauer. Alte Klavier-Musik. 2d series. Part 4.
Organ music.
In: Anthologia antiqua. Vol.2.
Sonata und Cembalo Concertate. Flöte und Violine.
In: Kammersonaten. No.12.
BACH, JOHANN ERNST, 1722–1777.
Selections.
In: Geiringer. Music of the Bach family.
Fantaisie et fugue.
In: Köhler. Les maîtres du clavecin. Heft 2.
Fantasie and fugue in F. Piano.
In: Roitzsch. Alte-Klavier Musik.
Keyboard music.
In: Clementi. Clementi's Selection of practical harmony. Vol.1.
In: Pauer. Alte Klavier-Musik. 2d series. Part 3.
In: Tagliapietra. Antologia di musica antica e moderna per pianoforte. Bd.13.
Passion.
In: Denkmäler deutscher Tonkunst. [1.Folge]. Vol.48.
Sonate D-dur für Klavier und Geige.
In: Nagels Musik-Archiv. No.2.
Songs.
In: Denkmäler deutscher Tonkunst. [1.Folge]. Vol.42.
BACH, JOHANN HEINRICH, 1614–1692.
Selections.
In: Geiringer. Music of the Bach family.
Altbachisches Archiv.
In: Das Erbe deutscher Musik. 1.Reihe. Vol.1–2.
Chorale prelude. Have mercy, O Lord God. Organ.
In: Dickinson. Historical recital series for organ. Vol.1, No.8.
Christ is risen. Organ.
In: The Liturgical Music Press, Inc. Masterpieces of organ music. Folio 19.
BACH, JOHANN LUDWIG, 1677–1731.
Selections.
In: Geiringer. Music of the Bach family.
Zwei Motetten.
In: Das Chorwerk. No.99.
BACH, JOHANN MICHAEL, 1648–1694.
Selections.
In: Geiringer. Music of the Bach family.
Altbachisches Archiv.
In: Das Erbe deutscher Musik. 1.Reihe. Vol.1–2.
Chorale prelude. When my last hour. Organ.
In: Dickinson. Historical recital series for organ. Vol.1, No.10.
Organ music.
In: Buszin. Organ series. Vol.1.
In: Dietrich. Elf Orgelchörale des siebzehnten Jahrhunderts.
In: Das Erbe deutscher Musik. 1.Reihe. Vol.9.
In: Keller. Achtzig Choralvorspiele deutscher Meister des 17. und 18. Jahrhunderts.
In: Klein. The first four centuries of music for the organ from Dunstable to Bach (1370–1749).
In: The Liturgical Music Press, Inc. Masterpieces of organ music. Folio 12.
In: The parish organist. Vol.1–4.
In: Straube. Choralvorspiele alter Meister.
BACH, JOHANN NIKOLAUS, 1669–1753.
Selections.
In: Geiringer. Music of the Bach family.

Der jenaische Wein- und Bierrufer.
In: Bach Family. Die Kunst des Bachsen Geschlechts. No.3.
Messe (Em) für gemischtem Chor mit Streichorchester und Pianoforte (Cembalo).
In: Bach Family. Die Kunst des Bachsen Geschlechts. No.2.
BACH, JOHANN SEBASTIAN, 1685–1750.
Werke. 61v. in 47.
—— Another issue. 60v. in 46. (bound in 47).
Veröffentlichungen. Jahrg.1– .
Die neue Bach-Ausgabe. 8 series.
Johann Sebastian Bach's Compositionen für die Orgel. 9v.
Complete organ works. 10v.
Complete organ works. 8v.
Oeuvres complètes pour orgue. 12v.
The complete organ works.
In: Lea pocket scores. No.31–38.
Klavierübung. 4v. in 5.
Klavierwerke. 23v.
Selections.
In: Crotch. Specimens of various styles of music. Vol.3.
Ach Golgatha, from the "St. Matthew Passion."
In: Parrish. Masterpieces of music before 1750. No.49.
Arie. Agnus.
In: Königliche Akademie der Künste. Auswahl vorzüglicher Musik-Werke. Appendix.
Arie aus Kantate 39, 119, 182, 142, 208, 161, 175.
In: Moecks gelbe Musikhefte. Vol.23, 24, 25, 26, 27, 28, 29.
Arioso "Betrachte meine Seel" aus der Johannes-Passion.
In: Gitarre-Kammermusik. No.38.
Badinage. Organ.
In: Dickinson. Historical recital series for organ. No.44.
The 6 Brandenburg concerti. (1–3, 4–6).
In: Lea pocket scores. No.27/28.
Canonic trio for oboe, violin (or two tenor recorders) and piano.
In: Music for wind instruments by 18th century masters. No.8.
Acht Canons aus dem "Musikalischen Opfer" für Streichinstrument.
In: Musikschätze der Vergangenheit.
Cantatas. Excerpts.
In: Parrish. Masterpieces of music before 1750. No.46, 47, 48.
Cantatas.
In: Lea pocket scores. No.79–85; 106–109.
Canzone für Streichorchester.
In: Rahter's Kammer-Orchester. No.12.
Capriccio in B-dur.
In: Musikalische Stundenbücher.
Capriccio. On the departure of his beloved brother. Organ.
In: Dickinson. Historical recital series for organ. Vol.1, No.12.
Choral music.
In: Antiqua Chorbuch. Vol.1. Heft 5; Vol.2. Heft 5.
In: Commer. Cantica sacra. Vol.1, No.13; Vol.2, No.14, 24, 25.
In: Dessoff choir series. No.26, 27.
In: Engel. Three centuries of choral music. Vol.4.
In: Nagels Männerchor-Blätter. No.4, 9, 10, 19.
In: Recueil de musique ancienne. Recueil des morceaux de musique ancienne. Bd.2, 4.
In: Rochlitz. Sammlung vorzüglicher Gesangstücke. Bd.3.
185 4-part chorales (C. P. E. Bach collection).
In: Lea pocket scores. No.75.
Chorale prelude. In dulci jubilo. Organ.
In: Dickinson. Historical recital series for organ. Vol.2, No.30.
4-Stimmige Choräle.
In: Zeitschrift für Spielmusik. No.14.
8 Choräle.
In: Zeitschrift für Spielmusik. No.137.
Sechzig Choralgesänge.
In: Musikalische Stundenbücher.
Chorus. Da pacem.
In: Ecclesiasticon. No.37.
The 16 Concerti for harpsichord (after Vivaldi and others).
In: Lea pocket scores. No.69.
The 2 Concerti for 3 claviers (D minor, C major).
In: Lea pocket scores. No.56.
Harpsichord concerti.
In: Lea pocket scores. No.97, 98.
Concerto grosso Form.
In: Einstein. Beispielsammlung zur älteren Musikgeschichte.
Contrapunctus III, from "Die Kunst der Fuge."
In: Parrish. Masterpieces of music before 1750. No.50.
Doch Jesus will . . . Arie aus Kantate 46.
In: Moecks gelbe Musikhefte. Vol.16.
Duette alter Meister.
In: Zeitschrift für Spielmusik. No.69.
Easter oratorio.
In: Lea pocket scores. No.78.
The 6 English and 6 French suites.
In: Lea pocket scores. No.9.
Fantaisie, C-moll, für Klavier.
In: Hausmusik. No.90.
Feiermusik.
In: Corona. Vol.30.
Fig. Choral. Ich lasse.
In: Königliche Akademie der Künste. Auswahl vorzüglicher Musik-Werke. No.11.
Fuge über ein Thema von Corelli für Streichorchester.
In: Rahter's Kammer-Orchester. No.13.
Fugen.
In: Musica instrumentalis. Vol.2.
2 Fugen für 4 Instrumente (aus den Orgelfugen).
In: Zeitschrift für Spielmusik. No.160.
2 Fugen aus der "Kunst der Fuge."
In: Zeitschrift für Spielmusik. No.139.
2 Spielgelfugen aus der "Kunst der Fuge."
In: Zeitschrift für Spielmusik. No.203.
The 3 gamba (or cello)-clavier sonatas; 7 flute-clavier sonatas.
In: Lea pocket scores. No.10.
Goldberg variations; Italian concerto; 15 2-part and 15 3-part inventions.

In: Lea pocket scores. No.21.
Hausmusik.
In: Zeitschrift für Spielmusik. No.135.
Clavier works. Vol.VI, VII, VIII.
In: Lea pocket scores. No.45/46, 68.
Keyboard music.
In: Clementi. Clementi's Selection of practical harmony. Vol.1, 2, 3.
In: Farrenc. Le trésor des pianistes. Vol.8.
In: Tagliapietra. Antologia di musica antica e moderna per pianoforte. Bd.11.
Konzert für Klavier (Cembalo), 2 Altblockflöten und 4stg. Streichorchester.
In: Corona. Vol.32.
Die Kunst der Fuge. (The art of fugue).
In: Lea pocket scores. No.73.
Largo aus dem Doppelkonzert.
In: Corona. Vol.24.
Lieder.
In: Moser. Alte Meister des deutschen Liedes. 46 Gesänge. No.24.
In: Reimann. Das deutsche Lied. Vol.2, 3, 4.
Magnificat and Appendix: Xmas interpolations.
In: Lea pocket scores. No.105.
Märsche.
In: Corona. Vol.11.
Menuette aus einer Serenate.
In: Corona. Vol.52.
The motets.
In: Lea pocket scores. No.76/77.
The musical offering; 3 Trio sonatas.
In: Lea pocket scores. No.26.
Aus Johann Sebastian Bachs Notenbüchlein für Anna Magdalena.
In: Zeitschrift für Spielmusik. No.142.
Vier Stücke aus dem Klavierbuche der Anna Magdalena Bach.
In: Moser. Das Musikkränzlein. No.7.
9 Stücke aus dem Notenbüchlein für Anna Magdalena Bach.
In: Zeitschrift für Spielmusik. No.129.
Anna Magdalena's march. Organ.
In: Dickinson. Historical recital series for organ. Vol.2. No.40.
Organ music.
In: Anthologia antiqua. Vol.1.
In: Bonnet. Historical organ-recitals. Vol.2.
In: Buszin. Organ series. Vol.3.
In: Caecilia; Sammlung von Choralvorspielen.
In: Guilmant. Concert historique d'orgue.
In: Keller. Achtzig Choralvorspiele deutscher Meister des 17. und 18. Jahrhunderts.
In: Keller. Orgelvorspiele.
In: Organ masters of the Baroque period. Vol.3.
In: The parish organist. Vol.1–4, 5–6, 7–8.
In: Pierront. Cent versets de Magnificat.
In: Rohr. Orgelspiel im Kirchenjahr.
In: Standard series of organ compositions (passim).
In: Straube. Alte Meister.
[Paraphrases extraites du recueil intitule l'Autograph de Leipzig]. Organ.
In: Orgue et liturgie. Vol.7.
The 6 Partitas; French overtures.
In: Lea pocket scores. No.22.
Passionschoräle.
In: Zeitschrift für Spielmusik. No.173.
Praeludium und Fuge H-moll für Orgel.
In: Musikalische Seltenheiten. Bd.6.
Prélude-Choral "Wir glauben all an einen Gott." Organ.
In: Guilmant. École classique de l'orgue. No.23.
Presto de la cantate Nr.35.
In: Guilmant. Répertoire des concerts du Trocadéro. Vol.4.
Ricercare aus dem "Musikalischen Opfer" für Streichinstrumente.
In: Musikschätze der Vergangenheit.
Sarabanden und andere Suitensätze. Für drei oder vier Streichinstrumente zum Solo-wie zum Chorspiel.
In: Musikschätze der Vergangenheit.
Sinfonia in C-dur, Ouvertüre in A-moll, Sinfonia in H-moll.
In: Corona. Vol.57.
Sinfonia D-dur aus der Kantate Nr.42.
In: Concertino.
Sinfonia et sonatina.
In: Guilmant. Répertoire des concerts du Trocadéro. Vol.3.
Sonate in G-moll für obligates Cembalo und Flöte.
In: Nagels Musik-Archiv. No.77.
Sonate en ut majeur, pour deux violons et continuo.
In: Flores musicae. Vol.2.
Songs and arias. (Sacred and other). Complete.
In: Lea pocket scores. No.74.
Fünf Stücke für kleines Orchester aus den Kirchenkantaten.
In: Musikschätze der Vergangenheit.
The four suites (overtures) for orchestra.
In: Lea pocket scores. No.55.
Trio-Sonate C-dur für 2 Violinen, Tasten-Instrument und Bass-Instrument ad lib.
In: Antiqua Edition. Von 3 Instrumenten an.
Triosonate D-moll für zwei Violinen, Klavier oder Orgel.
In: Nagels Musik-Archiv. No.49.
Unschuld, kleinod Reiner Seelen. Arie für Sopran, Flauto traverso, Oboe, Viola und Violine.
In: Hortus musicus. No.1.
Violin concerti.
In: Lea pocket scores. No.96.
6 Violin solo sonatas and 6 Cello solo suites.
In: Lea pocket scores. No.2.
The 6 Violin-clavier sonatas.
In: Lea pocket scores. No.4.
Virga Jesse floruit. Duett für Sopran, Bass und Continuo aus dem Magnificat.
In: Hortus musicus. No.80.
Weihnachts-Choräle.
In: Zeitschrift für Spielmusik. No.272.
Ein kleines Weihnachtsoratorium.
In: Zeitschrift für Spielmusik. No.144, 145.
The well-tempered clavier. Parts I, II.
In: Lea pocket scores. No.1a/b.
BACH, WILHELM FRIEDEMANN, 1710–1784.
Ausgewählte Instrumentalwerke. 1 v.
Complete works for organ. 32p.
Selections.

In: Geiringer. Music of the Bach family.
Capriccio, Fugue, Sonate.
In: Köhler. Les maîtres du clavecin. Heft 1.
Chorale prelude. We thank Thee, Lord. Organ.
In: Dickinson. Historical recital series for organ. Vol.1, No.13.
Concert D-moll. Organ.
In: Guilmant. École classique de l'orgue. No.8.
Concerto C-moll für Cembalo (Klavier) und Streichorchester.
In: Antiqua Edition. Solo-Instrument mit Begleitung.
Solo-Konzert G-dur. Piano.
In: Organum. 5.Reihe. Nr.27.
Fantasie C-dur. Piano.
In: Organum. 5.Reihe. Nr.31.
Fuge (Cm).
In: Pauer. Alte Meister. No.8.
8 Fugues sans pedale. Organ.
In: Orgue et liturgie. Vol.45.
Keyboard music.
In: Clementi. Clementi's Selection of practical harmony. Vol.3.
In: Farrenc. Le trésor des pianistes. Vol.10.
In: Georgii. Keyboard music of the Baroque and Rococo. Vol.3.
In: Herrmann. Lehrmeister und Schüler Joh. Seb. Bachs. Vol.2.
In: Pauer. Alte Klavier-Musik. 2d series. Part 2.
In: Tagliapietra. Antologia di musica antica e moderna per pianoforte. Bd.12.
Organ music.
In: Das Erbe deutscher Musik. 1.Reihe. Vol.9.
In: Königliche Akademie der Künste. Auswahl vorzüglicher Musik-Werke. No.6.
In: The Liturgical Music Press, Inc. Masterpieces of organ music. Folio 12.
In: Orgue et liturgie. Vol.37.
In: Schweiger. A brief compendium of early organ music.
In: Straube. Choralvorspiele alter Meister.
Sechs Polonaisen.
In: Hausmusik. No.98.
Sonate (C).
In: Pauer. Alte Meister. No.24.
Sonata Es-dur für zwei Flöten.
In: Nagels Musik-Archiv. No.39.
Zwei Sonaten für zwei Flöten (Violinen) allein.
In: Nagels Musik-Archiv. No.120.
Klaviersonaten. Heft I–II, Nr.1–3, 4–6.
In: Nagels Musik-Archiv. No.63, 78.
Sonaten für Klavier. Nr.7–9.
In: Nagels Musik-Archiv. No.156.
Sonate in D. Piano.
In: Roitzsch. Alte Klavier-Musik.
Trio in B dur. Für 2 Violinen, Violoncell und Klavier.
In: Riemann. Collegium musicum. No.45.

BACH, WILHELM FRIEDRICH ERNST, 1759–1845.
Selections.
In: Geiringer. Music of the Bach family.
Trio G-dur für zwei Querflöten und Viola.
In: Hortus musicus. No.57.

BACH FAMILY.
Geiringer. Music of the Bach family. 248p.
Die Kunst des Bachsen Geschlechts. 4v.

BACHMETIEFF.
Vocal music.
In: Sammlung russischer Romanzen. No.53, 54, 62, 63, 181, 182, 263.

BACHOFEN, THOMAS.
Motetten.
In: Das Chorwerk. No.69.

BÄCK, KNUT, 1868–1953.
Theme and variations for piano, Op.2.
In: Musikaliska konstföreningen. 1895.
Tomten. Op.5.
In: Musikaliska konstföreningen. 1900.

BÄCK, SVEN ERIK, 1919– .
String quartet, No.2.
In: Musikaliska konstföreningen. 1957.

BACON, ERNST, 1898– .
Seven canons.
In: Music Press, Inc. [Choral series]. Vol.114.
The Lord star.
In: Music Press, Inc. [Choral series]. Vol.125.
6 Songs.
In: New music. Vol.15. No.2. Jan.1942.

BADINGS, HENK, 1907– .
Divertimento für 3 Blockflöten oder Geigen.
In: Zeitschrift für Spielmusik. No.217.

BAI, TOMMASO, ca.1650–1714.
Sacred music.
In: Proske. Musica divina. Annus primus. Tom 2.

BAÏF, JEAN ANTOINE DE, 1532–1589.
(var. sp.: Jan Antoine de Baïf).
Chansonnettes mesurées.
In: Expert. Les maîtres musiciens de la Renaissance française. Vol.10.
Psaumes mesurés.
In: Expert. Florilège du concert vocal de la Renaissance. No.7.

BAILDON.
Sacred music.
In: Page. Harmonia sacra. Vol.2.

BAILEY, PARKER, 1902– .
Sonata for flute and piano.
In: Society for the Publication of American Music. Publications. 10th season. 1928–29.

BAILEY, WILLIAM H.
Idless, for piano and violin.
In: New music. Vol.10. No.2. Jan.1937.

BAKER, ROBERT.
Computer cantata.
In: New music. To be pub.

BAKFARK, V., *see* GREFF, VALENTIN.

BALAKIREV, MILIĬ ALEKSEEVICH, 1836–1910.
(var. sp.: Balakireff).
Complete piano works. v.1– .
Vocal music.
In: Sammlung russischer Romanzen. No.112, 259, 274.

BALBASTRE, CLAUDE, 1729–1799.
Organ music.
In: Biggs. A treasury of shorter organ classics.
In: Raugel. Les maîtres français de l'orgue. Vol.1.

In: Raugel. Les maîtres français de l'orgue aus XVIIème et XVIIIème siècles.
Prelude on two French noels. Organ.
In: Dickinson. Historical recital series for organ. No.47.
BALLADES.
In: Turin. Biblioteca Nazionale. Mss. (J.II.9). The Cypriot-French repertory. Vol.3.
BALLARD, ROBERT.
Bibliographie des éditions.
In: Société Française de Musicologie, Paris. Ser.II. Bd.9.
BALLARINI.
Airs.
In: Prunières. Les maîtres du chant. Recueil 5.
BALLET, WILLIAM, 16th CENTURY.
Lute music.
In: Chilesotti. Lautenspieler des XVI Jahrhunderts.
BALLETTI, BERNARDINO.
Intabolatura de lauto.
In: Lefkoff. Five sixteenth century Venetian lute books.
BALTAZARINI, *see* BEAUJOYEULX, BALTHASARD DE.
BAMBERG, MANUSCRIT ED.IV.6 DE.
In: Aubry. Cent motets du XIIe siècle publiés d'après le Manuscrit Ed.IV.6 de Bamberg. 3v.
BANCHIERI, ADRIANO, ca.1567–1634.
Selections.
In: Documenta historica musicae.
In: Torchi. L'arte musicale in Italia. Bd.3, 4.
Aus den "Canzoni alla Francese."
In: Zeitschrift für Spielmusik. No.294.
Festino nella sera . . . 1608.
In: Somma. Capolavori polifonici del secolo XVI. Vol.1.
Instrumental music.
In: Wasielewski. Instrumentalsätze vom Ende des XVI. bis Ende des XVII. Jahrhunderts.
Keyboard music.
In: Apel. Musik aus früher Zeit für Klavier. Bd.1.
In: Tagliapietra. Antologia di musica antica e moderna per pianoforte. Bd.3.
Musiche corali.
In: I classici della musica italiana. Vol.1.
In: I classici della musica italiana. Raccolta nazionale delle musiche italiane. Quad.1–3.
Organ music.
In: Fuser. Classici italiani dell'organo.
In: Klein. The first four centuries of music for the organ from Dunstable to Bach (1370–1749).
In: Liber organi. Bd.4.
La pazzia senile.
In: Somma. Capolavori polifonici del secolo XVI. Vol.6.
BANGERT, EMILIUS, 1883– .
Jeg Vaelger mig April. Koncertouverture. Op.7.
In: Samfundet til Udgivelse af dansk Musik. Ser.III. No.52.
Kantate.
In: Samfundet til Udgivelse af dansk Musik. Ser.III. No.26.
BANKS.
Sacred music.
In: Page. Harmonia sacra. Vol.3.
BANKS, DON.
Piano music.
In: Contemporary British piano music.
BANNER, FILIPPO, fl.1700.
Sonate für Violoncello und Klavier (Cembalo).
In: Nagels Musik-Archiv. No.160.
BARBE, ANTOINE, d.1564.
Choral music.
In: Commer. Collectio operum musicorum batavorum saeculi XVI. Bd.12.
BARBELLA, EMANUELE, ca.1725–1777.
Sonate (Gm). Violin and piano.
In: Moffat. Meister-Schule der alten Zeit. Violin-Sonaten. No.19.
BARBETTA, GIULIO CESARE, 16th CENTURY.
(var. sp.: J. C. Barbetta).
Lute music.
In: Chilesotti. Lautenspieler des XVI. Jahrhunderts.
BARBICE, C.
Part music.
In: Hullah. Part music. Class B.1.
BARBIERI, FRANCISCO ASENJO Y, *see* ASENJO Y BARBIERI, FRANCISCO.
BARBIREAU, JACQUES, ca.1420–1491.
(var. sp.: Jacobus Barbireau).
Opera omnia. 2v.
Choral music.
In: Smijers. Van Ockeghem tot Sweelinck. Aflg.2.
BARBOGLES, MARIOS.
Aye Varvara; prélude symphonique.
In: Institut Français d'Athènes. Collection. Série musicale. Vol.2.
BARCROFT, GEORGE, 16th–17th CENTURIES.
Church music.
In: Motett Society. [Collection of ancient church music]. Division 2, 3.
BARFARK, V., *see* GREFF, VALENTIN.
BARI, ITALY–MUSIC.
In: Istituto Italiano per la Storia della musica. Pubblicazioni. 2. Antologie e raccolte. Vol.1.
In: Monumenta musicae sacrae. Vol.1
BARKHAUSEN, ALBERT.
Kleine Stücke für drei Blockflöten.
In: Musica practica. No.53.
BARNARDELLO, BERNARDO GIANONCELLI DELLO IL.
Lute music.
In: Chilesotti. Lautenspieler des XVI. Jahrhunderts.
BARNEKOW, CHRISTIAN, 1837–1913.
8 Finnish folk poems.
In: Samfundet til Udgivelse af dansk Musik. Suppl. 1895.
4 Folksongs from the Russian. Op.14.
In: Samfundet til Udgivelse af dansk Musik. Suppl. 1905.
Idyller for Strygeorkester. Op.29.
In: Samfundet til Udgivelse af dansk Musik. Ser.II. No.32.
Kvintet for 2 Violiner, Bratsch og 2 Violonceller. Op.20.

In: Samfundet til Udgivelse af dansk Musik. Ser.II. No.26.
Nocturnes. Op.19.
In: Samfundet til Udgivelse af dansk Musik. Suppl.1905.
BARRA, HOTINET.
Motets.
In: Attaingnant. Treize livres de motets. Livre 5, 7, 12.
BARRE, JOSEPH DE LA.
Organ music.
In: Raugel. Les maîtres français de l'orgue. Vol.2.
BARRE, MICHEL DE LA, ca.1674–ca.1744.
Sonate dite L'inconnue en sol majeur pour flûte (ou hautbois ou violin), clavier et basse.
In: Musiques françaises. Vol.17.
Suite, G-dur, für zwei Flöten oder andere Melodieinstrumente.
In: Florilegium musicum. Vol.8.
BARRETT, JOHN, ca.1674–ca.1735.
Harpsichord music.
In: Fuller-Maitland. The contemporaries of Purcell. Vol.6–7.
In: Hermann. Contemporaries of Purcell.
Organ music.
In: Tallis to Wesley. Vol.21.
BARRIÈRE, JEAN, 17th CENTURY.
Keyboard sonatas.
In: Newman. Thirteen keyboard sonatas of the 18th and 19th centuries.
BARTHEL, RUDOLF.
Weihnachtsweisen mit Variationen.
In: Zeitschrift für Spielmusik. No.247.
BARTHÉLEMON, FRANÇOIS HIPPOLYTE, 1741–1808.
Organ music.
In: The Liturgical Music Press, Inc. Masterpieces of organ music. Folio 42.
BARTHOLDY, CONRAD JOHAN, 1853–1904.
Solomons Sang i Vingaarden. Op.15.
In: Samfundet til Udgivelse af dansk Musik. Suppl.1906.
Tannhäuser.
In: Samfundet til Udgivelse af dansk Musik. Suppl.1906.
BARTHOLOMAEUS DE BONONIA.
Sacred music.
In: Plainsong and Mediaeval Music Society. Publications. (Borren).
BARTHOLOMEUS DE FLORENTIA.
Selections.
In: Ambros. Auserwählte Tonwerke.
In: Pirrotta. The music of fourteenth-century Italy. Vol.1.
BARTHOLOMEW, MARSHALL, 1885– . ed.
Ten glees, madrigals, and airs. [1600–1765].
In: Music Press, Inc. [Choral series]. Vol.121.
BARTLET, JOHN, fl.1606–1610.
(var. sp.: John Bartlett).
Book of ayres.
In: Fellowes. The English school of lutenist song writers. 2d series. Vol.3.
Madrigals.
In: Euterpe. Vol.11; 2d ed., No.1.
BARTÓK, BÉLA, 1881–1945.
Keyboard music.
In: Musica hungarica.
Zehn leichte Stücke für Streichorchester.
In: Concertino.
Vier kleine Tanzstücke und Sechs ungarische Volkslieder für Streichorchester.
In: Concertino.
Ungarische Volksweisen.
In: Zeitschrift für Spielmusik. No.152.
BARTOLINO DA PADUA, 15th CENTURY.
(var. sp.: Bartolino da Padova).
Credo.
In: Van. Les monuments de l'ars nova. I. No.2.
BARTOLUCCI DA ASSISI, RUFINO, *see* ASSISI, RUFINO BARTOLUCCI DA.
BASIRON, PHILIPPE, 15th CENTURY.
(var. sp.: Phil. Bassiron).
Choral music.
In: Commer. Collectio operum musicorum batavorum saeculi XVI. Bd.8.
In: Smijers. Van Ockeghem tot Sweelinck. Aflg.1.
Missa super l'homme armé.
In: Monumenta polyphoniae liturgicae sanctae ecclesiae romanae. Ser.1. Tomus 1. Fasc.8.
BASSA.
Selections.
In: Pedrell. Teatro lirico español anterior al siglo XIX. Bd.3.
BASSANI, GIOVANNI BATTISTA, ca.1657–1716.
Selections.
In: Torchi. L'arte musicale in Italia. Bd.7.
Airs.
In: Prunières. Les maîtres du chant. Recueil 5.
Arias.
In: Parisotti. Arie antiche. Bd.2.
Cantate a una voce.
In: I classici della musica italiana. Raccolta nazionale delle musiche italiane. Quad. 4–8.
Canzoni.
In: I classici della musica italiana. Vol.2.
Leichte Fantasien. Für drei Gamben oder andere Melodieinstrumente.
In: Hortus musicus. No.64.
Instrumental music.
In: Wasielewski. Instrumentalsätze vom Ende des XVI. bis Ende des XVII. Jahrhunderts.
Nascere, Nascere, Dive Puellule. Alt und B.C.
In: Cantio sacra. No.2.
Organ music.
In: Bossi. Sammlung von Stücken alter italienischer Meister für die moderne Orgel.
In: Cantantibus organis. Vol.11.
In: The Liturgical Music Press, Inc. Masterpieces of organ music. Folio 25.
Part music.
In: Hullah. Part music. Class A.1; Vol.2.
Sacred music.
In: Latrobe, C. I. Selection of sacred music.
In: Latrobe, J. A. The music of the church.
Sonata a tre per due violini e basso continuo. Op.V/9.
In: Hausmusik. No.176.
Sieben Trios für Violine/Viola/Viola da Gamba.

In: Hortus musicus. No.16.
BASSETT, LESLIE RAYMOND.
Five pieces for string quartet.
In: Society for the Publication of American Music. Publications. 41st season. 1960–61.
BASSIRON, PHILIPPE, *see* BASIRON, PHILIPPE.
BASTON, JOSQUIN, 16th CENTURY.
Selections.
In: Maldéghem. Trésor musical.
Choral music.
In: Commer. Collectio operum musicorum batavorum saeculi XVI. Bd.12.
BATAVIA–MUSIC.
In: Musica antiqua batava.
BATESON, THOMAS, ca.1590–1630.
A collection of anthems.
In: Musical Antiquarian Society. Publications. Vol.14.
Madrigals.
In: Arion. Vol.3.
In: Euterpe. Vol.1, 12; 2d ed., No.2–3.
In: Fellowes. The English madrigal school. Vol.21, 22.
In: Musical Antiquarian Society. Publications. Vol.17.
In: Squire. Ausgewählte Madrigale und mehrstimmige Gesänge. No.6, 7.
In: The triumphs of Oriana.
BATTEN, ADRIAN, ca.1590–1637.
Sacred music.
In: Boyce. Cathedral music. Vol.2; 1849, Vol.2, 3.
BATTISHILL, JONATHAN, 1738–1801.
Organ music.
In: Elkan-Vogel organ series. Vol.2.
Sacred music.
In: Page. Harmonia sacra. Vol.1, 2, 3.
Vocal music.
In: Hullah. Vocal scores. II. Secular.
BAUCH, C. W.
String quartet, G major.
In: Musikaliska konstföreningen. 1863.
BAUER, FRANZ.
Sätze für 3 gleiche Streichinstrumente.
In: Moecks Kammermusik. Vol.203.
Sätze für 3 Sopran-Blockflöten oder andere Instrumente.
In: Zeitschrift für Spielmusik. No.16.
Suite Nr.1 für Alt-Blockflöte und Tasteninstrument.
In: Moecks gelbe Musikhefte. Vol.5.
Suite Nr.2 für Alt-Blockflöte und Tasteninstrument.
In: Moecks gelbe Musikhefte. Vol.9.
Variationen über "Im Märzen der Bauer die Rosslein einspannt."
In: Zeitschrift für Spielmusik. No.63.
7 Variationen über ein bretonisches Volkslied.
In: Zeitschrift für Spielmusik. No.143.
6 Variationen über ein eigenes Thema für 1 Melodieinstrument und Klavier.
In: Zeitschrift für Spielmusik. No.127.
7 Variationen über ein Thema von J. Ph. Krieger.
In: Zeitschrift für Spielmusik. No.35.
BAUER, MARION, 1887–1955.
Música de cámera.
In: Boletín latino-americano de música. Vol.5.
Sonata. Viola and piano. Op.22.
In: Society for the Publication of American Music. Publications. 31st season. 1949–50.
BAUERNFEIND, HANS.
Festliches Spiel, für zwei Klaviere.
In: Hausmusik. No.163.
Heiteres Spiel, auf drei Instrumenten, Streicher oder Holzbläser.
In: Hausmusik. No.35.
BAULDEWIJN, NOËL, d.ca.1529.
(var. sp.: Noël Bauldewyn).
Chanson.
In: Brown. Theatrical chansons of the 15th and early 16th centuries.
Polyphonic music.
In: Monumenta musicae belgicae. Vol.9.
BAUMANN, HERBERT.
Kleines Quartett.
In: Zeitschrift für Spielmusik. No.222.
BAUMANN, MAX.
Divertimento.
In: Zeitschrift für Spielmusik. No.271.
BAUR, JÜRG, 1918– .
Concertino.
In: Collegium musicae novae. No.44.
BAUSTETTER, J. T.
Organ music.
In: Peeters. Oudnederlandse meesters. Vol.1.
BAVARIA–MUSIC.
In: Denkmäler deutscher Tonkunst. [2.Folge]. Denkmäler der Tonkunst in Bayern.
In: Das Taghorn.
In: Zeitschrift für Spielmusik. No.26.
BAZIRON.
Chanson.
In: Copenhagen Kongelige Bibliotek. Mss. (Thottske Samling 291[8]). Der kopenhagener Chansonnier.
BAZYLIK, CYPRIAN, 1535–1591.
Pieśni.
In: Denkmäler altpolnischer Musik. Vol.34.
BEACH, MRS. H. H. A., 1867–1944.
Prelude on an old folk tune. Organ.
In: Contemporary organ series. No.15.
BEACH, JOHN PARSONS, 1877–1953.
Songs; Piano music.
In: The Wa-Wan series of American compositions.
BEALE, JAMES.
Second piano sonata. Op.8.
In: Washington (State) University. Music series. No.3.
BEAUJOYEULX, BALTHASARD DE, d.ca.1587.
(var. sp.: Baltazarini; Beaujoyeux).
Le ballet-comique de la reine.
In: Les chefs d'oeuvres classiques de l'opéra français.
BEAUSSE, LA, *see* LA BEAUSSE.
BEAUVARLET-CHARPENTIER, JEAN JACQUES, *see* CHARPENTIER, JEAN JACQUES BEAUVARLET.
BEBER, AMBROSIUS.
Markus-Passion.
In: Das Chorwerk. No.66.

BECCHI, ANTONIO DI, 16th CENTURY.
(var. sp.: Antonio di Becchi Parmegiano).
Libro primo da leuto.
In: Lefkoff. Five sixteenth century Venetian lute books.
BECHGAARD, JULIUS ANDREAS, 1843–1917.
Selected characteristic pieces. Piano.
In: Samfundet til Udgivelse af dansk Musik. Suppl.1897.
BECK, FRANZ, 1723–1809.
Orchestral music.
In: Riemann. Mannheim symphonists. Vol.2.
Sinfonia D-moll für Streichorchester und Basso Continuo, Op.III, Nr.5.
In: Nagels Musik-Archiv. No.193.
Sinfonie Nr.1, G-moll; Nr.2, Es-dur. Sinfonia Grande, Nr.3, G-moll.
In: Sondheimer. Werke aus dem 18. Jahrhundert. Nr.20/21, 43.
BECK, HERMANN. ed.
The suite.
In: Anthology of music. Vol.26.
BECKER, DIETRICH, 17th CENTURY.
Musikalische Frühlingsfrüchte. Sonata a 3; Sonata a 4; Sonata a 5.
In: Rahter's Kammer-Orchester. No.5, 6, 7.
BECKER, HEINRICH.
Klarinetten-Duette.
In: Riemann. Collegium musicum. No.106.
BECKER, HEINZ. ed.
History of instrumentation.
In: Anthology of music. Vol.24.
BECKER, JOHN J., 1886– .
Concerto for horn in F and orchestra.
In: New music. Orchestra series. No.17.
Concerto arabesque, for piano and orchestra.
In: New music. Orchestra series. No.7.
Fantasia tragica. Organ.
In: Contemporary organ series. No.29.
Soundpiece No.2 (Homage to Haydn).
In: New music. Orchestra series. No.23.
Soundpiece No.4, second string quartet.
In: New music. Vol.22. No.1. Oct.1948.
Soundpiece No.5. A short sonata for piano.
In: New music. Special edition.
Symphonia brevis; Symphony No.3. Arr. for piano.
In: New music. Vol.3. No.2. Jan.1930.
BECKERATH, ALFRED VON, 1901– .
Ambacher Quartett.
In: Zeitschrift für Spielmusik. No.77.
Kuckucks im Duett und andere Bicinien.
In: Zeitschrift für Spielmusik. No.191.
Sonate in einem Satz für Alt-Blockflöte und Klavier.
In: Moecks gelbe Musikhefte. Vol.7.
Sonatine für Alt-Blockflöte und Tasteninstrument.
In: Moecks gelbe Musikhefte. Vol.31.
Sonatine für 2 Blas- oder Streichinstrumente und Klavier.
In: Moecks Kammermusik. Vol.18.
Kleine Stücke für Sopran-Blockflöte und Tasteninstrument.
In: Zeitschrift für Spielmusik. No.52.
Tag für Tag. Kleine Spielmusiken.
In: Zeitschrift für Spielmusik. No.57.
Neue Tänze.
In: Zeitschrift für Spielmusik. No.118.
Weisensonate für Violine und Klavier.
In: Moecks Kammermusik. Vol.104.
BECKMAN, BROR, 1866–1929.
Om lyckan. Op.10. Tone poem.
In: Musikaliska konstföreningen. 1904.
Sonata for violin and piano, Op.1, A minor.
In: Musikaliska konstföreningen. 1893.
BEČVAŘOVSKÝ, ANTONÍN FELIX, 1754–1823.
Piano music.
In: Musica antiqua bohemia. Vol.14.
BEECKE, IGNAZ VON, 1733–1803.
Streichquartett, G dur, Nr.6.
In: Hortus musicus. No.170.
BEETHOVEN, LUDWIG VAN, 1770–1827.
Werke. 25 series.
—— Another issue. 25 series in 24v.
Veröffentlichungen des Beethovenhauses in Bonn. 9v.
Veröffentlichungen des Beethovenhauses in Bonn. Neue Folge. v.1– .
[Unvollendete Gesamtausgabe erschienen in:] Ser.1– .
Werke. 20v.
Sämtliche Werke. 14 series.
—— Supplemente. v.1– .
Klavierstücke. 7v.
Oeuvres inédites.
In: Société Française de Musicologie, Paris. Publications. Ser.I. Bd.2.
Adagio sostenuto (Moonlight sonata). Organ.
In: Dickinson. Historical recital series for organ. Vol.1. No.15.
Allegro und Menuett für eine Flötenuhr.
In: Zeitschrift für Spielmusik. No.279.
Andante, für Klavier zu zwei Händen.
In: Hausmusik. No.106.
Bagatellen.
In: Musikalische Stundenbücher.
Chamber music for winds.
In: Lea pocket series. No.100.
Zwölf Contretänze für Orchester.
In: Concertino.
Drei Duos (C-dur, F-dur, B-dur) für Klarinette in B und Fagott.
In: Hausmusik. No.41.
Feiermusik.
In: Corona. Vol.30.
Piano pieces. Complete.
In: Lea pocket scores. No.65.
Keyboard music.
In: Hausmusik. No.107.
In: Tagliapietra. Antologia di musica antica e moderna per pianoforte. Bd.14.
6 Ländlerische Tänze.
In: Hausmusik. No.127.
Sechs ländlerische Tänze für zwei Violinen und Bass.
In: Concertino.
Lieder.
In: Lea pocket scores. No.60.
In: Reimann. Das deutsche Lied. Vol.1.
Märsche.
In: Corona. Vol.11.
6 Gesellschafts-Menuette für 2 Violinen und Bass (Violoncello). Klavier ad lib.
In: Antiqua Edition. Von 3 Instrumenten an.

Zwölf Menuette für Orchester.
In: Nagels Musik-Archiv. No.183.
Motets.
In: Concerts spirituels ou recueil de motets.
Organ music.
In: The Liturgical Music Press, Inc. Masterpieces of organ music. Folio 48, Suppl.
Präludium.
In: Hausmusik. No.105.
Präludium und Fuge. C-dur, F-dur, E-moll.
In: Nagels Musik-Archiv. No.186, 187, 188.
The 17 string quartets. Complete.
In: Lea pocket scores. No.61–64.
Rondo. A-dur, C-dur, für Klavier zu zwei Händen.
In: Hausmusik. No.108.
Streichquartett in F-dur. Op.14/1.
In: Diletto musicale. No.105.
Keyboard music: Sonates.
In: Farrenc. Le trésor des pianistes. Vol.19, 20, 21.
The 32 piano sonatas.
In: Lea pocket scores. No.11–15.
2 Sonates. Piano. Op.31, Nr.1 und 2; 2 Sonates. Op.13, Pathétique. Op.31, Nr.3.
In: Répertoire des clavicinistes. Heft 5, 11.
Sonate. Op.27, Nr.2.
In: Musikalische Seltenheiten. Bd.1.
Grande sonate. Op.53. Waldstein–Sonata. Piano.
In: Répertoire des clavecinistes. Heft 15.
Deutsche Tänze.
In: Zeitschrift für Spielmusik. No.229.
Zwölf deutsche Tänze.
In: Corona. Vol.9.
Trio, für zwei Oboen und englisch Horn (zwei Violinen und Viola), Op.87.
In: Hausmusik. No.29.
Violin sonatas 1–6, 7–10.
In: Lea pocket scores. No.3a/b.
The 5 Cello-piano sonatas.
In: Lea pocket scores. No.18.
String trios. Complete.
In: Lea pocket scores. No.99.
Variations: Op.34; Op.35 (Eroica); Op.76; Op.120 (Diabelli); Grove 191 (C minor); Grove 189.
In: Lea pocket scores. No.30.
Vocal music.
In: Delsarte. Archives du chant. Livr.15. No.1.
BÈGUE, NICOLAS ANTOINE LE, ca.1630–1702.
(var. sp.: Nicolas Antoine Lebègue; Antoine Nicolas Lebègue).
Oeuvres de clavecin. 89p.
Fugue for piano, in F.
In: Königliche Akademie der Künste. Auswahl vorzüglicher Musik-Werke. No.48.
Grand-messe. Organ.
In: Orgue et liturgie. Vol.29.
Keyboard music.
In: Farrenc. Le trésor des pianistes. Vol.3.
In: Georgii. Keyboard music of the Baroque and Rococo. Vol.1.
In: Grovlez. Les plus belles pièces de clavessin de l'école française. Vol.1.
In: Tagliapietra. Antologia di musica antica e moderna per pianoforte. Bd.8.
Noëls varies. Organ.
In: Orgue et liturgie. Vol.16.
Oeuvres complètes d'orgue.
In: Guilmant. Archives des maîtres de l'orgue. Vol.9.
Organ music.
In: Bonnet. An anthology of early French organ music.
In: Bonnet. Historical organ-recitals. Vol.1.
In: Cantantibus organis. Vol.1.
In: Klein. The first four centuries of music for the organ from Dunstable to Bach (1370–1749).
In: Liber organi. Bd.1.
In: The parish organist. Vol.5–6.
In: Pierront. Cent versets de Magnificat.
In: Raugel. Les maîtres français de l'orgue. Vol.1, 2.
In: Raugel. Les maîtres français de l'orgue aux XVIIème et XVIIIème siècles.
In: Schweiger. A brief compendium of early organ music.
BEL, FIRMIN LE, *see* LE BEL, FIRMIN.
BELCHER, SUPPLY, 1751–1836.
Selections.
In: Goldman. Landmarks of early American music, 1760–1800.
Choruses from The harmony of Maine.
In: Music Press, Inc. [Choral series]. Vol.115.
BELGIUM–MUSIC (*see also* BRUSSELS–MUSIC).
In: Monumenta leodiensium musicorum. Vol.1.
In: Monumenta musicae belgicae.
In: Société Belge de Musicologie. Publications. Flores musicales belgicae.
BELKNAP, DANIEL, 1771–1815.
Selections.
In: Goldman. Landmarks of early American music, 1760–1800.
BELLA, DOMENICO DELLA, 16th–17th CENTURIES.
Sonata für Violoncello und unbezifferten Bass.
In: Nagels Musik-Archiv. No.83.
BELLE, JAN, 16th CENTURY.
Choral music.
In: Musica antiqua batava. MA–1, 2.
BELLENGUES, RICHARD DE, 1380–1470.
(var. sp.: Cardot de Bellengues).
Selections.
In: Reaney. Early fifteenth-century music. Vol.2.
BELL'HAVER, VINCENZO, d.1587.
Selections.
In: Torchi. L'arte musicale in Italia. Bd.1, 3.
BELLI, DOMENICO, 16th–17th CENTURIES.
Vocal music.
In: Gevaert. Les gloires de l'Italie. Vol.1.
BELLINI, VINCENZO, 1801–1835.
Composizioni giovanili inedite.
In: Reale Accademia d'Italia, Rome. Musica. Vol.6.
Concerto in E flat (oboe solo, strings).
In: Antica musica strumentale italiana. Ser.I. Vol.5.
Norma.
In: Reale Accademia d'Italia, Rome. Musica. Vol.5.
BENCINI, GIUSEPPE, 18th CENTURY.

Selections.
In: Torchi. L'arte musicale in Italia. Bd.3.
Organ music.
In: Fuser. Classici italiani dell'organo.
BENCINI, PIETRO PAOLO.
Jesu redemptor omnium. Sopran-Solo, gemischt. Chor und B.C.
In: Die Kantate. No.9.
BENDA, FRANZ, 1709–1786.
(var. sp.: František Benda).
Sonata. Flauto, violoncello e cembalo.
In: Musica antiqua bohemica. Vol.60.
Sonata (A). Violin and piano.
In: Moffat. Meister-Schule der alten Zeit. Violin-Sonaten. No.22.
Violin and piano.
In: Musica antiqua bohemica. Vol.11.
In: Schering. Alte Meister des Violinspiels.
BENDA, GEORG, *see* BENDA, JIŘÍ ANTONÍN.
BENDA, JAN JIŘÍ, 1715–1752.
Violin and piano.
In: Musica antiqua bohemica. Vol.11.
BENDA, JIŘÍ ANTONÍN, 1722–1795.
(var. sp.: Georg Benda).
3 Concerti.
In: Musica antiqua bohemica. Vol.45.
Konzert für Cembalo und Streichorchester in G-dur.
In: Nagels Musik-Archiv. No.144.
Concerto sol minore.
In: Musica antiqua bohemica. Vol.10.
Erschallet ihr Himmel. Kantate.
In: Organum. 1.Reihe. Nr.32.
Der Jahrmarkt.
In: Denkmäler deutscher Tonkunst. [1.Folge]. Vol.64.
Keyboard music.
In: Farrenc. Le trésor des pianistes. Vol.14.
In: Georgii. Keyboard music of the Baroque and Rococo. Vol.3.
In: Musica antiqua bohemica. Vol.14, 17.
In: Newman. Thirteen keyboard sonatas of the 18th and 19th centuries.
In: Pauer. Alte Klavier-Musik. 2d series. Part 3.
In: Tagliapietra. Antologia di musica antica e moderna per pianoforte. Bd.13.
Largo und Presto. (F).
In: Pauer. Alte Meister. No.20.
Sinfonie 1–3. Part I.
In: Musica antiqua bohemica. Vol.58.
Sinfonie B-dur für Streicher.
In: Sondheimer. Werke aus dem 18. Jahrhundert. Nr.24.
Sonate I–XVI. Piano.
In: Musica antiqua bohemica. Vol.24.
Sonate No.5, Largo, Presto.
In: Köhler. Les maîtres du clavecin. Heft 5.
Sonate für Querflöte und obligates Cembalo.
In: Nagels Musik-Archiv. No.154.
Sonata per 2 violini e clavicembalo.
In: Musica antiqua bohemica. Vol.2.
Sonatine. I–XXXIV. Piano.
In: Musica antiqua bohemica. Vol.37.
12 Sonatinas. 1 Sonata. Piano.
In: Oberdörffer. Deutsche Klaviermusik das 17. und 18. Jahrhunderts. Vol.6.
4 Sonatas. Violino e quartetto d'archi.
In: Musica antiqua bohemica. Vol.57.
Violin and piano.
In: Musica antiqua bohemica. Vol.11.
BENDER, JAKOB, 1798–1844.
Choral music.
In: Nagels Männerchor-Blätter. No.9, 20.
BENDER, JAN, 1909– .
Organ music.
In: The parish organist. Vol.1–4, 5–6, 7–8.
BENDIX, VICTOR EMANUEL, 1851–1926.
Fjeldstigning. Symphoni. Op.16.
In: Samfundet til Udgivelse af dansk Musik. Ser.I. No.17.
Sommerklange fra Syd-Rusland.
In: Samfundet til Udgivelse af dansk Musik. Ser.II. No.3.
Symphoni Nr.3. Op.25.
In: Samfundet til Udgivelse af dansk Musik. Ser.II. No.19.
BENDUSI, FRANCESCO.
Keyboard music.
In: Apel. Musik aus früher Zeit für Klavier. Bd.1.
BENEDICAMUS DOMINO.
In: Van. Les monuments de l'ars nova. I. No.5.
BENEDICAMUS DOMINO.
3 Dreistimmige Organa aus der Zeit um 1200 für Singstimmen oder hohe Instrumente.
In: Antiqua Edition. Instrumente mit Singstimmen.
BENEDICT, JULIUS, 1804–1885.
Part music.
In: Hullah. Part music. Class A.2. Vol.2.
BENEDICTUS, *see* APPENZELLER, BENEDICTUS.
BENET, JOHN, 15th CENTURY.
Madrigal.
In: The triumphs of Oriana.
BENEVOLI, ORAZIO, 1605–1672.
Opera omnia. 13v.
Works.
In: Monumenta liturgiae polychoralis sanctae ecclesiae romanae. Ser.I– .
Choral music.
In: Recueil de musique ancienne. Recueil des morceaux de musique ancienne. Bd.11.
In: Rochlitz. Sammlung vorzüglicher Gesangstücke. Bd.2.
In: Societas Polyphonica Romanae. Repertorium. Vol.4.
Ego autem pro Te, Domine. Sopran (Tenor) und B.C.
In: Cantio sacra. No.22.
Festmesse and Hymnus.
In: Denkmäler der Tonkunst in Österreich. Vol.20. (Jg.X/1).
Sacred music.
In: Documenta liturgiae polychoralis sanctae ecclesiae romanae. No.1, 2, 3, 4, 5.
BENINCASA, ANTONIO.
Sacred music.
In: Jeppesen. Italia sacra musica. Vol.2.
BENKER, HEINZ, 1921– .
Colloquium musicale.
In: Collegium musicae novae. No.32.
Concerto colorito für Orchester.
In: Collegium musicae novae. No.49.

Praeludium pastorale.
In: Collegium musicae novae. No.29.
Rondo scherzando für Flöte und Streicher.
In: Collegium musicae novae. No.40.
Triplum humanum.
In: Collegium musicae novae. No.26.
Der Wächter aus dem Turme sass.
In: Collegium musicae novae. No.20.
BENN, JOHANNES.
Missae concertatae.
In: Schweizerische Musikdenkmäler. Vol.4.
BENNET, JOHN, 16th–17th CENTURIES.
Madrigals.
In: Fellowes. The English madrigal school. Vol.23.
In: Musical Antiquarian Society. Publications. Vol.15.
Organ music.
In: Tallis to Wesley. Vol.34.
Part music.
In: Hullah. Part music. Class A.2. Vol.1, 2; Class B.2.
Thyrsis, sleepest thou?
In: Parrish. Masterpieces of music before 1750. No.28.
Vocal music.
In: Hullah. Vocal scores. II. Secular.
BENNETT, WILLIAM STERNDALE, 1816–1875.
Part music.
In: Hullah. Part music. 1868 ed.
Vocal music.
In: Hullah. Vocal scores. II. Secular.
BENOIST, FRANÇOIS, 1794–1878.
Organ music.
In: Raugel. Les maîtres français de l'orgue. Vol.2.
BENOIT.
Selections.
In: Reaney. Early fifteenth-century music. Vol.3.
BENSON, L. S.
Long time ago. S.A.T.B.
In: Arion. Vol.2.
BENTZON, JØRGEN, 1897–1951.
Kammerkoncert. No.3. Op.39.
In: Samfundet til Udgivelse af dansk Musik. Ser.III. No.77.
Mikrofoni. Nr.1. Op.44.
In: Samfundet til Udgivelse af dansk Musik. Ser.III. No.100.
Songs.
In: Samfundet til Udgivelse af dansk Musik. Suppl. 1925–26.
Symfonisk Trio. Op.18.
In: Samfundet til Udgivelse af dansk Musik. Ser.III. No.30.
BENTZON, NILES VIGGO, 1919– .
Sonate for violoncel og klaver. Op.43.
In: Samfundet til Udgivelse af dansk Musik. Ser.III. No.93.
BENVENUTI, GIACOMO, 1885–1943. ed.
Andrea e Giovanni Gabrieli e la musica strumentale in San Marco. Vol.1–2.
In: Istituzioni e monumenti dell'arte musicale italiana. Vol.1–2.
BERANECK.
Offertorium.
In: Ecclesiasticon. No.78.
BERCHEM, JACHET DE, d.1580.
(var. sp.: Jacob van Berchem; Jacques Berchem).
Selections.
In: Maldéghem. Trésor musical.
Chansons.
In: Publikationen älterer praktischer und theoretischer Musikwerke. Jahrg.27.
O Jesu Christe.
In: Music Press, Inc. [Choral series]. No.74.
BERG.
Part music.
In: Hullah. Part music. Class A.1. Vol.2; Class B.2.
BERG, CARL NATANAEL, 1879–1957.
Höga Visan.
In: Musikaliska konstföreningen. 1926.
BERG, GUNNAR.
For clarinet og violin.
In: Samfundet til Udgivelse af dansk Musik. Ser.III. No.155.
BERGAMO, PIETRO LOCATELLI DA, *see* LOCATELLI DA BERGAMO, PIETRO.
BERGER, ARTHUR VICTOR, 1912– .
3 Poems of Yeats, from "Words for music, perhaps." For flute, clarinet, voice, and violoncello.
In: New music. Vol.24. No.1. Oct.1950.
BERGER, GREGOR.
Aus sommerlichen Tagen.
In: Zeitschrift für Spielmusik. No.140.
Sonate in G für Alt-Blockflöte und Tasteninstrument.
In: Moecks gelbe Musikhefte. Vol.41.
BERGER, OLOF WILHELM PETERSON–, *see* PETERSON-BERGER, OLOF WILHELM.
BERGH, ARTHUR, 1882– .
Song.
In: The Wa-Wan series of American compositions.
BERGSMA, WILLIAM, 1921– .
First string quartet.
In: Society for the Publication of American Music. Publications. 26th season. 1944–45.
Quartet, No.3, for strings.
In: Society for the Publication of American Music. Publications. 40th season. 1959–60.
BERHANDIZKI, ROCHUS.
Lute music.
In: Denkmäler der Tonkunst in Österreich. Vol.50. (Jg.XXV/2).
BERLIN, JOHAN DANIEL, ca.1711–1787.
Sonatina for Klaver.
In: Oslo. Universitet. Bibliotek. Norsk musikksamling. Nr.1.
BERLIOZ, HECTOR, 1803–1869.
Werke. 20v.
Ausgewählte Lieder.
In: Musikalische Stundenbücher.
BERMEISER, VIKTOR.
Kleine Stücke, 1–3. Für Violine mit Klavier.
In: Hausmusik. No.101.
BERMUDO, G.
Keyboard music.

In: Tagliapietra. Antologia di musica antica e moderna per pianoforte. Bd.1.
BERMUDO, JUAN, 16th CENTURY.
Oeuvres d'orgue.
In: Orgue et liturgie. Vol.47.
Organ music.
In: Elkan-Vogel organ series. Vol.5.
Songs.
In: Bal y Gay. Romances y villancicos españoles del signo XVI.
BERNABEI.
Choral music.
In: Rochlitz. Sammlung vorzüglicher Gesangstücke. Bd.2.
BERNABEI, ERCOLE, ca.1620–1687.
Heu me miseram et infelicem. Sopran (Tenor) und B.C.
In: Cantio sacra. No.44.
In hymnis et canticis. Sopran (Tenor) und B.C.
In: Cantio sacra. No.52.
BERNABEI, GIUSEPPE ANTONIO, 1649–1732.
Sacred music.
In: Proske. Musica divina. Annus primus. Tom 2, 3, 4; Annus secundus. Tom 3.
In: Proske. Selectus novus missarum. Annus secundus. Tom 3.
BERNAL, ANTONIO, 16th CENTURY.
Sacred music.
In: Eslava y Elizondo. Lira sacro-hispana. 16th century. i.1.
BERNAL, JOSEPH.
Sacred music.
In: Rubio. Antologia polifonica sacra. Vol.1.
BERNARDI, STEFFANO, d.ca.1637.
(var. sp.: Stefano Bernardi; Bernard).
Church music.
In: Denkmäler der Tonkunst in Österreich. Vol.69. (Jg.XXXVI/1).
Hoheliedmotette.
In: Cantio sacra. No.23.
Sacred music.
In: Messner. Alte salzburger Meister des kirchlichen Tonkunst. Heft 1, 10, 13.
Vocal music.
In: Delsarte. Archives du chant. Livr.11. No.1.
BERNART DE VENTADORN, d.1195.
Selections.
In: Gleason. Examples of music before 1400.
Be m'an perdut.
In: Parrish. A treasury of early music. No.6.
BERNER.
Part music.
In: Hullah. Part music. Class C. Sacred.
BERNHARD, CHRISTOPH, 1627–1692.
Kurzmessen.
In: Das Chorwerk. No.16.
Selected vocal works.
In: Denkmäler deutscher Tonkunst. [1.Folge]. Vol.6.
BERNIER, NICOLAS, 1664–1734.
Selections.
In: Expert. Répertoire classique de musique. 1re année.
Nicolas Bernier. (Philip Nelson).
In: Institute of Mediaeval Music. Musical theorists in translation. Vol.5.
BERTANI, L.
Ch'ami la vita mia.
In: Arion. Vol.1.
BERTI, GIOVANNI PIETRO, d.1638.
Songs.
In: Jeppesen. La flora. Vol.2.
BERTONI, FERDINANDO GIUSEPPE, 1725–1813.
Composizioni.
In: I classici della musica italiana. Vol.16.
Keyboard music.
In: Benvenuti. Cembalisti italiani del settecento.
In: Tagliapietra. Antologia di musica antica e moderna per pianoforte. Bd.13.
Composizioni per pianoforte e quattro mani.
In: I classici della musica italiana. Raccolta nazionale della musiche italiane. Quad. 205.
Quartetto No.3, riduzione per pianoforte a 4 mani.
In: I classici della musica italiana. Raccolta nazionale della musiche italiana. Quad. 155–156.
BERTRAM, HANS GEORG, 1936– .
Tanzende Intervalle.
In: Collegium musicae novae. No.53.
BERTRAND, ANTHOINE DE, ca.1540–ca.1581.
Premier et second livre des amours de Pierre de Ronsard.
In: Expert. Monuments de la musique française au temps de la Renaissance. Vol.4–5, 6.
Troisième livre de chansons.
In: Expert. Monuments de la musique française au temps de la Renaissance. Vol.7.
BERWALD, FRANZ, 1796–1868.
Älvlek. Tone picture.
In: Musikaliska konstföreningen. 1921.
Duo for violin and piano, D major.
In: Musikaliska konstföreningen. 1898.
Estrella de Soria.
In: Musikaliska konstföreningen. 1883.
Grand septet.
In: Musikaliska konstföreningen. 1893.
Symphony, G minor (sérieuse). Score.
In: Musikaliska konstföreningen. 1874.
Symphony, G minor (sérieuse). Arr. for piano, 4 hands.
In: Musikaliska konstföreningen. 1874.
Symphonie singulière.
In: Musikaliska konstföreningen. 1905.
BERXES.
Selections.
In: Pedrell. Teatro lirico español anterior al siglo XIX. Bd.4/5.
BESARD, JEAN BAPTISTE, b.ca.1567.
(var. sp.: G. B. Besardo; Joh. Bapt. Besardus; Johann Baptiste Besardus).
Airs de court (secolo XVI) dal Thesaurus harmonicus.
In: Chilesotti. Biblioteca di rarità musicali. Vol.7.
Keyboard music.
In: Apel. Musik aus früher Zeit für Klavier. Bd.2.
Lute music.

In: Chilesotti. Lautenspieler des XVI. Jahrhunderts.
Madrigali, villanelle ed arie di danza del cinquecento.
In: Chilesotti. Biblioteca di rarità musicali. Vol.9.
BEUERLE, H.
Choral music.
In: Nagels Männerchor-Blätter. No.4, 12, 23.
BEVIN, ELWAY, 16th–17th CENTURIES.
Part music.
In: Hullah. Part music. Class A.1. Vol.2.
Sacred music.
In: Boyce. Cathedral music. Vol.1; 1849, Vol.1.
BEYER, JOHANN SAMUEL, 1669–1744.
Weihnachtskantate, für Sopran- oder Tenorsolo.
In: Nagels Musik-Archiv. No.54.
BEYER, JOHANNA M.
IV.
In: New music. Orchestra series. No.18.
BEZANSON, PHILIP.
String quartet, No.1.
In: Society for the Publication of American Music. 45th season. 1965.
BEZE, THÉODORE DE.
Vocal music.
In: Delsarte. Archives du chant. Livr.4. No.2.
BIALAS, GÜNTER, 1907– .
Die alte Weise im neuen Satz.
In: Bausteine für Musikerziehung und Musikpflege. B 103.
Rhythmische Miniaturen.
In: Zeitschrift für Spielmusik. No.186.
Veni Creator Spiritus.
In: Christophorus-Chorwerk. Heft 15.
BIANCO, PIETRO ANTONIO, ca.1540–1611.
Selections.
In: Denkmäler der Tonkunst in Österreich. Vol.90.
BIANCOSI, GERARDO.
Songs.
In: Jeppesen. La flora. Vol.2.
BIBER, CARL HEINRICH, 1681–1749.
Church music.
In: Denkmäler der Tonkunst in Österreich. Vol.80. (Jg.XLIII/1).
BIBER, HEINRICH IGNAZ FRANZ VON, 1644–1704.
Harmonia artificiosa-ariosa.
In: Denkmäler der Tonkunst in Österreich. Vol.92.
Lute music.
In: Denkmäler der Tonkunst in Österreich. Vol.50. (Jg.XXV/2).
Mensa sonora; Fidicinium sacro-profanum.
In: Denkmäler der Tonkunst in Österreich. Vol.96, 97.
Missa Sti Henrici.
In: Denkmäler der Tonkunst in Österreich. Vol.49. (Jg.XXV/1).
Requiem.
In: Denkmäler der Tonkunst in Österreich. Vol.59. (Jg.XXX/1).
Oelberg-Sonate.
In: Messner. Alte salzburger Meister der kirchlichen Tonkunst. Heft 8.
Serenade für fünf Streichinstrumente. (Nachtwächter-Bass) und Cembalo.
In: Nagels Musik-Archiv. No.112.
Sonatae tam aris quam aulis servientes.
In: Denkmäler der Tonkunst in Österreich. Vol.106/107.
Violin sonatas.
In: Denkmäler der Tonkunst in Österreich. Vol.11. (Jg.V/2); Vol.25. (Jg.XII/2).
BIBLIOTHÈQUE DE L'ARSENAL À PARIS.
Catalogue des livres de musique.
In: Société Française de Musicologie, Paris. Publications. Sér.II. Bd.7.
Le chansonnier de l'Arsenal.
In: Paris. Bibliothèque de l'Arsenal. Mss. (No.5198). Le chansonnier de l'Arsenal.
BIBLIOTHÈQUE DU CONSERVATOIRE DE MUSIQUE DE PARIS.
Inventaire du Fonds Blancheton.
In: Société Française de Musicologie, Paris. Publications. Sér.II. Bd.1–2.
BICHAEL, M. ALFRED, 1909– .
Organ music.
In: The parish organist. Vol.1–4.
BICINIA OF THE RENAISSANCE.
Für zwei gleiche Instrumente.
In: Hortus musicus. No.27.
Für zwei ungleiche Instrumente.
In: Hortus musicus. No.28.
BICKHAM, GEORGE.
The musical entertainer. (1740). Facsimile.
In: Monuments of music and music literature. First series. No.6.
BIEBL, FRANZ, 1906– .
Neue bayerische Tänze.
In: Zeitschrift für Spielmusik. No.26.
Was wir gerne tun.
In: Bausteine für Musikerziehung und Musikpflege. B 134.
BIECHTELER, M. S.
Church music.
In: Denkmäler der Tonkunst in Österreich. Vol.80. (Jg.XLIII/1).
BIGAGLIA, DIOGENIO, 18th CENTURY.
Sonate en si ♭ majeur.
In: L'école du violon au XVIIe et XVIIIe siècle. No.1265.
BILHON, JEAN DE, 15th–16th CENTURIES.
(var. sp.: Jo. de Billon).
Motets.
In: Attaingnant. Treize livres de motets. Livre 6.
BILLART, ALBERT (?), 14th–15th CENTURIES.
Sacred music.
In: Plainsong and Mediaeval Music Society. Publications. (Borren).
BILLINGS, WILLIAM, 1746–1800.
The continental harmony. 201p.
Selections.
In: Fisher. The music that Washington knew.
In: Goldman. Landmarks of early American music, 1760–1800.
Choral music.
In: Music Press, Inc. [Choral series]. No.62, 63, 64, 88, 89, 101, 102, 123, 124.
Songs.

In: Siegmeister. Songs of early America, 1620–1830.
BILLON, JEAN DE, *see* BILHON, JEAN DE.
BINCHOIS, EGIDIUS, ca.1400–1460.
(var. sp.: Gillis Binchois; Gilles de Binche).
Selections.
In: Marix. Les musiciens de la cour de Bourgogne au XVe siècle (1420–1467).
Adieu m'amour.
In: Parrish. Masterpieces of music before 1750. No.16.
Die Chansons von Gillis Binchois.
In: Musikalische Denkmäler Bd.2.
Choral music.
In: Droz. Poètes et musiciens du XVe siècles.
In: Engel. Three centuries of choral music. Vol.1.
Sechzehn weltliche Lieder.
In: Das Chorwerk. No.22.
Missa de angelis.
In: Documenta polyphoniae liturgiae sanctae ecclesiae romanae. Ser.1. No.5.
Organ music.
In: Cantantibus organis. Vol.4.
Sacred music.
In: Plainsong and Mediaeval Music Society. Publications. (Borren).
Solus ortus cardine.
In: Dessoff choir series. No.38.
Songs.
In: Riemann. Hausmusik aus alter Zeit.
BINDER, CHRISTLIEB SIEGMUND, 1723–1789.
Instrumental music.
In: Schmid. Musik am sächsischen Hofe. Bd.6.
Keyboard music.
In: Schmid. Musik am sächsischen Hofe. Bd.4.
Sonate G-dur für Violine und Klavier (Cembalo).
In: Hortus musicus. No.62.
BINGHAM, SETH, 1882– .
Pastorale. (Op.16). Organ.
In: Contemporary organ series. No.11.
BIORDI.
Sacred music.
In: Proske. Musica divina. Annus primus. Tom 2, 3, 4.
BIRCKENSTOCK, JOHANN ADAM, 1687–1733.
Sonata B dur, Op.1, Nr.2, für Violine und Basso Continuo.
In: Nagels Musik-Archiv. No.25.
Sonate (Em). Violoncello and piano.
In: Moffat. Meister-Schule der alter Zeit. Violoncello-Sonaten. No.3.
Violin and piano.
In: Schering. Alte Meister des Violinspiels.
BIRD, WILLIAM, *see* BYRD, WILLIAM.
BISCHOFF, HEINZ.
Salzburger Sonatine in F.
In: Zeitschrift für Spielmusik. No.91.
BISHOP, JOHN, ca.1665–1737.
Vocal music.
In: Hullah. Vocal scores. I. Sacred.
BJERCKE, OLE.
Romeriks-svite. Fem danser.
In: Oslo. Universitet. Bibliotek. Norsk musikksamling. Nr.2.
BJERRE, JENS, 1903– .
Mosaïque musicale. Trio.
In: Samfundet til Udgivelse af dansk Musik. Ser.III. No.119.
Sonate for violoncel.
In: Samfundet til Udgivelse af dansk Musik. Ser.III. No.141.
BLACKWOOD, EASLEY.
String quartet, No.1. [Op.4].
In: Society for the Publication of American Music. Publications. 39th season. 1958.
BLAKE, BENJAMIN, 1761–1827.
Sacred music.
In: Page. Harmonia sacra. Vol.2.
BLANC, DIDIER LE, *see* LE BLANC, DIDIER.
BLANGINI, GIUSEPPE MARCO MARIA FELICE, 1781–1841.
Arias.
In: Parisotti. Arie antiche. Bd.3.
BLASON, THIBAUT DE, *see* THIBAUT DE BLASON.
BLAVET, MICHEL, 1700–1768.
Les caquets.
In: L'école du violon au XVIIe et XVIIIe siècle. No.1343.
Ciciliana.
In: L'école du violon au XVIIe et XVIIIe siècle. No.1344.
L'invincible.
In: L'école du violon au XVIIe et XVIIIe siècle. No.1340.
Le Marc-Antoine.
In: L'école du violon au XVIIe et XVIIIe siècle. No.1347.
Pièces pour flûte.
In: Musiques françaises. Vol.5.
Les regrets.
In: L'école du violon au XVIIe et XVIIIe siècle. No.1339.
Sarabande.
In: L'école du violon au XVIIe et XVIIIe siècle. No.1336.
Tendres badinages.
In: L'école du violon au XVIIe et XVIIIe siècle. No.1341.
BLEYER, NIKOLAUS, 1590–1658.
Variationen über "Est ce Mars."
In: Organum. 3.Reihe. Nr.27.
BLITHEMAN, WILLIAM, d.1591.
Keyboard music.
In: The Fitzwilliam virginal book.
In: Schott's Anthology of early keyboard music. Vol.2.
BLOCH, WALDEMAR, 1906– .
Ricercar über den Namen Bach. Organ.
In: Orgelmusik steirischer Komponisten.
Sonate für Violine und Gitarre.
In: Gitarre-Kammermusik. No.16.
Sonatine in E.
In: Marckhl. Klavierwerke steiermärkischer Komponisten. Vol.1.
BLONDEL DE NESLE, 12th CENTURY.
Selections.
In: Gleason. Examples of music before 1400.
BLOTZHEIM, A. GLUTZ-, *see* GLUTZ-BLOTZHEIM, A.

BLOW, JOHN, 1649–1708.
Complete organ works. 66p.
Selections.
In: Crotch. Specimens of various styles of music. Vol.2.
In: Smith. Musica antiqua.
Amphion anglicus. (1700). Facsimile.
In: Monuments of music and music literature. First series. No.2.
Church music.
In: Motett Society. [Collection of ancient church music]. Division 2.
Coronation anthems.
In: Musica Britannica. Vol.7.
Jubilate Deo.
In: Parrish. A treasury of early music. No.43.
Keyboard music.
In: English keyboard music. [No.10].
In: Fuller-Maitland. The contemporaries of Purcell. Vol.1–2.
In: Herrmann. Contemporaries of Purcell.
In: Oesterle. Early keyboard music. Vol.1.
In: Pauer. Old English composers for the virginals and harpsichord.
Organ music.
In: Liber organi. Bd.10.
In: Tallis to Wesley. Vol.21.
Part music.
In: Hullah. Part music. Class A.1. Vol.2.
Parthenia. Facsimile.
In: Monuments of music and music literature. First series. No.11.
Sacred music.
In: Boyce. Cathedral music. Vol.1, 2, 3; 1849 ed., Vol.2, 3 and Appendix, Vol.3.
In: Page. Harmonia sacra. Vol.2.
Songs.
In: Arkwright. The Old English edition. Vol.23.
In: Potter. Reliquary of English song. Vol.1.
Venus and Adonis.
In: Arkwright. The Old English edition. Vol.25.
BLUMENTHAL, JACOB, 1829–1908.
White-heart cherries.
In: Arion. Vol.2.
BLUNCK, ADOLF.
Kleine Hausmusik.
In: Zeitschrift für Spielmusik. No.72.
BOATWRIGHT, HOWARD.
Quartet for clarinet and strings.
In: Society for the Publication of American Music. Publications. 42nd season. 1961–62.
BOCCHERINI, LUIGI, 1743–1805.
Selections.
In: Crotch. Specimens of various styles of music. Vol.3.
Konzert für Flöte und kleines Streichorchester.
In: Nagels Musik-Archiv. No.172.
Concerto for violoncello and string orchestra.
In: Smith College music archives. No.3.
3 Stucke für Klavier.
In: Sondheimer. Werke aus dem 18. Jahrhundert. Nr.9.
Largo aus Op.12, Nr.1, für Streichquintett.
In: Sondheimer. Werke aus dem 18. Jahrhundert. Nr.4.
Menuett für Violine und Klavier.
In: Sondheimer. Werke aus dem 18. Jahrhundert. Nr.11.
Pastorale, Menuett und Trio aus der Sinfonia. (Cm).
In: Thouret. Musik am preussischen Hofe. No.4.
Quintettino "The military nightwatch in Madrid" für 2 Violinen, Viola, und 2 Violoncelli.
In: Musikschätze der Vergangenheit.
Vier quintettini, Op.30. Sechs quartettini, Op.33.
In: Classici italiani della musica. Vol.1.
Op.60/1. Quintetto in C-dur.
In: Diletto musicale. No.99.
Quintetto. Op.60/2, Op.60/3, Op.60/5, Op.60/6.
In: Diletto musicale. No.101, 102, 103, 104.
Quintetto. Op.62/1, Op.62/2, Op.62/3, Op.62/4, Op.62/6.
In: Diletto musicale. No.114, 115, 116, 147, 149.
Streichquintett Es-dur, Op.12, Nr.2.
In: Sondheimer. Werke aus dem 18. Jahrhundert. Nr.3.
Sacred music.
In: Latrobe, C. I. Selection of sacred music.
In: Latrobe, J. A. The music of the church.
Sinfonie C-dur, Op.16, Nr.3; Sinfonie D-moll; Sinfonie D-dur; Sinfonie A-dur; Sinfonia funèbre B-dur.
In: Sondheimer. Werke aus dem 18. Jahrhundert. Nr.1, 32, 36, 44/45.
Sonate.
In: I classici della musica italiana. Vol.3.
Sonate (Cm); Sonate (Es).
In: Moffat. Trio-Sonaten alter Meister. No.13, 28.
Sonate (G). Violoncello and piano.
In: Moffat. Meister-Schule der alter Zeit. Violoncello Sonaten. No.1.
Sonate Op.5 per cembalo con violino obbligato.
In: I classici musicali italiani. Vol.4.
Sonate per violoncello e piano.
In: I classici della musica italiana. Raccolta nazionale delle musiche italiane. Quad. 164–165.
Symphonies. Op.37, Op.21/3.
In: Classici italiani della musica. Vol.4.
5 Leichte Tänzweisen für 2 Violinen, Viola, Violoncello I und Violoncello II ad lib.
In: Antiqua Edition. Von 4 Instrumenten an.
Trio. Op.54. Nr.2.
In: Nagels Musik-Archiv. No.55.
6 Trios für 2 Violinen und Violoncello, Op.35.
In: Antiqua Edition. Von 3 Instrumenten an.
Trio, Op.54, Nr.3, für zwei Violinen und Violoncello.
In: Nagels Musik-Archiv. No.152.
BÖDDECKER, PHILIPP FRIEDRICH, 1615–1683.
Sonata sopra "La monica."
In: Organum. 3.Reihe. Nr.33.
Weihnachtskonzert.
In: Nagels Musik-Archiv. No.57.
BODENSCHATZ, L. H.
Organ music.
In: Caecilia; Sammlung von Choralvorspielen.

BODINUS, SEBASTIAN, 18th CENTURY.
Sonate E für 2 Querflöten oder Violinen.
In: Moecks Kammermusik. Vol.43.
Trio Sonate für 2 Oboen oder Violinen und B.C.
In: Musikschätze der Vergangenheit.
BODKY, ERWIN, 1896– . ed.
Das Charakterstück.
In: Musikalische Formen in historischen Reihen. Bd.12.
BOEDDECKER, PHILIPP FRIEDRICH, *see* BÖDDECKER, PHILIPP FRIEDRICH.
BOEHM, GEORG, *see* BÖHM, GEORG.
BOËLLMANN, LÉON, 1862–1897.
Organ music.
In: Bedell. The French organist. Vol.1, 2.
BOELSCHE, JAKOB, *see* BÖLSCHE, JAKOB.
BOËLY, ALEXANDRE PIERRE FRANCOIS, 1785–1858.
Organ music.
In: Bonnet. Historical organ-recitals. Vol.3.
In: Guilmant. Concert historique d'orgue.
In: Raugel. Les maîtres français de l'orgue. Vol.2.
BOERENLIEDJES AND CONTRADANSES, OLD DUTCH. VIOLIN WITH PIANO ACCOMPANIMENT.
In: Vereniging voor Nederlandsche Muziekgeschiedenis. Uitgave. No.20, 23, 33, 36.
BOESI, JOSÉ ANTONIO CARO DE, *see* CARO DE BOESI, JOSÉ ANTONIO.
BOËSSET, ANTOINE, SIEUR DE VILLEDIEU, ca.1585–1643.
Airs.
In: Prunières. Les maîtres du chant. Recueil 4.
Songs.
In: Expert. Chants de France et d'Italie. Ser.2.
BOHEMIA–MUSIC.
In: Documenta historica musicae.
In: Musica antiqua bohemica.
In: Musica viva historica.
In: Orgelwerke. Altböhmischer Meister.
BÖHM, GEORG, 1661–1733.
(var. sp.: Boehm).
Sämtliche Werke. Klavier- und Orgelwerke. v.1– .
Sämtliche Werke. Vol.1–2.
In: Kirchenmusikalisches Institut der Evangelisch-Lutherischen Landeskirche in Sachsen am Landeskonservatorium der Musik. Veröffentlichungen. No.1, 3.
Choral music.
In: Rochlitz. Sammlung vorzüglicher Gesangstücke. Bd.1. Pt.2.
Elmenhorst's Geistliche Lieder.
In: Denkmäler deutscher Tonkunst. [1.Folge]. Vol.45.
Keyboard music.
In: Buchmayer. Aus Richard Buchmayers historischen Klavierkonzerten. Vol.4, 5.
In: Georgii. Keyboard music of the Baroque and Rococo. Vol.1.
In: Herrmann. Lehrmeister und Schüler Joh. Seb. Bachs. Vol.1.
Organ music.
In: Buszin. Organ series. Vol.1.
In: Keller. Achtzig Choralvorspiele deutscher Meister des 17. und 18. Jahrhunderts.
In: Klein. The first four centuries of music for the organ from Dunstable to Bach (1370–1749).
In: The Liturgical Music Press, Inc. Masterpieces of organ music. Folio 6, 19, 28, 56.
In: Muziek voor de eredienst. Vol.1.
In: Organum. 4.Reihe. Nr.4.
In: The parish organist. Vol.5–6.
In: Peeters. Anthologia pro organo. Vol.2, 4.
In: Straube. Alte Meister.
In: Straube. Alte Meister des Orgelspiels.
In: Straube. Choralvorspiele alter Meister.
BOIELDIEU, FRANÇOIS ADRIEN, 1775–1834.
Sonates pour piano.
In: Société Française de Musicologie, Paris. Publications. Sér.I. Bd.11–12.
BOISMORTIER, JOSEPH BODIN DE, ca.1691–1755.
Pièces pour flûte.
In: Musiques françaises. Vol.5.
Rokoko-Duette für 2 Violoncelli, Gamben, Fideln, oder Fagotte.
In: Moecks Kammermusik. Vol.39, 45.
Sonate No.5 pour basson (ou violoncelle) et clavier.
In: Musiques françaises. Vol.12.
Sonate à deux flûtes traversières sans basse. Oeuvre VI, No.6.
In: Hortus musicus. No.85.
Sonate E-moll, Op.XXXVII/2, für Querflöte (Oboe, Violine), Gambe (Fagott, Violoncello), und Basso Continuo.
In: Hortus musicus. No.160.
Sonate für drei Melodie-Instrumente. E-moll, Op.34/3; A-moll, Op.34/6.
In: Concertino.
Trio D-dur, Op.50, Nr.6, für Violine, Violoncello und Basso Continuo.
In: Nagels Musik-Archiv. No.143.
BOLOGNA, JACOPO DA, *see* JACOPO DA BOLOGNA.
BOLOGNA, MARCO ANTONIO (CAVAZZONI) DA, *see* CAVAZZONI, MARCO ANTONIO.
BOLOGNA–MUSIC.
In: Maestri bolognesi.
BÖLSCHE, JAKOB.
(var. sp.: Boelsche).
Präambulum. Organ.
In: Die Rogel. Reihe II. Nr.4.
BOLZIUS, T.
Threnodier, 1632.
In: Musikaliska konstföreningen. 1932.
BONAMICO, PEDRO.
Laudate Dominum.
In: Messner. Alte salzburger Meister der kirchlichen Tonkunst. Heft 4.
BONI, GUILLAUME, 16th CENTURY.
Chansons.
In: Lesure. Anthologie de la chanson parisienne au XVIe siècle.
BONNET, PIERRE, 16th CENTURY.
Airs et villanelles.

In: Expert. Florilège du concert vocal de la Renaissance. No.5.
Chansons.
In: Lesure. Anthologie de la chanson parisienne au XVIe siècle.
BONNO, GIUSEPPE, 1710–1788.
Sacred music.
In: The Fitzwilliam music. Bd.3.
BONONCINI, GIOVANNI BATTISTA, 1670–1747.
(var. sp.: Giovanni Battista Buononcini).
Airs.
In: Prunières. Les maîtres du chant. Recueil 5.
Arias.
In: Landshoff. Alte Meister des Bel Canto. Eine Sammlung von Arien. Vol.1–2, 3.
In: Parisotti. Arie antiche. Bd.2.
Chamber music.
In: Riemann. Old chamber music. Vol.4.
Choral music.
In: Recueil de musique ancienne. Recueil des morceaux de musique ancienne. Bd.8.
Divertimento da Camera für Alt-Blockflöte und Basso Continuo.
In: Moecks Kammermusik. Vol.9.
Sacred music.
In: The Fitzwilliam music. Bd.1, 3.
Vocal music.
In: Gevaert. Les gloires de l'Italie. Vol.1, 2.
BONONCINI, GIOVANNI MARIA, 1642–1678.
Arias.
In: Parisotti. Arie antiche. Bd.1.
Sonata a tre, per due violini e basso continuo. Op.I/6.
In: Hausmusik. No.130.
BONONIA, BARTHOLOMAEUS DE, *see* BARTHOLOMAEUS DE BONONIA.
BONPORTI, FRANCESCO.
Concerto in B flat, Op.11, No.3 (violin solo, strings, cembalo).
In: Antica musica strumentale italiana. Ser.I. Vol.6.
Concerto in B flat, Op.11, No.4 (violin solo, strings, cembalo).
In: Antica musica strumentale italiana. Ser.I. Vol.7.
Inventionen für Violine und Basso Continuo. Op.10.
In: Hortus musicus. No.44–45, 77.
Sonate (C).
In: Moffat. Trio-Sonaten alter Meister. No.21.
Sonata a tre, per due violini e basso continuo. Op.IV/2.
In: Hausmusik. No.174.
BONTEMPO, JOÃO DOMINGOS.
Sinfonia, No.1/Op.11.
In: Portugaliae musica. Ser.B. Vol.8.
BOOM, JAN VAN, 1807–1872.
Grand sonata for piano.
In: Musikaliska konstföreningen. 1861.
BORCHGREVINCK, MELCHIOR, d.1632.
(var. sp.: Melchior Borchgreving).
"Paduanen" and "Galliarden."
In: Vereniging voor Nederlandsche Muziekgeschiedenis. Uitgave. No.34.
BORNEFELD, HELMUT, 1906– .
Choral music.
In: Nagels Männerchor-Blätter. No.15.
Neue Musik.
In: Spielstücke für Blockflöten, Geigen, Lauten oder andere Instrumente. Heft 7.
BORODĪN, ALEKSANDR PORFĪREVĪCH, 1833–1887.
Vocal music.
In: Sammlung russischer Romanzen. No.207–209.
BØRRESEN, HAKON, 1876–1954.
Kaddara. Opera.
In: Samfundet til Udgivelse af dansk Musik. Ser.III. No.4.
Mod Døden. For Strygere.
In: Samfundet til Udgivelse af dansk Musik. Ser.III. No.56.
Nordiske Folketoner. For Strygeorkester.
In: Samfundet til Udgivelse af dansk Musik. Ser.III. No.116.
Raadhus-Intrada.
In: Samfundet til Udgivelse af dansk Musik. Suppl. 1930.
Strygekvartet. For 2 Violiner, Viola og Violoncel.
In: Samfundet til Udgivelse af dansk Musik. Ser.III. No.70.
Serenade for Horn, Strygeorkester og Pauker.
In: Samfundet til Udgivelse af dansk Musik. Ser.III. No.78.
Symphonie Nr.3, C dur, Op.21.
In: Samfundet til Udgivelse af dansk Musik. Ser.III. No.37.
BORRI, B.
Sacred music.
In: Latrobe, C. I. Selection of sacred music.
In: Latrobe, J. A. The music of the church.
BORRIS, SIEFFRIED, 1906– .
Choral music.
In: Nagels Männerchor-Blätter. No.24.
BORRONO DA MILANO, P. PAUOLO.
La intabolatura de lauto.
In: Lefkoff. Five sixteenth century Venetian lute books.
BORUP-JØRGENSEN, AXEL.
Musik for slagtoj og viola. Op.18.
In: Samfundet til Udgivelse af dansk Musik. Ser.III. No.150.
To Sange. Op.49.
In: Samfundet til Udgivelse af dansk Musik. Ser.III. No.164.
BOSCOOP, CORNELIS, ca.1520–1573.
(var. sp.: Cornelius Boskoop).
50 Psalms. (1568).
In: Vereniging voor Nederlandsche Muziekgeschiedenis. Uitgave. No.22.
BOSKOOP, CORNELIUS, *see* BOSCOOP, CORNELIS.
BOSMANS, ARTURO, 1908– .
Sonata en colores. (Piano).
In: Instituto Interamericano de Musicologia. Publicaciónes. No.41.
BOSQUET, 15th CENTURY.
Selections.
In: Reaney. Early fifteenth-century music. Vol.2.
BOSSI, MARCO ENRICO, 1861–1925.
Ausgewählte Kompositionen für die Orgel. 2v.

Organ music.
In: Bonnet. Historical organ-recitals. Vol.5.
BOSSI-BEDELL.
Organ music.
In: Standard series of organ compositions. No.53.
BOSSINENSIS, FRANCISCUS.
Le frottole per canto e liuto intabulate.
In: Istituzioni e monumenti dell' arte musicale italiana. Nuova serie. Vol.3.
Keyboard music.
In: Apel. Musik aus früher Zeit für Klavier. Bd.1.
BOSSLER, KURT.
Heut singt die liebe Christenheit. Choralpartita für Orgel.
In: Die Orgel. Reihe I. Nr.6.
Sonatine für Alt-Blockflöte und Violine.
In: Zeitschrift für Spielmusik. No.155.
BOTTEGARI LUTEBOOK.
In: The Wellesley edition. No.8.
BOTTRIGARI, ERCOLE, 1531–1612.
Il desiderio.
In: Hirsch. Veröffentlichungen. [Bd.] 5.
BOULNOIS, M.
3 Pièces sur des thèmes de la Fête du Saint-Sacrement. Organ.
In: Orgue et liturgie. Vol.18.
BOUMAN, PAUL, 1918– .
Organ music.
In: The parish organist. Vol.1–4.
BOURGEOIS, LOYS, ca.1510–ca.1561.
24 Psaumes a 4 voix.
In: Schweizerische Musikdenkmäler. Vol.3.
BOURGOGNE, BIBLIOTHÈQUE DE.
Le manuscrit dit Des basses danses.
In: Basses danses. Le manuscrit.
BOURGUIGNON.
Chansons.
In: Publikationen älterer praktischer und theoretischer Musikwerke. Jahrg.27.
Motets.
In: Attaingnant. Treize livres de motets. Livre 12.
BOUTEILLER.
Chanson.
In: Brown. Theatrical chansons of the 15th and early 16th centuries.
BOUTEILLIER.
Motets.
In: Attaingnant. Treize livres de motets. Livre 1, 2.
BOUTMY, JOSSE, 1697–1779.
Werken voor klavecimbel.
In: Monumenta musicae belgicae. Vol.5.
BOUVARD, FRANÇOIS, ca.1670–d.after 1756.
Sonate en fa majeur.
In: L'école du violon au XVIIe et XVIIIe siècle. No.1271.
BOWLES, PAUL FREDERIC, 1910– .
Cafe sin nombre. Piano.
In: New music. Vol.8. No.3. Apr.1935.
Danger de mort, Letter to Freddy, Scènes d'Anabase.
In: New music. Vol.8. No.3. Apr.1935.
Piano music.
In: Boletín latino-americano de música. Vol.5.
BOYCE, WILLIAM, 1710–1779.
Selections.
In: Fisher. The music that Washington knew.
Organ music.
In: Butcher. English organ music of the eighteenth century. Vol.1.
In: Liber organi. Bd.10.
In: Tallis to Wesley. Vol.1, 26.
Overtures.
In: Musica Britannica. Vol.13.
Part music.
In: Hullah. Part music. Class A.1. Vol.1; Class A.2. Vol.2; Class B.1; Class C.
Sacred music.
In: Arnold. Cathedral music. Vol.3.
In: Page. Harmonia sacra. Vol.1, 3.
Sonate (Cm).
In: Moffat. Trio-Sonaten alter Meister. No.24.
Songs.
In: Potter. Reliquary of English song. Vol.2.
Acht Symphonien.
In: Diletto musicale. No.150–157.
BOYVIN, JACQUES, b.ca.1706.
Chansons.
In: Lesure. Anthologie de la chanson parisienne au XVIe siècle.
Oeuvres complètes d'orgue.
In: Guilmant. Archives des maîtres de l'orgue. Vol.6.
Organ music.
In: Keller. Orgelvorspiele.
In: Raugel. Les maîtres français de l'orgue. Vol.1, 2.
In: Raugel. Les maîtres français de l'orgue aux XVIIème et XVIIIème siècles.
BRACK, JÖRG, 16th CENTURY.
Songs.
In: Aich. Das Liederbuch.
BRADLEY, WILL.
The deep quarry.
In: New music. Vol.21. No.4. July 1948.
Honeysuckle and clover. For brass choir.
In: New music. Vol.21. No.4. July 1948.
BRAGA, FRANCISCO, 1868–1945.
Música de cámara.
In: Boletín latino-americano de música. Vol.6.
BRAHMS, JOHANNES, 1833–1897.
Sämtliche Werke. 26v.
—— Another issue. 26v.
—— Neuauflage.
Complete organ works. 2v.
The organ works. 2v.
Klavierwerke. 2v.
Piano works. 3v.
Choral music.
In: Nagels Männerchor-Blätter. No.18.
Keyboard music. Op.76, 79, 116, 117, 118, 119.
In: Lea pocket scores. No.66.
Keyboard music.
In: Tagliapietra. Antologia di musica antica e moderna per pianoforte. Bd.17.
Drei Lieder.
In: Musikalische Seltenheiten. Bd.3.
Organ music.
In: Bonnet. Historical organ-recitals. Vol.5.

In: The parish organist. Vol.1–4, 5–6, 7–8.
In: Standard series of organ compositions. No.6.
12 Préludes de chorals. Organ.
In: Orgue et liturgie. Vol.21.
Sonatas. Piano. Complete.
In: Lea pocket scores. No.57.
The violin-piano sonatas. Complete.
In: Lea pocket scores. No.6.
The 2 Cello-piano sonatas; The 2 Clarinet-piano sonatas.
In: Lea pocket scores. No.7.
Piano variations; Op.9 (Schumann); Op.21; Op.24 (Händel); Op.35 (Paganini); Op.56b (Haydn).
In: Lea pocket scores. No.19.
BRANCHE.
Sonate en sol mineur.
In: L'école du violon au XVIIe et XVIIIe siècle. No.1254.
BRANDÃO, JOSÉ VIEIRA.
Música de cámara.
In: Boletín latino-americano de música. Vol.6.
BRANDT, JOBST VOM, 1517–1570.
(var. sp.: Jobst vom Brant).
Choral music.
In: Antiqua Chorbuch. Vol.1. Heft 2; Vol.2. Heft 1.
BRANDTS, JODOCUS VON.
Gesänge.
In: Wolf. Chor- und Hausmusik aus älter Zeit. Vol.1.
BRANSCOMBE, GENA, 1881– .
Songs.
In: The Wa-Wan series of American compositions.
BRANT, HENRY DREYFUSS, 1913– .
Ice age, for clarinet, glockenspiel and piano.
In: New music. Vol.27. No.4. July 1954.
Música de cámara.
In: Boletín latino-americano de música. Vol.5.
"Variations" for 4 instruments. "Two sarabandes" for keyboard instrument.
In: New music. Vol.4. No.4. July 1931.
BRANT, JOBST VOM, *see* BRANDT, JOBST VOM.
BRASART, JOHANNES, *see* BRASSART, JOHANNES.
BRASCH.
Vocal music.
In: Sammlung russischer Romanzen. No.210, 211.
BRASSART, JOHANNES, 15th CENTURY.
(var. sp.: Johannes Brasart).
Opera omnia. 2v.
Sechs Motetten.
In: Musik alter Meister. Heft 13.
O flos flagrans.
In: Dessoff choir series. No.28.
Sacred music.
In: Plainsong and Mediaeval Music Society. Publications. (Borren).
BRASSETTI.
Part music.
In: Hullah. Part music. Class A.1. Vol.2.
Sacred music.
In: Latrobe, C. I. Selection of sacred music.
In: Latrobe, J. A. The music of the church.
BRASSICANUS, JOHANNES.
Sechs Choralbearbeitungen und das Quodlibet "Was wölln wir aber heben am?"
In: Musik alter Meister. Heft 2.
BRÄTEL, ULRICH, d.1544 (or 5).
(var. sp.: Ulrich Brätels).
Gesänge.
In: Wolf. Chor- und Hausmusik aus älter Zeit. Vol.1.
BRATT, L.
Six intimate songs for voice and piano.
In: Musikaliska konstföreningen. 1923.
BRÄUTIGAM, HELMUT, 1914–1942.
Festliche Musik für Bläser und Streicher.
In: Collegium musicae novae. No.47.
Fröhliche Musik für Flöte, Oboe und 3 Violinen.
In: Collegium musicae novae. No.1.
Kleine Musik für Streicher.
In: Collegium musicae novae. No.14.
Musik für Flöte und Streichorchester, Op.55b.
In: Collegium musicae novae. No.15.
Tänzerische Spielmusik.
In: Bausteine für Musikerziehung und Musikpflege. B 111.
BRAVO, J. DE.
Sacred music.
In: Eslava y Elizondo. Lira sacro-hispana. 18th century. i.1.
BRAZIL–MUSIC.
In: Lange. Archivo de música religiosa.
In: New music. Vol.16. No.1. Oct.1942.
BREITENGRASER, WILHELM, ca.1495–1542.
(var. sp.: Wilhelm Breytengraser).
Lieder.
In: Publikationen älterer praktischer und theoretischer Musikwerke. Jahrg.1–3.
BRENE, ERLING, 1896–
Sonatine for Klaver.
In: Samfundet til Udgivelse af dansk Musik. Ser.III. No.84.
To Gange tre smaa Klaverstykker.
In: Samfundet til Udgivelse af dansk Musik. Ser.III. No.53.
BRESCIANELLO, GIUSEPPE ANTONIO, ca.1690–1757.
Concerti a tre, für zwei Violinen und Bass.
In: Hortus musicus. No.66–68.
BRESGEN, CESAR, 1913– .
Die Bettlerhochzeit.
In: Bausteine für Musikerziehung und Musikpflege. B 104.
Das improvisierte Chorlied.
In: Bausteine für Musikerziehung und Musikpflege. B 138.
Morgenmusik.
In: Bausteine für Musikerziehung und Musikpflege. B 144.
Der Morgenstern ist aufgegangen.
In: Zeitschrift für Spielmusik. No.185.
Das Riesenpiel.
In: Bausteine für Musikerziehung und Musikpflege. B 119.
Das Schlaraffenland.

In: Bausteine für Musikerziehung und Musikpflege. B 130.
Sonne, Sonne, scheine.
In: Bausteine für Musikerziehung und Musikpflege. B 115.
Tagesmusik für den Morgen, den Mittag und den Abend.
In: Zeitschrift für Spielmusik. No.93.
Uns ist kommen ein liebe Zeit.
In: Bausteine für Musikerziehung und Musikpflege. B 127.
Weihnachtsmusiken.
In: Bausteine für Musikerziehung und Musikpflege. B 118.
BRESLAU CODEX MF. 2016.
Missa anonyma II.
In: Das Chorwerk. No.56.
BREUER, FRANZ JOSEF.
Blockflötenbüchlein für Wolfgang und Angelica.
In: Zeitschrift für Spielmusik. No.126.
BREVAL, JEAN BAPTISTE, 1756–1825.
Sonate (G). Violoncello and piano.
In: Moffat. Meister-Schule der alten Zeit. Violoncello-Sonaten. No.4.
BREVI, GIOVANNI BATTISTA, 17th CENTURY.
Catenae terrenae. Bass und B.C.
In: Cantio sacra. No.11.
Deliciae terrenae. Sopran (Tenor) und B.C.
In: Cantio sacra. No.25.
O spiritus angelici. Alt und B.C.
In: Cantio sacra. No.34.
BRÉVIO.
Sonate en la majeur. (2 violons et piano).
In: L'école du violon au XVIIe et XVIIIe siècle. No.1282.
BREYTENGRASER, WILHELM, *see* BREITENGRASER, WILHELM.
BRIANT, DENIS.
Motets.
In: Attaingnant. Treize livres de motets. Livre 9.
BRIDGE, FRANK, 1879–1941.
Organ music.
In: Standard series of organ compositions. No.16.
BRIEGEL, WOLFGANG CARL, 1626–1712.
Acht Fugen durch die Kirchentöne und Fuga super "Dies sind die heiligen zehn Gebot." Organ.
In: Die Orgel. Reihe II. Nr.19.
Kirchenmusik.
In: Kirchenmusik der Darmstädter Meister des Barock. Vol.3, 4, 5, 6.
Organ music.
In: Muziek voor de eredienst. Vol.2.
Songs.
In: Commer. Geistliche und weltliche Lieder aus dem XVI.–XVII. Jahrhundert.
BRIGNOLI, G.
Organ music.
In: Cantantibus organis. Vol.11.
In: Peeters. Anthologia pro organo. Vol.3.
BRIHUEGA.
Choral music.
In: Engel. Three centuries of choral music. Vol.5.
BRIQUET, 15th CENTURY.
Selections.
In: Reaney. Early fifteenth-century music. Vol.2.
BRISSIO, G. F.
Sacred music.
In: Proske. Musica divina. Annua primus. Tom 2.
BRIXI, FRANTIŠEK XAVER, 1732–1771.
Concerto Fa maggiore.
In: Musica antiqua bohemica. Vol.26.
Keyboard music.
In: Musica antiqua bohemica. Vol.14.
Organ music.
In: Musica antiqua bohemica. Vol.12.
In: Orgelwerke. Altböhmischer Meister. Vol.3.
BROLLO, BARTHOLOMEUS.
Sacred music.
In: Plainsong and Mediaeval Music Society. Publications. (Borren).
BROOKS, ERNEST.
Toccata, from third piano sonata.
In: New music. Vol.9. No.4. July 1936.
BROS, JUAN, 1776–1852.
Sacred music.
In: Eslava y Elizondo. Lira sacro-hispana. 19th century. i.2.
BROSSARD, SÉBASTIEN DE, 1655–1730.
O plenus irarum dies. Bass und B.C.
In: Cantio sacra. No.24.
Quemadmodum desiderat cervus. Tenor (Sopran) und B.C.
In: Cantio sacra. No.13.
Sonitus armorum. Alt und B.C.
In: Cantio sacra. No.29.
BROUCK, JACOB VON, ca.1540/1550–ca.1590.
Selections.
In: Denkmäler der Tonkunst in Österreich. Vol.90.
BROUNO, W.
Organ music.
In: Guilmant. Archives des maîtres de l'orgue. Vol.10.
BROWN, HAROLD.
Piano music.
In: Boletín latino-americano de música. Vol.5.
BROWN, MERTON.
Arioso for piano.
In: New music. Special edition.
Cantabile, for string orchestra.
In: New music. Vol.19. No.2. 1946.
Choral for strings.
In: New music. Special edition.
BROWN, WILLIAM, 18th CENTURY.
Selections.
In: Engel. Music from the days of George Washington.
BRUCH-REIMANN-BEDELL.
Organ music.
In: Standard series of organ compositions. No.21.
BRUCK, ARNOLD VON, ca.1470–1554.
(var. sp.: Arnoldus de Bruck).
Selections.
In: Ambros. Auserwählte Tonwerke.
Choral music.

In: Antiqua Chorbuch. Vol.1. Heft 2; Vol.2. Heft 2.
In: Chorbuch für die Kirchenchöre Sachsens.
Gesänge.
In: Wolf. Chor- und Hausmusik aus älter Zeit. Vol.1.
Lieder.
In: Denkmäler der Tonkunst in Österreich. Vol.72. (Jg.XXXVII/2).
In: Publikationen älterer praktischer und theoretischer Musikwerke. Jahrg.1–3.
Motets.
In: Denkmäler der Tonkunst in Österreich. Vol.99.
BRUCKNER, ANTON, 1824–1896.
Sämtliche Werke. v.1– .
—— Entwürfe und Skizzen zur IX Symphonie. 144p.
—— Another issue. Studienpartitur. (Neuauflage 1949–). v.1– .
Sämtliche Werke. [2.Revidierte Ausgabe]. v.1– .
BRUDIEU, JOAN, d.1591.
Choral music.
In: Engel. Three centuries of choral music. Vol.5.
Els madrigals.
In: Barcelona. Biblioteca Central. Sección de Música. Publicaciones. Vol.1.
BRUHNS, NIKOLAUS, ca.1665–1697.
Gesammelte Werke.
In: Das Erbe deutscher Musik. 2.Reihe. Schleswig-Holstein und Hansestädte. Vol.1–2.
Complete organ works. p.1– .
La fugue au XVIIIe siècle. Organ.
In: Orgue et liturgie. Vol.15.
Organ music.
In: Klein. The first four centuries of music for the organ from Dunstable to Bach (1370–1749).
In: Organ masters of the Baroque period. Vol.2.
In: Organum. 4.Reihe. Nr.8.
In: Straube. Alte Meister des Orgelspiels.
Prélude-choral "Nun komm der Heiden Heiland." Organ.
In: Guilmant. École classique de l'orgue. No.3.
BRULEZ, GACES.
Selections.
In: Smith. Musica antiqua.
BRUMANN, CONRAD, d.1526.
(var. sp.: Konrad Brumann).
Organ music.
In: Moser. Frühmeister der deutschen Orgelkunst.
BRUMEL, ANTOINE, ca.1480–ca.1520.
Opera omnia. 8v.(in progress).
Selections.
In: Ambros. Auserwählte Tonwerke.
In: Maldéghem. Trésor musical.
Choral music.
In: Smijers. Van Ockeghem tot Sweelinck. Aflg.5, 6.
Missa pro defunctis.
In: Das Chorwerk. No.68.
Organ music.
In: Peeters. Oudnederlandse meesters. Vol.2, 3.
In: Schering. Alte Meister aus der Frühzeit des Orgelspiels.
Sicut lilium.
In: Dessoff choir series. No.41.
BRUN, LE, *see* LE BRUN.
BRUNA, PAU, 17th CENTURY.
Organ music.
In: Muset. Early Spanish organ music.
BRUNCKHORST, ARNOLD MELCHIOR, ca.1670–1720.
Organ music.
In: Organum. 4.Reihe. Nr.7.
BRUNETTI, DOMENICO, 16th CENTURY.
Airs.
In: Prunières. Les maîtres du chant. Recueil 3.
Vocal music.
In: Delsarte. Archives du chant. Livr.8, 18.
BRUNETTI, GAETANO, ca.1740–1808.
Symphonies. No.33, 22.
In: Classici italiani della musica. Vol.3.
BRUSSELS–MUSIC (*see also* BELGIUM–MUSIC).
In: Monumenta musicae belgicae. Vol.12.
BRUYER.
Lieder.
In: Publikationen älterer praktischer und theoretische Musikwerke. Jahrg.1–3.
BRYAN.
Sacred music.
In: Arnold. Cathedral music. Vol.2.
BUCHNER, HANS (VON CONSTANZ), 1483–1538.
Fundamentbuch. p.1–192.
Organ music.
In: Froidebise. Anthologie de l'orgue. Vol.1.
In: Moser. Frühmeister der deutschen Orgelkunst.
In: Schering. Alte Meister aus der Frühzeit des Orgelspiels.
BÜCKEBURG–MUSIC.
In: Fürstliches Institut für Musikwissenschaftliche Forschung. Veröffentlichungen. Reihe 3.
BULACHOFF.
Vocal music.
In: Sammlung russischer Romanzen. No.18, 26, 51, 52, 134, 135, 168, 298–300, 311.
BULL, JOHN, 1562–1628.
Fantasias.
In: English instrumental music of the 16th and 17th centuries from manuscripts in the New York Public Library. No.2.
Keyboard music.
In: Apel. Musik aus früher Zeit für Klavier. Bd.2.
In: English keyboard music. [No.8, 14, 19].
In: Elizabethan virginal composers. Vol.1.
In: Farrenc. Le trésor des pianistes. Vol.2.
In: The Fitzwilliam virginal book.
In: The Fitzwilliam virginal book. Ausgewählte Stücke. Vol.2.
In: Fuller-Maitland. Twenty-five pieces for keyed instruments from Benjamin Cosyn's Virginal book.

In: Georgii. Keyboard music of the Baroque and Rococo. Vol.1.
In: Glyn. Twenty-one Old English compositions of the 16th and 17th centuries.
In: Musica Britannica. Vol.14, 19.
In: Oesterle. Early keyboard music. Vol.1.
In: Parthenia.
In: Pauer. Alte Klavier-Musik. 2d series. Part 6.
In: Pauer. Old English composers for the virginals and harpsichord.
In: Tagliapietra. Antologia di musica antica e moderna per pianoforte. Bd.3.
The king's hunt. Organ.
In: Dickinson. Historical recital series for organ. Vol.1. No.6.
The king's hunting jigg.
In: Köhler. Les maîtres du clavecin. Heft 13.
Organ music.
In: Biggs. Treasury of early organ music.
In: Bonnet. Historical organ-recitals. Vol.1.
In: Klein. The first four centuries of music for the organ from Dunstable to Bach (1370–1749).
In: Peeters. Anthologia pro organo. Vol.1, 3.
Parthenia–Music for virginals.
In: Musical Antiquarian Society. Publications. Vol.18.
Pavana for the virginal.
In: Parrish. A treasury of early music. No.30.
Sacred music.
In: Boyce. Cathedral music. Vol.3; 1849, Vol.3.
Virginal music.
In: Elizabethan virginal composers. Vol.1.
BULTEL, JACOBUS.
Selections.
In: Maldéghem. Trésor musical.
BUNAKOFF.
Vocal music.
In: Sammlung russischer Romanzen. No.136.
BUNJES, PAUL, 1914– .
Organ music.
In: The parish organist. Vol.1–4.
BUONAUGURIO DA TIVOLI, GIULIANO.
Sacred music.
In: Jeppesen. Italia sacra musica. Vol.1, 2.
BUONONCINI, GIOVANNI BATTISTA, *see* BONONCINI, GIOVANNI BATTISTA.
BURANELLO, *see* GALUPPI, BALDASSARE.
BURCH, CORNELIUS.
Geistliche Konzerte zu vier Stimmen, 1630.
In: Denkmäler rheinischer Musik. Vol.6, 9.
BURCK, JOACHIM À, 1546–1610.
(var. sp.: Joachim von Burck).
Choral music.
In: Antiqua Chorbuch. Vol.1. Heft 3.
Lieder und Passionen.
In: Publikationen älterer praktischer und theoretischer Musikwerke. Jahrg.26.
BUREK.
Gesänge.
In: Musica sacra. ca.1842–1896. Vol.11.
BURGUNDY–MUSIC.
In: Marix. Les musiciens de la cour de Bourgogne au XVe siècle (1420–1467).
BURKHART, FRANZ, 1902– .
Drei Adventlieder.
In: Gitarre-Kammermusik. No.3.
Toccata für 2 Gitarren.
In: Gitarre-Kammermusik. No.14.
BURKHART–SCHEIT.
Volksliederbuch zur Gitarre.
In: Gitarre-Kammermusik.
BURLIN, NATALIE CURTIS, 1875–1921.
Songs.
In: The Wa-Wan series of American compositions.
BURNETT, DUNCAN.
Keyboard music.
In: English keyboard music. [No.15].
BURNEY, CHARLES, 1726–1814.
Organ music.
In: The Liturgical Music Press, Inc. Masterpieces of organ music. Folio 60.
In: Tallis to Wesley. Vol.34.
BUSATTI, CHERUBINO.
Songs.
In: Jeppesen. La flora. Vol.1, 2.
BUSBY, THOMAS, 1755–1838.
Sacred music.
In: Page. Harmonia sacra. Vol.3.
BUSCHMANN, RAINER GLEN.
Vier Stücke für Blockflöten-Quartett.
In: Zeitschrift für Spielmusik. No.288.
BUSNOIS, ANTHOINE, d.1492.
(var. sp.: Antonius Busnois; Antonius Busnoys).
Chansons.
In: Copenhagen Kongelige Bibliotek. Mss. (Thottske Samling 291^8). Der kopenhagener Chansonnier.
Choral music.
In: Smijers. Van Ockeghem tot Sweelinck. Aflg.1, 6.
Missa super l'homme armé.
In: Monumenta polyphoniae liturgicae sanctae ecclesiae romanae. Ser.1. Tomus I. Fasc.2.
BUSONI, FERRUCCIO BENVENUTO, 1866–1924.
Keyboard music.
In: Tagliapietra. Antologia di musica antica e moderna per pianoforte. Bd.18.
BUSSY, N. DE, 16th CENTURY.
Chansons.
In: Cauchie. Quinze chansons françaises du XVIe siècle.
In: Lesure. Anthologie de la chanson parisienne au XVIe siècle.
BUTTSTEDT, FRANZ VOLLRATH, 1735–1814.
Keyboard music.
In: Farrenc. Le trésor des pianistes. Vol.14.
BUTTSTETT, JOHANN HEINRICH, 1666–1727.
Organ music.
In: Dietrich. Elf Orgelchörale des siebzehnten Jahrhunderts.
In: Das Erbe deutscher Musik. 1.Reihe. Vol.9.
In: Keller. Achtzig Choralvorspiele deutscher Meister des 17. und 18. Jahrhunderts.
In: Klein. The first four centuries of music for the organ from Dunstable to Bach (1370–1749).
In: The Liturgical Music Press, Inc. Masterpieces of organ music. Folio 26.

In: Muziek voor de eredienst. Vol.1, 2.
In: The parish organist. Vol.1–4.
In: Rohr. Orgelspiel im Kirchenjahr.
In: Straube. Choralvorspiele alter Meister.
BUUS, JACQUES, d.1565.
Chanson.
In: Brown. Theatrical chansons of the 15th and early 16th centuries.
Choral music.
In: Commer. Collectio operum musicorum batavorum saeculi XVI. Bd.8.
BUXHEIMER ORGELBUCH.
Das Buxheimer Orgelbuch. 111[1]p.
—— Facsimile edition. 167L.
Buxheimer Orgelbuch. 2v.
In: Documenta musicologica. 2.Reihe. Vol.1.
In: Das Erbe deutscher Musik. 1.Reihe. Vol.37/38/39.
In: Institute of Mediaeval Music. Musicological studies. Vol.6.
Selections.
In: Apel. Musik aus früher Zeit für Klavier. Bd.1.
In: Cantantibus organis. Vol.4, 8.
BUXTEHUDE, DIETRICH, 1637–1707.
Werke. v.1– .
Dietrich Buxtehude's Orgelcompositionen. 2v.
Ausgewählte Orgelwerke. 2v.
Orgelwerke. 4v.
Sämtliche Orgelwerke. 2v.
"Abendmusiken" and church cantatas.
In: Denkmäler deutscher Tonkunst. [1.Folge]. Vol.14.
Alles, was ihr tut mir Worten oder mit Werken.
In: Organum. 1.Reihe. Nr.22.
Cantata.
In: Eitner. Cantaten des 17. und 18. Jahrhunderts. Part 2, Part 3.
Choral music.
In: Antiqua Chorbuch. Vol.1. Heft 5.
In: Engel. Three centuries of choral music. Vol.4.
Choralvorspiele.
In: Zeitschrift für Spielmusik. No.169.
Choralvorspiele für Alt-Blockflöte und Orgel oder Klavier.
In: Moeck's Kammermusik. Vol.33.
Fugue C. Organ.
In: Guilmant. École classique de l'orgue. No.22.
Ihr lieben Christen, freut euch nun.
In: Organum. 1.Reihe. Nr.16.
Kantaten.
In: Berlin. Institut für Musikforschung. Veröffentlichungen. Reihe 1. Heft 1–37.
4 Latinske Kantater.
In: Samfundet til Udgivelse af dansk Musik. Ser.III. No.138.
Keyboard music.
In: Georgii. Keyboard music of the Baroque and Rococo. Vol.1.
In: Herrmann. Lehrmeister und Schüler Joh. Seb. Bachs. Vol.1.
In: Oesterle. Early keyboard music. Vol.1.
In: Tagliapietra. Antologia di musica antica e moderna per pianoforte. Bd.8.
A mighty fortress is our God. Organ.
In: The Liturgical Music Press, Inc. Commemoration folio.
Min Gud er med Mig. Cantata.
In: Samfundet til Udgivelse af dansk Musik. Ser.III. No.89.
Missa brevis. Kyrie-Gloria.
In: Dessoff choir series. No.23.
Nun komm, der Heiden Heiland.
In: Parrish. A treasury of early music. No.41.
Organ music.
In: Anthologia antiqua. Vol.5, 8.
In: Biggs. Treasury of early organ music.
In: Bonnet. Historical organ-recitals. Vol.1.
In: Buszin. Organ series. Vol.1.
In: Dietrich. Elf Orgelchörale des siebzehnten Jahrhunderts.
In: Elkan-Vogel organ series. Vol.4.
In: Gerhardt. Album nordischer Komponisten für Orgel. Vol.2.
In: Guilmant. Concert historique d'orgue.
In: Keller. Achtzig Choralvorspiele deutscher Meister des 17. und 18. Jahrhunderts.
In: Klein. The first four centuries of music for the organ from Dunstable to Bach (1370–1749).
In: Liber organi. Bd.6.
In: The Liturgical Music Press, Inc. Masterpieces of organ music. Folio 2, 14, 17, 20, 30, 71.
In: Organ masters of the Baroque period. Vol.3.
In: The parish organist. Vol.1–4, 5–6.
In: Peeters. Anthologia pro organo. Vol.2, 4.
In: Pierront. Cent versets de Magnificat.
In: Rohr. Orgelspiel im Kirchenjahr.
In: Schweiger. A brief compendium of early organ music.
In: Standard series of organ compositions. No.37, 42, 47, 63.
In: Straube. Alte Meister.
In: Straube. Alte Meister des Orgelspiels.
In: Straube. Choralvorspiele alter Meister.
Prélude et fugue G-moll. Organ.
In: Guilmant. École classique de l'orgue. No.2.
Prelude and fugue in F. Organ; Chorale prelude "Praise God, Ye Christians." Organ.
In: Dickinson. Historical recital series for organ. No.41, 42.
Sonatas for violin, violoncello, and harpsichord.
In: Denkmäler deutscher Tonkunst. [1.Folge]. Vol.11.
Sonate A-moll, Op.1, Nr.3, für Violine, Viola da Gamba, Cembalo (Klavier) und Bass-Instrument ad lib.; für Violine (Flöte), Violoncello, Cembalo (Klavier) und Bass-Instrument ad lib.
In: Antiqua Edition. Von 3 Instrumenten an.
Sonate in D dur. Für Violine, Viola da Gamba (oder Violoncell) und Klavier.
In: Riemann. Collegium musicum. Vol.53.
Sonate (D-dur). Op.2 (1696), Nr.2 für Violine, Gambe (Violoncello) und Cembalo.
In: Organum. 3.Reihe. Nr.6.
Sonate E-dur, Op.2, Nr.6.. Für Violine, Viola da Gamba (oder Violoncello) und Cembalo (oder Klavier).

In: Nagels Musik-Archiv. No.117.
Sonate E-moll für Violine, Gambe (Violoncell) und Cembalo. Op.1, Nr.7.
In: Organum. 3.Reihe. Nr.21.
Udvalgte Kompositioner.
In: Samfundet til Udgivelse af dansk Musik. Ser.II. No.31.

BUZZOLENI, GIOVANNI.
Songs.
In: Jeppesen. La flora. Vol.1, 2.

BYRD, WILLIAM, 1542 (or 3)–1623.
(var. sp.: William Bird).
The collected vocal works. v.1– .
—— New edition. v.1– .
Forty-five pieces for keyboard instruments. 142p.
My Ladye Nevells booke. 245p.
—— Reprint.
Selections.
In: Crotch. Specimens of various styles of music. Vol.2.
In: Documenta historica musicae.
In: The music with the form and order of the service to be performed at the coronation of . . . Queen Elizabeth II.
In: Smith. Musica antiqua.
The battell, a suite. Organ.
In: The Liturgical Music Press, Inc. Commemoration folio.
Choral music.
In: Engel. Three centuries of choral music. Vol.3.
Church music.
In: Motett Society. [Collection of ancient church music]. Division 1. Division 3.
In: Tudor church music. Vol.2.
Ego sum panis vivus.
In: Parrish. Masterpieces of music before 1750. No.25.
Fantasias.
In: English instrumental music of the 16th and 17th centuries from manuscripts in the New York Public Library. No.2.
Gradualia I, II.
In: Tudor church music. Vol.7.
Keyboard music.
In: Apel. Musik aus früher Zeit für Klavier. Bd.2.
In: English keyboard music. [No.4, 19].
In: Farrenc. Le trésor des pianistes. Vol.2.
In: The Fitzwilliam virginal book.
In: The Fitzwilliam virginal book. Ausgewählte Stücke. Vol.1.
In: Fuller-Maitland. Twenty-five pieces for keyed instruments from Benjamin Cosyn's Virginal book.
In: Georgii. Keyboard music of the Baroque and Rococo. Vol.1.
In: Glyn. Twenty-one Old English compositions of the 16th and 17th centuries.
In: Oesterle. Early keyboard music. Vol.1.
In: Parthenia.
In: Pauer. Alte Klavier-Musik. 2d series. Part 6.
In: Pauer. Old English composers for the virginals and harpsichord.
In: Tagliapietra. Antologia di musica antica e moderna per pianoforte. Bd.2.
Compositions for the lute.
In: Schott's Series of early lute music. Vol.3.
Madrigals.
In: Euterpe. Vol.1, 13; 2d ed., No.4–6.
In: Fellowes. The English madrigal school. Vol.14, 15, 16.
In: Squire. Ausgewählte Madrigale und mehrstimmige Gesänge. No.12, 27.
Masses, cantiones, and motets.
In: Tudor church music. Vol.9.
A mass for 5 voices; Book 1 of Cantiones sacrae for 5 voices; Parthenia–Music for virginals.
In: Musical Antiquarian Society. Publications. Vol.1, 6, 18.
Organ music.
In: Guilmant. Concert historique d'orgue.
In: Klein. The first four centuries of music for the organ from Dunstable to Bach (1370–1749).
In: Liber organi. Bd.10.
In: Peeters. Anthologia pro organo. Vol.1, 3.
In: Raugel. Quarante-six pièces pour orgue ou harmonium.
In: Tallis to Wesley. Vol.8.
Part music.
In: Hullah. Part music. Class B.2; Class C. Sacred.
Parthenia. Facsimile.
In: Monuments of music and music literature. First series. No.11.
Prélude et The carman's whistle.
In: Köhler. Les maîtres du clavecin. Heft 13.
Sacred music.
In: Boyce. Cathedral music. Vol.2, 3; 1849. Vol.1, 2, and Vol.2, Appendix.
Two sacred songs in 5 parts.
In: Music Press, Inc. [Choral series]. Vol.92.
Two sacred songs in 4 parts.
In: Music Press, Inc. [Choral series]. Vol.51.
Songs of sundry natures.
In: Arkwright. The Old English edition. Vol.7–9.
Vocal music.
In: Hullah. Vocal scores. I. Sacred; II. Secular.

BYSTRÖM, OSCAR FREDRIK BERNADOTTE, 1821–1909.
String quartet, No.2.
In: Musikaliska konstföreningen. 1937.
Symphony, D minor. Arr. for piano, 4 hands.
In: Musikaliska konstföreningen. 1897.

BYZANTINE ELEMENTS IN EARLY SLAVIC CHANT.
In: Monumenta musicae byzantinae. Subsidia. Vol.4. Pt.1–2.

BYZANTINE MUSIC.
In: Anthology of music. Vol.13.
In: Études de paléographie musicale byzantine.
In: Monumenta musicae byzantinae.
In: Wellesz. Trésor de musique byzantine.

CABALLERO, MANUEL FERNÁNDEZ, *see* FERNÁNDEZ CABALLERO, MANUEL.

CABANILLES, JUAN, 1644–1712.
(var. sp.: Johannis Cabanilles; Joan Cabanilles).

Opera selecta pro organo. 3v.
Musici organici. Opera omnia.
In: Barcelona. Biblioteca Central. Sección de Música. Publicaciones. Vol.4, 8, 13.
Organ music.
In: Bonnet. Historical organ-recitals. Vol.6.
In: Muset. Early Spanish organ music.
In: Pedrell. Antología de organistas clásicos españoles (siglos XVI, XVII y XVIII).
In: Peeters. Anthologia pro organo. Vol.2, 4.
In: Piedelievre. Les anciens maîtres espagnols.

CABEZÓN, ANTONIO DE, 1510–1566.
(var. sp.: Antonius de Cabezón).
Collected works.
In: Institute of Mediaeval Music. Collected works. Vol.4.
Composiciones.
In: Pedrell. Hispaniae schola musica sacra. Bd.3–4.
Composiciones a cinco y seis partes I, II.
In: Pedrell. Hispaniae schola musica sacra. Bd.7–8.
Keyboard music.
In: Apel. Musik aus früher Zeit für Klavier. Bd.2.
In: Kastner. Silva iberica.
In: Tagliapietra. Antologia di musica antica e moderna per pianoforte. Bd.1.
Organ music.
In: Auler. Spielbuch für Kleinorgel. Vol.1.
In: Bonnet. Historical organ-recitals. Vol.1, 6.
In: Elkan-Vogel organ series. Vol.5.
In: Klein. The first four centuries of music for the organ from Dunstable to Bach (1370–1749).
In: Liber organi. Bd.3.
In: Muset. Early Spanish organ music.
In: Orgue et liturgie. Vol.30, 34.
In: Pedrell. Antología de organistas clásicos españoles (siglos XVI, XVII y XVIII).
In: Peeters. Anthologia pro organo. Vol.1, 3.
In: Piedelievre. Les anciens maîtres espagnols.
In: Pierront. Cent versets de Magnificat.
In: Raugel. Quarante-six pièces pour orgue ou harmonium.
In: Straube. Alte Meister des Orgelspiels.

CABILLIAU.
Selections.
In: Maldéghem. Trésor musical.

CABO, FRANCISCO JAVIER, 1768–1832.
Sacred music.
In: Eslava y Elizondo. Lira sacro-hispana. 19th century. i.1.

CABRERA, F. V.
Sacred music.
In: Eslava y Elizondo. Lira sacro-hispana. 18th century. i.1.

CACCE, 14th CENTURY.
In: Marrocco. Fourteenth-century Italian cacce.

CACCINI, FRANCESCA, 1588–ca.1640.
Selections.
In: Torchi. L'arte musicale in Italia. Bd.5.
Arias.
In: Landshoff. Alte Meister des Bel Canto. Eine Sammlung von Arien. Vol.1–2.
La liberazione di Ruggiero dall' isola d'Alcina.
In: Smith College music archives. No.7.

CACCINI, GIULIO, d.ca.1618.
Airs.
In: Prunières. Les maîtres du chant. Recueil 3.
Arias.
In: I classici della musica italiana. Vol.4.
In: Parisotti. Arie antiche. Bd.2, 3.
Choral music.
In: Rochlitz. Sammlung vorzüglicher Gesangstücke. Bd.2.
Dovrò dunque morire.
In: Parrish. Masterpieces of music before 1750. No.30.
Euridice.
In: Publikationen älterer praktischer und theoretischer Musikwerke. Jahrg.9.
Le nuove musiche.
In: I classici della musica italiana. Raccolta nazionale delle musiche italiane. Quad. 9–12.
In: Mantica. Prime fioriture del melodramma italiano. Vol.2.
In: Reale Accademia d'Italia, Rome. Musica. Vol.4.
Songs.
In: Jeppesen. La flora. Vol.1, 3.
In: The Tudor edition of old music. Ser.B. No.2.
Vocal music.
In: Gevaert. Les gloires de l'Italie. Vol.1, 2.

CADÉAC, PIERRE, 16th CENTURY.
Chansons.
In: Publikationen älterer praktischer und theoretischer Musikwerke. Jahrg.27.
Mass.
In: Stein. Twelve Franco-Flemish masses of the early 16th century.
Motets.
In: Attaingnant. Treize livres de motets. Livre 13.

CADZOW, DOROTHY, 1916– .
Prelude for strings.
In: Washington (State) University. Music series. No.2.

CAESAR, JOHANN MELCHIOR, ca.1645–1692.
Ballett-Suite für Streichquartett (Streichorchester) und Basso Continuo.
In: Nagels Musik-Archiv. No.204.

CAFARO, PASQUALE, 1706–1787.
Sacred music.
In: The Fitzwilliam music. Bd.2.
In: Latrobe, C. I. Selection of sacred music.
In: Latrobe, J. A. The music of the church.

CAGE, JOHN, 1912– .
Amores, for piano and percussion.
In: New music. Vol.16. No.4. July 1943.

CAIX D'HERVELOIS, LOUIS DE, ca.1670–ca.1760.
Moulinet.
In: L'école du violon au XVIIe et XVIIIe siècle. No.1333.
Sonate (Am) Violoncello and piano.
In: Moffat. Meister-Schule der alter Zeit. Violoncello-Sonaten. No.9.

CALAHORRA, R. O.
Sacred music.
In: Eslava y Elizondo. Lira sacro-hispana. 19th century. ii.2.
CALDARA, ANTONIO, ca.1670–1736.
Selections.
In: Expert. Répertoire classique de musique. 1re année.
Arias.
In: Landshoff. Alte Meister des Bel Canto. Eine Sammlung von Arien. Vol.1–2, 3.
In: Parisotti. Arie antiche. Bd.1.
Chamber music.
In: Denkmäler der Tonkunst in Österreich. Vol.75. (Jg.XXXIX).
Choral music.
In: Musica sacra. 1839– . Vol.2, 3.
In: Rochlitz. Sammlung vorzüglicher Gesangstücke. Bd.2.
Church compositions.
In: Denkmäler der Tonkunst in Österreich. Vol.26. (Jg.XIII/1).
Dafne.
In: Denkmäler der Tonkunst in Österreich. Vol.91.
Fugue, Et in saecula.
In: Königliche Akademie der Künste. Auswahl vorzüglicher Musik-Werke. No.41.
Haec est regina virginum. Sopran, 2 Violinen und B.C.
In: Die Kantate. No.11.
Kirchensonate.
In: Einstein. Beispielsammlung zur älteren Musikgeschichte.
Lauda anima mea.
In: Messner. Alte salzburger Meister der kirchlichen Tonkunst. Heft 2.
Ein Madrigal und achtzehn Kanons.
In: Das Chorwerk. No.25.
Motets.
In: Denkmäler der Tonkunst in Österreich. Vol.101/102.
Organ music.
In: Commer. Compositionen für Orgel aus dem 16., 17., und 18. Jahrhundert. Heft 3.
In: Pierront. Cent versets de Magnificat.
Sacred music.
In: Latrobe, C. I. Selection of sacred music.
In: Latrobe, J. A. The music of the church.
Sonata a tre per due violini, violoncello e basso continuo. Op.I/5.
In: Hausmusik. No.59.
Sonata a tre per due violini, violoncello e basso continuo. Op.I/9.
In: Hausmusik. No.121.
Sonata da camera, Op.2/3.
In: Hausmusik. No.85.
Triosonaten.
In: Nagels Musik-Archiv. No.5, 12.
Veni, dilecte, veni. Sopran (Tenor) und B.C.
In: Cantio sacra. No.27.
CALESTANI, VINCENZIO, 16th–17th CENTURIES.
Songs.
In: Jeppesen. La flora. Vol.1, 3.
CALISTA, LELIO, 17th CENTURY.
(var. sp.: Lelio Colista).
Sonata IV in D major.
In: Seventeenth-century chamber music. No.5.
Sonata terza per due violini, violoncello e basso continuo.
In: Hausmusik. No.139.
Triosonate A-dur für 2 Violinen, Violoncello und Basso Continuo.
In: Hortus musicus. No.172.
CALL, LEONHARD VON, ca.1768–1815.
(var. sp.: Leonhard De Call).
Leichtes Trio für 3 Gitarren. Op.26.
In: Albert. Die Gitarre in der Haus- und Kammermusik vor 100 Jahren (1780–1820). No.12.
Notturno, Op.93, für Flöte, Viola, und Gitarre.
In: Musikschätze der Vergangenheit.
Part music.
In: Hullah. Part music. Class C. Secular.
Trio, C dur, für Violine oder Flöte, Viola und Gitarre. Op.134.
In: Albert. Die Gitarre in der Haus- und Kammermusik vor 100 Jahren (1780–1820). No.10.
CALLCOTT, JOHN WALL, 1766–1821.
Part music.
In: Hullah. Part music. Class A.1. Vol.2; Class A.2. Vol.2; Class C. Secular.
Vocal music.
In: Hullah. Vocal scores. I. Sacred; II. Secular.
CALVI, LORENZO.
Victimae paschali laudes.
In: Die Motette. No.3.
CALVISIUS, SETHUS, 1556–1615.
Choral music.
In: Antiqua Chorbuch; Vol.1. Heft 3.
In: Chorbuch für die Kirchenchöre Sachsens.
In: Nagels Männerchor-Blätter. No.11.
Joseph, lieber Joseph mein.
In: Arion. Vol.3.
CÁMARA, JUAN ANTONIO, 1917– .
Suite (Flauta, clarinete y fagot).
In: Instituto Interamericano de Musicologia. Publicaciónes. No.44.
CAMARGO, MIGUEL GÓMEZ, *see* GÓMEZ CAMARGO, MIGUEL.
CAMBEFORTE, JEAN DE, 1605–1661.
Airs.
In: Prunières. Les maîtres du chant. Recueil 4.
CAMBERT, ROBERT, 1628–1677.
Les peines & les plaisirs de l'amour; Pomone.
In: Les chefs d'oeuvres classiques de l'opéra français.
CAMBINI, GIOVANNI GIUSEPPE, 1746–1825.
Concerto in G, Op.15, No.3 (piano solo, strings).
In: Antica musica strumentale italiana. Ser.I. Vol.8.
Quintet No.3 for flute, oboe, clarinet, bassoon, and horn.
In: Music for wind instruments by 18th century masters. No.12.
CAMERACO, JO, 15th CENTURY.
Selections.
In: Reaney. Early fifteenth-century music. Vol.2.
CAMERLOHER, PLACIDUS VON, 1718–1782.
Orchesterquartett F-dur.

In: Corona. Vol.40.
Drei Freisinger Sinfonien.
In: Corona. Vol.36.
4 Sonaten für 2 Violinen und Klavier, Bass-Instrument ad lib.
In: Antiqua Edition. Von 3 Instrumenten an.
CAMPAGNOLI, BARTOLOMMEO, 1751–1827.
6 Fugues pour violon seul.
In: L'école du violon au XVIIe et XVIIIe siècle. No.1296.
CAMPBELL-TIPTON, LOUIS, *see* TIPTON, LOUIS CAMPBELL- .
CAMPIAN, THOMAS, 1567–1619/20.
(var. sp.: Thomas Campion).
Selections.
In: Smith. Musica antiqua.
Book of airs.
In: Fellowes. The English school of lutenist song writers. 2d series. Vol.1, 2, 10, 11.
Songs from Rosseter's Book of airs.
In: Fellowes. The English school of lutenist song writers. 1st series. Vol.4, 13.
Madrigals.
In: Euterpe. Vol.4, 7, 10, 12, 13; 2d ed. No.7–11.
Masque in honour of the marriage of Lord Hayes.
In: Arkwright. The Old English edition. Vol.1.
CAMPION, FRANÇOIS, ca.1686–1748.
Pièces pour le luth.
In: Orgue et liturgie. Vol.13.
CAMPION, THOMAS, *see* CAMPIAN, THOMAS.
CAMPIONI, CARLO ANTONIO, 1720–1793.
Sonate (Gm).
In: Moffat. Trio-Sonaten alter Meister. No.26.
CAMPRA, ANDRÉ, 1660–1744.
Selections.
In: Expert. Répertoire classique de musique. 1re année.
Airs.
In: Prunières. Les maîtres du chant. Recueil 6.
Domine, Dominus noster. Sopran, Flöte (Viol) und B.C.
In: Die Kantate. No.3.
L'Europe galante; Les fêtes vénitiennes; Tancrède.
In: Les chefs d'oeuvres classiques de l'opéra français.
Exaltabo Te. Deus meus, Rex. Bass und B.C.
In: Cantio sacra. No.9.
Les fêtes vénitiennes. Chaconne.
In: Parrish. A treasury of early music. No.45.
Jubilate Deo. Sopran (Tenor) und B.C.
In: Cantio sacra. No.32.
Musette.
In: L'école du violon au XVIIe et XVIIIe siècle. No.1341.
O dulcis amor. Sopran (Tenor) und B.C.
In: Cantio sacra. No.17.
Organ music.
In: Biggs. A treasury of shorter organ classics.
Quam dulce est. Inhaerere Tibi. Alt und B.C.
In: Cantio sacra. No.6.
Quemadmodum desiderat cervus. Sopran (Tenor) und B.C.
In: Cantio sacra. No.56.
CANCIONEROS.
In: Asenjo y Barbieri. Cancionero musical de los siglos XV y XVI. 636, [2] p.
In: Joaquim. O cancioneiro musical e poetico da Biblioteca Públia Hortênsia.
In: La Sablonare. Cancionero musical y poético del siglo XVII.
In: Monumentos de la música española. Vol.5, 8, 10.
In: Villancicos de diuersos autores. Cancionero de Upsala.
CANCIONES.
In: Oller. Madrigales y canciones polifónicas.
CANIS, CORNELIUS, d.1561.
Choral music.
In: Commer. Collectio operum musicorum batavorum saeculi XVI. Bd.8.
CANNABICH, CHRISTIAN, 1731–1798.
Orchestral music.
In: Riemann. Mannheim symphonists. Vol.2.
Sinfonie G-dur.
In: Sondheimer. Werke aus dem 18. Jahrhundert. Nr.35.
CANNICIARI, POMPEO, 1670–1744.
(var. sp.: Pompeo Cannicciari).
Missa cum organo. S.A.T.B. & organ.
In: Basilica. 1954.
Sacred music.
In: Documenta liturgiae polychoralis sanctae ecclesiae romanae. No.10, 11, 14, 15.
In: Proske. Musica divina. Annus primus. Tom 2.
CANNING, THOMAS, 1911– .
Organ music.
In: The parish organist. Vol.1–4.
CANTALLOS.
Sonatas. Piano.
In: Nin y Castellano. Seize sonates anciennes d'auteurs espagnols.
CANTATAS.
In: Eitner. Cantaten des 17. und 18. Jahrhunderts.
In: Die Kantate.
In: Lea pocket scores. No.79–85, 106–109.
CANTIGAS.
In: Barcelona. Biblioteca Central. Sección de Música. Publicaciones. Vol.15.
CAPIROLA, VINCENZO, b.1474.
Compositione. Lute-book (circa.1517).
In: La Société de Musique d'Autrefois. Publications. Tome 1.
O mia cieca e dura sorte.
In: Parrish. A treasury of early music. No.21.
CAPORALE, ANDREA, d.ca.1756.
Sonate (Dm) Violoncello and piano.
In: Moffat. Meister-Schule der alter Zeit. Violoncello-Sonaten. No.11.
CAPPELEN, CHR.
Organ music.
In: Gerhardt. Album nordischer Komponisten für Orgel. Vol.1.
CAPRIOLI, CARLO, 17th CENTURY.
Selections.
In: Torchi. L'arte musicale in Italia. Bd.5.
CAPRIOLI, GIOVANNI PAOLO.
Drei geistliche Konzerte. Sopran (Tenor) und B.C.

In: Cantio sacra. No.46.
CAPRON, HENRI, 18th CENTURY.
Selections.
In: Engel. Music from the days of George Washington.
CAPUT MASSES. (PLANCHART, ALEJANDRO, ed.).
In: Collegium musicum. Vol.5.
CARA, MARCHETTO, d.ca.1527.
O mia cieca e dura sorte.
In: Parrish. A treasury of early music. No.20.
Sacred music.
In: Jeppesen. Italia sacra musica. Vol.2.
CARAFA DE COLOBRANO, MICHELE ENRICO, 1787–1872.
Part music.
In: Hullah. Part music. Class B.1.
CARDOSO, FREI MANUEL, 1571–1650.
(var. sp.: Emmanuel Cardoso).
Selections.
In: Santos. A polifonia clássica portuguesa.
Liber primus missarum. Vol.1, 2.
In: Portugaliae musica. Sér.A. Vol.5, 6.
Sacred music.
In: Proske. Musica divina. Annus primus. Tom 2.
In: Rubio. Antologia polifonica sacra. Vol.1.
CARDOT DE BELLENGUES, *see* BELLENGUES, RICHARD DE.
CARÊME, DU.
Vocal music.
In: Delsarte. Archives du chant. Livr.9. No.1.
CARESANO.
Keyboard music.
In: Clementi. Clementi's Selection of practical harmony. Vol.1.
CAREY, HENRY, ca.1687–1743.
Selections.
In: Fisher. The music that Washington knew.
Songs.
In: Potter. Reliquary of English song. Vol.2.
CARILLO, JULIÁN, 1875– .
Preludio a Cristobal Colón.
In: New music. Vol.17. No.3. Apr.1944.
CARISSIMI, GIACOMO, ca.1604–1674.
Selections.
In: Crotch. Specimens of various styles of music. Vol.2.
In: Expert. Répertoire classique de musique. 1re année.
In: Torchi. L'arte musicale in Italia. Bd.5.
Afferti gladium, from "Judicium Salomonis."
In: Parrish. Masterpieces of music before 1750. No.32.
Airs.
In: Prunières. Les maîtres du chant. Recueil 5.
Arias.
In: Landshoff. Alte Meister des Bel Canto. Eine Sammlung von Arien. Vol.1–2.
In: Parisotti. Arie antiche. Bd.1, 3.
Choral music.
In: Documenta liturgiae polychoralis sanctae ecclesiae romanae. No.18.
In: Recueil de musique ancienne. Recueil des morceaux de musique ancienne. Bd.6, 8, 11.
In: Rochlitz. Sammlung vorzüglicher Gesangstücke. Bd.2.
In: Societas Polyphonica Romanae. Repertorium. Vol.4.
Daniele.
In: Istituto Italiano per la Storia della Musica. 1. Monumenti III. Vol.7.
Domine, Deus meus. Sopran (Tenor) und B.C.
In: Cantio sacra. No.8.
Lucifer. Bass und B.C.
In: Cantio sacra. No.37.
Messe e motetti.
In: Istituto Italiano per la Storia della Musica. 1. Monumenti III. Vol.6.
O quam pulchra es. Sopran (Tenor) und B.C.
In: Cantio sacra. No.57.
O vulnera doloris. Bass und B.C.
In: Cantio sacra. No.16.
Oratorios.
In: I classici della musica italiana. Vol.5.
In: I classici della musica italiana. Raccolta nazionale delle musiche italiane. Quad.13–18.
In: Denkmäler der Tonkunst. Vol.2.
In: Istituto Italiano per la Storia della Musica. 1. Monumenti III. Vol.1–5.
Organ music.
In: Commer. Compositionen für Orgel aus dem 16., 17., und 18. Jahrhundert. Heft 1.
In: Pierront. Cent versets de Magnificat.
Part music.
In: Hullah. Part music. Class C. Sacred.
Sacred music.
In: The Fitzwilliam music. Bd.1, 4, 5.
Salve, salve, Puellule. Sopran (Tenor) und B.C.
In: Cantio sacra. No.48.
Songs.
In: Jeppesen. La flora. Vol.1, 3.
Vocal music.
In: Gervaert. Les gloires de l'Italie. Vol.1, 2.
In: Hullah. Vocal scores. I. Sacred.
CARLOS V, LA MÚSICA EN LA CORTE DE. (HIGINI ANGLÉS).
In: Monumentos de la música española. Vol.2.
CARLTON, NICHOLAS, 16th CENTURY.
(var. sp.: Nicholas Carleton).
Keyboard music.
In: Schott's Anthology of early keyboard music. Vol.4.
CARLTON, RICHARD, ca.1558–ca.1638.
Madrigals.
In: Fellowes. The English madrigal school. Vol.27.
In: The triumphs of Oriana.
CARMEN, JOHANNES, 14th–15th CENTURIES.
Works.
In: Reaney. Early fifteenth-century music. Vol.1.
Sacred music.
In: Plainsong and Mediaeval Music Society. Publications. (Borren).
CARMINA.
In: Nagels Musik-Archiv. No.53.
CARMINA BURANA.
In: Institute of Mediaeval Music. Publications. Vol.9.

CARMINA GERMANICA ET GALLICA.
In: Hortus musicus. No.137, 138.
CARNAZZI.
Choral music.
In: Musica sacra. 1839– . Vol.2, 3.
CARNIVAL SONGS, RENAISSANCE.
In: Das Chorwerk. No.43.
CARO DE BOESI, JOSÉ ANTONIO, d.1814.
Christus factus est.
In: Archivo de musica colonial venezolana. No.8.
CAROLS.
In: Music Press, Inc. [Choral series]. Vol.59.
In: Musica Britannica. Vol.4.
CARON, PHILIPPE, 15th CENTURY.
(var. sp.: Firminus Caron).
Choral music.
In: Smijers. Van Ockeghem tot Sweelinck. Aflg.2.
Missa super l'homme armé.
In: Monumenta polyphoniae liturgicae sanctae ecclesiae romanae. Ser.1. Tomus I. Fasc.3.
An introduction to Caron. (Thomson).
In: Institute of Mediaeval Music. Musicological studies. Vol.9.
CAROSO, FABRIZIO, 16th–17th CENTURIES.
(var. sp.: Fabritio Caroso).
Lute music.
In: Chilesotti. Lautenspieler des XVI. Jahrhunderts.
Nobilità di Dame.
In: Chilesotti. Biblioteca di rarità musicali. Vol.1.
CARPENTRAS, *see* GENET, ELZÉAR.
CARPIO, LOPE FÉLIX DE VEGA, *see* VEGA CARPIO, LOPE FÉLIX DE.
CARPIO VALDÉS, ROBERTO, 1900– .
Selections.
In: Boletín latino-americano de música. Vol.3.
In: Instituto Interamericano de Musicologia. Publicaciónes. No.13.
CARRASSI-MATTEO.
Op.17. Variationen auf "Le songe de Rousseau" für Laute oder Gitarre.
In: Musikschätze der Vergangenheit.
CARREÑO, CAYETANO.
Tristis est; In Monte Oliveti.
In: Archivo de musica colonial venezolana. No.3, 6.
CARTER, ELLIOTT, 1908– .
Choral music.
In: Music Press, Inc. [Choral series]. Vol.119, 120.
Pastoral, for piano and viola [or] English horn or clarinet.
In: New music. Vol.18. No.3. Apr.1945.
Piano music.
In: Boletín latino-americano de música. Vol.5.
Sonata for violoncello and piano.
In: Society for the Publication of American Music. Publications. 34th season. 1952–53.
CARULLI, FERDINANDO, 1770–1841.
Sonata A dur und D dur für Gitarre und Hammerklavier. Op.21. Nr.1–2.
In: Albert. Die Gitarre in der Haus- und Kammermusik vor 100 Jahren (1780–1820). No.2–3.
CARVAJAL, ARMANDO, 1893– .
3 Pieces for children. Piano.
In: New music. Vol.12. No.4. July 1939.
CARVALHO, DINORÁ DE.
Música de câmara.
In: Boletín latino-americano de música. Vol.6.
CARVALHO, JOÃO DE SOUSA, 1745–1798.
L'amore industrioso.
In: Portugaliae musica. Sér.B. Vol.2.
Keyboard music.
In: Kastner. Cravistas portuguezes.
In: Kastner. Silva iberica.
CARVER, ROBERT, b.ca.1491.
Collected works. v.1– .
CASANOVAS, NARCIS, 1747–1799.
(var. sp.: Narcis Casanoves).
Instrumental music.
In: Mestres de l'escolania de Montserrat. (Pujol, ed. Musica instrumental. Vol.1).
Keyboard music.
In: Nin y Castellano. Dix-sept sonates et pièces anciennes d'auteurs espagnols.
Organ music.
In: Muset. Early Spanish organ music.
CASCIA, GIOVANNI DA, *see* GIOVANNI DA CASCIA (JOHANNES DE FLORENTIA).
CASCIOLINI, CLAUDIO, b.ca.1670.
Sacred music.
In: Proske. Musica divina. Annus primus. Tom 2; Annus secundus. Tom 2.
In: Proske. Selectus novus missarum. Annus secundus. Tom 2.
CASEDA, DIEGO, d.1723.
Sacred music.
In: Eslava y Elizondo. Lira sacro-hispana. 17th century. i.1.
CASEDA, J. DE.
Sacred music.
In: Eslava y Elizondo. Lira sacro-hispana. 18th century. i.1.
CASELLA, ALFREDO, 1883–1947.
Keyboard music.
In: Tagliapietra. Antologia di musica antica e moderna per pianoforte. Bd.18.
CASELLA, ENRIQUE M.
Songs with piano.
In: Boletín latino-americano de música. Vol.1.
CASERTA, ANTHONELLO DA, 14th CENTURY.
(var. sp.: Anthonellus de Caserta; Anthonello de Caserta).
Notes pour moi.
In: Parrish. A treasury of early music. No.17.
Secular music.
In: Apel. French secular music of the late fourteenth century.
CASIMIRI, RAFFAELE CASIMIRO, 1880–1943. ed.
Missa: Cantantibus organis. Caecilia.
In: Monumenta polyphoniae italicae. Vol.1.
CASINI, GIOVANNI MARIA, ca.1670–ca.1715.
Selections.
In: Torchi. L'arte musicale in Italia. Bd.3.
Organ music.
In: Fuser. Classici italiani dell' organo.

In: Guilmant. Archives des maîtres de l'orgue. Vol.10.
Sacred music.
In: Proske. Musica divina. Annus primus. Tom 2, 3.
CASOLA, FRANCESCO.
Quam candidus es. Sopran (Tenor) und B.C.
In: Cantio sacra. No.53.
CASSEL, BIBLIOTHÈQUE DE.
Manuscrit.
In: Écorcheville. Vingt suites d'orchestre du XVIIe siècle français.
CASTELLO, DARIO, 16th–17th CENTURIES.
Zwei Sonaten für Violine und Klavier.
In: Diletto musicale. No.37.
CASTELNUOVO-TEDESCO, MARIO, 1895– .
Fanfare. Organ.
In: Contemporary organ series. No.28.
Keyboard music.
In: Tagliapietra. Antologia di musica antica e moderna per pianoforte. Bd.18.
CASTILETI, JOAN, *see* GUYOT, JEAN.
CASTILLEJA, PEDRO FERNÁNDEZ DE, *see* FERNÁNDEZ DE CASTILLEJA, PEDRO.
CASTILLO, DIEGO DEL, 16th CENTURY.
O altitudo divitiarum.
In: Polifonía española. Vol.7.
Sacred music.
In: Eslava y Elizondo. Lira sacro-hispana. 16th century. i.2.
CASTRO, JEAN DE, 16th CENTURY.
(var. sp.: Joannes de Castro).
Sacred music.
In: Rubio. Antologia polifonica sacra. Vol.1.
CASTRO, JOSÉ MARÍA, 1892– .
Piano music.
In: Boletín latino-americano de música. Vol.4.
CASTRO, JUAN JOSÉ, 1895– .
Piano music.
In: Boletín latino-americano de música. Vol.1.
CASTRO, SERGIO FEDERICO DE, 1922– .
Canciones.
In: Instituto Interamericano de Musicologia. Publicaciónes. No.22.
CASTRUCCI, PIETRO, 1679–1752.
Sonata (D). Violin and piano.
In: Moffat. Meister-Schule der alten Zeit. Violin-Sonaten. No.35.
Sonate a violino, violine e cembalo: Sonata in sol minore, Op.1.
In: Somma. Musiche vocali e strumentali sacre e profane, Sec.XVII–XVIII–XIX. Vol.25.
CATALUNYA–MUSIC.
In: Barcelona. Biblioteca Central. Sección de Música. Publicaciones. Vol.10.
CATEL, CHARLES SIMON, 1773–1830.
Les bayadères.
In: Les chefs d'oeuvres classiques de l'opéra français.
CATHEDRAL MUSIC, *see* ENGLAND–CATHEDRAL MUSIC; ITALY–CATHEDRAL MUSIC.
CATHOLIC CHURCH, ROMAN. LITURGY AND RITUAL.
In: Plainsong and Mediaeval Music Society. Publications.
CATHOLIC CHURCH, ROMAN. LITURGY AND RITUAL. GRADUAL.
In: Publikationen älterer Musik. Jahrg.5, 7.
CATO, DIOMEDES, 16th–17th CENTURIES.
Organ music.
In: Corpus of early keyboard music. Vol.10. Pt.4.
Preludes, fantasies, dances and madrigals for lute.
In: Denkmäler altpolnischer Musik. Vol.24.
CATURLA, ALEJANDRO GARCIA, 1906–1940.
Canciones.
In: Instituto Interamericano de Musicologia. Publicaciónes. No.29.
Comparsa (Negro dance). From the Second suite of Cuban dances.
In: New music. Vol.10. No.3. Apr.1937.
Preludio corto. Sonata corta. Piano.
In: New music. Vol.7. No.4. July 1934.
Primero suite Cubana. Winds and piano.
In: New music. Orchestra series. No.10.
Yambambó. Canto negro para voz y piano.
In: New music. Vol.10. No.3. Apr.1937.
CAURROY, FRANÇOIS EUSTACHE DU, SIEUR DE ST. FRÉMIN, 1549–1609.
(var. sp.: Cauroy).
Chansons.
In: Lesure. Anthologie de la chanson parisienne au XVIe siècle.
Choral music.
In: Recueil de musique ancienne. Recueil des morceaux de musique ancienne. Bd.10.
Mélanges.
In: Expert. Les maîtres musiciens de la Renaissance française. Vol.17.
Organ music.
In: Bonnet. An anthology of early French organ music.
In: Raugel. Les maîtres français de l'orgue. Vol.2.
In: Raugel. Quarante-six pièces pour orgue ou ou harmonium.
CAVACCIO, GIOVANNI, ca.1556–1626.
Selections.
In: Torchi. L'arte musicale in Italia. Bd.3.
Organ music.
In: Cantantibus organis. Vol.11.
CAVALIERI, EMILIO DEL, ca.1550–1602.
(var. sp.: Emilio de Cavalieri).
Selections.
In: Crotch. Specimens of various styles of music. Vol.2.
Choral music.
In: Engel. Three centuries of choral music. Vol.2.
Rappresentazione di anima e di corpo.
In: I classici della musica italiana. Vol.10.
In: I classici della musica italiana. Raccolta nazionale delle musiche italiane. Quad. 35–36.
In: Mantica. Prime fioriture del melodramma italiano. Vol.1.
In: Parrish. A treasury of early music. No.37.
CAVALLI, PIETRO FRANCESCO, 1602–1676.
Arias.
In: Parisotti. Arie antiche. Bd.2, 3.
Il giasone.
In: Publikationen älterer praktischer und

theoretischer Musikwerke. Jahrg.11..
Vier Marianische Antiphonen.
In: Musica divina. Vol.1, 2, 3, 4.
Songs.
In: Jeppesen. La flora. Vol.1, 3.
Vocal music.
In: Gevaert. Les gloires de l'Italie. Vol.1, 2.
CAVALLOS, FRANCISCO.
Exaudiat.
In: Polifonía española. Vol.15.
CAVAZZONI, GIROLAMO, ca.1520–1560.
(var. sp.: Cavassoni).
Selections.
In: Torchi. L'arte musicale in Italia. Bd.3.
Composizioni.
In: I classici della musica italiana. Vol.6.
Dal I e II libro di intavolature per organo.
In: I classici della musica italiana. Raccolta nazionale delle musiche italiane. Quad.23–27.
Keyboard music.
In: Apel. Musik aus früher Zeit für Klavier. Bd.1.
In: Tagliapietra. Antologia di musica antica e moderna per pianoforte. Bd.1.
Organ music.
In: Cantantibus organis. Vol.4.
In: Elkan-Vogel organ series. Vol.1.
In: Froidebise. Anthologie de l'orgue. Vol.1.
In: Fuser. Classici italiani dell'organo.
In: Klein. The first four centuries of music for the organ from Dunstable to Bach (1370–1749).
In: Peeters. Anthologia pro organo. Vol.3.
In: Pierront. Cent versets de Magnificat.
CAVAZZONI, MARCO ANTONIO, 15th CENTURY.
(var. sp.: Marco Antonio [Cavazzoni] da Bologna).
Two French chansons and a recercar.
In: Early Italian keyboard music. No.2.
Organ music.
In: I classici musicali italiani. Vol.1.
In: Froidebise. Anthologie de l'orgue. Vol.1.
In: Fuser. Classici italiani dell'organo.
In: Jeppesen. Die italienische Orgelmusik am Anfang des Cinquecento.
CAVENDISH, MICHAEL, ca.1565–1628.
Madrigals.
In: Fellowes. The English madrigal school. Vol.36, 37.
In: The triumphs of Oriana.
Songs.
In: Fellowes. The English school of lutenist song writers. 2d series. Vol.7.
CAVOS, CATTERINO, 1775–1840.
Vocal music.
In: Sammlung russischer Romanzen. No.240.
CAZA, F.
Tractato vulgare de canto figurato.
In: Hirsch. Veröffentlichungen. [Bd.] 1.
CAZDEN, NORMAN, 1914– .
Piano music.
In: Boletín latino-americano de música. Vol.5.
Sonatina. Op.7. Piano.
In: New music. Vol.13. No.2. Jan.1940.
CAZZATI, MAURITIO.
Capriccio a tre, per due violini e basso continuo, Op.L/29. "Il Giustavilani."
In: Hausmusik. No.145.
Dulcis amor. Bass und B.C.
In: Cantio sacra. No.55.
In Calvaria rupe. Bass und B.C.
In: Cantio sacra. No.19.
Triosonate D-moll für zwei Violinen und Basso Continuo.
In: Hortus musicus. No.34.
CEBALLOS, FRANCISCO, *see* CEVALLOS, FRANCISCO.
CEBALLOS, RODRIGO (RODERICUS), *see* CEVALLOS, RODRIGO.
CEREROLS, JOAN, 1618–1676.
Works. [v.] 1–3.
In: Mestres de l'escolania de Montserrat.
ČERNOHORSKÝ, BOHUSLAV, *see* CZERNOHORSKÝ, BOHUSLAV.
CERTON, PIERRE, d.1572.
Selections.
In: Smith. Musica antiqua.
Chansons.
In: Bordes. Chansonnier du XVe siècle.
In: Cauchie. Quinze chansons françaises du XVIe siècle.
In: Das Chorwerk. No.82.
In: Einstein. Beispielsammlung zur älteren Musikgeschichte.
In: Lesure. Anthologie de la chanson parisienne au XVIe siècle.
In: Publikationen älterer praktischer und theoretischer Musikwerke. Jahrg.27.
Choral music.
In: Commer. Collectio operum musicorum batavorum saeculi XVI. Bd.12.
In: Engel. Three centuries of choral music. Vol.1.
In: Der Kammerchor. Vol.1.
Church music.
In: Motett Society. [Collection of ancient church music]. Division 3.
Messes à 4 voix.
In: Expert. Monuments de la musique française au temps de la Renaissance. Vol.2.
Motets.
In: Attaingnant. Treize livres de motets. Livre 7.
CERVETTO, GIACOMO BASSEVI, 1682–1783.
Sonate (G). Violoncello and piano.
In: Moffat. Meister-Schule der alten Zeit. Violoncello-Sonaten. No.10.
CESARI, GAETANO, 1870–1934. ed.
La musica in Cremona, nella seconda metà del secolo XVI e I primordi dell'arte Monteverdiana.
In: Istituzioni e monumenti dell'arte musicale italiana. Vol.6.
CESARINI, C. FR.
Arias.
In: Landshoff. Alte Meister des Bel Canto. Eine Sammlung von Arien. Vol.1–2, 3.
CESARIS, JOHANNES, 15th CENTURY.
Works.
In: Reaney. Early fifteenth-century music. Vol.1.
Sacred music.
In: Plainsong and Mediaeval Music Society. Publications. (Borren).

CESTI, MARC' ANTONIO, 1623–1669.
Selections.
In: Crotch. Specimens of various styles of music. Vol.2.
Airs.
In: Prunières. Les maîtres du chant. Recueil 5.
Arias.
In: Landshoff. Alte Meister des Bel Canto. Eine Sammlung von Arien. Vol.1–2, 3.
In: Parisotti. Arie antiche. Bd.1, 2.
Cantatas.
In: The Wellesley edition. No.5.
La dori.
In: Publikationen älterer praktischer und theoretischer Musikwerke. Jahrg.11.
Il pomo d'oro.
In: Denkmäler der Tonkunst in Österreich. Vol.6. (Jg.III/2); Vol.9. (Jg.IV/2).
Vocal music.
In: Gevaert. Les gloires de l'Italie. Vol.1, 2.
CEUALLOS, *see* CEVALLOS, RODRIGO.
CEVALLOS, FRANCISCO, d.1571.
(var. sp.: F. Ceballos).
Sacred music.
In: Eslava y Elizondo. Lira sacro-hispana. 16th century. i.1.
CEVALLOS, RODRIGO, 16th CENTURY.
(var. sp.: Rodrigo Ceballos; Rodericus Ceballos; Ceuallos).
Motets.
In: Elúsitiza. Antología musical.
Psalmodia modulata.
In: Pedrell. Hispaniae schola musica sacra. Bd.6.
Sacred music.
In: Rubio. Antologia polifonica sacra. Vol.1.
CHABRAN, FRANCESCO, b.1723.
La chasse.
In: L'école du violon au XVIIe et XVIIIe siècle. No.1334.
CHAIKOVSKIĬ, PETR IL'ICH, *see* TCHAIKOVSKIĬ, PETER ILICH.
CHAIX, CHARLES, 1885– .
Organ music.
In: Bedell. The French organist. Vol.2.
CHAMBER MUSIC AND MUSIC FOR STRING INSTRUMENTS–MISCELLANEOUS COLLECTIONS.
See also chamber works in the various Denkmäler series.
See also chamber works in the various Das Erbe deutscher Musik series.
In: Alte Musik.
In: Antiqua Edition.
In: Bausteine.
In: Collegium musicae novae.
In: Concertino.
In: Contemporary Japanese music series. No.9, 12, 22, 27, 28, 30, 32.
In: Corona.
In: Diletto musicale.
In: Flores musicae.
In: Für Kenner und Liebhaber.
In: Hortus musicus.
In: Kammersonaten.
In: Lea pocket scores.
In: Mitteldeutsches Musikarchiv. Reihe II.
In: Moecks Kammermusik.
In: Moffat. Kammer-Sonaten für Violine und Pianoforte des 17. und 18. Jahrhunderts.
In: Moffat. Meister-Schule der alter Zeit. Sammlung klassischer Violin-Sonaten.
In: Moffat. Meister-Schule der alter Zeit. Sammlung klassicher Violoncello-Sonaten.
In: Moffat. Trio-Sonaten alter Meister.
In: Music for wind instruments by 18th century masters.
In: Musica practica.
In: Musikschätze der Vergangenheit.
In: Nagels Musik-Archiv.
In: Organum. 3.Reihe.
In: Rahter's Kammer-Orchester.
In: Riemann. Collegium musicum.
In: Riemann. Old chamber music.
In: Schering. Perlen alter Kammermusik deutscher und italienischer Meister.
In: Seventeenth-century chamber music.
In: Society for the Publication of American music.
In: Sondheimer. Werke aus dem 18. Jahrhundert.
In: Spielstücke für Blockflöten, Geigen, Lauten oder andere Instrumente.
In: Volk Musiziert.
In: Wasielewski. Instrumentalsätze vom Ende des XVI. bis Ende des XVII. Jahrhunderts.
In: Wasielewski. Instrumentalsätze vom Ende des XVI. bis Ende des XVII. Jahrhunderts. Neuer mit einem Inhaltsverzeichnis versehen Abdruck.
CHAMBONNIÈRES, JACQUES CHAMPION DE, ca.1602–ca.1672.
Oeuvres complètes. 132p.
—— Reprint. [1967]. 139p.
Keyboard music.
In: Apel. Musik aus früher Zeit für Klavier. Bd.2.
In: Farrenc. Le trésor des pianistes. Vol.2.
In: Georgii. Keyboard music of the Baroque and Rococo. Vol.1.
In: Grovlez. Les plus belles pièces de clavessin de l'école française. Vol.1.
In: Köhler. Les maîtres du clavecin. Heft 12.
In: Monuments of music and music literature. First series. No.3.
In: Oesterle. Early keyboard music. Vol.1.
In: Pauer. Alte Klavier-Musik. 1st series. Part 6.
In: Pessl. The art of the suite.
In: Selva. Pièces de clavecin des XVIIme et XVIIIme siècles.
In: Tagliapietra. Antologia di musica antica e moderna per pianoforte. Bd.7.
Organ music.
In: Bonnet. An anthology of early French organ music.
In: Raugel. Les maîtres français de l'orgue. Vol.1.
In: Raugel. Les maîtres français de l'orgue aux XVIIème et XVIIIème siècles.
CHAMPIGNY.
Selections.

In: Crotch. Specimens of various styles of music. Vol.3.
CHANCY, FRANÇOIS DE, 17th CENTURY.
Songs.
In: Prunières. Les maîtres du chant. Recueil 4.
LE CHANSONNIER CANGÉ.
In: Beck. Anthologie de cent chansons de trouvères et de troubadours des XIIe et XIIIe siècles.
In: Beck. Les chansonniers des troubadours et des trouvères.
CHANSONNIER D'ARRAS.
Le chansonnier d'Arras. 19p.
CHANSONNIERS.
In: Aich. Das Liederbuch des Arnt von Aich.
In: Beck. Anthologie de cent chansons de trouvères et de troubadours des XIIe et XIIIe siècles.
In: Beck. Les chansonniers des troubadours et des trouvères.
In: Bordes. Chansonnier du XVe siècle.
In: Chansonnier d'Arras. Le chansonnier d'Arras.
In: Codex Escorial. Chansonnier. Ms. V.III.24.
In: Copenhagen Kongelige Bibliotek. Mss. (Thottske Samling 291^8). Der kopenhagener Chansonnier).
In: Droz. Trois chansonniers français du XVe siècle.
In: Paris. Bibliothèque de l'Arsenal. Mss. (No.5198). Le chansonnier de l'Arsenal.
CHANSONS (*see also* FRANCE–MUSIC; SONGS, FRENCH).
In: Attaingnant. Chansons und Tänze.
In: Attaingnant. Transcriptions of chansons for keyboard.
In: Brown. Theatrical chansons of the 15th and early 16th centuries.
In: Cauchie. Quinze chansons françaises du XVIe siècle.
In: Collegium musicum. Vol.2.
In: Documenta historica musicae.
In: Der Kammerchor.
In: Lesure. Anthologie de la chanson parisienne au XVIe siècle.
In: Music Press, Inc. [Choral series]. Vol.54.
In: Weckerlin. Échos du temps passé.
CHANT (PLAIN, GREGORIAN, ETC.).
In: Anthology of music. Vol.18.
In: Crotch. Specimens of various styles of music. Vol.2.
In: Paléographie musicale.
In: Paléographie musicale. Sér.2.
In: Plainsong and Mediaeval Music Society. Publications.
In: Soderlund. Examples illustrating the development of melodic line and contrapuntal style, from Greek melody to Mozart.
In: Soderlund. Examples of Gregorian chant and works by Orlandus Lassus and Giovanni Pierluigi Palestrina.
In: Soderlund. Examples of Gregorian chant and works by Orlandus Lassus, Giovanni Pierluigi Palestrina and Marc Antonio Ingegneri.
THE CHARACTER PIECE. (KAHL).
In: Anthology of music. Vol.8.
CHARITÉ, 15th CENTURY.
Selections.
In: Reaney. Early fifteenth-century music. Vol.2.
CHARLEMAGNE, 742–814.
Vocal music.
In: Delsarte. Archives du chant. Livr.13. No.1.
CHARPENTIER, JEAN JACQUES BEAUVARLET, 1734–1794.
Organ music.
In: Raugel. Les maîtres français de l'orgue. Vol.2.
Sonata. Piano. Op.II, No.6.
In: Reeser. De klaviersonate.
CHARPENTIER, MARC ANTOINE, 1634–1704.
Oeuvres. v.1– .
Selections.
In: Expert. Répertoire classique de musique. 1re année.
Airs.
In: Prunières. Les maîtres du chant. Recueil 4.
Concert pour quatre parties de violes.
In: Musiques françaises. Vol.16.
Vier Elevations. Sopran (Tenor) und B.C., Tenor (Sopran) und B.C., Alt und B.C.
In: Cantio sacra. No.26.
Judicium Salomonis.
In: Recent researches in the music of the Baroque era. Vol.1.
Sieben Motetten. Sopran (Tenor) und B.C., Tenor (Sopran) und B.C.
In: Cantio sacra. No.30.
Nuit. Extrait de "In nativitatem domini."
In: Musiques françaises. Vol.8.
Transcriptions pour orgue.
In: Orgue et liturgie. Vol.53.
Pie Jesus–Magnificat.
In: Flores musicae. Vol.1. Pt.1–2.
Le reniement de St. Pierre.
In: Parrish. A treasury of early music. No.42.
Suite für Streichorchester.
In: Concertino.
CHAUMONT.
Livre d'orgue.
In: Monumenta leodiensium musicorum. Vol.1.
CHAUVIGNY, DE, *see* DE CHAUVIGNY.
CHAVARRI, EDUARDO LOPEZ, 1875– .
Keyboard music.
In: Guenther. Collection espagnole.
CHÁVEZ, CARLOS, 1899– .
Arbolucu.
In: Music Press, Inc. [Choral series]. Vol.113.
7 Pieces for piano.
In: New music. Vol.10. No.1. Oct.1936.
Sonata for piano.
In: New music. Vol.6. No.2. Jan.1933.
Sonatina; Violin and piano.
In: New music. Vol.1. No.4. July 1928.
Spiral movement for violin and piano.
In: New music. Vol.8. No.3. Apr.1935.
36, for piano.
In: New music. Vol.4. No.1. Oct.1930.
CHÉDEVILLE, ESPRIT PHILIPPE, d.1782.
Sechs galante Duos für zwei gleiche Melodieinstrumente.
In: Hortus musicus. No.81.

CHÉDEVILLE, NICOLAS, LE CADET, 18th CENTURY.
? La chicane.
In: L'école du violon au XVIIe et XVIIIe siècle. No.1342.
Zwei Pastoral-Sonaten, für zwei Quer- oder Blockflöten.
In: Nagels Musik-Archiv. No.26.
Sixtième sonate. Extraite des six sonates pour hautboix (flute ou violon) avec la basse.
In: Musiques françaises. Vol.14.
? Le tapage.
In: L'école du violon au XVIIe et XVIIIe siècle. No.1347.
CHÉDEVILLE, PIERRE L'AINÉ, *see* AINÉ, PIERRE CHÉDEVILLE L'.
CHERUBINI, LUIGI, 1760–1842.
Selections.
In: Expert. Collection d'ordre lyrique.
Arias.
In: Parisotti. Arie antiche. Bd.3.
Arie per canto e pianoforte.
In: I classici della musica italiana. Raccolta nazionale delle musiche italiane. Quad. 172–173.
Le duo giornate.
In: I classici della musica italiana. Vol.7.
Fugue in C. Piano.
In: Roitzsch. Alte Klavier-Musik.
Keyboard music.
In: Köhler. Les maîtres du clavecin. Heft 7.
In: Tagliapietra. Antologia di musica antica e moderna per pianoforte. Bd.14.
Offertorium; Graduale to Mass No.4; Regina coeli; Tantum ergo und Genitori.
In: Ecclesiasticon. No.25–31, 32, 33, 34.
Part music.
In: Hullah. Part music. Class A.2. Vol.1.
Sonate No.3. (B flat).
In: Pauer. Alte Meister. No.17.
CHIERISY, 15th CENTURY.
Sacred music.
In: Plainsong and Mediaeval Music Society. Publications. (Borren).
CHILD, WILLIAM, 1606–1697.
Selections.
In: Crotch. Specimens of various styles of music. Vol.2.
In: Smith. Musica antiqua.
Anthems.
In: Music Press, Inc. [Choral series]. No.61.
Part music.
In: Hullah. Part music. Class A.1. Vol.1, 2.
Sacred music.
In: Arnold. Cathedral music. Vol.1.
In: Boyce. Cathedral music. Vol.1, 2, 3; 1849, Vol.1, 2, 3.
CHILESOTTI, OSCAR, 1848–1916. ed.
Musica del passato.
In: Chilesotti. Biblioteca di rarità musicali. Vol.8.
CHILIANDORICA PALAEOSLAVICA.
In: Monumenta musicae byzantinae. Série-principale. Vol.5. Pt.1–2.
CHINA–MUSIC.
In: Crotch. Specimens of various styles of music. Vol.1.
CHINZER, GIOVANNI, ca.1695–1750.
(var. sp.: Giovanni Chintzer).
Andante.
In: L'école du violon au XVIIe et XVIIIe siècle. No.1294.
CHIRBURY.
Selections.
In: Plainsong and Mediaeval Music Society. Publications. (Old Hall manuscript).
CHOIR BOOKS.
In: Liturgical choir books.
CHOPIN, FRYDERYK FRANCISZEK, 1810–1849.
Werke. 14v.
Complete works. v.1– .
Oeuvres complètes. v.1– .
Complete works for the piano. 15v.
Sämtliche Werke. 3v.
Sämtliche Werke. Neue Ausgabe. 12v.
The 4 Ballades and the 4 Scherzi.
In: Lea pocket scores. No.67.
Études complete. (Op.10, 25, Op.posth.).
In: Lea pocket scores. No.44.
Keyboard music.
In: Farrenc. Le trésor des pianistes. Vol.23.
In: Tagliapietra. Antologia di musica antica e moderna per pianoforte. Bd.15.
The mazurkas and polonaises.
Complete.
In: Lea pocket scores. No.119/120.
The complete nocturnes (19) and rondos (3).
In: Lea pocket scores. No.93.
The 25 Preludes (Op.28, 45); 2 Piano sonatas (Op.35, 58); Fantasy in f (Op.49).
In: Lea pocket scores. No.5.
The complete waltzes (15) and impromptus (4).
In: Lea pocket scores. No.94.
CHORAL MUSIC–MISCELLANEOUS COLLECTIONS.
See also choral works in the various Denkmäler series.
See also choral works in the various Das Erbe deutscher Musik series.
In: Anthology of music. Vol.3, 10.
In: Antiqua Chorbuch. 2v.
In: Arion. 3v.
In: Billings. The continental harmony.
In: Cantio sacra.
In: Capella.
In: Casimiri. Anthologia polyphonica auctorum saeculi XVI paribus vocibus. 2v.
In: Chor-Archiv.
In: Chorbuch für die Kirchenchöre Sachsens.
In: Das Chorwerk.
In: Christophorus-Chorwerk.
In: Clément. Chants de la Sainte-Chapelle tirés de manuscrits du XIIIe siècle.
In: Commer. Cantica sacra.
In: Commer. Collectio operum musicorum batavorum saeculi XVI.
In: Concerts spirituels ou recueil de motets.
In: Contemporary Japanese music series. No.24.
In: Dargomizhsky. Complete vocal ensembles and choruses.
In: Dehn. Sammlung älterer Musik aus dem XVI. und XVII. Jahrhundert.
In: Dessoff choir series.

In: Droz. Poètes et musiciens du XVe siècles.
In: Early Bodleian music. [I–III].
In: Ecclesiasticon.
In: Engel. Three centuries of choral music: Renaissance to Baroque.
In: Eslava y Elizondo. Lira sacro-hispana.
In: Ghisi. Feste musicali della Firenze Medicea (1480–1589).
In: Hullah. Part music.
In: Hullah. Vocal scores.
In: Der Kammerchor.
In: Latrobe, C. I. Selection of sacred music from the works of some of the most eminent composers of Germany and Italy.
In: Latrobe, J. A. The music of the church considered in its various branches, congregational and choral.
In: Maldéghem. Trésor musical.
In: Moser. Die Kantorei der Spätgotik.
In: Motett Society. [Collection of ancient church music].
In: Music Press, Inc. [Choral series].
In: Musica antiqua batava.
In: Musica practica.
In: Musica sacra.
In: Nagels Männerchor-Blätter.
In: Nagels Musik-Archiv.
In: Organum. 1.Reihe. 2.Reihe.
In: Page. Harmonia sacra.
In: Petrucci. Harmonice musices Odhecaton A.
In: Pistone. Capalavori della polifonia italiana.
In: Plainsong and Mediaeval Music Society. Publications.
In: Proske. Musica divina.
In: Proske. Selectus novus missarum.
In: Recueil de musique ancienne. Recueil des morceaux de musique ancienne.
In: Riemann. Hausmusik aus alter Zeit.
In: Rochlitz. Sammlung vorzüglicher Gesangstücke.
In: Rubio. Antologia polifonica sacra.
In: Schering. Einstimmige Chor- und Sololieder des XVI. Jahrhunderts mit Instrumental-Begleitung.
In: Schmidt-Garre. Benedicamus Domino. v.1– .
In: Schöberlein. Schatz des liturgischer Chor- und Gemeindegesanges.
In: Schweizer Sing- und Spielmusik.
In: Smijers. Van Ockeghem tot Sweelinck.
In: Smith. Musica antiqua.
In: Societas Polyphonica Romanae. Repertorium.
In: Squire. Ausgewählte Madrigale und mehrstimmige Gesänge berühmter Meister des 16., 17. Jahrhundert.
In: Staatliche Akademie für Kirchen- und Schulmusik, Berlin. Veröffentlichungen.
In: Stein. Twelve Franco-Flemish masses of the early 16th century.
In: Surzyński. Monumenta musicae sacrae in Polonia.
In: Tucher. Kirchengesänge der berühmtesten älteren Meister.
In: Tucher. Schatz des evangelischen Kirchengesanges.
In: Van. Les monuments de l'ars nova.
In: Winterfeld. Der evangelische Kirchengesang.
In: Wolf. Chor- und Hausmusik aus älter Zeit.
In: Zahn. Die Melodien der deutschen evangelischen Kirchenlieder.

CHORALE, LUTHERAN.
In: Zahn. Die Melodien der deutschen evangelischen Kirchenlieder.

CHOU, WEN-CHUNG, 1923– .
7 Poems of T'ang dynasty.
In: New music. Vol.25. No.4. July 1952.

CHRISTENIUS, JOHANN, ca.1600.
Choral music.
In: Antiqua Chorbuch. Vol.1. Heft 4.

CHRISTENSEN, BERNHARD, 1906– .
Karneval. Orchestra.
In: Samfundet til Udgivelse af dansk Musik. Ser.III. No.111.

CHRISTIANOWITSCH.
Vocal music.
In: Sammlung russischer Romanzen. No.87.

CHRISTIANSEN, CHRISTIAN.
Songs.
In: Samfundet til Udgivelse af dansk Musik. Suppl. 1925–26.

CHRISTIANSEN, HENNING.
Sonate, Op.13.
In: Samfundet til Udgivelse af dansk Musik. Ser.III. No.173.

CHRISTMAS CAROLS FROM ANCIENT SOURCES FOR UNISON OR MIXED VOICES.
In: Music Press, Inc. [Choral series]. No.59.

CHYBIŃSKI, ADOLF, 1880–1952.
36 Dances from the Tablature by Jan de Lublin.
In: Denkmäler altpolnischer Musik. Vol.20.

CIAIA, AZZOLINO BERNARDINO DELLA, *see* DELLA CIAIA, AZZOLINO BERNARDINO.

CIAMPI, FRANCESCO, ca.1695–d.after 1735.
Sacred music.
In: Latrobe, C. I. Selection of sacred music.
In: Latrobe, J. A. The music of the church.

CIBULKA, MATOUS ALOIS, 1768–1845.
Keyboard music.
In: Musica antiqua bohemica. Vol.14.

CICONIA, JOHANNES, 14th–15th CENTURIES.
Sacred music.
In: Plainsong and Mediaeval Music Society. Publications. (Borren).

CIFRA, ANTONIO, 1584–1629.
Missa s'allor che più sperai. S.A.T.B.
In: Basilica. 1953.
Songs.
In: Jeppesen. La flora. Vol.3.

CILÈA, FRANCESCO, 1866–1950.
Keyboard music.
In: Tagliapietra. Antologia di musica antica e moderna per pianoforte. Bd.18.

CIMA, ANDREA, 17th CENTURY.
Organ music.
In: Fuser. Classici italiani dell'organo.

CIMA, GIOVANNI PAOLO, 16th–17th CENTURIES.
Selections.

In: Torchi. L'arte musicale in Italia. Bd.3.
CIMAROSA, DOMENICO, 1749–1801.
Arias.
In: Landshoff. Alte Meister des Bel Canto. Eine Sammlung von Arien. Vol.1–2.
In: Parisotti. Arie antiche. Bd.3.
Vocal music.
In: Gevaert. Les gloires de l'Italie. Vol.1, 2.
CIRRI, GIOVANNI BATTISTA, b.ca.1740.
Concerto in A, Op.14, No.1. (violoncello solo, strings).
In: Antica musica strumentale italiana. Ser.I. Vol.9.
Part music.
In: Hullah. Part music. Class C. Sacred.
CIVITATE, ANTONIUS DE, *see* ANTONIUS DE CIVITATE.
CLARI, GIOVANNI CARLO MARIA, 1677–1754.
Choral music.
In: Recueil de musique ancienne. Recueil des morceaux de musique ancienne. Bd.3, 8.
Sacred music.
In: The Fitzwilliam music. Bd.1, 2, 3, 4, 5.
CLARINET.
In: Das Erbe deutscher Musik. 1.Reihe. Vol.41.
CLARKE, JEREMIAH, ca.1673–1707.
Keyboard music.
In: Fuller-Maitland. The contemporaries of Purcell. Vol.5.
In: Herrmann. Contemporaries of Purcell.
Part music.
In: Hullah. Part music. Class A.1. Vol.1, 2; Class C. Sacred.
Sacred music.
In: Arnold. Cathedral music. Vol.1.
In: Boyce. Cathedral music. Vol.2, 3; 1849, Vol.2, 3.
In: Page. Harmonia sacra. Vol.1, 2.
THE CLASSICS. (STEPHENSON).
In: Anthology of music. Vol.6.
CLAUDE DE SERMISY, *see* SERMISY, CLAUDE DE.
CLAUDE LE JEUNE, *see* LE JEUNE, CLAUDE.
CLAUDIN, *see* LE JEUNE, CLAUDE.
CLAUSING, FRANZ.
Introitus, Sequenz und Psalm.
In: Christophorus-Chorwerk. Heft 20.
CLAVICHORD MUSIC, *see* KEYBOARD MUSIC–CLAVICHORD, HARPSICHORD, PIANO, VIRGINAL.
CLEGHORN, JAMES.
How do you like this? Three ironies for piano.
In: New music. Vol.11. No.4. July 1938.
CLEMENS NON PAPA, *see* CLÉMENT, JACQUES.
CLÉMENT, CHARLES FRANÇOIS, b.ca.1720.
Sonata. Piano. Op.I, No.6.
In: Reeser. De klaviersonate.
CLÉMENT, JACQUES, 16th CENTURY.
(var. sp.: Clemens non Papa; Clement non Papa).
Opera omnia. v.1– .
Selections.
In: Maldéghem. Trésor musical.
In: Smith. Musica antiqua.
Chansons.
In: Publikationen älterer praktischer und theoretischer Musikwerke. Jahrg.27.
Choral music.
In: Antiqua Chorbuch. Vol.2. Heft 2.
In: Commer. Collectio operum musicorum batavorum saeculi XVI. Bd.1, 2, 3, 5, 8, 10, 11, 12.
In: Music Press, Inc. [Choral series]. Vol.126.
La, la, Maistre Pierre.
In: Arion. Vol.3.
Mass.
In: Stein. Twelve Franco-Flemish masses of the early 16th century.
Motets.
In: Das Chorwerk. No.72.
In: Vereniging voor Nederlandsche Muziekgeschiedenis. Uitgave. No.44.
Sacred music.
In: Proske. Musica divina. Annus primus. Tom 2.
Works arr. by Molinaro.
In: Molinaro. Intavolatura di liuto.
CLEMENTI, MUZIO, 1752–1832.
Works for pianoforte. v.1– .
Selections.
In: Crotch. Specimens of various styles of music. Vol.3.
Concerto in C.
In: Antica musica strumentale italiana. In preparation.
Fugue for piano in F.
In: Königliche Akademie der Künste. Auswahl vorzüglicher Musik-Werke. No.12.
Keyboard music.
In: Esposito. Early Italian piano music.
In: Farrenc. Le trésor des pianistes. Vol.16.
In: Tagliapietra. Antologia di musica antica e moderna per pianoforte. Bd.13.
Piano sonatas.
In: I classici della musica italiana. Vol.8.
In: I classici della musica italiana. Raccolte nazionale delle musiche italiane. Quad. 176–181.
In: Organum. 5.Reihe. Nr.1, 4.
In: Répertoire des clavicinistes. Heft 1, 10.
Sonate B-dur, Op.14, Nr.1.
In: Organum. 5.Reihe. Nr.18.
Sonate G-moll, Op.7, Nr.3; Sonate F-moll, Op.14, Nr.3.
In: Organum. 5.Reihe. Nr.15, 16.
Sonate H-moll, Op.40, Nr.2.
In: Organum. 5.Reihe. Nr.20.
Symphony in B flat, Op.44 (formerly Op.18).
In: Antica musica strumentale italiana. Ser.II. Vol.12.
Symphony in D, Op.44 (formerly Op.18).
In: Antica musica strumentale italiana. Ser.III. Vol.21.
Toccata in B flat. Piano.
In: Roitzsch. Alte Klavier-Musik.
CLÉRAMBAULT, LOUIS NICOLAS, 1676–1749.
Selections.
In: Expert. Répertoire classique de musique. 1re année.
Airs.
In: Prunières. Les maîtres du chant. Recueil 6.
Keyboard music.

In: Grovlez. Les plus belles pièces de clavessin de l'école française. Vol.2.
In: Herrmann. Lehrmeister und Schüler Joh. Seb. Bachs. Vol.1.
Organ music.
In: Anthologia antiqua. Vol.1.
In: Biggs. Treasury of early organ music.
In: Bonnet. Historical organ-recitals. Vol.1.
In: Guilmant. Archives des maîtres de l'orgue. Vol.3.
In: Guilmant. Concert historique d'orgue.
In: Klein. The first four centuries of music for the organ from Dunstable to Bach (1370–1749).
In: Liber organi. Bd.2.
In: The Liturgical Music Press, Inc. Masterpieces of organ music. Folio 31.
In: Peeters. Anthologia pro organo. Vol.2, 4.
In: Raugel. Les maîtres français de l'orgue. Vol.2.
Prelude in D minor. Organ.
In: Dickinson. Historical recital series for organ. Vol.2. No.31.
Sonate en sol majeur (2 violons et piano).
In: L'école du violon au XVIIe et XVIIIe siècle. No.1286.
CLÉREAU, PIERRE, 16th CENTURY.
Chansons.
In: Lesure. Anthologie de la chanson parisienne au XVIe siècle.
CLEVE, JOHANNES DE, ca.1529–1582.
(var. sp.: Joannes de Cleve).
Selections.
In: Denkmäler der Tonkunst in Österreich. Vol.90.
In: Maldéghem. Trésor musical.
Choral music.
In: Commer. Collectio operum musicorum batavorum saeculi XVI. Bd.4.
Missa, Rex Babylonis venit ad lacum.
In: Musik alter Meister. Heft 12.
Missa, Vous perdes temps.
In: Musik alter Meister. Heft 1.
CLODIENSI, J.
Sacred music.
In: Proske. Musica divina. Annus secundus. Tom 2.
In: Proske. Selectus novus missarum. Annus secundus. Tom 2.
CLUZEAU MORTET, LUIS, 1893–1957.
Selections.
In: Boletín latino-americano de música. Vol.3.
Mar de luna. (Canto y piano).
In: Instituto Interamericano de Musicologia. Publicaciónes. No.2.
COBBOLD, WILLIAM, 1560–1639.
Madrigal.
In: The triumphs of Oriana.
Vocal music.
In: Hullah. Vocal scores. II. Secular.
COCCHI, GIOACCHINO, ca.1715–1804.
Vocal music.
In: Gevaert. Les gloires de l'Italie. Vol.1.
COCLICO, ADRIAN PETIT, ca.1500–ca.1563.
Consolationes piae. Musica reservata. 1552.
In: Das Erbe deutscher Musik. 1.Reihe. Vol.42.
COCQ, JOAN LE, *see* LE COCQ, JOAN.
CODAX, MARTIN, 14th CENTURY.
Las siete canciones de amor. 14p., 10L.
CODEX: 339, 121, VI–34.
In: Paléographie musicale. Bd.I, IV, XV.
CODEX BIBL. LAURENTIANAE ASHBURNHAMENSIS.
In: Monumenta musicae byzantinae. Série-principale. Vol.4.
CODEX BRESLAU. MF. 2016.
Missa anonyma II.
In: Das Chorwerk. No.56.
CODEX CRYPTENSIS E, GAMMA, II.
In: Monumenta musicae byzantinae. Série-principale. Vol.3.
DER CODEX DES MAGISTER NICOLAUS APEL VON KÖNIGSHOFEN.
In: Das Erbe deutscher Musik. 1.Reihe. Vol.32/33/34.
CODEX ESCORIAL.
Codex Escorial. Chansonnier. 62 numb. leaves, [5] p.
In: Documenta musicologica. 2.Reihe. Vol.2.
CODEX MONASTERII HIBERORUM 470.
In: Monumenta musicae byzantinae. Série-principale. Vol.2.
CODEX VATICAN ROSSI 215.
In: Pirrotta. The music of fourteenth-century Italy. Vol.2.
CODEX VINCOBONENSIS THEOL. GR.181.
In: Monumenta musicae byzantinae. Série-principale. Vol.1.
COELHO, MANUEL RODRIGUES, b.before 1583–d.after 1623.
Flores de musica. Vol.1, 2.
In: Portugaliae musica. Sér.A. Vol.1, 3.
Keyboard music.
In: Kastner. Cravistas portuguezes.
COELHO NETTO, MARCOS.
Selections.
In: Lange. Archivo de música religiosa.
COENEN, JOHANNES MEINARDUS, 1824–1899.
(var. sp.: Hans Coenen).
Kinderzirkus Bum. Szenische Spielmusik.
In: Zeitschrift für Spielmusik. No.199.
Das Märchen vom Dicken.
In: Zeitschrift für Spielmusik. No.180.
COHEN, ALBERT.
Guillaume Gabriel Nivers.
In: Institute of Mediaeval Music. Musical theorists in translation. Vol.3.
COINCI, GAUTIER DE, 1177 (78)–1236.
Les chansons à la Vierge.
In: Société Française de Musicologie, Paris. Publications. Sér.I. Bd.15.
COKER, WILSON.
Woodwind quintet in three movements.
In: Society for the Publication of American Music. 43d season. 1963.
COLASSE, PASCAL, 1649–1709.
Les saisons; Thétis et Pélée.
In: Les chefs d'oeuvres classiques de l'opera français.
Vocal music.
In: Delsarte. Archives du chant. Livr.2. No.8.
COLE, JOHN.
Selections.
In: Smith. Musica antiqua.

Songs.
In: Plainsong and Mediaeval Music Society. Publications. (A collection of songs and madrigals . . .).
COLE, ULRIC, 1905– .
Quintet for piano and strings.
In: Society for the Publication of American Music. 22d season. 1940–41.
Sonata. Violin and piano.
In: Society for the Publication of American Music. 11th season. 1929–30.
COLEMAN, MARK.
Keyboard music.
In: Fuller-Maitland. The contemporaries of Purcell. Vol.6–7.
COLIN, PIERRE GILBERT, 16th CENTURY.
Chansons.
In: Publikationen älterer praktischer und theoretischer Musikwerke. Jahrg.27.
COLISTA, LELIO, *see* CALISTA, LELIO.
COLLEGRANO, ROSSO DA, *see* ROSSO DA COLLEGRANO.
COLLETT, JOHN, 18th CENTURY.
Sonate (B). Violin and piano.
In: Moffat. Meister-Schule der alten Zeit. Violin-Sonaten. No.34.
Sonata C-dur für Violine und Pianoforte.
In: Moffat. Kammer-Sonaten für Violine und Pianoforte. No.27.
COLMARER HANDSCHRIFT, DIE SANGESWEISEN DER.
In: Runge. Die Sangesweisen der Colmarer Handschrift und die Liederhandschrift Donaueschingen.
COLOBRANO, MICHELE ENRICO CARAFA DE, *see* CARAFA DE COLOBRANO, MICHELE ENRICO.
COLOMA, RAPHAEL.
Sacred music.
In: Rubio. Antologia polifonica sacra. Vol.1.
COLÓN, PEDRO NOLASCO, *see* NOLASCO COLÓN, PEDRO.
COLONNA, GIOVANNI PAOLO, 1637–1695.
Choral music.
In: Recueil de musique ancienne. Recueil des morceaux de musique ancienne. Bd.8.
Church music.
In: Motett Society. [Collection of ancient church music]. Division 2.
Sacred music.
In: The Fitzwilliam music. Bd.5.
Songs.
In: Jeppesen. La flora. Vol.3.
COMES, JUAN BAUTISTA, 1568–1643.
Danzas del Santísimo Corpus Christi. 144p.
Sacred music.
In: Eslava y Elizondo. Lira sacro-hispana. 17th century. i.1.
COMMETTE, EDOUARD, 1883– .
Organ music.
In: Bedell. The French organist. Vol.1.
In: Standard series of organ compositions. No.22.
COMPÈRE, LOYSET, d.1518.
Opera omnia. v.1– .
Selections.
In: Ambros. Auserwählte Tonwerke.
In: Maldéghem. Trésor musical.
Chanson.
In: Brown. Theatrical chansons of the 15th and early 16th centuries.
Choral music.
In: Droz. Poètes et musiciens du XVe siècles.
In: Smijers. Van Ockeghem tot Sweelinck. Aflg.4.
Karnevalslieder der Renaissance.
In: Das Chorwerk. No.43.
Missa "Alles regrets."
In: Das Chorwerk. No.55.
Motetten.
In: Chor-Archiv.
Le renvoy.
In: Dessoff choir series. No.42.
COMPONIMENTI MUSICALE. (1739?). (MUFFAT). FACSIMILE.
In: Monuments of music and music literature. First series. No.8.
THE CONCERTO GROSSO. (ENGEL).
In: Anthology of music. Vol.23.
CONDUCTUS, AN ANTHOLOGY OF POLYPHONIC. (KNAPP).
In: Collegium musicum. [Vol.7].
CONFORTO, GIOVANNI LUCA, b.ca.1560.
Breue et facile maniera d'essercitarsi a far passagi.
In: Hirsch. Veröffentlichungen. [Bd.].2.
CONGRÈS INTERNATIONAUX.
La musique dans les Congrès Internationaux. (1835–1939).
In: Société Française de Musicologie, Paris. Ser.II. Bd.10.
CONRAD, JOHANN CHRISTOPH.
Organ music.
In: Muziek voor de eredienst. Vol.2.
CONSERVATOIRE DE MUSIQUE DE PARIS, see BIBLIOTHÈQUE DU CONSERVATOIRE DE MUSIQUE DE PARIS.
CONSILIUM, JOANNES, 16th CENTURY.
Chansons.
In: Expert. Les maîtres musiciens de la Renaissance française. Vol.5.
Motets.
In: Attaingnant. Treize livres de motets. Livre 2, 4, 7, 8, 11, 12.
CONSORT MUSIC.
In: English instrumental music of the 16th and 17th centuries from manuscripts in the New York Public Library.
In: Morley. The first book of consort lessons.
In: Musica Britannica. Vol.9, 21, 22.
CONSTANTINI, A.
Sacred music.
In: Proske. Musica divina. Annus primus. Tom 2.
CONSTANTINI, F.
Sacred music.
In: Proske. Musica divina. Annus primus. Tom 2.
CONTACARIUM ASHBURNHAMENSE. CODEX BIBL. LAURENTIANAE ASHBURNHAMENSIS.
In: Monumenta musicae byzantinae. Série-principale. Vol.4.
CONTACARIUM PALAEOSLAVICUM. MOSQUENSE.

In: Monumenta musicae byzantinae. Série-principale. Vol.6.
CONTI, FRANCESCO.
Motets.
In: Denkmäler der Tonkunst in Österreich. Vol.101/102.
CONTI, GIUSEPPE.
Sacred music.
In: The Fitzwilliam music. Bd.4.
CONTRADANSES, OLD DUTCH BOERENLIEDJES AND.
In: Vereniging voor Nederlandsche Muziekgeschiedenis. Uitgave. No.20, 23, 33, 36.
CONVERSI, GIROLAMO, 16th CENTURY.
(var. sp.: Converso).
Vocal music.
In: Hullah. Vocal scores. II. Secular.
CONVERT.
Chansons.
In: Copenhagen Kongelige Bibliotek. Mss. (Thottske Samling 291[8]). Der kopenhagener Chansonnier.
COOKE, BENJAMIN, 1734–1793.
Selections.
In: Plainsong and Mediaeval Music Society. Publications. (Old Hall manuscript).
Part music.
In: Hullah. Part music. Class A.1. Vol.1, 2; Class A.2. Vol.1; Class A.2. Vol.2; Class C. Sacred. Class C. Secular.
Vocal music.
In: Hullah. Vocal scores. II. Secular.
COOPER, JOHN (COPERARIO), *see* COPERARIO, JOHN.
COPENHAGEN CHANSONNIER.
In: Copenhagen Kongelige Bibliotek. Mss. (Thottske Samling 291[8]). Der kopenhagener Chansonnier.
COPERARIO, JOHN, ca.1575–1626.
(var. sp.: Giovanni Coperario, Jo. Coprario, John Cooper).
Funerall teares.
In: Fellowes. The English school of lutenist song writers. Vol.17.
Songs.
In: Plainsong and Mediaeval Music Society. Publications. (A collection of songs and and madrigals . . .).
Violenmusik.
In: Giesbert. Violenmusik. Vol.1.
COPLAND, AARON, 1900– .
As it fell upon a day; Song for soprano, with flute and clarinet acc.
In: New music. Vol.2. No.4. Oct. 1929.
Episode. Organ.
In: Contemporary organ series. No.7.
Piano music.
In: Boletín latino-americano de música. Vol.5.
COPPINUS, ALEXANDER.
Vocal music.
In: Ghisi. Feste musicali della Firenze Medicea.
COPPOLA, PIER ANTONIO, 1793–1877.
Keyboard music.
In: Tagliapietra. Antologia di musica antica e moderna per pianoforte. Bd.18.
COPRARIO, JO., *see* COPERARIO, JOHN.
CORBEIL, PIERRE DE, *see* PIERRE DE CORBEIL.
CORDANS, BARTOLOMMEO, ca.1700–1757.
Choral music.
In: Musica sacra. 1839– . Vol.2, 3.
CORDIER, BAUDE, 15th CENTURY.
Works.
In: Reaney. Early fifteenth-century music. Vol.1.
Songs.
In: Riemann. Hausmusik aus alter Zeit.
CORELLI, ARCANGELO, 1653–1713.
Les oeuvres. 5v.
Selections.
In: Crotch. Specimens of various styles of music. Vol.2.
Concerti grossi.
In: I classici della musica italiana. Raccolta nazionale delle musiche italiane. Quad. 289, 290.
In: Nagels Musik-Archiv. No.42.
In: Schering. Perlen alter Kammermusik.
Concertino für 2 B-Trompeten und Streicher.
In: Concertino.
Duette alter Meister.
In: Zeitschrift für Spielmusik. No.69.
La folia.
In: L'école du violon au XVIIe et XVIIIe siècle. No.1276.
Kammer-Sonaten.
In: Moffat. Kammer-Sonaten für Violine und Pianoforte. No.8.
In: Musikschätze der Vergangenheit.
In: Organum. 3.Reihe. Nr.2.
Keyboard music.
In: Tagliapietra. Antologia di musica antica e moderna per pianoforte. Bd.9.
2 Kirchensonaten (C, D) für 2 Violinen, Tasten-Instrument und Bass-Instrument ad lib.
In: Antiqua Edition. Von 3 Instrumenten an.
Konzertante Weihnachtsmusik.
In: Nagels Musik-Archiv. No.182.
Organ music.
In: Anthologia antiqua. Vol.1.
In: Peeters. Anthologia pro organo. Vol.4.
Pastorale aus der Weihnachtsmusik. (Concerto grosso, Nr.8).
In: Schering. Perlen alter Kammermusik.
Preludio.
In: Guilmant. Répertoire des concerts du Trocadéro. Vol.3.
Sonata E-moll, Op.5/8.
In: Gitarre-Kammermusik. No.19.
Sonate en fa majeur.
In: L'école du violon au XVIIe et XVIIIe siècle. No.1281.
Sonata a tre, Op.4/3.
In: Gitarre-Kammermusik. No.1.
Sonata a tre, Op.4/5.
In: Gitarre-Kammermusik. No.4.
Sonate Op.5, Nr.8. Concerto grosso. (Francesco Geminiari).
In: Nagels Musik-Archiv. No.211.
Sonata da chiesa.
In: Organum. 3.Reihe. Nr.1.
In: Parrish. Masterpieces of music before 1750. No.39.

In: Riemann. Collegium musicum. No.54.
Sonate II nach den Concerti grossi für 2 Alt-Blockflöten und Basso Continuo.
In: Moecks Kammermusik. Vol.38.
Sonatas. Violin.
In: I classici della musica italiana. Vol.9.
In: I classici della musica italiana. Raccolta nazionale delle musiche italiane. Quad. 28–34.
In: Moffat. Meister-Schule der alter Zeit. Violin-Sonaten. No.13, 33.
In: Sondheimer. Werke aus dem 18. Jahrhundert. Nr.39/41.
Sonaten für 2 Violinen, Violoncello und Bass.
In: Denkmäler der Tonkunst. Vol.3.
Sonate en ré majeur. (2 violons et piano).
In: L'école du violon au XVIIe et XVIIIe siècle. No.1288.
Trio-Sonate (Dm); 6 Sonaten.
In: Moffat. Trio-Sonaten alter Meister. No.1, 5–10.
Variations on La follia, Op.5, No.12, for alto recorder (flute, oboe) and piano.
In: Music for wind instruments by 18th century masters. No.9.
Violin and piano.
In: Schering. Alte Meister des Violinspiels.
Weihnachtskonzert. (Concerto grosso Nr.8).
In: Schering. Perlen alter Kammermusik.
CORETTE, MICHEL, *see* CORRETTE, MICHEL.
CORFE.
Vocal music.
In: Hullah. Vocal scores. II. Secular.
CORKINE, WILLIAM, 16th–17th CENTURIES.
Book of ayres.
In: Fellowes. The English school of lutenist song writers. 2d series. Vol.12, 13.
CORNAZZANO, FELINO.
Sacred music.
In: Proske. Musica divina. Annus secundus. Tom 3.
In: Proske. Selectus novus missarum. Annus secundus. Tom 3.
CORNELIUS, PETER, 1824–1874.
Musikalische Werke. 5v.
Weihnachtslieder und Trauer und Trost.
In: Musikalische Stundenbücher.
CORNET, PIETER, 16th–17th CENTURIES.
(var. sp.: Peter Cornet).
Organ music.
In: Bonnet. Historical organ-recitals. Vol.1.
In: Guilmant. Archives des maîtres de l'orgue. Vol.10.
In: Peeters. Altniederländische Meister für Orgel oder Harmonium.
In: Peeters. Anthologia pro organo. Vol.1, 3.
In: Peeters. Oudnederlandse Meesters. Vol.1, 2, 3.
CORNISH, WILLIAM, ca.1468–1523.
(var. sp.: William Cornyshe).
Songs.
In: Plainsong and Mediaeval Music Society. Publications. (A collection of songs and madrigals . . .).
CORNYSHE, WILLIAM, *see* CORNISH, WILLIAM.
CORRADINE, NICOLÒ.
Organ music.
In: Fuser. Classici italiani dell'organo.
CORREA DE ARAUXO, FRANCISCO, ca.1575–1663.
(var. sp.: Pedro de Araújo).
Selections.
In: Pedrell. Teatro lirico español anterior al signo XIX. Bd.3.
Facultad orgánica.
In: Monumentos de la música española. Vol.6, 12.
Keyboard music.
In: Kastner. Cravistas portuguezes.
Organ music.
In: Bonnet. Historical organ-recitals. Vol.6.
In: Pedrell. Antología de organistas clásicos españoles. (siglos XVI, XVII y XVIII).
CORRETTE, GASPARD.
Messe du 8e ton pour l'orgue.
In: Orgue et liturgie. Vol.50–51.
Organ music.
In: Raugel. Les maîtres français de l'orgue. Vol.2.
CORRETTE, MICHEL, 18th CENTURY.
(var. sp.: Michel Corette).
Airs pour flûte et clavier.
In: Musiques françaises. Vol.1.
Konzert D-moll, Op.XXVI, Nr.6, für Cembalo oder Orgel.
In: Nagels Musik-Archiv. No.201.
Keyboard music.
In: Grovlez. Les plus belles pièces de clavessin de l'école française. Vol.2.
Noël allemand. 5me concerto pour le flûte (ou violon) avec la basse continuo.
In: Musiques françaises. Vol.10.
Organ music.
In: Raugel. Les maîtres français de l'orgue. Vol.2.
Rokoko-Duette für 2 Violoncelli, Gamben, Fideln oder Fagotte.
In: Moecks Kammermusik. Vol.45.
CORSINI, BONAIUTUS.
Selections.
In: Pirrotta. The music of fourteenth-century Italy. Vol.5.
CORTECCIA, FRANCESCO DI BERNARDO, 1504–1591.
Selections.
In: Maldéghem. Trésor musical.
In: Torchi. L'arte musicale in Italia. Bd.1.
Hinnario secondo l'vso della chiesa romana et fiorentina. No.1–5, 6–10.
In: Musica liturgica. Vol.1. Fasc.4; Vol.2. Fasc.2.
Vocal music.
In: Ghisi. Feste musicali della Firenze Medicea.
COSME, LUIS, 1908– .
(var. sp.: Luiz Cosme).
Canção do Tio Barnabé. (Piano).
In: Instituto Interamericano de Musicologia. Publicaciónes. No.18.
Música de câmara.
In: Boletín latino-americano de música. Vol.6.
COSTA DE LISBOA, JOÃO DA.
Tenção.

In: Portugaliae musica. Sér.A. Vol.7.
COSTANTINI, ALESSANDRO, 17th CENTURY.
Selections.
In: Torchi. L'arte musicale in Italia. Bd.5.
COSTELEY, GUILLAUME, 1531–1606.
Arreste un peu, mon coeur.
In: Expert. Florilège du concert vocal de la Renaissance. No.4.
Chansons.
In: Bordes. Chansonnier du XVe siècle.
In: Cauchie. Quinze chansons françaises du XVIe siècle.
In: Lesure. Anthologie de la chanson parisienne au XVIe siècle.
Choral music.
In: Engel. Three centuries of choral music. Vol.1.
In: Der Kammerchor. Vol.1.
Musique.
In: Expert. Les maîtres musiciens de la Renaissance française. Vol.3, 18–19.
COSYN, BENJAMIN, 17th CENTURY.
The goldfinch. Organ.
In: Dickinson. Historical recital series for organ. No.45.
Keyboard music.
In: Fuller-Maitland. Twenty-five pieces for keyed instruments from Benjamin Cosyn's Virginal book.
In: Gibbons. Ten pieces arranged for modern organ from the virginal book of Benjamin Cosyn.
COUCY, RAOUL DE.
Selections.
In: Smith. Musica antiqua.
COUILLART.
Motets.
In: Attaingnant. Treize livres de motets. Livre 1.
COUPER, MILDRED.
Dirge, for 2 pianos. Second piano tuned one quarter tone higher than the first.
In: New music. Vol.10. No.2. Jan. 1937.
COUPERIN, ARMAND LOUIS, 1725–1789.
Sonata. Piano. Op.II, No.3.
In: Reeser. De klaviersonate.
COUPERIN, FRANÇOIS, 1668–1735.
Oeuvres complètes. 12v.
Pièces de clavecin. 4v.
Pièces de clavecin (1713–1730). Facsimile.
In: Monuments of music and music literature. First series. No.9.
Selections.
In: Expert. Répertoire classique de musique. 1re année.
La bandoline. Les agrémens.
In: Pauer. Alte Meister. No.14.
La bersan, L'ausonienne (allemande), Les charmes, Le bavolet flottant.
In: Pauer. Alte Meister. No.38.
La florentine, La Terpsichore, La garnière, La tendre Fanchon, La lugubre, Passepied.
In: Pauer. Alte Meister. No.42.
La galante.
In: Parrish. Masterpieces of music before 1750. No.40.
Keyboard music.
In: Denkmäler der Tonkunst. Vol.4.
In: Farrenc. Le trésor des pianistes. Vol.4, 5.
In: Georgii. Keyboard music of the Baroque and Rococo. Vol.2.
In: Grovlez. Les plus belles pièces de clavessin de l'école française. Vol.1.
In: Herrmann. Lehrmeister und Schüler Joh. Seb. Bachs. Vol.1.
In: Köhler. Les maîtres du clavecin. Heft 10.
In: Nagels Musik-Archiv. No.94.
In: Oesterle. Early keyboard music. Vol.2.
In: Pauer. Alte Klavier-Musik. 1st series. Part 6.
In: Pessl. The art of the suite.
In: Roitzsch. Alte Klavier-Musik.
In: Tagliapietra. Antologia di musica antica e moderna per pianoforte. Bd.10.
Lament. Organ.
In: Dickinson. Historical recital series for organ. Vol.1. No.7.
Leçons de ténèbres. Premier, Seconde leçon. Sopran (Tenor) und B.C.
In: Cantio sacra. No.3, 4.
Leçons de ténèbres. Troisième leçon.
In: Dessoff choir series. No.14.
In: Die Kantate. No.10.
Organ music.
In: Anthologia antiqua. Vol.4, 7.
In: Biggs. Treasury of early organ music.
In: Bonnet. An anthology of early French organ music.
In: Bonnet. Historical organ-recitals. Vol.1.
In: Guilmant. Archives des maîtres de l'orgue. Vol.5.
In: Klein. The first four centuries of music for the organ from Dunstable to Bach (1370–1749).
In: Liber organi. Bd.1, 2.
In: The Liturgical Music Press, Inc. Masterpieces of organ music. Folio 29, 33, 37.
In: The parish organist. Vol.7–8.
In: Peeters. Anthologia pro organo. Vol.2, 4.
Qui tollis peccata mundi. Organ.
In: Dickinson. Historical recital series for organ. No.48.
Sarabande et fughette.
In: Guilmant. Répertoire des concerts du Trocadéro. Vol.3.
Sarabande grave.
In: Guilmant. Répertoire des concerts du Trocadéro. Vol.4.
Soeur Monique. Organ.
In: Dickinson. Historical recital series for organ. Vol.2. No.32.
In: Guilmant. Répertoire des concerts du Trocadéro. Vol.2.
Suite (Gm). (Allemande. Courante I, II. Sarabande. Gavotte. Gigue).
In: Pauer. Alte Meister. No.41.
Vocal music.
In: Delsarte. Archives du chant. Livr.22. No.1; Livr.23. No.1.
COUPERIN, LOUIS, ca.1626–1661.
Oeuvres complètes. 151p.
Pièces de clavecin. 135p.
Keyboard music.

In: Apel. Musik aus früher Zeit für Klavier. Bd.2.
In: Farrenc. Le trésor des pianistes. Vol.3.
In: Georgii. Keyboard music of the Baroque and Rococo. Vol.1.
In: Oesterle. Early keyboard music. Vol.1.
In: Tagliapietra. Antologia di musica antica e moderna per pianoforte. Bd.8.
Organ music.
In: Bonnet. An anthology of early French organ music.
In: Orgue et liturgie. Vol.6.
In: Raugel. Les maîtres français de l'orgue. Vol.2.
COURTOIS, JEAN, 16th CENTURY.
(var. sp.: Courtoys).
Selections.
In: Maldéghem. Trésor musical.
Chansons.
In: Expert. Les maîtres musiciens de la Renaissance française. Vol.5.
In: Publikationen älterer praktischer und theoretischer Musikwerke. Jahrg.27.
Motets.
In: Attaingnant. Treize livres de motets. Livre 4.
COURTOYS, JEAN, *see* COURTOIS, JEAN.
COURVILLE.
Chansons.
In: Lesure. Anthologie de la chanson parisienne au XVIe siècle.
COUSSER, JOHANN SIGISMUND, *see* KUSSER, JOHANN SIGISMUND.
COUSU, ANTOINE DE, ca.1600–1658.
Organ music.
In: Raugel. Quarante-siz pièces pour orgue ou harmonium.
COUTREMAN, 15th CENTURY.
Selections.
In: Reaney. Early fifteenth-century music. Vol.2.
COVERSI, G.
Sola soletta.
In: Squire. Ausgewählte Madrigale und mehrstimmige Gesänge. No.47.
COWELL, HENRY DIXON, 1897–1965.
American muse.
In: Music Press, Inc. [Choral series]. No.57.
Hilarious curtain opener, and Ritournelle. From incidental music for "Les Maries de la Tour Eiffel." Piano.
In: New music. Vol.19. No.1. 1945.
Maestoso, for piano.
In: New music. Vol.14. No.1. Oct. 1940.
Ostinato pianissimo (for percussion band).
In: New music. Vol.26. No.1. Oct. 1952.
Piano music.
In: Boletín latino-americano de música. Vol.5.
Processional. Organ.
In: Contemporary organ series. No.16.
Sunset. Rest. Two songs for low voice.
In: New music. Special edition.
Two woofs. Piano.
In: New music. Vol.21. No.1. Oct. 1947.
United quartet; for string art.
In: New music. Special edition.
COX, HARRY, 1923– .
2 Flämische Suiten für Sopran– und Alt-Blockflöte.
In: Zeitschrift für Spielmusik. No.167.
CRAEN, NIKOLAUS, 16th CENTURY.
(var. sp.: Nicolas Craen).
Choral music.
In: Smijers. Van Ockeghem tot Sweelinck. Aflg.4.
CRAMER, JOHANN BAPTIST, 1771–1858.
Keyboard music.
In: Farrenc. Le trésor des pianistes. Vol.18.
In: Tagliapietra. Antologia di musica antica e moderna per pianoforte. Bd.14.
Les menus plaisirs. Piano.
In: Organum. 5.Reihe. Nr.10.
3 Sonates. Piano.
In: Répertoire des clavicinistes. Heft 2.
Toccatina in A flat. Piano.
In: Roitzsch. Alte Klavier-Musik.
CRAPPIUS, ANDREAS, ca.1542–1623.
Works.
In: Das Erbe deutscher Musik. 2.Reihe. Niedersachsen. Vol.2.
Choral music.
In: Antiqua Chorbuch. Vol.1. Heft 3.
CRAWFORD, RUTH PORTER, 1901–1953.
Música de cámara.
In: Boletín latino-americano de música. Vol.5.
CRECQUILLON, THOMAS, d.1557.
(var. sp.: T. Crequillon; Thom. Creyquillon).
Selections.
In: Maldéghem. Trésor musical.
Choral music.
In: Commer. Collectio operum musicorum batavorum saeculi XVI. Bd.10, 12.
Lieder.
In: Publikationen älterer praktischer und theoretischer Musikwerke. Jahrg.1–3.
Mass.
In: Stein. Twelve Franco-Flemish masses of the early 16th century.
Pour ung plaisir.
In: Parrish. Masterpieces of music before 1750. No.20.
Works arr. by Molinaro.
In: Molinaro. Intavolatura di liuto.
CREMA, JOAN MARIA DA.
Intavolatura di liuto. 64p.
CREMONA, ITALY–MUSIC.
In: Istituzioni e monumenti dell'arte musicale italiana. Vol.6.
CREQUILLON, T., *see* CRECQUILLON, THOMAS.
CRESTON, PAUL, 1906– .
Música de cámara.
In: Boletín latino-americano de música. Vol.5.
7 Theses for piano.
In: New music. Vol.8. No.2. Jan. 1935.
In: New music. Vol.13. No.2. Jan. 1940.
Suite, for E alto saxophone or B clarinet and piano.
In: New music. Vol.11. No.3. Apr. 1938.
CREYGHTON, ROBERT, ca.1639–1734.
Selections.

In: Crotch. Specimens of various styles of music. Vol.2.
Part music.
In: Hullah. Part music. Class A.1. Vol.1.
Sacred music.
In: Boyce. Cathedral music. Vol.2, 3; 1849, Vol.2 and Vol.II, Appendix.
CREYQUILLON, THOM, *see* CRECQUILLON, THOMAS.
CRISPI, PIETRO MARIA, 1737–1797.
Selections.
In: Crotch. Specimens of various styles of music. Vol.3.
CROCE, GIOVANNI, ca.1557–1609.
Selections.
In: Musica sacra. 1839– . Vol.15, 16.
In: Torchi. L'arte musicale in Italia. Bd.2.
Choral music.
In: Societas Polyphonica Romanae. Repertorium. Vol.6.
Church music.
In: Motett Society. [Collection of ancient church music]. Division 1. Division 3.
Cinthia il tuo dolce canto.
In: Squire. Ausgewählte Madrigale und mehrstimmige Gesänge. No.48.
Madrigal.
In: The triumphs of Oriana.
Part music.
In: Hullah. Part music. Class A.1. Vol.1, 2.
Sacred music.
In: Proske. Musica divina. Annus primus. Tom 2, 4; Annus secundus. Tom 2.
Triaca musicale, 1596.
In: Somma. Capolavori polifonici del secolo XVI. Vol.3.
Vocal music.
In: Hullah. Vocal scores. I. Sacred. II. Secular.
CROFT, WILLIAM, 1678–1727.
Selections.
In: Crotch. Specimens of various styles of music. Vol.2.
Keyboard music.
In: Fuller-Maitland. The contemporaries of Purcell. Vol.3–4.
In: Herrmann. Contemporaries of Purcell.
Part music.
In: Hullah. Part music. Class A.1. Vol.1, 2.
Sacred music.
In: Arnold. Cathedral music. Vol.1, 2.
In: Boyce. Cathedral music. Vol.2; 1849. Vol.3.
In: Page. Harmonia sacra. Vol.1, 2, 3.
Vocal music.
In: Hullah. Vocal scores. I. Sacred.
CROME, FRITZ, 1879–1948.
Zwei Lieder. Op.29.
In: Samfundet til Udgivelse af dansk Musik. Ser.III. No.25.
CRONETS, PIERRE DES.
Selections.
In: Maldéghem. Trésor musical.
CROTCH, WILLIAM, 1775–1847.
Part music.
In: Hullah. Part music. 1868 ed.
Vocal music.
In: Hullah. Vocal scores. I. Sacred.
CRÜGER, JOHANN, 1598–1662.
Choral music.
In: Antiqua Chorbuch. Vol.1. Heft 5.
Neun geistliche Lieder.
In: Chor-Archiv.
CRUSELL, BERNHARD HENRIK, 1775–1838.
Quatuor No.2, in E flat.
In: Für Kenner und Liebhaber. No.27.
CRUZ, AGOSTINHO DA, ca.1590–ca.1633.
Keyboard music.
In: Kastner. Silva iberica.
CRUZ, DOMINGO SANTA, *see* SANTA CRUZ, DOMINGO.
CUELLAR, RAMÓN, 1777–1833.
Sacred music.
In: Eslava y Elizondo. Lira sacro-hispana. 19th century. i.l.
CUI, CÉSAR ANTONOVITCH, 1835–1918.
(var. sp.: Cuy).
Vocal music.
In: Sammlung russischer Romanzen. No.267–269.
CUNHA LUZ, BRASÍLIO ITIBERE DA, *see* ITIBERE DA CUNHA LUZ, BRASÍLIO.
CURIE, JOHANNES DE ALTE (HAUCOURT), 15th CENTURY.
Selections.
In: Reaney. Early fifteenth-century music. Vol.2.
CURSCHMANN, KARL FRIEDRICH, 1804–1841.
Lied.
In: Riemann. Das deutsche Lied. Vol.2.
CUSTER, ARTHUR.
Colloquy for string quartet.
In: Society for the Publication of American Music. 44th season. 1963–64.
CUY, CÉSAR, *see* CUI, CÉSAR ANTONOVITCH.
CYBOT.
Motets.
In: Attaingnant. Treize livres de motets. Livre 5.
THE CYPRIOT-FRENCH REPERTORY.
In: Turin. Biblioteca Nazionale. Mss. (J.II.9). The Cypriot-French repertory.
CZAJANEK.
Klavierstücke. Nr.1, Ballett. Nr.2, Intermezzo.
In: Hausmusik. No.93.
CZECH MUSIC.
In: Zeitschrift für Spielmusik. No.267.
CZERMÁK, A. G.
Streichquartett. Die drohende Gefahr oder Die Vaterlandsliebe.
In: Diletto musicale. No.134.
CZERNOHORSKÝ, BOHUSLAV, 1684–1742.
(var. sp.: Bohuslav Černohorský).
Fugue D-moll. Organ.
In: Guilmant. École classique de l'orgue. No.18.
Organ music.
In: Musica antiqua bohemica. Vol.12.
In: Peeters. Anthologia pro organo. Vol.2.
In: Raugel. Quarante-six pièces pour orgue ou harmonium.
Varhanní skladby. Organ.
In: Musica antiqua bohemica. Vol.3.

CZERNOZORSKY, GOTTLOB.
Organ music.
In: Orgelwerke. Altböhmischer Meister. Vol.1.
CZERNY, CARL, 1791–1857.
Six graduales. Op.318.
In: Ecclesiasticon. No.63.
Keyboard music.
In: Tagliapietra. Antologia di musica antica e moderna per pianoforte. Bd.15.

DA BOLOGNA, JACOPO, *see* JACOPO DA BOLOGNA.
DACA, ESTABAN, *see* DAZA, ESTABAN.
DA CASERTA, ANTHONELLO, *see* CASERTA, ANTHONELLO DA.
DA COSTA DE LISBOA, JOÃO, *see* COSTA DE LISBOA, JOÃO DA.
DA FERRARA, SIMON, *see* FERRARA, SIMON DA.
DA GAGLIANO, GIOVANNI BATTISTA, *see* GAGLIANO, GIOVANNI BATTISTA DA.
DA GAGLIANO, MARCO, *see* GAGLIANO, MARCO DA.
DAGINCOURT, FRANÇOIS, ca.1684–1758.
(var. sp.: François d'Agincour; Perrin d'Angincourt; J. A. Dagincourt; Perrin Dangecourt).
Selections.
In: Gleason. Examples of music before 1400.
In: Smith. Musica antiqua.
Keyboard music.
In: Grovlez. Les plus belles pièces de clavessin de l'école française. Vol.2.
In: Selva. Pièces de clavecin des XVIIme et XVIIIme siècles.
Pièces d'orgue.
In: Orgue et liturgie. Vol.31.
Organ music.
In: Raugel. Les maîtres français de l'orgue. Vol.2.
DAHL, INGOLF, 1912– .
Divertimento. Viola and piano.
In: Society for the Publication of American Music. Publications. 31st season. 1949–50.
Variations on a Swedish folktune. For flute solo.
In: New music. Vol.19. No.4. July 1946.
DAHL, VIKING, 1895–1945.
Selections.
In: Svensk sanglyrik. Vol.1.
DALAYRAC, NICOLAS, 1752–1809.
Selections.
In: Échos de France. Vol.1–3.
In: Expert. Collection d'ordre lyrique.
Arias.
In: Parisotti. Arie antiche. Bd.3.
Vocal music.
In: Delsarte. Archives du chant. Livr.18. No.11; Livr.23. No.6; Livr.25. No.7.
DALL'ABACO, EVARISTO FELICE, *see* ABACO, EVARISTO FELICE DALL'.
DALZA, JOAN AMBROSIO, 16th CENTURY.
Keyboard music.
In: Apel. Musik aus früher Zeit für Klavier. Bd.1.
DAMAN, WILLIAM, d.1591.
Anthems and motets.
In: Arkwright. The Old English edition. Vol.21.
DAMETT.
Selections.
In: Plainsong and Mediaeval Music Society. Publications. (Old Hall manuscript.)
DAMIAN, P. S. P., d.1729.
Veni Consolator.
In: Denkmäler altpolnischer Musik. Vol.13.
D'AMIENS, GUILLAUME, *see* AMIENS, GUILLAUME D'.
DAMON, JULIA.
Song.
In: The Wa-Wan series of American compositions.
D'ANA, FRANCESCO, *see* ANA, FRANCESCO D'.
DANBY, JOHN, 1757–1798.
Part music.
In: Hullah. Part music. Class A.2. Vol.1; Class B.2.
Vocal music.
In: Hullah. Vocal scores. II. Secular.
THE DANCE. (REICHERT).
In: Anthology of music. Vol.27.
DANCES.
In: Attaingnant. Chansons und Tänze.
In: Chilesotti. Biblioteca di rarità musicali.
In: Corpus of early keyboard music. Vol.8.
In: Diletto musicale. No.128.
In: English keyboard music. [No.2].
In: Moecks gelbe Musikhefte. Vol.8, 37.
In: The Penn state music series. No.12.
In: Playford. The English dancing master.
In: Playford. Old English dance tunes.
In: Vereniging voor Nederlandsche Muziekgeschiedenis. Uitgave. No.25, 27.
In: The Wellesley edition. No.6.
In: Zeitchrift für Spielmusik. passim.
In: Źroda do historii muzyki polskiej. Vol.1, 2, 6.
DANDRIEU, JEAN FRANÇOIS, 1682–1738.
Choral music.
In: Droz. Poètes et musiciens du XVe siècle.
Gavotte.
In: L'école du violon au XVIIe et XVIIIe siècle. No.1295.
Keyboard music.
In: Farrenc. Le trésor des pianistes. Vol.9.
In: Georgii. Keyboard music of the Baroque and Rococo. Vol.2.
In: Grovlez. Les plus belles pièces de clavessin de l'école française. Vol.1, 2.
In: The Penn state music series. No.6.
In: Tagliapietra. Antologia di musica antica e moderna per pianoforte. Bd.11.
Organ music.
In: Anthologia antiqua. Vol.2.
In: Cantantibus organis. Vol.8.
In: Guilmant. Archives des maîtres de l'orgue. Vol.7.
In: Guilmant. Concert historique d'orgue.
In: Keller. Orgelvorspiele.
In: Klein. The first four centuries of music for the organ from Dunstable to Bach (1370–1749).
In: The Liturgical Music Press, Inc. Masterpieces of organ music. Folio 72.

In: The parish organist. Vol.5–6, 7–8.
In: Pierront. Cent versets de Magnificat.
In: Raugel. Les maîtres français de l'orgue. Vol.1, 2.
In: Raugel. Les maîtres français de l'orgue aux XVIIème et XVIIIème siècles.
Sonata a tre per due violini e basso continuo. Op.I/6.
In: Hausmusik. No.171.
Sonate en sol majeur; Sonate en mi mineur (2 violons et piano).
In: L'école du violon au XVIIe et XVIIIe siècle. No.1269, 1270.
Sonate pour 2 violons, violoncelle et piano.
In: Musiques françaises. Vol.22.
DANDRIEU, PIERRE, ca.1660–1733.
Organ music.
In: Raugel. Les maîtres français de l'orgue. Vol.2.
In: Raugel. Quarante-six pièces pour orgue ou harmonium.
DANGECOURT, PERRIN, *see* DAGINCOURT, FRANÇOIS.
D'ANGLEBERT, JEAN HENRI, *see* ANGLEBERT, JEAN HENRI D'.
DANICAN-PHILIDOR, A., *see* PHILIDOR, FRANÇOIS ANDRÉ DANICAN.
DANIEL, JOHN, ca.1565–ca.1630.
Songs for the lute, viol and voice.
In: Fellowes. The English school of lutenist song writers. 2d series. Vol.8.
DANISH NATIONAL ANTHEMS [2].
In: Samfundet til Udgivelse af dansk Musik. Ser.III. No.98.
DANNSTRÖM, ISIDOR, 1812–1897.
Three songs for tenor and mixed chorus.
In: Musikaliska konstföreningen. 1875.
DANZI, FRANZ, 1763–1826.
Blaserquintett, B-dur, Op.56, Nr.1. (Weigelt).
In: Alte Musik. (Reihe "Leuckartiana")
Blaserquintett, G-moll, Op.56, Nr.2. (Weigelt).
In: Alte Musik. (Reihe "Leuckartiana").
Duos (2). Viola and violoncello.
In: Für Kenner und Liebhaber. No.23.
Quintet, Op.86, No.1.
In: Für Kenner und Liebhaber. No.24.
Quintet for flute, oboe, clarinet, bassoon, horn. Op.67, No.2.
In: Für Kenner und Liebhaber. No.8.
Sacred music.
In: Latrobe. C. I. Selection of sacred music.
In: Latrobe, J. A. The music of the church.
DA PERUGIA, NICCOLÒ, *see* NICCOLÒ DA PERUGIA.
DAQUIN, LOUIS CLAUDE, 1694–1772.
Keyboard music.
In: Farrenc. Le trésor des pianistes. Vol.9.
In: Georgii. Keyboard music of the Baroque and Rococo. Vol.2.
In: Grovlez. Les plus belles pièces de clavessin de l'école française. Vol.1, 2.
In: Pessl. The art of the suite.
In: Tagliapietra. Antologia di musica antica e moderna per pianoforte. Bd.12.
Nouveau livre de Noëls.
In: Guilmant. Archives des maîtres de l'orgue. Vol.3.
In: Orgue et liturgie. Vol.27–28.
Organ music.
In: Biggs. Treasury of early organ music.
In: Bonnet. Historical organ-recitals. Vol.3.
In: Cantantibus organis. Vol.1.
In: Liber organi. Bd.2.
In: The parish organist. Vol.5–6.
In: Raugel. Les maîtres français de l'orgue. Vol.1.
In: Raugel. Les maîtres français de l'orgue aux XVIIème et XVIIIème siècles.
D'AREZZO, GUIDO, *see* GUIDO D'AREZZO.
DARGOMIZHSKY, ALEXANDER, 1813–1869.
Complete piano works. v.1– .
Complete romances and songs. 2v.
Complete vocal ensembles and choruses. 288p.
Vocal music.
In: Sammlung russischer Romanzen. passim.
DARMSTADT–MUSIC, *see also* ARIAS, GERMAN; FOLKSONGS, GERMAN; GERMANY–MUSIC; SONGS, GERMAN.
In: Kirchenmusik der Darmstädter Meister des Barock.
DA ROCHA, FRANCISCO GOMES, *see* GOMES DA ROCHA, FRANCISCO.
D'ARRAS, MONIOT, *see* ARRAS, MONIOT D'.
DASER, LUDWIG, ca.1525–1589.
Motetten.
In: Das Erbe deutscher Musik. 1.Reihe. Vol.47.
Passion.
In: Berg. Patrocinium musices. Vol.6.
D'ASTORGA, EMANUELE GIOACCHINO CESARE RINCÓN, BARON, *see* ASTORGA, EMANUELE GIOACCHINO CESARE RINCÓN, BARON D'.
DATTARI, GHINOLFO, ca.1540–1617.
Le villanelle. (1568).
In: Maestri bolognesi. Vol.3.
DAUPHIN.
Le coucou.
In: L'école du violon au XVIIe et XVIIIe siècle. No.1293.
DAUVERGNE, ANTOINE, 1713–1797.
Sonate en sol majeur.
In: L'école du violon au XVIIe et XVIIIe siècle. No.1257.
DA VALLERANO, A., *see* VALLERANO, A. DA.
DAVID.
Vocal music.
In: Delsarte. Archives du chant. Livr.14. No.1.
DAVID, HANS THEODORE, 1902– .
French chansons of the sixteenth century.
In: Music Press, Inc. [Choral series]. No.54.
DAVID, JOHANN NEPOMUK, 1895– .
Choralwerk. v.1– .
Deutsche Tänze. Variationen über ein eigenes Thema für Streichorchester.
In: Collegium musicae novae. No.2.
DAVID, THOMAS CHRISTIAN, 1925– .
Serenade für Streichorchester, Op.10.
In: Collegium musicae novae. No.34.
DAVIDENKO, ALEXANDER ALEXANDROVITCH, 1899–1934.
Song of a shepherd perishing in the mountains. Chorus, a cappella.

In: New music. Vol.8. No.1. Oct. 1934.
DAVIDSON, HAROLD GIBSON, 1893– .
Auto accident.
In: New music. Orchestra series. No.18.
DAVY, JOHN, 1763–1824.
Songs.
In: Potter. Reliquary of English song. Vol.2.
DAWIDOWICZ, ANTON.
Sechs Variationen über "Valet will ich der geben."
In: Hausmusik. No.71.
DAZA, ESTABAN, 16th CENTURY.
(var. sp.: Daca).
Lute music.
In: Morphy. Les luthistes espagnols du XVIe siècle. Vol.2.
Organ music.
In: Cantantibus organis. Vol.8.
DE ALBA, ALONSO, *see* ALONSO DE ALBA.
DE ANCHIETA, JUAN, *see* ANCHIETA, JUAN DE.
DE ARIMINO, VINCENTIUS, *see* VINCENTIUS DE ARIMINO.
DE BELLENGUES, RICHARD, *see* BELLENGUES, RICHARD DE.
DE BERCHEM, JACHET, *see* BERCHEM, JACHET DE.
DE BEZE, THÉODORE, *see* BEZE, THÉODORE DE.
DE BOESI, JOSÉ ANTONIO CARO, *see* CARO DE BOESI, JOSÉ ANTONIO.
DE BOISMORTIER, JOSEPH BODIN, *see* BOISMORTIER, JOSEPH BODIN DE.
DE BONONIA, BARTHOLOMAEUS, *see* BARTHOLOMAEUS DE BONONIA.
DE BROSSARD, SÉBASTIEN, *see* BROSSARD, SÉBASTIEN DE.
DE BRUCK, ARNOLD, *see* BRUCK, ARNOLD VON.
DE BUSSY, N., *see* BUSSY, N. DE.
DE CABEZÓN, ANTONIO, *see* CABEZÓN, ANTONIO DE.
DE CALL, LEONHARD, *see* CALL, LEONHARD VON.
DE CASTILLEJO, PEDRO FERNÁNDEZ, *see* FERNÁNDEZ DE CASTILLEJA, PEDRO.
DE CASTRO, JEAN, *see* CASTRO, JEAN DE.
DE CHAMBONNIÈRES, JACQUES CHAMPION, *see* CHAMBONNIÈRES, JACQUES CHAMPION DE.
DE CHANCY, FRANÇOIS, *see* CHANCY, FRANÇOIS DE.
DE CHAUVIGNY.
La maladie de Monseigneur le Dauphin.
In: L'école du violon au XVIIe et XVIIIe siècle. No.1337.
DECIUS, NIKOLAUS, ca.1485–1546.
Part music.
In: Hullah. Part music. Class A.1. Vol.2.
DE CIVITATE, ANTONIUS, *see* ANTONIUS DE CIVITATE.
DECKER, JOACHIM, ca.1600.
Choral music.
In: Antiqua Chorbuch. Vol.1. Heft 4.
Organ music.
In: Organum. 4.Reihe. Nr.2.
DE CLEVE, JOHANNES, *see* CLEVE, JOHANNES DE.
DE COUCY, RAOUL, *see* COUCY, RAOUL DE.
DE COUSU, ANTOINE, *see* COUSU, ANTOINE DE.
DEDEKIND, CONSTANTIN CHRISTIAN, 1628–1715.
Choral music.
In: Chorbuch für die Kirchenchöre Sachsens.
Vier geistliche Konzerte, für eine Altstimme mit Basso Continuo.
In: Nagels Musik-Archiv. No.43.
Lieder.
In: Moser. Alte Meister des deutschen Liedes. 30 Gesänge. No.8–10.
In: Moser. Alt Meister des deutschen Liedes. 46 Gesänge. No.12, 13, 14, 15.
DEDEKIND, HENNING, d.ca.1630.
Choral music.
In: Antiqua Chorbuch. Vol.2. Heft 4.
DE ELDUAYEN, P. TOMÁS, *see* ELDUAYEN, P. TOMÁS DE.
DE ERAUZQUIN, JOSÉ ANTONIO, *see* ERAUZQUIN, JOSÉ ANTONIO DE.
DEERING, RICHARD, *see* DERING, RICHARD.
DE FALLA, MANUEL, *see* FALLA, MANUEL DE.
DE FERARE, *see* FERARE, DE.
DE FESCH, WILLEM, *see* FESCH, WILLEM DE.
DE FEVIN, ANTOINE, *see* FEVIN, ANTOINE DE.
DE FLORENTIA, BARTHOLOMEUS, *see* BARTHOLOMEUS DE FLORENTIA.
DE FLORENTIA, PAOLO, *see* PAOLO DE FLORENTIA.
DE FOSSA, JOANNES, *see* FOSSA, JOANNES DE.
DE FRUMERIE, GUNNAR FREDRIK, *see* FRUMERIE, GUNNAR FREDRIK DE.
DE FUENLLANA, MIGUEL, *see* FUENLLANA, MIGUEL DE.
DEGEN, HELMUT, 1911– .
Kleine symphonische Musik.
In: Collegium musicae novae. No.54.
DE GIARDINI, FELICE, *see* GIARDINI, FELICE DE.
DE GOUY, JACQUES, *see* GOUY, JACQUES DE.
DE GRIGNY, NICOLAS, *see* GRIGNY, NICOLAS DE.
DE HASPRE, JOHANNES SIMON, *see* HASPRE, JOHANNES SIMON DE.
DE HOLLANDE, JEAN, *see* HOLLANDE, JEAN DE.
DE INSULA, FRANCUS, *see* INSULA, FRANCUS DE.
DE KERLE, JACOB, *see* KERLE, JACOBUS DE.
DE LA BARRE, JOSEPH, *see* BARRE, JOSEPH DE LA.
DE LA BARRE, MICHEL, *see* BARRE, MICHEL DE LA.
DE LA FAGE, JUSTE ADRIEN LENOIR, *see* FAGE, JUSTE ADRIEN LENOIR DE LA.
DE LA GROTTE, NICOLAS, *see* LA GROTTE, NICOLAS DE.
DA LA HALLE, ADAM, *see* ADAM DE LA HALLE.
DELALANDE, MICHEL RICHARD, *see* LALANDE, MICHEL RICHARD DE.
DE LA LAURENCIE, LIONEL, *see* LA LAURENCIE, LIONEL DE.
DELANEY, ROBERT.
Música de cámara.
In: Boletín latino-americano de música. Vol.5.
DE LANTINS, ARNOLD, *see* LANTINS, ARNOLD DE.
DE LANTINS, HUGO, *see* LANTINS, HUGO DE.
DE LA RUE, PIERRE, *see* LA RUE, PIERRE DE.
DE LA SABLONARA, CLAUDIO, *see* LA SABLONARA, CLAUDIO DE.

DE LAS INFANTUS, FERNANDO, *see* INFANTUS, FERNANDO DE LAS.
DE LA TORRE, FRANCESCO, *see* TORRE, FRANCESCO DE LA.
DELÂTRE, JEAN PETIT CLAUDE, d.ca.1589.
(var. sp.: Jehan de Latre; Petit Jan de Lattre).
Selections.
In: Smith. Musica antiqua.
Choral music.
In: Commer. Collectio operum musicorum batavorum saeculi XVI. Bd.8.
DE LAYOLLE, FRANCISCUS, *see* LAYOLLE, FRANCISCUS DE.
DEL CASTILLO, DIEGO, *see* CASTILLO, DIEGO DEL.
DEL CAVALIERI, EMILIO, *see* CAVALIERI, EMILIO DEL.
DEL ENCINA, JUAN, *see* ENCINA, JUAN DEL.
DE L'ESCUREL, JOHANNOT, *see* ESCUREL, JOHANNOT DE L'.
DELIN.
Aria.
In: L'école du violon au XVIIe et XVIIIe siècle. No.1291.
DE LINGY.
Chanson à boire.
In: L'école du violon au XVIIe et XVIIIe siècle. No.1337.
DELIUS, FREDERICK, 1862–1934.
Complete works. v.1– .
DELLA BELLA, DOMENICO, *see* BELLA, DOMENICO DELLA.
DELLA CIAIA, AZZOLINO BERNARDINO, 1671–1755.
(var. sp.: A. B. Della Ciaja).
Keyboard music.
In: Tagliapietra. Antologia di musica antica e moderna per pianoforte. Bd.10.
DELLA PORTA, FRANCESCO, ca.1590–1666.
Church music.
In: Motett Society. [Collection of ancient church music]. Division 1. Division 3.
DELL'ARPA, ORAZIO, *see* ARPA, ORAZIO DELL'.
DELLA VIOLA, ALFONSO, *see* VIOLA, ALFONSO DELLA.
DELLER, FLORIAN JOHANN, 1729–1773.
Ballets.
In: Denkmäler deutscher Tonkunst. [1.Folge]. Vol.43–44.
DEL LEUTO, ARCANGELO, *see* LEUTO, ARCANGELO DEL.
DEL MEL, RENATUS, *see* MEL, RENATUS DEL.
DE LUCA, S., *see* LUCA, S. DE.
DE LUPRANO, FILIPPO, *see* LUPRANO, FILIPPO DE.
DEL ZOCHOLO, PRESBYTER P., *see* ZOCHOLO, PRESBYTER P. DEL.
DE MACHAUT, GUILLAUME, *see* GUILLAUME DE MACHAUT.
DEMACHI, GIUSEPPE, 18th CENTURY.
Trio Nr.1 für 3 Flöten oder 3 Violinen.
In: Diletto musicale. No.141.
DE MACQUE, GIOVANNI, *see* MACQUE, GIOVANNI (JEAN DE).
DE MAJO, F., *see* MAJO, GIAN FRANCESCO DE.
DEMANTIUS, JOHANN CHRISTOPH, 1567–1643.
Choral music.
In: Antiqua Chorbuch. Vol.1. Heft 4; Vol.2. Heft 3.
In: Der Kammerchor. Vol.5.
4 Galliarden.
In: Zeitschrift für Spielmusik. No.86.
Neue teutsche weltliche Lieder.
In: Das Erbe deutscher Musik. 2.Reihe. Sudetenland, Böhmen und Mähren. Vol.1.
In: Das Erbe deutscher Musik. Sonderreihe. Vol.1.
Vier deutsche Motetten.
In: Das Chorwerk. No.39.
Passion nach dem Evangelisten Johannes.
In: Das Chorwerk. No.27.
Polnischer und teutscher art Täntze.
In: Zeitschrift für Spielmusik. No.210.
Der 116. Psalm.
In: Das Chorwerk. No.36.
Sacred music.
In: Proske. Musica divina. Annus primus. Tom 3.
Deutsche Tänze für Streichquartett oder Streichorchester.
In: Hortus musicus. No.148.
DE MANTUA, JACHET, *see* JACHET DE MANTUA.
DE MARLE, NICOLAS, *see* MARLE, NICOLAS DE.
DE MARTELAERE, JOANNES, *see* MARTELAERE, JOANNES DE.
DE MEZQUITA, JOSÉ JOAQUIM EMERICO LOBO, *see* LOBO DE MEZQUITA, JOSÉ JOAQUIM EMERICO.
DE MOLIER, LOUIS, *see* MOLIER, LOUIS DE.
DE MONDONVILLE, JEAN JOSEPH CASSANEA, *see* MONDONVILLE, JEAN JOSEPH CASSANEA DE.
DE MONTE, LAMBERTUS, *see* MONTE, LAMBERTUS DE.
DE MONTE, PHILIPPE, *see* MONTE, PHILIPPE DE.
DE MONTÉCLAIR, MICHEL PINOLET, *see* MONTÉCLAIR, MICHEL PINOLET DE.
DEMOPHON, ALESSANDRO.
Selections.
In: Torchi. L'arte musicale in Italia. Bd.1.
DE MUDARRA, A., *see* MUDARRA, ALONSO DE.
DE NARVÁEZ, LUIS, *see* NARVÁEZ, LUIS DE.
DENCKE, JEREMIAH, 1725–1795.
Sacred songs.
In: Music of the Moravians in America. Vol.1.
DE NEGRI, GIULIO SANTO PIETRO, *see* NEGRO, GIULIO SANTO PIETRO DEL.
DE NESLE, BLONDEL, *see* BLONDEL DE NESLE.
DEN GHEYN, MATTHIAS VAN, *see* GHEYN, MATTHIAS VAN DEN.
DENHÖFF, JOACHIM.
Du bist min.
In: Christophorus-Chorwerk. Heft 36.
Missa brevis.
In: Christophorus-Chorwerk. Heft 23.
DENIS, JEAN.
Organ music.
In: Raugel. Les maîtres français de l'orgue. Vol.2.
Sonate en la mineur.

In: L'école du violon au XVIIe et XVIIIe siècle. No.1261.
DEN KERCKHOVEN, ABRAHAM VAN, *see* KERCKHOVEN, ABRAHAM VAN DEN.
DENMARK–MUSIC.
In: Crotch. Specimen of various styles of music. Vol.1.
In: Samfundet til Udgivelse af dansk Musik.
In: Zeitschrift für Spielmusik. No.1, 188.
DENTE, JOSEPH GOTTLIEB, 1838–1905.
Symphony, D minor. Score.
In: Musikaliska konstföreningen. 1890.
Symphony, D minor. Arr. for piano, 4 hands.
In: Musikaliska konstföreningen. 1890.
DENTICE, FABRIZIO, 16th CENTURY.
Sacred music.
In: Proske. Musica divina. Annus primus. Tom 4.
DE ORTO, MARBRIANO, *see* ORTO, MARBRIANO DE.
DEPRÈS, JOSQUIN, d.1521.
(var. sp.: De Près; De Prez; Des Près; Des Prez; Du Près; Desprès; Josquin).
Werken. v.1– .
Opera omnia. v.1– .
Ausgewählte Kompositionen.
In: Publikationen älterer praktischer und theoretischer Musikwerke. Jahrg.5.
Selections.
In: Ambros. Auserwählte Tonwerke.
In: Crotch. Specimens of various styles of music. Vol.2.
In: Documenta historica musicae.
In: Maldéghem. Trésor musical.
Choral music.
In: Capella. Vol.1.
In: Commer. Collectio operum musicorum batavorum saeculi XVI. Bd.6, 7, 8, 12.
In: Dessoff choir series. No.25, 39, 43–48.
In: Engel. Three centuries of choral music. Vol.1.
In: Der Kammerchor. Vol.1.
In: Music Press, Inc. [Choral series]. Vol.93.
In: Musica antiqua batava. MA–7.
In: Recueil de musique ancienne. Recueil des morceaux de musique ancienne. Bd.5.
In: Rochlitz. Sammlung vorzüglicher Gesangstücke. Bd.1. Pt.1.
In: Smijers. Van Ockeghem tot Sweelinck. Aflg.5.
In: Societas Polyphonica Romanae. Repertorium. Vol.2.
Drei Evangelien-Motetten.
In: Das Chorwerk. No.23.
Weltliche Lieder.
In: Das Chorwerk. No.3.
Lied– und Choralmotetten.
In: Das Chorwerk. No.30.
Missa da pacem.
In: Das Chorwerk. No.20.
Missa de Beata Virgine.
In: Das Chorwerk. No.42.
Missa "Pange lingua."
In: Das Chorwerk. No.1.
Motets.
In: Attaingnant. Treize livres de motets. Livre 4, 12.
In: Chor-Archiv.
In: Das Chorwerk. No.18, 54, 57.
In: Müller-Blattau. Musica reservata. Vol.2.
In: Parrish. Masterpieces of music before 1750. 1750. No.19.
In: Vereniging voor Nederlandsche Muziekgeschiedenis. Uitgave. No.44.
Organ music.
In: Cantantibus organis. Vol.4, 6, 8.
In: Klein. The first four centuries of music for the organ from Dunstable to Bach (1370–1749).
In: Liber organi. Bd.8.
In: The Liturgical Music Press, Inc. Masterpieces of organ music. Folio 65.
In: Peeters. Anthologia pro organo. Vol.1.
In: Peeters. Oudnederlandse Meesters. Vol.1, 2, 3.
In: Schering. Alte Meister aus der Frühzeit des Orgelspiels.
Petite camusette.
In: Arion. Vol.3.
La plus des plus.
In: Zeitschrift für Spielmusik. No.234.
Psalms.
In: Das Chorwerk. No.33, 64.
Sequenz "Ave Maria" für vier Stimmen.
In: Christophorus-Chorwerk. Heft 1.
DE PSALINIS, UBERTUS, *see* SALINIS, UBERTUS DE.
DE QUATRIS, JOHANNES, *see* QUATRIS, JOHANNES DE.
DERFELDT.
Vocal music.
In: Sammlung russischer Romanzen. No.55, 287.
DE RIBERA, ANTONIO, *see* RIBERA, ANTONIO DE.
DE RIMINI, VINCENZO, *see* RIMINI, VINCENZO DE.
DERING, RICHARD, ca.1580–1630.
(var. sp.: Richard Deering).
The cries of London.
In: The Penn state music series. No.5.
Madrigals.
In: Musica Britannica. In process.
DE RORE, CIPRIANO, *see* RORE, CIPRIANO DE.
DE ROUCOURT, *see* ROUCOURT, DE.
DE RUCTIS, AR., *see* RUCTIS, AR. DE.
DER VOGELWEIDE, WALTER VON, *see* VOGELWEIDE, WALTER VON DER.
DERWIS.
Vocal music.
In: Sammlung russischer Romanzen. No.170.
DE SARTO, JOHANNES, *see* SARTO, JOHANNES DE.
DES CRONETS, PIERRE, *see* CRONETS, PIERRE DES.
DE SERMISY, CLAUDE, *see* SERMISY, CLAUDE DE.
DE SILVA, ANDREAS, *see* SILVA, ANDREAS DE.
DESLOUGES, PHILIPPE.
Chansons.
In: Expert. Les maîtres musiciens de la Renaissance française. Vol.5.
DE SOTO, PEDRO, *see* SOTO, PEDRO DE.
D'ESPINOSA, JUAN, *see* ESPINOSA, JUAN D'.

DESPRÈS, JOSQUIN, *see* DEPRÈS, JOSQUIN.
DESTOUCHES, ANDRÉ CARDINAL, 1672–1749.
(var. sp.: Destouche).
Airs.
In: Prunières. Les maîtres du chant. Recueil Recueil 6.
Les éléments; Issé; Omphale.
In: Les chefs d'oeuvres classiques de l'opéra français.
Vocal music.
In: Delsarte. Archives du chant. Livr.1. No.11; Livr.3. No.10; Livr.18. No.6.
DETHIER, GASTON MARIE, 1875– .
Organ music.
In: Bedell. The French organist. Vol.2.
DE TOLESA, P. NICOLÁS, *see* TOLESA, P. NICOLÁS DE.
DE TORNACO, PASSET, *see* PASSET DE TORNACO.
DE TORRIJOS, DIEGO, *see* TORRIJOS, DIEGO DE.
DEUTEROMELIA, SELECTIONS FROM.
In: Euterpe. 2d ed. No.40, 41.
DE VALDERRÁBANO, ENRIQUE, ENRIQUEZ, *see* ENRIQUEZ DE VALDERRÁBANO, ENRIQUE.
DE VAQUIERAS, REIMBAUTZ, *see* VAQUIERAS, REIMBAUTZ DE.
DE VAUX, RAULIN, *see* VAUX, RAULIN DE.
DE VENTADORN, BERNART, *see* BERNART DE VENTADORN.
DE VENTO, IVO, *see* VENTO, IVO DE.
DEVIENNE, FRANÇOIS, 1759–1803.
Three duos concertantes.
In: Für Kenner und Liebhaber. No.29.
Duo concertant Nr.1 für 2 Klarinetten.
In: Diletto musicale. No.136.
Trio, Op.66, No.2.
In: Für Kenner und Liebhaber. No.19.
DE VILLIERS, PIERRE, *see* VILLIERS (VUILLERS), PIERRE DE.
D'EVRY, E., *see* EVRY, E. D'.
DE WERT, GIACHES, *see* WERT, GIACHES DE.
DIABELLI, ANTON, 1781–1858.
Sonate, Op.68.
In: Hausmusik. No.46.
Sonatine A dur für Gitarre und Hammerklavier. Op.68.
In: Albert. Die Gitarre in der Haus- und Kammermusik vor 100 Jahren (1780–1820). No.1.
Trio für Flöte oder Violine, Viola (2 Violine) und Gitarre.
In: Hausmusik. No.62.
DIAMOND, DAVID LEO, 1915– .
Piano music.
In: Boletín latino-americano de música. Vol.5. Vol.5.
Quintet in B minor. Flute, string trio, and piano.
In: Society for the Publication of American Music. Publications. 23d season. 1941–42.
Sonata for violoncello and piano.
In: New music. Vol.13. No.1. Oct. 1939.
Young Joseph.
In: Music Press, Inc. [Choral series]. Vol.105.
DIBDIN, CHARLES, 1745–1814.
Songs.
In: Potter. Reliquary of English song. Vol.2.
DIEPENBROCK, ALPHONS, 1862–1921.
De musikale handschriften.
In: Vereniging voor Nederlandsche Muziekgeschiedenis. Uitgave. No.43.
DIESNER, GERHARD.
Keyboard music.
In: Fuller-Maitland. The contemporaries of Purcell. Vol.6–7.
DIETRICH, SIXTUS, ca.1490–1548.
Hymnen. 178p.
Selected works.
In: Das Erbe deutscher Musik. 1.Reihe. Vol.23.
In: Publikationen älterer Musik. Jahrg.3. Pt.2.
Choral music.
In: Antiqua Chorbuch. Vol.1. Heft 1.
Lieder.
In: Publikationen älterer praktischer und theoretischer Musikwerke. Jahrg.1–3.
Novum ac insigne opus musicum 36 antiphonarum 1541.
In: Rhaw. Musikdrucke. Vol.7.
DIETRICHSTEIN, MORIZ VON.
Selections.
In: Denkmälter der Tonkunst in Österreich. Vol.79. (Jg.XLII/2).
DIEUPART, CHARLES, ca.1670–1740.
Collection. 2v.
Keyboard music.
In: Herrmann. Lehrmeister und Schüler Joh. Seb. Bachs. Vol.1.
In: Pessl. The art of the suite.
Suite I–II für Tenor-Blockflöte und Basso Continuo.
In: Moecks Kammermusik. Vol.2, 3.
DI FERRARA, DOMENICO, *see* FERRARA, DOMENICO DI.
DIJON [MS. NO.517 DE LA BIBLIOTHÈQUE DE LA VILLE DE DIJON (ANCIEN 296)].
In: Droz. Trois chansonniers français du XVe siècle.
DIOMEDES, CATO, *see* CATO, DIOMEDES.
DIRUTA, GIROLAMO, b.ca.1550.
Selections.
In: Torchi. L'arte musicale in Italia. Bd.3.
Keyboard music.
In: Apel. Musik aus früher Zeit für Klavier. Bd.1.
Organ music.
In: Fuser. Classici italiani dell'organo.
In: Klein. The first four centuries of music for the organ from Dunstable to Bach (1370–1749).
DI SALE, FRANCESCO, *see* SALE, FRANCESCO DI.
DISTLER, HUGO, 1908–1942.
Choral music.
In: Nagels Männerchor-Blätter. No.6.
Organ music.
In: The parish organist. Vol.5–6.
DITTERS VON DITTERSDORF, KARL, 1739–1799.
Ausgewählte Orchesterwerke. 11v.

Instrumental works.
In: Denkmäler der Tonkunst in Österreich. Vol.81. (Jg.XLIII/2).
Keyboard music.
In: Newman. Thirteen keyboard sonatas of the 18th and 19th centuries.
Konzert, A-dur, für Cembalo, zwei Violinen und Violoncello.
In: Nagels Musik-Archiv. No.41.
Konzert in C-dur für zwei Violinen und Streichorchester.
In: Concertino.
Konzert in E-moll.
In: Corona. Vol.54.
Drei Partiten für Bläser, 2 Oboen, 2 Hörner und Fagott oder 3 Violinen, Viola und Cello.
In: Riemann. Collegium musicum. No.101.
Sinfonia. Die vier Weltalter.
In: Diletto musicale. No.117.
6 Streichtrios für zwei Violinen, Violoncello.
In: Hortus musicus. No.92.
DITTMER, LUTHER A.
Anonymous IV; Robert de Handlo.
In: Institute of Mediaeval Music. Musical theorists in translation. Vol.1, 2.
A central source of Notre-Dame polyphony.
In: Institute of Mediaeval Music. Publications. Vol.3.
Facsimile reproduction of the manuscript Madrid 20486.
In: Institute of Mediaeval Music. Publications. Vol.1.
Firenze Biblioteca Mediceo-Laurenziana, Pluteo 29, I.
In: Institute of Mediaeval Music. Publications. Vol.10–11.
Oxford, Latin liturgical d 20 and Chicago 654 app.
In: Institute of Mediaeval Music. Publications. Vol.6.
Paris 13521 and 11411.
In: Institute of Mediaeval Music. Publications. Vol.4.
Wolfenbüttel 1099.
In: Institute of Mediaeval Music. Publications. Vol.2.
Worcester Add. 68.
In: Institute of Mediaeval Music. Publications. Vol.5.
Auszug aus The Worcester music fragments.
In: Institute of Mediaeval Music. Musicological studies. Vol.1.
DIVITIS, ANTONIUS, 16th CENTURY.
Missa "Quem dicunt homines."
In: Das Chorwerk. No.83.
Motets.
In: Attaingnant. Treize livres de motets. Livre 6, 10.
DLUGORAJ, ADALBERT WOJCIECH, b.ca.1550.
Fantasies and villanellas for flute.
In: Denkmäler altpolnischer Musik. Vol.23.
DMITRIEFF.
Vocal music.
In: Sammlung russischer Romanzen. No.64, 65.
DOHNÁNYI, ERNÖ, 1877– .
Keyboard music.
In: Musica hungarica.
DOLAR.
Selections.
In: Cvetko. Skladatelji Gallus, Plautzius [in] Dolar.
DOLES, JOHANN FRIEDRICH, 1715–1797.
Organ music.
In: Buszin. Organ series. Vol.1.
DONATH, GUSTAV, 1878– .
Trio für zwei Violinen und Klavier, im alten Stil.
In: Hausmusik. No.17.
DONATI, BALDASSARE, ca.1530–1603.
(var. sp.: Donato).
Selections.
In: Torchi. L'arte musicale in Italia. Bd.1.
Choral music.
In: Nagels Männerchor-Blätter. No.25.
In: Recueil de musique ancienne. Recueil des morceaux de musique ancienne. Bd.10.
Part music.
In: Hullah. Part music. Class A.2. Vol.1.
DONATO, ANTHONY, 1909– .
Quartet in E minor.
In: Soçiety for the Publication of American Music. Publications. 28th season. 1946–47.
DONATUS DE FLORENTIA, 14th CENTURY.
Selections.
In: Pirrotta. The music of fourteenth-century Italy. Vol.3.
DONAÜROFF.
Vocal music.
In: Sammlung russischer Romanzen. No.169, 212, 233.
DON CARLO GESUALDO, PRINCE DE VENOSA, *see* GESUALDO, CARLO, PRINCIPE DI VENOSA.
DON JOÃO IV, *see* JOHN IV, KING OF PORTUGAL.
DON JUAN IV, *see* JOHN IV, KING OF PORTUGAL.
DONOSTÍA, JOSÉ ANTONIO DE, 1886–1956.
Obras musicales. v.1– .
DONOVAN, RICHARD FRANK, 1891– .
Choral music.
In: Music Press, Inc. [Choral series]. Vol.104.
Paignion. Organ.
In: Contemporary organ series. No.18.
Serenade for oboe, violin, viola, and violoncello.
In: New music. Vol.14. No.3. Apr.1941.
Suite for piano.
In: New music. Vol.6. No.3. Apr.1933.
DOPPELBAUER, JOSEF FRIEDRICH, 1918– .
Fünf kleine Motetten.
In: Christophorus-Chorwerk. Heft 10.
DORNEL, LOUIS ANTOINE, ca.1685–1765.
Keyboard music.
In: Grovlez. Les plus belles pièces de clavessin de l'école française. Vol.1.
Organ music.
In: Raugel. Les maîtres français de l'orgue. Vol.2.
Première suite pour la flûte traversière (violon ou hautbois) avec la basse (1709).
In: Musiques françaises. Vol.9.
DOSTAL, VIKTOR. comp.
Der Weg zur Orgel.
In: Hausmusik. No.52.

DOWLAND, JOHN, 1563–1626.
Selections.
In: Crotch. Specimens of various styles of music. Vol.2.
In: Smith. Musica antiqua.
Ayres for 4 voices.
In: Musica Britannica. Vol.6.
Book of airs.
In: Fellowes. The English school of lutenist song writers. 1st series. Vol.1–2, 5–6, 10–11, 12, 14.
Choral music.
In: Engel. Three centuries of choral music. Vol.3.
The first set of songs.
In: Musical Antiquarian Society. Publications. Vol.12.
Lachrimae.
In: Nagels Musik-Archiv. No.173.
In: The Tudor edition of old music. Ser.A. No.1.
Lachrymae paran. Organ.
In: Dickinson. Historical recital series for organ. Vol.2. No.21.
Madrigals.
In: Euterpe. Vol.3, 4, 5, 7, 10, 12, 13; 2d ed. No.12–23.
In: Squire. Ausgewählte Madrigale und mehrstimmige Gesänge. No.3, 12.
My thoughts are wing'd with hope.
In: Parrish. A treasury of early music. No.34.
Part music.
In: Hullah. Part music. Class A.2. Vol.1; Class A.2. Vol.2.
Songs.
In: Potter. Reliquary of English song. Vol.1.
Vocal music.
In: Hullah. Vocal scores. II. Secular.
DOWLAND, ROBERT, 1586–1641.
Varietie of lute lessons.
In: Schott's Series of early lute music. Vol.1.
DOYAGÜE, MANUEL, 1755–1842.
Sacred music.
In: Eslava y Elizondo. Lira sacro-hispana. 19th century. i.1. and Appendix.
DRAGHI, ANTONIO, 1635–1700.
Church music (masses, sequences, hymns).
In: Denkmäler der Tonkunst in Österreich. Vol.46. (Jg.XXIII/1).
DRAGHI, GIOVANNI BATTISTA, b.ca.1640.
Keyboard music.
In: English keyboard music. [No.10].
DRAGONETTI, DOMENICO, 1763–1846.
Solo in D-dur für Kontrabass und Klavier; Solo in D-moll für Kontrabass und Klavier.
In: Diletto musicale. No.118, 120.
DREISSLER, J.
Choral music.
In: Nagels Männerchor-Blätter. No.20.
DRESSLER, GALLUS, b.1533.
Selections.
In: Musica sacra. 1839– . Vol.15.
Choral music.
In: Antiqua Chorbuch. Vol.1. Heft 3.
Gesänge.
In: Musica sacra. ca.1842–1896. Vol.11.
Motets.
In: Das Chorwerk. No.28.
In: Publikationen älterer praktischer und theoretischer Musikwerke. Jahrg.28.
DRUZECKÝ, J.
Serenate Boeme.
In: Musica antiqua bohemica. Vol.35.
DÜBEN, ANDREAS, ca.1590–1662.
Organ music.
In: Organum. 4.Reihe. Nr.21.
Pugna troumphalis, 1634.
In: Musikaliska konstföreningen. 1932.
DÜBEN, GUSTAF, 1624–1690.
Odae svecicae; Sinfonia a 4; Veni Sancte Spiritus.
In: Monumenta musicae svecicae.
THE DUBLIN VIRGINAL MANUSCRIPT.
In: The Wellesley edition. No.3.
DUBOIS, FRANÇOIS CLÉMENT THÉODORE, 1837–1924.
Organ music.
In: Bedell. The French organist. Vol.1.
DÜBÜQUE.
Vocal music.
In: Sammlung russischer Romanzen. No.23, 66, 67, 91–98, 162, 213, 214.
DU CARÊME, *see* CARÊME, DU.
DU CAURROY, FRANÇOIS EUSTACHE, *see* CAURROY, FRANÇOIS EUSTACHE DU, SIEUR DE ST. FRÉMIN.
DUCIS, BENEDICTUS, ca.1490–1544.
(var. sp.: Benedict Ducis; Benedictus Hertoghs).
Selections.
In: Ambros. Auserwählte Tonwerke.
In: Maldéghem. Trésor musical.
Choral music.
In: Antiqua Chorbuch. Vol.1. Heft 1; Vol.2. Heft 1.
Missa de beata Virgine.
In: Musik alter Meister. Heft 11.
Zwei Psalmmotetten
In: Musik alter Meister. Heft 6.
DUDOSO, DAN.
Sacred music.
In: Eslava y Elizondo. Lira sacro-hispana. 18th century. i.1.
DUFAY, GUILLAUME, ca.1400–1474.
Opera omnia. v.1– .
Early Bodleian music. [I]. Dufay and his contemporaries. 207p.
Selections.
In: Documenta historica musicae.
Choral music.
In: Capella. Vol.1.
In: Engel. Three centuries of choral music. Vol.1.
In: Music Press, Inc. [Choral series]. Vol.116.
In: Rochlitz. Sammlung vorzüglicher Gesangstücke. Bd.1. Pt.1.
Hymns.
In: Sämtliche Hymnen.
In: Das Chorwerk. No.49.
Kyrie (I) from the Mass "Se la face ay pale."
In: Parrish. Masterpieces of music before 1750. No.15.
Magnificat in the eighth mode.
In: Dessoff choir series. No.29.
Masses.
In: Documenta polyphoniae liturgicae sanctae

ecclesiae romanae. Ser.I. No.1, 3, 4, 7, 10.
In: Monumenta polyphoniae liturgicae sanctae ecclesiae romanae. Ser.I. Tomus I. Fasc.1; Tomus II. Fasc.1, 2, 4.
Vierstimmige Messe "Se la face ay pale." 1951.
In: Capella. Vol.2.
Messesatz.
In: Einstein. Beispielsammlung zur älteren Musikgeschichte.
Motetten.
In: Chor-Archiv.
Organ music.
In: Cantantibus organis. Vol.6.
In: Klein. The first four centuries of music for the organ from Dunstable to Bach (1370–1749).
In: Liber organi. Bd.8.
In: Peeters. Anthologia pro organo. Vol.1, 3.
In: Peeters. Oudnederlandse meesters. Vol.2, 3.
Songs.
In: Riemann. Hausmusik aus alter Zeit.
Zwölf geistliche und weltliche Werke.
In: Das Chorwerk. No.19.
DUFOUR.
Organ music.
In: Raugel. Les maîtres français de l'orgue. Vol.2.
DU HAMEL, *see* HAMEL, DU.
DULICHIUS, PHILIPPUS, 1562–1631.
Centuriae.
In: Denkmäler deutscher Tonkunst. [1.Folge]. Vol.31, 41.
DULOT, FRANÇOIS, 16th CENTURY.
(var. sp.: François Du Lot).
Chansons.
In: Expert. Les maîtres musiciens de la Renaissance française. Vol.5.
Motets.
In: Attaingnant. Treize livres de motets. Livre 2, 5.
DU MAGE, PIERRE, ca.1676–1751.
Livre d'orgue. 20p.
Organ music.
In: Bonnet. Historical organ-recitals. Vol.1.
In: Guilmant. Archives des maîtres de l'orgue. Vol.3.
In: Klein. The first four centuries of music for the organ from Dunstable to Bach (1370–1749).
In: The Liturgical Music Press, Inc. Masterpieces of organ music. Folio 38.
In: Raugel. Les maîtres français de l'orgue. Vol.2.
DU MONT, HENRI, 1610–1684.
Meslanges divers. 57p.
Selections.
In: Expert. Répertoire classique de musique. 1re année.
Airs.
In: Prunières. Les maîtres du chant. Recueil 4.
Keyboard music.
In: Oesterle. Early keyboard music. Vol.1.
In: Pauer. Alte Klavier-Musik. 1st series. Part 6.
In: Tagliapietra. Antologia di musica antica e moderna per pianoforte. Bd.7.
Organ music.
In: Raugel. Les maîtres français de l'orgue. Vol.1, 2.
In: Raugel. Les maîtres français de l'orgue aus XVIIème et XVIIIème siècles.
Part music.
In: Hullah. Part music. Class A.1. Vol.1.
Suite de pièces.
In: Köhler. Les maîtres du clavecin. Heft 12.
DUNAEVSKIĬ, ISAAK OSIPOVICH, 1900–1955.
Complete works. v.1– .
DUNI, 18th CENTURY.
(var. sp.: Duny).
Vocal music.
In: Delsarte. Archives du chant. Livr.8, No.9; Livr.10, No.8; Livr.12, No.10; Livr.15, No.11; Livr.19, No.3.
DUNSTABLE, JOHN, ca.1370–1453.
Complete works.
In: Musica Britannica. Vol.8.
Selections.
In: Documenta historica musicae.
Choral music.
In: Capella. Vol.1.
In: Engel. Three centuries of choral music. Vol.3.
Gloria e Credo.
In: Documenta polyphoniae liturgicae sanctae ecclesiae romanae. Ser.1. No.8.
Organ music.
In: Biggs. Treasury of early organ music.
In: Klein. The first four centuries of music for the organ from Dunstable to Bach (1370–1749).
Veni Sancte Spiritus.
In: Parrish. A treasury of early music. No.18.
DUNY, *see* DUNI.
DUPHLY, JACQUES, 1715–1789.
Keyboard music.
In: Farrenc. Le trésor des pianistes. Vol.14.
In: Grovlez. Les plus belles pièces de clavessin de l'école française. Vol.2.
DUPONT-HANSEN, GEORGE.
Pieces for piano, Op.1.
In: Samfundet til Udgivelse af dansk Musik. Suppl.1899.
DUPORT, JEAN PIERRE, 1741–1818.
Sonate (Am). Violoncello and piano.
In: Moffat. Meister-Schule der alter Zeit. Violoncello-Sonaten. No.2.
DUPORT, PIERRE LANDRIN.
Selections.
In: Engel. Music from the days of George Washington.
DU PRÈS, JOSQUIN, *see* DEPRÈS, JOSQUIN.
DUPUIS, THOMAS SANDERS, 1733–1796.
Cathedral music in score. v.1– .
Organ music.
In: Butcher. English organ music of the eighteenth century. Vol.1.
In: Tallis to Wesley. Vol.22.
Psalmen.
In: Musica sacra. ca.1842–1896. Vol.8–10.
Sacred music.
In: Arnold. Cathedral music. Vol.3.

In: Page. Harmonia sacra. Vol.1.
DUPUITS, JEAN BAPTISTE.
Sonate en ré majeur.
In: L'école du violon au XVIIe et XVIIIe siècle. No.1284.
DU PUY, JEAN BAPTISTE EDOUARD, 1770–1822.
Ouverture "Ungdom og Galskab" til Syngestykket.
In: Samfundet til Udgivelse af dansk Musik. Ser.III. No.105.
DÜR.
Vocal music.
In: Sammlung russischer Romanzen. No.99.
DURAN, *see* DURÓN, SEBASTIÁN.
DURAND.
Le retour du printemps.
In: L'école du violon au XVIIe et XVIIIe siècle. No.1336.
DURANTE, FRANCESCO, 1684–1755.
Selections.
In: Crotch. Specimens of various styles of music. Vol.2.
In: Expert. Répertoire classique de musique. 1re année.
Arias.
In: Parisotti. Arie antiche. Bd.2.
Aria, Ingemisco.
In: Königliche Akademie der Künste. Auswahl vorzüglicher Musik-Werke. Appendix.
Choral music.
In: Commer. Cantata sacra. Vol.1, No.7, 8.
In: Musica sacra. 1839– . Vol.2, 3.
In: Recueil de musique ancienne. Recueil des morceaux de musique ancienne. Bd.6.
In: Rochlitz. Sammlung vorzüglicher Gesangstücke. Bd.2.
Keyboard music.
In: Esposito. Early Italian piano music.
In: Farrenc. Le trésor des pianistes. Vol.9.
In: Pauer. Alte Klavier-Musik. 2d series. Part 1.
In: Tagliapietra. Antologia di musica antica e moderna per pianoforte. Bd.11.
Part music.
In: Hullah. Part music. Class A.1. Vol.2.
Sacred music.
In: The Fitzwilliam music. Bd.1, 4.
In: Latrobe, C. I. Selection of sacred music.
In: Latrobe, J. A. The music of the church.
Sonate, toccate e divertimenti.
In: I classici della musica italiana. Vol.11.
In: I classici della musica italiana. Raccolta nazionale delle musiche italiane. Quad.40–42, 303.
Songs.
In: Jeppesen. La flora. Vol.3.
In: Musica sacra. 1839– . Vol.4.
Studio.
In: Köhler. Les maîtres du clavecin. Heft 7.
Vocal music.
In: Delsarte. Archives du chant. Livr.7. No.11.
DURÓN, SEBASTIÁN, ca.1650–1716.
(var. sp.: Duran).
Selections.
In: Pedrell. Teatro lirico español anterior al siglo XIX. Bd.3, 4/5.
Sacred music.
In: Eslava y Elizondo. Lira sacro-hispana. 17th century. ii.1. and Appendix.
DUŠEK, FRANTIŠEK XAVER, 1731–1799.
Keyboard music.
In: Musica antiqua bohemica. Vol.14, 17.
Serenate Boeme.
In: Musica antiqua bohemica. Vol.35.
Sonate per il clavicembalo.
In: Musica antiqua bohemica. Vol.8.
DUSÍK, JAN LADISLAV, *see* DUSSEK, JAN LADISLAV.
DUSSEK, JAN LADISLAV, 1760–1812.
(var. sp.: Jan Ladislav Dušek; Jan Ladislav Dusík).
Keyboard music.
In: Farrenc. Le trésor des pianistes. Vol.18.
In: Musica antiqua bohemica. Vol.17, 20, 21.
In: Tagliapietra. Antologia di musica antica e moderna per pianoforte. Bd.14.
Sonate. Part I–III.
In: Musica antiqua bohemica. Vol.46, 53, 59.
3 Sonates. Piano.
In: Répertoire des clavecinistes. Heft 3.
Sonate B-dur, Op.45, Nr.1. Piano.
In: Organum. 5.Reihe. Nr.12.
Sonate C-moll, Op.35, Nr.3. Piano.
In: Organum. 5.Reihe. Nr.22.
Sonate G-moll, Op.10, Nr.2. Piano; Sonate Es-dur (The farewell), Op.44. Piano.
In: Organum. 5.Reihe. Nr.3, 6.
Sonate. Op.69, No.1, 2. Violino e piano.
In: Musica antiqua bohemica. Vol.41.
6 Sonatines pour la harpe.
In: Musica antiqua bohemica. Vol.22.
Songs.
In: Documenta historica musicae.
Violin and piano.
In: Musica antiqua bohemica. Vol.11.
DUTCH EAST INDIES–MUSIC.
In: Musicologisch onderzoek.
DUTCH MUSIC, *see* NETHERLANDS–MUSIC.
A DUTCH MUSIC-BOOK (1572).
In: Vereniging voor Nederlandsche Muziekgeschiedenis. Uitgave. No.26.
DU TERTRE, GUILLAUME, *see* TERTRE, GUILLAUME DU.
DÜTSCH.
Vocal music.
In: Sammlung russischer Romanzen. No.260, 308.
DÜTSCH-WARLAMOFF.
Vocal music.
In: Sammlung russischer Romanzen.
DU VAL, FRANÇOIS, ca.1673–1728.
La girouette.
In: L'école du violon au XVIIe et XVIIIe siècle. No.1293.
Papillon.
In: L'école du violon au XVIIe et XVIIIe siècle. No.1343.
Sonate en la majeur.
In: L'école du violon au XVIIe et XVIIIe siècle. No.1251.
DVOŘÁK, ANTONÍN, 1841–1904.
Kritische Gesamtausgabe. 7 series.
A Slavonic cradle song. S.A.T.B.

In: Arion. Vol.2.
DYCKERHOFF, W.
Organ music.
In: Muziek voor de eredienst. Vol.1.
DYSON, GEORGE, 1883– .
Selections.
In: The music with the form and order of the service to be performed at the coronation of . . . Queen Elizabeth II.

EARLY AMERICAN HYMN TUNES, 1800–1860.
In: Music Press, Inc. [Choral series]. No.55.
EARLY TUDOR MAGNIFICATS. VOL.1.
In: Early English church music. Vol.5.
EARLY TUDOR MASSES. VOL.1, 2.
In: Early English church music. Vol.1, 4.
EARSDEN, JOHN, 16th–17th CENTURIES.
Selections.
In: Smith. Musica antiqua.
Ayres. (1618).
In: Fellowes. The English school of lutenist song writers. 2d series. Vol.18.
EAST, MICHAEL, ca.1580–1648.
(var. sp.: Michael Este).
A collection of anthems.
In: Musical Antiquarian Society. Publications. Vol.14.
Madrigals.
In: Fellowes. The English madrigal school. Vol.29, 30, 31.
In: The triumphs of Oriana.
Vocal music.
In: Hullah. Vocal scores. II. Secular.
EAST, THOMAS, ca.1540–ca.1609.
(var. sp.: Easte, Este, Est).
The whole book of psalms.
In: Musical Antiquarian Society. Publications. Vol.11.
EASTERN ORTHODOX CHURCH. LITURGY AND RITUAL, *see* ORTHODOX EASTERN CHURCH. LITURGY AND RITUAL.
EBART, SAMUEL, 1655–1684.
Miserere, Christe, mei.
In: Organum. 1.Reihe. Nr.23.
EBELING, JOHANN GEORG, 1637–1676.
(var. sp.: Johann Georg Eberling).
Choral music.
In: Antiqua Chorbuch. Vol.1. Heft 5.
Zwölf geistliche Lieder.
In: Chor-Archiv.
EBERL, ANTON.
Selections.
In: Denkmäler der Tonkunst in Österreich. Vol.79. (Jg.XLII/2).
EBERLIN, JOHANN ERNST, 1702–1762.
Der blutschwitzende Jesus.
In: Denkmäler der Tonkunst in Österreich. Vol.55. (Jg.XXVIII/1).
Church music.
In: Denkmäler der Tonkunst in Österreich. Vol.80. (Jg.XLIII/1).
Keyboard music.
In: Clementi. Clementi's Selection of practical harmony. Vol.1, 2.
In: Farrenc. Le trésor des pianistes. Vol.11.
In: Pauer. Alte Klavier-Music. 2d series. Part 2.
Organ music.
In: Biggs. A treasury of shorter organ classics.
In: Cantantibus organis. Vol.3.
In: Organ masters of the Baroque period. Vol.3.
In: Raugel. Quarante-six pièces pour orgue ou harmonium.
Prélude et fugue.
In: Köhler. Les maîtres du clavecin. Heft 5.
Prelude and fugue in E minor. Piano.
In: Roitzsch. Alte Klavier-Musik.
EBERLING, JOHANN GEORG, *see* EBELING, JOHANN GEORG.
EBNER, WOLFGANG, ca.1610–1665.
Keyboard music.
In: Tagliapietra. Antologia di musica antica e moderna per pianoforte. Bd.7.
ECCARD, JOHANN, 1553–1611.
Choral music.
In: Antiqua Chorbuch. Vol.1. Heft 3; Vol.2. Heft 4.
In: Der Kammerchor. Vol.5.
Neue geistliche und weltliche Lieder.
In: Publikationen älterer praktischer und theoretischer Musikwerke. Jahrg.25.
ECCLES, HENRY, 1670–1742.
Sonata E-moll (La Guitate) für Violine und Pianoforte.
In: Moffat. Kammer-Sonaten für Violine und Pianoforte. No.28.
Sonate (Fm). Violoncello and piano.
In: Moffat. Meister-Schule der alten Zeit. Violoncello-Sonaten. No.7.
ECCLES, JOHN, ca.1650–1735.
Keyboard music.
In: Fuller-Maitland. The contemporaries of Purcell. Vol.6–7.
In: Herrmann. Contemporaries of Purcell.
ECKARD, JOHANN GOTTFRIED, 1735–1809.
Oeuvres complètes pour le clavecin ou le pianoforte. 94p.
ECKEL, MATTHIAS, 16th CENTURY.
(var. sp.: Mathias Eckel).
Choral music.
In: Moser. Die Kantorei der Spätgotik.
Lieder.
In: Publikationen älterer praktischer und theoretischer Musikwerke. Jahrg.1–3.
ECKHARDT-GRAMATTÉ, SOPHIE CARMEN, 1902– .
Duo. Nr.2.
In: Hausmusik. No.76.
EDELMANN, JOHANN FRIEDRICH, 1749–1794.
Sonata. Piano. Op.VIII, No.1.
In: Reeser. De klaviersonate.
EDER, HELMUT, 1916– .
Musica semplice. Op.23, Nr.1.
In: Collegium musicae novae. No.28.
Musik für zwei Trompeten und Streichorchester, Op.23, Nr.2.
In: Collegium musicae novae. No.46.
EDWARDS, RICHARD, ca.1522–1566.
(var. sp.: Edwardes).
Madrigals.
In: Fellowes. The English madrigal school. Vol.36, 37.
Part music.

In: Hullah. Part music. Class A.2. Vol.1.
EFFINGER, CECIL, 1914– .
Prelude and fugue. Organ.
In: Contemporary organ series. No.17.
EGUINO, JOSÉ MARÍA NEMESIO OTAÑO, Y, *see* OTAÑO Y EGUINO, JOSÉ MARÍA NEMESIO.
EHRHARDT-PITSCH, ELSE.
5 Flötensprünge.
In: Zeitschrift für Spielmusik. No.113.
EICHNER, ERNST, 1740–1777.
Duette für Violine und Bratsche, Op.10.
In: Nagels Musik-Archiv. No.125, 128.
Orchestral music.
In: Riemann. Mannheim symphonists. Vol.2.
Sonata F-dur für Violine und Klavier.
In: Sondheimer. Werke aus dem 18. Jahrhundert. Nr.15.
EIJL, ANNA MARIA VAN, *see* EYL, ANNA MARIA VAN.
EINSTEIN, ALFRED, 1880–1952. ed.
Canzoni sonetti strambotti et frottole, libro tertio.
In: Smith College music archives. No.4.
EISEL, GÜNTHER.
Klaviersonate.
In: Marckhl. Klavierwerke steiermärkischer Komponisten. Vol.2.
Kleine Fuge. Organ.
In: Orgelmusik steirischer Komponisten.
EISLER, HANNS, 1898–1962.
Lieder und Kantaten. v.1– .
EITELWEIN, HEINRICH, ca.1520.
Choral music.
In: Antiqua Chorbuch. Vol.2. Heft 1.
EIZENBERGER, JOSEF.
Österreichische Tanzsuite.
In: Zeitschrift für Spielmusik. No.67.
ELDUAYEN, P. TOMÁS DE.
Organ music.
In: Organ album of ten pieces by Spanish composers.
ELER, ANDREAS.
Quartett. Streicher. Op.2, Nr.3.
In: Organum. 3.Reihe. Nr.49.
ELGAR, SIR EDWARD WILLIAM, 1857–1934.
Organ music.
In: Standard series of organ compositions. No.49.
ELIAS, FR. MANUEL DE SANTO, 18th CENTURY.
Keyboard music.
In: Kastner. Silva iberica.
ELIAS, JOSEPH, 1675–1749.
Organ music.
In: Muset. Early Spanish organ music.
ELIZABETH II, QUEEN OF GREAT BRITAIN, 1926– .
Coronation music.
In: The music with the form and order of the service to be performed at the coronation of . . . Queen Elizabeth II.
ELIZABETHAN CONSORT SONGS.
In: Musica Britannica. Vol.22.
ELLIOTT, KENNETH. ed.
Music of Scotland, 1500–1700.
In: Musica Britannica. Vol.15.
ELMENHORST, HEINRICH, 1632–1704.
Lieder.
In: Denkmäler deutscher Tonkunst. [1.Folge]. Vol.45.
In: Organum. 2.Reihe. No.9.
EMBORG, JENS LAURSØN, 1876–1957.
Concerto for Orgel med Strygere og Klaver. Op.49.
In: Samfundet til Udgivelse af dansk Musik. Ser.III. No.20.
Concerto for Strygere og Piano. Op.72.
In: Samfundet til Udgivelse af dansk Musik. Ser.III. No.45.
Kammer-Koncert. Op.57.
In: Samfundet til Udgivelse af dansk Musik. Ser.III. No.83.
De Tolv Masker. Op.50.
In: Samfundet til Udgivelse af dansk Musik. Ser.III. No.99.
ENCINA, JUAN DEL, ca.1468–ca.1530.
Soy contento y vos servido.
In: Parrish. A treasury of early music. No.19.
ENGEL, CARL, 1818–1882.
Psalmen.
In: Musica sacra. ca.1842–1896. Vol.8–10.
ENGEL, HANS. ed.
The concerto grosso.
In: Anthology of music. Vol.23.
The sixteenth-century part song in Italy, France, England and Spain.
In: Anthology of music. Vol.3.
The solo concerto.
In: Anthology of music. Vol.25.
ENGEL, LEHMAN, 1910– .
4 Excerpts from "Job." Op.3. Voice and piano.
In: New music. Vol.6. No.1. Oct.1932.
Piano music.
In: Boletín latino-americano de música. Vol.5.
Sonata for violoncello and piano.
In: Society for the Publication of American Music. Publications. 27th season. 1945–46.
ENGELBRECHT, RICHARD.
Selections.
In: Instituto Interamericano de Musicologia. Publicaciónes. No.3, 26.
ENGELMANN, GEORG, 16th–17th CENTURIES.
Chamber music.
In: Riemann. Old chamber music. Vol.2.
ENGLAND–CATHEDRAL MUSIC.
In: Arnold. Cathedral music.
In: Boyce. Cathedral music.
In: Dupuis. Cathedral music in score.
In: Page. Harmonia sacra.
ENGLAND–MUSIC (*see also* FOLKSONGS, ENGLISH; SONGS, ENGLISH).
In: Arkwright. The Old English edition.
In: Butcher. English organ music of the eighteenth century. 2v.
In: Chappell. The ballad literature and popular music of the olden time.
In: Chappell. Old English popular music.
In: Chappell. Old English popular music. A new ed.
In: Contemporary British piano music.
In: Crotch. Specimens of various styles of music. Vol.1.
In: Early English church music.
In: Elizabethan virginal composers.

In: English instrumental music of the 16th and 17th centuries from manuscripts in the New York Public Library.
In: English keyboard music.
In: English songs.
In: Glyn. Twenty-one Old English compositions of the 16th and 17th centuries.
In: Hullah. 58 English songs of the 17th and 18th century.
In: The music with the form and order of the service to be performed at the coronation of . . . Queen Elizabeth II.
In: Musica Britannica.
In: Musical Antiquarian Society. Publications.
In: Parthenia.
In: Parthenia-in-Violata.
In: Pauer. Old English composers for the virginals and harpsichord.
In: Plainsong and Mediaeval Music Society. Publications. (Glyn. Madrigals by English composers).
In: Playford. The English dancing master.
In: Playford. Old English dance tunes.
In: Potter. Reliquary of English song.
In: Rimbault. The rounds, catches and canons of England.
In: Schott's Series of early lute music. Vol.2.
In: Tallis to Wesley.
In: The triumphs of Oriana.
In: Tudor church music.
In: West. Old English organ music.
In: Zeitschrift für Spielmusik. No.92, 262.

ENRIQUEZ DE VALDERRÁBANO, ENRIQUE, 16th CENTURY.
Choral music.
In: Engel. Three centuries of choral music. Vol.5.
Keyboard music.
In: Apel. Musik aus früher Zeit für Klavier. Bd.2.
Lute music.
In: Morphy. Les luthistes espagnols du XVIe siècle. Vol.2.
Songs.
In: Bal y Gay. Romances y villancicos españoles del signo XVI.

ENSINA, JUAN DEL.
Choral music.
In: Engel. Three centuries of choral music. Vol.5.

EPISCOPIUS, LUDOVICUS, ca.1520–1595.
Selections.
In: Maldéghem. Trésor musical.
Choral music.
In: Musica antiqua batava. MA–4, 5.

ERARS, JEHAN.
Selections.
In: Smith. Musica antiqua.

ERARS, THOMAS.
Selections.
In: Smith. Musica antiqua.

ERAUZQUIN, JOSÉ ANTONIO DE.
Organ music.
In: Organ album of ten pieces by Spanish composers.

ERBACH, CHRISTIAN, 1573–1635.
Selected works.
In: Denkmäler deutscher Tonkunst. [2.Folge]. Vol.4 (ii).
Canzona "La paglia" für 3 Violinen und 2 Violoncello.
In: Hortus musicus. No.156.
Keyboard music.
In: Tagliapietra. Antologia di musica antica e moderna per pianoforte. Bd.3.
Organ music.
In: Cantantibus organis. Vol.1, 2, 4, 8.
In: Liber organi. Bd.6.
In: The Liturgical Music Press, Inc. Masterpieces of organ music. Folio 44.
Drei Introitus mit Versus. Organ.
In: Die Orgel. Reihe II. Nr.11.

ERBACH, FRIEDRICH KARL, GRAF ZU, 1680–1731.
Divertissement melodieux D-dur für 2 Violinen und Generalbass.
In: Organum. 3.Reihe. Nr.60.
6 Duos für 2 Violoncello (oder Fagotte).
In: Hortus musicus. No.122.

ERDMANN, DIETRICH, 1917– .
Serenade für Streichorchester und Bläser.
In: Collegium musicae novae. No.21.

EREDIA, PIETRO.
Selections.
In: Torchi. L'arte musicale in Italia. Bd.4.

ERICH, DANIEL, 17th–18th CENTURIES.
Organ music.
In: Dietrich. Elf Orgelchoräle des siebzehnten Jahrhunderts.
In: Straube. Choralvorspiele alter Meister.

ERIKSSON, JOSEF, 1872– .
Selections.
In: Svensk sanglyrik. Vol.1.

ERLEBACH, PHILIPP HEINRICH, 1657–1714.
Ausgewählte Arien und Duette.
In: Organum. 2.Reihe. Nr.8.
3 Arien für mittlere Singstimme, 2 Alt-Blockflöten und Basso Continuo.
In: Moecks gelbe Musikhefte. Vol.3.
Choral music.
In: Antiqua Chorbuch. Vol.1. Heft 5.
Harmonische Freunde.
In: Denkmäler deutscher Tonkunst. [1.Folge]. Vol.46–47.
Der Herr hat offenbaret. Kantate.
In: Organum. 1.Reihe. Nr.33.
Ouvertüren-Suite. C-dur; D-moll. Für Streicher (Ouvertüren, 1693, Nr.3–4).
In: Organum. 3.Reihe. Nr.15, 16.
Sonate (E-moll) (1694) für Violine, Gambe (oder Violoncello) und Cembalo.
In: Organum. 3.Reihe. Nr.5.
Sonate 1, D-dur, für Violine, Gambe und Basso Continuo; Sonate III, A-dur, für Violine, Gambe und Basso Continuo.
In: Hortus musicus. No.117, 118.

ERRECART, HÉCTOR A. TOSAR, *see* TOSAR ERRECART, HÉCTOR A.

ERTEL.
Organ music.
In: Cantantibus organis. Vol.7.

ERYTHRÄUS, GOTTHARD, ca.1560–1617.
Choral music.
In: Antiqua Chorbuch. Vol.1. Heft 3.

ESCOBAR, JUAN.
Choral music.
In: Engel. Three centuries of choral music. Vol.5.
ESCOBAR, PEDRO DE, 16th CENTURY.
Selections.
In: Monumentos de la música española. Vol.1.
Motets.
In: Elúsitiza. Antología musical.
ESCOBEDO, BARTOLOMEO, ca.1515–1563.
(var. sp.: Bartolomé Escobedo).
Selections.
In: Ambros. Auserwählte Tonwerke.
Exsurge, quare obdormis; Immutemur.
In: Polifonía española. Vol.13, 14.
Sacred music.
In: Eslava y Elizondo. Lira sacro-hispana. 16th century. i.1.
ESCUREL, JEHANNOT DE L'., 14th CENTURY.
Collected works. p.1– .
Selections.
In: Gleason. Examples of music before 1400.
ESLAVA Y ELIZONDO, HILARIÓN, 1807–1878.
Sacred music.
In: Eslava y Elizondo. Lira sacro-hispana. 19th century. ii.1.
ESNAOLA, J. P.
Selections.
In: Antologia de compositores argentinos.
ESPINOSA, JUAN D', 16th CENTURY.
Choral music.
In: Engel. Three centuries of choral music. Vol.5.
ESPOSITO, MICHELE, 1855–1929.
Keyboard music.
In: Tagliapietra. Antologia di musica antica e moderna per pianoforte. Bd.17.
ESQUIVEL, JUAN BARAHONA DE, 16th–17th CENTURIES.
(var. sp.: Joannes Esquivel).
Sacred music.
In: Rubio. Antologia polifonica sacra. Vol.1.
ESTE, MICHAEL, *see* EAST, MICHAEL.
ESTE, THOMAS, *see* EAST, THOMAS.
ESTEVE, PABLO, d.1794.
Selections.
In: Pedrell. Teatro lirico español anterior al siglo XIX. Bd.2.
ESTOCART, PASCHAL DE L', b.1540.
Premier livre des octonaires de la vanité du monde.
In: Expert. Monuments de la musique française du temps de la Renaissance. Vol.10.
Second livre des octonaires de la vanité du monde.
In: Expert. Monuments de la musique française du temps de la Renaissance. Vol.11.
ESTRADA, CARLOS, 1909– .
Caminos tristes.
In: Instituto Interamericano de Musicologia. Publicaciónes. No.4.
ETLER, ALVIN BERARD, 1913– .
Piano music.
In: Boletín latino-americano de música. Vol.5.
THE ETON CHOIR BOOK.
In: Musica Britannica. Vol.10, 11, 12.
ETT, CASPAR, 1788–1847.
Organ music.
In: Cantantibus organis. Vol.3.
EUGENIEFF.
Vocal music.
In: Sammlung russischer Romanzen. No.137.
EUROPEAN FOLKSONGS. (WIORA).
In: Anthology of music. Vol.4.
THE EUTERPE ROUND BOOK.
In: Euterpe. 2d ed. No.56.
EVANGELIARIUM.
In: Monumenta musicae byzantinae. Lectionaria. Vol.2. Fasc.1.
EVRY, E.D'.
Organ music.
In: Standard series of organ compositions. No.30.
EWALDT.
Organ music.
In: Corpus of early keyboard music. Vol.10, Pt.1.
EXAUDET, ANDRÉ JOSEPH, ca.1710–1762.
Sonate en ut mineur.
In: L'école du violon au XVIIe et XVIIIe siècle. No.1289.
EYBLER, JOSEPH, 1765–1846.
3 Menuette.
In: Hausmusik. No.49.
EYL, ANNA MARIA VAN.
(var. sp.: Van Eijl).
Klavier-Boek.
In: Monumenta musica Neerlandica. Vol.2.
Old Dutch clavier music from the Music-book of . . .
In: Vereniging voor Nederlandsche Muziekgeschiedenis. Uitgave. No.37.
EZNARRIAGA, CÁNDIDO, 17th CENTURY.
Organ music.
In: Muset. Early Spanish organ music.

FABER, FRANK.
Eine kleine Weihnachtskantate für 2 Singstimmen und 3 Blockflöten.
In: Zeitschrift für Spielmusik. No.50.
Eine neuer Tag ist angebrochen.
In: Zeitschrift für Spielmusik. No.80.
FABER, JOHANN CHRISTOPH, fl.1730.
Partita für drei Blockflöten oder andere Melodieinstrumente.
In: Nagels Musik-Archiv. No.88.
FABINI, F. EDUARDO, 1883–1950.
Songs with piano.
In: Boletín latino-americano de música. Vol.1.
FABRIANESE, TIBERIO, 16th CENTURY.
La canzon della Gallina.
In: Squire. Ausgewählte Madrigale und mehrstimmige Gesänge. No.28.
FABRICUS, J.
Brogede Blade. Piano.
In: Samfundet til Udgivelse af dansk Musik. Suppl.1918.
FABRIS, STEPHANI.
Choral music.
In: Monumenta liturgiae polychoralis sanctae ecclesiae romanae. Ser.IV. No.11, 12.
FACOLI, MARCO.
Collected works.
In: Corpus of early keyboard music. Vol.2.

FACSIMILES.
In: Aich. Das Liederbuch des Arnt von Aich.
In: Attaingnant. Chansons und Tänze.
In: Aubry. Cent motets du XVIIIe siècle.
In: Bach, J. S. Werke. Vol.44.
In: Bannister. Monumenti Vaticani di paleografia musicale latina.
In: Barcelona. Biblioteca Central. Sección de Música. Publicaciones. Vol.6, 15.
In: Basses danses. Le manuscrit dit Des basses danses de la Bibliothèque de Bourgogne. [46] p.
In: Beck. Les chansonniers des troubadours et des trouvères.
In: Billings. The continental harmony.
In: Buxheimer Orgelbuch. Das Buxheimer Orgelbuch.
In: Catholic Church, Roman. Liturgy and ritual. Troper. The Winchester troper.
In: Chansonnier d'Arras. Le chansonnier d'Arras.
In: Codax. Las siete canciones de amor.
In: Codex Escorial. Chansonnier. Ms.V.III.24.
In: Copenhagen Kongelige Bibliotek. Mss. (Thottske Samling 291^{8}). Der kopenhagener Chansonnier.
In: Early Bodleian music. [II] and [III].
In: Écorcheville. Vingt suites d'orchestre du XVIIe siècle français.
In: Fantini. Modo per imparare a sonare di tromba tanto di gverra quanto musicalmente in organo.
In: Fauvel. Le roman de Fauvel.
In: Fürstliches Institut für Musikwissenschaftliche Forschung. Veröffentlichung. [Nr.] 1.
In: Fürstliches Institut für Musikwissenschaftliche Forschung. Veröffentlichungen. 2.Reihe. [Nr.] 2, 3.
In: Institute of Mediaeval Music. Publications.
In: Jenaer Liederhandschrift. Die Jenaer Liederhandschrift. Facsimile ed.
In: Liuzzi. La lauda.
In: Das Locheimer Liederbuch. Das Locheimer Liederbuch und Fundamentum organisandi des Conrad Paumann.
In: Mantica. Prime fioriture del melodramma italiano.
In: Montpellier, France. Université. Faculté de Médicine. Bibliothèque. Mss. (H 196). Polyphonies du XIIIe siècle.
In: Monumenta musicae byzantinae. Série principale.
In: Monumenta musicae sacrae.
In: Monuments of music and music literature. First series.
In: Musikalische Seltenheiten.
In: Paléographie musicale.
In: Państwowa Wyższa Szkoła Muzyczna w Katowicach.
In: Parthenia.
In: Parthenia-in-Violata.
In: Petrucci. Harmonice musices Odhecaton A.
In: Plainsong and Mediaeval Music Society. Publications.
In: Publikationen älterer praktischer und theoretischer Musikwerke. Jahrg.10, 12.
In: Radino. Il primo libro d'intavolatura di balli d'arpicordo.
In: Reale Accademia d'Italia, Rome. Musica.
In: Runge. Die Sangesweisen der Colmarer Handschrift und die Liederhandschrift Donaueschingen.
In: Schlick. Tabulaturen etlicher Lobgesang und Lidlein uff die Orgeln und Lauten.
In: Société Française de Musicologie, Paris. Publications. Ser.I. Bd.6, 7.
In: Stanley. Voluntaries for the organ.
In: Summa musicae medii aevi. Vol.5, 6, 11.
In: Thibaut. Monuments de la notation ekphonétique et neumatic de l'église latine.
In: Wienhäuser Liederbuch. Das Wienhäuser Liederbuch.
In: Wolfenbüttel. Herzog-August-Bibliothek. Mss. (677 [Helmst 628]). An old St. Andrews music book.
In: Zagiba. Die ältesten musikalischen Denkmäler zu Ehren des heiligen Leopold, Herzog und Patron von Österreich.
FAGE, JUSTE ADRIEN LENOIR DE LA, 1805–1862.
Motets.
In: Attaingnant. Treize livres de motets. Livre 3, 4, 11.
FAIGNIENT, NOËL, 16th CENTURY.
Selections.
In: Maldéghem. Trésor musical.
FAIRFAX, ROBERT, *see* FAYRFAX, ROBERT.
FALCONE, ACHILLE.
Selections.
In: Torchi. L'arte musicale in Italia. Bd.2.
FALCONIERO, ANDREA, 1586–1656.
Selections.
In: Torchi. L'arte musicale in Italia. Bd.7.
Arias.
In: Parisotti. Arie antiche. Bd.2, 3.
Songs.
In: Jeppesen. La flora. Vol.2, 3.
FALK, GEORG PAUL.
Instrumental music.
In: Denkmäler der Tonkunst in Österreich. Vol.86.
FALLA, MANUEL DE, 1876–1946.
Keyboard music.
In: Guenther. Collection espagnole.
FALLAMERO, GABRIEL, 16th CENTURY.
Lute music.
In: Chilesotti. Lautenspieler des XVI. Jahrhunderts.
FANO, FABIO. ed.
La camerata fiorentina: Vincenzo Galilei, 1520? –1591.
In: Istituzioni e monumenti dell'arte musicale italiana. Vol.4.
Le origini e il primo maestro di cappella: Matteo da Perugia.
In: Istituzioni e monumenti dell'arte musicale italiana. Nuova serie. Vol.1.
FANTASIAS.
In: English instrumental music of the 16th and 17th centuries from manuscripts in the New York Public Library. No.2.
In: Hortus musicus. No.14, 18, 19, 64.

FANTINI, GIROLAMO, fl.1638.
Modo per imparare a sonare di tromba. 86p.
FARINA, CARLO.
Chamber music.
In: Riemann. Old chamber music. Vol.2, 3.
FARMER, JOHN, fl.1591–1601.
Choral music.
In: Engel. Three centuries of choral music. Vol.3.
Madrigals.
In: Fellowes. The English madrigal school. Vol.8.
In: Squire. Ausgewählte Madrigale und mehrstimmige Gesänge. No.39.
In: The triumphs of Oriana.
FARNABY, GILES, ca.1560–1640.
Giles Farnaby's dreame. Organ.
In: Dickinson. Historical recital series for organ. Vol.2. No.25.
Keyboard music.
In: English keyboard music. [No.11].
In: The Fitzwilliam virginal book.
In: The Fitzwilliam virginal book. Ausgewählte Stücke. Vol.2.
In: Georgii. Keyboard music of the Baroque and Rococo. Vol.1.
In: Tagliapietra. Antologia di musica antica e moderna per pianoforte. Bd.2.
Loth to depart.
In: Parrish. Masterpieces of music before 1750. No.29.
Madrigals.
In: Fellowes. The English madrigal school. Vol.20.
FARNABY, RICHARD, 16th–17th CENTURIES.
Keyboard music.
In: The Fitzwilliam virginal book.
FARRANT, RICHARD, ca.1530–1581.
Selections.
In: Crotch. Specimens of various styles of music. Vol.2.
Church music.
In: Motett Society. [Collection of ancient church music]. Division 3.
Part music.
In: Hullah. Part music. Class A.1. Vol.1.
Sacred music.
In: Boyce. Cathedral music. Vol.1, 2; 1849, Vol.1, 2.
In: Page. Harmonia sacra. Vol.1.
Vocal music.
In: Hullah. Vocal scores. I. Sacred.
FARWELL, ARTHUR, 1872–1952.
Songs. Piano music.
In: The Wa-Wan series of American compositions.
FASCH, JOHANN FRIEDRICH, 1688–1758.
Compositions.
In: Das Erbe deutscher Musik. 1.Reihe. Vol.11.
Canon/Sonata a 3, F-dur, für Alt-Blockflöte, Violine und Basso Continuo.
In: Moecks Kammermusik. Vol.46.
Duette alter Meister.
In: Zeitschrift für Spielmusik. No.69.
Fugue, Meine Zunge.
In: Königliche Akademie der Künste. Auswahl vorzüglicher Musik-Werke. No.2.
Keyboard music.
In: Clementi. Clementi's Selection of practical harmony. Vol.1.
Konzert in D-dur.
In: Corona. Vol.65.
Konzert D-moll für Oboe oder Sopranblockflöte.
In: Corona. Vol.77.
Sinfonie in G-dur.
In: Corona. Vol.43, 59.
Sonata for bassoon (cello) and figured bass.
In: Music for wind instruments by 18th century masters. No.11.
Sonata a 4, für Altblockflöte, Oboe und Violine, Violoncello und ausgesetzten Generalbass.
In: Nagels Musik-Archiv. No.148.
Sonata a 4 in D moll. Für 2 Violinen, Viola und Violoncell.
In: Riemann. Collegium musicum. No.13.
Sonate B-dur für Blockflöte, Oboe (Violine), Violine und Basso Continuo.
In: Hortus musicus. No.26.
Sonate G-dur für Querflöte, 2 Alt-Blockflöten und Basso Continuo.
In: Moecks Kammermusik. Vol.40.
Sonate für zwei Violinen und Basso Continuo.
In: Nagels Musik-Archiv. No.169.
Trios. Strings and piano.
In: Riemann. Collegium musicum. No.8, 9, 10, 11, 12.
Triosonate. Nr.1.
In: Nagels Musik-Archiv. No.56.
FASCH, KARL FRIEDRICH CHRISTIAN, 1736–1800.
Sämmtliche Werke. 2v. in 7 pts.
Ariette. Andantino.
In: Nagels Musik-Archiv. No.38.
Concert fugue. Organ.
In: Dickinson. Historical recital series for organ. Vol.2. No.24.
Keyboard music.
In: Farrenc. Le trésor des pianistes. Vol.15.
FASOLO, GIOVANNI BATTISTA, 17th CENTURY.
Arias.
In: Parisotti. Arie antiche. Bd.2, 3.
Keyboard music.
In: Tagliapietra. Antologia di musica antica e moderna per pianoforte. Bd.6.
Organ.
In: Cantantibus organis. Vol.1, 4, 8.
In: Klein. The first four centuries of music for the organ from Dunstable to Bach (1370–1749).
In: Liber organi. Bd.4.
In: Pierront. Cent versets de Magnificat.
FATTORINI, GABRIELE, 16th–17th CENTURIES.
(var. sp.: Gabriel Fatorini).
Selections.
In: Torchi. L'arte musicale in Italia. Bd.3.
FAUCHARD, A.
Le mystère de Noël. Organ.
In: Orgue et liturgie. Vol.12.
FAUGUES, GUILLAUME, 15th CENTURY.
Opera omnia. Complete edition of facsimiles.
In: Institute of Mediaeval Music. Publications. Vol.7.
Collected works. Transcriptions of all of the compositions.

In: Institute of Mediaeval Music. Collected works. Vol.1.
Missa super l'homme armé.
In: Monumenta polyphoniae liturgicae sanctae ecclesiae romanae. Ser.1. Tomus I. Fasc.4.
FAUGUES, AN INTRODUCTION TO. (GEORGE C. SCHÜTZE).
In: Institute of Mediaeval Music. Musicological studies. Vol.2.
FAUVEL.
Le roman de Fauvel. 220p.
Le roman de Fauvel. 7p., facsim.: 95 pl.
The roman de Fauvel.
In: Schrade. Polyphonic music of the fourteenth century. Vol.1.
FAUXBOURDON, AN HISTORICAL SURVEY. I. (E. TRUMBLE).
In: Institute of Mediaeval Music. Musicological studies. Vol.3.
FAUXBOURDONS.
In: Plainsong and Mediaeval Music Society. Publications.
FAYRFAX, ROBERT, ca.1465–1521.
(var. sp.: Robert Fairfax).
Collected works. v.1– .
Missa "Tecum principium."
In: Das Chorwerk. No.97.
Songs.
In: Plainsong and Mediaeval Music Society. Publications. (A collection of songs and madrigals . . .).
FECKER, ADOLF.
Das dreistimmige Blockflötenspiel aus dem Stegreif.
In: Moecks gelbe Musikhefte. Vol.10.
Lustige Hamburger Flötenstücke.
In: Zeitschrift für Spielmusik. No.162.
FEDELI, VITO, 1866–1933. ed.
Le cappelle musicali di Novara, dal secolo XVI a primordi dell'ottocento.
In: Istituzioni e monumenti dell'arte musicale italiana. Vol.3.
FEGERS, KARL.
Sechs kleine Weisen.
In: Bausteine für Musikerziehung und Musikpflege. B 142.
FELDMAN, MORTON.
Illusions for piano.
In: New music. Vol.23. No.4. July 1950.
FELICI, ALESSANDRO, 18th CENTURY.
Sacred music.
In: Latrobe, C. I. Selection of sacred music.
In: Latrobe, J. A. The music of the church.
FELLERER, KARL GUSTAV. ed.
Pre-classical polyphony.
In: Anthology of music. Vol.28.
FELSZTYŃSKI, SEBASTIAN VON, 15th–16th CENTURIES.
Prosa ad rorate. Tempore Paschali.
In: Surzyński. Monumenta musicae sacrae in Polonia. Vol.2.
FEO, FRANCESCO, ca.1691–1761.
Gratias and Deux Pater.
In: Königliche Akademie der Künste. Auswahl vorzüglicher Musik-Werke. Appendix.
FEO, SER.
Selections.
In: Pirrotta. The music of fourteenth-century Italy. Vol.5.
FERAGUT, BELTRAME, 15th CENTURY.
(var. sp.: Baltrame Feragu).
Sacred music.
In: Plainsong and Mediaeval Music Society. Publications. (Borren).
FERAND, ERNST THOMAS, 1887– . ed.
Improvisation.
In: Anthology of music. Vol.12.
FERARE, DE.
(var. sp.: Jo de Ferrare).
Motets.
In: Attaingnant. Treize livres de motets. Livre 3, 8.
FERDINAND III, HOLY ROMAN EMPEROR, 1608–1657.
Works.
In: Musikalische Werke der Kaiser Ferdinand III, Leopold I, und Joseph I. 2v.
FERDINAND, JOHANN KASPAR, ca.1670–ca.1738.
Organ music.
In: The parish organist. Vol.5–6.
FERNANDEZ, OSCAR LORENZO, 1897–1948.
Batuque. Negro dance from the opera "Malazarte."
In: New music. Orchestra series. No.26.
Keyboard music.
In: Guenther. Collection espagnole.
Moda. Piano.
In: New music. Vol.16. No.1. Oct.1942.
Música de cámara.
In: Boletín latino-americano de música. Vol.6.
Songs with piano.
In: Boletín latino-americano de música. Vol.1.
FERNÁNDEZ, P.
Sacred music.
In: Eslava y Elizondo. Lira sacro-hispana. 16th century. i.1.
FERNÁNDEZ CABALLERO, MANUEL, 1835–1906.
Sacred music.
In: Eslava y Elizondo. Lira sacro-hispana. 19th century. ii.2.
FERNÁNDEZ DE CASTILLEJA, PEDRO, ca.1490–1574.
Dispersit; Heu mihi.
In: Polifonía española. Vol.10, 11.
FERNANDEZ-LAVIE, FERNAND.
Gitarrespiel im Überblick. Einführung.
In: Moecks gelbe Musikhefte. Vol.49.
FERNSTRÖM, JOHN AXEL, 1897– .
Selections.
In: Svensk sanglyrik. Vol.1.
FERODI.
Sacred music.
In: The Fitzwilliam music. Bd.1.
FERRABOSCO, ALFONSO, ca.1575–1628.
Ayres.
In: Fellowes. The English school of lutenist song writers. 2d series. Vol.16.
Choral music.

In: Dehn. Sammlung älterer Musik aus dem XVI. und XVII. Jahrhundert.
Fantasias.
In: English instrumental music of the 16th and 17th centuries from manuscripts in the New York Public Library. No.2.
Madrigals from Musica transalpina.
In: Arkwright. The Old English edition. Vol.11–12.
Italienische Madrigale.
In: Das Chorwerk. No.58.
Organ music.
In: Cantantibus organis. Vol.6.
FERRABOSCO, MATTHIA, 1550–1616.
Selections.
In: Denkmäler der Tonkunst in Österreich. Vol.90.
FERRARA, DOMENICO DI.
Songs.
In: Riemann. Hausmusik aus alter Zeit.
FERRARA, SIMON DA.
Sacred music.
In: Jeppesen. Italia sacra musica. Vol.2.
FERRARE, *see* FERARE, DE.
FERRARESE, SIMON.
Selections.
In: Torchi. L'arte musicale in Italia. Bd.1.
FERRARIO.
Sacred music.
In: Proske. Musica divina. Annus primus. Tom 4.
FERRER, GUILLERMO, 18th CENTURY.
Selections.
In: Pedrell. Teatro lirico español anterior al siglo XIX. Bd.2, 3.
FERRER, MATEO, 1788–1864.
Sonatas. Piano.
In: Nin y Castellano. Seize sonates anciennes d'auteurs espagnols.
FERRY-REBEL, JEAN, *see* REBEL, JEAN FERRY.
FESCA, ALEXANDER ERNST, 1820–1849.
Lied.
In: Reimann. Das deutsche Lied. Vol.2.
FESCA, FRIEDRICH ERNST, 1789–1826.
Fugue, Lobet seinen Namen.
In: Königliche Akademie der Künste. Auswahl vorzüglicher Musik-Werke. No.8.
FESCH, WILLEM DE, 1687–1761.
(var. sp.: William de Fesch, William Defesch).
Konzert D-dur für Querflöte, Streicher und Basso Continuo. Op.X. Nr.7.
In: Nagels Musik-Archiv. No.195.
Sechs Sonaten für Violine und Basso Continuo.
In: Hortus musicus. No.127, 128.
Sonate (F). Violoncello and piano.
In: Moffat. Meister-Schule der alten Zeit. Violoncello-Sonaten. No.8.
Sonaten für 2 Violoncelli, Op.8, Nr.7–9, 10–12.
In: Moecks Kammermusik. Vol.19, 20.
Songs.
In: Potter. Reliquary of English song. Vol.2.
FESTA, COSTANZO, d.1545.
Opera omnia. v.1– .
Selections.
In: Maldéghem. Trésor musical.
In: Torchi. L'arte musicale in Italia. Bd.1.
Hymni per totum annum.
In: Monumenta polyphoniae italicae. Vol.3.
Italienische Madrigale.
In: Das Chorwerk. No.58.
Sacrae cantiones 3, 4, 5, 6 vocibus.
In: Monumenta polyphoniae italicae. Vol.2.
Sacred music.
In: Jeppesen. Italia sacra musica. Vol.1, 2.
Te Deum a 4.
In: Alfieri. Raccolta di musica sacra. Vol.7.
FESTA, SEBASTIANO.
Sacred music.
In: Jeppesen. Italia sacra musica. Vol.2.
FESTING, MICHAEL CHRISTIAN, ca.1680–1752.
Concerto a 7, D-dur, für zwei Flöten, Streicher und Basso Continuo, Op.3, Nr.10.
In: Nagels Musik-Archiv. No.203.
Sonate en si mineur.
In: L'école du violon au XVIIe et XVIIIe siècle. No.1274.
FETLER, PAUL, 1920– .
Three pieces for violin and piano.
In: Society for the Publication of American Music. Publications. 34th season. 1952–53.
FEVIN, ANTOINE DE, ca.1474–1512.
(var. sp.: Antonius Fevin).
Selections.
In: Ambros. Auserwählte Tonwerke.
Chanson.
In: Brown. Theatrical chansons of the 15th and early 16th centuries.
Descende in hortum meum.
In: Musica spiritualis. Ser.IIB. No.13.
Motets.
In: Attaingnant. Treize livres de motets. Livre 5, 10, 11.
Sacred music.
In: Eslava y Elizondo. Lira sacro-hispana. 16th century. i.1.
FÉVRIER, PIERRE.
Organ music.
In: Raugel. Les maîtres français de l'orgue. Vol.2.
FEYS, ARNOLDUS.
Selections.
In: Maldéghem. Trésor musical.
FIBICH, ZDENĚK, 1850–1900.
[Works]. v.1– .
Paradise. Organ.
In: Dickinson. Historical recital series for organ. Vol.2. No.29.
FICHER, JACOBO, 1896– .
Sonatina. Piano, trumpet, alto saxophone.
In: New music. Vol.12. No.1. Oct.1938.
FIEBIG, KURT, 1908– .
Concertino für Violine und Streichorchester.
In: Collegium musicae novae. No.3.
FIELD, JOHN, 1782–1837.
Concertos. Piano.
In: Musica Britannica. Vol.17.
Keyboard music.
In: Tagliapietra. Antologia di musica antica e moderna per pianoforte. Bd.14.
Rondo in E. Piano.
In: Roitzsch. Alte Klavier-Musik.
FILCIK, J. N. J.
Duette für 2 Violinen.

In: Musica viva historica. Vol.11.
FILLIMARINO, FABRIZIO.
Keyboard music.
In: Corpus of early keyboard music. Vol.24.
FILS, ANTONÍN, *see* FILTZ, ANTON.
FILTZ, ANTON, ca.1730–1760.
(var. sp.: Antonín Fils, Anton Filz).
Böhmische Sinfonie A-dur.
In: Sondheimer. Werke aus dem 18. Jahrhundert. Nr.23.
Concerto Re maggiore. Flauto e piano.
In: Musica antiqua bohemica. Vol.18.
Orchestral music.
In: Riemann. Mannheim symphonists. Vol.1, 2.
6 Sinfonie per orchestra. Op.2.
In: Musica antiqua bohemica. Vol.44.
Symphonies.
In: Denkmäler deutscher Tonkunst. [2.Folge]. Vol.3 (i).
Trio in Es dur. Op.3, Nr.5. Für 2 Violinen, Violoncell und Klavier.
In: Riemann. Collegium musicum. No.17.
FILZ, ANTON, *see* FILTZ, ANTON.
FINCK, HEINRICH, 1445–1527.
Ausgewählte Werke.
In: Das Erbe deutscher Musik. 1.Reihe. Vol.57.
Ausgewählte Kompositionen.
In: Publikationen älterer praktischer und theoretischer Musikwerke. Jahrg.7.
Selections.
In: Ambros. Auserwählte Tonwerke.
Choral music.
In: Antiqua Chorbuch. Vol.1. Heft 1; Vol.2. Heft 1.
In: Capella. Vol.1.
In: Moser. Die Kantorei der Spätgotik.
Hymnen.
In: Das Chorwerk. No.9, 32.
Instrumental music.
In: Nagels Musik-Archiv. No.53.
Lieder.
In: Denkmäler der Tonkunst in Österreich. Vol.72. (Jg.XXXVII/2).
In: The Penn state music series. No.4.
Missa in summis.
In: Das Chorwerk. No.21.
In: Denkmäler der Tonkunst in Württemberg. Heft 1.
Organ music.
In: Cantantibus organis. Vol.8.
In: Schering. Alte Meister aus der Frühzeit des Orgelspiels.
FINE, IRVING GIFFORD, 1914– .
String quartet.
In: Society for the Publication of American Music. Publications. 35th season. 1953–54.
FINE, VIVIAN, 1913– .
The great wall of China. For voice and flute.
In: New music. Vol.21. No.3. Apr.1948.
Música de cámara.
In: Boletín latino-americano de música. Vol.5.
4 Songs.
In: New music. Vol.6. No.4. July 1933.
FINETTI, J.
Sacred music.
In: Proske. Musica divina. Annus primus. Tom 4.
FINGER, GOTTFRIED GODFREY, b.ca.1660.
Sonate für zwei f-Blockflöten oder Blockflöte und Violine (Oboe) und B.C.
In: Musica practica. No.26.
2 Sonaten für 2 Alt-Blockflöten oder Querflöten.
In: Moecks Kammermusik. Vol.7.
FINKBEINER, REINHOLD, 1929– .
Sinfonia piccola.
In: Collegium musicae novae. No.43.
FINNEY, ROSS LEE, 1906– .
String quartet. No.4.
In: Society for the Publication of American Music. Publications. 30th season. 1948–49.
Piano sonata.
In: New music. Vol.11. No.1. Oct.1937.
Vocal music.
In: Boletín latino-americano de música. Vol.5.
FIOCCO, JOSEPH HECTOR, 1703–1741.
(var. sp.: Gioseffo Hectore Fiocco; Jozef Hector Fiocco).
Werken voor clavecimbel.
In: Monumenta musicae belgicae. Vol.3.
Lamentatio prima. Sopran, 2 Violoncelli (Viola da Gamba) und B.C.
In: Die Kantate. No.13.
Lamentatio secunda. Sopran, Violoncello (Viola da Gamba) und B.C.
In: Die Kantate. No.6.
Lamentatio tertia. Sopran (Tenor) und B.C.
In: Cantio sacra. No.33.
Concerting motets.
In: Monumenta musicae belgicae. Vol.11.
Organ music.
In: Peeters. Oudnederlandse meesters. Vol.1, 2.
FIORILLO, FEDERIGO, 1755–d.after 1823.
28e caprice.
In: L'école du violon au XVIIe et XVIIIe siècle. No.1346.
FIRENZE, GHIRARDELLO DA, *see* GHERARDELLO (GHIRARDELLUS DE FLORENTIA).
FIRENZE, GIOVANNI DA, *see* GIOVANNI DA CASCIA (JOHANNES DE FLORENTIA).
FIRENZE, LORENZO DA, *see* LORENZO DE FLORENTIA.
FISCHER, HANS. ed.
Die Sonate.
In: Musikalische Formen in historischen Reihen. Bd.18.
Die Variation.
In: Musikalische Formen in historischen Reihen. Bd.2.
FISCHER, JOHANN CASPAR FERDINAND, 1650–1746.
(var. sp.: J. K. F. Fischer).
Sämtliche Werke für Klavier und Orgel. 125p.
—— Reprint. 1965.
Selections.
In: Leichtentritt. Deutsche Hausmusik aus vier Jahrhunderten.

Feiermusik.
In: Corona. Vol.30.
Festliche Suite in B-dur (aus "Tafel-Musik," 1702).
In: Schering. Perlen alter Kammermusik.
Fugen.
In: Musica instrumentalis. Vol.1.
Journal des Printemps.
In: Denkmäler deutscher Tonkunst. [1.Folge]. Vol.10.
Klavier-Suite.
In: Einstein. Beispielsammlung zur älteren Musikgeschichte.
Keyboard music.
In: Georgii. Keyboard music of the Baroque and Rococo. Vol.1.
In: Herrmann. Lehrmeister und Schüler Joh. Seb. Bachs. Vol.1.
In: Pessl. The art of the suite.
In: Tagliapietra. Antologia di musica antica e moderna per pianoforte. Bd.10.
Organ music.
In: Elkan-Vogel organ series. Vol.3.
In: Keller. Achtzig Choralvorspiele deutscher Meister des 17. und 18. Jahrhunderts.
In: Keller. Orgelvorspiele.
In: Klein. The first four centuries of music for the organ from Dunstable to Bach (1370–1749).
In: Liber organi. Bd.7.
In: The Liturgical Music Press, Inc. Masterpieces of organ music. Folio 7, 55.
In: The parish organist. Vol.7–8.
In: Raugel. Quarante-six pièces pour orgue ou harmonium.
In: Rohr. Orgelspiel im Kirchenjahr.
In: Schweiger. A brief compendium of early organ music.
Vier Suiten, für Blockflöte (Violine, Flöte, Oboe, Viola) mit Basso Continuo.
In: Hortus musicus. No.59.
Tafelmusik Ouvertürensuite.
In: Hortus musicus. No.17.
FISCHER, KARL VON. ed.
The variation.
In: Anthology of music. Vol.11.
FISCHER, MICHAEL GOTTHARDT, 1773–1829.
Introduction and fugue for organ.
In: Königliche Akademie der Künste. Auswahl vorzüglicher Musik-Werke. No.45.
Organ music.
In: Caecilia; Sammlung von Choralvorspielen.
FITINGHOFF.
Vocal music.
In: Sammlung russischer Romanzen. No.160.
THE FITZWILLIAM VIRGINAL BOOK.
In: English keyboard music. [No.4, 11, 14, 16].
FLACKTON, WILLIAM, 1709–1793.
Sonata für Viola und Klavier. C-dur, D-dur, G-dur.
In: Diletto musicale. No.62, 63, 64.
Sonata für Violoncello und Klavier. C-dur, B-dur, F-dur.
In: Diletto musicale. No.68, 69, 70.
FLAGG, JOSIAH, 1737–ca.1795.
Selections.
In: Goldman. Landmarks of early American music, 1760–1800.
FLANDERS-MUSIC.
In: Das Chorwerk. No.92.
In: Peeters. Altniederländische Meister für Orgel oder Harmonium.
In: Peeters. Oudnederlandse meesters.
In: Stein. Twelve Franco-Flemish masses of the early 16th century.
In: Zeitschrift für Spielmusik. No.167, 275.
FLECHA, MATEO.
(var. sp.: Matteo Flecha).
Selections.
In: Denkmäler der Tonkunst in Österreich. Vol.77. (Jg.XLI).
Choral music.
In: Engel. Three centuries of choral music. Vol.5.
FLEISCHER, HEINRICH, 1912– .
Organ music.
In: The parish organist. Vol.1–4.
FLEITES, VIRGINIA, 1916– .
Pequeña suite. (Piano).
In: Instituto Interamericano de Musicologia. Publicaciónes. No.46.
FLEMISH MUSIC, *see* FLANDERS-MUSIC.
FLETCHER, P.
Organ music.
In: Standard series of organ compositions. No.23, 24.
FLEURET, DANIEL.
Organ music.
In: Bedell. The French organist. Vol.2.
FLOR, CHRISTIAN, 1626–1697.
Organ music.
In: The Liturgical Music Press, Inc. Masterpieces of organ music. Folio 45.
In: Organum. 4.Reihe. Nr.2.
FLORENTIA, BARTHOLOMEUS DE, *see* BARTHOLOMEUS DE FLORENTIA.
FLORENTIA, DONATUS DE, *see* DONATUS DE FLORENTIA.
FLORENTIA, GHIRARDELLUS DE, *see* GHERARDELLO (GHIRARDELLUS DE FLORENTIA).
FLORENTIA, JOHANNES DE, *see* GIOVANNI DA CASCIA (JOHANNES DE FLORENTIA).
FLORENTIA, LORENZO DE, *see* LORENZO DE FLORENTIA.
FLORENTIA, PAOLO DE, *see* PAOLO DE FLORENTIA.
FLORIGAL, V.
Hymnen.
In: Das Chorwerk. No.32.
FLORIO, GIOVANNI.
(var. sp.: Florius).
Choral music.
In: Dehn. Sammlung älterer Musik aus dem XVI. und XVII. Jahrhundert.
FLUTE.
In: Das Erbe deutscher Musik. 1.Reihe. Vol.51.
In: Florilegium musicum.
In: Musiques françaises. Vol.1, 3, 4, 5, 6, 9, 10, 13, 14, 17, 19.
In: New Music (passim).
In: Zeitschrift für Spielmusik (passim).
FOGGIA, ANTONIO.
O quam fulgido splendore. Sopran (Tenor) und B.C.

In: Cantio sacra. No.10.
FOGGIA, FRANCESCO, 1604–1688.
Cessate, deh, cessate. Sopran (Tenor) und B.C.
In: Cantio sacra. No.38.
De valle lacrimarum. Sopran (Tenor) und B.C.
In: Cantio sacra. No.28.
Vocal music.
In: Hullah. Vocal scores. I. Sacred.
FOGLIANO, JACOBO.
Composizioni per organo.
In: I classici musicali italiani. Vol.1.
Sacred music.
In: Jeppesen. Italia sacra musica. Vol.1.
FOGLIANO, LODIVICO, d.1539.
(var. sp.: Ludovico Fogliano).
Sacred music.
In: Jeppesen. Italia sacra musica. Vol.2.
FOLK MUSIC.
In: Volk Musiziert.
In: Zeitschrift für Spielmusik (passim).
FOLKSONGS.
In: Möller. Das Lied der Völker.
FOLKSONGS, AMERICAN, *see* FOLKSONGS, U.S.
FOLKSONGS, DUTCH, *see* FOLKSONGS, NETHERLAND.
FOLKSONGS, ENGLISH (*see also* ENGLAND–MUSIC; SONGS, ENGLISH).
In: Chappell. The ballad literature and popular music of the olden time.
In: Chappell. Old English popular music.
In: Chappell. Old English popular music. A new ed.
FOLKSONGS, EUROPEAN.
In: Anthology of music. Vol.4.
FOLKSONGS, GERMAN (*see also* ARIAS. GERMAN; DARMSTADT–MUSIC; GERMANY–MUSIC; SONGS, GERMAN).
In: Leichtentritt. Deutsche Hausmusik aus vier Jahrhunderten.
In: Reimann. Das deutsche geistliche Lied.
In: Reimann. Das deutsche Lied.
In: Das Rostocker Liederbuch.
FOLKSONGS, HUNGARIAN (*see also* HUNGARY–MUSIC).
In: Corpus musicae popularis hungaricae.
FOLKSONGS, NETHERLAND (*see also* NETHERLANDS–MUSIC; SONGS, NETHERLAND).
In: Duyse. Het oude nederlandsche Lied.
FOLKSONGS, NORWEGIAN (*see also* NORWAY–MUSIC).
In: Music Press, Inc. [Choral series]. Vol.97.
FOLKSONGS, SCOTTISH (*see also* SCOTLAND–MUSIC).
In: Dauney. Ancient Scotish melodies.
FOLKSONGS, SPANISH (*see also* SONGS, SPANISH; SPAIN–MUSIC).
In: Asenjo y Barbieri. Cancionero musical de los siglos XV y XVI.
In: Música hispana. Serie A.
In: Ribera y Tarragó. La música andaluza medieval en las canciones de trovadores, troveros y minnesinger.
FOLKSONGS, SWISS (*see also* SWITZERLAND–MUSIC).
In: Music Press, Inc. [Choral series]. Vol.86, 87.
FOLKSONGS, U.S. (*see also* SONGS, AMERICAN; U.S.–MUSIC).
In: Downes. A treasury of American song.
In: Music Press, Inc. Choral series]. Vol.94–99.
FONTAINE, PIERRE, 15th CENTURY.
Selections.
In: Marix. Les musiciens de la cour de Bourgogne au XVe siècle (1420–1467).
FONTANA, FABRIZIO.
Selections.
In: Torchi. L'arte musicale in Italia. Bd.3.
Keyboard music.
In: Tagliapietra. Antologia di musica antica e moderna per pianoforte. Bd.6.
Organ music.
In: Fuser. Classici italiani dell'organo.
In: Guilmant. Archives des maîtres de l'orgue. Vol.10.
FONTANA, GIOVANNI BATTISTA, d.1630.
Selections.
In: Torchi. L'arte musicale in Italia. Bd.7.
Instrumental music.
In: Wasielewski. Instrumentalsätze vom Ende des XVI. bis Ende des XVII. Jahrhunderts.
Sechs Sonaten für Violine und Klavier. Heft 1–3. Nr.1–6.
In: Diletto musicale. No.13, 14, 15.
Sonata a tre, per due violini, fagotto e basso continuo. [Nr.14].
In: Hausmusik. No.169.
FORCER, FRANCIS, ca.1650–1705.
Keyboard music.
In: English keyboard music. [No.10].
FORCK, WILHELM.
Introduktion und Doppelfuge in der lydischen Tonart.
In: Zeitschrift für Spielmusik. No.71.
FORD, THOMAS, ca.1580–1648.
Airs to the lute from "Musicke of sundrei kindes."
In: Fellowes. The English school of lutenist song writers. 1st series. Vol.3.
A collection of anthems.
In: Musical Antiquarian Society. Publications. Vol.14.
Madrigals.
In: Euterpe. Vol.12; 2d ed. No.24.
Part music.
In: Hullah. Part music. Class A.1. Vol.1; Class A.2. Vol.1.
FORKEL, JOHANN NIKOLAUS, 1749–1818.
Sonate D-dur für Klavier.
In: Organum. 5.Reihe. Nr.11.
Sonate D-moll für Klavier.
In: Organum. 5.Reihe. Nr.17.
FORNSETE, JOHN OF, *see* JOHN OF FORNSETE.
FÖRSTER, CHRISTOPH, 1693–1745.
Suite (mit Ouvertüre) in G dur.
In: Riemann. Collegium musicum. No.22.
Trio für 2 Violinen (Flöten) Violoncell und Cembalo.
In: Organum. 3.Reihe. Nr.14.
FÖRSTER, EMANUEL ALOYS, 1748–1823.
Chamber music.
In: Denkmäler der Tonkunst in Österreich. Vol.67. (Jg.XXXV/1).
Streichquartett in C-dur. Op.2/1.

In: Diletto musicale. No.2.
FORSTER, GEORG, ca.1510–1568.
Choral music.
In: Antiqua Chorbuch. Vol.1. Heft 2; Vol.2. Heft 1.
Frische teutsche Liedlein. 1.Teil.
In: Das Erbe deutscher Musik. 1.Reihe. Vol.20.
Frische teutsche Liedlein. (Teil III bis V).
In: Das Chorwerk. No.63.
Kurzweilige . . . Liedlein. 2.Teil.
In: Publikationen älterer praktischer und theoretischer Musikwerke. Jahrg.33.
FORTHING, THOMAS.
Songs.
In: Plainsong and Mediaeval Music Society. Publications. (A collection of songs and madrigals . . .).
FOSS, LUKAS, 1922– .
String quartet in G.
In: Society for the Publication of American Music. Publications. 29th season. 1947–48.
FOSSA, JOANNES DE, 17th CENTURY.
Selections.
In: Maldéghem. Trésor musical.
Missa super Theutonicam Cantionem "Ich segge â dieu."
In: Musica divina. Vol.13.
Sacred music.
In: Proske. Musica divina. Annus primus. Tom 4.
FOSTER, STEPHEN COLLINS, 1826–1864.
Songs, compositions and arrangements. 3v.
FOUR HUNDRED YEARS OF EUROPEAN KEYBOARD MUSIC. (GEORGII).
In: Anthology of music. Vol.1.
FRANCE–MUSIC (*see also* CHANSONS; SONGS, FRENCH).
In: Apel. French secular music of the late fourteenth century.
In: Bedell. The French organist.
In: Bonnet. An anthology of early French organ music.
In: Brunold. Anthologie des maîtres français du clavecin des XVIIe et XVIIIe siècles.
In: Cauchie. Quinze chansons françaises du XVIe siècle.
In: Crotch. Specimens of various styles of music. Vol.1.
In: Échos de France.
In: Écorcheville. Vingt suites d'orchestre du XVIIe siècle français.
In: Expert. Chants de France et d'Italie.
In: Expert. Les maîtres musiciens de la Renaissance française. [Sec.1].
In: Expert. Les maîtres musiciens de la Renaissance française. [Sec.2].
In: Expert. Monuments de la musique française au temps de la Renaissance.
In: Grovlez. Les plus belles pièces de clavessin de l'école française.
In: Lesure. Anthologie de la chanson parisienne au XVIe siècle.
In: Musiques françaises.
In: Raugel. Les maîtres français de l'orgue aux XVIIème et XVIIIème siècles.
In: Raugel. Quarante-six pièces pour orgue ou harmonium d'anciens auteurs.
In: Reeser. De klaviersonate.
In: Société Française de Musicologie, Paris. Publications.
In: Stäblein-Harder. Fourteenth-century mass music in France.
In: Stein. Twelve Franco-Flemish masses of the early 16th century.
In: Turin. Biblioteca Nazionale. Mss. (J.II.9). The Cypriot-French repertory.
In: Weckerlin. Échos du temps passé.
In: Zeitschrift für Spielmusik. No.165, 212, 257, 284.
FRANCESCO DA MILANO, ca.1497–ca.1573.
Lute music.
In: Chilesotti. Lautenspieler des XVI. Jahrhunderts.
FRANCHOYS, JOHANNES.
Gloria e Credo.
In: Documenta polyphoniae liturgicae sanctae ecclesiae romanae. Ser.1. No.11.
Sacred music.
In: Plainsong and Mediaeval Music Society. Publications. (Borren).
FRANCISCO DE PEÑALOSA, *see* PEÑALOSA, FRANCISCO.
FRANCISQUE, ANTOINE, fl.1600.
Le trésor d'Orphée. 80p.
FRANCK, CÉSAR AUGUSTE, 1822–1890.
Oeuvres complètes pour orgue. n.d. 4v.
Oeuvres complètes pour orgue. cop.1955– . 4v.
The organ works. 6v.
Orgelwerke. 4v.
Organ music.
In: Bonnet. Historical organ-recitals. Vol.5.
In: The parish organist. Vol.5–6, 7–8.
FRANCK, JOHANN WOLFGANG, b.ca.1641.
Die drey Töchter Cecrops'.
In: Das Erbe deutscher Musik. 2.Reihe. Bayern. Vol.2.
Elmenhorst's "Geistliche Lieder."
In: Denkmäler deutscher Tonkunst. [1.Folge]. Vol.45.
Ausgewählte "geistreiche" Lieder Heinrich Elmenhorsts.
In: Organum. 2.Reihe. Nr.9.
Lieder.
In: Moser. Alte Meister des deutschen Liedes. 30 Gesänge. No.14, 15.
In: Moser. Alte Meister des deutschen Liedes. 46 Gesänge. No.22, 23.
FRANCK, MELCHIOR, 1573–1639.
Altdeutsche Tanzsätze.
In: Nagels Musik-Archiv. No.80.
Chamber music.
In: Riemann. Old chamber music. Vol.2.
Choral music.
In: Antiqua Chorbuch. Vol.1. Heft 5; Vol.2. Heft 5.
In: Engel. Three centuries of choral music. Vol.4.
Dank sagen wir alle Gott.
In: Chor-Archiv.
Deutsche weltliche Gesänge und Täntze.
In: Zeitschrift für Spielmusik. No.28.
Fünf Hohelied-Motetten.

In: Das Chorwerk. No.24.
Selected instrumental compositions.
In: Denkmäler deutscher Tonkunst. [1.Folge]. Vol.16.
Zwei Intraden aus "Neue Musicalische Intraden auff allerhand Instrumenten."
In: Schering. Perlen alter Kammermusik.
Geistliches Lied: Jesu, du zartes Kindelein.
In: Musica sacra . . . between 1892–1897. No.4.
Lied.
In: Reimann. Das deutsche Lied. Vol.1.
Musikalische Bergreihen.
In: Das Chorwerk. No.38.
Drei Quodlibets.
In: Das Chorwerk. No.53.
4-stimmige Suite. (1614).
In: Zeitschrift für Spielmusik. No.32.
Zwei deutsche Tänze für vier Instrumente.
In: Musica practica. No.18.
Whoso doth love must suffer.
In: Arion. Vol.1.

FRANCO.
Selections.
In: Crotch. Specimens of various styles of music. Vol.2.

FRANCOEUR, FRANÇOIS, 1698–1787.
Kammer-Sonaten, für Violine und Pianoforte.
In: Moffat. Kammer-Sonaten für Violine und Pianoforte. No.14, 26.
Sonate (Em). Violin and piano.
In: Moffat. Meister-Schule der alten Zeit. Violin-Sonaten. No.6.
Sonate en mi mineur.
In: L'école du violon au XVIIe et XVIIIe siècle. No.1262.
Sonate en sol mineur.
In: L'école du violon au XVIIe et XVIIIe siècle. No.1248.

FRANCOEUR, LOUIS JOSEPH, 1738–1804.
Sarabande.
In: L'école du violon au XVIIe et XVIIIe siècle. No.1291.

FRANCUS DE INSULA, *see* INSULA, FRANCUS DE.

FRANK, MARCO.
Drittes Streichquartett.
In: Hausmusik. No.110.

FRAUENHOLTZ, JOHANN CHRISTOPH, 1684–1754.
Der Herr Gedenkt an uns. Kantate.
In: Organum. 1.Reihe. Nr.31.
Verbirg nicht deine Holden Strahlen. Kantate.
In: Organum. 1.Reihe. Nr.30.

FRECK.
Part music.
In: Hullah. Part music. Class C. Sacred.

FREDERICI, DANIEL, b.before 1600.
Choral music.
In: Nagels Männerchor-Blätter. No.9.

FREDERICK II, THE GREAT, KING OF PRUSSIA, *see* FRIEDRICH II, DER GROSSE, KING OF PRUSSIA.

FREE.
Keyboard music.
In: The Fitzwilliam virginal book.

FREED, ISADORE, 1900– .
Triptych. Violin, viola, violoncello and piano.
In: Society for the Publication of American Music. Publications. 25th season. 1943–44.

FREER, ELEANOR EVEREST, 1864–1942.
Songs.
In: The Wa-Wan series of American compositions.

FREIXANET, 18th CENTURY.
Keyboard music.
In: Kastner. Silva iberica.
In: Nin y Castellano. Dix-sept sonates et pièces anciennes d'auteurs espagnols.

FRENCH, JACOB, b.1754.
Selections.
In: Goldman. Landmarks of early American music, 1760–1800.

FRESCOBALDI, GIROLAMO, 1583–1644.
Ausgewählte Orgelsätze. 2v.
Ausgewählte Orgelwerke. 2v.
Orgel- und Klavierwerke. v.1– .
Fiori musicali. 101p.
Selections.
In: Torchi. L'arte musicale in Italia. Bd.3.
Gerolamo Frescobaldi. (Luigi Ronga).
In: Istituzioni e monumenti dell'arte musicale italiana. Nuova serie.
Arie musicali.
In: Musikalische Denkmäler. Bd.4.
Canzonen.
In: Diletto musicale. No.87, 88, 89.
Fünf Canzonen für zwei beliebige hohe Instrumente (Streicher, Bläser oder gemischt), Tasten-Instrument und Bass-Instrument ad lib.
In: Antiqua Edition. Von 3 Instrumenten an.
Capriccio G moll.
In: Musica instrumentalis. Vol.3.
Chamber music.
In: Riemann. Old chamber music. Vol.1.
Correnti. Canzone.
In: Köhler. Les maîtres du clavecin. Heft 7.
Douze fantaisies. Organ.
In: Orgue et liturgie. Vol.32, 35.
Fugue G-moll. Organ.
In: Guilmant. École classique de l'orgue. No.7.
Keyboard music.
In: Apel. Musik aus früher Zeit für Klavier. Bd.1.
In: Clementi. Clementi's Selection of practical harmony. Vol.2.
In: Esposito. Early Italian piano music.
In: Farrenc. Le trésor des pianistes. Vol.2.
In: Georgii. Keyboard music of the Baroque and Rococo. Vol.1.
In: Herrmann. Lehrmeister und Schüler Joh. Seb. Bachs. Vol.1.
In: Oesterle. Early keyboard music. Vol.1.
In: Pauer. Alte Klavier-Musik. 1st series. Part 1.
In: Selva. Pièces de clavecin des XVIIme et XVIIIme siècles.
In: Tagliapietra. Antologia di musica antica e moderna per pianoforte. Bd.4, 5.
Nove toccate inedite.
In: Monumenti di musica italiana. Ser.I. Vol.2.

Composizione per organo e cembalo.
In: I classici della musica italiana. Raccolta nazionale delle musiche italiane. Quad.43–47.
Organ music.
In: Auler. Spielbuch für Kleinorgel. Vol.1.
In: Biggs. Treasury of early organ music.
In: Bonnet. Historical organ-recitals. Vol.1.
In: Bossi. Sammlung von Stücken alter italienischer Meister für die moderne Orgel.
In: Cantantibus organis. Vol.6.
In: Commer. Compositionen für Orgel aus dem 16., 17. und 18. Jahrhundert. Heft 2.
In: Elkan-Vogel organ series. Vol.1.
In: Fuser. Classici italiani dell'organo.
In: Guilmant. Concert historique d'orgue.
In: Guilmant. École classique de l'orgue. No.17, 26.
In: Keller. Orgelvorspiele.
In: Klein. The first four centuries of music for the organ from Dunstable to Bach (1370–1749).
In: Königliche Akademie der Künste. Auswahl vorzüglicher Musik-Werke. No.42.
In: Liber organi. Bd.4, 5.
In: The Liturgical Music Press, Inc. Masterpieces of organ music. Folio 24, 71.
In: Organ masters of the Baroque period. Vol.2.
In: The parish organist. Vol.1–4, 7–8.
In: Peeters. Anthologia pro organo. Vol.1, 3.
In: Pierront. Cent versets de Magnificat.
In: Raugel. Quarante-six pièces pour orgue ou harmonium.
In: Schweiger. A brief compendium of early organ music.
In: Straube. Alte Meister des Orgelspiels.
Partite sopra La romanesca, La monicha, Ruggiero e La follia.
In: Chilesotti. Biblioteca di rarità musicali. Vol.6.
Ricercar.
In: Parrish. Masterpieces of music before 1750. No.34.
Sonate.
In: I classici della musica italiana. Vol.12.
Songs.
In: Jeppesen. La flora. Vol.1, 3.
Douze toccatas. Organ.
In: Orgue et liturgie. Vol.26.
Toccatas. IIe fascicule. Organ.
In: Orgue et liturgie. Vol.41.
Toccatas. No.1–12.
In: Pauer. Alte Meister. No.61–66.
Toccata e Canzone für Cembalo und Bass.
In: Diletto musicale. No.49.
Toccata per spinettina e violino.
In: Diletto musicale. No.46.
FREUNDT, CORNELIUS, 1535–1591.
Choral music.
In: Antiqua Chorbuch. Vol.1. Heft 3.
FRIBERTH, CARL, 1736–1812.
Songs.
In: Denkmäler der Tonkunst in Österreich. Vol.54. (Jg.XXVII/2).
FRICKER, PETER RACINE, 1920– .
(var. sp.: P. Racini Fricker).
Piano music.
In: Contemporary British piano music.
FRIDERICI, DANIEL, 1584–1638.
(var. sp.: Daniel Friederici).
As Cupid once.
In: Arion. Vol.1.
Choral music.
In: Antiqua Chorbuch. Vol.2. Heft 5.
Ausgewählte Kirchengesänge.
In: Das Erbe deutscher Musik. 2.Reihe. Mecklenburg und Pommern. Vol.2.
FRIEDLAENDER, MAX, 1852–1934. ed.
Neujahrsgrüsse empfindsamer Seelen.
In: Hirsch. Veröffentlichungen. [Bd.] 3.
FRIEDRICH II, DER GROSSE, KING OF PRUSSIA, 1712–1786.
(var. sp.: Frederick II, the Great, King of Prussia).
Musikalische Werke. 7 parts in 4v.
Arioso aus der Flöten-Sonate (Gm).
In: Thouret. Musik am preussischen Hofe. No.1.
Music in Berlin at the time of Frederick the Great.
In: Oberdörffer. Deutsche Klaviermusik des 17. und 18. Jahrhunderts.
Sinfonie D-dur für zwei Flöten, zwei Oboen, zwei Hörner, Streicher und Cembalo (Oboen und Hörner nach Belieben).
In: Nagels Musik-Archiv. No.110.
1.Symphonie; 2.Symphonie; 4.Symphonie; Andante für 2.Symphonie; Recitative und Aria "Nota V'e Quesya Dea" aus Il re pastore.
In: Musikschätze der Vergangenheit.
FRITSCH, BALTHASAR, 16th CENTURY.
Vierstimmige Tänze aus "Primitia musicales."
In: Zeitschrift für Spielmusik. No.285.
FRITZ, KASPAR (GASPARO), ca.1716–1782.
Sonata, violin and piano, Op.2, No.4.
In: Verein schweizerischer Tonkünstler. Musikalische Werke. Heft 2.
FROBERGER, JOHANN JAKOB, 1616–1667.
(var. sp.: Johann Jakob Frohberger).
Selections.
In: Leichtentritt. Deutsche Hausmusik aus vier Jahrhunderten.
Fantasie. Organ.
In: Dickinson. Historical recital series for organ. Vol.1. No.18.
Keyboard music.
In: Farrenc. Le trésor des pianistes. Vol.3.
In: Georgii. Keyboard music of the Baroque and Rococo. Vol.1.
In: Herrmann. Lehrmeister und Schüler Joh. Seb. Bachs. Vol.1.
In: Oesterle. Early keyboard music. Vol.1.
In: Pauer. Alte Klavier-Musik. 1st series. Pt.3.
In: Pessl. The art of the suite.
In: Selva. Pièces de clavecin des XVIIme et XVIIIme siècles.
In: Tagliapietra. Antologia di musica antica e moderna per pianoforte. Bd.6.
Organ and clavier works.
In: Denkmäler der Tonkunst in Österreich. Vol.8. (Jg.IV/1); Vol.13. (Jg.VI/2); Vol.21. (Jg.X/2).

Organ music.
In: Auler. Spielbuch für Kleinorgel. Vol.1.
In: Biggs. Treasury of early organ music.
In: Bonnet. Historical organ-recitals. Vol.1.
In: Elkan-Vogel organ series. Vol.3.
In: Guilmant. Concert historique d'orgue.
In: Klein. The first four centuries of music for the organ from Dunstable to Bach (1370–1749).
In: Liber organi. Bd.5.
In: The Liturgical Music Press, Inc. Masterpieces of organ music. Folio 35, 62.
In: Organ masters of the Baroque period. Vol.2.
In: Organum. 4.Reihe. Nr.11.
In: The parish organist. Vol.7–8.
In: Peeters. Anthologia pro organo. Vol.1, 3.
In: Raugel. Quarante-six pièces pour orgue ou harmonium.
In: Straube. Alte Meister des Orgelspiels.
Suite in E minor.
In: Parrish. Masterpieces of music before 1750. No.35.
2 Toccatas.
In: Köhler. Les maîtres du clavecin. Heft 4.
Toccata. (Dm).
In: Pauer. Alte Meister. No.21.
FROEHLICH, JOHANNES FREDERIK, *see* FRÖHLICH, JOHANNES FREDERICK.
FROHBERGER, JOHANN JAKOB, *see* FROBERGER, JOHANN JAKOB.
FRÖHLICH, JOHANNES FREDERIK, 1806–1860.
(var. sp.: Froehlich; J. F. Frölich).
Erik Menveds Barndom. Ballet. Op.51.
In: Samfundet til Udgivelse af dansk Musik. Ser.I. No.15.
Majgildet. Ouverture.
In: Samfundet til Udgivelse af dansk Musik. Ser.III. No.130.
Riberhus march. Orchestra.
In: Samfundet til Udgivelse af dansk Musik. Ser.III. No.135.
FRÖLICH, JOHANNES FREDERIK, *see* FRÖHLICH, JOHANNES FREDERIK.
FROMM, ANDREAS, 1621–1683.
Actus musicus de Divite et Lazaro.
In: Denkmäler der Musik in Pommern. Heft 5.
Lazarus, das erste deutsche Oratorium.
In: Engel. Drei Werke pommerscher Komponisten.
FRONCIACO, 14th CENTURY.
Kyrie Jhesu dulcissime.
In: Parrish. A treasury of early music. No.14.
FROTSCHER, GOTTHOLD, 1897– .
Der Volksliedvogel.
In: Zeitschrift für Spielmusik. No.219.
FROTTOLE.
In: Jeppesen. Die italienische Orgelmusik am Anfang des Cinquecento.
In: Publikationen älterer Musik. Vol.8.
In: Smith College music archives. No.4.
FRUMERIE, GUNNAR FREDRIK DE, 1908– .
Selections.
In: Svensk sanglyrik. Vol.1.
Four Chinese poems.
In: Musikaliska konstföreningen. 1935.
Piano quartet.
In: Musikaliska konstföreningen. 1948.
Piano trio, No.2.
In: Musikaliska konstföreningen. 1955.
Sonata for violin and piano.
In: Musikaliska konstföreningen. 1935.
Violin sonata, No.2.
In: Musikaliska konstföreningen. 1950.
FRYE, WALTER, 15th CENTURY.
Opera omnia. 83p.
FRYKLÖF, HAROLD LEONARD, 1882–1919.
Selections.
In: Svensk sanglyrik. Vol.1.
Fugue for piano.
In: Musikaliska konstföreningen. 1910.
Passacaglia for organ.
In: Musikaliska konstföreningen. 1929.
Sonata à la legenda.
In: Musikaliska konstföreningen. 1919.
Symphonic piece for organ.
In: Musikaliska konstföreningen. 1926.
FUCHS, ARNO, 1909– .
Tres canciones.
In: Instituto Interamericano de Musicologia. Publicaciónes. No.49.
FUCHS, FRANZ.
Kleine Suite über Wie Schön leuchtet der Morgenstern, für Flöte, zwei Geigen, und Bratsche.
In: Hausmusik. No.36.
FUENLLANA, MIGUEL DE, 16th CENTURY.
Keyboard music.
In: Apel. Musik aus früher Zeit für Klavier. Bd.2.
In: Tagliapietra. Antologia di musica antica e moderna per pianoforte. Bd.1.
Lute music.
In: Morphy. Les luthistes espagnols du XVIe siècle. Vol.2.
Organ music.
In: Elkan-Vogel organ series. Vol.5.
FUENTES, PASCUAL, d.1768.
Sacred music.
In: Eslava y Elizondo. Lira sacro-hispana. 18th century. i.1.
THE FUGUE. VOL.1. (ADRIO).
In: Anthology of music. Vol.19.
FUHRMANN, LEOPOLD, 17th CENTURY.
Kinderlieder.
In: Zeitschrift für Spielmusik. No.179.
FULDA, ADAM VON, *see* ADAM VON FULDA.
FUMAGALLI, ADOLFO, 1828–1856.
Keyboard music.
In: Tagliapietra. Antologia di musica antica e moderna per pianoforte. Bd.17.
FUNCK, DAVID, d.ca.1690.
Sonaten-Suite für vier Gamben.
In: Organum. 3.Reihe. Nr.34.
FUNCKE, FRIEDRICH.
Matthäuspassion für Solostimmen.
In: Das Chorwerk. No.78/79.
FURCHHEIM, JOHANN WILHELM, ca.1635–1682.
Sonate. Für 2 Violinen, 2 Violen, Violon, und Basso Continuo.
In: Riemann. Collegium musicum. No.60.
Suite für 5 Streicher und Generalbass.
In: Organum. 3.Reihe. Nr.26.

FURLONI, GAETANO.
Sonata I und II für Violinen, Gambe; Sonata III und IV für 2 Violinen, Gambe.
In: Moecks Kammermusik. Vol.106, 107.
FÜRSTENAU, KASPAR, 1772–1819.
Kompositionen für Flöte und Gitarre. Op.34, 35.
In: Nagels Musik-Archiv. No.118, 31.
FUSS, JOHANN.
Selections.
In: Denkmäler der Tonkunst in Österreich. Vol.79. (Jg.XLII/2).
FUSSAN, WERNER, 1912– .
Concertino für Flöte und Streichorchester.
In: Concertino.
Kleine Suite für Streichorchester und Bläser.
In: Collegium musicae novae. No.38.
Suite für Streicher.
In: Collegium musicae novae. No.24.
FUX, JOHANN JOSEPH, 1660–1741.
Sämtliche Werke. 8 series (v.1–).
Canon. Kyrie.
In: Königliche Akademie der Künste. Auswahl vorzüglicher Musik-Werke. No.10.
Capriccio und Fuge für Cembalo. K.V.404.
In: Diletto musicale. No.106.
Choral music.
In: Rochlitz. Sammlung vorzüglicher Gesangstücke. Bd.2.
Church sonatas and overtures.
In: Denkmäler der Tonkunst in Österreich. Vol.19. (Jg.IX/2).
Concentus musico-instrumentalis.
In: Denkmäler der Tonkunst in Österreich. Vol.47. (Jg.XXIII/2).
Costanza e fortezza.
In: Denkmäler der Tonkunst in Österreich. Vol.34–35. (Jg.XVII).
In: Smith College music archives. No.2.
Drei Einzelstücke für Klavier.
In: Hausmusik. No.22.
Works for keyboard instruments.
In: Denkmäler der Tonkunst in Österreich. Vol.85.
Märsche.
In: Corona. Vol.11.
Masses.
In: Denkmäler der Tonkunst in Österreich. Vol.1. (Jg.I/1).
Zwölf Menuette für Klavier.
In: Hausmusik. No.23.
8 Menuette für ein Melodieinstrument und ein Tasteninstrument.
In: Zeitschrift für Spielmusik. No.146.
Missa Sancti Ioannis.
In: Musica divina. Vol.12.
Motets.
In: Denkmäler der Tonkunst in Österreich. Vol.3. (Jg.II/1); Vol.101/102.
Nürnberger Partita.
In: Corona. Vol.18.
Organ music.
In: The Liturgical Music Press, Inc. Masterpieces of organ music. Folio 30.
Ouvertüre in C.
In: Diletto musicale. No.110.
Partita a tre, per due violini e basso continuo. K.V.322.
In: Hausmusik. No.159.
Partiten, G-dur und F-dur, für zwei Violinen und Bass.
In: Hortus musicus. No.51.
Sacred music.
In: Proske. Musica divina. Annus primus. Tom 2, 3.
Sinfonia a tre, per due violini e basso continuo. K.V.330.
In: Hausmusik. No.164.
Sinfonia, für Flauto, Hautbois et Basso (Cembalo).
In: Nagels Musik-Archiv. No.146.
Sonate (Kanon) für zwei Viola da Gamba (Bratschen) und Basso Continuo.
In: Hortus musicus. No.30.
Sonata a tre für 3 Violinen.
In: Antiqua Edition. Von 3 Instrumenten an.
Sonata pastorale a tre, per due violini e basso continuo. K.V.397.
In: Hausmusik. No.158.
Suite in D-moll, aus dem "Concertus musico-Instrumentalis" für kleines Streichorchester und Cembalo (Klavier).
In: Musikschätze der Vergangenheit.
Tänze für 2 Violinen, Viola bzw. Sopran- und Alt-Blockflöten oder Streichorchester und Basso Continuo.
In: Moecks Kammermusik. Vol.50.

GABRIELI, ANDREA, ca.1510–1586.
Andrea e Giovanni Gabrieli e la musica strumentale in San Marco.
In: Istituzioni e monumenti dell'arte musicale italiana. Vol.1–2.
Selections.
In: Denkmäler der Tonkunst in Österreich. Vol.77. (Jg.XLI).
In: Torchi. L'arte musicale in Italia. Bd.2, 3.
Canzone francese deta Pour ung plaisir.
In: Parrish. Masterpieces of organ music before 1750. No.21.
Chamber music.
In: Riemann. Old chamber music. Vol.1.
Choral music.
In: Engel. Three centuries of choral music. Vol.2.
In: Recueil de musique ancienne. Recueil des morceaux de musique ancienne. Bd.11.
In: Societas Polyphonica Romanae. Repertorium. Vol.6.
Keyboard music.
In: Tagliapietra. Antologia di musica antica e moderna per pianoforte. Bd.1, 5.
Madrigals.
In: Einstein. The golden age of the madrigal.
Magnificat octavi toni.
In: Musica sacra ... between 1892–97. No.7.
Drei Motetten.
In: Das Chorwerk. No.96.
Musiche di chiesa.
In: I classici musicali italiani. Vol.5.
Organ music.
In: Biggs. Treasury of early organ music.
In: Bonnet. Historical organ-recitals. Vol.1.
In: Cantantibus organis. Vol.2.
In: Froidebise. Anthologie de l'orgue. Vol.1.

In: Fuser. Classici italiani dell'organo.
In: Guilmant. Archives des maîtres de l'orgue. Vol.10.
In: Klein. The first four centuries of music for the organ from Dunstable to Bach (1370–1749).
In: The Liturgical Music Press, Inc. Masterpieces of organ music. Folio 66.
In: Peeters. Anthologia pro organo. Vol.1.
Quem vidistis pastores?
In: Chor-Archiv.
Sacred music.
In: Proske. Musica divina. Annus primus. Tom 1, 2; Annus secundus. Tom 2.
In: Proske. Selectus novus missarum. Annus primus. Tom 2; Annus secundus. Tom 2.
GABRIELI, DOMENICO, ca.1655–1690.
Arias.
In: Landshoff. Alte Meister des Bel Canto. Eine Sammlung von Arien. Vol.3.
Balletto a tre, per due violini e basso continuo. Op.I/9.
In: Hausmusik. No.149.
Kammerkantate.
In: Einstein. Beispielsammlung zur älteren Musikgeschichte.
GABRIELI, GIOVANNI, 1557–1612.
(var. sp.: Ioanne Gabrieli).
Opera omnia. v.1– .
Andrea e Giovanni Gabrieli e la musica strumentale in San Marco.
In: Istituzioni e monumenti dell'arte musicale italiana. Vol.1–2.
Selections.
In: Documenta historica musicae.
In: Gabrieli. Music of Gabrieli and his time.
In: Musica sacra . . . 1839– . v.15, 16.
In: Torchi. L'arte musicale in Italia. Bd.2, 3.
Canzoni per sonar.
In: Antiqua Edition. Von 4 Instrumenten an.
Chamber music.
In: Riemann. Old chamber music. Vol.1.
Choral music.
In: Der Kammerchor. Vol.3.
In: Musica sacra . . . 1839– . Vol.2, 3.
In: Recueil de musique ancienne. Recueil des morceaux de musique ancienne. Bd.6, 9.
? In: Rochlitz. Sammlung vorzüglicher Gesangstücke. Bd.1. Pt.2.
Church music.
? In: Motett Society. [Collection of ancient church music]. Division 2.
Instrumental music.
In: Wasielewski. Instrumentalsätze vom Ende des XVI. bis Ende des XVII. Jahrhunderts.
Keyboard music.
In: Apel. Musik aus früher Zeit für Klavier. Bd.1.
In: Tagliapietra. Antologia di musica antica e moderna per painoforte. Bd.2.
Madrigals.
In: Einstein. The golden age of the madrigal.
Missa brevis.
In: Musica spiritualis. Ser.IA. No.1.
Motetten.
In: Das Chorwerk. No.10, 67.
Organ music.
In: Cantantibus organis. Vol.2.
In: Fuser. Classici italiani dell'organo.
? In: Guilmant. Concert historique d'orgue.
In: Klein. The first four centuries of music for the organ from Dunstable to Bach (1370–1749).
In: Raugel. Quarante-six pièces pour orgue ou harmonium.
Sacred music.
In: Proske. Musica divina. Annus secundus. Tom 4.
In: Proske. Selectus novus missarum. Annus secundus. Tom 4.
Sonate für drei Violinen und Basso Continuo.
In: Hortus musicus. No.70.
Venezianische Motette.
In: Einstein. Beispielsammlung zur älteren Musikgeschichte.
Vocal music.
In: Hullah. Vocal scores. I. Sacred.
GABURO, KENNETH.
Ideas and transformations, for violin and viola.
In: New music. March 1964.
GADE, NIELS WILHELM, 1817–1890.
Baldurs Drøm. Choral work.
In: Samfundet til Udgivelse af dansk Musik. Ser.II. No.10.
Et Folkesagn.
In: Samfundet til Udgivelse af dansk Musik. Ser.II. No.8.
Organ music.
In: Gerhardt. Album nordischer Komponisten für Orgel. Vol.2.
Sanct Hansaften-Spil. Choral work.
In: Samfundet til Udgivelse af dansk Musik. Ser.II. No.37.
GADSCH, HERBERT.
Spatzenlügen.
In: Zeitschrift für Spielmusik. No.289.
Die undankbare Flunder.
In: Zeitschrift für Spielmusik. No.266.
GAENSBACHER, JOHANN, *see* GÄNSBACHER, JOHANN.
GAFFI, BERNARDO, 17th–18th CENTURIES.
Arias.
In: Landshoff. Alte Meister des Bel Canto. Eine Sammlung von Arien. Vol.3.
GAFFURIO, FRANCHINO, 1451–1522.
(var. sp.: Franchino Gafori).
Collected musical works. v.1– .
Magnificat. Motetti.
In: Archivium musices metropolitanum mediolanense. Vol.4, 5.
Messe.
In: Archivium musices metropolitanum mediolanense. Vol.1, 2, 3.
Theorica musical.
In: Reale Accademia d'Italia, Rome. Musica. Vol.1.
GAGLIANO, GIOVANNI BATTISTA DA, ca.1585–ca.1650.
Songs.
In: Jeppesen. La flora. Vol.2, 3.
GAGLIANO, MARCO DA, ca.1575–1642.
Selections.

In: Torchi. L'arte musicale in Italia. Bd.4.
Arias.
In: Landshoff. Alte Meister des Bel Canto. Eine Sammlung von Arien. Vol.1–2.
Dafne.
In: Publikationen älterer praktischer und theoretischer Musikwerke. Jahrg.9.
Kammerduette.
In: Landshoff. Alte Meister des Bel Canto. Italienische Kammerduette.
Madrigals.
In: Einstein. The golden age of the madrigal.
Songs.
In: Jeppesen. Le flora. Vol.1, 2, 3.
Vocal music.
In: Gevaert. Les gloires de l'Italie. Vol.1, 2.
GAGNEBIN, HENRI, 1886– .
Sonata. Organ.
In: Orgue et liturgie. Vol.9.
GAIL, EDMÉE SOPHIE, 1775–1819.
Selections.
In: Échos de France. Vol.1–3.
GÁL, HANS, 1890– .
Capriccio, für Mandolinenorchester.
In: Hausmusik. No.56.
Kleine Suite, für 2 Violinen und Violoncello, Klavier ad lib. Op.49a.
In: Hausmusik. No.13.
Musik für Streichorchester, Op.73.
In: Collegium musicae novae. No.33.
Trio. Op.49b.
In: Hausmusik. No.14.
GALEAZZO.
Keyboard music.
In: The Fitzwilliam virginal book.
GALENO, GIOVANNI BATTISTA, 1550/55–d. after 1626.
Selections.
In: Denkmäler der Tonkunst in Österreich. Vol.90.
GALEOTTI, STEFANO, 18th CENTURY.
Sonate (Cm). Violoncello and piano.
In: Moffat. Meister-Schule der alten Zeit. Violoncello-Sonaten. No.6.
GALILEI, VINCENZO, d.1591.
(var. sp.: Vincentio Galilei).
La Camerata Fiorentina.
In: Istituzioni e monumenti dell'arte musicale italiana. Vol.4.
Contrapunti a due voci.
In: Smith College music archives. No.8.
Dialogo della musica.
In: Reale Accademia d'Italia, Rome. Musica. Vol.2.
Lute music.
In: Chilesotti. Lautenspieler des XVI. Jahrhunderts.
GALLÉS, PADRE JOSÉ, 1761–1836.
Keyboard music.
In: Nin y Castellano. Dix-sept sonates et pièces anciennes d'auteurs espagnols.
GALLIARD, JOHANN ERNEST, 1687–1749.
Hornpipe.
In: L'école du violon au XVIIe et XVIIIe siècle. No.1294.
Six sonatas for bassoon or cello and piano.
In: Music for wind instruments by 18th century masters. No.2.
Sonate en mi mineur.
In: L'école du violon au XVIIe et XVIIIe siècle. No.1279.
Sonate (F). Violoncello and piano.
In: Moffat. Meister-Schule der alten Zeit. Violoncello-Sonaten. No.5.
Songs.
In: Potter. Reliquary of English song. Vol.2.
GALLICULUS, JOHANNES, 16th CENTURY.
(var. sp.: Johannes Hähnel).
Ostermesse, über das Lied "Christ ist erstanden."
In: Das Chorwerk. No.44.
Weihnachtsmagnificat.
In: Das Chorwerk. No.85.
GALLO, R., 15th CENTURY.
Selections.
In: Reaney. Early fifteenth-century music. Vol.2.
GALLUS, JACOBUS, *see* HANDL, JACOB.
GALUPPI, BALDASSARE, 1706–1785.
(var. sp.: Buranello).
Concerto a quattro. Nr.1, 2.
In: Diletto musicale. No.94, 95.
Concerto No.6 in C minor (strings).
In: Antica musica strumentale italiana. Ser.II. Vol.13.
L'ero cincese for oboes, horns, strings.
In: Antica musica strumentale italiana. In preparation.
Il filosofo di campagna.
In: I classici della musica italiana. Vol.13.
In: I classici della musica italiana. Raccolta nazionale delle musiche italiane. Quad.54–58.
Keyboard music.
In: Benvenuti. Cembalisti italiani del settecento.
In: Esposito. Early Italian piano music.
In: Georgii. Keyboard music of the Baroque and Rococo. Vol.3.
In: Pauer. Alte Klavier-Musik. 1st series. Pt.2.
In: Selva. Pièces de clavecin des XVIIme et XVIIIme siècles.
In: Tagliapietra. Anthologia di musica antica e moderna per pianoforte. Bd.12.
Rapida cerva, fuge. Sopran, Streicher und B.C.
In: Die Kantate. No.12.
Sacred music.
In: Latrobe, C. I. Selection of sacred music.
In: Latrobe, J. A. The music of the church.
Sonate.
In: Köhler. Les maîtres du clavecin. Heft 7.
Sonate (Cm); Sonate (Am).
In: Pauer. Alte Meister. No.48, 49.
Sonate. Cembalo o pianoforte.
In: Paoli. Sonate italiane del secolo XVIII per cembalo o pianoforte.
Vocal music.
In: Delsarte. Archives du chant. Livr.8. No.6.
In: Gevaert. Les gloires de l'Italie. Vol.1, 2.
GANASSI, SYLVESTRO DI, 15th–16th CENTURIES.

Regola Rubertina.
In: Fürstliches Institut für Musikwissenschaftliche Forschung. Veröffentlichungen. 2.Reihe. [No.] 3.
GÄNSBACHER, JOHANN, 1778–1844.
(var. sp.: Gaensbacher).
Sacred music.
In: Latrobe, C. I. Selection of sacred music.
In: Latrobe, J. A. The music of the church.
GARAT, PIERRE JEAN, 1762–1823.
Selections.
In: Échos de France. Vol.1–3.
GARCIA, FRANCISCO JAVIER, 1731–1809.
Sacred music.
In: Eslava y Elizondo. Lira sacro-hispana. 19th century. i.1.
GARCIA, MANUEL DEL POPOLO VICENTE, 1775–1832.
Sacred music.
In: Eslava y Elizondo. Lira sacro-hispana. 19th century. ii.2.
GARCÍA MORILLO, ROBERTO, 1911– .
Selections.
In: Boletín latino-americano de música. Vol.4.
In: Instituto Interamericano de Musicologia. Publicatiónes. No.17, 39.
GARDANO, ANTONIO, 16th CENTURY.
(var. sp.: Antoine Gardane).
Chansons.
In: Lesure. Anthologie de la chanson parisienne au XVIe siècle.
Duos.
In: Expert. Florilège du concert vocal de la Renaissance. No.8.
GARNIER, FRANÇOIS JOSEPH, 1755–1825.
Chansons.
In: Publikationen älterer praktischer und theoretischer Musikwerke. Jahrg.27.
GASCONGNE, MATHIEU, 16th CENTURY.
(var. sp.: Gascogne; Mattheus Gascongne).
Chansons.
In: Bordes. Chansonnier du XVe siècle.
In: Brown. Theatrical chansons of the 15th and early 16th centuries.
In: Expert. Les maîtres musiciens de la Renaissance française. Vol.5.
Mass.
In: Stein. Twelve Franco-Flemish masses of the early 16th century.
Motets.
In: Attaingnant. Treize livres de motets. Livre 1, 2, 6, 9, 11.
Polyphonic music.
In: Monumenta musicae belgicae. Vol.9.
GASPAR.
Selections.
In: Ambros. Auserwählte Tonwerke.
GASPARINI, FRANCESCO, 1668–1727.
Arias.
In: Parisotti. Arie antiche. Bd.2, 3.
GASPARINI, QUIRINO, d.1778.
Adoramus Te, Christe.
In: Die Motette. No.2.
GASPAR VAN WEERBECKE, *see* WEERBECKE, GASPAR VAN.
GASS, MICHAEL, 16th CENTURY.
Choral music.
In: Moser. Die Kantorei der Spätgotik.
GASSMANN, FLORIAN LEOPOLD, 1729–1774.
Church music.
In: Denkmäler der Tonkunst in Österreich. Vol.83. (Jg.XLV).
La Contessina.
In: Denkmäler der Tonkunst in Österreich. Vol.42–44. (Jg.XXI/1).
Divertimento a tre, per due violini e basso continuo, C-dur.
In: Hausmusik. No.161.
Fugue for 4tet, A minor.
In: Königliche Akademie der Künste. Auswahl vorzüglicher Musik-Werke. No.36.
Partita.
In: Diletto musicale. No.130.
Sinfonia (Ouvertüre) "Issipile."
In: Diletto musicale. No.28.
Trio (Sonate) B-dur. Für Flöte, Violine (ou 2 Violinen) und Viola; Trio (Sonate) G-dur. Für Flöte, Violine, und Viola.
In: Organum. 3.Reihe. Nr.45, 48.
Trio-Sonatas.
In: Organum. 3.Reihe. Nr.51, 53, 55, 58.
GASTOLDI, GIOVANNI GIACOMO, d.ca.1622.
Selections.
In: Documenta historica musicae.
In: Torchi. L'arte musicale in Italia. Bd.2.
Al mormorar.
In: Squire. Ausgewählte Madrigale und mehrstimmige Gesänge. No.5.
7 Ballette.
In: Zeitschrift für Spielmusik. No.33.
Choral music.
In: Der Kammerchor. Vol.3.
In: Nagels Männerchor-Blätter. No.17.
In: Recueil de musique ancienne. Recueil des morceaux de musique ancienne. Bd.10.
Un nuovo Cacciator.
In: Squire. Ausgewählte Madrigale und mehrstimmige Gesänge. No.38.
Spielstücke für zwei gleiche Instrumente.
In: Hortus musicus. No.23.
Spielstücke für zwei ungleiche Instrumente.
In: Hortus musicus. No.24.
Tanslied.
In: Einstein. Beispielsammlung zur älteren Musikgeschichte.
GATTO, SIMONE, ca.1540/1550–1594/95.
Selections.
In: Denkmäler der Tonkunst in Österreich. Vol.90.
GAULTIER, DENIS, d.1672.
Keyboard music.
In: Apel. Musik aus früher Zeit für Klavier. Bd.2.
La rhétorique des dieux.
In: Société Française de Musicologie, Paris. Publications. Ser.I. Bd.6, 7.
Tombeau de Mademoiselle Gaultier.
In: Parrish. A treasury of early music. No.39.
GAULTIER, J.
Keyboard music.
In: Tagliapietra. Antologia di musica antica e moderna per pianoforte. Bd.7.

GAULTIER DE MARSEILLE, PIERRE, 1642–1697.
Suite en sol pour flûte à bec ou traversière et clavier.
In: Musiques françaises. Vol.13.
GAVALDÁ, MIGUEL QUEROL, *see* QUEROL GAVALDÁ, MIGUEL.
GAVEAUX, PIERRE, 1761–1825.
Selections.
In: Échos de France. Vol.1–3.
GEBEL, GEORG, JR., 1709–1753.
Triosonate für 2 Violinen (Flöten), Violoncell und Cembalo.
In: Organum. 3.Reihe. Nr.12, 13.
GEBHARD, HANS, 1897– .
Konzert. Op.62.
In: Collegium musicae novae. No.30.
GEBHARDI, LUDWIG ERNST, 1787–1862.
Organ music.
In: Caecilia; Sammlung von Choralvorspielen.
GEHRKE, HUGO, 1912– .
Organ music.
In: The parish organist. Vol.1–4, 5–6.
GEIGER.
Mass.
In: Ecclesiasticon. No.68.
GEIST, CHRSTIAN, d.1711.
Ausgewählte Kirchenkonzerte.
In: Das Erbe deutscher Musik. 1.Reihe. Vol.48.
GELINEK, JOSEPH, 1758–1825.
(var. sp.: Jelinek).
Klaviertrio Es-dur.
In: Musica viva historica. Vol.6.
GELLI, VINCENZO, fl.1817.
Drei Divertimenti, für Flöte oder Violine und Gitarre. Op.2.
In: Nagels Musik-Archiv. No.139.
GEMINIARI, FRANCESCO, ca.1687–1762.
Selections.
In: Crotch. Specimens of various styles of music. Vol.3.
In: Smith. Musica antiqua.
Allegretto.
In: L'école du violon au XVIIe et XVIIIe siècle. No.1292.
Concerto grosso. Op.2. No.4, 5, 6.
In: Moser. Das Musikkränzlein. No.8, 9, 10.
Concerto grosso, Op.VII, Nr.1, für zwei Violinen, Viola und Violoncello.
In: Nagels Musik-Archiv. No.202.
Concerto grosso B-dur, Op.3, Nr.5, um 1735.
In: Schering. Perlen alter Kammermusik.
Concerto grosso C-dur aus Sonate Op.5, Nr.8 von Corelli.
In: Nagels Musik-Archiv. No.211.
Kammer-Sonaten für Violine und Pianoforte.
In: Moffat. Kammer-Sonaten für Violine und Pianoforte. No.2.
Twelve sonatas for violin and piano.
In: Smith College music archives. No.1.
Sonata A-dur op.I/1 für Violine und Basso Continuo; Sonata D-dur Op.I/4 für Violine und Basso Continuo.
In: Hortus musicus. No.173, 174.
Sonata E-moll für Oboe (Querflöte, Violine) und Basso Continuo.
In: Hortus musicus. No.178.
Sonate (Hm). Violin and piano.
In: Moffat. Meister-Schule der alter Zeit. Violin-Sonaten. No.23.
Sonate, pour deux violons, un violoncelle et la basse continue.
In: Flores musicae. Vol.8.
GENDRE, JEAN LE, *see* LE GENDRE, JEAN.
GENET, ELZÉAR, ca.1470–1548.
(var. sp.: Eleazar Genet genannt Carpentras).
Selections.
In: Ambros. Auserwählte Tonwerke.
Lamentatio a 4.
In: Alfieri. Raccolta di musica sacra. Vol.7.
GENISCHTA.
Vocal music.
In: Sammlung russischer Romanzen. No.175.
GENNRICH, FRIEDRICH, 1883– . ed.
Musikwissenschaftliche Studien-bibliothek. v.1– .
Ein altfranzösischer Motettenkodex.
In: Summa musicae medii aevi. Vol.6.
Bibliographie der ältesten französischen und lateinischen Motetten.
In: Summa musicae medii aevi. Vol.2.
Die musikalische Nachlass der Troubadours.
In: Summa musicae medii aevi. Vol.3–4.
Niedhart-Lieder.
In: Summa musicae medii aevi. Vol.9.
Troubadours, trouveres, minnesang and meistergesang.
In: Anthology of music. Vol.2.
Die Wimpfener Fragmente.
In: Summa musicae medii aevi. Vol.5.
GENTIAN.
Chansons.
In: Publikationen älterer praktischer und theoretischer Musikwerke. Jahrg.27.
GENZMER, HARALD, 1909– .
Fünf Bagatellen.
In: Zeitschrift für Spielmusik. No.230.
Divertimento giocoso, für zwei Holzbläzer und Streichorchester.
In: Concertino.
Musik für Flieger-Orchester.
In: Platzmusik. Nr.9.
GEOFFROY, JEAN NICOLAS.
Organ music.
In: Raugel. Les maîtres français de l'orgue. Vol.2.
GEORGET, M.
Motets.
In: Attaingnant. Treize livres de motets. Livre 12.
GEORGI, G.
Sacred music.
In: Monumenta liturgiae polychoralis sanctae ecclesiae romanae. Ser.VIII–IX.
Two masses.
In: Monumenta liturgiae polychoralis sanctae ecclesiae romanae. Ser.VI. No.2.
GEORGII, WALTER, 1887– . ed.
Four hundred years of European keyboard music.
In: Anthology of music. Vol.1.
GEORGIIS, JOANNIS DE.
Catalogus thematicus et bibliographicus.
In: Monumenta liturgiae polychoralis sanctae ecclesiae romanae. Ser.X. No.1.

GERBER, HEINRICH NICOLAUS, 1702–1775.
Organ music.
In: Das Erbe deutscher Musik. 1.Reihe. Vol.9.
GERDES, F.
Selections.
In: Boletín latino-americano de música. Vol.3.
GERHARD, FRITZ CHRISTIAN, 1911– .
Concertino für Streichorchester.
In: Collegium musicae novae. No.27.
Rhapsodisches Konzert.
In: Collegium musicae novae. No.42.
GERLE, HANS, 16th CENTURY.
Laute mit oder ohne Singstimme.
In: Musica practica. No.17b.
GERMAN ARIAS FROM COMEDIES (1754–8).
In: Denkmäler der Tonkunst in Österreich. Vol.64. (Jg.XXXIII/1).
THE GERMAN "GESELLSCHAFTSLIED" IN AUSTRIA, 1480–1550.
In: Denkmäler der Tonkunst in Österreich. Vol.72. (Jg.XXXVII/2).
THE GERMAN PART SONG (OSTHOFF).
In: Anthology of music. Vol.10.
THE GERMAN SOLO SONG AND THE BALLAD. (MOSER).
In: Anthology of music. Vol.14.
GERMANY–MUSIC (*see also* ARIAS, GERMAN; DARMSTADT–MUSIC; FOLKSONGS, GERMAN; SONGS, GERMAN).
In: Crotch. Specimens of various styles of music. Vol.1.
In: Denkmäler deutscher Tonkunst. [1.Folge].
In: Das Erbe deutscher Musik.
In: Hagen. Minnesinger.
In: Leichtentritt. Deutsche Hausmusik aus vier Jahrhunderten.
In: Moser. Alte Meister des deutschen Liedes. 30 Gesänge.
In: Moser. Alte Meister des deutschen Liedes. 46 Gesänge.
In: Moser. Frühmeister der deutschen Orgelkunst.
In: Moser. Die Kantorei der Spätgotik.
In: Oberdörffer. Deutsche Klaviermusik des 17. und 18. Jahrhunderts.
In: Reimann. Das deutsche geistliche Lied.
In: Reimann. Das deutsche Lied.
In: Das Rostocker Liederbuch. Das Rostocker Liederbuch.
In: Straube. Alte Meister.
In: Straube. Alte Meister des Orgelspiels.
In: Straube. Choralvorspiele alter Meister.
GERO, JHAN, 16th CENTURY.
(var. sp.: Jan Gero).
Selections.
In: Smith. Musica antiqua.
In: Torchi. L'arte musicale in Italia. Bd.1.
GERSCHEFSKI, EDWIN, 1909– .
Música de cámara.
In: Boletín latino-americano de música. Vol.5.
GERVAISE, CLAUDE, 16th CENTURY.
Danceriès.
In: Expert. Les maîtres musiciens de la Renaissance française. Vol.23.
Tänze.
In: Zeitschrift für Spielmusik. No.11.
Tanzsätze.
In: Musica practica. No.44, 46.
GESIUS, BARTHOLOMAUS, d.1613.
Choral music.
In: Antiqua Chorbuch. Vol.1. Heft 3.
Gesänge.
In: Musica sacra . . . ca.1842–1896. Vol.13.
GESUALDO, CARLO, PRINCIPE DI VENOSA, ca.1560–1613.
Sämtliche Werke. v.1– .
Sämtliche Madrigale. 6v.
Selections.
In: Documenta historica musicae.
In: Torchi. L'arte musicale in Italia. Bd.4.
Choral music.
In: Engel. Three centuries of choral music. Vol.2.
In: Der Kammerchor. Vol.3.
In: Recueil de musique ancienne. Recueil des morceaux de musique ancienne. Bd.5.
Felice primavera.
In: Squire. Ausgewählte Madrigale und mehrstimmige Gesänge. No.46.
Keyboard music.
In: Corpus of early keyboard music. Vol.24.
Madrigals.
In: I classici della musica italiana. Vol.14.
In: I classici della musica italiana. Raccolta nazionale delle musiche italiane. Quad.59–62.
In: Istituto italiano per la storia della musica. I. Monumenti I. Vol.1–3.
Moro lasso.
In: Parrish. A treasury of early music. No.33.
DER GETREUE MUSIKMEISTER. (G. P. TELEMANN).
In: Hortus musicus. No.6–13, 175.
GETTY, ALICE.
Song.
In: The Wa-Wan series of American compositions.
GEUSS.
8 Duette für 2 Querflöten oder Violinen.
In: Moecks Kammermusik. Vol.44.
GEUZELIEDJES, SONGS OF THE "GUEUX" DURING THE SPANISH OPPRESSION.
In: Vereniging voor nederlandsche Musikgeschiedenis. Uitgave. No.4.
GHEERKIN, *see* HONDT, GHEERKIN.
GHERARDELLO (GHIRARDELLUS DE FLORENTIA), 14th CENTURY.
(var. sp.: Ghirardello da Firenze).
Selections.
In: Gleason. Examples of music before 1400.
In: Pirrotta. The music of fourteenth-century Italy. Vol.1.
Cacce.
In: Marrocco. Fourteenth-century Italian cacce.
Gloria; Agnus Dei.
In: Van. Les monuments de l'Ars Nova. I. No.1, 4.
GHEYN, MATTHIAS VAN DEN, 1721–1785.
(var. sp.: Mathias van den Gheyn).
Carillon et fugue. Organ.
In: Dickinson. Historical recital series for organ. Vol.2. No.36.

Keyboard music.
In: Clavecinistes flamands. Vol.1.
Organ music.
In: Peeters. Anthologia pro organo. Vol.2, 4.
In: Peeters. Oudnederlandse meesters. Vol.2, 3.
In: Raugel. Quarante-six pièces pour orgue ou harmonium.
GHIRARDELLUS DE FLORENTIA, *see* GHERARDELLO (GHIRARDELLUS DE FLORENTIA).
GHISELIN-VERBONNET, JOHANNES, 15th–16th CENTURIES.
(var. sp.: Johannes Ghiselin).
Opera omnia. v.1– .
Selections.
In: Ambros. Auserwählte Tonwerke.
GHIZEGHEM, HAYNE VAN, 15th CENTURY.
Selections.
In: Maldéghem. Trésor musical.
In: Marix. Les musiciens de la cour de Bourgogne au XVe siècle (1420–1467).
Chanson.
In: Copenhagen Kongelige Bibliotek. Mss. (Thottske Samling 291^8). Der kopenhagener Chansonnier.
Choral music.
In: Droz. Poètes et musiciens du XVe siècles.
In: Smijers. Van Ockeghem tot Sweelinck. Aflg.5.
GIACOBBI, GIROLAMO, 1567–1629.
L'Aurora ingannata.
In: Maestri bolognesi. Vol.1.
GIANNEO, LUIS, 1897– .
Piano music.
In: Boletín latino-americano de música. Vol.1.
GIANNINI, VITTORIO, 1903– .
Quintet for piano and strings.
In: Society for the Publication of American Music. Publications. 13th season. 1931–32.
GIANONCELLI DELLO IL BARNARDELLO, BERNARDO, *see* BARNARDELLO, BERNARDO GIANONCELLI DELLO IL.
GIANSETTI, GIOVANNI BATTISTA.
Blandire puero. Sopran und B.C.
In: Cantio sacra. No.43.
GIARDINI, FELICE DE, 1716–1796.
Kammer-Sonaten für Violine und Pianoforte.
In: Moffat. Kammer-Sonaten für Violine und Pianoforte. No.9.
Quartetti Op.23, Nr.3 e 4.
In: I classici musicali italiani. Vol.6.
Sonate (Em). Violin and piano.
In: Moffat. Meister-Schule der alten Zeit. Violin-Sonaten. No.29.
Sonate per cembalo con violino o flauto traverso. Op.3.
In: I classici musicali italiani. Vol.3.
Weihnachtspastoralen.
In: Zeitschrift für Spielmusik. No.236.
GIBBONS, CHRISTOPHER, 1615–1676.
Cupid and Death.
In: Musica Britannica. Vol.2.
GIBBONS, ELLIS, 1573–1603.
Madrigals.
In: The triumphs of Oriana.
GIBBONS, ORLANDO, 1583–1625.
Complete keyboard works. 5v.
Ten pieces arranged for modern organ from the virginal book of Benjamin Cosyn. 36p.
Selections.
In: Crotch. Specimens of various styles of music. Vol.1, 2.
In: Documenta historica musicae.
In: The music with the form and order of the service to be performed at the coronation of . . . Queen Elizabeth II.
In: Smith. Musica antiqua.
Concerted anthems.
In: Documents of the musical past. Vol.3.
Anthems.
In: Early English church music. Vol.3.
Choral music.
In: Engel. Three centuries of choral music. Vol.3.
In: Recueil de musique ancienne. Recueil des morceaux de musique ancienne. Bd.11.
Church music.
In: Motett Society. [Collection of ancient church music]. Division 3.
In: Tudor church music. Vol.4.
2 Fantasias.
In: Musikschätze der Vergangenheit.
In nomine.
In: Parrish. A treasury of early music. No.36.
Keyboard music.
In: Elizabethal virginal composers. Vol.1.
In: English keyboard music. [No.17, 19].
In: Farrenc. Le trésor des pianistes. Vol.2.
In: The Fitzwilliam virginal book.
In: Fuller-Maitland. Twenty-five pieces for keyed instruments from Benjamin Cosyn's virginal book.
In: Glyn. Twenty-one old English compositions of the 16th and 17th centuries.
In: Musica Britannica. Vol.20.
In: Oesterle. Early keyboard music. Vol.1.
In: Parthenia.
In: Pauer. Alte Klavier-Musik. 2d series. Pt.6.
In: Pauer. Old English composers for the virginals and harpsichord.
In: Schott's Anthology of early keyboard music. Vol.4.
In: Tagliapietra. Antologia di musica antica e moderna per pianoforte. Bd.3.
Londoner Strassenrufe für fünf Instrumente.
In: Antiqua Edition. Instrumente mit Singstimmen.
Madrigals and motets.
In: Euterpe. 2d ed. No.25.
In: Fellowes. The English madrigal school. Vol.5.
In: Musical Antiquarian Society. Publications. Vol.3, 9, 18.
In: Squire. Ausgewählte Madrigale und mehrstimmige Gesänge. No.21, 25.
Organ music.
In: Klein. The first four centuries of music for the organ from Dunstable to Bach (1370–1749).
In: Liber organi. Bd.10.

In: The Liturgical Music Press, Inc. Masterpieces of organ music. Folio 21, 35, 73.
In: Raugel. Quarante-six pièces pour orgue ou harmonium.
In: Tallis to Wesley. Vol.9.
Part music.
In: Hullah. Part music. Class A.1. Vol.1, 2; 1868 edition.
Parthenia. Facsimile.
In: Monuments of music and music literature. First series. No.11.
Sacred music.
In: Boyce. Cathedral music. Vol.1, 2, 3; 1849, Vol.1, 2, and Vol.2, Appendix; Vol.3.
Trust not too much.
In: Arion. Vol.1.
Violenmusik.
In: Giesbert. Altenglische Violenmusik. Vol.1, 2.
Vocal music.
In: Hullah. Vocal scores. I. Sacred; II. Secular.
GIDEON, MIRIAM, 1906– .
Canzona. For piano solo.
In: New music. Vol.20. No.2. Jan.1947.
GIEGLING, FRANZ, 1921– . ed.
The solo sonata.
In: Anthology of music. Vol.15.
GIGAULT, NICOLAS, ca.1624–1707.
Keyboard music.
In: Tagliapietra. Antologia di musica antica e moderna per pianoforte. Bd.7.
Organ music.
In: Guilmant. Archives des maîtres de l'orgue. Vol.4.
In: Klein. The first four centuries of music for the organ from Dunstable to Bach (1370–1749).
In: Liber organi. Bd.1.
In: The parish organist. Vol.1–4.
In: Raugel. Les maîtres français de l'orgue. Vol.1, 2.
In: Raugel. Les maîtres français de l'orgue aus XVIIème et XVIIIème siècles.
GIGOUT, EUGÈNE, 1844–1925.
Organ music.
In: Bedell. The French organist. Vol.1, 2.
In: Bonnet. Historical organ-recitals. Vol.5.
GILBERT, HENRY FRANKLIN BELKNAP, 1868–1928.
Songs; Piano music.
In: The Wa-Wan series of American compositions.
GILLE, JACOB EDWARD, 1814–1880.
Mass No.7, A major.
In: Musikaliska konstföreningen. 1863.
Trio for violin, violoncello, and piano.
In: Musikaliska konstföreningen. 1863.
GILLES DE BINCHE, *see* BINCHOIS, EGIDIUS.
GILMAN, LAWRENCE, 1878–1939.
Songs.
In: The Wa-Wan series of American compositions.
GINASTERA, ALBERTO EVARISTO, 1916– .
Impresiones de la puna.
In: Instituto Interamericano de Musicologia. Publicaciónes. No.12.
The lamentations of Jeremiah.
In: Music Press, Inc. [Choral series]. Vol.103.
GINDELE, CORBINIAN.
Gregorianische Choralvorspiele für die Orgel. 1. Proprium de Tempore. 2. Proprium Sanctorum.
In: Musica divina. Vol.7, 8.
Orgelintonationen in den acht Kirchentonarten.
In: Musica divina. Vol.6.
Kleine Orgelstücke.
In: Musica divina. Vol.14.
GINÉS PÉREZ, JUAN, 1548–1612.
(var. sp.: Joannes Ginesius Pérez).
Composiciones.
In: Pedrell. Hispaniae schola musica sacra. Bd.5.
Domine Deus.
In: Polifonía española. Vol.17.
Gloria laus et honor.
In: Polifonía española. Vol.20.
Miseremini fideles animorum; Parce mihi, Domine.
In: Polifonía española. Vol.3, 4.
Sacred music.
In: Rubio. Antologia polifonica sacra. Vol.1.
GINTZLER, SIMON, 16th CENTURY.
Lute music.
In: Chilesotti. Lautenspieler des XVI. Jahrhunderts.
In: Denkmäler der Tonkunst in Österreich. Vol.37 (Jg.XVIII/2).
GIORDANI, GIUSEPPE, ca.1753–1798.
Arias.
In: Parisotti. Arie antiche. Bd.2.
Konzert für Klavier und Streichorchester.
In: Nagels Musik-Archiv. No.157.
GIORDANI, TOMMASO, d.1806.
Concerto No.3 in C (cembalo solo, strings).
In: Antica musica strumentale italiana. Ser.II. Vol.14.
Concerto No.5 in D (cembalo solo, strings).
In: Antica musica strumentale italiana. Ser.II. Vol.15.
GIORGI, GIOVANNI.
Improperium exspectavit.
In: Documenta liturgiae polychoralis sanctae ecclesiae romanae. No.19.
Laetentur coeli.
In: Die Motette. No.1.
Liturgia paschalis; Liturgia pentecostes.
In: Monumenta liturgiae polychoralis sanctae ecclesiae romanae. Ser.VIII. No.1, 2.
Missa.
In: Documenta maiora liturgiae polychoralis sanctae ecclesiae romanae. No.6, 7, 8.
O sacrum convivium; Et manducantibus illus.
In: Documenta liturgiae polychoralis sanctus ecclesiae romanae. No.12, 13.
Officium de beata Virgine.
In: Monumenta liturgiae polychoralis sanctae ecclesiae romanae. Ser.IX. No.1. Pt.1–2.
GIORNI, AURELIO, 1895–1938.
Sonate for violoncello (or viola) and piano.
In: Society for the Publication of American Music. Publications. 6th season. 1924–25.

GIORNOVICCHI, GIOVANNI MANE, ca.1740–1804.
(var. sp.: Giornovichi; Jarnowich).
Konzert Nr.1 in A-dur, für Violine und Orchester.
In: Concertino.
GIOVANNELLI, RUGGIERO, 1560–1625.
(var. sp. : Ruggero Giovanelli).
Selections.
In: Torchi. L'arte musicale in Italia. Bd.2.
Organ music.
In: Cantantibus organis. Vol.6.
Sacred music.
In: Proske. Musica divina. Annus primus. Tom 3; Annus secundus. Tom 2.
In: Proske. Selectus novus missarum. Annus secundus. Tom 2.
GIOVANNI DA CASCIA (JOHANNES DE FLORENTIA), 14th CENTURY.
(var. sp.: Giovanni da Firenze).
Selections.
In: Documenta historica musicae.
In: Pirrotta. The music of fourteenth-century Italy. Vol.1.
Cacce.
In: Marrocco. Fourteenth-century Italian cacce.
Con brachi assai.
In: Parrish. A treasury of early music. No.16.
GIRGENSOHN, AREND.
Variationen über "Schwesterlein, Schwesterlein, wann geh'n wir nach Haus."
In: Zeitschrift für Spielmusik. No.65.
GIROD, M. L.
Triptyque sur l'hymne sacris solemnis. Organ.
In: Orgue et liturgie. Vol.18.
GISTOU, NICOLAUS, 16th CENTURY.
(var. sp.: Nicolaus Gistow).
"Paduanen" and "Galliarden."
In: Vereniging voor nederlandsche Muziekgeschiedenis. Uitgave. No.34.
GIULIANI, MAURO, 1728–1828.
Sonate für Violine und Gitarre. Op.25.
In: Albert. Die Gitarre in der Haus- und Kammermusik vor 100 Jahren (1780–1820). No.7.
Trio für 3 Gitarren. Op.71.
In: Albert. Die Gitarre in der Haus- und Kammermusik vor 100 Jahren (1780–1820). No.14.
GLAREANUS, HENRICUS, 1488–1563.
Dodecachord in deutscher übersetzung.
In: Publikationen älterer praktischer und theoretischer Musikwerke. Jahrg.16–18.
GLASS, LOUIS CHRISTIAN AUGUST, 1864–1936.
Fantasi for Klavier. Op.35.
In: Samfundet til Udgivelse af dansk Musik. Ser.III. No.3.
Fantasi for Pianoforte og Orkester. Op.47.
In: Samfundet til Udgivelse af dansk Musik. Ser.III. No.12.
Klaverstykker. Op.66.
In: Samfundet til Udgivelse af dansk Musik. Ser.III. No.33.
Skovsymfoni. Op.30.
In: Samfundet til Udgivelse af dansk Musik. Ser.II. No.23; Ser.III. No.19.
Sommerliv. Suite for orchestra. Op.27.
In: Samfundet til Udgivelse af dansk Musik. Ser.II. No.12.
Symfoni Nr.4, E-moll, Op.43.
In: Samfundet til Udgivelse af dansk Musik. Ser.II. No.34.
GLASSE.
Part music.
In: Hullah. Part music. Class B.1.
GLEES.
In: Music Press, Inc. [Choral series]. Vol.121.
GLETLE, JOHANN MELCHIOR, d.before 1684.
Werke.
In: Verein schweizerischer Tonkünstler. Musikalische Werke. Heft 4.
Ausgewählte Kirchenmusik.
In: Schweizerische Musikdenkmäler. Vol.2.
Zwölf kleine Duos . . . aus Blockflöten.
In: Schweizer Sing- und Spielmusik. Heft 6.
Wein und Musik; Neu und Alt.
In: Schweizer Sing- und Spielmusik. Heft 10.
Wer da will frisch und gesund auf Erden länger elben.
In: Organum. 2.Reihe. Nr.19.
GLINKA, MICHAEL IVANOVITCH, 1803–1857.
Complete works. v.1– .
Complete works for piano solo and piano 4 hands. 442p.
Vocal music.
In: Sammlung russischer Romanzen. No.13–17, 35, 60–61, 68–69, 100–102, 117–119, 189–192, 215–220, 236–237, 261, 279, 281, 296–297.
GLOGAUER LIEDERBUCH.
In: Antiqua Chorbuch. Vol.1. Heft 1; Vol.2. Heft 1.
In: Cantantibus organis. Vol.8.
In: Das Erbe deutscher Musik. 1.Reihe. Vol.4, 8.
GLÖTZNER, KARL HERMANN.
Spielmusik.
In: Zeitschrift für Spielmusik. No.74.
Vetter Florian.
In: Zeitschrift für Spielmusik. No.62.
GLUCK, CHRISTOPH WILLIBALD, RITTER VON, 1714–1787.
Sämtliche Werke. 1v.
Werke. v.1– .
Sämtliche Werke. 6 Abteilung.
Selections.
In: Crotch. Specimens of various styles of music. Vol.1, 3.
In: Échos de France. Vol.1–3.
Arias.
In: Landshoff. Alte Meister des Bel Canto. Eine Sammlung von Arien. Vol.1–2.
In: Parisotti. Arie antiche. Bd.1.
Ballettmusik.
In: Corona. Vol.5.
Choral music.
? In: Recueil de musique ancienne. Recueil des morceaux de musique ancienne. Bd.3.
Don Juan. (Pantomime ballet).
In: Denkmäler der Tonkunst in Österreich. Vol.60. (Jg.XXX/2).
3 Festival marches.
In: Musikschätze der Vergangenheit.
L'innocenza giustificata.

In: Denkmäler der Tonkunst in Österreich. Vol.82. (Jg.XLIV).
Lied.
In: Reimann. Das deutsche Lied. Vol.3.
Märsche.
In: Corona. Vol.11.
Motets.
In: Concerts spirituels ou recueil de motets.
Nozze d'Ercole de d'Ebe.
In: Denkmäler deutscher Tonkunst. [2.Folge]. Vol.14. (ii).
Orfeo e Euridice.
In: Denkmäler der Tonkunst in Österreich. Vol.44a. (Jg.XXI/2).
Part music.
In: Hullah. Part music. Class A.2. Vol.1; Class A.2. Vol.2.
Sacred music.
In: Latrobe, C. I. Selection of sacred music.
In: Latrobe, J. A. The music of the church.
Sinfonie (G-dur).
In: Corona. Vol.6.
Sonate (F).
In: Moffat. Trio-Sonaten alter Meister. No.11.
Trio. Für 2 Violinen, Violoncell und Klavier. No.1–7.
In: Riemann. Collegium musicum. No.32–38.
Triosonaten.
In: Nagels Musik-Archiv. No.205, 206, 207, 208.
Triosonate, G-moll, für 2 Violinen und Cembalo (Klavier).
In: Nagels Musik-Archiv. No.158.
Vocal music.
In: Delsarte. Archives du chant (passim).
In: Gevaert. Les gloires de l'Italie. Vol.1, 2.
GLUTZ-BLOTZHEIM, A.
Waltzes. Voice and piano. Op.10. Arr. for 2 violins.
In: Schweizer Sing- und Spielmusik. Heft 7.
GNATTALI, RADAMÉS, 1906– .
Selections.
In: Boletín latino-americano de música. Vol.3.
Chôro. Piano.
In: New music. Vol.16. No.1. Oct.1942.
Música de cámara.
In: Boletín latino-americano de música. Vol.6.
GODARD, 16th CENTURY.
Chanson.
In: Brown. Theatrical chansons of the 15th and early 16th centuries.
In: Cauchie. Quinze chansons française du XVIe siècle.
In: Publikationen älterer praktischer und theoretischer Musikwerke. Jahrg.27.
GODEBRYE, JACQUES, *see* JACOTIN (REAL NAME JACQUES GODEBRYE).
GODSKE-NIELSEN, SVEND, 1867–1935.
Strygekvartet. Op.14.
In: Samfundet til Udgivelse af dansk Musik. Ser.III. No.38.
GOERNER, JOHANN VALENTIN, *see* GÖRNER, JOHANN VALENTIN.
GOETHE, JOHANN WOLFGANG VON, 1749–1832.
Lied.
In: Das Erbe deutscher Musik. 1.Reihe. Vol.58.
GOLĄBEK, J.
Partita. (Blasinstrumenten-Ensemble).
In: Źródła do historii muzyki polskiej. Vol.4.
Sinfonien.
In: Źródla do historii muzyki polskiej. Vol.3.
GOLD, ERNEST.
String quartet, No.1.
In: Society for the Publication of American Music. Publications. 37th season. 1956.
GOLDBERG, JOHANN GOTTLIEB, ca.1727–1756.
Kantaten.
In: Das Erbe deutscher Musik. 1.Reihe. Vol.35.
Keyboard music.
In: Herrmann. Lehrmeister und Schüler Joh. Seb. Bachs. Vol.2.
Trio in G-moll für zwei Violinen und Basso Continuo.
In: Nagels Musik-Archiv. No.198.
GOLDBERG, SZYMON, 1909– .
Trio in A-moll, für zwei Violinen und Basso Continuo.
In: Nagels Musik-Archiv. No.185.
GOLDBERG, THÉOPHILE.
Keyboard music.
In: Farrenc. Le trésor des pianistes. Vol.11.
GOLDMAN, RICHARD FRANKO, 1910– .
Hymn for brass choir.
In: New music. Vol.15. No.1. Oct.1941.
GOLDMARK, RUBIN, 1872–1936.
Song.
In: The Wa-Wan series of American compositions.
GOLDWIN, JOHN, d.1719.
Sacred music.
In: Arnold. Cathedral music. Vol.1.
In: Boyce. Cathedral music. Vol.2; 1849. Vol.3.
In: Page. Harmonia sacra. Vol.1, 2.
GOLINELLI, STEFANO, 1818–1891.
Keyboard music.
In: Tagliapietra. Antologia di musica antica e moderna per pianoforte. Bd.16.
GOMBERT, NICOLAS, fl.1520–1552.
(var. sp.: Nicolaus Gombert).
Opera omnia. v.1– .
Selections.
In: Ambros. Auserwählte Tonwerke.
In: Maldéghem. Trésor musical.
Choral music.
In: Commer. Collectio operum musicorum batavorum saeculi XVI. Bd.8, 12.
In: Engel. Three centuries of choral music. Vol.1.
In: Smijers. Van Ockeghem tot Sweelinck. Aflg.7.
Lieder.
In: Publikationen älterer praktischer und theoretischer Musikwerke. Jahrg.1–3.
Mass.
In: Stein. Twelve Franco-Flemish masses of the early 16th century.

Motets.
In: Attaingnant. Treize livres de motets. Livre 1, 2, 4, 7, 8, 12, 13.
In: Das Chorwerk. No.94.
GOMES DA ROCHA, FRANCISCO.
Selections.
In: Lange. Archivo de música religiosa.
GÓMEZ CAMARGO, MIGUEL, 16th CENTURY.
Himno de Santiago apostol.
In: Polifonía española. Vol.16.
Sacred music.
In: Eslava y Elizondo. Lira sacro-hispana. 16th century. i.2.
GOMÓLKA, MIKOLAY (NICOLAS), b.ca.1535.
(var. sp.: Nikolaus Gomólka; Nicolai Gomólka).
Selections.
In: Gieburowski. Cantica selecta musices sacrae in Polonia saeculi XVI et XVII.
"Melodies for Polish Psalter."
In: Denkmäler altpolischer Musik. Vol.47, 48, 49.
Psalmen.
In: Cichocki. Chants d'église à plusieurs voix des anciens compositeurs polonais. Vol.1.
GONZALEZ, LE TOMBEAU DE. ORGAN.
In: Orgue et liturgie. Vol.38.
GONZALO, GISELA HERNÁNDEZ, *see* HERNÁNDEZ GONZALO, GISELA.
GORCZYCKI, GREGOR GERNASIUS, ca.1664–1734.
(var. sp.: Gregor Gerwazy Gorczyki; Greg. Gorczyski).
Selections.
In: Gieburowski. Cantica selecta musices sacrae in Polonia saeculi XVI et XVII.
Choral music.
In: Surzyński. Monumenta musicae sacrae in Polonia. Vol.2.
Completorium.
In: Zródła do historii muzyki polskiej. Vol.7.
Illuxit sol.
In: Denkmäler altpolnischer Musik. Vol.14.
Laetatus sum.
In: Denkmäler altpolnischer Musik. Vol.37.
Messen.
In: Cichocki. Chants d'église à plusieurs voix des anciens compositeurs polonais. Vol.2.
Missa paschalis.
In: Denkmäler altpolnischer Musik. Vol.7.
GORIGOYTÍA, HÉCTOR MELO, *see* MELO GORIGOYTÍA, HÉCTOR.
GÖRNER, JOHANN VALENTIN, 1702–1762.
(var. sp.: Goerner).
Lieder.
In: Moser. Alte Meister des deutschen Liedes. 46 Gesänge. No.25.
Odes and songs.
In: Denkmäler deutscher Tonkunst. [1.Folge]. Vol.57.
In: Organum. 2.Reihe. Nr.15.
GORZANIS, JACOMO, 16th CENTURY.
Lute music.
In: Chilesotti. Lautenspieler des XVI. Jahrhunderts.
GOSSE.
Chanson.
In: Brown. Theatrical chansons of the 15th and early 16th centuries.
Motets.
In: Attaingnant. Treize livres de motets. Livre 7, 9.
GOSSEC, FRANÇOIS JOSEPH, 1734–1829.
Part music.
In: Hullah. Part music. Class A.1. Vol.2.
Sacred music.
In: Latrobe, C. I. Selection of sacred music.
In: Latrobe, J. A. The music of the church.
Sinfonie C-dur.
In: Sondheimer. Werke aus dem 18. Jahrhundert. Nr.42.
Sinfonia in G major. Op.XII, No.2. For two oboes, two horns, and strings.
In: Early symphonies and concertos. Vol.1.
Trio in Es-dur, Op.9, Nr.1. Für 2 Violinen, und Violoncell.
In: Riemann. Collegium musicum. No.47.
GOSSWIN, ANTON, 16th CENTURY.
(var. sp.: Gosswinus).
Choral music.
In: Antiqua Chorbuch. Vol.2. Heft 2.
In: Dehn. Sammlung älterer Musik aus dem XVI. und XVII. Jahrhundert.
Newe teutsche Lieder.
In: Das Chorwerk. No.75.
GOSTENA, GIOVANNI BATTISTA DALLA, d.before 1605.
Intavolatura di liuto. 75p.
Lute music.
In: Chilesotti. Lautenspieler des XVI. Jahrhunderts.
GOTT, RUDOLPH.
Oboe and piano.
In: The Wa-Wan series of American compositions.
GOTTRON, ADAM BERNHARD, 1889– .
Musik am Mainzer Hof: für Streicher und Basso Continuo, Cembalo (Pianoforte), Violoncello (Viola da gamba) ad lib.
In: Concertino.
GÖTTSCHING, R. ed.
Das Soldatenlied.
In: Musikalische Formen in historischen Reihen. Bd.20.
GOUDIMEL, CLAUDE, ca.1505–1572.
Collected works.
In: Institute of Mediaeval Music. Collected works. Vol.3.
Selections.
In: Maldéghem. Trésor musical.
Chansons.
In: Cauchie. Quinze chansons françaises du XVIe siècle.
In: Lésure. Anthologie de la chanson parisienne au XVIe siècle.
Choral music.
In: Engel. Three centuries of choral music. Vol.1.
In: Rochlitz. Sammling vorzüglicher Gesangstücke. Bd.1. Pt.1.
In: Societas Polyphonica Romanae. Repertorium. Vol.5.
Festmotetten zu 4 und 6 Stimmen.
In: Das Chorwerk. No.103.

Messes à quatre voix.
In: Expert. Monuments de la musique française au temps de la Renaissance. Vol.9.
Mon Dieu me paist. 1564, 1565.
In: Parrish. A treasury of early music. No.25, 26.
Motet a 4.
In: Alfieri. Raccolta di musica sacra. Vol.7.
Les 140 pseaumes de David.
In: Expert. Les maîtres musiciens de la Renaissance française. Vol.2, 4, 6.
Ps. CV.
In: Arion. Vol.3.
GOUY, JACQUES DE, 17th CENTURY.
Vocal music.
In: Hullah. Vocal scores. I. Sacred.
GRABBE, JOHANN, 16th–17th CENTURIES.
Madrigale.
In: Das Chorwerk. No.35.
GRABNER, HERMANN, 1886– .
Op.44. Burgmusik.
In: Platzmusik. Nr.1.
Firlefei.
In: Platzmusik. Nr.4.
Media Vita in Morte sumus.
In: Die Orgel. Reihe I. Nr.2.
Meditationen für Orgel.
In: Die Orgel. Reihe I. Nr.7.
Der 66. Psalm "Jauchzt, alle Lande, Gott zu Ehren," für Orgel.
In: Die Orgel. Reihe I. Nr.5.
GRADEHAND, FRIED.
Organ music.
In: Musiek voor de eredienst. Vol.2.
DAS GRADUALE DER ST. THOMASKIRCHE ZU LEIPZIG.
In: Publikationen älterer Musik. Jahrg.5, 7.
GRAETZER, GUILLERMO, 1914– .
Tres tocatas. (Para piano).
In: Instituto Interamericano de Musicologia. Publicaciónes. No.9.
GRÄFE, JOHANN FRIEDRICH, 1711–1787.
Lied.
In: Reimann. Das deutsche Lied. Vol.4.
GRAFF, J.
Violinsonate. Op.1. Nr.3. D dur.
In: Organum. 3.Reihe. Nr.3.
GRAGNANI, FILIPPO, b.ca.1767.
Sonate. Violine und Gitarre. Op.8. Nr.1–3.
In: Albert. Die Gitarre in der Haus- und Kammermusik vor 100 Jahren (1780–1820). No.4–6.
Trio für 3 Gitarren. Op.12.
In: Albert. Die Gitarre in der Haus- und Kammermusik vor 100 Jahren (1780–1820). No.13.
GRAM, PEDER, 1881–1956.
Koncert for Violin og Orkester. Op.20.
In: Samfundet til Udgivelse af dansk Musik. Ser.III. No.8.
Ouverture i C dur. Op.21.
In: Samfundet til Udgivelse af dansk Musik. Ser.III. No.50.
Poëme lyrique for Orkester. Op.9.
In: Samfundet til Udgivelse af dansk Musik. Ser.III. No.108.
Prolog. Til et Drama af Shakespeare. Op.27.
In: Samfundet til Udgivelse af dansk Musik. Ser.III. No.61.
Strygekvartet. Nr.3. Op.30.
In: Samfundet til Udgivelse af dansk Musik. Ser.III. No.75.
Symphonie Nr.2. Op.25.
In: Samfundet til Udgivelse af dansk Musik. Ser.III. No.21.
GRAMATGES, HAROLD, 1918– .
Dúo en la bemol.
In: Instituto Interamericano de Musicologia. Publicaciónes. No.48.
GRANADOS, ENRIQUE, 1867–1916.
Keyboard music.
In: Guenther. Collection espagnole.
GRANADOS, V.
Keyboard music.
In: Guenther. Collection espagnole.
GRANDI, ALESSANDRO, d.1630.
Selections.
In: Expert. Répertoire classique de musique. 1re Année.
Drei geistliche Konzerte. Sopran (Tenor) und B.C.
In: Cantio sacra. No.18.
Hoheliedmotette.
In: Cantio sacra. No.23.
Kammerduette.
In: Landshoff. Alte Meister des Bel Canto. Italienische Kammerduette.
Drei konzertierende Motetten.
In: Das Chorwerk. No.40.
GRANT, GUILLAUME LE, *see* LE GRANT, GUILLAUME.
GRANT, JOHANNES LE, *see* LE GRANT, JOHANNES.
GRAST.
Part music.
In: Hullah. Part music. Class A.2. Vol.2.
GRATIANI, BONIFATIO, *see* GRAZIANI, BONIFAZIO.
GRATIOSUS DE PADUA, 15th CENTURY.
Gloria; Sanctus.
In: Van. Les monuments de l'Ars Nova. II. No.6, 7.
GRÄTZ.
Organ music.
In: Cantantibus organis. Vol.3.
GRAUN, JOHANN GOTTLIEB, ca.1703–1771.
Christe.
In: Königliche Akademie der Künste. Auswahl vorzüglicher Musik-Werke. No.17.
Concerto C-dur für Alt-Blockflöte, Violine und Streicher.
In: Moecks Kammermusik. Vol.68.
Fugue. Tu Rex.
In: Königliche Akademie der Künste. Auswahl vorzüglicher Musik-Werke. No.1.
Sacred music.
? In: Latrobe, C. I. Selection of sacred music.
? In: Latrobe, J. A. The music of the church.
Sonate. Viola und Cembalo.
In: Kammersonaten. No.10, 11.
Trio in F dur; Trio in G dur; Trio in C moll.
In: Riemann. Collegium musicum. No.24–26.

Vocal music.
In: Hullah. Vocal scores. I. Sacred.
GRAUN, KARL HEINRICH, 1704–1759.
(var. sp.: Carl H. Graun).
Selections.
? In: Crotch. Specimens of various styles of music. Vol.2.
Arias.
In: Landshoff. Alte Meister des Bel Canto. Eine Sammlung von Arien. Vol.1–2.
Choral music.
? In: Commer. Cantica sacra. Vol.1. No.10, 11; Vol.2. No.8, 22.
? In: Rochlitz. Sammlung vorzüglicher Gesängstücke. Bd.3.
Cantata.
In: Eitner. Cantaten des 17. und 18. Jahrhunderts. Part 3.
Gigue.
In: Köhler. Les maîtres du clavecin. Heft 3.
In: Pauer. Alte Meister. No.32.
Konzert C-moll.
In: Corona. Vol.60.
Lieder.
In: Moser. Alte Meister des deutschen Liedes. 30 Gesänge. No.21.
In: Moser. Alte Meister des deutschen Liedes. 46 Gesänge. No.32.
In: Reimann; Das deutsche Lied. Vol.2.
Montezuma.
In: Denkmäler deutscher Tonkunst. [1.Folge]. Vol.15.
GRAUPNER, CHRISTOPH, 1683–1760.
Ausgewählte Werke. v.1– .
Christoph Graupner als Kirchenkomponist. (Friedrich Noack).
In: Denkmäler deutscher Tonkunst. [1.Folge]. Reprint. Suppl. Vol.51/52.
Selected cantatas.
In: Denkmäler deutscher Tonkunst. [1.Folge]. Vol.51–52.
Instrumental concertos.
In: Denkmäler deutscher Tonkunst. [1.Folge]. Vol.29–30.
Kirchenmusik.
In: Kirchenmusik der Darmstädter Meister des Barock. Vol.1, 2.
Konzert.
In: Corona. Vol.27.
Konzert für Oboe, Streicher und Cembalo.
In: Nagels Musik-Archiv. No.168.
Märsche.
In: Corona. Vol.11.
Acht Partiten für Cembalo oder Klavier.
In: Mitteldeutsches Musikarchiv. Reihe I. Bd.2.
Zwei Sonaten. Für Cembalo (Klavier) und Violin oder Flöte.
In: Hortus musicus. No.121.
Sonata G-dur für Streichquartett oder Streichorchester.
In: Hortus musicus. No.120.
GRAY, A.
The midhour of night. S.A.T.B.
In: Arion. Vol.2.
GRAZIANI, BONIFAZIO, d.1664.
(var. sp.: Bonifatio Gratiani).
Gaudia, Pastores, Optate. Sopran (Tenor) und B.C.
In: Cantio sacra. No.1.
Pastores, dum custodistis. Sopran (Tenor) und B.C.
In: Cantio sacra. No.41.
Salve, Regina. Sopran (Tenor) und B.C.
In: Cantio sacra. No.39.
GRAZIANI, CARLO, 18th CENTURY.
Sei sonate per violoncello e basso continuo. Op.3.
In: I classici musicali italiani. Vol.15.
GRAZIOLI, GIOVANNI BATTISTA, ca.1750–ca.1820.
Dodici sonate per cembalo.
In: I classici musicali italiani. Vol.12.
Keyboard music.
In: Esposito. Early Italian piano music.
In: Tagliapietra. Antologia di musica antica e moderna per pianoforte. Bd.13.
Sonate.
In: Köhler. Les maîtres du clavecin. Heft 8.
Sonate. No.5 (G).
In: Pauer. Alte Meister. No.35.
GREAVES, THOMAS, 16th–17th CENTURIES.
Madrigals.
In: Fellowes. The English madrigal school. Vol.36, 37.
In: Squire. Ausgewählte Madrigale und mehrstimmige Gesänge. No.44.
Songs of sundrie kindes. (1604).
In: Fellowes. The English school of lutenist song writers. 2d series. Vol.18.
Three songs.
In: The Tudor edition of old music. Series B. No.1.
GREECE–MUSIC.
In: Institut Français d'Athènes.
GREEN, RAY, 1909– .
Compositions; 2 Madrigals; Sonatina for piano; 2 Songs.
In: New music. Vol.7. No.3. Apr.1934.
Three inventories of Casey Jones.
In: New music. Orchestra series. No.18.
GREENE, MAURICE, 1695–1755.
Forty select anthems in score. 2v.
Organ music.
In: Liber organi. Bd.10.
In: Peeters. Anthologia pro organo. Vol.4.
In: Tallis to Wesley. Vol.4, 15.
Part music.
In: Hullah. Part music. Class A.1. Vol.2; Class B.2.
Sacred music.
In: Arnold Cathedral music. Vol.2, 3.
In: Page. Harmonia sacra. Vol.1, 2, 3.
GREFF, VALENTIN, 1507–1576.
(var. sp.: Bakfarc (Greffus); Bakfark; Barfark).
Der Lautenist V. Barfark, 1507–1576. 166p. and 32p.
Lute music.
In: Denkmäler der Tonkunst in Österreich. Vol.37 (Jg.XVIII/2).
Organ music.
In: Cantantibus organis. Vol.6.
GREFINGER, WOLFGANG, 15th CENTURY.
Choral music.
In: Antiqua Chorbuch. Vol.2. Heft 1.

Lied.
In: Denkmäler der Tonkunst in Österreich. Vol.72 (Jg.XXXVII/2).
Songs.
In: Aich. Das Liederbuch.
GREGORIAN CHANT, *see* CHANT (PLAIN, GREGORIAN, ETC.).
GREGORY, SAINT, 6th CENTURY.
(var. sp.: Saint Grégoire le Grand).
Vocal music.
In: Delsarte. Archives du chant. Livr.2. No.1.
GREITER, MATTHIAS, d.1550.
(var. sp.: Matthes Greiter).
Selections.
In: Ambros. Auserwählte Tonwerke.
Choral music.
In: Antiqua Chorbuch. Vol.2. Heft 1.
Sämtliche weltliche Lieder.
In: Das Chorwerk. No.87.
GRELL, EDUARD AUGUST, 1800–1886.
Psalmen.
In: Musica sacra . . . ca.1842–1896. Vol.8–10.
GRENIER.
Chansons.
In: Publikationen älterer praktischer und theoretischer Musikwerke. Jahrg.27.
GRENON, NICOLAS, 15th CENTURY.
Selections.
In: Marix. Les musiciens de la cour de Bourgogne au XVe siècle. (1420–1467).
Sacred music.
In: Plainsong and Mediaeval Music Society. Publications. (Borren).
Songs.
In: Riemann. Hausmusik aus alter Zeit.
GREP, BENEDICTUS, ca.1600.
Paduanen and Galliarden.
In: Vereniging voor Nederlandsche Muziekgeschiedenis. Uitgave. No.34.
GRÉTRY, ANDRÉ ERNEST MODESTE, 1741–1813.
Collection complète des oeuvres de Grétry. 49v.
Selections.
In: Crotch. Specimens of various styles of music. Vol.3.
In: Échos de France. Vol.1–3.
La Caravane du Caire; Céphale & Procris.
In: Les chefs d'oeuvres classiques de l'opéra français.
Vocal music.
In: Delsarte. Archives du chant (passim).
GRIEG, EDVARD HAGERUP, 1843–1907.
Sämtliche Klavierwerke. 3v.
The bearhunter. S.A.T.B.
In: Arion. Vol.2.
I host. Op.11.
In: Musikaliska konstföreningen. 1867.
Organ music.
In: Gerhardt. Album nordischer Komponisten für Orgel. Vol.2.
GRIGNY, NICOLAS DE, 1671–1703.
Premier livre d'orgue. 101p.
Keyboard music.
In: Herrmann. Lehrmeister und Schüler Joh. Seb. Bachs. Vol.1.
Organ music.
In: Bonnet. An anthology of early French organ music.
In: Bonnet. Historical organ-recitals. Vol.1.
In: Cantantibus organis. Vol.1.
In: Guilmant. Archives des maîtres de l'orgue. Vol.5.
In: Klein. The first four centuries of music for the organ from Dunstable to Bach (1370–1749).
In: Liber organi. Bd.2.
In: Peeters. Anthologie pro organo. Vol.2, 4.
In: Raugel. Les maîtres français de l'orgue. Vol.1, 2.
In: Raugel. Les maîtres français de l'orgue aus XVIIème et XVIIIème siècles.
GRILLO, GIOVANNI BATTISTA, 17th CENTURY.
Choral music.
In: Dehn. Sammlung älterer Musik aus dem XVI und XVII Jahrhundert.
GRIMM.
Choral music.
In: Sammlung vorzüglicher Gesängstücke. Bd.2.
GRONAU, D. M.
Organ music.
In: The Liturgical Music Press, Inc. Masterpieces of organ music. Folio 15.
GRØNDAHL, LAUNY, 1886– .
Koncert for Fagot og Orkester.
In: Samfundet til Udgivelse af dansk Musik. Ser.III. No.82.
Koncert for Trombone og Orkester.
In: Samfundet til Udgivelse af dansk Musik. Ser.III. No.124.
Koncert for Violin og Orkester.
In: Samfundet til Udgivelse af dansk Musik. Ser.III. No.49.
GRÖNING, HERBERT.
Kleine Stücke für eine Blockflöte allein.
In: Zeitschrift für Spielmusik. No.130.
Kleine Stücke für 1 Streichinstrument allein oder zum Unisonospiel von Geige, Bratsche und Cello.
In: Moecks Kammermusik. Vol.201.
GROSSI DA VIADANA, LUDOVICO, *see* VIADANA, LODOVICO DA.
GROSSIN, ESTIENNE.
Selections.
In: Reaney. Early fifteenth-century music. Vol.3.
GROTTE, NICOLAS DE LA, *see* LA GROTTE, NICOLAS DE.
GRUA, CARLO LUIGI PIETRO, b.ca.1665.
(var. sp.: Carlo Pietragrua),
Songs.
In: Jeppesen. La flora. Vol.1.
GRUNENWALD, J. J.
Noël [de Scheidt] Organ.
In: Orgue et liturgie. Vol.4.
GRÜNWALD, J. J., ca.1780.
Songs.
In: Denkmäler der Tonkunst in Österreich. Vol.54 (Jg.XXVII/2).
GUAMI, GIOSEFFO, ca.1540–1611.
(var. sp.: Giuseppe Guamo; Guammi).
Selections.

In: Torchi. L'arte musicale in Italia. Bd.3.
Choral music.
In: Dehn. Sammlung älterer Musik aus dem XVI. und XVII. Jahrhundert.
Organ music.
In: Cantantibus organis. Vol.2.
In: Fuser. Classici italiani dell'organo.
Works arr. by Molinaro.
In: Molinaro. Intavolatura di liuto.
GUARNIERI, MOZART CAMARGO, 1907– .
Choral music.
In: Music Press, Inc. [Choral music]. Vol.109–112.
Música de cámara.
In: Boletín latino-americano de música. Vol.6.
Songs with piano.
In: Boletín latino-americano de música. Vol.1.
Valsa. Piano.
In: New music. Vol.16. No.1. Oct.1942.
GUDMUNDSEN-HOLMGREEN, PELLE.
Chronos (22–24 musicians).
In: Samfundet til Udgivelse af dansk Musik. Ser.III. No.166.
2 improvisations. Op.9.
In: Samfundet til Udgivelse af dansk Musik. Ser.III. No.154.
GUÉDRON, PIERRE, 1565–1621.
Selections.
In: Échos de France. Vol.1–3.
Airs.
In: Prunières. Les maîtres du chant. Recueil 4.
Songs.
In: Expert. Chants de France et l'Italie. Ser.2.
Vocal music.
In: Delsarte. Archives du chant. Livr.1. No.2.
GUÉNIN, MARIE ALEXANDRE, 1744–1819.
Sonata. Piano. Op.V, No.3.
In: Reeser. De klaviersonate.
GUERAU, MICHAEL.
Sacred music.
In: Rubio. Antologia polifonica sacra. Vol.1.
GUERRERO, FRANCISCO, 1527–1599.
Opera omnia.
In: Monumentos de la música española. Vol.16, 19.
Composiciones.
In: Pedrell. Hispaniae schola musica sacra. Bd.2.
Ave virgo sanctissima; Trahe me post te, Virgo Maria.
In: Polifonía española. Vol.21, 22.
Choral music.
In: Engel. Three centuries of choral music. Vol.5.
Falsum bordonem in IV tono.
In: Pedrell. Hispaniae schola musica sacra. Bd.6.
Motets.
In: Elúsitiza. Antología musical.
Sacred music.
In: Eslava y Elizondo. Lira sacro-hispana. 16th century. i.2.
In: Rubio. Antologia polifonica sacra. Vol.1.
GUERRERO, PEDRO, 16th CENTURY.
Motets.
In: Elúsitiza. Antología musical.
GUIDETTI, GIOVANNI DOMENICO, d.1592.
(var. sp.: Guidelli).
Sacred music.
In: Proske. Musica divina. Annus primus. Tom 4.
GUIDO D'AREZZO, ca.990–1050.
Selections.
In: Crotch. Specimens of various styles of music. Vol.2.
In: Gleason. Examples of music before 1400.
GUIGNON, JEAN PIERRE, 1702–1774.
Chasse.
In: L'école du violon au XVIIe et XVIIIe siècle. No.1295.
Sonate en sol majeur.
In: L'école du violon au XVIIe et XVIIIe siècle. No.1252.
Tambourin.
In: L'école du violon au XVIIe et XVIIIe siècle. No.1342.
GUILAIN, JEAN ADAM, 18th CENTURY.
Organ music.
In: Liber organi. Bd.2.
In: Pierront. Cent versets de magnificat.
Pièces d'orgue pour le magnificat.
In: Guilmant. Archives des maîtres de l'orgue. Vol.7.
GUILIELMUS DE FRANCIA.
Selections.
In: Pirrotta. The music of fourteenth-century Italy. Vol.5.
GUILLAUME D'AMIENS, *see* AMIENS, GUILLAUME D'.
GUILLAUME DE MACHAUT, d.1377.
(var. sp.: Machault; Guglielmi de Mascaudio).
Musikalische Werke. v.1– .
—— Reprint. 4v.
Opera. 30p.
Musikalische Werke. Bd.1–3.
In: Publikationen älterer Musik. Jahrg.1, Pt.1; Jahrg.3, Pt.1; Jahrg.4, Pt.2.
Works.
In: Schrade. Polyphonic music of the fourteenth century. Vol.2, 3.
Selections.
In: Documenta historica musicae.
In: Gleason. Examples of music before 1400.
Agnus Dei (I) from the Mass.
In: Parrish. Masterpieces of music before 1750. No.13.
Choral music.
In: Engel. Three centuries of choral music. Vol.1.
Double hoquet.
In: Van. Les monuments de l'Ars Nova.
La Messe de Nostre-Dame.
In: Summa musicae medii aevi. Vol.1.
Songs.
In: Riemann. Hausmusik aus alter Zeit.
GUILLAUME LE GRANT, *see* LE GRANT, GUILLAUME.
GUILLAUME LE HEURTEUR, *see* HEURTEUR, GUILLAUME LE.

GUILLEMAIN, GABRIEL, 1705–1770.
La chasse.
In: L'école du violon au XVIIe et XVIIIe siècle. No.1336.
Conversation galante et amusante entre une flûte, un violon, une basse de viole et basse continue. Op.12. Nr.1,
In: Riemann. Collegium musicum. No.58.
Sonata. Piano. Op.XIII, no.2.
In: Reeser. De klaviersonate.
GUILLET, CHARLES, 17th CENTURY.
Werken voor orgel of 4 speeltuigen.
In: Monumenta musicae belgicae. Vol.4.
Organ music.
In: Peeters. Altniederländische Meister für Orgel oder Harmonium.
In: Peeters. Oudnederlandse meesters. Vol.2, 3.
GUILMANT, ALEXANDRE, 1837–1911.
Organ music.
In: Bonnet. Historical organ-recitals. Vol.5.
GUITAR.
In: Albert. Die Gitarre in der Haus- und Kammermusik vor 100 Jahren (1780–1820).
In: Gitarre-Kammermusik.
In: Hausmusik. No.47.
In: Moecks gelbe Musikhefte. Vol.40, 49, 69, 70.
In: Musik alter Meister. Heft 10.
In: Zeitschrift für Spielmusik (passim).
GÜMBEL, MARTIN.
Fünf kurze Stücke.
In: Zeitschrift für Spielmusik. No.251.
GUMPELZHAIMER, ADAM, 1559–1625.
(var. sp.: A. Gumpeltzheimer).
Selected works.
In: Denkmäler deutscher Tonkunst. [2.Folge].Vol.10. (ii).
Choral music.
In: Antiqua Chorbuch. Vol.1. Heft 4; Vol.2. Heft 4.
In: Chorbuch für die Kirchenchöre Sachsens.
Gesänge.
In: Musica sacra . . . ca.1842–1896. Vol.11.
GURDJIEFF, GEORGES IVANOVITCH, 1872–1949.
Works. v.1– .
GURILEFF, ALEXANDER LWOWITSCH, 1803–1858.
Vocal music.
In: Sammlung russischer Romanzen (passim).
GUSTAVUS II, ADOLPHUS, 1594–1632.
Sorgemusik med anledning av Gustav II Adolfs död.
In: Musikaliska konstföreningen. 1932.
GUYARD.
Chanson.
In: Brown. Theatrical chansons of the 15th and early 16th centuries.
GUYON.
Motets.
In: Attaingnant. Treize livres de Motets. Livre 9.
GUYOT, JEAN, 1512–1588.
(var. sp.: Joan Castileti).
Choral music.
In: Commer. Collectio operum musicorum batavorum saeculi XVI. Bd.12.
GYROWETZ, ADALBERT, 1763–1850.
(var. sp.: Vojtěch Jírovec).
Divertissement für Klavier, Violine und Cello. Op.50.
In: Organum. 3.Reihe. Nr.43.
Keyboard music.
In: Musica antiqua bohemica. Vol.14.
Quartett für zwei Violinen, Viola und Violoncello.
In: Hausmusik. No.18.

HAAG, HEINZ.
Alte Lothringer Lieder.
In: Zeitschrift für Spielmusik. No.95.
HAAGER, MAX.
Fünf Klavierstücke. Werk 2b.
In: Marckhl. Klavierwerke steiermärkischer Komponisten. Vol.1.
Spielmusik, Op.6a.
In: Hausmusik. No.60.
Spielmusik für drei Instrumente, Geigen, Flöten, usw. Werk 6a.
In: Hausmusik. No.20.
HAAK, C. G.
Caprice and variations. Piano.
In: Répertoire des clavicinistes. Heft 6.
HABERT, JOHANNES EVANGELISTA, 1833–1896.
Werke. v.1– .
HACHIMURA, YOSHIO.
Improvisation for piano.
In: Contemporary Japanese music series. No.29.
HACKEL, JOHANN CHRISTOPH, 1758–1814.
Songs.
In: Denkmäler der Tonkunst in Österreich. Vol.54. (Jg.XXVII/2).
HAENDEL, GEORG FRIEDRICH, *see* HÄNDEL, GEORG FRIEDRICH.
HAESER, AUGUST FERDINAND, *see* HÄSER, AUGUST FERDINAND.
HAESSLER, JOHANN WILHELM, *see* HÄSSLER, JOHANN WILHELM.
HÄFNER, WOLFGANG ERICH.
2 Präludien mit Fugen.
In: Zeitschrift für Spielmusik. No.78.
HAGEN, PETER ALBRECHT VON, Jr., 18th–19th CENTURIES.
Selections.
In: Goldman. Landmarks of early American music. 1760–1800.
HAGIUS RINTELEUS, CUNRADUS, 16th CENTURY.
(var. sp.: Conrad Hagius).
Choral music.
In: Antiqua Chorbuch. Vol.2. Heft 3.
Die Psalmen Davids nach Kaspar Ulenberg (Köln 1582).
In: Denkmäler rheinischer Musik. Vol.3.
HÄHNEL, JOHANNES, *see* GALLICULUS, JOHANNES.
HAIBEL, JAKOB, 1761–1826.
Aus der komischen Oper "Der Tiroler Wastel."
In: Diletto musicale. No.158–163.
HAIDEN, HANS CHRISTOPH, 1572–1617.
(var. sp.: Hanns Christoph Haiden).
Choral music.
In: Antiqua Chorbuch. Vol.2. Heft 4.

Mach mir ein lustige Liedelein.
In: Squire. Ausgewählte Madrigale und mehrstimmige Gesänge. No.8.
HAIDMAYER, KARL.
VII. Sonate für Klavier.
In: Marckhl. Klavierwerke steiermärkischer Komponisten. Vol.2.
HAINDL, FRANZ SEBASTIAN, 1727–1812.
Instrumental music.
In: Denkmäler der Tonkunst in Österreich. Vol.86.
HAINES, EDMUND THOMAS.
Slow dance, for organ.
In: New music. Vol.21. No.4. July 1948.
HAINLEIN, PAUL.
12 Monatslieder.
In: Zeitschrift für Spielmusik. No.131.
HÅKANSON, KNUT ALGOT, 1887–1929.
(var. sp.: Knut Håkansson).
Selections.
In: Svensk sanglyrik. Vol.1.
Ten variations and fugue for piano, op.37.
In: Musikaliska konstföreningen. 1930.
HALBIG, HERMANN, 1890–1942. ed.
Geistliche Musik bis zum Ausgang des 16. Jahrhunderts.
In: Musikalische Formen in historischen Reihen. Bd.5.
Die Ouverture.
In: Musikalische Formen in historischen Reihen. Bd.16.
HALL.
Sacred music.
In: Arnold. Cathedral music. Vol.3.
HALLE, ADAM DE LA, *see* ADAM DE LA HALLE.
HALLÉN, JOHAN ANDREAS, 1846–1925.
A Christmas oratorio.
In: Musikaliska konstföreningen. 1905.
Den unge herr Sten Sture. Op.35.
In: Musikaliska konstföreningen. 1916.
En sommarsaga. Op.36. Symphonic concert piece.
In: Musikaliska konstföreningen. 1892.
Skogsrået. Op.33.
In: Musikaliska konstföreningen. 1898.
HALLNÄS, JOHAN HILDING, 1903– .
Sonata for viola and piano, Op.19.
In: Musikaliska konstföreningen. 1945.
HALLSTRÖM, IVAR, 1826–1901.
Blommornas undran.
In: Musikaliska konstföreningen. 1860.
Cantata for the 25 years' jubilee of the reign of King Oskar II.
In: Musikaliska konstföreningen. 1897.
HAMEL, DU.
Motets.
In: Attaingnant. Treize livres de motets. Livre 6.
HAMERIK, EBBE, 1898–1951.
Kvintet for fløjte, obo, clarinet, horn og fagot.
In: Samfundet til Udgivelse af dansk Musik. Ser.III. No.79.
Orkester variationer.
In: Samfundet til Udgivelse af dansk Musik. Ser.III. No.44.
HAMILTON, IAIN, 1922– .
Piano music.
In: Contemporary British piano music.
HAMMER, FRANZ XAVER, ca.1750–ca.1813.
Sonate D-dur (Nr.5).
In: Antiqua Edition. Von 2 Instrumenten an.
HAMMERSCHMIDT, ANDREAS, 1611 or 12–1675.
Selected works.
In: Denkmäler deutscher Tonkunst. [1.Folge]. Vol.40.
Ballet & Canzone.
In: Moecks Kammermusik. Vol.24–27.
Choral music.
In: Antiqua Chorbuch. Vol.1. Heft 5.
In: Chorbuch für die Kirchenchöre Sachsens.
Dialogi.
In: Denkmäler der Tonkunst in Österreich. Vol.16. (Jg.VIII/1).
Instrumentalwerke zu fünf und drei Stimmen.
In: Das Erbe deutscher Musik. 1.Reihe. Vol.49.
Lieder.
In: Moser. Alte Meister des deutschen Liedes. 30 Gesänge. No.4, 5.
In: Moser. Alte Meister des deutschen Liedes. 46 Gesänge. No.7, 8, 9.
Weltliche Oden.
In: Das Erbe deutscher Musik. 1.Reihe. Vol.43.
HÄNDEL, GEORG FRIEDRICH, 1685–1759.
(var. sp.: Frédéric Haendel).
Werke. 96v. and 6 supplements.
—— Reprint. 1965.
The works of Handel. 180 installments.
The works of Handel. 14v.
Veröffentlichungen der Händel-Gesellschaft. 10 nos.
Hallische Händel-Ausgabe. 5 series.
Kompositionen für Klavier. 4v.
The vocal works . . . arr. for the organ or pianoforte. v.1– .
Selections.
In: Crotch. Specimens of various styles of music. Vol.1, 2.
In: Fisher. The music that Washington knew.
In: The music with the form and order of the service to be performed at the coronation of . . . Queen Elizabeth II.
Ach Herr, mich armen Sünder.
In: Organum. 1.Reihe. Nr.12.
Ah, che troppo ineguali. Sopran, Streicher und B.C.
In: Die Kantate. No.7.
9 Sätze aus der Oper "Almira" für Sopran-Blockflöten oder Violine und Basso Continuo.
In: Moecks Kammermusik. Vol.34.
Arias.
In: Landshoff. Alte Meister des Bel Canto. Eine Sammlung von Arien. Vol.3.
In: Parisotti. Arie antiche. Bd.1, 3.
Arie für Sopran (Tenor).
In: Organum. 2.Reihe. Nr.4–5, 10–11.
Neun deutsche Arien.
In: Musikalische Stundenbücher.
Bourrée.
In: L'école du violon au XVIIe et XVIIIe siècle No.1295.
Capriccio (G).
In: Pauer. Alte Meister. No.26.

Choral music.
In: Antiqua Chorbuch. Vol.2. Heft 5.
In: Commer. Cantica sacra (passim).
In: Recueil de musique ancienne. Recueil des morceaux de musique ancienne. Bd.3.
In: Rochlitz. Sammlung vorzüglicher Gesängstücke. Bd.3.
Coelestis dum spirat aura. Sopran, 2 Violinen, und B.C.
In: Die Kantate. No.2.
Concert.
In: Guilmant. Répertoire des concerts du Trocadéro. Vol.1, 2.
Concert I a 4 D-moll; Concerto II a 4 D-dur.
In: Antiqua Edition. Von vier Instrumenten an.
Concerto für Harfe (Orgel, Klavier) und Streicher; Tanz- und Spielmusik; Ouvertüre zu "Esther;" Kleine Stück für Streichinstrumente und Continuo (Klavier).
In: Musikschätze der Vergangenheit.
Konzert für Flöte und 4stg. Streichorchester und Generalbass.
In: Corona. Vol.31.
Konzert, B-dur.
In: Corona. Vol.66.
Konzert B-dur; Konzert G moll für Oboe.
In: Corona. Vol.74, 75.
Konzert B-dur, Op.4, Nr.6, für Klavier (Cembalo oder Orgel) zwei Violinen und Violoncello oder Kleines Orchester.
In: Nagels Musik-Archiv. No.136.
Konzert Es-dur für Solo-Oboe, Streichorchester und Cembalo.
In: Das weltliche Konzert im 18. Jahrhundert. Heft 4.
Konzert F-dur in zwei Sätzen.
In: Schering. Perlen alter Kammermusik.
Concerti grossi.
In: Lea pocket scores. No.54, 71/72.
Concerto grosso B-dur.
In: Corona. Vol.72.
Concerto grosso in C major, first movement; Cara sposa from "Rinaldo"; Draw the tears, from "Solomon."
In: Parrish. Masterpieces of music before 1750. No.43, 44, 45.
Duet XVIII: Beato in ver chi puo.
In: Dessoff choir series. No.30.
Duette alter Meister.
In: Zeitschrift für Spielmusik. No.69.
9 Duette nach den "Pieces for harpsichord."
In: Zeitschrift für Spielmusik. No.76.
Feiermusik.
In: Corona. Vol.29, 30.
Ouverture aus der Feuerwerksmusik. (Concerto grosso Nr.20).
In: Platzmusik. Nr.8.
In: Zeitschrift für Spielmusik. No.249.
Festliche Ouvertüre in B-dur (zum Oratorium "Salomo"); Ouvertüre zum Oratorium "Herakles"; Ouvertüre zu "Theodora."
In: Schering. Perlen alter Kammermusik.
Festmusik (B-dur). (Ouvertüre und Tänze) aus der Oper "Alcina."
In: Corona. Vol.1.
11 Fugues. Organ.
In: Guilmant. École classique de l'orgue. No.1.
Fugue. "Halleluja."
In: Königliche Akademie der Künste. Auswahl vorzüglicher Musik-Werke. No.4.
Zwei Gesänge.
In: Gitarre-Kammermusik. No.27.
Das grosse Halleluja aus "Messias."
In: Thouret. Musik am preussischen Hofe. No.18.
Herz, der Liebe susser Born . . . Arie aus "Acis und Galatea."
In: Moecks gelbe Musikhefte. Vol.17.
Hornpipe.
In: L'école du violon au XVIIe et XVIIIe siècle. No.1291.
Kammer-Sonaten. Violine und Pianoforte.
In: Moffat. Kammer-Sonaten für Violine und Pianoforte. No.4.
Keyboard music.
In: Antiqua Edition. Ein Tasten-Instrument allein.
In: Clementi. Clementi's Selection of practical harmony. Vol.1, 2.
In: Farrenc. Le trésor des pianistes. Vol.5.
In: Lea pocket scores. No.86.
In: Tagliapietra. Antologia di musica antica e moderna per pianoforte. Bd.11.
Look down, harmonious Saint. Cantata.
In: The Penn state music series. No.1.
Märsche.
In: Corona. Vol.11.
Zwölf Märsche, für Streichorchester mit Bläsern nach Belieben.
In: Nagels Musik-Archiv. No.108.
Meine Selle hört in Sehen.
In: Organum. 2.Reihe. Nr.20.
Messiah. Part I and II.
In: Documents of the musical past. Vol.6.
Mirtillo-Suite.
In: Schering. Perlen alter Kammermusik.
Nel dolce del oblio.
In: Gitarre-Kammermusik. No.28.
O my Irene. (Theodora).
In: Königliche Akademie der Künste. Auswahl vorzüglicher Musik-Werke. Appendix.
O qualis de coeli sonus. Sopran, 2 Violinen und B.C.
In: Die Kantate. No.1.
Organ music.
In: Anthologia antiqua. Vol.2.
In: Bonnet. Historical organ-recitals. Vol.3.
In: Butcher. English organ music of the eighteenth century. Vol.1.
In: Keller. Orgelvorspiele.
In: Lea pocket scores. No.125–126.
In: The Liturgical Music Press, Inc. Masterpieces of organ music. Folio 49, 50, 69/70.
In: The parish organist. Vol.1–4.
In: Schweiger. A brief compendium of early organ music.
In: Standard series of organ compositions. No.12, 36, 58.
In: Tallis to Wesley. Vol.12, 19, 33.
Drei Ouvertüren.
In: Corona. Vol.55.

Pastorella, vagha bella.
In: Organum. 2.Reihe. Nr.18.
Rinaldo. Suite.
In: Corona. Vol.26.
Sacred music.
In: Page. Harmonia sacra. Vol.2, 3.
Sieben Spielstücke.
In: Zeitschrift für Spielmusik. No.261.
Sinfonia de Saul.
In: Guilmant. Répertoire des concerts du Trocadéro. Vol.4.
Vier Original-Sonaten für Altblockflöte und Cembalo (Klavier).
In: Nagels Musik-Archiv. No.122.
Sonata A-moll.
In: Gitarre-Kammermusik. No.23.
Sonate (B).
In: Moffat. Trio-Sonaten alter Meister. No.23.
Sonata C-dur.
In: Gitarre-Kammermusik. No.37.
Sonata C-moll.
In: Gitarre-Kammermusik. No.26.
Sonate D-moll.
In: Gitarre-Kammermusik. No.24.
Sonata F-dur.
In: Gitarre-Kammermusik. No.9.
Sonata G-moll.
In: Gitarre-Kammermusik. No.29.
Sonate für Alt-Blockflöte und Basso Continuo. G-moll, F-dur, C-dur, A-moll.
In: Moecks gelbe Musikhefte. Vol.11–14.
15 Sonatas, Op.1 (Flute, Violin, Oboe). 3 early flute sonatas. Gamba sonata.
In: Lea pocket scores. No.70.
Sonate D-dur, für Flöte (Oboe, Violine) und Basso Continuo.
In: Hortus musicus. No.3.
Sonate für Gambe und obl. Cembalo.
In: Hortus musicus. No.112.
Sonate. Oboe (Flôte, Violine) und Basso Continuo.
In: Florilegium musicum. Vol.4, 5.
Sonate (A). Violin and piano.
In: Moffat. Meister-Schule der alter Zeit. Violin-Sonaten. No.2.
Sonate en fa majeur.
In: L'école du violon au XVIIe et XVIIIe siècle. No.1278.
Sonata en sol mineur (2 violons et piano).
In: L'école du violon au XVIIe et XVIIIe siècle. No.1283.
Songs.
In: Jeppesen. La flora. Vol.1, 2, 3.
In: Potter. Reliquary of English song. Vol.2.
Suite mit dem Marsch für 2 Violinen, Violoncello (Kontrabass) und Klavier.
In: Corona. Vol.10.
Trio. Für Altblockflöte, Violine und Cembalo.
In: Nagels Musik-Archiv. No.150.
Triosonate, B dur für Oboe, Violine (oder 2 Violinen) und Basso Continuo.
In: Hortus musicus. No.15.
Trio-Sonata F-dur, Óp.5 VI, für zwei Violinen, Tasten-Instrument und Bass-Instrument ad lib.
In: Antiqua Edition. Von 3 Instrumenten an.
Vocal music.
In: Delsarte. Archives du chant. Livr.13. No.8; Livr.15. No.4; Livr.22. No.3, 4, 5; Suppl. No.5.
In: Gevaert. Les gloires de l'Italie. Vol.2.
Aus der "Wassermusik."
In: Zeitschrift für Spielmusik. No.241.
Suite from Water music. Organ.
In: Anthologia antiqua. Vol.3.
Weihnachtsarie: "Und siehe! Der Engel des Herrn kam über sie."
In: Nagels Musik-Archiv. No.104.
Weihnachtsmusik. Konzertante.
In: Nagels Musik-Archiv. No.182.
Weihnachts-Pastorale aus dem "Messias."
In: Schering. Perlen alter Kammermusik.
Weihnachtspastoralen.
In: Zeitschrift für Spielmusik. No.236.
Xerxes. Ouvertüre.
In: Corona. Vol.35.

HANDL, JACOB, 1550–1591.
(var. sp.: Jacobus Gallus).
Selections.
In: Ambros. Auserwählte Tonwerke.
In: Cvetko. Skladetelji Gallus, Plautzius [in] Dolar.
In: Documants historica musicae.
In: Musica sacra . . . 1839– . Vol.15.
Choral music.
In: Antiqua Chorbuch. Vol.1. Heft 3.
In: Music Press, Inc. [Choral series]. No.67, 68.
In: Recuil de musique ancienne. Recueil des morceaux de musique ancienne. Bd.6.
In: Rochlitz. Sammlung vorzüglicher Gesangstücke. Bd.1. Pt.2.
Gesänge.
In: Musica sacra . . . ca.1842–1896. Vol.12.
Masses.
In: Denkmäler der Tonkunst in Österreich. Vol.78. (Jg.XLII/1); Vol.94/95.
Natus est nobis.
In: Musica spiritualis. Serie IB. No.8.
Opus musicum, motets.
In: Denkmäler der Tonkunst in Österreich. Vol.12. (Jg.VI/1); Vol.24. (Jg.XII/1); Vol.30. (Jg.XV/1); Vol.40. (Jg.XX/1); Vol.48. (Jg.XXIV); Vol.51–52. (Jg.XXVI).
Repleti sunt; Trahe me post te; Regnum mundi.
In: Dessoff choir series. No.31, 32, 33.
Sacred music.
In: Proske. Musica divina. Annus primus. Tom 2, 4; Annus secundus. Tom 2.
In: Proske. Selectus novus missarum. Annus secundus. Tom 2.

HANDLO, ROBERT DE, 13th CENTURY.
(Luther A. Dittmer).
In: Institute of Mediaeval Music. Musical theorists in translation. Vol.2.

HANFF, JOHANN NIKOLAUS, 1630–1706.
Organ music.
In: The Liturgical Music Press, Inc. Masterpieces of organ music. Folio 61.
In: Straube. Choralvorspiele alter Meister.

HANSEN, CHRISTIAN JULIUS, 1814–1875.
Koncert-Ouverture.

In: Samfundet til Udgivelse af dansk Musik. Ser.I. No.8.
HANSEN, GEORGE DUPONT-, *see* DUPONT-HANSEN, GEORGE.
HANSEN, JOHAN GOTFRED MATTHISON-, *see* MATTHISON-HANSEN, JOHAN GOTFRED.
HAQUINIUS, ALGOT, 1886– .
Selections.
In: Svensk sanglyrik. Vol.1.
String quartet, A minor.
In: Musikaliska konstföreningen. 1931.
HARDCASTLE, ARTHUR E.
Prelude, No.4. Piano.
In: New music. Vol.6. No.3. Apr.1933.
HARINGTON, HENRY, 1727–1816.
(var. sp.: Harrington).
Part music.
In: Hullah. Part music. Class A.1. Vol.2; Class C. Secular.
HARK, FRIEDRICH, 1914–1943.
Erntedank-Kantate aus Texte von Conrad Ferdinand Meyer, Georg Trakl, und Matthias Claudius.
In: Zeitschrift für Spielmusik. No.82.
Organ music.
In: The parish organist. Vol.1–4.
HARMONICE MUSICES ODHECATON (1501). (PETRUCCI). FACSIMILE.
In: Monuments of music and music literature. First series. No.10.
HARMONY.
In: Plainsong and Mediaeval Music Society. Publications. (Hughes, Wooldridge).
HARNISCH, OTTO SIEGFRIED, 16th–17th CENTURIES.
Choral music.
In: Antiqua Chorbuch. Vol.1. Heft 4; Vol.2. Heft 3.
Gesänge.
In: Wolf. Chor- und Hausmusik aus älter Zeit. Vol.1.
HARPSICHORD MUSIC, *see* KEYBOARD MUSIC–CLAVICHORD, HARPSICHORD, PIANO, VIRGINAL.
HARRER, JOHANN GOTTLOB, 1703–1755.
Fugue. "Halleluja."
In: Königliche Akademie der Künste. Auswahl vorzüglicher Musik-Werke. No.47.
HARRINGTON, HENRY, *see* HARINGTON, HENRY.
HARRIS, ROY, 1898– .
Trio for piano, violin, and violoncello.
In: New music. Vol.9. No.3. Apr.1936.
HARRIS, WILLIAM HENRY, 1883– .
Selections.
In: The music with the form and order of the service to be performed at the coronation of . . . Queen Elizabeth II.
HARRISON, LOU, 1917– .
Alleluia. For orchestra.
In: New music. Vol.21. No.2. Jan.1948.
Sarabande and prelude. Piano.
In: New music. Vol.11. No.4. July 1938.
6 Sonatas for cembalo or pianoforte.
In: New music. Vol.17. No.1. Oct.1943.
Spring in Nak Yang, for mixed chorus and orchestra.
In: New music. To be published.
HART, PHILIP, d.1749.
Organ music.
In: Tallis to Wesley. Vol.34.
HARTMANN, EMIL, 1836–1898.
Selected songs.
In: Samfundet til Udgivelse af dansk Musik. Suppl. 1898.
Symphoni Nr.3. Op.42.
In: Samfundet til Udgivelse af dansk Musik. Ser.II. No.2.
HARTMANN, HEINRICH, 16th–17th CENTURIES.
Motetten.
In: Das Chorwerk. No.98.
HARTMANN, JOHAN ERNST, 1726–1793.
Balders Død. Singspiel.
In: Samfundet til Udgivelse af dansk Musik. Ser.I. No.9.
Musik til "Fiskerne." Singspiel.
In: Samfundet til Udgivelse af dansk Musik. Ser.I. No.21.
HARTMANN, JOHANN PETER EMIL, 1805–1900.
Cantate ved Universitetets Fest. Op.84.
In: Samfundet til Udgivelse af dansk Musik. Ser.I. No.24.
Et Folkesagn.
In: Samfundet til Udgivelse af dansk Musik. Ser.II. No.8.
Hakon Jarl. Op.40. Tragedy.
In: Samfundet til Udgivelse af dansk Musik. Ser.I. No.4.
Koncert-Indledning. Choral work.
In: Samfundet til Udgivelse af dansk Musik. Ser.II. No.18.
Korsarerne. Opera. Op.16.
In: Samfundet til Udgivelse af dansk Musik. Ser.I. No.16.
La Légende de Thrym. Op.67.
In: Samfundet til Udgivelse af dansk Musik. Ser.II. No.5.
Organ music.
In: Gerhardt. Album nordischer Komponisten für Orgel. Vol.1.
Orla Lehmann. Choral work.
In: Samfundet til Udgivelse af dansk Musik. Ser.II. No.40.
Ouverture til Correggio. Op.59.
In: Samfundet til Udgivelse af dansk Musik. Ser.III. No.120.
Ouverture "Hakon Jarl." Op.40.
In: Samfundet til Udgivelse af dansk Musik. Ser.III. No.39.
Ouverture til "Yrsa."
In: Samfundet til Udgivelse af dansk Musik. Ser.III. No.90.
Rhythmische Szenen.
In: Zeitschrift für Spielmusik. No.227.
Syvsoverdag. Comedy.
In: Samfundet til Udgivelse af dansk Musik. Ser.I. No.2.
Undine. Fairy-play. Op.33.
In: Samfundet til Udgivelse af dansk Musik. Ser.I. No.11.
Valkyrien. Op.62.
In: Samfundet til Udgivelse af dansk Musik. Ser.II. No.14.
HARTZER, BALTHASAR, *see* RESINARIUS BALTHASAR.

HARUM, GÜNTHER.
Fuge für Streichquartett. Op.31.
In: Hausmusik. No.38.
HARWOOD, BASIL, 1859–1949.
Organ music.
In: Bonnet. Historical organ-recitals. Vol.5.
HARZER, BALTHASAR, *see* RESINARIUS, BALTHASAR.
HÄSER, AUGUST FERDINAND, 1779–1844.
(var. sp.: Haeser).
Part music.
In: Hullah. Part music. 1868 edition.
Sacred music.
In: Latrobe, C. I. Selection of sacred music.
In: Latrobe, J. A. The music of the church.
Vocal music.
In: Hullah. Vocal scores. I. Sacred.
HASLER, HANS LEO, *see* HASSLER, HANS LEO.
HASPRE, JOHANNES SIMON DE, 15th CENTURY.
Selections.
In: Reaney. Early fifteenth-century music. Vol.2.
HASSE, JOHANN ADOLPH, 1699–1783.
Ausgewählte Werke.
In: Schmid. Musik am sächsischen Hofe. Bd.2, 7–8.
Selections.
In: Crotch. Specimens of various styles of music. Vol.2.
Airs.
In: Prunières. Les maîtres du chant. Recueil 1.
Allegro. (B flat).
In: Pauer. Alte Meister. No.23.
Arias.
In: Landshoff. Alte Meister des Bel Canto. Eine Sammlung von Arien. Vol.1–2.
Aria, Pietà Signore.
In: Königliche Akademie der Künste. Auswahl vorzüglicher Musik-Werke. Appendix.
Arminio I–II Teil.
In: Das Erbe deutscher Musik. 1.Reihe. Vol.27–28.
Cantata.
In: Eitner. Cantaten des 17. und 18. Jahrhunderts. Part 3.
Choral music.
In: Commer. Cantaca sacra. Vol.1. No.2, 3, 23.
In: Rochlitz. Sammlung vorzüglicher Gesangstücke. Bd.3.
Konzert G-dur, für Flöte, Streicher und Basso Continuo.
In: Nagels Musik-Archiv. No.194.
Concerto in G-dur.
In: Musikschätze der Vergangenheit.
Conversione di Sant' Agostino.
In: Denkmäler deutscher Tonkunst. [1.Folge]. Vol.20.
Duette alter Meister.
In: Zeitschrift für Spielmusik. No.69.
Fugue; Christe.
In: Königliche Akademie der Künste. Auswahl vorzüglicher Musik-Werke. No.19.
Instrumental concertos.
In: Denkmäler deutscher Tonkunst. [1.Folge]. Vol.29–30.
Instrumental music.
In: Schmid. Musik am sächsischen Hofe. Bd.6.
Keyboard music.
In: Pauer. Alte Klavier-Musik. 1st series. Pt.4.
In: Tagliapietra. Antologia di musica antica e moderna per pianoforte. Bd.12.
Ouvertüre zur Oper "Euristeo."
In: Schering. Perlen alter Kammermusik.
Sacred music.
In: Latrobe, C. I. Selection of sacred music.
In: Latrobe, J. A. The music of the church.
Sonata Op,7, Allegro.
In: Köhler. Les maîtres du clavecin. Heft 6.
Sonata a tre, Op.3/6.
In: Hausmusik. No.166.
Sonate Nr.1, D-dur, für Flöte und bezifferten Bass.
In: Nagels Musik-Archiv. No.99.
Songs.
In: Musica sacra . . . 1839– . Vol.4.
Triosonate D-dur, für zwei Flöten (oder Violinen) mit Fagott oder Violoncello (ad lib.) und Generalbass.
In: Nagels Musik-Archiv. No.159.
Triumph-Marsch aus der Oper "Ezio"; Arie des Ezio aus der oper "Ezio." Te Deum laudamus.
In: Schmid. Musik aus sächsischen Hofe. Bd.1.
Vocal music.
In: Gevaert. Les gloires de l'Italie. Vol.1, 2.
HASSE, NIKOLAUS, 17th CENTURY.
(var. sp.: Nicolaus Hasse).
Organ chorales.
In: Corpus of early keyboard music. Vol.10, Pt.1.
HASSE, PETER, d.1640.
Organ music.
In: Organum. 4.Reihe. Nr.21.
HASSLER, HANS LEO, 1564–1612.
(var. sp.: Hans Leo Hasler; Hans Leo von Hassler).
Sämtliche Werke. v.1– .
Selected works.
In: Denkmäler deutscher Tonkunst. [2.Folge]. Vol.4 (ii), 5, 11 (i).
Selections.
In: Ambros. Auserwählte Tonwerke.
In: Leichtentritt. Deutsche Hausmusik aus vier Jahrhunderten.
In: Musica sacra . . . 1839– . Vol.13, 14.
Ad dominum cum tribularer.
In: Dessoff choir series. No.2.
Ave Maris stella.
In: Musica spiritualis. Serie IB. No.7.
Beata es Virgo Maria.
In: Musica spiritualis. Serie IIB. No.14.
Cantiones sacrae.
In: Denkmäler deutscher Tonkunst. [1.Folge]. Vol.2.
Choral music.
In: Antiqua Chorbuch. Vol.1. Heft 4; Vol.2. Heft 4.
In: Chor-Archiv.
In: Engel. Three centuries of choral music. Vol.4.
In: Der Kammerchor. Vol.2.

In: Nagels Männerchor-Blätter. No.3.
In: Rochlitz. Sammlung vorzüglicher Gesangstücke. Bd.2.
Fantasie in C minor. Piano.
In: Roitzsch. Alte Klavier-Musik.
Gesänge.
In: Musica sacra . . . ca.1842–1896. Vol.12, 13.
Keyboard music.
In: Tagliapietra. Antologia di musica antica e moderna per pianoforte. Bd.3.
Kirchengesange, Psalmen und geistliche Lieder.
In: Corona. Vol.49.
Laudate Dominum.
In: Parrish. A treasury of early music. No.28.
Lied.
In: Reimann. Das deutsche Lied. Vol.1, 3.
Luce negli' occhi.
In: Squire. Ausgewählte Madrigale und mehrstimmige Gesänge. No.11.
Lustgarten.
In: Publikationen älterer praktischer und theoretischer Musikwerke. Jahrg.15.
Intraden aus dem "Lustgarten."
In: Hortus musicus. No.73.
In: Schering. Perlen alter Kammermusik.
Masses.
In: Denkmäler deutscher Tonkunst. [1.Folge]. Vol.7.
Mass Dixit Maria.
In: The Penn state music series. No.11.
Missa et motettum dixit Maria.
In: Musica spiritualis. Serie IA. No.3.
Motetten.
In: Das Chorwerk. No.14.
Organ music.
In: Cantantibus organis. Vol.2.
In: Klein. The first four centuries of music for the organ from Dunstable to Bach (1370–1749).
In: The Liturgical Music Press, Inc. Masterpieces of organ music. Folio 34.
In: Schweiger. A brief compendium of early organ music.
Sacred music.
In: Proske. Musica divina. Annus primus. Tom 1, 2, 3; Annus secundus. Tom 1.
In: Proske. Selectus novus missarum. Annus primus. Tom 1; Annus secundus. Tom 1.
Sacri concentus.
In: Denkmäler deutscher Tonkunst. [1.Folge]. Vol.24–25.
HÄSSLER, JOHANN WILHELM, 1747–1822.
(var. sp.: Johann Wilhelm Haessler).
Keyboard music.
In: Farrenc. Le trésor des pianistes. Vol.16.
In: Georgii. Keyboard music of the Baroque and Rococo. Vol.3.
In: Tagliapietra. Antologia di musica antica e moderna per pianoforte. Bd.13.
Klaviersonaten.
In: Organum. 5.Reihe. Nr.26, 28, 30.
Organ music.
In: Caecilia; Sammlung von Choralvorspielen.
Sonaten für Klavier und Flöte oder Violine; Sonaten für Klavier zu drei und zu vier Händen; Sonaten für Klavier.
In: Nagels Musik-Archiv. No.11, 19, 20.
Sonate (Am).
In: Pauer. Alte Meister. No.18.
Sonate.
In: Köhler. Les maîtres du clavecin. Heft 4.
HAUCOURT, *see* CURIE, JOHANNES DE ALTE (HAUCOURT).
HAUSSMAN, VALENTIN, 16th CENTURY.
(var. sp.: Valentin Haussmann).
Choral music.
In: Antiqua Chorbuch. Vol.2. Heft 4.
Selected instrumental compositions.
In: Denkmäler deutscher Tonkunst. [1.Folge]. Vol.16.
Gesänge.
In: Wolf. Chor- und Hausmusik aus älter Zeit. Vol.2.
Deutsche Tänze.
In: Musica practica. No.4.
In: Nagels Musik-Archiv. No.80.
Neue artige und liebliche Tänze.
In: Zeitschrift für Spielmusik. No.56.
HAVER, VINCENZO BELL', *see* BELL'HAVER, VINCENZO.
HAVINGHA, GERHARDUS, 1696–1753.
Werken voor clavecimbel.
In: Monumenta musicae belgicae. Vol.7.
HAYAMA, MITSUAKI.
Piano sonata.
In: Contemporary Japanese music series. No.10.
HAYDN, JOSEPH, 1732–1809.
(var. sp.: Giuseppe Haydn).
Oeuvres complètes. 12v.
Werke. 11v. in 10.
Kritische Gesamtausgabe. v.1– .
Werke. v.1– .
Sämtliche Klavierwerke. 6v.
Selections.
In: Crotch. Specimens of various styles of music. Vol.1, 3.
Eine Abendmusik (Tassatio in Es).
In: Musikschätze der Vergangenheit.
Cantata "Miseri noi, misera patria."
In: Diletto musicale. No.17.
Capriccio in A-dur. Hoboken XV:35.
In: Diletto musicale. No.93.
Cassatio.
In: Diletto musicale. No.47, 56, 66.
Cassation für 5stg. Streichorchester.
In: Corona. Vol.51.
Cassation C-dur.
In: Gitarre-Kammermusik. No.31.
Choral music.
In: Commer. Cantica sacra. Vol.1, No.5; Vol.2, No.4, 6.
In: Music Press, Inc. [Choral series]. Vol.83, 84.
In: Recueil de musique ancienne. Recueil des morceaux de musique ancienne. Bd.4.
Concertino in C-dur. Hoboken XIV:11.
In: Diletto musicale. No.21.
Concerto.
In: Diletto musicale. No.41–45, 78, 79, 80.
Divertimenti.
In: Corona. Vol.62, 63, 64.
In: Diletto musicale. No.1, 22, 23, 29–33, 57, 84–86, 91, 92.

In: Gitarre-Kammermusik. No.25.
In: Hortus musicus. No.65, 94, 95.
In: Musica viva historica. Vol.1.
In: Nagels Musik-Archiv. No.52, 84.
In: The Wellesley edition. No.4.
In: Zeitschrift für Spielmusik. No.98.
Zwei italienische Duette.
In: Diletto musicale. No.35.
Einleitung zu "Die sieben letzten Worte unserers Erlösers am Kreuz."
In: Sondheimer. Werke aus dem 18. Jahrhundert. Nr.19.
Feiermusik.
In: Corona. Vol.30.
Fugue from 4tet, F min.
In: Königliche Akademie der Künste. Auswahl vorzüglicher Musik-Werke. No.3.
The holy ten commandments.
In: Dessoff choir series. No.10.
Keyboard music.
In: Clementi. Clementi's Selection of practical harmony. Vol.1.
In: Farrenc. Le trésor des pianistes. Vol.15.
In: Tagliapietra. Antologia di musica antica e moderna per pianoforte. Bd.13.
Konzert C-dur für Klavier (Cembalo) und Streicher.
In: Nagels Musik-Archiv. No.200.
Konzert F-dur. Hoboken XVIII:3.
In: Concertino.
Konzert in G-dur, für Cembalo oder Pianoforte mit Begleitung von Streichern und Blasern ad lib.
In: Nagels Musik-Archiv. No.86.
Werke für das Laufwerk. (Flötenuhr).
In: Nagels Musik-Archiv. Sonderausgabe. No.1.
Lieder.
In: Gitarre-Kammermusik. No.22.
In: Reimann. Das deutsche Lid. Vol.1, 2, 4.
Die Londoner Trios.
In: Nagels Musik-Archiv. No.71.
March für The Royal Society of Musicians. Hoboken VIII:3 bis.
In: Diletto musicale. No.98.
Märsche für Blasinstrumente.
In: Diletto musicale. No.34.
Sechs Menuette und Trios.
In: Zeitschrift für Spielmusik. No.242.
Notturno Nr.1 in C-dur.
In: Diletto musicale. No.48.
Opernsinfonie, Die wahre Bestandigkeit. "La vera costanza."
In: Corona. Vol.61.
Oratorien; Fragment "Mare clausum."
In: Diletto musicale. No.90.
Ouvertüre "Lo Speziale." Hoboken Ia:10.
In: Diletto musicale. No.18, 39, 51, 55, 58–60.
Part music.
In: Hullah. Part music. Class A.1. Vol.1.
Quartett D-dur.
In: Gitarre-Kammermusik. No.32.
Quartetto in G, op.5/4.
In: Gitarre-Kammermusik. No.36.
Quartett, G-dur, für Flöte (Violine), Violine, Viola und bezifferten Bass. Op.5, Nr.IV.
In: Nagels Musik-Archiv. No.129.
Streichquartett.
In: Diletto musicale. No.5, 6, 7, 8.
In: Hortus musicus. No.98.
Streichquintett.
In: Diletto musicale. No.122, 123.
Sacred music.
In: Latrobe, C. I. Selection of sacred music.
In: Latrobe, J. A. The music of the church.
Scena di Berenice für Sopran und Orchester.
In: Diletto musicale. No.129.
Sechs Scherzandi. Hoboken II:33–38.
In: Diletto musicale. No.71–76.
Schottische Volkslieder.
In: Zeitschrift für Spielmusik. No.281.
Selection of Scots Airs.
In: Musikalische Seltenheiten. Bd.2.
Sinfonia in B-dur. Hoboken I:107.
In: Diletto musicale. No.167.
Sinfonia (Overture) in D-dur. Hoboken Ia:7.
In: Diletto musicale. No.77.
Sinfonia (Parthia). Hoboken I:108.
In: Diletto musicale. No.50.
Die Sinfonien. Hoboken I:1–49.
In: Diletto musicale. No.201–249.
"Son pietosa, son bonina." Arie der Lindora in Cimarosas. "La Circe."
In: Diletto musicale. No.19.
The 52 piano sonatas.
In: Lea pocket scores. No.101–104.
Klavier-Sonate in Es-dur. Hoboken XVI:52.
In: Diletto musicale. No.168.
Sonate. Violine und Viola. Hoboken VI:1, 2, 3.
In: Diletto musicale. No.10, 11, 12, 124, 125, 126.
Sonatenform.
In: Einstein. Beispielsammlung zur älteren Musikgeschichte.
Symphony No.3.
In: Für Kenner und Liebhaber. No.17.
Symphony No.12 in E.
In: Für Kenner und Liebhaber. No.5.
Symphony No.39 in F minor.
In: Für Kenner und Liebhaber. No.10.
Symphony No.63.
In: Für Kenner und Liebhaber. No.15.
Symphony No.70.
In: Für Kenner und Liebhaber. No.33.
Symphony No.84.
In: Für Kenner und Liebhaber. No.22.
Symphony No.87 in A major.
In: Smith College music archives. No.10.
Zwölf deutsche Tänze.
In: Corona. Vol.7.
Sechs deutsche Tänze für Orchester.
In: Diletto musicale. No.52.
Zwölf deutsche Tänze für zwei Violinen und Violoncello.
In: Hortus musicus. No.41.
Zwölf deutsche Tänze für Orchester.
In: Moser. Das Musikkränzlein. No.4.
The 31 piano trios.
In: Lea pocket scores. No.121–124.
Klaviertrio in F-dur. Hoboken XV:40.
In: Diletto musicale. No.4.
Trio. Für 2 Violinen und Violoncell.
In: Riemann. Collegium musicum. No.62.
Variationen.

In: Hausmusik. No.104.
Violoncellokonzert C-dur. Hoboken VIIb:1.
In: Musica viva historica Vol.12.
Vocal music.
In: Delsarte. Archives du chant. Livr.15, No.10; Livr.16, No.8, 9.
In: Gevaert. Les gloires de l'Italie. Vol.2.
Sechs Weinzirler Trios.
In: Corona. Vol.15.
Wiener Hofball-Menuette; Divertimenti, Nr.109, C-dur; No.113, D-dur.
In: Antiqua Edition. Von 3 Instrumenten an.
Sechs leichte Wiener Trios.
In: Corona. Vol.20.
HAYDN, MICHAEL, 1737–1806.
Choral music.
In: Rochlitz. Sammlung vorzüglicher Gesangstücke. Bd.3.
Church compositions.
In: Denkmäler der Tonkunst in Österreich. Vol.62. (Jg.XXXII/1).
Divertimento in B-dur; G-dur.
In: Diletto musicale. No.24–25.
Divertimento C-dur, für Violine, Violoncello (Viola) und Violine (Kontrabass oder Violoncello II).
In: Antiqua Edition. Von 3 Instrumenten an.
Divertimento, D-dur, für zwei Violinen, Viola und Bass. (Violoncello).
In: Nagels Musik-Archiv. No.7.
Duo für Violine und Viola. Nr.1, C-dur; Nr.2, E-dur; Nr.3, F-dur; Nr.4, D-dur.
In: Hausmusik. No.43, 44, 109, 125.
Fugue. "Quam olim."
In: Königliche Akademie der Künste. Auswahl vorzüglicher Musik-Werke. No.20.
Graduales.
In: Ecclesiasticon. No.1–20, 41–62.
Instrumental works.
In: Denkmäler der Tonkunst in Österreich. Vol.29. (Jg.XIV/2).
Konzert in B-dur.
In: Diletto musicale. No.3.
Masses.
In: Denkmäler der Tonkunst in Österreich. Vol.45. (Jg.XXII).
Notturno in F-dur. Perger-Kat. 106.
In: Diletto musicale. No.26.
Part music.
In: Hullah. Part music. Class A.1. Vol.1, 2.
Quintett C-dur; G-dur, F-dur. Für 2 Violinen, 2 Violen, und Violoncello.
In: Organum. 3.Reihe. Nr.38, 40, 42.
Sacred music.
In: Latrobe, C. I. Selection of sacred music.
In: Latrobe, J. A. The music of the church.
Sinfonia.
In: Diletto musicale. No.20, 143, 144, 145.
Te Deum in C (1770).
In: Collegium musicum. Vol.3.
Tenebrae factae sunt; Gott, ich falle Dir zu füssen.
In: Messner. Alte salzburger Meister der kirchlichen Tonkunst. Heft 3, 11.
HAYES, WILLIAM, 1705–1777.
Part music.
In: Hullah. Part music. Class B.1; Class B.2; Class C. Sacred.
Vocal music.
In: Hullah. Vocal scores. II. Secular.
HAYNE VAN GHIZEGHEM, *see* GHIZEGHEM, HAYNE VAN.
HE'S GONE AWAY. Folk song from the Southern Appalachians. (Arr. by A. Lief).
In: Music Press, Inc. [Choral series]. Vol.94.
HEATH, JOHN, 16th CENTURY.
Selections.
In: Smith. Musica antiqua.
HEBREO.
Kammerduette.
In: Landshoff. Alte Meister des Bel Canto. Italienische Kammerduette.
HEBREW MUSIC.
In: Anthology of music. Vol.20.
In: Hebräisch-Orientalischer Melodienschatz.
HEER, HANS.
Das Liederbuch.
In: Schweizerische Musikdenkmäler. Vol.5.
HEIDORN, PETER.
Fuga (um 1683). Organ.
In: Die Orgel. Reihe II. Nr.4.
HEIDUCZEK, ALOIS.
Uns in dem Schneegebirge. Kleine Instrumentalmusiken.
In: Zeitschrift für Spielmusik. No.190.
HEILMAN, WILLIAM CLIFFORD, 1877–1946.
Piano trio.
In: Society for the Publication of American music. Publications. 4th season. 1922–23.
HEILNER, IRWIN.
Second rhapsody for tenor and piano (4 hands).
In: New music. Vol.8. No.4. July 1935.
HEINICHEN, JOHANN DAVID, 1683–1729.
Compositions.
In: Das Erbe deutscher Musik. 1.Reihe. Vol.11.
Concerto a 8 C-dur für 4 Alt-Blockflöten, Streicher und Basso Continuo.
In: Moecks Kammermusik. Vol.69.
Instrumental music.
In: Schmid. Musik am sächsischen Hofe. Bd.6.
Konzert in G-dur.
In: Corona. Vol.58.
Konzert in G-dur für Flöte oder Oboe, zwei Violinen und Continuo.
In: Musikschätze der Vergangenheit.
Sonate.
In: Riemann. Collegium musicum. No.78.
HEINRICH, ALBERT.
Cantata.
In: Eitner. Cantaten des 17. und 18. Jahrhunderts. Pt.1.
HEINTZ, WOLFF, 16th CENTURY.
Choral music.
In: Antiqua Chorbuch. Vol.2. Heft 1.
HEINTZE, GUSTAF HJALMAR, 1879–1946.
Grand sonata for piano.
In: Musikaliska konstföreningen. 1871.
Piano trio, op.17.
In: Musikaliska konstföreningen. 1944.
HEISE, PETER ARNOLD, 1830–1879.
Musik til "Palnatoke." Tragedy.
In: Samfundet til Udgivelse af dansk Musik. Ser.I. No.14.
Ouverture til "Marsk Stig."

In: Samfundet til Udgivelse af dansk Musik. Ser.II. No.13.
Rus-Kantate.
In: Samfundet til Udgivelse af dansk Musik. Ser.II. No.17.
Tornerose. Choral work.
In: Samfundet til Udgivelse af dansk Musik. Ser.I. No.5.
HELD, JAN THEOBALD, 1770–1851.
Piano music.
In: Musica antiqua bohemica. Vol.14.
HELLENDALL, PIETER, 1721–1799.
Concerti grossi. Op.3.
In: Monumenta musica neerlandica. Vol.1.
HELLER, JAMES GUTHEIM, 1892– .
Three aquatints for string quartet.
In: Society for the Publication of American Music. Publications. 10th season. 1928–29.
HELLINCK, JOANNES LUPUS, d.1541.
(var. sp.: Lupus Hellingk; Johannes Lupi).
Chanson.
In: Brown. Theatrical chansons of the 15th and early 16th centuries.
In: Publikationen älterer praktischer und theoretischer Musikwerke. Jahrg.27.
Choral music.
In: Antiqua Chorbuch. Vol.1. Heft 1.
In: Commer. Collectio operum musicorum batavorum saeculi XVI. Bd.12.
In: Musica antiqua batava. MA–6.
In: Recueil de musique ancienne. Recueil des morceaux de musique ancienne. Bd.6.
In: Smijers. Van Ockeghem tot Sweelinck. Aflg.7.
Zehn weltliche Lieder.
In: Das Chorwerk. No.15.
Lieder.
In: Publikationen älterer praktischer und theoretischer Musikwerke. Jahrg.1–3.
Mass.
In: Stein. Twelve Franco-Flemish masses of the early 16th century.
Motets.
In: Attaingnant. Treize livres de motets. Livre 1, 8, 9, 13.
HELMONT, CHARLES JOSEPH VAN, 1715–1790.
Werken voor orgel en/of clavecimbel.
In: Monumenta musicae belgicae. Vol.6.
Organ music.
In: Peeters. Altniederländische Meister für Orgel oder Harmonium.
HELSTED, GUSTAV, 1857–1924.
Koncert for Violin og Orkester. Op.27.
In: Samfundet til Udgivelse af dansk Musik. Ser.III. No.1.
Sonate (D-dur) for Orgel. Op.29.
In: Samfundet til Udgivelse af dansk Musik. Ser.III. No.13.
Strygekvartet 1 F-moll. Op.33.
In: Samfundet til Udgivelse af dansk Musik. Ser.III. No.7.
Vort Land. Op.30. Choral work.
In: Samfundet til Udgivelse af dansk Musik. Ser.II. No.35.
HEMMERLEY, GEORG.
Motetten.
In: Das Chorwerk. No.69.
HENARES, ALCALÁ DE, *see* VENEGAS DE HENESTROSA, LUYS.
HENESTROSA, LUYS VENEGAS DE, *see* VENEGAS DE HENESTROSA, LUYS.
HENKEL, MICHAEL, 1780–1851.
Sonate für Flöte oder Violine und Gitarre, Op.9.
In: Nagels Musik-Archiv. No.138.
HENLEY.
Sacred music.
In: Page. Harmonia sacra. Vol.3.
HENNEBERG, R.
Serenade. Octet.
In: Musikaliska konstföreningen. 1916.
HENNING.
Fugue, for 4tet in C.
In: Königliche Akademie der Künste. Auswahl vorzüglicher Musik-Werke. No.39.
HENRICHSEN, ROGER, 1876–1926.
Sct. Hans Hymne. Op.9. Choral work.
In: Samfundet til Udgivelse af dansk Musik. Ser.II. No.33.
4 Klaverstykker. Op.23.
In: Samfundet til Udgivelse af dansk Musik. Ser.III. No.17.
HENRIQUES, FINI VALDEMAR, 1867–1940.
Strygekvartet.
In: Samfundet til Udgivelse af dansk Musik. Ser.III. No.43.
HENRY VIII, KING OF ENGLAND, 1491–1547.
Songs, ballads and instrumental pieces. 68p.
Selections.
In: Smith. Musica antiqua.
Choral music.
In: Engel. Three centuries of choral music. Vol.3.
Part music.
In: Hullah. Part music. Class A.1. Vol.1.
Sacred music.
In: Boyce. Cathedral music. Vol.2.
Songs.
In: Plainsong and Mediaeval Music Society. Publications. (A collection of songs and madrigals . . .).
Music at the Court of Henry VIII.
In: Musica Britannica. Vol.18.
HENSCHEL, SIR GEORGE, 1850–1934.
To music. S.S.A.T.B.
In: Arion. Vol.2.
HENSE, ALFRED.
Thema mit Variationen für Sopran-oder Tenor-Blockflöte.
In: Zeitschrift für Spielmusik. No.8.
HERBING, AUGUST BERNHARD VALENTIN, 1735–1766.
Die Haushaltung.
In: Moser. Alte Meister des deutschen Liedes. 46 Gesänge. No.34.
Songs.
In: Denkmäler deutscher Tonkunst. [1.Folge]. Vol.42.
HERBST, JOHANN ANDREAS, 1588–1666.
Drei mehrchörige Festkonzerte für die Freie Reichsstadt.
In: Das Erbe deutscher Musik. 2.Reihe. Rhein-Main-Gebiet. Vol.1.
HERBST, JOHANNES, 1735–1812.

Sacred songs.
In: Music of the Moravians in America. Vol.1.
HERÉDIA, SEBASTIAN AGUILERA DE, *see* AGUILERA DE HERÉDIA, SEBASTIAN.
HERISSANT, JEAN, 16th CENTURY.
Mass.
In: Stein. Twelve Franco-Flemish masses of the early 16th century.
HÉRITIER, JEAN L', 16th CENTURY.
(var. sp.: Jo Lhéritier).
Motets.
In: Attaingnant. Treize livres de motets. Livre 1, 2, 6, 8, 9, 12, 13.
HERMANN, PAUL.
Flötenmusik über ein Nachtigallenlied.
In: Zeitschrift für Spielmusik. No.116.
HERNÁNDEZ GONZALO, GISELA, 1912– .
Suite coral.
In: Instituto Interamericano de Musicologia. Publicaciónes. No.42.
HEROLD, JOHANN THEODOR.
Lute music.
In: Denkmäler der Tonkunst in Österreich. Vol.50. (Jg.XXV/2).
HEROLD, JOHANNES.
Historia des Leidens und Sterbens unsers Herrn und Heilands.
In: Musik alter Meister. Heft 4.
HERRMANN, BERNARD, 1911– .
Sinfonietta for string orchestra.
In: New music. Orchestra series. No.19.
HERRMANN, WILLY. ed.
Der Walzer.
In: Musikalische Formen in historischen Reihen. Bd.8.
HERRMANN.
Süddeutsche Dorfmusiken.
In: Platzmusik. Nr.5.
HERTEL, JOHANN WILHELM, 1727–1789.
Sonata in D-moll, für Cembalo oder Klavier.
In: Hortus musicus. No.49.
HERTOGHS, BENEDICTUS, *see* DUCIS, BENEDICTUS.
HERVELOIS, CAIX DE, *see* CAIX D'HERVELOIS, LOUIS DE.
HESDIN, PIERRE, 16th CENTURY.
Chansons.
In: Expert. Les maîtres musiciens de la Renaissance française. Vol.5.
In: Lesure. Anthologie de la chanson parisienne au XVIe siècle.
In: Publikationen älterer praktischer und theoretischer Musikwerke. Jahrg.27.
Motets.
In: Attaingnant. Treize livres de Motets. Livre 3, 4, 5, 7, 8.
HESSE, ADOLF FRIEDRICH, 1809–1863.
Organ music.
In: Caecilia; Sammlung von Choralvorspielen.
HESSEN, LANDGRAF MORITZ VON, *see* MORITZ, LANDGRAF OF HESSE-CASSEL.
HESSEN, LUDWIG V., LÄNDGRAF, *see* LUDWIG V. HESSEN, LÄNDGRAF.
HEURTEUR, GUILLAUME LE, 16th CENTURY.
Chansons.
In: Brown. Theatrical chansons of the 15th and early 16th centuries.
In: Publikationen älterer praktischer und theoretischer Musikwerke. Jahrg.27.
Duos.
In: Expert. Florilège du concert vocal de la Renaissance. No.8.
Mass.
In: Stein. Twelve Franco-Flemish masses of the early 16th century.
Motets.
In: Attaingnant. Treize livres de motets. Livre 3, 4, 5, 6, 7, 9.
HEWITT, JAMES, 1770–1827.
Selections.
In: Engel. Music from the days of George Washington.
In: Goldman. Landmarks of early American music, 1760–1800.
HEYDEN, REINHOLD.
Choral music.
In: Musica practica. No.7.
Geistliche Morgenlieder.
In: Nagels Musik-Archiv. No.46.
Variationen über "Grün sind alle meine Kleider" für 2 Blockflöten.
In: Zeitschrift für Spielmusik. No.134.
HEYMAN, KATHERINE RUTH WILLOUGHBY, 1877–1944.
Song.
In: The Wa-Wan series of American compositions.
HIDALGO, JUAN, 17th CENTURY.
Selections.
In: Pedrell. Teatro lirico espanol anterior al siglo XIX. Bd.3, 4/5.
Celos aun del aire matan.
In: Barcelona. Biblioteca Central. Sección de Música. Publicaciones. Vol.11.
HILDNER, VICTOR, 1917– .
Organ music.
In: The parish organist. Vol.1–4.
HILL, EDWARD BURLINGHAME, 1872– .
Música de cámara.
In: Boletín latino-americano de música. Vol.5.
Piano music.
In: The Wa-Wan series of American compositions.
Sextet for flute, oboe, clarinet, horn, bassoon, and piano. Op.39.
In: Society for the Publication of American music. Publications. 19th season. 1937–38.
Sonata. Piano and clarinet (or violin).
In: Society for the Publication of American music. Publications. 8th season. 1926–27.
HILLENDAAL, P.
Vier sonates voor violoncel en bicijferde bas.
In: Vereniging voor nederlandsche Muziekgeschiedenis. Uitgave. No.41.
HILLER, JOHANN ADAM, 1728–1804.
Lieder.
In: Moser. Alte Meister des deutschen Liedes. 46 Gesänge. No.36, 37.
In: Reimann. Das deutsche Lied. Vol.4.
Part music.
? In: Hullah. Part music. Class C. Secular.
Psalmen.

? In: Musica sacra . . . ca.1842–1896. Vol.8–10.
HILLER, LEJAREN A., JR.
Computer cantata.
In: New music. To be published.
Illiac suite for string quartet.
In: New music. Vol.30. No.3. 1957.
HILTON, JOHN, 1599–1657.
Ayres or fa las.
In: Musical Antiquarian Society. Publications. Vol.13.
Madrigal.
In: The triumphs of Oriana.
Part music.
In: Hullah. Part music. Class B.2; Class C. Secular.
Tricinien.
In: Zeitschrift für Spielmusik. No.87.
Vocal music.
In: Hullah. Vocal scores. II. Secular.
HILTSCHER, WOLFGANG, 1913–1941.
Organ music.
In: The parish organist. Vol.7–8.
HIMMEL, FRIEDRICH HEINRICH, 1765–1814.
Lied.
In: Reimann. Das deutsche Lied. Vol.1, 3, 4.
Part music.
In: Hullah. Part music. Class A.1. Vol.1.
Wiegenlied.
In: Thouret. Musik am preussischen Hofe. No.11.
HINDEMITH, PAUL, 1895–1963.
Wer sich die Musik erkiest.
In: Bausteine für Musikerziehung und Musikpflege. B 107.
HINE, WILLIAM, 1687–1730.
Sacred music.
In: Arnold. Cathedral music. Vol.3.
In: Page. Harmonia sacra. Vol.2, 3.
HINTERLEITHNER, FERDINAND IGNAZ.
Lute music.
In: Denkmäler der Tonkunst in Österreich. Vol.50. (Jg.XXV/2).
THE HIRMOLOGION.
In: Monumenta musicae byzantinae. Subsidia. Vol.4. Pt.1–2.
HIRMOLOGION, JERUSALEM. SABA 83.
In: Monumenta musicae byzantinae. Série-principale. Vol.7.
HIRMOLOGIUM, THE HYMNS OF THE.
In: Monumenta musicae byzantinae. Transcripta. Vol.6, 8.
HIRMOLOGIUM, TWENTY CANONS FROM THE TRINITY.
In: Monumenta musicae byzantinae. Transcripta. Vol.4.
HIRMOLOGIUM ATHOUM. (RÉPRODUCTION INTÉGRALE DU CODEX MONASTERII HIBERORUM 470).
In: Monumenta musicae byzantinae. Série-principale. Vol.2.
HIRMOLOGIUM CRYPTENSE. (RÉPRODUCTION INTÉGRALE DU CODEX CRYPTENSIS E, GAMMA, II).
In: Monumenta musicae byzantinae. Série-principale. Vol.3.
HISTORICAL MUSICOLOGY. (L. SPIESS).
In: Institute of Mediaeval Music. Musicological studies. Vol.4.
HISTORY OF INSTRUMENTATION. (BECKER).
In: Anthology of music. Vol.24.
HOBRECHT, JACOB, *see* OBRECHT, JACOB.
HÖCKH, KARL.
Partita a tre, due violini e basso continuo. Nr.2.
In: Hausmusik. No.170.
HÖCKNER, HILMAR, 1891– .
Violin-Übung am Volkslied.
In: Bausteine für Musikerziehung und Musikpflege. B 121.
HØEG, CARSTEN, 1896– .
La notation ekphonetique.
In: Monumenta musicae byzantinae. Subsidia. Vol.1. Fasc.2.
HOEGNER, FRIEDRICH, 1897– .
Organ music.
In: The parish organist. Vol.5–6.
HOELTY-NICKEL, THEODORE CARL, 1894– .
Organ music.
In: The parish organist. Vol.1–4.
HØFFDING, FINN, 1899– .
"Det er Ganske Vist." Symfonisk Fantasi for Orkester. Op.37.
In: Samfundet til Udgivelse af dansk Musik. Ser.III. No.80.
Evolution. Fantasi for Orkester. Op.31.
In: Samfundet til Udgivelse af dansk Musik. Ser.III. No.97.
Fantasia sinfonica. Op.54.
In: Samfundet til Udgivelse af dansk Musik. Ser.III. No.129.
Kammermusik. Op.11.
In: Samfundet til Udgivelse af dansk Musik. Ser.III. No.145.
Sinfonia Concertante for Kammerorkester. Op.23.
In: Samfundet til Udgivelse af dansk Musik. Ser.III. No.62.
Symphonie Nr.3. Op.12.
In: Samfundet til Udgivelse af dansk Musik. Ser.III. No.36.
HOFFER, JOHANN JOSEF, 17th–18th CENTURIES.
Dance music.
In: Denkmäler der Tonkunst in Österreich. Vol.56. (Jg.XXVIII/2).
HÖFFER, PAUL, 1895–1949.
Fliegermorgen.
In: Platzmusik. Nr.7.
Heitere Bläser-Sinfonie.
In: Platzmusik. Nr.10.
HOFFHEIMER, PAULUS, *see* HOFHAIMER, PAUL.
HOFFMANN, ERNST THEODOR AMADEUS, 1776–1822.
Musikalische Werke. 3 parts.
Divertimento a tre.
In: Hausmusik. No.156.
Keyboard sonatas.
In: Newman. Thirteen keyboard sonatas of the 18th and 19th centuries.
HOFFMEISTER, FRANZ ANTON, 1754–1812.
Quartett.
In: Diletto musicale. No.131.
Quintett in Es-dur für Horn und Streichquartett.
In: Diletto musicale. No.109.
Serenade in E flat.

In: Für Kenner und Liebhaber. No.34. (Score).
In: Für Kenner und Liebhaber. No.32. (Parts).
Sinfonie C-dur.
In: Sondheimer. Werke aus dem 18. Jahrhundert. Nr.33.
Songs.
In: Denkmäler der Tonkunst in Österreich. Vol.54. (Jg.XXVII/2).
HÖFFNER.
Fliegermusik.
In: Platzmusik. Nr.2.
Musik zu einem Volkspiel.
In: Platzmusik. Nr.3.
HOFHAIMER, PAUL, 1459–1537.
(var. sp.: Paulus Hoffheimer; Paul Hofhaymer).
Einundneunzig gesammelte Tonsätze. 194p.
Selections.
In: Ambros. Auserwählte Tonwerke.
In: Leichtentritt. Deutsche Hausmusik aus vier Jahrhunderten.
Choral music.
In: Antiqua Chorbuch. Vol.2. Heft 1.
Lieder.
In: Aich. Das Liederbuch.
In: Denkmäler der Tonkunst in Österreich. Vol.72. (Jg.XXXVII/2).
In: Publikationen älterer praktischer und theoretischer Musikwerke. Jahrg.8.
Organ music.
In: Bonnet. Historical organ-recitals. Vol.1.
In: Cantantibus organis. Vol.11.
In: Klein. The first four centuries of music for the organ from Dunstable to Bach (1370–1749).
In: Liber organi. Bd.8.
In: The Liturgical Music Press, Inc. Masterpieces of organ music. Folio 65.
In: Moser. Frühmeister der deutschen Orgelkunst.
HOFLAND, SIGVART A., 1889– .
Organ music.
In: The parish organist. Vol.1–4.
HOFMANN, LEOPOLD, 1738–1793.
Songs.
In: Denkmäler der Tonkunst in Österreich. Vol.54. (Jg.XXVII/2).
HOFMEISTER.
Part music.
In: Hullah. Part music. Class B.1.
HØGENHAVEN JENSEN, KNUD, 1928– .
Danse triomphale. Orchestra.
In: Samfundet til Udgivelse af dansk Musik. Ser.III. No.134.
Lamento for Strygeorkester. Op.9.
In: Samfundet til Udgivelse af dansk Musik. Ser.III. No.113.
HOHLFELD, CHRISTOPH, 1922– .
Kleines Konzert.
In: Collegium musicae novae. No.41.
HOHN, WILHELM.
Stücke für 3 Blockflöten.
In: Zeitschrift für Spielmusik. No.37.
HOLBORNE, WILLIAM, 17th CENTURY.
Madrigals.
In: Fellowes. The English madrigal school. Vol.36.
HOLDEN, DAVID JUSTIN, 1911– .
Music for piano and strings.
In: Society for the Publication of American music. Publications. 20th season. 1938–39.
HOLDEN, OLIVER, 1765–1844.
Selections.
In: Goldman. Landmarks of early American music, 1760–1800.
HOLGUÍN, GUILLERMO URIBE-, *see* URIBE-HOLGUÍN, GUILLERMO.
HOLLANDE, JEAN DE, 16th CENTURY.
Selections.
In: Maldéghem. Trésor musical.
HOLLANDER, CHRISTIAN JANSZOON, 16th CENTURY.
Choral music.
In: Antiqua Chorbuch. Vol.1. Heft 2.
In: Commer. Collectio operum musicorum batavorum saeculi XVI. Bd.1, 4, 5, 6, 9.
Lied- und Choralmotetten.
In: Das Chorwerk. No.30.
Lieder.
In: Commer. Geistliche und weltliche Lieder aus dem XVI.–XVII. Jahrhundert.
HOLLANDER, SEB.
Choral music.
In: Commer. Collectio operum musicorum batavorum saeculi XVI. Bd.1.
HOLLINS, ALFRED, 1865–1942.
Organ music.
In: Standard series of organ compositions. No.4, 5, 65.
HOLM, MOGENS WINKEL.
Concerto Piccolo for Orkester. (1961).
In: Samfundet til Udgivelse af dansk Musik. Ser.III. No.176.
HOLMBOE, VAGN, 1909– .
Kammerkoncert. Nr.2.
In: Samfundet til Udgivelse af dansk Musik. Ser.III. No.74.
Sonate for Violin og Klaver.
In: Samfundet til Udgivelse af dansk Musik. Ser.III. No.54.
HOLMES, JOHN, d.1602.
Madrigal.
In: The triumphs of Oriana.
Sacred music.
In: Page. Harmonia sacra. Vol.3.
HOLMGREEN, PELLE GUDMUNDSEN-, *see* GUDMUNDSEN-HOLMGREEN, PELLE.
HOLYOKE, SAMUEL, 1762–1820.
Selections.
In: Goldman. Landmarks of early American music, 1760–1800.
HOLZBAUER, IGNAZ, 1711–1783.
Günther von Schwarzburg.
In: Denkmäler deutscher Tonkunst. [1.Folge]. Vol.8–9.
Ausgewählte Kammermusik.
In: Das Erbe deutscher Musik. 1.Reihe. Vol.24.
Orchestral music.
In: Riemann. Mannheim symphonists. Vol.2.
Sinfonia, Mi majeur, für Streichorchester.
In: Rahter's Kammer-Orchester. No.14.
Sinfonia a tre für 2 Violinen und Bass.

In: Antiqua Edition. Von 3 Instrumenten an.
Sinfonia in D-dur.
In: Diletto musicale. No.166.
HOLZER, JOHANN, ca.1779.
Songs.
In: Denkmäler der Tonkunst in Österreich. Vol.54. (Jg.XXVII/2).
HOLZMANN, RUDOLPH, 1910– .
Pequeña suite. (Piano).
In: Instituto Interamericano de Musicologia. Publicaciónes. No.33.
HOMBERGER, PAUL, d.1634.
Brautgesänge für vier-bzw. fünfstimmigen gemischten Chor.
In: Musik alter Meister. Heft 7.
HOMILIUS, GOTTFRIED AUGUST, 1714–1785.
Choral music.
In: Rochlitz. Sammlung vorzüglicher Gesangstücke. Bd.3.
Fünf Choralbearbeitungen. Organ.
In: Die Orgel. Reihe II. Nr.1.
Sechs Choralvorspiele. Organ.
In: Die Orgel. Reihe II. Nr.2.
Motetten.
In: Das Chorwerk. No.89.
Motet. Hilf Herr.
In: Königliche Akademie der Künste. Auswahl vorzüglicher Musik-Werke. No.34.
Organ music.
In: Biggs. Treasury of early organ music.
Part music.
In: Hullah. Part music. 1868 edition.
Vocal music.
In: Hullah. Vocal scores. I. Sacred.
HONAUER, LEONTZI, 18th CENTURY.
Sonata. Piano. Op.III, No.4.
In: Reeser. De klaviersonate.
HONDT, GHEERKIN, 16th CENTURY.
Selections.
In: Maldéghem. Trésor musical.
HOOK, JAMES, 1746–1827.
Songs.
In: Potter. Reliquary of English song. Vol.2.
HOOPER, EDMUND, ca.1553–1621.
Church music.
In: Motett Society. [Collection of ancient church music]. Division 3.
Keyboard music.
In: The Fitzwilliam virginal book.
HOPKINS, EDWARD JOHN, 1818–1901.
Part music.
In: Hullah. Part music. 1868 edition.
HOPKINSON, FRANCIS, 1737–1791.
Selections.
In: Engel. Music from the days of George Washington.
In: Fisher. The music that Washington knew.
In: Goldman. Landmarks of early American music, 1760–1800.
HORNEMAN, CHRISTIAN FREDERIK EMIL, 1841–1906.
Aladdin. Opera.
In: Samfundet til Udgivelse af dansk Musik. Ser.II. No.6.
Aladdin. Ouverture.
In: Samfundet til Udgivelse af dansk Musik. Ser.III. No.109.
Kalanus. Tragedy.
In: Samfundet til Udgivelse af dansk Musik. Ser.II. No.20.
Kampen med Muserne. Drama.
In: Samfundet til Udgivelse af dansk Musik. Ser.II. No.25.
Strygekvartet, No.1, G-moll.
In: Samfundet til Udgivelse af dansk Musik. Ser.III. No.81.
HÖRSCHELMANN, OTTMAR.
Weihnachtsliederspiel für eine Singstimme und 3 Instrumente.
In: Zeitschrift für Spielmusik. No.73.
HORSLEY, WILLIAM, 1774–1858.
Canon. Sanctus and Hosanna.
In: Königliche Akademie der Künste. Auswahl vorzüglicher Musik-Werke. No.29.
Part music.
In: Hullah. Part music. Class A.1. Vol.1, 2; Class A.2. Vol.1, 2; Class B.2; 1868 edition.
Vocal music.
In: Hullah. Vocal scores. II. Secular.
HORZALKA.
Missa solennis. Op.27.
In: Ecclesiasticon. No.21.
HOTHBY, JOHN, 1415–1487.
The musical works. v.1– .
HOTINET, *see* BARRA, HOTINET; HUTINET.
HOTTETERRE, JACQUES, d.ca.1761.
Sonate en ré majeur pour hautbois (flûte ou violon) et basse continue.
In: Musiques Françaises. Vol.6.
HOTTETERRE, LOUIS, 17th CENTURY.
Suite. D dur.
In: Nagels Musik-Archiv. No.48.
HOVHANESS, ALAN, 1911– .
Mihr (Ancient Armenian fire god), for 2 pianos.
In: New music. Vol.19. No.3. Apr.1946.
HOWARD, SAMUEL, 1710–1782.
Songs.
In: Potter. Reliquary of English song. Vol.2.
HOWE, MARY, 1882– .
Elegy. Organ.
In: Contemporary organ series. No.21.
Música de cámara.
In: Boletín latino-americano de música. Vol.5
HOWELLS, HERBERT NORMAN, 1892– .
Selections.
In: The music with the form and order of the service to be performed at the coronation of . . . Queen Elizabeth II.
HOYOUL, BAUDOIN, 1548–1594.
(var. sp.: Balduin Hoyoul).
Choral music.
In: Antiqua Chorbuch. Vol.1. Heft 2.
HÜBSCH, HANNS. ed.
Hänsel und Gretel.
In: Zeitschrift für Spielmusik. No.197.
LAS HUELGAS DE BURGOS, SPAIN.
El còdex musical.
In: Barcelona. Biblioteca Central. Sección de Música. Publicaciones. Vol.6.
HUGALDE, C. J.
Sacred music.
In: Eslava y Elizondo. Lira sacro-hispana. 19th century. ii.2.

HUGL.
Organ music.
In: Cantantibus organis. Vol.3, 11.
HUGUENOT.
Air badin.
In: L'école du violon au XVIIe et XVIIIe siècle. No.1345.
HUGUENOT PSAUTIER DU XVIe SIÈCLE.
In: Expert. Psautier Huguenot du XVIe siècle.
In: Pidoux. Le Psautier Huguenot du XVIe siècle.
HULLAH, JOHN PYKE, 1812–1884.
Part music.
In: Hullah. Part music. Class A.1. Vol.1, 2; Class A.2. Vol.2; Class C. Sacred; 1868 edition.
Vocal music.
In: Hullah. Vocal scores. II. Secular.
HÜLLMANDEL, NICOLAS JOSEPH, 1751–1823.
Selections.
In: Crotch. Specimens of various styles of music. Vol.3.
Sonata. Piano. Op.I, No.2; Op.VI, No.3.
In: Reeser. De klaviersonate.
HULSE, CAMIL CAN, 1897– .
Organ music.
In: The parish organist. Vol.1–4.
HUMFREY, PELHAM, 1647–1674.
(var. sp.: Pelham Humphrey).
Selections.
In: Smith. Musica antiqua.
Part music.
In: Hullah. Part music. Class A.1. Vol.2.
Sacred music.
In: Boyce. Cathedral music. Vol.2, 3; 1849 ed., Vol.3.
Songs.
In: Potter. Reliquary of English song. Vol.1.
HUMMEL, JOHANN NEPOMUK, 1778–1837.
Keyboard music.
In: Farrenc. Le trésor des pianistes. Vol.22.
In: Tagliapietra. Antologia di musica antica e moderna per pianoforte. Bd.14.
Sacred music.
In: Latrobe, C. I. Selection of sacred music.
In: Latrobe, J. A. The music of the church.
Op.5/1. Sonate in B-dur für Violine und Klavier.
In: Diletto musicale. No.100.
Sonate in D-dur für Flöte und Klavier. Op.50.
In: Diletto musicale. No.148.
Op.5/3. Sonate in Es-dur für Viola und Klavier.
In: Diletto musicale. No.65.
Variationen über ein Thema aus Glucks "Armida." Piano.
In: Organum. 5.Reihe. Nr.8.
HUMPERT, HANS, 1901–1943.
Psalm 60 und 121.
In: Christophorus-Chorwerk. Heft 14.
Psalm 67 und 24. Psalm 90.
In: Christophorus-Chorwerk. Heft 17, 18
HUMPHREY, DORIS, 1895–1958.
Dance rhythms.
In: New music. Orchestra series. No.18.
HUMPHREY, PELHAM, *see* HUMFREY, PELHAM.
HUMPHRIES, JOHN.
Sonate en ut mineur.
In: L'école du violon au XVIIe et XVIIIe siècle. No.1273.
HUNGARY–MUSIC (*see also* FOLKSONGS, HUNGARIAN).
In: Corpus musicae popularis hungaricae.
In: Melodiarium Hungariae medii aevi.
In: Monumenta hungariae musica.
In: Musica hungarica.
In: Zeitschrift für Spielmusik. No.268.
HUNT, THOMAS, 16th–17th CENTURIES.
Madrigal.
In: The triumphs of Oriana.
HURÉ, JEAN, 1877–1930.
Organ music.
In: Standard series of organ compositions. No.15.
HURLEBUSCH, CONRAD FRIEDRICH, 1696–1765.
(var. sp.: Corrado Federigo Hurlebusch; Konrad Friedrich Hurlebusch).
Compositioni musicali per il cembalo.
In: Vereniging voor Nederlandsche Muziekgeschiedenis. Uitgave. No.32.
Instrumental concertos.
In: Denkmäler deutscher Tonkunst. [1.Folge]. Vol.29–30.
Lieder.
In: Moser. Alte Meister des deutschen Liedes. 30 Gesänge. No.19, 20.
In: Moser. Alte Meister des deutschen Liedes. 46 Gesänge. No.30, 31.
HUSMANN, HEINRICH, 1908– . ed.
Die drei- und vierstimmigen Notre-Dame-Organa.
In: Publikationen älterer Musik. Jahrg.11.
Medieval polyphony.
In: Anthology of music. Vol.9.
HUSS, HENRY HOLDEN, 1862–1953.
String quartet.
In: Society for the Publication of American Music. Publications. 2d season. 1920–21.
HUTCHINSON.
Vocal music.
In: Hullah. Vocal scores. II. Secular.
HUTINET (HOTINET?).
Selections.
In: Maldéghem. Trésor musical.
HUYGENS, CONSTANTIN, 1596–1687.
Pathodia sacra et profana.
In: Vereniging voor Nederlandsche Muziekgeschiedenis. Uitgave. No.11.
Constantyn Huygens. (Ericka Smit-Vanrotte).
In: Institute of Mediaeval Music. Musical theorists in translation. Vol.4.
HYLÉN, O. W.
String quartet, D major.
In: Musikaliska konstföreningen. 1870.
HYMNS.
In: Melodiarium hungariae medii aevi. Vol.1.
In: Monumenta monodica medii aevi.
In: Monumenta polyphoniae italicae. Vol.3.
In: Music Press, Inc. [Choral series]. Vol.55.
In: Plainsong and Mediaeval Music Society. Publications.
HYMNS, GERMAN.
In: Bäumker. Das katholische deutsche Kirchenlied in seinen Singweisen von den frühesten Zeiten.
HYMNS, ITALIAN.
In: Liuzzi. La Lauda.

HYMNS (ORGAN).
In: Orgue et liturgie. Vol.8.

IDE, CHESTER EDWARD, 1878– .
Songs; Piano music.
In: The Wa-Wan series of American compositions.
IGLESIAS VILLOUD, HÉCTOR, 1913– .
Catamarqueña.
In: Instituto Interamericano de Musicologia. Publicaciónes. No.15.
IMBERT.
Vocal music.
In: Sammlung russischer Romanzen. No.309.
IMMLER.
Part music.
In: Hullah. Part music. Class B.1.
IMPROVISATION. (FERAND).
In: Anthology of music. Vol.12.
INDIA, SIGISMONDO D', *see* SIGISMONDO D'INDIA, CAVALIERE.
INFANTUS, FERNANDO DE LAS, 1534–d.after 1607.
Choral music.
In: Dehn. Sammlung älterer Musik aus dem XVI. und XVII. Jahrhundert.
Sacred music.
In: Eslava y Elizondo. Lira sacro-hispana. 16th century. i.2.
Victimae paschali.
In: Polifonía española. Vol.9.
INGEGNERI, MARC ANTONIO, d.1592.
(var. sp.: Ingegnerius).
Selections.
In: Musica sacra . . . 1839– . Vol.15.
Chant.
In: Soderlund. Examples of Gregorian chant and works by Orlandus Lassus, Giovanni Pierluigi Palestrina and Marc Antonio Ingegneri.
Choral music.
In: Dehn. Sammlung älterer Musik aus dem XVI. und XVII. Jahrhundert.
In: Societas Polyphonica Romanae. Repertorium. Vol.4.
INGLOTT, WILLIAM, 1554–1621.
(var. sp.: William Inglot).
Keyboard music.
In: The Fitzwilliam virginal book.
INNOCENT III, POPE, d.1216.
Vocal music.
In: Delsarte. Archives du chant. Livre 3.
INSULA, FRANCUS DE, 15th CENTURY.
Selections.
In: Reaney. Early fifteenth-century music. Vol.2.
INZAURRAGA, ALEJANDRO.
Vocal music.
In: Boletín latino-americano de música. Vol.4.
IPPOLITO.
Keyboard music.
In: Corpus of early keyboard music. Vol.24.
IRELAND–MUSIC.
In: Crotch. Specimens of various styles of music. Vol.1.
IRUARRÍZAGA, LUIS, 1891–1927.
Obras completas. 1.ed. de voces solas. 431p.
ISAAC, HEINRICH, ca.1450–1517.
(var. sp.: Heinrich Isaak; Henricus Isaac).
Choralis Constantinus. Book III. 456p.
Choralis Constantinus.
In: Denkmäler der Tonkunst in Österreich. Vol.10. (Jg.V/1); Vol.32. (Jg.XVI/1).
Secular compositions.
In: Denkmäler der Tonkunst in Österreich. Vol.28. (Jg.XIV/1).
Selections.
In: Ambros. Auserwählte Tonwerke.
In: Documenta historica musicae.
Choral music.
In: Antiqua Chorbuch. Vol.1. Heft 1; Vol.2. Heft 1.
In: Engel. Three centuries of choral music. Vol.4.
In: Smijers. Van Ockeghem tot Sweelinck. Aflg.6.
Instrumental music. (Carmina).
In: Nagels Musik-Archiv. No.53.
Dreistimmige Instrumentalstücke.
In: Zeitschrift für Spielmusik. No.58.
Sechs Instrumentalsätze für vier Streich- oder Blasinstrumente.
In: Hortus musicus. No.29.
Zwei Instrumentalsätze zu drei Stimmen für Streich- oder Bläser Trio.
In: Musica practica. No.9.
Vierstimmige Instrumentalsätze.
In: Zeitschrift für Spielmusik. No.9.
Introiten I zu 6 Stimmen.
In: Das Chorwerk. No.81.
Karnevalslieder der Renaissance.
In: Das Chorwerk. No.43.
Lieder.
In: Aich. Das Liederbuch.
In: Publikationen älterer praktischer und theoretischer Musikwerke. Jahrg.1–3, 8.
In: Reimann. Das deutsche Lied. Vol.1.
Vier "Marienmotetten."
In: Das Chorwerk. No.100.
Messe.
In: Archivium musices metropolitanum mediolanense. Vol.10.
Missa Carminum.
In: Das Chorwerk. No.7.
Organ music.
In: Klein. The first four centuries of music for the organ from Dunstable to Bach (1370–1749).
In: Liber organi. Bd.8.
In: Moser. Frühmeister der deutschen Orgelkunst.
In: Peeters. Anthologia pro organo. Vol.3.
In: Peeters. Oudnederlandse meesters. Vol.1, 2, 3.
In: Schering. Alte Meister aus der Frühzeit des Orgelspiels.
Proprium missae.
In: Christophorus-Chorwerk. Heft 8.
ISAACSON, LEONARD M.
Illiac suite for string quartet.
In: New music. Vol.30. No.3. 1957.
ISAAK, HEINRICH, *see* ISAAC, HEINRICH.
ISAMITT, CARLOS, 1887– .
Keyboard music.

In: Boletín latino-americano de música. Vol.1, 4.
In: Guenther. Collection espagnole.
Música de cámara.
In: Boletín latino-americano de música. Vol.5.
ISHIKETA, MAREO.
Sonata II for violoncello and pianoforte.
In: Contemporary Japanese music series. No.23.
ISNARDI, PAOLO, 16th CENTURY.
Missa angelus Domini.
In: Musica liturgica. Vol.1. Fasc.5.
ITALIAN MUSICIANS, 1567–1625; 1564–1590.
In: Denkmäler der Tonkunst in Österreich. Vol.77. (Jg.XLI); Vol.90.
THE ITALIAN TRIO SONATA. (SCHENK).
In: Anthology of music. Vol.7.
ITALY–CATHEDRAL MUSIC.
In: Jeppesen. Italia sacra musica.
ITALY–MUSIC (*see also* SONGS, ITALIAN).
In: Antica musica strumentale italiana.
In: Benevenuti. Cembalisti italiani del settecento.
In: Boghen. Antichi maestri italiani.
In: Bossi. Sammlung von Stücken alter italienischer Meister für die moderne Orgel.
In: I classici della musica italiana.
In: I classici della musica italiana. Raccolta nazionale delle musiche italiane.
In: Classici italiani della musica.
In: I classici musicali italiani.
In: Crotch. Specimens of various styles of music. Vol.1.
In: Denkmäler der Tonkunst in Österreich. Vol.77. (Jg.XLI); Vol.90.
In: Early Italian keyboard music.
In: Einstein. The golden age of the madrigal.
In: Esposito. Early Italian piano music.
In: Expert. Chants de France et d'Italie.
In: Fuser. Classici italiani dell'organo.
In: Gevaert. Les gloires de l'Italie.
In: Istituto italiano per la storia della musica. Pubblicazioni.
In: Istituzioni e monumenti dell' arte musicale italiana.
In: Istituzioni e monumenti dell' arte musicale italiana. Nuova serie.
In: Jeppesen. La flora.
In: Jeppesen. Italia sacra musica.
In: Jeppesen. Die italienische Orgelmusik am Anfang des Cinquecento.
In: Jeppesen. Die mehrstimmige italienische Laude um 1500.
In: Kastner. Alt-italienische Versetten.
In: Kastner. Silva iberica.
In: Landshoff. Alte Meister des Bel Canto. Italienische Kammerduette.
In: Landshoff. I classici del Bel Canto.
In: Madrigalisti italiani.
In: Mantica. Prime fioriture del melodramma italiano.
In: Marrocco. Fourteenth-century Italian cacce.
In: Monumenta polyphoniae italicae.
In: Monumenti di musica italiana.
In: Paoli. Sonate italiane del sec.: XVIII per cembalo o pianoforte.
In: The Penn state music series. No.12.
In: Pirrotta. The music of fourteenth-century Italy.
In: Pistone. Capalavori della polifonia italiana.
In: Squarcialupi Codex. Der Squarcialupi-Codex, Pal.87.
In: Torchi. L'arte musicale in Italia.
In: Zeitschrift für Spielmusik. No.94.
ITIBERE DA CUNHA LUZ, BRASÍLIO, 1896– .
Música de cámara.
In: Boletín latino-americano de música. Vol.6.
IVES, CHARLES EDWARD, 1874–1954.
Calcium light, for orchestra.
In: New music. Vol.26. No.4. July 1953.
The fourth of July. Orchestra.
In: New music. Orchestra series. No.3.
The gong on the hook and ladder.
In: New music. Vol.26. No.4. July 1953.
Lincoln, the great commoner.
In: New music. Vol.26. No.2. Jan.1953.
In: New music. Orchestra series. No.1.
Música de cámara.
In: Boletín latino-americano de música. Vol.5.
A set of pieces for theater or chamber orchestra.
In: New music. Vol.5. No.2. Jan.1932.
In: New music. Orchestra series. No.5.
Sonata No.3 for piano and violin.
In: New music. Vol.24. No.2. Jan.1951.
18 [i.e.19] Songs.
In: New music. Vol.9. No.1. Oct.1935.
34 Songs.
In: New music. Vol.7. No.1. Oct.1933.
Symphony "Holidays." First movement. Orchestra.
In: New music. Orchestra series. No.20.
Fourth symphony. (Second movement).
In: New music. Vol.2. No.2.
In: New music. Orchestra series. No.15.
Three protests. Piano.
In: New music. Vol.21. No.1. Oct.1947.
IVES, SIMON, 1600–1662.
Selections.
In: Smith. Musica antiqua.
Fantasias.
In: English instrumental music of the 16th and 17th centuries from manuscripts in the New York Public Library. No.2.
Vocal music.
In: Hullah. Vocal scores. I. Sacred.

JACCHINI, GIUSEPPE, 17th–18th CENTURIES.
Op.5. No.3. Triosonate G-dur.
In: Musikschätze der Vergangenheit.
JACHET DE MANTUA, ca.1495–1559.
Selections.
In: Maldéghem. Trésor musical.
JACINTO, FREI.
Keyboard music.
In: Kastner. Cravistas portuguezes.
JACKSON.
Part music.
In: Hullah. Part music. Class B.1.
JACKSON, GEORGE K., 1758–1822.
Selections.
In: Goldman. Landmarks of early American music, 1760–1800.

JACOBEAN CONSORT MUSIC.
In: Musica Britannica. Vol.9.
JACOBI, FREDERICK, 1891–1952.
Prelude. Organ.
In: Contemporary organ series. No.6.
Three quiet preludes. Organ.
In: Contemporary organ series. No.24.
String quartet, No.1. (On Indian themes).
In: Society for the Publication of American Music. Publications. 7th season. 1925–26.
String quartet, No.2.
In: Society for the Publication of American Music. Publications. 16th season. 1934–35.
Vocal music.
In: Boletín latino-americano de música. Vol.5.
JACOBI, MICHAEL, 17th CENTURY.
Choral music.
In: Antiqua Chorbuch. Vol.2. Heft 5.
JACOBI, WOLFGANG, 1894– .
5 Studien für Flauto dolce und Klavier oder Cembalo.
In: Moecks Kammermusik. Vol.503.
JACOBS, CHARLES.
Tempo notation in Renaissance Spain.
In: Institute of Mediaeval Music. Musicological studies. Vol.8.
JACOBSEN, KARSTEN.
Niederdeutsche Präludien.
In: Zeitschrift für Spielmusik. No.106.
JACOBSSON, JOHN.
(var. sp.: J. Jacobson).
Cavatina. For tenor and orchestra.
In: Musikaliska konstföreningen. 1888.
Three pieces for clarinet, viola, and piano, op.45.
In: Musikaliska konstföreningen. 1896.
JACOBUS DE BONONIA.
Selections.
In: Pirrotta. The music of fourteenth-century Italy. Vol.4.
JACOPO DA BOLOGNA, 14th CENTURY.
The music of Jacopo da Bologna. 162p.
Selections.
In: Gleason. Examples of music before 1400.
In: Pirrotta. The music of fourteenth-century Italy. Vol.4.
In: Torchi. L'arte musicale in Italia. Bd.1.
Cacce.
In: Marrocco. Fourteenth-century Italian cacce.
Lux purpurata radiis; Non al suo Amante.
In: Van. Les monuments de l'Ars Nova.
JACOTIN (REAL NAME JACQUES GODEBRYE), ca.1445–1529.
(var. sp.: Jacquet).
Selections.
In: Maldéghem. Trésor musical.
Chansons.
In: Brown. Theatrical chansons of the 15th and early 16th centuries.
In: Expert. Les maîtres musiciens de la Renaissance française. Vol.5.
In: Lesure. Anthologie de la chanson parisienne au XVIe siècle.
In: Publikationen älterer praktischer und theoretischer Musikwerke. Jahrg.27.
Motets.
In: Attaingnant. Treize livres de motets. Livre 5, 6, 9, 10, 13.
JACQUIN, EMILIAN GOTTFRIED VON.
Selections.
In: Denkmäler der Tonkunst in Österreich. Vol.79. (Jg.XLII/2).
JAKOWIEFF-GLINKA.
Vocal music.
In: Sammlung russischer Romanzen. No.241, 289.
JAMES, PHILIP, 1890– .
Pantomime. Organ.
In: Contemporary organ series. No.8.
JANEQUIN, CLÉMENT, *see* JANNEQUIN, CLÉMENT.
JANIEWICZ, FELIX, 1762–1848.
Andante "Erhell' deinen Blick."
In: Florilegium musicae antiquae. Vol.12.
JANITSCH, JOHANN GOTTLIEB, 1708–1763.
Kammersonate "Echo" für Flaute traverso, Oboe (Viol oder Flauto), Viola da Braccio (oder da Gamba) und Cembalo und Violoncell.
In: Riemann. Collegium musicum. No.68.
JANNACONI, GIUSEPPE, 1741–1816.
Part music.
In: Hullah. Part music. Class A.1. Vol.2.
JANNEQUIN, CLÉMENT, 16th CENTURY.
(var. sp.: Clément Janequin).
Selections.
In: Documenta historica musicae.
In: Maldéghem. Trésor musical.
Chansons.
In: Bordes. Chansonnier du XVe siècle.
In: Brown. Theatrical chansons of the 15th and early 16th centuries.
In: Cauchie. Quinze chansons françaises du XVIe siècle.
In: Das Chorwerk. No.73.
In: Expert. Les maîtres musiciens de la Renaissance française. Vol.5, 7.
In: Lesure. Anthologie de la chanson parisienne au XVIe siècle.
In: Publikationen älterer praktischer und theoretischer Musikwerke. Jahrg.27.
Chantons, sonnons, trompétes; Les cris de Paris.
In: Expert. Florilège du concert vocal de la Renaissance. No.1, 3.
Choral music.
In: Commer. Collectio operum musicorum batavorum saeculi XVI. Bd.12.
In: Engel. Three centuries of choral music. Vol.1.
In: Der Kammerchor. Vol.1.
In: Recueil de musique ancienne. Recueil des morceaux de musique ancienne. Bd.5, 11.
Petite nymphe folastre.
In: Squire. Ausgewählte Madrigale und mehrstimmige Gesänge. No.18.
JAN Z LUBLINA, fl.1540.
(var. sp.: Johannes de Lublin; Jana z Lublina).
Tablature.
In: Corpus of early keyboard music. Vol.6. Pt.1, 2, 3.
In: Denkmäler altpolnischer Musik. Vol.20.
In: Monumenta musicae in Polonia. Ser.B.1.

JAPAN–MUSIC.
In: Contemporary Japanese music series.
In: Die geschichtlichen Denkmäler der japanischen Tonkunst.
JAPART, JOHANNES, 15th–16th CENTURIES.
Chanson.
In: Brown. Theatrical chansons of the 15th and early 16th centuries.
JARECKI, TADEUZ, 1889– .
String quartet.
In: Society for the Publication of American Music. Publications. 3d season. 1921–22.
JARNOWICH, GIOVANNI MANE, *see* GIORNOVICCHI, GIOVANNI MANE.
JARSINS, G.
Motets.
In: Attaingnant. Treize livres de motets. Livre 13.
JARZEBSKI, ADAM, ca.1590–ca.1649.
Bentrovala.
In: Denkmäler altponischer Musik. Vol.27.
Canzoni.
In: Denkmäler altponischer Musik. Vol.39.
Chromatica.
In: Denkmäler altponischer Musik. Vol.21.
Concerti a 2, No.1–4. 2 instruments and continuo.
In: Denkmäler altpolnischer Musik. Vol.51.
Nova casa.
In: Denkmäler altpolnischer Musik. Vol.15.
Sentinella.
In: Denkmäler altpolnischer Musik. Vol.32.
Tamburitta.
In: Denkmäler altpolnischer Musik. Vol.11.
JEANROY, ALFRED, 1859– . ed.
Lais et descorts français du XIIIe siècle.
In: Mélanges de musicologie critique. Vol.3.
JEEP, JOHANN, 1581–1644.
Dreistimmige Lieder.
In: Zeitschrift für Spielmusik. No.46.
Studentengärtlein. 1614.
In: Das Erbe deutscher Musik. 1.Reihe. Vol.29.
JELICH, VINCENZ, b.ca.1595.
Sechs Motetten aus Arion Primus.
In: Musik alter Meister. Heft 5.
JELINEK, JOSEPH, *see* GELINEK, JOSEPH.
JEMNITZ, ALEXANDER, 1890– .
Second sonata for violin alone.
In: New music. Vol.15. No.1. Oct.1941.
JENAER LIEDERHANDSCHRIFT.
Die Jenaer Liederhandschrift. 2v.
—— Reprint. 1966.
—— [1896] [266]p.
Die Jenaer Liederhandschrift.
In: Summa musicae medii aevi. Vol.11.
JENKINS, JOHN, 1592–1678.
Fancies and ayres.
In: The Wellesley edition. No.1, 10.
Selections.
In: Smith. Musica antiqua.
Fantasias.
In: English instrumental music of the 16th and 17th centuries from manuscripts in the New York Public Library. No.2.
7 Fantasien für 3 Gamben.
In: Hortus musicus. No.149.
Fantasy suite No.5 in C major; Fantasy suite No.4 in G major.
In: Seventeenth-century chamber music. No.4, 21.
JERSILD, JÖRGEN, 1913– .
Alice in Wonderland. A musical fairy-tale.
In: Samfundet til Udgivelse af dansk Musik. Ser.III. No.140.
JERUSALEM HIRMOLOGION SABA 83.
In: Monumenta musicae byzantinae. Série-principale. Vol.7.
JEUNE, CLAUDE LE, *see* LE JEUNE, CLAUDE.
JEWISH MUSIC.
In: Crotch. Specimens of various styles of music. Vol.1.
In: The library of the Goldmark School.
JEWSEJEFF.
Vocal music.
In: Sammlung russischer Romanzen. No.72.
JIMENEZ.
Organ music.
In: Piedelievre. Les anciens maîtres espagnols.
JIRÁNEK, ANTON, 1712–1761.
Trio in A dur. Für 2 Violinen, Violoncell und Klavier.
In: Riemann. Collegium musicum. No.15.
JÍROVEC, VOJTĚCH, *see* GYROWETZ, ADALBERT.
JOÃO IV, DON, *see* JOHN IV, KING OF PORTUGAL.
JOCELIN, SIMEON, 1746–1823.
Selections.
In: Goldman. Landmarks of early American music, 1760–1800.
JÖDE, FRITZ, 1887– .
Egon Kraus. Der Fünfton.
In: Bausteine für Musikerziehung und Musikpflege. B 123.
Der Kanon.
In: Musikalische Formen in historischen Reihen. Bd.17.
Kleine Ulfiaden. Männerloten. Der kleinen Ulfiaden andere Teil.
In: Zeitschrift für Spielmusik. No.111, 123.
Männerloten.
In: Zeitschrift für Spielmusik. No.123.
Die Musikantenfibel. (Neuausgabe).
In: Bausteine für Musikerziehung und Musikpflege. B 109.
Der Singkreisel.
In: Bausteine für Musikerziehung und Musikpflege. B 101.
JODON.
Motets.
In: Attaingnant. Treize livres de motets. Livre 13.
JOHANNES DE FLORENTIA, *see* GIOVANNI DA CASCIA (JOHANNES DE FLORENTIA).
JOHANNES DE LUBLIN, *see* JAN Z LUBLINA.
JOHANNES LE GRANT, *see* LE GRANT, JOHANNES.
JOHANNESPASSION.
In: Monumenta musicae svecicae. Vol.3.
JOHN IV, KING OF PORTUGAL, 1604–1656.
(var. sp.: Don João IV; Don Juan IV).
Selections.
In: Santos. A polifonia clássica portuguesa.

Choral music.
In: Recueil de musique ancienne. Recueil des morceaux de musique ancienne. Bd.6.
JOHN BULL VIRGINAL BOOK.
In: English keyboard music. [No.14].
JOHN OF FORNSETE, b.1239.
Selections.
In: Documenta historica musicae.
JOHNSON, EDWARD, 16th CENTURY.
Keyboard music.
In: The Fitzwilliam virginal book.
Madrigal.
In: The triumphs of Oriana.
JOHNSON, ROBERT, d.1633.
Selections.
In: Smith. Musica antiqua.
Ayres, songs, and dialogues.
In: Fellowes. The English school of lutenist song writers. 2d series. Vol.17.
Keyboard music.
In: The Fitzwilliam virginal book.
In: The Fitzwilliam virginal book. Ausgewählte Stücke. Vol.2.
JOMMELLI, NICCOLÒ, 1714–1774.
(var. sp.: Jomelli).
Selections.
In: Crotch. Specimens of various styles of music. Vol.3.
Arias.
In: Parisotti. Arie antiche. Bd.1.
Choral music.
In: Commer. Cantica sacra. Vol.1. No.15, 25.
In: Rochlitz. Sammlung vorzüglicher Gesangstücke. Bd.3.
Fetonte.
In: Denkmäler deutscher Tonkunst. [1.Folge]. Vol.32–33.
Fugue. Tune imponent.
In: Königliche Akademie der Künste. Auswahl vorzüglicher Musik-Werke. No.35.
La Passione di Gesù Cristo.
In: I classici della musica italiana. Vol.15.
In: I classici della musica italiana. Raccolta nazionale delle musiche italiane. Quad. 63–66.
Sacred music.
In: The Fitzwilliam music. Bd.3.
In: Latrobe, C. I. Selection of sacred music.
In: Latrobe, J. A. The music of the church.
Songs.
In: Musica sacra . . . 1839– . Vol.4.
Vocal music.
In: Delsarte. Archives du chant. Livr.12. No.5.
In: Gevaert. Les gloires de l'Italie. Vol.1, 2.
JONCKERS, GOESSEN, 16th CENTURY.
(var. sp.: Gossen Junckers).
Selections.
In: Maldéghem. Trésor musical.
JONES, CHARLES, 1910– .
Sonatine for violin and piano.
In: Society for the Publication of American Music. Publications. 26th season. 1944–45.
JONES, RICHARD, 18th CENTURY.
Sonate (Am). Violin and piano.
In: Moffat. Meister-Schule der alten Zeit. Violin-Sonaten. No.12.
JONES, ROBERT, 16th–17th CENTURIES.
Selections.
In: Smith. Musica antiqua.
Book of ayres.
In: Fellowes. The English school of lutenist song writers. 2d series. Vol.4, 5, 6, 14, 15.
Four duets.
In: The Tudor edition of old music. Series B. No.3.
Madrigals.
In: Euterpe. Vol.12; 2d ed., No.26.
In: Fellowes. The English madrigal school. Vol.35, pt.1.
In: The triumphs of Oriana.
JONGEN, JOSEPH, 1873–1953.
Organ music.
In: Bedell. The French organist. Vol.1, 2.
JONSSON, JOSEF, 1887– .
Selections.
In: Svensk sanglyrik. Vol.1.
Korallrevet. Op.10. Symphonic poem.
In: Musikaliska konstföreningen. 1919.
Missa Solemnis. Op.37.
In: Musikaliska konstföreningen. 1938.
JØRGENSEN, AXEL BORUP-, *see* BORUP-JØRGENSEN, AXEL.
JØRGENSEN, ERIK.
Figure in Tempo per Violoncello e Piano.
In: Samfundet til Udgivelse af dansk Musik. Ser.III. No.175.
JORIS, CORNEILLE.
Motets.
In: Attaingnant. Treize livres de motets. Livre 13.
JOSEPH I. HOLY ROMAN EMPEROR, 1678–1711.
Works.
In: Musikalische Werke der Kaiser Ferdinand III, Leopold I, und Joseph I. 2v.
JOSQUIN DES PRÈS, *see* DEPRÈS, JOSQUIN.
JOVANELLI.
Sacred music.
In: Proske. Musica divina. Annus secundus. Tom 2.
JOYE, GILLES.
Selections.
In: Marix. Les Musiciens de la cour de Bourgogne au XVe siècle. (1420–1467).
JUAN IV, *see* JOHN IV, KING OF PORTUGAL.
JUAREZ, A.
Sacred music.
In: Eslava y Elizondo. Lira sacro-hispana. 17th century. i.1.
JUATO.
Selections.
In: Pedrell. Teatro lirico espanol anterior al siglo XIX. Bd.4/5.
JUDENKÜNIG, HANS, d.ca.1526.
Keyboard music.
In: Apel. Musik aus früher Zeit für Klavier. Bd.1.
Lute music.
In: Denkmäler der Tonkunst in Österreich. Vol.37. (Jg.XVIII/2).
JULIÁ, B.
Sacred music.

In: Eslava y Elizondo. Lira sacro-hispana. 18th century. i.1.
JULLIEN, GILLES, d.1703.
Organ music.
In: Raugel. Les maîtres français de l'orgue. Vol.1.
In: Raugel. Les maîtres français de l'orgue aus XVIIème et XVIIIème siècles.
In: Société Française de Musicologie, Paris. Publications. Ser.I. Bd.13.
JUMIÈGES, FRANCE–MUSIC.
In: Monumenta musicae sacrae. Vol.2.
JUNCKERS, GOSSEN, *see* JONCKERS, GOESSEN.
JURAFSKY, ABRAHAMA.
Vocal music.
In: Boletín latino-americano de música. Vol.4.

KAESTNER.
Das erste Spiel auf der Schulflöte.
In: Bausteine für Musikerziehung und Musikpflege. B 108.
KAHL, WILLI, 1893– .
The character piece.
In: Anthology of music. Vol.8.
KAINZ, WALTER.
Sonatine in E.
In: Marckhl. Klavierwerke steiermärkischer Komponisten. Vol.2.
KALABIN.
Vocal music.
In: Sammlung russischer Romanzen. No.285.
KALDENBACH, CHRISTOPH, 1613–1698.
Preussische Festlieder.
In: Das Erbe deutscher Musik. 2.Reihe. Ostpreussen und Danzig. Vol.1.
KALKBRENNER, AUG.
Short Troop.
In: Thouret. Musik am preussischen Hofe. No.10.
KALKBRENNER, FRIEDRICH WILHELM MICHAEL, 1785–1849.
Keyboard music.
In: Tagliapietra. Antologia di musica antica e moderna per pianoforte. Bd.15.
KALLSTENIUS, EDVIN, 1881– .
Selections.
In: Svensk sanglyrik. Vol.1.
KAMMEIER, HANS.
Quartettino.
In: Zeitschrift für Spielmusik. No.233.
KAMMEL, E.
Serenate Boeme.
In: Musica antiqua bohemica. Vol.35.
KAPSBERGER, JOHANN HIERONYMUS, d.ca. 1640.
(var. sp.: G. H. Kapsperger).
Airs.
In: Prunières. Les maîtres du chant. Recueil 3.
KARG-ELERT, SIGFRID, 1877–1933.
Organ music.
In: Standard series of organ compositions. No.1, 3, 7, 10, 27.
KARGES, WILHELM, 17th–18th CENTURIES.
Organ music.
In: Organum. 4.Reihe. Nr.21.
KARL II.
Netherland and Italian musicians of the Graz court orchestra of Karl II, 1564–1590.
In: Denkmäler der Tonkunst in Österreich. Vol.90.
KAROW, C.
Organ music.
In: Caecilia; Sammlung von Choralvorspielen.
KÄSTNER, JEAN GEORGES, 1810–1867.
Psalmen.
In: Musica sacra . . . ca.1842–1896. Vol.8–10.
KAUDER, HUGO, 1888– .
Quartet for oboe, clarinet, horn, and bassoon.
In: New music. Vol.22. No.3. Apr.1949.
KAUFFMANN, GEORG FRIEDRICH, 1679–1735.
(var. sp.: G. F. Kaufmann).
Organ music.
In: Das Erbe deutscher Musik. 1.Reihe. Vol.9.
In: Keller. Achtzig Choralvorspiele deutscher Meister des 17. und 18. Jahrhunderts.
In: Klein. The first four centuries of music for the organ from Dunstable to Bach (1370–1749).
In: The Liturgical Music Press, Inc. Masterpieces of organ music. Folio 17, 18.
In: Muziek voor de eredienst. Vol.1.
In: The parish organist. Vol.1–4, 5–6.
KAUFMANN, ARMIN, 1902– .
Drei Stücke, Violoncello und Klavier.
In: Hausmusik. No.140.
KAUFMANN, GEORG FRIEDRICH, *see* KAUFFMANN, GEORG FRIEDRICH.
KAY, ULYSSES SIMPSON, 1917– .
Two meditations. Organ.
In: Contemporary organ series. No.27.
KAYSER, LEIF, 1919– .
Kong Kristian Stod. Koncertouverture. Op.5.
In: Samfundet til Udgivelse af dansk Musik. Ser.III. No.114.
3 Salmi per contralto solo e organo.
In: Samfundet til Udgivelse af dansk Musik. Ser.III. No.137.
KECZER, ANNA SZIRMAY–, *see* SZIRMAY-KECZER, ANNA.
KEEBLE, JOHN, 1711–1786.
Organ music.
In: Butcher. English organ music of the eighteenth century. Vol.2.
In: Tallis to Wesley. Vol.22.
KEHRER, A.
Organ music.
In: Caecilia; Sammlung von Choralvorspielen.
KEISER, REINHARD, 1674–1739.
Selections.
In: Leichtentritt. Deutsche Hausmusik aus vier Jahrhunderten.
Aria from Croesus. "Hoffe noch."
In: Parrish. A treasury of early music. No.46.
Cantata.
In: Eitner. Cantaten des 17. und 18. Jahrhunderts. Pt.1.
Duette alter Meister.
In: Zeitschrift für Spielmusik. No.69.
Fugue, Gott ist Offenbaret, Kyrie.

In: Königliche Akademie der Künste. Auswahl vorzüglicher Musik-Werke. No.13, 14.
"Krösus" and selection from "L'inganno felice".
In: Denkmäler deutscher Tonkunst. [1.Folge]. Vol.37–38.
Der lächerliche Prinz Jodelet.
In: Publikationen älterer praktischer und theoretischer Musikwerke. Jahrg.21–22.
Lied.
In: Reimann. Das deutsche Lied. Vol.1.
Sonata a tre.
In: Nagels Musik-Archiv. No.68, 114, 132.
Weihnachtspastoralen.
In: Zeitschrift für Spielmusik. No.236.
KELLER, H.
Fantasy and fugue. Organ.
In: Contemporary organ series. No.22.
KELLER, HEINRICH MICHAEL, 1638–1710.
Organ music.
In: Das Erbe deutscher Musik. 1.Reihe. Vol.9.
KELLER, WILHELM, 1920– .
Kleine Vogelpredigt für 3 Blockflöten oder andere hohe Blasinstrumente.
In: Zeitschrift für Spielmusik. No.204.
Quibus, quabus.
In: Bausteine für Musikerziehung und Musikpflege. B 124.
KELLEY, EDGAR STILLMAN, 1857–1944.
Songs.
In: The Wa-Wan series of American compositions.
KELLNER, JOHANN PETER, 1705–1772.
Ausgewählte Orgelwerke.
In: Die Orgel. Reihe II. Nr.7.
Organ music.
In: Straube. Choralvorspiele alter Meister.
KELZ, MATTHIAS, 17th CENTURY.
Fugue for 4tet in C.
In: Königliche Akademie der Künste. Auswahl vorzüglicher Musik-Werke. No.27.
KEMPIS, NICOLAUS À, 17th CENTURY.
Chamber music.
In: Riemann. Old chamber music. Vol.4.
KENT, JAMES, 1700–1776.
Sacred music.
In: Arnold. Cathedral music. Vol.1, 3.
In: Page. Harmonia sacra. Vol.1.
KERCKHOVEN, ABRAHAM VAN DEN, 17th CENTURY.
Werken voor orgel.
In: Monumenta musicae belgicae. Vol.2.
Organ music.
In: Peeters. Altniederländische Meister für Orgel oder Harmonium.
In: Peeters. Anthologia pro organo. Vol.1, 3.
In: Peeters. Oudnederlandse meesters. Vol.1, 2, 3.
KERLE, JACOBUS DE, 1531/32–1591.
(var. sp.: Gaspard de Kerl; Jacob de Kerle).
Selected works. Pt.1.
In: Denkmäler deutscher Tonkunst. [2.Folge]. Vol.26.
Selections.
In: Maldéghem. Trésor musical.
Choral music.
In: Antiqua Chorbuch. Vol.1. Heft 2.
Keyboard music.
? In: Farrenc. Le trésor des pianistes. Vol.3.
Sacred music.
In: Proske. Musica divina. Annus primus. Tom 2.
KERLL, JOHANN CASPAR, 1627–1693.
(var. sp.: Johann Kaspar Kerll; Kerl).
Selected works.
In: Denkmäler deutscher Tonkunst. [2.Folge]. Vol.2 (ii).
Keyboard music.
In: Oesterle. Early keyboard music. Vol.1.
? In: Pauer. Alte Klavier-Musik. 1st series. Pt.3.
In: Tagliapietra. Antologia di musica antica e moderna per pianoforte. Bd.7.
Masses.
In: Denkmäler der Tonkunst in Österreich. Vol.49. (Jg.XXV/1).
Missa superba.
In: Recent researches in the music of the Baroque era. Vol.3.
Organ music.
In: Auler. Spielbuch für Kleinorgel. Vol.1.
In: Cantantibus organis. Vol.2.
In: Guilmant. École classique de l'orgue. No.12.
In: Klein. The first four centuries of music for the organ from Dunstable to Bach (1370–1749).
In: The Liturgical Music Press, Inc. Masterpieces of organ music. Folio 10, 60.
In: Pierront. Cent versets de magnificat.
In: Straube. Alte Meister.
In: Straube. Alte Meister des Orgelspiels.
Requiem.
In: Denkmäler der Tonkunst in Österreich. Vol.59. (Jg.XXX.1).
KERN, FRIDA.
Tierbilder; fünf Stücke für Klavier. Op.54.
In: Hausmusik. No.116.
KERR, HARRISON, 1899– .
Música de cámara.
In: Boletín latino-americano de música. Vol.5.
Notations on a sensitized plate, for voice, clarinet, string quartet and piano.
In: New music. Orchestra series. No.25.
Study for violoncello (unacc.).
In: New music. Vol.14. No.3. Apr.1941.
Trio, for clarinet, violoncello and piano.
In: New music. Vol.13. No.3. Apr.1940.
KESSLER, JOSEPH CHRISTOPH, 1800–1872.
Keyboard music.
In: Tagliapietra. Antologia di musica antica e moderna per pianoforte. Bd.15.
KEUTZENHOFF, JOHANNES.
Motetten.
In: Das Chorwerk. No.69.
KEWITSCH, THEODOR.
Preussischer Armeemarsch.
In: Thouret. Musik am preussischen Hofe. No.17.
KEYBOARD MUSIC OF THE FOURTEENTH AND FIFTEENTH CENTURIES. (W. APEL).
In: Corpus of early keyboard music. Vol.1.

KEYBOARD MUSIC–CLAVICHORD, HARPSICHORD, PIANO, VIRGINAL.
See also keyboard works in the various Denkmäler series.
See also keyboard works in the various Das Erbe deutscher Musik series.
In: Anthology of music. Vol.1.
In: Apel. Musik aus früher Zeit für Klavier.
In: Attaingnant. Transcriptions of chansons for keyboard.
In: Bach, C. P. E. Die sechs Sammlungen von Sonaten, Freien Fantasien und Rondos für Kenner und Liebhaber.
In: Bach, J. S. Klavierwerke.
In: Bach, J. S. Klavierübung.
In: Balakirev. Complete piano works.
In: Beethoven. Klavierstücke.
In: Bègue. Oeuvres de clavecin.
In: Benvenuti. Cembalisti italiani del settecento.
In: Boghen. Antichi maestri italiani.
In: Böhm. Sämtliche Werke. Klavier- und Orgelwerke.
In: Brahms. Klavierwerke.
In: Brahms. Piano works.
In: Brunold. Anthologie des maîtres français du clavecin des XVIIe et XVIIIe siècles.
In: Buchmayer. Aus Richard Buchmayers historischen Klavierkonzerten.
In: Byrd. Forty-five pieces for keyboard instruments.
In: Byrd. My Ladye Nevells booke.
In: Chilesotti. Biblioteca di rarità musicali.
In: Chopin. Complete works for the piano.
In: Chopin. Sämtliche Werke. 3v.
In: Chopin. Sämtliche Werke. Neue Ausgabe. 12v.
In: I classici della musica italiana. Vol.8, 11, 18, 22, 27, 28, 29, 31, 33, 36.
In: I classici della musica italiana. Raccolta nazionale delle musiche italiane. Quad.40, 42, 303, 72–75, 85, 88, 114–119, 304–305, 126–130, 176–181, 266–267, 276–281, 284, 286–288.
In: I classici musicali italiani. Vol.3, 4, 11, 12, 13.
In: Clavecinistes flamands.
In: Clementi. Clementi's Selection of practical harmony.
In: Clementi. Works for pianoforte.
In: Contemporary British piano music.
In: Contemporary Japanese music series. No.10, 11, 14, 25, 26, 29.
In: Corpus of early keyboard music.
In: Couperin, F. Pièces de clavecin.
In: Couperin, L. Pièces de clavecin.
In: Dargomizhsky. Complete piano works.
In: Early Italian keyboard music.
In: Eckard. Oeuvres complètes pour le clavecin ou le pianoforte.
In: Elizabethan virginal composers.
In: English keyboard music.
In: Esposito. Early Italian piano music.
In: Farrenc. Le trésor des pianistes.
In: Fischer. Sämtliche Werke für Klavier und Orgel.
In: The Fitzwilliam virginal book.
In: The Fitzwilliam virginal book. Ausgewählte Stücke.
In: Frescobaldi. Orgel- und Klavierwerke.
In: Fuller-Maitland. The contemporaries of Purcell.
In: Fuller-Maitland. Twenty-five pieces for keyed instruments from Benjamin Cosyn's virginal book.
In: Georgii. Keyboard music of the Baroque and Rococo.
In: Gibbons. Complete keyboard works.
In: Gibbons. Ten pieces arranged for modern organ from the virginal book of Benjamin Cosyn.
In: Glinka. Complete works for piano solo and piano 4 hands.
In: Glyn. Twenty-one old English compositions of the 16th and 17th centuries.
In: Grieg. Sämtliche Klavierwerke.
In: Grovlez. Les plus belles pièces de clavessin de l'école française.
In: Guenther. Collection espagnole.
In: Händel. Kompositionen für Klavier.
In: Händel. The vocal works . . . arr. for the organ or pianoforte.
In: Hausmusik (passim).
In: Haydn. Sämtliche Klavierwerke.
In: Herrmann. Contemporaries of Purcell.
In: Herrmann. Klaviermusik des 17. und 18. Jahrhunderts.
In: Herrmann. Lehrmeister und Schüler Joh. Seb. Bachs.
In: Jeppesen. Balli antichi Veneziano per cembalo.
In: Kastner. Alt-italienische Versetten.
In: Kastner. Cravistas portuguezes.
In: Kastner. Silva iberica.
In: Köhler. Les maîtres du clavecin.
In: Liszt. Werke für Klavier.
In: Marckhl. Klavierwerke steiermärkischer Komponisten.
In: Mendelssohn-Bartholdy. Complete piano works.
In: Mendelssohn-Bartholdy. Sämtliche Klavierwerke.
In: Mitteldeutsches Musikarchiv. Reihe I.
In: Monumenta musica neerlandica. Vol.3.
In: Monumenta musicae belgicae.
In: Monumenti di musica italiana. Ser.I.
In: Moscheles. Collection complète des oeuvres composés pour le piano.
In: Mozart. Werke für Klavier.
In: Musica Britannica. Vol.5, 14, 19.
In: Musica hungarica.
In: Musical Antiquarian Society. Publications. Vol.18.
In: Musik in Goethes Haus. Vol.1.
In: Nagels Musik-Archiv. No.3.
In: New music (passim).
In: Newman. Thirteen keyboard sonatas of the 18th and 19th centuries.
In: Nin y Castellano. Dix-sept sonates et pièces anciennes d'auteurs espagnols.
In: Nin y Castellano. Seize sonates anciennes d'auteurs espagnols.
In: Oberdörffer. Deutsche Klaviermusik des 17. und 18. Jahrhunderts.
In: Oesterle. Early keyboard music.
In: Organum. 5.Reihe.

In: Paoli. Sonate italiane del secolo XVIII per cembalo o pianoforte.
In: Parthenia.
In: Parthenia in-Violata.
In: Pauer. Alte Klavier-Musik.
In: Pauer. Alte Meister.
In: Pauer. Old English composers for the virginals and harpsichord.
In: Pessl. The art of the suite.
In: Purcell. Suites, lessons, and pieces for the harpsichord.
In: Rameau. Pièces de clavecin.
In: Reeser. De klaviersonate.
In: Rehberg. Alte Hausmusik für Klavier (1550–1780).
In: Repertoire des clavecinistes. Repertoire des clavecinistes.
In: Roitzsch. Alte Klavier-Musik.
In: Roux. Pieces for harpsichord.
In: Scarlatti, D. Opere complete per clavicembalo.
In: Scheidt. Ausgewählte Werke für Orgel und Klavier.
In: Scheidt. Das Görlitzer Tabulaturbuch vom Jahre 1650.
In: Schott's Anthology of early keyboard music.
In: Schubert. Klavier-Werke.
In: Schubert. Werke für Klavier.
In: Schumann. Complete works for piano solo.
In: Schumann. Sämtliche Werke für Klavier.
In: Selva. Pièces de clavecin des XVIIme et XVIIIme siècles.
In: Skriabin. Complete piano works.
In: Société Française de Musicologie, Paris. Publications. Ser.I. Bd.8–9, 11–12.
In: Sweelinck. Ausgewählte Werke für Orgel und Klavier.
In: Tagliapietra. Antologia di musica antica e moderna per pianoforte.
In: Tallis. Complete keyboard works.
In: Tchaikovskiĭ. Ausgewählte Klavierwerke.
In: Tchaikovskiĭ. Werke für Klavier.
In: Tisdall. Complete keyboard works.
In: Vereniging voor Nederlandsche Muziekgeschiedenis. Uitgave. No.32, 37.
In: The Wa-Wan series of American compositions.
In: Weber. Sämtliche Werke für Pianoforte.
In: The Wellesley edition. No.3.

KEYBOARD MUSIC–ORGAN.
See also keyboard works in the various Denkmäler series.
See also keyboard works in the various Das Erbe deutscher Musik series.
In: Alain. L'oeuvre d'orgue.
In: Annibale Padovano. Ricercari.
In: Anthologia antiqua.
In: Auler. Spielbuch für Kleinorgel.
In: Bach, J. S. Johann Sebastian Bach's Compositionen für die Orgel.
In: Bach, J. S. Complete organ works. 10v.
In: Bach, J. S. Complete organ works. 8v.
In: Bach, J. S. Oeuvres complètes pour orgue.
In: Bach, W. F. Complete works for organ.
In: Bedell. The French organist.
In: Biggs. Treasury of early organ music.
In: Biggs. A treasury of shorter organ classics.
In: Blow. Complete organ works.
In: Böhm. Sämtliche Werke. Klavier- und Orgelwerke.
In: Bonnet. An anthology of early French organ music.
In: Bonnet. Historical organ-recitals.
In: Bossi. Ausgewählte Kompositionen für die Orgel.
In: Bossi. Sammlung von Stücken alter italienischer Meister für die moderne Orgel.
In: Brahms. Complete organ works.
In: Brahms. The organ works.
In: Bruhns. Complete organ works.
In: Buchner. Fundamentbuch.
In: Buszin. Organ series.
In: Butcher. English organ music of the eighteenth century.
In: Buxheimer Orgelbuch. Das Buxheimer Orgelbuch.
In: Buxtehude. Orgelcompositionen.
In: Buxtehude. Orgelwerke.
In: Buxtehude. Ausgewählte Orgelwerke.
In: Cabanilles. Opera selecta pro organo.
In: Caecilia.
In: Cantantibus organis.
In: I classici della musica italiana. Vol.6, 12, 26, 36.
In: I classici della musica italiana. Raccolta nazionale delle musiche italiane. Quad.23–27, 43–47, 70–71, 110–113, 145–150.
In: I classici musicali italiani. Vol.1.
In: Clementi. Clementi's Selection of practical harmony.
In: Commer. Compositionen für Orgel aus dem 16., 17., und 18. Jahrhundert.
In: Contemporary organ series.
In: David. Choralwerk.
In: Dickinson. Historical recital series for organ.
In: Dietrich. Elf Orgelchoräle des siebzehnten Jahrhunderts.
In: Du Mage. Livre d'orgue.
In: Elkan-Vogel organ series.
In: Eslava y Elizondo. Museo orgánico español.
In: Fischer. Sämtliche Werke für Klavier und Orgel.
In: Franck. Oeuvres complètes pour orgue. n.d. 4v.
In: Franck. Oeuvres complètes pour orgue. cop. 1955– . 4v.
In: Franck. The organ works. 6v.
In: Franck. Orgelwerke. 4v.
In: Frescobaldi. Ausgewählte Orgelwerke. 2v.
In: Frescobaldi. Ausgewählte Orgelsätze. 2v.
In: Frescobaldi. Fiori musicali.
In: Frescobaldi. Orgel- und Klavierwerke.
In: Froidebise. Anthologie de l'orgue.
In: Fuser. Classici italiani dell' organo.
In: Gerhardt. Album nordischer Komponisten für Orgel.
In: Gibbons. Ten pieces arranged for modern organ from the virginal book of Benjamin Cosyn.
In: Grigny. Premier livre d'orgue.
In: Guilmant. Archives des maîtres de l'orgue des XVIe et XVIIe et XVIIIe siècles.
In: Guilmant. Concert historique d'orgue.
In: Guilmant. École classique de l'orgue.

In: Händel. The vocal works . . . arr. for the organ or pianoforte.
In: Hofhaimer. Einundneunzig gesammelte Tonsätze.
In: Jeppesen. Die italienische Orgelmusik am Anfang des Cinquecento.
In: Keller. Achtzig Choralvorspiele deutscher Meister des 17. und 18. Jahrhunderts.
In: Keller. Orgelvorspiele.
In: Klein. The first four centuries of music for the organ from Dunstable to Bach (1370–1749).
In: Krebs. Gesammt-Ausgabe der Tonstücke für Orgel.
In: Krebs. Orgelwerke.
In: Krieger. Ausgewählte Orgelstücke.
In: Liber organi.
In: Liszt. Orgelkompositionen.
In: The Liturgical Music Press, Inc. Commemoration folio.
In: The Liturgical Music Press, Inc. Masterpieces of organ music.
In: Das Locheimer Liederbuch. Das Locheimer Liederbuch.
In: Lübeck. Orgelwerke.
In: Martini. 20 composizioni originali per organo.
In: Mendelssohn-Bartholdy. Complete organ works.
In: Monumenta leodiensium musicorum. Vol.1.
In: Monumenta musicae belgicae.
In: Monumenti di musica italiana. Ser.I.
In: Moser. Frühmeister der deutschen Orgelkunst.
In: Muffat. Apparatus musico-organisticus.
In: Muset. Early Spanish organ music.
In: Musica sacra . . . 1839– . v.1– .
In: Musica sacra . . . [cop.1931–1932] 2v.
In: Musik alter Meister. Heft 9.
In: Musikalische Denkmäler. Bd.3.
In: Muziek voor de eredienst.
In: Organ album of ten pieces by Spanish composers.
In: Organ masters of the Baroque period.
In: Organum. 4.Reihe.
In: Die Orgel.
In: Orgelmusik steirischer Komponisten.
In: Orgelwerke. Altböhmischer Meister.
In: Orgue et liturgie.
In: The parish organist.
In: Pedrell. Antología de organistas clásicos españoles (siglos XVI, XVII y XVIII).
In: Peeters. Altniederländische Meister für Orgel oder Harmonium.
In: Peeters. Anthologia pro organo.
In: Peeters. Oudnederlandse meesters.
In: Piedelievre. Les anciens maîtres espagnols.
In: Pierront. Cent versets de magnificat.
In: Plainsong and Mediaeval Music Society. Publications. (Glyn).
In: Praetorius. Sämtliche Orgelwerke.
In: Purcell. Organ works.
In: Raugel. 46 pieces pour orgue.
In: Raugel. Les maîtres français de l'orgue aus XVIIème et XVIIIème siècles. [1925?] and [cop.1951].
In: Raugel. Quarante-six pièces pour orgue ou harmonium d'anciens auteurs.
In: Recent researches in the music of the Baroque era. Vol.2.
In: Rohr. Orgelspiel im Kirchenjahr.
In: Roseingrave. Fifteen voluntaries & fugues for the organ.
In: Scheidt. Ausgewählte Werke für Orgel und Klavier.
In: Scheidt. Das Görlitzer Tabulaturbuch vom Jahre 1650.
In: Schering. Alte Meister aus der Frühzeit des Orgelspiels.
In: Schlick. Spiegel der Orgelmacher und Organisten.
In: Schlick. Tabulaturen etlicher Lobgesang und Lidlein uff die Orgeln und Lauten.
In: Schweiger. A brief compendium of early organ music.
In: Shannon. The free organ compositions from the Lueneburg organ tablatures.
In: Société Française de Musicologie, Paris. Publications. Ser.I. Bd.1, 5, 13, 14; Ser.2. Bd.5–6.
In: Staatliche Akademie für Kirchen- und Schulmusik, Berlin. Veröffentlichungen. [Nr.] 1.
In: Standard series of organ compositions.
In: Stanley. Voluntaries for the organ.
In: Straube. Alte Meister.
In: Straube. Alte Meister des Orgelspiels.
In: Straube. Choralvorspiele alter Meister.
In: Sweelinck. Ausgewählte Werke für Orgel und Klavier.
In: Tallis to Wesley.
In: Tappert. Sang und Klang aus alter Zeit.
In: Telemann. Zwölf leichte Choralvorspiele, für Orgel.
In: Vereniging voor Nederlandsche Muziekgeschiedenis. Uitgave. No.3, 47.
In: West. Old English organ music.

KEYBOARD MUSIC–PIANO, 4 HANDS.
In: I classici della musica italiana. Vol.16.
In: I classici della musica italiana. Raccolta nazionale delle musiche italiane. Quad.155–156, 205.
In: Glinka. Complete works for piano solo and piano 4 hands.
In: Vereniging voor nederlandsche Muziekgeschiedenis. Uitgave. No.10, 21, 25, 27.

KHACHATURIAN, ARAM ILYICH, 1903– .
Dance, No.3. Piano.
In: New music. Vol.8. No.1. Oct.1934.

KICKSTAT, PAUL, 1893– .
Organ music.
In: The parish organist. Vol.5–6.

KILLMAYER, WILHELM, 1927– .
Balletto.
In: Zeitschrift für Spielmusik. No.245.

KIMBALL, JACOB, JR., 1761–1826.
Selections.
In: Goldman. Landmarks of early American music, 1760–1800.
Down east spirituals.
In: Music Press, Inc. [Choral series]. Vol.122.

KINDERMANN, JOHANN ERASMUS, 1616–1655.
Selected works.
In: Denkmäler deutscher Tonkunst. [2.Folge]. Vol.13, 21–24.
Choral music.

In: Chorbuch für die Kirchenchöre Sachsens.
Keyboard music.
In: Apel. Musik aus früher Zeit für Klavier. Bd.1.
In: Tagliapietra. Antologia di musica antica e moderna per pianoforte. Bd.7.
Organ music.
In: Keller. Achtzig Choralvorspiele deutscher Meister des 17. und 18. Jahrhunderts.
In: Klein. The first four centuries of music for the organ from Dunstable to Bach (1370–1749).
In: The parish organist. Vol.1–4.
Sonetta und zwei Arien für drei Blockflöten.
In: Musica practica. No.43.
Tanzstücke für Klavier. (Cembalo, Clavichord oder andere Tasteninstrumente).
In: Hortus musicus. No.61.
KING, CHARLES, 1687–1748.
Part music.
In: Hullah. Part music. Class B.1.
Sacred music.
In: Arnold. Cathedral music. Vol.1, 2, 3.
In: Page. Harmonia sacra. Vol.1, 2.
KING, ROBERT, 17th CENTURY.
Harpsichord music.
In: Fuller-Maitland. The contemporaries of Purcell. Vol.6–7.
KINLOCH, WILLIAM.
Keyboard music.
In: English keyboard music. [No.15].
KIRBYE, GEORGE, d.1634.
Anthems and motets.
In: Arkwright. The Old English edition. Vol.21.
Madrigals.
In: Arkwright. The Old English edition. Vol.3–5.
In: Fellowes. The English madrigal school. Vol.24.
In: The triumphs of Oriana.
KIRCHHOFF, GOTTFRIED, 1685–1746.
Kantaten.
In: Das Erbe deutscher Musik. 1.Reihe. Vol.35.
Piano music.
In: Nagels Musik-Archiv. No.3.
KIRMSSE, HERBERT.
Divertimento zu 3 Stimmen.
In: Zeitschrift für Spielmusik. No.221.
KIRNBERGER, JOHANN PHILIPP, 1721–1783.
Driestimmige Fuge. (Dm). Zweistimmige Fuge. (Dm).
In: Pauer. Alte Meister. No.2, 3.
Fugue for piano, B flat.
In: Königliche Akademie der Künste. Auswahl vorzüglicher Musik-Werke. No.9.
Keyboard music.
In: Clementi. Clementi's Selection of practical harmony. Vol.1.
In: Farrenc. Le trésor des pianistes. Vol.14.
In: Herrmann. Lehrmeister und Schüler Joh. Seb. Bachs. Vol.2.
In: Köhler. Les maîtres du clavecin. Heft 6.
In: Pauer. Alte Klavier-Musik. 1st series. Pt.5.
In: Tagliapietra. Antologia di musica antica e moderna per pianoforte. Bd.13.
Lied.
In: Reimann. Das deutsche Lied. Vol.2.
Motetten.
In: Das Chorwerk. No.89.
Organ music.
In: Guilmant. École classique de l'orgue. No.19.
In: Die Orgel. Reihe II. Nr.14.
In: Rohr. Orgelspiel im Kirchenjahr.
Prelude and fugue in C sharp minor. Piano.
In: Roitzsch. Alte Klavier-Musik.
Recueil d'Airs de Danse caractéristiques.
In: Zeitschrift für Spielmusik. No.270.
KITTEL, JOHANN CHRISTIAN, 1732–1809.
Organ music.
In: Caecilia; Sammlung von Choralvorspielen.
KITTL, JAN BEDŘICH.
Symfonie Es dur.
In: Documenta historica musicae.
KITTLER, RICHARD.
Sonate für Flöte und Klavier.
In: Hausmusik. No.186.
KJERULF, HALFDAN, 1815–1868.
Keyboard music.
In: Tagliapietra. Antologia di musica antica e moderna per pianoforte. Bd.16.
KLAUSS, V.
Organ music.
In: Caecilia; Sammlung von Choralvorspielen.
KLEBER, LEONHARD, ca.1490–1556.
Keyboard music.
In: Apel. Musik aus früher Zeit für Klavier. Bd.1.
Organ music.
In: Froidebise. Anthologie de l'orgue. Vol.1.
In: Moser. Frühmeister der deutschen Orgelkunst.
KLEIN, BERNHARD, 1793–1832.
Ave Maria.
In: Königliche Akademie der Künste. Auswahl vorzüglicher Musik-Werke. No.38.
Lied.
In: Reimann. Das deutsche Lied. Vol.2.
Part music.
In: Hullah. Part music. 1868 edition.
Vocal music.
In: Hullah. Vocal scores. I. Sacred.
KLEIN, RICHARD RUDOLF.
Das Bauernjahr.
In: Bausteine für Musikerziehung und Musikpflege. B 112.
Lobe den Herren.
In: Christophorus-Chorwerk. Heft 21.
Sieben geistliche Chorlieder.
In: Christophorus-Chorwerk. Heft 29.
Tänze und Spielweisen.
In: Zeitschrift für Spielmusik. No.232.
KLEMM.
Vocal music.
In: Sammlung russischer Romanzen. No.277, 282.
KLIMOFFSKY.
Vocal music.
In: Sammlung russischer Romanzen. No.103, 103a.
KLINGENBERG, FRIEDRICH GOTTLIEB, 17th CENTURY.

Hochzeitsarien und Kantaten.
In: Das Erbe deutscher Musik. 2.Reihe. Mecklenburg und Pommern. Vol.1.
KLINT, F. W.
String quartet, Op.25, No.2, A major.
In: Musikaliska konstföreningen. 1882.
KLOSTERNEUBURG MONASTERY.
Compositions.
In: Zagiba. Die ältesten musikalischen Denkmäler zu Ehren des heiligen Leopold, Herzog und Patron von Österreich.
KLOTZ, HANS, 1900– .
Organ music.
In: The parish organist. Vol.1–4.
KNAPP, ARNO, 1913–1957.
Concertino für Klavier und Streichorchester.
In: Collegium musicae novae. No.4.
Neue Suite zu dritt.
In: Zeitschrift für Spielmusik. No.278.
Suite zu dritt.
In: Zeitschrift für Spielmusik. No.196.
KNAPP, JANET. ed.
An anthology of polyphonic conductus.
In: Collegium musicum. [Vol.7].
KNECHT, JUSTIN HEINRICH, 1752–1817.
Organ music.
In: Caecilia; Sammlung von Choralvorspielen.
KNEFFEL, JOHANNES, 16th CENTURY.
(var. sp.: Knefel, Knöfel, Knöffel, Knofelius).
Chorlieder.
In: Christophorus-Chorwerk. Heft 5.
KNELLER, ANDREAS, 1649–1724.
Organ music.
In: Organum. 4.Reihe. Nr.7.
KNILLER, ANTON.
Organ music.
In: Straube. Choralvorspiele alter Meister.
KNÖFEL, JOHANN, *see* KNEFFEL, JOHANNES.
KNORR, ERNST LOTHAR VON, 1896– .
Choral music.
In: Nagels Männerchor-Blätter. No.5, 13, 23, 28.
KNOWLTON, FANNY SNOW, 1859–1926.
Song.
In: The Wa-Wan series of American compositions.
KNÜPFER, SEBASTIAN, 1632–1676.
Church cantatas.
In: Denkmäler deutscher Tonkunst. [1.Folge]. Vol.58–59.
KOCH, ERLAND VON, 1910– .
Selections.
In: Svensk sanglyrik. Vol.2.
String quartet, No.2, Op.28.
In: Musikaliska konstföreningen. 1946.
KOCH, JOHANNES HERMANN ERNST, 1918– .
Capriccio für 3 Blockflöten oder andere Instrumente.
In: Zeitschrift für Spielmusik. No.211.
Choral music.
In: Nagels Männerchor-Blätter. No.31.
KOCH, SIGURD VON, 1879–1919.
Selections.
In: Svensk sanglyrik. Vol.1.
KOCH-BEDELL.
Organ music.
In: Standard series of organ compositions. No.46.
KODÁLY, ZOLTÁN, 1882–1967.
Keyboard music.
In: Musica hungarica.
Ungarische Volksweisen.
In: Zeitschrift für Spielmusik. No.152.
KOELLREUTTER, H. J., 1915– .
Música 1941. (Piano).
In: Instituto Interamericano de Musicologia. Publicaciónes. No.14.
KOERPPEN, ALFRED, *see* KÖRPPEN, ALFRED.
KÖGLER, WALTER.
Choralfantasie über "O Haupt voll Blut und Wunden." Organ.
In: Orgelmusik steirischer Komponisten.
KOHAUT, CARL.
Concerto in F-dur für Laute, 2 Violinen, und Violoncello.
In: Musikschätze der Vergangenheit.
KOHS, ELLIS, 1916– .
Passacaglia. (Organ and piano duet).
In: Contemporary organ series. No.26.
KOLB, GEORG.
Preussische Festlieder.
In: Das Erbe deutscher Musik. 2.Reihe. Ostpreussen und Danzig. Vol.1.
KOLB, KARLMANN, 1703–1765.
Organ music.
In: Cantantibus organis. Vol.3.
In: The Liturgical Music Press, Inc. Masterpieces of organ music. Folio 45.
KÖLER, DAVID, d.1565.
Selections.
In: Ambros. Auserwählte Tonwerke.
Drei deutsche Psalmen.
In: Das Chorwerk. No.71.
KÖLN, ANNA VON, *see* ANNA VON KÖLN.
KÖLZ, ERNST.
Kleine Spielmusik für zwei Blockflöten.
In: Hausmusik. No.97.
KOMITAS KEVORKIAN, *VARTABED*, 1869–1935.
Collected works. Vol.1– .
KÖNIGSPERGER, MARIAN, 1708–1769.
Organ music.
In: Cantantibus organis. Vol.1, 5.
KONINK, SERVAAS VAN, 17th–18th CENTURIES.
Sonata IX, VII, X, für Alt-Blockflöte und Basso Continuo.
In: Moecks Kammermusik. Vol.4, 8.
KONTSKY.
Vocal music.
In: Sammlung russischer Romanzen. No.120, 121.
KOPPEL, HERMAN DAVID, 1908– .
Concertino No.2 for Strygeorkester. Op.66.
In: Samfundet til Udgivelse af dansk Musik. Ser.III. No.151.
Divertimento pastorale. For Obo, Viola og Violoncel. Op.61.
In: Samfundet til Udgivelse af dansk Musik. Ser.III. No.131.
Fest-Orkester. Op.33.
In: Samfundet til Udgivelse af dansk Musik. Ser.III. No.94.

Strygekvartet No.2. Op.34.
In: Samfundet til Udgivelse af dansk Musik. Ser.III. No.72.
Suite for Klaver. Op.21.
In: Samfundet til Udgivelse af dansk Musik. Ser.III. No.47.
KOPPEL, THOMAS.
Quartetto d'archi No.2, Op.12.
In: Samfundet til Udgivelse af dansk Musik. Ser.III. No.171.
KOPRŽIWA, KARL, 1756–1785.
(var. sp.: Karel Blazej Kopřiva, C. Kopřiwa).
Fugue As, F-moll. Organ.
In: Guilmant. École classique de l'orgue. No.13.
Organ.
In: Musica antiqua bohemica. Vol.12.
KOPRZYWNICA, HIERONIM VON.
Veni Sancte Spiritus.
In: Florilegium musicae antiquae. Vol.4.
KORDA, VICTOR, 1900– .
Vier Feiermusiken.
In: Hausmusik. No.160.
Flieg her, flieg hin; Variationen über ein altes Dragonerlied.
In: Zeitschrift für Spielmusik. No.117, 121.
Serenade für Mandolinenorchester; Wir lernen Hausmusik.
In: Hausmusik. No.57, 58.
Suite im alten Stil.
In: Zeitschrift für Spielmusik. No.36.
10 leichte Volksliedsätze.
In: Zeitschrift für Spielmusik. No.10.
KÖRLING, A.
Håtunaleken.
In: Musikaliska konstföreningen. 1896.
KORNAUTH, EGON, 1891– .
Drei Canons. Klavier zu zwei Händen.
In: Hausmusik. No.131.
Kleine Hausmusik für Streichquartett, Op.41a.
In: Hausmusik. No.96.
KÖRPPEN, ALFRED, 1926– .
(var. sp.: Koerppen).
Concerto in D für Streichorchester.
In: Collegium musicae novae. No.5.
Zwei Sätze über den Choral "Wir glauben all'an einen Gott."
In: Collegium musicae novae. No.48.
KORSAKOFF, R.
(possibly Rimskiĭ-Korsakov).
Peaceful and still. S.A.T.B.
In: Arion. Vol.2.
KOSELUH, *see* KOZELUCH, LEOPOLD ANTONÍN.
KOTSCHUBEI.
Vocal music.
In: Sammlung russischer Romanzen. No.50, 50a, 122, 123, 222.
KOTTER, HANS, ca.1485–1541.
Keyboard music.
In: Apel. Musik aus früher Zeit für Klavier. Bd.1.
Organ music.
In: Moser. Frühmeister der deutschen Orgelkunst.
KOUTNÍK, TOMÁŠ NORBERT, 1698–1775.
Selections.
In: Musica antiqua bohemica. Vol.23.
KOUTZEN, BORIS, 1901– .
String quartet, No.2.
In: Society for the Publication of American Music. Publications. 25th season. 1943–44.
KOYAMA, KIYOSHIGE.
Ainu no Uta for string orchestra.
In: Contemporary Japanese music series. No.27.
KOZELUCH, LEOPOLD ANTONÍN, 1752–1818.
(var. sp.: Koseluh, Kozebuch).
Selections.
In: Crotch. Specimens of various styles of music. Vol.3.
Keyboard music.
In: Musica antiqua bohemica. Vol.14, 17.
Op.32/I. Quartetto d'archi Si♭ maggiore.
In: Musica antiqua bohemica. Vol.15.
Op.12, Nr.1. Sonate für Klavier, Violine und Violoncello.
In: Organum. 3.Reihe. Nr.59.
Sonate D-moll, Op.51, Nr.3. Piano.
In: Organum. 5.Reihe. Nr.23.
Sonate Es-dur, Op.51, Nr.2. Piano.
In: Organum. 5.Reihe. Nr.5.
Songs.
In: Denkmäler der Tonkunst in Österreich. Vol.54. (Jg.XXVII/2).
Klavier-Trio G-moll. Op.12, Nr.3.
In: Organum. 3.Reihe. Nr.41.
Trio(Sonate) Op.12, Nr.2. Für Violine, Violoncello und Cembalo.
In: Organum. 3.Reihe. Nr.54.
KOZINA, MARJAN.
Selections.
In: Slovenska Akademija Znanosti in Umetnosti. Vol.5, 10, 11, 16, 17, 20, 22.
KOZLOW.
Vocal music.
In: Sammlung russischer Romanzen. No.234, 265.
KRAFT, ANTON, 1752–1820.
Sonata, Op.2, No.2, for cello and piano or 2 celli alone.
In: Music for wind instruments by 18th century masters. No.5.
Violoncello-Konzert C-dur (Piano reduction).
In: Musica viva historica. Vol.2.
KRAMÁŘ, FRANTIŠEK VINCENC, *see* KROMMER, FRANTIŠEK VINCENC.
KRAMER, *see* KROMMER, FRANTIŠEK VINCENC.
KRAUS, EGON, 1912– ed.
Sechs Fugen. Vier Fugen.
In: Musica instrumentalis. Vol.1, 2.
KRAUS, JOSEPH MARTIN, 1756–1792.
Sinfonie C-moll.
In: Monumenta musicae svecicae. Vol.2.
Sonata a Flauto traverso e Viola.
In: Nagels Musik-Archiv. No.76.
Stella caeli.
In: Monumenta musicae svecicae.
KREBS, JOHANN LUDWIG, 1713–1780.
Gesammt-Ausgabe der Tonstücke für Orgel. 4 Abt.
Orgelwerke. 70p.
Choral music.
In: Music Press, Inc. [Choral series]. Vol.117.
Fantasie für Oboe und Orgel.

In: Kammersonaten. No.14.
Keyboard music.
In: Farrenc. Le trésor des pianistes. Vol.9.
In: Herrmann. Lehrmeister und Schüler Joh. Seb. Bachs. Vol.2.
In: Pauer. Alte Klavier-Musik. 1st series. Pt.5.
In: Tagliapietra. Antologia di musica antica e moderna per pianoforte. Bd.12.
Motetten.
In: Das Chorwerk. No.89.
Organ music.
In: Biggs. A treasury of shorter organ classics.
In: Bonnet. Historical organ-recitals. Vol.3.
In: Buszin. Organ series. Vol.1.
In: Dickinson. Historical recital series for organ. Vol.2. No.33.
In: Elkan-Vogel organ series. Vol.3.
In: Erbe deutscher Musik. 1.Reihe. Vol.9.
In: Guilmant. École classique de l'orgue. No.10, 15.
In: Keller. Achtzig Choralvorspiele deutscher Meister des 17. und 18. Jahrhunderts.
In: Keller. Orgelvorspiele.
In: The Liturgical Music Press, Inc. Masterpieces of organ music. Folio 9, 18, 43.
In: Muziek voor de eredienst. Vol.1, 2.
In: Die Orgel. Reihe II. Nr.18, 20.
In: Straube. Choralvorspiele alter Meister.
Partita, No.2; Partita, No.6.
In: Köhler. Les maîtres du clavecin. Heft 3.
Partita, No.2. (B flat); Partita, No.6. (E flat).
In: Pauer. Alte Meister. No.11, 12.
Prélude-Choral "Wir glauben all an einen Gott." Organ.
In: Guilmant. École classique de l'orgue. No.23.
Sonate A-moll für zwei Violinen mit Basso Continuo.
In: Nagels Musik-Archiv. No.109.
Trio (Suite mit Ouvertüre) in D dur. Für Flöte (1. Violine), Violine, Violoncell und Klavier.
In: Riemann. Collegium musicum. No.31.
Triosonate H-moll für 2 Querflöten (oder 2 Violinen) und Generalbass.
In: Organum. 3.Reihe. Nr.62.
KREBS, JOHANN TOBIAS, 1690–1728.
Organ music.
In: Das Erbe deutscher Musik. 1.Reihe. Vol.9.
KREIDER, NOBLE W.
Piano music.
In: The Wa-Wan series of American compositions.
KŘENEK, ERNST, 1900– .
Sonata. Op.92. Organ.
In: Contemporary organ series. No.10.
KRETZSCHMAR, PAUL, 1905– .
Organ music.
In: The parish organist. Vol.1–4.
KREUTZER.
Etude marche.
In: L'École du violon au XVIIe et XVIIIe siècle. No.1347.
KREUTZER, CONRADIN, 1780–1849.
Selections.
In: Denkmäler der Tonkunst in Österreich. Vol.79. (Jg.XLII/2).
Lied.
In: Reimann. Das deutsche Lied. Vol.2.
Part music.
In: Hullah. Part music. Class A.1. Vol.2; Class B.2; Class C. Secular.
KREUTZER, JEAN NICOLAS AUGUSTE, 1778–1832.
Trio A dur für Flöte, Klarinette und Gitarre.
In: Albert. Die Gitarre in der Haus– und Kammermusik vor 100 Jahren (1780–1820). No.9.
KREUTZER , JOSEPH, ca.1800.
Trio D-dur, Op.9/3.
In: Gitarre-Kammermusik. No.33.
KRIEGER, ADAM, 1634–1666.
Selections.
In: Leichtentritt. Deutsche Hausmusik aus vier Jahrhunderten.
Arien.
In: Denkmäler deutscher Tonkunst. [1.Folge]. Vol.19.
Ausgewählte Arien für Sopran.
In: Organum. 2.Reihe. Nr.7.
Deutsches Lied.
In: Einstein. Beispielsammlung zur älteren Musikgeschichte.
Lieder.
In: Moser. Alte Meister des deutschen Liedes. 30 Gesänge. No.11–13.
In: Moser. Alte Meister des deutschen Liedes. 46 Gesänge. No.16–21.
In: Reimann. Das deutsche Lied. Vol.1.
KRIEGER, JOHANN, 1651–1735.
Selected works.
In: Denkmäler deutscher Tonkunst. [2.Folge]. Vol.18.
Keyboard music.
In: Georgii. Keyboard music of the Baroque and Rococo. Vol.1.
In: Tagliapietra. Antologia di musica antica e moderna per pianoforte. Bd.9.
Organ music.
In: Auler. Spielbuch für Kleinorgel. Vol.2.
In: Das Erbe deutscher Musik. 1.Reihe. Vol.9.
In: Keller. Achtzig Choralvorspiele deutscher Meister des 17. und 18. Jahrhunderts.
In: Klein. The first four centuries of music for the organ from Dunstable to Bach (1370–1749).
In: The Liturgical Music Press, Inc. Commemoration folio.
In: The Liturgical Music Press, Inc. Masterpieces of organ music. Folio 15, 17, 20, 35, 40, 45, 47, 57.
In: Muziek voor de eredienst. Vol.2.
In: Die Orgel. Reihe II. Nr.3.
In: The parish organist. Vol.1–4.
In: Raugel. Quarante-six pièces pour orgue ou harmonium.
In: Rohr. Orgelspiel im Kirchenjahr.
KRIEGER, JOHANN PHILIPPE, 1649–1725.
(var. sp.: Johann Philipp Krieger).
Ausgewählte Orgelstücke. p.1– .
Selected works.
In: Denkmäler deutscher Tonkunst. [2.Folge]. Vol.18.

Selected church compositions.
In: Denkmäler deutscher Tonkunst. [1.Folge]. Vol.53–54.
Die Gerechten werden weggerafft.
In: Organum. 1.Reihe. Nr.6.
Vierundzwanzig Lieder und Arien. Heft 1. Nr.1–12; Heft II. Nr. 13–24.
In: Nagels Musik-Archiv. No.174, 175.
Organ music.
In: Auler. Spielbuch für Kleinorgel. Vol.2.
In: Organum. 4.Reihe. Nr.17.
Partie F-dur "Feldmusik" 1704. No.III, für Bläser und Streicher mit Cembalo.
In: Organum. 3.Reihe. Nr.9.
Rufet nicht die Weischeit.
In: Organum. 1.Reihe. Nr.10.
Sonate (D-moll) für Violine, Gambe (Violoncello) und Cembalo (Op.II, 1693, Nr.2).
In: Organum. 3.Reihe. Nr.10.
Sonate F-dur für 2 Violinen und Generalbass (Op.1, Nr.3. 1688).
In: Organum. 3.Reihe. Nr.11.
Sonate à trois, pour deux violons et le clavecin.
In: Flores musicae. Vol.7.
Suite F-dur aus "Lustige Feldmusik."
In: Schering. Perlen alter Kammermusik.
Triosonate A moll, für Violine, Viola da Gamba und Cembalo.
In: Nagels Musik-Archiv. No.135.
Wo wilt du hin, weil's Abend ist.
In: Organum. 1.Reihe. Nr.3.
KROEGER, ERNEST RICHARD, 1862–1934.
Songs.
In: The Wa-Wan series of American compositions.
KROMMER, FRANTIŠEK VINCENC, 1759–1831.
(var. sp.: Kramář, Kramer).
Concerto, Op.36, Fa maggiore, oboe e piano.
In: Musica antiqua bohemica. Vol.27.
Concerto Mi ♭ maggiore. Clarinetto e piano.
In: Musica antiqua bohemica. Vol.13.
Klarinetten-konzert Es-dur, Op.36.
In: Musica viva historica. Vol.7.
Il quartetti.
In: Musica antiqua bohemica. Vol.42.
Quartetto. Op.5. No.1.
In: Musica antiqua bohemica. Vol.5.
Violinduett in A-dur.
In: Hausmusik. No.173.
KRONSTEINER, JOSEF, 1910– .
(var. sp.: Joseph Kronsteiner).
Partita für 2 Gitarren.
In: Gitarre-Kammermusik. No.30.
Vier Rilke-Lieder; für Alt, Bratsche, Klavier.
Zwei Hymnen, für Alt und Klavier, nach Gedichten von Karl Kleinschmidt.
In: Hausmusik. No.183.
KRUFFT, NIKLAS VON.
Selections.
In: Denkmäler der Tonkunst in Österreich. Vol.79. (Jg.XLII/2).
KRUMPHOLTZ, JOHANN BAPTIST, 1745–1790.
Selections.
In: Crotch. Specimens of various styles of music. Vol.3.
Sonate, für Flöte (oder Violine) und Harfe (oder Klavier).
In: Nagels Musik-Archiv. No.98.
KRYGELL, JOHANN ADAM, 1835–1915.
Organ music.
In: Gerhardt. Album nodischer Komponisten für Orgel. Vol.1, 2.
KRYŠTOF HARANT Z POLŽIC A BEZDRUŽIC.
Opera omnia.
In: Documenta historica musicae.
KUBIK, GAIL, 1914– .
Quiet piece. Organ.
In: Contemporary organ series. No.19.
Sonatina. Violin and piano.
In: Society for the Publication of American Music. Publications. 24th season. 1942–43.
KUBIZEK, K. M.
Sonate für Oboe und Klavier.
In: Hausmusik. No.185.
KUCHAŘ, JAN KŘTITEL, 1751–1829.
Organ.
In: Musica antiqua bohemica. Vol.12.
KUGELMANN, HANS, d.1542.
(var. sp.: Johann Kugelmann).
Choral music.
In: Antiqua chorbuch. Vol.1. Heft 1.
Concentus novi. 1540.
In: Das Erbe deutscher Musik. Sonderreihe. Vol.2.
Kleine Messe.
In: Zeitschrift für Spielmusik. No.21.
KUGELMANN, PAUL, 16th CENTURY.
Sieben teutsche Liedlein.
In: Chor-Archiv.
KUHLAU, FRIEDRICH, 1786–1832.
Concerto for Klaver og Orkester. Oeuvre 7.
In: Samfundet til Udgivelse af dansk Musik. Ser.III. No.136.
Elverhøj Ouverture; 4–5. Akt.
In: Samfundet til Udgivelse af dansk Musik. Ser.III. No.11, 163.
Kvintet Op.51. Nr.1. For Fløjte, Violin, Viola I–II og Violoncel.
In: Samfundet til Udgivelse af dansk Musik. Ser.III. No.143.
Ouverture til "Eurydice i Tartarus." Op.47.
In: Samfundet til Udgivelse af dansk Musik. Ser.I. No.10.
Ouverture til Syngestykket. "Røverborgen."
In: Samfundet til Udgivelse af dansk Musik. Ser.III. No.101.
Ouverture til "Trillingbrødrene fra Damask." Op.115.
In: Samfundet til Udgivelse af dansk Musik. Ser.I. No.18.
Ouverture til "Wilhelm Shakespeare." Op.74.
In: Samfundet til Udgivelse af dansk Musik. Ser.III. No.57
William Shakespeare. Op.74. Drama.
In: Samfundet til Udgivelse af dansk Musik. Ser.I. No.3.
KÜHMSTEDT, FRIEDRICH, 1809–1858.
Organ music.
In: Caecilia; Sammlung von Choralvorspielen.
KUHNAU, JOHANN, 1660–1722.
(var. sp.: Jean Kuhnau).
Church cantatas.

In: Denkmäler deutscher Tonkunst. [1.Folge]. Vol.58–59.
Ich habe Lust abzuscheiden.
In: Organum. 1.Reihe. Nr.14.
Keyboard music.
In: Denkmäler deutscher Tonkunst. [1.Folge]. Vol.4.
In: Farrenc. Le trésor des pianistes. Vol.3.
In: Georgii. Keyboard music of the Baroque and Rococo. Vol.1.
In: Herrmann. Lehrmeister und Schüler Joh. Seb. Bachs. Vol.1.
In: Oesterle. Early keyboard music. Vol.1.
In: Pauer. Alte Klavier-Musik. 1st series. Part 3.
In: Tagliapietra. Antologia di musica antica e moderna per pianoforte. Bd.10.
Organ music.
In: Bonnet. Historical organ-recitals. Vol.1.
In: Organum. 4.Reihe. Nr.19.
In: The parish organist. Vol.1–4.
In: Straube. Choralvorspiele alter Meister.
Sonate No.2. (D).
In: Pauer. Alte Meister. No.9.
Suite No.3, Sonate.
In: Köhler. Les maîtres du clavecin. Heft 4.
KÜHNEL, AUGUST, b.1645.
Drei Sonaten (Nr.7–9) für Viola da Gamba, Cembalo (Klavier) und Bass-Instrument ad lib.
In: Antiqua Edition. Von 2 Instrumenten an.
KÜHNHAUSEN, JOHANNES GEORG, fl.1714.
Passion nach dem Evangelisten Matthäus.
In: Das Chorwerk. No.50.
KUKUCK, FELICITAS, 1914– .
Komm, wir wollen tanzen.
In: Bausteine für Musikerziehung und Musikpflege. B 114.
KULLA, HANS.
Lateinisches Proprium vom Ostermontag.
In: Christophorus-Chorwerk. Heft 37.
KUNGSPERGER, URBANUS.
Hymnen.
In: Das Chorwerk. No.32.
KUNST, JAAP, 1891–1960. ed.
Over zelzame fluiten en veelstemmige muziek in het Ngada– en Naheh-gebied. (West Flores).
In: Musicologisch onderzoek. No.1.
Songs of North New Guinea.
In: Musicologisch onderzoek. No.2.
KUNTNER, LEOPOLD.
Sonatine in D-für Violine mit Klavier.
In: Hausmusik. No.82.
2 Suiten für 2 Blockflöten oder andere Instrumente.
In: Zeitschrift für Spielmusik. No.68.
KUNTZ, MICHAEL.
Kleine Passacaglia auf ein altdeutsches Volkslied.
In: Zeitschrift für Spielmusik. No.100.
KUNZEN, F. L. AE., 1761–1817.
Gyrithe. Drama.
In: Samfundet til Udgivelse af dansk Musik. Ser.I. No.1.
KUSCHELEFF-BESBARODKO.
Vocal music.
In: Sammlung russischer Romanzen. No.142.
KUSSER, JOHANN SIGISMUND, 1660–1727.
(var. sp.: Cousser).
Arien, Duette und Chöre aus Erindo, oder Die unsträfliche Liebe.
In: Das Erbe deutscher Musik. 2.Reihe. Schleswig-Holstein und Hansestädte. Vol.3.
Ouverture IV, aus "Composition de Musique" (1682).
In: Nagels Musik-Archiv. No.100.
KUTTENBERGER MENUETT.
In: Musica viva historica. Vol.3.

LA BARRE, JOSEPH DE, *see* BARRE, JOSEPH DE LA.
LA BARRE, MICHEL DE, *see* BARRE, MICHEL DE LA.
L'ABBÉ, JOSEPH BARNABÉ SAINT-SEVIN, 1727–1803.
Sonate en ré majeur.
In: L'école du violon au XVIIe et XVIIIe siècle. No.1249.
LA BEAUSSE, 15th CENTURY.
Selections.
In: Reaney. Early fifteenth-century music. Vol.2.
LA FAGE, JUSTE ADRIEN LENOIR DE, *see* FAGE, JUSTE ADRIEN LENOIR DE LA.
L'AFFILARD, MICHEL, *see* AFFILARD, MICHEL L'.
LA GROTTE, NICOLAS DE, 16th CENTURY.
Chansons.
In: Lesure. Anthologie de la chanson parisienne au XVIe siècle.
LA HALLE, ADAM DE, *see* ADAM DE LA HALLE.
LAHUSEN, CHRISTIAN, 1886– .
Choral music.
In: Nagels Männerchor-Blätter. No.12.
L'AINÉ, PIERRE CHÉDEVILLE, *see* AINÉ, PIERRE CHÉDEVILLE L'.
LAJOVIC, ANTON, 1878– .
Selections.
In: Slovenska Akademija Znanosti in Umetnosti. Vol.1, 4, 8, 12, 14, 23.
LALANDE, MICHEL RICHARD DE, 1657–1726.
Selections.
In: Expert. Répertoire classique de musique. 1re année.
Motets. 20v.
Suite factice. Organ.
In: Orgue et liturgie. Vol.36.
LA LAURENCIE, LIONEL DE, 1861–1933.
Mélanges.
In: Société Française de Musicologie, Paris. Ser.II. Bd.3–4.
LAMAS, J. A.
Popule meus.
In: Archivo de musica colonial venezolana. No.7.
Salve Regina.
In: Archivo de musica colonial venezolana. No.5.
Tres lecciones para el oficio de difuntos.
In: Archivo de musica colonial venezolana. No.2.
LAMB, HUBERT.
Six scenes from the Protevangelion.
In: The Wellesley edition. No.2.
LAMBARDO, FRANCESCO.
Keyboard music.

In: Corpus of early keyboard music. Vol.24.
LAMBE.
Selections.
In: Plainsong and Mediaeval Music Society. Publications. (Old Hall manuscript).
LAMBERT, MICHEL, ca.1610–1696.
Airs.
In: Prunières. Les maîtres du chant. Recueil 4.
Vocal music.
In: Delsarte. Archives du chant. Livr.4. No.6
LAMBORD, BENJAMIN, 1879–1915.
Piano music.
In: The Wa-Wan series of American compositions.
LANCIANI, F.
Airs.
In: Prunières. Les maîtres du chant. Recueil 5.
LANDAETA, JUAN JOSÉ.
Pésame a la Vírgen.
In: Archivo de música colonial venezolana. No.1.
Salve Regina.
In: Archivo de música colonial venezolana. No.11.
LANDI, STEFANO, ca.1590–ca.1655.
Selections.
In: Torchi. L'arte musicale in Italia. Bd.5.
LANDINO, FRANCESCO, ca.1325–1397.
(var. sp.: Landini).
Works. 316p.
Works.
In: Schrade. Polyphonic music of the fourteenth century. Vol.4.
Selections.
In: Documenta historica musicae.
In: Gleason. Examples of music before 1400.
Cacce.
In: Marrocco. Fourteenth-century Italian cacce.
Chi più le vuol sapere.
In: Parrish. Masterpieces of music before 1750. No.14.
Choral music.
In: Engel. Three centuries of choral music. Vol.2.
Organ music.
In: Raugel. Quarante-six pièces pour orgue ou harmonium.
Songs.
In: Riemann. Hausmusik aus alter Zeit.
LANGE, FRANCISCO CURT, 1903– .
Música de cámara.
In: Boletín latino-americano de música. Vol.6.
LANGE, GREGOR, ca.1540–1587.
Choral music.
In: Antiqua Chorbuch. Vol.2. Heft 3.
Newe deudsche Lieder.
In: Zeitschrift für Spielmusik. No.54.
LANGE-MÜLLER, PETER ERASMUS, 1850–1926.
Agnete og Havmanden. Op.73. Choral work.
In: Samfundet til Udgivelse af dansk Musik. Ser.II. No.28.
H. C. Andersen-Kantate. Op.71.
In: Samfundet til Udgivelse af dansk Musik. Ser.II. No.22.
Industri,-Landbrugs-og Kunst-Udstillings. Op.37.
In: Samfundet til Udgivelse af dansk Musik. Ser.II. No.1.
"1848." Kantate. Op.60.
In: Samfundet til Udgivelse af dansk Musik. Ser.III. No.2.
Middelalderlig. Op.55. Melodrama.
In: Samfundet til Udgivelse af dansk Musik. Ser.II. No.16.
Stavnsbaandskantate. Op.36.
In: Samfundet til Udgivelse af dansk Musik. Ser.II. No.29.
Tove. Singspiel. Op.7.
In: Samfundet til Udgivelse af dansk Musik. Ser.I. No.12.
LANGENAU, JOHANN LEONHARD VON, b.ca.1500.
Choral music.
In: Antiqua Chorbuch. Vol.2. Heft 1.
LANGGAARD, RUED IMMANUEL, 1893–1952.
(var. sp.: Rud Langgaard).
Det Himmelrivende. Symfoni. Nr.6.
In: Samfundet til Udgivelse af dansk Musik. Ser.III. No.87.
Strygekvartet, Nr.3.
In: Samfundet til Udgivelse af dansk Musik. Ser.III. No.34.
LANGIUS, GREGOR, d.1587.
Sammlung von Motetten.
In: Publikationen älterer praktischer und theoretischer Musikwerke. Jahrg.29.
LANGLAIS, JEAN, 1907– .
Pâques [de Pachelbel]. Organ.
In: Orgue et liturgie. Vol.1.
LANIERE,NICHOLAS, 1588–1666.
Selections.
In: Smith. Musica antiqua.
LANNER, JOSEPH FRANZ KARL, 1801–1843.
Werke. 8v.
Ausgewählte Walzer.
In: Musikalische Stundenbücher.
Ländler und Walzer.
In: Corona. Vol.17.
In: Denkmäler der Tonkunst in Österreich. Vol.65. (Jg.XXXIII/2).
LANTINS, ARNOLD DE, 15th CENTURY.
(var. sp.: Arnoldus de Lantins).
Sacred music.
In: Plainsong and Mediaeval Music Society. Publications. (Borren).
LANTINS, HUGO DE, 15th CENTURY.
(var. sp.: Ugo de Lantins).
Sacred music.
In: Plainsong and Mediaeval Music Society. Publications. (Borren).
LAPICIDA, ERASMUS, 15th–16th CENTURIES.
Choral music.
In: Antiqua Chorbuch. Vol.2. Heft 1.
Lieder.
In: Denkmäler der Tonkunst in Österreich. Vol.72. (Jg.XXXVII/2).
In: The Penn state music series. No.4.
Songs.
In: Aich. Das Liederbuch.
LAPPERDEY, PHILIPPE.
Selections.
In: Maldéghem. Trésor musical.

LARSSON, LARS ERIK, 1908– .
Förklädd gud Klaverutdrag. Op.24.
In: Musikaliska konstföreningen. 1941.
String quartet, No.1, Op.31.
In: Musikaliska konstföreningen. 1956.
LA RUE, PIERRE DE, d.1518.
Liber missarum. 223p.
Selections.
In: Ambros. Auserwählte Tonwerke.
In: Maldéghem. Trésor musical.
Chansons.
In: Cauchie. Quinze chansons françaises du XVIe siècle.
In: Publikationen älterer praktischer und theoretischer Musikwerke. Jahrg.27.
Choral music.
In: Engel. Three centuries of choral music. Vol.1.
In: Smijers. Van Ockeghem tot Sweelinck. Aflg.4, 5.
Magnificat quinti toni.
In: The Penn state music series. No.8.
Drei missen.
In: Monumenta musicae belgicae. Vol.8.
Missa ave sanctissima.
In: Documenta polyphoniae liturgicae sanctae ecclesiae romanae. Serie 1.B. No.1.
Vier Motetten.
In: Das Chorwerk. No.91.
Requiem und eine Motetten.
In: Das Chorwerk. No.11.
Sicut cervus. Pourquoy non.
In: Dessoff choir series. No.36, 37.
LA SABLONARA, CLAUDIO DE, fl. 1599.
Cancionero musical y poetico del siglo XVII. 340p.
LASCEUX, GUILLAUME, 1740–1829.
Organ music.
In: Raugel. Les maîtres français de l'orgue. Vol.1, 2.
In: Raugel. Les maîtres français de l'orgue aux XVIIème et XVIIIème siècles.
LASERNA, BLAS, 1751–1816.
Selections.
In: Pedrell. Teatro lirico espanol anterior al siglo XIX. Bd.2.
LAS INFANTUS, FERNANDO DE, *see* INFANTUS, FERNANDO DE LAS.
LASSO, ORLANDO DI, *see* LASSUS, ORLAND DE.
LASSO, RUDOLF DI, b.1625.
Choral music.
In: Antiqua Chorbuch. Vol.1. Heft 4.
Sacred music.
In: Proske. Musica divina. Annus primus. Tom 2.
LASSON, M.
Motets.
In: Attaingnant. Treize livres de motets. Livre 8, 11, 13.
LASSUS, FERDINAND DE, d.1609.
Choral music.
In: Dehn. Sammlung älterer Musik aus dem XVI. und XVII. Jahrhundert.
LASSUS, ORLAND DE, d.1594.
(var. sp.: Orlando di Lasso; Orland Lasso; Orlandus Lassus; Roland de Lassus).
Sämtliche Werke. 21v.
Sämtliche Werke. Neue Reihe. v.1– .
Selections.
In: Documenta historica musicae.
In: Gabrieli. Music of Gabrieli and his time.
In: Leichtentritt. Deutsche Hausmusik aus vier Jahrhunderten.
In: Maldéghem. Trésor musical.
In: Musica sacra . . . 1839– . Vol.5–12.
In: Smith. Musica antiqua.
Anthems.
In: Music Press, Inc. [Choral series]. No.72.
Bicinien.
In: Zeitschrift für Spielmusik. No.18.
Bicinien, zum Singen und Spielen auf Streich– und Blasinstrumenten.
In: Hortus musicus. No.2.
Busstränen des Heiligen Petrus.
In: Das Chorwerk. No.34, 37, 41.
Chansons.
In: Bordes. Chansonnier du XVe siècle.
Chant.
In: Soderlund. Examples of Gregorian chant and works of Orlandus Lassus and Giovanni Pierluigi Palestrina.
In: Soderlund. Examples of Gregorian chant and works by Orlandus Lassus, Giovanni Pierluigi Palestrina and Marc Antonio Ingegneri.
Choral music.
In: Antiqua Chorbuch. Vol.1. Heft 3; Vol.2. Heft 3.
In: Chor-Archiv.
In: Commer. Collectio operum musicorum batavorum saeculi XVI. Bd.7, 8, 10, 12.
In: Dehn. Sammlung älterer Musik aus dem XVI. und XVII. Jahrhundert.
In: Dessoff choir series. No.8, 9, 11, 16, 21, 22.
In: Engel. Three centuries of choral music. Vol.4.
In: Der Kammerchor. Vol.1, 2, 3.
In: Music Press, Inc. [Choral series]. No.73, 76, 80.
In: Recueil de musique ancienne. Recuiel des morceaux de musique ancienne. Bd.2, 5, 6, 9.
In: Rochlitz. Sammlung vorzüglicher Gesangstücke. Bd.1. Pt.1.
In: Societas Polyphonica Romanae. Repertorium. Vol.1, 2, 5.
Choral music.
In: Motett Society. [Collection of ancient church music]. Division 1. Division 3.
Sechs Fantasien für Violine und Viola oder andere Streich– oder Blasinstrumente besonders für Blockflöten.
In: Hortus musicus. No.19.
Sechs Fantasien für zwei Violinen oder andere Streich– oder Blasinstrumente besonders für Blockflöten.
In: Hortus musicus. No.18.
Gesänge.
In: Musica sacra . . . ca.1842–1896. Vol.12.
Jubilate–Factus est. Tibi laus.
In: Musica spiritualis. Serie IB. No.6.
Madrigale und Chansons.

In: Das Chorwerk. No.13.
Madrigal. Quand non mari.
In: Squire. Ausgewählte Madrigale und mehrstimmige Gesänge. No.9.
Les Meslanges.
In: Expert. Les maîtres musiciens de la Renaissance française. Vol.1.
Missen.
In: Basilica. 1954.
In: Musica divina. Vol.9.
In: Musica spiritualis. Serie IIA. No.10, 11, 12.
Motetten.
In: Das Chorwerk. No.14.
In: Müller-Blattau. Musica reservata. Vol.1, 2.
In: Parrish. Masterpieces of music before 1750. No.23.
O let me look on thee; I know a young maiden.
In: Arion. Vol.1.
O temps divers.
In: Expert. Florilège du concert vocal de la renaissance. No.2.
Organ music.
In: Cantantibus organis. Vol.1, 2, 6, 8.
In: The parish organist. Vol.1–4.
In: Peeters. Oudnederlandse meesters. Vol.2, 3.
Prophetiae Sibyllarum.
In: Das Chorwerk. No.48.
Sacred music.
In: Berg. Patrocinium musices. Vol.1, 2, 3, 4, 5, 7, 8.
In: The Fitzwilliam music. Bd.4.
In: Proske. Musica divina. Annus primus. Tom 1, 2, 3, 4; Annus secundus. Tom 2, 3.
In: Proske. Selectus novus missarum. Annus primus. Tom 1, 2; Annus secundus. Tom 2, 3.
In: Rubio. Antologia polifonica sacra. Vol.1.
Vocal music.
In: Delsarte. Archives du chant. Livr.7, No.10; Livr.16, No.1, 2; Livr.18, No.1.
LATILLA, GAETANO, 1711–1791.
Airs.
In: Prunières. Les maîtres du chant. Recueil 1.
LA TORRE, FRANCESCO DE, *see* TORRE, FRANCESCO DE LA.
LATRE, JEHAN DE, *see* DELÂTRE, JEAN PETIT CLAUDE.
LATTRE, PETIT JAN DE, *see* DELÂTRE, JEAN PETIT CLAUDE.
LAUDE.
In: Jeppesen. Die mehrstimmige italienische Laude um 1500.
In: Liuzzi. La Lauda.
LAURENCIE, LIONEL DE LA, *see* LA LAURENCIE, LIONEL DE.
LAVIE, FERNAND FERNANDEZ– , *see* FERNANDEZ-LAVIE, FERNAND.
LAW, ANDREW, 1749–1821.
Selections.
In: Goldman. Landmarks of early American music, 1760–1800.
LAWES, HENRY, 1596–1662.
Ten ayres for contralto (or baritone) and keyboard.
In: English songs. No.1.
Dialogues, for two voices and continuo.
In: The Penn state music series. No.3.
Part music.
In: Hullah. Part music. Class A.1. Vol.1.
Songs.
In: Potter. Reliquary of English song. Vol.1.
LAWES, WILLIAM, 1602–1645.
Selections.
In: Smith. Musica antiqua.
Consort music.
In: Musica Britannica. Vol.21.
Dialogues, for two voices and continuo.
In: The Penn state music series. No.3.
Fantasy suite No.5 in D minor.
In: Seventeenth-century chamber music. No.3, 20.
Sacred music.
In: Boyce. Cathedral music. Vol.2; 1849, Vol.3.
Songs.
In: Potter. Reliquary of English song. Vol.1.
Vocal music.
In: Hullah. Vocal scores. I. Sacred.
LAWTON, EDWARD. ed.
Catches.
In: Music Press, Inc. [Choral series]. Vol.108.
LAYOLLE, FRANCISCUS DE, 16th CENTURY.
Selections.
In: Ambros. Auserwählte Tonwerke.
LEBÈGUE, NICOLAS ANTOINE, *see* BÈGUE, NICOLAS ANTOINE LE.
LE BEL, FIRMIN, 16th CENTURY.
Choral music.
In: Societas Polyphonica Romanae. Repertorium. Vol.1.
LEBERMANN, WALTER. ed.
Flöten-Konzerte des 18. Jahrhunderts.
In: Das Erbe deutscher Musik. 1.Reihe. Vol.51.
LEBERTOUL, FRANCHOYS, 14th–15th CENTURIES.
(var. sp.: Franchois Lebertoul).
Selections.
In: Reaney. Early fifteenth-century music. Vol.2.
Sacred music.
In: Plainsong and Mediaeval Music Society. Publications. (Borren).
LE BLANC, DIDIER, 16th CENTURY.
Airs de plusiers musiciens.
In: Expert. Monuments de la musique française au temps de la Renaissance. Vol.3.
La Chasse.
In: L'école du violon au XVIIe et XVIIIe siècle. No.1338.
Sonate en mi ♭ majeur.
In: L'école du violon au XVIIe et XVIIIe siècle. No.1264.
LE BRUN.
Motets.
In: Attaingnant. Treize livres de motets. Livre 5, 8.
LECHNER, LEONHARD, ca.1550–1606.

Werke. 15v.
Choral music.
In: Antiqua Chorbuch. Vol.1. Heft 3; Vol.2. Heft 3.
In: Chor-Archiv.
In: Dehn. Sammlung älterer Musik aus dem XVI. und XVII. Jahrhundert.
In: Der Kammerchor. Vol.2.
Chorlieder.
In: Christophorus-Chorwerk. Heft 7.
LECHTHALER, JOSEF, 1891–1948.
Suite für 2 Gitarren.
In: Gitarre-Kammermusik. No.8.
Weihnachtsbüchlein. Op.62.
In: Hausmusik. No.28.
LECLAIR, JEAN MARIE, 1697–1764.
Allegro.
In: L'école du violon au XVIIe et XVIIIe siècle. No.1346, 1347.
Aria.
In: L'école du violon au XVIIe et XVIIIe siècle. No.1340.
La Chasse.
In: L'école du violon au XVIIe et XVIIIe siècle. No.1337.
Ciaconna.
In: L'école du violon au XVIIe et XVIIIe siècle. No.1341.
Kammer-Sonaten für Violine und Pianoforte.
In: Moffat. Kammer-Sonaten für Violine und Pianoforte. No.5, 22.
Konzert A-moll für Violine, Streichorchester und Basso Continuo. Op.VII, Nr.5.
In: Nagels Musik-Archiv. No.209.
Konzert C-dur, Op.VII, 3.
In: Florilegium musicum. Vol.6.
Largo.
In: L'école du violon au XVIIe et XVIIIe siècle. No.1293, 1333, 1338.
Musette.
In: L'école du violon au XVIIe et XVIIIe siècle. No.1344.
Prestissimo.
In: L'école du violon au XVIIe et XVIIIe siècle. No.1342.
Presto.
In: L'école du violon au XVIIe et XVIIIe siècle. No.1345.
Sarabanda.
In: L'école du violon au XVIIe et XVIIIe siècle. No.1343.
12 Sonaten und 1 Trio.
In: Publikationen älterer praktischer und theoretischer Musikwerke. Jahrg.31.
Sonate VIII D-dur aus op.2.
In: Antiqua Edition. Von 3 Instrumenten an.
Sonate No.XI pour flûte et clavier.
In: Musiques françaises. Vol.19.
Sonate. G-dur, für Flöte (Violine), Cembalo (Klavier) und Bass-Instrument ad lib.
In: Antiqua Edition. Von 2 Instrumenten an.
Sonate. Violin and piano.
In: Moffat. Meister-Schule der alter Zeit. Violin-Sonaten. No.4, 32.
Sonate en trio, pour deux violons et la basse continuo.
In: Flores musicae. Vol.4.
Sonate à trois, avec une Flûte allemande ou un violon, une viole et le clavecin.
In: Flores musicae. Vol.5.
Tambrin de la 10e sonate.
In: L'école du violon au XVIIe et XVIIIe siècle. No.1336.
LE COCQ, JOAN, 16th CENTURY.
(var. sp.: Jean Le Cocq).
Choral music.
In: Commer. Collectio operum musicorum batavorum Saeculi XVI. Bd.12.
LECUONA, ERNESTO, 1896– .
Keyboard music.
In: Guenther. Collection espagnole.
LEDESMA, MARIANO RODRIGUEZ DE, 1779–1848.
Sacred music.
In: Eslava y Elizondo. Lira sacro-hispana. 19th century. i.2.
LEDESMA, N.
Sacred music.
In: Eslava y Elizondo. Lira sacro-hispana. 19th century. i.2.
LEE, NOËL.
Dialogues for violin and piano.
In: New music. 1962.
LEFEVRE, JEAN XAVIER, 1763–1829.
(var. sp.: Jacques Lefevre).
Aime-moi bergère.
In: Arion. Vol.3.
Sonate III pour clarinette et basse. Op.XII; 5ème sonate pour clarinette et clavier.
In: Musiques françaises. Vol.15, 2.
Sonate No.2 pour clarinette, cello et clavier.
In: Musiques françaises. Vol.20.
LEFFLOTH.
Konzert D-dur für obligates Cembalo und Flöte oder Violine.
In: Nagels Musik-Archiv. No.184.
LE GENDRE, JEAN, 16th CENTURY.
Chansons.
In: Publikationen älterer praktischer und theoretischer Musikwerke. Jahrg. 27.
LE GRANT, GUILLAUME, 14th–15th CENTURIES.
(var. sp.: Legrant).
Selections.
In: Reaney. Early fifteenth-century music Vol.2.
Sacred music.
In: Plainsong and Mediaeval Music Society. Publications. (Borren).
LE GRANT, JOHANNES, 15th CENTURY.
Selections.
In: Reaney. Early fifteenth-century music. Vol.2.
LEGRENZI, GIOVANNI, 1626–1690.
(var. sp.: Legrenzy).
Selections.
In: Expert. Répertoire classique de musique. 1re Année.
Arias.
In: Landshoff. Alte Meister des Bel Canto. Eine Sammlung von Arien. Vol.1–2.
In: Parisotti. Arie antiche. Bd.1.
Chamber music.
In: Riemann. Old chamber music. Vol.4.
Instrumental music.

In: Wasielewski. Instrumentalsätze vom Ende des XVI. bis Ende des XVII. Jahrhunderts.
3 sonatas from the opera La Cetra, for strings, basso continuo.
In: Antica musica strumentale italiana. In preparation.
Sonate für Violine und Violoncello mit Basso Continuo. Op.10, 1. Nr.4.
In: Hortus musicus. No.84.
Sonata für vier Violinen mit Basso Continuo. Op.10, 3. Nr.1.
In: Hortus musicus. No.83.
Sonata a tre, per due violini e basso continuo, Op.IV/1. [La Bernarda].
In: Hausmusik. No.74.
Triosonate G-dur für zwei Violinen und Basso Continuo.
In: Hortus musicus. No.31.
Vocal music.
In: Gevaert. Les gloires de l'Italie. Vol.1, 2.
LE HEURTEUR, GUILLAUME, *see* HEURTEUR, GUILLAUME LE.
LEIBL, CARL, 1784–1870.
Festkantate.
In: Denkmäler rheinischer Musik. Vol.5.
LEIDING, GEORG DIETRICH.
Praeludium in B. Organ.
In: Die Orgel. Reihe II. Nr.15.
LEISRING, VOLKMAR, d.1637.
Choral music.
In: Recueil de musique ancienne. Recueil des morceaux de musique ancienne. Bd.2.
In: Rochlitz. Sammlung vorzüglicher Gesangstücke. Bd.2.
Geistliches Lied; Parvus pu ellus produit; Uns ist geboren ein Kindelein.
In: Musica sacra . . . between 1892–1897. No.5.
Vocal music.
In: Hullah. Vocal scores. I. Sacred.
LE JEUNE, CLAUDE, d.1600.
(var. sp.: Claudin).
Airs. 4v.
Selections.
In: Maldéghem. Trésor musical.
Chansons.
In: Bordes. Chansonnier du XVe siècle.
In: Lesure. Anthologie de la chansons parisienne au XVIe siècle.
Choral music.
In: Commer. Collectio operum musicorum batavorum saeculi XVI. Bd.12.
In: Engel. Three centuries of choral music. Vol.1.
In: Music Press, Inc. [Choral series]. No.56.
Dodecacorde; Le Printemps; Mélanges; Pseames an vers mezurez.
In: Expert. Le maîtres musiciens de la Renaissance française. Vol.11, 12–14, 16, 20–22.
Trois fantaisies instrumentales. Organ.
In: Orgue et liturgie. Vol.39.
Las! ou vas-tu sans moy.
In: Expert. Florilège du concert vocal de la Renaissance. No.6.
Motets.
In: Attaingnant. Treize livres de motets. Livre 1, 2, 3, 5, 6, 7, 9, 10, 11, 12, 13.
O Vilanella quand a l'aqua vai; O occhi manza mia.
In: Squire. Ausgewählte Madrigale und mehrstimmige Gesänge. No.9, 18.
Octonaires de la vanité et inconstance du monde. (I–VIII, IX–XII).
In: Expert. Monuments de la musique française au temps de la Renaissance. Vol.1, 8.
Part music.
In: Hullah. Part music. Class A.1. Vol.1.
LE MAISTRE, MATTHEUS (MATTHAEUS), *see* MAISTRE, MATTHEUS LE.
LEMBCKE, G. A.
Selected songs.
In: Samfundet til Udgivelse af dansk Musik. Suppl. 1901.
LEMLIN, LORENZ, 16th CENTURY.
Choral music.
In: Antiqua Chorbuch. Vol.2. Heft 1.
LEMMENS, NICOLAS JACQUES, 1823–1881.
Oeuvres inédites. 4v.
Organ music.
In: Bonnet. Historical organ-recitals. Vol.5.
In: Guilmant. Concert historique d'orgue.
LEMOS, IBERE.
Música de cámara.
In: Boletín latino-americano de música. Vol.6.
LE MOYNE, *see* MOYNE, LE.
LENAERTS, RENÉ BERNARD, 1902– . ed.
Music of the Netherlands.
In: Anthology of music. Vol.22.
LENEL, LUDWIG, 1914– .
Organ music.
In: The parish organist. Vol.1–4, 5–6, 7–8.
LENFANT.
Motets.
In: Attaingnant. Treize livres de motets. Livre 10.
LENG, ALFONSO, 1884– .
Piano music.
In: Boletín latino-americano de música. Vol.4.
LENTE-FILM COMPOSITIES NEDERLANDSCHE BOERENDANSEN.
In: Vereniging voor Nederlandsche Muziekgeschiedenis. Uitgave. No.40.
LEO, LEONARDO, 1694–1744.
Selections.
In: Crotch. Specimens of various styles of music. Vol.2.
In: Expert. Répertoire classique de musique. 1re Année.
Airs.
In: Prunières. Les maîtres du chant. Recueil 1.
Arias.
In: Landshoff. Alte Meister des Bel Canto. Eine Sammlung von Arien. Vol.1–2.
In: Parisotti. Arie antiche. Bd.1.
Choral music.
In: Commer. Cantica sacra. Vol.1. No.6, 21; Vol.2. No.16.

In: Recueil de musique ancienne. Recueil des morceaux de musique ancienne. Bd.8.
In: Rochlitz. Sammlung vorzüglicher Gesangstücke. Bd.3.
Concerto for cello and strings.
In: Antica musica strumentale italiana. In preparation.
Keyboard music.
In: Tagliapietra. Antologia di musica antica e moderna per pianoforte. Bd.12.
Konzert für 4 Violinen und Bass.
In: Musikschätze der Vergangenheit.
Praebo, Virgo, Benignas aures. Motette a canto solo con organo obligato.
In: Cantio sacra. No.15.
Sacred music.
In: The Fitzwilliam music. Bd.1, 2, 3, 4, 5.
In: Latrobe, C. I. Selection of sacred music.
In: Latrobe, J. A. The music of the church,
Salve Regina. Sopran, 2 Violinen und B.C.
In: Die Kantate. No.4.
Sinfonie D-dur zu "Amor vuol sofferenze"; Sinfonie G-moll zu "S. Elena al Calvario."
In: Sondheimer. Werke aus dem 18. Jahrhundert. Nr.46/47.
Trio. Dominus.
In: Königliche Akademie der Künste. Auswahl vorzüglicher Musik-Werke. Appendix.
Vocal music.
In: Gevaert. Les gloires de l'Italie. Vol.1, 2.
LEONEL.
Selections.
In: Plainsong and Mediaeval Music Society. Publications. (Old Hall manuscript).
Missa super. Fuit homo missus.
In: Documenta polyphoniae liturgicae sanctae ecclesiae romanae. Serie I. No.9.
LEONI, LEONE, 16th–17th CENTURIES.
Selections.
In: Torchi. L'arte musicale in Italia. Bd.2.
LEONIN, 12th CENTURY.
Viderunt omnes.
In: Parrish. A treasury of early music. No.9.
LEOPOLD I. HOLY ROMAN EMPEROR, 1640–1705.
Works.
In: Musikalische Werke der Kaiser Ferdinand III, Leopold I, und Joseph I. 2v.
LEOPOLD III, SAINT, MARGRAVE OF AUSTRIA, ca.1073–1136.
Selections.
In: Zagiba. Die ältesten musikalischen Denkmäler zu Ehren des heiligen Leopold, Herzog und Patron von Österreich.
LEOPOLITA, MARTINUS (MARCIN ZE LWOWA), ca.1540–1589.
(var. sp.: Martin Leopolity, Marcin z Lwowa, Martin de Leopol).
"Missa paschalis."
In: Denkmäler altpolnischer Musik. Vol.35.
In: Surzyński. Monumenta musicae sacrae in Polonia. Vol.3.
LERCHE, C. A.
Six songs.
In: Samfundet til Udgivelse af dansk Musik. Suppl. 1899.
LERICH, RUDOLF.
Spiele zu zweien.
In: Moecks Kammermusik. Vol.202.
In: Zeitschrift für Spielmusik. No.103.
LE ROUX, GASPARD, *see* ROUX, GASPARD LE.
LE ROY, ADRIAN, d.ca.1589.
Bibliographie des éditions.
In: Société Française de Musicologie, Paris. Sér.II. Bd.9.
LE ROY, G., *see* ROY, G LE.
LERPERGER, KURT.
Andante für Violine mit Klavier.
In: Hausmusik. No.99.
L'ESCUREL, JEHANNOT DE, *see* ESCUREL, JEHANNOT DE L'.
L'ESTOCART, PASCHAL DE, *see* ESTOCART, PASCHAL DE L'.
LESUEUR, JEAN FRANCOIS, 1760–1837.
(var. sp.: Le Sueur).
Ossian ou les Bardes.
In: Les chefs d'oeuvres classiques de l'opéra français.
LETELIER LLONA, ALFONSO, 1912– .
Canciones.
In: Instituto Interamericano de Musicologia. Publicaciónes. No.7, 30.
LEUTO, ARCANGELO DEL.
Arias.
In: Parisotti. Arie antiche. Bd.2.
Vocal music.
In: Gevaert. Les gloires de l'Italie. Vol.1.
LEVANT, OSCAR, 1906– .
Nocturne.
In: New music. Orchestra series. No.24.
LEVARIE, SIEGMUND, 1914– .
Fundamentals of music.
In: Institute of Mediaeval Music. Musicological studies. Vol.5.
LEVERIDGE, RICHARD, b.ca.1670–1758.
Songs.
In: Potter. Reliquary of English Song. Vol.2.
LEYDING, GEORG DIETRICH, 1664–1710.
Organ music.
In: Organum. 4.Reihe. Nr.7.
LHÉRITIER, JEAN, *see* HÉRITIER, JEAN L'.
LIBERT, GUALTERIUS, 14th–15th CENTURIES.
(var. sp.: Gautier Libert).
Selections.
In: Reaney. Early fifteenth-century music. Vol.2.
LIBERT, HENRI, 1869–1937.
Organ music.
In: Bedell. The French organist. Vol.1.
LIBERT, R.
Selections.
In: Reaney. Early fifteenth-century music. Vol.3.
LICHFIELD, HENRY, 16th–17th CENTURIES.
(var. sp.: Lichfild).
All yee that sleepe in pleasure.
In: Arion. Vol.1.
Choral music.
In: Engel. Three centuries of choral music. Vol.3.
Madrigals.
In: Euterpe. Vol.3; 2d ed. No.27, 69–70.
In: Fellowes. The English madrigal school. Vol.17.

In: Squire. Ausgewählte Madrigale und mehrstimmige Gesänge. No.29, 30.
LIDARTI, CRISTIANO GIUSEPPE, 18th CENTURY.
Part music.
In: Hullah. Part music. Class C. Secular.
LIDHOLM, INGVAR, 1921– .
Selections.
In: Svensk sanglyrik. Vol.2.
LIDON, JOSÉ, 1752–1827.
Keyboard music.
In: Kastner. Silva iberica.
Sacred music.
In: Eslava y Elizondo. Lira sacro-hispana. 18th century. ii.1.
LIEBMANN, AXEL.
Humoreske. (Elskov en Jaegerdreng).
In: Samfundet til Udgivelse af dansk Musik. Unnumbered.
LIÉGE, FRANCE-MUSIC.
In: Société Française de Musicologie, Paris. Publications.
LILIUS, FRANCISZEK, d.1657.
Jubilate Deo omnis terra.
In: Denkmäler altpolnischer Musik. Vol.40.
LILJA, BERNHARD.
Selections.
In: Svensk sanglyrik. Vol.2.
Andante religioso for organ.
In: Musikaliska konstföreningen. 1940.
LILJEFORS, INGEMAR, 1906– .
Selections.
In: Svensk sanglyrik. Vol.2.
LIMMERT, ERICH, 1909– .
Russische Miniaturen.
In: Collegium musicae novae. No.55.
Suite concertante.
In: Collegium musicae novae. No.57.
LINDBERG, OSKAR FREDRIK, 1887–1955.
Selections.
In: Svensk sanglyrik. Vol.2.
Jungfru Maria.
In: Musikaliska konstföreningen. 1934.
Requiem.
In: Musikaliska konstföreningen. 1929.
LINDBLAD, ADOLF FREDRIK, 1801–1878.
Allegro, Andante, Scherzo. For violin and piano.
In: Musikaliska konstföreningen. 1892.
Quintet for 2 violins, 2 violas, and violoncello; Arr. for piano, 4 hands.
In: Musikaliska konstföreningen. 1885, 1885.
LINDEGREN, JOHAN, 1842–1908.
Fugue in free style for piano.
In: Musikaliska konstföreningen. 1866.
Grand sonata, canon, for piano. Op.2.
In: Musikaliska konstföreningen. 1867.
Quintet for 2 violins, 2 violas, and violoncello.
In: Musikaliska konstföreningen. 1908.
LINDEMAN, LUDVIG MATHIAS, 1812–1887.
(var. sp.: Lindemann).
Aeldre og nyere Fjeldmelodier.
In: Oslo. Universitet. Bibliotek. Norsk musikksamling. Nr.3.
Organ music.
In: Gerhardt. Album nordischer Komponisten für Orgel. Vol.1.
LINDEMAN, OLE ANDREAS, 1769–1857.
(var. sp.: Lindemann).
Keyboard music.
In: Farrenc. Le trésor des pianistes. Vol.16.
LINDROTH, A. F.
Andante and Bolero for violin and piano.
In: Musikaliska konstföreningen. 1884.
Five studies for violin solo.
In: Musikaliska konstföreningen. 1865.
LINEK, JIŘÍ IGNÁC, 1725–1791.
Selections.
In: Musica antiqua bohemica. Vol.23.
Organ music.
In: Musica antiqua Bohemica. Vol.12.
LINGY, DE, *see* DE LINGY.
LINLEY, THOMAS, SR., 1733–1795.
Sacred music.
In: Page. Harmonia sacra. Vol.3.
Songs.
In: Potter. Reliquary of English song. Vol.2.
LISBOA, JOÃO DA COSTA, *see* COSTA DE LISBOA, JOÃO DA.
LISLEY, JOHN, 16th–17th CENTURIES.
Madrigal.
In: The triumphs of Oriana.
LISTE, ANTOINE, 1774–1832.
2 sonates. Piano; Grande Sonate. Piano.
In: Répertoire des clavecinistes. Heft 9, 17.
LISTENIUS, MAGISTER NIKOLAUS, b.ca.1500.
Musica Nicolai Listenii ab Authore denuo recognita multisque novis regulis et exemplis adaucta.
In: Hirsch. Veröffentlichungen. [Bd.].8.
LISZT, FRANZ, 1811–1886.
Musikalische Werke. v.1– .
Liszt society publications. v.1– .
Orgelkompositionen. 2v.
Werke für Klavier zu 2 Händen. 12v.
Keyboard music.
In: Musica hungarica.
In: Tagliapietra. Antologia di musica antica e moderna per pianoforte. Bd.16.
Organ music.
In: Bonnet. Historical organ-recitals. Vol.4.
In: Dickinson. Historical recital series for organ. Vol.2. No.35.
LITAIZE, GASTON GILBERT, 1909– .
Organ music.
In: Orgue et liturgie. Vol.9, 20, 29, 42.
LITERES, ANTONIO, b.ca.1670–1747.
Selections.
In: Pedrell. Teatro lirico espanol anterior al siglo. Bd.2, 4/5.
Sacred music.
In: Eslava y Elizondo. Lira sacro-hispana. 18th century. i.1.
LITTLE, ALFRED E.
Song.
In: The Wa-Wan series of American compositions.
LITTLE, ARTHUR REGINALD.
Songs; Piano music.
In: The Wa-Wan series of American compositions.
LLISSÁ, FRANCISCO, 18th CENTURY.
Organ music.
In: Piedelievre. Les anciens maîtres espagnols.
LLONA, ALFONSO LETELIER, *see* LETELIER LLONA, ALFONSO.

LLUSÁ, FRANCESCO, 17th–18th CENTURIES.
Organ music.
In: Muset. Early Spanish organ music.
LOBO, ALONSO, d.1617.
Sacred music.
In: Eslava y Elizondo. Lira sacro-hispana. 17th century. i.1.
LOBO, DUARTE, 1540–1643.
Composições polifónicas. v.1– .
Selections.
In: Santos. A polifonia clássica portuguesa.
LOBO, ILDEPHONSUS, fl.1601.
Sacred music.
In: Rubio. Antologia polifonica sacra. Vol.1.
LOBO DE MEZQUITA, JOSÉ JOAQUIM EMERICO.
Selections.
In: Lange. Archivo de música religiosa.
LOCATELLI DA BERGAMO, PIETRO, 1695–1764.
(var. sp.: Pietro Antonio Locatelli).
Composizioni.
In: I classici della musica italiana. Vol.16.
In: I classici della musica italiana. Raccolta nazionale delle musiche italiane. Quad.205.
Concerto grosso F-moll mit Pastorale (Nr.8 aus Op.1, 1721).
In: Schering. Perlen alter Kammermusik.
Concerto grosso in G minor, Op.1, No.2. (strings).
In: Antica musica strumentale italiana. Ser.III. Vol.25.
Op.1. No.6. Concerto grosso. Für Streichorchester mit Klavier.
In: Musikschätze der Vergangenheit.
Kammer-Sonaten für Violine und Pianoforte.
In: Moffat. Kammer-Sonaten für Violine und Pianoforte. No.18.
Opera quarta prima parte.
In: Monumenta musica neerlandica. Vol.4.
Il pianto di Arianna, for strings.
In: Antica musica strumentale italiana. In preparation.
Sinfonia.
In: Gitarre-Kammermusik. No.11.
Sonata D-dur.
In: Gitarre-Kammermusik. No.34.
Sonate en ré majeur.
In: L'école du violon au XVIIe et XVIIIe siècle. No.1280.
Drei Sonaten, für Querflöte und Basso Continuo.
In: Hortus musicus. No.35.
Sonatas. Violin and piano.
In: Moffat. Meister-Schule der alten Zeit. Violin-Sonaten. No.7.
In: Vereniging voor Nederlandsche Muziekgeschiedenis. Uitgave. No.31.
Sei sonate da camera per violino e basso. Op.6.
In: I classici musicali italiani. Vol.14.
Sonate à deux violons ou deux flûtes traversières.
In: Flores musicae. Vol.6.
Trauersymphonie. Zwei Violinen, Viola, Violoncello, Orgel.
In: Schering. Perlen alter Kammermusik.
Trio in G dur. Op.3. Nr.1. Für 2 Violinen (Flöten), Violoncell und Klavier.
In: Riemann. Collegium musicum. No.21.
Trio-Sonaten.
In: Moffat. Trio-Sonaten alter Meister. No.2, 22.
In: Organum. 3.Reihe. Nr.46, 50, 52.
Violin and piano.
In: Schering. Alte Meister des Violinspiels.
DAS LOCHEIMER LIEDERBUCH.
Das Locheimer Liederbuch. p.1–234.
—— 1925. [2], 92, [2]p. 24p.
—— 1926. 94p.
—— 1926. 32p.
In: Antiqua Chorbuch. Vol.2. Heft 1.
LOCKE, J.
Duette für 2 Gamben.
In: Hortus musicus. No.167.
LOCKE, MATTHEW, ca.1630–1677.
Selections.
In: Smith. Musica antiqua.
Consort zu 4 Stimmen (6 Suiten) für Violen- und Blockflötenchor oder Streichquartett.
In: Antiqua Edition. Von 4 Instrumenten an.
Cupid and Death.
In: Musica Britannica. Vol.2.
Organ music.
In: Tallis to Wesley. Vol.6.
Sacred music.
Boyce. Cathedral music. Vol.2; 1849, Vol.3.
Four suites made from consort music.
In: English instrumental music of the 16th and 17th centuries from manuscripts in the New York Public Library. No.7.
Suite. Organ voluntaries.
In: English keyboard music. [No.6, 7].
LOCKWOOD, NORMAND, 1906– .
String quartet, no.3.
In: Society for the Publication of American Music. Publications. 27th season. 1945–46.
LOEFFLER, CHARLES MARTIN, 1861–1935.
Music for four stringed instruments.
In: Society for the Publication of American Music. Publications. 4th season. 1922–23.
LOEILLET, JEAN BAPTISTE, 1680–1730.
(var. sp.: L'Oeillet de Gant; Loeilly).
Werken voor clavecimbel.
In: Monumenta musicae belgicae. Vol.1.
Keyboard music.
In: Herrmann. Contemporaries of Purcell.
In: Oesterle. Early keyboard music. Vol.1.
In: Tagliapietra. Antologia di musica antica e moderna per pianoforte. Bd.10.
Organ music.
In: Peeters. Oudnederlandse meesters. Vol.1, 2, 3.
Quintett H-moll für 2 f'-Blockflöte, Querflöte und Basso Continuo.
In: Hortus musicus. No.133.
Sonata A-moll, Op.1/1.
In: Gitarre-Kammermusik. No.13.
Sonate Op.1. Nr.1, 4, 6, 8; Op.2. Nr.5; Op.4. Nr.6. Für Alt-Blockflöte und Basso Continuo.
In: Moecks Kammermusik. Vol.28–32.
Drei Sonaten, für Flöte (Geige-Oboe) und Generalbass.
In: Hortus musicus. No.43.
Sonaten für Querflöte und Basso Continuo. Heft 2, 3.
In: Hortus musicus. No.162, 165.
Sonate (Em). Violin and piano.
In: Moffat. Meister-Schule der alten Zeit. Violin-Sonaten. No.21.

Sonate en la majeur.
In: L'école du violon au XVIIe et XVIIIe siècle. No.1277.
Suite.
In: Köhler. Les maîtres du clavecin. Heft 12.
Suite (Gm).
In: Pauer. Alte Meister. No.28.
Triosonate für f'-Blockflöte (Querflöte), Oboe (Violine) und Basso Continuo.
In: Hortus musicus. No.166, 176.
LOEWE, JOHANN JAKOB, 1629–1703.
Neuen Arien mit Ritornellen.
In: Nagels Musik-Archiv. No.32.
Zwei Suiten.
In: Nagels Musik-Archiv. No.67.
LOEWE, KARL, 1796–1869.
Werke. 17v.
Keyboard sonatas.
In: Newman. Thirteen keyboard sonatas of the 18th and 19th centuries.
Ouverture zu "Die Zerstörung von Jerusalem." Op.30.
In: Sondheimer. Orchesterwerke aus dem 19. Jahrhundert. Nr.350.
LOGI, GRAF.
Lute music.
In: Denkmäler der Tonkunst in Österreich. Vol.50. (Jg.XXV/2).
LOMBART, 16th CENTURY.
Chansons.
In: Expert. Les maîtres musiciens de la Renaissance française. Vol.5.
LONATI, CARLO AMBROGIO, b.ca.1655.
Arias.
In: Landshoff. Alte Meister des Bel Canto. Eine Sammlung von Arien. Vol.1–2.
LONGAS, FEDERICO, 1895– .
Keyboard music.
In: Guenther. Collection espagnole.
LONGO, ALESSANDRO, 1864–1945.
Keyboard music.
In: Tagliapietra. Antologia di musica antica e moderna per pianoforte. Bd.17.
LONGUEVAL, JEAN.
Selections.
In: Maldéghem. Trésor musical.
Motets.
In: Attaingnant. Treize livres de motets. Livre 11.
LOOMIS, HARVEY WORTHINGTON, 1865–1930.
Songs; Piano music.
In: The Wa-Wan series of American compositions.
LOPES MORAGO, ESTÊVAO.
Várias obras de música religiosa.
In: Portugaliae musica. Ser.A. Vol.4.
LÓPEZ, FRAY MIGUEL.
Organ music.
In: Piedelievre. Les anciens maîtres espagnols.
In: Pierront. Cent versets de magnificat.
LÓPEZ, MIQUEL, 1669–1723.
Instrumental music.
In: Mestres de l'escolania de Montserrat. (Pujol, ed. Musica instrumental. Vol.1).
Organ music.
In: Muset. Early Spanish organ music.
LOQUEVILLE, RICHARD, d.1418.
(var. sp.: Richardus Loqueville).
Selections.
In: Reaney. Early fifteenth-century music. Vol.3.
Sacred music.
In: Plainsong and Mediaeval Music Society. Publications. (Borren).
LORENZ, KARL ADOLF, 1837–1923.
Herzdame.
In: Zeitschrift für Spielmusik. No.171.
Orchesterausgabe.
In: Moecks gelbe Musikhefte. Vol.15.
LORENZO DE FLORENTIA.
(var. sp.: Laurentius Masii de Florentia; Lorenzo da Firenze).
Selections.
In: Pirrotta. The music of fourteenth-century Italy. Vol.3.
Cacce.
In: Marrocco. Fourteenth-century Italian cacce.
Sanctus.
In: Van. Les monuments de l'Ars Nova. I. No.3.
LORET, CLÉMENT.
Organ music.
In: Bedell. The French organist. Vol.1.
LOSY VON LOSYMTHAL, JOHANN ANTON, ca.1645–1721.
(var. sp.: Jan Antonín Losy z Losimtálu).
Pièces de guitarre.
In: Musica antiqua bohemica. Vol.38.
LOT, FRANÇOIS DU, *see* DULOT, FRANÇOIS.
LOTTI, ANTONIO, ca.1667–1740.
Arias.
In: Parisotti. Arie antiche. Bd.1.
Arie des Evander, Arie der Silvia, aus der Oper "Ascanio."
In: Schmid. Musik am sächsischen Hofe. Bd.1.
Choral music.
In: Commer. Cantica sacra. Vol.1. No.4.
In: Musica sacra . . . 1839– . Vol.2, 3.
In: Recueil de musique ancienne. Recueil des morceaux de musique ancienne. Bd.5, 10, 11.
In: Rochlitz. Sammlung vorzüglicher Gesangstücke. Bd.2.
Masses.
In: Denkmäler deutscher Tonkunst. [1.Folge]. Vol.60.
Part music.
In: Hullah. Part music. Class A.1. Vol.1; Class A. 2. Vol.1; 1868 edition.
Sacred music.
In: Latrobe, C. I. Selection of sacred music.
In: Latrobe, J. A. The music of the church.
In: Proske. Musica divina. Annus primus. Tom 1, 3.
Vocal music.
In: Gevaert. Les gloires de l'Italie. Vol.1.
In: Hullah. Vocal scores. I. Sacred.
LOUIS FERDINAND, PRINCE OF PRUSSIA. 1772–1806.
Musikalische Werke. 7v.

LOUVET, G.
Motets.
In: Attaingnant. Treize livres de motets. Livre 10.
LØVENSKIOLD, HERMAN SEVERIN, 1815–1870.
Fra Skoven ved Furesø. Concert-Ouverture. Op.29.
In: Samfundet til Udgivelse af dansk Musik. Ser.I. No.6.
LÜBECK, VINCENT, 1654–1740.
(var. sp.: Luebeck).
Musikalische Werke. 122p.
Orgelwerke. 51p.
Choral music.
In: Chorbuch für die Kirchenchöre Sachsens.
Organ music.
In: Klein. The first four centuries of music for the organ from Dunstable to Bach (1370–1749).
In: The Liturgical Music Press, Inc. Masterpieces of organ music. Folio 13, 52.
In: Organum. 4.Reihe. Nr.9.
In: Peeters. Anthologia pro organo. Vol.2, 4.
In: Straube. Choralvorspiele alter Meister.
Six préludes et fugues. Organ.
In: Orgue et liturgie. Vol.17.
Weihnachtsmusik. Für Klavier oder Orgel.
In: Nagels Musik-Archiv. No.95.
LUBLIN, JOHANNES DE, *see* JAN Z LUBLINA.
LUC, JACQUES DE SAINT.
Lute music.
In: Denkmäler der Tonkunst in Österreich. Vol.50. (Jg.XXV/2).
LUCA, S. DE.
Arias.
In: Parisotti. Arie antiche. Bd.2.
LUDFORD, NICHOLAS, ca.1485–ca.1557.
Collected works. 3v.
LUDWIG, FRIEDRICH, 1872–1930.
Repertorium organorum recentioris et motetorum vetustissimi stili.
In: Institute of Mediaeval Music. Musicological studies. Vol.7.
In: Summa musicae medii aevi. Vol.7, 8.
LUDWIG, WENZEL.
Lute music.
In: Denkmäler der Tonkunst in Österreich. Vol.50. (Jg.XXV/2).
LUDWIG V. HESSEN, LÄNDGRAF.
Leichte Suite.
In: Corona. Vol.28.
LUEBECK, VINCENT, *see* LÜBECK, VINCENT.
LUENENBURG, *see* LÜNEBURG.
LUENING, OTTO, 1900– .
8 Preludes for piano.
In: New music. Vol.15. No.3. Apr.1942.
Fantasia brevis, for clarinet and piano.
In: New music. Vol.10. No.4. July 1937.
Piano music.
In: Boletín latino-americano de música. Vol.5.
Only themselves understand themselves. Voice and piano.
In: New music. Vol.8. No.4. July 1935.
LUETKEMAN, PAUL.
Choralfantasien.
In: Engel. Drei Werke pommerscher Komponisten.
Fantasien über Kirchenmelodien der pommerschen Reformationzeit.
In: Denkmäler der Musik in Pommern. Heft 2.
LUISE, QUEEN OF PRUSSIA.
Lieblingswalzer.
In: Thouret. Musik am preussischen Hofe. No.3.
LULLY, JEAN BAPTISTE DE, 1632–1687.
Oeuvres complètes. 10v.
Selections.
In: Échos de France. Vol.1–3.
In: Expert. Répertoire classique de musique. 1re année).
Airs.
In: Prunières. Les maîtres du chant. Recueil 2.
Allemande, Sarabande et Gigue.
In: Köhler. Les maîtres du clavecin. Heft 8.
Armide.
In: Publikationen älterer praktischer und theoretischer Musikwerke. Jahrg.13.
Overture to "Armide."
In: Parrish. Masterpieces of music before 1750. No.36.
Ballettsuite "Le triomphe de l'amour."
In: Diletto musicale. No.16.
Keyboard music.
In: Oesterle. Early keyboard music. Vol.1.
In: Pauer. Alte Klavier-Musik. 1st series. Pt.1.
In: Selva. Pièces de clavecin des XVIIme et XVIIIme siècles.
In: Tagliapietra. Antologia di musica antica e moderna per pianoforte. Bd.7.
"Des Königs Musikanten."
In: Moser. Das Musikkränzlein. No.11a.
Menuet du bourgeois gentilhomme.
In: L'école du violon au XVIIe et XVIIIe siècle. No.1338.
Operas.
In: Les chefs d'oeuvres classiques de l'opéra français.
Organ music.
In: Anthologia antiqua. Vol.2.
Vocal music.
In: Delsarte. Archives du chant. Livr.1–17, 20–22, Suppl.
LUMBYE, HANS CHRISTIAN, 1810–1874.
Champagne Galop. Op.14. Orchestra.
In: Samfundet til Udgivelse af dansk Musik. Ser.III. No.91.
Concert-polka for 2 Violiner.
In: Samfundet til Udgivelse af dansk Musik. Ser.III. No.127.
Danse. Suite. Nr.1. For Orkester.
In: Samfundet til Udgivelse af dansk Musik. Ser.III. No.126.
LUNDBERG, LENNART ARVID, 1863–1931.
Piano sonata, D minor, Op.33.
In: Musikaliska konstföreningen. 1915.
LUNDH, L. A.
Requiem.
In: Musikaliska konstföreningen. 1891.

LÜNEBURG ORGAN TABULATURES.
In: Das Erbe deutscher Musik. 1.Reihe. Vol.36.
In: Shannon. The free organ compositions from the Lüneberg organ tablatures.
LUPA.
Church music.
In: Motett Society. [Collection of ancient church music]. Division 1.
LUPI, EDWARDI.
Sacred music.
In: The Fitzwilliam music. Bd.5.
LUPI, JOHANNES, *see* HELLINCK, JOANNES LUPUS.
LUPO, THOMAS, ca.1610.
Leichte Fantasien. Für drei Gamben oder andere Melodieinstrumente.
In: Hortus musicus. No.64.
Violenmusik.
In: Giesbert. Altenglische Violenmusik. Vol. 1, 2.
LUPRANO, FILIPPO DE, 15th–16th CENTURIES.
(var. sp.: Filippus de Lurano).
Sacred music.
In: Jeppesen. Italia sacra musica. Vol.2.
LUPUS, JOANNES, *see* HELLINCK, JOANNES LUPUS.
LURANO, FILIPPUS DE, *see* LUPRANO, FILIPPO DE.
LUSCINIUS (ACTUALLY OTTOMAR NACHTGALL), 1487–1537.
(var. sp.: Othomar Nachtigall).
Organ music.
In: Moser. Frühmeister der deutschen Orgelkunst.
LUTE MUSIC.
In: Attaingnant. Zwei– und dreistimmige Solostücke für die Laute.
In: Bruger. Alte Lautenkunst aus drei Jahrhundertern.
In: Chilesotti. Da un codice Lauten-Buch del cinquecento.
In: Chilesotti. Lautenspieler des XVI. Jahrhunderts.
In: Collegium musicum. Vol.4.
In: Crema. Intavolatura di liuto.
In: Denkmäler der Tonkunst in Österreich. Vol.37. (Jg.XVIII/2); Vol.50. (Jg.XXV/2); Vol.84.
In: Das Erbe deutscher Musik. 1.Reihe. Vol.12.
In: Das Erbe deutscher Musik. 2.Reihe. Alpen– und Donau Reichsgave. Vol.1. (Same as Denkmäler der Tonkunst in Österreich. Vol.84).
In: Fellowes. The English school of lutenist song writers. Ser.1–2; Rev. ed. The English lutesongs. Ser.2.
In: Francisque. Le trésor d'Orphée.
In: Gostena. Intavolatura di liuto.
In: Greff. Der Lautenist V. Bakfark, 1507–1576.
In: Hofhaimer. Einundneunzig gesammelte Tonsätze.
In: Lefkoff. Five sixteenth century Venetian lute books.
In: Martínez Torner. Colección de vihuelistas españoles del siglo XVI.
In: Moecks gelbe Musikhefte. Vol.40.
In: Molinaro. Intavolatura di liuto.
In: Monumenta musicae belgicae. Vol.10.
In: Monumentos de la música española. Vol.3, 7.
In: Morphy. Les luthistes espagnols du XVIe siècle.
In: Parrish. Masterpieces of music before 1750. No.22.
In: Parrish. A treasury of early music. No.21, 34, 39.
In: Radino. Intavolatura di balli per sonar di liuto.
In: Radino. Il primo libro d'intavolatura di balli d'arpicordo.
In: Schlick. Tablaturen etlicher Lobgesang und Lidlein uff die Orgeln und Lauten.
In: Schott's Series of early lute music.
In: La Société de Musique d'Autrefois. Publications. Tome 1.
In: Société Française de Musicologie, Paris. Publications. Sér.I. Bd.3–4, 6–7, 16.
In: Spielstücke für Blockflöten, Geigen, Lauten oder andere Instrumente.
In: Tappert. Sang und Klang aus alter Zeit.
In: Vereniging voor Nederlandsche. Muziekgeschiedenis. Uitgave. No.2.
In: The Wellesley edition. No.8.
LUTHER, MARTIN, 1483–1546.
Selections.
In: Crotch. Specimens of various styles of music. Vol.2.
Choral music.
In: Rochlitz. Sammlung vorzüglicher Gesangstücke. Bd.1. Pt.2.
Deutsche Messe. 1526.
In: Hirsch. Veröffentlichungen. [Bd.].11.
Part music.
In: Hullah. Part music. Class A.1. Vol.1; Class B.1.
Vocal music.
In: Delsarte. Archives du chant. Livr.14. No.2.
LUTOSLAWSKI, WITOLD, 1913– .
Sechs polnische Weihnachtslieder.
In: Zeitschrift für Spielmusik. No.259.
LUTTENBERGER, WILHELM, 1900–1933.
Gesamtausgabe (1926–1933). v.1– .
LUYTHON, KAREL, ca.1556–1620.
(var. sp.: Carolus Luython, Carlo Luyton).
Selections.
In: Denkmäler der Tonkunst in Österreich. Vol.77. (Jg.XLI).
Werken voor orgel of 4 speeltuigen.
In: Monumenta musicae belgicae. Vol.4.
Organ music.
In: Peeters. Altniederländsche Meister für Orgel oder Harmonium.
In: Peeters. Oudnederlandse meesters. Vol.2, 3.
LUZZASCHI, LUZZASCO, ca.1545–1607.
Selections.
In: Torchi. L'arte musicale in Italie. Bd.3.
Keyboard music.
In: Tagliapietra. Antologia di musica antica e moderna per pianoforte. Bd.2.
Madrigals.
In: Einstein. The golden age of the madrigal.
Organ music.
In: Fuser. Classici italiani dell'organo.
In: Klein. The first four centuries of music for the organ from Dunstable to Bach (1370–1749).
LVOV, ALEXIS FEODOROVICH, 1798–1870.
(var. sp.: Lvoff).

Part music.
In: Hullah. Part music. Class A.1. Vol.1.
Vocal music.
In: Sammlung russischer Romanzen. No.2, 29, 159.
LYON, JAMES, 1735–1794.
Selections.
In: Goldman. Landmarks of early American music, 1760–1800.

MAASZ, GERHARD, 1906– .
Choral music.
In: Nagels Männerchor-Blätter. No.1, 20, 21, 22.
Klingende Jahreszeiten.
In: Bausteine für Musikerziehung und Musikpflege. B 106.
Maienzeit.
In: Zeitschrift für Spielmusik. No.175.
O musica.
In: Zeitschrift für Spielmusik. No.213.
Scherzo für Blockflöten-Quartett.
In: Zeitschrift für Spielmusik. No.265.
Weihnachtsmusiken.
In: Bausteine für Musikerziehung und Musikpflege. B 118.
McCOY, WILLIAM J., 1848–1926.
Song.
In: The Wa-Wan series of American compositions.
MACÉ, DENIS, 17th CENTURY.
Airs.
In: Prunières. Les maîtres du chant. Recueil 4.
MACERO, TEO.
Canzona no.1. For 4 saxophones and 1 trumpet.
In: New music. Vol.27. No.3. Apr.1954.
MACFARREN, SIR GEORGE ALEXANDER, 1813–1887.
Part music.
In: Hullah; Part music. Class A.2. Vol.1, 2.
Vocal music.
In: Hullah. Vocal scores. II. Secular.
MACHADO, AUGUSTO, 1845–1924.
Selections.
In: Pedrell. Teatro lirico espanol anterior al siglo XIX. Bd.4/5.
MACHAUT, GUILLAUME DE, *see* GUILLAUME DE MACHAUT.
MACHINGER (MALCHINGER).
Lieder.
In: Publikationen älterer praktischer und theoretischer Musikwerke. Jahrg.8.
MACHOTIN.
Vocal music.
In: Sammlung russischer Romanzen. No.235, 264.
McKAY, GEORGE FREDERICK.
Dance suite No.2. Piano.
In: New music. Vol.13. No.2. Jan. 1940.
String quartet, No.2.
In: Washington (State) University. Music series. No.5a/b.
McMURDIE, JOSEPH, 1792–1878.
Part music.
In: Hullah. Part music. 1868 edition.
Vocal music.
In: Hullah. Vocal scores. I. Sacred; II. Secular.
McPHEE, COLIN, 1901– .
Concerto for piano with wind octette.
In: New music. Vol.4. No.2. Jan. 1931.
4 Iroquois dances.
In: New music. Vol.18. No.4. July 1945.
Kinesis, Invention. Piano.
In: New music. Vol.3. No.2. Jan. 1930.
MACQUE, GIOVANNI (JEAN DE), ca.1550–1614.
(var. sp.: Joannes de Macque).
Selections.
In: Maldéghem. Trésor musical.
Canzon alla francese.
In: Einstein. Beispielsammlung zur älteren Musikgeschichte.
Werken voor orgel of 4 speeltuigen.
In: Monumenta musicae belgicae. Vol.4.
Organ music.
In: Peeters. Altniederländsche Meister für Orgel oder Harmonium.
In: Peeters. Oudnederlandse meesters. Vol.1, 2, 3.
MADLSEDER, NONNOSUS, 1730–1797.
Instrumental music.
In: Denkmäler der Tonkunst in Österreich. Vol.86.
MADRID 20486. FACSIMILE REPRODUCTION OF THE MANUSCRIPT. (LUTHER A. DITTMER).
In: Institute of Mediaeval Music. Publications. Vol.1.
MADRIGALS.
In: Arion. 3v.
In: Arkwright. The Old English edition.
In: Chor-Archiv.
In: Das Chorwerk.
In: I classici della musica italiana. Vol.14, 21.
In: I classici della musica italiana. Raccolta nazionale delle musiche italiane. Quad. 59–62, 82–84.
In: I classici musicali italiani. Vol.10.
In: Documenta historica musicae.
In: Einstein. The golden age of the madrigal.
In: Euterpe.
In: Fellowes. The English madrigal school; Rev. ed. The English madrigalists. Ser.2.
In: Fellowes. The English school of lutenist song writers. Ser.1–2; Rev. ed. The English lutesongs. Ser.2.
In: Gesualdo. Sämtliche Madrigale.
In: Istituto italiano per la storia della musica. Pubblicazioni. 1. Monumenti I. Vol.1–3; 1. Monumenti II. Vol.1.
In: Der Kammerchor.
In: Madrigalisti italiani.
In: Marrocco. Fourteenth-century Italian cacce.
In: Monumenta musica neerlandica. Vol.5.
In: Music Press, Inc. [Choral series]. Vol.58, 118, 121.
In: Musical Antiquarian Society. Publications. Vol.2, 3, 8, 15, 16, 17.
In: Oller. Madrigales y canciones polifónicas.
In: Pistone. Capalavori della polifonia italiana.
In: Plainsong and Mediaeval Music Society. Publications.
In: Publikationen älterer Musik. Jahrg.10.
In: Smith College music archives. No.6.

In: Squire. Ausgewählte Madrigale und mehrstimmige Gesänge berühmter Meister des 16., 17. Jahrhundert.
In: The triumphs of Oriana.
In: Vereniging voor Nederlandsche Muziekgeschiedenis. Uitgave. No.5, 24, 45.
MAEGAARD, JAN, 1926– .
Kammerkoncert Nr.2. (1962).
In: Samfundet til Udgivelse af dansk Musik. Ser.III. No.161a.
Oktomeri (1962).
In: Samfundet til Udgivelse af dansk Musik. Ser.III. No.161b.
5 preludes for solo violin.
In: Samfundet til Udgivelse af dansk Musik. Ser.III. No.144.
Trio for obo, clarinet og fagot.
In: Samfundet til Udgivelse af dansk Musik. Ser.III. No.123.
MAFFONI, HIERONIMO.
Sacred music.
In: Jeppesen. Italia sacra musica. Vol.1, 2.
MAGDELAIN.
Chansons.
In: Publikationen älterer praktischer und theoretischer Musikwerke. Jahrg.27.
MAGE, PIERRE DU, *see* DU MAGE, PIERRE.
MAGNI, BENEDETTO, 17th CENTURY.
Motetto: Giligam te Domine.
In: Musica sacra . . . between 1892–1897. No.8.
MAGNI, GIOAN BATTISTA.
Instrumental music.
In: Wasielewski. Instrumentalsätze vom Ende des XVI. bis Ende des XVII. Jahrhunderts.
MAGNIFICATS.
In: Early English church music. Vol.5.
MAHLER, GUSTAV, 1860–1911.
Sämtliche Werke. v.1– .
MAHU, STEPHAN, 16th CENTURY.
(var. sp.: Steffan Mahu).
Selections.
In: Musica sacra . . . 1839– . Vol.17, 18.
Choral music.
In: Antiqua Chorbuch. Vol.1. Heft 1; Vol.2. Heft 1.
Lieder.
In: Denkmäler der Tonkunst in Österreich. Vol.72. (Jg.XXXVII/2).
In: Publikationen älterer praktischer und theoretischer Musikwerke. Jahrg.1–3.
MAIER, A. E.
Violin sonata, B minor.
In: Musikaliska konstföreningen. 1878.
MAILLARD.
Chansons.
In: Publikationen älterer praktischer und theoretischer Musikwerke. Jahrg.27.
MAILLARD, JEAN, 16th CENTURY.
Mass.
In: Stein. Twelve Franco-Flemish masses of the early 16th century.
MAILLART.
Choral music.
In: Recueil de musique ancienne. Recueil des morceaux de musique ancienne. Bd.11.
MAINERIO, DON GIORGIO, 16th CENTURY.
Il primo libro di balli.
In: Musikalische Denkmäler. Bd.5.
MAISTRE, MATTHEUS LE, ca.1505–1577.
(var. sp.: Matthaeus le Maistre, Meister).
Selections.
In: Ambros. Auserwählte Tonwerke.
In: Maldéghem. Trésor musical.
Choral music.
In: Antiqua Chorbuch. Vol.1. Heft 2; Vol.2. Heft 2.
In: Commer. Collectio operum musicorum batavorum saeculi XVI. Bd.8.
In: Der Kammerchor. Vol.5.
Lied– und Choralmotetten.
In: Das Chorwerk. No.30.
MAJO, GIAN FRANCESCO DE, 1732–1770.
Arias.
In: Landshoff. Alte Meister des Bel Canto. Eine Sammlung von Arien. Vol.1–2.
Sicut cerva, quae per valles. Sopran und Konzertierende Orgel.
In: Cantio sacra. No.36.
MAJONE, ASCANIO, 16th–17th CENTURIES.
Selections.
In: Torchi. L'arte musicale in Italia. Bd.3.
Organ music.
In: Fuser. Classici italiani dell'organo.
MALAGA, CARLOS SÁNCHEZ.
Piano music.
In: Boletín latino-americano de música. Vol.4.
MALBECQUE, GUILLERMUS, 15th CENTURY.
Selections.
In: Reaney. Early fifteenth-century music. Vol.2.
MALEINGREAU, PAUL DE, 1887–1956.
Organ music.
In: Bedell. The French organist. Vol.2.
MALER, WILHELM, 1902– .
Choral music.
In: Nagels Männerchor-Blätter. No.6.
MALLING, JØRGEN HENRIK, 1836–1905.
Küwala. Choral work.
In: Samfundet til Udgivelse af dansk Musik. Ser.II. No.15.
Eight Scottish folksongs, Op.2.
In: Samfundet til Udgivelse af dansk Musik. Suppl. 1897.
MALLING, OTTO VALDEMAR, 1848–1915.
Det hellige Land. Op.46. Choral work.
In: Samfundet til Udgivelse af dansk Musik. Ser.II. No.9.
Oktet. Op.50.
In: Samfundet til Udgivelse af dansk Musik. Ser.II. No.24.
Organ music.
In: Gerhardt. Album nordischer Komponisten für Orgel. Vol.1, 2.
In: Standard series of organ compositions. No.11.
Prolog til "Den gyldne Legende." Op.25. Choral work.
In: Samfundet til Udgivelse af dansk Musik. Ser.II. No.4.
Symfoni, D moll, Op.17.
In: Samfundet til Udgivelse af dansk Musik. Ser.I. No.20.

MALVEZZI, CRISTOFORO, 1547–1597.
Organ music.
In: Fuser. Classici italiani dell' organo.
MALZAT, JOHANN M.
Quintett Nr.5, Es-dur.
In: Hausmusik. No.63.
MAMIYA, MICHIO.
Composition for male chorus.
In: Contemporary Japanese music series. No.24.
Three movements for wind quintet. Quartet for shakuhachi, sangen and two kotos.
In: Contemporary Japanese music series. No.9.
MANALT, FRANCISCO.
Sonatas I–II, III–IV para violin y piano.
In: Musica hispana. Ser.C. No.2, 7.
MANCHICOURT, PIERRE DE, ca.1510–1564.
(var. sp.: Peter de Manchichourt).
Chanson.
In: Brown. Theatrical chansons of the 15th and early 16th centuries.
Choral music.
In: Commer. Collectio operum musicorum batavorum saeculi XVI. Bd.12.
Mass.
In: Stein. Twelve Franco-Flemish masses of the early 16th century.
Motets.
In: Attaingnant. Treize livres de motets. Livre 5, 7, 13, 14.
MANCINI, FRANCESCO, 1679–1739.
Airs.
In: Prunières. Les maîtres du chant. Recueil 1.
Songs.
In: Jeppesen. La flora. Vol.2.
MANEI.
Vocal music.
In: Sammlung russischer Romanzen. No.124.
MANFREDINI, FRANCESCO, b.1688.
(var. sp.: Vincenzo Manfredini).
Concerto grosso, Op.3, Nr.11.
In: Nagels Musik-Archiv. No.153.
Keyboard music.
In: Benvenuti. Cembalisti italiani del settecento.
Konzertante Weihnachtsmusik.
In: Nagels Musik-Archiv. No.182.
12a sinfonia pastorale.
In: Somma. Musiche vocali e strumentali sacre e profane, sec. XVII–XVIII–XIX. Vol.22.
Il sinfonie dell' Op.2.
In: Somma. Musiche vocali e strumentali sacre e profane, sec. XVII–XVIII–XIX. Vol.11–21.
Weihnachtskonzert. (Concerto grosso per il santissimo natale).
In: Schering. Perlen alter Kammermusik.
Weihnachtssymphonie (Pastorale aus dem Weihnachtskonzert).
In: Schering. Perlen alter Kammermusik.
MANGEAN.
Sonate en fa majeur
In: L'école du violon au XVIIe et XVIIIe siècle. No.1287.
MANGIAGALLI, RICCARDO PICK-, *see* PICK-MANGIAGALLI, RICCARDO.
MANKELL, HENNING, 1868–1930.
Andante and variations for piano, Op.57.
In: Musikaliska konstföreningen. 1943.
Barcarolle for piano, Op.60, No.1.
In: Musikaliska konstföreningen. 1936.
MANN, ALFRED.
Kleine Schulmusik.
In: Moecks Kammermusik. Vol.203.
In: Zeitschrift für Spielmusik. No.59.
MANN, JOHANN CHRISTOPH.
Instrumental music.
In: Denkmäler der Tonkunst in Österreich. Vol.39. (Jg.XIX/2).
MANNA, GIUSEPPE.
Vocal music.
In: Gevaert. Les gloires de l'Italie. Vol.1.
MANNELLI, CARLO.
Selections.
In: Torchi. L'arte musicale in Italia. Bd.5.
MANNHEIM CHAMBER MUSIC, 18th CENTURY.
In: Denkmäler deutscher Tonkunst. [2.Folge]. Vol.15–16.
MANNHEIM SYMPHONIES.
In: Denkmäler deutscher Tonkunst. [2.Folge]. Vol.3 (i), 7 (ii), 8 (ii).
In: Riemann. Mannheim symphonists.
MANTUA, JACHET DE, *see* JACHET DE MANTUA.
MANTUA COMPOSERS.
Madrigals.
In: Das Chorwerk. No.80.
LE MANUSCRIT DU ROI.
In: Beck. Les chansonniers des troubadours et des trouvères. Vol.2.
MANZIA, LUIGI.
Songs.
In: Jeppesen. La flora. Vol.1.
MARAIS, MARIN, 1656–1728.
Suite D-moll für Viola da Gamba, Cembalo (Klavier) und Bass Instrument ad lib.
In: Antiqua Edition. Von 2 Instrumenten an.
MARAZZOLI, MARCO, ca.1619–1662.
Kammerduette.
In: Landshoff. Alte Meister des Bel Canto. Italienische Kammerduette.
MARBECK, JOHN, ca.1510–ca.1585.
(var. sp.: John Merbecke).
Church music.
In: Tudor church music. Vol.10.
MARCELLO, ALESSANDRO, ca.1684–ca.1750.
Konzert D-moll für Oboe.
In: Corona. Vol.76.
Largo aus einem Concerto grosso.
In: Schering. Perlen alter Kammermusik.
MARCELLO, BENEDETTO, 1686–1739.
Selections.
In: Crotch. Specimens of various styles of music. Vol.2.
Arianna.
In: Chilesotti. Biblioteca di rarità musicali. Vol.4.
Arias.
In: Landshoff. Alte Meister des Bel Canto. Eine Sammlung von Arien. Vol.1–2.
In: Parisotti. Arie antiche. Bd.1, 2.
Cantate.
In: I classici della musica italiana. Vol.17.
In: I classici della musica italiana. Raccolta nazionale delle musiche italiane. Quad. 67–69.

Cantate per contralto e per soprano.
In: I classici musicali italiani. Vol.2.
Choral music.
In: Recueil de musique ancienne. Recueil des morceaux de musique ancienne. Bd.3, 5.
In: Rochlitz. Sammlung vorzüglicher Gesangstücke. Bd.2.
Composizioni per cembalo od organo.
In: I classici della musica italiana. Raccolta nazionale della musiche italiane. Quad. 70–71.
Concerto, Op.1, No.3.
In: Antica musica strumentale italiana. In preparation.
Concerto No.5 in F, Op.1, No.4. (strings, cembalo).
In: Antica musica strumentale italiana. Ser.III. Vol.22.
Fugue. "Mai non turbarsi."
In: Königliche Akademie der Künste. Auswahl vorzüglicher Musik-Werke. No.37.
Gioàz.
In: I classici musicali italiani. Vol.8.
Keyboard music.
In: Esposito. Early Italian piano music.
In: Farrenc. Le trésor des pianistes. Vol.9.
In: Tagliapietra. Antologia di musica antica e moderna per pianoforte. Bd.11.
Organ music.
In: Biggs. Treasury of early organ music.
In: Biggs. A treasury of shorter organ classics.
Psaume.
In: Guilmant. Répertoire des concerts du Trocadéro. Vol.3.
Recitative and Aria from Stravaganze d'Amore. "Amor tu sei."
In: Parrish. A treasury of early music. No.49.
Sacred music.
In: Alfieri. Raccolta di musica sacra. Vol.1.
In: Latrobe, C. I. Selection of sacred music.
In: Latrobe, J. A. The music of the church.
In: Page. Harmonia sacra. Vol.2.
Sonata (B).
In: Pauer. Alte Meister. No.45.
Sonaten für f'-Blockflöte und Basso Continuo.
In: Hortus musicus. No.142, 151, 152.
Sonaten II und V für 2 Violoncelli und Basso Continuo.
In: Moecks Kammermusik. Vol.56.
Songs.
In: Jeppesen. La flora. Vol.3.
Vocal music.
In: Delsarte. Archives du chant. Livr.20. No.1; Livr.21. No.1.
In: Gevaert. Les gloires de l'Italie. Vol.1.
In: Hullah. Vocal scores. I. Sacred.
MARCELLO-DUBOIS-BEDELL.
Organ music.
In: Standard series of organ compositions. No.28.
MARCHAND, LOUIS, 1669–1732.
Keyboard music.
In: Grovlez. Les plus belles pièces de clavessin de l'école française. Vol.1.
In: Tagliapietra. Antologia di musica antica e moderna per pianoforte. Bd.10.
Organ music.
In. Bonnet. Historical organ-recitals. Vol.1.
In: Guilmant. Archives des maîtres de l'orgue. Vol.3, 5.
In: Klein. The first four centuries of music for the organ from Dunstable to Bach (1370–1749).
In: Liber organi. Bd.1.
In: The Liturgical Music Press, Inc. Masterpieces of organ music. Folio 48.
In: Raugel. Les maîtres français de l'orgue. Vol.2.
MARCHANT.
Keyboard music.
In: The Fitzwilliam virginal book.
MARCHARD, JOSEPH, LE FILS.
Suite sonate.
In: L'école du violon au XVIIe et XVIIIe siècle. No.1259.
MARCHES.
In: Moecks gelbe Musikhefte. Vol.8, 37.
In: Thouret. Musik am preussischen Hofe.
In: Vereniging voor Nederlandsche Muziekgeschiedenis. Uitgave. No.21.
MARCIN Z LWOWA, *see* LEOPOLITA, MARTINUS (MARCIN ZE LWOWA).
MARCKHL, ERICH.
Klaviersonate in F.
In: Marckhl. Klavierwerke steiermärkischer Komponisten. Vol.3.
Plomberger Haustänze, für Violine und Klavier.
In: Hausmusik. No.30.
Zwei kleine Choraltrios. Organ.
In: Orgelmusik steirischer Komponisten.
MARCO, GIOVANNI, *see* RUTINI, GIOVANNI MARIA PLACIDO.
MARCO DA GAGLIANO, *see* GAGLIANO, MARCO DA.
MARELLA.
Part music.
In: Hullah. Part music. Class C. Secular.
MARENZIO, LUCA, ca.1553–1599.
(var. sp.: L. Marentius).
Sämtliche Werke. Bd.1–2.
In: Publikationen älterer Musik. Jahrg.4, Pt.1; Jahrg.6.
Selections.
In: Crotch. Specimens of various styles of music. Vol.2.
In: Documenta historica musicae.
In: Gabrieli. Music of Gabrieli and his time.
In: Musica sacra . . . 1839– . Vol.16.
In: Torchi. L'arte musicale in Italia. Bd.2.
Choral music.
In: Engel. Three centuries of choral music. Vol.2.
In: Der Kammerchor. Vol.3.
In: Music Press, Inc. [Choral series]. No.50, 77.
In: Recueil de musique ancienne. Recueil des morceaux de musique ancienne. Bd.11.
In: Societas Polyphonica Romanae. Repertorium. Vol.2, 4, 5, 6.
Giovane Donna.
In: The Penn state music series. No.13.
Madrigals.
In: Einstein. Beispielsammlung zur älteren Musikgeschichte.

In: Einstein. The golden age of the madrigal.
In: Madrigalisti italiani. Vol.1.
In: Squire. Ausgewählte Madrigale und mehrstimmige Gesänge. No.16, 24.
Organ music.
In: Cantantibus organis. Vol.6.
Part music.
In: Hullah. Part music. Class A.2. Vol.1.
Sacred music.
In: Page. Harmonia sacra. Vol.3.
In: Proske. Musica divina. Annus primus. Tom 2, 3; Annus secundus. Tom 2.
In: Proske. Selectus novus missarum. Annus secundus. Tom 2.
S'io parto, i'moro.
In: Parrish. Masterpieces of music before 1750. No.27.
2 Villanellen, zu singen oder zu spielen.
In: Zeitschrift für Spielmusik. No.33.
MARESCHAL, SAMUEL.
Selected works.
In: Corpus of early keyboard music. Vol.27.
MARGOT, COLIN.
Motets.
In: Attaingnant. Treize livres de motets. Livre 13.
MARIA, FRAY TOMÁS DE SANTA, *see* SANTA MARIA, FRAY TOMÁS DE.
MARIN, JOSÉ, 1619–1699.
Selections.
In: Pedrell. Teatro lirico espanol anterior al siglo XIX. Bd.3, 4/5.
MARIN, MERSENNE.
Lute music.
In: Chilesotti. Lautenspieler des XVI. Jahrhunderts.
MARINI, BIAGIO, ca.1595–1665.
Selections.
In: Torchi. L'arte musicale in Italia. Bd.7.
Chamber music.
In: Riemann. Old chamber music. Vol.3.
Instrumental music.
In: Wasielewski. Instrumentalsätze vom Ende des XVI. bis Ende des XVII. Jahrhunderts.
Sonate D-moll für Violine und Basso Continuo.
In: Hortus musicus. No.129.
Sonate für 2 Violine und Basso Continuo.
In: Hortus musicus. No.143.
MARKEVITCH, IGOR, 1912– .
(var. sp.: Markewitsch).
Vocal music.
In: Sammlung russischer Romanzen. No.56.
MARKWORTH, HENRY J., 1900– .
Organ music.
In: The parish organist. Vol.1–4.
MARLE, NICOLAS DE.
Chansons.
In: Publikationen älterer praktischer und theoretischer Musikwerke. Jahrg.27.
MAROT, CLÉMENT, 1496–1544.
Les chansons.
In: Société Française de Musicologie, Paris. Publications. Sér.III. Bd.1.
Vocal music.
In: Delsarte. Archives du chant. Livr.20, Suppl.
MARPURG, FRIEDRICH WILHELM, 1718–1795.
Op.1. Capriccio. (F).
In: Pauer. Alte Meister. No.4.
Capriccio. Op.1. Prélude et capriccio.
In: Köhler. Les maîtres du clavecin. Heft 6.
Fugue for piano, D minor.
In: Königliche Akademie der Künste. Auswahl vorzüglicher Musik-Werke. No.15.
Keyboard music.
In: Clementi. Clementi's Selection of practical harmony. Vol.1.
In: Pauer. Alte Klavier-Musik. 1st series. Pt.5.
In: Tagliapietra. Antologia di musica antica e moderna per pianoforte. Bd.13.
Organ music.
In: The Liturgical Music Press, Inc. Masterpieces of organ music. Folio 71.
Preludio e capriccio. Organ.
In: Dickinson. Historical recital series for organ. Vol.1. No.16.
MARRIGUES, JEAN NICOLAS.
Organ music.
In: Raugel. Les maîtres français de l'orgue. Vol.2.
MARSEILLE, PIERRE GAULTIER DE, *see* GAULTIER DE MARSEILLE, PIERRE.
MARSH, JOHN, ca.1752–1828.
Sacred music.
In: Page. Harmonia sacra. Vol.3.
MARSON, GEORGE, ca.1573–1632.
Madrigal.
In: The triumphs of Oriana.
MARTELAERE, JOANNES DE, 16th CENTURY.
(var. sp.: Joanne Matelart).
Selections.
In: Maldéghem. Trésor musical.
Lute music.
In: Chilesotti. Lautenspieler des XVI. Jahrhunderts.
MARTELLI, HENRI, 1895– .
Melodien für Flauto dolce und Klavier.
In: Moecks Kammermusik. Vol.505, 508.
Provençalische Lieder und Tänze.
In: Zeitschrift für Spielmusik. No.293.
MARTENS, HENRICH, 1876– . ed.
Das Melodram; Das Menuett; Polonaise und Mazurka.
In: Musikalische Formen in historischen Reihen. Bd.11, 1, 19.
MARTI.
Selections.
In: Pedrell. Teatro lirico espanol anterior al siglo XIX. Bd.4/5.
MARTIENSSEN, CARL ADOLF, 1881–1955. ed.
Die individualle Klaviertechnik.
In: Kirchenmusikalisches Institut der Evangelisch-Lutherischen Landeskirche in Sachsen am Landeskonservatorium der Musik. Veröffentlichungen. No.2.
MARTIN DE LEOPOL, *see* LEOPOLITA, MARTINUS (MARCIN ZE LWOWA).
MARTINEZ, M. A.
Sonate (E); Sonate (A).
In: Pauer. Alte Meister. No.59, 60.
MARTINI, GIOVANNI BATTISTA, 1706–1784.
(var. sp.: Johannes Martini).

20 Composizioni originali per organo. 55p.
Selections.
In: Échos de France. Vol.1–3.
In: Expert. Répertoire classique de musique. 1re année.
Arias.
In: Parisotti. Arie antiche. Bd.1.
Concerti per cembalo e orchestra.
In: I classici musicali italiani. Vol.11.
Gavotte.
In: L'école du violon au XVIIe et XVIIIe siècle. No.1344.
Gavotte F do la 12me sonata.
In: Guilmant. Répertoire des concerts du Trocadéro. Vol.1.
Gavotte, Ballet, Prélude, Fugue et Allegro.
In: Köhler. Les maîtres du clavecin. Heft 7.
Drei geistliche Gesänge.
In: Das Chorwerk. No.46.
Keyboard music.
In: Clementi. Clementi's Selection of practical harmony. Vol.1, 2, 4.
In: Esposito. Early Italian piano music.
In: Farrenc. Le trésor des pianistes. Vol.9.
In: Georgii. Keyboard music of the Baroque and Rococo. Vol.3.
In: Pauer. Alte Klavier-Musik. 1st series. Pt.2.
In: Tagliapietra. Antologia di musica antica e moderna per pianoforte. Bd.12.
Magnificat e Messe.
In: Archivium musices metropolitanum mediolanense. Vol.12.
Organ music.
In: Bonnet. Historical organ-recitals. Vol.3.
In: Bossi. Sammlung von Stücken alter italienischer Meister für die moderne Orgel.
In: Elkan-Vogel organ series. Vol.1.
In: Fuser. Classici italiani dell' organo.
In: Peeters. Anthologia pro organo. Vol.2, 4.
In: Schering. Alte Meister aus der Frühzeit des Orgelspiels.
Präludium, Fuge und Allegro. (Em).
In: Pauer. Alte Meister. No.10.
Sacred music.
In: The Fitzwilliam music. Bd.1, 4.
Sonata F-moll. Organ.
In: Guilmant. École classique de l'orgue. No.24.
Sonata. Piano.
In: I classici della musica italiana. Vol.18.
In: I classici della musica italiana. Raccolta nazionale delle musiche italiana. Quad.72–75.
In: Paoli. Sonate italiane del secolo XVIII per cembalo o pianoforte.
Sechs Sonaten für Cembalo oder Klavier.
In: Mitteldeutsches Musikarchiv. Reihe I. Bd.5.
Sonate (F).
In: Pauer. Alte Meister. No.52.
Vocal music.
In: Gevaert. Les gloires de l'Italie. Vol.2.
MARTUCCI, GIUSEPPE, 1856–1909.
Keyboard music.
In: Tagliapietra. Antologia di musica antica e moderna per pianoforte. Bd.17.
MARUTA, SHOZO.
Divertissement for brass quintet.
In: Contemporary Japanese music series. No.30.
MARX, KARL, 1897– .
Choral music.
In: Nagels Männerchor-Blätter. No.1, 2, 10, 14, 22, 23, 27, 29, 30.
Deutsches Proprium.
In: Christophorus-Chorwerk. Heft 2.
Es liegt ein Schloss in Österreich.
In: Zeitschrift für Spielmusik. No.282.
Der Morgenstern ist aufgegangen.
In: Zeitschrift für Spielmusik. No.185.
MASCAUDIO, GUGLIELMI DE, *see* GUILLAUME DE MACHAUT.
MASCHERA, FLORENTIO, 16th CENTURY.
Instrumental music.
In: Wasielewski. Instrumentalsätze vom Ende des XVI. bis Ende des XVII. Jahrhunderts.
Organ music.
In: Auler. Spielbuch für Kleinorgel. Vol.1.
In: Fuser. Classici italiani dell'organo.
MASCITTI, MICHELE, b.1663 or 1664.
Adagio religioso.
In: L'école du violon au XVIIe et XVIIIe siècle. No.1341.
Forlana.
In: L'école du violon au XVIIe et XVIIIe siècle. No.1333.
Kammer-Sonaten für Violine und Pianoforte.
In: Moffat. Kammer-Sonaten für Violine und Pianoforte. No.7.
Sarabande.
In: L'école du violon au XVIIe et XVIIIe siècle. No.1334, 1339.
Sonate (A). Violin and piano.
In: Moffat. Meister-Schule der alter Zeit. Violin-Sonaten. No.24.
Les Vents.
In: L'école du violon au XVIIe et XVIIIe siècle. No.1345.
MAŠEK, VINCENZ, 1755–1831.
Serenate Boeme.
In: Musica antiqua bohemica. Vol.35.
MASERA.
Church music.
In: Motett Society. [Collection of ancient church music]. Division 1.
MASETTI, ENZO, 1893– .
Keyboard music.
In: Tagliapietra. Antologia di musica antica e moderna per pianoforte. Bd.18.
MASON, DANIEL GREGORY, 1873–1953.
Three pieces for flute, harp, and string quartet. Op.13.
In: Society for the Publication of American Music. Publications. 4th season. 1922–23.
Serenade for string quartet. Op.31.
In: Society for the Publication of American Music. Publications. 15th season. 1933–34.
Sonata for clarinet (or violin) and piano. Op.14.
In: Society for the Publication of American Music. Publications. 1st season. 1919–20.

String quartet on Negro themes. Op.19.
In: Society for the Publication of American Music. Publications. 11th season. 1929–30.
MASON, GEORGE, 16th–17th CENTURIES.
Selections.
In: Smith. Musica antiqua.
Ayres (1618).
In: Fellowes. The English school of lutenist song writers. 2d series. Vol.18.
Sacred music.
In: Page. Harmonia sacra. Vol.1.
MASQUES.
In: Arkwright. The Old English edition. Vol.1.
MASSAINO, TIBURTIO, 16th–17th CENTURIES. (var. sp.: Tiburzio Massaino).
Selections.
In: Denkmäler der Tonkunst in Österreich. Vol.110.
In: Smith. Musica antiqua.
Vocal music.
In: Ghisi. Feste musicali della Firenze Medicae.
MASSES.
In: Alfieri. Raccolta di musica sacra.
In: Anthologie des maîtres religieux primitifs des XVe, XVIe et XVIIe siècles.
In: Archivium musices metropolitanum mediolanense.
In: Arkwright. The Old English edition. Vol.10.
In: Basilica.
In: Catholic Church, Roman. Liturgy and ritual. Missal. Missa Tornacensis.
In: Chor-Archiv.
In: Das Chorwerk.
In: Christophorus-Chorwerk.
In: Collegium musicum. Vol.5.
In: Coussemaker. Messe du XIIIe siècle.
In: Denkmäler der Tonkunst in Österreich. Vol.1. (Jg.I/1); Vol.45. (Jg.XXII); Vol.49. (Jg.XXV/1); Vol.78. (Jg.XLII/1); Vol.94/95.
In: Denkmäler deutscher Tonkunst. [1.Folge]. Vol.7, 60.
In: Documenta maiora liturgiae polychoralis sanctae ecclesiae romanae.
In: Documenta polyphoniae liturgicae sanctae ecclesiae romanae.
In: Early English church music. Vol.1, 4.
In: Das Erbe deutscher Musik. 1.Reihe. Vol.5, 57.
In: Monumenta liturgiae polychoralis sanctae ecclesiae romanae.
In: Monumenta musicae belgicae. Vol.8.
In: Monumenta polyphoniae italicae. Vol.1.
In: Monumenta polyphoniae liturgicae sanctae ecclesiae romanae.
In: Musica liturgica.
In: Musica spiritualis.
In: Musik alter Meister. Heft 1, 11, 12.
In: Plainsong and Mediaeval Music Society. Publications.
In: Recent researches in the music of the Renaissance. Vol.4.
In: Stäblein-Harder. Fourteenth-century mass music in France.
In: Stein. Twelve Franco-Flemish masses of the early 16th century.
In: Summa musicae medii aevi. Vol.1.
In: Turin. Biblioteca Nazionale. Mss. (J.II.9). The Cypriot-French repertory. Vol.1.
In: Vereniging voor Nederlandsche Muziekgeschiedenis. Uitgave. No.9.
MATCHETT, CLEMENT.
Clement Matchett's virginal book.
In: English keyboard music. [No.9].
MATELART, JOANNE, *see* MARTELAERE, JOANNES DE.
MATHIAS.
Motets.
In: Attaingnant. Treize livres de motets. Livre 2, 4.
MATHO, S. B.
Airs.
In: Prunières. Les maîtres du chant. Recueil 6.
MATIELLI, GIOVANNI ANTONIO, 18th CENTURY.
Gigue, Adagio, Allegro.
In: Köhler. Les maîtres du clavecin. Heft 8.
In: Pauer. Alte Meister. No.33.
MATIJEGKA, W.
Serenade für Flöte, Viola und Gitarre. Op.26.
In: Albert. Die Gitarre in der Haus– und Kammermusik vor 100 Jahren (1780–1820). No.11.
MATSUSHITA, SHIN-ICHI.
Canzona da sonate No.1. [for piano and percussion].
In: Contemporary Japanese music series. No.11.
Music for soprano and chamber ensemble.
In: Contemporary Japanese music series. No.22.
MATTEIS, NICOLA, 17th CENTURY.
Arias.
In: Landshoff. Alte Meister des Bel Canto. Eine Sammlung von Arien. Vol.1–2.
MATTEO-CARRASSI, *see* CARRASSI-MATTEO.
MATTESON, JEAN.
Keyboard music.
In: Farrenc. Le trésor des pianistes. Vol.11.
MATTHÄI, KONRAD, 17th CENTURY. (var. sp.: Konrad Matthaei).
Preussische Festlieder.
In: Das Erbe deutscher Musik. 2.Reihe. Ostpreussen und Danzig. Vol.1.
MATTHESON, JOHANN, 1681–1764.
Vier Giguen.
In: Pauer. Alte Meister. No.13.
Pièces de clavecin. (1714). facsimile.
In: Monuments of music and music literature. First series. No.5.
Keyboard music.
In: Oesterle. Early keyboard music. Vol.2.
In: Pauer. Alte Klavier-Musik. 1st series. Pt.4.
In: Tagliapietra. Antologia di musica antica e moderna per pianoforte. Bd.10.
Suite. No.5. (Cm).
In: Pauer. Alte Meister. No.37.
Suite. No.5. 4 Gigues, Allemande, Courante, Gigue, Sarabande avec 3 Variations.
In: Köhler. Les maîtres du clavecin. Heft 5.
Tanzsätze.
In: Zeitschrift für Spielmusik. No.5.
Die wohlklingende Fingersprache. Für Cembalo oder Klavier.

In: Mitteldeutsches Musikarchiv. Reihe I. Bd.1.
MATTHISON-HANSEN, JOHAN GOTFRED, 1832–1909.
Album for piano.
In: Samfundet til Udgivelse af dansk Musik. Suppl. 1895.
Drapa. For orkester.
In: Samfundet til Udgivelse af dansk Musik. Ser.II. No.36.
Organ music.
In: Gerhardt. Album nordischer Komponisten für Orgel. Vol.1, 2.
MAUDUIT, JACQUES, 1557–1627.
Chansonnettes mesurées de Jan Antoine de Baïf.
In: Expert. Les maîtres musiciens de la Renaissance française. Vol.10.
Psaumes mesurés à l'antique de J.–A. de Baïf.
In: Expert. Florilège du concert vocal de la Renaissance. No.7.
Vocal music.
In: Delsarte. Archives du chant. Livr.2. No.2.
MAURICE, THE LEARNED, LANDGRAVE OF HESSE-CASSEL, *see* MORITZ, LANDGRAF OF HESSE-CASSEL.
MAXXAFERRATA.
(possibly Mazzaferrata).
Instrumental music.
In: Wasielewski. Instrumentalsätze vom Ende des XVI. bis Ende des XVII. Jahrhunderts.
MAY, O.
Part music.
In: Hullah. Part music. 1868 edition.
Vocal music.
In: Hullah. Vocal scores. II. Secular.
MAYER, MARTIN.
Das Weihnachtsevangelium.
In: Nagels Musik-Archiv. No.164.
MAYER, RUDOLF.
Kleine Stücke.
In: Hausmusik. No.79.
Kleines Quartett für Violinen.
In: Hausmusik. No.115.
MAYONE, ASCANIO.
Keyboard music.
In: Corpus of early keyboard music. Vol.24.
MAYR, ANTON.
Kleine Suite.
In: Hausmusik. No.32.
MAYR, RUPERT IGNAZ, 1646–1712.
Ausgewählte Kirchenmusik.
In: Das Erbe deutscher Musik. 2.Reihe. Bayern. Vol.1.
Organ music.
In: Cantantibus organis. Vol.11.
MAZZAFERRATA, GIOVANNI BATTISTA, d.1691 (*see also* Maxxaferrata).
Sonata a tre, per due violini, violoncello e basso continuo, Op.V/6.
In: Hausmusik. No.148.
MAZZOCCHI, DOMENICO, 1592–1665.
(var. sp.: Mazocchi).
Airs.
In: Prunières. Les maîtres du chant. Recueil 3.
Arias.
In: Landshoff. Alte Meister des Bel Canto. Eine Sammlung von Arien. Vol.1–2.
Acht Madrigalen.
In: Das Chorwerk. No.95.
MAZZOCCHI, VIRGILIO, 1597–1646.
Selections.
In: Torchi. L'arte musicale in Italia. Bd.5.
MEDIEVAL POLYPHONY. (HUSMAN).
In: Anthology of music. Vol.9.
MEDTNER, NIKOLAI KARLOVITCH, 1880–1951.
Collected works. v.1– .
MEERT, C. F. VAN.
Organ music.
In: Peeters. Oudnederlandse meesters. Vol.3.
MÉHUL, ET. HENRI.
Sonate. Op.1. No.3.
In: Köhler. Les maîtres du clavecin. Heft 12.
In: Pauer. Alte Meister. No.5.
MÉHUL, ÉTIENNE NICOLAS, 1763–1817.
Selections.
In: Échos de France. Vol.1–3.
In: Expert. Collection d'ordre lyrique.
Keyboard music.
In: Georgii. Keyboard music of the Baroque and Rococo. Vol.3.
MEILAND, JACOB, 1542–1577.
Choral music.
In: Der Kammerchor. Vol.5.
Trinklieder.
In: Christophorus-Chorwerk. Heft 11.
MEJIA, ESTANISLAO.
Choral music.
In: Boletín latino-americano de música. Vol.4.
MEL, RENATUS DEL, 16th CENTURY.
(var. sp.: Rinaldo del Mel).
Selections.
In: Maldéghem. Trésor musical.
In: Musica sacra . . . 1839– . Vol.16.
Church music.
In: Motett Society. [Collection of ancient church music]. Division 3.
Sacred music.
In: Proske. Musica divina. Annus secundus. Tom 3.
In: Proske. Selectus novus missarum. Annus secundus. Tom 3.
MELANDE, GEORGIO.
Sonate (Am). Violin and piano.
In: Moffat. Meister-Schule der alten Zeit. Violin-Sonaten. No.8.
MELANI, ALESSANDRO, d.1703.
Songs.
In: Jeppesen. La flora. Vol.2.
MELANI, JACOPO, 1623–1676.
Arias.
In: Landshoff. Alte Meister des Bel Canto. Eine Sammlung von Arien. Vol.1–2.
MELCHERS, HENRIK MELCHER, 1882– .
Selections.
In: Svensk sanglyrik. Vol.2.
Sonata for violin and piano, Op.22, G major.
In: Musikaliska konstföreningen. 1932.
Sonata for violoncello and piano, Op.20.
In: Musikaliska konstföreningen. 1940.
MELCHIOR, FRANCK.
Zwei Galliarden für vier und fünf Blockflöten.
In: Musica practica. No.3.
MELDART, LEONHARD.
Choral music.

In: Der Kammerchor. Vol.2.
MELDERT, LEONARD VAN.
Selections.
In: Maldéghem. Trésor musical.
MELISMATA, THREE SONGS FROM.
In: Euterpe. Vol.5; 2d ed. No.42–44.
MELK MONASTERY.
Compositions.
In: Zagiba. Die ältesten musikalischen Denkmäler zu Ehren des heiligen Leopold, Herzog und Patron von Österreich.
MELO GORIGOYTÍA, HÉCTOR, 1899– .
Manchas de color.
In: Instituto Interamericano de Musicologia. Publicaciónes. No.25.
MELONI, ANNIBALE, 16th CENTURY.
Choral music.
In: Dehn. Sammlung älterer Musik aus dem XVI. und XVII. Jahrhundert.
MENALT, GABRIEL, d.1687.
Organ music.
In: Muset. Early Spanish organ music.
MENDELSSOHN-BARTHOLDY, FELIX, 1809–1847.
Werke. 19 series.
Leipziger Ausgabe. v.1– .
Complete organ works. p.1– .
Complete piano works. 5v.
Sämtliche Klavierwerke. 5v.
Complete works for organ.
In: Lea pocket scores. No.48.
Keyboard music.
In: Farrenc. Le trésor des pianistes. Vol.23.
In: Tagliapietra. Antologia di musica antica e moderna per pianoforte. Bd.15.
Lieder ohne Worte.
In: Musikalische Stundenbücher.
Organ music.
In: Bonnet. Historical organ-recitals. Vol.4.
In: Guilmant. Concert historique d'orgue.
In: Standard series of organ compositions. No.55.
In: Tallis to Wesley. Vol.14.
Psalmen.
In: Musica sacra . . . ca.1842–1896. Vol.8–10.
Schweizer Sinfonie C-moll.
In: Corona. Vol.80.
Songs without words. (complete)
In: Lea pocket scores. No.47.
Vocal music.
In: Hullah. Vocal scores. II. Secular.
MENDOZA, VICENTE T., 1894– .
Canto funeral.
In: Instituto Interamericano de Musicologia. Publicaciónes. No.34.
MERBECKE, JOHN, *see* MARBECK, JOHN.
MERIAN, WILHELM, 1889–1952.
Geistliche Werke des XVI. Jahrhunderts.
In: Verein schweizerischer Tonkünstler Musikalische Werke. Heft 1.
MERULA, TARQUINIO, 16th–17th CENTURIES.
Selections.
In: Torchi. L'arte musicale in Italia. Bd.3.
Chamber music.
In: Riemann. Old chamber music. Vol.3.
Composizioni per organo e cembalo.
In: Monumenti di musica italiana. Ser.I. Vol.1.
Instrumental music.
In: Wasielewski. Instrumentalsätze vom Ende des XVI. bis Ende des XVII. Jahrhunderts.
Keyboard music.
In: Tagliapietra. Antologia di musica antica e moderna per pianoforte. Bd.6.
MERULO, CLAUDIO, 1533–1604.
Selections.
In: Gabrieli. Music of Gabrieli and his time.
In: Musica sacra . . . 1839– . Vol.16.
In: Torchi. L'arte musicale in Italia. Bd.1, 3.
Keyboard music.
In: Farrenc. Le trésor des pianistes. Vol.2.
In: Tagliapietra. Antologia di musica antica e moderna per pianoforte. Bd.2.
Madrigals.
In: Einstein. The golden age of the madrigal.
Organ music.
In: Cantantibus organis. Vol.2.
In: Fuser. Classici italiani dell'organo.
In: Guilmant. Archives des maîtres de l'orgue. Vol.10.
In: Guilmant. Concert historique d'orgue.
In: Klein. The first four centuries of music for the organ from Dunstable to Bach (1370–1749).
In: Organ masters of the Baroque period. Vol.2.
Ricercar.
In: Einstein. Beispielsammlung zur älteren Musikgeschichte.
Four toccatas.
In: Early Italian keyboard music. No.1.
Toccata quinta, secondo tuono. Organ.
In: Parrish. A treasury of early music. No.29.
MÉSANGEAU.
Organ music.
In: Raugel. Les maîtres français de l'orgue. Vol.1.
In: Raugel. Les maîtres français de l'orgue aus XVIIème et XVIIIème siècles.
METON, V.
Sacred music.
In: Eslava y Elizondo. Lira sacro-hispana. 19th century. ii.2.
METSCH.
Organ music.
In: Cantantibus organis. Vol.5.
METZGER, HANS ARNOLD, 1914– .
Organ music.
In: The parish organist. Vol.1–4, 5–6, 7–8.
METZLER, FRIEDRICH, 1910– .
Die güldene Sonne.
In: Bausteine für Musikerziehung und Musikpflege. B 117.
MEYER, D.
Organ music.
In: Organum. 4.Reihe. Nr.2.
MEYER, GREGOR, 16th CENTURY.
Organ music.
In: The Liturgical Music Press, Inc. Masterpieces of organ music. Folio 67.
In: Schering. Alte Meister aus der Frühzeit des Orgelspiels.
MEYER, OTTO.
Herzlich tut mich erfreuen die fröhlich Sommerzeit.

In: Zeitschrift für Spielmusik. No.55.
MEYERBEER, GIACOMO, 1791–1864.
Psalmen.
In: Musica sacra . . . ca.1842–1896. Vol.8–10.
MEZQUITA, JOSÉ JOAQUIM EMERICO LODO DE, *see* LOBO DE MEZQUITA, JOSÉ JOAQUIM EMERICO.
MIASKOVSKY, NIKOLAI, 1881–1950.
Collected works. v.1– .
Fragment lyrique. Orchestra.
In: New music. Orchestra series. No.12.
MÍČA, FRANTIŠEK ADAM, 1746–1811.
II. Quartetto Do maggiore.
In: Musica antiqua bohemica. Vol.6.
Concertino notturno.
In: Musica antiqua bohemica. Vol.19.
MICHAEL, CHRISTIAN, d.1637.
Organ music.
In: The Liturgical Music Press, Inc. Masterpieces of organ music. Folio 60.
MICHAEL, ROGIER, ca.1550–1619.
(var. sp.: Roger).
Selections.
In: Ambros. Auserwählte Tonwerke.
Choral works.
In: Chor-Archiv.
Motets.
In: Attaingnant. Treize livres de motets. Livre 13.
MICHALIČKA, JAN.
Selections.
In: Musica antiqua bohemica. Vol.23.
MICHEL, DON.
Sacred music.
In: Jeppesen. Italia sacra musica. Vol.2.
MICHEL, G.
Airs.
In: Prunières. Les maîtres du chant. Recueil 4.
MICHELET.
Chanson.
In: Copenhagen Kongelige Bibliotek. Mss. (Thottske Samling 291[8]). Der kopenhagener Chansonnier.
MICHL, ARTUR.
Choralvorspiel über "Wie schön leuchtet uns der Morgenstern." Organ.
In: Orgelmusik steirischer Komponisten.
Sonatine für Violine und Klavier. Op.13.
In: Hausmusik. No.84.
MIEDLAR, MARIAN.
Schule für Violoncello. Heft I, II, III.
In: Moecks gelbe Musikhefte. Vol.54, 55, 56.
MIELCZEWSKI, MARCIN, d.1651.
Canzone.
in: Denkmäler altponischer Musik. Vol.6, 29.
Deus in nomine tuo.
In: Denkmäler altponischer Musik. Vol.2.
Veni Domine.
In: Denkmäler altponischer Musik. Vol.38.
Vesperae Dominicales. Soloists, chorus, instruments and continuo.
In: Denkmäler altpolnischer Musik. Vol.42.
MIES, PAUL, 1889– . ed.
Das kölnische Volks– und Karnevalslied.
In: Denkmäler rheinischer Musik. Vol.2.
MIGNONE, FRANCISCO, 1897– .
Lenda sertaeja No.9. Piano.
In: New music. Vol.16. No.1. Oct. 1942.
Música de cámara.
In: Boletín latino-americano de música. Vol.6.
Songs with piano.
In: Boletín latino-americano de música. Vol.1.
MILÁN, LUIS, 16th CENTURY.
Keyboard music.
In: Apel. Musik aus früher Zeit für Klavier. Bd.2.
Libro de musica de vihuela de mano.
In: Publikationen älterer Musik. Jahrg.2.
Lute music.
In: Morphy. Les luthistes espagnols du XVIe siècle. Vol.1.
Organ music.
In: Elkan-Vogel organ series. Vol.5.
Songs.
In: Bal y Gay. Romances y villancicos españoles del signo XVI.
MILAN, ITALY–MUSIC.
In: Istituzioni e monumenti dell' arte musicale italiana. Nuova serie. Vol.1, 3.
MILANO, FRANCESCO DA, *see* FRANCESCO DA MILANO.
MILANS, TOMAS.
Drei Motetten. Sopran (Tenor) und B.C., Bass und B. C.
In: Cantio sacra. No.12.
MILČINSKÝ, DANIEL ALOIS FRANTIŠEK, 1732–1808.
Selections.
In: Musica antiqua bohemica. Vol.23.
MILES, GEORGE TH., 1913– .
Organ music.
In: The parish organist. Vol.1–4, 5–6, 7–8.
MILHAUD, DARIUS, 1892– .
Pastorale. Organ.
In: Contemporary organ series. No.9.
Sonata. Organ.
In: Contemporary organ series. No.23.
MILLÁN.
Choral music.
In: Engel. Three centuries of choral music. Vol.5.
MILLOT.
Chansons.
In: Lesure. Anthologie de la chanson parisienne au XVIe siècle.
MILLOT, NICOLAS.
Chansons.
In: Cauchie. Quinze chansons françaises du XVIe siècle.
MILTON, JOHN, ca.1563–1647.
Six anthems.
In: Arkwright. The Old English edition. Vol.22.
Madrigal.
In: The triumphs of Oriana.
MILWID, A.
Alla Polacca Sub tuum praesidium.
In: Florilegium musicae antiquae. Vol.3.
MINNESINGERS.
In: Denkmäler der Tonkunst in Österreich. Vol.18. (Jg.IX/1); Vol.41. (Jg.XX/2).

In: Hagen. Minnesinger.
In: Jenaer Liederhandschrift. Die Jenaer Liederhandschrift.
In: Ribera y Tarragó. La música antaluza medieval en las canciones de trovadores, troveros y minnesinger.
In: Runge. Die Sangesweisen der Colmarer Handschrift und die Liederhandschrift Donaueschingen.
In: Das Taghorn.
MISCELLANEOUS COLLECTIONS.
In: Ambros. Auserwählte Tonwerke der berühmtesten Meister des 15. und 16. Jahrhunderts.
In: Anthology of music.
In: Arion.
In: Arnold. Cathedral music.
In: Boyce. Cathedral music.
In: Buchner. Fundamentbuch.
In: Clementi. Clementi's Selection of practical harmony.
In: Commer. Cantica sacra.
In: Commer. Collectio operum musicorum batavorum saeculi XVI.
In: Coussemaker. L'art harmonique aux XIIe et XIIIe siècles.
In: Crotch. Specimens of various styles of music.
In: Dauney. Ancient Scotish melodies.
In: Davison. Historical anthology of music.
In: Einstein. Beispielsammlung zur älteren Musikgeschichte.
In: Eslava y Elizondo. Lira sacro-hispana.
In: Gleason. Examples of music before 1400.
In: Hullah. Part music.
In: Hullah. Vocal scores.
In: Jeppesen. La flora.
In: Maldéghem. Trésor musical.
In: Musikalische Formen in historischen Reihen.
In: Parrish. Masterpieces of music before 1750.
In: Parrish. A treasury of early music.
In: Riemann. Musikgeschichte in Beispielen.
In: Schering. Einstimmige Chor- und Sololieder des XVI. Jahrhunderts mit Instrumental-Begleitung.
In: Schering. Geschichte der Musik in Beispielen.
In: Soderlund. Examples illustrating the development of melodic line and contrapuntal style, from Greek melody to Mozart.
In: Soderlund. Examples of Gregorian chant and works by Orlandus Lassus and Giovanni Pierluigi Palestrina.
In: Soderlund. Examples of Gregorian chant and works by Orlandus Lassus, Giovanni Pierluigi Palestrina and Marc Antonio Ingegneri.
In: Steinitzer. Musikgeschichtlicher Atlas.
In: Tappert. Sang und Klang aus alter Zeit.
In: Thibaut. Monuments de la notation ekphonétique et neumatic de l'église latine.
In: Torchi. L'arte musicale in Italia.
In: Wolf. Music of earlier times.
In: Wolf. Sing- und Spielmusik aus älterer Zeit.
MITTANTIER.
Chansons.
In: Publikationen älterer praktischer und theoretischer Musikwerke. Jahrg.27.
MIXA, FRANZ, 1902– .
Klaviersonate.
In: Marckhl. Klavierwerke steiermärkischer Komponisten. Vol.3.
Sechs Lieder im Volkston. Nr.1–3, 4–6.
In: Hausmusik: No.94.
MIYAKE, HARUNA.
Quartet for clarinet, violin, violoncello and piano.
In: Contemporary Japanese music series. No.32.
MIYOSHI, AKIRA.
En blanc; four poems by Chika Sagawa.
In: Contemporary Japanese music series. No.13.
MODERNE, JACQUES, 16th CENTURY.
Zwölf französische Lieder aus Jacques Moderne: Le parangon des chansons (1538).
In: Das Chorwerk. No.61.
MOHLER, PHILIPP, 1908– .
Shakespeare-Suite.
In: Concertino.
MOLAN, L.
Keyboard music.
In: Tagliapietra. Antologia di musica antica e moderna per pianoforte. Bd.1.
MOLIER, LOUIS DE, 17th CENTURY.
(var. sp.: L. de Mollier).
Airs.
In: Prunières. Les maîtres du chant. Recueil 4.
MOLINARO, SIMONE, fl.1600.
Intavolatura di liuto. 115p.
Selections.
In: Musica sacra . . . 1839– . Vol.15, 16.
Lute music.
In: Chilesotti. Lautenspieler des XVI. Jahrhunderts.
MOLINET, JEHAN, 15th–16th CENTURIES.
Chanson.
In: Copenhagen Kongelige Bibliotek. Mss. (Thottske Samling 291[8]). Der kopenhagener Chansonnier.
Choral music.
In: Droz. Poètes et musiciens du XVe siècles.
MOLINO, FRANCESCO, ca.1775–ca.1847.
Trio D dur für Flöte, Viola und Gitarre. Op.45.
In: Albert. Die Gitarre in der Haus– und Kammermusik vor 100 Jahren (1780–1820). No.8.
MØLLER, SVEND-OVE, 1903–1949.
Gak under Jesu Kors at Stå. Op.40. Passionskantate.
In: Samfundet til Udgivelse af dansk Musik. Ser.III. No.122.
Orgel Te Deum. Op.56.
In: Samfundet til Udgivelse af dansk Musik. Ser.III. No.106.
22 Sange. Op.18.
In: Samfundet til Udgivelse af dansk Musik. Ser.III. No.160.
MOLLIER, LOUIS DE, *see* MOLIER, LOUIS DE.
MONARD.
Organ music.
In: Raugel. Les maîtres français de l'orgue. Vol.1.
In: Raugel. Les maîtres français de l'orgue aux XVIIème et XVIIIème siècles.
MONDONVILLE, JEAN JOSEPH CASSANEA DE, 1711–1772.
Airs.

In: Prunières. Les maîtres du chant. Recueil 6.
La Chasse.
In: L'école du violon au XVIIe et XVIIIe siècle. No.1335.
Menuet et variations.
In: L'école du violon au XVIIe et XVIIIe siècle. No.1294.
Pièces de clavecin en sonates.
In: Société Française de Musicologie, Paris. Publications. Sér.I. Bd.9.
Sarabande.
In: L'école du violon au XVIIe et XVIIIe siècle. No.1292.
Sonata. Piano. Op.III, No.3.
In: Reeser. De klaviersonate.
Sonate en fa mineur.
In: L'école du violon au XVIIe et XVIIIe siècle. No.1260.
MONFERRATO, NATALE, d.1685.
Alma redemptoris mater. Sopran (Tenor) und B.C.
In: Cantio sacra. No.49.
MONIUSZKO, STANISLAW, 1819–1872.
(var. sp.: Moniuschko).
Vocal music.
In: Sammlung russischer Romanzen. No.125, 126, 193–195, 223–224.
MONJO.
Selections.
In: Pedrell. Teatro lirico espanol anterior al siglo XIX. Bd.4/5.
MONK OF STRATFORD, *see* PARKER, MONK OF STRATFORD.
MÖNKEMEYER, HELMUT.
Ein Bündel bekannter Kernlieder in Sätzen.
In: Zeitschrift für Spielmusik. No.19.
Handlietung für das Spiel der Alt-Blockflöte in f.
In: Moecks gelbe Musikhefte. Vol.33.
Hohe Schule des Blockflötenspiels.
In: Moecks gelbe Musikhefte. Vol.1.
Ich wollt gern singen. Alte Weisen zu singen oder zu spielen.
In: Zeitschrift für Spielmusik. No.193.
Instrumentale Liedsätze um 1500; Italienische Meister um 1600; Meister des 16., und 17. Jahrhunderts.
In: Musica instrumentalis. Vol.5, 6, 4.
Die Quintfidel. Heft I, II, III, IV.
In: Moecks gelbe Musikhefte. Vol.45, 46, 47, 48.
Schule für Sopran-Gambe; Schule für Alt-Tenor-Gambe; Schule für Tenor-Bass-Gambe.
In: Moecks gelbe Musikhefte. Vol.42, 43, 44.
Das Spiel aus der Bass-Blockflöte.
In: Moecks gelbe Musikhefte. Vol.38.
Das Spiel auf der Blockflöte in C-moll.
In: Moecks gelbe Musikhefte. Vol.6, 51, 52, 53.
MONN, GEORG MATTHIAS, 1717–1750.
(var. sp.: Matthias George Monn).
Instrumental music.
In: Denkmäler der Tonkunst in Österreich. Vol.31. (Jg.XV/2); Vol.39. (Jg.XIX/2).
MONOD, JACQUES LOUIS.
Passacaille, for soprano and 7 instruments. Op.1.
In: New music. Vol.25. No.2. Jan. 1952.
MONRO, GEORGE, 18th CENTURY.
Songs.
In: Potter. Reliquary of English song. Vol.2.
MONSIGNY, PIERRE ALEXANDRE, 1729–1817.
Selections.
In: Échos de France. Vol.1–3.
In: Expert. Collection d'order lyrique.
Vocal music.
In: Delsarte. Archives du chant. Heft 6, 11, 12, 19, 21, 24, suppl.
MONT, HENRI DU, *see* DU MONT, HENRI.
MONTANOS, FRANCISCO DI, 16th CENTURY.
Motets.
In: Elúsitiza. Antología musical.
MONTE, LAMBERTUS DE.
Selections.
In: Maldéghem. Trésor musical.
MONTE, PHILIPPE DE, 1521–1603.
(var. sp.: Philippus de Monte; Filippo di Monte; Filip de Monte).
Complete works. 32v.
Selections.
In: Denkmäler der Tonkunst in Österreich. Vol.77. (Jg.XLI).
In: Maldéghem. Trésor musical.
Choral music.
In: Commer. Collectio operum musicorum batavorum saeculi XVI. Bd.6.
In: Dehn. Sammlung älterer Musik aus dem XVI. und XVII. Jahrhundert.
In: Engel. Three centuries of choral music. Vol.1.
Madrigals.
In: Einstein. The golden age of the madrigal.
Missa ad modulum benedicta.
In: Vereniging voor Nederlandsche Muziekgeschiedenis. Uitgave. No.38.
Missa sine nomine. S.S.A.T.B.B.
In: Basilica. 1952.
Organ music.
In: Peeters. Oudnederlandse meesters. Vol.1.
MONTÉCLAIR, MICHEL PINOLET DE, ca.1667–1737.
Airs.
In: Prunières. Les maîtres du chant. Recueil 6.
MONTELLA, GIAN DOMENICO.
Keyboard music.
In: Corpus of early keyboard music. Vol.24.
MONTEMAYOR, F. DE.
Sacred music.
In: Eslava y Elizondo. Lira sacro-hispana. 17th century. ii.1.
MONTESINOR, A.
Sacred music.
In: Eslava y Elizondo. Lira sacro-hispana. 19th century. i.1.
MONTEVERDI, CLAUDIO, 1567–1643.
Tutte de opere. 16v.
Selections.
In: Documenta historica musicae.
In: Expert. Répertoire classique de musique. 1re année.
In: Gabrieli. Music of Gabrieli and his time.
In: Torchi. L'arte musicale in Italia. Bd.4, 6.
Airs.
In: Prunières. Les maîtres du chant. Recueil 3.
Arias.
In: Landshoff. Alte Meister des Bel Canto. Eine Sammlung von Arien. Vol.1–2.

In: Parisotti. Arie antiche. Bd.2, 3.
Canzonetten.
In: Chor-Archiv.
Choral music.
In: Engel. Three centuries of choral music. Vol.2.
Il Combattimento di Tancredi e Clorinda.
In: I classici della musica italiana. Vol.19.
In: I classici della musica italiana. Raccolta nazionale delle musiche italiane. Quad. 224–225.
Composizioni varie: Lamento d'Arianna.
In: I classici della musica italiana. Raccolta nazionale delle musiche italiane. Quad.79.
Hoheliedmotette.
In: Cantio sacra. No.23.
Hor ch'el ciel e la terra.
In: The Penn state music series. No.7.
Kammerduette.
In: Landshoff. Alte Meister des Bel Canto. Italienische Kammerduette.
L'Orfeo.
In: I classici musicali italiani. Vol.9.
In: Publikationan älterer praktischer und theoretischer Musikwerke. Jahrg.9.
Il Ritorna d'Ulisse in Patria.
In: Denkmäler der Tonkunst in Österreich. Vol.57. (Jg.XXIX/1).
Sacrae cantiunculae, nos.12 and 16.
In: Dessoff choir series. No.24.
Salmo; Messe a quattro voci.
In: Somma. Musiche vocali e strumentali sacre e profane, sec. XVII–XVIII–XIX. Vol.6, 9.
Salve, O regina. Tenor (Sopran) und B.C.
In: Cantio sacra. No.7.
Songs.
In: Jeppesen. La flora. Vol.1, 2, 3.
Tu se' morta, from "Orfeo."
In: Parrish. Masterpieces of music before 1750. No.31.
Vocal music.
In: Gevaert. Les gloires de l'Italie. Vol.2.
MONTEVIDEO–MUSIC.
In: Boletín latino-americano de música.
MONTONA, ANDREA ANTICO DA, *see* ANTIQUUS, ANDREAS.
MONTPELLIER, FRANCE. UNIVERSITÉ. FACULTÉ DE MÉDICINE. BIBLIOTHÈQUE. MSS. (H 196).
Polyphonies du XIIIe siècle. 4v.
MONTPELLIER MANUSCRIPT.
In: Coussemaker. L'Art harmonique aux XIIe et XIIIe siècles.
MONTSERRAT (BENEDICTINE ABBEY).
In: Mestres de l'escolania de Montserrat.
MOORE, DOUGLAS STUART, 1893– .
Dirge. (Passacaglia). Organ.
In: Contemporary organ series. No.4.
Quintet for winds.
In: Society for the Publication of American Music. Publications. 28th season. 1946–47.
String quartet.
In: Society for the Publication of American Music. Publications. 19th season. 1937–38.
MORAGO, ESTEVÃO LOPES, *see* LOPES MORAGO, ESTEVÃO.
MORALES, CRISTÓBAL, ca.1500–1553.
Opera omnia.
In: Monumentos de la música española. Vol.11, 13, 15, 17, 20, 21.
Selections.
In: Ambros. Auserwählte Tonwerke.
In: Smith. Musica antiqua.
Choral music.
In: Engel. Three centuries of choral music. Vol.5.
In: Rochlitz. Sammlung vorzüglicher Gesangstücke. Bd.1. Pt.1.
Composiciones.
In: Pedrell. Hispaniae schola musica sacra. Bd.1.
Cuatro motetes.
In: Polifonía española. Vol.1.
Magnificat octavi toni.
In: Parrish. A treasury of early music. No.23.
Misa De Beata Virgine; Misa Quaeramus cum pastoribus; Selección de motetes.
In: Música hispana. Ser.B. No.1, 2, 3.
Motet a 5.
In: Alfieri. Raccolta di musica sacra. Vol.7.
Motets.
In: Elúsitiza. Antología musical.
Organ music.
In: Cantantibus organis. Vol.6.
Sacred music.
In: Eslava y Elizondo. Lira sacro-hispana. 16th century. i.1.
In: Proske. Musica divina. Annus primus. Tom 3.
In: Rubio. Antologia polifonica sacra. Vol.1.
Songs.
In: Bal y Gay. Romances y villancicos españoles de signo XVI.
MORARI.
Choral music.
In: Dehn. Sammlung älterer Musik aus dem XVI. und XVII. Jahrhundert.
Sacred music.
In: Latrobe, C. I. Selection of sacred music.
In: Latrobe, J. A. The music of the church.
MORAVIAN MUSIC.
In: Music of the Moravians in America.
MOREL, CLEMENT.
Chansons.
In: Publikationen älterer praktischer und theoretischer Musikwerke. Jahrg.27.
MORENO, JUAN, d.1776.
Organ music.
In: Muset. Early Spanish organ music.
MORGAN, JUSTIN, 1747–1798.
Selections.
In: Goldman. Landmarks of early American music, 1760–1800.
MORIARI.
Sacred music.
In: Latrobe, C. I. Selection of sacred music.
In: Latrobe, J. A. The music of the church.
MORILLO, ROBERTO GARCÍA, *see* GARCÍA MORILLO, ROBERTO.
MORIN, JEAN BAPTISTE, ca.1677–1745.
Ad mensam coelitus paratam. Sopran (Tenor) und B.C.
In: Cantio sacra. No.45.

Venite, exsultemus Domino. Sopran (Tenor) und B.C.
In: Cantio sacra. No.50.
MORITZ, LANDGRAF OF HESSE-CASSEL, 1572–1632.
(var. sp.: Maurice, the Learned, Landgrave of Hesse-Cassel; Moritz von Hessen, Landgraf).
Ausgewählte Werke.
In: Das Erbe deutscher Musik. 2.Reihe. Kurhessen. Vol.1. t.1–2.
Chamber music.
In: Riemann. Old chamber music. Vol.1.
Vier Fugen (vierstimmig) auszuführen auf allerlei Instrumenten.
In: Rahler's Kammer-Orchester. No.1.
Pavanen, Gaillarden, Intraden, auszuführen auf allerlei Instrumenten. Heft 1–2.
In: Rahter's Kammer-Orchester. No.2–2a.
MORLACCHI, FRANCESCO, 1784–1841.
Agnus Dei aus der E-dur-Messe.
In: Schmid. Musik am sächsischen Hofe. Bd.1.
MORLEY, THOMAS, 1557–ca.1603.
The first book of consort lessons. 194p.
Selections.
In: Crotch. Specimens of various styles of music. Vol.2.
First book of airs.
In: Fellowes. The English school of lutenist song writers. 1st series. Vol.16.
The first set of ballets for five voices.
In: Musical Antiquarian Society. Publications. Vol.5.
Choral music.
In: Engel. Three centuries of choral music. Vol.3.
In: Der Kammerchor. Vol.4.
Leichte Fantasien. Für drei Gamben oder andere Melodieinstrumente.
In: Hortus musicus. No.64.
9 Fantasien für 2 Gamben.
In: Hortus musicus. No.136.
Keyboard music.
In: English keyboard music. [No.12, 13].
In: The Fitzwilliam virginal book.
In: The Fitzwilliam virginal book. Ausgewählte Stücke. Vol.1.
In: Tagliapietra. Antologia di musica antica e moderna per pianoforte. Bd.2.
Madrigals.
In: Euterpe. Vol.6, 11, 12; 2d ed. No.27–31, 60.
In: Fellowes. The English madrigal school. Vol.1, 2, 3, 4, 32.
In: Squire. Ausgewählte Madrigale und mehrstimmige Gesänge. No.15, 17.
In: The triumphs of Oriana.
Three motets in four parts.
In: Music Press, Inc. [Choral series]. No.53.
Part music.
In: Hullah. Part music. Class A.2. Vol.1.
Sacred music.
In: Boyce. Cathedral music. Vol.1; 1849, Vol.1.
Songs.
In: Potter. Reliquary of English song. Vol.1.
Vocal music.
In: Hullah. Vocal scores. II. Secular.
MORNABLE, ANTOINE.
Chansons.
In: Publikationen älterer praktischer und theoretischer Musikwerke. Jahrg.27.
Motets.
In: Attaingnant. Treize livres de motets. Livre 5, 7.
MORNINGTON, GARRETT COLLEY WELLESLEY, EARL OF, 1735–1781.
Part music.
In: Hullah. Part music. Class A.2. Vol.1; Class A.2. Vol.2; Class C. Secular; 1868 edition.
Vocal music.
In: Hullah. Vocal scores. II. Secular.
MOROCCO-MUSIC.
In: Morocco. Service des Arts Indigenes. Corpus de musique marocaine.
MOROSS, JEROME, 1913– .
Biguine.
In: New music. Orchestra series. No.9.
Paeans. Orchestra.
In: New music. Orchestra series. No.8.
Suite for chamber orchestra.
In: New music. Orchestra series. No.27.
MORRIS, HAROLD, 1890– .
Trio No.2 for violin, violoncello and piano.
In: Society for the Publication of American Music. Publications. 32nd season. 1950–51.
MORTARO, ANTONIO, 16th–17th CENTURIES.
Organ music.
In: Raugel. Quarante-six pièces pour orgue ou harmonium.
MORTENSEN, OTTO, 1907– .
Strygekvartet. 1937.
In: Samfundet til Udgivelse af dansk Musik. Ser.III. No.64.
MORTET, L. CLUZEAU, *see* CLUZEAU MORTET, LUIS.
MORTON, ROBERT, 15th CENTURY.
Selections.
In: Marix. Les musiciens de la cour de Bourgogne au XVe siècle.
Chansons.
In: Copenhagen Kongelige Bibliotek. Mss. (Thottske Samling 291^8). Der kopenhagener Chansonnier.
MOSCHELES, IGNAZ, 1794–1870.
Collection complète des oeuvres. 5v.
Keyboard sonatas.
In: Newman. Thirteen keyboard sonatas of the 18th and 19th centuries.
Keyboard music.
In: Tagliapietra. Antologia di musica antica e moderna per pianoforte. Bd.15.
Part music.
In: Hullah. Part music. Class A.2. Vol.1.
MOSER, HANS, JOACHIM, 1889– . ed.
Die Ballade.
In: Musikalische Formen in historischen Reihen. Bd.3.
Frühmeister der deutschen Orgelkunst. Die mehrstimmige Vertonung des Evangeliums.
In: Staatliche Akademie für Kirchen- und Schulmusik. Berlin. Veröffentlichungen. [Nr].1–2.

The German solo song and the ballad.
In: Anthology of music. Vol.14.
MOSER, RUDOLF, 1892– .
Organ music.
In: The parish organist. Vol.1–4, 5–6, 7–8.
MÖSLER, KARL HEINRICH.
1 Duo.
In: Zeitschrift für Spielmusik. No.78.
MOSSI, GIOVANNI, 17th CENTURY.
Sonate (Cm). Violin and piano.
In: Moffat. Meister-Schule der alten Zeit. Violin-Sonaten. No.5.
MOSSOLOV, ALEXANDER VASSILIEVITCH, 1900– .
A Turkmenian lullaby. Chorus.
In: New music. Vol.8. No.1. Oct.1934.
MOTETS.
In: Alfieri. Raccolta di musica sacra.
In: Anthologie des maîtres religieux primitifs des XVe, XVIe et XVIIe siècles.
In: Archivium musices metropolitanum mediolanense.
In: Arkwright. The Old English edition. Vol.21.
In: Attaingnant. Treize livres de motets.
In: Aubry. Cent motets du XIIIe siècle.
In: Basilica.
In: Chor-Archiv.
In: Das Chorwerk.
In: Christophorus-Chorwerk.
In: Concerts spirituels ou recueil de motets recueil.
In: Denkmäler der Tonkunst in Österreich. Vol.3. (Jg.II/1); Vol.12. (Jg.VI/1); Vol.24. (Jg.XII/1); Vol.30. (Jg.XV/1); Vol.40. (Jg.XX/1); Vol.48. (Jg.XXIV); Vol.51–52. (Jg.XXVI); Vol.99; Vol.101/102.
In: Denkmäler deutscher Tonkunst. [1.Folge]. Vol.49–50.
In: Du Mont. Melanges divers.
In: The earliest motets (13th century).
In: Elúsitiza. Antología musical.
In: Das Erbe deutscher Musik. 1.Reihe. Vol.13, 47, 57.
In: Expert. Répertoire classique de musique.
In: Gastoué. Motets choises des maîtres du XVe au XVIIIe siècle.
In: Lalande. Motets.
In: Monumenta musicae belgicae. Vol.11.
In: Motett Society. [Collection of ancient church music].
In: Die Motette.
In: Müller-Blattau. Musica reservata.
In: Music Press, Inc. [Choral series]. Vol.53.
In: Musik alter Meister. Heft 5, 6, 12, 13, 15.
In: Organum. 1.Reihe. Nr.19–20.
In: Publikationen älterer praktischer und theoretischer Musikwerke. Jahrg.28, 29.
In: Recent researches in the music of the Renaissance. Vol.2.
In: Société Française de Musicologie, Paris. Publications. Sér.I. Bd.5, 17.
In: Société Française de Musicologie, Paris. Publications. Sér.I. Bd.17.
In: Summa musicae medii aevi. Vol.2, 6.
In: Turin. Biblioteca Nazionale. Mss. (J.II.9). The Cypriot-French repertory. Vol.2.
In: Vereniging voor Nederlandsche Muziekgeschiedenis. Uitgave. No.44.
MOTLEY, RICHARD.
Keyboard music.
In: English keyboard music. [No.10].
MOTZER, FRANZ.
Lateinisches Proprium von Allerheiligen.
In: Christophorus-Chorwerk. Heft 38.
Proprium vom 4. Fastensonntag.
In: Christophorus-Chorwerk. Heft 26.
MOULINIÉ, ESTIENNE, 17th CENTURY.
Airs.
In: Prunières. Les maîtres du chant. Recueil 4.
MOULU, PIERRE, 16th CENTURY.
Chanson.
In: Brown. Theatrical chansons of the 15th and early 16th centuries.
Motets.
In: Attaingnant. Treize livres de motets. Livre 10, 12.
MOURET, JEAN JOSEPH, 1682–1738.
Airs.
In: Prunières. Les maîtres du chant. Recueil 6.
Deux divertissements. Pour cor et clavier.
In: Musiques françaises. Vol.11.
MOUSSORGSKIĬ, MODEST PETROVICH, *see* MUSORGSKIĬ, MODEST PETROVICH.
MOUTON, JEAN, ca.1475–1522.
(var. sp.: Joan Mouton).
Ave Maria.
In: Dessoff choir series. No.40.
Chanson.
In: Brown. Theatrical chansons of the 15th and early 16th centuries.
Choral music.
In: Commer. Collectio operum musicorum batavorum saeculi XVI. Bd.8.
In: Engel. Three centuries of choral music. Vol.1.
In: Music Press, Inc. [Choral series]. Vol.91.
In: Smijers. Van Ockeghem tot Sweelinck. Aflg.7.
Missa "Alleluya."
In: Das Chorwerk. No.70.
Motets.
In: Attaingnant. Treize livres de motets. Livre 1, 2, 3, 6, 7, 8, 9, 11.
In: Das Chorwerk. No.76.
MOYNE, LE.
Chansons.
In: Cauchie. Quinze chansons françaises du XVIe siècle.
MOZÁRABE, EL CANTO.
In: Barcelona. Biblioteca Central. Sección de Música. Publicaciones. Vol.5.
MOZART, JOHANN GEORG LEOPOLD, 1719–1787.
Selected works.
In: Denkmäler deutscher Tonkunst. [2.Folge]. Vol.9 (ii).
Divertimenti.
In: Concertino.
In: Musikschätze der Vergangenheit.
In: Organum. 3.Reihe. Nr.30.
Zwölf Duette für zwei Violinen.
In: Hortus musicus. No.78.
12 Hochzeitsmenuette.
In: Zeitschrift für Spielmusik. No.218.
Konzert in D-dur.
In: Organum. 3.Reihe. Nr.29.

Sacred music.
In: Messner. Alte Salzburger Meister der kirchlichen Tonkunst. Heft 5, 6.
Sinfonia Burlesca.
In: Diletto musicale. No.83.
Sonata a tre, per due violini e basso continuo. Nr.4.
In: Hausmusik. No.177.
12 Spielstücke.
In: Zeitschrift für Spielmusik. No.60.
Kleine Stücke für 2 gleiche Streichinstrumente.
In: Moecks Kammermusik. Vol.202.
8 Tänze aus Leopold Mozarts Notenbuch für Wolfgang.
In: Zeitschrift für Spielmusik. No.141.
Trumpet concerto.
In: Für Kenner und Liebhaber. No.1.
MOZART, WOLFGANG AMADEUS, 1756–1791.
Sämtliche Werke. 24 series.
—— Another issue. 24 series.
Oeuvres complettes. 17v.
Neue Ausgabe sämtliche Werke. 10 series.
Werke für Klavier. 5v.
W. A. Mozart's Handschrift in zeitlich geordneten Nachbildungen.
In: Fürstliches Institut für musikwissenschaftliche Forschung. Veröffentlichung. [No.] 1.
Selections.
In: Crotch. Specimens of various styles of music. Vol.3.
Adagio B-dur, K.V.411. Für Flöte, Oboe, Klarinette, Horn und Fagott. (Weigelt).
In: Alte Musik. (Reihe "Leuckartiana").
Adagio. K.580a.
In: Für Kenner und Liebhaber. No.25.
Andante der Urfassung der 1. Pariser Symphonie. K.V.297.
In: Diletto musicale. No.53.
Fünf Contretänze für Zwei Violinen, Violoncello, Contrabass, Flöte und Trommel.
In: Musikschätze der Vergangenheit.
Divertimento Nr.8, F-dur, K.V.213. Für Flöte, Oboe, Klarinette, Horn und Fagott. (Weigelt).
In: Alte Musik. (Reihe "Leuckartiana").
Divertimento Nr.9, B-dur, K.V.240. Für Flöte, Oboe, Klarinette, Horn und Fagott. (Weigelt).
In: Alte Musik. (Reihe "Leuckartiana").
Divertimento Nr.13, F-dur, K.V.253. Für Flöte, Oboe, Klarinette, Horn und Fagott. (Weigelt).
In: Alte Musik. (Reihe "Leuckartiana").
Divertimento Nr.14, B-dur, K.V.270. Für Flöte, Oboe, Klarinette, Horn und Fagott. (Weigelt).
In: Alte Musik. (Reihe "Leuckartiana").
12 Duette für 2 Bassetthörner K.V.487. Ausgabe für Violine und Viola.
In: Hortus musicus. No.115.
Twelve duos for two French horns, K.487.
In: Hausmusik. No.21.
In: Music for wind instruments by 18th century masters. No.4.
Duetten für 2 Hörner.
In: Zeitschrift für Spielmusik. No.238.
Duos. Violin and Viola.
In: Hausmusik. No.5, 8, 113, 114.
Feiermusik.
In: Corona. Vol.30.
Fuge G moll (K.V.401). Aus den Londoner Skizzenbuch.
In: Zeitschrift für Spielmusik. No.207, 208.
Zwei Fugen und eine Fantaste, für 4stg. Streichorchester.
In: Corona. Vol.33.
Fugue for piano in C.
In: Königliche Akademie der Künste. Auswahl vorzüglicher Musik-Werke. No.21.
Keyboard music.
In: Clementi. Clementi's Selection of practical harmony. Vol.1, 2.
In: Farrenc. Le trésor des pianistes. Vol.17.
In: Tagliapietra. Antologia di musica antica e moderna per pianoforte. Bd.13.
Kontratänze und Menuette.
In: Zeitschrift für Spielmusik. No.29.
Sechs Kontretänze für Zwei Violinen und Bass (Violoncello). K.V.462.
In: Hausmusik. No.53.
Konzert B-dur für Fagott.
In: Das weltliche Konzert im 18. Jahrhundert. Heft 2.
Konzert-Rondo A-dur K.V.386.
In: Concertino.
Konzerte für Cembalo (Klavier) mit Streichorchester.
In: Antiqua Edition. Von 5 Instrumenten an.
Sechs Ländlerische Tänze, für zwei Violinen und Bass (Violoncello) K.V.606.
In: Hausmusik. No.24.
Lieder.
In: Hausmusik. No.150a-b.
In: Lea pocket scores. No.59.
In: Musikalische Stundenbücher.
In: Nagels Musik-Archiv. No.66.
In: Reimann. Das deutsche Lied. Vol.1, 2.
Die Mailänder Quartette; 6 Quartetti capricciosi.
In: Antiqua Edition. Von 4 Instrumenten an.
Märsche.
In: Corona. Vol.11.
Menuette mit Trio für zwei Violinen und Bass. K.V.65a, K.V.585.
In: Hausmusik. No.7, 69.
Motets.
In: Concerts spirituels ou recueil de motets.
Ombra felice. (K.255).
In: Für Kenner und Liebhaber. No.11.
Organ music.
In: Biggs. A treasury of shorter organ classics.
In: Bonnet. Historical organ-recitals. Vol.3.
In: Keller. Orgelvorspiele.
In: Raugel. Quarante-six pièces pour orgue ou harmonium.
Pantalon und Colombine.
In: Corona. Vol.53.
Part music.
In: Hullah. Part music. Class B.2.
The ten celebrated quartets.
In: Hirsch. Veröffentlichungen. [Bd.].12.
Streichquartett in G-dur. K.V.80.
In: Diletto musicale. No.9.
The 2 quartets for piano and strings; Quintet for piano and winds, E flat.
In: Lea pocket scores. No.90.
Quartettstücke nach Duetten für 2 Hörner.

In: Zeitschrift für Spielmusik. No.220, 238.
Complete string quintets.
In: Lea pocket scores. No.91/92.
Regina coeli; Tremendum; Offertorium in F; Sancti in Justi.
In: Ecclesiasticon. No.24, 65, 72, 75.
Zwei Rondos, D-dur und A-moll.
In: Musikalische Seltenheiten. Bd.5.
Sacred music.
In: Latrobe, C. I. Selection of sacred music.
In: Latrobe, J. A. The music of the church.
In: Messner. Alte salzburger Meister der kirchlichen Tonkunst. Heft 7, 9, 12.
Drei salzburger Sinfonien ohne Bläser.
In: Corona. Vol.25.
Serenade in C.
In: Zeitschrift für Spielmusik. No.119.
Serenade, Eine kleine Nachtmusik. K.V.525.
In: Hausmusik. No.12.
Fünf Wiener Serenaden.
In: Corona. Vol.22.
Sonate für Fagott und Violoncello, K.V.292, auch für zwei Violoncelli.
In: Hausmusik. No.6.
The piano sonatas and fantasies, I & II.
In: Lea pocket scores. No.39/40.
Violin-piano sonatas. Vol.I/II/III.
In: Lea pocket scores. No.16a/b/c.
5 Spielstücke.
In: Zeitschrift für Spielmusik. No.164.
Zwölf deutsche Tänze.
In: Corona. Vol.8.
Sechs deutsche Tänze für Klavier. K.V.509.
In: Diletto musicale. No.27.
3 Terzette.
In: Zeitschrift für Spielmusik. No.99.
The piano trios (1–4, 5–8).
In: Lea pocket scores. No.49/50.
Trio, K.V.266.
In: Hausmusik. No.9.
Trio for 2 violins and cello. K.266.
In: Musikschätze der Vergangenheit.
Piano variations. Complete.
In: Lea pocket scores. No.89.
Vocal music.
In: Delsarte. Archives du chant. Livr.5, 10, 14, 15, 16, 24, suppl.
In: Hullah. Vocal scores. II. Secular.
MUDARRA, ALONSO DE, 16th CENTURY.
Keyboard music.
In: Kastner. Silva iberica.
In: Tagliapietra. Antologia di musica antica e moderna per pianoforte. Bd.1.
Lute music.
In: Morphy. Les luthistes espagnols du XVIe siècle. Vol.2.
Organ music.
In: Cantantibus organis. Vol.4.
Tres libros de música en cifra para vihuela.
In: Monumentos de la música española. Vol.7.
MUELAS, D.
Sacred music.
In: Eslava y Elizondo. Lira sacro-hispana. 18th century. i.1.
MUELLER, *see* MÜLLER.
MUELLER, GOTTFRIED, 1914– .
Organ music.
In: The parish organist. Vol.1–4, 7–8.
MUENNICH, RICHARD, *see* MÜNNICH, RICHARD.
MUFFAT, GEORGE, d.1704.
Apparatus musico-organisticus. 75p.
Armonico tributo 1682.
In: Denkmäler der Tonkunst in Österreich. Vol.89.
Auserlesene. Instrumental music.
In: Denkmäler der Tonkunst in Österreich. Vol.23. (Jg.XI/2).
Florilegium primum.
In: Denkmäler der Tonkunst in Österreich. Vol.2. (Jg.I/2).
Florilegium secundum.
In: Denkmäler der Tonkunst in Österreich. Vol.4. (Jg.II/2).
Keyboard music.
In: Farrenc. Le trésor des pianistes. Vol.2.
In: Georgii. Keyboard music of the Baroque and Rococo. Vol.1.
?In: Pauer. Alte Klavier-Musik. 1st series. Pt.4.
?In: Tagliapietra. Antologia di musica antica e moderna per pianoforte. Bd.8, 12.
Lute music.
In: Denkmäler der Tonkunst in Österreich. Vol.50. (Jg.XXV/2).
Organ music.
In: Bonnet. Historical organ-recitals. Vol.1.
?In: Cantantibus organis. Vol.1, 3, 8.
?In: Guilmant. Concert historique d'orgue.
?In: Guilmant. École classique de l'orgue. No.11.
In: Klein. The first four centuries of music for the organ from Dunstable to Bach (1370–1749).
In: Liber organi. Bd.5.
In: Organ masters of the Baroque period. Vol.2.
In: Orgue et liturgie. Vol.10.
In: Straube. Alte Meister.
In: Straube. Alte Meister des Orgelspiels.
Respectable Wedding.
In: Musikschätze der Vergangenheit.
MUFFAT, GOTTLIEB, 1690–1770.
Componimenti Musicali.
In: Denkmäler der Tonkunst in Österreich. Vol.7. (Jg.III/3).
In: Monuments of music and music literature. First series. No.8.
Sechs Fugen. Organ.
In: Die Orgel. Reihe II. Nr.17.
Gigue (B flat) und Allegro spirituoso (D).
In: Pauer. Alte Meister. No.40.
Keyboard music.
In: Georgii. Keyboard music of the Baroque and Rococo. Vol.2.
In: Oesterle. Early keyboard music. Vol.2.
In: Pessl. The art of the suite.
In: Selva. Pièces de clavecin des XVIIme et XVIIIme siècles.
2 Menuets et Courante, Gigue, Allegro spirituoso.
In: Köhler. Les maîtres du clavecin. Heft 4.
Organ music.
In: Liber organi. Bd.5, 6.
In: The Liturgical Music Press, Inc. Masterpieces of organ music. Folio 58.
In: The parish organist. Vol.1–4.
Works for organ and piano.
In: Denkmäler der Tonkunst in Österreich. Vol.58. (Jg.XXIX/2).

Zwölf kleine Praeludien. Organ.
In: Die Orgel. Reihe II. Nr.16.
Drei Toccaten. Organ.
In: Die Orgel. Reihe II. Nr.10.
Drei Toccaten und Capriccios. Neue Folge.
In: Die Orgel. Reihe II. Nr.13.
Toccata, Fuge und Capriccio. Organ.
In: Die Orgel. Reihe II. Nr.8.
Weihnachtsmusik. Für Klavier oder Orgel.
In: Nagels Musik-Archiv. No.95.
MUFFAT, THÉOPHILE.
Keyboard music.
In: Farrenc. Le trésor des pianistes. Vol.10.
MULET, HENRI.
Organ music.
In: Bedell. The French organist. Vol.2.
MULET-BEDELL, S.
Organ music.
In: Standard series of organ compositions. No.50.
MÜLLER, FRIEDRICH EWALD.
Thema mit Variationen.
In: Zeitschrift für Spielmusik. No.23.
MÜLLER, GEORG GOTTFRIED, 1762–1821.
Sacred songs.
In: Music of the Moravians in America. Vol.1.
MÜLLER, GOTTFRIED, *see* MUELLER, GOTTFRIED.
MÜLLER, JOHANN.
Lieder.
In: Publikationen älterer praktischer und theoretischer Musikwerke. Jahrg.1–3.
MÜLLER, PETER ERASMUS LANGE-, *see* LANGE-MÜLLER, PETER ERASMUS.
MÜLLER, SIGFRID WALTHER, 1905–1946.
Weihnachtsmusik. Op.38b.
In: Collegium musicae novae. No.45.
MULLINER BOOK.
In: English keyboard music. [No.3].
In: Musica Britannica. Vol.1.
In: Schott's Anthology of early keyboard music. Vol.2.
In: Tallis to Wesley. Vol.3.
MUNDY, JOHN, d.1630.
(var. sp.: John Munday).
Keyboard music.
In: The Fitzwilliam virginal book.
In: The Fitzwilliam virginal book. Ausgewählte Stücke. Vol.2.
In: Tagliapietra. Antologia di musica antica e moderna per pianoforte. Bd.3.
Madrigals.
In: Euterpe. Vol.4, 5, 12; 2d ed. no.32–34, 59, 63–64.
In: Fellowes. The English madrigal school. Vol.35, pt.2.
In: The triumphs of Oriana.
MUNDY, WILLIAM, ca.1529–ca.1591.
Latin antiphons and psalms.
In: Early English church music. Vol.2.
Sacred music.
In: Boyce. Cathedral music. 1849. Vol.2.
MÜNNICH, RICHARD, 1877– . ed.
Die Suite.
In: Musikalisches Formen in historischen Reihen. Bd.9.
MUREAU, G.
Choral music.
In: Droz. Poètes et musiciens du XVe siècles.
MURSCHHAUSER, FRANZ XAVER ANTON, 1663–1738.
Selected works.
In: Denkmäler deutscher Tonkunst. [2.Folge]. Vol.18.
Aria pastoralis variata. Piano music.
In: Köhler. Les maîtres du clavecin. Heft 5.
Keyboard music.
In: Oesterle. Early keyboard music. Vol.2.
In: Pauer. Alte Klavier-Musik. 2d series. Pt.2.
In: Tagliapietra. Antologia di musica antica e moderna per pianoforte. Bd.10.
Organ music.
In: Auler. Spielbuch für Kleinorgel. Vol.2.
In: Cantantibus organis. Vol.2, 3.
In: Commer. Compositionen für Orgel aus dem 16., 17., und 18. Jahrhundert. Heft 4.
In: The parish organist. Vol.1–4, 5–6.
In: Raugel. Quarante-six pièces pour orgue ou harmonium.
Praeambulum, arpeggiata, fuga. Organ.
In: Guilmant. École classique de l'orgue. No.16.
Weihnachtsmusik. Für Klavier oder Orgel.
In: Nagels Musik-Archiv. No.95.
MUSELLA, S.
Keyboard music.
In: Tagliapietra. Antologia di musica antica e moderna per pianoforte. Bd.18.
THE MUSIC OF THE BYZANTINE CHURCH. (WELLESZ).
In: Anthology of music. Vol.13.
MUSIC OF THE NETHERLANDS. (LENAERTS).
In: Anthology of music. Vol.22.
LA MÚSICA EN LA CORTE DE CARLOS V. (HIGINI ANGLÉS).
In: Monumentos de la música española. Vol.2.
LA MÚSICA EN LA CORTE DE LOS REYES CATÓLICOS.
In: Monumentos de la música española. Vol.1, 5, 10.
MUSICA RESERVATA. I–II.
In: Chor-Archiv.
THE MUSICAL ENTERTAINER. (1740). FACSIMILE. (BICKHAM).
In: Monuments of music and music literature. First series. No.6.
THE MUSICA MISCELLANY. (1729–1731). FACSIMILE.
In: Monuments of music and music literature. First series. No.12.
MUSICK'S HAND-MAID. II.
In: English keyboard music. [No.10].
MUSORGSKIĬ, MODEST PETROVICH, 1839–1881.
(var. sp.: Moussorgskiĭ).
Sämtliche Werke. v.1– .
Complete works. v.1– .
Complete romances and songs. 387p.
MÜTHEL, JOHANN GOTTFRIED, 1718–1788.
Zwei Ariosi mit zwölf Variationen für Klavier.
In: Mitteldeutsches Musikarchiv. Reihe I. Bd.7.
Keyboard music.

In: Herrmann. Lehrmeister und Schüler Joh. Seb. Bachs. Vol.2.
Drei Sonaten für Klavier.
In: Mitteldeutsches Musikarchiv. Reihe I. Bd.6.
Sonata (Duett). Zwei Klaviere.
In: Nagels Musik-Archiv. No.176.
Sonate B-dur mit sechs Variationen. Piano.
In: Organum. 5.Reihe. Nr.29.
MUTUS.
Sacred music.
In: Jeppesen. Italia sacra musica. Vol.1.
MYSLIVEČEK, JOSEF, 1737–1781.
Keyboard music.
In: Musica antiqua bohemica. Vol.17.
3 octets, oboe, 2 clarinets, 2 trumpets, 2 bassoons.
In: Musica antiqua bohemica. Vol.55.
3 Quintetti d'archi.
In: Musica antiqua bohemica. Vol.31.
Trio in B dur. Op.1. Nr.4. Für Flöte (1.Violine), Violine, Violoncello und Klavier.
In: Riemann. Collegium musicum. No.20.
Violin and piano.
In: Musica antiqua bohemica. Vol.11.

NACHTIGALL, OTHOMAR, *see* LUSCINIUS (ACTUALLY OTTOMAR NACHTGALL).
NÄGELI, HANS GEORG, 1773–1836.
Lied
In: Reimann. Das deutsche Lied. Vol.4.
Part music.
In: Hullah. Part music. Class C. Sacred.
NAICH, ROBERT.
Lieder.
In: Publikationen älterer praktischer und theoretischer Musikwerke. Jahrg.1–3.
NANCARROW, CONLON, 1912– .
Blues, for piano.
In: New music. Vol.11. No.2. Jan. 1938.
Prelude, for piano.
In: New music. Vol.11. No.2. Jan. 1938.
Rhythm study No.1, for player piano.
In: New music. Vol.25. No.1. Oct. 1951.
Toccata for violin and piano.
In: New music. Vol.11. No.2. Jan. 1938.
NANINI.
Choral music.
In: Recueil de musique ancienne. Recueil des morceaux de musique ancienne. Bd.6.
Church music.
In: Motett Society. [Collection of ancient church music]. Division 1.
Vocal music.
In: Delsarte. Archives du chant. Livr. 15. No.2.
NANINI, GIOVANNI BERNARDINO, ca.1560–1623.
(var. sp.: Bernardinus Nanini).
Sacred music.
In: Proske. Musica divina. Annus primus. Tom 3; Annus secundus. Tom 2.
In: Proske. Selectus novus missarum. Annus secundus. Tom 2.
In: Rubio. Antologia polifonica sacra. Vol.1.
NANINI, GIOVANNI MARIA, ca.1545–1607.
(var. sp.: G. M. Nanino).
Selections.
In: Torchi. L'arte musicale in Italia. Bd.2.
Choral music.
In: Engel. Three centuries of choral music. Vol.2.
In: Rochlitz. Sammlung vorzüglicher Gesangstücke. Bd.1. Pt.2.
Kirchengesänge.
In: Tucher. Kirchengesänge der berühmtesten älteren italienischen Meister.
Il primo libro delle canzonette a tre voci miste.
In: Somma. Polifonia vocale sacra e profana. Sec.XVI. Vol.2.
Sacred music.
In: Proske. Musica divina. Annus primus. Tom 2, 4.
Vienn' Himeneo.
In: Squire. Ausgewählte Madrigale und mehrstimmige Gesänge. No.26.
NAPIERSKY, HERBERT.
Fröhliche Musik.
In: Zeitschrift für Spielmusik. No.81.
NAPLES, ITALY–MUSIC.
In: Istituzioni e monumenti dell' arte musicale italiana. Vol.5.
In: Istituzioni e monumenti dell' arte musicale italiana. Nuova serie.
NAPRAWNIK, EDUARD FRANZEWITSCH, 1839–1916.
Vocal music.
In: Sammlung russischer Romanzen. No.270, 271.
NARDINI, PIETRO, 1722–1793.
Adagio.
In: L'école du violon au XVIIe et XVIIIe siècle. No.1342.
Adagio en mi.
In: L'école du violon au XVIIe et XVIIIe siècle. No.1346.
Adagio en ré.
In: L'école du violon au XVIIe et XVIIIe siècle. No.1335.
Kammer-Sonaten für Violine und Pianoforte.
In: Moffat. Kammer-Sonaten für Violine und Pianoforte. No.15.
Seche Streichquartette. No.1–6.
In: Riemann. Collegium musicum. No.63/65.
Sonate. Violin and piano.
In: Moffat. Meister-Schule der alten Zeit. Violin-Sonaten. No.14, 25.
NARES, JAMES, 1715–1783.
Part music.
In: Hullah. Part music. Class A.1. Vol.2.
Sacred music.
In: Arnold. Cathedral music. Vol.3.
In: Page. Harmonia sacra. Vol.2.
Vocal music.
In: Hullah. Vocal scores. I. Sacred.
NARVÁEZ, LUIS DE, 16th CENTURY.
El Delphin de musica.
In: Martínez Torner. Colección de vihuelistas españoles del siglo XVI. Cuad. 1.
Keyboard music.
In: Apel. Musik aus früher Zeit für Klavier. Bd.2.
Los seys libros del Delphin de música de cifra para tañer vihuela.
In: Monumentos de la música española. Vol.3.

Lute music.
In: Morphy. Les luthistes espagnols du XVIe siècle. Vol.1.
Songs.
In: Bal y Gay. Romances y villancicos españoles del signo XVI.
Tema y variaciones sobre un aire popular.
In: Asociación Patriótica Española. Clásicos españoles de la música. Vol.1.
NASCO, GIOVAN.
Italienische Madrigale.
In: Das Chorwerk. No.58.
Madrigale.
In: Das Chorwerk. No.88.
NAUBAUER, JOHANN.
Chamber music.
In: Riemann. Old chamber music. Vol.2.
NAUDOT, JEAN JACQUES, 18th CENTURY.
Konzert G-dur für f'-Blockflöte (Querflöte, Oboe), 2 Violinen und Basso Continuo.
In: Hortus musicus. No.153.
Pièces pour flûte.
In: Musiques françaises. Vol.5.
Prémiere fête rustique. Extraite des "Six fêtes rustiques." Op.VIII.
In: Musiques françaises. Vol.4.
NAUMANN, EMIL, 1827–1888.
Psalmen.
In: Musica sacra . . . ca.1842–1896. Vol.8–10.
NAUMANN, JOHANN GOTTLIEB, 1741–1801.
Ballet-Suite aus der "Protesitao"; Medea Suite.
In: Sondheimer. Werke aus dem 18. Jahrhundert. Nr.30/31.
Sechs leichte Duette für zwei Violinen.
In: Hortus musicus. No.90.
Fugue. Di l'alimenta.
In: Königliche Akademie der Künste. Auswahl vorzüglicher Musik-Werke. No.5.
Instrumental music.
In: Schmid. Musik am sächsischen Hofe. Bd.6.
Kyrie aus der As-dur-Messe; Agnus Dei aus der D-moll-(Pastoral-) Messe.
In: Schmid. Musik am sächsischen Hofe. Bd.1.
2 Lieder für eine Singstimme mit Klavierbegleitung.
In: Sondheimer. Werke aus dem 18. Jahrhundert. Nr.16.
Sacred music.
In: Latrobe, C. I. Selection of sacred music.
In: Latrobe, J. A. The music of the church.
Scena (Davidde pen).
In: Königliche Akademie der Künste. Auswahl vorzüglicher Musik-Werke. Appendix.
Sonaten für Klavier.
In: Sondheimer. Werke aus dem 18. Jahrhundert. Nr.17.
10 Stücke für Klavier.
In: Sondheimer. Werke aus dem 18. Jahrhundert. Nr.7.
NAVARRO, JUAN, ca.1530–1580.
Selections.
In: Pedrell. Teatro lirico espanol anterior al siglo XIX. Bd. 4/5.
Choral music.
In: Engel. Three centuries of choral music. Vol.5.
Lauda Jerusalem.
In: Polifonía española. Vol.19.
Motets.
In: Elúsitiza. Antología musical.
Sacred music.
In: Eslava y Elizondo. Lira sacro-hispana. 16th century. i.2.
NAVAS, JUAN, 17th CENTURY.
Selections.
In: Pedrell. Teatro lirico espanol anterior al siglo XIX. Bd.3, 4/5.
NEBRA, JOSÉ DE, ca.1688–1768.
Sacred music.
In: Eslava y Elizondo. Lira sacro-hispana. 18th century. ii.1.
NEBRA, M. B. DE.
Keyboard sonatas.
In: Newman. Thirteen keyboard sonatas of the 18th and 19th centuries.
NEEFE, CHRISTIAN GOTTLOB, 1748–1798.
Keyboard music.
In: Newman. Thirteen keyboard sonatas of the 18th and 19th centuries.
Lieder.
In: Moser. Alte Meister des deutschen Liedes. 30 Gesänge. No.23, 24.
In: Moser. Alte Meister des deutschen Lieder. 46 Gesänge. No.38, 39.
In: Reimann. Das deutsche Lied. Vol.2.
Partita in Es.
In: Denkmäler rheinischer Musik. Vol.1.
Zwölf Klavier-Sonaten. (Nr.I–VI).
In: Denkmäler rheinischer Musik. Vol.10.
NEGRET, SAMUEL.
Piano music.
In: Boletín latino-americano de música. Vol.4.
NEGRETE WOOLCOCK, SAMUEL, 1892– .
Ritmica. (Piano).
In: Instituto Interamericano de Musicologia. Publicaciónes. No.21.
NEGRI, CESARE, b.ca.1546.
Lute music.
In: Chilesotti. Lautenspieler des XVI. Jahrhunderts.
Sacred music.
In: Latrobe, C. I. Selection of sacred music.
In: Latrobe, J. A. The music of the church.
NEGRO, GIULIO SANTO PIETRO DEL, 16th CENTURY.
(var. sp.: S. P. de Negri).
Airs.
In: Prunières. Les maîtres du chant. Recueil 3.
NEIDHARDT VON REUENTHAL, 12th–13th CENTURIES.
(var. sp.: Neidhart von Reuental; Neidhart von Reuenthal).
Selections.
In: Gleason. Examples of music before 1400.
In: Leichtentritt. Deutsche Hausmusik aus vier Jahrhunderten.
Lieder.
In: Denkmäler der Tonkunst in Österreich. Vol.71. (Jg.XXXVII/1).
In: Summa musicae medii aevi. Vol.9.
Willekommen Mayenschein.
In: Parrish. Masterpieces of music before 1750. No.5.

NEITHARDT, AUGUST HEINRICH, 1793–1861.
(var. sp.: Neithart).
Part music.
In: Hullah. Part music. Class A.2. Vol.1.
Psalmen.
In: Musica sacra . . . ca.1842–1896. Vol.8–10.
NELSON, PHILIP.
Nicolas Bernier.
In: Institute of Mediaeval Music. Musical theorists in translation. Vol.5.
NEMIROFF, ISAAC, 1912– .
Sonata, No.2, for violin and piano.
In: New music. Oct. 1963.
NENNA, POMPONIA, ca.1550–ca.1618.
(var. sp.: Pomponio Nenna).
Madrigals.
In: Istituto italiano per la storia della musica. 1. Monumenti II. Vol.1.
Sacred music.
In: Proske. Musica divina. Annus secundus. Tom 2.
In: Proske. Selectus novus missarum. Annus secundus. Tom 2.
NERESCHEIMER ORGELBUCH.
Organ music.
In: Cantantibus organis. Vol.8.
NERI, MASSIMILIANO, 17th CENTURY.
Instrumental music.
In: Wasielewski. Instrumentalsätze vom Ende des XVI. bis Ende des XVII. Jahrhunderts.
NERUDA, FRANZ XAVER, 1843–1915.
Organ music.
In: Gerhardt. Album nordischer Komponisten. Vol.2.
NESLE, BLONDEL DE, *see* BLONDEL DE NESLE.
NETHERLANDS–MUSIC (*see also* FOLKSONGS, NETHERLAND; SONGS, NETHERLAND).
In: Anthology of music. Vol.22.
In: Denkmäler der Tonkunst in Österreich. Vol.90.
In: Duyse. Het oude nederlandsche lied.
In: Monumenta musica neerlandica.
In: Monumenta musicae belgicae.
In: Organum. 1.Reihe. Nr.19–20.
In: Peeters. Oudnederlandse meesters.
In: Smijers. Van Ockeghem tot Sweelinck.
In: Vereniging voor Nederlandsche Muziekgeschiedenis. Uitgave.
In: Zeitschrift für Spielmusik. No.1.
NETTO, MARCOS COELHO, *see* COELHO NETTO, MARCOS.
NEUBAUER, JOHANN, 17th CENTURY.
Chamber music.
In: Riemann. Old chamber music. Vol.2.
NEUBAUR, FRANZ CHRISTOPH, 1760–1795.
Duetten.
In: Nagels Musik-Archiv. No.85.
NEUKOMM, SIGMUND.
Selections.
In: Denkmäler der Tonkunst in Österreich. Vol.79. (Jg.XLII/2).
Part music.
In: Hullah. Part music. Class A.1. Vol.2.
Sacred music.
In: Latrobe, C. I. Selection of sacred music.
In: Latrobe, J. A. The music of the church.
NEUMARK, GEORG, 1621–1681.
Choral music.
In: Chorbuch für die Kirchenchöre Sachsens.
NEUMEYER, FRITZ, 1900– .
Choral music.
In: Nagels Männerchor-Blätter. No.3.
NEUSIEDLER, HANS, d.1563.
(var. sp.: Hans Newsidler).
Keyboard music.
In: Apel. Musik aus früher Zeit für Klavier. Bd.1.
Laute mit oder ohne Singstimme.
In: Musica practica. No.17b.
Lute music.
In: Chilesotti. Lautenspieler des XVI. Jahrhunderts.
In: Denkmäler der Tonkunst in Österreich. Vol.37. (Jg.XVIII/2).
NEWARK, WILLIAM, ca.1450–1509.
Songs.
In: Plainsong and Mediaeval Music Society. Publications. (A collection of songs and madrigals . . .).
NEW GUINEA–MUSIC.
In: Musicologisch onderzoek. [No].2.
NEWSIDLER, HANS, *see* NEUSIEDLER, HANS.
NIBBIO, STEFANO VENTURI DEL, *see* VENTURI DEL NIBBIO, STEFANO.
NICCOLÒ DA PERUGIA.
Cacce.
In: Marrocco. Fourteenth-century Italian cacce.
NICHELMANN, CHRISTOPH, 1717–1762.
La gaillarde, La tendre, Sarabande, Gigue.
In: Köhler. Les maîtres du clavecin. Heft 3.
Keyboard music.
In: Farrenc. Le trésor des pianistes. Vol.10.
In: Herrmann. Lehrmeister und Schüler Joh. Seb. Bachs. Vol.2.
In: Pauer. Alte Klavier-Musik. 2d series. Pt.3.
Konzert für Cembalo und Streichorchester.
In: Nagels Musik-Archiv. No.145.
Suite. Organ.
In: Dickinson. Historical recital series for organ. Vol.2. No.22.
NICKEL, THEODORE CARL HOELTY-, *see* HOELTY-NICKEL, THEODORE CARL.
NICOLAI, OTTO, 1810–1849.
Psalmen.
In: Musica sacra . . . ca.1842–1896. Vol.8–10.
NICOLAUS À KEMPIS, *see* KEMPIS, NICOLAUS À.
NICOLSON, RICHARD.
Madrigal.
In: The triumphs of Oriana.
NIEDERSACHSISCHE DORFTÄNZE.
In: Corona. Vol.16.
NIELSEN, CARL AUGUST, 1865–1931.
Commotio. Op.58. Organ.
In: Samfundet til Udgivelse af dansk Musik. Ser.III. No.40.
Helios. Ouverture. Op.17.
In: Samfundet til Udgivelse af dansk Musik. Ser.II. No.21.
Koncert for Clarinet og Orkester. Op.57.
In: Samfundet til Udgivelse af dansk Musik. Ser.III. No.32.
Koncert for Fløjte og Orkester.
In: Samfundet til Udgivelse af dansk Musik. Ser.III. No.117.

Kvintet for Strygere, G-dur, 1888.
In: Samfundet til Udgivelse af dansk Musik. Ser.III. No.167.
Organ music.
In: Gerhardt. Album nordischer Komponisten für Orgel. Vol.2.
Ouverture til "Maskerade."
In: Samfundet til Udgivelse af dansk Musik. Ser.III. No.27.
Preludio e presto per Violino solo, Op.52.
In: Samfundet til Udgivelse af dansk Musik. Ser.III. No.169.
Symfoni Nr.2 "The four temperaments." Op.16.
In: Samfundet til Udgivelse af dansk Musik. Ser.II. No.39.
Symfoni Nr.5. Op.50.
In: Samfundet til Udgivelse af dansk Musik. Ser.III. No.18.
Symfoni Nr.6 for Orkester. "Sinfonia semplice."
In: Samfundet til Udgivelse af dansk Musik. Ser.III. No.60.
Symfoni Nr.6, "Sinfonia semplice." Rev. ed. (cf.No.60).
In: Samfundet til Udgivelse af dansk Musik. Ser.III. No.133.
Tre Klaverstykker. Op. posth. 59.
In: Samfundet til Udgivelse af dansk Musik. Ser.III. No.168.
NIELSEN, HANS, 17th CENTURY.
Madrigale.
In: Das Chorwerk. No.35.
NIELSEN, LUDOLF, 1876–1939.
Dronning Margrethe. Op.50. Choral work.
In: Samfundet til Udgivelse af dansk Musik. Ser.III. No.5.
Lackschmi oder Ein indisches Liebesmärchen.
In: Samfundet til Udgivelse af dansk Musik. Ser.III. No.10.
Ouverture "Isbella". Op.10.
In: Samfundet til Udgivelse af dansk Musik. Ser.III. No.24.
Strygekvartet Nr.3, C dur.
In: Samfundet til Udgivelse af dansk Musik. Ser.III. No.29.
Symfoni Nr.2, E-dur, Op.19.
In: Samfundet til Udgivelse af dansk Musik. Ser.II. No.30.
NIELSEN, SVEND GODSKE-, *see* GODSKE-NIELSEN, SVEND.
NIETZSCHE, FRIEDRICH WILHELM, 1844–1900.
Musikalische Werke. 1v.
NIGETTI, FRANCESCO.
Selections.
In: Torchi. L'arte musicale in Italia. Bd.5.
NITSCHE, PAUL EDUARD, 1909– .
Die Pflege der Kinderstimme II.
In: Bausteine für Musikerziehung und Musikpflege. B 120.
NIVERS, GUILLAUME GABRIEL, ca.1617–1714.
Guillaume Gabriel Nivers. (Albert Cohen).
In: Institute of Mediaeval Music. Musical theorists in translation. Vol.3.
Keyboard music.
In: Herrmann. Lehrmeister und Schüler Joh. Seb. Bachs. Vol.1.
Organ music.
In: Klein. The first four centuries of music for the organ from Dunstable to Bach (1370–1749).
In: Raugel. Les maîtres français de l'orgue. Vol.1, 2.
In: Raugel. Les maîtres français de l'orgue aux XVIIème et XVIIIème siècles.
In: Raugel. Quarante-six pièces pour orgue ou harmonium.
In: Société Française de Musicologie, Paris. Sér.I. Bd.14.
NJIRIC, NIKSA.
Die schöne Jana.
In: Zeitschrift für Spielmusik. No.253.
NOACK, FRIEDRICH, 1890–1958.
Christoph Graupner als Kirchenkomponist.
In: Denkmäler deutscher Tonkunst. [1.Folge]. Reprint. Suppl. Vol.51/52.
NODAH, TERYUKI.
Trio for violin, violoncello and piano.
In: Contemporary Japanese music series. No.28.
NOEHREN, ROBERT, 1910– .
Organ music.
In: The parish organist. Vol.7–8.
NOLA, GIAN DOMENICO DA, 16th CENTURY.
Selections.
In: Torchi. L'arte musicale in Italia. Bd.1.
Karnevalslieder der Renaissance.
In: Das Chorwerk. No.43.
Mascherata.
In: Einstein. Beispielsammlung zur älteren Musikgeschichte.
NOLASCO COLÓN, PEDRO.
Lloral Mortales.
In: Archivo de musica colonial venezolana. No.9.
NOORDT, ANTHONI VAN, d.1675.
Organ music.
In: Klein. The first four centuries of music for the organ from Dunstable to Bach (1370–1749).
In: Peeters. Oudnederlandse meesters. Vol.2.
Tabulaturbuch. Psalms and fantasias.
In: Vereniging voor Nederlandsche Muziekgeschiedenis. Uitgave. No.19.
NORCOME, DANIEL, d.before 1626.
Madrigal.
In: The triumphs of Oriana.
NORDIC MUSIC.
In: Gerhardt. Album nordischer Komponisten für Orgel.
In: Zeitschrift für Spielmusik. No.90.
NORDQVIST, GUSTAV LAZARUS, 1886–1949.
Dryaden. Three songs.
In: Musikaliska konstföreningen. 1931.
NORDRAAK, RIKAR, 1842–1866.
Samlede verker. v.1– .
NØRGAARD, HELMER.
Serenade to young man with a horn.
In: Samfundet til Udgivelse af dansk Musik. Ser.III. No.174.
NØRHOLM, IB.
Kenotafium for Sopran, Kor og Orkester. Op.23.
In: Samfundet til Udgivelse af dansk Musik. Ser.III. No.165.

Trio for Klaver, Violin og Violoncel. Op.22.
In: Samfundet til Udgivelse af dansk Musik. Ser.III. No.153.
NORMAN, FREDRICK VILHELM LUDVIG, 1831–1885.
Concert overture, Op.21. Arr. for piano, 4 hands.
In: Musikaliska konstföreningen. 1895.
Three overtures for orchestra.
In: Musikaliska konstföreningen. 1911.
Symphony, No.2, E flat major, Op.40. Score; Arr. for piano, 4 hands.
In: Musikaliska konstföreningen. 1873, 1873.
Symphony, No.3, D minor, Op.58. Score; Arr. for piano, 4 hands.
In: Musikaliska konstföreningen. 1885, 1885.
Trio, No.2, B minor, Op.38.
In: Musikaliska konstföreningen. 1911.
NÖRMIGER, AUGUSTUS.
Keyboard music.
In: Apel. Musik aus früher Zeit für Klavier. Bd.1.
NORRMAN, JOHN.
Selections.
In: Svensk sanglyrik. Vol.2.
NORWAY–MUSIC (*see also* FOLKSONGS, NORWEGIAN).
In: Crotch. Specimens of various styles of music. Vol.1.
In: Oslo. Universitet. Bibliotek. Norsk musikksamling.
NOSKE, FRITS RUDOLF, 1920– .
The solo song outside German-speaking countries.
In: Anthology of music. Vol.16.
NOTATION.
In: Plainsong and Mediaeval Music Society. Publications. (The musical notation of the Middle Ages).
In: Thibaut. Monuments de la notation ekphonétique et neumatic de l'église latine.
NOTRE-DAME-ORGANA, DIE DREI- UND VIERSTIMMIGEN.
In: Publikationen älterer Musik. Jahrg.11.
NOTRE-DAME POLYPHONY, A CENTRAL SOURCE OF. (LUTHER A. DITTMER).
In: Institute of Mediaeval Music. Publications. Vol.3.
NOVÁK, VÍTĚZSLAV, 1870–1949.
In the church. (From "Slovak suite"). Organ.
In: Dickinson. Historical recital series for organ. Vol.2. No.28.
NOVARA, ITALY–MUSIC.
In: Istituzioni e monumenti dell' arte musicale italiana. Vol.3.
NOWAK, LEOPOLD, 1904– .
Bicinien der Renaissance.
In: Spielstücke für Blockflöten, Geigen, Lauten oder andere Instrumente. Heft 3, 4.
Sonata for solo violin.
In: New music. Vol.25. No.3. Apr. 1952.
NOWAKOWSKI, D.
Prayer. (Ancient Hebrew melody). Organ.
In: Dickinson. Historical recital series for organ. No.46.
NOWIKOFF.
Vocal music.
In: Sammlung russischer Romanzen. No.73.
NUCETI.
Selections.
In: Musica sacra . . . 1839– . Vol.15.
NUCIUS, JOHANNES, ca.1556–1620.
Zwei Hohelied-Motetten.
In: Christophorus-Chorwerk. Heft 9.
Mariä Verkündigung.
In: Christophorus-Chorwerk. Heft 12.
Drei Psalmen. (112, 123 und 8).
In: Christophorus-Chorwerk. Heft 19.
Salve regina.
In: Christophorus-Chorwerk. Heft 35.
NUREMBERG MASTERS OF THE 17th CENTURY.
In: Denkmäler deutscher Tonkunst. [2.Folge]. Vol.6 (i).
NURNBERG–MUSIC.
In: Musik alter Meister. Heft 3.
NYSTROEM, GÖSTA, 1890– .
Selections.
In: Svensk sanglyrik. Vol.2.
String quartet, 1956.
In: Musikaliska konstföreningen. 1958.

OBERBORBECK, FELIX, 1900– .
Ich ging durch einen grasgrünen Wald. Kleine Kantate.
In: Zeitschrift für Spielmusik. No.150.
Kirchlintler Weihnachtsgeschichte.
In: Zeitschrift für Spielmusik. No.132.
Nun ruhen alle Wälder.
In: Zeitschrift für Spielmusik. No.133.
Steinbacher Tageskreis.
In: Zeitschrift für Spielmusik. No.200.
Variationen über "Der Mai, der lustige Mai."
In: Zeitschrift für Spielmusik. No.163.
Vechtaer Adventkantate.
In: Zeitschrift für Spielmusik. No.182.
OBOE.
In: Florilegium musicum.
OBRECHT, JACOB, ca.1430–1505.
(var. sp.: Jacob Hobrecht).
Werken. 30v.
Opera omnia. v.1– .
Selections.
In: Ambros. Auserwählte Tonwerke.
In: Documenta historica musicae.
In: Maldéghem. Trésor musical.
In: Smith. Musica antiqua.
Choral music.
In: Capella. Vol.1.
In: Engel. Three centuries of choral music. Vol.1.
In: Smijers. Van Ockeghem tot Sweelinck. Aflg.2, 3.
Mass Fortuna desperata.
In: Vereniging voor Nederlandsche Muziekgeschiedenis. Uitgave. No.9.
Motets.
In: Parrish. Masterpieces of music before 1750. No.18.
In: Vereniging voor Nederlandsche Muziekgeschiedenis. Uitgave. No.44.
Organ music.
In: Klein. The first four centuries of music for the organ from Dunstable to Bach (1370–1749).

In: Peeters. Oudnederlandse meesters. Vol.1, 2, 3.
In: Schering. Alte Meister aus der Frühzeit des Orgelspiels.
Passio Domini. (St. Matthew), for four voices.
In: Vereniging voor Nederlandsche Muziekgeschiedenis. Uitgave. No.18.
OCKEGHEM, JEAN DE, d.ca.1496.
(var. sp.: Jan Ockeghem, Jean Ockeghem, Johannes Ockeghem, Jean de Okeghem, Joannes Okeghem, Johannes Okeghem).
Collected works. v.1– .
Sämtliche Werke. Bd.1.
In: Publikationen älterer Musik. Jahrg.1, pt.2.
Selections.
In: Ambros. Auswerwählte Tonwerke.
In: Documenta historica musicae.
In: Maldéghem. Trésor musical.
In: Smith. Musica antiqua.
Chansons.
In: Copenhagen Kongelige Bibliotek. Mss. (Thottske Samling 291[8]). Der kopenhagener Chansonnier.
Choral music.
In: Engel. Three centuries of choral music. Vol.1.
In: Rochlitz. Sammlung vorzüglicher Gesangstücke. Bd.1. Pt.1.
In: Smijers. Van Ockeghem tot Sweelinck. Aflg.1.
Missa Mi-Mi.
In: Das Chorwerk. No.4.
Missa super l'homme armé.
In: Monumenta polyphoniae liturgicae sanctae ecclesiae romaniae. Ser.I. Tomus I. Fasc.VI.
Motetten.
In: Chor-Archiv.
Organ music.
In: Klein. The first four centuries of music for the organ from Dunstable to Bach (1370–1749).
In: Peeters. Oudnederlandse meesters. Vol.1.
Sanctus from the "Missa Protationum."
In: Parrish. Masterpieces of music before 1750. No.17.
OCTOECHUS, THE HYMNS OF THE.
In: Monumenta musicae byzantinae. Transcripta. Vol.3, 5.
ODHECATON A.
In: Petrucci. Harmonica musices Odhecaton A.
ODINGTON, WALTER DE, 14th CENTURY.
Selections.
In: Gleason. Examples of music before 1400.
OEGLIN, ERHART, 16th CENTURY.
Liederbuch zu 4 St. Augsburg 1512.
In: Publikationen älterer praktischer und theoretischer Musikwerke. Jahrg.8.
OEVERING, RYNOLDUS POPMA VAN, 1692–1782.
6 suites voor klavier. Op.1.
In: Vereninging voor Nederlandsche Muziekgeschiedenis. Uitgave. No.46.
OHLSSON, RICHARD, 1874–1940.
String quartet, No.3.
In: Musikaliska konstföreningen. 1934.
OKEGHEM, JEAN DE, *see* OCKEGHEM, JEAN DE.
OKUMURA, HAJIME.
Third, fourth sonatina for piano.
In: Contemporary Japanese music series. No.26, 14.
OLAGUÉ, FR. BERM. EU DE, 17th CENTURY.
Keyboard music.
In: Kastner. Silva iberica.
OLD BANG 'AM.
In: Music Press, Inc. [Choral series]. Vol.95.
OLD HALL MANUSCRIPT.
The Old Hall manuscript.
In: Plainsong and Mediaeval Music Society. Publications. (Old Hall manuscript).
OLDBERG, ARNE, 1874– .
Piano music.
In: The Wa-Wan series of American compositions.
OLDFIELD, THOMAS, 16th–17th CENTURIES.
Keyboard music.
In: The Fitzwilliam virginal book.
OLEY, JOHANN CHRISTOPH, 1738–1789.
Organ music.
In: Muziek voor de eredienst. Vol.2.
In: The parish organist. Vol.1–4.
OLIVARES, J. M.
Salve.
In: Archivo de música colonial venezolana. No.4.
OLIVER.
Selections.
In: Plainsong and Mediaeval Music Society. Publications. (Old Hall manuscript).
OLLETA, D.
Sacred music.
In: Eslava y Elizondo. Lira sacro-hispana. 19th century. ii.2.
OLSEN, POUL ROVSING, *see* ROVSING OLSEN, POUL.
OLSSON, OTTO EMANUEL, 1879– .
Six Latin hymns for chorus a cappella.
In: Musikaliska konstföreningen. 1917.
Six Latin hymns for mixed chorus a cappella.
In: Musikaliska konstföreningen. 1954.
String quartet, No.2, G major, Op.27.
In: Musikaliska konstföreningen. 1912.
Te Deum. Op.25.
In: Musikaliska konstföreningen. 1912.
OLSSON-BEDELL.
Organ music.
In: Standard series of organ compositions. No.31.
OLTER, MARCUS.
Organ music.
In: Organum. 4.Reihe. Nr.2.
ONGUEVAL, VAN.
Selections.
In: Maldéghem. Trésor musical.
ONSLOW, GEORGE, 1784–1853.
Blaserquintett, F-dur, Op.81. Nr.3. (Redel).
In: Alte Musik. (Reihe "Leuckartiana").
OPERA–FRANCE.
In: Les chefs d'oeuvres classiques de l'opéra français.
OPERA FROM ITS BEGINNINGS TO THE BEGINNING OF THE NINETEENTH CENTURY. (ABERT).
In: Anthology of music. Vol.5.

ORBÓN, JULIÁN, 1925– .
Tocata. (Piano).
In: Instituto Interamericano de Musicologia. Publicaciónes. No.38.
ORCHESTRATION, HISTORY OF. (BECKER).
In: Anthology of music. Vol.24.
OREFICE, GIACOMO, 1865–1922.
Keyboard music.
In: Tagliapietra. Antologia di musica antica e moderna per pianoforte. Bd.17.
ORGAN MUSIC, *see* KEYBOARD MUSIC–ORGAN.
ORIANA.
In: The triumphs of Oriana.
ORNSTEIN, LEO, 1895– .
The corpse, for voice and piano.
In: New music. Vol.1. No.3. Apr.1928.
OROLOGIO, ALESSANDRO.
Selections.
In: Denkmäler der Tonkunst in Österreich. Vol.77. (Jg.XLI).
ORPHEUS BRITANNICUS (1698 and 1702). FACSIMILE. (Purcell).
In: Monuments of music and music literature. First series. No.1.
ORTELLS.
Sacred music.
In: Eslava y Elizondo. Lira sacro-hispana. 17th century. ii.1.
ORTHODOX EASTERN CHURCH. LITURGY AND RITUAL.
In: Monumenta musicae byzantinae. Transcripta.
ORTIZ, DIEGO, b.ca.1525.
Pereat dies.
In: Polifonía española. Vol.8.
Recercada. (Ricercare).
In: Antiqua Edition. Von 4 Instrumenten an.
Sacred music.
In: Eslava y Elizondo. Lira sacro-hispana. 16th century. i.2.
In: Proske. Musica divina. Annus primus. Tom 3, 4.
In: Rubio. Antologia polifonica sacra. Vol.1.
ORTO, MARBRIANO DE, d.1529.
Selections.
In: Ambros. Auserwählte Tonwerke.
Missa super l'homme armé.
In: Monumenta polyphoniae liturgicae sanctae ecclesiae romanae. Ser.I. Tomus I. Fasc.VII.
Organ music.
In: Cantantibus organis. Vol.6.
In: Schering. Alte Meister aus der Frühzeit des Orgelspiels.
OSIANDER, LUCAS, 1534–1604.
Choral music.
In: Antiqua Chorbuch. Vol.1. Heft 3.
OSTHOFF, HELMUTH, 1896– . ed.
The German part song.
In: Anthology of music. Vol.10.
OSTIA, PETRUS DE, *see* PETRUS DE OSTIA.
OSWALD, JAMES, d.1769.
Songs.
In: Potter. Reliquary of English song. Vol.2.
OTAÑO Y EGUINO, JOSÉ MARÍA NEMESIO, 1880–1956.
Organ music.
In: Organ album of ten pieces by Spanish composers.
OTHMAYR, KASPAR, 1515–1553.
(var. sp.: Caspar Othmayr, Caspar Othmayer).
Ausgewählte Werke.
In: Das Erbe deutscher Musik. 1.Reihe. Vol.16, 26.
Choral music.
In: Antiqua Chorbuch. Vol.2. Heft 2.
Geistliche Lieder zu vier Stimmen.
In: Chor-Archiv.
Organ music.
In: The parish organist. Vol.5–6.
OTT, JOHANNES, 16th CENTURY.
Mehrstimmiges deutsches Liederbuch von 1544; Liederbuch die Einleitung, Biographien, Texte und Melodien.
In: Publikationen älterer praktischer und theoretischer Musikwerke. Jahrg.1–3, 4. Pt.1.
OTTO, STEPHAN, b.ca.1594.
Choral music.
In: Antiqua Chorbuch. Vol.1. Heft 5.
OTTO, VALERIUS, 17th CENTURY.
Chamber music.
In: Riemann. Old chamber music. Vol.2.
Intrada.
In: Rahter's Kammer-Orchester. No.4.
OVALLE, JAYME.
Música de cámara.
In: Boletín latino-americano de música. Vol.6.
OVERTON, HALL.
Second string quartet.
In: Society for the Publication of American Music. Publications. 41st season. 1960–61.
OXFORD, LATIN LITURGICAL D 20 AND CHICAGO 654 APP. (LUTHER A. DITTMER).
In: Institute of Mediaeval Music. Publications. Vol.6.
OXINAGAS, JOAQUIN, 18th CENTURY.
Organ music.
In: Muset. Early Spanish organ music.
In: Piedelievre. Les anciens maîtres espagnols.
OYSTERMAYRE, JEHAN, 16th CENTURY.
Keyboard music.
In: The Fitzwilliam virginal book.
OZI, ÉTIENNE, 1754–1813.
Bassoon and piano works.
In: Musiques françaises. Vol.7, 21.

PACELLI, ASPRILIO, ca.1570–1623.
Opera omnia. v.1– .
PACHELBEL, CARL THEODORUS, 1690–1750.
Magnificat for double chorus and organ. p.1– .
PACHELBEL, JOHANN, 1653–1706.
Christmas pastorale. From heaven high. Organ.
In: Dickinson. Historical recital series for organ. Vol.2. No.34.
Fugen.
In: Musica instrumentalis. Vol.2.
Fugue for organ in C.
In: Königliche Akademie der Künste. Auswahl vorzüglicher Musik-Werke. No.24.
Kanon und Gigue für drei Violinen mit Generalbass.

In: Organum. 3.Reihe. Nr.24.
Keyboard music.
In: Denkmäler deutscher Tonkunst. [2.Folge]. Vol.2 (i).
In: Georgii. Keyboard music of the Baroque and Rococo. Vol.1.
In: Herrmann. Lehrmeister und Schüler Joh. Seb. Bachs. Vol.1.
In: Oesterle. Early keyboard music. Vol.1.
In: Tagliapietra. Antologia di musica antica e moderna per pianoforte. Bd.9.
Organ music.
In: Auler. Spielbuch für Kleinorgel. Vol.1, 2.
In: Biggs. Treasury of early organ music.
In: Bonnet. Historical organ-recitals. Vol.1.
In: Buszin. Organ series. Vol.1.
In: Denkmäler der Tonkunst in Österreich. Vol.17. (Jg.VIII/2).
In: Denkmäler deutscher Tonkunst. [2.Folge]. Vol.4 (i).
In: Einstein. Beispielsammlung zur älteren Musikgeschichte.
In: Elkan-Vogel organ series. Vol.3.
In: Guilmant. Concert historique d'orgue.
In: Guilmant. École classique de l'orgue. No.5.
In: Keller. Achtzig Choralvorspiele deutscher Meister des 17. und 18. Jahrhunderts.
In: Klein. The first four centuries of music for the organ from Dunstable to Bach (1370–1749).
In: Liber organi. Bd.5, 6.
In: The Liturgical Music Press, Inc. Masterpieces of organ music. Folio 1, 5, 17, 27, 45, 55.
In: Organ masters of the Baroque period. Vol.1.
In: Organum. 4.Reihe. Nr.12, 13, 14.
In: The parish organist. Vol.1–4, 5–6, 7–8.
In: Peeters. Anthologia pro organo. Vol.2,4.
In: Pierront. Cent versets de magnificat.
In: Raugel. Quarante-six pièces pour orgue ou harmonium.
In: Rohr. Orgelspiel im Kirchenjahr.
In: Straube. Alte Meister.
In: Straube. Alte Meister des orgelspiels.
In: Straube. Choralvorspiele alter Meister.
Partie für 5 Streicher und Generalbass.
In: Organum. 3.Reihe. Nr.22.
Toccata in E minor.
In: Parrish. Masterpieces of music before 1750. No.37.
Triosuiten für zwei Geigen und Basso Continuo. Heft I, II, III.
In: Hortus musicus. No.54, 55, 56.
Weihnachtsmusik. Für Klavier oder Orgel.
In: Nagels Musik-Archiv. No.95.
PACHELBEL, WILHELM HIERONYMUS, ca.1685–1764.
Keyboard music.
In: Denkmäler deutscher Tonkunst. [2.Folge]. Vol.2 (i).
Organ music.
In: Auler. Spielbuch für Kleinorgel. Vol.2.
In: Biggs. Treasury of early organ music.
In: Denkmäler deutscher Tonkunst. [2.Folge]. Vol.4 (i).
In: Liber organi. Bd.5.
In: Organ masters of the Baroque period. Vol.3.
PACIOTTI, PIETRO PAOLO, 16th–17th CENTURIES.
Sacred music.
In: Proske. Selectus novus missarum. Annus primus. Tom 2.
PADBRUÉ, CORNELIS THYMONS, 17th CENTURY.
I. V. Vondels Kruisbergh, op musijck gebraght door Cornelis Padbrué.
In: Vereniging voor Nederlandsche Muziekgeschiedenis. Uitgave. No.42.
Nederlandse Madrigalen.
In: Monumenta musica neerlandica. Vol.5.
PADOVANO, ANNIBALE, *see* ANNIBALE PADOVANO.
PADRÓS, JAIME.
Katalanische und kastellanische Volkslieder.
In: Christophorus-Chorwerk. Heft 27.
PADUA, BARTOLINO DA, *see* BARTOLINO DA PADUA.
PADUA, GRATIOSUS DE, *see* GRATIOSUS DE PADUA.
PAESIELLO, GIOVANNI, *see* PAISIELLO, GIOVANNI.
PAEZ, J.
Sacred music.
In: Eslava y Elizondo. Lira sacro-hispana. 18th century. i.l.
PAGANELLI, GIUSEPPE ANTONIO, 1710–1760.
(var. sp.: Giovanni Antonio Paganelli).
Keyboard music.
In: Benvenuti. Cembalisti italiani del settecento.
In: Tagliapietra. Antologia di musica antica e moderna per pianoforte. Bd.12.
Sonate (F).
In: Pauer. Alte Meister. No.50.
PAGANINI, NICCOLÒ, 1782–1840.
Quartetto für Violine, Viola, Violoncello und Gitarre (oder Cembalo).
In: Antiqua Edition. Von 4 Instrumenten an.
PAGIN, ANDRÉ NOËL, b.1721.
Sonate en ré majeur.
In: L'école du violon au XVIIe et XVIIIe siècle. No.1258.
PAGNIER (PAIGNIER).
(var. sp.: Paignier).
Chansons.
In: Publikationen älterer praktischer und theoretischer Musikwerke. Jahrg.27.
PAISIBLE, JAMES, d.1721.
(var. sp.: Jacques Paisible).
Sonata 1–5 für 2 Alt-Blockflöten und Basso Continuo.
In: Moecks Kammermusik. Vol.12–15.
PAISIELLO, GIOVANNI, 1740–1816.
(var. sp.: Paesiello).
Arias.
In: Landshoff. Alte Meister des Bel Canto. Eine Sammlung von Arien. Vol.1–2.
In: Parisotti. Arie antiche. Bd.1.
Concerto in F for 2 horns, strings, cembalo.
In: Antica musica strumentale italiana. In preparation.

Dalla "Nina."
In: I classici della musica italiana. Raccolta nazionale delle musiche italiane. Quad. 80–81.
La pazza per amore.
In: I classici della musica italiana. Vol.20.
Vocal music.
In: Delsarte. Archives du chant. Livr.18. No.12.
In: Gevaert. Les gloires de l'Italie. Vol.1, 2.
PAIX, JAKOB, 16th CENTURY.
Organ music.
In: Cantantibus organis. Vol.2, 6.
PALADINI, GIOVANNI PAOLO, 16th CENTURY.
(var. sp.: Giuseppe Paladini).
Keyboard music.
In: Benvenuti. Cembalisti italiani del settecento.
PALAFUTI, VINCENZO, 18th CENTURY.
Organ music.
In: Bossi. Sammlung von Stücken alter italienischer Meister für die moderne Orgel.
PALAVICINO, CARLO, *see* PALLAVICINO, CARLO.
PALERO, FRANCISCO FERNANDEZ, 16th CENTURY.
Organ music.
In: Cantantibus organis. Vol.4, 6.
In: Muset. Early Spanish organ music.
In: Piedelievre. Les anciens maîtres espagnols.
PALESTRINA, GIOVANNI BATTISTA PIERLUIGI DA, d.1594.
Werke. 33v.
Le opere complete. v.1– .
Raccolta di musica sacra. 7v.
Selections.
In: Crotch. Specimens of various styles of music. Vol.2.
In: Documenta historica musicae.
In: Gabrieli. Music of Gabrieli and his time.
Agnus Dei (I) from the Mass "Veni sponsa Christi."
In: Parrish. Masterpieces of music before 1750. No.24.
Canzonette e madrigali.
In: I classici della musica italiana. Vol.21.
Chant.
In: Soderlund. Examples of Gregorian chant and works by Orlandus Lassus and Giovanni Pierluigi Palestrina.
In: Soderlund. Examples of Gregorian chant and works by Orlandus Lassus, Giovanni Pierluigi Palestrina, and Marc Antonio Ingegneri.
Choral music.
In: Dehn. Sammlung älterer Musik aus dem XVI. und XVII. Jahrhundert.
In: Dessoff choir series. No.1, 12.
In: Engel. Three centuries of choral music. Vol.2.
In: Der Kammerchor. Vol.3.
In: Music Press, Inc. [Choral series]. No.75.
In: Musica sacra . . . 1839– . Vol.2, 3.
In: Recueil de musique ancienne. Recueil des morceaux de musique ancienne. Bd.1, 5, 7, 9, 10.
In: Rochlitz. Sammlung vorzüglicher Gesangstücke. Bd.1. Pt.2; Appendix.
In: Societas Polyphonica Romanae. Repertorium. Vol.1, 2, 3, 4, 5, 6.
Church music.
In: Motett Society. [Collection of ancient church music]. Division 1, 2, 3.
Gesänge.
In: Musica sacra . . . ca.1842–1896. Vol.12.
Kirchengesänge.
In: Tucher. Kirchengesänge der berühmtesten älteren italienischen Meister.
Madrigals.
In: I classici della musica italiana. Raccolta nazionale delle musiche italiane. Quad. 82–84.
In: Music Press, Inc. [Choral series]. No.58.
Masses.
In: Anthologie des maîtres religieux primitifs des XVe, XVIe et XVIIe siècles.
In: Monumenta polyphoniae italicae. Vol.1.
Missa aeterna Christi munera.
In: Musica spiritualis. Serie IA. No.2.
Missa brevis. S.A.T.B.
In: Basilica. 1952.
Missa brevis quatuor vocum.
In: Somma. Polifonia vocale sacra e profana. Sec. XVI. Vol.4.
Missa iste confessor. S.A.T.B.
In: Basilica. 1958.
Missa Papae Marcelli.
In: Musikalische Stundenbücher.
In: Somma. Polifonia vocale sacra e profana. Sec.XVI. Vol.3.
Mori quasi il mio core.
In: Arion. Vol.1.
Motecta festorum.
In: Denkmäler der Tonkunst. Vol.1.
Motet (a 6) Tu es Petrus.
In: Königliche Akademie der Künste. Auswahl vorzüglicher Musik-Werke. No.28.
Organ music.
In: Bonnet. Historical organ-recitals. Vol.1.
In: Cantantibus organis. Vol.1, 6.
In: Guilmant. Concert historique d'orgue.
In: Klein. The first four centuries of music for the organ from Dunstable to Bach (1370–1749).
In: The Liturgical Music Press, Inc. Masterpieces of organ music. Folio 22, 55.
In: Peeters. Anthologia pro organo. Vol.3.
In: Raugel. Quarante-six pièces pour orgue ou harmonium.
Part music.
In: Hullah. Part music. Class A.1. Vol.1, 2; Class B.1; Class C. Sacred; 1868 edition.
Prayer. Organ.
In: Dickinson. Historical recital series for organ. Vol.1. No.17.
Ricercari.
In: Antiqua edition. Von 4 Instrumenten an.
In: Orgue et liturgie. Vol.3.
Sacred music.
In: Alfieri. Raccolta di musica sacra. Vol.1–7.
In: The Fitzwilliam music. Bd.1.
In: Proske. Musica divina. Annus primus. Tom 1, 2, 3, 4.
In: Proske. Selectus novus missarum. Annus primus. Tom 1, 2; Annus secundus. Tom 1, 2.

Sicut cervus; Sitivit anima mea.
In: Musica spiritualis. Ser.IB. No.5.
Vocal music.
In: Hullah. Vocal scores. I. Sacred.
PALIKAROVA VERDEIL, R., *see* VERDEIL, R. PALIKAROVA.
PALLAVICINO, BENEDETTO, d.1601.
Selections.
In: Torchi. L'arte musicale in Italia. Bd.2.
Madrigale.
In: Das Chorwerk. No.80.
PALLAVICINO, CARLO, 1630–1688.
(var. sp.: Carlo Palavicino).
La Gerusalemme liberata.
In: Denkmäler deutscher Tonkunst. [1.Folge]. Vol.55.
PALMER, ROBERT, 1915– .
Piano quartet.
In: Society for the Publication of American Music. Publications. 30th season. 1948–49.
PALUSELLI, STEFAN.
Instrumental musik.
In: Denkmäler der Tonkunst in Österreich. Vol.86.
PAMER, M.
Zwölf Walzer.
In: Corona. Vol.19.
PAMINGER, LEONHARD, 1495–1567.
Choral music.
In: Antiqua Chorbuch. Vol.1. Heft 1.
Lieder.
In: Publikationen älterer praktischer und theoretischer Musikwerke. Jahrg.1–3.
Sacred music.
In: Proske. Musica divina. Annus primus. Tom 4.
Weihnachtsmotette.
In: Chor-Archiv.
PANDION, FRANZ. ed.
Lieder niederösterreichischer Komponisten. Singstimme (Mittel) und Klavier.
In: Hausmusik. No.137.
PANNAIN, GUIDO, 1891– . ed.
L'oratorio dei Filippini e la scuola musicale di Napoli.
In: Istituzioni e monumenti dell' arte musicale italiana. Nuova serie. In preparation.
In: Istituzioni e monumenti dell' arte musicale italiana. Nuova serie.
PAOLO DE FLORENTIA.
Songs.
In: Riemann. Hausmusik aus alter Zeit.
PAOLO TENORISTA, DON, 15th CENTURY.
Paolo Tenorista in a new fragment of the Italian Ars Nova. 83p.
PAPA, CLEMENS NON, *see* CLÉMENT, JACQUES.
PARADIES, PIETRO DOMENICO, 1707–1791.
(var. sp.: Pietro Domenico Paradisi).
Selections.
In: Crotch. Specimens of various styles of music. Vol.3.
Arias.
In: Parisotti. Arie antiche. Bd.2.
Keyboard music.
In: Benvenuti. Cembalisti italiani del settecento.
In: Esposito. Early Italian piano music.
In: Farrenc. Le trésor des pianistes. Vol.14.
In: Georgii. Keyboard music of the Baroque and Rococo. Vol.3.
In: Pauer. Alte Klavier-Musik. 1st series. Pt.2.
In: Selva. Pièces de clavecin des XVIIme et XVIIIme siècles.
In: Tagliapietra. Antologia di musica antica e moderna per pianoforte. Bd.12.
2 Sonates.
In: Köhler. Les maîtres du clavecin. Heft 8.
Sonata. Piano.
In: I classici della musica italiana. Vol.22.
In: I classici della musica italiana. Raccolta nazionale delle musiche italiane. Quad. 85, 88, 304–305.
In: Paoli. Sonate italiane del sec.: XVIII per cembalo o pianoforte.
Sonate. No.10. (D).
In: Pauer. Alte Meister. No.15.
Sonate. (G). (F). (C).
In: Pauer. Alte Meister. No.53, 54, 55.
Songs.
In: Denkmäler der Tonkunst in Österreich. Vol.54. (Jg.XXVII/2).
PARADISI, PIETRO DOMENICO, *see* PARADIES, PIETRO DOMENICO.
PAREJA, BARTOLOMÉ RAMOS DE, *see* RAMOS DE PAREJA, BARTOLOMÉ.
PARIS 13521 AND 11411. (LUTHER A. DITTMER).
In: Institute of Mediaeval Music. Publications. Vol.4.
PARISIENSIS, MAGISTER ALBERTUS.
Selections.
In: Gleason. Examples of music before 1400.
PARKER, MONK OF STRATFORD.
Selections.
In: Smith. Musica antiqua.
PARMEGIANO, ANTONIO DI BECCHI, *see* BECCHI, ANTONIO DI.
PARRY, SIR CHARLES HUBERT HASTINGS, BART., 1848–1918.
Selections.
In: The music with the form and order of the service to be performed at the coronation of . . . Queen Elizabeth II.
PARSLEY, OSBERT, 1511–1585.
Church music.
In: Tudor church music. Vol.10.
PARSONS, JOHN, d.1623.
Sacred music.
In: Boyce. Cathedral music. 1849. Vol.1. Appendix.
PARSONS, ROBERT, d.1570.
Keyboard music.
In: The Fitzwilliam virginal book.
PART-SONGS, *see* CHORAL MUSIC–MISCELLANEOUS COLLECTIONS.
PARTHENIA.
In: English keyboard music. [No.19].
In: Farrenc. Le trésor des pianistes. Vol.2.
In: Glyn. Twenty-one old English compositions of the 16th and 17th centuries.
In: Monuments of music and music literature. First series. No.11.

In: Musical Antiquarian Society. Publications. Vol.18.
PASCHKOFF.
Vocal music.
In: Sammlung russischer Romanzen. No.4, 104, 163.
PASQUALI, NICOLÒ, d.1757.
Menuet de la 5e sonate.
In: L'école du violon au XVIIe et XVIIIe siècle. No.1335.
PASQUINI, BERNARDO, 1637–1710.
Selections.
In: Torchi. L'arte musicale in Italia. Bd.3.
Arias.
In: Landshoff. Alte Meister des Bel Canto. Eine Sammlung von Arien. Vol.1–2.
Introduzione e pastorale; Toccata con lo scherzo.
In: Somma. Musiche vocali e strumentali sacre e profane, sec. XVII–VXIII–XIX. Vol.4, 5.
Collected works for keyboard.
In: Corpus of early keyboard music. Vol.5. Pt.1– .
Keyboard music.
In: Esposito. Early Italian piano music.
In: Farrenc. Le trésor des pianistes. Vol.3.
In: Georgii. Keyboard music of the Baroque and Rococo. Vol.1.
In: Kastner. Silva iberica.
In: Oesterle. Early keyboard music. Vol.1.
In: Tagliapietra. Antologia di musica antica e moderna per pianoforte. Bd.8.
Organ music.
In: Elkan-Vogel organ series. Vol.1.
In: Fuser. Classici italiani dell' organo.
Partitas. Clavicembalo or piano.
In: Boghen. Antichi maestri italiani.
Sonata D-moll.
In: Gitarre-Kammermusik. No.18.
Songs.
In: Jeppesen. La flora. Vol.1, 2.
PASQUINI, ERCOLE, b.ca.1580.
Selections.
In: Torchi. L'arte musicale in Italia. Bd.3.
Keyboard music.
In: Corpus of early keyboard music. Vol.12.
In: Esposito. Early Italian piano music.
PASSERAT.
Vocal music.
In: Delsarte. Archives du chant. Livr.10. No.6.
PASSEREAU, 15th–16th CENTURIES.
Chansons.
In: Cauchie. Quinze chansons françaises du XVIe siècle.
In: Lesure. Anthologie de la chanson parisienne au XVIe siècle.
In: Publikationen älterer praktischer und theoretischer Musikwerke. Jahrg.27.
Choral music.
In: Der Kammerchor. Vol.1.
Motets.
In: Attaingnant. Treize livres de motets. Livre 11.
PASSET DE TORNACO, 15th CENTURY.
Selections.
In: Reaney. Early fifteenth-century music. Vol.2.
PASTERWITZ, GEORG VON, 1730–1803.
Choral music.
In: Rochlitz. Sammlung vorzüglicher Gesangstücke. Bd.3.
Fugue for organ, in B flat.
In: Königliche Akademie der Künste. Auswahl vorzüglicher Musik-Werke. No.30.
Organ music.
In: Cantantibus organis. Vol.5.
PATAVUS, LAURUS.
Sacred music.
In: Jeppesen. Italia sacra musica. Vol.1.
PATIÑO, CARLOS, d.1683.
Selections.
In: Pedrell. Teatro lirico espanol anterior al siglo XIX. Bd.3, 4/5.
Sacred music.
In: Eslava y Elizondo. Lira sacro-hispana. 17th century. ii.1.
PATTRICK, NATHANIEL, d.1595.
(var. sp.: Patrick).
Sacred music.
In: Arnold. Cathedral music.
PAUFFER.
Vocal music.
In: Sammlung russischer Romanzen. No.49, 196, 197.
PAULLET, 14th–15th CENTURIES.
Selections.
In: Reaney. Early fifteenth-century music. Vol.2.
PAULSON, GUSTAF, 1898– .
Selections.
In: Svensk sanglyrik. Vol.2.
PAUMANN, CONRAD, ca.1410–1473.
Fundamentum organisandi.
In: Das Locheimer Liederbuch. Das Locheimer Liederbuch.
Keyboard music.
In: Apel. Musik aus früher Zeit für Klavier. Bd.1.
Organ music.
In: Buxheimer Orgelbuch. Das Buxheimer Orgelbuch.
PAUMGARTNER.
Keyboard music.
In: Apel. Musik aus früher Zeit für Klavier. Bd.1.
PAXTON, STEPHEN, 1735–1787.
Part music.
In: Hullah. Part music. Class A.1. Vol.2; Class A.2. Vol.1, 2; Class C. Secular; 1868 edition.
PAXTON, WILLIAM, 1737–1781.
Part music.
In: Hullah. Part music. Class A.1. Vol.2; Class A.2. Vol.1, 2; Class C. Secular; 1868 edition.
PAZ, JUAN CÁRLOS, 1897– .
Selections.
In: Boletín latino-americano de música. Vol.1, 4.
In: Instituto Interamericano de Musicologia. Publicaciónes. No.10, 27.
3a composicion en los 12 tonos, for clarinet in B and piano.
In: New music. Vol.16. No.2. Jan.1943.
PEARSALL, ROBERT LUCAS DE, 1795–1856.
Part music.

In: Hullah. Part music. Class A.2. Vol.1.
PEDERSØN, MOGENS, d.1623.
Madrigale.
In: Das Chorwerk. No.35.
1. Pratum spirituale. 2. Madrigali a cinque voci, libro primo.
In: Samfundet til Udgivelse af dansk Musik. Ser.IV. Dania sonans. No.1.
PEDRELL, FELIPE, 1841–1922.
Catàleg dels manuscrits musicals de la collecció Pedrell.
In: Barcelona. Biblioteca Central. Sección de Música. Publicaciones. Vol.2.
Els madrigals i la missa de difunts d'en Brudieu.
In: Barcelona. Biblioteca Central. Sección de Música. Publicaciones. Vol.1.
PEDRO DE ESCOBAR, *see* ESCOBAR, PEDRO DE.
PEERSON, MARTIN, ca.1572–1650.
Keyboard music.
In: The Fitzwilliam virginal book.
In: The Fitzwilliam virginal book. Ausgewählte Stücke. Vol.2.
Organ music.
In: Elkan-Vogel organ series. Vol.2.
PEIXE, CÉSAR GUERRA.
Música de cámara.
In: Boletín latino-americano de música. Vol.6.
PEKIEL, BARTLOMIEJ, d.ca.1670.
(var. sp.: Bartolomäus Pekiel).
Audite Mortales.
In: Denkmäler altpolnischer Musik. Vol.4.
2 Latin carols for S.A.T.B. a cappella.
In: Denkmäler altpolnischer Musik. Vol.19.
Lute music.
In: Denkmäler altpolnischer Musik. Vol.30.
In: Moecks gelbe Musikhefte. Vol.40.
Missa pulcherrima.
In: Denkmäler altpolnischer Musik. Vol.17.
In: Surzyński. Monumenta musicae sacrae in Polonia. Vol.4.
2 Patrem. Male or mixed chorus a cappella.
In: Denkmäler altpolnischer Musik. Vol.52.
PELETIER.
Duos.
In: Expert. Florilège du concert vocal de la Renaissance. No.8.
PELLEGRINI, DOMENICO.
Dicite, morales. Sopran (Tenor) und B. C.
In: Cantio sacra. No.54.
PELLEGRINI, VINCENZO, d.1636.
Selections.
In: Torchi. L'arte musicale in Italia. Bd.3.
Organ music.
In: Fuser. Classici italiani dell' organo.
In: Peeters. Anthologia pro organo. Vol.3.
PEÑALOSA, FRANCISCO, 15th–16th CENTURIES.
Selections.
In: Monumentos de la musica espagñola. Vol.1.
Motets.
In: Elúsitiza. Antología musical.
Sacred music.
In: Eslava y Elizondo. Lira sacro-hispana. 16th century. i.1.
Sancta Mater.
In: Polifonía española. Vol.28.
PENET, HILAIRE, 15th–16th CENTURIES.
Motets.
In: Attaingnant. Treize livres de motets. Livre 3, 5.
PENTECOSTARIUM, THE HYMNS OF THE.
In: Monumenta musicae byzantinae. Transcripta. Vol.7.
PEPUSCH, JOHANN CHRISTOPH, 1667–1752.
Sonaten I–VIII für Alt-Blockflöte und Basso Continuo.
In: Moecks Kammermusik. Vol.11, 21, 22, 23.
3 Sonaten für Violine und Basso Continuo.
In: Moecks Kammermusik. Vol.105.
Sonata D-moll, G-dur.
In: Gitarre-Kammermusik. No.10, 12.
Sonate A-moll, für Violine, Viola da Gamba (Viola) und Basso Continuo.
In: Nagels Musik-Archiv. No.190.
Sonata de Camera, G-moll für Querflöte (Blockflöte, Violin oder Oboe), Violine (Oboe) und Generalbass.
In: Organum. 3.Reihe. Nr.67.
Triosonate D-moll für Querflöte (f'-Blockflöte, Violine), Viola (Gambe) und Basso Continuo.
In: Hortus musicus. No.161.
Sechs Triosonaten für Violine, Oboe und Basso Continuo. Teil 1–2.
In: Mitteldeutsches Musikarchiv. Reihe II. Bd.1–2.
Triosonaten. 2 Violinen oder 2 Oboen und Generalbass.
In: Organum. 3.Reihe. Nr.56, 57, 61.
PER SPELMANN.
Norwegian folk song from Minnesota. Arr. by M. Dodd.
In: Music Press, Inc. [Choral series]. Vol.97.
PERAZA, FRANCISCO, 1564–1598.
Organ music.
In: Muset. Early Spanish organ music.
PERCEVEL, JULIO.
Piano music.
In: Boletín latino-americano de música. Vol.4.
PEREIRA, ARTHUR.
Música de cámara.
In: Boletín latino-americano de música. Vol.6.
PÉREZ, JUAN GINÉS, *see* GINÉS PÉREZ, JUAN.
PÉREZ, VICENTE RIPOLLÉS, *see* RIPOLLÉS PÉREZ, VICENTE.
PEREZ Y ALVAREZ, J.
Sacred music.
In: Eslava y Elizondo. Lira sacro-hispana. 19th century. ii.2.
PERGAMENT, MOSES.
Selections.
In: Svenck sanglyrik. Vol.2.
Duo for violin and violoncello, op.28.
In: Musikaliska konstföreningen. 1947.
PERGOLESI, GIOVANNI BATTISTA, 1710–1736.
Opera omnia. 25(26)v.
Opere.
In: I classici della musica italiana. Vol.23.
Selections.
In: Crotch. Specimens of various styles of music. Vol.2.
Airs.
In: Prunières. Les maîtres du chant. Recueil 1.
Arias.

In: Landshoff. Alte Meister des Bel Canto. Eine Sammlung von Arien. Vol.1–2.
In: Parisotti. Arie antiche. Bd.1, 3.
Choral music.
In: Rochlitz. Sammlung vorzüglicher Gesangstücke. Bd.3.
Concertino in E flat; Concertino no.1 in G. Strings.
In: Antica musica strumentale italiana. Series II. Vol.16, 17.
Concerto a cinque.
In: Diletto musicale. No.146.
Livietta e tracollo.
In: I classici della musica italiana. Raccolta nazionale delle musiche italiane. Quad. 91–92.
Recitative and Aria from Livietta e Tracollo. Misero.
In: Parrish. A treasury of early music. No.50.
Sacred music.
In: The Fitzwilliam music. Bd.2, 3.
In: Latrobe, C. I. Selection of sacred music.
In: Latrobe, J. A. The music of the church.
Salve Regina.
In: Königliche Akademie der Künste. Auswahl vorzüglicher Musik-Werke. Appendix.
La serva padrona.
In: I classici della musica italiana. Raccolta nazionale delle musiche italiane. Quad. 89–90.
Sonata a tre, per due violini e basso continuo. Nr.11.
In: Hausmusik. No.168.
Stabat mater.
In: I classici della musica italiana. Raccolta nazionale delle musiche italiane. Quad. 93, 94, 306, 307.
In: Somma. Musiche vocali e strumentali sacre e profane, sec. XVII–XVIII–XIX. Vol.7, 8.
Tänze.
In: Zeitschrift für Spielmusik. No.252.
Trio Nr.1. in G dur; Nr.2 in B dur. Für 2 Violinen, Violoncell und Klavier.
In: Riemann. Collegium musicum. No.29, 30.
Zwei Triosonaten für zwei Violinen und Basso Continuo.
In: Nagels Musik-Archiv. No.107.
Vocal music.
In: Delsarte. Archives du chant. Livr. 13, No.7; Livr.14. No.3; Livr.18. No.8.
In: Gevaert. Les gloires de l'Italie. Vol.1, 2.
PERI, JACOPO, 1561–1633.
Selections.
In: Crotch. Specimens of various styles of music. Vol.2.
In: Torchi. L'arte musicale in Italia. Bd.5, 6.
Arias.
In: Parisotti. Arie antiche. Bd.3.
Euridice.
In: I classici della musica italiana. Vol.24.
In: I classici della musica italiana. Raccolta nazionale delle musiche italiane. Quad. 95–96.
In: Reale Accademie d'Italia, Rome. Musica. Vol.3.
Motet. O d'immenso.
In: Königliche Akademie der Künste. Auswahl vorzüglicher Musik-Werke. No.46.
Songs.
In: Jeppesen. La flora. Vol.2.
Vocal music.
In: Gevaert. Les gloires de l'Italie. Vol.1.
PERIAÑEZ, P.
Sacred music.
In: Eslava y Elizondo. Lira sacro-hispana. 16th century. i.2.
PERLE, GEORGE, 1915– .
Hebrew melodies, for unaccompanied violoncello. Op.19.
In: New music. Vol.22. No.2. Jan.1949.
Piano music.
In: Boletín latino-americano de música. Vol.5.
Quartet no.3. Strings.
In: New music. Vol.23. No.1. Oct.1949.
Sonata. (Viola solo). Op.12.
In: Instituto Interamericano de Musicologia. Publicaciónes. No.31.
PERONI, GIUSEPPE, ca.1700.
Concerto a tre.
In: Gitarre-Kammermusik. No.5.
PEROTI, PADRE FULGENZIO.
Keyboard music.
In: Benvenuti. Cembalisti italiani del settecento.
PEROTINUS, MAGNUS, 12th–13th CENTURIES. (var. sp.: Pérotin le Grand).
Selections.
In: Gleason. Examples of music before 1400.
Alleluya (12th century).
In: Parrish. Masterpieces of music before 1750. No.9.
Organ music.
In: Bonnet. An anthology of early French organ music.
In: Peeters. Anthologia pro organo. Vol.1, 3.
PERRACHIO, LUIGI, 1883– .
Keyboard music.
In: Tagliapietra. Antologia di musica antica e moderna per pianoforte. Bd.18.
PERTI, GIACOMO ANTONIO, 1661–1756.
Arias.
In: Landshoff. Alte Meister des Bel Canto. Eine Sammlung von Arien. Vol.1–2.
Keyboard music.
In: Clementi. Clementi's Selection of practical harmony. Vol.1.
Laudate pueri.
In: The Penn state music series. No.10.
Sacred music.
In: The Fitzwilliam music. Bd.3.
Songs.
In: Jeppesen. La flora. Vol.2.
PERUGIA, MATTEO DA.
Le origini e il primo maestro di cappella: Matteo da Perugia. (Fabio Fano).
In: Istituzioni e monumenti dell' arte musicale italiana. Nuova serie. Vol.1.
PERUGIA, NICCOLÒ DA, *see* NICCOLÒ DA PERUGIA.
PERUSIO, MATHEUS DE.
Gloria in excelsis.
In: Van. Les monuments de l'Ars Nova.
Secular music.

In: Apel. French secular music of the late fourteenth century.
PESCETTI, GIOVANNI BATTISTA, ca.1704–ca. 1766.
Keyboard music.
In: Benvenuti. Cembalisti italiani del settecento.
In: Farrenc. Le trésor des pianistes. Vol.9.
In: Tagliapietra. Antologia di musica antica e moderna per pianoforte. Bd.12.
Organ music.
In: Bossi. Sammlung von Stücken alter italienischer Meister für die moderne Orgel.
Sonate (Cm).
In: Pauer. Alte Meister. No.51.
PESCHIN, GREGOR.
Lied.
In: Denkmäler der Tonkunst in Österreich. Vol.72. (Jg.XXXVII/2).
PESENTI, MARTINO, ca.1600–ca.1648.
Selections.
In: Torchi. L'arte musicale in Italia. Bd.7.
Ballata.
?In: Einstein. Beispielsammlung zur älteren Musikgeschichte.
Songs.
In: Jeppesen. La flora. Vol.2.
Tänze für Violine und Klavier.
?In: Diletto musicale. No.36.
PESENTI, MICHELE, 16th CENTURY.
Karnevalslieder der Renaissance.
In: Das Chorwerk. No.43.
PETER, H. A.
Stücke für ein Melodieinstrument und Klavier.
In: Hausmusik. No.89.
PETER, JOHANN FRIEDRICH, 1746–1813.
(var. sp.: John Frederick Peter).
Six quintets.
In: Music of the Moravians in America. Vol.2.
Sacred songs.
In: Music of the Moravians in America. Vol.1.
PETER, SIMON, 1743–1819.
Sacred songs.
In: Music of the Moravians in America. Vol.1.
PETERSON-BERGER, OLOF WILHELM, 1867–1942.
Cantata for the 150 years' jubilee of the Royal Theatre, Stockholm.
In: Musikaliska konstföreningen. 1942.
PETRARCA, FRANCESCO, 1304–1374.
Madrigale auf Texte von Francesco Petrarca.
In: Das Chorwerk. No.88.
PETRESCU, JOAN D., 1884– .
Les Idiomèles et le canon de l'office de Noël.
In: Études de paleógraphie musicale Byzantine. [Tome 1].
PETROFF.
Vocal music.
In: Sammlung russischer Romanzen. No.143, 232.
[PETRUCCI, OTTAVIANO DEI] 1466–1539. pub.
Harmonice musices odhecaton A. 103 numb.L.
—— 1942. 421p.
Frottole, Buch I und IV.
In: Publikationen älterer Musik. Jahrg.8.
Le Frottole nell' edizione principe.
In: Instituta et monumenta. Vol.1.
Harmonice musices odhecaton (1501). Facsimile.
In: Monuments of music and music literature. First series. No.10.
Laudenbuch.
In: Jeppesen. Die mehrstimmige italienische Laude um 1500.
PETRUS DE OSTIA.
Sacred music.
In: Jeppesen. Italia sacra musica. Vol.1.
PETTI, PAOLO.
Missa in Honorem S. Ceciliae. 1670.
In: Monumenta liturgiae polychoralis sanctae ecclesiae romanae. Series I. No.6.
PETYREK, FELIX, 1892–1951.
Sonatine, C-dur, 1947. Klavier au zwei Händen.
In: Hausmusik. No.124.
PETZ, JOHANN CHRISTOPH, 1664–1716.
(var. sp.: Johann Christoph Pez).
Selected works.
In: Denkmäler deutscher Tonkunst. [2.Folge]. Vol.27–28.
Concerto Pastorale in Einfacher oder Chorischer besetzung mit Cembalo (Klavier).
In: Musikschätze der Vergangenheit.
Ouvertüren-Suite, A-moll.
In: Concertino.
Triosonate, für zwei Blockflöten und Basso Continuo.
In: Nagels Musik-Archiv. No.111.
PETZOLD, CHRISTIAN, 1677–1733.
Instrumental music.
In: Schmid. Musik am sächsischen Hofe. Bd.6.
PEUERL, PAUL, 16th–17th CENTURIES.
(var. sp.: Paul Peurl).
Chamber music.
In: Riemann. Old chamber music. Vol.2.
Choral music.
In: Antiqua Chorbuch. Vol.2. Heft 5.
Instrumental and vocal compositions.
In: Denkmäler der Tonkunst in Österreich. Vol.70. (Jg.XXXVI/2).
2 Suiten.
In: Zeitschrift für Spielmusik. No.24.
Tänze.
In: Zeitschrift für Spielmusik. No.239.
PEVERNAGE, ANDRIES, 1543–1591.
(var. sp.: And. Peverage).
Selections.
In: Maldéghem. Trésor musical.
Choral music.
In: Commer. Collectio operum musicorum batavorum saeculi XVI. Bd.8.
PEYER, JOHANN GOTTHARD.
Lute music.
In: Denkmäler der Tonkunst in Österreich. Vol.50. (Jg.XXV/2).
PEYRÓ, JOSÉ, 16th–17th CENTURIES.
Selections.
In: Pedrell. Teatro lirico espanol anterior al siglo XIX. Bd.3.
PEZ, JOHANN CHRISTOPH, *see* PETZ, JOHANN CHRISTOPH.
PEZEL, JOHANN CHRISTOPH, 1639–1694.
Feierliche Musik (E-moll) aus der "Musica Vespertina."

In: Corona. Vol.2.
Suite G-moll aus "Delitiae musicales oder Lust-Music."
In: Schering. Perlen alter Kammermusik.
Turnmusiken.
In: Denkmäler deutscher Tonkunst. [1.Folge]. Vol.63.
PFANNENSTIEL, EKKEHART.
Altstädter Suite für 4 gleiche Instrumente.
In: Zeitschrift für Spielmusik. No.138.
PFEIFFER, JOHANN, 1697–1761.
Konzert für Cembalo, zwei Violinen und Violoncello ad lib.
In: Nagels Musik-Archiv. No.79.
Sonate D-dur, für Viola da Gamba und Konzertierendes Cembalo.
In: Nagels Musik-Archiv. No.142.
PFLEGER, AUGUSTIN, 17th CENTURY.
Geistliche Konzerte. Nr.1–11.
In: Das Erbe deutscher Musik. 1.Reihe. Vol.50.
Passionsmusik über die Sieben Worte Jesu Christi am Kreuz.
In: Das Chorwerk. No.52.
PHALÈSE, PIERRE, ca.1510–ca.1573.
(var. sp.: Phalesius).
Lute music.
In: Monumenta musicae belgicae. Vol.10.
Tanzsätze
In: Musica practica. No.44, 45, 46.
PHILE, PHILIP, ca.1734–1793.
Selections.
In: Engel. Music from the days of George Washington.
In: Fisher. The music that Washington knew.
PHILIDOR, FRANÇOIS ANDRÉ DANICAN, 1726–1795.
(var. sp.: Phylidor).
Selections.
?In: Expert. Collection d'ordre lyrique.
Airs.
In: Prunières. Les maîtres du chant. Recueil 6.
Ernélinde.
In: Les chefs d'oeuvres classiques de l'opéra français.
Pièces pour flûte.
In: Musiques Françaises. Vol.5.
Sonate D-moll für f'-Blockflöte (Querflöte, Oboe) und Basso Continuo.
In: Hortus musicus. No.139.
Vocal music.
In: Delsarte. Archives du chant. Livr.9, 11, 12, 20.
PHILIPPI, PIETRO.
Organ music.
In: Guilmant. Archives des maîtres de l'orgue. Vol.10.
PHILIPS, PETER, 1561–1628.
Choral music.
In: Engel. Three centuries of choral music. Vol.3.
Dispiegate guancie amate.
In: Squire. Ausgewählte Madrigale und mehrstimmige Gesänge. No.31.
Keyboard music.
In: The Fitzwilliam virginal book.
In: The Fitzwilliam virginal book. Ausgewählte Stücke. Vol.2.
In: Tagliapietra. Antologia di musica antica e moderna per pianoforte. Bd.2.
Madrigals.
In: Euterpe. 2d ed. No.35.
In: Musica Britannica. In process.
Organ music.
In: Peeters. Oudnederlandse meesters. Vol.2, 3.
Trios. Organ.
In: Guilmant. Archives des maîtres de l'orgue. Vol.10.
PHILIPS, THOMAS, *see* PHILIPPS, THOMAS.
PHILLIPON.
Choral music.
?In: Smijers. Van Ockeghem tot Sweelinck. Aflg.2.
PHILLIPS, ARTHUR, 1605–1695.
Keyboard music.
In: Schott's Anthology of early keyboard music. Vol.4.
PHILLIPS, BURRILL, 1907– .
(var. sp.: Burril Phillips).
Música de cámara.
In: Boletín latino-americano de música. Vol.5.
PHILLIPS, THOMAS, 15th CENTURY.
(var. sp.: Thomas Philips).
Songs.
In: Plainsong and Mediaeval Music Society. Publications. (A collection of songs and madrigals . . .).
PHINOT, DOMINICUS, 16th CENTURY.
Choral music.
In: Commer. Collectio operum musicorum batavorum saeculi XVI. Bd.8, 9.
PHYLIDOR, FRANÇOIS, *see* PHILIDOR, FRANÇOIS ANDRÉ DANICAN.
PIANELAIO, JACOPO.
Selections.
In: Pirrotta. The music of fourteenth-century Italy. Vol.5.
PIANO MUSIC, *see* KEYBOARD MUSIC–CLAVICHORD, HARPSICHORD, PIANO, VIRGINAL.
PIANO MUSIC OF BRAZIL.
In: New music. Vol.16. No.1. Oct.1942.
PIANO, 4 HANDS, *see* KEYBOARD MUSIC–PIANO, 4 HANDS.
PIAZZA, GAETANO.
Tonat coelum cum furore. Sopran und Konzertierende Orgel.
In: Cantio sacra. No.42.
PÍČ (PITSCH), KAREL FRANTIŠEK, 1786–1858.
Organ music.
In: Musica antiqua bohemica. Vol.12.
PICCHI, GIOVANNI, 16th–17th CENTURIES.
(var. sp.: Giovanni Pichi).
Balli d'arpicordo.
In: Chilesotti. Biblioteca di rarità musicali. Vol.2.
Keyboard music.
In: The Fitzwilliam virginal book.
In: Tagliapietra. Antologia di musica antica e moderna per pianoforte. Bd.5.
PICCINNI, NICCOLÒ, 1728–1800.
(var. sp.: Niccola Piccini).
Selections.
In: Échos de France. Vol.1–3.

Arias.
In: Landshoff. Alte Meister des Bel Canto. Eine Sammlung von Arien. Vol.1–2.
In: Parisotti. Arie antiche. Bd.1, 2.
La buona figliola.
In: I classici musicali italiani. Vol.7.
Didon; Roland.
In: Les chefs d'oeuvres classiques de l'opéra français.
Motets.
In: Concerts spirituels ou recueil de motets.
Vocal music.
In: Gevaert. Les gloires de l'Italie. Vol.1.
PICCIONI, GIOVANNI, 16th–17th CENTURIES.
(var. sp.: Giovanni Pizzoni).
Duo begl' occhi lucenti.
In: Squire. Auswählte Madrigale und mehrstimmige Gesänge. No.28.
PICHL, WENZEL VÁCLAV, 1741–1805.
Sei fughe con un preludio fugato. Per un violino solo.
In: Musica antiqua bohemica. Vol.7.
6 fugues pour violon seul.
In: L'école du violon au XVIIe et XVIIIe siècle. No.1272.
PICINETTI, FELICE MARIA, fl.1700.
Sonate, für Violoncello und Klavier. (Cembalo).
In: Nagels Musik-Archiv. No.161.
PICK-MANGIAGALLI, RICCARDO, 1882–1949.
Keyboard music.
In: Tagliapietra. Antologia di musica antica e moderna per pianoforte. Bd.18.
PIERNÉ, GABRIEL, 1863–1937.
Organ music.
In: Bedell. The French organist. Vol.1.
PIERO, MAGISTER, 14th CENTURY.
(var. sp.: Pierro).
Selections.
In: Pirrotta. The music of fourteenth-century Italy. Vol.2.
Cacce.
In: Marrocco. Fourteenth-century Italian cacce.
PIERRE DE CORBEIL, d.1222.
Office de Pierre de Corbeil. 244p.
PIERRO, *see* PIERO, MAGISTER.
PIERSIG, FRITZ, 1900– .
Das Rondo.
In: Musikalische Formen in historischen Reihen. Bd.4.
PIÉTON, LOYSET, 15th–16th CENTURIES.
Motets.
In: Attaingnant. Treize livres de motets. Livre 3.
PIETRAGRUA, CARLO, *see* GRUA, CARLO LUIGI PIETRO.
PIFFET LE FILS.
La choix d'un berger.
In: L'école du violon au XVIIe et XVIIIe siècle. No.1343.
Le pastor fido.
In: L'école du violon au XVIIe et XVIIIe siècle. No.1346.
PIGOTT, FRANCIS, d.1704.
(var. sp.: Francis Piggott).
Keyboard music.
In: Fuller-Maitland. The contemporaries of Purcell. Vol.6–7.
PILATI, MARIO, 1903–1938.
Keyboard music.
In: Tagliapietra. Antologia di musica antica e moderna per pianoforte. Bd.18.
PILKINGTON, FRANCIS, d.1638.
Selections.
In: Smith. Musica antiqua.
Book of airs.
In: Arkwright. The Old English edition. Vol.18–20.
In: Fellowes. The English school of lutenist song writers. 1st series. Vol.7, 15.
Choral music.
In: Engel. Three centuries of choral music. Vol.3.
Madrigals.
In: Euterpe. Vol.8, 11, 13; 2d ed. No.36–38, 65.
In: Fellowes. The English madrigal school. Vol.25, 26.
In: The triumphs of Oriana.
Part music.
In: Hullah. Part music. 1868 edition.
Vocal music.
In: Hullah. Vocal scores. II. Secular.
PIONNIER, JEAN.
Motette.
In: Das Chorwerk. No.94.
PIPELARE, MATTHAEUS, ca.1500.
(var. sp.: Mattheus Pipelare).
Opera omnia. 3v. (proposed).
Selections.
In: Maldéghem. Trésor musical.
Songs.
In: Aich. Das Liederbuch.
PIROYE, CHARLES.
Organ music.
In: Raugel. Les maîtres français de l'orgue. Vol.2.
PISADOR, DIEGO, ca.1508–ca.1557.
Lute music.
In: Morphy. Les luthistes espagnols du XVIe siècle. Vol.2.
Songs.
In: Bal y Gay. Romances y villancicos españoles del signo XVI.
PISANO, BERNARDO.
Opera omnia. v.1– .
PISARI, PASQUALE, 1725–1778.
Dixit Dominus. No.8.
In: Monumenta liturgiae polychoralis sanctae ecclesiae romanae. Series IV. No.8.
PISENDEL, JOHANN GEORG, 1687–1755.
Instrumental concertos.
In: Denkmäler deutscher Tonkunst. [1.Folge]. Vol.29–30.
Konzert Es-dur für Violine, Streichorchester und Basso Continuo.
In: Nagels Musik-Archiv. No.196.
Sonate für Violine allein.
In: Hortus musicus. No.91.
Sonate für Violine und Cembalo (Klavier).
In: Antiqua Edition. Von 2 Instrumenten an.
Violin and piano.
In: Schering. Alte Meister des Violinspiels.
PISK, PAUL AMADEUS, 1893– .
5 Sketches for piano. Op.39.

In: New music. Vol.15. No.3. Apr.1942.
Meadow-Saffrons. For contralto, clarinet and bass clarinet.
In: New music. Vol.28. No.2. Jan.1955.
Sonatina, (Piano).
In: Instituto Interamericano de Musicologia. Publicaciónes. No.36.
PISTON, WALTER, 1894– .
Chromatic study on the name of Bach. Organ.
In: Contemporary organ series. No.3.
Música de cámara.
In: Boletín latino-americano de música. Vol.5.
3 Pieces for flute, clarinet, and bassoon.
In: New music. Vol.6. No.4. July 1933.
PITONI, GIUSSEPPE OTTAVIO, 1657–1743.
(var. sp.: Josepho Octavio Pitoni).
Dixit Dominus. No.5, 6, 7.
In: Monumenta liturgiae polychoralis sanctae ecclesiae romanae. Series IV. No.5, 6, 7.
Misericordia Domini; Beata es Virgo; Justorum animae; Introito, Kyrie, Offertorio.
In: Documenta liturgiae polychoralis sanctus ecclesiae romanae. No.6, 7, 8, 9.
Missa.
In: Documenta maiora liturgiae polychoralis sanctae ecclesiae romanae. No.1, 2, 3, 4, 5.
In: Monumenta liturgiae polychoralis sanctae ecclesiae romanae. Series I. No.5, 7.
Sacred music.
In: Proske. Musica divina. Annus primus. Tom 1, 2, 3, 4.
Vocal music.
In: Delsarte. Archives du chant. Livr.19. No.1.
PITSCH, KAREL FRANTIŠEK, *see* PÍČ (PITSCH), KAREL FRANTIŠEK.
PIXÉRÉCOURT MANUSCRIPT.
Music from the Pixérécourt manuscript. 95p.
PIZZONI, GIOVANNI, *see* PICCIONI, GIOVANNI.
PLA, JOSÉ.
Trio No.6 for two oboes or flutes and figured bass.
In: Music for wind instruments by 18th century masters. No.13.
PLACIDO, GIOVANNI, *see* RUTINI, GIOVANNI MARIA PLACIDO.
PLAINSONG, *see* CHANT (PLAIN, GREGORIAN, ETC.).
PLAMENAC, DRAGAN, 1895– . ed.
Sevilla, 5–I–43 and Paris, Nouv. Acq. Frç. 4379.
In: Institute of Mediaeval Music. Publications. Vol.8.
PLANCHART, ALEJANDRO. ed.
Three Caput masses.
In: Collegium musicum. Vol.5.
PLANSON.
Chansons.
In: Lesure. Anthologie de la chanson parisienne au XVIe siècle.
PLATTI, GIOVANNI, ca.1690–1763.
Giovanni Benedetto Platti e la sonata moderna (Fausto Torrefranca).
In: Istituzioni e monumenti dell'arte musicale italiana. Nuova serie. Vol.2.
Keyboard music.
In: Newman. Thirteen keyboard sonatas of the 18th and 19th centuries.
Ricercari für Violine und Violoncello. Nr.1–4.
In: Hortus musicus. No.87–88.
Sonaten für Flöte oder Violine, Klavier und Bass-Instrument ad lib. Nr.1–3.
In: Antiqua Edition. Von 2 Instrumenten an.
Sonate D-dur, für Flauto traverso und Basso Continuo.
In: Florilegium musicum. Vol.9.
Zwölf Sonaten für Cembalo oder Klavier. Teil 1–2.
In: Mitteldeutsches Musikarchiv. Reihe I. Bd.3, 4.
Le sonate per tastiera.
In: Istituzioni e monumenti dell' arte musicale italiana. Vol.7.
PLAUTZIUS.
Selections.
In: Cvetko. Skladatelji Gallus, Plautzius [in] Dolar.
PLEYEL, IGNAZ JOSEPH, 1757–1831.
Selections.
In: Crotch. Specimens of various styles of music. Vol.3.
Zwölf Duette für 2 Flöten.
In: Diletto musicale. No.137–140.
Part music.
In: Hullah. Part music. Class B.1.
Quartett für Flöte, Violine, Viola und Violoncello. Op.20, Nr.1–3.
In: Organum. 3.Reihe. Nr.39, 44, 47.
Sonate für Klavier, Flöte (Violine) und Violoncello. Op.16, Nr.1, 2, 5.
In: Organum. 3.Reihe. Nr.35, 36, 37.
PLOWDEN, MRS.
Songs.
In: Potter. Reliquary of English song. Vol.2.
PODBIELSKI, JAN, 17th CENTURY.
(var. sp.: Jacobus Podbielski).
Organ music.
In: Corpus of early keyboard music. Vol.10. Pt.4.
Praeludium for organ or harpsichord.
In: Denkmäler altpolnischer Musik. Vol.18.
POGLIETTI, ALESSANDRO, d.1683.
Capriccio über dass Hennengeschrey. Harpsichord.
In: Parrish. A treasury of early music. No.40.
Dance music.
In: Denkmäler der Tonkunst in Österreich. Vol.56. (Jg.XXVIII/2).
Keyboard music.
In: Georgii. Keyboard music of the Baroque and Rococo. Vol.1.
In: The Penn state music series. No.9.
In: Tagliapietra. Antologia di musica antica e moderna per pianoforte. Bd.8.
Zwölf Ricercare. 1.–2.Folge. Nr.1–6, 7–12. Organ.
In: Die Orgel. Reihe II. Nr.5–6.
POHANKA, JAROSLAV.
Dějiny českí hudby.
In: Documenta historica musicae.
POHL, WILHELM, ca.1780.
Songs.
In: Denkmäler der Tonkunst in Österreich. Vol.54. (Jg.XXVII/2).
POHLÉNZ, CHRISTIAN AUGUST, 1790–1843.
Part music.
In: Hullah. Part music. Class B.2.

POLACI.
Sinfonie in D-dur.
In: Sondheimer. Werke aus dem 18. Jahrhundert. Nr.6.
POLAK, J.
Preludes, fantasies and dances for lute.
In: Denkmäler altpolnischer Musik. Vol.22.
POLAND–MUSIC.
In: Antiquitates musicae in Polonia.
In: Chomiński. Music of the Polish Renaissance.
In: Cichocki. Chants d'église à plusieurs voix des anciens compositeurs polonais.
In: Corpus of early keyboard music. Vol.10.
In: Crotch. Specimens of various styles of music. Vol.1.
In: Denkmäler altpolnischer Musik.
In: Florilegium musicae antiquae.
In: Gieburowski. Cantica selecta musices sacrae in Polonia.
In: Monumenta musicae in Polonia.
In: Państwowa Wyższa Szkoła Muzyczna w Katowicach.
In: Surzyński. Monumenta musicae sacrae in Polonia.
In: Zeitschrift für Spielmusik. No.210, 244, 259.
In: Źródła do historii muzyki polskiej.
POLAROLI, CARLO FRANCESCO, *see* POLLAROLO, CARLO FRANCESCO.
POLETZKY, ERWIN.
Fünf Inventionen für Flauto dolce und Klavier.
In: Moecks Kammermusik. Vol.506.
Tanzporträts.
In: Zeitschrift für Spielmusik. No.240.
POLLAROLO, CARLO FRANCESCO, 1653–1722.
(var. sp.: C. F. Pollaroli, C. F. Polaroli).
Selections.
In: Torchi. L'arte musicale in Italia. Bd.3.
Keyboard music.
In: Esposito. Early Italian piano music.
In: Tagliapietra. Antologia di musica antica e moderna per pianoforte. Bd.9.
Organ music.
In: Bossi. Sammlung von Stücken alter italienischer Meister für die moderne Orgel.
POLLINI, FRANCESCO GIUSEPPE, 1763–1846.
Keyboard music.
In: Tagliapietra. Antologia di musica antica e moderna per pianoforte. Bd.14.
Variations et rondeaux. Piano.
In: Répertoire des clavicinistes. Vol.13.
POLOVINKIN, LEONID ALEXEJEWITSCH, 1894–1949.
Humoresque philosophique. Piano.
In: New music. Vol.8. No.1. Oct.1934.
POLYPHONY.
In: Anthology of music. Vol.9, 28.
In: Montpellier, France. Université. Faculté de Médicine. Bibliothèque. Mss. (H 196). Polyphonies du XIIIe siècle.
In: Music Press, Inc. [Choral series]. No.72.
POMASANSKI.
Vocal music.
In: Sammlung russischer Romanzen. No.258.
POMERANIA–MUSIC.
In: Denkmäler der Musik in Pommern.
In: Engel. Drei Werke pommerscher Komponisten.
POMPONIO NENNA, *see* NENNA, POMPONIA.
PONCE, JUAN.
Choral music.
In: Engel. Three centuries of choral music. Vol.5.
PONCE, MANUEL M., 1886– .
Selections.
In: Instituto Interamericano de Musicologia. Publicaciónes. No.5, 19, 23.
PONS, JOSÉ, 1768–1818.
Sacred music.
In: Eslava y Elizondo. Lira sacro-hispana. 19th century. i.1.
PONTAC, D.
Sacred music.
In: Eslava y Elizondo. Lira sacro-hispana. 17th century. ii.1.
PONTE, JACOB VAN.
Selections.
In: Maldéghem. Trésor musical.
PONZIO.
Organ music.
In: Cantantibus organis. Vol.11.
POPE INNOCENT III, *see* INNOCENT III, POPE.
PORPORA, NICOLA ANTONIO, 1686–1768.
(var. sp.: Nicolo Porpora; Niccolò Porpora; Niccola Porpora).
Selections.
In: Torchi. L'arte musicale in Italia. Bd.3.
Arias.
In: Landshoff. Alte Meister des Bel Canto. Eine Sammlung von Arien. Vol.1–2.
2 Fugues.
In: Köhler. Les maîtres du clavecin. Heft 9.
Kammer-Sonaten für Violine und Pianoforte.
In: Moffat. Kammer-Sonaten für Violine und Pianoforte. No.19.
Keyboard music.
In: Clementi. Clementi's Selection of practical harmony. Vol.1.
In: Esposito. Early Italian piano music.
In: Farrenc. Le trésor des pianistes. Vol.8.
In: Pauer. Alte Klavier-Musik. 1st series. Pt.1.
In: Tagliapietra. Antologia di musica antica e moderna per pianoforte. Bd.11.
Organ music.
In: Fuser. Classici italiani dell' organo.
In: Raugel. Quarante-six pièces pour orgue ou harmonium.
Sinfonia da camera, Op.2/6.
In: Hausmusik. No.136.
Sinfonia for recorder (flute, oboe, violin) and piano.
In: Music for wind instruments by 18th century masters. No.10.
Sonata. Violin and piano.
In: I classici della musica italiana. Vol.25.
In: I classici della musica italiana. Raccolta nazionale delle musiche italiane. Quad. 104–107.
In: Moffat. Meister-Schule der alten Zeit. Violin-Sonaten. No.15, 27.
Songs.
In: Jeppesen. La flora. Vol.1, 2.
Trio in D dur. (Op.2. Concerto IV). Für 2 Violinen, Violoncell und Klavier.

In: Riemann. Collegium musicum. No.23.
Vigilate, oculi mei. Sopran (Tenor) und B.C.
In: Cantio sacra. No.20.
Violin and piano.
In: Schering. Alte Meister des Violinspiels.
PORTA, COSTANZO, ca.1530–1601.
Selections.
In: Torchi. L'arte musicale in Italia. Bd.1.
Choral music.
?In: Dehn. Samlung älterer Musik aus dem XVI. und XVII. Jahrhundert.
Madrigals.
In: Einstein. The golden age of the madrigal.
Missa "La sol fa re mi."
In: Das Chorwerk. No.93.
Missa tertii Toni.
In: Musica divina. Vol.5.
Musica in introitus missarum. Nos.1–4, 5–8.
In: Musica liturgica. Vol.1. Fasc.3; Vol.2. Fasc.3.
Sacred music.
In: Proske. Musica divina. Annus primus. Tom 2, 3; Annus secundus. Tom 2.
In: Proske. Selectus novus missarum. Annus secundus. Tom 2.
PORTA, FRANCESCO DELLA, *see* DELLA PORTA, FRANCESCO.
PORTER, QUINCY, 1897– .
Canon and fugue. Organ.
In: Contemporary organ series. No.12.
Música de cámara.
In: Boletín latino-americano de música. Vol.5.
Sonata, No.2. Violin and piano.
In: Society for the Publication of American Music. Publications. 14th season. 1932–33.
String quartet, No.3, 6.
In: Society for the Publication of American Music. Publications. 17th season. 1935–36; 23rd season. 1941–42.
PORTINARO, FRANCESCO.
Selections.
In: Denkmäler der Tonkunst in Österreich. Vol.77. (Jg.XLI).
PORTUGAL, MARCOS ANTONIO DA FONSECA, 1762–1830.
Il duca di foix.
In: Portugaliae musica. Sér.B. Vol.9.
PORTUGAL–MUSIC.
In: Joaquim. O cancioneiro musical e poetico da Biblioteca Públia Hortênsia.
In: Kastner. Cravistas portuguezes.
In: Kastner. Silva iberica.
In: Portugaliae musica.
In: Santos. A polifonia clássica portuguesa.
POSADA AMADOR, CARLOS, 1908– .
Selections.
In: Boletín latino-americano de música. Vol.4.
In: Instituto Interamericano de Musicologia. Publicaciónes. No.20.
POSCH, ISAAC, 16th–17th CENTURIES.
Instrumental and vocal compositions.
In: Denkmäler der Tonkunst in Österreich. Vol.70. (Jg.XXXVI/2).
POSER, HANS.
Dreizehn Kanons.
In: Zeitschrift für Spielmusik. No.250.
Kleine Serenade für Alt-Blockflöte und Gitarre.
In: Zeitschrift für Spielmusik. No.274.
Tanzbüchlein.
In: Zeitschrift für Spielmusik. No.214.
Weihnachtspartita.
In: Zeitschrift für Spielmusik. No.237.
POSS, GEORG.
Drei Motetten für zwei vierstimmige gemischte Chöre.
In: Musik alter Meister. Heft 15.
POWELL, MEL, 1923– .
Divertimento for five winds; flute, oboe, clarinet in B flat, trumpet in B flat, bassoon.
In: Society for the Publication of American Music. Publications. 38th season. 1957.
POWELL, NEWMAN W., 1919– .
Organ music.
In: The parish organist. Vol.1–4.
POWER, LIONEL, d.1445.
Missa super alma redemptoris mater.
In: Documenta polyphoniae liturgicae sanctae ecclesiae romanae. Ser.1. No.2.
PRAAG, HENRI C. VAN.
Kleine Dialoge.
In: Zeitschrift für Spielmusik. No.201.
PRACTICAL POLYPHONY. Five easy anthems of the 16th century.
In: Music Press, Inc. [Choral series]. No.72.
PRÁDANOS, H.
Sacred music.
In: Eslava y Elizondo. Lira sacro-hispana. 19th century. ii.2.
PRADO, GERMAN. ed.
El canto Mozárabe.
In: Barcelona. Biblioteca Central. Sección de Música. Publicaciones. Vol.5.
PRAENESTINUS, J. P. A.
Sacred music.
In: Proske. Musica divina. Annus secundus. Tom 1, 2.
In: Rubio. Antologia polifonica sacra. Vol.1.
PRAETORIUS, BARTHOLOMAEUS, 17th CENTURY.
Keyboard music.
In: Tagliapietra. Antologia di musica antica e moderna per pianoforte. Bd.3.
PRAETORIUS, HIERNONYMUS, 1560–1629.
Selected compositions.
In: Denkmäler deutscher Tonkunst. [1.Folge]. Vol.23.
Choral music.
In: Antiqua Chorbuch. Vol.1. Heft 4.
Gesänge.
In: Musica sacra . . . ca.1842–1896. Vol.12, 13.
Motetten.
In: Das Chorwerk. No.14.
Organ magnificats. On the eight tones.
In: Corpus of early keyboard music. Vol.4.
PRAETORIUS, JAKOB, 1586–1651.
Organ music.
In: The Liturgical Music Press, Inc. Masterpieces of organ music. Folio 45.
In: Organum. 4.Reihe. Nr.2.

PRAETORIUS, MICHAEL, 1571–1621.
Gesamtausgabe der musikalischen Werke. 21v. in 22.
Sämtliche Orgelwerke. 105p.
Choral music.
In: Antiqua Chorbuch. Vol.1. Heft 4; Vol.2. Heft 4.
In: Chor-Archiv.
In: Chorbuch für die Kirchenchöre Sachsens.
In: Dehn. Sammlung älterer Musik aus dem XVI. und XVII. Jahrhundert.
In: Nagels Männerchor-Blätter. No.11.
In: Rochlitz. Sammlung vorzüglicher Gesangstücke. Bd.1. Pt.2; Bd.1. Appendix.
Choräle.
In: Zeitschrift für Spielmusik. No.195.
Fantasie über "Ein feste Burg ist unser Gott" für Orgel.
In: Nagels Musik-Archiv. No.40.
Organ music.
In: Keller. Achtzig Choralvorspiele deutscher Meister des 17. und 18. Jahrhunderts.
In: Klein. The first four centuries of music for the organ from Dunstable to Bach (1370–1749).
In: The Liturgical Music Press, Inc. Masterpieces of organ music. Folio 36.
In: The parish organist. Vol.1–4.
In: Peeters. Anthologia pro organo. Vol.3.
In: Rohr. Orgelspiel im Kirchenjahr.
In: Straube. Alte Meister des Orgelspiels.
Syntagma Musici. Tomus 2.
In: Publikationen älterer praktischer und theoretischer Musikwerke. Jahrg.12.
Sechs Tanzfolgen.
In: Corona. Vol.13, 14.
Teutsche Liedlein.
In: Das Chorwerk. No.51.
PRATENSIS, JODOCUS.
Selections.
In: Smith. Musica antiqua.
PRAUSNITZ, FREDERICK.
Episode.
In: New music. Vol.22. No.2. Jan.1949.
PRE-CLASSICAL POLYPHONY. (FELLERER).
In: Anthology of music. Vol.28.
PRÈS, JOSQUIN DE, *see* DEPRÈS, JOSQUIN.
PRESTON, THOMAS, 16th CENTURY.
Organ music.
In: Cantantibus organis. Vol.8.
PREUSSISCHE FESTLIEDER.
In: Das Erbe deutscher Musik. 2.Reihe. Ostpreussen und Danzig. Vol.1.
PRIENTO, J.
Sacred music.
In: Eslava y Elizondo. Lira sacro-hispana. 19th century. i.1.
PRIORIS, JOHANNES, 15th–16th CENTURIES.
Chanson.
In: Copenhagen Kongelige Bibliotek. Mss. (Thottske Samling 291[8]). Der kopenhagener Chansonnier.
PRIULI, GIOVANNI.
Selections.
In: Denkmäler der Tonkunst in Österreich. Vol.77. (Jg.XLI).
PROKOFIEFF, SERGE, 1891–1953.
Complete works. v.1– .
PROPERS.
In: Monumenta polyphoniae liturgicae sanctae ecclesiae romanae. Ser.2. Vol.1.
PROPHETOLOGIUM.
In: Monumenta musicae byzantinae. Lectionaria. Vol.1. Fasc.1–5.
LE PROSAIRE D'AIX-LA-CHAPELLE.
In: Monumenta musicae sacrae. Vol.3.
LE PROSAIRE DE LA SAINTE-CHAPELLE.
In: Monumenta musicae sacrae. Vol.1.
PROTEVANGELION.
In: The Wellesley edition. No.2.
PROVENZALE, FRANCESCO.
Arias.
In: Landshoff. Alte Meister des Bel Canto. Eine Sammlung von Arien. Vol.1–2, 3.
PROWO, P., 18th CENTURY.
Concerto a 6 für 2 Alt-Blockflöten, 2 Oboen, 2 Violoncelli und Cembalo.
In: Moecks Kammermusik. Vol.75.
Sonata Nr.5, 6 a tre für 2 Alt-Blockflöten und Basso Continuo.
In: Moecks Kammermusik. Vol.16, 17.
PRUSSIA–MUSIC.
In: Thouret. Musik am preussischen Hofe.
PSALINIS, UBERTUS DE, *see* SALINIS, UBERTUS DE.
PSALMS.
In: Early English church music. Vol.2.
In: Early psalmody in 17th century America.
In: Musica sacra . . . ca.1842–1896. Vol.8–10, 16.
PSALMS, ENGLISH.
In: Musical Antiquarian Society. Publications. Vol.11.
PSAUTIER HUGUENOT DU XVIe SIÈCLE.
In: Expert. Psautier Huguenot du XVIe siècle.
In: Pidoux. Le Psautier Huguenot du XVIe siècle.
PUCCINI, DOMENICO, 1771–1815.
Concerto in B flat (piano, orchestra).
In: Antica musica strumentale italiana. Ser.II. Vol.18.
PUDELKO, W. ed.
Zehn leichte Duette. Zwölf leichte Duette.
Alte Musik. Aus dem Baltischen Lautenbuch.
In: Spielstücke für Blockflöten, Geigen, Lauten oder andere Instrumente. Heft 1, 2, 6, 9.
PUGNANI, GAETANO, 1731–1798.
Andantino.
In: L'école du violon au XVIIe et XVIIIe siècle. No.1291.
Sonate (C).
In: Moffat. Trio-Sonaten alter Meister. No.15.
Sonata a tre due violini e basso continuo. Op.I/3.
In: Hausmusik. No.172.
PUJOL, DAVID, 1894– . ed.
Musica instrumental. Vol.1–2.
In: Mestres de l'escolania de Montserrat.
PUJOL, JOAN, 1573–1626.
(var. sp.: Johannis Pujol).
Opera omnia.

In: Barcelona. Biblioteca Central. Sección de Música. Publicaciones. Vol.3, 7.
PURCELL, DANIEL, ca.1660–1717.
Selections.
In: Smith. Musica antiqua.
Keyboard music.
In: Fuller-Maitland. The contemporaries of Purcell. Vol.6–7.
In: Herrmann. Contemporaries of Purcell.
PURCELL, HENRY, 1658 (or 9)–1695.
Complete works. v.1– .
Organ works. 20p.
Suites, lessons, and pieces for the harpsichord. 4v.
Selections.
In: Crotch. Specimens of various styles of music. Vol.2.
In: Smith. Musica antiqua.
Choral works.
In: Chor-Archiv.
Choral music.
In: Music Press, Inc. [Choral series]. No.52.
Christmas anthem.
In: Documents of the musical past. Vol.2.
Dido and Aeneas; Bonduca; King Arthur; Ode.
In: Musical Antiquarian Society. Publications. Vol.4, 7, 10, 19.
Fantasien, für Streichinstrumente. Heft I–II.
In: Nagels Musik-Archiv. No.58, 113.
Fröhliche Kanons.
In: Zeitschrift für Spielmusik. No.45.
Frühlingslied für 4 Instrumente oder 3 Instrumente mit Singstimme.
In: Zeitschrift für Spielmusik. No.174.
Fünf geistliche Chöre.
In: Das Chorwerk. No.17.
"Herr, zu dir will ich schrein." Für Bass, Streicher und Basso Continuo.
In: Hortus musicus. No.163.
In the midst of Life; Lord, how long wilt Thou be angry.
In: Dessoff choir series. No.34, 35.
Sechs Instrumentalstücke aus Opern-und Schauspielmusiken.
In: Zeitschrift für Spielmusik. No.269.
Keyboard music.
In: English keyboard music. [No.5, 10].
In: Farrenc. Le trésor des pianistes. Vol.3.
In: Georgii. Keyboard music of the Baroque and Rococo. Vol.1.
In: Herrmann. Contemporaries of Purcell.
In: Oesterle. Early keyboard music. Vol.1.
In: Pauer. Old English compositions for the virginal and harpsichord.
In: Pessl. The art of the suite.
In: Tagliapietra. Antologia di musica antica e moderna per pianoforte. Bd.9.
Die Nacht. 3 Arien für hohe St. und Streichquartett.
In: Hortus musicus. No.141.
A new ground.
In: Parrish. Masterpieces of music before 1750. No.38.
Organ music.
In: Biggs. A treasury of shorter organ classics.
In: Bonnet. Historical organ-recitals. Vol.1.
In: Klein. The first four centuries of music for the organ from Dunstable to Bach (1370–1749).
In: Liber organi. Bd.10.
In: The Liturgical Music Press, Inc. Masterpieces of organ music. Folio 10.
In: Peeters. Anthologia pro organo. Vol.2.
In: Standard series of organ compositions. No.2.
In: Tallis to Wesley. Vol.10.
Orpheus Britannicus. (1698 and 1702). Facsimile.
In: Monuments of music and music literature. First series. No.1.
Part music.
In: Hullah. Part music. Class A.1. Vol.1, 2; Class A.2. Vol.1; Class C. Secular.
Pavane und Chaconne für drei hohe Instrumente.
In: Antiqua Edition. Von 4 Instrumenten an.
Sacred music.
In: Arnold. Cathedral music. Vol.1.
In: Boyce. Cathedral music. Vol.2, 3; 1849, Vol.2, 3.
In: Page. Harmonia sacra. Vol.1, 2.
Sonata I. Sonata X.
In: Seventeenth-century chamber music. No.1, 2.
Sonate (Gm). Violin and Piano.
In: Moffat. Meister-Schule der alten Zeit. Violin-Sonaten. No.1.
Sonate, G moll.
In: Riemann. Collegium musicum. No.102.
Songs.
In: Arkwright. The Old English edition. Vol.24.
In: Potter. Reliquary of English song. Vol.1.
Spielmusik zum Sommernachtstraum, für vier Streich- oder Blasinstrumente und Basso Continuo.
In: Hortus musicus. No.50, 58.
Zwei Trio-Sonaten.
In: Antiqua Edition. Von 3 Instrumenten an.
Trio-Stücke.
In: Zeitschrift für Spielmusik. No.243.
Trumpet voluntary. Organ.
In: Dickinson. Historical recital series for organ. Vol.2. No.39.
"Wie wonnig ist's auf blumigen Gefild," für Sopran, Tenor, 2 f'-Blockflöte, Basso Continuo.
In: Hortus musicus. No.164.
PURCELL, THOMAS, d.1682.
Selections.
In: Crotch. Specimens of various styles of music. Vol.2.
PÜRINGER, ANTON.
Sonatine für Violine mit Klavier.
In: Hausmusik. No.83.
PUXOL, LUCAS.
Keyboard music.
In: Kastner. Silva iberica.
PUY, JEAN BAPTISTE EDOUARD DU, *see* DU PUY, JEAN BAPTISTE EDOUARD.

QUAGLIATI, PAOLO, ca.1555–1628.
Selections.
In: Torchi. L'arte musicale in Italia. Bd.3.
Arias.

In: Landshoff. Alte Meister des Bel Canto. Eine Sammlung von Arien. Vol.1–2.
La Sfera armoniosa. (1623) and Il Carro di fedeltà d'amore. (1611).
In: Smith College music archives. No.13.
QUACK, ERHARD, 1904– .
Die Geburt des Herrn.
In: Christophorus-Chorwerk. Heft 33.
QUANTZ, JOHANN JOACHIM, 1697–1773.
Arioso.
In: Dickinson. Historical recital series for organ. Vol.1. No.3.
Arioso aus dem Flöten-Konzert. (F).
In: Thouret. Musik am preussischen Hofe. No.2, 6.
Konzert.
In: Corona. Vol.39, 56.
In: Hortus musicus. No.76.
Presto. (Sonata 333). Organ.
In: Dickinson. Historical recital series for organ. Vol.1. No.4.
Sonate E moll. (Flöte und Klavier).
In: Kammersonaten. No.9.
Sonate für drei Flöten (oder Violinen und andere Instrumente) ohne Bass.
In: Nagels Musik-Archiv. No.116.
Trio-Sonate C-dur. Für Blockflöte (oder Querflöte, Geige), Querflöte (oder Geige) und Basso Continuo.
In: Hortus musicus. No.60.
Trio-sonate. D-dur.
In: Organum. 3.Reihe. Nr.32.
Triosonate A-moll für 2 Querflöten (Violinen) und Generalbass.
In: Organum. 3.Reihe. Nr.65.
QUATRIS, JOHANNES DE.
Sacred music.
In: Plainsong and Mediaeval Music Society. Publications. (Borren).
QUEF, CHARLES, 1873–1931.
Organ music.
In: Bedell. The French organist. Vol.1.
QUEROL GAVALDÁ, MIGUEL, 1912– .
Cancionero musical de la casa de Medinaceli. I–II. Polifonía profana.
In: Monumentos de la música española. Vol.8–9.
Romances y letras a tres voces. Siglo XVII.
In: Monumentos de la música española. Vol.18.
QUINTIANI, L.
At sound of his sweet voice.
In: Arion. Vol.1.

RAASTED, NIELS OTTO, 1888– .
Kristi Fødsel. Op.67. Cantata.
In: Samfundet til Udgivelse af dansk Musik. Ser.III. No.51.
Kuvia suomesta. Symfonisk suite for orkester. Op.56.
In: Samfundet til Udgivelse af dansk Musik. Ser.III. No.31.
Orgelsonate. Nr.3. Op.33.
In: Samfundet til Udgivelse af dansk Musik. Ser.III. No.9.
Passionsmusik. Oratorio. Op.86.
In: Samfundet til Udgivelse af dansk Musik. Ser.III. No.115.
Primavera. Trio. Op.96.
In: Samfundet til Udgivelse af dansk Musik. Ser.III. No.142.
Sangen om København. Op.60. Chorus.
In: Samfundet til Udgivelse af dansk Musik. Ser.III. No.65.
Serenade für Flöte, Oboe, Viola und Violoncell. Op.40.
In: Samfundet til Udgivelse af dansk Musik. Ser.III. No.16.
Sinfonia da chiesa. Op.76.
In: Samfundet til Udgivelse af dansk Musik. Ser.III. No.96.
Sonata for klaver. Op.109.
In: Samfundet til Udgivelse af dansk Musik. Ser.III. No.162.
Songs.
In: Samfundet til Udgivelse af dansk Musik. Suppl. 1925–26.
RABASSA, P.
Sacred music.
In: Eslava y Elizondo. Lira sacro-hispana. 18th century. i.1.
RACQUET, CHARLES.
Organ music.
In: Raugel. Les maîtres français de l'orgue. Vol.2.
RADINO, GIOVANNI MARIA, fl.1579–1598.
Intavolatura di balli per sonar di liuto. 20p.
Il primo libro d'intavolatura di balli d'arpicordo. facsim. (28p.) 31–75p.
RADOLT, FREIHERR VON.
Lute music.
In: Denkmäler der Tonkunst in Österreich. Vol.50. (Jg.XXV/2).
RAFF, JOSEPH JOACHIM, 1822–1882.
Keyboard music.
In: Tagliapietra. Antologia di musica antica e moderna per pianoforte. Bd.17.
RAICK, DIEUDONNÉ, 1702–1764.
Organ music.
In: Peeters. Oudnederlandse meesters. Vol.1, 2, 3.
Werken voor orgel en/of clavecimbel.
In: Monumenta musicae belgicae. Vol.6.
RAISON, ANDRÉ, 17th–18th CENTURIES.
Organ music.
In: Biggs. Treasury of early organ music.
In: Bonnet. Historical organ-recitals. Vol.1.
In: Guilmant. Archives des maîtres de l'orgue. Vol.2.
In: Keller. Orgelvorspiele.
In: Klein. The first four centuries of music for the organ from Dunstable to Bach (1370–1749).
In: Orgue et liturgie. Vol.55–56, 58–59.
In: The parish organist. Vol.1–4, 7–8.
In: Raugel. Les maîtres français de l'orgue. Vol.1, 2.
In: Raugel. Les maîtres français de l'orgue aus XVIIème et XVIIIème siècles.
RAMEAU, JEAN PHILIPPE, 1683–1764.
(var. sp.: J. Philip Rameau).
Oeuvres complètes. 18v.
Pièces de clavecin. 3v.

Pièces de clavecin. Complete.
In: Lea pocket scores. No.87.
Selections.
In: Échos de France. Vol.1–3.
In: Expert. Répertoire classique de musique. 1re année.
Scene from "Castor et Pollux."
In: Parrish. Masterpieces of music before 1750. No.41.
Gavotte und Variationen. (Am).
In: Pauer. Alte Meister. No.1.
Keyboard music.
In: Farrenc. Le trésor des pianistes. Vol.8.
In: Georgii. Keyboard music of the Baroque and Rococo. Vol.2.
In: Grovlez. Les plus belles pièces de clavessin de l'école française. Vol.2.
In: Köhler. Les maîtres du clavecin. Heft 11.
In: Monuments of music and music literature. First series. No.7.
In: Oesterle. Early keyboard music. Vol.2.
In: Pauer. Alte Klavier-Music. 2d series. Pt.5.
In: Tagliapietra. Antologia di musica antica e moderna per pianoforte. Bd.11.
La livri, L'agaçante, La timide.
In: Pauer. Alte Meister. No.27.
Minuet and gigue. Organ.
In: Dickinson. Historical recital series for organ. Vol.2. No.23.
Nouvelles suites de pièces de clavecin. (1727). Facsimile.
In: Monuments of music and music literature. First series. No.13.
Operas.
In: Les chefs d'oeuvres classiques de l'opéra français.
Organ music.
In: Anthologia antiqua. Vol.4.
Prélude, musette et rondeau, air majestueux.
In: Guilmant. Répertoire des concerts du Trocadéro. Vol.4.
Suite (Am). (Allemande. Courante. Sarabande. Les trois mains. Fanfarinette. La triomphante).
In: Pauer. Alte Meister. No.43.
Tambourin in E minor. Piano.
In: Roitzsch. Alte Klavier-Musik.
Les troubillons (rondeau). L'indifférente. La villageoise (rondeau). L'entretien des muses. Les soupirs.
In: Pauer. Alte Meister. No.44.
Vocal music.
In: Delsarte. Archives du chant (passim).
RAMOS DE PAREJA, BARTOLOMÉ, b.ca.1440.
Sacred music.
In: Eslava y Elizondo. Lira sacro-hispana. 16th century. i.1.
RANGSTRÖM, TURE, 1884–1947.
Den Utvalda. Lyrical scene.
In: Musikaliska konstföreningen. 1939.
Hennes ord. Three songs.
In: Musikaliska konstföreningen. 1937.
Un notturno. String quartet.
In: Musikaliska konstföreningen. 1949.
Four poems (songs).
In: Musikaliska konstföreningen. 1930.
Six songs.
In: Musikaliska konstföreningen. 1916.
Trolltyg. Two ballads.
In: Musikaliska konstföreningen. 1937.
RAPHAEL, GÜNTER ALBERT RUDOLF, 1903–1960.
(var. sp.: Guenter Raphael).
Organ music.
In: The parish organist. Vol.7–8.
Die vier Jahreszeiten, vier Variations-Reihen für Streichorchester, Op.77. Teil I–II.
In: Collegium musicae novae. No.6, 16.
RASCH, KURT, 1902– .
Moritat.
In: Collegium musicae novae. No.22.
RASELIUS, ANDREAS, ca.1563–1602.
Choral music.
In: Antiqua Chorbuch. Vol.1. Heft 4.
Sacred songs.
In: Denkmäler deutscher Tonkunst. [2.Folge]. Vol.29–30.
Vater unser im Himmelreich; Christ unser Herr zum Jordan kam.
In: Musica sacra . . . between 1892–1897. No.1, 2.
RASMUSEN, P.
Organ music.
In: Gerhardt. Album nordischer Komponisten für Orgel. Vol.1.
RATHAUS, KAROL, 1895–1954.
Fourth string quartet.
In: Society for the Publication of American Music. Publications. 36th season. 1954–55.
RATHGEBER, VALENTIN, 1682–1750.
Augsburger Tafelconfect.
In: Das Erbe deutscher Musik. 1.Reihe. Vol.19. (a).
Lieder.
In: Moser. Alte Meister des deutschen Liedes. 30 Gesänge. No.16.
In: Moser. Alte Meister des deutschen Liedes. 46 Gesänge. No.26, 27.
Musikalischer Zeitvertreib aus dem Klavier.
In: Nagels Musik-Archiv. No.105.
Pastorellen vor die Weynacht-Zeit.
In: Zeitschrift für Spielmusik. No.258.
Weihnachtsmusik. Für Klavier oder Orgel.
In: Nagels Musik-Archiv. No.95.
RATTI, BARTOLOMMEO, b.1593.
Sacred music.
In: Proske. Musica divina. Annus secundus. Tom 3.
In: Proske. Selectus novus mussarum. Annus secundus. Tom 3.
RAUCH, ANDREAS, ca.1600.
Choral music.
In: Antiqua Chorbuch. Vol.1. Heft 4; Vol.2. Heft 4.
RAULIN DE VAUX, *see* VAUX, RAULIN DE.
RAVENSCROFT, JOHN, d.ca.1745.
Trio da chiesa in H moll. Für 2 Violinen, Violoncell und Klavier. Op.1. Nr.2.
In: Riemann. Collegium musicum. No.44.
RAVENSCROFT, THOMAS, ca.1590–ca.1633.
Choral music.
In: Engel. Three centuries of choral music. Vol.3.

Madrigals.
In: Euterpe. Vol.5; 2d ed. No.39–44.
RAVNKILDE, N.
Four pieces for piano, Op.2.
In: Samfundet til Udgivelse af dansk Musik. Suppl. 1902.
Four songs.
In: Samfundet til Udgivelse af dansk Musik. Suppl. 1902.
READ, DANIEL, 1757–1836.
Selections.
In: Goldman. Landmarks of early American music, 1760–1800.
READING, JOHN.
Organ music.
In: Tallis to Wesley. Vol.21.
Part music.
In: Hullah. Part music. Class A.2. Vol.2.
REALI.
La follia.
In: Antica musica strumentale italiana. In preparation.
REBEL, JEAN FERRY, 1661–1747.
Sonate en ré mineur.
In: L'école du violon au XVIIe et XVIIIe siècle. No.1253.
Violin and piano.
In: Schering. Alte Meister des Violinspiels.
REBOULOT, ANTOINE.
Ricercari de Luzzaschi. Organ.
In: Orgue et liturgie. Vol.5.
RECKZEH, ADOLPH.
Short Troop.
In: Thouret. Musik am preussischen Hofe. No.10.
RECORDER.
In: Hortus musicus.
In: Moecks gelbe Musikhefte.
In: Moecks Kammermusik.
In: Musica practica.
In: Nagels Musik-Archiv.
In: Spielstücke für Blockflöten, Geigen, Lauten oder andere Instrumente.
In: Zeitschrift für Spielmusik.
REDFORD, JOHN, d.1547.
Selections.
In: The music with the form and order of the service to be performed at the coronation of . . . Queen Elizabeth II.
Church music.
In: Motett Society. [Collection of ancient church music]. Division 1.
Keyboard music.
In: Schott's Anthology of early keyboard music. Vol.2.
Organ music.
In: Biggs. Treasury of early organ music.
In: Cantantibus organis. Vol.1.
In: Klein. The first four centuries of music for the organ from Dunstable to Bach (1370–1749).
In: Liber organi. Bd.10.
In: The Liturgical Music Press, Inc. Masterpieces of organ music. Folio 73.
REESEN, EMIL, 1887– .
Gaucho-Suite. Orchestra.
In: Samfundet til Udgivelse af dansk Musik. Ser.III. No.102.
Variationer for Orkester. Over et tema af Schubert.
In: Samfundet til Udgivelse af dansk Musik. Ser.III. No.69.
REESER, EDUARD, 1908– .
De muzikale handschriften van Alphons Diepenbrock.
In: Vereniging voor Nederlandsche Muziekgeschiedenis. Uitgave. No.43.
Drei oud-nederlandsche Motetten.
In: Vereniging voor Nederlandsche Muziekgeschiedenis. Uitgave. No.44.
REEVE, WILLIAM, 1757–1815.
Songs.
In: Potter. Reliquary of English song. Vol.2.
REGER, MAX, 1873–1916.
Sämtliche Werke. 35v.
Organ music.
In: Bonnet. Historical organ-recitals. Vol.5.
In: The parish organist. Vol.1–4.
In: Standard series of organ compositions. No.43, 48.
REGIS, JOHANNES, 15th CENTURY.
Opera omnia. 2v.
Missa super l'homme armé.
In: Monumenta polyphoniae liturgicae sanctae ecclesiae romanae. Ser.1. Tomus I. Fasc.5.
REGNART, FRANÇOIS.
Poésies de P. de Ronard.
In: Expert. Les maîtres musiciens de la Renaissance française. Vol.15.
REGNART, GIACOMO.
Selections.
In: Denkmäler der Tonkunst in Österreich. Vol.77. (Jg.XLI).
REGNART, JACOB, ca.1540–1599.
Selections.
In: Leichtentritt. Deutsche Hausmusik aus vier Jahrhunderten.
Choral music.
In: Antiqua Chorbuch. Vol.2. Heft 3.
Dreistimmige deutsche Lieder nebst Leonh. Lechner's Bearbeitung.
In: Publikationen älterer praktischer und theoretischer Musikwerke. Jahrg.23.
Einsmals in einem Tiefen Tal.
In: Chor-Archiv.
Herzlich tut mich erfreuen.
In: Squire. Ausgewählte Madrigale und mehrstimmige Gesänge. No.50.
Kurtzweilige teutsche Lieder, zu singen oder zu spielen. 1. Heft. 2. Heft.
In: Zeitschrift für Spielmusik. No.6, 17.
Lied- und Choralmotetten.
In: Das Chorwerk. No.30.
Newe deudsche Lieder.
In: Zeitschrift für Spielmusik. No.54.
REICHA, ANTON, 1770–1836.
Organ music.
In: Raugel. Quarante-six pièces pour orgue ou harmonium.
Woodwind quartet, Op.91, No.1.
In: Für Kenner und Liebhaber. No.28.
Blaserquintett B-dur, Op.88, Nr.5. (Seydel).
In: Alte Musik. (Reihe "Leuckartiana").

Blaserquintett Es-dur, Op.88, Nr.2. (Weigelt).
In: Alte Musik. (Reihe "Leuckartiana").
Quintet Op.91, No.5 (A).
In: Für Kenner und Liebhaber. No.31.
Wind quintet. Op.100, No.4.
In: Für Kenner und Liebhaber. No.20.
Woodwind quintet in D, Op.91, No.3.
In: Für Kenner und Liebhaber. No.13.
REICHARDT, CHRISTIAN.
Duet and Chorus. (Morgengesang). Solo and Chorus. (Morgengesang).
In: Königliche Akademie der Künste. Auswahl vorzüglicher Musik-Werke. Appendix.
Organ music.
In: Das Erbe deutscher Musik. 1.Reihe. Vol.9.
REICHARDT, G.
Part music.
In: Hullah. Part music. Class A.2. Vol.2.
REICHARDT, JOHANN FRIEDRICH, 1752–1814.
Goethes Lieder, Oden, Balladen und Romanzen mit Musik.
In: Das Erbe deutscher Musik. 1.Reihe. Vol.58.
Keyboard sonatas.
In: Newman. Thirteen keyboard sonatas of the 18th and 19th centuries.
Stücke für Klavier.
In: Musik in Goethes Haus. Vol.1.
Konzert in Es-dur für Violine und Streichorchester.
In: Nagels Musik-Archiv. No.181.
Lieder.
In: Moser. Alte Meister des deutschen Liedes. 30 Gesänge. No.28, 29.
In: Moser. Alte Meister des deutschen Liedes. 46 Gesänge. No.44, 45.
In: Reimann. Das deutsche Lied. Vol.2, 4.
Lieder und Oden in Auswahl.
In: Nagels Musik-Archiv. No.37.
Sinfonia in G-dur.
In: Diletto musicale. No.97.
Sonaten.
In: Nagels Musik-Archiv. No.64.
Trio in Es dur. Für 2 Violinen, Violoncell und Klavier.
In: Riemann. Collegium musicum. No.52.
REICHARDT, LUISE.
Lied.
In: Reimann. Das deutsche Lied. Vol.4.
REICHEL, BERNHARD, 1901– .
Organ music.
In: The parish organist. Vol.5–6, 7–8.
REICHENBACH, HERMAN. ed.
Canons.
In: Music Press, Inc. [Choral series]. No.65, 66, 85.
REICHERT, ERNST. ed.
The dance.
In: Anthology of music. Vol.27.
Sechs Gesänge, nach Texten von Hermann Hesse. Für hohe Stimme und Klavier.
In: Hausmusik. No.184.
Lieder Salzburg Komponisten.
In: Hausmusik. No.180.
REIN, WALTER, 1893–1955.
Choral music.
In: Nagels Männerchor-Blätter. No.2, 18, 26.
Dreikönigsmusik.
In: Moser. Das Musikkränzlein. No.5.
Der Morgenstern ist aufgegangen.
In: Zeitschrift für Spielmusik. No.185.
REINAGLE, ALEXANDER, 1756–1809.
Selections.
In: Engel. Music from the days of George Washington.
In: Goldman. Landmarks of early American music, 1760–1800.
REINAGLE, JOSEPH, 1762–1825.
12 leichte Violoncello-Duette.
In: Moecks Kammermusik. Vol.48, 49.
REINCKEN, JAN ADAMS, *see* REINKEN, JAN ADAMS.
REINER, ADAM, *see* RENER, ADAM.
REINER, JACOB, ca.1560–1606.
Chorlieder.
In: Christophorus-Chorwerk. Heft 5.
Sacred music.
In: Proske. Musica divina. Annus secundus. Tom 2.
In: Proske. Selectus novus missarum. Annus secundus. Tom 2.
REINHARD, A.
Organ music.
In: Caecilia; Sammlung von Choralvorspielen.
REINKEN, JAN ADAMS, 1623–1722.
(var. sp.: Reincken).
Hortus musicus.
In: Riemann. Collegium musicum. No.77
In: Vereninging voor Nederlandsche Muziekgeschiedenis. Uitgave. No.13.
Keyboard music.
In: Buchmayer. Aus Richard Buchmayers historischen Klavierkonzerten. Vol.3, 4.
In: Georgii. Keyboard music of the Baroque and Rococo. Vol.1.
In: Herrmann. Lehrmeister und Schüler Joh. Seb. Bachs. Vol.1.
In: Tagliapietra. Antologia di musica antica e moderna per pianoforte. Bd.7.
Organ music.
In: Klein. The first four centuries of music for the organ from Dunstable to Bach (1370–1749).
In: The Liturgical Music Press, Inc. Masterpieces of organ music. Folio 40.
In: Organum. 4.Reihe. Nr.5.
Partite diverse sopra l'Aria: Schweiget mir von Weiber nehmen.
In: Vereniging voor Nederlandsche Muziekgeschiedenis. Uitgave. No.14.
Triosuite für 2 Violinen, Gambe (Violoncell) und Cembalo.
In: Organum. 3.Reihe. Nr.20.
REINTHALER, KARL MARTIN, 1822–1896.
Psalmen.
In: Musica sacra . . . ca.1842–1896. Vol.8–10.
REISER, ALOIS, 1887– .
String quartet. Op.16.
In: Society for the Publication of American Music. Publications. 1st season. 1919–20.

REISSIGER, KARL GOTTLIEB, 1798–1859.
Credo aus der As-dur-Messe.
In: Schmid. Musik am sächsischen Hofe. Bd.1.
Fughetta, Cum sancto.
In: Königliche Akademie der Künste. Auswahl vorzüglicher Musik-Werke. No.44.
Grand mass in E flat.
In: Ecclesiasticon. No.64.
Psalmen.
In: Musica sacra . . . ca.1842–1896. Vol.8–10.
REITER, ALBERT, 1905– .
Sonatine für Violine und Gitarre.
In: Gitarre-Kammermusik. No.7.
Sonatine in einem Satz.
In: Hausmusik. No.81.
Kleine Suite für Streicher.
In: Hausmusik. No.37.
REJCHA, ANTONÍN JOSEF, 1770–1836.
L'art de varier. Op.57. Piano.
In: Musica antiqua bohemica. Vol.50.
Keyboard music.
In: Musica antiqua bohemica. Vol.20.
Organ music.
In: Musica antiqua bohemica. Vol.12.
3 Quintetti. Op.88, No.3; Op.91, No.9; Op.91. No.11.
In: Musica antiqua bohemica. Vol.33.
REMBT, JOHANN ERNST, 1749–1810.
Organ music.
In: Caecilia; Sammlung von Choralvorspielen.
RENDALL, E. D.
Ballet madrigal. S.S.A.T.B.
In: Arion. Vol.2.
Dame music. S.A.T.B. Spring the sweet spring. S.A.T.B.
In: Arion. Vol.2.
RENE, H.
Chansons.
In: Publikationen älterer praktischer und theoretischer Musikwerke. Jahrg.27.
RENER, ADAM, ca.1485–ca.1520.
(var. sp.: Adam Reiner).
Collected works.
In: Institute of Mediaeval Music. Collected works. Vol.2.
Lieder.
In: Aich. Das Liederbuch.
In: Publikationen älterer praktischer und theoretischer Musikwerke. Jahrg.8.
Missa Carminum zu 4 Stimmen.
In: Das Chorwerk. No.101.
REPERTORIUM ORGANORUM RECENTIORIS ET MOTETORUM VETUSTISSIMI STILI. (FRIEDRICH LUDWIG).
In: Institute of Mediaeval Music. Musicological studies. Vol.7.
RESINARIUS, BALTHASAR, 16th CENTURY.
(var. sp.: Balthasar Hartzer, Balthasar Harzer).
Choral music.
In: Antiqua Chorbuch. Vol.1. Heft 1.
In: Chorbuch für die Kirchenchöre Sachsens.
Hymnen.
In: Das Chorwerk. No.32.
Responsoriorum numero octoginta. Vol.1–2.
In: Rhaw. Musikdrucke. Vol.1, 2.
Summa passions secundum Johannem.
In: Das Chorwerk. No.47.
RESON, JOHANNES.
Selections.
In: Reaney. Early fifteenth-century music. Vol.2.
REUENTHAL, NEIDHARDT VON, *see* NEIDHARDT VON REUENTHAL.
REUSCH, FRITZ, 1896– .
Das Christkindelspiel.
In: Bausteine für Musikerziehung und Musikpflege. B 113.
Elementares Musikschaffen. Band I, II.
In: Bausteine für Musikerziehung und Musikpflege. B 110, B 116.
REUSNER, ESAJAS, 1636–1679.
(var. sp.: Essias Reusner).
Ausgewählte Werke.
In: Das Erbe deutscher Musik. 1.Reihe. Vol.12.
REUTER.
Sudetendeutsche Suite.
In: Platzmusik. Nr.6.
REUTTER, JOHANN ADAM KARL GEORG, 1708–1772.
Church compositions.
In: Denkmäler der Tonkunst in Österreich. Vol.88.
Instrumental music.
In: Denkmäler der Tonkunst in Österreich. Vol.31. (Jg.XV/2).
REVUELTAS, SILVESTRE, 1899– .
Dos canciones.
In: Instituto Interamericano de Musicologia. Publicaciónes. No.50.
REYNOLDS.
Part music.
In: Hullah. Part music. Class A.1. Vol.2.
Sacred music.
In: Page. Harmonia sacra. Vol.1.
REYTTER, OSWALD, ca.1520.
Choral music.
In: Antiqua Chorbuch. Vol.2. Heft 1.
Lieder.
In: Publikationen älterer praktischer und theoretischer Musikwereke. Jahrg.1–3.
RHAW, GEORG, 1488–1548. pub.
(var. sp.: Georg Rhau).
Musikdrucke. v.1– .
Bicinia Germanica.
In: Zeitschrift für Spielmusik. No.112.
Sacrorum hymnorum Liber Primus I–II.
In: Das Erbe deutscher Musik. 1.Reihe. Vol.21, 25.
RHEINECK, CHRISTOPH, 1748–1797.
Lieder.
In: Moser. Alte Meister des deutschen Liedes. 30 Gesänge. No.25.
In: Moser. Alte Meister des deutschen Liedes. 46 Gesänge. No.41.
RHENISH MUSIC.
In: Denkmäler rheinischer Musik.
RIBERA, ANTONIO DE, 15th–16th CENTURIES.
Choral music.
In: Engel. Three centuries of choral music. Vol.5.

RIBERA, BERNARDINO DE, 16th CENTURY.
Rex autem David.
In: Polifonía española. Vol.12.
Sacred music.
In: Eslava y Elizondo. Lira sacro-hispana. 16th century. i.1.
RICCI, LUIGI, 1805–1859.
Sacred music.
In: Latrobe, C. I. Selection of sacred music.
In: Latrobe, J. A. The music of the church.
RICCIO, GIOVANNI BATTISTA, 17th CENTURY.
Jubilent omnes.
In: Nagels Musik-Archiv. No.75.
RICCIOTTI, CARLO, 1681–1756.
Selections.
In: Crotch. Specimens of various styles of music. Vol.3.
Concertini für vier Violinen, Viola alta, Violoncello und Basso Continuo.
In: Hortus musicus. No.82, 144, 154, 155, 158, 159.
RICERCARI-ORGAN.
In: Annibale Padovano. Ricercari.
In: Corpus of early keyboard music. Vol.9.
RICHAFORT, JEAN, ca.1480–1547.
Selections.
In: Maldéghem. Trésor musical.
In: Smith. Musica antiqua.
Chanson.
In: Brown. Theatrical chansons of the 15th and early 16th centuries.
Choral music.
In: Commer. Collectio operum musicorum batavorum saeculi XVI. Bd.12.
In: Smijers. Van Ockeghem tot Sweelinck. Aflg.7.
Lieder.
In: Publikationen älterer praktischer und theoretischer Musikwerke. Jahrg.1–3.
Mass.
In: Stein. Twelve Franco-Flemish masses of the early 16th century.
Motets.
In: Attaingnant. Treize livres de motets. Livre 1, 2, 4, 6, 8, 12.
In: Das Chorwerk. No.94.
RICHARD II, KING OF ENGLAND, 1367–1400.
(var. sp.: Richard the Lion-Hearted).
Selections.
In: Gleason. Examples of music before 1400.
Organ music.
In: Biggs. A treasury of shorter organ classics.
RICHARD, ÉTIENNE.
Organ music.
In: Raugel. Les maîtres français de l'orgue. Vol.1.
In: Raugel. Les maîtres français de l'orgue aus XVIIème et XVIIIème siècles.
In: Raugel. Quarante-six pièces pour orgue ou harmonium.
RICHARDSON, FERDINAND, ca.1558–1618.
(var. sp.: Ferdinando Richardson).
Keyboard music.
In: The Fitzwilliam virginal book.
In: Tagliapietra. Antologia di musica antica e moderna per pianoforte. Bd.2.
RICHARDSON, VAUGHAN, d.1729.
Part music.
In: Hullah. Part music. Class A.1. Vol.1.
Sacred music.
In: Page. Harmonia sacra. Vol.1.
RICHTER, ERNST FRIEDRICH EDUARD, 1808–1879.
Psalmen.
In: Musica sacra . . . ca.1842–1896. Vol.8–10.
RICHTER, FERDINAND TOBIAS, 1649–1711.
Keyboard music.
In: Georgii. Keyboard music of the Baroque and Rococo. Vol.1.
RICHTER, FRANZ XAVER, 1709–1789.
Concerto in E-moll; Symphonie in G-dur.
In: Musikschätze der Vergangenheit.
Sechs Kammersonaten, Op.2. Für obligates Cembalo (Klavier), Flöte (Violine), und Violoncello. Heft I.
In: Hortus musicus. No.86.
Orchestral music.
In: Riemann. Mannheim symphonists. Vol.1.
Streichquartett in C dur. Op.5. Nr.1.
In: Riemann. Collegium musicum. No.51.
Sinfonia da Camera für vierstimmiges Streichorchester und Continuo.
In: Nagels Musik-Archiv. No.72.
Sinfonie C-moll.
In: Sondheimer. Werke aus dem 18. Jahrhundert. Nr.25.
Drei Sinfonien für 4stg. streichorchester.
In: Corona. Vol.41.
Sonate in G für Flöte (Violine) und Cembalo (Klavier).
In: Antiqua Edition. Von 2 Instrumenten an.
Sonata da camera in A dur. Für Violine (Flöte), Violoncell und obligat Klavier.
In: Riemann. Collegium musicum. No.18.
Symphonies.
In: Denkmäler deutscher Tonkunst. [2.Folge]. Vol.3 (i).
RIEGGER, WALLINGFORD, 1885– .
3 Canons for woodwinds. Op.9.
In: New music. Vol.5. No.4. July 1932.
Dichotomy. Op.12. For chamber orchestra.
In: New music. Orchestra series. No.4.
Op.35. Duos for 3 woodwinds.
In: New music. Vol.17. No.4. July 1944.
Suite for flute alone.
In: New music. Vol.3. No.4. July 1930.
Trio for piano and strings in B minor.
In: Society for the Publication of American Music. Publications. 14th season. 1932–33.
Vocal music.
In: Boletín latino-americano de música. Vol.5.
RIEMSDIJK, JOHAN CORNELIS MARIUS VAN, 1841–1895.
Old Dutch dances arranged for piano (four hands).
In: Vereniging voor Nederlandsche Muziekgeschiedenis. Uitgave. No.10.
RIES, FERDINAND, 1784–1838.
Keyboard music.
In: Farrenc. Le trésor des pianistes. Vol.23.
In: Tagliapietra. Antologia di musica antica e moderna per pianoforte. Bd.14.
RIETZ, JULIUS, 1812–1877.
Concertino (Oboe, Viola, Streicher).
In: Collegium musicae novae. No.60.

RIGEL, HENRI JEAN, 1772–1852.
Adagio für Violine und Klavier.
In: Sondheimer. Werke aus dem 18. Jahrhundert. Nr.12.
Andante G-dur, Nr.1–2. Violine und Klavier.
In: Sondheimer. Werke aus dem 18. Jahrhundert. Nr.14, 18.
Overture in F major to "Le Savatier et le Financier."
In: Sondheimer. Werke aus dem 18. Jahrhundert. Nr.52.
Sinfonie in D-dur; Sinfonie C-moll, Op.12, Nr.4; Sinfonie G-dur, Op.12. Nr.2.
In: Sondheimer. Werke aus dem 18. Jahrhundert. Nr.5, 50, 51.
RIGHINI, VINCENZO, 1756–1812.
Sacred music.
In: Latrobe, C. I. Selection of sacred music.
In: Latrobe, J. A. The music of the church.
RIISAGER, KNUDÅGE, 1897– .
Darduse. Suite for Orkester.
In: Samfundet til Udgivelse af dansk Musik. Ser.IV. No.121.
Finalegalop for Orkester.
In: Samfundet til Udgivelse af dansk Musik. Ser.III. No.88.
Kvartet for Fløjte, Obo, Clarinet og Fagot. Op.40a.
In: Samfundet til Udgivelse af dansk Musik. Ser.III. No.112.
Månerenen. Ballet.
In: Samfundet til Udgivelse af dansk Musik. Ser.III. No.156.
Ouverture "Erasmus Montanus."
In: Samfundet til Udgivelse af dansk Musik. Ser.III. No.23.
Primavera. Koncertouverture.
In: Samfundet til Udgivelse af dansk Musik. Ser.III. No.95.
Sonate pour violon et piano.
In: Samfundet til Udgivelse af dansk Musik. Ser.III. No.14.
Songs.
In: Samfundet til Udgivelse af dansk Musik. Suppl. 1925–26.
Tre danske Peblingeviser for Orkester.
In: Samfundet til Udgivelse af dansk Musik. Ser.III. No.63.
RIIS-MAGNUSSEN, AD.
Songs.
In: Samfundet til Udgivelse af dansk Musik. Suppl. 1925–26.
RIMINI, VINCENZO DE, *see* VINCENTIUS DE ARIMINO.
RIMSKIĬ-KORSAKOV, NIKOLAĬ ANDREEVICH, 1844–1908.
(*see also* Korsakoff, R.)
[Works]. v.1– .
RINALDO.
Keyboard music.
In: Corpus of early keyboard music. Vol.24.
RINCK, JOHANN CHRISTIAN HEINRICH, 1770–1846.
Organ music.
In: Caecilia; Sammlung von Choralvorspielen.
Rondo (From Concerto for flute stop). Organ.
In: Dickinson. Historical recital series for organ. Vol.2. No.38.
RINTELEUS, CUNRADUS HAGIUS, *see* HAGIUS RINTELEUS, CUNRADUS.
RIPA, ALBERTO DA, 1529–1551.
Sacred music.
In: Eslava y Elizondo. Lira sacro-hispana. 18th century. ii.1.
RIPOLLÉS PÉREZ, VICENTE, 1867–1943.
El villancico i la cantata del segle XVIII e València.
In: Barcelona. Biblioteca Central. Sección de Música. Publicaciones. Vol.12.
RITTER, CHRISTIAN, ca.1640–ca.1720.
Gott hat Jesum erwecket.
In: Organum. 1.Reihe. Nr.9.
Keyboard music.
In: Buchmayer. Aus Richard Buchmayers historischen Klavierkonzerten. Vol.5.
Organ music.
In: The Liturgical Music Press, Inc. Masterpieces of organ music. Folio 25.
In: Organum. 4.Reihe. Nr.5.
RIVAFIECHA.
Motets.
In: Elúsitiza. Antología musical.
ROBERDAY, FRANÇOIS, ca.1620–ca.1690.
Fugues and caprices.
In: Guilmant. Archives des maîtres de l'orgue. Vol.3.
Fugue D-moll. Organ.
In: Guilmant. École classique de l'orgue. No.18.
Keyboard music.
In: Tagliapietra. Antologia di musica antica e moderna per pianoforte. Bd.7.
Organ music.
In: Klein. The first four centuries of music for the organ from Dunstable to Bach (1370–1749).
In: Liber organi. Bd.2.
In: Raugel. Les maîtres français de l'orgue. Vol.2.
ROBERTSON, LEROY, 1896– .
Quintet in A minor for piano and strings.
In: Society for the Publication of American Music. Publications. 17th season. 1935–36.
ROBINSON, EARL, 1910– .
Piano music.
In: Boletín latino-americano de música. Vol.5.
ROBLEDO, MELCHOR, d.1587.
Ave Maris Stella.
In: Polifonía española. Vol.6.
Motets.
In: Elúsitiza. Antología musical.
Sacred music.
In: Eslava y Elizondo. Lira sacro-hispana. 16th century. i.1.
In: Rubio. Antologia polifonica sacra. Vol.1.
ROBLES, DANIEL ALOMIA, 1871–1942.
Keyboard music.
In: Guenther. Collection espagnole.
ROCHA, FRANCISCO GOMES DA, *see* GOMES DA ROCHA, FRANCISCO.
ROCHBERG, GEORGE, 1918– .
String quartet.
In: Society for the Publication of American Music. Publications. 37th season. 1956.

ROCK, MICHAEL, d.1809.
Part music.
In: Hullah. Part music. 1868 edition.
Vocal music.
In: Hullah. Vocal scores. II. Secular.
RODRÍGUEZ, FELIPE, 1759–1814.
(var. sp.: Felip Rodríguez).
Instrumental music.
In: Mestres de l'escolania de Montserrat. (Pujol. Musica instrumental. Vol.2).
Keyboard music.
In: Nin y Castellano. Dix-sept sonates et pièces anciennes d'auteurs espagnols.
RODRIGUEZ, VICENTE, ca.1685–1761.
Keyboard music.
In: Nin y Castellano. Dix-sept sonates et pièces anciennes d'auteurs espagnols.
RODRIGUEZ DE LEDESMA, MARIANO, *see* LEDESMA, MARIANO RODRIGUEZ DE.
ROESELING, KASPAR, 1894–1960.
Kleine Anzeigen der Stadtzeitung.
In: Christophorus-Chorwerk. Heft 13.
Missa in Honorem Sanctorum Trium Regum.
In: Christophorus-Chorwerk. Heft 3.
Psalmen und Gesänge zum Advent. Psalmen und Gesänge zur Fastenzeit.
In: Christophorus-Chorwerk. Heft 40, 41.
2 Sonaten für Flauto dolce solo.
In: Moecks Kammermusik. Vol.504.
Tänzerische Suite in A-moll.
In: Zeitschrift für Spielmusik. No.235.
ROGER, *see* MICHAEL, ROGIER.
ROGERS, BENJAMIN, 1614–1698.
Selections.
In: Crotch. Specimens of various styles of music. Vol.2.
Anthems.
In: Music Press, Inc. [Choral series]. No.61.
Keyboard music.
In: Fuller-Maitland. The contemporaries of Purcell. Vol.6–7.
Part music.
In: Hullah. Part music. Class A.1. Vol.1, 2; Class C. Secular.
Sacred music.
In: Boyce. Cathedral music. Vol.1, 2, 3.
In: Page. Harmonia sacra. Vol.3.
ROGERS, ELIZABETH.
Virginal book. Selections.
In: Schott's Anthology of early keyboard music. Vol.5.
ROGERS, SIR JOHN, ca.1780–1847.
Part music.
In: Hullah. Part music. Class A.1. Vol.2; Class A.2. Vol.2.
Vocal music.
In: Hullah. Vocal scores. II. Secular.
ROGIER, PHILIPPE, ca.1560–1596.
Selections.
In: Maldéghem. Trésor musical.
Eleven motets.
In: Recent researches in the music of the Renaissance. Vol.2.
ROGIER (PATHIE).
Chansons.
In: Publikationen älterer praktischer und theoretischer Musikwerke. Jahrg.27.
ROGIER-PATHIE, MAITRE.
Selections.
In: Maldéghem. Trésor musical.
ROHACZEWSKI, A.
Canzon a 4. Organ (or 4 string or wind instruments) and continuo.
In: Denkmäler altpolnischer Musik. Vol.43.
Crucifixus surrexit. Mixed chorus.
In: Denkmäler altpolnischer Musik. Vol.46.
ROHDE, MICHAEL.
Hochzeitsarien und Kantaten.
In: Das Erbe deutscher Musik. 2.Reihe. Mecklenburg und Pommern. Vol.1.
ROHWER, JENS, 1914– .
Einfache Singsätze.
In: Bausteine für Musikerziehung und Musikpflege. B 125.
Heptameron, eine vierstimmige Suite.
In: Collegium musicae novae. No.7.
Kammerkonzert.
In: Collegium musicae novae. No.52.
Drei hübsche Mädchen.
In: Bausteine für Musikziehung und Musikpflege. B 136.
Der Morgenstern ist ausgegangen.
In: Zeitschrift für Spielmusik. No.185.
Wach auf, wach auf, 's ist höchste Zeit.
In: Collegium musicae novae. No.23.
ROI, LE MANUSCRIT DU, *see* LE MANUSCRIT DU ROI.
ROJO, CASIANO, 1877–1931.
El canto Mozárabe.
In: Barcelona. Biblioteca Central. Sección de música. Publicaciones. Vol.5.
ROLDÁN, AMADEO, 1900–1939.
(var. sp.: Amadee Roldán).
Motivos de son.
In: New music. Vol.7. No.2. Jan.1934.
In: New music. Orchestra series. No.16.
ROLDAN, J. P.
Sacred music.
In: Eslava y Elizondo. Lira sacro-hispana. 18th century. i.1.
ROLLA, ALESSANDRO, 1757–1841.
Drei Duos für Violine und Violoncello. Nr.1–3.
In: Antiqua Edition. Von 2 Instrumenten an.
ROLLE, JOHANN HEINRICH, 1718–1785.
Choral music.
In: Commer. Cantica sacra. Vol.2. No.10, 12.
In: Rochlitz. Sammlung vorzüglicher Gesangstücke. Bd.3.
Part music.
In: Hullah. Part music. Class C. 1868 edition.
Sacred music.
In: Latrobe, C. I. Selection of sacred music.
In: Latrobe, J. A. The music of the church.
Sonate.
In: Köhler. Les maîtres du clavecin. Heft 6.
Sonate (Es).
In: Pauer. Alte Meister. No.25.
Vocal music.
In: Hullah. Vocal scores. II. Sacred.
ROMAN, JOHAN HELMICH, 1694–1758.
Selections.
In: Svenska samfundet för musikforskning. Äldre svensk musik. No.1–5, 8–9.
Assaggi a violino solo.

In: Monumenta musicae svecicae. Vol.1.
Sinfonien 1–3.
In: Monumenta musicae svecicae.
2 Sonaten für Querflöte und Basso Continuo.
In: Hortus musicus. No.101.
THE ROMAN DE FAUVEL.
Le roman de Fauvel. 220p.
Le roman de Fauvel. 7p., facsim.: 95 pl.
The roman de Fauvel.
In: Schrade. Polyphonic music of the fourteenth century. Vol.1.
ROMANINI, ANTONIO.
Selections.
In: Torchi. L'arte musicale in Italia. Bd.3.
ROMANTICISM IN MUSIC. (STEPHENSON).
In: Anthology of music. Vol.21.
ROMBERG.
Vocal music.
In: Sammlung russischer Romanzen. No.127.
ROMERO, MATEO, d.1647.
Selections.
In: Pedrell. Teatro lirico espanol anterior al siglo XIX. Bd.3.
Sacred music.
In: Eslava y Elizondo. Lira sacro-hispana. 17th century. i.1.
RÖMHILD, JOHANN THEODERICH, 1684–1757.
Das neue Jahr ist kommen.
In: Hortus musicus. No.89.
RON, JEAN MARTIN DE, 1789–1817.
Streichquartett in F.
In: Svenska samfundet för musikforskning. Äldre svensk musik. No.6.
RONDEAUX.
In: Summa musicae medii aevi. Vol.10.
In: Turin. Biblioteca Nazionale. Mss. (J.II.9). The Cypriot-French repertory. Vol.4.
RONGA, LUIGI, 1901– .
Gerolamo Frescobaldi.
In: Istituzioni e monumenti dell'arte musicale italiana. Nuova serie. In preparation.
RONSARD, PIERRE DE, 1524–1585.
Bibliographie des poésies.
In: Société Française de Musicologie, Paris. Publications. Sér.II. Bd.8.
RONTANI, RAFFAELLO, d.1622.
(var. sp.: Rafaello Rontani).
Arias.
In: Landshoff. Alte Meister des Bel Canto. Eine Sammlung von Arien. Vol.1–2.
In: Parisotti. Arie antiche. Bd.2, 3.
Songs.
In: Jeppesen. La flora. Vol.2.
ROPARTZ, JOSEPH GUY MARIE, 1864–1955.
Organ music.
In: Bedell. The French organist. Vol.1, 2.
In: Bonnet. Historical organ-recitals. Vol.5.
ROPER, VIRGINIA.
Piano music.
In: The Wa-Wan series of American compositions.
RORE, CIPRIANO DE, 1516–1565.
Opera omnia. v.1– .
Selections.
In: Documenta historica musicae.
In: Maldéghem. Trésor musical.
Chansons.
In: Lesure. Anthologie de la chanson parisienne au XVIe siècle.
Choral music.
In: Commer. Collectio operum musicorum batavorum saeculi XVI. Bd.7, 12.
In: Dehn. Sammlung älterer Musik aus dem XVI. und XVII. Jahrhundert.
Keyboard music.
In: Tagliapietra. Antologia di musica antica e moderna per pianoforte. Bd.1.
Madrigals.
In: Einstein. The golden age of the madrigal.
In: Smith College music archives. No.6.
Vergil-Motetten.
In: Das Chorwerk. No.54.
ROREM, NED, 1923– .
Madrigals.
In: Music Press, Inc. [Choral series]. Vol.118.
ROSA, SALVATORE, 1615–1673.
Selections.
In: Crotch. Specimens of various styles of music. Vol.2.
Arias.
In: Parisotti. Arie antiche. Bd.3.
ROSEINGRAVE, THOMAS, 1690–1766.
Fifteen voluntaries & fugues for the organ. 42p.
Compositions for organ and harpsichord.
In: The Penn state music series. No.2.
Ten organ pieces.
In: English keyboard music. [No.18].
Organ music.
In: Raugel. Quarante-six pièces pour orgue ou harmonium.
Part music.
In: Hullah. Part music. Class C. Sacred.
ROSEN, HENRICUS JACOBUS.
Aus einem Klavierbuch.
In: Moecks Kammermusik. Vol.251.
ROSENBERG, HILDING CONSTANTIN, 1892– .
Selections.
In: Svensk sanglyrik. Vol.2.
Fantasia and fugue for organ.
In: Musikaliska konstföreningen. 1953.
ROSENFELD, LEOPOLD, 1850–1909.
Bjergpigen. Choral work.
In: Samfundet til Udgivelse af dansk Musik. Ser.II. No.38.
Henrik og Else. Op.25. Choral work.
In: Samfundet til Udgivelse af dansk Musik. Ser.I. No.23.
ROSENMÜLLER, JOHANN, ca.1619–1684.
Choral music.
In: Commer. Cantica sacra. Vol.2, No.18, 20.
Dialog von Tobias und Raguel.
In: Organum. 1.Reihe. Nr.21.
Feiermusik.
In: Corona. Vol.30.
In hac misera valle.
In: Organum. 1.Reihe. Nr.24.
Kammersonate.
In: Zeitschrift für Spielmusik. No.114.
Lamentationes Jeremiae prophetae.
In: Nagels Musik-Archiv. No.27–28.
Der 134. Psalm.
In: Nagels Musik-Archiv. No.81.

Der 138. Psalm.
In: Nagels Musik-Archiv. No.59.
Sonate G-moll; Sonate F-moll. Für zwei Violinen mit beziffertem Bass.
In: Nagels Musik-Archiv. No.29, 30.
Sonate da camera.
In: Denkmäler deutscher Tonkunst. [1.Folge]. Vol.18.
Studenten-Musik.
In: Nagels Musik-Archiv. No.61.
In: Zeitschrift für Spielmusik. No.158.
Suite C-moll aus "Studenten-Musik."
In: Schering. Perlen alter Kammermusik.
ROSENSTENGEL, ALBRECHT, 1912– .
Concertino.
In: Collegium musicae novae. No.35.
Kleine Musik für Glockenspiel (Vibraphon) und Streicher.
In: Collegium musicae novae. No.51.
Klingende Miniaturen.
In: Zeitschrift für Spielmusik. No.292.
Der Rätselzoo.
In: Zeitschrift für Spielmusik. No.277.
Vater und Sohn.
In: Zeitschrift für Spielmusik. No.286.
ROSETTI, FRANCESCO ANTONIO, *see* RÖSSLER, FRANZ ANTON.
ROSIER, KARL, 1640–1725.
(var. sp.: Carl Rosier).
Ausgewählte Instrumentalwerke.
In: Denkmäler rheinischer Musik. Vol.7.
RÖSLER, JOHANN JOSEF, 1771–1813.
Songs.
In: Documenta historica musicae.
ROSSELLI, FRANCESCO, 16th CENTURY.
Anthems.
In: Music Press, Inc. [Choral series]. No.72.
Sacred music.
In: Proske. Musica divina. Annus primus. Tom 4.
ROSSETER, PHILIP, ca.1575–1623.
Madrigals.
In: Euterpe. Vol.4; 2d ed. No.55, 55a.
Songs from book of airs.
In: Fellowes. The English school of lutenist song writers. 1st series. Vol.8, 9.
ROSSETTI, STEFFANO, 16th CENTURY.
(var. sp.: Stephano Rossetti).
Madrigale.
In: Das Chorwerk. No.88.
ROSSI, GIUSEPPE DA.
Graduale di S. Cecilia per soli, coro ed istrumenti. 1715.
In: Documenta maiora liturgiae polychoralis sanctae ecclesiae romanae. No.10.
ROSSI, LUIGI, 1598–1653.
Selections.
In: Crotch. Specimens of various styles of music. Vol.2.
In: Torchi. L'arte musicale in Italia. Bd.5.
Airs.
In: Prunières. Les maîtres du chant. Recueil 3, 5.
Arias.
In: Landshoff. Alte Meister des Bel Canto. Eine Sammlung von Arien. Vol.1–2.
Organ music.
In: Raugel. Quarante-six pièces pour orgue ou harmonium.
Vocal music.
In: Gevaert. Les gloires de l'Italie. Vol.1, 2.
ROSSI, MICHAEL ANGELO, 17th CENTURY.
(var. sp.: Michelangelo Rossi).
Selections.
In: Torchi. L'arte musicale in Italia. Bd.3.
Composizioni.
In: I classici della musica italiana. Vol.26.
Airs.
In: Prunières. Les maîtres du chant. Recueil 3.
Andantino. Allegro.
In: Köhler. Les maîtres du clavecin. Heft 8.
In: Pauer. Alte Meister. No.29.
Keyboard music.
In: Corpus of early keyboard music. Vol.15.
In: Esposito. Early Italian piano music.
In: Oesterle. Early keyboard music. Vol.1.
In: Tagliapietra. Antologia di musica antica e moderna per pianoforte. Bd.6.
Composizioni per organo e cembalo.
In: I classici della musica italiana. Raccolta nazionale della musiche italiane. Quad. 110–113.
Organ music.
In: Fuser. Classici italiani dell' organo.
In: Raugel. Quarante-six pièces pour orgue ou harmonium.
ROSSI, SALOMONE, ca.1570–ca.1630.
Chamber music.
In: Riemann. Old chamber music. Vol.3.
Kammerduette.
In: Landshoff. Alte Meister des Bel Canto. Italienische Kammerduette.
Sonata detta la Moderna für 2 Violinen und Basso Continuo.
In: Hortus musicus. No.110.
ROSSINI, GIOACCHINO ANTONIO, 1792–1868.
Quaderni Rossiniani. v.1– .
Motets.
In: Concerts spirituels ou recueil de motets.
Part music.
In: Hullah. Part music. Class A.1. Vol.1.
RÖSSLER, FRANZ ANTON, 1746–1792.
(var. sp.: Giovanni Antonio Rosetti; Anton Rosetti; Francesco Antonio Rosetti; František Antonín Rössler-Rosetti).
Selected works.
In: Denkmäler deutscher Tonkunst. [2.Folge]. Vol.12 (ii), 25.
Ad festa, fideles. Bass und B. C.
In: Cantio sacra. No.31.
Notturno in D.
In: Musica antiqua bohemica. Vol.32.
Parthia (Partita) for wind septet.
In: Für Kenner und Liebhaber. No.6.
Parthia.
In: Für Kenner und Liebhaber. No.26.
Symphonies.
In: Denkmäler deutscher Tonkunst. [2.Folge]. Vol.12 (ii).
Woodwind quintet, E flat.
In: Für Kenner und Liebhaber. No.30.
ROSSO DA COLLEGRANO.
Selections.

In: Pirrotta. The music of fourteenth-century Italy. Vol.3.
ROSTHIUS, JOHANN KASPAR NIKOLAUS, 16th–17th CENTURIES.
(var. sp.: Nicolaus Rosthius).
Choral music.
In: Antiqua Chorbuch. Vol.2. Heft 4.
DAS ROSTOCKER LIEDERBUCH.
Das Rostocker Liederbuch. p.[193]–306.
ROTA, ANDREA, ca.1553–1597.
Selections.
In: Musica sacra . . . 1839– . Vol.16.
In: Torchi. L'arte musicale in Italia. Bd.1.
ROTENBUCHER, ERASMUS, 16th CENTURY.
Schöne und liebliche Zweigesänge. Für zwei Melodieinstrumente.
In: Hortus musicus. No.74.
ROUCOURT, DE.
Choral music.
In: Commer. Collectio operum musicorum batavorum saeculi XVI. Bd.12.
ROUNDS, CATCHES, CANONS.
In: Music Press, Inc. [Choral series]. Vol.65, 66, 85, 108, 114.
In: Rimbault. The rounds, catches and canons of England.
ROUSÉE.
Motets.
In: Attaingnant. Treize livres de motets. Livre 7, 8, 12.
ROUSSEAU, JEAN JACQUES, 1712–1778.
Minuet (From Le Devin du village). Organ.
In: Dickinson. Historical recital series for organ. Vol.1. No.5.
Part music.
In: Hullah. Part music. Class A.1. Vol.1.
ROUX, GASPARD LE, 1660–1705.
Pieces for harpsichord. 77p.
Keyboard music.
In: Herrmann. Lehrmeister und Schüler Joh. Seb. Bachs. Vol.1.
ROVIGO, FRANCESCO.
Selections.
In: Denkmäler der Tonkunst in Österreich. Vol.77. (Jg.XLI), 90.
ROVSING OLSEN, POUL, 1922– .
Prolana. Op.33.
In: Samfundet til Udgivelse af dansk Musik. Ser.III. No.157.
Schicksalslieder für Singstimmen mit Instrumentalgruppe. Op.28.
In: Samfundet til Udgivelse af dansk Musik. Ser.III. No.147.
Variations symphoniques. Op.27.
In: Samfundet til Udgivelse af dansk Musik. Ser.III. No.128.
ROY, ADRIAN, LE, *see* LE ROY, ADRIAN.
ROY, BARTHELEMY VAN.
Selections.
In: Maldéghem. Trésor musical.
ROY, G. LE.
Motets.
In: Attaingnant. Treize livres de motets. Livre 7.
ROY, OTTO.
Die Fuge; Der Volkstanz.
In: Musikalische Formen in historischen Reihen. Bd.7, 14.
ROYER.
Vocal music.
In: Delsarte. Archives du chant. Livr.11. No.6.
RÓZSA, BÉLA.
Sonate for piano.
In: New music. Vol.9. No.2. Jan.1936.
RÓZYCKI, JACEK HYACINTHUS, d.ca.1700.
Exsultemus omnes. S.S.B. soli and continuo.
In: Denkmäler altpolnischer Musik. Vol.44.
Hymni ecclesiastici.
In: Denkmäler altpolnischer Musik. Vol.3.
Magnificemus in cantico.
In: Denkmäler altpolnischer Musik. Vol.16.
RSCHEWSKY.
Vocal music.
In: Sammlung russischer Romanzen. No.286, 310.
RUBENSON, ALBERT, 1826–1901.
En Natt bland fjellen. Operetta.
In: Musikaliska konstföreningen. 1887.
Selection from the music to Halte-Hulda.
In: Musikaliska konstföreningen. 1902.
Symphonic intermezzo, No.1.
In: Musikaliska konstföreningen. 1902.
RUBINSTEIN, ANTON GRIGOREVICH, 1830–1894.
Keyboard music.
In: Tagliapietra. Antologia di musica antica e moderna per pianoforte. Bd.17.
Vocal music.
In: Sammlung russischer Romanzen. No. 144–146, 226, 227.
RUBIO, SAMUEL. ed.
Canciones espirituales polifónicas.
In: Polifonía española. Vol.2.
RUCTIS, AR. DE.
Sacred music.
In: Plainsong and Mediaeval Music Society. Publications. (Borren).
RUDBECK, OLOF DER ÄLTERE, 1630–1702.
Trauer- und Klagegesang zur Beerdigung Axel Oxenstiernas.
In: Monumenta musicae svecicae.
RUDHYAR, DANE, 1895– .
Granites. Piano.
In: New music. Vol.8. No.4. July 1935.
3 Paeans for piano.
In: New music. Vol.1. No.2. Jan.1928.
Sinfonietta.
In: New music. Orchestra series. No.13.
5 Stanzas for strings' ensemble.
In: New music. Orchestra series. No.22.
RUDOLPH, JOHANN JOSEPH RAINER, ARCHDUKE OF AUSTRIA, 1788–1831.
Ballets.
In: Denkmäler deutscher Tonkunst. [1.Folge]. Vol.43–44.
RUE, PIERRE DE LA, *see* LA RUE, PIERRE DE.
RUFFO, VINCENZO, d.1587.
Selections.
In: Torchi. L'arte musicale in Italia. Bd.1.
Anthems.
In: Music Press, Inc. [Choral series]. No.72.
Choral music.
In: Music Press, Inc. [Choral series]. No.78.
Missa sine nomine.

In: Musica liturgica. Vol.1. Fasc.1.
Part music.
In: Hullah. Part music. Class A.2. Vol.1.
RUGGIERI, G. M.
Sonata prima-decima, aus Sonate da chiesa, Op.3.
In: Hausmusik. No.64–67, 122–123, 129, 135, 141–142.
RUGGLES, CARL, 1876– .
Angels for brass or strings.
In: New music. Vol.16. No.3. Apr.1943.
Evocations. 3 Chants for piano.
In: New music. Vol.16. No.3. Apr.1943.
Evocations no.4. Chant for piano.
In: New music. Vol.18. No.2. Jan.1945.
Organum. Large orchestra.
In: New music. Special edition.
Organum. Piano.
In: New music. Vol.21. No.1. Oct.1947.
Portals, for full string orchestra.
In: New music. Vol.3. No.3. Apr.1930.
Sun treader. Orchestra.
In: New music. Orchestra series. No.14.
Symphonic ensemble. Men and mountains.
In: New music. Vol.1. No.1. Oct.1927.
RUMANIA–MUSIC.
In: Zeitschrift für Spielmusik. No.209.
RUNG, FREDERIK, 1854–1914.
Den trekantede Hat. Opera.
In: Samfundet til Udgivelse af dansk Musik. Ser.II. No.11.
RUNGENHAGEN, CARL FRIEDRICH, 1778–1851.
Fugue. Tu ad dexteram.
In: Königliche Akademie der Künste. Auswahl vorzüglicher Musik-Werke. No.32.
Lied.
In: Reimann. Das deutsche Lied. Vol.2.
RUPINI.
Vocal music.
In: Sammlung russischer Romanzen. No.176.
RUPRECHT, MARTIN, 1758–1800.
Songs.
In: Denkmäler der Tonkunst in Österreich. Vol.54. (Jg.XXVII/2).
RUPSCH, KONRAD, d.after 1525.
Choral music.
In: Moser. Die Kantorei der Spätgotik.
RUSSELL, WILLIAM.
Fugue. 8 percussion instruments.
In: New music. Orchestra series. No.6.
3 Dance movements. For piano and percussion instruments.
In: New music. Vol.28. No.3. Apr.1955.
3 Dance movements.
In: New music. Orchestra series. No.18.
RUSSIA–MUSIC.
In: Crotch. Specimens of various styles of music. Vol.1.
In: New music. Vol.8. No.1. Oct.1934.
In: Sammlung russischer Romanzen.
RUST, FRIEDRICH WILHELM, 1739–1796.
Werke für Klavier und Streichinstrumente.
In: Das Erbe deutscher Musik. 2.Reihe. Mitteldeutschland. Vol.1.
Lied.
In: Reimann. Das deutsche Lied. Vol.3.
Sonate in D-moll.
In: Musikschätze der Vergangenheit.
RUTINI, GIOVANNI MARIA PLACIDO, 1723–1797.
(var. sp.: Giovanni Marco; Giovanni Placido).
Keyboard music.
In: Benvenuti. Cembalisti italiani del settecento.
In: Tagliapietra. Antologia di musica antica e moderna per pianoforte. Bd.13.
Sonate. Cembalo o pianoforte.
In: Paoli. Sonate italiane del sec.: XVIII per cembalo o pianoforte.
Sonate. Pianoforte.
In: I classici della musica italiana. Vol.27.
In: I classici della musica italiana. Raccolta nazionale delle musiche italiane. Quad. 276–281.
Sonate (C). (A). (C).
In: Pauer. Alte Meister. No.56, 57, 58.
RUYNEMAN, DANIEL, 1886– .
Sonata for chamber choir.
In: New music. Vol.7. No.2. Jan.1934.

SABADINI, BERNARDO.
Selections.
In: Torchi. L'arte musicale in Italia. Bd.3.
SABBATINI, GALEAZZO, d.1662.
Sacred music.
?In: Latrobe, C. I. Selection of sacred music.
?In: Latrobe, J. A. The music of the church.
SABEL, HANS.
Kleine Musik für Sopran-Blockflöte und Klavier.
In: Zeitschrift für Spielmusik. No.183.
SABIO, KING OF CASTILE AND LEON, ALFONSO X, EL, *see* ALFONSO X, EL SABIO, KING OF CASTILE AND LEON.
SABLONARA, CLAUDIO DE LA, *see* LA SABLONARA, CLAUDIO DE.
SACCHINI, ANTONIO MARIA GASPARO, 1730–1786.
Selections.
In: Échos de France. Vol.1–3.
Chimène ou le Cid; Renaud.
In: Les chefs d'oeuvres classiques de l'opéra français.
Keyboard music.
In: Tagliapietra. Antologia di musica antica e moderna per pianoforte. Bd.13.
Motets.
In: Concerts spirituels ou recueil de motets.
Sonate.
In: Köhler. Les maîtres du clavecin. Heft 9.
Sonate (F).
In: Pauer. Alte Meister. No.22.
Triosonate in G dur, Op.1. Für 2 Violinen, Violoncell und Klavier.
In: Riemann. Collegium musicum. No.46.
Vocal music.
In: Delsarte. Archives du chant. Livr.19. No.5; Livr.21. No.9.
In: Gevaert. Les gloires de l'Italie. Vol.1, 2.
SACH, J. PH.
Lieder.
In: Moser. Alte Meister des deutschen Liedes. 30 Gesänge. No.22.
SACHS, HANS, 1494–1576.
Gesangweise.
In: Parrish. A treasury of early music. No.22.

SACHS, ILSE.
Berliner Sonatine in G.
In: Zeitschrift für Spielmusik. No.161.
Weihnachtsmusiken.
In: Bausteine für Musikerziehung und Musikpflege. B 118.
SACK, JOHANN PHILIPP, 1722–1763.
Lieder.
In: Moser. Alte Meister des deutschen Liedes. 46 Gesänge. No.35.
SAGGIONE, GIOSEPPE FEDELI.
Sonate en mi majeur.
In: L'école du violon au XVIIe et XVIIIe siècle. No.1285.
A ST. ANDREWS MUSIC BOOK.
In: Wolfenbüttel. Herzog-August-Bibliothek. Mss. (677 [Helmst 628]). An old St. Andrews music book.
SAINT-CHAPELLE, LE PROSAIRE DE LA.
In: Monumenta musicae sacrae. Vol.1.
SAINT GRÉGOIRE LE GRAND, *see* GREGORY, SAINT.
ST. JOHN'S PASSION.
In: Monumenta musicae svecicae. Vol.3.
SAINT-SAËNS, CAMILLE, 1835–1921.
Organ music.
In: Bonnet. Historical organ-recitals. Vol.5.
SAINT-VICTOR, ADAM DE, *see* ADAM DE SAINT-VICTOR.
SALA.
Sacred music.
In: Latrobe, C. I. Selection of sacred music.
In: Latrobe, J. A. The music of the church.
SALAZAR, JUAN GARCÍA DE, d.1710.
Sacred music.
In: Eslava y Elizondo. Lira sacro-hispana. 17th century, ii.1.
SALE, FRANCESCO DI.
(var. sp.: Franciscus Sale).
Selections.
In: Maldéghem. Trésor musical.
Office. Mass.
In: Berg. Patrocinium musices. Vol.9, 12.
SALEM, BERNHARD V.
Organ music.
In: Moser. Frühmeister der deutschen Orgelkunst.
SALES, PIETRO POMPEO, 1729–1797.
Keyboard music.
In: Benvenuti. Cembalisti italiani del settecento.
SALIERI, ANTONIO, 1750–1825.
Benedictus, etc.
In: Königliche Akademie der Künste. Auswahl vorzüglicher Musik-Werke. No.31.
Zwei Bläserserenaden.
In: Diletto musicale. No.132.
Concerto. C dur. D dur.
In: Diletto musicale. No.54, 135.
Les danaïdes; Tarare.
In: Les chefs d'oeuvres classiques de l'opéra français.
Part music.
In: Hullah. Part music. Class B.1.
Scherzi istrumentali a quattro di stile fugato (Streichquartett).
In: Diletto musicale. No.67.
Symphony in D (Patron Saints' Day).
In: Antica musica strumentale italiana. Ser.III. Vol.24.
Symphony in D (Veneziana).
In: Antica musica strumentale italiana. Ser.III. Vol.23.
SALINIS, UBERTUS DE, 14th–15th CENTURIES.
(var. sp.: Ubertus de Psalinis).
Sacred music.
In: Plainsong and Mediaeval Music Society. Publications. (Borren).
SALOMON, KAREL, 1897– .
Drei Miniaturen.
In: Zeitschrift für Spielmusik. No.263.
SALVATORE, GIOVANNI, ca.1610–ca.1675.
Collected keyboard works.
In: Corpus of early keyboard music. Vol.3.
Sacred music.
In: Latrobe, C. I. Selection of sacred music.
In: Latrobe, J. A. The music of the church.
SALZBURG–MUSIC.
In: Denkmäler der Tonkunst in Österreich. Vol.80. (Jg.XLIII/1).
In: Hausmusik. No.95.
In: Messner. Alte salzburger Meister der kirchlichen Tonkunst.
In: Zeitschrift für Spielmusik. No.91.
SALZEDO, CARLOS, 1885–1961.
Sonata for harp and piano.
In: Society for the Publication of American Music. Publications. 6th season. 1924–25.
SAMBETH, HEINRICH.
Das Blockflötchen.
In: Moecks gelbe Musikhefte. Vol.4.
SAMIN, VULFRAN.
Mass.
In: Stein. Twelve Franco-Flemish masses of the early 16th century.
SAMMARTINI, GIOVANNI BATTISTA, ca.1700–1775.
Introduzione, D dur. Violine und Klavier.
In: Sondheimer. Werke aus dem 18. Jahrhundert. Nr.13.
Kammer-Sonaten für Violine und Pianoforte.
In: Moffat. Kammer-Sonaten für Violine und Pianoforte. No.16.
Keyboard music.
In: Benvenuti. Cembalisti italiani del settecento.
In: Tagliapietra. Antologia di musica antica e moderna per pianoforte. Bd.12.
Organ music.
In: Anthologia antiqua. Vol.2.
Sinfonie D-dur.
In: Sondheimer. Werke aus dem 18. Jahrhundert. Nr.49.
Sonate.
In: I classici della musica italiana. Vol.28.
Sonate (Gm).
In: Moffat. Trio-Sonaten alter Meister. No.12.
Sonate notturne. Op.VII.
In: I classici della musica italiana. Raccolta nazionale delle musiche italiane. Quad. 114–119.
Four symphonies.

In: Collegium musicum. [Vol.6].
Trio in A moll. Op.3. Nr.9; Trio in Es dur. Op.1. Nr.3. Für 2 Violinen, Violoncell und Klavier.
In: Riemann. Collegium musicum. No.27, 28.
Trio C-dur; Trio Es-dur.
In: Sondheimer. Werke aus dem 18. Jahrhundert. Nr.37/38.
SAMOILOFF.
Vocal music.
In: Sammlung russischer Romanzen. No.288.
SAMTER, WENZEL VON.
Selections.
In: Gieburowski. Cantica selecta musices sacrae in Polonia saeculi XVI et XVII.
SANCES, GIOVANNI FELICE, ca.1600–1679.
Songs.
In: Jeppesen. La flora. Vol.2, 3.
SANCHEZ, DIEGO, fl.1616.
Motets. (Collections signed by Diego Sanchez).
In: Elúsitiza. Antología musical.
SANCHEZ, MICHAEL.
Sacred music.
In: Rubio. Antologia polifonica sacra. Vol.1.
SANDBERG NIELSEN, OTTO, 1900–1941.
Praeludium, Trio, Ciacona. Op.11.
In: Samfundet til Udgivelse af dansk Musik. Ser.III. No.58.
SANDERS, ROBERT L., 1906– .
Choral music.
In: Music Press, Inc. [Choral series]. Vol.107.
SANDONI, PIER GIUSEPPE, d.1750.
Sonate. Cembalo.
In: I classici della musica italiana. Vol.29.
In: I classici della musica italiana. Raccolta nazionale delle musiche italiane. Quad. 266–267.
SANDOVAL, MIGUEL, 1903–1953.
Keyboard music.
In: Guenther. Collection espagnole.
SANDRIN, P.
Chansons.
In: Cauchie. Quinze chansons françaises du XVIe siècle.
In: Lesure. Anthologie de la chanson parisienne au XVIe siècle.
In: Publikationen älterer praktischer und theoretischer Musikwerke. Jahrg.27.
SANJUAN, N.
Sacred music.
In: Eslava y Elizondo. Lira sacro-hispana. 18th century. i.1.
SANTA CRUZ, DOMINGO, 1899– .
Piano music.
In: Boletín latino-americano de música. Vol.4.
3 Pieces for violin and piano.
In: New music. Vol.12. No.3. Apr.1939.
SANTA MARIA, FRAY TOMÁS DE, d.1570.
(var. sp.: Thomas de Sancta Maria).
Fabordon del i tono.
In: Polifonía española. Vol.5.
Organ music.
In: Bonnet. Historical organ-recitals. Vol.6.
In: Klein. The first four centuries of music. for the organ from Dunstable to Bach (1370–1749).
In: Liber organi. Bd.3.
In: Muset. Early Spanish organ music.
In: Orgue et liturgie. Vol.49.
In: Peeters. Anthologia pro organo. Vol.1, 3.
Psalmodia variata.
In: Pedrell. Hispaniae schola musica sacra. Bd.6.
SANTOLIQUIDO, FRANCESCO, 1883– .
Keyboard music.
In: Tagliapietra. Antologia di musica antica e moderna per pianoforte. Bd.18.
SANTORO, CLAUDIO, 1919– .
Selections.
In: Instituto Interamericano de Musicologia. Publicaciónes. No.8, 43.
Música de cámara.
In: Boletín latino-americano de música. Vol.6.
SANTÓRSOLA, GUIDO, 1904– .
Agonia.
In: Instituto Interamericano de Musicologia. Publicaciónes. No.16.
SARRI, DOMENICO, 1679–1744.
Arias.
In: Landshoff. Alte Meister des Bel Canto. Eine Sammlung von Arien. Vol.1–2.
In: Parisotti. Arie antiche. Bd.2.
SARTI, GIUSEPPE, 1729–1802.
Allegro.
In: Köhler. Les maîtres du clavecin. Heft 9.
In: Pauer. Alte Meister. No.34.
Sacred music.
In: Latrobe, C. I. Selection of sacred music.
In: Latrobe, J. A. The music of the church.
Vocal music.
In: Gevaert. Les gloires de l'Italie. Vol.2.
SARTO, JOHANNES DE, 15th CENTURY.
Sacred music.
In: Plainsong and Mediaeval Music Society. Publications. (Borren).
SARTORIO, ANTONIO, b.ca.1620.
Arias.
In: Parisotti. Arie antiche. Bd.3.
Sinfonia zur Oper "L'Adelaide."
In: Nagels Musik-Archiv. No.141.
SARTORIUS, PAUL, 16th–17th CENTURIES.
Choral music.
In: Antiqua Chorbuch. Vol.2. Heft 4.
Gesänge.
In: Wolf. Chor- und Hausmusik aus älter Zeit. Vol.2.
SÁS, ANDRÉS, 1900– .
Vocal music.
In: Boletín latino-americano de música. Vol.4.
In: Instituto Interamericano de Musicologia. Publicaciónes. No.6.
SAVAGE, WILLIAM, 1720–1789.
Sacred music.
In: Arnold. Cathedral music. Vol.3.
SAVASTA, A.
Keyboard music.
In: Tagliapietra. Antologia di musica antica e moderna per pianoforte. Bd.18.
SAVILE, JEREMY, 17th CENTURY.
(var. sp.: Saville).
Part music.
In: Hullah. Part music. Class A.2. Vol.1.
SAXONY–MUSIC.
In: Corona. Vol.16.

In: Schmid. Musik am sächsischen Hofe.
SAYVE, LAMBERT DE, ca.1549–1614.
Selections.
In: Denkmäler der Tonkunst in Österreich. Vol.77. (Jg.XLI), 90.
Teutsche Liedlein.
In: Das Chorwerk. No.51.
Vier Motetten.
In: Das Chorwerk. No.86.
SCALABRINI, PABLO, 1713–1806.
Kaerlighed uden Strømper. Tragedy.
In: Samfundet til Udgivelse af dansk Musik. Ser.II. No.27.
SCANDELLO, ANTONIO, 1517–1580.
(var. sp.: Antonius Scandellus).
Selections.
In: Ambros. Auserwählte Tonwerke.
In: Musica sacra. 1839– . Vol.15.
Choral music.
In: Antiqua Chorbuch. Vol.1. Heft 2.
In: Der Kammerchor. Vol.2, 5.
Chorlieder.
In: Christophorus-Chorwerk. Heft 5.
Geistliches Lied; Lobet den Herren, denn er ist sehr freundlich.
In: Musica sacra ... between 1892–1897. No.6.
Lieder.
In: Commer. Geistliche und weltliche Lieder aus dem XVI.–XVII. Jahrhundert.
Missa super Eptiaphium Mauritii.
In: Das Chorwerk. No.65.
Organ music.
In: Cantantibus organis. Vol.11.
Trinklieder.
In: Christophorus-Chorwerk. Heft 11.
SCANDINAVIA–MUSIC.
In: Crotch. Specimens of various styles of music. Vol.1.
In: Zeitschrift für Spielmusik. No.48.
SCARLATTI, ALESSANDRO, 1660–1725.
Gli oratorii. v.1– .
Selections.
In: Crotch. Specimens of various styles of music. Vol.2.
In: Torchi. L'arte musicale in Italia. Bd.5.
Airs.
In: Prunières. Les maîtres du chant. Recueil 1, 5.
Arias.
In: Landshoff. Alte Meister des Bel Canto. Eine Sammlung von Arien. Vol.1–2, 3.
In: Parisotti. Arie antiche. Bd.1, 2, 3.
Ariette a una voce, con e senza stromenti.
In: Flores musicae. Vol.9.
Le Caduta de decem viri. Sinfonia.
In: Parrish. A treasury of early music. No.44.
Cantate.
In: I classici della musica italiana. Vol.30.
In: I classici della musica italiana. Raccolta nazionale delle musiche italiane. Quad. 120–125.
Choral music.
In: Music Press, Inc. [Choral series]. No.71.
?In: Recueil de musique ancienne. Recueil des morceaux de musique ancienne. Bd.2.
In: Rochlitz. Sammlung vorzüglicher Gesangstücke. Bd.2.
Concerto A-moll für Alt-Blockflöte, 2 Violinen und Basso Continuo.
In: Moecks Kammermusik. Vol.35.
Concerto in F.
In: Antica musica strumentale italiana. In preparation.
Concerto No.6 in E (2 violin soli, strings, cembalo).
In: Antica musica strumentale italiana. Ser.II. Vol.19.
Sechs Concerti Grossi für Streichorchester mit Cembalo. Erstes und zweites Konzert. Drittes Konzert in F-dur.
In: Musikschätze der Vergangenheit.
Concerto grosso F-moll.
In: Schering. Perlen alter Kammermusik.
Domine, Refugium factus es.
In: Die Motette. No.4.
Fugue.
In: Köhler. Les maîtres du clavecin. Heft 9.
Infirmata vulnerata. Alt, 2 Violinen und B.C.
In: Die Kantate. No.5.
Keyboard music.
In: Clementi. Clementi's Selection of practical harmony. Vol.2.
In: Esposito. Early Italian piano music.
In: Farrenc. Le trésor des pianistes. Vol.3.
In: Oesterle. Early keyboard music. Vol.1.
In: Pauer. Alte Klavier-Musik. 2d series. Part 1.
In: Tagliapietra. Antologia di musica antica e moderna per pianoforte. Bd.9.
Part music.
?In: Hullah. Part music. Class A.2. Vol.1.
Passio Domini nostri Jesu Christi secundum Joannem.
In: Collegium musicum. Vol.1.
Primo e secondo libro di toccate.
In: I classici musicali italiani. Vol.13.
La rosaura.
In: Publikationen älterer praktischer und theoretischer Musikwerke. Jahrg.14.
Sacred music.
In: Proske. Musca divina. Annus primus. Tom 2.
Sinfonien, für Kammerorchester.
In: Hortus musicus. No.48, 116, 125.
Sinfonie II D-dur für KammerOrchester.
In: Hortus musicus. No.146.
Sinfonie XII C-moll für KammerOrchester.
?In: Hortus musicus. No.168.
Sonate für 3 Alt-Blockflöten, und Basso Continuo.
In: Moecks Kammermusik. Vol.36.
Sonate A-dur für 2 Querflöten, 2 Violinen und Basso Continuo.
In: Moecks Kammermusik. Vol.37.
Songs.
In: Jeppesen. La flora. Vol.1, 2.
Toccata. No.11.
In: Somma. Musiche vocali e strumentali sacre e profane, sec. XVII–XVIII–XIX. Vol.2.
Vocal music.
In: Delsarte. Archives du chant. Livr.16. No.5.
In: Gevaert. Les gloires de l'Italie. Vol.1.
SCARLATTI, DOMENICO, 1685–1757.
Opere complete per clavicembalo. 10v. and Suppl.

—— Indice tematico delle sonate per clavicembalo. 36, [1] p.
Selections.
In: Crotch. Specimens of various styles of music. Vol.1.
Airs.
In: Prunières. Les maîtres du chant. Recueil.1.
Arias.
In: Parisotti. Arie antiche. Bd.1.
Composizioni.
In: I classici della musica italiana. Vol.31.
Keyboard music.
In: Clementi. Clementi's Selection of practical harmony. Vol.2.
In: Esposito. Early Italian piano music.
In: Farrenc. Le trésor des pianistes. Vol.6/7.
In: Georgii. Keyboard music of the Baroque and Rococo. Vol.2.
In: Oesterle. Early keyboard music. Vol.2.
In: Pauer. Alte Klavier-Musik. 2d series. Pt.1.
In: Roitzsch. Alte Klavier-Musik.
In: Tagliapietra. Antologia di musica antica e moderna per pianoforte. Bd.11.
Organ music.
In: Cantantibus organis. Vol.6.
Sonate. Cembalo o pianoforte.
In: Paoli. Sonate italiane del secolo XVIII per cembalo o pianoforte.
Sonate per pianoforte.
In: I classici della musica italiana. Raccolta nazionale delle musiche italiane. Quad. 126–130.
Sonata in C minor.
In: Parrish. Masterpieces of music before 1750. No.42.
Stabat Mater; Quattro sonate.
In: Somma. Musiche vocali e strumenti sacre a profane, sec. XVII–XVIII–XIX. Vol.1, 3.
2 Studien.
In: Pauer. Alte Meister. No.36.
2 Terzette und Duett; 8 Arien. Aus der Oper "Tetyde auf Skyros."
In: Florilegium musicae antiquae. Vol.5, 6.
SCHAERER, MELCHIOR, ca.1600.
(var. sp.: Schärer).
Choral music.
In: Antiqua Chorbuch. Vol.1. Heft 4; Vol.2. Heft 3.
Newe deudsche Lieder.
In: Zeitschrift für Spielmusik. No.54.
SCHÄFER.
Kinderlieder.
In: Zeitschrift für Spielmusik. No.179.
SCHAFFRATH, CHRISTOPH, 1709–1763.
Keyboard music.
In: Farrenc. Le trésor des pianistes. Vol.11.
Sonate in A-dur. Für obligates Cembalo und Viola da Gamba.
In: Kammersonaten. No.15.
Trio in Do magg per 3 Violini.
In: Riemann. Collegium musicum. No.71.
SCHALLER, ERWIN.
Hirtenlieder aus dem oberösterreichischen Salzkammergut.
In: Hausmusik. No.78.
Der Jahreskreis.
In: Hausmusik. No.33, 45, 54, 55.
Lieder um Ostern; Volkslieder um Satz für eine Singstimme und zwei bis drei instrumente
In: Hausmusik. No.132.
Lieder um Weihnacht.
In: Hausmusik. No.134.
Totenlieder; Volkslieder im Satz für zwei Knaben- oder Frauenstimmen.
In: Hausmusik. No.73.
SCHAPF, GEORG.
Organ music.
In: Raugel. Quarante-six pièces pour orgue ou harmonium.
SCHARFF, ERICH.
Alte Lieder.
In: Zeitschrift für Spielmusik. No.66.
Weihnacht.
In: Zeitschrift für Spielmusik. No.15.
SCHASCHIN.
Vocal music.
In: Sammlung russischer Romanzen. No.147, 172.
SCHEDEL, DR. HARTMANN.
Das Liederbuch.
In: Das Erbe deutscher Musik. 1.Reihe. Vol.40.
SCHEDELSCHES LIEDERBUCH.
In: Antiqua Chorbuch. Vol.2. Heft 1.
SCHEIBE, JOHANN ADOLF, 1708–1776.
Concerto a 4 für Alt-Blockflöte, 2 Violinen und Basso Continuo.
In: Moecks Kammermusik. Vol.41.
SCHEIDEMANN, HEINRICH, ca.1596–1663.
Keyboard music.
In: Tagliapietra. Antologia di musica antica e moderna per pianoforte. Bd.6.
Organ music.
In: Buszin. Organ series. Vol.1.
In: Corpus of early keyboard music. Vol.10, Pt.2.
In: Dietrich. Elf Orgelchörale des siebzehnten Jahrhunderts.
In: Keller. Achtzig Choralvorspiele deutscher Meister des 17. und 18. Jahrhunderts.
In: Klein. The first four centuries of music for the organ from Dunstable to Bach (1370–1749).
In: Organum. 4.Reihe. Nr.1.
In: The parish organist. Vol.7–8.
In: Straube. Choralvorspiele alter Meister.
SCHEIDLER, CHRISTIAN GOTTLIEB, 18th CENTURY.
Sonata, D-dur.
In: Hausmusik. No.40.
SCHEIDT, SAMUEL, 1587–1654.
Werke. v.1–
Ausgewählte Werke für Orgel und Klavier. 145p.
Das Görlitzer Tabulaturbuch vom Jahre 1650. 81p.
Cantilena anglica fortuna. Organ.
In: Guilmant. École classique de l'orgue. No.14.
Canzon Bergamasca für 3 Violine, Viola, Violoncello.
In: Hortus musicus. No.96.
Canzon super Intradem Aechiopicam für 3 Violinen, Viola, Violoncello.
In: Hortus musicus. No.140.
Chamber music.
In: Riemann. Old chamber music. Vol.2.
Choral music.

In: Chor-Archiv.
In: Engel. Three centuries of choral music. Vol.4.
Gelobet seist du, Jesu Christ.
In: Zeitschrift für Spielmusik. No.246.
Keyboard music.
In: Apel. Musik aus früher Zeit für Klavier. Bd.1.
In: Tagliapietra. Antologia di musica antica e moderna per pianoforte. Bd.6.
Organ music.
In: Auler. Spielbuch für Kleinorgel. Vol.1.
In: Bonnet. Historical organ-recitals. Vol.1.
In: Buszin. Organ series. Vol.1.
In: Dietrich. Elf Orgelchörale des siebzehnten Jahrhunderts.
In: Guilmant. Concert historique d'orgue.
In: Keller. Achtzig Choralvorspiele deutscher Meister des 17. und 18. Jahrhunderts.
In: Klein. The first four centuries of music for the organ from Dunstable to Bach (1370–1749).
In: Liber organi. Bd.6.
In: The Liturgical Music Press, Inc. Masterpieces of organ music. Folio 4, 5, 15, 17, 18, 19, 53.
In: Organum. 4.Reihe. Nr.21.
In: The parish organist. Vol.1–4, 5–6, 7–8.
In: Peeters. Anthologia pro organo. Vol.1, 3.
In: Pierront. Cent versets de magnificat.
In: Rohr. Orgelspiel im Kirchenjahr.
In: Schweiger. A brief compendium of early organ music.
In: Straube. Alte Meister.
In: Straube. Alte Meister des Orgelspiels.
In: Straube. Choralvorspiele alter Meister.
In: Vereniging voor Nederlandsche Muziekgeschiedenis. Uitgave. No.3.
Zwei Paduanen für drei Blockflöten, Gambe (Laute, Cello) und B.C.
In: Musica practica. No.19.
Spielmusik. Heft I, II.
In: Nagels Musik-Archiv. No.179, 180.
Suite für fünf Streicher oder Bläser und Generalbass.
In: Nagels Musik-Archiv. No.137.
15 Symphonien für 2 Violinen (oder andere Melodie-Instrumente), Violoncello, Bass ad lib., Klavier (Orgel).
In: Antiqua Edition. Von 3 Instrumenten an.
Tabulatura nova for organ.
In: Denkmäler deutscher Tonkunst. [1.Folge]. Vol.1.
Fünfstimmige Tänze.
In: Zeitschrift für Spielmusik. No.184.
Weihnachtsmusik. Für Klavier oder Orgel.
In: Nagels Musik-Archiv. No.95.
SCHEIFFELHUT, JAKOB, 1647-1709.
Siebente Suite aus dem "Lieblichen frühlings Anfang."
In: Musikschätze der Vergangenheit.
SCHEIN, JOHANN HERMANN, 1586–1630.
Sämtliche Werke. 7v.
Neue Ausgabe sämtliche Werke. v.1– .
Selections.
In: Leichtentritt. Deutsche Hausmusik aus vier Jahrhunderten.
Chamber music.
In: Riemann. Old chamber music. Vol.2.
Choral music.
In: Antiqua chorbuch. Vol.1. Heft 5; Vol.2. Heft 5.
In: Chorbuch für die Kirchenchöre Sachsens.
In: Engel. Three centuries of choral music. Vol.4.
Christmas chorale; Who with grieving soweth.
In: Dessoff choir series. No.7, 19.
Erschienen ist der herrliche Tag.
In: Parrish. A treasury of early music. No.38.
Motets.
In: Das Chorwerk. No.12, 14.
Der 116. Psalm.
In: Das Chorwerk. No.36.
2 Fünfstimmige Suiten.
In: Zeitschrift für Spielmusik. No.43.
Suite aus "Banchetto Musicale."
In: Schering. Perlen alter Kammermusik.
4-stimmige Suitensätze.
In: Zeitschrift für Spielmusik. No.49.
Waldliederlein.
In: Zeitschrift für Spielmusik. No.89.
SCHELLE, JOHANN, d.1701.
Church cantatas.
In: Denkmäler deutscher Tonkunst. [1.Folge]. Vol.58–59.
SCHENK, ERICH, 1902– . ed.
The Italian trio sonata.
In: Anthology of music. Vol.7.
Salzburger Triosonate.
In: Hausmusik. No.95.
SCHENK, JOHANN, 17th CENTURY.
Der Dorfbarbier.
In: Denkmäler der Tonkunst in Österreich. Vol.66. (Jg.XXXIV).
Konzert in Es-dur für Harfe und Orchester.
In: Diletto musicale. No.113.
Le Nymphe di Rheno.
In: Das Erbe deutscher Musik. 1.Reihe. Vol.44.
Quartett für Flöte, 2 Englischhörner und Fagott.
In: Diletto musicale. No.142.
Scherzi musicali per la viola da gamba.
In: Vereniging voor Nederlandsche Muziekgeschiedenis. Uitgave. No.28.
SCHEREMETIEFF.
Vocal music.
In: Sammlung russischer Romanzen. No.312.
SCHERER, SEBASTIAN ANTON, 1631–1712.
Oeuvres d'orgue.
In: Guilmant. Archives des maîtres de l'orgue. Vol.8.
SCHETKY, JOHANN GEORG CHRISTOPH, 1740–1824.
12 Violoncello-Duette. Heft I–II.
In: Moecks Kammermusik. Vol.70, 71.
SCHEURE, D'OUDE.
Selections.
In: Maldéghem. Trésor musical.
SCHIASSI, GAETANO MARIA, d.1754.
(var. sp.: Schiasse).
Concerto.
In: Nagels Musik-Archiv. No.101.
Konzertante Weihnachtsmusik.
In: Nagels Musik-Archiv. No.182.

Weihnachts-Symphonie für Streichorchester und Orgel oder Cembalo.
In: Musikschätze der Vergangenheit.
SCHIBLER, ARMIN, 1920– .
Elegische Musik. Op.52.
In: Collegium musicae novae. No.37.
Festlicher Introitus (2 Flöte, 2 Klarinette, Klavier/ Cembalo, Streicher).
In: Collegium musicae novae. No.59.
Kleine konzertante Suite für Streichorchester.
In: Collegium musicae novae. No.25.
SCHICKHARD, JOHANN CHRISTIAN, 18th CENTURY.
(var. sp.: Johann Chr. Schickhardt).
Sonate (Cm).
In: Moffat. Trio-Sonaten alter Meister. No.18.
Sonate (Dm). Violin and piano.
In: Moffat. Meister-Schule der alten Zeit. Violin-Sonaten. No.31.
Trio-Sonate F-dur.
In: Gitarre-Kammermusik. No.15.
SCHIEFFERDECKER, JOHANN CHRISTIAN, 1679–1732.
Organ music.
In: Das Erbe deutscher Musik. 1.Reihe. Vol.9.
SCHIERBECK, POUL, 1888–1949.
Adrienne Lecouvreur. Radio-Rapsodi, op.49.
In: Samfundet til Udgivelse af dansk Musik. Ser.III. No.104.
Akademisk Festmusik. Op.17.
In: Samfundet til Udgivelse af dansk Musik. Ser.III. No.41.
Fête galante. Op.25. Opera.
In: Samfundet til Udgivelse af dansk Musik. Ser.III. No.118.
Haxa. For Sopran solo or Orkester med Orgel. Op.48.
In: Samfundet til Udgivelse af dansk Musik. Ser.III. No.148.
Kantate. Op.16.
In: Samfundet til Udgivelse af dansk Musik. Ser.III. No.41.
Natten. For Klaver og Orkester. Op.41.
In: Samfundet til Udgivelse af dansk Musik. Ser.III. No.139.
Ouverture "Fête galante." Op.25.
In: Samfundet til Udgivelse af dansk Musik. Ser.III. No.73.
Songs.
In: Samfundet til Udgivelse af dansk Musik. Suppl. 1925–26.
Tre italienske Duetter. Op.28.
In: Samfundet til Udgivelse af dansk Musik. Ser.III. No.55.
SCHIERI, FRITZ, 1922– .
Deutsche Ordinariumsmesse.
In: Christophorus-Chorwerk. Heft 45.
Die Eigengesänge des Christkönigsfestes.
In: Christophorus-Chorwerk. Heft 32.
Zwei Pfingstchöre "Heiliger Geist!"
In: Christophorus-Chorwerk. Heft 4.
Proprium in Festo Corporis Christi.
In: Christophorus-Chorwerk. Heft 25.
SCHIFF.
Vocal music.
In: Sammlung russischer Romanzen. No.74.
SCHIKHARDT, JEAN CHRISTIAN.
Ciacona.
In: L'école du violon au XVIIe et XVIIIe siècle. No.1295.
SCHILDT, MELCHIOR, 1592–1667.
Organ music.
In: Keller. Orgelvorspiele.
In: The Liturgical Music Press, Inc. Masterpieces of organ music. Folio 45.
In: Organum. 4.Reihe. Nr.2.
SCHILLING, HANS LUDWIG.
Suite für Sopran- Blockflöten oder Oboe und Klavier.
In: Moecks Kammermusik. Vol.502.
SCHILOFFSKY.
Vocal music.
In: Sammlung russischer Romanzen. No.166.
SCHINCK, ADOLPH.
Grosser Tusch und Fantaren auf "Der Zauber der weissen Rose."
In: Thouret. Musik am preussischen Hofe. No.12.
SCHINDLER, WALTER.
Partita über den Choral "Nun ruhen alle Wälder."
In: Die Orgel. Reihe I. Nr.4.
Praeludium und Ricercare für Orgel.
In: Die Orgel. Reihe I. Nr.3.
Kleine Toccata für die Orgel.
In: Die Orgel. Reihe I. Nr.1.
SCHISKE, KARL, 1916– .
Erstes Streichquartett, Op.4.
In: Hausmusik. No.34.
Drei kleine Suiten, Op.15a–c.
In: Hausmusik. No.88.
Kleine Suite, für Klavier. Op.1.
In: Hausmusik. No.126.
SCHLENSOG, MARTIN, 1897– .
Festliche Musik.
In: Zeitschrift für Musik. No.189.
Der Jahreskreis.
In: Zeitschrift für Musik. No.13.
Bei Schäfern und Hirten.
In: Zeitschrift für Musik. No.41.
3 Stücke für 2 Blockflöten und Klavier.
In: Zeitschrift für Spielmusik. No.25.
7 Tanzweisen für Sopran-Blockflöte und Klavier.
In: Zeitschrift für Spielmusik. No.22.
SCHLICK, ARNOLD, fl.1512.
(var. sp.: Arnolt Schlick).
Spiegel der Orgelmacher und Organisten. 1932, 1937, 1951. 49p., 39p., 47p.
Tabulaturen etlicher Lobgesang und Lidlein uff die Orgeln und Lauten. 61p.
Organ music.
In: Klein. The first four centuries of music for the organ from Dunstable to Bach (1370–1749).
In: The Liturgical Music Press, Inc. Masterpieces of organ music. Folio 51.
In: Orgue et liturgie. Vol.2.
In: Straube. Alte Meister des Orgelspiels.
SCHLÖGER, MATTHAEUS.
Instrumental music.
In: Denkmäler der Tonkunst in Österreich. Vol.31. (Jg.XV/2).
SCHLÜTER, GUSTAV.
Ein niederdeutscher Tageskreis.
In: Zeitschrift für Spielmusik. No.64.

SCHMEITZEL, WOLFGANG, ca.1500–1561.
Choral music.
In: Antiqua Chorbuch. Vol.2. Heft 2.
SCHMELZER, JOHANN HEINRICH, ca.1630–1680.
Dance music.
In: Denkmäler der Tonkunst in Österreich. Vol.56. (Jg.XXVIII/2).
Duodena selectarum sonatarum. (1659).
In: Denkmäler der Tonkunst in Österreich. Vol.105.
Masses.
In: Denkmäler der Tonkunst in Österreich. Vol.49. (Jg.XXV/1).
Sacro-profanus concentus musices fidium aliorumque instrumentorum (1662).
In: Denkmäler der Tonkunst in Österreich. Vol.111/112.
Violin sonatas.
In: Denkmäler der Tonkunst in Österreich. Vol.93.
SCHMID, BERNHARD DER ÄLTERE, 1528–1592.
Organ music.
In: Cantantibus organis. Vol.6.
SCHMID, BERNHARD DER JÜNGERE, b.1548.
Organ music.
In: Cantantibus organis. Vol.6.
SCHMID, BERNHARD.
Gagliarda.
In: Guilmant. Répertoire des concerts du Trocadéro. Vol.4.
Organ music.
In: Cantantibus organis. Vol.7, 8.
In: Raugel. Quarante-six pièces pour orgue ou harmonium.
SCHMIDT, HEINRICH, 1861–1923.
Märsche und Signale der deutschen Wehrmacht.
In: Musikalische Formen in historischen Reihen. Bd.15.
SCHMIDT, JOHANN CHRISTOPH, d.1728.
Instrumental music.
In: Schmid. Musik am sächsischen Hofe. Bd.6.
SCHMIERER, JOHANN ABRAHAM, 17th CENTURY.
Zodiacus.
In: Denkmäler deutscher Tonkunst. [1.Folge]. Vol.10.
In: Organum. 3.Reihe. Nr.31.
SCHMITZ, FRANZ ARNOLD, 1893– . ed.
Oberitalienische Figuralpassionen des 16. Jahrhunderts.
In: Musikalische Denkmäler. Bd.1.
SCHNEIDER, EDWARD FABER, 1872–1950.
Violin and piano music.
In: The Wa-Wan series of American compositions.
SCHNEIDER, FRIEDRICH, 1786–1853.
Kyrie.
In: Königliche Akademie der Künste. Auswahl vorzüglicher Musik-Werke. No.25.
Vocal music.
In: Hullah. Vocal scores. I. Sacred.
SCHNEIDER, JOHANN, 1702–1787.
Organ music.
In: Das Erbe deutscher Musik. 1.Reihe. Vol.9.
In: The Liturgical Music Press, Inc. Masterpieces of organ music. Folio 17.
SCHNEIDER, LORENZ.
3 Duos für 2 Violinen.
In: Musikschätze der Vergangenheit.
SCHNITTELBACH, NATAN, 1633–1667.
Suite für Streicher und Cembalo.
In: Organum. 3.Reihe. Nr.17.
SCHOBERT, JOHANN, d.1767.
Selected works.
In: Denkmäler deutscher Tonkunst. [1.Folge]. Vol.39.
Selections.
In: Crotch. Specimens of various styles of music. Vol.3.
Keyboard music.
In: Georgii. Keyboard music of the Baroque and Rococo. Vol.3.
Minuette. Allegro molto.
In: Köhler. Les maîtres du clavecin. Heft 12.
In: Pauer. Alte Meister. No.39.
Quartet in F moll. Op.7, Nr.2. Für 2 Violinen, Violoncell und Klavier.
In: Riemann. Collegium musicum. No.50.
Sechs Sinfonien für Cembalo mit Begleitung von Violine und Hörnern ad libitum. Op.9. und Op.10.
In: Das Erbe deutscher Musik. Sonderreihe. Vol.4.
Sonata. Piano. Op.I, No.2; Op.XVII, No.2.
In: Reeser. De klaviersonate.
Sonata A-dur für Konzertierendes Cembalo und Violine, Op.9, Nr.2.
In: Nagels Musik-Archiv. No.199.
Klaviertrio Es-dur. Für Klavier, Violine und Violoncello. Op.6, Nr.1.
In: Nagels Musik-Archiv. No.197.
Klaviertrio F-dur, Op.16, Nr.4.
In: Nagels Musik-Archiv. No.134.
SCHOEFFER, PETER, *see* SCHÖFFER, PETER.
SCHOENBERG, ARNOLD, *see* SCHÖNBERG, ARNOLD.
SCHOENDLINGER, ANTON, *see* SCHÖNDLINGER, ANTON.
SCHOENFELD, JOHANN PHILIPP, *see* SCHÖNFELD, JOHANN PHILIPP.
SCHOENFELDER, GEORG, *see* SCHÖNFELDER, GEORG.
SCHÖFFER, PETER, 16th CENTURY.
(var. sp.: Schoeffer).
Liederbuch. (1513).
In: Das Chorwerk. No.29.
Alte Liedsätze, aus Peter Schöffers Liederbuch.
In: Nagels Musik-Archiv. No.97.
Fünfzehn deutsche Lieder.
In: Denkmäler der Tonkunst in Württemberg. Heft 2.
SCHOLLUM, ROBERT, 1913– .
Im Frühtau zu Berge.
In: Hausmusik. No.42.
Klavierwerke oberösterreichischer Komponisten.
In: Hausmusik. No.182.
Konturen. Op.59b.
In: Collegium musicae novae. No.39.
SCHOLTZE, JOHANN SIGISMUND, *see* SCHOLZE, JOHANN SIGISMUND.
SCHOLZ, A. J.

6 Quartettini, 1–3, 4–6.
In: Hausmusik. No.15, 27.
SCHOLZE, JOHANN SIGISMUND, 1705–1750.
(var. sp.: Johann Sigismund Scholtze; Sperontes, pseud.).
Lieder.
In: Moser. Alte Meister des deutscher Liedes. 30 Gesänge. No.17, 18.
In: Moser. Alte Meister des deutschen Liedes. 46 Gesänge. No.28, 29.
Singende Muse an der Pleisse.
In: Denkmäler deutscher Tonkunst. [1.Folge]. Vol.35–36.
In: Organum. 2.Reihe. Nr.13–14.
In: Zeitschrift für Spielmusik. No.101.
SCHÖNBERG, ARNOLD, 1874–1951.
(var. sp.: Schoenberg).
The complete works. 29v.
Klavierstück.
In: New music. Vol.5. No.3. Apr. 1932.
Variations on a recitative. Organ.
In: Contemporary organ series. No.13.
SCHÖNDLINGER, ANTON.
(var. sp.: Schoendlinger).
Partita über "O Heiland, reiss die Himmel auf."
In: Zeitschrift für Spielmusik. No.260.
SCHÖNFELD, JOHANN PHILIPP, 1742–1790.
(var. sp.: Schoenfeld).
Marsch des Regiments.
In: Thouret. Musik am preussischen Hofe. No.8.
SCHÖNFELDER, GEORG, ca.1520.
(var. sp.: Schoenfelder).
Choral music.
In: Antiqua Chorbuch. Vol.2. Heft 1.
SCHOP, JOHANN, d.ca.1664.
Vom Himmel hoch, da komm ich her.
In: Nagels Musik-Archiv. No.69.
SCHREM, JOH.
Organ music.
In: Moser. Frühmeister der deutschen Orgelkunst.
SCHREYER, WILHELM.
Kleine Abendkantate.
In: Zeitschrift für Spielmusik. No.70.
Kleine Weihnachtsmusik.
In: Zeitschrift für Spielmusik. No.51.
SCHROEDER, HERMANN, 1904– .
Organ music.
In: The parish organist. Vol.7–8.
Uns kommt ein Schiff gefahren.
In: Bausteine für Musikerziehung und Musikpflege. B 145.
Die Weihnachtsgeschichte.
In: Bausteine für Musikerziehung und Musikpflege. B 132.
SCHROETER, JOHANN SAMUEL, *see* SCHRÖTER, JOHANN SAMUEL.
SCHROETER, LEONHART, *see* SCHRÖTER, LEONHART.
SCHRÖTER, JOHANN SAMUEL, d.1788.
(var. sp.: Schroeter).
Konzert C-dur, für Klavier und Streichorchester, Op.3, Nr.3.
In: Concertino.
SCHRÖTER, LEONHART, ca.1532–ca.1601.
(var. sp.: Schroeter; Leonhard Schröter).
Selections.
In: Ambros. Auserwählte Tonwerke.
Choral music.
In: Antiqua Chorbuch. Vol.1. Heft 2.
Wo der Herr nicht das Haus Bauet. Der 127. Psalm.
In: Chor-Archiv.
SCHTSCHERBATSCHOW, WLADIMIR WLADIMIROWITSCH, 1889–1952.
(var. sp.: Schtscherbatscheff).
Vocal music.
In: Sammlung russischer Romanzen. No.228.
SCHUBART, CHRISTIAN FRIEDRICH DANIEL, 1739–1791.
Lieder.
In: Moser. Alte Meister des deutschen Liedes. 30 Gesänge. No.26.
In: Moser. Alte Meister des deutschen Liedes. 46 Gesänge. No.42.
SCHUBERT, FRANZ PETER, 1797–1828.
Werke. 10v.
Werke. 21v. and Revisionsbericht.
—— Reprint. [1965–].
Neue Ausgabe sämtlicher Werke. 8 series.
Klavier-Werke. 7v.
Werke für Klavier. 5v.
Atzenbrugger Tänze für Klavier.
In: Diletto musicale. No.169.
Fünf Deutsche mit Coda und sieben Trios für Streicher.
In: Concertino.
Deutsche Tanze, Ländler, Walzer, Menuette, Ecossaisen.
In: Corona. Vol.23.
Feiermusik.
In: Corona. Vol.30.
Piano pieces. (Complete). Vol.II.
In: Lea pocket scores. No.58.
Keyboard music.
In: Tagliapietra. Antologia di musica antica e moderna per pianoforte. Bd.15.
Lieder. Vol.I–VII.
In: Lea pocket scores. No.23, 24, 112–116.
Fünf erste Lieder.
In: Musikalische Seltenheiten. Bd.4.
Lieder der Liebe.
In: Hausmusik. No.16.
Part music.
In: Hullah. Part music. Class A.2. Vol.2.
All string quartets. (1–6, 7–11, 12–15).
In: Lea pocket scores. No.51/52/53.
Piano quintet in A. ("Trout"), Op.114; String quintet in C. Op.163.
In: Lea pocket scores. No.111.
Salva regina.
In: Für Kenner und Liebhaber. No.14.
Serenade (Ständchen, Op.135).
In: Dessoff choir series. No.15.
The piano sonatas. (1–8, 9–12, 13–15).
In: Lea pocket scores. No.41/42/43.
Tänze.
In: Zeitschrift für Spielmusik. No.264.
Wiener Tänze.
In: Zeitschrift für Spielmusik. No.107.
The piano trios. (Op.99, 100, 148).
In: Lea pocket scores. No.110.
Siebzehn Valses Sentimentales. Op.50a.

In: Moser. Das Musikkränzlein. No.11.
Complete violin-piano works.
In: Lea pocket scores. No.17.
Wanderer fantasy, Op.15; Eight impromptus, Op.90, 142; Moments musicaux, Op.94.
In: Lea pocket scores. No.29.
SCHUBERT, HEINO.
Ich bin das Brot des Lebens.
In: Christophorus-Chorwerk. Heft 34.
Missa für dreistimmigen gemischten Chor und obligate Orgel.
In: Christophorus-Chorwerk. Heft 24.
Drei Motetten.
In: Christophorus-Chorwerk. Heft 43.
SCHUBERT, KURT, 1891– . ed.
Die Programm-Musik.
In: Musikalische Formen in historischen Reihen. Bd.13.
SCHUBIGER, ANSELM, 1815–1888.
Musikalische Spizilegien.
In: Publikationen älterer praktischer und theoretischer Musikwerke. Jahrg.4, Pt.2.
SCHUCKIN' OF THE CORN.
Folk song from Tennessee. Arr. by W. Preston.
In: Music Press, Inc. [Choral series]. Vol.96.
SCHUELER, KARL, *see* SCHÜLER, KARL.
SCHUERMANN, GEORG CASPAR, *see* SCHÜRMANN, GEORG CASPAR.
SCHUETZ, HEINRICH, *see* SCHÜTZ, HEINRICH.
SCHUETZE, G., *see* SCHÜTZE, G.
SCHUIJT.
Three madrigals.
In: Vereniging voor Nederlandsche Muziekgeschiedenis. Uitgave. No.5.
SCHÜLER, KARL.
(var. sp.: Schueler).
Es waren zwei Königskinder.
In: Zeitschrift für Spielmusik. No.7.
Klänge von unterwegs.
In: Zeitschrift für Spielmusik. No.110, 115.
SCHULTZ, CHRISTOPH, 1606–1683.
Das bittere Leiden und Sterben unsers Herren und Erlösers Jesu Christi.
In: Hirsch. Veröffentlichungen. [Bd.].10.
SCHULTZ, FERDINAND, *see* SCHULZ, FERDINAND.
SCHULTZ, HELMUT, 1904–1945.
Das Madrigal als formideal.
In: Publikationen älterer Musik. Jahrg.10.
SCHULTZ, JOHANN ABRAHAM PETER, 1747–1800.
(var. sp.: Schulz).
Christi Død. Oratorium.
In: Samfundet til Udgivelse af dansk Musik. Ser.I. No.13.
Lieder.
In: Moser. Alte Meister des deutschen Liedes. 46 Gesänge. No.40.
In: Reimann. Das deutsche Lied. Vol.1, 3, 4.
Serenata in Walde zu singen.
In: Moecks gelbe Musikhefte. Vol.50.
SCHULTZ, JOHANNES, d.1653.
(var. sp.: Johann Schultz).
Choral music.
In: Antiqua Chorbuch. Vol.2. Heft 5.
Musikalischer Lüstgarte.
In: Das Erbe deutscher Musik. 2.Reihe. Niedersachsen. Vol.1.
Aus dem "Musikalischen Lustgarten".
In: Zeitschrift für Spielmusik. No.147.
SCHULTZ, SVEND S., 1913– .
Job. Symfonisk Oratorium.
In: Samfundet til Udgivelse af dansk Musik. Ser.III. No.92.
Sonate for Klaver.
In: Samfundet til Udgivelse af dansk Musik. Ser.III. No.66.
Storstrømsbroen. Orchestra.
In: Samfundet til Udgivelse af dansk Musik. Ser.III. No.110.
Strygekvartet. Nr.4.
In: Samfundet til Udgivelse af dansk Musik. Ser.III. No.158.
SCHULTZE, JOHANN CHRISTOPH, ca. 1733–1813.
Ouvertüre (Suite) I F-dur für 2 Alt-Blockflöten und Basso Continuo.
In: Moecks Kammermusik. Vol.6.
Ouvertüre (Suite) II B-dur; Ouvertüre (Suite) III A-moll.
In: Moecks Kammermusik. Vol.61, 62.
SCHULZ, FERDINAND, 1821–1897.
(var. sp.: Schultz).
Psalmen.
In: Musica sacra . . . ca.1842–1896. Vol.8–10.
SCHULZ, JOHANN ABRAHAM PETER, *see* SCHULTZ, JOHANN ABRAHAM PETER.
SCHUMAN, WILLIAM HOWARD, 1910– .
Música de cámera.
In: Boletín latino-americano de música. Vol.5.
SCHUMANN, ROBERT ALEXANDER, 1810–1856.
Werke. 14v.
Complete works for piano solo. 7v.
Sämtliche Werke für Klavier. 5v.
Album for the young, Op.68; Three sonatas for the young, Op.118; Forest scenes, Op.82.
In: Lea pocket scores. No.95.
Carnaval. Op.9; Fantasiestücke, Op.12; Symphonic etudes, Op.13; Fantasy, Op.17.
In: Lea pocket scores. No.8.
Humoresque, Op.20; Davidsbündler, Op.6; Kinderszenen, Op.15; Kreisleriana, Op.16; Toccata, Op.7.
In: Lea pocket scores. No.20.
Keyboard music.
In: Tagliapietra. Antologia di musica antica e moderna per pianoforte. Bd.16.
Lieder. Vol.I–III.
In: Lea pocket socres. No.25, 117, 118.
Organ music.
In: Bonnet. Historical organ-recitals. Vol.4.
In: Schweiger. A brief compendium of early organ music.
In: Standard series of organ compositions. No.8, 56.
The 3 piano sonatas. (Op.11, 14, 22).
In: Lea pocket scores. No.88.
SCHÜRMANN, GEORG CASPAR, ca.1672–1751.
(var. sp.: Schuermann).

Cantata.
In: Eitner. Cantaten des 17. und 18. Jahrhunderts. Pt.2.
Ludovicus Pius oder Ludwig der Fromme.
In: Publikationen älterer praktischer und theoretischer Musikwerke. Jahrg.19–20.
SCHUSTER, JOSEPH, 1748–1812.
Ave Maria.
In: Schmid. Musik am sächsischen Hofe. Bd.1.
SCHÜTZ, HEINRICH, 1585–1672.
(var. sp.: Schuetz).
Sämtliche Werke. 18v.
Neue Ausgabe sämtliche Werke. 30v.
Selections.
In: Gabrieli. Music of Gabrieli and his time.
Bringt her dem Herren.
In: Schmid. Musik am Sächsischen Hofe. Bd.1.
Choral music.
In: Antiqua Chorbuch. Vol.1. Heft 5; Vol.2. Heft 5.
In: Chor-Archiv.
In: Chorbuch für die Kirchenchöre Sachsens.
In: Dessoff choir series. No.6, 13, 17, 18, 20.
In: Engel. Three centuries of choral music. Vol.4.
In: Rochlitz. Sammlung vorzüglicher Gesangstücke. Bd.2.
Der Herr ist mein Licht.
In: Nagels Musik-Archiv. No.102.
Konzertierende Motette.
In: Einstein. Beispielsammlung zur älteren Musikgeschichte.
Liebster.
In: Organum. 2.Reihe. Nr.17.
Madrigals.
In: Organum. 2.Reihe. Nr.16.
Die Markus-Passion.
In: Moecks gelbe Musikhefte. Vol.34, 35.
Motet. Was betrübst.
In: Königliche Akademie der Künste. Auswahl vorzüglicher Musik-Werke. No.22.
O Herr, hilf.
In: Parrish. Masterpieces of music before 1750. No.33.
Psalm 18, Herzlich lieb hab ich dich, O Herr.
In: Nagels Musik-Archiv. No.17.
Vom reichen Manne und armen Lazarus.
In: Organum. 1.Reihe. Nr.8.
SCHÜTZE, G.
An introduction to Faugues.
In: Institute of Mediaeval Music. Musicological studies. Vol.2.
SCHUYLER, WILLIAM.
Song.
In: The Wa-Wan series of American compositions.
SCHUYT, CORNELIS, 1557–1616.
Vijfstemmige madrigalen. Bundel 1–2.
In: Vereniging voor Nederlandsche Muziekgeschiedenis. Uitgave. No.45.
SCHWANENBERG, JOHANN GOTTFRIED, 1740–1804.
Keyboard music.
In: Farrenc. Le trésor des pianistes. Vol.18.
SCHWARZ-SCHILLING, REINHARD, 1904– .
Choral music.
In: Nagels Männerchor-Blätter. No.8.
SCHWINDEL, FRIEDRICH, 1737–1786.
Quartett in G-dur, für Flöte, Violine (oder für zwei Violinen), Viola und Violoncello.
In: Musikschätze der Vergangenheit.
SCOTLAND–MUSIC (*see also* FOLKSONGS, SCOTTISH).
In: Crotch. Specimens of various styles of music. Vol.1.
In: Dauney. Ancient Scotish melodies.
In: English keyboard music. [No.15].
In: Musica Britannica. Vol.15.
In: Zeitschrift für Spielmusik. No.281.
SCOTUS, PAULUS.
Selections.
In: Ambros. Auserwählte Tonwerke.
Karnevalslieder.
In: Das Chorwerk. No.43.
SCRIABIN, ALEXANDER, *see* SKRIABIN, ALEKSANDR NIKOLAEVICH.
SCRONX, FR.
Organ music.
In: Guilmant. Archives des maîtres de l'orgue. Vol.10.
SCRONX, GHERARDUS.
Organ music.
In: Peeters. Oudnederlandse meesters. Vol.2, 3.
SEARCH, FREDERICK PRESTON, 1889– .
Sextet in F minor for strings.
In: Society for the Publication of American Music. Publications. 15th Season. 1933–34.
SEARLE, HUMPHREY, 1915– .
Piano music.
In: Contemporary British piano music.
SEAY, ALBERT. ed.
Thirty chansons for three and four voices, from Attaingnant's collections.
In: Collegium musicum. Vol.2.
SEBASTIANI, JOHANN, 1622–1683.
Passion-settings.
In: Denkmäler deutscher Tonkunst. [1.Folge]. Vol.17.
Preussische Festlieder.
In: Das Erbe deutscher Musik. 2.Reihe. Ostpreussen und Danzig. Vol.1.
SECANILLA, F.
Sacred music.
In: Eslava y Elizondo. Lira sacro-hispana. 18th century. i.l. and Appendix.
SECHTER, SIMON, 1788–1867.
Mass, Graduale, etc.; Salve regina and Ave Maria; Missa solennis in C.
In: Ecclesiasticon. No.39, 66, 74.
SEEBOTH, MAX, 1904– .
Andreana. Suite für vier Streicher.
In: Collegium musicae novae. No.8.
SEEGER, CHARLES LOUIS, 1886– .
The letter, song for solo voice. Psalm 137. Recitation for solo voice.
In: New music. Vol.26. No.3. Apr.1953.
Música de cámera.
In: Boletín latino-americano de música. Vol.5.

SEEGER, JOSEPH FERDINAND NORBERT, 1716–1782.
(var. sp.: Seegner, Seegr, Josef Ferdinand Norbert Seger).
Fugue F-moll. Organ.
In: Guilmant. École classique de l'orgue. No.13.
Mass in F; Grand mass in E flat; Mass in D.
In: Ecclesiasticon. No.73, 76, 77.
Composizioni per organo. Pt.I, II.
In: Musica antiqua bohemica. Vol.51, 56.
Organ music.
In: Guilmant. École classique de l'orgue. No.21.
In: Musica antiqua bohemica. Vol.12.
In: Organum. 4.Reihe. Nr.22.
In: Orgelwerke. Altböhmischer Meister. Vol.2.
SEEGER, RUTH PORTER (CRAWFORD), 1901–1953.
Diaphonic suite (1930) for solo flute or oboe.
In: New music. Vol.26. No.3. Apr.1953.
Piano study in mixed accents.
In: New music. Vol.6. No.1. Oct.1932.
4 Preludes for piano.
In: New music. Vol.2. No.1. Oct.1928.
String quartet. 1931.
In: New music. Vol.14. No.2. Jan.1941.
SEGER, JOSEF FERDINAND NORBERT, *see* SEEGER, JOSEPH FERDINAND NORBERT.
SEGNI, GIULIO, 1498–1561.
(var. sp.: Julio Segni).
Composizioni per organo.
In: I classici musicali italiani. Vol.1.
SEIFFERT, MAX, 1868–1948.
Georg Philipp Telemann.
In: Denkmäler deutscher Tonkunst. [1.Folge]. Reprint. Suppl. Vol.61/62.
SEIXAS, JOSÉ ANTONIO CARLOS DE, 1704–1742.
Keyboard music.
In: Kastner. Cravistas portuguezes.
80 Sonatas para instrumentos de tecla.
In: Portugaliae musica. Sér.A. Vol.10.
SÉJAN, LOUIS.
Organ music.
In: Raugel. Les maîtres français de l'orgue. Vol.1.
In: Raugel. Les maîtres français de l'orgue aux XVIIème et XVIIIème siècles.
SÉJAN, NICOLAS, 1745–1819.
Organ music.
In: Raugel. Les maîtres français de l'orgue. Vol.2.
SELBY, WILLIAM, 1738–1798.
Organ music.
In: Biggs. A treasury of shorter organ classics.
SELESNEFF.
Vocal music.
In: Sammlung russischer Romanzen. No.150.
SELIMER, J.
Trios. S.S.A.
In: Arion. Vol.2.
SELLE, THOMAS, 1599–1663.
Lieder.
In: Moser. Alte Meister des deutschen Liedes. 30 Gesänge. No.1.
In: Moser. Alte Meister des deutschen Liedes. 46 Gesänge. No.2, 3.
Zwei Kurzmessen.
In: Das Chorwerk. No.90.
Passion nach dem Evangelisten Johannes.
In: Das Chorwerk. No.26.
Vocal Concerto Nr.3, 4.
In: Musikschätze der Vergangenheit.
SENAILLÉ, JEAN BAPTISTE, 1687–1730.
(var. sp.: Senaillié, Senallié).
Allegro.
In: L'école du violon au XVIIe et XVIIIe siècle. No.1293.
Kammer-Sonaten für Violine und Pianoforte.
In: Moffat. Kammer-Sonaten für Violine und Pianoforte. No.11, 25.
Sonate en mi majeur; Sonate en ut mineur.
In: L'école du violon au XVIIe et XVIIIe siècle. No.1250, 1263.
Sonate. Violin and piano.
In: Moffat. Meister-Schule der alten Zeit. Violin-Sonaten. No.20, 26, 30.
SENFL, LUDWIG, ca.1492–1555.
Sämtliche Werke. v.1– .
Works. Vol.1.
In: Denkmäler deutscher Tonkunst. [2.Folge]. Vol.3 (ii).
Selections.
In: Ambros. Auserwählte Tonwerke.
In: Das Erbe deutscher Musik. 1.Reihe. Vol.5, 10, 13, 15, 19b.
Choral music.
In: Antiqua Chorbuch. Vol.1. Heft 1; Vol.2. Heft 2.
In: Engel. Three centuries of choral music. Vol.4.
In: Moser. Die Kantorei der Spätgotik.
In: Rochlitz. Sammlung vorzüglicher Gesangstücke. Bd.1. Pt.1.
Gesänge.
In: Wolf. Chor- und Hausmusik aus älter Zeit. Vol.1.
Instrumental music. (Carmina).
In: Nagels Musik-Archiv. No.53.
Deutsches Lied.
In: Einstein. Beispielsammlung zur älteren Musikgeschichte.
Lieder.
In: Parrish. A treasury of early music. No.32.
In: Publikationen älterer praktischer und theoretischer Musikwerke. Jahrg. 1–3, 8.
In: Schweizer Sing- und Spielmusik. Heft 3.
Motetten.
In: Chor-Archiv. Musica reservata. I, II.
In: Das Chorwerk. No.62.
In: Müller-Blattau. Musica reservata. Vol.1, 2.
Organ music.
In: Klein. The first four centuries of music for the organ from Dunstable to Bach (1370–1749).
In: Liber organi. Bd.8.
In: The Liturgical Music Press, Inc. Masterpieces of organ music. Folio. 65.
In: Musik alter Meister. Heft 9.

SENLECHES.
Secular music.
In: Apel. French secular music of the late fourteenth century.
SENSTIUS; KAI, 1889– .
Concertino for Fløjte and Orkester. Op.5.
In: Samfundet til Udgivelse af dansk Musik. Ser.III. No.46, 59.
Fantasia i D-mol for Orgel.
In: Samfundet til udgivelse af dansk Musik. Ser.III. No.85.
Serenade for Obo, Viola og Fagot. Op.36.
In: Samfundet til Udgivelse af dansk Musik. Ser.III. No.125.
Strygekvartet, 1 A-mol. Op.28.
In: Samfundet til Udgivelse af dansk Musik. Ser.III. No.107.
SEQUENCES.
In: Melodiarium hungariae medii aevi. Vol.1.
SERAPHIN, FRANCISCUS.
Sacred music.
In: Jeppesen. Italia sacra musica. Vol.1.
SERDIN, EBERHARD.
Quartettstücke nach W. A. Mozart's Duetten für 2 Hörner. II.Teil.
In: Zeitschrift für Spielmusik. No.238.
SERINI, GIOVANNI BATTISTA, 18th CENTURY.
Keyboard music.
In: Benvenuti. Cembalisti italiani del settecento.
Sacred music.
In: Latrobe, C. I. Selection of sacred music.
In: Latrobe, J. A. The music of the church.
Sonate.
In: I classici della musica italiana. Vol.29.
In: I classici della musica italiana. Raccolta nazionale delle musiche italiane. Quad. 284.
SERMISY, CLAUDE DE, ca.1490–1562.
(var. sp.: Claudin de Sermisy; Claudin [Sermisy]).
Selections.
In: Maldéghem. Trésor musical.
Chansons.
In: Bordes. Chansonnier du XVe siècle.
In: Brown. Theatrical chansons of the 15th and early 16th centuries.
In: Cauchie. Quinze chansons françaises du XVIe siècle.
In: Expert. Les maîtres musiciens de la Renaissance française. Vol.5.
In: Lesure. Anthologie de la chanson parisienne au XVIe siècle.
In: Musik alter Meister. Heft 1.
In: Publikationen älterer praktischer und theoretischer Musikwerke. Jahrg.27.
Choral music.
In: Engel. Three centuries of choral music. Vol.1.
In: Der Kammerchor. Vol.1.
Duos.
In: Expert. Florilège du concert vocal de la Renaissance. No.8.
Mass.
In: Stein. Twelve Franco-Flemish masses of the early 16th century.
Missa pro defunctis.
In: Musica liturgica. Vol.1. Fasc. 2.
Motets.
In: Attaingnant. Treize livres de motets. Livre 1.
SEROCKI, KAZIMIERZ, 1922– .
Improvisationen für Blockflöten-Quartett.
In: Zeitschrift für Spielmusik. No.255.
SERQUEYRA.
Selections.
In: Pedrell. Treatro lirico español anterior al siglo XIX. Bd.4/5.
SERRANO, BLAS.
Sonatas. Piano.
In: Nin y Castellano. Seize sonates anciennes d'auteurs espagnols.
SESSIONS, ROGER HUNTINGTON, 1896– .
Chorale. (No.1). Organ.
In: Contemporary organ series. No.2.
Duo, for violin and piano.
In: New music. Vol.20. No.4. July 1947.
SEVILLA, 5–I–43 AND PARIS, NOUV. ACQ. FRÇ. 4397. (D. PLAMENAC).
In: Institute of Mediaeval Music. Publications. Vol.8.
SGAMBATI, GIOVANNI, 1841–1914.
Keyboard music.
In: Tagliapietra. Antologia di musica antica e moderna per pianoforte. Bd.17.
SHELLEY, HARRY ROWE, 1858–1947.
Organ music.
In: Bonnet. Historical organ-recitals. Vol.5.
SHEPHERD, ARTHUR, 1880–1958.
Choral music.
In: Music Press, Inc. [Choral series]. Vol.106.
String quartet in E minor.
In: Society for the Publication of American Music. Publications. 16th season. 1934–35.
Songs; Piano music.
In: The Wa-Wan series of American compositions.
Triptych. Soprano and string quartet.
In: Society for the Publication of American Music. Publications. 8th season. 1926–27.
SHEPHERD, JOHN, ca.1520–ca.1563.
Church music.
In: Motett Society. [Collection of ancient church music]. Division 3.
Sechs Responsorien.
In: Das Chorwerk. No.84.
SHIELD, WILLIAM, 1748–1829.
Selections.
In: Engel. Music from the days of George Washington.
In: Fisher. The music that Washington knew.
Part music.
In: Hullah. Part music. Class B.2.
Songs.
In: Potter. Reliquary of English song. Vol.2.
SHIFRIN, SEYMOUR.
4 Canons, for piano.
In: New music. Vol.23. No.4. July 1950.
SICARD, MR., fl.1785.
Selections.
In: Goldman. Landmarks of early American music, 1760–1800.

SICCARDI, HONORIO.
Piano music.
In: Boletín latino-americano de música. Vol.4.
SICHER, FRIDOLIN, 1490–1546.
Organ music.
In: Cantantibus organis. Vol.6, 8.
In: The Liturgical Music Press, Inc. Masterpieces of organ music. Folio 67.
In: Moser. Frühmeister der deutschen Orgelkunst.
In: The parish organist. Vol.5–6.
SIDERITS, JOSEPH.
Vom Schulgesang zur Hansmusik; kleine Stücke für drei Violinen.
In: Hausmusik. No.25.
SIDEROFF.
Vocal music.
In: Sammlung russischer Romanzen. No.177, 178.
SIDON, SAMUEL PETER, *see* SIDOW, SAMUEL PETER.
SIDOW, SAMUEL PETER, 17th CENTURY.
(var. sp.: Samuel Peter Sidon).
Sonate mit Suite für Violine und Generalbass.
In: Organum. 3.Reihe. Nr.23.
SIEBERT, HANS.
Lobt Gott, ihr Christen.
In: Zeitschrift für Spielmusik. No.170.
SIEFERT, PAUL, 1586–1666.
Organ music.
In: Organum. 4.Reihe. Nr.20.
SIEGL, OTTO, 1896– .
Cellomappe I, II.
In: Hausmusik. No.114, 113.
Zwei Chöre zur Muttertagsfeier.
In: Hausmusik. No.80.
Duo-sonatine, Op.138.
In: Hausmusik. No.75.
Geigerstücke, Op.148, 1; Op.148, 2.
In: Hausmusik. No.91, 92.
Lieder steirischer Komponisten, für eine Singstimme und Klavier.
In: Hausmusik. No.112.
Orgelmusik steirischer Komponisten.
In: Hausmusik. No.143.
Sonatine D-moll für Violine und Gitarre.
In: Gittarre-Kammermusik. No.2.
Toccata. Organ.
In: Orgelmusik steirischer Komponisten.
Trio in B-dur, Op.130.
In: Hausmusik. No.77.
Erstes Trio für zwei Violinen und Viola, Op.134a.
In: Hausmusik. No.86.
SIEGMEISTER, ELIE, 1909– .
The strange funeral, for baritone and piano.
In: New music. Vol.9. No.4. July 1936.
SIEPRAWSKI, P.
Fragment aus der Motette "Justus germinavit."
In: Florilegium musicae antiquae. Vol.1.
SIES, JOHANN.
Lied.
In: Denkmäler der Tonkunst in Österreich. Vol.72. (Jg.XXXVII/2).
SIGISMONDO D'INDIA, CAVALIERE, b.end 16th CENTURY.
Airs.
In: Prunières. Les maîtres du chant. Recueil 3.
Madrigal.
In: I classici musicali italiani. Vol.10.
SILCHER, FRIEDRICH, 1789–1860.
Ausgewählte Werke. 10v.
SILVA, ANDREAS DE, 15th–16th CENTURIES.
Lieder.
In: Publikationen älterer praktischer und theoretischer Musikwerke. Jahrg.1–3.
Motets.
In: Attaingnant. Treize livres de motets. Livre 3, 4, 12.
SILVA, PAULO.
Música de cámara.
In: Boletín latino-americano de música. Vol.6.
SIMON DE HASPRE, JOHANNES, *see* HASPRE, JOHANNES SIMON DE.
SIMPSON, CHRISTOPHER, ca.1610–1669.
Variationen über zwei Bassthemen für Viola da Gamba und Cembalo (Klavier).
In: Antiqua Edition. Von 2 Instrumenten an.
SIMPSON, THOMAS, 17th CENTURY.
Chamber music.
In: Riemann. Old chamber music. Vol.2.
"Taffel Consort", 1621.
In: Zeitschrift für Spielmusik. No.273.
SINDING, CHRISTIAN, 1856–1941.
Organ music.
In: Gerhardt. Album nordischer Komponisten für Orgel. Vol.2.
SIQUEIRA, JOSÉ, 1907– .
Música de camara.
In: Boletín latino-americano de música. Vol.6.
SIRET, NICOLAS.
Organ music.
In: Raugel. Les maîtres français de l'orgue. Vol.1.
In: Raugel. Les maîtres français de l'orgue aux XVIIème et XVIIIème siècles.
SIROLI.
Sacred music.
In: Latrobe, C. I. Selection of sacred music.
In: Latrobe, J. A. The music of the church.
SIXTEENTH CENTURY ITALIAN DANCES.
From British Museum Royal Appendix Ms. 59–62.
In: The Penn state music series. No.12.
THE SIXTEENTH-CENTURY PART SONG IN ITALY, FRANCE, ENGLAND AND SPAIN. (ENGEL).
In: Anthology of music. Vol.3.
SJÖBERG, SVANTE LEONARD, 1873–1935.
Sonata for violin and piano, A minor, Op.2.
In: Musikaliska konstföreningen. 1899.
SJÖGREN, JOHANN GUSTAV EMIL, 1853–1918.
Six hymns and psalms.
In: Musikaliska konstföreningen. 1908.
Islandsfärd. Op.18. Men's chorus and orchestra.
In: Musikaliska konstföreningen. 1925.
Organ music.
In: Gerhardt. Album nordischer Komponisten für Orgel. Vol.1.
Five poems for voice and piano, Op.63.
In: Musikaliska konstföreningen. 1914.
Sonata for piano, No.2, A major, Op.44.

In: Musikaliska konstföreningen. 1904.
Seven songs for voice and piano, Op.3.
In: Musikaliska konstföreningen. 1880.
Violin sonata, No.5, A minor, Op.61.
In: Musikaliska konstföreningen. 1914.
SKALKOTTAS, NIKOS, 1904–1943.
Quatre danses grecques.
In: Institut français d'Athènes. Collection. Série musicale. Vol.3.
SKENE MANUSCRIPT.
In: Dauney. Ancient Scotish melodies.
ŠKERJANC, LUCIJAN MARIA, 1900– .
Selections.
In: Slovenska Akademija Znanosti in Umetnosti. Vol.2, 3, 6, 7, 9, 13, 18, 21, 24.
SKÖLD, YNGVE, 1899–
Selections.
In: Svensk sanglyrik. Vol.2.
Fantasy for viola and organ, Op.12.
In: Musikaliska konstföreningen. 1941.
Preludio e fuga. Op.20. For piano.
In: Musikaliska konstföreningen. 1927.
Sonatina for violin and piano, Op.23.
In: Musikaliska konstföreningen. 1927.
SKORZENY, FRITZ, 1900– .
Trio für Flöte, Viola und Gitarre.
In: Gitarre-Kammermusik. No.35.
SKRIABIN, ALEKSANDR NIKOLAEVICH, 1872–1915.
(var. sp.: Alexander Scriabin).
Complete piano works. v.1– .
ŠKROUP, FRANTIŠEK, 1801–1862.
Keyboard music.
In: Musica antiqua bohemica. Vol.20.
SLONIMSKY, NICOLAS, 1894– .
Studies in black and white. Piano.
In: New music. Vol.3. No.1. Oct.1929.
Suite. Arr. of studies in black and white for small ensemble.
In: New music. Special edition.
SLOVAKIA–MUSIC.
In: Slovenska Akademija Znanosti in Umetnosti.
In: Zeitschrift für Spielmusik. No.267.
SMETANA, BEDŘICH, 1824–1884.
Souborná. 4v.
Blanik. ("My country"). Organ.
In: Dickinson. Historical recital series for organ. Vol.2. No.27.
Tabor. ("My country"). Organ.
In: Dickinson. Historical recital series for organ. Vol.2. No.26.
SMIT-VANROTTE, ERICKA.
Constantyn Huygens.
In: Institute of Mediaeval Music. Musical theorists in translation. Vol.4.
SMITH, CHRISTOPHE.
Keyboard music.
In: Farrenc. Le trésor des pianistes. Vol.11.
SMITH, DAVID STANLEY, 1877–1949.
String quartet. Op.46.
In: Society for the Publication of American Music. Publications. 3d season. 1921–22.
String quartet. No.6, in C major.
In: Society for the Publication of American Music. Publications. 18th season. 1936–37.
Sonata for piano and oboe. Op.43.
In: Society for the Publication of American Music. Publications. 7th season. 1925–26.
Sonata. Piano and violin. Op.51.
In: Society for the Publication of American Music. Publications. 5th season. 1923–24.
SMITH, JOHN STAFFORD, ca.1750–1836.
Selections.
In: Fisher. The music that Washington knew.
Part music.
In: Hullah. Part music. 1868 edition.
Vocal music.
In: Hullah. Vocal scores. II. Secular.
SNOW, [MOSES].
Keyboard music.
In: English keyboard music. [No.10].
SODERINI, AGOSTINO, 17th CENTURY.
Selections.
In: Torchi. L'arte musicale in Italia. Bd.3.
Organ music.
In: Fuser. Classici italiani dell'organo.
SÖDERMAN, JOHAN AUGUST, 1832–1876.
(var. sp.: Soederman).
Catholic mass.
In: Musikaliska konstföreningen. 1881.
Ode till glädjen. Men's chorus and orchestra.
In: Musikaliska konstföreningen. 1891.
Qvarnruinen. Ballad for baritone and orchestra.
In: Musikaliska konstföreningen. 1866.
Signe lill's färd. Concert poem.
In: Musikaliska konstföreningen. 1892.
Tannhäuser.
In: Musikaliska konstföreningen. 1860.
SOEDERMAN, JOHANN A., *see* SÖDERMAN, JOHAN AUGUST.
SOHIER.
Chansons.
In: Expert. Les maîtres musiciens de la Renaissance française. Vol.5.
Motets.
In: Attaingnant. Treize livres de motets. Livre 12.
SOKOLOFF, NICOLAI.
Vocal music.
In: Sammlung russischer Romanzen. No.151, 164, 171, 173, 174, 179, 180, 198–200, 229, 306, 307.
SOLAGE.
Secular music.
In: Apel. French secular music of the late fourteenth century.
SOLER, ANTONIO, PADRE, 1729–1783.
Sonatas para instrumentos de tecla. 6v.
Concierto para dos instrumentos de tecla. I–VI.
In: Música hispana. Ser.C. No.3, 4, 1, 5, 6, 8.
Introito and offertoria de defuntos.
In: Eslava y Elizondo Lira sacro-hispana. 18th century. i.l.
Keyboard music.
In: Nin y Castellano. Dix-sept sonates et pièces ancienne d'auteurs espagnols.
Organ music.
In: Biggs. A treasury of shorter organ classics.
In: Pedrell. Antología de organistas clásicos españoles (siglos XVI, XVII y XVIII).
In: Piedelievre. Les anciens maîtres espagnols.

Sis quintets per a instruments d'arc i orgue o clave obligat.
In: Barcelona. Biblioteca Central. Sección de Música. Publicaciones. Vol.9.
Sonatas.
In: Nin y Castellano. Seize sonates anciennes d'auteurs espagnols.
THE SOLO CONCERTO. (ENGEL).
In: Anthology of music. Vol.25.
THE SOLO SONATA. (GIEGLING).
In: Anthology of music. Vol.15.
THE SOLO SONG OUTSIDE GERMAN-SPEAKING COUNTRIES. (NOSKE).
In: Anthology of music. Vol.16.
SOMIS, GIOVANNI BATTISTA, 1686–1763.
Kammersonate.
In: Einstein. Beispielsammlung zur älteren Musikgeschichte.
Sonate en sol majeur.
In: L'école du violon au XVIIe et XVIIIe siècle. No.1275.
Tambourin.
In: L'école du violon au XVIIe et XVIIIe siècle. No.1340.
SOMIS, LORENZO, 1688–1775.
Sonate (G). Violin and piano.
In: Moffat. Meister-Schule der alten zeit. Violin-Sonaten. No.16.
SOMMER, HANS, 1837–1922.
Lied.
In: Reimann. Das deutsche Lied. Vol.1.
SONGS.
In: Anthology of music. Vol.16. (The solo song outside German-speaking countries).
In: Commer. Geistliche und weltliche Lieder aus dem XVI.–XVII. Jahrhundert.
SONGS, AMERICAN (*see also* FOLKSONGS, U.S.; U.S.–MUSIC).
In: Downes. A treasury of American song.
In: The Wa-Wan series of American compositions.
SONGS, DUTCH, *see* SONGS, NETHERLAND.
SONGS, ENGLISH (*see also* ENGLAND-MUSIC; FOLKSONGS, ENGLISH).
In: Arkwright. The Old English edition.
In: Chappell. The ballad literature and popular music of the olden time.
In: Chappell. Old English popular music.
In: Chappell. Old English popular music. A new edition.
In: English songs. No.1– .
In: Hullah. 58 English songs of the 17th and 18th century.
In: Plainsong and Mediaeval Music Society. Publications. (A collection of songs and madrigals.).
In: Potter. Reliquary of English song.
SONGS, FLEMISH.
In: Das Chorwerk. No.92.
SONGS, FRENCH (*see also* CHANSONS; FRANCE–MUSIC).
In: Das Chorwerk. No.61.
SONGS, GERMAN (*see also* ARIAS, GERMAN; DARMSTADT–MUSIC; FOLKSONGS, GERMAN; GERMANY–MUSIC).
In: Anthology of music. Vol.14.
In: Jenaer Liederhandschrift. Der Jenaer Liederhandschrift.
In: Moser. Alte Meister des deutschen Liedes. 30 Gesänge.
In: Moser. Alte Meister des deutschen Liedes. 46 Gesänge.
In: Reimann. Das deutsche geistliche Lied.
In: Reimann. Das deutsche Lied.
In: Das Rostocker Liederbuch. Das Rostocker Liederbuch.
In: Schlick. Tabulaturen etlicher Lobgesang und Lidlein uff die Orgeln und Lauten.
SONGS, ITALIAN (*see also* ITALY–MUSIC).
In: Jeppesen. La flora.
In: Squarcialupi Codex. Der Squarcialupi-Codex, Pal.87.
SONGS, NETHERLAND (*see also* FOLKSONGS, NETHERLAND; NETHERLANDS–MUSIC).
In: Vereniging voor Nederlandsche Muziekgeschiedenis. Uitgave. No.16, 30.
SONGS, SPANISH (*see also* FOLKSONGS, SPANISH: SPAIN–MUSIC).
In: Asenjo y Barbieri. Cancionero musical de los siglos XV y XVI.
In: Bal y Gay. Romances y villancicos españoles del signo XVI.
SONNLEITHNER, CHRISTOPH VON, 1734–1786.
Divertimento in Es dur.
In: Hausmusik. No.19.
SOR, (REAL NAME SORS), FERNANDO, 1778–1839.
(var. sp.: Fernando Sors).
Duo, für zwei Gitarren, Op.34.
In: Hausmusik. No.175.
[Stücke]. Op.25, 35.
In: Hausmusik. No.102.
SORGE, GEORG ANDREAS, 1703–1778.
Organ music.
In: Auler. Spielbuch für Kleinorgel. Vol.2.
SORIANO, FRANCESCO, *see* SURIANO, FRANCESCO.
SOTO, PEDRO DE, 16th CENTURY.
Organ music.
In: Muset. Early Spanish organ music.
SOURWOOD MOUNTAIN.
Folk song from the Appalachians. Arr. by A. Lief.
In: Music Press, Inc. [Choral series]. Vol.99.
SOUSA CARVALHO, JOÃO DE, *see* CARVALHO, JOÃO DE SOUSA.
SOUTHERN, E.
The Buxheim organ book.
In: Institute of Mediaeval Music. Musicological studies. Vol.6.
SOWERBY, LEO, 1895– .
String quartet. Serenade in G major.
In: Society for the Publication of American Music. Publications. 2d season. 1920–21.
Quintet for flute, oboe, clarinet, horn, and bassoon.
In: Society for the Publication of American Music. Publications. 12th season. 1930–31.
Sonata for clarinet (or viola) and piano.
In: Society for the Publication of American Music. Publications. 24th season. 1942–43.
Toccata. Organ.
In: Contemporary organ series. No.1.
Whimsical variations. Organ.

In: Contemporary organ series. No.25.
SPAETH.
Part music.
In: Hullah. Part music. Class C. Sacred.
SPAIN–MUSIC (*see also* FOLKSONGS, SPANISH; SONGS, SPANISH).
In: Asenjo y Barbieri. Cancionero musical de los siglos XV y XVI.
In: Asociación Patriótica Española. Clásicos españoles de la música.
In: Bal y Gay. Romances y villancicos españoles del siglo XVI.
In: Barcelona. Biblioteca Central. Sección de Música. Publicaciones.
In: Cantio sacra. No.21, 35.
In: Das Chorwerk. No.60.
In: Crotch. Specimens of various styles of music. Vol.1.
In: Elúsitiza. Antología musical.
In: Eslava y Elizondo. Lira sacro-hispana.
In: Eslava y Elizondo. Museo orgánico español.
In: Guenther. Collection espagnole.
In: Kastner. Silva iberica.
In: Martínez Torner. Colección de vihuelistas españoles del siglo XVI.
In: Monumentos de la música española.
In: Morphy. Les luthistes espanols du XVIe siècle.
In: Muset. Early Spanish organ music.
In: Música hispana.
In: Nin y Castellano. Dix-sept sonates et pièces anciennes d'auteurs espagnols.
In: Nin y Castellano. Seize sonates anciennes d'auteurs espagnols.
In: Organ album of ten pieces by Spanish composers.
In: Pedrell. Antología de organistas clásicos españoles (siglos XVI, XVII y XVIII).
In: Pedrell. Hispaniae schola musica sacra.
In: Pedrell. Teatro lirico espanol anterior al siglo XIX.
In: Piedelievre. Les anciens maîtres espagnols.
In: Polifonía española.
In: Rubio. Antologia polifonica sacra.
In: Villancicos de diuersos autores. Cancionero de Upsala.
In: Zeitschrift für Spielmusik. No.178, 231.
SPATARO, GIOVANNI, ca.1458–1541.
Selections.
In: Torchi. L'arte musicale in Italia. Bd.1.
Dilucide et Probatissime Demonstratione de Maestro Zoanne Spatario.
In: Hirsch. Veröffentlichungen. [Bd.] 7.
Sacred music.
In: Jeppesen. Italia sacra musica. Vol.1.
SPENDIAROV, ALEKSANDR AFANAS'EVICH, 1871–1928.
[Works]. v.1– .
SPERINDIO, BERTOLDO.
Selections.
In: Torchi. L'arte musicale in Italia. Bd.3.
SPERONTES, PSEUD., *see* SCHOLZE, JOHANN SIGISMUND.
SPERVOGEL.
Tritt ein reines Weib.
In: Arion. Vol.3.
SPETH, JOHANN, d.1709.
Organ music.
In: Commer. Compositionen für Orgel aus dem 16., 17., und 18. Jahrhundert. Heft 5–6.
In: Liber organi. Bd.9.
SPIESS, LINCOLN BUNCE.
Historical musicology.
In: Institute of Mediaeval Music. Musicological studies. Vol.4.
SPINNER, LEOPOLD.
Trio for violin, violoncello and piano.
In: New music. Vol.28. No.4. July 1955.
SPITTA, HEINRICH, 1902– .
Der Marsch.
In: Musikalische Formen in historischen Reichen. Bd.6.
SPOFFORTH, REGINALD, 1770–1827.
Vocal music.
In: Hullah. Vocal scores. II. Secular.
SPOHR, LOUIS, 1784–1859.
Ausgewählte Werke. v.1– .
Neue Auswahl der Werke. v.1– .
Fugue, Lasst uns.
In: Königliche Akademie der Künste. Auswahl vorzüglicher Musik-Werke. No.26.
Lied.
In: Riemann. Das deutsche Lied. Vol.2.
Part music.
In: Hullah. Part music. 1868 edition.
Vocal music.
In: Hullah. Vocal scores. I. Sacred.
SPONTINI, GASPARO, 1774–1851.
Arias.
In: Parisotti. Arie antiche. Bd.3.
SPONTONE, BARTOLOMEO, 16th CENTURY.
Selections.
In: Torchi. L'arte musicale in Italia. Bd.2.
Part music.
In: Hullah. Part music. Class A.2. Vol.2.
Vieni soave e dilettoso Maggio.
In: Squire. Ausgewählte Madrigale und mehrstimmige Gesänge. No.32.
SPORER, THOMAS, ca.1534.
Die erhaltenen Tonwerke des Alt-Strassburger Meisters Thomas Sporer, 1534. 24p.
SQUARCIALUPI CODEX.
Der Squarcialupi-Codex, Pal.87. 359p.
SSJEROFF.
Vocal music.
In: Sammlung russischer Romanzen. No.256, 257, 273.
STABILE, ANNIBALE, 16th CENTURY.
Selections.
In: Musica sacra . . . 1839– . Vol.16.
Io non sò.
In: Arion. Vol.3.
Masses.
In: Monumenta polyphoniae italicae. Vol.1.
STADEN, JOHANN, 1581–1634.
Selected works.
In: Denkmäler deutscher Tonkunst. [2.Folge] Vol.7 (i), 8 (i).
Altdeutsche Tanzsätze.
In: Nagels Musik-Archiv. No.80.
Choral music.
In: Antiqua Chorbuch. Vol.1. Heft 5; Vol.2. Heft 5.

In: Chorbuch für die Kirchenchöre Sachsens. Fünfzehn vier- und fünfstimmige Instrumentalsätze aus dem "Venus-Kraentzlein".
In: Nagels Musik-Archiv. No.119.
STADLER, MAXIMILIAN, 1748–1833.
Selections.
In: Ecclesiasticon. No.22, 23, 35, 36.
2 Sonates suivies d'une fugue. Piano.
In: Répertoire des clavicinistes. Heft 8.
STADLMAIR, HANS, 1929– .
Introduktion und Fuge für Streicher.
In: Collegium musicae novae. No.56.
STADLMAYR, JOHANN, d.1648.
Hymns.
In: Denkmäler der Tonkunst in Österreich. Vol.5 (Jg.III/1).
STAEPS, HANS ULRICH.
Auf unserm Hof daheim; Spielmusik.
In: Hausmusik. No.70.
Rondelli.
In: Zeitschrift für Spielmusik. No.280.
STAGGINS, NICHOLAS, d.1700.
Selections.
In: Smith. Musica antiqua.
STAHLKNECHT.
Psalmen.
In: Musica sacra . . . ca.1842–1896. Vol.8–10.
STAMIC, JAN VÁCLAV, 1717–1757.
Op.6a. Sonata sol maggiore.
In: Musica antiqua bohemica. Vol.28.
STAMITZ, JOHANN WENZEL ANTON, 1717–1757.
Two divertimenti in two parts for one unaccompanied violin.
In: Music for wind instruments by 18th century masters. No.7.
Konzert für Violine in G-dur.
In: Concertino.
Drei Mannheimer Sinfonien.
In: Corona. Vol.38.
Orchestertrios.
In: Antiqua Edition. Von 3 Instrumenten an.
In: Riemann. Collegium musicum. No.1–6, 7, 48, 49.
Orchestral music.
In: Riemann. Mannheim symphonists. Vol.1.
Quartett B-dur.
In: Sondheimer. Werke aus dem 18. Jahrhundert. Nr.2.
Sinfonia pastorale D-dur. Op.4. Nr.2.
In: Musikschätze der Vergangenheit.
Sinfonie A-dur (Frühlingssinfonie); Sinfonie D-dur (Reiter-sinfonie); Sinfonie B-dur.
In: Sondheimer. Werke aus dem 18. Jahrhundert. Nr.27/28, 48.
Sonate (G).
In: Moffat. Trio-Sonaten alter Meister. No.25.
2 Stücke für Violine und Klavier.
In: Sondheimer. Werke aus dem 18. Jahrhundert. Nr.10.
Symphonies.
In: Denkmäler deutscher Tonkunst. [2.Folge]. Vol.3 (i).
STAMITZ, KARL, 1745–1801.
(var. sp.: Carl Stamitz).
Andante. Organ.
In: Dickinson. Historical recital series for organ. Vol.1. No.1.
Andantino aus der Symphonie (Es).
In: Thouret. Musik am preussische Hofe. No.5.
Blaserquintett Es-dur, Op.8, Nr.2. (Weigelt).
In: Alte Music. (Reihe "Leuckartiana").
Concertos. Violoncello.
In: Hortus musicus. No.79, 104, 105.
Duette. Op.27. Nr.1–3, 4–6. Für zwei Flöten (oder Violinen).
In: Nagels Musik-Archiv. No.62, 178.
Duo für Violine und Viola. Op.10/1; Op.10/2.
In: Diletto musicale. No.108, 119.
Orchestral music.
In: Riemann. Mannheim symphonists. Vol.2.
Two quartets for clarinet or flute or oboe, violin, viola, and cello or string quartet.
In: Music for wind instruments by 18th century masters. No.3.
Quartett D-dur für Querflöte, Violine, Viola (Horn in F), Violoncello. Op.VIII/1.
In: Hortus Musicus. No.109.
Quartetto concertante G-dur für Streicher.
In: Concertino.
Orchester-Quartett C-dur für zwei Violinen, Viola und Violoncello.
In: Concertino.
Orchesterquartett A-dur; G-dur.
In: Corona. Vol.67, 68.
Sinfonie Es-dur; Sonate in F-dur.
In: Musikschätze der Vergangenheit.
Sonate D-dur für Viola d'amore und Cembalo (Klavier). Bass-Instrument ad lib.
In: Antiqua Edition. Von 2 Instrumenten an.
Symphonie concertante.
In: Für Kenner und Liebhaber. No.12, 21.
Trio G-dur für 2 Querflöte und Violoncello.
In: Hortus musicus. No.106.
Trio für Flöte, Violine (oder zwei Violinen) und bezifferten Bass, Op.14, Nr.1.
In: Nagels Musik-Archiv. No.33.
Trio-sonata für Flöte, Violine, Violoncell, und Klavier.
In: Riemann. Collegium musicum. No.70.
STANDLEY, 15th CENTURY.
Missa ad fugam reservatam.
In: Documenta polyphoniae liturgicae sanctae ecclesiae romanae. Ser.1. No.6.
Quae est ista.
In: Documenta polyphoniae liturgicae sanctae ecclesiae romanae. Ser.4. No.1.
STANFORD, SIR CHARLES VILLIERS, 1852–1924.
Selections.
In: The music with the form and order of the service to be performed at the coronation of . . . Queen Elizabeth II.
STANLEY, CHARLES JOHN, 1713–1786.
Voluntaries for the organ. 3v.
Organ music.
In: Butcher. English organ music of the eighteenth century. Vol.1.
In: Liber organi. Bd.10.
In: The Liturgical Music Press, Inc. Masterpieces of organ music. Folio 10, 46, 60.

In: Peeters. Anthologia pro organo. Vol.2, 4.
In: Tallis to Wesley. Vol.1, 11, 34.
Sonata G dur für Violine und Pianoforte.
In: Moffat. Kammer-Sonaten für Violine und Pianoforte. No.29.
STAPPEN, CRISPINUS VAN.
Choral music.
In: Smijers. Van Ockeghem tot Sweelinck. Aflg.6.
STARZER, JOSEF, 1726–1787.
Divertimento für Streichquartett oder Streichorchester.
In: Musikschätze der Vergangenheit.
Instrumental music.
In: Denkmäler der Tonkunst in Österreich. Vol.31 (Jg.XV/2).
Konzert in F-dur für Violine und Streichorchester.
In: Diletto musicale. No.82.
STASOV, VLADIMIR VASILIEVITCH, 1824–1906.
Collected works. 3v. (4th vol. added in 1905).
STEFANI, ANDREA.
Selections.
In: Pirrotta. The music of fourteenth-century Italy. Vol.5.
STEFANINI, GIOVANNI BATTISTA, 16th–17th CENTURIES.
(var. sp.: G. Stefani; Steffanini).
Selections.
In: Musica sacra . . . 1839– . Vol.15.
Affetti amorosi.
In: Chilesotti. Biblioteca di rarità musicali. Vol.3.
STEFFAN, JOSEPH ANTON, 1726–1797.
Songs.
In: Denkmäler der Tonkunst in Österreich. Vol.54 (Jg.XXVII/2).
STEFFANI, AGOSTINO, 1654–1728.
Selected compositions.
In: Denkmäler deutscher Tonkunst. [2.Folge]. Vol.6 (ii).
Selections.
In: Crotch. Specimens of various styles of music. Vol.2.
Alarico; Selected operas.
In: Denkmäler deutscher Tonkunst. [2.Folge]. Vol.11 (ii), 12 (i).
Arias.
In: Landshoff. Alte Meister des Bel Canto. Eine Sammlung von Arien. Vol.3.
Duet, Occhi perche.
In: Königliche Akademie der Künste. Auswahl vorzüglicher Musik-Werke. Appendix.
Kammerduette.
In: Denkmäler der Tonkunst. Vol.6.
Ouverture zu Oper "Enrico Leone."
In: Nagels Musik-Archiv. No.141.
Eight songs.
In: Smith College music archives. No.11.
Tassilone.
In: Denkmäler rheinischer musik. Vol.8.
STEFFANINI, GIOVANNI, *see* STEFANINI, GIOVANNI BATTISTA.
STEIBELT, DANIEL, 1765–1823.
Keyboard music.
In: Farrenc. Le trésor des pianistes. Vol.18.
In: Tagliapietra. Antologia di musica antica e moderna per pianoforte. Bd.14.
Rondo C-dur für Klavier.
In: Organum. 5.Reihe. Nr.14.
2 Sonates. Piano.
In: Répertoire des clavicinistes. Heft 4.
STEIGLEDER, ADAM, 17th CENTURY.
Organ music.
In: Auler. Spielbuch für Kleinorgel. Vol.1.
STEIGLEDER, JOHANN ULRICH, 1593–1635.
Organ music.
In: The Liturgical Music Press, Inc. Masterpieces of organ music. Folio 17.
STEINBAUER, OTHMAR.
Die Ros' ist ohn' Warum.
In: Hausmusik. No.72.
STEINER, LUIS.
Kleine Hirtenkantate.
In: Zeitschrift für Spielmusik. No.226.
STELLA, SCIPIONE.
Keyboard music.
In: Corpus of early keyboard music. Vol.24.
STELLHORN, MARTIN, 1914– .
Organ music.
In: The parish organist. Vol.1–4.
STELZER, THEODORE G., 1892– .
Organ music.
In: The parish organist. Vol.1–4.
STEMMELIO, E. G.
Sacred music.
In: Proske. Musica divina. Annus secundus. Tom 3.
In: Proske. Selectus novus missarum. Annus secundus. Tom 3.
STENHAMMAR, PER ULRIK, 1829–1875.
David och Saul. Oratorio.
In: Musikaliska konstföreningen. 1899–1900.
Four songs with piano.
In: Musikaliska konstföreningen. 1861.
STENHAMMAR, WILHELM, 1871–1927.
Ithaka. Op.21.
In: Musikaliska konstföreningen. 1906.
Sången. Op.44. Symphonic cantata.
In: Musikaliska konstföreningen. 1924.
Five songs for voice and piano.
In: Musikaliska konstföreningen. 1928.
String quartet, No.6, D minor, Op.35.
In: Musikaliska konstföreningen. 1928.
ŠTĚPÁN, JOSEF ANTONÍN, 1726–1797.
Concerto in D.
In: Musica antiqua bohemica. Vol.39.
Keyboard music.
In: Musica antiqua bohemica. Vol.14.
Menuette für Klavier.
In: Musica viva historica. Vol.9.
STEPHENS, DAPHNE E. R. ed.
The Wickhambrook lute manuscript.
In: Collegium musicum. Vol.4.
STEPHENSON, KURT, 1899– . ed.
The classics.
In: Anthology of music. Vol.6.
Romanticism in music.
In: Anthology of music. Vol.21.
STERN, ALFRED, arr.
Schweizer Lieder.

In: Schweizer Sing- und Spielmusik.
Heft 1, 2, 4, 5, 8, 11, 12.
STETSENKO, KYRYLO HRYHOROVYCH, 1882–1922.
[Works]. v.1– .
STEVENS, HALSEY, 1908– .
Quintet for flute, strings, and piano.
In: Society for the Publication of American Music. Publications. 29th season. 1947–48.
STEVENS, RICHARD JOHN SAMUEL, 1757–1837.
Part music.
In: Hullah. Part music. Class A.2. Vol.1; Class A.2. Vol.2; Class C. Secular; 1868 edition.
Songs.
In: Potter. Reliquary of English song. Vol.2.
Vocal music.
In: Hullah. Vocal scores. II. Secular.
STICH, JAN VÁCLAV, 1746–1803.
(var. sp.: Johann Wenzel Stich).
Quartet für Horn, Geige, Bratsche, und Violoncello.
In: Hortus musicus. No.93.
Quartett Op.XVIII/1, für Horn, Violine, Viola, Violoncello.
In: Hortus musicus. No.171.
STICHERARIUM, THE HYMNS OF THE.
In: Monumenta musicae byzantinae. Transcripta. Vol.1–2, 10.
STICHERARIUM (REPRODUCTION INTEGRALE DU CODEX VINDOBONENSIS THEOL. GR. 181).
In: Monumenta musicae byzantinae. Série-principale. Vol.1.
STILL, WILLIAM GRANT, 1895– .
Dismal swamp.
In: New music. Orchestra series. No.21.
STINGL, ANTON.
O Herr, mein Gott, wie bist du gross!
In: Christophorus-Chorwerk. Heft 28.
STOBAEUS, JOHANN, *see* STOBÄUS, JOHANN.
STOBÄUS, JOHANN, 1580–1646.
(var. sp.: Johann Stobaeus).
Choral music.
In: Antiqua Chorbuch. Vol.1. Heft 5.
Motetten.
In: Chor-Archiv. Musica Reservata. I.
In: Müller-Blattau. Musica reservata. Vol.1.
Preussische Festlieder.
In: Das Erbe deutscher Musik. 2.Reihe. Ostpreussen und Danzig. Vol.1.
STOCKER, CLARA.
2 Little pieces. Piano.
In: New music. Vol.10. No.3. Apr.1937.
STOESSEL, ALBERT, 1894–1943.
Suite antique. Two violins and piano.
In: Society for the Publication of American Music. Publications. 5th season. 1923–24.
STOKHEM, JOHANNES.
Chanson.
In: Brown. Theatrical chansons of the 15th and early 16th centuries.
STOLTE, SIEGFRIED.
Kleines Konzert für 2 Blockflöten und Klavier.
In: Zeitschrift für Spielmusik. No.224.
STOLTZER, THEODOR.
Zwei Liedsätze.
In: Musica practica. No.17a.
STOLTZER, THOMAS, d.1526.
(var. sp.: Thomas Stolzer).
Ausgewählte Werke.
In: Das Erbe deutscher Musik. 1.Reihe. Vol.22.
Selections.
In: Ambros. Auserwählte Tonwerke.
Choral music.
In: Antiqua Chorbuch. Vol.1. Heft 1; Vol.2. Heft 1.
Fantasien für fünf beliebige Instrumente.
?In: Antiqua Edition. Von 5 Instrumenten an.
Gesänge.
?In: Wolf. Chor- und Hausmusik aus älter Zeit. Vol.1.
Complete collection of Latin hymns and psalms.
In: Denkmäler deutscher Tonkunst. [1.Folge]. Vol.65.
Lieder.
In: Denkmäler der Tonkunst in Österreich. Vol.72. (Jg.XXXVII/2).
In: The Penn state music series. No.4.
In: Publikationen älterer praktischer und theoretischer Musikwerke. Jahrg.1–3.
Ostermesse.
In: Das Chorwerk. No.74.
Der 37. Psalm, erzürne dich nicht.
In: Das Chorwerk. No.6.
STÖLZEL, GOTTFRIED HEINRICH, 1690–1749.
(var. sp.: G. H. Stoelzel).
Cantata.
In: Eitner. Cantaten des 17. und 18. Jahrhunderts. Pt.1.
Choral music.
In: Rochlitz. Sammlung vorzüglicher Gesangstücke. Bd.3.
Enharmonische Sonate.
In: Denkmäler thuringischer Musik. Heft 2.
Instrumental concertos.
In: Denkmäler deutscher Tonkunst. [1.Folge]. Vol.29–30.
Lob und Dank. Kantate.
In: Organum. 1.Reihe. Nr.29.
Sonata a 3; Sonate für Oboe, Violine und Generalbass; Sonate F dur.
In: Riemann. Collegium musicum. No.72, 76, 79.
Triosonate F-moll, für zwei Violinen oder Oboen und Basso Contino.
In: Nagels Musik-Archiv. No.133.
Weihnachtskantate. Kundlich gross ist das Gottselige Geheimnis.
In: Organum. 1.Reihe. Nr.28.
STOLZER, THOMAS, *see* STOLTZER, THOMAS.
STONARD, WILLIAM, d.1630.
Church music.
In: Motett Society. [Collection of ancient church music]. Division 2.
STORACE, BERNARDO, 17th CENTURY.
Selva di varie compositioni d'intavolatura per cimbalo ed organo.
In: Corpus of early keyboard music. Vol.7.
STORACE, STEPHEN, 1763–1796.

Selections.
In: Engel. Music from the days of George Washington.
No.1. Quick-March "The Duke" of York's Favourite. No.2. Marsch aus der Oper "The Siège of Belgrad."
In: Thouret. Musik am preussischen Hofe. No.9.
No song, no supper.
In: Musica Britannica. Vol.16.
Songs.
In: Potter. Reliquary of English song. Vol.2.
STRADELLA, ALESSANDRO, 1642–1682.
Selections.
In: Crotch. Specimens of various styles of music. Vol.2.
Arias.
In: Landshoff. Alte Meister des Bel Canto. Eine Sammlung von Arien. Vol.1–2, 3.
In: Parisotti. Arie antiche. Bd.2, 3.
Cantatas.
In: The Wellesley edition. No.7.
Choral music.
In: Recueil de musique ancienne. Recueil des morceaux de musique ancienne. Bd.3.
Sacred music.
In: The Fitzwilliam music. Bd.4.
Songs.
In: Jeppesen. La flora. Vol.1.
Vocal music.
In: Delsarte. Archives du chant. Livr. 17. No.2.
In: Gevaert. Les gloires de l'Italie. Vol.1.
STRANDQVIST, ALFRED, 1886–1936.
Davids 84. Psalme.
In: Samfundet til Udgivelse af dansk Musik. Ser.III. No.35.
STRANG, GERALD, 1908– .
11. 15. Piano.
In: New music. Vol.7. No.4. July 1934.
Intermezzo (second movement of a symphony).
In: New music. Vol.14. No.4. July 1941.
Mirrorrorrim. Piano.
In: New music. Vol.5. No.4. July 1932.
Música de cámara.
In: Boletín latino-americano de música. Vol.5.
Percussion music.
In: New music. Orchestra series. No.18.
3 Pieces for flute and piano.
In: New music. Vol.10. No.4. July 1937.
Sonatina for clarinet alone.
In: New music. Vol.10. No.4. July 1937.
STRATFORD, PARKER, MONK OF, *see* PARKER, MONK OF STRATFORD.
STRAUS, CHRISTOPH, 17th CENTURY.
Requiem.
In: Denkmäler der Tonkunst in Österreich. Vol.59 (Jg.XXX/1).
STRAUSS, JOHANN, SR., 1804–1849.
Sämtliche Werke. 7 Bde.
Valses.
In: Denkmäler der Tonkunst in Österreich. Vol.68. (Jg.XXXV/2).
STRAUSS, JOHANN, JR., 1825–1899.
Tänze.
?In: Thouret. Musik am preussischen Hofe. No.20.
Three valses.
In: Denkmäler der Tonkunst in Österreich. Vol.63. (Jg.XXXII/2).
STRAUSS, JOSEF, 1827–1870.
Three valses.
In: Denkmäler der Tonkunst in Österreich. Vol.74. (Jg.XXXVIII/2).
STRAUSS, RICHARD, 1864–1949.
Lieder. 4v.
STRAVINSKIĬ, IGOR' FEDOROVICH, 1882– .
Rondo des Princesses (From "The fire bird"). Organ.
In: Dickinson. Historical recital series for organ. Vol.1. No.2.
STRIGGIO, ALESSANDRO, ca.1535–ca.1587.
Selections.
In: Documenta historica musicae.
In: Torchi. L'arte musicale in Italia. Bd.1.
Il cicalamento delle Donne al Bucato.
In: Somma. Capolavori polifonici del secolo XVI. Vol.4.
Madrigale.
In: Das Chorwerk. No.80.
STROGERS, NICHOLAS, 16th–17th CENTURIES.
Keyboard music.
In: The Fitzwilliam virginal book.
STROHBACH, SIEGFRIED, 1929– .
Festliche Ouvertüre für drei Geigen und Violoncello.
In: Collegium musicae novae. No.9.
Unser Metronom: Kommet all herbei.
In: Musikalischer Spielplatz. Vol.1.
STRONGIN, THEODORE.
4 Duos for 2 flutes.
In: New music. Vol.21. No.3. Apr.1948.
STROUD, CHARLES, ca.1705–1726.
Sacred music.
In: Page. Harmonia sacra. Vol.1.
STROZZI, BARBARA, b.ca.1620.
Songs.
In: Jeppesen. La flora. Vol.2.
STROZZI, GREGORIO.
Capricci da sonare cembali et organi.
In: Corpus of early keyboard music. Vol.11.
STRUNGK, DELPHIN, 1601–1694.
Organ music.
In: Klein. The first four centuries of music for the organ from Dunstable to Bach (1370–1749).
In: The Liturgical Music Press, Inc. Masterpieces of organ music. Folio 64.
In: Die Orgel. Reihe II. Nr.12.
In: Straube. Alte Meister.
In: Straube. Choralvorspiele alter Meister.
STRUNGK, NICOLAUS ADAM, 1640–1700.
Concerto I. G-dur für Violoncello und KammerOrchester; Sonata für 3 Violinen, 2 Viola, Violoncello, Basso Continuo.
In: Hortus musicus. No.103.
Keyboard music.
In: Tagliapietra. Antologia di musica antica e moderna per pianoforte. Bd.7.
Organ music.
In: The Liturgical Music Press, Inc. Masterpieces of organ music. Folio 64.

In: Organum. 4.Reihe. Nr.18.
In: Pierront. Cent versets de magnificat.
In: Schweiger. A brief compendium of early organ music.
Triosonate für 2 Violinen, Gambe (Violoncell) und Orgel.
In: Organum. 3.Reihe. Nr.18.
STUCK, JEAN BAPTISTE, ca.1680–1755.
Vocal music.
In: Delsarte. Archives du chant. Livr.3. No.11.
STURGEON.
Selections.
In: Plainsong and Mediaeval Music Society. Publications. (Old Hall manuscript).
STÜRMER, BRUNO, 1892–1958.
Choral music.
In: Nagels Männerchor-Blätter. No.31.
STUTZMANN.
Vocal music.
In: Sammlung russischer Romanzen. No.75, 106, 149.
STYRIAN MUSIC.
In: Hausmusik. No.143, 165, 178, 181.
In: Marckhl. Klavierwerke steiermärkischer Komponisten.
In: Orgelmusik steirischer Komponisten.
In: Zeitschrift für Spielmusik. No.157, 187.
SUEUR, JEAN FRANÇOIS LE, *see* LESUEUR, JEAN FRANÇOIS.
SUFFERN, CARLOS, 1905– .
Keyboard music.
In: Boletín latino-americano de música. Vol.4.
In: Guenther. Collection espagnole.
In: Instituto Interamericano de Musicologia. Publicaciónes. No.1.
SUIDELL.
Sacred music.
In: Latrobe, C. I. Selection of sacred music.
In: Latrobe, J. A. The music of the church.
THE SUITE. (BECK).
In: Anthology of music. Vol.26.
SUMNER, JEZANIAH.
Songs.
In: Siegmeister. Songs of early America, 1620–1830.
SURIANO, FRANCESCO, 1549– d.after 1621. (var. sp.: Francesco Soriano).
Choral music.
In: Engel. Three centuries of choral music. Vol.2.
Masses.
In: Monumenta polyphoniae italicae. Vol.1.
Sacred music.
In: Proske. Musica divina. Annus primus. Tom 3, 4.
In: Proske. Selectus novus missarum. Annus primus. Tom 1, 2.
SUSATO, TYLMAN, d.before 1564.
First music-book.
In: Vereniging voor Nederlandsche Muziekgeschiedenis. Uitgave. No.29.
Organ music.
In: Froidebise. Anthologie de l'orgue. Vol.1.
Tanzsätze.
In: Musica practica. No.44.
SÜSSMAYR, FRANZ XAVER, 1766–1803.
Quintett in D-dur.
In: Diletto musicale. No.112.
SVENDSEN, JOHAN SEVERIN, 1840–1911.
Organ music.
In: Gerhardt. Album nordischer Komponisten für Orgel. Vol.1.
SWAN, TIMOTHY, 1758–1842.
Selections.
In: Goldman. Landmarks of early American music, 1760–1800.
SWEDEN–MUSIC.
In: Monumenta musicae svecicae.
In: Musikaliska konstföreningen.
In: Plainsong and Mediaeval Music Society. Publications. (Ruuta).
In: Svensk sanglyrik.
In: Svenska samfundet för musikforskning. Äldre svensk musik.
SWEELINCK, JAN PIETERS, 1562–1621.
Werken. 12v. in 10.
—— 1943– . v.1– .
Ausgewählte Werke für Orgel und Klavier. 2v.
Supplement zu Teil I der Gesamtausgabe Werke für Orgel und Cembalo.
In: Vereniging voor Nederlandsche Muziekgeschiedenis. Uitgave. No.47.
Chansons.
In: Organum. 2.Reihe. Nr.1–3.
In: Vereniging voor Nederlandsche Muziekgeschiedenis. Uitgave. No.5, 7.
Choral music.
In: Engel. Three centuries of choral music. Vol.4.
In: Musica antiqua batava. MA–9, 10, 11, 12, 13.
Fantaisie D-moll. Organ.
In: Guilmant. École classique de l'orgue. No.6.
Hodie Christus natus est.
In: Organum. 1.Reihe. Nr.11.
In: Vereniging voor Nederlandsche Muziekgeschiedenis. Uitgave. No.15.
Keyboard music.
In: The Fitzwilliam virginal book.
In: Georgii. Keyboard music of the Baroque and Rococo. Vol.1.
In: Tagliapietra. Antologia di musica antica e moderna per pianoforte. Bd.3.
Motetten.
In: Das Chorwerk. No.14.
O sacrum convivium. 5-part motet.
In: Vereniging voor Nederlandsche Muziekgeschiedenis. Uitgave. Without no.
Organ music.
In: Auler. Spielbuch für Kleinorgel. Vol.1.
In: Biggs. Treasury of early organ music.
In: Bonnet. Historical organ-recitals. Vol.1.
In: Guilmant. Archives des maîtres de l'orgue. Vol.10.
In: Klein. The first four centuries of music for the organ from Dunstable to Bach (1370–1749).
In: The Liturgical Music Press, Inc. Masterpieces of organ music. Folio 10, 32.
In: Musikalische Denkmäler. Bd.3.
In: Peeters. Altniederländische Meister für Orgel oder Harmonium.

In: Peeters. Anthologia pro organo. Vol.1, 3.
In: Peeters. Oudnederlandse meesters. Vol.1, 2, 3.
In: Schweiger. A brief compendium of early organ music.
In: Straube. Alte Meister des Orgelspiels.
In: Vereniging voor Nederlandsche Muziekgeschiedenis. Uitgave. No.3.
Poi che voi non volete; Madonna con questi occhi.
In: Squire. Ausgewählte Madrigale und mehrstimmige Gesänge. No.1, 2.
Psalms.
In: Dessoff choir series. No.3–5.
In: Vereniging voor Nederlandsche Muziekgeschiedenis. Uitgave. No.6, 12, 17.
Regina coeli.
In: Vereniging voor Nederlandsche Muziekgeschiedenis. Uitgave. No.1.
Rimes françaises et italiennes à deux parties.
In: Hortus musicus. No.75.
Tu es tout seul.
In: Arion. Vol.1.
Weltliche Lieder und Tänze.
In: Zeitschrift für Spielmusik. No.276.
Zwiegesänge.
In: Zeitschrift für Spielmusik. No.96.
SWITZERLAND–MUSIC (*see also* FOLKSONGS, SWISS).
In: Crotch. Specimens of various styles of music. Vol.1.
In: Music Press, Inc. [Choral series]. Vol.86, 87.
In: Schweizer Sing- und Spielmusik.
In: Schweizerische Musikdenkmäler.
In: Verein schweizerischer Tonkünstler. Musikalische Werke schweizerischer Komponisten des XVI., XVII. und XVIII. Jahrhunderts.
SYDOW, KURT.
Jagdliedvariationen.
In: Zeitschrift für Spielmusik. No.168.
SYLVA, JOHANN ELIAS DE.
Instrumental music.
In: Denkmäler der Tonkunst in Österreich. Vol.86.
SYMON, MAGISTER.
Chanson.
In: Copenhagen Kongelige Bibliotek. Mss. (Thottske Samling 291^8). Der kopenhagener Chansonnier.
SYMON, P.
Chansons.
In: Publikationen älterer praktischer und theoretischer Musikwerke. Jahrg.27.
SYMPHONIAE JUCUNDAE.
In: Rhaw. Musikdrucke. Vol.3.
SZADEK, TOMASZ, ca.1550–ca.1611.
Dies est laetitiae.
In: Denkmäler altpolnischer Musik. Vol.33.
Missa in melodiam moteti Pisneme.
In: Surzyński. Monumenta musicae sacrae in Polonia. Vol.1.
SZAMOTULSKI, WAZLAW, *see* WACHAW OF SZAMOTULY.
SZARZYŃSKI, STANISLAW SYLWESTER, 17th-18th CENTURIES.
Ad hymnos ad cantus.
In: Denkmäler altpolnischer Musik. Vol.26.
Ave Regina.
In: Denkmäler altpolnischer Musik. Vol.25.
Jesu spes mea.
In: Denkmäler altpolnischer Musik. Vol.10.
Pariendo non gravaris.
In: Denkmäler altpolnischer Musik. Vol.5.
Sonata for 2 violins and organ.
In: Denkmäler altpolnischer Musik. Vol.1.
Veni Sancte Spiritus. Soprano, 2 violins and continuo.
In: Denkmäler altpolnischer Musik. Vol.50.
SZELIGOWSKI, TADEUSZ, 1896– .
Polnische Liebeslieder.
In: Zeitschrift für Spielmusik. No.244.
SZIRMAY-KECZER, ANNA.
Polnische Tänze aus der Sammlung.
In: Źródła do historii muzyki polskiej. Vol.6.
SZYMANOWSKI, KAROL, 1882–1937.
Études pour piano, Op.33.
In: Państwowa Wyższa Szkoła Muzyczna w Katowicach. Biblioteka. Faksymilia. Nr.1.

TACK, FRANZ, 1908– . ed.
Gregorian chant.
In: Anthology of music. Vol.18.
TAFALLA, P.
Sacred music.
In: Eslava y Elizondo. Lira sacro-hispana. 17th century. i.l.
TAGLIA, PIETRO, 16th CENTURY.
Madrigale.
In: Das Chorwerk. No.88.
TAKÁCS, JENÖ, 1902– .
Kleine Stücke, Op.50, 1–8. Für Violine mit Klavier.
In: Hausmusik. No.100.
TALLARD, GRAF.
Lute music.
In: Denkmäler der Tonkunst in Österreich. Vol.50. (Jg.XXV/2).
TALLIS, THOMAS, ca.1505–1585.
(var. sp.: Talys).
Selections.
In: Crotch. Specimens of various styles of music. Vol.2.
In: Smith. Musica antiqua.
Choral music.
In: Engel. Three centuries of choral music. Vol.3.
In: Music Press, Inc. [Choral series]. No.60.
In: Recueil de musique ancienne. Recueil des morceaux de musique ancienne. Bd.6.
In: Rochlitz. Sammlung vorzüglicher Gesangstücke. Bd.1. Pt.1.
Church music.
In: Motett Society. [Collection of ancient church music]. Division 1. Division 3.
In: Tudor church music. Vol.6.
Heare the voyce and prayer of thy servaunts.
In: Parrish. A treasury of early music. No.27.
Complete keyboard works. 42p.
Keyboard music.
In: The Fitzwilliam virginal book.
In: Schott's Anthology of early keyboard music. Vol.2.

Organ music.
In: Biggs. Treasury of early organ music.
In: Cantantibus organis. Vol.1.
In: Tallis to Wesley. Vol.1, 2, 3.
Part music.
In: Hullah. Part music. Class A.1. Vol.1.
Sacred music.
In: Arnold. Cathedral music. Vol.1, 3.
In: Boyce. Cathedral music. Vol.1, 2.
Vocal music.
In: Hullah. Vocal scores. I. Sacred.
TALYS, *see* TALLIS, THOMAS.
TANAKA, TOSHIMITSU.
Adagio and allegro for piano quartet.
In: Contemporary Japanese music series. No.25.
TAPISSIER, JEAN, 15th CENTURY.
Works.
In: Reaney. Early fifteenth-century music. Vol.1.
TARCHI, ANGELO, d.1814.
Vocal music.
In: Gevaert. Les gloires de l'Italie. Vol.1.
TARINI.
Kammer-Sonaten. Für Violine und Pianoforte.
In: Moffat. Kammer-Sonaten für Violine und Pianoforte. No.1.
TARNOFFSKY.
Vocal music.
In: Sammlung russischer Romanzen. No.158, 266.
TARP, SVEND ERIK, 1908– .
Concertino for Fløjte og Orkester. Op.30.
In: Samfundet til Udgivelse af dansk Musik. Ser.III. No.68.
Lystspilouverture.
In: Samfundet til Udgivelse af dansk Musik. Ser.III. No.76.
Serenade for Fløjte, Klarinet, Violin, Viola og Violoncel.
In: Samfundet til Udgivelse af dansk Musik. Ser.III. No.42.
Symfoni i Es. Op.50.
In: Samfundet til Udgivelse af dansk Musik. Ser.III. No.103.
Te Deum. Op.33.
In: Samfundet til Udgivelse af dansk Musik. Ser.III. No.86.
TARTINI, GIUSEPPE, 1692–1770.
Selections.
In: Crotch. Specimens of various styles of music. Vol.3.
Concerto.
In: Antica musica strumentale italiana. In preparation.
Concerto in A minor. Concerto in F major.
In: Smith College music archives. No.9.
Kammer-Sonaten für Violine und Pianoforte.
In: Moffat. Kammer-Sonaten für Violine und Pianoforte. No.21.
Organ music.
In: Anthologia antiqua. Vol.2.
Sinfonia Pastorale.
In: Schering. Perlen alter Kammermusik.
Sinfonie oder Streichquartett in A.
In: Hortus musicus. No.53.
Sonate. Violin and piano.
In: I classici della musica italiana. Vol.32.
In: I classici della musica italiana. Raccolta nazionale delle musiche italiane. Quad. 131–136.
In: Moffat. Meister-Schule der alten Zeit. Violin-Sonaten. No.18.
Sonata a tre, per due violini e basso continuo, Op.VIII/6.
In: Hausmusik. No.167.
Violin and piano.
In: Schering. Alte Meister des Violinspiels.
TAVERNER, JOHN, ca.1495–1545.
Choral music.
In: Engel. Three centuries of choral music. Vol.3.
Church music.
In: Tudor church music. Vol.1, 3.
TCHAIKOVSKIĬ, PETER ILICH, 1840–1893.
(var. sp.: Chaikovskiĭ; Tschaikowskiĭ).
[Complete works]. v.1– .
Ausgewählte Klavierwerke. 3v.
Werke für Klavier. 3v.
Valse. (From Symphony V). Organ.
In: Dickinson. Historical recital series for organ. Vol.1. No.19.
Vocal music.
In: Sammlung russischer Romanzen. No.249–255, 272.
TECHELMANN, FRANZ MATHIAS, ca.1649–1714.
Suiten für Tasteninstrumente.
In: Denkmäler der Tonkunst in Österreich. Vol.115.
TEDESCO, MARIO CASTELNUOVO– , *see* CASTELNUOVO–TEDESCO, MARIO.
TELEMANN, GEORG PHILIPP, 1681–1767.
Musikalische Werke. v.1– .
Selections.
In: Das Erbe deutscher Musik. 1.Reihe. Vol.11.
In: Leichtentritt. Deutsche Hausmusik aus vier Jahrhunderten.
Choral music.
In: Rochlitz. Sammlung vorzüglicher Gesangstücke. Bd.3.
Zwölf leichte Choralvorspiele, für Orgel. 24p.
Forty-eight chorale preludes for organ.
In: Recent researches in the music of the Baroque era. Vol.2.
Concerto Nr.1; Concerto Nr.2; Don-Quichotte Suite; Divertimenti; Konzert in B-dur; Ouvertüre (Suite) G-dur; Sinfonia Melodica C-dur.
In: Musikschätze der Vergangenheit.
Concert A-moll.
In: Concertino.
Concerto A-moll und C-dur für Alt-Blockflöte, Streicher und Basso Continuo.
In: Moecks Kammermusik. Vol.64, 65.
Concerto a 4 (A-moll); Sonata a 3 (D-moll) für Alt-Blockflöte, Violine une Basso Continuo.
In: Moecks Kammermusik. Vol.66, 67.
Konzert.
In: Corona. Vol.21, 37.
Konzert E-moll für f'-Blockflöte, Querflöte, Streicher und Basso Continuo.
In: Hortus musicus. No.124.

Konzert F-dur für f'-Blockflöte, Streich und Basso Continuo.
In: Hortus musicus. No.130.
Konzert G-dur für Querflöte, 2 Violinen, Basso Continuo.
In: Hortus musicus. No.131.
Konzert A-moll, für zwei Soloflöten, Streichorchester und Basso Continuo.
In: Nagels Musik-Archiv. No.167.
Konzert F-moll, für Solo-Oboe mit Begleitung von Streichorchester und Cembalo (Klavier).
In: Das weltliche Konzert im 18. Jahrhundert. Heft 1.
Konzert G-dur, für Viola und Streichorchester mit Basso Continuo.
In: Hortus musicus. No.22.
Konzert A-moll für Violine und Streichorchester mit Basso Continuo.
In: Hortus musicus. No.32.
Concerto per Violino, Orchestra di Strumenti ad Arco e Continuo.
In: Rahter's Kammer-Orchester. No.10.
Concerto a 4 für 4 Violinen.
In: Antiqua Edition. Von 4. Instrumenten an.
Konzert für vier Violinen ohne Basso Continuo.
In: Hortus musicus. No.20.
Concerto D-dur, eine kleine Tanzsuite für Streichorchester mit Cembalo oder Streichorchester mit Cembalo oder Streichquartett.
In: Hortus musicus. No.52.
Konzertsuite.
In: Corona. Vol.34.
Konzertsuite für Altblockflöte, Streicher und Basso Continuo (Klavier).
In: Nagels Musik-Archiv. No.177.
Konzertsuite A-dur für Violine· Konzert G-dur für Violine.
In: Corona. Vol.78, 79.
Das Darmstädter Trio für Violine, Viola (Gamba) und Basso Continuo.
In: Nagels Musik-Archiv. No.151.
Duett G-dur, für Flöte und Violine.
In: Nagels Musik-Archiv. No.16.
Duette alter Meister.
In: Zeitschrift für Spielmusik. No.69.
Fantaisies pour le Clavessin.
In: Hirsch. Veröffentlichungen. [Bd.].4.
Fantasie for violin solo.
In: Parrish. A treasury of early music. No.48.
Festliche Suite (A-dur).
In: Corona. Vol.12.
XX Kleine Fugen, So wohl auf der Orgel.
In: Nagels Musik-Archiv. No.13.
Fugue. Piano, A minor.
In: Königliche Akademie der Künste. Auswahl vorzüglicher Musik-Werke. No.18.
Der getreue Musikmeister.
In: Hortus musicus. No.6–13, 175.
Instrumental concertos.
In: Denkmäler deutscher Tonkunst. [1.Folge]. Vol.29–30.
Die kleine Kammermusik. Sechs Partiten für Violine (Querflöte/Oboe/Blockflöte/Diskantgambe u.A.) und Basso Continuo.
In: Hortus musicus. No.47.
Kammer-Sonaten für Violine und Pianoforte.
In: Moffat. Kammer-Sonaten für Violine und Pianoforte. No.17.
Keyboard music.
In: Clementi. Clementi's Selection of practical harmony. Vol.1.
In: Farrenc. Le trésor des pianistes. Vol.9.
In: Georgii. Keyboard music of the Baroque and Rococo. Vol.2.
In: Tagliapietra. Antologia di musica antica e moderna per pianoforte. Bd.10.
Klingende Geographie; Ouverturensuite.
In: Corona. Vol.70–71.
Lieder.
In: Moser. Alte Meister des deutschen Liedes. 46 Gesänge. No.33.
In: Organum. 2.Reihe. Nr.12.
In: Reimann. Das deutsche Lied. Vol.4.
Lustige Suite (C-dur).
In: Corona. Vol.3.
Märsche.
In: Corona. Vol.11.
7 Menuette von Melante für 1 Melodieinstrumente und Bass.
In: Zeitschrift für Spielmusik. No.12.
Odes and songs.
In: Denkmäler deutscher Tonkunst. [1.Folge]. Vol.57.
Organ music.
In: The Liturgical Music Press, Inc. Masterpieces of organ music. Folio 5, 11, 30, 59.
In: The parish organist. Vol.1–4.
In: Raugel. Quarante-six pièces pour orgue ou harmonium.
Overtures. No.1–3, 4–6. Piano.
In: Oberdörffer. Deutsche Klaviermusik des 17. und 18. Jahrhunderts. Vol.4/5.
Ouvertüre in G-dur für 4stg. Streichorchester.
In: Corona. Vol.42.
Ouvertüren-Suite. (Hinnenthal).
In: Alte Musik. (Reihe "Leuckartiana").
Pimpinone, oder Die ungleiche Heirat.
In: Das Erbe deutscher Musik. 1.Reihe. Vol.6.
Polnische Suite.
In: Florilegium musicae antiquae. Vol.11.
Presto, Flauto (Violino Solo), 2 Violinen, Viola (3d Violino), Violoncello e Continuo.
In: Rahter's Kammer-Orchester. No.9.
Der 117. Psalm.
In: Chor-Archiv.
Quadro G-moll für Alt-Blockflöte, Violine, Viola und Basso Continuo.
In: Moecks Kammermusik. Vol.42.
Quartett in D moll für Flauto, zwei Querflöten, Cembalo und Violoncell.
In: Riemann. Collegium musicum. No.59.
Quartett in E-moll, für Flöte, Violine, Violoncello und Basso Continuo; Quartett H moll, für Flöte, Violine, Violoncello und Basso Continuo.
In: Nagels Musik-Archiv. No.10, 24.
Quartett für Violine, Flöte, Violoncell obligat und Klavier.
In: Riemann. Collegium musicum. No.56.
Streichquartett A-dur.
In: Hortus musicus. No.108.
Sacred music.

In: Latrobe, C. I. Selection of sacred music.
In: Latrobe, J. A. The music of the church.
Sonata.
In: Antiqua Edition. Von 4 Instrumenten an.
Sonate F-dur für Alt-Blockflöte und Oboe und Basso Continuo.
In: Moecks Kammermusik. Vol.10.
Sonate F-dur, für Alt-Blockflöte und Klavier; Sonate, D-dur für Flöte und Basso Continuo.
In: Nagels Musik-Archiv. No.8, 163.
Sonata à tre in F moll für Alt-Blockflöte, Violine und Basso Continuo.
In: Moecks Kammermusik. Vol.1.
Sonate 1 für 2 Alt-Blockflöten.
In: Zeitschrift für Spielmusik. No.128.
Sonate für Flöte oder Violine mit Cembalobegleitung.
In: Organum. 3.Reihe. Nr.7, 8.
Sonate in G für Flöte (Violine) und Cembalo (oder Klavier). Bass-Instrument ad lib.
In: Antiqua Edition. Von 2 Instrumenten an.
Sonate in H moll. Für Flöte und Cembalo.
In: Kammersonaten. No.5.
Sonate für 2 Flöten und Cembalo.
In: Riemann. Collegium musicum. No.69.
Sonata à flûte, violon, alto et basse.
In: Flores musicae. Vol.3.
Sonate in G moll.
In: Kammersonaten. No.8.
Sonata in C moll. Violin (Oboe) Solo.
In: Kammersonaten. No.13.
Sonate I–VI für Violine und Basso Continuo.
In: Moecks Kammermusik. Vol.101, 102, 103.
Sonate für 3 Violine und Basso Continuo.
In: Hortus musicus. No.97.
Sonate D-dur, für Violoncell und Basso Continuo.
In: Nagels Musik-Archiv. No.23.
Sonate im Kanon.
In: Gitarre-Kammermusik. No.17.
Sonate in Kanonform.
In: Hausmusik. No.68.
Sonata Polonese I; Sonata Polonoise II.
In: Nagels Musik-Archiv. No.50, 51.
11 Stücke.
In: Zeitschrift für Spielmusik. No.38.
Suite A-moll; Suite G-moll.
In: Schering. Perlen alter Kammermusik.
Suite G-moll. ("Der getreue Musikmeister") für Violine (Oboe) und Basso Continuo.
In: Hortus musicus. No.175.
Zwei Suiten.
In: Musica instrumentalis. Vol.7.
Kleine Suite D-dur für 2 Violinen, 2 Viola, Basso Continuo (oder 3 Violinen, Viola, Basso Continuo).
In: Hortus musicus. No.107.
Suite Baroque. Arr. organ.
In: Anthologia antiqua. Vol.6.
Tafelmusik.
In: Denkmäler deutscher Tonkunst. [1.Folge]. Vol.61–62.
Tag des Gerichte. Ino.
In: Denkmäler deutscher Tonkunst. [1.Folge]. Vol.28.
Tänze.
In: Zeitschrift für Spielmusik. No.44.
Tre Trietti melodiche e tre Scherzi.
In: Riemann. Collegium musicum. No.73–75.
Trio F-dur für Flauto dolce, Viola da Gamba und Basso Continuo.
In: Nagels Musik-Archiv. No.131.
Trio für Flöte, Oboe, Violoncell und Klavier.
In: Riemann. Collegium musicum. No.55.
Trio in Es dur. Für 2 Violinen, Violoncell und Klavier.
In: Riemann. Collegium musicum. No.14.
Trio-Sonate (Em).
In: Moffat. Trio-Sonaten alter Meister. No.3.
Trio-Sonate in F-dur; Trio-Sonate in C-dur.
In: Riemann. Collegium musicum. No.66, 67.
Triosonate E-moll für Altblockflöte (Querflöte/Violine), Oboe (Querflöte/Violine) und Basso Continuo.
In: Hortus musicus. No.25.
Trio-Sonate F-dur für Alt-Blockflöte, Violine und Basso Continuo.
In: Moecks Kammermusik. Vol.5.
Triosonate B-dur für Blockflöte (Querflöte/Violine) konzertierender Cembalo (Klavier) und Basso Continuo.
In: Hortus musicus. No.36.
Triosonate, E-dur, für Flöte, Violine und Continuo.
In: Nagels Musik-Archiv. No.47.
Triosonate B-dur für Oboe (Querflöte), Violin und Basso Continuo.
In: Hortus musicus. No.179.
Vocal music.
In: Hullah. Vocal scores. I. Sacred.
Georg Philipp Telemann. (Max Seiffert).
In: Denkmäler deutscher Tonkunst. [1.Folge]. Reprint. Suppl. Vol.61/62.
TEMPO NOTATION IN RENAISSANCE SPAIN. (CHARLES JACOBS).
In: Institute of Mediaeval Music. Musicological studies. Vol.8.
TEN CHRISTMAS CAROLS FROM ANCIENT SOURCES. For Unison or Mixed Voices.
In: Music Press, Inc. [Choral series]. No.59.
TENAGLIA, ANTONIO FRANCESCO, 17th CENTURY.
Arias.
In: Parisotti. Arie antiche. Bd.2, 3.
TERRADELLAS, DOMINGO, 1713–1751.
La merope.
In: Barcelona. Biblioteca Central. Sección de Música. Publicaciones. Vol.14.
TERRY, FRANCES.
Sonata. Violin and piano. Op.15.
In: Society for the Publication of American Music. Publications. 12th season. 1930–31.
TERTRE, GUILLAUME DU.
Chansons.
In: Cauchie. Quinze chansons françaises du XVIe siècle.
In: Publikationen älterer praktischer und theoretischer Musikwerke. Jahrg.27.
TERZI, GIOVANNI ANTONIO, 16th–17th CENTURIES.
Lute music.

In: Chilesotti. Lautenspieler des XVI. Jahrhunderts.
TERZIANI, PIETRO.
Salve, regina. Sopran und Konzertierende Orgel.
In: Cantio sacra. No.47.
TESSARINI, CARLO, 1690–ca.1765.
Kammer-Sonaten für Violine und Pianoforte.
In: Moffat. Kammer-Sonaten für Violine und Pianoforte. No.3, 24.
Sonate (G).
In: Moffat. Trio-Sonaten alter Meister. No.19.
Sonate (C). Violin and piano.
In: Moffat. Meister-Schule der alten Zeit. Violin-Sonaten. No.11.
Sonate en ré majeur.
In: L'école du violon au XVIIe et XVIIIe siècle. No.1266.
TESSIER, CHARLES, b.ca.1550.
Au joli bois.
In: Arion. Vol.1.
Chansons.
In: Lesure. Anthologie de la chanson parisienne au XVIe siècle.
Songs.
In: Expert. Chants de France et d'Italie. Ser.2.
Vocal music.
In: Delsarte. Archives du chant. Livr.7 No.6.
TEUSCHER, HANS.
Sonata A-moll für 2 Blockflöten oder andere Instrumente.
In: Zeitschrift für Spielmusik. No.159.
Sonata G-moll für 2 Blockflöten oder andere Instrumente.
In: Zeitschrift für Spielmusik. No.120.
TEYBER, ANTON.
Selections.
In: Denkmäler der Tonkunst in Österreich. Vol.79. (Jg.XLII/2).
THALBERG, SIGISMUND, 1812–1871.
Keyboard music.
In: Tagliapietra. Antologia di musica antica e moderna per pianoforte. Bd.16.
THATE, ALBERT, 1903– .
Organ music.
In: The parish organist. Vol.5–6.
THEILE, JOHANN, 1646–1724.
Kurzmessen.
In: Das Chorwerk. No.16.
Passion-settings.
In: Denkmäler deutscher Tonkunst. [1.Folge]. Vol.17.
Suite für Violine, 2 Violen, Violoncell und Cembalo.
In: Organum. 3.Reihe. Nr.19.
THIBAUT IV, KING OF NAVARRE AND COUNT OF CHAMPAGNE, 1201–1253.
Selections.
In: Smith. Musica antiqua.
THIBAUT DE BLASON.
Selections.
In: Smith. Musica antiqua.
THIEL, JÖRN.
Ene mene Tintenfass.
In: Bausteine für Musikerziehung und Musikpflege. B 131.
THIELE, ALFRED.
Die Vogelhochzeit.
In: Zeitschrift für Spielmusik. No.254.
THIERRES.
Selections.
In: Smith. Musica antiqua.
THOMAS, KURT, 1904– .
Erste Spielmusik, Op.18a; Zweite Spielmusik, Op.22.
In: Collegium musicae novae. No.10, 17.
THOMAS AQUINAS, 1227–1274.
Hymne du XIIIème siècle.
In: Delsarte. Archives du chant. Livr.4. No.1; Livr.5. No.1.
THOMSON, E.
An introduction to Caron.
In: Institute of Mediaeval Music. Musicological studies. Vol.9.
THOMSON, VIRGIL, 1896– .
Capital, capitals. For 4 men and a piano.
In: New music. Vol.20. No.3. Apr.1947.
Pastorale on a Christmas plainsong. Organ.
In: Contemporary organ series. No.14.
Sonata da chiesa. Clarinet, trumpet, viola, horn, and trombone.
In: New music. Vol.18. No.1. Oct.1944.
THURINGIA–MUSIC.
In: Denkmäler deutscher Tonkunst. [1.Folge]. Vol.49–50.
In: Denkmäler thuringischer Musik.
THYBO, LEIF, 1922– .
Concerto per Organo.
In: Samfundet til Udgivelse af dansk Musik. Ser.III. No.132.
Concerto per archi.
In: Samfundet til Udgivelse af dansk Musik. Seri.III. No.152.
TIECK.
Part music.
In: Hullah. Part music. 1868 edition.
Vocal music.
In: Hullah. Vocal scores. II. Secular.
TILLYARD, HENRY JULIUS WETENHALL, 1881– .
Handbook of the middle Byzantine musical notation.
In: Monumenta musicae byzantinae. Subsidia. Vol.1. Fasc.1.
TINCTORIS, JOHANNES, ca.1435–1511.
Opera omnia. v.1– .
Choral music.
In: Smijers. Van Ockeghem tot Sweelinck. Aflg.4.
Missa super l'homme armé.
In: Monumenta polyphoniae liturgicae sanctae ecclesiae romanae. Ser.1. Tomus 1. Fasc.9.
TINTORI, GIAMPIERO. ed.
Sacre rappresentazioni.
In: Instituta et Monumenta. Vol.2.
TIPTON, LOUIS CAMPBELL– , 1877–1921.
Songs; Piano music.
In: The Wa-Wan series of American compositions.
TIROLER INSTRUMENTAL MUSIC IN THE 18th CENTURY.
In: Denkmäler der Tonkunst in Österreich. Vol.86.

TISCH, LUSTIG VOR.
Altmärkische Volkstänze.
In: Zeitschrift für Spielmusik. No.122.
TISDALL, WILLIAM, 16th CENTURY.
Complete keyboard works. 12p.
Complete keyboard works.
In: English keyboard music. [No.14].
Keyboard music.
In: The Fitzwilliam virginal book.
TITELOUZE, JEAN, 1563–1633.
Oeuvres complètes.
In: Guilmant. Archives des maîtres de l'orgue. Vol.1.
Keyboard music.
In: Tagliapietra. Antologia di musica antica e moderna per pianoforte. Bd.3.
Organ music.
In: Bonnet. An anthology of early French organ music.
In: Bonnet. Historical organ-recitals. Vol.1.
In: Cantantibus organis. Vol.1, 8.
In: Guilmant. Concert historique d'orgue.
In: Keller. Orgelvorspiele.
In: Klein. The first four centuries of music for the organ from Dunstable to Bach (1370–1749).
In: Liber organi. Bd.1, 2.
In: The Liturgical Music Press, Inc. Masterpieces of organ music. Folio 23.
In: The parish organist. Vol.7–8.
In: Peeters. Anthologia pro organo. Vol.1, 3.
In: Pierront. Cent versets de magnificat.
In: Raugel. Les maîtres français de l'orgue. Vol.2.
In: Straube. Alte Meister des Orgelspiels.
TITOFF.
Vocal music.
In: Sammlung russischer Romanzen. No.31, 36, 77, 78.
TITTEL, ERNST, 1910– .
Sonate für drei gleiche oder ungleiche Stimmen. Op.30.
In: Hausmusik. No.39.
TIVOLI, GIULIANO BUONAUGURIO DA, *see* BUONAUGURIO DA TIVOLI, GIULIANO.
THE TOCCATA, (VALENTIN).
In: Anthology of music. Vol.17.
TOCH, ERNST, 1887– .
Fugue from the Geographie. S.A.T.B.
In: New music, Vol.23. No.2. Jan.1950.
TOESCHI, G.
Sonata für Viola d'amore und Cembalo.
In: Diletto musicale. No.127.
TOESCHI, JOSEPH.
Orchestral music.
In: Riemann. Mannheim symphonists. Vol.2.
TOFFT, ALFRED, 1865–1931.
Airs melancoliques. Quatre pièces pour piano. Op.36.
In: Samfundet til Udgivelse af dansk Musik. Unnumbered.
10 Danske Sange for blandet Kor. Op.64.
In: Samfundet til Udgivelse af dansk Musik. Ser.III. No.22.
Vifandaka. Opera.
In: Samfundet til Udgivelse af dansk Musik. Ser.III. No.6.
Ouverture til "Vifandaka."
In: Samfundet til Udgivelse af dansk Musik. Ser.III. No.15.
TOKUNAGA, HIDENORI.
3 Interludes for piano.
In: New music. Aug.1963.
TOLAR, JAN KŘTITEL, 17th CENTURY.
Balletti e sonate.
In: Musica antiqua bohemica. Vol.40.
TOLESA, P. NICOLÁS DE.
Organ music.
In: Organ album of ten pieces by Spanish composers.
TOLLIUS, JAN, ca.1550–ca.1603.
Six-part madrigals.
In: Vereniging voor Nederlandsche Muziekgeschiedenis. Uitgave. No.24.
TOLSTOY.
Vocal music.
In: Sammlung russischer Romanzen. No.76.
TOMÁS DE SANTA MARÍA, FRAY, *see* SANTA MARÍA, FRAY TOMÁS DE.
TOMASCHECK, JOHANN WENZEL, *see* TOMÁŠEK, VÁCLAV JAN.
TOMÁŠEK, VÁCLAV JAN, 1774–1850.
(var. sp.: Johann Wenzel Tomascheck).
Keyboard music.
In: Musica antiqua bohemica. Vol.20.
Op.65. Piano.
In: Musica antiqua bohemica. Vol.29.
Sonate et rondeau. Piano.
In: Répertoire des clavecinistes. Heft 14.
LE TOMBEAU DE GONZALEZ. Organ.
In: Orgue et liturgie. Vol.38.
TOMKINS, JOHN, 16th–17th CENTURIES.
Keyboard music.
In: Schott's Anthology of early keyboard music. Vol.4.
TOMKINS, THOMAS, ca.1575–1656.
Verse anthems. I.
In: Early English church music. Vol.6.
Keyboard music.
In: The Fitzwilliam virginal book.
In: Musica Britannica. Vol.5.
In: Schott's Anthology of early keyboard music. Vol.4.
Madrigals.
In: Euterpe. 2d ed. No.61.
In: Fellowes. The English madrigal school. Vol.18.
In: Squire. Ausgewählte Madrigale und mehrstimmige Gesänge. No.10, 20, 45.
In: The triumphs of Oriana.
Musica deo sacra: I.
In: Early English church music. Vol.5.
Organ music.
In: English keyboard music. [No.1, 2].
In: Liber organi. Bd.10.
In: Tallis to Wesley. Vol.17.
Sacred music.
In: Boyce. Cathedral music. 1849. Vol.1. Appendix; Vol.2. Appendix.
Services.
In: Tudor church music. Vol.8.
TOMKINS MANUSCRIPT.
In: Schott's Anthology of early keyboard music. Vol.4.

TONSOR, MICHAEL, 16th CENTURY.
Selections.
In: Musica sacra . . . 1839– . Vol.15.
TORELLI, GASPARO, 16th–17th CENTURIES.
(var. sp.: Gaspare Torelli).
Selections.
In: Torchi. L'arte musicale in Italia. Bd.4.
TORELLI, GIUSEPPE, 1658–1709.
Arias.
In: Landshoff. Alte Meister des Bel Canto. Eine Sammlung von Arien. Vol.3.
Concerti musicali Op.VI. No.1.
In: Somma. Musiche vocali e strumentale sacre e profane, sec. XVII–XVIII–XIX. Vol.23.
Concerto.
In: Gitarre-Kammermusik. No.6.
I fidi amanti.
In: Somma. Capolavori polifonici del secolo XVI. Vol.7.
Instrumental music.
In: Wasielewski. Instrumentalsätze vom Ende des XVI. bis Ende des XVII. Jahrhunderts.
Konzert, Op.6, Nr.10, für vier Streichinstrumente und Orgel oder Cembalo.
In: Nagels Musik-Archiv. No.70.
Konzert für Streichorchester, Op.VI, Nr.1.
In: Concertino.
Sinfonia E-moll (Nr.6 aus "Concerti Musicali", Op.6, Bologna 1698).
In: Schering. Perlen alter Kammermusik.
Sonata a cinque Nr.1 für Trompete und Streicher; Sonata a cinque Nr.2 für Trompete und Streicher.
In: Diletto musicale. No.164, 165.
Sonate in G-dur, für Violoncello und Klavier (Cembalo).
In: Hortus musicus. No.69.
Weihnachtskonzert. Concert a 4, in forma di Pastorale per il santissimo natale. Aus Op.8, Bologna 1709.
In: Schering. Perlen alter Kammermusik.
TORNACENSIS, MISSA.
In: Catholic Church, Roman. Liturgy and ritual. Missal. Missa Tornacensis.
TORNACO, PASSET DE, *see* PASSET DE TORNACO.
TORRE, FRANCESCO DE LA.
Selections.
In: Pedrell. Teatro lirico espanol anterior al siglo XIX. Bd.3.
Choral music.
In: Engel. Three centuries of choral music. Vol.5.
TORREFRANCO, FAUSTO, 1883–1955.
Giovanni Benedetto Platti e la sonata moderna.
In: Istituzioni e monumenti dell' arte musicale italiana. Nuova serie. Vol.2.
TORRENTES, A. DE.
Sacred music.
In: Eslava y Elizondo. Lira sacro-hispana. 16th century. i.l.
TORRES, EDUARDO, 1872–1934.
Organ music.
In: Organ album of ten pieces by Spanish composers.
TORRI, PIETRO, ca.1665–1737.
Selected works.
In: Denkmäler deutscher Tonkunst. [2.Folge]. Vol.19–20.
TORRIJOS, DIEGO DE, 1640–1691.
Organ music.
In: Muset. Early Spanish organ music.
TOSAR ERRECART, HÉCTOR A., 1923– .
Canciones.
In: Instituto Interamericano de Musicologia. Publicaciónes. No.24.
TOSCANO, GIAN.
Selections.
In: Pirrotta. The music of fourteenth-century Italy. Vol.5.
TOULOUZE, MICHEL.
L'art et instruction de bien dancer.
In: The Wellesley edition. No.6.
TOURNAI MASS. (14th CENTURY).
Agnus Dei.
In: Parrish. A treasury of early music. No.13.
TOURNEMIRE, CHARLES, 1870–1939.
Organ music.
In: Bedell. The French organist. Vol.1, 2.
In: Bonnet. Historical organ-recitals. Vol.5.
Symphonie sacrée pour orgue.
In: Orgue et liturgie. Vol.44.
Triple choral. Organ.
In: Orgue et liturgie. Vol.54.
TOURONT.
Choral music.
In: Capella. Vol.1.
TOYAMA, YUZO.
Sonate for violin and piano.
In: Contemporary Japanese music series. No.21.
TOZZI, V.
Missa octo vocum.
In: Monumenta liturgiae polychoralis sanctae ecclesiae romanae. Series VI. No.2.
TRABACI, GIOVANNI MARIA, ca.1580–1647.
Selections.
In: Torchi. L'arte musicale in Italia. Bd.3.
Keyboard music.
In: Apel. Musik aus früher Zeit für Klavier. Bd.1.
In: Tagliapietra. Antologia di musica antica e moderna per pianoforte. Bd.5.
Organ music.
In: Fuser. Classici italiani dell' organo.
TRÄDER, WILLI.
Singt im Chor.
In: Bausteine für Musikerziehung und Musikpflege. B 140.
Über Jahr und Tag.
In: Bausteine für Musikerziehung und Musikpflege. B 128.
TRAETTA, TOMMASO, 1727–1779.
Selected works.
In: Denkmälter deutscher Tonkunst. [2.Folge]. Vol.14 (i), 17.
Arias.
In: Parisotti. Arie antiche. Bd.1, 3.
TRAPP, KLAUS, 1931– .
Kleine Streichersinfonie.
In: Collegium musicae novae. No.31.
TRAVERS, JOHN, ca.1703–1758.
Organ music.

In: The Liturgical Music Press, Inc. Masterpieces of organ music. Folio 16.
In: Tallis to Wesley. Vol.22.
Sacred music.
In: Arnold. Cathedral music. Vol.2, 3.
In: Page. Harmonia sacra. Vol.2.
TREBOR.
Secular music.
In: Apel. French secular music of the late fourteenth century.
TREMAIS.
Violin and piano.
In: Schering. Alte Meister des Violinspiels.
TREMBLAY, GEORGE, 1911– .
2 Piano sonatas, Op.8, No.1 and 2.
In: New music. Vol.12. No.2. Jan.1939.
TRENT, COUNCIL OF. (Kerle. Selected works. Pt.1).
In: Denkmäler deutscher Tonkunst. [2.Folge]. Vol.26.
TRENT CODICES.
In: Denkmäler der Tonkunst in Österreich. Vol.14–15. (Jg.VII); Vol.22. (Jg.XI/1); Vol.38. (Jg.XIX/1); Vol.53. (Jg.XXVII/1); Vol.61. (Jg.XXXI); Vol.76. (Jg.XL).
TRÉSOR D'APT, LE MANUSCRIT.
In: Société Française de Musicologie, Paris. Publications. Sér.I. Bd.10.
TRIMBLE, LESTER.
String quartet, No.1.
In: Society for the Publication of American Music. Publications. 44th season. 1963–64.
TRINITY HIRMOLOGIUM, TWENTY CANONS FROM.
In: Monumenta musicae byzantinae. Transcripta. Vol.4.
THE TRIUMPHS OF ORIANA. 1601.
In: Fellowes. The English madrigal school. Vol.32.
TROMBETTI, ASCANIO, 16th–17th CENTURIES.
Selections.
In: Torchi. L'arte musicale in Italia. Bd.1.
Il primo libro delle Napolitane (1573).
In: Maestri bolognesi. Vol.4.
TROMBONCINO, BARTOLOMEO, 15th–16th CENTURIES.
Selections.
In: Torchi. L'arte musicale in Italia. Bd.1.
TROPES.
In: Catholic Church, Roman. Litugy and Ritual. Troper. The Winchester troper. 248p.
TROUBADOURS AND TROUVÈRES.
In: Adam de la Halle. Oeuvres complètes.
In: Anthology of music. Vol.2.
In: Beck. Anthologie de cent chansons de trouvères et de troubadours des XIIe et XIIIe siècles.
In: Beck. Les chansonniers des troubadours et des trouvères.
In: Ribera y Tarragó. La música andaluza medieval en las canciones de trovadores, troveros y minnesinger.
In: Summa musicae medii aevi. Vol.3–4.
TROYER, CARLOS, 1837–1920.
Songs; Piano music.
In: The Wa-Wan series of American compositions.
TRUBETZKOY.
Vocal music.
In: Sammlung russischer Romanzen. No.128.
TRUMBLE, E.
Fauxbourdon, an historical survey. I.
In: Institute of Mediaeval Music. Musicological studies. Vol.3.
TRUMPET.
In: Das Erbe deutscher Musik. 1.Reihe. Vol.7.
In: Fantini. Modo per imparare a sonare di tromba tanto di gverra quanto musicalment in organo.
TSCHAIKOWSKIĬ, PETER ILICH, *see* TCHAIKOVSKIĬ, PETER ILICH.
TUCKER, WILLIAM, d.1679.
Sacred music.
In: Page. Harmonia sacra. Vol.1.
TUCKEY, WILLIAM, 1708–1781.
Selections.
In: Goldman. Landmarks of early American music. 1760–1800.
TUDOR MAGNIFICATS. Vol.1.
In: Early English church music. Vol.4.
TUDOR MASSES. I.
In: Early English church music. Vol.1.
TUDWAY, THOMAS, ca.1650–1726.
Sacred music.
In: Arnold. Cathedral music. Vol.2.
TŮMA, FRANTIŠEK, 1704–1774.
(var. sp.: Franz Tuma).
Partita a tre, Nr.7.
In: Hausmusik. No.155.
Stabat mater.
In: Documenta historica musicae.
TUNDER, FRANZ, 1614–1667.
Arie: Ach Herr, lass deine lieben Engelein.
In: Organum. 1.Reihe. Nr.7.
Solo cantatas and choral works.
In: Denkmäler deutscher Tonkunst. [1.Folge]. Vol.3.
Choral music.
In: Chorbuch für die Kirchchöre Sachsens.
Feiermusik.
In: Corona. Vol.30.
Ein' feste Burg ist unser Gott.
In: Organum. 1.Reihe. Nr.15.
Fugen.
In: Musica instrumentalis. Vol.2.
Keyboard music.
In: Buchmayer. Aus Richard Buchmayers historischen Klavierkonzerten. Vol.2, 3.
Ein kleines Kindelein.
In: Organum. 1.Reihe. Nr.4.
Organ music.
In: Corpus of early keyboard music. Vol.10, Pt.2.
In: Klein. The first four centuries of music for the organ from Dunstable to Bach (1370–1749).
In: The Liturgical Music Press, Inc. Masterpieces of organ music. Folio 45, 63.
In: Organum. 4.Reihe. Nr.6.
In: Straube. Alte Meister des Orgelspiels.
In: Straube. Choralvorspiele alter Meister.
Wachet auf! Ruft uns die Stimme.
In: Organum. 1.Reihe. Nr.13.
TÜRCK, DANIEL, *see* TÜRK, DANIEL GOTTLOB.

TURIN. BIBLIOTECA NAZIONALE. MSS. (J.II.9).
The Cypriot-French repertory. 4v.
TURINA, JOAQUIN, 1882–1949.
Keyboard music.
In: Guenther. Collection espagnole.
TURINI, FERDINANDO, 1749–1812.
(var. sp.: F. Turrini).
Keyboard music.
In: Clementi. Clementi's Selection of practical harmony. Vol.1.
In: Esposito. Early Italian piano music.
In: Tagliapietra. Antologia di musica antica e moderna per pianoforte. Bd.13.
Presto. Sonate. No.6.
In: Köhler. Les maîtres du clavecin. Heft 9.
Presto. (Gm). Sonate. (D flat).
In: Pauer. Alte Meister. No.30.
Sonate.
In: I classici della musica italiana. Vol.33.
In: I classici della musica italiana. Raccolta nazionale delle musiche italiane. Quad. 286–288.
TURINI, FRANCESCO, ca.1595–1656.
Sacred music.
In: Proske. Musica divina. Annus primus. Tom 2.
TURINI, GREGORIO, ca.1560–ca.1600.
Sacred music.
In: Proske. Musica divina. Annus primus. Tom 2, 3, 4.
TÜRK, DANIEL GOTTLOB, 1756–1813.
(var. sp.: Türck).
Kleine Handstücke. Klavier.
In: Nagels Musik-Archiv. No.93.
Sacred music.
In: Latrobe, C. I. Selection of sacred music.
In: Latrobe, J. A. The music of the church.
Sonate A-moll für Klavier.
In: Organum. 5.Reihe. Nr.19.
Sonate C-dur für Klavier.
In: Organum. 5.Reihe. Nr.13.
Sonate D-dur.
In: Organum. 5.Reihe. Nr.24.
Sonate E-moll für Klavier.
In: Organum. 5.Reihe. Nr.9.
TURKEY–MUSIC.
In: Crotch. Specimens of various styles of music. Vol.1.
TURNER, WILLIAM, 1651–1740.
Keyboard music.
In: English keyboard music. [No.10].
In: Fuller-Maitland. The contemporaries of Purcell. Vol.6–7.
Sacred music.
In: Boyce. Cathedral music. Vol.3; 1849 ed., Vol.3.
TURRINI, FERDINANDO, *see* TURINI, FERDINANDO.
TWITTENHOFF, WILHELM, 1904– .
Das erste Spiel auf der Schulflöte.
In: Bausteine für Musikerziehung und Musikpflege. B 108.
Kleine Tanzstücke.
In: Zeitschrift für Spielmusik. No.136.
Weihnachtsmusiken.
In: Bausteine für Musikerziehung und Musikpflege. B 118.
TYE, CHRISTOPHER, ca.1500–ca.1573.
Selections.
In: Crotch. Specimens of various styles of music. Vol.2.
Choral music.
In: Engel. Three centuries of choral music. Vol.3.
Church music.
In: Motett Society. [Collection of ancient church music]. Division 3.
Instrumental music.
In: Recent reserches in the music of the Renaissance. Vol.3.
Mass to six voices. "Euge Bone".
In: Arkwright. The Old English edition. Vol.10.
Organ music.
In: The Liturgical Music Press, Inc. Masterpieces of organ music. Folio 73.
Part music.
In: Hullah. Part music. Class A.1. Vol.1, 2.
Sacred music.
In: Boyce. Cathedral music. Vol.2; 1849 ed. Vol.2.
In: Page. Harmonia sacra. Vol.3.
Vocal music.
In: Hullah. Vocal scores. I. Sacred.
TYPP.
Selections.
In: Plainsong and Mediaeval Music Society. Publications. (Old Hall manuscript).

UCCELLININI, MARCO, b.ca.1610.
Selections.
In: Torchi. L'arte musicale in Italia. Bd.7.
Chamber music.
In: Riemann. Old chamber music. Vol.4.
Instrumental music.
In: Wasielewski. Instrumentalsätze vom Ende des XVI. bis Ende des XVII. Jahrhunderts.
Sinfonia a tre, per due violini e basso continuo. Op.9/7.
In: Hausmusik. No.151.
The wedding of the hen and the cuckoo.
In: Musikschätze der Vergangenheit.
UDDÉN, ÅKE.
Selections.
In: Svensk sanglyrik. Vol.2.
String trio.
In: Musikaliska konstföreningen. 1952.
UHL, ALFRED, 1909– .
Erstes Streichquartett, für zwei Violinen, Viola und Violoncello.
In: Hausmusik. No.119–120.
So ruhig . . . aus Frühlingsstimmen.
In: Hausmusik. No.146.
ULENBERG, KASPAR.
Die Psalmen Davids.
In: Denkmäler rheinischer Musik. Vol.3.
UMLAUFF, IGNAZ, 1746–1796.
Die Bergknappen.
In: Denkmäler der Tonkunst in Österreich. Vol.36. (Jg.XVIII/1).

UMSTATT.
Keyboard music.
In: Clementi. Clementi's Selection of practical harmony. Vol.1.
U.S.–MUSIC (*see also* FOLKSONGS, U.S; SONGS, AMERICAN).
In: Downes. A treasury of American song.
In: Engel. Music from the days of George Washington.
In: Fisher. The music that Washington knew.
In: Goldman. Landmarks of early American music, 1760–1800.
In: Marrocco. Music in America.
In: Music Press, Inc. [Choral series]. Vol.55.
In: Siegmeister. Songs of early America, 1620–1830.
In: Society for the Publication of American Music. Publications.
In: The Wa-Wan series of American compositions.
In: Zeitschrift für Spielmusik. No.290.
UNKEL, ROLF, 1912– .
Organ music.
In: The parish organist. Vol.1–4.
UPSALA, CANCIONERO DE.
In: Villancicos de diuersos autores. Cancionero de Upsala.
URAY, ERNST LUDWIG, 1906– .
Variationen und Fuge.
In: Gitarre-Kammermusik. No.21.
URIBE-HOLGUÍN, GUILLERMO, 1880– .
(var. sp.: Guilermo Uribe-Holguín).
Preludio. Op.49, No.1, Op.56, No.1.
In: New music. Vol.12. No.4. July 1939.
Vocal music.
In: Boletín latino-americano de música. Vol.4.
URIO, FRANCESCO ANTONIO, b.ca.1660.
Te Deum.
In: Denkmäler der Tonkunst. Vol.5.
URREDA, JUAN, 15th CENTURY.
(var. sp.: Juan Urrede).
Choral music.
In: Engel. Three centuries of choral music. Vol.5.
URTEAGA, LUIS.
Organ music.
In: Organ album of ten pieces by Spanish composers.
UTENDAL, ALEXANDER, ca.1530–1581.
(var. sp.: Alexander Uttendal).
Choral music.
In: Antiqua Chorbuch. Vol.2. Heft 2.
In: Der Kammerchor. Vol.2.
Lied- und Choralmotetten.
In: Das Chorwerk. No.30.
Lieder.
In: Commer. Geistliche und weltliche Lieder aus dem XVI.–XVII. Jahrhundert.
Madrigals.
In: Squire. Ausgewählte Madrigale und mehrstimmige Gesänge. No.42, 49.
Sacred music.
In: Proske. Musica divina. Annus primus. Tom 4.
UTTENDAL, A., *see* UTENDAL, ALEXANDER.

VACHON, PIERRE, 1731–1802.
Violin and piano.
In: Schering. Alte Meister des Violinspiels.
VACQUERAS, BELTRAME, 15th–16th CENTURIES.
(var. sp.: Vaqueras).
Chanson.
In: Brown. Theatrical chansons of the 15th and early 16th centuries.
Missa super l'homme armé.
In: Monumenta polyphoniae liturgicae sanctae ecclesiae romanae. Ser.1. Tomus 1. Fasc.10.
VACTOR, DAVID VAN, *see* VAN VACTOR, DAVID.
VAET, JACOBUS, 1529–1567.
Complete works. I, II, III, IV, V.
In: Denkmäler der Tonkunst in Österreich. Vol.98, 100, 103/104, 108/109, 113/114.
Selections.
In: Maldéghem. Trésor musical.
Choral music.
In: Commer. Collectio operum musicorum batavorum saeculi XVI. Bd.2, 4, 5, 9.
Zwei Hymnen.
In: Musik alter Meister. Heft 8.
Sechs Motetten.
In: Das Chorwerk. No.2.
Motette Rex Babylonis venit ad lacum.
In: Musik alter Meister. Heft 12.
VAL, FRANÇOIS DU, *see* DU VAL, FRANÇOIS.
VALCÁRCEL, THEODORO, 1900– .
Danza del combate. (Piano).
In: Instituto Interamericano de Musicologia. Publicaciónes. No.32.
VALDERRÁBANO, ENRIQUE, ENRIQUEZ DE, *see* ENRIQUEZ DE VALDERRÁBANO, ENRIQUE.
VALDÉS, ROBERTO CARPIO, *see* CARPIO VALDÉS, ROBERTO.
VALENCIA–MUSIC.
In: Comes. Danzas del Santísimo Corpus Christi.
VALENCIANO.
Selections.
In: Pedrell. Treatro lirico espanol anterior al siglo XIX. Bd.4/5.
VALENTE, ANTONIO, b.ca.1520.
(var. sp.: Antonio Valento).
Selections.
In: Torchi. L'arte musicale in Italia. Bd.3.
Keyboard music.
In: Kastner. Silva iberica.
Organ music.
In: Fuser. Classici italiani dell' organo.
VALENTIN, ERICH, 1906– . ed.
The toccata.
In: Anthology of music. Vol.17.
VALENTIN, K.
Eight songs for voice and piano, Op.7.
In: Musikaliska konstföreningen. 1886.
VALENTINI, GIOVANNI, d.1649.
Chamber music.
In: Riemann. Old chamber music. Vol.3.
VALENTINI, GIUSEPPE, ca.1681–ca.1740.
Concerto No.3 in C (oboe, violin soli, strings, cembalo).
In: Antica musica strumentale italiana. Ser.II. Vol.20.
Kammer-Sonaten für Violine und Pianoforte.
In: Moffat. Kammer-Sonaten für Violine und Pianoforte. No.23.
Sonate. (G). Sonate. (D).
In: Moffat. Trio-Sonaten alter Meister. No.20, 27.

Weihnachts-Pastorale.
In: Schering. Perlen alter Kammermusik.
VALENTINO, ROBERTO, fl.1730.
Drei Sonaten für Block- oder Querflöte und Basso Continuo.
In: Nagels Musik-Archiv. No.149.
Sonate. (Am). Violin and piano.
In: Moffat. Meister-Schule der alten Zeit. Violin-Sonaten. No.17.
VALENTO, ANTONIO, *see* VALENTE, ANTONIO.
VALENZUELA, PEDRO, 16th CENTURY.
La verginella.
In: Squire. Ausgewählte Madrigale und mehrstimmige Gesänge. No.36.
VALERANO, GIOVANNI MARIA NANINI DA, *see* NANINI, GIOVANNI MARIA.
VALERIUS, ADRIANUS, ca.1575–1625.
Old Dutch songs.
In: Vereninging voor Nederlandsche Muziekgeschiedenis. Uitgave. No.2.
VALLADOLID CODEX.
Missa pro defunctis.
In: Musica liturgica. Vol.2. Fasc.1.
VALLEDOR, JACINTO.
Selections.
In: Pedrell. Teatro lirico espanol anterior al siglo XIX. Bd.1.
VALLERANO, A. DA.
Keyboard music.
In: Clementi. Clementi's Selection of practical harmony. Vol.1.
VALLS, FRANCISCO, 1665–1747.
Sacred music.
In: Eslava y Elizondo. Lira sacro-hispana. 18th century. i.l.
VAN BOOM, JAN, *see* BOOM, JAN VAN.
VAN DEN GHEYN, MATTHIAS, *see* GHEYN, MATTHIAS VAN DEN.
VAN DEN KERCKHOVEN, ABRAHAM, *see* KERCKHOVEN, ABRAHAM VAN DEN.
VAN EYL, ANNA MARIA, *see* EYL, ANNA MARIA VAN.
VAŇHAL, JAN KŘTITEL, *see* WANHAL, JOHANN BAPTIST.
VANHALL, JOHANN BAPTIST, *see* WANHAL, JOHANN BAPTIST.
VAN HELMONT, CHARLES JOSEPH, *see* HELMONT, CHARLES JOSEPH VAN.
VAN HULSE, CAMIL, *see* HULSE, CAMIL VAN.
VAN KONINK, SERVAAS, *see* KONINK, SERVAAS VAN.
VAN MELDERT, LEONARD, *see* MELDERT, LEONARD VAN.
VAN NOORDT, ANTHONI, *see* NOORDT, ANTHONI VAN.
VAN OEVERING, RYNOLDUS POPMA, *see* OEVERING, RYNOLDUS POPMA VAN.
VAN ONGUEVAL, *see* ONGUEVAL, VAN.
VAN PONTE, JACOB, *see* PONTE, JACOB VAN.
VAN RIEMSDIJK, JOHANN CORNELIS MARIUS, *see* RIEMSDIJK, JOHANN CORNELIS MARIUS, VAN.
VANROTTE, ERICKA SMIT– ., *see* SMIT-VANROTTE, ERICKA.
VAN ROY, BARTHELEMY, *see* ROY, BARTHELEMY VAN.
VAN VACTOR, DAVID, 1906– .
Música de cámara.
In: Boletín latino-americano de música. Vol.5.
Quintet for flute and strings.
In: Society for the Publication of American Music. Publications. 22d season. 1940-41.
Vocal works.
In: New music. Vol.17. No.2. Jan.1944.
VAN WESTERHOUT, NICCOLÒ, *see* WESTERHOUT, NICCOLÒ VAN.
VAQUERAS, *see* VACQUERAS, BELTRAME.
VAQUIERAS, REIMBAUTZ DE.
Selections.
In: Gleason. Examples of music before 1400.
VARÈSE, EDGAR, 1885– .
(var. sp.: Edgard Varèse).
Density 21.5. For flute solo
In: New music. Vol.19. No.4. July 1946.
Ionisation, for percussion ensemble of 13 players.
In: New music. Orchestra series. No.11.
VARGAS, U. DE.
Sacred music.
In: Eslava y Elizondo. Lira sacro-hispana. 17th century. i.l.
THE VARIATION. (FISCHER).
In: Anthology of music. Vol.11.
VAROTTI, MICHELE, 16th CENTURY.
(var. sp.: Varoti).
Selections.
In: Musica sacra . . . 1839– . Vol.15, 16.
VÁSQUEZ, JUAN, 16th CENTURY.
Recopilación de sonetos y villancicos a quatro y a cinco.
In: Monumentos de la música española. Vol.4.
Songs
In: Bal y Gay. Romances y villancicos españoles del signo XVI.
VASURTO.
Organ music.
In: Cantantibus organis. Vol.8.
VAUGHAN WILLIAMS, RALPH, 1872–1958.
Selections.
In: The music with the form and order of the service to be performed at the coronation of . . . Queen Elizabeth II.
VAUTOR, THOMAS, 16th–17th CENTURIES.
Choral music.
In: Engel. Three centuries of choral music. Vol.3.
Madrigals.
In: Euterpe. Vol.2, 9; 2d ed. No.45–46.
In: Fellowes. The English madrigal school. Vol.34.
In: Squire. Ausgewählte Madrigale und mehrstimmige Gesänge. No.35.
VAUX, RAULIN DE, 15th CENTURY.
Selections.
In: Reaney. Early fifteenth-century music. Vol.2.
VEANA, M.
Sacred music.
In: Eslava y Elizondo. Lira sacro-hispana. 17th century. i.l.
VECCHI, ORAZIO, ca.1550–1605.
(var. sp.: Vecchio).
Selections.
In: Documenta historica musicae.

In: Musica sacra . . . 1839– . Vol.16.
In: Smith. Musica antiqua.
In: Torchi. L'arte musicale in Italia. Bd.2, 4.
L'Amfiparnasso.
In: Publikationen älterer praktischer und theoretischer Musikwerke. Jahrg.30.
In: Somma. Capolavori polifonici del secolo XVI. Vol.5.
Arie, canzonette e balli.
In: Chilesotti. Biblioteca di rarità musicali. Vol.5.
Choral music.
In: Engel. Three centuries of choral music. Vol.2.
Convito musicale, a 3, 4, 5, 6, 7 et 8 voci.
In: Somma. Capolavori polifonici del secolo XVI. Vol.8.
Leggiadretto Clorino.
In: Arion. Vol.3.
Madrigals.
In: Einstein. The golden age of the madrigal.
In: Squire. Ausgewählte Madrigale und mehrstimmige Gesänge. No.23, 34.
O bella, O bianca.
In: Arion. Vol.3.
Sacred music.
In: Proske. Musica divina. Annus primus. Tom 2.
In: Proske. Selectus novus missarum. Annus primus. Tom 2.
Le Veglie di Siena.
In: Somma. Capolavori polifonici del secolo XVI. Vol.2.
Vocal music.
In: Ghisi. Feste musicali della Firenze Medicea.
VEGA CARPIO, LOPE FÉLIX DE, 1562–1635.
Treinta canciones. 109p.
VEJVANOVSKÝ, PAVEL JOSEF, ca.1643–ca. 1693.
Serenate e sonate per orchestra.
In: Musica antiqua bohemica. Vol.36.
VELÁSQUEZ, JOSÉ FRANCISCO.
Niño mío; Tercera lección de difuntos.
In: Archivo de musica colonial venezolana. No.10, 12.
VELJVANOVSKY.
Composizioni per orchestra. Pt.I–III.
In: Musica antiqua bohemica. Vol.47–49.
VELUT, GILET, 15th CENTURY.
Selections.
In: Reaney. Early fifteenth-century music. Vol.2.
Sacred music.
In: Plainsong and Mediaeval Music Society. Publications. (Borren).
VENEGAS DE HENESTROSA, LUYS, 16th CENTURY.
(var. sp.: Alcalá de Henares).
Libro de cifra nueva para tecla, harpa y vihuela.
In: Monumentos de la música española. Vol.2.
Lute music.
In: Morphy. Les luthistes espanols du XVIe siècle. Vol.2.
VENEZUELA–MUSIC.
In: Archivo de música colonial venezolana.
VENICE–MUSIC.
In: Jeppesen. Balli antichi veneziano per cembalo.
In: Lefkoff. Five sixteenth century Venetian lute books.
VENTADORN, BERNART DE, *see* BERNART DE VENTADORN.
VENTO, IVO DE, d.1575.
Choral music.
In: Antiqua Chorbuch. Vol.1. Heft 3; Vol.2. Heft 3.
Lied- und Choralmotetten.
In: Das Chorwerk. No.30.
Weltliche Chorlieder.
In: Christophorus-Chorwerk. Heft 6.
Lieder.
In: Commer. Geistliche und weltliche Lieder aus dem XVI.–XVII. Jahrhundert.
VENTURI DEL NIBBIO, STEFANO, 16th–17th CENTURIES.
Selections.
In: Musica sacra . . . 1839– . Vol.16.
VEPES, *see* YEPES.
VEPRIK, ALEXANDER MOISEYEVITCH, 1899–
Stalinstan. Chorus with piano acc.
In: New music. Vol.8. No.1. Oct.1934.
VERACINI, ANTONIO, b.ca.1650.
Instrumental music.
In: Wasielewski. Instrumentalsätze vom Ende des XVI. bis Ende des XVII. Jahrhunderts.
VERACINI, FRANCESCO MARIA, ca.1690–ca.1750.
Kammer-Sonaten für Violine und Pianoforte.
In: Moffat. Kammer-Sonaten für Violine und Pianoforte. No.6, 13.
Konzert D-dur für Violine und Streicher.
In: Hortus musicus. No.169.
Sonate.
In: I classici della musica italiana. Vol.34.
In: I classici della musica italiana. Raccolta nazionale delle musiche italiane. Quad. 139–144.
Sonate (Dm). Violin and piano.
In: Moffat. Meister-Schule der alten Zeit. Violin-Sonaten. No.3.
Violin and piano.
In: Schering. Alte Meister des Violinspiels.
VERBONNET, JOHANNES GHISELIN–, *see* GHISELIN-VERBONNET, JOHANNES.
VERDEIL, R. PALIKAROVA.
La musique byzantine chez les Bulgares et les Russes.
In: Monumenta musicae byzantinae. Subsidia. Vol.3.
VERDELOT, PHILIPPE, d.ca.1565.
Opera omnia. v.1– .
Selections.
In: Maldéghem. Trésor musical.
I vostr'-acuti dardi.
In: Arion. Vol.3.
Lieder.
In: Publikationen älterer praktischer und theoretischer Musikwerke. Jahrg.1–3.
Motets.
In: Attaingnant. Treize livres de motets. Livre 1, 2, 3, 4, 10, 11.

Sacred music.
In: Jeppesen. Italia sacra musica. Vol.1.
VERDELOTTO, F.
Keyboard music.
In: Tagliapietra. Antologia di musica antica e moderna per pianoforte. Bd.1.
VERDIER.
Keyboard music.
In: English keyboard music. [No.10].
VERDONCK, CORNELIUS, ca.1563–1625.
Selections.
In: Maldéghem. Trésor musical.
Sacred music.
In: Proske. Musica divina. Annus secundus. Tom 2.
In: Proske. Selectus novus missarum. Annus secundum. Tom 2.
VERELST, THEO.
Polyphonic music.
In: Monumenta musicae belgicae. Vol.9.
VERETTI, ANTONIO, 1900– .
Keyboard music.
In: Tagliapietra. Antologia di musica antica e moderna per pianoforte. Bd.18.
VERMONT, PIERRE, 16th CENTURY.
Chansons.
In: Expert. Les maîtres musiciens de la Renaissance française. Vol.5.
Motets.
In: Attaingnant. Treize livres de motets. Livre 1, 3, 4, 7, 9, 11, 12.
VERRALL, JOHN, 1908– .
Four pieces for piano.
In: Washington (State) University. Music series. No.4.
VERT, G. DE, *see* WERT, GIACHES DE.
VERVOILLE, C.
Part music.
In: Hullah. Part music. 1868 edition.
VESPERORUM PRECUM OFFICIA.
In: Rhaw. Musikdrucke. Vol.4.
VETTER, ANDREAS NIKOLAUS, 1666–1710.
(var. sp.: Andreas Nicolaus Vetter).
Organ music.
In: Buszin. Organ series. Vol.1.
In: Dietrich. Elf Orgelchörale des siebzehnten Jahrhunderts.
In: Das Erbe deutscher Musik. 1.Reihe. Vol.9.
In: Keller. Achtzig Choralvorspiele deutscher Meister des 17. und 18. Jahrhunderts.
In: Klein. The first four centuries of music for the organ from Dunstable to Bach (1370–1749).
VIADANA, LODOVICO DA, 1564–1645.
(var. sp.: Ludovico Grossi da Viadana).
Chamber music.
In: Riemann. Old chamber music. Vol.1.
Choral music.
In: Societas Polyphonica Romanae. Repertorium. Vol.4.
Drei geistliche Konzerte. Alt und B.C.
In: Cantio sacra. No.40.
Drei geistliche Konzerte. Bass und B.C.
In: Cantio sacra. No.5.
Drei geistliche Konzerte. Sopran und B.C.
In: Cantio sacra. No.51.
Missa Dominicalis.
In: Musica divina. Vol.10.
Sacred music.
In: Proske. Musica divina. Annus primus. Tom 3, 4; Annus secundus. Tom 3.
In: Proske. Selectus novus missarum. Annus secundus. Tom 3.
VIANNA, FRUCTUOSO, 1896– .
Música de cámara.
In: Boletín latino-americano de música. Vol.6.
Piano music.
In: Boletín latino-americano de música. Vol.4.
VICENTINO, NICOLA, 1511–1572.
Collected works. 160p.
Selections.
In: Torchi. L'arte musicale in Italia. Bd.1.
VICTOR, ADAM DE SAINT, *see* ADAM DE SAINT-VICTOR.
VICTORIA, TOMÁS LUIS DE, d.1611.
(var. sp.: T. L. da Vittoria).
Opera omnia. 8v.
——Reprint 1965.
Ave Maria.
In: Musica spiritualis. Serie IB. No.7.
Choral music.
In: Engel. Three centuries of choral music. Vol.2, 5.
In: Music Press, Inc. [Choral series]. No.69, 70, 79.
In: Recueil de musique ancienne. Recueil des morceaux de musique ancienne. Bd. 2, 6, 10.
In: Rochlitz. Sammlung vorzüglicher Gesangstücke. Bd.1. Pt.2.
In: Societas Polyphonica Romanae. Repertorium. Vol.1, 3, 5.
Church music.
In: Motett Society. [Collection of ancient church music]. Division 1, 2, 3.
Falsum bordonem.
In: Pedrell. Hispaniae schola musica sacra. Bd.6.
Kirchengesänge.
In: Tucher. Kirchengesänge der berühmtesten älteren italienischen Meister.
Missa Ave maris stella.
In: Musica spiritualis. Ser.IIA. No.9.
Missa pro defunctis cum responsorio, Libera me Domine 1605.
In: Musica divina. Vol.15.
Missa quarti toni.
In: Musica spiritualis. Ser.IA. No.4.
O magnum mysterium.
In: Musica spiritualis. Ser.IB. No.8.
Organ music.
In: Cantantibus organis. Vol.6.
Sacred music.
In: Eslava y Elizondo. Lira sacro-hispana. 16th century. i.2.
In: The Fitzwilliam music. Bd.5.
In: Musica spiritualis. Ser.IIB. No.13, 14.
In: Polifonía española. Vol.18, 23, 24, 25, 26, 27.
In: Proske. Musica divina. Annus primus.

Tom 1, 2, 3, 4; Annus secundus.
Tom 1, 2.
In: Proske. Selectus novus missarum. Annus primus. Tom 1, 2; Annus secundus. Tom 1, 2, 3.
In: Rubio. Antologia polifonica sacra. Vol.1.

VICTORINUS, S.
Sacred music.
In: Proske. Musica divina. Annus primus. Tom 4.

VIDE, JACQUES, 15th CENTURY.
Selections.
In: Marix. Les musiciens de la Cour de Bourgogne au XVe siècle (1420–1467).

VIDES, PEDRO ARANAZ Y., *see* ARANAZ Y VIDES, PEDRO.

VIENNA–MUSIC.
In: Denkmäler der Tonkunst in Österreich. Vol.27. (Jg.XIII/2); Vol.31. (Jg.XV/2); Vol.39. (Jg.XIX/2); Vol.54. (Jg.XXVII/2); Vol.56. (Jg.XXVIII/2); Vol.79. (Jg. XLII/2); Vol.84.
In: Das Erbe deutscher Musik. 2.Reihe. Alpen- und Donau Reichsgaue. Vol.1. (Same as Denkmäler der Tonkunst in Österreich. Vol.84).

VIERDANCK, JOHANN, 17th CENTURY.
Capricci mit zwei oder drei Instrumenten.
In: Hortus musicus. No.21.
Der Herr hat seinen Engeln befahlen. (Psalm 91).
In: Engel. Drei Werke pommerscher Komponisten.
Siehe, wie fein und lieblich, aus "Erster Theil geistlicher Concerten."
In: Denkmäler der Musik in Pommern. Heft 4.
Spielmusik für zwei und drei Violinen oder andere Melodieninstrumente.
In: Denkmäler der Musik in Pommern. Heft 1.
Triosuite für 2 Violinen, Violoncello und Klavizimbel.
In: Organum. 3.Reihe. Nr.4.
Weihnachtskonzert "Ich verkündige euch grosse Freude" aus "Erster Theil geistlicher Concerten."
In: Denkmäler der Musik in Pommern. Heft 3.

VIERLING, JOHANN GOTTFRIED, 1750–1813.
Fugue, Timentibus.
?In: Königliche Akademie der Künste. Auswahl vorzüglicher Musik-Werke. No.40.
Organ music.
In: Caecilia; Sammlung von Choralvorspielen.

VIERNE, LOUIS, 1870–1937.
Organ music.
In: Bedell. The French organist. Vol.1, 2.
In: Bonnet. Historical organ-recitals. Vol.5.

VIERNE-BEDELL.
Organ music.
In: Standard series of organ compositions. No.54.

VILA, PEDRO ALBERTO, 1517–1582.
Organ music.
In: Muset. Early Spanish organ music.

VILLAFLOR.
Selections.
In: Pedrell. Teatro lirico espanol anterior al siglo XIX. Bd.4/5.

VILLAIN, M. F.
Motets.
In: Attaingnant. Treize livres de motets. Livre 13.

VILLALAR.
Motets.
In: Elúsitiza. Antología musical.

VILLA-LOBOS, HEITOR, d.1959.
Canciones.
In: Boletín latino-americano de música. Vol.1.
Keyboard music.
In: Boletín latino-americano de música. Vol.1, 4.
In: Guenther. Collection espagnole.
Melodia de Montanha. Piano.
In: New music. Vol.16. No.1. Oct. 1942.
Música da cámara.
In: Boletín latino-americano de música. Vol.6.
New York sky-line. Piano.
In: New music. Vol.16. No.1. Oct. 1942.
O pião. (Band).
In: Instituto Interamericano de Musicologia. Publicaciónes. No.37.

VILLANCICOS.
In: Asenjo y Barbieri. Cancionero musical de los siglos XV y XVI.
In: Bal y Gay. Romances y villancicos españoles del signo XVI.
In: Barcelona. Biblioteca Central. Sección de Música. Publicaciones. No.12.
In: Monumentos de la música española. Vol.4.
In: Villancicos de diversos autores. Cancionero de Upsala.

VILLANUEVA, FR. MARTINUS DE.
Sacred music.
In: Rubio. Antologia polifonica sacra. Vol.1.

VILLEBOIS.
Vocal music.
In: Sammlung russischer Romanzen. No.130–132.

VILLIERS (VUILLERS), PIERRE DE.
Chansons.
In: Publikationen älterer praktischer und theoretischer Musikwerke. Jahrg.27.

VILLOUD, HÉCTOR OGLESIAS, *see* IGLESIAS VILLOUD, HÉCTOR.

VINCENTIUS DE ARIMINO.
(var. sp.: Vincenzo de Rimini).
Selections.
In: Pirrotta. The music of fourteenth-century Italy. Vol.4.
Cacce.
In: Marrocco. Fourteenth-century Italian cacce.

VINCI, LEONARDO, 1690–1730.
Selections.
?In: Crotch. Specimens of various styles of music. Vol.3.
Arias.
In: Parisotti. Arie antiche. Bd.3.
Vocal music.
In: Gevaert. Les gloires de l'Italie. Vol.1, 2.

VINCI, PIETRO, ca.1535–1584.

Selections.
In: Torchi. L'arte musicale in Italia. Bd.1.
VINCO.
Organ music.
In: Cantantibus organis. Vol.11.
VINTZ, GEORG.
Altdeutsche Tanzsätze.
In: Nagels Musik-Archiv. No.80.
VINYALS, JOSEP.
Instrumental music.
In: Mestres de l'escolania de Montserrat. (Pujol, ed. Musica instrumental. Vol.2.).
VIOLA, ALFONSO DELLA, ca.1508–ca.1570.
Italienische Madrigale.
In: Das Chorwerk. No.58.
VIOLA, ANSELM, 1739–1798.
Instrumental music.
In: Mestres de l'escolania de Montserrat. (Pujol, ed. Musica instrumental. Vol.2.).
Organ music.
In: Muset. Early Spanish organ music.
VIOLA.
In: Contemporary Japanese music series. No.21.
In: Giesbert. Altenglische Violenmusik zu drei Stimmen.
VIOLIN.
In: L'école du violon au XVIIe et XVIIIe siècle.
In: Hausmusik (passim).
In: Hortus musicus (passim).
In: Moffat. Kammer-Sonaten für Violine und Pianoforte des 17. und 18. Jahrhunderts.
In: Moffat. Meister-Schule der alten Zeit. Sammlung klassischer Violin-Sonaten.
In: New music (passim).
In: Schering. Alte Meister des Violinspiels.
In: Spielstücke für Blockflöten, Geigen, Lauten oder andere Instrumente.
VIOLONCELLO.
In: Contemporary Japanese music series. No.23.
In: Hortus musicus (passim).
In: Moecks gelbe Musikhefte. Vol.54–57.
In: Moffat. Meister-Schule der alten Zeit. Sammlung klassischer Violoncello-Sonaten.
In: New music (passim).
VIOTTI, GIOVANNI BATTISTA, 1753–1824.
Concerto in G minor (piano solo, orchestra).
In: Antica musica strumentale italiana. Ser.I. Vol.10.
Concerto No.19 in G minor for violin, orchestra.
In: Antica musica strumentale italiana. In preparation.
VIRDUNG, SEBASTIAN, 15th–16th CENTURIES.
Musica Getutscht.
In: Publikationen älterer praktischer und theoretischer Musikwerke. Jahrg.10.
VIRELAIS.
In: Summa musicae medii aevi. Vol.10.
In: Turin. Biblioteca Nazionale. Mss. (J.II.9). The Cypriot-French repertory. Vol.4.
VIRGINAL MANUSCRIPT, THE DUBLIN.
In: The Wellesley edition. No.3.
VIRGINAL MUSIC, *see* KEYBOARD MUSIC–CLAVICHORD, HARPSICHORD, PIANO, VIRGINAL.
VIRGINAL PIECES.
In: Schott's Anthology of early keyboard music. Vol.3, 5.
VISCONTI, GASPARO, 17th–18th CENTURIES.
Sonate (A). Violoncello and piano.
In: Moffat. Meister-Schule der alten Zeit. Violoncello-Sonaten. No.12.
VITALI, FILIPPO, d.1653.
Songs.
In: Jeppesen. La flora. Vol.2, 3.
Vocal music.
In: Gevaert. Les gloires de l'Italie. Vol.1.
VITALI, GIOVANNI BATTISTA, ca.1644–1692.
Selections.
In: Torchi. L'arte musicale in Italia. Bd.7.
Artifici musicali. Op.XIII.
In: Smith College music archives. No.14.
Chamber music.
In: Riemann. Old chamber music. Vol.4.
In: Instrumental music.
In: Wasielewski. Instrumentalsätze vom Ende des XVI. bis Ende des XVII. Jahrhunderts.
Sonata a tre, per due violini e basso continuo, Op.II/6.
In: Hausmusik. No.147.
Sonata in F major, Op.5, No.8. (La Guidoni).
In: Seventeenth-century chamber music. No.6.
VITALI, TOMMASO ANTONIO, 17th CENTURY.
Concerto di sonate, Op.4, for violin, violoncello, and continuo.
In: Smith College music archives. No.12.
Sonate für Violine/Violoncello und Cembalo.
In: Hortus musicus. No.38.
VITÁSEK, JAN AUGUSTIN, 1770–1839.
Drei Vortragsstücke für Klavier.
In: Musica viva historica. Vol.4.
Keyboard music.
In: Musica antiqua bohemica. Vol.14.
VITRY, PHILIPPE DE, 1291–1361.
Works.
In: Schrade. Polyphonic music of the fourteenth century. Vol.1.
VITTORIA, T. L. da, *see* VICTORIA, TOMÁS LUIS DE.
VIVALDI, ANTONIO, ca.1675–1743.
Le opere. v.1– .
Airs.
In: Prunières. Les maîtres du chant. Recueil.1.
Arias.
In: Parisotti. Arie antiche. Bd.1.
Capriccio.
In: L'école du violon au XVIIe et XVIIIe siècle. No.1339.
Concerto G dur.
In: Sondheimer. Werke aus dem 18. Jahrhundert. Nr.26.
Concerto in Do maggiore. Concerto in Fa maggiore. Concerti di Dresda.
In: Classici italiani della musica. Vol.2.
Violin concerto, Op.7/II/2.
In: Lea pocket scores. No.69.
Concerto grosso. Op.3. Nr.3.
In: Musikschätze der Vergangenheit.
Duette alter Meister.
In: Zeitschrift für Spielmusik. No.69.
La fide Ninfa.
In: Instituta et monumenta. Vol.3.
Juditha triumphans.

In: Somma. Musiche vocali e strumentali sacre e profane, sec. XVII–XVIII–XIX. Vol.10.
Kammer-Sonaten für Violine und Pianoforte.
In: Moffat. Kammer-Sonaten für Violine und Pianoforte. No.10.
Keyboard music.
In: Tagliapietra. Antologia di musica antica e moderna per pianoforte. Bd.10.
Konzert für Flauto traverso, Streichorchester und Cembalo. Op.10; Konzert D-dur für Violoncello, Streichorchester und Cembalo.
In: Antiqua Edition. Solo-Instrument mit Begleitung.
Konzert für Violine mit Streichorchester und Basso Continuo. Op.6, Nr.1. G moll.
In: Nagels Musik-Archiv. No.106.
Konzert A-moll für Violoncello und Streichorchester.
In: Nagels Musik-Archiv. No.166.
Largo aus einer Violinsonate. Largo aus einem Violinkonzert.
In: Schering. Perlen alter Kammermusik.
Il pastor fido. 6 Sonaten für ein Holzblasinstrumente oder Violine und Basso Continuo.
In: Hortus musicus. No.135.
Il pastor fido. Sonata No.VI in G minor for flute, or oboe, or violin, and piano.
In: Music for wind instruments by 18th century masters. No.1.
Pastorale, für Flöte (Violine, Oboe) obligates Violoncello und Orgel (Cembalo).
In: Nagels Musik-Archiv. No.18.
La primavera. (Allegro).
In: Parrish. A treasury of early music. No.47.
Drei Sonaten.
In: Kammersonaten. No.16.
Sonate für Oboe und Basso Continuo; Sonaten für Violine und Klavier, Violoncello ad lib.
In: Antiqua Edition. Von 2 Instrumenten an.
Vier Sonaten für Violine und Basso Continuo, Op.5, Nr.1–4.
In: Nagels Musik-Archiv. No.162.
Sonate. Violin and piano.
In: Moffat. Meister-Schule der alten Zeit. Violin-Sonaten. No.10, 36.
Sonate G-moll für Violine und Basso Continuo.
In: Hortus musicus. No.102.
Sonate in G moll. Für Violine und Cembalo (Klavier) mit Violoncell ad lib.
In: Kammersonaten. No.17.
Sonata G-moll für Violine und Gitarre.
In: Gitarre-Kammermusik. No.20.
Sonate en la majeur.
In: L'école du violon au XVIIe et XVIIIe siècle. No.1268.
Zwei Sonaten, Op.2, für Violine, Cembalo (Klavier) und Bass-Instrument.
In: Antiqua Edition. Von 3 Instrumenten an.
Zwei Sonaten für zwei Violinen und Basso Continuo, Op.5, Nr.5–6. (Cembalo und Violoncello).
In: Nagels Musik-Archiv. No.171.
Sonata a tre, Op.5/5.
In: Hausmusik. No.138.
Sonata a tre, per due violini e basso continuo.
In: Hausmusik. No.51.
Songs.
In: Jeppesen. La flora. Vol.3.
Le stagioni.
In: I classici della musica italiana. Vol.35.
Concerti delle stagioni. Op.VIII.
In: I classici della musica italiana. Raccolta nazionale delle musiche italiane. Quad. 294–297.
Trio für Alt-Blockflöte, Violine und Basso Continuo.
In: Moecks Kammermusik. Vol.47.
Trio-Sonate (Dm); Sonate (Em).
In: Moffat. Trio-Sonaten alter Meister. No.4, 14.
Triosonate, Op.1, Nr.2, E-moll, für zwei Violinen und Basso Continuo.
In: Nagels Musik-Archiv. No.147.
Violin and piano.
In: Schering. Alte Meister des Violinspiels.
Weihnachtspastoralen.
In: Zeitschrift für Spielmusik. No.236.
VIVANCO, SEBASTIANUS.
Sacred music.
In: Eslava y Elizondo. Lira sacro-hispana. 17th century. i.l.
In: Rubio. Antologia polifonica sacra. Vol.1.
VOCAL MUSIC–MISCELLANEOUS COLLECTIONS.
In: Bausteine.
In: Delsarte. Archives du chant.
In: Landshoff. Alte Meister des Bel Canto. Eine Sammlung von Arien.
In: Landshoff. I classici del Bel Canto.
In: Parisotti. Arie antiche.
In: Plainsong and Mediaeval Music Society. Publications. (Ruuta).
In: Potter. Reliquary of English song.
In: Prunières. Les maîtres du chant.
In: Publikationen älterer praktischer und theoretischer Musikwerke. Jahrg.27.
In: Sammlung russischer Romanzen.
In: Weckerlin. Échos du temps passé.
VODICKA, V.
Sinfonia für Streichquartett. (Cembalo ad lib.).
In: Musica viva historica. Vol.14.
6 Sonate. Violino e piano.
In: Musica antiqua bohemica. Vol.54.
VOGEL.
Selections.
In: Crotch. Specimens of various styles of music. Vol.3.
VOGELWEIDE, WALTER VON DER, ca.1170–ca.1230.
Selections.
In: Gleason. Examples of music before 1400.
VOGLER, GEORG JOSEPH, 1749–1814.
Konzert für Cembalo (Klavier), 2 Violinen und Cello-Bass.
In: Musikschätze der Vergangenheit.
Organ music.
?In: Cantantibus organis. Vol.3.
Variationen und Capriccio über "Malbrough s'en va-t-en guerre" für Klavier (Cembalo) und kleines Kammerorchester.
In: Antiqua Edition. Solo-Instrument mit Begleitung.
VOGLER, JOHANN KASPAR, 1696–1765.
(var. sp.: Johann Caspar Vogler).
Organ music.
In: Straube. Choralvorspiele alter Meister.

Sacred music.
?In: Latrobe, C. I. Selection of sacred music.
?In: Latrobe, J. A. The music of the church.
VOIGTLÄNDER, GABRIEL, d.1643.
Lieder.
In: Moser. Alte Meister des deutschen Liedes. 30 Gesänge. No.6, 7.
In: Moser. Alte Meister des deutschen Liedes. 46 Gesänge. No.10, 11.
VOISON, BON.
Chansons.
In: Publikationen älterer praktischer und theoretischer Musikwerke. Jahrg.27.
VOLCKMAR, TOBIAS, 1678–1756.
Organ music.
In: Buszin. Organ series. Vol.1.
In: Das Erbe deutscher Musik. 1.Reihe. Vol.9.
In: The Liturgical Music Press, Inc. Masterpieces of organ music. Folio 19.
In: The parish organist. Vol.7–8.
VOM BRANDT, JOBST, *see* BRANDT, JOBST VOM.
VON AICH, ARNT, *see* AICH, ARNT VON.
VON BECKERATH, ALFRED, *see* BECKERATH, ALFRED VON.
VON BEECKE, IGNAZ, *see* BEECKE, IGNAZ VON.
VON BROUCK, JACOB, *see* BROUCK, JACOB VON.
VON BRUCK, ARNOLD, *see* BRUCK, ARNOLD VON.
VON BURCK, JOACHIM, *see* BURCK, JOACHIM À.
VON CALL, LEONHARD, *see* CALL, LEONHARD VON.
VON CAMERLOHER, PLACIDUS, *see* CAMERLOHER, PLACIDUS VON.
VON DER VOGELWEIDE, WALTER, *see* VOGELWEIDE, WALTER VON DER.
VON FULDA, ADAM, *see* ADAM VON FULDA.
VON HAGEN, PETER ALBRECHT, *see* HAGEN, PETER ALBRECHT VON, JR.
VON HASSLER, HANS LEO, *see* HASSLER, HANS LEO.
VON KNORR, ERNST LOTHAR, *see* KNORR, ERNST LOTHAR VON.
VON KOCH, ERLAND, *see* KOCH, ERLAND VON.
VON KOCH, SIGURD, *see* KOCH, SIGURD VON.
VON LANGENAU, JOHANN LEONHARD, *see* LANGENAU, JOHANN LEONHARD VON.
VON REUENTHAL, NEIDHARDT, *see* NEIDHARDT VON REUENTHAL.
VON SAMTER, WENZEL, *see* SAMTER, WENZEL VON.
VON WESTHOFF, JEAN PAUL, *see* WESTHOFF, JOHANN PAUL VON.
VON WINTER, PETER, *see* WINTER, PETER VON.
VON WOLKENSTEIN, OSWALD, *see* WOLKENSTEIN, OSWALD VON.
VOŘÍŠEK, JAN HUGO, 1791–1825.
(var. sp.: Jan Václav Voříšek; Johann Hugo Woržischek).
Impromptus. Op.7. Pour le pianoforte.
In: Musica antiqua bohemica. Vol.1.
Keyboard music.
In: Musica antiqua bohemica. Vol.17, 20, 52.
Offertorium.
In: Ecclesiasticon. No.67.
Sinfonia Re maggiore.
In: Musica antiqua bohemica. Vol.34.
Sonata. Op.5. Violino e piano.
In: Musica antiqua bohemica. Vol.30.
Sonata. Op.20. Pour le pianoforte.
In: Musica antiqua bohemica. Vol.4.
Songs.
In: Documenta historica musicae.
Violin and piano.
In: Musica antiqua bohemica. Vol.11.
VRANICKÝ, ANTONÍN, 1761–1820.
(var. sp.: Anton Wranitzky).
Concerto Si♭ maggiore. Violino e piano.
In: Musica antiqua bohemica. Vol.16.
VRANICKÝ, PAVEL, 1756–1808.
(var. sp.: Paul Wranitzky).
Keyboard music.
In: Musica antiqua bohemica. Vol.14.
Op.15–III. Quartetto d'archi Si♭ maggiore.
In: Musica antiqua bohemica. Vol.25.
VUILDRE, PHILIPPE DE, *see* WILDER, PHILIPPE VAN.
VUILLERS, PIERRE DE, *see* VILLIERS (VUILLERS), PIERRE DE.
VULPIUS, MELCHIOR, ca.1560–1615.
Choral music.
In: Antiqua Chorbuch. Vol.1. Heft 3; Vol.2. Heft 4.
In: Recueil de musique ancienne. Recueil des morceaux de musique ancienne. Bd.6.
In: Rochlitz. Sammlung vorzüglicher Gesangstücke. Bd.1. Pt.2.
Passions-Music.
In: Denkmäler thuringischer Musik. Heft 1.
Von der Geburt Jesu Christ.
In: Nagels Musik-Archiv. No.44.

WACLAW OF SZAMOTULY, d.1567/68.
(var. sp.: Wachaw z Szamotul; Wazlaw Szamotulski).
Ego sum pastor bonus.
In: Surzyński. Monumenta musicae sacrae in Polonia. Vol.2.
In te Domine speravi.
In: Denkmäler altpolnischer Musik. Vol.9.
Piesni.
In: Denkmäler altpolnischer Musik. Vol.28.
WAELRANT, HUBERT, ca.1517–1595.
Selections.
In: Maldéghem. Trésor musical.
Choral music.
In: Commer. Collectio operum musicorum batavorum saeculi XVI. Bd.1.
Musiciens qui chantez.
In: Squire. Ausgewählte Madrigale und mehrstimmige Gesänge. No.14.
Part music.
In: Hullah. Part music. Class A.2. Vol.1.
WAGENAAR, BERNARD, 1894– .
Eclogue. Organ.
In: Contemporary organ series. No.5.
String quartet, No.3.
In: Society for the Publication of American Music. Publications. 21st season. 1939–40.
Sonata. Violin and piano.
In: Society for the Publication of American Music. Publications. 9th season. 1927–28.

WAGENSEIL, GEORG CHRISTOPH, 1715–1777.
Concerto in A-dur für Violoncello, Streichorchester und Cembalo.
In: Diletto musicale. No.61.
Concerto in C-dur.
In: Musikschätze der Vergangenheit.
Concerto in C-dur für Violoncello und Orchester.
In: Diletto musicale. No.121.
Vier Divertimenti.
In: Nagels Musik-Archiv. No.36.
Das Glockengeläute.
In: Hausmusik. No.50.
Instrumental music.
In: Denkmäler der Tonkunst in Österreich. Vol.31. (Jg.XV/2).
Keyboard music.
In: Georgii. Keyboard music of the Baroque and Rococo. Vol.3.
Sinfonie in D-dur.
In: Sondheimer. Werke aus dem 18. Jahrhundert. Nr.22.
Sonate.
In: Köhler. Les maîtres du clavecin. Heft 3.
Op.4. Sonate. (F).
In: Pauer. Alte Meister. No.19.
Sonata a tre per due violini e basso continuo, Op.I/3.
In: Hausmusik. No.157.
WAGNER, RICHARD, 1813–1883.
Musikalische Werke. 10v.
Eingamschor aus dem "Liebesmal der Apostel."
In: Schmid. Musik am sächsischen Hofe. Bd.1.
Zehn Lieder aus den Jahren 1838–1858.
In: Musikalische Stundenbücher.
WAGNER-BENNETT.
Organ music.
In: Standard series of organ compositions. No.19.
WALCH, JOHANN HEINRICH, ca.1775–1855.
Marsch aus den Befreiungskriegen 1813–1815.
In: Thouret. Musik am preussischen Hofe. No.8.
WALDSTEIN, FERDINAND ERNST GABRIEL, GRAF VON, 1762–1823.
Sinfonie in D.
In: Denkmäler rheinischer Musik. Vol.1.
WALDSTEIN, WILHELM, 1897– .
Variationen über ein Thema von Mozart, für Streichquintett. Op.11.
In: Hausmusik. No.133.
WALES–MUSIC.
In: Crotch. Specimens of various styles of music. Vol.1.
WALKER, CAROLINE HOLME.
Songs.
In: The Wa-Wan series of American compositions.
WALLER, HENRY.
Song.
In: The Wa-Wan series of American compositions.
WALLISER, CHRISTOPH THOMAS, 1568–1648.
Selections.
In: Ambros. Auserwälte Tonwerke.
In: Musica sacra . . . 1839– . Vol.15.
Choral music.
In: Rochlitz. Sammlung vorzüglicher Gesangstücke. Bd.1. Pt.2.
WALLOON MUSIC.
In: Zeitschrift für Spielmusik. No.287.
WALMISLEY, THOMAS ATTWOOD, 1814–1856.
Part music.
In: Hullah. Part music. 1868 edition.
Vocal music.
In: Hullah. Vocal scores. I. Sacred.
WALMISLEY, THOMAS FORBES, 1783–1866.
Part music.
In: Hullah. Part music. Class A.1. Vol.2.
Vocal music.
In: Hullah. Vocal scores. I. Sacred; II. Secular.
WALOND, WILLIAM, 1725–1770.
Organ music.
In: Biggs. Treasury of early organ music.
In: Butcher. English organ music of the eighteenth century. Vol.2.
In: Tallis to Wesley. Vol.1, 20, 32.
WALTER, JOHANN, *see* WALTHER, JOHANN.
WALTER.
Kleine Suite für Bläser und Pauken.
In: Platzmusik. Nr.11.
WALTER VON DER VOGELWEIDE, *see* VOGELWEIDE, WALTER VON DER.
WALTHER, JOHANN, 1496–1570.
(var. sp.: Johann Walter).
Sämtliche Werke. v.1– .
Selections.
In: Ambros. Auserwählte Tonwerke.
Choral music.
In: Antiqua Chorbuch. Vol.1. Heft 2; Vol.2. Heft 1.
In: Engel. Three centuries of choral music. Vol.4.
In: Rochlitz. Sammlung vorzüglicher Gesangstücke. Bd.1. Pt.2.
Fugues.
In: Spielstücke für Blockflöten, Geigen, Lauten oder andere Instrumente. Heft 5, 8.
Herr Christ, der einig Gotts Sohn; Wol dem, der in Gottes furchte steht.
In: Schmid. Musik am sächsischen Hofe. Bd.1.
Kanons in den Kirchentönen zu 2 und 3 Stimmen.
In: Hortus musicus. No.63.
Komm, Gott Schöpfer, heiliger Geist.
In: Parrish. A treasury of early music. No.24.
Wittenbergisch Gesangbuch von 1524.
In: Publikationen älterer praktischer und theoretischer Musikwerke. Jahrg.6.
WALTHER, JOHANN GOTTFRIED, 1684–1748.
Choralvorspiele.
In: Zeitschrift für Spielmusik. No.169.
Complete organ works.
In: Denkmäler deutscher Tonkunst. [1.Folge]. Vol.26–27.
Organ music.
In: Auler. Spielbuch für Kleinorgel. Vol.2.
In: Buszin. Organ series. Vol.1, 2.
In: Guilmant. École classique de l'orgue. No.4.

In: Keller. Choralvorspiele deutscher Meister des 17. und 18. Jahrhunderts.
In: Keller. Orgelvorspiele.
In: Klein. The first four centuries of music for the organ from Dunstable to Bach (1370–1749).
In: The Liturgical Music Press, Inc. Commemoration folio.
In: The Liturgical Music Press, Inc. Masterpieces of organ music. Folio 3, 5, 18, 19, 39, 54, 71.
In: Organ masters of the Baroque period. Vol.2.
In: Organum. 4.Reihe. Nr.15.
In: The parish organist. Vol.1–4, 5–6, 7–8.
In: Peeters. Anthologia pro organo. Vol.2, 4.
In: Rohr. Orgelspiel im Kirchenjahr.
In: Schweiger. A brief compendium of early organ music.
In: Straube. Alte Meister.
In: Straube. Choralvorspiele alter Meister.

WALTHER, JOHANN JAKOB, b.1650.
Scherzi da Violino solo.
In: Das Erbe deutscher Musik. 1.Reihe. Vol.17.
Sonate C-dur für Violine und Basso Continuo.
In: Nagels Musik-Archiv. No.89.
Sonate mit Suite für Violine und Generalbass.
In: Organum. 3.Reihe. Nr.28.
Violin and piano.
In: Schering. Alte Meister des Violinspiels.

WALTON, SIR WILLIAM TURNER, 1902– .
Selections.
In: The music with the form and order of the service to be performed at the coronation of . . . Queen Elizabeth II.

WANHAL, JOHANN BAPTIST, 1739–1813.
(var. sp.: Jan Křtitel Vanhal; Johann Baptist Vanhall).
Selections.
In: Crotch. Specimens of various styles of Music. Vol.3.
Bratschenkonzert C-dur. (Piano reduction).
In: Musica viva historica. Vol.10.
Keyboard music.
In: Musica antiqua bohemica. Vol.17.
Organ music.
In: Musica antiqua bohemica. Vol.12.
Sinfonia in G-moll.
In: Diletto musicale. No.38.
Sinfonie C-dur.
In: Sondheimer. Werke aus dem 18. Jahrhundert. Nr.29.
Sonata for clarinet (violin, flute, or oboe) and piano.
In: Music for wind instruments by 18th century masters. No.6.
Violin and piano.
In: Musica antiqua bohemica. Vol.11.

WANNENMACHER, JOHANNES, d.ca.1551.
Lieder.
In: Publikationen älterer praktischer und theoretischer Musikwerke. Jahrg.1–3.
Psaumes et cantiques.
In: Verein schweizerischer Tonkünstler. Musikalische Werke. Heft 3.

WANNING, JOHANNES, ca.1542–ca.1604.
Selections from "LII Sententiae."
In: Vereniging voor Nederlandsche Muziekgeschiedenis. Uitgave. No.8.

WANSKI, JOHANN.
Zwei Sinfonien.
In: Źródła do historii muzyki polskiej. Vol.5.

WARD, JOHN, d. before 1641.
Choral music.
In: Der Kammerchor. Vol.4.
Madrigals.
In: Fellowes. The English madrigal school. Vol.19.
In: Squire. Ausgewählte Madrigale und mehrstimmige Gesänge. No.4.
Vocal music.
In: Hullah. Vocal scores. II. Secular.

WARD, JOHN, 1917– . ed.
The Dublin virginal manuscript.
In: The Wellesley edition. No.3.

WARLAMOW, ALEXANDER JEGOROWITSCH, 1801–1848.
(var. sp.: Warlamoff).
Vocal music.
In: Sammlung russischer Romanzen (passim).

WARNER, THEODOR, 1903– .
Vier Capricen für drei Bläser und Streichorchester.
In: Collegium musicae novae. No.36.

WARROCK, THOMAS, *see* WARWICK, THOMAS.

WARTECKI, MARCIN, 16th CENTURY.
Organ music.
In: Corpus of early keyboard music. Vol.10, Pt.4.

WARWICK, THOMAS, 16th–17th CENTURIES.
(var. sp.: Thomas Warrock).
Keyboard music.
In: The Fitzwilliam virginal book.

WASSILEFF.
Vocal music.
In: Sammlung russischer Romanzen. No.109, 100.

WATKINSON, GERD.
Vier musikantische Spielstücke; Aufzug und Abendmusik.
In: Musica practica. No.60, 61.

WEBBE, SAMUEL.
Selections.
In: Engel. Music from the days of George Washington.
Part music.
In: Hullah. Part music. Class A.2. Vol.1, 2; Class B.1; Class C. Secular.
Vocal music.
In: Hullah. Vocal scores. II. Secular.

WEBER, BEN, 1916– .
5 Bagatelles for piano.
In: New music. Vol.13. No.4. July 1940.
Closing piece, for organ. Op.36.
In: New music. Vol.28. No.1. Oct. 1954.
Dance, for unaccompanied violoncello. Op.28.
In: New music. Vol.22. No.2. Jan. 1949.
Nocturne for flute, violoncello, and celeste.
In: New music. Aug. 1962.
4 Songs. For soprano or tenor with solo violoncello. Op.40.
In: New music. Vol.27. No.2. Jan. 1954.

WEBER, BERNHARD ANSELM, 1766–1821.
Lied.

In: Reimann. Das deutsche Lied. Vol.1.
WEBER, CARL MARIA FRIEDRICH ERNST, FREIHERR VON, 1786–1826.
Musikalische Werke. 3v.
Compositionen. v.1– .
Sämtliche Werke für Pianoforte. 3v.
Choral music.
In: Nagels Männerchor-Blätter. No.7.
Op.26. Concertino für Klarinette und Klavier in Es-dur.
In: Diletto musicale. No.111.
Divertimento für Gitarre und Klavier. Op.38.
In: Hausmusik. No.47.
Dritte grosse Sonate D-moll.
In: Musikalische Stundenbücher.
Keyboard music.
In: Farrenc. Le trésor des pianistes. Vol.23.
In: Tagliapietra. Antologia di musica antica e moderna per pianoforte. Bd.14.
Lied.
In: Reimann. Das deutsche Lied. Vol.1.
Motets.
In: Concerts spirituels ou recueil de motets.
Part music.
In: Hullah. Part music. 1868 edition.
Schlusschor aus der Jubel-Cantate (Op.58); Sanctus aus der Es-dur– Messe; Benedictus aus der G-dur– (Jubel-) Messe.
In: Schmid. Musik am sächsischen Hofe. Bd.1.
WEBER, HANNS JOACHIM.
Einem jeden gefällt seine Art wohl.
In: Zeitschrift für Spielmusik. No.177.
Marienauer Weihnachtsmusik.
In: Zeitschrift für Spielmusik. No.194.
WEBERN, ANTON VON, 1883–1945.
Geistlicher Volkstext.
In: New music. Vol.4. No.1b. Oct. 1930.
WECKMANN, JAKOB.
Wenn der Herr die Gefangenen zu Zion.
In: Organum. 1.Reihe. Nr.2.
WECKMANN, MATTHIAS, 1619–1674.
Ausgewählte Werke.
In: Das Erbe deutscher Musik. 2.Reihe. Schleswig-Holstein und Hansestädte. Vol.4.
Keyboard music.
In: Buchmayer. Aus Richard Buchmayers historischen Klavierkonzerten. Vol.1, 2, 3.
In: Georgii. Keyboard music of the Baroque and Rococo. Vol.1.
Organ music.
In: Auler. Spielbuch für Kleinorgel. Vol.1.
In: Buszin. Organ series. Vol.1.
In: Dietrich. Elf Orgelchörale des siebzehnten Jahrhunderts.
In: Keller. Achtzig Choralvorspiele deutscher Meister des 17. und 18. Jahrhunderts.
In: Klein. The first four centuries of music for the organ from Dunstable to Bach (1370–1749).
In: The Liturgical Music Press, Inc. Masterpieces of organ music. Folio 35.
In: Organum. 4.Reihe. Nr.3.
In: The parish organist. Vol.7–8.
In: Straube. Choralvorspiele alter Meister.
Selected vocal works.
In: Denkmäler deutscher Tonkunst. [1.Folge]. Vol.6.
Weine nicht! es hat überwunden.
In: Organum. 1.Reihe. Nr.18.
Wie liegt die Stadt so wüste.
In: Organum. 1.Reihe. Nr.1.
Zion spricht: der Herr hat mich verlassen.
In: Organum. 1.Reihe. Nr.17.
THE WEE COOPER OF FIFE.
Folk song from North Carolina. Arr. by. A. Lief.
In: Music Press, Inc. [Choral series]. Vol.98.
WEELKES, THOMAS, d.1623.
Selections.
In: Documenta historica musicae.
In: Smith. Musica antiqua.
Choral music.
In: Engel. Three centuries of choral music. Vol.3.
In: Der Kammerchor. Vol.4.
Lady your eie.
In: Arion. Vol.1.
Loe countrie sports.
In: Arion. Vol.3.
Madrigals.
In: Arkwright. The Old English edition. Vol.13–15, 16–17.
In: Euterpe. Vol.6, 7; 2d ed. No.47–49, 57–58, 66–68.
In: Fellowes. The English madrigal school. Vol.9, 10, 11, 12, 13.
In: Musical Antiquarian Society. Publications. Vol.8, 14.
In: Squire. Ausgewählte Madrigale und mehrstimmige Gesänge. No.41, 43.
In: The triumphs of Oriana.
Sacred music.
In: Musica Britannica. In process.
Vocal music.
In: Hullah. Vocal scores. I. Sacred. II. Secular.
WEERBECKE, GASPAR VAN, ca.1440–1514.
Choral music.
In: Smijers. Van Ockeghem tot Sweelinck. Aflg.6.
Messe e mottetti.
In: Archivium musices metropolitanum mediolanense. Vol.11.
WEHRLI, WERNER, 1892–1944.
Tafelmusik.
In: Schweizer Sing- und Spielmusik. Heft 9.
WEICHENBERGER, JOHANN GEORG.
Lute music.
In: Denkmäler der Tonkunst in Österreich. Vol.50. (Jg.XXV/2).
WEICHMANN, JOHANN, 1620–1652.
Preussische Festlieder.
In: Das Erbe deutscher Musik. 2.Reihe. Ostpreussen und Danzig. Vol.1.
WEILAND, JULIUS JOHANNES, d.1663.
Jauchzet Gott, alle Lande.
In: Nagels Musik-Archiv. No.14.
WEINER, LEO, 1885–1960.
Keyboard music.
In: Musica hungarica.
WEINLICH, CHR.
Lied.

In: Reimann. Das deutsche Lied. Vol.4.
WEIS, FLEMMING, 1898– .
Concertino for Orgel.
In: Samfundet til Udgivelse af dansk Musik. Ser.III. No.149.
Concertino for Strygeorkester.
In: Samfundet til Udgivelse af dansk Musik. Ser.III. No.159.
Musik for Fløjte, Clarinet og Fagot.
In: Samfundet til Udgivelse af dansk Musik. Ser.III. No.28.
Sonate for Clarinet og Klaver.
In: Samfundet til Udgivelse af dansk Musik. Ser.III. No.48.
WEISMANN, WILHELM, 1900– .
Organ music.
In: The parish organist. Vol.7–8.
WEISS, ADOLPH, 1891– .
American life. Scherzaso jazzoso for large orchestra. (1929).
In: New music. Orchestra series. No.2.
Música de cámara.
In: Boletín latino-americano de música. Vol.5.
6 Preludes for piano.
In: New music. Vol.2. No.3. Apr. 1929.
Sonate for flute and viola.
In: New music. Vol.4. No.la. Oct. 1930.
WEISS, HELMUT.
Serenade.
In: Zeitschrift für Spielmusik. No.104.
WEISS, SYLVIUS LEOPOLD, 1686–1750.
Ausgewählte Werke.
In: Das Erbe deutscher Musik. 1.Reihe. Vol.12.
Menuet, Sarabande, Menuet. Adapted for guitar; Tombeau sur la mort de Mr. Comte d'Logy arrivée 1721. Adapted for guitar.
In: Hausmusik. No.128a, 128b.
WEISS, W.
Lied.
In: Reimann. Das deutsche Lied. Vol.3.
WEISSHAUS, IMRE.
6 Pieces for solo voice.
In: New music. Vol.1. No.3. Apr. 1928.
WELDON, JOHN, 1676–1736.
Sacred music.
In: Arnold. Cathedral music. Vol.1, 2.
In: Boyce. Cathedral music. Vol.2; 1849. Vol.3.
In: Page. Harmonia sacra. Vol.1.
Songs.
In: Potter. Reliquary of English song. Vol.2.
WELLEJUS, HENNING.
Det har Slet ingen Hast for Den, Som Tror. Ouverture, Op.13.
In: Samfundet til Udgivelse af dansk Musik. Ser.III. No.146.
WELLESZ, EGON, 1885– .
Eastern elements in western chant.
In: Monumenta musicae byzantinae. Subsidia. Vol.2.
The music of the Byzantine church.
In: Anthology of music. Vol.13.
WEMAN, NILS HENRY PAUL, 1897– .
Selections.
In: Svensk sanglyrik. Vol.2.
WENDLING, JOHANN BAPTIST, ca.1720–1797.
Quartett G-dur, Op.10, Nr.4, für Flöte, Violine, Viola und Violoncello.
In: Nagels Musik-Archiv. No.191.
WENNERBERG, GUNNAR, 1817–1901.
Jesu födelse.
In: Musikaliska konstföreningen. 1862.
Stabat Mater.
In: Musikaliska konstföreningen. 1894.
WERBA, ERIK, 1918– .
Hochzeits-Spruch. Gesang und Klavier, Mittel.
In: Hausmusik. No.152.
WERDIN, EBERHARD, 1911– .
Festliche Musik für zwei Instrumentalchöre.
In: Concertino.
Die Heinzelmännchen.
In: Bausteine für Musikerziehung und Musikpflege. B 126.
Kommt, ihr G'spielen.
In: Bausteine für Musikerziehung und Musikpflege. B 105.
Muntere Runde. 5 Tanzweisen.
In: Zeitschrift für Spielmusik. No.166.
4 Tanzstücke.
In: Zeitschrift für Spielmusik. No.151.
Verzierte Volksliedsätze.
In: Bausteine für Musikerziehung und Musikpflege. B 137.
WERNER, ERIC, 1901– . ed.
Hebrew music.
In: Anthology of music. Vol.20.
WERNER, GREGOR JOSEPH, ca.1695–1766.
Instrumentalkalender. Der Mai.
In: Hausmusik. No.87.
Neuer und sehr Curios-musikalischer Instrumentalkalender.
In: Das Erbe deutscher Musik. 1.Reihe. Vol.31.
Part music.
In: Hullah. Part music. Class C. Secular.
Salve, Regina. Bass, 2 Violinen und B.C.
In: Die Kantate. No.8.
Wienerischer Tandelmarkt.
In: Diletto musicale. No.81.
WERNER, JOHANN GOTTLIEB, 1777–1822.
October; December.
In: Musikschätze der Vergangenheit.
WERNICKE, J.G.,
Keyboard music.
In: Farrenc. Le trésor des pianistes. Vol.18.
WERSTOWSKI, A.
Vocal music.
In: Sammlung russischer Romanzen. No.33, 57–59, 129, 188.
WERT, GIACHES DE, 1535–1596.
(var. sp.: G. de Vert).
Opera omnia. v.1– .
Selections.
In: Smith. Musica antiqua.
Choral music.
In: Dehn. Sammlung alterer Musik aus dem XVI. und XVII. Jahrhundert.
Madrigals.
In: Das Chorwerk. No.80.
In: Einstein. The golden age of the madrigal.
In: Squire. Ausgewählte Madrigale und mehrstimmige Gesänge. No.19, 40.

Part music.
In: Hullah. Part music. Class A.2. Vol.2.
WESLEY, CHARLES, 1757–1834.
Organ music.
In: Tallis to Wesley. Vol.5, 24.
Sacred music.
In: Page. Harmonia sacra. Vol.2.
WESLEY, SAMUEL, 1766–1837.
Organ music.
In: Bonnet. Historical organ-recitals. Vol.3.
In: Liber organi. Bd.10.
In: Standard series of organ compositions. No.14.
In: Tallis to Wesley. Vol.5, 7, 14, 18, 24.
Sacred music.
In: Page. Harmonia sacra. Vol.2.
WESLEY, SAMUEL SEBASTIAN, 1810–1876.
Selections.
In: The music with the form and order of the service to be performed at the coronation of . . . Queen Elizabeth II.
Organ music.
In: Standard series of organ compositions. No.25.
In: Tallis to Wesley. Vol.5, 13, 24.
WESSTRÖM, ANDERS, ca.1720–1781.
Streichquartett in E.
In: Svenska Samfundet för Musikforskning. Äldre svensk musik. No.7.
WEST, JOHN EBENEZER, 1863–1929.
Organ music.
In: Standard series of organ compositions. No.18, 26.
WESTERGAARD, SVEND.
Sinfonia, Op.21.
In: Samfundet til Udgivelse af dansk Musik. Ser.III. No.172.
WESTERHOUT, NICCOLÒ VAN, 1857–1898.
Keyboard music.
In: Tagliapietra. Antologia di musica antica e moderna per pianoforte. Bd.17.
WESTHOFF, JOHANN PAUL VON, 1656–1705.
(var. sp.: Jean Paul von Westhoff).
Aria.
In: L'école du violon au XVIIe et XVIIIe siècle. No.1334.
WETZEL, JUSTUS HERMANN, 1879– . ed.
Die Liedformen.
In: Musikalische Formen in historischen Reihen. Bd.10.
WEYSE, CHRISTOPH ERNST FRIEDRICH, 1774–1842.
Allegri di bravura. Piano.
In: Répertoire des clavicinistes. Heft 7, 16.
Festen paa Kenilworth. Opera.
In: Samfundet til Udgivelse af dansk Musik. Ser.I. No.7.
Reformations-Kantate.
In: Samfundet til Udgivelse af dansk Musik. Ser.I. No.19.
WHITE, COOL.
Songs.
In: Siegmeister. Songs of early America, 1620–1830.
WHITE, ERNEST. ed.
Anthems.
In: Music Press, Inc. [Choral series]. No.61.
WHITE, ROBERT, ca.1530–1574.
(var. sp.: Robert Whyte).
Anthems and motets.
In: Arkwright. The Old English edition. Vol.21.
Church music.
In: Tudor church music. Vol.5.
Madrigals.
In: Euterpe. Vol.8; 2d ed. No.50.
WHYTE, ROBERT, *see* WHITE, ROBERT.
WHYTHORNE, THOMAS, b.ca.1528.
Choral music.
In: Engel. Three centuries of choral music. Vol.3.
In: Music Press, Inc. [Choral series]. Vol.90.
THE WICKHAMBROOK LUTE MANUSCRIPT.
In: Collegium musicum. Vol.4.
WIDMANN, ERASMUS, 1572–1634.
Ausgewählte Werke.
In: Das Erbe deutscher Musik. Sonderreihe. Vol.3.
Chamber music.
In: Riemann. Old chamber music. Vol.2.
Choral music.
In: Antiqua Chorbuch. Vol.2. Heft 4.
Chorlieder.
In: Christophorus-Chorwerk. Heft 5.
Trinklieder.
In: Christophorus-Chorwerk. Heft 11.
WIDOR, CHARLES MARIE, 1845–1937.
Organ music.
In: Bedell. The French organist. Vol.1, 2.
In: Bonnet. Historical organ-recitals. Vol.5.
WIELHORSKY.
Vocal music.
In: Sammlung russischer Romanzen. No.85, 86.
WIENHÄUSER LIEDERBUCH.
Das Wienhäuser Liederbuch. 2v.
WIENHORST, RICHARD, 1920– .
Organ music.
In: The parish organist. Vol.1–4.
WIENIAWSKI, HENRI, 1835–1880.
Oeuvres. 9v. (in progress).
WIGGLESWORTH, FRANK, 1918– .
Duo for oboe and viola.
In: New music. To be published.
WIKANDER, DAVID, 1884–1955.
Selections.
In: Svensk sanglyrik. Vol.2.
Mass for mixed choir a cappella.
In: Musikaliska konstföreningen. 1947.
WIKLUND, ADOLF, 1879–1950.
Selections.
In: Svensk sanglyrik. Vol.2.
WIKMANSON, JOHAN, 1753–1800.
Streichquartett. Nr.1, 2.
In: Monumenta musicae svecicae.
WILBYE, JOHN, 1574–1638.
Anthems and motets.
In: Arkwright. The Old English edition. Vol.21.
Choral music.
In: Der Kammerchor. Vol.4.
Madrigals.
In: Arion. Vol.1, 3.
In: Euterpe. Vol.2, 9, 13; 2d ed. No.51–53.

In: Fellowes. The English madrigal school. Vol.6, 7.
In: Musical Antiquarian Society. Publications. Vol.2, 16.
In: Squire. Ausgewählte Madrigale und mehrstimmige Gesänge. No.13, 33, 37.
In: The triumphs of Oriana.
Part music.
In: Hullah. Part music. Class A.2. Vol.2; Class B.2.
Vocal music.
In: Hullah. Vocal scores. II. Secular.
WILDER, PHILIPPE VAN, 16th CENTURY.
(var. sp.: Philippe de Vuildre).
Chanson.
In: Brown. Theatrical chansons of the 15th and early 16th centuries.
WILHELM, GRETE.
Besinnliches Singen.
In: Christophorus-Chorwerk. Heft 30.
Sechs Chöre.
In: Christophorus-Chorwerk. Heft 44.
WILHELMER, AMBROS.
Sonatine, für drei Trompeten.
In: Hausmusik. No.48.
WILKES, JOSUÉ TEÓFILO, 1883– .
Songs with piano.
In: Boletín latino-americano de música. Vol.1.
WILKINSON, MARC.
3 Pieces for violoncello and piano.
In: New music. Vol.24. No.4. July 1951.
WILKOMIRSKI, KAZIMIERZ, 1901– .
(var. sp.: Kasimir Wilkomirski).
12 Etuden für Violoncello.
In: Moecks gelbe Musikhefte. Vol.57.
WILLAERT, ADRIAN, ca.1480–1562.
(var. sp.: Adriano Willaert).
Opera omnia. 15v. (in progress).
Sämtliche Werke. Bd.1.
In: Publikationen älterer Musik. Jahrg.9.
Selections.
In: Ambros. Auserwählte Tonwerke.
In: Documenta historica musicae.
In: Maldéghem. Trésor musical.
In: Smith. Musica antiqua.
Chanson.
In: Brown. Theatrical chansons of the 15th and early 16th centuries.
Choral music.
In: Commer. Collectio operum musicorum batavorum saeculi XVI. Bd.1, 2.
In: Engel. Three centuries of choral music. Vol.2.
Keyboard music.
In: Tagliapietra. Antologia di musica antica e moderna per pianoforte. Bd.1.
Volkstümliche italienische Lieder.
In: Das Chorwerk. No.8.
Italienische Madrigale.
In: Das Chorwerk. No.5.
Missa super benedicta.
In: Vereniging voor Nederlandsche Muziekgeschiedenis. Uitgave. No.35.
Motets.
In: Attaingnant. Treize livres de motets. Livre 1, 2, 4, 7, 8, 11, 12.
In: Das Chorwerk. No.54, 59.
Niederländische Motette.
In: Einstein. Beispielsammlung zur älteren Musikgeschichte.
Organ music.
In: Klein. The first four centuries of music for the organ from Dunstable to Bach (1370–1749).
In: Peeters. Oudnederlandse meesters. Vol.1, 2, 3.
Neun Ricercari für drei beliebige Instrumente.
In: Antiqua Edition. Von 3 Instrumenten an.
Vocal music.
In: Hullah. Vocal scores. I. Sacred.
WILLAN, HEALEY, 1880– .
Selections.
In: The music with the form and order of the service to be performed at the coronation of . . . Queen Elizabeth II.
Organ music.
In: The parish organist. Vol.1–4, 7–8.
WILLFORT, EGON STUART.
Duos für Jedermann, für Klavier zu vier Händen.
In: Hausmusik. No.153–154.
Waldsuite, für Klavier zu vier Händen.
In: Hausmusik. No.26.
WILSON, GEORGE BALCH.
String quartet in G.
In: Society for the Publication of American Music. Publications. 33rd season. 1951–52.
WILSON, JOHN, 1595–1674.
Songs.
In: Potter. Reliquary of English song. Vol.1.
Vocal music.
In: Hullah. Vocal scores. II. Secular.
DIE WIMPFENER FRAGMENTE.
Der Hessischen Landesbibliothek Darmstadt. (Gennrich).
In: Summa musicae medii aevi. Vol.5.
THE WINCHESTER TROPER.
In: Catholic Church, Roman. Liturgy and ritual. Troper. The Winchester troper.
WIND INSTRUMENTS–MISCELLANEOUS COLLECTIONS.
In: Alte Musik.
In: Music for wind instruments by 18th century masters.
In: Musiques françaises.
In: Nagels Musik-Archiv.
In: Platzmusik.
In: Das weltliche Konzert im 18. Jahrhundert.
WINDING, AUGUST, 1835–1899.
"Genrebilleder" for piano. (from Op.15).
In: Samfundet til Udgivelse af dansk Musik. Suppl. 1900.
Koncert-Ouverture. Op.14.
In: Samfundet til Udgivelse af dansk Musik. Ser.I. No.22.
Songs from Op.2 and Op.14.
In: Samfundet til Udgivelse af dansk Musik. Suppl. 1900.
Symphonie. Op.39.
In: Samfundet til Udgivelse af dansk Musik. Ser.II. No.7.
WINTELROY, JOAN, 16th CENTURY.
Choral music.

In: Musica antiqua batava. MA–8.
WINTER, PETER VON, 1754–1825.
Dominus Israel.
?In: Ecclesiasticon. No.38.
Lied.
In: Reimann. Das deutsche Lied. Vol.1.
Sacred music.
In: Latrobe, C. I. Selection of sacred music.
In: Latrobe, J. A. The music of the church.
WINTER, RICHARD, 1902– .
Lieder für eine Singstimme und Klavier (mittel).
In: Hausmusik. No.117a-b.
WIORA, WALTER, 1906– .
European folksongs.
In: Anthology of music. Vol.4.
WIRÉN, DAG IVAR, 1905– .
Selections.
In: Svensk sanglyrik. Vol.2.
Sonatina for violin and piano, Op.15.
In: Musikaliska konstföreningen. 1949.
Triptyk, for orchestra.
In: Musikaliska konstföreningen. 1959.
WISE, MICHAEL, ca.1648–1687.
Sacred music.
In: Boyce. Cathedral music. Vol.2, 3; 1849 ed., Vol.3.
WITT, CHRISTIAN FRIEDRICH, ca.1660–1716.
(var. sp.: Witte).
Organ music.
In: Das Erbe deutscher Musik. 1.Reihe. Vol.9.
Suite in F-dur. Für drei Blockflöten (zwei f', eine c') oder andere Blas- oder Streichinstrumente und Basso Continuo.
In: Hortus musicus. No.99.
Drei Märsche für vier Streichinstrumente oder Blockflöten.
In: Musica practica. No.14.
WITTE, GERD.
Sieben kanonische Sätze über alte Weihnachsweisen.
In: Zeitschrift für Spielmusik. No.248.
WITTENBERGISCH GESANGBUCH VON 1524. (Johann Walther).
In: Publikationen älterer praktischer und theoretischer Musikwerke. Jahrg.6.
WIZLAV, PRINCE, d.1325.
(var. sp.: Wizlaw Fürst von Rugen).
Selections.
In: Leichtentritt. Deutsche Hausmusik aus vier Jahrhunderten.
Mancher Thor.
In: Arion. Vol.3.
WOCKENFUSS, PETER LAURENTIUS, 17th CENTURY.
Elmenhorst's Geistliche Lieder.
In: Denkmälter deutscher Tonkunst. [1.Folge]. Vol.45.
WOELFL, JOSEPH, *see* WÖLFL, JOSEPH.
WOELKE, KONRAD, *see* WÖLKE, KONRAD.
WOLF, ERNST WILHELM, 1735–1792.
Choral music.
?In: Rochlitz. Sammlung vorzüglicher Gesangstücke. Bd.3.
Zwei leichte Klaviersonaten, D-moll und E-dur; C-moll. Piano.
In: Organum. 5.Reihe. Nr.7, 25.
Sacred music.
?In: Latrobe, C. I. Selection of sacred music.
?In: Latrobe, J. A. The music of the church.
Zwei leichte Sonaten in G-dur und F-dur. Piano.
In: Organum. 5.Reihe. Nr.21.
WOLF, HUGO, 1860–1903.
Sämtliche Werke. v.1– .
Nachgelassene Werke. v.1– .
WOLF, JOHANNES, 1869–1947.
Musikalische Schrifttafeln.
In: Fürstliches Institut für musikwissenschaftliche Forschung. Veröffentlichungen. 2.Reihe. [No.] 2.
WOLFENBÜTTEL 1099. (LUTHER A. DITTMER).
In: Institute of Mediaeval Music. Publications. Vol.2.
WOLFF, HELLMUTH CHRISTIAN, 1906– .
For prepared piano.
In: New music. Vol.24. No3. Apr. 1951.
WOLFF, MARTIN, ca.1500.
Choral music.
In: Antiqua Chorbuch. Vol.1. Heft 1.
WÖLFL, JOSEPH, 1773–1812.
(var. sp.: Woelfl).
Keyboard sonatas.
In: Newman. Thirteen keyboard sonatas of the 18th and 19th centuries.
Sonate für Violoncello und Klavier. Op.31.
In: Hortus musicus. No.111.
Sonate précédée d'une introduction et fugue. Piano.
In: Répertoire des clavicinistes. Heft 12.
WÖLKE, KONRAD.
(var. sp.: Woelke).
Reinickendorfer Flötenmusik.
In: Zeitschrift für Spielmusik. No.225.
WOLKENSTEIN, OSWALD VON, ca.1377–1445.
Selections.
In: Leichtentritt. Deutsche Hausmusik aus vier Jahrhunderten.
Lieder.
In: Denkmäler der Tonkunst in Österreich. Vol.18. (Jg.IX/1).
WOLL, ERNA, 1917– .
Herz-Mariä-Kantate.
In: Christophorus-Chorwerk. Heft 31.
Lass den Stern mich finden.
In: Christophorus-Chorwerk. Heft 42.
Messe in E.
In: Christophorus-Chorwerk. Heft 16.
Und alles preist dich, Gott, den Herrn.
In: Christophorus-Chorwerk. Heft 22.
WOLPE, STEFAN, 1902– .
Passacaglia. For piano solo.
In: New music. Vol.20. No.1. Oct.1946.
WOLPERT, FRANZ ALFONS, 1917– .
Banchetto musicale, Nr.1, Op.25.
In: Collegium musicae novae. No.11.
WOLTZ, JOHANN, 16th–17th CENTURIES.
Organ music.
In: Cantantibus organis. Vol.7.
WOOD.
Sacred music.
In: Page. Harmonia sacra. Vol.2.
WOOD, CARL PAIGE.
Winter winds; for women's voices and strings.

Arr. for women's voices and piano.
In: Washington (State) University. Music series. No.1.
WOOLCOCK, SAMUEL NEGRETE, *see* NEGRETE WOOLCOCK, SAMUEL.
WORCESTER ADD. 68. (LUTHER A. DITTMER).
In: Institute of Mediaeval Music. Publications. Vol.5.
THE WORCESTER FRAGMENTS.
In: Dittmer. The Worcester fragments.
In: Institute of Mediaeval Music. Musicological studies. Vol.1.
WORK, HENRY CLAY, 1832–1884.
Songs. 180p.
WORONOFF, WLADIMIR, 1903– .
Sonnet, for Dallapiccolo. Piano.
In: New music. Vol.23. No.3. Apr. 1950.
WORONZOFF.
Vocal music.
In: Sammlung russischer Romanzen. No.231.
WORŽISCHEK, JOHANN HUGO, *see* VOŘÍŠEK, JAN HUGO.
WRANITZKY, ANTON, *see* VRANICKÝ, ANTONÍN.
WRANITZKY, PAUL, *see* VRANICKÝ, PAVEL.
WRIGHT, LOUISE DRAKE.
Song.
In: The Wa-Wan series of American compositions.
WUORINEN, CHARLES.
Into the organ pipes and steeples. For antiphonal orchestra.
In: New music. Vol.30. No.2. Jan. 1957.
Movement for wind quintet.
In: New music. Jan. 1961.
Sonatina for woodwind quartet.
In: New music. Vol.29. No.4. July 1956.
WÜRTTEMBERG–MUSIC.
In: Denkmäler der Tonkunst in Württemberg.

YEPES, 16th CENTURY.
(var. sp.: Vepes).
Keyboard music.
In: Kastner. Silva iberica.
YOULL, HENRY, 16th–17th CENTURIES.
Madrigals.
In: Euterpe. Vol.9; 2d ed. No.54.
In: Fellowes. The English madrigal school. Vol.28.
YVER, A.
Selections.
In: Maldéghem. Trésor musical.

ZACCARIA, CESARE DE, 16th CENTURY.
(var. sp.: Caesar de Zacchariis; Cesare de Zachariis).
Cacce.
In: Marrocco. Fourteenth-century Italian cacce.
Intonationes.
In: Berg. Patrocinium musices. Vol.11.
Sacred music.
In: Proske. Musica divina. Annus primus. Tom 3.
In: Proske. Selectus novus missarum. Annus secundus. Tom 3.
ZACCHARIIS, CAESAR DE, *see* ZACCARIA, CESARE DE.
ZACH, JAN (JOHANN), 1699–ca.1773.
5 Sinfonie d'archi.
In: Musica antiqua bohemica. Vol.43.
Konzert für Cembalo mit begleitung von Streichorchester.
In: Nagels Musik-Archiv. No.165.
Organ music.
In: Musica antiqua bohemica. Vol.12.
In: Orgelwerke. Altböhmischer Meister. Vol.3.
2 Sinfonien für 2 Violinen und Basso Continuo.
In: Hortus musicus. No.145.
Sonata a 3 stromenti. Per 2 violini e basso.
In: Musica antiqua bohemica. Vol.9.
ZACHARIAS, NICOLAUS.
Sacred music.
In: Plainsong and Mediaeval Music Society. Publications. (Borren).
ZACHARIIS, CESARE DE, *see* ZACCARIA, CESARE DE.
ZACHAU, FRIEDRICH WILHELM, 1663–1712.
(var. sp.: Zachow).
Selected compositions.
In: Denkmäler deutscher Tonkunst. [1.Folge]. Vol.21–22.
Choralvorspiele.
In: Zeitschrift für Spielmusik. No.169.
Fantasia für Streichorchester; 2 Stücke.
In: Musikschätze der Vergangenheit.
Herr, wenn ich nur dich habe.
In: Organum. 1.Reihe. Nr.5.
Kammertrio für Flöte (Oboe), Fagott und Generalbass.
In: Organum. 3.Reihe. Nr.25.
Organ music.
In: Buszin. Organ series. Vol.1.
In: Keller. Achtzig Choralvorspiele deutscher Meister des 17. und 18. Jahrhunderts.
In: Klein. The first four centuries of music for the organ from Dunstable to Bach (1370–1749).
In: The Liturgical Music Press, Inc. Masterpieces of organ music. Folio 8.
In: Muziek voor de eredienst. Vol.1.
In: Organ masters of the Baroque period. Vol.3.
In: Organum. 4.Reihe. Nr.16.
In: The parish organist. Vol.1–4, 5–6, 7–8.
In: Raugel. Quarante-six pièces pour orgue ou harmonium.
In: Rohr. Orgelspiel im Kirchenjahr.
In: Straube. Choralvorspiele alter Meister.
Weihnachtsmusik. Für Klavier oder Orgel.
In: Nagels Musik-Archiv. No.95.
ZACHOW, FRIEDRICH WILHELM, *see* ZACHAU, FRIEDRICH WILHELM.
ZANELLA, AMILCARE, 1873–1949.
Keyboard music.
In: Tagliapietra. Antologia di musica antica e moderna per pianoforte. Bd.18.
ZANETI, FRANCESCO MARIA, ca.1680.
Songs.
In: Jeppesen. La flora, Vol.2.
ZANG, NIC, *see* ZANGIUS, NICOLAUS.
ZANGIUS, NICOLAUS, d.1618 or 1619.
(var. sp.: Zang).
Choral music.

In: Antiqua Chorbuch. Vol.1. Heft 4.
Lieder.
In: Commer. Geistliche und weltliche Lieder aus dem XVI.–XVIII. Jahrhundert.
Sacred and secular songs.
In: Denkmäler der Tonkunst in Österreich. Vol.87.
ZANOSKAR, HUBERT.
Das Spiel auf der Altfidel.
In: Bausteine für Musikerziehung und Musikpflege. B 122.
ZANOTTI, CAMILLO.
Selections.
In: Denkmäler der Tonkunst in Österreich. Vol.77 (Jg.XLI).
ZARLINO, GIOSEFFO, 1517–1590.
(var. sp.: Giuseppe Zarlino).
Selections.
In: Smith. Musica antiqua.
In: Torchi. L'arte musicale in Italia. Bd.1.
Choral music.
In: Engel. Three centuries of choral music. Vol.2.
Drei Motetten und ein geistliches Madrigal.
In: Das Chorwerk. No.77.
ZBINDEN, JULIEN FRANCOIS, 1917– .
Suite Française für Streichorchester, Op.23.
In: Collegium musicae novae. No.18.
ZEISL, ERIC, 1905– .
Stücke für Barbara.
In: Hausmusik. No.61.
ŻELECHOWSKI, PIOTR, 17th CENTURY.
Organ music.
In: Corpus of early keyboard music. Vol.10, Pt.4.
ZELENKA, JAN DISMAS, 1679–1745.
(var. sp.: Johann Dismas Zelenka).
Choral music.
In: Rochlitz. Sammlung vorzüglicher Gesangstücke. Bd.3.
Instrumental music.
In: Schmid. Musik am sächsischen Hofe. Bd.6.
Sonate I, IV, V, VI für 2 Oboen (Violinen), Fagotte (Violoncello), und Basso Continuo.
In: Hortus musicus. No.126, 147, 157, 132.
Sonata III B-dur für Violine, Oboe (Violine), Fagott (Violoncello) und Basso Continuo.
In: Hortus musicus. No.177.
ZELTER, CARL FRIEDRICH, 1758–1832.
(var. sp.: K. F. Zelter).
Choral works.
In: Chor-Archiv.
In: Nagels Männerchor-Blätter. No.13.
Fig. Choral, Ewiger lob.
In: Königliche Akademie der Künste. Auswahl vorzüglicher Musik-Werke. No.23.
Die Gunst des Augenblicks.
In: Nagels Musik-Archiv. No.92.
Johanna Sebus (Goethe) für Singstimmen am Pianoforte.
In: Nagels Musik-Archiv. No.91.
Lieder.
In: Hirsch. Veröffentlichungen. [Bd.] 6.
In: Moser. Alte Meister des deutschen Liedes. 30 Gesänge. No.30.
In: Moser. Alte Meister des deutsches Liedes. 46 Gesänge. No.46.
In: Reimann. Das deutsche Lied. Vol.2, 3, 4.
Lieder, Balladen und Romanzen in Auswahl.
In: Nagels Musik-Archiv. No.60.
ZENCK, HERMANN, 1898–1950.
Sixtus Dietrich.
In: Publikationen älterer Musik. Jahrg.3, Pt.2.
ZENDER, HANS, 1936– .
Divertimento, Op.7b.
In: Collegium musicae novae. No.19.
Fünf leichte Stücke für Streichorchester, Op.7a.
In: Collegium musicae novae. No.12.
ZESSO, JOHANN BAPTIST.
Selections.
In: Ambros. Auserwählte Tonwerke.
Karnevalslieder der Renaissance.
In: Das Chorwerk. No.43.
ZEUNER, MARTIN, 17th CENTURY.
82 Geistliche Kirchenlieder.
In: Publikationen älterer praktischer und theoretischer Musikwerke. Jahrg.32.
ZIANI, MARC' ANTONIO.
Motets.
In: Denkmäler der Tonkunst in Österreich. Vol.101/102.
ZIANI, PIETRO ANDREA, ca.1620–1684.
Organ music.
In: Cantantibus organis. Vol.11.
ZIELEŃSKI, MIKOLAJ (NIKOLAUS), ca.1550–ca. 1615.
(var. sp.: Nikolaus Zieleński).
Selections.
In: Gieburowski. Cantica selecta musices sacrae in Polonia saeculi XVI et XVII.
Choral music.
In: Surzyński. Monumenta musicae sacrae in Polonia. Vol.1, 2.
Communiones. Soprano and organ.
In: Denkmäler altpolnischer Musik. Vol.45.
Domus mea.
In: Denkmäler altpolnischer Musik. Vol.31.
Exiit sermo inter fratres and Si consurrexistis cum Christo.
In: Denkmäler altpolnischer Musik. Vol.36.
Justus ut palma florebit.
In: Denkmäler altpolnischer Musik. Vol.41.
Vox in Rama.
In: Denkmäler altpolnischer Musik. Vol.12.
ZIEMS, H.
Kammerkonzert. (Klarinette, Streicher).
In: Collegium musicae novae. No.58.
ZINGARELLI, NICOLA ANTONIO, 1752–1837.
Part music.
In: Hullah. Part music. Class A.1. Vol.1, 2; 1868 edition.
Vocal music.
In: Hullah. Vocal scores. I. Sacred.
ZIPOLI, DOMENICO, 1688–1726.
(var. sp.: Dominique Zipoli).
Selections.
In: Torchi. L'arte musicale in Italia. Bd.3.
Composizioni.
In: I classici della musica italiana. Vol.36.
Composizioni per organo e cembalo.

In: I classici della musica italiana. Raccolta nazionale delle musiche italiane. Quad. 145–150.
Keyboard music.
In: Esposito. Early Italian piano music.
In: Farrenc. Le trésor des pianistes. Vol.11.
In: Tagliapietra. Antologia di musica antica e moderna per pianoforte. Bd.10.
Organ music.
In: Bossi. Sammlung von Stücken alter italienischer Meister für die moderne Orgel.
In: Fuser. Classici italiani dell' organo.
In: Guilmant. École classique de l'orgue. No.9.
In: Klein. The first four centuries of music for the organ from Dunstable to Bach (1370–1749).
In: Liber organi. Bd.4.
In: The Liturgical Music Press, Inc. Masterpieces of organ music. Folio 25.
In: Raugel. Quarante-six pièces pour orgue ou harmonium.
Partita. Clavicembalo or piano.
In: Boghen. Antichi maestri italiani.
Prelude, Courante, Sarabande, Gigue.
In: Köhler. Les maîtres du clavecin. Heft 9.
Preludio, Corrente, Sarabanda und Giga. (Gm).
In: Pauer. Alte Meister. No.16.
Suite (Hm). (Preludio. Corrente. Aria. Gavotte); Partita (A minor). (Arie mit 12 Variationen).
In: Pauer. Alte Meister. No.46, 47.
ZIPP, FRIEDRICH, 1914– .
Fest und Feier.
In: Bausteine für Musikerziehung und Musikpflege. B 133.
Fröhlicher Jahrmarkt.
In: Bausteine für Musikerziehung und Musikpflege. B 141.
Heiteres Tierliederspiel.
In: Bausteine für Musikerziehung und Musikpflege. B 129.
Kein schöner Lied.
In: Bausteine für Musikerziehung und Musikpflege. B 102.
Musik für Orchester.
In: Concertino.
ZOCHOLO, PRESBYTER P. DEL.
Sacred music.
In: Plainsong and Mediaeval Music Society. Publications. (Borren).
ZOELLNER, KARL HEINRICH, *see* ZÖLLNER, KARL HEINRICH.
ZOILO, ANNIBALE, ca.1537–1592.
(var. sp.: Annibale Zoile).
Selections.
In: Torchi. L'arte musicale in Italia. Bd.1.
Sacred music.
In: Proske. Musica divina. Annus primus. Tom 4.
ZÖLLNER, KARL HEINRICH, 1792–1836.
(var. sp.: Zoellner)
Organ music.
In: Caecilia; Sammlung von Choralvorspielen.
ZORITA, NICASIUS.
Sacred music.
In: Rubio. Antología polifónica sacra. Vol.1.
ZUCHINO, G.
Sacred music.
In: Proske. Musica divina. Annus primus. Tom 4.
ZUMSTEEG, JOHANN RUDOLF, 1760–1802.
Kleine Balladen und Lieder in Auswahl.
In: Nagels Musik-Archiv. No.82.
Lied.
In: Reimann. Das deutsche Lied. Vol.2.
ZUYLEN VAN NYEVELT, WILLEM VAN.
Souterliedekens.
In: Duyse. Het oude Nederlandsche lied. 1.Vervolg.
ZWIERZCHOWSKI, M.
Polonäse "Tuba mirum" aus "Requiem."
In: Florilegium musicae antiquae. Vol.2.